ECONOMIC THEORY IN RETROSPECT

Fourth edition

This is a fully revised fourth edition of a book that has made a name for itself as a unique textbook on the history of economic thought. Teachers who have long deplored the antiquarian flavor of so many books in this field will welcome a text such as this one which studies theories rather than theorists, and which focuses on the logical coherence and explanatory value of the mainstream of economic ideas, undiluted by biographical coloring or historical digressions.

Students who have grown weary of reading secondhand commentaries on the great economists, which really bring them no nearer to the original masterpieces of economics, will derive fresh inspiration from the detailed Reader's Guides provided here: chapter by chapter, and sometimes paragraph by paragraph, the author takes us through the leading works of Adam Smith, David Ricardo, John Stuart Mill, Karl Marx, Alfred Marshall, Philip Wicksteed, and Knut Wicksell. A series of annotated bibliographies then guide the student through the enormous literature that has grown uparound these classics.

For the present edition, the later chapters of the book on monetary theory and macroeconomics have been entirely rewritten to take account of the rise of monetarism and rational expectations. The continuous debate on what-Keynes-really-meant has resulted in a thorough revision of the Keynes chapter, marking the successive stages in what is now a history of interpretations of Keynes over a period of almost 50 years. There is an entirely new chapter on the history of location theory, a subject almost totally neglected in rival histories of economic thought. There are minor additions to the earlier chapters on Ricardo and Marx and major additions to the middle chapters on marginal productivity theory and welfare economics, such as new sections on the history of the concept of entrepreneurship and recent developments in the never-ending controversy about marginal cost pricing of public utilities. And, of course, the Notes on Further Readings have been thoroughly updated.

ECONOMIC THEORY IN RETROSPECT

Fourth edition

MARK BLAUG

*University of London Institute of Education
and University of Buckingham*

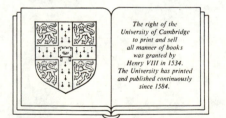

The right of the
University of Cambridge
to print and sell
all manner of books
was granted by
Henry VIII in 1534.
The University has printed
and published continuously
since 1584.

CAMBRIDGE UNIVERSITY PRESS

CAMBRIDGE
NEW YORK   NEW ROCHELLE
MELBOURNE   SYDNEY

330. 1
B64e4

Published by the Press Syndicate of the University of Cambridge
The Pitt Building, Trumpington Street, Cambridge CB2 1RP
32 East 57th Street, New York, NY 10022, USA
10 Stamford Road, Oakleigh, Melbourne 3166, Australia

First edition © Richard D. Irwin. Inc. 1962
Second edition © Richard D. Irwin. Inc. 1968
Third edition © Mark Blaug 1978
Fourth edition © Mark Blaug 1985

First published by Richard D. Irwin. Inc. 1962
Second edition 1968
Third edition published by the Cambridge University Press 1978
Fourth edition published by the Cambridge University Press 1985
Reprinted 1986, 1987, 1988

Printed in Great Britain at Woolnough Bookbinding, Irthlingborough

British Library Cataloguing in Publication Data

Blaug, Mark
Economic theory in retrospect. – 4th ed.
1. Economics – History
I. Title

Library of Congress Cataloguing in Publication Data

Blaug, Mark
Economic theory in retrospect.
Includes bibliographical references and indexes
1. Economics – History. I. Title.
HB75.B664 1977 330.1′09   *MB*

ISBN 0 521 30354 0 hard covers
ISBN 0 521 31644 8 paperback

Someone said: 'The dead writers are remote from us because we know so much more than they did.' Precisely, and they are that which we know.

T. S. ELIOT

We hold that for the mastery of a speculative controversial science a certain multiplication of authorities is desirable. The false tendency of teachers to inculcate, and pupils to learn by rote, the very phrases and metaphors of a favourite author can only be corrected by dividing the allegiance of those who, like the Romans of old, 'rush to slavery'. Hence the history of theory is particularly instructive in political economy as in philosophy. History and literature, dialectics and all that the Greeks comprehensively called 'words,' seem the best correction of the narrow prejudices and deceptive associations which are sure to be contracted by those who have been confined to a single school or system.

F. Y. EDGEWORTH

To my son, David Ricardo

Preface

First edition

This book is a study of the logical coherence and explanatory value of what has come to be known as orthodox economic theory. The history of this body of received doctrine goes back at least as far as Adam Smith. I am not concerned, however, with historical antecedents for their own sake. My purpose is to teach contemporary economic theory. But contemporary theory wears the scars of yesterday's problems now resolved, yesterday's blunders now corrected, and cannot be fully understood except as a legacy handed down from the past. It is for this reason that I have adopted a historical presentation. Nevertheless, the focus is on theoretical analysis, undiluted by entertaining historical digressions or biographical coloring.

Students are often told of the inspiration to be derived from the study of the history of economics. They are not so often reminded of the inspiration which the historian of economic thought derives from a study of contemporary economic theory. In truth, one should no more study modern price theory without knowing Adam Smith than one should read Adam Smith without having learned modern price theory. There is a mutual interaction between past and present economic thinking for, whether we set it down in so many words or not, the history of economic thought is being rewritten every generation.

The study of the history of economics must derive its *raison d'être* from the extent to which it encourages a student to become acquainted at first hand with some of the great works of the subject. It is for this reason that I have included Reader's Guides to the works of Smith, Ricardo, Mill, Marx, Marshall, Wicksteed, and Wicksell. The importance of reading original sources in a subject such as economics cannot be overemphasized. We must all have had the experience, after reading a commentary on some great book, of going back to the text itself and finding how much more there is in it than we had been led to expect. Commentaries are tidy and consistent, great books are not. This is why great books are worth reading.

I wish to express my gratitude to H. Barkai, B. Balassa, W. Fellner, T. W. Hutchison, R. L. Meek, and G. Shepherd who read parts of the manuscript and made many helpful suggestions. I am also grateful to my graduate students, too numerous to mention, who from time to time argued me off some of my pet hobbyhorses. Further, I must thank Miss Margaret Lord for her stylistic improvements and Mrs A. Granger for the efficient typing of the manuscript.

I am indebted to the following publishers for permission to quote from works published by them: Harper and Brothers – J. Viner, *Studies in the Theory of International Trade*, copyright 1937; University of Chicago Press – *Adam Smith, 1776–1926*, ed. J. M. Clark, and others, copyright 1928 by the University of Chicago, and G. J. Stigler, 'The Development of Utility Theory, II', *Journal of Political Economy*, October, 1950; Harcourt, Brace and World – J. M. Keynes, *The Economic Consequences of the Peace*, copyright 1919; *Review of Economic Studies* – O. Lange, 'Marxian Economics and the Modern Economic Theory', *Review of Economic Studies*, June, 1935; The Macmillan Company – A. Marshall, *The Principles of Economics*, copyright 1930, and K. Wicksell, *Lectures in Political Economy*, copyright 1934; and Routledge and Kegan Paul – P. Wicksteed, *The Common Sense of Political Economy*, copyright 1934.

New Haven, Conn.   M. BLAUG
November, 1961

Preface

Second edition

What I have tried to do in this book has been so frequently misunderstood that I would like to restate my aims. Presented with the ultra-Marxist thesis that the economic theory of a given period is nothing but a reflection of the prevailing historical and political circumstances, I have wondered whether the diametrically opposite thesis – economic theory for economic theory's sake – is no less misleading. Suppose one were to read a history of economics which contained no reference whatever to nontheoretical events: would it be less enlightening than a typical Marxist or quasi-Marxist presentation? Of course it would be limited and inadequate, but that is true of all monocausal interpretations of intellectual history. It is perfectly obvious that much of what we think of as economics had its origin in intellectual responses to major unsettled policy questions: Adam Smith and mercantilist restrictions, David Ricardo and the difficulty of raising Britain's food supply from domestic resources, Keynes and the treatment of mass unemployment in the 1930s are favourite examples. But equally obviously, it must be insisted, great chunks of the history of economic thought are about mistakes in logic and gaps in analysis, having no connection with contemporary events. And so, without pretending that this is the whole story, or even the best part of the story, but merely that it is a part rarely told, I have tried to write a history of economic analysis which pictures it as evolving out of previous analysis, propelled forward by the desire to refine, to improve, to perfect, a desire which economists share with all other scientists. There is a danger in this sort of treatment. As Francis Bacon said over 300 years ago:

'For the wit and mind of man, if it work upon matter, which is the contemplation of the creatures of God, worketh according to the stuff and is limited thereby; but if it work upon itself, as the spider worketh his web, then it is endless, and brings forth indeed cobwebs of learning, admirable for the fineness of thread and work, but of no substance or profit' (*The Advancement of Learning*, London: 1865, page 32).

This book is all about those 'cobwebs of learning' but we shall be asking continually: 'of no substance or profit'?

As in the first edition, we begin with the mercantilist writers of the 18th century, not with the medieval schoolmen or with Plato and Aristotle. No doubt, the Greeks made contributions to the history of economic thought, but their economic ideas were so intimately associated with other preoccupations that only a full-scale treatment of Greek philosophy, and particularly Greek political theory, can do them justice. Similarly, scholastic analysis of usury is fascinating in its own right but the background that is required in medieval catholic doctrine to prevent misunderstanding of scholastic reasoning would absorb more space than is warranted in a book of this kind. Economics, as a separate discipline of inquiry, did not emerge until the 17th century, perhaps because in preceding centuries economic transactions were not integrated on a national or even a regional basis, perhaps because economic institutions were severely circumscribed by military and political considerations, perhaps because economic motives were prevented from affecting more than a limited aspect of social behaviour. It is not obvious why all economic reasoning before the 17th century was *ad hoc*, unsystematic and devoid of the recognition of an autonomous sphere of economic activity, but that it was so is hardly ever controverted. And since this is a book about economics rather than economists, we will ignore what might be described as the 'paleontology' of the subject.

As before, the story is carried down to our own times, roughly 1960, although there is more material on activity analysis, economic dynamics, welfare economics, growth models, and technical change – topics that have dominated economics in recent years – in this edition than in the first. To put all my cards on the table, new sections have been added to the chapters on Adam Smith and John Stuart Mill, dealing with their views on the role of the public sector; the notion of the 'single tax' is now discussed in some detail in the chapter on population and rent; the treatment of Harrod-Domar growth models in the chapter on Say's Law has been extended; a new section on the Leninist theory of imperialism has been added to the Marx chapter; a new section on the theory of monopolistic competition has been added to the second Marshall chapter; the chapter on marginal productivity theory has been thoroughly revised and now contains a new section on innovations and relative shares; the chapters on Walras, Pareto, and Keynes have been extensively rewritten; the last chapter of the book, 'A Methodological Postscript', has been expanded into an essay on the future prospects of scientific economics; and almost every page of the first edition has undergone some amendment and, I like to think, improvement. It is now a better book; it is for others to say whether it was a good book in the first place.

In order to encourage students to doubt all commentators, including the author of this book, this edition, like the first one, contains detailed Reader's Guides to seven major works in the history of economic thought. But as some reviewers of the first edition felt that these were more welcomed as heaven-sent cribs than as stimuli to consult the original writers, I should warn readers again that the Guides are neither summaries nor *précis*; they are running commentaries and more concerned with what the great economists might have meant than with what they actually said. In short, they are expressly designed to be provocative and the student who uses them as a substitute for the originals is like a connoisseur of vintage wines who has seen old bottles but has never tasted the contents.

I wish to thank K. Kubota, E. Kuska, and R. M. Olsen for making specific suggestions that have entered into this revision. I owe a particular debt to Miss

R. Towse and Miss M. Woodhall for their ruthless combing of the entire manuscript: we were friends when we started and, surprisingly enough, we are still friends.

London, England   MARK BLAUG
January, 1968

Preface

Third edition

The first edition of this book appeared in 1962, by which time the history of economic thought had virtually disappeared as a teaching subject in British and American universities. In a perceptive article published in that year, entitled 'What Price the History of Economic Thought?', Donald Winch explained why most economists knew little and cared even less about the history of their own discipline: owing to recent developments in modern economics, economists had increasingly come to feel that at long last they were beginning to provide new answers to new problems, or, at any rate, better answers to old problems; such a confident state of mind naturally tends to discourage an interest in predecessors and forerunners. The complacency of the 1960s, however, has given way to the nail-biting of the 1970s. There is nowadays a pervasive and repeatedly expressed sense of 'crisis' in economics. In part this reflects the failure to come to grips with such outstanding contemporary economic problems as stagflation, pollution, and sex and race discrimination in labour markets. This failure to tackle the major economic problems of the day has in turn given rise to such alternative economic doctrines as radical political economy, neo-Marxian economics, and post-Keynesian economics, all of which purport to throw light on these unsolved problems, in the course of which they first criticize and then reject mainstream modern economics. If there is anything to the Winch thesis, we may expect that the current anxiety about the state of modern economics will bring about a revival of interest in the history of economic thought. And, indeed, it is possible to discern definite signs of such a renaissance in the flood of articles and books that has appeared on the history of economics in the last few years, not to mention the reappearance of history-of-thought courses in economics departments around the world.

What has been revived, however, is not quite the good old history of economic thought that we knew fifteen or twenty years ago. Some have argued in recent years that we have long misrepresented the historical evolution of modern economics: the so-called Marginal Revolution of the 1870s was not the great breakthrough that marked the advent of modern analytical techniques but a detour from the more fruitful line of attack charted by Ricardo and Marx; starting from Ricardo and Marx on the one hand and from Keynes on the other, a wholly different economics can be constructed than that which rules the textbooks of today, resting as it does on the shoulders of Walras and Marshall. Alternatively, modern economic analysis can be married to Marx or Veblen to produce a strikingly new framework with which to replace the prevailing orthodoxy. Others have no quarrel with Walras and Marshall but take the view that Keynesian macroeconomics has been misunderstood in modern textbooks and that Keynesian economics as we know it bears little resemblance to the economics of Keynes himself. These sorts of arguments open up questions in the history of economic thought that many had long considered closed. Suffice it to say that the history of economic thought now seems to be becoming the arena in which some of these controversial questions will be fought out. In short, the subject is back on the map and any book on it, such as the present one written as long ago as 1962, stands in need of drastic revision and updating.

Most of the changes have come in the last two chapters of the book dealing with Keynesian economics and economic methodology. Indeed, these chapters have been entirely rewritten in the light of recent debates on the Clower-Leijonhufvud disequilibrium interpretation of Keynes and the structure of scientific revolutions among philosophers of science. I still believe that questions about the meaning of economics must be asked at the end and not at the beginning of the study of the history of economic thought. Nevertheless, an increasing number of methodological issues are now raised throughout the text, pointing forward to the final 'Methodological Postscript' which closes the book. Apart from drastic revisions in the last two chapters, chapter 4 on Ricardo is now followed by a discussion of Sraffa's classic book, *Production of Commodities by Means of Commodities* (1960), which may be justly described as Ricardo in modern dress. Chapter 7 on Marx is likewise revised here and there to take account of the remarkable rejuvenation of Marxian economics in recent years. The post-Keynesian theory of distribution of Robinson, Kaldor, and Pasinetti has made us think again about the so-called 'marginal productivity theory of distribution', thereby producing further changes in chapter 11. Similarly, the reswitching debate that has filled the journals over the last few years has altered our perspective of the Austrian theory of capital interest and this new perspective is reflected in a sharpening of issues raised in chapter 12. The final outcome is a book in the same spirit as the original but geared to the theoretical concerns of the 1970s rather than those of the 1960s.

In 1962, bibliographies in the history of economic thought were few and far between and my extensive 'Notes on Further Reading' at the end of every chapter may be said to have filled a real need. Since then, however, the appearance of *History of Political Economy*, the first English specialist journal in the history of economic thought, and the book lists and abstracts of articles in the *Journal of Economic Literature*, coupled with the published *Index to Economic Journals* in fourteen volumes (spanning the period 1886 to 1972 by author and subject), have simplified the problem of keeping up with the literature. Nowadays, a student in search of reading material would be better advised to skip my Notes and go straight to the 135 pages of bibliographical notes appended to H. W. Spiegel, *The Growth of Economic Thought* (1971), which includes almost everything that I cite and much more besides. Nevertheless, I have not discarded the 'Notes on Further Reading' in this third edition of the book, partly because a reader may wish to check my personal preferences among the secondary literature and partly because the Notes serve me as footnotes, listing not only what I recommend to others but also what has particularly influenced me in the course of writing this book. However, in revising and updating these bibliographical essays, I have become more selective than before in the knowledge that obsessive readers have other places to go for encyclopaedic lists of books and articles.

Over the years I have had many unsolicited but welcome reactions from various readers, some of whom have pointed to errors, misprints, and downright mistakes in the text. Their names are too many to mention but I owe a particular debt to D. Hamblin for his careful reading of the previous edition and to S. P. Hersey for similar diligence applied to the present one.

London, England   MARK BLAUG
December, 1976

Preface

Fourth edition

I have sometimes been asked: How should this book be read? 'From beginning to end' is my answer. Nevertheless, this answer never satisfies readers with the maddening habit of dipping into books, browsing through a chapter here and a chapter there. To those readers, I must insist that the arguments build up slowly and that later chapters take for granted knowledge conveyed in earlier ones: I have provided numerous summaries of what has gone before but, nevertheless, cannot hope to make every chapter truly self-contained. Thus, the browser pays a heavy price.

However, for those who persist in starting in the middle of books, the natural breaks in this work are chapters 2–7 on the classical economists, chapters 8–14 on the neoclassical economists, and chapters 1, 5, 15 and 16 on monetary theory and macroeconomics. Chapter 17, the last chapter, stands by itself as a commentary on 250 years of economic theorizing.

The major changes in this edition come in the later chapters of the book on the quantity theory of money and Keynesian economics. I have now taken account of the rise of 'monetarism' and the 'new classical macroeconomics', emphasizing the connections between these recent developments and the older monetary economics of Hume and Ricardo. The persistent debate on 'what Keynes really meant' has accelerated in the 1970s, almost as if the passage of time has aggravated rather than alleviated the problem of making sense of Keynes' arguments. This has resulted in a significant revision of my chapter on Keynes, marking the successive stages in what is now a history of interpretations of Keynes over a period of almost 50 years. I have drastically cut the final chapter on methodology because it duplicates a more detailed discussion of these issues in my book, *The Methodology of Economics* (1980). There is an entirely new chapter on the history of location theory, a subject almost totally neglected in rival histories of economic thought, which is of great interest in its own right and also serves to explain the recent emergence of urban and regional economics as specialized fields of study. There are minor additions to the earlier chapters on Ricardo and Marx and major additions to the middle chapters on marginal productivity and welfare economics, such as new sections on the history of the concept of entrepreneurship and recent developments in the never-ending controversy about marginal cost pricing of public utilities. And, of course, the Notes on Further Readings have been scrupulously updated. Over and above such specific changes, the text in this edition has been pruned and simplified in various places where earlier versions left something to be desired in the way of clarity.

I had hoped to make the fourth edition shorter than the third edition but so great are the pleasures of adding and so great are the pains of cutting that, at the end of the day, I was only too pleased to discover that I had not actually lengthened what is already a much too long book.

London, England   MARK BLAUG
February, 1984

Contents

xvii

Glossary of mathematical symbols in order of appearance

M	=	the stock of money
V	=	the number of times M turns over per time period
T	=	the volume of trade per time period
P	=	the average level of prices in a time period
X_i	=	the annual output of an industry or sector
a_{ij}	=	the input-output coefficient
Y	=	money income
N	=	the number of workers
W	=	total money wages
w	=	the money wage rate
r	=	the rate of profit or the rate of interest
p_i	=	money prices of goods and services
t	=	time
$\bar{W}$	=	total real wages
$\bar{w}$	=	the real wage rate
K	=	the stock of physical capital
$\bar{R}$	=	total real rentals of land
$\bar{\pi}_i$	=	total real profits in an industry or sector
π	=	total money profits
AP	=	the average product of a factor
MP	=	the marginal product of a factor
ε	=	the elasticity of a production function
η	=	the elasticity of an average product function
D_i	=	the demand for goods and services
S_i	=	the supply of goods and services
D_n	=	the demand for money
S_n	=	the supply of money
ED_i	=	the excess demand for commodities
ES_i	=	excess supply of commodities
ED_n	=	excess demand for money
λ	=	an arbitrary positive constant
m	=	the degree of a homogeneous function

κ	=	the demand for cash balances as a fraction of total transactions or total income
M_1	=	the transactions demand for active money balances
M_2	=	the speculative demand for inactive money balances
S	=	planned saving
I	=	ΔK = planned investment
s'	=	the average propensity to save
z	=	the incremental capital-output ratio
G	=	the actual rate of growth of income
u	=	the fraction of the real wages bill spent on luxuries and personal services
ω	=	elasticity of the average revenue function or price elasticity of demand
AR	=	the average revenue of a product
MR	=	marginal revenue of a product
c_i	=	'constant capital'
v_i	=	'variable capital'
k_i	=	$c_i + v_i$
$t_{c,v}$	=	turnover rate of 'constant and variable capital'
$d_{c,v}$	=	durability of 'constant and variable capital'
C	=	fixed capital
V	=	working capital
s	=	'surplus value'
σ	=	'rate of surplus value' per time period
q	=	'organic composition of capital'
q_0	=	the average organic composition of capital in the economy as a whole
Q	=	capital-labour ratio
o_i	=	output of a sector in Marx
t_r	=	turnover rate of raw materials
t_f	=	turnover rate of fixed assets
s_v	=	proportion of 'surplus value' spent on labour
s_c	=	proportion of 'surplus value' spent on consumer goods
s_k	=	proportion of 'surplus value' spent on capital goods
$\bar{s}$	=	disposable 'surplus value'
$\bar{v}$	=	'variable capital' minus salaries
e'	=	'rate of rent'
U	=	total utility
MU	=	marginal utility
MU_n	=	marginal utility of money
MU_e	=	marginal utility of expenditures
MRS	=	marginal rate of substitution of pairs of commodities or factors
MP_N	=	marginal product of labour
MP_K	=	marginal product of capital
p_N	=	price of a unit of labour
p_K	=	price of a unit of capital
MC	=	marginal cost

A	=	total factor productivity
α	=	elasticity of the production function with respect to labour
β	=	elasticity of the production function with respect to capital
$\bar{n}$	=	the real rental per unit of capital
n	=	the money rental per unit of capital
ϕ	=	elasticity of substitution between factors
TR	=	total revenue
TC	=	total cost
ψ	=	elasticity of total costs
AC	=	average cost
τ	=	elasticity of average costs
θ	=	the average period of production
PV	=	present value of future income streams
i	=	the internal rate of return
V_y	=	the income velocity of money
Y_e	=	earned income
Y_d	=	disposable income
Y_p	=	planned income
Y_r	=	realized income
H	=	hoarding
$\dot{p}$	=	the rate of change of prices per time period

Abbreviations:
Journals and anthologies

IEP	–	*International Economic Papers*
IESS	–	*International Encyclopedia of the Social Sciences*, ed. D.L. Sills (1968)
ISSB	–	*International Social Science Bulletin*
JEI	–	*Journal of Economic Issues*
JEL	–	*Journal of Economic Literature*
JHI	–	*Journal of the History of Ideas*
JLE	–	*Journal of Law and Economics*
JMCB	–	*Journal of Money, Credit and Banking*
JMKCA	–	*John Maynard Keynes: Critical Assessments*, ed. J.C. Wood (1983)
JPE	–	*Journal of Political Economy*
JPUE	–	*Journal of Public Economics*
JRS	–	*Journal of Regional Science*
JWH	–	*Journal of World History*
KYK	–	*Kyklos*
MeEc	–	*Metroeconomica*
MME	–	*Marx and Modern Economics*, ed. D. Horowitz (1968)
MS	–	*Manchester School of Economic and Social Studies*
OEP	–	*Oxford Economic Papers*
PDPE	–	*Palgrave's Dictionary of Political Economy*, ed. H. Higgs (1963)
PS	–	*Population Studies*
QJE	–	*Quarterly Journal of Economics*
REA	–	*Readings in Economic Analysis*, ed. R.V. Clemence (1950)
REP	–	*Revue d'économie politique*
REStat	–	*Review of Economics and Statistics*
REStud	–	*Review of Economic Studies*
RHET	–	*Readings in the History of Economic Thought*, ed. I.H. Rima (1970)
RRPE	–	*Review of Radical Political Economics*
RSE	–	*Review of Social Economy*
RPE	–	*Rivista di Politica Economica*
SAJE	–	*South African Journal of Economics*
SEHR	–	*Scandinavian Economic History Review*
SEJ	–	*Southern Economic Journal*
SJPE	–	*Scottish Journal of Political Economy*
SQ	–	*Southwestern Social Science Quarterly*
SR	–	*Social Research*
SS	–	*Science and Society*
SZV	–	*Schweizerische Zeitschrift für Volkswirtschaft*
TEC	–	*The Eighteenth Century. Theory and Interpretation*
UT	–	*Utility Theory. A Book of Readings*, ed. A.N. Page (1968)
WA	–	*Weltwirtschaftliches Archiv*
WEJ	–	*Western Economic Journal*
WP	–	*World Politics*
ZN	–	*Zeitschrift für Nationalœkonomie*

Introduction. Has economic theory progressed?

This is a critical study of the theories of the past: it concentrates on the theoretical analysis of leading economists, neglecting their lives, their own intellectual develop-ment, their precursors, and their propagators. Criticism implies standards of judg-ment, and my standards are those of modern economic theory. This would hardly be worth saying were it not for the fact that some writers on the history of economic thought have held out the prospect of judging past theory in its own terms. Literally speaking, this is an impossible accomplishment for it implies that we can erase from our minds knowledge of modern economics. What they have meant to say, however, is that ideas should be weighed sympathetically in the context of their times, lest the history of economic thought degenerate into a boring exercise in omniscience. The danger of arrogance toward the writers of the past is certainly a real one – but so is ancestor worship. Indeed, there are always two sorts of dangers in evaluating the work of earlier writers: on the one hand, to see only their mistakes and defects without appreciating the limitations both of the analysis they inherited and of the historical circumstances in which they wrote; and, on the other hand, to expand their merits in the eagerness to discover an idea in advance of their own times, and frequently their own intentions. To put it somewhat differently: there is the anthropomorphic sin of judging older writers by the canons of modern theory, but there is also what Samuelson once called 'the sophisticated-anthropomorphic sin of not recognizing the equivalent content in older writers; because they do not use the terminology and symbols of the present'. For an example of the former, take Pigou's reaction when asked to review a work on the *Theories of Value before Adam Smith*: 'These antiquarian researches have no great attraction for one who finds it difficult enough to read what is now thought on economic problems, without spending time in studying confessedly inadequate solutions that were offered centuries ago.' For an example of the latter, take the opening page of any doctoral dissertation on the works of a neglected forerunner.

The conflict between those who regard earlier economic doctrine as simply 'the wrong opinions of dead men' and those who view it as the repository of a series of prescient insights goes deeper than economics. It is a fundamental division of attitude toward intellectual history as such. With a little training in German philosophy it is possible to represent the conflict in terms of two polar opposites:

absolutism and relativism. The relativist regards every single theory put forward in the past as a more or less faithful reflection of contemporary conditions, each theory being in principle equally justified in its own context; the absolutist has eyes only for the strictly intellectual development of the subject, regarded as a steady progression from error to truth. Relativists cannot rank the theories of different periods in terms of better or worse; absolutists cannot help but do so. Now, of course, few commentators have ever held either of these positions in such an extreme form, but almost every historian of economic thought can be placed near one or the other pole of what is in fact a continuum of attitudes to the theories of the past.

Either of the two positions is capable of further subdivision. One version of the relativist position, for example, is that the ideas of economists are nothing more than the rationalization of class or group interests, or, to go one step further, the motivated pleadings of people with a political axe to grind. This is the doctrine of 'ideology' or 'false consciousness' which in its Marxist form is forever equating ideological bias with apologetic intent, though the two are by no means equivalent. The first edition of E. Roll's *History of Economic Thought* (1939) perfectly exemplifies this approach, although in later editions the author goes no further than claiming that changes in economic institutions are 'major influences' – a question-begging phrase! – on economic thinking. Relativism is driven to extremes in W. Stark's *History in Its Relation to Social Development* (1944) which views theories as little more than a mirror reflection of the contemporary world: we are asked to believe, to open the book at random, that Ricardo was justified in advocating a labour theory of value in 1817 because fixed capital was little used at the time, but when he qualified the theory three years later he simply 'yielded to the victorious march of mechanization'.[1] A singularly untenable version of the relativist interpretation is to be found in L. Rogin's study *The Meaning and Validity of Economic Theory* (1956). In appraising the validity of an economic theory, relativists are always likely to ignore considerations of internal coherence and explanatory scope and to fix attention solely on congruence with the historical and political environment. But Rogin goes further and argues that the objective meaning of a particular economic theory lies in its practical policy recommendations; what is worse, he seems to mean by this, not the logical implications of a theory for the policy problems of its time, but rather the policy implications as they appear to a 20th-century economist writing under the influence of the Great Depression. The trouble with the entire thesis is that economic theories are seldom devised to reach specific policy conclusions: time and time again, economists have recommended diametrically opposed policies while appealing to the same theory for authority.

In its moderate versions, the relativist interpretation can yield a really valuable fusion of the history of economic thought with the history of political and moral philosophy against the background of economic and political history. One of the best examples of this broad approach is W. C. Mitchell's lecture notes on *Types of Economic Theory* (1949), which deliberately plays down 'the passing on of ideas

---

[1] Stark's later book, *The Sociology of Knowledge* (1959), a really stimulating work, suggests that he no longer adheres to this extreme position.

from one to another and the development of these ideas by successive generations' as 'an intellectual stunt'. The same viewpoint is upheld in A. Gray's delightful introductory survey, *The Development of Economic Doctrine* (1931): 'Economic science, if it be a science, differs from other sciences in this, that there is no inevitable advance from less to greater certainty; there is no ruthless tracking down of truth which, once unbared, shall be truth to all times to the complete confusion of any contrary doctrine.' A glance at the latter portions of Mitchell's or Gray's book, dealing with the period after 1870, shows immediately what is wrong with the argument. Economics only became an academic subject in the 1880s, and thereafter, for the first time perhaps, 'the passing on of ideas from one to another' did dominate the development of the subject. No relativist has been able to carry the institutional or historical interpretation beyond the classical era that ended around 1870; and so, like Mitchell and Gray, they either neglect the modern period or, like Roll and Rogin, shift grounds in their treatment of economic ideas after 1870.

Speaking generally, it is absurd to think that economic and social history alone can furnish the key to intellectual variations in a discipline like economics. Many relativists claim only that economists write always *sub specie temporis* and that a knowledge of the prevailing historical context 'illuminates' the theories of the past. This is obviously true, but one wonders why it is necessary to argue this so insistently unless it is subtly designed to make us forget that ideas have a momentum of their own. As Jacob Viner observed, relativism frequently amounts to a kind of whitewashing with historical necessity:

> The economic historians seem to derive from their valid doctrine, that if sufficient information were available the prevalence in any period of a particular theory could be *explained* in the light of the circumstances then prevailing, the curious corollary that they can also be *justified* by appeal to these special circumstances. There are some obvious obstacles to acceptance of this point of view. It would lead to the conclusion that no age, except apparently the present one, is capable of serious doctrinal error. It overlooks the fact that one of the historical circumstances which has been undergoing an evolution has been the capacity of economic analysis (*Studies in the Theory of International Trade*, p. 110.)

No assumptions about economic behavior are absolutely true and no theoretical conclusions are valid for all times and places, but would anyone seriously deny that in the matter of techniques and analytical constructs there has been progress in economics? Adam Smith, for example, had a firm grasp of the way in which the market mechanism is capable of coordinating the independent decisions of buyers and sellers, but anything so fundamental as the functional relationship of demand and price escaped him. It never occcurred to him that it was possible to demonstrate precisely in what sense a decentralized economy produces optimum results and it took a hundred years before Walras, Marshall, Pigou, and Pareto worked out the logic of Smith's convictions about the workings of 'the invisible hand'. Thoughts such as these produce the absolutist who, looking down from present heights at the errors of the ancients, cannot help but conclude that truth is largely concentrated in the marginal increment to economic knowledge.

It is very likely that absolutists are created by reading the works of too many relativists. It is difficult nowadays to appreciate the freshness of Cannan's iconoclastic approach in his famous book *The History of the Theories of Production and Distribution* (1893) – a veritable catalog of the elementary blunders of great economists – to a generation nurtured on the relativist texts of Blanqui, Roscher, Ingram and Cossa. Nevertheless, the recognition that economic theory has indeed progressed should not be allowed to obscure the highly uneven rate of improvement which has typified the history of analytical progress in economics. General insights into the pure logic of the price system make their appearance embedded in a particular theoretical framework associated with conditions and problems peculiar to the times. As the body of ideas gives way under criticism, much of what is still valuable gets discarded in an enthusiasm over the latest novelty. As a result, the history of economics is not so much the chronicle of a continuous accumulation of theoretical achievements as the story of exaggerated intellectual revolutions in which truths already known are neglected in favour of new revelations. Indeed, sometimes it seems as if economics has been propelled forward by a sense of symmetry which demands that every new theory should always be the exact reverse of the old.

In the first half of the 19th century, economics itself was regarded as an investigation of 'the nature and causes of the wealth of nations' (Smith), 'the laws which regulate the distribution of the produce of the earth' (Ricardo), and 'the laws of motion of capitalism' (Marx). After 1870, however, economics came to be regarded as a science that analyzed 'human behaviour as a relationship between given ends and scarce means which have alternative uses' – an apt definition formulated in 1932 by Robbins, which, if taken strictly, would deny that much of what had gone before was economics. After two centuries of being concerned with the growth of resources and the rise of wants, economics after 1870 became largely a study of the principles that govern the efficient allocation of resources when both resources and wants are given. Classical economic theory was as much macro as microeconomics; neoclassical theory was nothing but microeconomics; macroeconomics came back into its own with Keynes and for a decade or so virtually replaced microeconomics. It is doubtful whether such dramatic shifts in the focus of attention can be explained solely in terms of intellectual forces – as absolutists are inclined to argue. In the final analysis, even pure economic theory is framed for the purpose of throwing light upon the actual workings of the economic system. A change of emphasis as drastic as 'the marginal revolution' or the Keynesian Revolution must surely have been associated with changes in the institutional structure of society and with the emergence of new practical problems?

One possibility is that such shifts in emphasis within economics are due to changes in philosophical attitudes or dominant modes of reasoning. It was in opposition to this relativist interpretation that Schumpeter insisted upon the strictly autonomous nature of scientific economics. Although the political preferences and philosophical value judgments of economists impinge upon the development of economics, he declared, they leave it fundamentally unaffected: 'economic analysis has not been shaped at any time by the philosophical opinions that economists happen to have'.

This piece of dogmatic 'positivism', put forward in the introduction to his erudite *History of Economic Analysis* (1954), is not in fact sustained in the body of the text, half of which is given over to narrative history, political theory, and philosophical climates of opinion, presumably because of their relevance to economic theory. Upon close inspection it turns out that Schumpeter did not mean that economic analysis is *logically* independent of philosophy but rather that the philosophical beliefs of economists are not relevant to the *validity* of the economic hypotheses they advance. The latter point is only too well taken. Witness the numerous pseudo-explanations that treat the history of economic thought in terms of a struggle between contending philosophical principles: 'individualism' versus 'universalism' – O. Spann, *The History of Economics* (1930); the biological view of the economic system as an organism versus the mechanical view of the system as a machine – E. Heimann, *History of Economic Doctrines* (1945); or, for that matter, value-free versus value-impregnated social science in G. Myrdal's brilliant *Political Element in the Development of Economic Thought* (1953), which ridicules the effort to free economics from value judgments and, by implication, deprecates every analytical insight that is found to be associated with philosophical or political preconceptions.

Indeed, why stop at philosophical or political bias? W. Weisskopf in *The Psychology of Economics* (1955) gets the great economists to lie down on the couch, discovering, for example, a new significance in Petty's famous remark that 'land is the mother and labour the father of value'. For Ricardo and Malthus, he observes, the fecundity of the human female and the niggardliness of Mother Earth are the roots of all economic ills, while the only source of value is the 'male' factor of labour. But this is just how we would expect people to think in a patriarchal civilization, he concludes triumphantly. Certainly it is conceivable that a knowledge of the psychological quirks of great economists might throw some light on their theories, but to infer the theories from the psychological association of words is to ignore the systematic logical character and empirical content of economic analysis.

It may be granted that, even in its purest form, economic theory has implications for policy and in that sense makes political propaganda of one kind or another. This element of propaganda is inherent in the subject and, even when a thinker studiously maintains a sense of Olympian detachment, philosophical and political preferences enter at the very beginning of the analysis in the formation of, as Schumpeter would have it, his 'vision': the preanalytical act of selecting certain features of reality for examination. The problem is not that of denying the presence of propaganda but that of separating the scientific ideas from the ideology in which they are invariably embedded and to submit these ideas to scientific tests of validation. Moreover, propaganda is not the same thing as lying: to say that Karl Marx wanted to discredit capitalism and began with preconceptions about its defects is not to imply that his analysis is for that reason worthless. Political prejudices may even assist scientific analysis: a critic of capitalism is likely to pay more attention to the real blemishes of the system and it is surely no accident, for example, that Marx's comments on business cycles were fifty years ahead of his time.

The task of the historian of economic thought is to show how definite preconceptions lead to definite kinds of analysis and then to ask whether the analysis stands up when it is freed from its ideological foundation. It is doubtful whether Ricardo would have developed his theory of international trade without a strong animus against the landed classes; but this theory survives the removal of his prejudices. When it came to proving that landlords would have no interest in making agricultural improvements, however, ideological bias prevented him from arriving at the correct result, correct, that is, in terms of his own assumptions. The history of economic thought is full of such examples, and nothing is gained by laying down flat generalizations about the relationship between the value judgments of individual economists and the quality of their theoretical work. Propaganda and ideology are always there, but so is the discipline exerted by rules of scientific procedure built into economics by generations of practitioners: economics is forever catching up with the biases of yesterday.

The problem that gave rise to economics in the first place, the 'mystery' that fascinated Adam Smith as much as it does a modern economist, is that of market exchange: there is a sense of order in the economic universe, and this order is not imposed from above but is somehow the outcome of the exchange transactions between individuals, each seeking to maximize his own gain. The history of economic thought, therefore, is nothing but the history of our efforts to understand the workings of an economy based on market transactions. But whereas received doctrine has always been concerned with the analysis of market economies, the structure of these economies has changed significantly over time and, in each generation, different concepts and methods of analysis have been employed to throw light on these changes. It is impossible to employ the findings of one method of analysis – appropriate to a particular economic environment – to pass judgment on the findings of another method appropriate to a different setting: one model cannot be used to judge another. Are we then driven into the arms of relativism? Surely, there are universal standards that can be applied to all theories?

Science, we have been told often enough, consists of the endless process of trying to falsify hypotheses. In that sense, the body of acceptable economic knowledge at any moment comprises all the theories that have not yet been falsified. But how are economic theories falsified? The great difficulty of testing economic theories, whether ancient or modern, is not so much the impossibility of making controlled experiments and thus disproving theories once and for all but rather that, lacking suitable labouratory conditions, economists (and for that matter all social scientists) cannot agree on definite empirical criteria for falsifying a hypothesis. Worse than that, they frequently disagree about the fundamental character of a theory. For example, was the neoclassical theory of perfect competition advanced as a hypothesis about how firms and households actually behave, or was it intended to furnish ideal standards for judging whether they behaved as they should? If the former is the correct interpretation, congruence with observed market behavior is indeed the test of the validity of the theory, but if the latter, the fact that no existing market structure corresponds to the conditions laid down in the theory is a challenge to economic policy. It may be, of course, that the theory of perfect competition is both a 'positive' and a 'normative' theory, depending on the purpose for which it is used. Positive theories about the social order cannot, in the nature of the case, be conclusively falsified by a single adverse result. An element of judgment inevitably enters into their evaluation and it is precisely for this reason that relativists and absolutists can continue to argue about the validity of the doctrine of comparative cost or the relevance of the labour theory of value. Normative theories, on the other hand, can never be evaluated by empirical tests. To make matters even more confusing, there are many examples in economics of theories which appear to be neither positive nor normative but merely taxonomic, providing an elabourate set of pigeonholes into which economic phenomena can be classified – Walrasian general equilibrium theory is a perfect example. Must we ruthlessly eliminate all such theories in the interest of 'the principle of falsifiability'?

The history of economic thought is a proving ground for answering such questions. How much economics is simply taxonomy travelling in disguise? How have economists reacted to normative theories? What positive theories have been falsified by comparing their predictions with the real world? The answers lie in what economics has been: the practice of past generations still shapes what economics now is.

We opened the chapter with the declaration: 'Criticism implies standards of judgment, and my standards are those of modern economic theory.' Enough has been said to show that even this innocent sentence is subject to a variety of interpretations, and indeed at times it is not at all obvious what it means to apply the standards of modern economics. Where are the standards that we all nowadays approve? Could this be why we still need to worry about the history of economic thought?

And so, has there been progress in economic theory? Clearly, the answer is yes: analytical tools have been continuously improved and augmented; empirical data have been increasingly marshalled to verify economic hypotheses, metaeconomic biases have been repeatedly exposed and separated from the core of testable propositions which they enmesh; and the workings of the economic system are better understood than ever before. And yet the relativists do have a point. The development of economic thought has not taken the form of a linear progression toward present truths. While it has progressed, many have been the detours imposed by the exigencies of time and place. Therefore, whether we adopt a relativist or absolutist interpretation of the subject depends entirely on the questions that we wish to raise. If a commentator is interested in explaining why certain people held certain ideas at certain times, he must look outside the sphere of intellectual debate for a complete answer. But if he wants to know why some economists in the past held a labour theory of value while others believed that value is determined by utility, and this is not only at the same time and in the same country but also in different countries generations apart, he is forced to concentrate on the internal logic of theory, willy-nilly becoming an absolutist.

If in the chapters that follow, there is little about *Zeitgeist*, social milieu, economic institutions and philosophical currents, it is not because these things are unimportant but because they fall outside the scope of our inquiry. What do economists know?

How much does economics explain? What are the standards by which economic
theories have been accepted or rejected? What features have characterized endurable economic ideas? What practical use is economic knowledge? These are the
questions to which this book is addressed. We will come back to these questions in
the last chapter. But, of course, the answers will keep turning up on every second
page of what follows.

NOTES ON FURTHER READING

The outstanding single reading on the various themes touched on in this introduction – why do
we bother with the history of economics?; is economics a science?; how does a history of
economic analysis differ from a history of economic thought? – is J.A. Schumpeter, *History of
Economic Analysis* (1954), Part I, chaps. 1, 2, 3, and 4, and particularly chap. 4. We shall refer
to this book so frequently that perhaps this is the place to say that this undoubted masterpiece is
full of prejudices and idiosyncrasies, and any student who finds himself overawed by it ought to
provide himself with antidotes: see the major review articles by J. Viner, *AER*, December,
1954, and L. Robins, *QJE*, 1955, reprinted in his *Evolution of Modern Economic Theory*
(1970), as well as the reactions of F.H. Knight, *SEJ*, January, 1954; O.H. Taylor, *REStat*,
February, 1955; I.M.D. Little, *EHR*, August, 1955; G.B. Richardson, *OEP*, June, 1955;
W. Stark, *KYK*, XII, 1, 1959; and R.L. Meek, *SJPE*, February, 1957. See also D.F. Gordon,
'The Role of the History of Economic Thought in the Understanding of Modern Economic
Theory', *AER*, May, 1965; and F.W. Fetter, 'The Relation of the History of Economic Thought
to Economic History', *ibid*.
    Those who wish to pursue the distinction between relativism and absolutism must compare
the differences in interpretation of specific authors and doctrines in the many available histories
of economics; the subject lacks critical surveys of this kind to which the student may be referred.
A good way to start is to consult O. Popescu, 'On the Historiography of Economic Thought: A
Bibliographical Survey', *JWH*, VIII, 1, 1964, which lists and discusses some one hundred
histories between 1824 and 1963. J.J. Spengler, 'Exogenous and Endogenous Influences in the
Formation of Post-1870 Economic Thought', *Events, Ideology, and Economic Theory*, ed.
R.V. Eagly (1968), argues persuasively that the professionalization of economics after 1870
strengthens the absolutist interpretation of modern economics. The argument is continued in
A.F. Chalk, 'Relativist and Absolutist Approaches to the History of Economic Theory', *SQ*,
48, 1967; J.J. Spengler, 'Economics: Its History, Themes, Approaches', *JEI*, March, 1968; and
C.D. Goodwin, 'Toward a Theory of the History of Economics', *HOPE*, Winter, 1980. The
opposition between relativist and absolutist interpretations is nicely exemplified by J. Robinson's *Economic Philosophy* (1962, and in paperback). This vigorous, opinionated little book
might serve as an introduction to the whole subject, provided the student is not discouraged by
its deeply cynical tone. Robinson traces the development of economics from the classical
writers through the neoclassical economists to the Keynesians, showing how economics
sometimes reflected social conditions, sometimes the policy preoccupations of the time, but
almost always – and this is her main thesis – underlying metaphysical assumptions and
ideological preconceptions. It all depends on what is meant by 'reflected'; in her approach it is
difficult to see what, if anything, is scientific as distinct from ideological economics.
    D.N. Winch, 'What Price the History of Economic Thought?', *SJPE*, November, 1962,
explains the waning of interest in the history of economic thought since World War II. He goes
on to deplore histories of economic analysis that leave out everything that would interest a
historian or a student of social thought – in other words, books such as the present one – which,
he argues, have encouraged indifference to the writings of the great economists. He is
supported in this view by L. Nabers, 'The Positive and Genetic Approaches', *The Structure of
Economic Science. Essays on Methodology*, ed. S.R. Krupp (1966), and W.J. Samuels, 'The

History of Economic Thought as Intellectual History', *HOPE*, Fall, 1974. B.A. Corry, 'Should Economists Abandon HOPE?', *ibid.*, Summer, 1975; K.E. Boulding, 'After Samuelson, Who Needs Adam Smith?', *ibid.*, 1971, reprinted in *ASCA*, III, and R.L. Heilbroner, 'Modern Economics as a Chapter in the History of Economic Thought', *ibid.*, Summer, 1979, argue a different case but all of them agree that part of the problem lies in the way that the history of economic thought has been studied. Suffice it to say that there is room for a variety of approaches to the history of economics and it is not at all obvious to me that narrow absolutism has done more harm to the subject than shallow relativism. But let the argument continue: that is what the history of economic thought ought to be about.

1

Pre-Adamite economics

MERCANTILISM

The term 'mercantilism' first acquired significance at the hands of Adam Smith. 'The different progress of opulence in different ages and nations has given occasion to two different systems of political economy, with regard to enriching the people', he noted: 'the system of commerce' or 'mercantile system' and 'the system of agriculture'. These two systems, however, are not quite on the same footing. Quesnay and his band of disciples, whom posterity has agreed to call the Physiocrats – *les économistes* was their own designation – presented a common front and formed a definite school of opinion. But the English pamphlet writers of the 17th and 18th centuries showed no awareness of contributing to any definite stream of ideas, much less to a tradition that Adam Smith attacked under the rubric of mercantilism. They had neither agreed principles nor common analytical tools. Nevertheless, throughout the three hundred years of uncoordinated intellectual effort, full of controversy and reflecting a great variety of practical circumstances, certain doctrinal threads appear again and again. It is these threads that we knit together into something called 'mercantilism', thereby imposing a far greater sense of unity and logical coherence upon the literature than it in fact possessed. In recent times, mercantilism, as a label for a phase in the history of economic policy, has been called a 'cumbersome portmanteau', 'a red-herring of historiography', and 'a gigantic theoretical balloon'. But as a description of a central tendency in economic thought from the close of the 16th to the middle of the 18th century, the label retains general validity. Certainly, for our purposes, there is great convenience in looking comprehensively at the predecessors of Adam Smith much in the same way that he did.

1. The-Balance-of-Trade Doctrine

The leading features of the mercantilist outlook are well known: gold bullion and treasure of every kind as the essence of wealth; regulation of foreign trade to produce an inflow of gold and silver; promotion of industry by inducing cheap raw-material imports; protective duties on imported manufactured goods; encouragement of exports, particularly finished goods; and an emphasis on population growth, keeping wages low. The core of mercantilism, of course, is the doctrine that a favourable balance of trade is desirable because it is somehow productive of national prosperity.

The question that immediately arises is how such a notion ever came to be held. Adam Smith gave the first and still the simplest answer: mercantilism is nothing but a tissue of protectionist fallacies foisted upon a venal Parliament by 'our merchants and manufacturers', grounded upon 'the popular notion that wealth consists in money'. Like an individual, a country must spend less than its income if its wealth is to increase. What tangible form does this surplus over consumption take? The mercantilist authors identified it with the acquisition of hard money or 'treasure'. Money was falsely equated with capital, and the favourable balance of trade with the annual balance of income over consumption. This was the gist of Adam Smith's critique of mercantilism.

Since the days of Adam Smith, commentators have never ceased to debate this question: did the mercantilists really equate money with capital, or, to use the old-fashioned words, specie with wealth? Considering the extraordinary looseness with which writers in those days used such common, everyday words, it is hardly surprising that the literature admits of more than one interpretation. 'Some of the best English writers on commerce', Smith conceded, citing Thomas Mun and John Locke, 'do set out with observing, that the wealth of a country consists, not in its gold and silver only, but in its lands, houses, and consumable goods of all different kinds; in the course of their reasoning, however, the lands, houses, and consumable goods seem to slip out of their memory, and the strain of their argument frequently supposes that all wealth consists in gold and silver.' In estimating the value of property in England at the close of the 17th century, William Petty concluded that the quantity of money comprised less than 3 percent of total property, and in his *Taxes and Contributions* (1662) he opposed the indefinite accumulation of bullion by appealing to what we will call the 'needs-of-trade doctrine' about the quantity of money: 'There is a certain measure and due proportion requisite to drive the trade of a Nation, more or less than which would prejudice the same.' Nevertheless, this did not stop later writers from making the quantity of money synonymous with national wealth or from calling for a permanently favourable balance of trade.

It is easy to cite moderate mercantilists who did not identify money with capital and who followed Aristotle in emphasizing the purely conventional nature of money, but it is also true that almost all mercantilist writers entertained the illusion that money is somehow *nervus rerum*. Money is 'the life of commerce', 'the vital spirit of trade', 'like muck', as Bacon put it, 'not good except it be spread'. Such animistic imagery was epitomized in the 18th-century doctrine that 'money stimulates trade', but it was current for centuries without any apparent theoretical justification. In the final analysis, it is pointless to argue the question because the absence of a technical vocabulary in the literature of the day makes it almost impossible to distinguish between the axiomatic identification of money with wealth and the broad suggestion that an increase of one will always cause an increase of the other.

2. The Specie-Flow Mechanism

If mercantilism in its more sophisticated formulations did not confuse money with capital, why the universal concern at that time with a favourable balance of trade?

What advantage was an excess of exports over imports supposed to confer upon a country? Once again, the lack of a common terminology and the preanalytic character of the literature makes it difficult to know what was meant when a writer gave expression to the desirability of an export surplus. Does it imply something as silly as that a favourable balance of trade is the only source of wealth for a nation, or that it is the sole advantage that a nation derives from foreign trade, or is it merely a way of speaking to justify measures which are regarded as advantageous on other grounds? Whatever the precise interpretation, the idea that an export surplus is *the* index of economic welfare may be described as the basic fallacy that runs through the whole of the mercantilist literature. The title of Thomas Mun's book puts it nicely: *England's Treasure by Forraign Trade, or the Ballance of our Forraign Trade Is the Rule of Our Treasure* (1664). But even this statement of the basic fallacy of mercantilism has been denied. One student of English mercantilism, E.A.J. Johnson, declared that 'the ultimate concern of the mercantilists was the creation of effective factors of production. Not ten per cent of English mercantilist literature is devoted to the ill-fated doctrine of the balance of trade', to which Viner retorted that 'on the basis of my turning of the pages of English mercantilist literature I venture the conclusion that not ten per cent of it was free from concern, expressed or clearly implied, in the state of the balance of trade and in the means whereby it could be improved'. It is, of course, no fallacy to be concerned with the balance of trade. What distinguishes mercantilist theory is a fixation on the balance of trade and a fixation on the objective of maintaining an imbalance of trade even in the long run.

The balance of *payments* must always be balanced, for it is merely a book-keeping identity of debits and credits (we do talk about 'deficits' and 'surpluses' in international payments but only by excluding certain debits and credits from a set of accounts which must always be in balance when taken as a whole). But the balance of *trade* need not be in balance. A country earns foreign exchange by either (1) visible commodity exports, (2) invisible exports of services, (3) export of precious metals, or (4) *im*ports of capital, either in the form of foreign investment at home, profits on its own foreign investment abroad, or loans granted by foreigners. A country spends foreign exchange by (1) visible imports, (2) invisible imports, (3) imports of precious metals, and (4) *ex*ports of capital in the general form of acquiring claims on foreigners. The four items always balance because if the first three do not, the difference appears as a capital export or import. When mercantilist authors speak of a surplus in the balance of *trade*, however, they mean an excess of exports, both visible and invisible, over imports, calling either for an inflow of gold or for the granting of credit to foreign countries, that is, capital exports. In other words, they were roughly thinking of what we would now call 'the current account' as distinct from 'the capital account' in the balance of payments.

The classical economists never doubted that the arguments of their predecessors in favour of a chronic export surplus were based from start to finish on an intellectual confusion: whatever the mercantilists hoped to achieve with a favourable balance of trade was bound to be short-lived. Thomas Mun, writing as early as 1630, had realized that an inflow of bullion raises domestic prices and that 'selling dear and buying cheap' tends to turn the balance of trade against a country. Cantillon and Hume restated this argument in the 18th century and for a century or more this 'specie-flow mechanism' provided the definitive refutation of mercantilist principles. Purely automatic forces, the argument ran, tend to establish a 'natural distribution of specie' between the trading countries of the world and levels of domestic prices in different countries such that each country's exports come to be equal to its imports. Any additional mining of gold in one country will raise its price level relative to those of other countries; the resulting import surplus must be financed by a specie outflow; this engenders the same reaction in the gold-receiving country; and the process continues until all trading nations have established a new equilibrium between exports and imports corresponding to the higher supply of gold. Since external trade and gold are akin to water in two connected vessels that is constantly seeking a common level, a policy aiming at a favourable balance of trade is simply self-defeating.

All the elements forming such a theory of the self-regulatory mechanism of specie distribution were already at hand in the 17th century. Thomas Mun had shown that any net deficit or surplus in the balance on current account, the visible plus invisible items, must be financed by the outflow or inflow of bullion and, hence, that the volume of exports and imports depends upon relative price levels in different countries. Writing in the 1690s, John Locke made it perfectly clear that prices vary in a definite proportion to the quantity of money in circulation. All that was required was to put these ideas together and it would follow that concern over the long-run state of the balance of trade was unnecessary. Although Adam Smith does not refer to the specie-flow mechanism in *The Wealth of Nations* – one of the great mysteries of the history of economic thought, as Viner observes, because he had discussed it in his earlier *Lectures* – it is this kind of reasoning that prompted the classical economists to dismiss the writings of the mercantilists as confused and self-contradictory.

The classical economists might have added that the hearty protectionist sentiments of the time caused many mercantilist writers to employ the 'balance-of-labour' argument in favour of import restrictions without any reference to the balance of trade, or else to invoke the latter only to reinforce the former. It was widely held that imports should consist of raw materials and semifabricated goods produced by capital-intensive methods, whereas exports should consist of finished goods produced by labour-intensive methods on the grounds that a net outflow of labour services sustains domestic employment and increases 'foreign-paid incomes'. To this familiar protectionist argument were added the military, the strategic and the infant-industry arguments. To a later age that had discovered the Law of Comparative Cost as well as the Automatic Specie-Flow Mechanism, this seemed like error compounded upon error.

3. The Defense of Mercantilism

The stern condemnation visited upon mercantilist errors by classical theory went unchallenged for a hundred years. The relativist interpretation of mercantilism had to wait upon the revival of protectionism in Europe and the rise of the German

Historical School. First, Roscher, Schmoller and then their English disciples, Cunningham and Ashley, rose to defend mercantilist policies as perfectly rational in the sense that they were appropriate means to achieve certain desired ends, namely, those of national autarky and the expansion of state power, and even these ends were now regarded as reasonable in and for their time. This interpretation came to be widely accepted by economic historians. When Adam Smith at one point commented carelessly that 'defence is more important than opulence', he was stating a position that mercantilist writers were said to have held seriously. This viewpoint helps to throw light on one of the central beliefs of the mercantilist age: the goal of state building can be achieved just as well, if not better, by weakening the economic powers of neighbors as by strengthening one's own. As Locke expressed it, 'riches' means not just more gold and silver but more in proportion to other countries. Indeed, most mercantilist writers subscribed to the view that the economic interests of nations are mutually antagonistic, as if there were a fixed quantity of resources in the world that one country could acquire only at the expense of another. This explains why they were not embarrassed to advocate beggar-my-neighbor policies or to deprecate domestic consumption as an objective of national policy.

Even if we grant that state power was the sole end of mercantilist policies, with wealth valued solely as a means thereto – an interpretation that Viner has called into question – little has been said to remove the stigma of intellectual error in mercantilist theory. For a full-blown defense we must go to Keynes's provocative 'Notes on Mercantilism' in *The General Theory* (1936). As soon as it is realized that an economic system does not automatically tend toward a state of full employment, Keynes argued, the whole of the classical case against protectionist policies, based upon the advantages of the international division of labour, loses much of its force: 'As a contribution to statecraft, which is concerned with the economic system as a whole and with securing the optimum employment of the system's entire resources, the methods of the early pioneers of economic thinking in the 16th and 17th centuries may have attained to fragments of practical wisdom which the unrealistic abstractions of Ricardo first forgot and then obliterated.' The preoccupation of the mercantilists with gold inflows was no 'puerile obsession', Keynes declared, but an intuitive recognition of the connection between plenty of money and low interest rates. Moreover, there has always been a 'chronic tendency throughout human history for the propensity to save to be stronger than the inducement to invest', and the mercantilists must be praised for recognizing that the weakness of the inducement to invest is the key to the economic problem. When direct public investment or monetary policy is out of the question, as it was before modern times, the best that could be done was to encourage inflation through a favourable balance of trade: the export surplus serves to keep up prices and the inflow of gold lowers interest rates, thus stimulating investment and employment by boosting the money supply. This, Keynes felt, was 'the element of scientific truth in mercantilist doctrine'.

4. Precursors of Keynes?
No doubt the English economists of the 17th and 18th centuries often sound like precursors of Keynes. They railed against 'locking up money', converting it into

'dead stock'; they urged spending on luxury goods and proposed public works programs to relieve 'supernumeraries'; and the frequency with which statements concerning the desirability of bullion were associated with a belief in its employment-producing effect is indeed striking. But this is not to say that the writers of the period had a pre-Keynesian appreciation of the problem of aggregate effective demand. Keynes's defense of mercantilism seems to rest in part on the modern inference that a persistently favourable balance of trade must be associated with the export of capital as an offsetting item, thus absorbing excess savings at home. But foreign investment plays no role in mercantilist analysis and there are no instances of arguments in favour of maintaining a steady flow of foreign investment before James Steuart, writing in the 1760s. The basic flaw in Keynes's interpretation, however, as Heckscher points out in his critique of Keynes's 'Notes on Mercantilism', is the belief that unemployment in the mercantilist era was similar in character to technological and cyclical unemployment recurrent in industrialized economies. Unemployment caused by a fall in fixed investment was virtually unknown before the Industrial Revolution. In 17th-century England, a predominantly rural economy, most unemployment was due to the seasonal nature of agriculture or to the incidence of poor harvests. Even in industry, much unemployment was seasonal, as winter ice or spring floods interrupted the functioning of the water-powered mills. A trade crisis might produce cyclical unemployment that called for special remedial measures, but the kind of unemployment that attracted the attention of the mercantilists was voluntary unemployment in the sense of a sheer disinclination to work in workshops and factories and a marked preference for leisure instead of higher earnings: the problem was not Keynesian involuntary unemployment but what was charmingly referred to as 'an idle and debauched populace'.

This brings up a distinction that will recur again in the course of our analysis: the distinction between what, for obvious reasons, has been called Keynesian and Marxian unemployment. Keynesian unemployment denotes a situation in which the flow of investment is insufficient to mop up the savings that would be forthcoming at full-employment levels of income. Because of relative overabundance of physical capital, rates of return are too low to call forth the investment required to produce full employment. Marxian unemployment, on the other hand, is the result of scarcity of capital relative to the labour supply; inappropriate resource endowments and the limited technical possibilities of substituting labour for capital make it impossible to absorb the labour that is available, even when the capital stock is used to capacity. Marxian unemployment is the result of either excessive population growth or income levels too low to produce an adequate flow of savings, combined with a primitive, rigid technology. Too little thrift, not insufficient effective demand, impedes the expansion of output. Marxian unemployment is a structural, not a cyclical, problem; and for that reason public investment of expansionary monetary policy, effective in curing Keynesian unemployment, will merely produce inflation without leading to full employment. The symptom is the same in either case, but the successful cure is not, since the nature of the illness is quite different. It follows that the analogy to the problem of unemployment as it appears in the mercantilist literature is not underemployment in a mature capitalist economy but actual or disguised unemployment in the now overpopulated underdeveloped countries of Asia, Africa, and Latin America. Keynes' interpretation of mercantilism is merely another example of his penchant to appraise all previous theories in terms of his own and to generalize the problems of his own times throughout human history.

When writers in the 17th and 18th centuries praised luxury spending on the part of the rich, their rationale was the belief that 'high living' on the part of the well-to-do generates wants and stimulates pecuniary incentives all round. An underdeveloped economy with rudimentary labour markets is very likely, as we know from modern experience, to develop the idea that the upper classes have an obligation to provide work by maintaining a large retinue of 'menial servants'. Dr Johnson expressed orthodox 18th-century opinion when he told Boswell: 'You cannot spend money in luxury without doing good to the poor. Nay, you do more good by spending it in luxury than by giving it; for by spending it you make them exert industry, whereas by giving it you keep them idle.' As for the mercantilist approval of public works, that was frequently based on nothing more than the typical belief in the magical efficacy of state action, simply because it is action undertaken in the public interest. Sometimes a trade depression caused a contemporary writer to advocate public works and, in the careless manner of the day, a recommendation designed to alleviate an immediate problem might get itself expressed as permanent advice. There is very little in the literature to suggest that concern over employment-promoting schemes stemmed from a recognition that underemployment was due to a failure of effective demand. Worse than that, schemes were recommended without any attention to the necessity of stimulating saving or of providing appropriate institutions to transmit such funds as were saved to potential investors.

5. Rational Elements in Mercantilist Theory

Despite Heckscher's cogent criticism of Keynes' unhistorical interpretation, his own analysis of mercantilism displays an almost absurd irritation with anything that smacks of economic determinism. He not only attributes every mercantilist proposition to the powerful hold of fallacious economic ideas but goes so far as to assert that 'there are no grounds whatever for supposing that the mercantilist writers constructed their system ... out of any knowledge of reality however derived' – a perfect example of the absolutist position. Now it is true that the mercantilists had indeed little interest in the practical use of precious metals for war chests or for final export; nor did they desire bullion to overcome a physical shortage of metal to mint coins. Certainly, 'scarcity of money' was a frequent complaint at the time, but even mercantilist writers realized that a genuine shortage of coin can be remedied by clipping or by issuing paper money and that such complaints frequently involve a confusion between a mismanaged currency – scarcity of coins of a particular denomination – and stringency of credit in periods of slack trade. But recently a British historian, Charles Wilson, has submitted evidence to show that the desire for hard money in the mercantilist era had merits under the then prevailing circumstances that it later lost: the conditions of British trade with the Baltics and the East Indies were such as to make it necessary to achieve international liquidity through acquisition of stocks of precious metals. England produced virtually nothing that could have been exported owing to the then underdeveloped international money market. To obtain Baltic wheat and Indian 'spices' – and 'spices' at that time meant not merely seasonings but all Oriental wares such as textiles, dyes, sugar, coffee, tea and saltpeter, items for which no adequate substitutes could be produced in Europe – Britain had to squeeze her colonial trade to yield precious metals. Thus the economic setting of the mercantilist world made free multilateral trade unworkable and required a system of bilateral controls. In his reply to this argument, Heckscher maintained that foreign exchange markets in the 16th and 17th centuries were sufficiently developed to permit currency exchange, but he admitted that the mercantilists had good reasons to be concerned about the Indian drain on bullion supplies. Be that as it may, this debate does suggest hitherto unsuspected elements of rationality in mercantilist thought.

One may wonder why the mercantilists themselves never drew attention to the peculiarities of trade with the Baltics and the East Indies. The answer, of course, is that they never recognized it as particularly unusual. As a matter of fact, the whole body of mercantilist theory involves unspoken assumptions about the real world, assumptions that may have been so obvious to observers at the time that they were not worth mentioning. The static conception of economic activity as a zero-sum game, so that one man's or one country's gain was another's loss, the tacit acceptance of limited wants, a prevailing inelastic demand, weak pecuniary incentives – these were all notions that one would expect to be held in a preindustrialized economy accustomed to a growth of output and population so slow as to be barely discernible. At a time when foreign trade was notable for windfall gains – those were the days of buccaneering imperialism – when domestic trade was confined to particular localities and carried on only sporadically, and when regularity of employment and factory discipline were virtually unknown, what was more natural than to think that only beggar-my-neighbor policies could enrich a nation, that a favourable trade balance constituted a net addition to sales on a more or less limited home market and that higher wages would decrease, not increase, the supply of labour? Such general attitudes to economic life are so firmly rooted in reality as hardly to need stating, but they alone explain why reasonable men could have held the doctrines that were advanced in that age.

This does not mean that misconceptions and even downright fallacies played no role. After all, the balance-of-trade doctrine was already current in the 15th century and had been espoused at various times as early as the 14th. The notion that bullion supplied 'the sinews of war' had genuine appeal in the days of Henry VIII and when Henry squandered the state treasure this idea persisted, fed by the rational fear of illiquidity in an era when credit institutions were little developed. Protectionist sentiment, popular in any age, but particularly in one that took state regulation of foreign trade for granted, clung easily to the innocent identification of money and capital encouraged by analogies between public and personal finance, the oldest of all economic fallacies. The undisciplined pamphleteers, swept along on the tide of public belief, found striking and sometimes cogent reasons for defending the mercantilist economics of the man in the street and, in grappling with the logical consequences of premises, they displayed economic theory in its infancy. There is plenty of room here for the relativist and the absolutist interpretation: a mercantilist 'vision' of reality, on the one hand, and, on the other, an essentially crude analysis, erring more often by omission than by commission.

THE 18TH-CENTURY PREDECESSORS

Since the days of Hume, students of English mercantilism have been puzzled by the failure of mercantilist writers to realize that their objectives were self-contradictory. Thomas Mun could write that 'all men do consent that plenty of money in a Kingdom doth make the native commodities dearer' and that 'as plenty of money makes wares dearer, so dear wares decline in their use and consumption', yet he did not hesitate to advocate the indefinite accumulation of hard money. One might be tempted to argue that Mun did not grasp the full meaning of the quantity theory of money. But in this case how was it that mercantilist ideas survived into the 18th century after Locke had demonstrated that the value of money varies inversely with its quantity? The mystery deepens when it is realized that very few mercantilists made the mistake of advocating a favourable balance of trade as a method of price inflation. Heckscher found more evidence of inflationary sentiments in the literature than did Viner, but the fact remains that even the 18th-century advocates of paper money and note-issuing banks did not really want higher prices.

6. The Mercantilist Dilemma and the Quantity Theory of Money

The resolution of the dilemma lies in the characteristic mercantilist doctrine that money 'quickens' trade by increasing the velocity of circulation of goods. According to the familiar Equation of Exchange, $MV \equiv PT$, the quantity of money (M) multiplied by the number of times it changes hands in a given time period (V) is identically equal to the total volume of trade (T) multiplied by the average prices of these goods (P). The identity becomes a theory by relating the variables in a definite way. The quantity *theory* of money is a doctrine linking M to P, with T somehow determined by 'real' forces and V given by the payment habits and financial institutions of the economy. This formulation does not begin to do justice to the complexity of the quantity theory of money in the 19th century but it will suffice for present purposes. The point is that the mercantilists emphasized the effect of M on T rather than on P. The quantity theory in the 17th and 18th centuries had at its center the proposition that 'money stimulates trade': an increase in the supply of money was thought to be attended by a rise in the demand for money, and hence the volume of trade and not prices would be directly affected by a specie inflow. The mercantilists did not take account of Hume's self-regulating mechanism because they did not interpret the quantity theory of money as he did.

As first formulated by Locke, the quantity 'theory' stated simply that the level of prices is always in proportion to the quantity of money, the quantity of money being understood to include 'the quickness of its circulation'. The particular proportion depends, of course, on the volume of trade. This is a truism rather than a theory, but it may be a useful truism because it emphasizes the function of money as a medium of exchange. It compares two flows, the total quantity of money in circulation in a given time period and the total volume of goods traded over the same time period and thus demonstrates that the absolute size of the money stock is of no significance to the wealth of a nation. Money is peculiar in that, serving only as a means of exchange, it has no 'intrinsic' value. The thesis is obviously destructive of mercantilist principles, but Locke nevertheless remained a mercantilist because he thought it was to a country's advantage to have a larger stock of money than any other country.

David Hume, failing to recognize that the quantity 'theory' as Locke stated it presupposes a different amount of money everything else being the same, that is, a *once-and-for-all* change in the money supply rather than a *temporal* process of increasing the money supply, introduced the notion of a causal relationship between M and P. He laid down this commonly accepted version: T and V being insensitive to monetary changes, M and P will vary proportionately. As long as money is merely a standard of value and a medium of exchange even this theoretical proposition is merely a tautology. But as soon as we consider the demand for money to hold as a store of value – the key to almost all disputes in monetary theory – M and P will not necessarily vary proportionately. It may be possible to show that P will vary proportionately with M when both the final and the original states being compared are in equilibrium: this is the modern, comparative static formulation of the quantity theory of money (of which more anon). It is doubtful whether Locke grasped this theory. In any case, Hume interpreted the Lockean argument in a dynamic sense and so did everyone else in the 18th century. The quantity 'theory', in the sense of a definite and fairly rigid connection between M and P, was understood at the time as a verifiable and indeed obvious statement about the real world. If nothing else, the 'price revolution' of the 16th century was taken as overwhelming evidence of a direct causal relationship between variations in M and variations in P. This confusion between comparative statics and dynamics is one which we will encounter time and time again in the history of economic analysis.

7. The Theory of Creeping Inflation

It is clear that by 1700 no writer could ignore the fact that the call for a permanent inflow of specie involves a contradiction in terms. Indeed, all 18th-century writers justify a permanently favourable balance of trade on the grounds that prices need not rise when the extra bullion is used to finance a greater volume of trade. Although the *amount* of money itself had no economic importance whatever, the *process* of increasing the amount of money in circulation might have a significant effect in promoting the growth of output. What they held was not so much a quantity theory of the value of money as a monetary theory of the volume of trade and employment.

Perhaps the best exponent of the doctrine that 'money stimulates trade' was the so-called 'paper-money mercantilist' John Law. The argument in his *Money and Trade Considered* (1705), as in Jacob Vanderlint's *Money Answers all Things* (1734) and in Bishop Berkeley's *Querist* (1737), is based in essence on profit inflation and the premise that 'an addition to the money will employ the people that are now idle'. It utilizes Petty's needs-of-trade doctrine to show that extra specie or paper money will be taken up by borrowers owing to abundant profit opportunities, while relying on income payments to the previously unemployed to give rise to new consumers' demand. As money is cheaper to borrow, realized profits and sales increase without leading to a rise in prices; indeed, Law thought that prices might actually fall. It is evident that Law's argument supposes that the supply of commodities is highly elastic, a small increase in price leading to large increases in the amount of goods offered. Law himself realized the necessity of making some such assumption. In the case of perishable goods, he explicitly assumes a horizontal supply curve so that 'as the demand for them increases or decreases their value continues equal or near the same', whereas, for durable goods, he assumes a negative elasticity of supply: they become 'less valuable' as the demand rises.

Law's doctrine, while apparently contradictory to the quantity theory of money, is of course perfectly compatible with some versions of that theory. Law stressed the necessity of a gradual increase in the money supply so as not to disrupt the level of wages and prices that had come about through the prevailing international distribution of specie. His doctrine that 'money stimulates trade' may be interpreted therefore to apply to 'transitional periods', calling, as it were, for a state of permanent disequilibrium. The demand for a continual inflow of precious metals amounts to a demand for continuous series of transitional periods. Even Hume allows for this possibility in his dynamic version of the quantity theory, a version that minimizes but does not deny the importance of the proposition that creeping inflation may promote economic growth. An inflow of gold, Hume observed, has a gradual effect on prices; 'at first, no alteration is perceived; by degrees the price rises, first of one commodity, then of another; till the whole at last reaches a just proportion with the new quantity of specie which is in the Kingdom. In my opinion, it is only in this interval or intermediate situation between the acquisition of money and the rise in prices, that the enhancing quantity of gold and silver is favourable to industry.'

8. Cantillon's Essay

A very different resolution of the mercantilist dilemma is to be found in Cantillon's *Essay on the Nature of Commerce*, written in the 1720s but published in 1755. This is the most systematic, the most lucid, and at the same time the most original of all the statements of economic principles before the *Wealth of Nations*. Cantillon is the first to leave absolutely no doubt that the effect of an increase in V is equivalent to an increase in M alone, and he put monetary analysis on its feet by showing that the effect of an increase in the quantity of money upon prices and incomes depends upon the manner in which cash is injected into the economy. 'Mr Locke has clearly seen that the abundance of money makes everything dear', Cantillon declared, 'but he has not considered how it does so. The great difficulty of this question consists in knowing in what way and in what proportion the increase of money raises prices.' In an oft-quoted passage, Cantillon describes how an increase in the output of domestic gold mines first affects incomes in that industry, then spending on consumer goods, then the price of foodstuffs, causing farming profits to rise and real wages to fall; this leads to an upward pressure on money wages and further cycles of increased expenditures and rising prices. He stressed the fact that an increase in M will not only raise the level of prices but will also alter the structure of prices, depending upon the initial recipients of the new cash and their relative demand for goods. The differential effect of a cash injection, as governed by the nature of the injection, will hereafter be called the Cantillon Effect; it was stated less explicitly by Hume in his essay 'On Money' (1752) and it is probably in this version, rather than in Cantillon's, that it was handed down to the classical economists. It has its modern counterpart in Keynes's analysis of 'the diffusion of price levels' in chapter 7 of *The Treatise on Money* (1930), namely, 'the fact that monetary changes do not affect all prices in the same way, in the same degree, or at the same time'.

Cantillon also gave an excellent account of the specie-flow mechanism and a sound critique of Law's doctrine that 'money stimulates trade' which, he noted, is much more likely to be true when the increase in specie is due to an export surplus than to increased production in gold mines at home; in the latter case, it is likely to raise prices directly without promoting an expansion of output. Still, Cantillon was a mercantilist who did not hesitate to say that 'the comparative power and wealth of states consists, other things being equal, in the greater or less abundance of money circulating in them' and that 'every state which has more money in circulation than its neighbor has an advantage over them so long as it maintains this abundance of money'. A specie inflow will indeed raise domestic prices to some extent, but this is all to the good. Selling dear and buying cheap means not only favourable barter terms of trade – a high ratio of export to import prices – but a favourable balance of payments as well, implying that foreign demand for domestic goods and the domestic demand for foreign goods is highly inelastic. Cantillon did not, however, propose to let the inflationary process run its natural course if demand should prove to be elastic. Following Petty, he recommended the policy of preventing imported specie from going into active circulation by lending it abroad or by melting it down in the form of plate and ornaments. Thus, on both theoretical and practical grounds, he saw no reason why a country should not continue indefinitely to import precious metals.

Cantillon's argument ignores the fact that the fall in the price level of foreign countries drained of bullion would in and of itself turn the balance of trade in their favour. Nevertheless, it is theoretically correct to say that a rise in domestic prices will produce a favourable, not an unfavourable, balance of trade if the sum of the elasticities of demand for imports at home and for exports abroad is less than unity. Whether Cantillon was empirically justified in assuming such low elasticities for imports and exports is another question. At any rate, Hume, writing only twenty-five years after him, treated demand as relatively elastic and hence produced a full-blown specie-flow argument that rang the death knell of mercantilism. Glancing backward, this created something we have labeled 'the mercantilist dilemma'. But, as we have seen, this was no real dilemma to the predecessors of Hume.

9. Monetary analysis

Enough has been said to show that monetary theory in the 18th century consisted of dynamic process analysis of a crude kind which was gradually extended to imply a macroeconomic theory of the general level of economic activity. In demonstrating that an increase in the supply of money generates additional purchasing power which stimulates output, the inflationists of the 18th century finally provided the theoretical justification for the notion that more gold and silver is the avenue by which wealth and power are to be attained, a notion that has been mouthed for over two hundred years without any explanation of what it really meant. Nevertheless, despite the remarkable advances in monetary theory in the 18th century, one may well doubt whether the belief in the benefits of gradual inflation was justified in the light of contemporary conditions. There is insufficient recognition in the writings of Law and Berkeley of the real problems of a dominantly agrarian economy, problems that cannot be cured simply by cranking the monetary pump. Adam Smith and Ricardo may have overemphasized thrift and enterprise, but their skepticism about monetary panaceas was well taken in the circumstances of an economy suffering from scarcity of capital and chronic structural unemployment.

The gradual emergence of real analysis in the 18th century and its victory over the monetary analysis of the early mercantilists is nowhere better expressed than in the development of the theory of interest. By 'monetary analysis', we mean any analysis that introduces the element of money at the outset of the argument and denies that the essential features of economic life can be represented by a barter model. By 'real analysis', we mean analysis that explains economic activity solely in terms of decisions about goods and services and the relations between them; money is a veil because a well-functioning monetary system permits analysis of trade as if it were barter. With these distinctions in mind, we can make short shrift of the so-called 'monetary theory of interest' of the mercantilists.

The idea that the rate of interest varies inversely with the quantity of money is found, among others, in Locke, Petty, and Law; it rested on the commonsense idea that since interest is the price paid for the hire of money, interest is lower when there is more money about, just as a commodity falls in price when it is less scarce. Adam Smith accused Locke and Law of believing that as the quantity of money increases and prices rise, the rate of interest must fall because any given sum of money will now buy fewer goods for borrowers; in other words, the demand for money will fall because the value of money over goods has declined. This error, Smith pointed out, had been 'fully exposed by Mr Hume': given that the only effect of an increased supply of money is to raise the level of prices, it is obvious that the rate of interest will not be affected because the interest rate is merely a ratio of two sums of money. However, it is unlikely that anyone ever held the point of view that Adam Smith attacked. Rather, as Cantillon stated, it is the 'common idea, received of all those who have written on trade that the increased quantity of currency in a State brings down the price of Interest there, because when Money is plentiful it is more easy to find some to borrow'. It is important to remember that the relationship between the quantity of money and the rate of interest was never considered in isolation from the normal course of economic progress. An increase in *M* leads to a reduction in the rate of interest because it is normally accompanied by an increase in real national wealth. Casual empiricism sufficed to establish this argument: everyone knew that the general level of the market rate of interest – the rate on first-class commercial loans – tended downward in the 17th century, and it was also a familiar fact that interest in such poor countries as Spain, Scotland, and Ireland was almost twice as high as in rich countries like Holland and England.

This is all there is to the mercantilist theory of interest, and it is extraordinary indeed that Keynes saw merit in this theory or, for that matter, in any *purely* monetary theory of interest. It is often forgotten, not least by Keynes himself, that the rate of interest in the complete Keynesian system is not determined merely by the quantity of money and the state of liquidity preferences but also by 'real' forces expressed in the investment-demand schedule and the consumption function. In short, the classical economists may have erred in neglecting the influence of monetary forces on the rate of interest but real analytical progress was made when they rejected explanations of the interest rate which run solely in terms of the quantity of money.

10. The Real Rate of Interest
Real theories of interest came to the fore with Cantillon, Hume, and Turgot. All three criticized the monetary theories of interest of their predecessors but admitted that an increase in the supply of money could depress the rate of interest temporarily. If prices rose in proportion to the increase in money, however, equilibrium was impossible unless the rate of interest resumed its former height: at higher prices, more money would have to be borrowed to finance any project; hence, the demand for money loans would be increased, and equilibrium implied that it would be increased in the same proportion as the supply of money loans. Generally speaking, however, the rate of interest was not thought to be uniquely related to the supply of money. The repercussions of an increase in the money supply could be traced by means of the Cantillon Effect: for example, if the new money flowed into the hands of entrepreneurs to be saved and invested, the rate of interest would probably fall; but, if it came first into the hands of landowners, it would be spent on consumption and the rise in consumers' demand would make entrepreneurs more willing and able to pay higher interest charges.

This contrast between the frugal merchant and the prodigal landlord is characteristic of all 18th-century theory, including that of Adam Smith. The rate of real saving and of net investment is not made a function of the rate of interest or even of the merchant's expectation of profits. Rather it is connected with the preponderance of certain classes in the community imbued with the philosophy of thrift. The rate of interest depends on the supply of and demand for loanable funds, with the profitability of investment and the prodigality of landlords governing the demand side and the wealth of the country and the distribution of that wealth governing the supply side. The old doctrine that advanced countries would have low interest rates was maintained, but the forces causing variations in demand and supply were now analyzed in detail. Economic expansion would increase the importance of the 'moneyed interests' and thereby augment the supply of loanable capital; agriculture would decline in importance, and hence consumption loans to landlords would dwindle away. Moreover, capital accumulation per se would reduce profit margins by increasing competition for an essentially limited number of available investment outlets. Since interest was a derived income – a deduction from business profits – this alone would reduce the yield on money loans. The changing proportions between lenders and borrowers would do the rest. This was the new classical explanation of why economic development is normally accompanied by a fall in the rate of interest.

PHYSIOCRACY

Adam Smith praised the physiocratic system 'with all its imperfections' as 'perhaps the nearest approximation to the truth that has yet been published upon the subject of Political Economy'. The physiocrats' attack on mercantilism and their proposals to remove tariff barriers roused his admiration; from them he drew the theme of wealth as 'the consumable goods annually reproduced by the labour of society', the doctrine of productive labour, and the emphasis on the essential circularity of the process of production and distribution. It comes as something of a shock, however, to realize that he refers only obliquely to the most notorious of physiocratic concepts, the single tax, and does not mention it at all in the chapter specifically devoted to the physiocrats. Moreover, he misrepresents the no less infamous notion of 'the sterile class' by condemning Quesnay for seeking 'to degrade the artificers, manufacturers, and merchants by the humiliating appellation of the barren or unproductive classes'. The physiocrats did not regard industry as useless but simply as a sector that produces no net additions to income: Turgot's 'stipendiary class' is indeed a happier expression than Quesnay's 'sterile class'. Ironically enough, Adam Smith had difficulty in upsetting the physiocratic doctrine that manufacturing is 'sterile'; in the end he was forced to argue that manufacturing *is* productive because its receipts are sufficient to pay wages and to replace worn-out capital, but that agriculture is *more* productive because it yields rent over and above wages and depreciation. But apart from a quibble on words, this concedes the whole of the physiocratic argument.

11. The Meaning of Physiocracy

Physiocracy, as Adam Smith suggested, should be understood as a reaction to the mercantilist policies of Colbert during the reign of Louis XIV. The glory of the age of the Sun King was the growth of French industry, and agriculture was consistently neglected. The War of the Spanish Succession and the magnificence of the Versailles court placed a severe burden upon taxable capacity and the land tax, being the chief source of revenue, was steadily increased. By the time of the death of Louis XIV in 1715, the plight of French agriculture had produced a wave of reactions against *Colbertisme*, fanned by the religious struggle against the Huguenots. Louis XV, instead of recouping losses at home, threw himself into the Seven Years' War with England, from which France emerged defeated, deprived of Canada and her

Oriental possessions, and reduced to a second-rate power in Europe. The stage was set for a back-to-nature movement, a return to rustic simplicity, of which the writings of Rousseau and the paintings of Boucher and Fragonard are familiar witnesses.

Inclined to emphasize agriculture, the physiocrats could hardly resist casting envious glances at England. The combination of smallholdings, antiquated methods and a maze of feudal obligations made it difficult for France to adopt the improvements effected by the much admired 'agricultural revolution' in England. The program of the physiocrats was to eliminate the vestiges of medieval parochialism in the countryside, to rationalize the fiscal system by reducing all taxes to a single levy on rent, to amalgamate smallholdings and to free the corn trade from all protectionist restrictions, in short, to emulate English agriculture. Placed in its historical context – the reader must forgive this brief lapse into relativism – there is nothing very surprising about all this. It was only the effort to provide agrarian reform with a watertight theoretical argument that produced conclusions which struck observers even at the time as slightly absurd.

12. The Tableau Economique

Quesnay's *Tableau Economique*, published three to four years after Cantillon's *Essay*, was regarded in its day as the crowning achievement of the physiocratic school. Mentioned but not explained by Adam Smith, it soon fell into oblivion and had to be rediscovered by Marx in the middle of the 19th century. Since that time it has never ceased to fascinate commentators and yet, despite its importance, it should not be regarded as the centerpiece of the physiocratic system. What it achieved was a vivid graphic picture of general interdependence by means of a drastic simplification of the economic system into three interacting sectors. Out of this emerged a conception of the closed 'stationary state' as a circular flow which in each period repeats itself, a conception that has ever since maintained a powerful grip upon the imagination of economists. But the conclusions of physiocratic theory are not deducible from the *Tableau*; on the contrary, they form the premises upon which the zigzag diagram of the stationary process is constructed. A discussion of the *Tableau*, however, serves to bring out the principal analytical weakness of Quesnay's system: not so much that it attributes the net return to economic activity to land alone but rather that it fails in any way to prove that land is productive of *value* . The *Tableau* most frequently reproduced is that printed at Versailles in 1758–59, being a combination of three earlier versions published by Quesnay. Long thought to be destroyed, a copy of the fourth version was discovered in 1894. This zigzag diagram, however, is not a macroeconomic table but rather an illustration of the circular flow involving the expenditure of one landlord. Later editions of the *Tableau* simplify the argument by giving the total annual receipts and expenditures of all the three participating classes. This is the form of the table presented in Quesnay's *Analysis* (1766) to which Marx first drew attention (see Figure 1–1).

Quesnay inaugurated the tradition of regarding capital as consisting of a series of 'advances'. First, there is fixed capital in the form of 'original advances' – livestock, buildings, and implements – interest on which at 10 percent is included as

Figure 1–1

(In thousands)

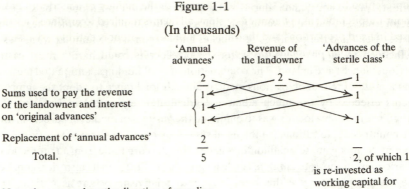

	'Annual advances'	Revenue of the landowner	'Advances of the sterile class'

Sums used to pay the revenue of the landowner and interest on 'original advances'

Replacement of 'annual advances'   2

Total.   5   2, of which 1 is re-invested as working capital for the following year

Note: the arrows show the direction of spending

depreciation in the table. Second, there is fixed capital in the form of 'landlord's advances' – drainage, fencing, and other permanent land improvements – which do not figure in the table as such. Last, there is working capital under the title of 'annual advances' – the wages of agricultural labour, seeds, and other recurring annual costs. The process of circulation is as follows: the gross value added by agriculture is 5 thousand, 3 thousand of which constitute costs of production incurred in cultivation. Farmers use two fifths of their own output for working capital; one fifth is sold to the 'sterile' artisans in exchange for goods required to replace worn-out fixed capital. Since farmers receive only 'wages of management' – it is land that is productive, not their labour – the remainder goes to landowners as rent. The landowners in turn exchange half of their 2 thousand revenue for manufactured articles, while the 'sterile' artisans purchase 2 thousand worth of raw materials and foodstuffs from the agricultural sector. The whole process may be conceived of in real terms, with three fifths of output entering into circulation, or, as Quesnay suggested, it may equally well be pictured in money terms. At the beginning of the process, the farmers are in possession of the entire money stock of the economy (2 thousand). They pay this to landowners to purchase 'rental services', who in turn spend it on foodstuffs and fabricated commodities; the farmers now spend the 1 thousand just received to replace fixed capital, and the artisans spend their total receipts of 2 thousand on agricultural products. At the end, the farmers have received 3 thousand and spent 1; they are back where they started. The net effect of the sterile sector is nil, and the 2 thousand of money is paid out once more to landowners as a new cycle of production begins.

The *Tableau* as conceived by Quesnay involves a one-period income-spending lag: landowners spend the previous period's rent, while the artisans always retain 1 thousand of the last period's receipts for spending in the following period. Presumably, Quesnay was thinking of output as identical with the annual harvest, the whole of which is consumed in the following 12 months. The *Tableau*, however, can also be pictured with leads as well as lags, each sector simply spending in each income period the receipts of the same period. In this case, the whole argument can be represented by a two-way transaction diagram in the manner of a modern Leontief input-output table: as in Leontief's system, all factors required to produce a good are used in fixed proportions and the value of a sector's output is entirely exhausted by the sector's total payments to other sectors (see Table 1–1).

Table 1–1

	Purchasing Sector			Annual Output
Producing Sector	I	II	III	
I. Farmers	2	1	2	5
II. Landowers	2	0	0	2
III. Artisans	1	1	0	2
Total Purchases	5	2	2	9

A three-sector closed Leontief model can be represented by three simultaneous equations:

$$(1-a_{11})X_1 \quad -a_{12}X_2 \quad -a_{13}X_3 = 0,$$
$$-a_{21}X_1 + (1-a_{22})X_2 \quad -a_{23}X_3 = 0,$$
$$-a_{31}X_1 \quad -a_{32}X_2 + (1-a_{33})X_3 = 0,$$

where the X's stand for the annual output of the three sectors and the a_{ij} coefficients for the input-output relations – the ith sectors product (read across the rows) is used as input to produce a unit of the jth sector's output (read down the columns). The equations state simply that if $(1 - a_{ij}) X_i$ stands for the amount of output a sector does not itself use up, this must be equal to the amounts purchased from it by the other sectors $(a_{ij}X_j)$. So, for example reading across the first row in Table 1–1, the total output of agriculture equals the amount retained by farmers, $(a_{11}X_1) = 2$, plus the amount sold to landowners and artisans, $(a_{12}X_2 + a_{13}X_3) = 3$; or the amount not retained by farmers, $(1 - a_{11}) X_1 = 3$, equals the amount sold to landowners and artisans, $a_{12}X_2 + a_{13}X_3 = 3$. Since $X_1 = 5$, $X_2 = 2$, and $X_3 = 2$, the input-output coefficients of the table are quickly computed in our simple case: $a_{11} = \frac{2}{5}$, $a_{12} = \frac{1}{2}$, $a_{13} = 1$, $a_{21} = \frac{2}{5}$, $a_{22} = 0$, $a_{23} = 0$, $a_{31} = \frac{1}{5}$, $a_{32} = \frac{1}{2}$, $a_{33} = 0$. When the a_{ij}s are substituted into the equations given above, we obtain:

$$+ 0.6(5) - 0.5(2) - 1(2) = 0,$$

$$- 0.4(5) + \quad 1(2) - \quad 0 = 0,$$

$$- 0.2(5) - 0.5(2) + 1(2) = 0.$$

This set of equations provides a scale model of the economy, given the output of the three sectors, the X_is, or, as Leontief would say, 'the final bill of goods'. The practical purpose of the construction is limited to evaluating the effects of changes in the final bill of goods small enough to leave the input coefficients unchanged. This is a limitation inherent in the *Tableau* itself, which has no other purpose than to illustrate the phenomenon of mutual interdependence between industries.

13. The Single Tax

There are obvious formal defects in the *Tableau*. The sterile sector is simply assumed to possess fixed capital, but no provision is made for its replacement. Competition is supposed to reduce the value of output of this sector to the sum of the wages of workers and managers, but no argument is supplied here or elsewhere to show why competition among the farmers for workers and seeds to apply to the land does not reduce rents to zero. Quesnay does not succeed either in showing that manufacturing is sterile or in demonstrating that agriculture necessarily yields a 'net product'.

The physiocrats regard rents as a perfectly legitimate income, a payment for costs incurred in clearing the land and for keeping up 'capital advances'. The bulk of receipts, however, was admittedly disposable, ready to provide the revenue of the state. And, indeed, since rent is at least in part a return for the use of a nonreproducible natural agent, the incidence of any tax will always fall upon landlords; the returns of all other classes consist of 'necessary' expenses of production. Thus, the physiocratic demand for a single tax aimed at minimizing collection costs by taxing directly those incomes that ultimately bear taxes. We shall come back to the idea of a 'single tax' in our discussion of Henry George [see chapter 3, section 11] but note for the moment that the physiocratic single tax is not a tax on 'the unearned increment' of rental values in response to rising population *à la* James and John Stuart Mill but a species of land value taxation in the form of a levy on pure rent, which Quesnay estimated to be about one third of the 'net product'.

14. Say's Law

The notion subsequently popularized by J. B. Say as the Law of Markets formed an integral part of the physiocratic critique of mercantilism. Mercier de La Rivière whose *L'Ordre naturel et essentiel* (1767) was cited by Smith as giving 'the most distinct and best connected account of physiocracy', remarks that 'no one is a buyer without being at the same time a seller', and it is a short step from Quesnay's 'all that is bought is sold, and all that is sold is bought' to Say's 'supply creates its own demand'. The central lesson of the *Tableau* is, after all, that money is merely a medium of exchange, that trade reduces essentially to barter exchange, and that the creation of output automatically generates the income whose disbursement makes it possible to enter upon another cycle of production. But, strangely enough, Say directed the Law of Markets against his physiocratic predecessors because they had argued that income received is not automatically restored to the income stream. The landlord's income, as Cantillon had stressed, is not necessarily balanced by a cost item and hence can be withheld, breaking the income stream. Here is the origin of the idea developed by Malthus that the balanced spending of landlords on luxury goods is the factor that maintains the circular flow and therefore economic prosperity [see chapter 5 section 13]. Here, too, is the origin of the underconsumptionist thesis, which passed from Quesnay to such English physiocrats as Thomas Spence and via Malthus to the Ricardian socialists, to issue at long last into a full-scale attack on capitalism by Marx.

15. Scholastic Influences: An Afterthought

The prehistory of economics, some commentators have insisted, starts in the 13th century with the scholastic pioneers in market analysis rather than with the 17th-century mercantilists. Schumpeter has even put forth the claim that the skeleton of Adam Smith's *Wealth of Nations* hails from the Schoolmen and the natural-law philosophers, not from the physiocrats and the British free-trade writers of the 18th century. This is not a historical question we can hope to settle in a few pages, but it may be worthwhile to touch upon it to round off the picture of pre-Adamite economics.

There can be no doubt that scholastic doctrines were transmitted to Adam Smith by way of the 17th-century natural-law philosophers, Hugo Grotius and Samuel von Pufendorf. Moreover, the writings of the physiocrats with which Smith was acquainted are replete with scholastic influences: Quesnay often sounds like an 18th-century version of Thomas Aquinas. For our purposes, the distinctive contributions of scholastic economics may be broken down into three elements: (1) an emphasis on utility as the principal source of value; (2) the notion of 'the just price'; and (3) the proposition that money capital is sterile.

On the first score, it is generally agreed now that the Doctors did develop a utility-cum-scarcity doctrine of value. This would have been denied a hundred years ago because of the interpretation given to the scholastic concept of the 'just price'. Aristotle had argued in the fifth book of the *Nicomachean Ethics* that commutative or contractual justice requires an 'exchange of equivalents'; Aquinas commented upon this passage, suggesting that 'equivalence' should be interpreted in terms of costs, chiefly labour costs. It was this commentary that led to the view that the scholastics held a labour theory of value, ignoring Aquinas' insistence that all goods are valued only in relation to human wants. Scholastic economics based value squarely on the satisfaction of wants and, in its later versions, related utility to the relative scarcity of a good. How much we should make of this is another question. A utility theory of value without a concept of diminishing utility to explain why demand at a given price is satiable hardly amounts to a satisfactory theory of price determination.

Next, there is the scholastic concept of 'the just price', which is often thought to reflect an underlying notion of the just wage. This seems to be a historical myth. There is no suggestion in the scholastic literature of a just price that corresponds to cost of production as determined by the producer's social status. The Schoolmen did not distinguish between short-run and long-run equilibrium and had no conception of how competition produces a long-run normal price that just covers costs. They seldom gave much attention to what constituted a just price, but usually they identified it with the current market price, the price given to an individual which he cannot himself affect. They did not question the right of the civil authorities to set and regulate prices and in that sense the just price is simply the price ruling at the moment, whether produced by competition or not.

Clearly, Adam Smith was in no way indebted to his scholastic predecessors in developing the fundamental distinction between the 'natural' and the 'market' price; and in deliberately rejecting the explanation of value along the lines of utility, he completely ignored scholastic thinking. It is hardly necessary to add that he also discarded the standard doctrine of the Church that interest is 'a breed of barren metal' and probably had read little of the scholastic literature dealing with the question of interest. If so, the loss was not great, for the bulk of scholastic writing on the subject dealt with the legal distinction between a loan and a partnership. To demand interest from a partner was never justified. A loan, however, was a voluntary contract and interest on loans could be demanded under certain conditions extraneous to the circumstances of the borrower. Two of these conditions were losses suffered by the lender as a result of the loan (*damnum emergens*) and a gain forgone by the lender on an alternative investment (*lucrum cessans*); this equates interest to the opportunity cost of liquid funds, an idea which must be put down as a genuine analytical insight. Ingenious apologists have found other nuggets in the literature but on the whole it is analytically sterile. There is a bizarre rationalization by Keynes who regarded the disquisitions of the Schoolmen as directed toward raising the marginal efficiency of capital, while using moral suasion to lower the rate of interest. But scholastic doctrine treats all interest on borrowed money as 'usury' and therefore in principle unjustified, and variations in the rate of interest play no part in scholastic analysis.

The scholastic writers always handle economic questions within the context of the types of contracts involved in transactions. This juristic approach to economic activity in the tradition of Roman Law is a distinctive feature of scholasticism and sets it apart from the mercantilist tradition. And, indeed, it was the mercantilists who, long before Adam Smith, broke with the canonical conception of market behavior as a moral problem and fashioned the concept of 'economic man'. The pamphleteers of the 17th century assumed as a matter of course that the profit motive was a controlling motive in economic conduct. They believed in the direct power of self-interest and in matters of domestic economic policy came near to advocating laissez-faire. Adam Smith was not the first to have confidence in the workings of the 'invisible hand'. Nor is it necessary to appeal to scholastic influences to account for his grasp of the determination of prices by demand and supply. One of the oldest British mercantilist tracts, John Hales' *Discourse of the Common Weal of This Realm of England*, written in 1549, already shows a fairly sophisticated understanding of the price mechanism as an efficient method of allocating resources. Only a few writers prior to Adam Smith were free traders, but all the basic elements of the classical approach to economic activity are embedded in the mercantilist literature.

One may doubt, therefore, whether recent work on scholastic economics required a revision of the history of economic thought prior to Adam Smith. The Schoolmen may have contributed ideas that passed through Grotius, Locke, and Pufendorf to Francis Hutcheson and Adam Smith, but we are hardly justified for that reason in following Schumpeter's reduction of mercantilism to a mere by-current in the forward march of economic analysis.

NOTES ON FURTHER READING

J. R. McCulloch's *Early English Tracts on Commerce*, reprinted for the Economic History of Society in 1952, contains T. Mun's *England's Treasure* (1664), D. North's *Discourses upon Trade* (1691), and H. Martin's *Considerations on the East India Trade* (1701), primary sources worth reading as expressive of mercantilist thinking. In a class by itself is a work that first appeared in 1720, I. Gervaise, *The System or Theory of the Trade of the World*, ed. J. Viner, with an introduction by J. M. Letiche (1954): this is the most brilliant statement of the liberal elements in English mercantilism, and provides an early example of the income approach to international economic equilibrium. A. E. Monroe, *Early Economic Thought* (1924) is another useful compendium of selections from 17th-century and 18th-century primary sources.

All critical study of mercantilism begins with Adam Smith, *The Wealth of Nations*, Book IV, chaps. 1–8. If a student had to confine himself to a single secondary source, the choice would naturally fall on the first two chapters of J. Viner, *Studies in the Theory of International Trade* (1937, reprinted 1955), and summed up in his 'Economic Thought: Mercantilist Thought', *IESS*, 4. Viner's incisive survey of mercantilist theory and policy proposals is profoundly critical in tone. By way of contrast, see Schumpeter's subtle defense of mercantilism: *History of Economic Analysis*, Part II, chap. 7.7. C.-Y. Wu, *An Outline of International Price Theories* (1939), chap. 2, complements Viner and Schumpeter in its treatment of mercantilist monetary theory.

The outstanding historical study of mercantilism in all its phases is E. F. Heckscher, *Mercantilism*, ed. E. F. Söderlund (1955). An appendix in this last edition of Heckscher's book criticizes Keynes's views on mercantilism as expounded in chap. 23 of Keynes' *General Theory*. For a quick summary of the book's general argument, see Heckscher's article on 'Mercantilism', *ESS*, reprinted in *DET*. A reading of Heckscher's book should be supplemented by H. Heaton's masterly review article (*JPE*, June, 1937) and D. C. Coleman's more recent criticism of Heckscher's fundamental approach: 'Eli Heckscher and the Idea of Mercantilism', *SEHR*, 1957, reprinted in *Revisions in Mercantilism*, ed. D. C. Coleman (1969), an indispensable collection of papers: it includes, among others, J. Viner, 'Power versus Plenty as Objectives of Foreign Policy in the Seventeenth and Eighteenth Centuries', *WP*, 1948, which attacks the stereotyped view that mercantilism was a system of ideas that aimed exclusively at national wealth as an end in itself. A recent bird's-eye view of this apparently endless debate on the meaning of mercantilism is W. R. Allen, 'The Position of Mercantilism and the Early Development of International Trade Theory', *Events, Ideology, and Economic Theory*, ed. Eagley, followed by the same author's 'Modern Defenders of Mercantilist Theory', *HOPE*, Fall, 1970, with a rebuttal by A. W. Coats, *ibid.*, Fall, 1973.

Those grown weary of reading about *the* mercantilist system will find support in E. A. J. Johnson, *Predecessors of Adam Smith* (1937), which denies any unifying characteristics in the economic writings of the 17th and 18th centuries. Johnson presents an intellectual portrait gallery of ten leading writers from Hales to Steuart and reconstructs their 'balance-of-work' doctrines. W. Letwin, *The Origins of Scientific Economics* (1963, and in paperback) vividly depicts the new style of economic reasoning of Petty, Locke, and North in contrast to the old style of Child and Barbon.

W. D. Grampp shows that the mercantilists anticipated almost every classical idea but that, unlike the classical authors, their economic objective was primarily to secure full employment: 'The Liberal Elements in English Mercantilism', *QJE*, 1952, reprinted in *EET* and in the author's *Economic Liberalism* (1965), I, chap. 2. J. M. Low presents a fascinating discussion of Scottish mercantilism in the early years of the 18th century: 'A Regional Example of the Mercantilist Theory of Economic Policy', *MS*, January, 1953.

Of the treatises published before *The Wealth of Nations*, Cantillon's *Essay on the Nature of Commerce* (1755, reprinted 1931) and Turgot's *Reflections on the Formation and Distribution of Wealth* (1700, reprinted in *Turgot on Progress, Sociology and Economics*, ed. R. L. Meek, 1973) can still be read with pleasure and occasional surprise. *The Economics of A. R. J. Turgot*, ed. P. Groenewegen (1977) reprints, other papers by Turgot, not found in the Meek volume. Hume's scintillating essays on economics are brought together for the first time in *David Hume: Writings on Economics*, ed. E. Rotwein (1955). Readers in a hurry can find extracts of all three, and more besides, in R. L. Meek's book of readings, *Precursors of Adam Smith* (1973).

On Cantillon, see F. A. v. Hayek's characteristically brilliant introduction to the German edition of Cantillon's *Essay* (1931) and the prolix but comprehensive discussion of the whole of the contents of the *Essay* by J. J. Spengler, 'Richard Cantillon: First of the Moderns', *JPE*, 1954, reprinted in *EET*. The recent French edition of Cantillon's book by A. Sauvy (1952) contains some important accompanying studies and commentaries. On Turgot, see Meek's introduction to *Turgot on Progress, Sociology and Economics* and P. D. Groenewegen, 'Turgot's Place in the History of Economic Thought: A Bicentenary Estimate', *HOPE*, Winter, 1983, besides his introduction to *The Economics of A. R. J. Turgot*. On Hume, see Rotwein's introduction to his economic writings; M. Arkin, 'The Economic Writings of David Hume – A Reassessment', *SAJE*, 1956, reprinted in *EET*; and M. I. Duke, 'David Hume and Monetary Adjustment', *HOPE*, Winter, 1979. A debate among Hume's personal friends on his ideas about economic development in relation to foreign trade is the subject of another splendid article by J. M. Low, 'An Eighteenth Century Controversy in the Theory of Economic Progress', *MS*, September, 1952.

C. H. Hull's introduction to *The Economic Writings of Sir William Petty* (1899) is still useful. K. I. Vaughn, *John Locke, Economist and Social Scientist* (1980) deals, among other things, with Locke's economic writings. A. S. Skinner, editor of the recent reprint of Steuart's *Principles of Political Oeconomy* (1966) considers the question of the neglect of Steuart's work even in his own lifetime in 'Sir James Steuart: Author of a System', *SJPE*, February, 1981. T. W. Hutchison gives an excellent *précis* of Berkeley's *Querist* and concludes with some controversial comments on the Keynesian aspect of pre-Adamite economics: *BJPS*, May, 1953. I. D. S. Ward takes exception to Hutchison's interpretation in an article whose title is self-explanatory: 'George Berkeley: Precursor of Keynes or Moral Economist on Underdevelopment?' *JPE*, February, 1959; see also the revealing exchange between Hutchison and Ward, *ibid.*, June, 1960 and Hutchison's more recent thoughts on the question in his *On Revolutions and Progress in Economic Knowledge* (1978), chap. 5. D. Vickers, *Studies in the Theory of Money*, 1690–1776 (1959), emphasizes the preoccupation of 18th-century authors with employment-generating schemes and lends support to Keynes's enthusiastic endorsement of mercantilist theory. J. M. Low's brilliant paper, 'The Rate of Interest: British Opinion in the Eighteenth Century', *MS*, May 1954, provides a healthy antidote to Keynesian exuberance, as do the first two chapters of G. S. L. Tucker, *Progress and Profits in British Economic Thought, 1650–1850* (1960). D. C. Coleman, 'Labour in the English Economy of the Seventeenth Century', *EHR*, April, 1956, argues that the employment theme in the literature of the period must be understood in the context of an underdeveloped economy. E. S. Furniss, *The Position of the Labourer in a System in Nationalism* (1920, reprinted 1957), the classic book on mercantilist labour policy, makes interesting reading in the light of later Keynesian interpretations of mercantilism.

On the emergence of the quantity theory of money, see the standard work by A. E. Monroe, *Monetary Theory before Adam Smith* (1923), and the incisive treatment of H. Hegeland, *The Quantity Theory of Money* (1951). Schumpeter deals brilliantly with the struggle between monetary and real analysis in the 18th century: *History of Economic Analysis*, Part II, chap. 6.

A selection of Quesnay's economic writings is available in English: *The Economics of Physiocracy* (1962) by R. L. Meek. Quesnay was a poor expositor and his writings abound in obscurities and inconsistencies. The detail, however, matters less than the amazing sweep of his ideas. *Quesnay's Tableau Economique*, eds. M. Kuczynski and R. L. Meek (1972), tells the extraordinary story of the appearance and disappearance of successive editions of Quesnay's *Tableau*. A recent French collection of essays, *François Quesnay et la Physiocratie*, ed. A. Sauvy (1958), depicts the physiocrats as premature economic liberals; N. J. Ware denied this thesis in a famous paper entitled: 'The Physiocrats: A Study in Economic Rationalization'. *AER*, December, 1931. Ware views physiocratic ideas as an expression of the interests of a new class of bourgeois landowners emerging from the French bureaucracy; this neo-Marxist interpretation makes an interesting contrast with Marx's own subtler explanation echoed in the last chapter of Meek's *Economics of Physiocracy*: 'the doctrine of the exclusive productivity of agriculture can be said to have "fitted the facts" with a reasonable degree of accuracy'; 'They [the physiocrats] were wrong not so much because they were bad scientists, as because they were bad prophets'.

A good brief treatment of physiocracy can be found in C. Gide and C. Rist, *A History of Economic Doctrines* (1948), chap. 1. L. Rogin in *The Meaning and Validity of Economic Theory* (1956), chap. 2, treats the physiocrats as agrarian reformers. Schumpeter, *History of Economic Analysis*, Part II, chap. 4, deals not only with the physiocrats but also with Petty and Cantillon. The contrast between the conditions of French and English agriculture, so important for grasping Smith's reaction to physiocracy, is well brought out by S. J. Brandenburg, 'The Place of Agriculture in British National Economy Prior to Adam Smith', *JPE*, June, 1931. A. I. Bloomfield shows how meager were the contributions of the physiocrats to the classical theory of the nature and gains of foreign trade: 'The Foreign Trade Doctrines of the Physiocrats', *AER*, 1938, reprinted in *EET*. On the input-output formulation of Quesnay's zigzag diagrams, see A. Phillips, 'The Tableau d'Economique as a Simple Leontief Model', *QJE*, 1955, reprinted in *ETHA*, and T. Barna, 'Quesnay's *Tableau* in Modern Guise', *EJ*, September, 1975. The definite review of the long history of attempts to read meaning into the *Tableau* is by R. L. Meek, 'The Interpretation of the "Tableau Economique"', *Ec*, 1960, reprinted in his *Economics of Physiocracy*, and in *ETHA*. But V. J. Tarascio, 'Quesnay's Tableau Economique: A Puzzle Unresolved', *HESB*, Summer, 1979, reminds us that only very generous interpretations can make Quesnay's diagrams internally consistent. See also the remarkably fresh discussion by W. A. Eltis, *The Classical Theory of Economic Growth* (1984), chaps. 1, 2, which comes closer to demystifying the *Tableau* than anything I know of.

T. P. Neill, 'Quesnay and Physiocracy', *JHI*, April, 1948, and 'The Physiocrats' Concept of Economics', *QJE*, November, 1949, provide a useful reminder that the physiocrats had no notion of economics as an autonomous science; they regarded their system as providing an all-embracing normative social science. For an acute analysis of the natural-law foundation of physiocratic thinking, see M. Albaum, 'Moral Defenses of Physiocrat's Laissez-Faire', *JHI*, April, 1955, and two articles by W. J. Samuels, 'The Physiocratic Theory of Property and State', *QJE*, February, 1961, and 'The Physiocratic Theory of Economic Policy', *ibid.*, February, 1962. On the natural-law philosophers, see O. H. Taylor's two well-known articles: 'Economics and the Idea of Natural Laws, I, II', *QJE*, 1929, 1930, reprinted in the author's *Economics and Liberalism* (1955). The first of these discusses the influence of natural-law doctrine in fostering analysis of the operation of a free market; the second deals in detail with the physiocrats and Adam Smith. British natural-law doctrine is treated by A. F. Chalk, 'Natural Law and the Rise of Economic Individualism in England', *JPE*, 1951, reprinted in *RHET*.

Adam Smith's strange notions of Chinese economic development (*Wealth of Nations*, Book IV, chap. 9) were apparently derived from Quesnay, who believed that China practised Mandarin despotism, esteemed agriculture, and allowed the natural order to prevail: see the fascinating study by L. A. Maverick, *China: a Model for Europe* (1946). Physiocratic ideas survived in England well into the 19th century and were taken up by the English underconsumptionists. Say's Law of Markets grew out of the debate between 'Physiocracy and Classicism in Britain'; see the article of that title by R. L. Meek, *EJ*, 1951, reprinted in his *Economics of Physiocracy* and in *RHET*, and J. J. Spengler, 'The Physiocrats and Say's Law of Markets', *JPE*, 1945, reprinted in *EET*.

My comments on scholastic economics lean heavily on a series of articles by R. A. De Roover, reprinted in *Business, Banking and Economic Thought in Late Medieval and Early Modern Europe: Selected studies of Raymond de Roover*, ed. V. Krishner (1974), and summarized in his 'Economic Thought: Ancient and Medieval Thought', *IESS*, 4. For a different view, see D. D. Friedman, 'In Defense of Thomas Aquinas and the Just Price', *HOPE*, Summer, 1980. J. T. Noonan, Jr., *The Scholastic Analysis of Usury* (1957), is also useful in dispelling the many misconceptions about scholastic doctrine that still prevail; of the many books available on scholastic usury doctrines, this is the most congenial to modern economists. For a succinct but excessively laudatory discussion of the subject, see Schumpeter, *History of Economic Analysis*, Part II, chap. 2, pp. 73–107. Scholastic economics forms part of the broad stream of premarginal utility theory that runs back to Aristotle and forward through Galiani, Condillac and Say to Gossen, Jevons, and Menger: see E. Kauder, 'Genesis of Marginal Utility Theory', *EJ*, 1953, reprinted in *EET*, L. Einaudi, 'Ferdinando Galiani', *SZV*, 1945, reprinted in *DET*, and H. R. Sewall, *The Theory of Value before Adam Smith* (1901), which is still the standard reference work on the subject, covering a long list of writers from Plato to Steuart, and tracing in detail the fluctuations of opinion that stressed now demand, now supply. O. Langholm's path-breaking book, *Price and Value Theory in the Aristotelian Tradition* (1979), reinterprets this entire literature and must be read by serious students of pre-Adamite economics. B. J. Gordon, *Economic Analysis Before Adam Smith: Hesiod to Lessius* (1975) is an informative but traditional recent book on Greek, Roman and scholastic economics. See also S. Todd Lowry, 'Recent Literature on Greek Economic Thought', *JEL*, March, 1979.

2

Adam Smith

The practice of reading the expensive tomes of the 18th century from cover to cover seems to have almost wholly died out. Nowadays we read selections of Gibbon, Johnson, and Hume and confine ourselves to the first ten chapters of the *Wealth of Nations*. But Glenn Morrow at the sesquicentennial commemoration of Smith's book told of someone who actually read the whole volume:

> Once upon a time there was a man who read the *Wealth of Nations*; not a summary, nor a volume of selected passages, but the *Wealth of Nations* itself. He began with the Introduction, he read the famous first chapter on the division of labour, the chapters on the origin and use of money, the prices of commodities, the wages of labour, the profits of stock, the rent of land, and all the other well-known economic portions of the first book, not omitting the long digression on the fluctuation in the value of silver during the last four centuries, and the statistical tables at the end. Having completed the first book he went on to the second, not deterred by the fact that it is supposed to contain an erroneous theory of capital and an untenable distinction between productive and unproductive labour. In Book III he found an account of the economic development of Europe since the fall of the Roman Empire, with digressions upon the various phases of medieval life and civilization. In the fourth book he came upon extended analyses and criticisms of the commercial and colonial policies of European nations, and a whole battery of free trade arguments. Finally, he attacked the long concluding book on the revenue of the sovereign. Here he found even more varied and unexpected matters: an account of the different methods of defense and of administering justice in primitive societies, and of the origin and growth of standing armies in Europe; a history of education in the Middle Ages and a criticism of eighteenth-century universities; a history of the temporal power of the church, of the growth of public debts in modern nations, of the mode of electing bishops in the ancient church; reflections as to the disadvantages of the division of labour, and – what is the main purpose of the book – an examination of principles of taxation and of systems of public revenue. Time is too short to enumerate all that he found here before he finally came to the concluding paragraphs, written during the opening events of the American Revolution, concerning the duty of colonies to contribute towards the expenses of the mother country.
>
> Now, of course I may have exaggerated somewhat. There probably never was any such man.

1. Adam Smith and the Industrial Revolution

Let us assume, in a triumph of hope over experience, that people who read Smith's entire volume are not as rare as is sometimes believed. Before turning to a detailed review of the contents of the *Wealth of Nations*, however, we must clear up one point. In his Introduction to the book, Adam Smith makes it clear that his leading theme is economic development: the long-term forces that govern the growth of the wealth of nations. It is evident that by 'wealth' he really means, not the community's capital at a given moment of time – a stock – but the community's income produced during a *period* of time – a flow – although he did not always adhere consistently to this conception. The growth of income is made dependent, in the first place, upon the scope of the division of labour in a society with division of labour so broadly defined as to include everything we would nowadays call technical progress. No sooner has he described division of labour in 'a very trifling manufacture' in the opening pages of the work than he notes that industry generally affords greater scope for specialization than does agriculture and that rich countries usually excel in manufacturing. 'The prophet of the Industrial Revolution', 'the spokesman of manufacturing interests', we are likely to mutter to ourselves. But this is all wrong! The whole book is directed against 'the mean rapacity, the monopolizing spirit of merchants and manufacturers, who neither are, nor ought to be, the rulers of mankind'. The merchants and master-manufacturers are the architects of the hated Mercantile System, and there is virtually no indication in the *Wealth of Nations* that these same men were even then launching England upon a new industrial age. Indeed, there is nothing in the book to suggest that Adam Smith was aware that he was living in times of extremely unusual economic change.

He speaks of 'the invention of all those machines which facilitate and abridge labour' but gives concrete examples of innovations dating back to the Middle Ages. He talks of iron ore smelted with charcoal, although it was generally smelted with coke by his time. And despite the fact that the last revised edition of the *Wealth of Nations* appeared in 1784, he nowhere mentions Kay's flying shuttle, Hargreaves' spinning jenny, Compton's mule, or Arkwright's water frame, inventions that were revolutionizing the textile industry in the 1780s. James Watt, the inventor of the steam engine, was a personal acquaintance, possibly a friend; the Boulton-Watt partnership was formed in 1775; yet Smith never refers to the successful commercial application of the steam engine to coal mining in the late 1770s. As a matter of fact, he took a dim view generally of the speculative trading of 'projectors' – 'innovators' we would call them – and in Book II of the *Wealth of Nations* condemned Scottish banks for extending credit too liberally to the 'spirited undertakings' that were being carried on at the time in Scotland. Is this the language of a prophet of the Industrial Revolution?

When Toynbee gave currency to the term 'Industrial Revolution' over seventy-five years ago, he dated the onset of the movement at 1760, the year in which the furnaces at the great Carron iron works in Scotland were first lighted. But if by an industrial revolution we mean, not a stampede on the Patent Office but a sudden acceleration in the rate of growth of output, we should move the date at which the Industrial Revolution started forward to 1790. No doubt, all the major inventions of the period had been patented by 1755 but it is only in the late 1780s that statistical series of production in Britain, and particularly the then available figures on exports and imports, began to show a sharp upward trend. There may have been an earlier and milder rise in the pace of economic progress in the 1740s, but the decisive turning point that marks the 'take-off' of British industry came in the last two decades of the 18th century, some years after the *Wealth of Nations* first saw the light of day. Of course, most contemporaries were slow to recognize what was happening, and even by the turn of the century there were still many acute observers who were unimpressed by the recent 'progress of the mechanical arts' in England. It is not surprising, therefore, that Adam Smith failed to anticipate the Industrial Revolution. We need to remember that when the book appeared, the typical water-driven factory held 300–400 workers, and there were only twenty or thirty such establishments in the whole of the British Isles. This helps to account for Adam Smith's neglect of fixed capital and for the conviction, which he never really abandoned, that agriculture and not manufacture was the principal source of Britain's wealth.

READER'S GUIDE TO 'WEALTH OF NATIONS'

2. Division of Labour

Book I contains the core of Smith's theory of value and distribution; it opens with a discussion of the advantages of the division of labour, understood in the sense of the specialization of tasks within an industrial enterprise – later, in Book V, this kind of specialization is admitted to have some disadvantages. But 'division of labour' may also mean the separation of different multiproduct enterprises by a process of horizontal or vertical disintegration, followed by concentration upon the production of single products. This sense of the term soon comes to overshadow the earlier conception. Indeed, the whole of Book I is constructed upon the grand theme of the *social* division of labour: the economic system is in essence a vast network of interrelations among specialized producers held together by 'the propensity to truck, barter, and exchange'. The last magnificent paragraph of **Book I, chapter 1** – a beautiful example of 18th-century prose – makes this plain enough and, in the next chapter, we are told that 'the certainty of being able to exchange all that surplus part of the produce of his own labour, which is over and above his own consumption, for such parts of the produce of other men's labour as he may have occasion for, encourages every man to apply himself to a particular occupation, and to cultivate and to bring to perfection whatever talent or genius he may possess for that particular species of business'. The characteristic 18th-century faith in the powerful influence of nurture as against nature explains why Smith neglects to cite the accommodation of different natural aptitudes as one of the advantages of the division of labour; but the 'territorial division of labour' is ignored without any apparent reason, although the idea had been broached frequently by previous writers. **Book I, chapter 3,** points out that 'division of labour is limited by the extent of the market'; in other words, nothing limits the length to which specialization can be carried except the marketable volume of output, a proposition which is by no means self-evident. The phrase '*extent* of the market' might suggest that he was aware of the notion of sales areas: it is not just a matter of the number of customers but also where they are actually located. But such ideas were to come into economics much later [see chapter 14, section 10]. Nevertheless, Smith's third chapter foreshadows all later discussions of the limits to increasing returns to scale. There is a striking emphasis throughout the discussion on the reductions in costs that are effected by improvements in the means of transportation and communication, a note that appears again a century later in Marshall's *Principles*.

3. The Measure and Cause of Value

So far, exchange is considered solely as barter exchange. In **Book I, chapter 4,** money is introduced and exchange value is distinguished from use value as illustrated by the water-diamond paradox; the chapter closes with an appeal to the reader's patience for the next three chapters, which investigate 'the principles which regulate the exchangeable value of commodities'. It is 'a subject extremely abstracted', Smith concedes, and it 'may perhaps, after the fullest explication which I am capable of giving it, appear still in some degree obscure'. Most readers would put this remark down as the greatest understatement in the history of economic thought; **Book I, chapter 5,** is particularly difficult to follow and has attracted a bewildering variety of interpretations, revolving around the distinction between the 'cause' and the 'measure' of exchange value, on the one hand, and the difference between a 'labour-commanded' and a 'labour-embodied' theory of value, on the other. The trouble lies in the fact that Smith himself was in two minds about the problem he was posing. 'In order to investigate the conditions which regulate the exchangeable value of commodities', he declared, 'I shall endeavor to shew

> First, what is the real measure of this exchangeable value; or, wherein consists the real price of all commodities.
>
> Secondly, what are the different parts of which this real price is composed or made up.
>
> And, lastly, what are the different circumstances which sometimes raise some or all of these different parts of prices above, and sometimes sink them below their natural or ordinary rate; or what are the causes which sometimes hinder the market price, that is, the actual price of commodities, from coinciding exactly with what may be called their natural price.'

This confuses two very different sorts of questions: what is the best measure of value and what is it that determines value? **Book I, chapter 5,** takes up the first question; and **Book I, chapters 6 and 7,** deal with the second question. For the sake of clarity, these two lines of inquiry ought to be kept strictly separate. Let us, therefore, pass over chapter 5 at this point and come back to it when we have dealt with the remainder of Book I.

4. Cost-of-Production Theory

Book I, chapters 6 and 7, take up the traditional problem of value theory: Why are relative prices what they are? At any moment of time, of course, the 'market price' is determined by demand and supply. But as the forces of demand and supply work themselves out, the daily and even hourly fluctuations of the market price tend constantly to be reduced to a 'normal' or, as Smith says, a 'natural' level. What he calls 'market price' and 'natural price' is identical to what Marshall calls the short-period and the long-period price and, like Marshall, Smith is essentially interested in explaining how prices are determined in the long run. To motivate his ultimate explanation, Smith begins by constructing a simple model in which only one factor of production is used to produce commodities; this is his 'early and rude state of society', where land is free and capital is nonexistent. In this one-factor world, relative prices are obviously governed by relative labour costs, and even the premium that skilled labour receives over unskilled labour is no more than a payment for the labour costs of extra training: in a society of hunters – presumably using their bare hands – one beaver will exchange for two deer when it takes twice as much labour to kill a beaver as it does to kill a deer. But this argument is designed to show only that the exchange value of a commodity in the real world cannot be determined simply by the labour expended on its production. The value of a commodity is the sum of the normal amounts payable to all the factors used in making it; hence, the 'natural price' of an article in the real world is determined by its money costs of production as made up of wages, rents and profits, themselves the 'natural price' of labour, land, and capital.

A cost-of-production theory of the value of a commodity is obviously empty and meaningless if it does not include some explanation of how the prices of productive services are determined. But Adam Smith had no consistent theory of wages and rents and no theory of profit or pure interest at all. To say that the normal price of an article is the price that just covers money costs is to explain prices by prices. In this sense, Adam Smith had no theory of value whatever. Be that as it may, it is clear that he had no *labour* theory of value, meaning by that the proposition that commodities exchange at ratios which – as in the beaver-deer example above – are the reciprocals of the quantity of labour expended in their production, including the labour embodied in the capital goods the labourers make use of. There is no suggestion in the *Wealth of Nations* that the different factors of production can be assimilated in terms of some common denominator other than money and, in particular, there is no suggestion that the value of capital goods can be reduced to labour expended on their production in the past; as we shall see, it is this 'reduction' which constitutes the *pons asinorum* of the labour theory of value. Indeed, the construction of **Book I, chapter 6,** shows clearly that it was meant to be a refutation of the labour-cost theory of value hinted at by so many of Smith's predecessors: he shows that such a theory is valid only under the special and artificial conditions of an 'early and rude state of society'.

5. Supply-Determined Prices
Book I, chapter 7, one of the high points of the book, is full of the kind of 'partial equilibrium analysis' that has always been the bread and butter of economists. His reference to the effect of a public mourning on the price of black cloth is a classic of its kind: a temporary shortage of black cloth raises the price of mourning cloth and

the wages of tailors but does not affect the wages of weavers because the scarcity is temporary, whereas it reduces the price of such goods as colored silk and the wages of workers producing them. It is only when the producers of an article are neither gaining excess profits nor suffering actual losses that the price corresponds to its normal value. The constant adjustment of demand and supply is forever tending to produce the long-run 'natural price' that just covers the cost of bringing the product to market. 'Effectual demand', Smith points out, is the demand of those 'who are willing to pay the natural price of a commodity'; it is the demand effective at the long-run equilibrium price. Now 'the *quantity* of every commodity brought to the market naturally suits itself to the effectual demand', but the long-run *price* of a commodity is said to be governed solely by the outlays of producers on the supply side of the market. When it comes to the determination of natural price, demand is supposed to have no influence.

Smith did not justify his neglect of demand; he lacked the apparatus to do so. But it is possible to justify the argument with the aid of Marshallian reasoning. Notice first, however, that his mention of 'the paradox of value' – useful goods like water are free, whereas useless goods like diamonds are expensive – is not an attempt to defend the neglect of demand. The passage begins with the remark that 'the word value has two different meanings', and the statement of the paradox drives home the distinction between use value and exchange value; exchange value is the proper subject of investigation, Smith concludes. It is evident to any modern reader that Smith means by 'use value' the total utility of a whole class of commodities instead of the marginal utility of individual units: he is thinking of utility not as the power to satisfy a particular want – clearly, diamonds are wanted – but as the power to satisfy a generalized biological or social need. He does not even trouble to say that use value is a prerequisite to exchange value; and, clearly, as he employs the words, it is not. This illustrates the importance of paying strict attention to the meaning of terms as employed by the older writers.

Moreover, long before Adam Smith, such writers as Locke, Law, and Harris had contrasted the value of water with that of diamonds to show that relative scarcity governs value irrespective of the usefulness of an article. And what governs relative scarcity? In the short run, demand and supply; this is exactly what Smith himself says later about the high price of precious stones (**Book I, chapter 11, part 2**). But in the long run, it was held, scarcity is governed solely by the cost of producing an article. This curious belief that only the short-run or current price of a commodity is the province of the forces of demand and supply is very character-istic of 18th-century economics, and it is a belief that was only destroyed by the marginal revolution of the 1870s. It rests, of course, on a misunderstanding. When we say that value is determined by demand and supply, we mean merely that they are the channels through which ultimate factors like cost or utility operate: whatever regulates value does so via its effect upon demand and supply. But this is not how the matter was regarded in Smith's time. It is not that these writers rejected a utility theory of value because they thought that utility was incapable of being quantitatively related to price, a difficulty that never occurred to them, but rather that they saw no relationship between utility, in their sense of the term, and demand.

If we look carefully at Smith's examples of price determination, we notice that he always assumes implicitly that the 'natural price' of a commodity does not vary with its rate of output. In other words, he assumes that the industry in question produces under conditions of constant costs: to make two units of an article costs twice as much as to make one unit of it; cost per unit remains constant regardless of the level of output. This is the case in which the long-run supply curve of the industry is perfectly horizontal and in which the level of demand governs the quantity of a commodity produced but has indeed no influence on price (see Figure 2–2a in contrast to Figure 2–2b). Without realizing it, Adam Smith investigated a special case of the Marshallian theory of value, the case in which price is determined by supply alone. Under exactly what conditions this case obtains we must leave until later [see chapter 10, section 3]. Suffice it to say that a good argument could be made for constant costs even now as the simplest general assumption. Still, the fact that we need Marshall to make sense of Smith affords an excellent illustration of what is meant by analytical progress in economics.

The advanced student of economics may benefit from the following justification of Smith's approach which borrows the tools of 20th-century economics to clarify the logic of the constant-costs case. Recall the two-commodity, one-factor society of hunters: let us express the rate at which deer can be converted via hunting into beavers by means of a production-transformation curve (Figure 2–1). Since there is only one scarce resource, the transformation curve is in fact a straight line: the ratio of deer gained per beavers sacrificed is the same no matter how many beavers or deer are killed; when there is only one factor of production, the scale of operations cannot affect costs per unit of output because a factor of production is defined as consisting of units of equal efficiency. It takes two hours to kill a beaver as against one hour for a deer. Hence, beavers should cost twice as much to buy as deer. But suppose the rate of exchange is one deer per beaver instead of two deer per beaver. In that case, a beaver producer will give up producing *one* beaver in two hours and produce two deer instead, with which he can then buy *two* beavers. Deer hunting

Figure 2–1

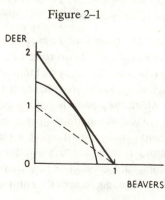

Figure 2–2

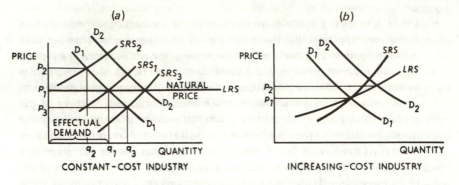

(a)

CONSTANT-COST INDUSTRY

(b)

INCREASING-COST INDUSTRY

will increase and beaver hunting will decline until the rate of exchange is once again equal to the production-transformation ratio; the price is entirely determined by supply considerations. It would not matter if we imposed a pattern of demand in the form of a family of convex indifference curves. Equilibrium would be found at the tangency point with the transformation curve and, once again, the market price ratio would necessarily have the same slope as the transformation line. Under conditions of constant costs, relative prices are not influenced by demand.

If, however, as we approached the deer axis, the beaver cost of deer rose because hunters have to go farther afield for them while beavers can be obtained nearer home, the transformation curve would become concave (as shown). Now the structure of demand – the position of the indifference curves – does help to determine relative price. In the latter case we have introduced an additional factor of production, namely land: and land and labour cannot be combined with equal efficiency regardless of the absolute amount of each required. This means that the constant-costs case is analogous to the case of a single factor: although several factors are used, they are employed in fixed proportions, so that we can talk of a composite dose varying in amount but unchanging in its composition.

It may be useful to present Smith's argument graphically in terms of a standard demand-and-supply diagram (Figure 2–2a). Consider the following passage in Smith interlarded with our own geometrical translations:

> When the quantity of any commodity which is brought to market falls short of the effectual demand [the short-run supply curve SRS_1 shifts back to SRS_2 along D_1] all those who are willing to pay the whole value of the rent, wages, and profit, which must be paid in order to bring it thither, cannot be supplied with the quantity which they want [which is q_1]. Rather than want it altogether, some of them will be willing to give more [to pay p_2]. A competition will immediately begin among them, and the market price will rise more or less above the natural price according as either the greatness of the deficiency, or the wealth and wanton luxury of the competitors, happen to animate more or less the eagerness of the competition ... When the quantity

brought to market exceeds the effectual demand [SRS_1 shifts forward to SRS_3], it cannot be all sold to those who are willing to pay the whole value of the rent, wages, and profit, which must be paid in order to bring it thither. Some part must be sold to those who are willing to pay less, and the low price which they give for it must reduce the price of the whole. The market price will sink more or less below the natural price [fall to p_3], according as the greatness of the excess increases more or less the competition of the sellers, or according as it happens to be more or less important to them to get immediately rid of the commodity ... When the quantity brought to market is just sufficient to supply the effectual demand and no more, the market price naturally comes to be either exactly, or as nearly as can be judged of, the same with the natural price. The whole quantity upon hand can be disposed of for this price, and cannot be disposed of for more. The competition of the different dealers obliges them all to accept of this price, but does not oblige them to accept of less.

It will be noticed that Smith thinks of demand and supply as referring to people's willingness to buy or sell at a particular price rather than at all possible prices; the former is expressed in actual amounts desired or offered, the latter in a schedule of amounts, each corresponding to a different price. Still, the whole of the passage given above has no real meaning unless demand at any rate is interpreted in the sense of a schedule, and a negatively inclined schedule at that. Here and elsewhere Smith intuitively gropes his way toward the right answer.

The common usage of the term 'competition' as denoting rivalry is reflected in Smith's remark that a reduced supply leads to 'competition' among buyers, which raises the price – a race to get limited supplies – while an excess supply leads to rivalry to get rid of the surplus, which causes the price to fall. He is aware of the fact that competition deprives the participants in the market process of the power to influence price and that the larger the number of sellers, the greater the obstacles to 'combinations'. In the course of **Book I, chapter 7,** he mentions not only many sellers but also perfect information and perfect mobility of resources as pre-requisites of effective competition; only homogeneity of the product is missing in a discussion that any modern textbook might envy. Nevertheless, Smith's analysis of competition is not equivalent to the modern concept of perfect competition: what he emphasizes is the *process* of rivalry that drives the market price towards the natural prices, and not, as in modern treatments, the properties of the final *state* of perfect competition, virtually achieved without the passage of time. Similarly his brief treatment of monopoly at the end of the chapter is decidedly old-fashioned: monopoly prevails for any articles in fixed supply. Nonreproducible commodities, such as valuable paintings or 'some vineyards in France', fall outside the scope of the theory of competitive price. But something like imperfect competition is hinted at when he remarks that 'secrets of manufacture' induce monopoly, meaning presumably that they give the manufacturer some power over the price. He concludes that 'the price of monopoly is upon every occasion the highest which can be squeezed out of the buyers', a misleading remark that nevertheless has the merit of recognizing that demand is responsive to price.

6. Wages

Book I, chapters 8–11, contain Smith's theory of distribution. Chapter 8 is simply a compendium of wage theories. In the space of a half-dozen pages, we meet the wages fund theory, the subsistence theory, the bargaining theory, something like a productivity theory, and even a residual-claimant theory, without any recognition of the fact that these cannot all hold true on the same level of analysis. From the outset, Smith adheres to the conception of capital or 'stock' as consisting of 'advances' to workmen to tide them over the period of production; hence, a connection is laid down between 'the demand for those who live by wages' and 'the funds which are destined for the payment of wages'. This relationship is not explored, but it is made the basis of the conviction that the growth of capital entails a constantly rising demand for labour. This short-run supply and demand theory – supply is given by the size of the labour force and demand by the size of the wages fund – is combined with a long-run minimum-of-existence theory. Smith is not very clear as to how this adjustment takes place but a Malthusian wages-population mechanism is implied [see chapter 3, section 5].

The argument is perfectly analogous to the determination of the normal price of a commodity (see Figure 2–3). The 'natural price' of labour is the subsistence wage rate, that minimum reward that workers insist on before they are willing to have children (we postpone the discussion of this very elusive concept to the next chapter); in short, labour itself is produced at constant cost. Let us start when the 'market price' of labour is w_1 and the labour force is at L_1. We have drawn the supply curve of labour to show that the same number of workers could supply more labour at a higher wage rate, say, by working longer hours; still, unless population grows, the supply curve of labour stays where it is, for it depicts the

Figure 2–3

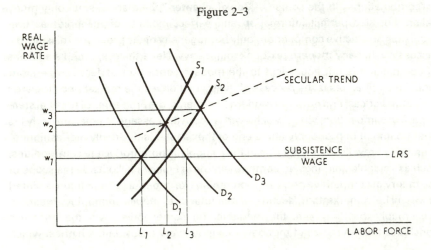

maximum quantity of labour that a given population is willing to offer at various wage rates.

Now suppose the demand for labour increases from D_1 to D_2; in the short run, wages rise to w_2 and, since 'the demand for men, like that of any other commodity, necessarily regulates the production of men', this will in time induce population growth to L_3; the supply curve will shift to the right (not shown) until wages fall back once again to w_1, the subsistence level. But if demand is continuously rising, population growth will lag behind: the rightward shifting supply curves (such as S_2, etc.) cannot catch up with the rightward shifting demand curves and the historical trend in real wages, which strictly speaking should be shown along a third axis depicting the passage of time, will be upward from w_2 to w_3. The subsistence theory of wages – a long-run theory of constant wages – is therefore perfectly compatible with a belief in the secular tendency of the going wage to rise indefinitely, and this quite apart from vertical upward shifts in the long-run supply curve as labour gradually changes its concept of what is a minimum acceptable level of subsistence.

As a matter of fact, Smith does say that wages in Great Britain are in excess of subsistence. Britain and North America are examples of the 'cheerful' progressive state where demand for labour outruns the supply. In 'dull' stationary countries like China, however, wages have sunk to the subsistence level. At this point, Smith makes an interesting slip in speaking of the minimum-of-existence wage as the lowest rate that 'common humanity' allows; it has, of course, nothing to do with the benevolence of employers, being a function of the elasticity of supply of labour in the long run. In fact, Smith never adopts a consistent subsistence theory of wages: it is only among 'inferior ranks of people', he observes, that population varies with the supply of food. Moreover, he emphasizes the very remote application of the subsistence theory to practical problems of wage determination: (1) although summer wages are invariably higher than winter wages because the demand for agricultural labour falls off in cold weather, the cost of a worker's maintenance is actually lower in the summer than in the winter; (2) although the price of 'provisions' fluctuates continually, money wages vary little and sometimes remain constant for as much as a half-century, presumably because of the influence of custom in setting wages, in consequence of which *real* wages fluctuate continually; (3) wages vary greatly in different parts of the country but the price of food is almost everywhere the same, owing to the fact that 'a man is of all sorts of luggage the most difficult to transport'; (4) wages and food prices often move in opposite directions because in years of bumper crops and low wheat prices, 'servants frequently leave their masters, and trust their subsistence to what they can make by their own industry' and the resulting shortage of labour then causes wages to rise; similarly, in years of dearth, wages fall as workmen flock back to the labour market. Adam Smith in effect makes the 'mode of subsistence' a result of the going wage rate rather than a cause of it. Certainly there is enough material here that points away from the subsistence theory.

In the earlier part of **Book I, chapter 8,** Smith remarks briefly, and almost as a matter of course, that the bargaining advantage in a labour market always lies on the side of the employer, employers 'being fewer in number' and able to 'hold out much longer'. Moreover, the law favours employers. Hence, 'masters' are 'always and everywhere in a sort of tacit, but constant and uniform combination, not to raise the wages of labour above their actual rate'. Taken strictly, this argument sits uneasily next to remarks about 'common humanity', and it flies in the face of the emphasis in the rest of the chapter upon the upward pull on demand for labour in a growing economy. But it has all the germs of the Marshallian thesis that there is indeterminacy in the labour market because the labour market is by its nature a noncompetitive market. Marshall, too, drew attention to the significance of fewness on the buying side in the labour market and noted, as did Smith, that workers lacked reserves for a protracted struggle with employers [see chapter 10, section 32].

Chapter 8 closes on an optimistic note. Wages have been rising in 'the course of the present century', and higher wages have not reduced incentives. The mercantilist notion that the short-run supply curve of labour is backward bending is strongly condemned: a rise in wages will tend to bring about an increase in the supply of labour services.

7. Profits

Book I, chapter 9, deals with the 'profits of stock' without saying very much about the nature of profit as income. Earlier, in chapter 6, Smith pointed out that profits are not to be confused with the wages of management, which vary with 'the quantity, the hardship, or the ingenuity of this supposed labour of inspection and direction'; more than this we are never told. The burden of chapter 9 is that the rate of profit tends to fall in the course of economic progress owing to 'mutual competition' as the 'stocks of many rich merchants are turned into the same trade.' But so long as output is growing, it is difficult to see why 'mutual competition' alone should lead to falling profit margins. It is only later, in **Book II, chapter 4,** that a satisfactory reason is given, namely, the increasing difficulty of finding new profitable investment outlets. Throughout this chapter, Smith speaks of profits as consisting of interest plus a risk premium. In such countries as Britain, he thinks, about one half of what is normally regarded as profits is pure interest on capital; the rest is a payment for superintendence and risk. The trend in the rate of profit, therefore, can be roughly inferred from movements in the market rate of interest. The rate of interest has been falling for centuries and seems everywhere inversely related to the degree of economic development of a country – a familiar piece of casual empiricism, 18th-century style. Generally, wages rise and profits fall in the process of capital accumulation; a new colony, however, may experience both rising wages and a rising rate of profit.

8. Relative Wages

Book I, chapter 10, part 1, digresses from the main theme to discuss the structure of wages. It is perhaps the best single piece of economic analysis in the *Wealth of*

Nations and, although it leans heavily on Cantillon, a reading of the corresponding chapters in Cantillon's *Essai* (chapters 7 and 8) is likely to raise one's respect for Adam Smith's analytical powers. Quite apart from its classic treatment of relative wage differences, this chapter has an important role to play in the general structure of Book I: indeed, without it the troublesome fifth chapter makes little sense. Smith traces all differences in daily or weekly wage rates in stationary equilibrium to differences in (1) the agreeableness of different occupations, (2) the cost of acquiring the skill to carry them on, (3) the degree of regularity of employment, (4) the trust and responsibility imposed upon those employed, and (5) the probability of actually obtaining anticipated earnings given the great uncertainty of success in some lines of employment.

The first reason for relative wage differentials is the common idea, later formalized by Jevons, that wages vary positively, everything else being the same, with the disutility of labour. Alas, wages in the real world, as John Stuart Mill was to say, seem if anything to vary inversely to the disutility of effort: the hardest, dirtiest jobs are generally the worst paid. However, the wages we observe are the results of the interaction of demand and supply and the disutility of labour is concerned solely with the supply side. It is perfectly conceivable, therefore, that elements on the demand side or other elements on the supply side will dominate considerations of disutility. The second reason for relative wage differentials, again on the supply side, contains the germ of an idea that is only now being fully exploited, namely, the concept of human capital. The cost of a man's education or training, Adam Smith conjectures, can be viewed as an investment in future earning capacity, analogous to investment in physical capital; this investment must be recouped over the lifetime of the student or trainee if it is to be economically justified. Thus, better educated and better trained people will generally earn more than those who lack education or training: 'The work which he [an educated man] learns to perform, it must be expected, over and above the usual wages of common labour, will replace to him the whole expense of his education, with at least the ordinary profits of an equally valuable capital'. This notion has given rise in recent years to numerous attempts to measure the rate of return on investment in education to check whether in fact such investments earn 'the ordinary profits of an equally valuable capital'. The third reason for wage differentials, again on the supply side, implies that workers will insist on higher wages if they cannot be promised secure employment; on the other hand, why should employers in casual, seasonal trades be able to pay higher wages than employers in stable, non-seasonal trades? Suffice it to say that here is the germ, but only the germ, of modern theories of the 'implicit contract' between workers and firms, according to which a bargain is struck about wages and employment between risk-averting workers and risk-neutral firms.

Next, the fourth reason does not clearly fall on one side or the other: it assumes either that the assumption of responsibility must be rewarded because responsibility is irksome, a supply-determined explanation, or that the higher wages of supervisors and executives are a sort of insurance policy against theft and the betrayal of confidences, a demand-determined explanation. The fifth reason, again from the side of supply, is particularly interesting because it clearly involves choice in the presence of uncertainty. Until fairly recently, these pages in Smith and a few pages in Marshall's *Principles* exhausted the content of the history of economic analysis of choices among unsure prospects. Smith uses casual evidence from lotteries and insurance to show that people tend to overvalue uncertain gains and to undervalue uncertain losses, that is, he assumes as a matter of course that people are 'risk-lovers'. This leads him to argue that all professions that hold out the prospect of relatively high but uncertain earnings for the few will show a mean rate of reward below that of comparable occupations whose earnings can be predicted with perfect certainty; people will always overestimate their chances of success in these risky professions (think of law and medicine) and so will overcrowd them. Smith then applies this line of reasoning with appropriate qualifications to differential rates of profit in different industries. Unfortunately, the opposite assumption that professionals are typically 'risk-averters' leads to exactly the opposite conclusion from that of Smith, namely, that high-risk professions will yield a higher average rate of return than low-risk professions. Again, surprisingly, it is only now that such hypotheses about occupational choice are being tested.

The general implication of the chapter is more important than matters of detail: while competition may not equalize the monetary returns to different occupations, it does equalize the 'net advantages' of different occupations to different individuals, that is, the sum of pecuniary and nonpecuniary rewards, each differential in monetary earnings being compensated by one or more of the five factors listed above. The market tends to reduce the various types of labour to a common measure: equal units of labour in the sense of equal amounts of disutility are at any one time compensated by equal amounts of money wages. This assumes, of course, that the labour market is perfectly competitive and, in particular, that there is perfect mobility of labour between different occupations; this is so obvious that Smith hardly bothers to say it, but he does add that net advantages are equalized only when there is adequate information about the monetary and nonmonetary alternatives of different occupations and when they are the sole employ of those who occupy them.

Remarkable as it is, Smith's analysis of the wage structure appears to be inadequate, if only because it has almost nothing to say about the demand for labour. Furthermore, Smith makes no distinction between time-wages and piece-rate wages, or between weekly wages and monthly salaries; it is conceivable that the occupational choices of salaried professionals are governed by factors other than income to a much greater degree than the occupational choices of wage earners, so that one theoretical framework cannot handle both phenomena. Besides, in the face of the imperfections that almost all labour markets exhibit, any analysis based on the postulate of perfect competition is unlikely to account for the wage and salary differentials that we actually observe. We must remember, however, that the purpose of Book I, chapter 10, was not so much to explain wage differentials as to show that despite subjective differences in people's inclination to work, the market mechanism left everyone equally well off no matter which occupation he entered.

Book I, chapter 10, part 2, on the 'Policy of Europe', may be passed over quickly, but it does contain some excellent economic history. It condemns the exclusive privileges of trading companies, the apprenticeship laws, the Settlements Acts and the Poor Laws in general for restricting the scope of competition and for interfering with the mobility of labour. The threat of monopolistic practices is ever present: 'people of the same trade seldom meet together but the conversation ends in a conspiracy to raise prices'.

9. Rent

Book I, chapter 11, deals formally with rent. Here rent is treated as a differential surplus and hence as price determined: 'high or low wages and profit, are the cause of high or low price; high or low rent is the effect of it'. Moreover, this surplus is made a function of both differences in fertility and differences in situation. The whole treatment is suggestive of the later Ricardian theory of rent. Earlier in the book, however, rent is regarded as price determining instead of price determined because land not receiving going rentals will be withdrawn from cultivation (**Book I, chapter 9**). Letting this contradiction stand for the moment, we turn to the conclusion of **Book I, chapter 11**. Parts 1–3 of chapter 11 can be skipped without too much loss, although part 2 contains a significant distinction between foodstuffs, the demand for which is highly inelastic, and luxury goods, the demand for which is generally elastic: 'The desire for food is limited in every man by the narrow capacity of the human stomach'. The concluding pages of chapter 11 declare without proof that economic progress entails rising money rentals, rising real rentals, and a rising rental share of national income. The interests of landowners, though they 'reap where they never sowed', are therefore inseparably connected with the general interest of society, whereas the interests of merchants and manufacturers are always anti-social: since the rate of profit declines as wealth accumulates, their interest is always 'to widen the market and to narrow the competition'. Any notion that Smith is an apologist for the bourgeoisie is dispelled by a reading of the acid sentence that closes Book I; a similarly acerbic sentiment appears at the end of Book IV, chapter 2.

10. A Social Unit of Accounting

We turn back now to **Book I, chapter 5,** entitled 'Of the Real and Nominal Price of Commodities, or of Their Price in Labour, and Their Price in Money'. This is concerned not with value theory but with welfare economics and, in particular, with the problem of an index number of welfare. The 'real price' of a thing is, of course, its purchasing power over all other goods: its nominal price corrected for changes in the value of money. Smith decides, however, to correct nominal prices for changes in money wage rates rather than changes in the average level of prices. This peculiar solution to the index-number problem is precisely the one adopted in our own times by Keynes who defined real income in terms of employment rather than physical output. By using a wage unit as a deflator – the money wage rate paid for an hour of common labour – Keynes obtained a one-to-one relationship between income and employment, given a constant share of wages in total income.[1] In the Keynesian short run, it makes little difference whether one corrects for price changes or for wage changes, but in the long run the choice of a deflator is a serious matter, for as the productivity of labour rises, prices will normally fall relative to wage rates. Unlike Keynes, Adam Smith did want to measure real income over long periods of time, and his choice of a labour standard was dictated not by any conviction that money wages are less subject to variation than prices in general but by his conception of the nature of economic welfare.

The purpose of an index number of welfare is that it enables us to estimate whether an individual or a society is better off over changes in time and place. Nowadays we assume that an increase in real income is tantamount to an improvement in welfare. But Adam Smith tried to go deeper, associating improvements in welfare with a reduction in the sacrifices required to obtain a given flow of real income. Labour is irksome and 'toil and trouble' is the ultimate scarce factor of production. An individual's 'wealth' is naturally measured by the ability to command other people's products, but the pursuit of wealth under the division of labour is motivated by the desire to save ourselves disagreeable labour and to impose it instead upon others; so a man values his wealth or a commodity that he possesses by the amount of other people's labour he can buy with it in the market. The 'real value' of a commodity is its labour price, meaning by labour, not a certain number of man-hours, but units of disutility, the psychological cost of work to the individual, and meaning by value, esteem value rather than exchange value.

With this much in mind, **Book I, chapter 5,** is plain sailing. In 'that rude and original state of society' when 'the whole produce of labour belongs to the labourer', the personal labour embodied in commodities coincides with their purchasing power over labour. A man is then rich or poor according to the value of his own labour services or his purchasing power over other men's labour services, for the two are identical. With the rise of property income, this coincidence is broken: the value of a commodity measured in current wage units – the quantity of labour that it can command in exchange – now exceeds the value of the labour embodied in its production by the whole value of profits and rents. Nevertheless, the 'real value' or effort price of a commodity is still to be measured by the units of 'toil and trouble' that it can purchase in the market at the going wage rate. But whose 'toil and trouble' is to be the invariant standard of subjective welfare? Different types of labour are not all equally disagreeable. Smith dismisses this problem in chapter 5 with a curt reference to 'the higgling and bargaining of the market', which will establish some 'sort of rough equality' between the esteem value of labour of different skills. Strangely enough, he does not refer the reader to **Book I, chapter 10,** where he demonstrates, as we have seen, that competition

---

[1] If Y = money income, N = employment, W = the money wage bill, and w = the money wage rate, then real income in Keynes = Y/w, labour's relative share = W/Y, and therefore $(Y/w)(W/Y)$ = W/w = N, from which follows the Keynesian relationship tying income rigidly to employment.

equalizes the monetary return to units of disutility of labour. In principle, therefore, it should be possible to construct a representative wage unit.

A standard of measurement, as Smith points out, must itself be invariable in order accurately to reflect changes in the things being measured. But is it true that the disutility of an hour of labour remains the same to individuals with the passage of time? Yes, Smith postulates, appealing to our intuitive feeling of pain cost: 'Equal quantities of labour, at all times and places, *may be said* to be of equal [esteem] value to the labourer' in that they represent 'the same proportion of his ease, liberty, and happiness'. Once this is granted, it can be argued that when a worker receives more wage goods per unit of effort, 'it is their [esteem] value which varies, not that of the labour which purchases them'; this remark, which has puzzled so many commentators, is perfectly logical in the context.

Having defended his labour standard of 'real value', Smith directs attention to the problem of selecting a stable yardstick in which to express the wage unit. For calendar periods of moderate lengths, a nominal wage unit in terms of silver will prove satisfactory owing to the relative stability of the value of silver 'from year to year' and even 'for half a century or a century together'. However for longer periods a corn-wage unit is more suitable: the price of corn fluctuates sharply in the short run and rarely in the same direction or with the same amplitude as money wages, but 'from century to century' corn prices are remarkably stable. As he explains in the 'Digression concerning the Variations of the Value of Silver', appended to Book I, the reason for this is that cost-reducing improvements in agriculture are 'more or less counterbalanced' by the rising price of cattle, 'the principal instruments of agriculture'. And since corn is 'the basic subsistence of the people', the money price of corn governs money wages in the long run. The argument is complete: the wage unit in real terms — the wages of common labour measured in corn — is invariant through time and reflects an invariant disutility of labour.

The burden of Smith's comments is that the labour-commanded standard provides a *positive* index of welfare: the higher the 'real price' of a commodity measured in wage units, the better off we are for having it; the more labour the total product commands, the 'richer' a nation is. This makes welfare a simple positive function of population: 'the most decisive mark of prosperity in any country is the increase of the number of its inhabitants'. But if money wages rise faster than the money value of output, that is, if labour's relative share of output rises, the total product will not necessarily yield a larger value expressed in terms of current wage units (see last footnote on Keynes). This shows only that Smith's wage unit must be held constant at its base-year value. Let us not be deceived, Smith seems to say, by a rise in money wages associated with a rise in output. What we want to know is how many hours of toil and trouble the larger output really represents, for the esteem value of an hour of toil and trouble never alters.

As soon as we drop the idea of a constant real wage rate, expressing a constant disutility of labour, Smith's argument may produce a *negative* index of economic welfare. If real wages are rising or prices are falling because of a rise in the productivity of labour, the number of current wage units commanded by the total product year after year may tend downward; in fact, the necessary condition for a negative index is a rise in real wages in excess of output per man. Actually, the negative index makes much better sense because a fall in the amount of labour which a commodity commands in exchange is the reciprocal of labour's purchasing power over a commodity. As the total product commands less labour, labour's purchasing power over real income rises. So interpreted, Smith's standard of welfare would give the same answer as the one that Ricardo was later to provide. Ricardo's standard of 'riches' makes improving welfare a negative function of human effort per unit of output; to put it plainly, we are better off if we work less to produce one unit of output. The practical difficulty of Smith's approach is the untenable assumption of a constancy in real wages, and this in turn reflects the heroic assumption of constant outlay of subjective sacrifice per unit of effort 'at all times'. Most of us would argue that a major element in the improvement of welfare in a growing economy is the falling effort price of income: as the workweek declines and real wages rise, the disutility of labour surely increases 'at all times'. An equal disutility of labour 'at all places' is probably a no more defensible assumption, although that is what is often assumed in making international comparisons of economic welfare. For instance, Soviet living standards may be compared with American living standards by asking how many hours of work, rewarded at the going rate, would be required to buy specific articles at current prices in each of the two countries. This procedure assumes, among other things, that the disutility of labour in the U.S.S.R. is the same as in the U.S.A.

It used to be said that Adam Smith tried to formulate a labour theory of value but got horribly confused between the 'labour commanded' by a product and the 'labour embodied' in its production. The origins of the legend are to be found in Ricardo's *Principles*, but the 'authorized version' is by Marx.

In a profit economy, the price of a commodity in terms of purchasing power over labour necessarily exceeds the labour required to produce it; hence, Marx implied that Smith failed to realise that price determination on the basis of the labour commanded by commodities gives quite different results from price determination on the basis of the labour required to produce them. The fallacy of such an argument is obvious: if two commodities exchange at ratios determined by the relative man-hours required to produce them, they will of course command the same labour, or apples, or nuts, or anything else; contrariwise, if two commodities exchange at a ratio determined by the labour they can command in exchange, they will of course embody the same man-hours required to produce them, at least if the man-hours embodied in capital goods have been allowed for and the rate of profit is the same in all lines of investment. However, what could it possibly mean to say that the exchange ratios of commodities are *determined* by the labour they command in exchange? This is like saying that the rate at which a thing exchanges for other things is governed by its purchasing power over other things, which is merely to repeat oneself in different words. The labour-commanded theory, whatever it is, cannot possibly be a theory of value, and to suggest that Adam Smith could have confused such different phenomena as the labour price of a product and its labour cost is simply absurd. Smith did not try to formulate anything properly called a labour theory of value: **Book I, chapter 5,** presents a labour theory of subjective welfare; **Book I, chapter 6,** toys with a primitive theory of price determination in the special case in which labour is the only factor of production; and **Book I, chapter 7,** offers a cost-of-production theory of relative prices. It is perfectly true that the *Wealth of Nations* starts with the sentence: 'The annual labour of every nation is the fund which originally supplied it with ... produce', but it is obvious that this is designed to emphasize the fact that wealth consists of real resources and not of money. Smith's phrase 'labour is the foundation and essence of wealth' was among the shibboleths of the time, a convenient weapon against mercantilist thinking.

11. The Trend of Prices

The 'Digression' on the value of silver in **Book I, chapter 11,** makes use of the labour standard in analyzing the history of prices. This is Adam Smith at his best as an economic historian. It begins with a study of the wheat price of silver between 1350 and 1750, an excellent example of the use of the quantity theory of money in its dynamic 18th-century version. After a brief and unimportant section on the relative value of gold and silver, he launches upon a lengthy and really masterful analysis of the price structure of wage goods. The general thesis is that agricultural products rise in price in the course of economic progress, while the price of manufactured articles tends naturally to fall. This is the origin of the famous classical notion that agriculture operates under conditions of diminishing returns, while industry enjoys increasing returns, returns being defined in a historical sense. The reader who skips this section because it is called a digression misses one of the most interesting sections of the *Wealth of Nations*.

12. Capital and Income

Book II deals with capital accumulation as the mainspring of economic progress. The introduction immediately lays down the conception that capital is in essence a stock of unfinished goods that permits the producer to span the time interval between the application of inputs and the emergence of final output. **Book II, chapter 1,** distinguishes between fixed and circulating capital and emphasizes the different proportions of fixed and working capital in different industries. Circulating capital, Smith argues, consists of those goods that yield a return to their owners by being sold in the course of a production cycle, in contrast to fixed capital goods, which take part in the productive process without changing hands. It is an essential characteristic of circulating capital goods that they embody a quantity of purchasing power that perpetually returns to their owner as he disposes of them; this led later writers to think of circulating capital in money terms, with disastrous results for the history of capital theory. But in Adam Smith, circulating capital is still conceived in real terms. Fixed capital he defined as including not only implements and buildings but also 'human capital', the capital value of 'the acquired and useful habits of all the members of society'. This follows quite rightly from the fact that capital stands for 'produced means of production': the acquired skills of workers are certainly 'produced' by the using up of material resources.

Book II, chapter 2, contains the bulk of Smith's theory of money and defines gross and net revenue. Gross revenue is apparently equal to what we now call gross national product; net revenue is equal to our net national product or gross revenue minus depreciation on fixed capital. At one point, Smith suggests that we should deduct the expenses of maintaining both fixed and circulating capital, that is, depreciation on buildings and equipment as well as the whole of the wages bill, but in the end he does not go as far as Ricardo who did confine net revenue to profits plus rent. But as a matter of logic, if the capital stock is defined to include human capital and wages are believed to tend toward subsistence levels, consistent social accounting demands that we net out all payments necessary to keep human capital intact, consisting of maintenance charges in the form of subsistence wages and depreciation and replacement allowances in the form of expenditures on the training of old workers and the rearing and education of new workers. All these may be said to represent 'real costs' in the sense of necessary outlays to make production physically possible. The physiocrats, and Ricardo after them, were quite right to deduct the whole of wages paid out from the final product to arrive at the 'net product', thus treating workers' consumption simply as intermediate products. If this sounds drastic to modern readers, it is only because we regard the net national product as a measure of social welfare, however inadequate, and value an increase in consumers' expenditures as an improvement in welfare even if it is unaccompanied by an increase in investment.

13. Banking

The function of banking, we are told by Smith, is to economize upon the stock of precious metals: paper money 'never can exceed the value of the gold and silver, of which it supplies the place' because excess paper will go abroad or be presented to banks in payment for gold; this is the Law of Reflux, which received a thorough airing in the monetary controversies over the Bank Charter Act of 1844 [see chapter 6, section 17]. But paper money, Smith contends, has been issued to excess owing to speculative 'over-trading of some bold projectors'. This would not have happened if banks had only discounted 'real bills of exchange'; here is the origin of the real-bills doctrine of commercial banking, which survived repeated criticism in the 19th century to be enshrined in the Federal Reserve Act of 1913, thus scoring high on the list of longest-lived economic fallacies of all times [see chapter 6, section 18]. **Book II, chapter 2,** closes with a brief discussion of Law's scheme to establish land banks, followed by a history of the Bank of England.

14. Productive and Unproductive Labour

Book II, chapter 3, introduces the concept of productive labour, followed by a powerful eulogy of saving and a hint of Say's Law of Markets. Smith's distinction between productive and unproductive labour is probably the most maligned concept in the history of economic doctrines. But unsatisfactory as is Smith's discussion, his meaning is perfectly clear and by no means nonsensical. The chapter is entitled 'Of the Accumulation of Capital, or of Productive and Unproductive Labour', and its subject matter cannot be understood independently of Smith's judgment that the rate of net investment must be maximized to secure economic progress. What he is driving at is the distinction between activity that results in capital accumulation and activity that services the needs of households. In a country poor in capital, the unproductive use of savings in service industries catering to the demand for luxuries may be as serious a block to economic development as insufficiency of saving itself. What Smith is saying is that saving should be used to create productive equipment or to improve technical facilities for the sake of adding to the capacity to generate income. And however unfashionable it has become to distinguish between productive and unproductive labour in this sense, the distinction is always revived during wartime when it is made the basis of drafting some people and deferring others.

Smith offers two definitions of productive labour. First, the 'value version': productive labour adds net value to the product, or, to use Smithian language, 'the price of that subject, can afterwards, if necessary, put into motion a quantity of labour equal to [or greater than] that which had originally produced it'. This is a very modern definition and would convey Smith's meaning if he had confined net revenue to profits plus rent. The second definition is the more famous 'storage version': productive labour 'realizes itself in some particular subject or vendible commodity', while the services of unproductive labour 'perish in the very instant of their performance'. Hence, the greater the proportion of labour force that is productively employed, the greater the tangible stock of means of production and the greater the economy's capacity to produce in the following year. This latter version comes closer to catching the spirit of Smith's argument, but it is hardly foolproof even on his own grounds: labour engaged in transmitting technical knowledge is unproductive on this score, but knowledge, however intangible, can be accumulated and does affect a society's rate of economic growth. But this is quibbling. Despite much criticism, Smith's distinction was retained by all the leading classical economists (although say, McCulloch, and other minor writers in the period abandoned it) and was handed down in the end to Marx to become the basis of present-day Soviet national income accounting.

Say's Law of Markets is suggested by Smith's paradoxical dictum that 'what is annually saved is as regularly consumed as what is annually spent, and nearly in the same time too; but it is consumed by a different set of people'. Now, what is saved is invested and hence not consumed; but Smith implies that investment results in income payments, which in turn get spent on consumption. Smith's way of putting the matter is positively misleading; nevertheless, these words were echoed and reechoed by two generations of economists. Properly understood, the dictum attacks the popular fallacy that saving necessarily destroys purchasing power; this is why it appealed to Smith's followers. Saving is not a problem as such, the argument ran, for it generates purchasing power as much as luxury spending. The operative proposition hidden away in Smith's phraseology is that saving is tantamount to investment because 'hoarding', the accumulation of idle money balances, is regarded as an exceptional occurrence. This is tied up in turn with the view, in evidence in the same chapter, that the medium-of-exchange function of money is the monetary function par excellence. In **Book I, chapter 4,** Smith had conceded that people do have a demand for money-to-hold for liquidity reasons: 'prudent men' will hold 'a certain quantity of some one commodity such as they imagined few people would be likely to refuse in exchange for the produce of their industry'. But typically he argued that money will be promptly spent because 'it is not for its own sake that men desire money, but for the sake of what they can purchase with it' (Book IV, chapter 1). By ruling out hoarding, money is indeed reduced to serving as a medium of exchange and no more: in consequence, saving or nonconsumption is necessarily identical to investment. The saving-is-spending theorem, therefore, implies a definite theory of money, and, contrariwise, a medium-of-exchange theory of money implies the saving-is-spending theorem [see chapter 5, section 3].

Smith never suggests that saving is a function of the rate of interest or of the size of net revenue. Saving habits are thought to be institutionally determined and dependent upon the prevalence of the Protestant Ethic. 'The principle which prompts to save, is the desire of bettering our condition', he says, which on the whole overcomes 'the principle which prompts to expense, the passion for present enjoyment'. In his view, bank credit is used to finance working capital, but increases in fixed capital depend upon reinvested earnings; hence, the frugal man, who is called a public benefactor, is invariably identified by him as a manufacturer, just as landowners are constantly pictured as prodigals. Near the end of the chapter Smith observes that contrary to popular opinion and the flood of pamphlets by 'very candid and intelligent people', the national income of England has been rising since the Restoration; that it was necessary to assert this emphatically tells us much about the lack of factual economic knowledge in the 18th century.

15. An Optimum Investment Pattern

In **Book II, chapter 4,** we come back to the theory of the declining rate of profit and a vigorous critique of monetary theories of interest. Smith gives qualified approval to the existing Usury Laws, which limited the rate of interest to 5 percent, because only 'prodigals and projectors' would give more than that: 'a great part of the capital of the country would thus be kept out of the hands which were more likely to make a profitable and advantageous use of it'. **Book II, chapter 5** defends middlemen and retailers as productive labourers and sketches an optimum investment policy for a country by an argument that has struck many commentators as tortuous in the extreme. The criterion invoked is the net value, measured in terms of wage units, added by equal quantities of capital in equal periods of time, that is, the reciprocal of the capital-labour ratio. At any rate, this is a modern translation of Smith's own terminology: the amount of labour 'put in motion' by a unit of capital. The so-called 'hierarchy of productivity of industries' is headed by agriculture, on the grounds that the value of the product of agriculture is sufficient to pay rent as well as wages and profits. This argument is wrong if we adopt Ricardo's notion of rent as a differential surplus; at the margin, agriculture no more yields rent than does manufacturing. Next in order of productivity comes manufacture, then inland trade, then foreign trade, and, last, the carrying trade. The only reason for placing inland trade ahead of foreign trade is that the turnover rate of domestic capital is greater in inland than in foreign trade: the inland trader reduces the turnover period of two domestic industries, while foreign trade reduces the turnover period of only one domestic producer. The carrying trade comes last because it neither economizes domestic capital nor implements productivity. The whole argument is employed against the mercantilist policy of favouring foreign commerce and manufacturing, and the sense of it seems to be that the natural stages in the evolution of a nation's industries are dictated by the practical need to minimize the capital-labour ratio: we are asked to believe that agriculture is the most productive sector of economic activity because here a unit of capital will set the maximum amount of labour in motion. An environment of severe capital scarcity is implicit throughout the discussion.

16. Synoptic History

Book III discusses 'the different progress of opulence in different nations' with a wealth of historical illustrations. In effect, it is a separate monograph on the development of agriculture in Europe since the fall of the Roman Empire. **Book IV,** as we already know, is devoted to mercantilist theory (chapter 1) and policy (chapters 2–8), including two badly placed and rather tedious monographs on 'Banks of Deposits' and the 'Corn Trade', closing with a chapter on the physiocrats. The introduction to Book IV defines political economy as a branch of statecraft, a definition in violent opposition to the whole tenor of the *Wealth of Nations*.

17. The Invisible Hand

Book IV, chapter 2, presents a simple argument in favour of free trade. It can never pay an individual to produce himself what he can buy more cheaply from someone else, and 'what is prudence in the conduct of every private family, can scarce be folly in that of a great Kingdom' – a fallacy of composition that Smith had earlier condemned in the mercantilists. He enlists the powerful motive of self-interest to show that the general welfare is best promoted by removing all restrictions on imports and exports. Intending only their own good, men are led by 'an invisible hand' to further social ends. The underlying thesis is that the interest of the community is simply the sum of the interests of the members who compose it: each man, if left alone, will seek to maximize his own wealth; therefore, all men, if unimpeded, will maximize aggregate wealth. But a legend has grown up that the whole of the *Wealth of Nations* rests on this kind of naive reasoning, the so-called doctrine of 'the spontaneous harmony of interests'. But 'the obvious and simple system of natural liberty', which is said to reconcile private interests and economic efficiency, turns out upon examination to be identical with the concept of competition; the 'invisible hand' is nothing more than the automatic equilibrating mechanism of the competitive market.

That competition does have optimizing characteristics is the fond belief of all economists. Primitive as is Smith's argument, he had shown earlier in the book that competition, by equalizing rates of return and by eroding excess gains, leads to an optimum allocation of labour and capital between industries. This is only part of a complete demonstration that competition maximizes welfare, but it is enough to exonerate Adam Smith from the charge of having indulged in naive philosophizing. Furthermore, if we draw up a list of the defects that Smith admits in the 'simple system of natural liberty' – the conflicts of interests, the cases where the pursuit of private gain leads to socially undesirable results – we should have sufficient ammunition, as Viner once said, for several socialist orations. For instance, in the chapter under discussion, given over to a plea for free trade, protectionist measures are justified in the case of infant industries and in retaliation against foreign tariffs; the Navigation Laws are defended because 'defence is of more importance than opulence'; and complete freedom of trade is regarded as a utopian dream, too much to hope for in view of the vested interests of manufacturers. And in **Book IV, chapter 9,** Smith notes that the state has 'three duties of great importance': the provision of military security, the administration of justice, and 'the duty of erecting and maintaining certain public works and certain public institutions, which it can never be for the interest of any individual, or small number of individuals, to erect and maintain; because the profit could neither repay the expense to any individual or small number of individuals, though it may frequently do much more than repay it to a great society'. As Pigou was to say later, the private costs of public works may greatly exceed the social costs owing to the presence of external economies for which the private investors cannot charge. The presence of external effects in production and consumption constitutes the chief source of nonoptimality under perfect competition: the whole is no longer the mere arithmetic sum of the individual parts [see chapter 13, section 13]. Of course, Adam Smith did not look at matters this way but, at the same time, he seems perfectly aware that laissez-faire creates only a presumption of maximum social welfare, not a complete program for its achievement.

It may be worth pointing out that Smith's vigorous attack on mercantilist policies conjures up a picture of severe government interference with industrial development in the 18th century. But as a matter of fact, most of the mercantilist statutes had become a dead letter by 1776; and, of course, there were no factory acts, sanitary laws, income taxes and the heavy poor rates that the 19th-century era of laissez-faire had to live with. In many respects, the policy of nonintervention in industrial activity was in operation long before Adam Smith, and his attacks would have been more relevant in the 16th than in the 18th century. Perhaps this accounts for the failure of his book to make much impact on the course of public policy in England. The tariff wall was not seriously reduced until the 1820s; the Law of Settlement was only repealed in 1834; the East India Company survived until the 1850s; and so forth. Indeed, apart from some reform of import duties under the younger Pitt in the 1780s, it is difficult to find any evidence that the *Wealth of Nations* made a difference to government policy in the 18th century.

Book IV, chapters 3 and **4**, warm to the task of exposing mercantilist legislation. **Chapter 5** notes that the influx of specie resulting from an export surplus tends to turn the balance of trade against a country, but the argument stops short of Hume's specie-flow proposition [see chapter 1, section 2]. Smith was, of course, acquainted with Hume's argument and set it out in some detail in the *Lectures of Jurisprudence*. He never mentions it, however, in the *Wealth of Nations*, possibly because he found, or thought he had found, persistent differences in the value of gold from country to country – a violation of the specie-flow mechanism. Thus, while conceding that 'the metals naturally fly from the worse to the better market', he hints in several places in the book that the movement of precious metals required to bring about an equilibrium distribution of gold and silver among the trading nations of the world would have to be of so large a magnitude as to be out of the question.

Book IV, chapter 6, comes back to a discussion of the Methuen Treaty and the mysteries of seignorage. **Book IV, chapter 7,** together with the closing remarks of Book V, spells out Smith's anticolonial position. **Book IV, chapter 8,** describes the prevailing system of customs and excises in England and concludes with a plea for consumers' sovereignty: 'in the mercantile system, the interest of the consumer is almost constantly sacrificed to that of the producer.'

18. Taxation and the Public Debt

Book V, covering one third of the total volume, is a self-contained treatise on public finance, composed of a historical analysis of state revenues and expenditures and an elementary theory of incidence. **Chapter 1, part 1,** provides a history of warfare since ancient times; **part 2** presents a 'Marxist' theory of the state; **part 3** deals with public works, such as 'good roads, bridges, navigable canals, harbors', followed by a typical Smithian digression on the education of the young. As one reads his analysis on the evolution of civil government, of justice, of standing armies, and of the human family, it becomes clear that he held definite views about the nature of the historical process. Like other Scottish writers of the time, such as Adam Ferguson, John Millar, William Robertson and even David Hume, he expounds a philosophy of history that attaches unique significance to the nature and distribution of property. It is no exaggeration to describe these men as forerunners of the Marxist theory of historical materialism.

Book V, chapter 2, is devoted to taxes, beginning with the famous four canons of taxation – it would be better to say beginning with the ability-to-pay theory and three administrative canons. The upshot of his theory of incidence is that all taxes fall ultimately on landlords because of their ownership of a fixed immobile resource. He mentions the 'ingenious theory' of the physiocrats and, without approving of *l'impôt unique*, nevertheless leans in the direction of favouring the taxation of ground rent. Taxes on wages raise wages by the full amount of the tax, except as disguised by a consequent fall in the demand for labour; this implies either that the demand for labour is perfectly inelastic – the crude wages fund doctrine – or that the long-run supply curve of labour is perfectly elastic – the subsistence theory of wages. The closing section of **Book V, chapter 2**, 'Taxes upon Consumable Commodities', is rich with implicit suggestions about the demand-elasticities of different types of goods.

Book V, chapter 3, on public debts, is strongly flavored by the classical prejudice against public expenditures and the 'Treasury View' that public spending financed by taxes or the sale of government bonds necessarily diverts productive labour into unproductive employment.

19. Adam Smith as an Economist

In the process of studying economics, every student is sooner or later made aware of the fact that the price system is a mechanism that imposes orderly rules of behavior on economic agents, and imposes them automatically, without central direction or collective design. Furthermore, when the price system is embedded in an appropriate institutional environment, it is the kind of mechanism that is capable of harmonizing the pursuit of private interests with the achievement of social goals. This insight comes to each of us in its own good time with all the thrill of a personal revelation. It is only later that we learn that we have rediscovered an ancient truth. Well, it is not too ancient: it is a truth that was first recognized about 300 years ago. And among the first to grasp it firmly, and certainly the first to understand its dramatic implications, was Adam Smith.

One cannot pretend that Adam Smith was the founder of political economy. Cantillon or Quesnay or Turgot have a better claim to that honor. But Cantillon's *Essay*, Quesnay's articles, and Turgot's *Reflections* are at best long pamphlets, dress rehearsals for a science rather than the real thing. *An Inquiry into the Nature and Causes of the Wealth of Nations* is the first full-scale treatise on economics, containing as it does a solid core of production and distribution theory, followed by a review of the past in the light of these abstract principles, and concluding with a battery of policy applications, the whole of it permeated by the high theme of 'the obvious and simple system of natural liberty' toward which Adam Smith saw the world moving.

The central theme that inspires the *Wealth of Nations* is the workings of 'the invisible hand'; it is not to the benevolence of the baker but to his self-interest that we owe our bread. Smith had caught sight of the pregnant consideration that under certain social arrangements, which we would nowadays describe as 'workable competition', private interests are indeed harmonized with social interests. Without collective regulation or single design, a market economy nevertheless conforms to orderly rules of behaviour. Each individual, being one among many, can exert only a negligible influence upon the total market situation; in effect, he takes prices as given and is free only to vary the quantity bought and sold at given prices, driven by the motive of maximizing his own gain. Yet the sum of all these separate actions determines prices; each person, viewed separately, is ruled by prices, and yet prices themselves are governed by the sum total of all individual reactions. The 'invisible hand' of the market in this way assures a social result that is independent of individual wills and intentions.

Moreover, these automatic market results have definite optimizing characteristics. The prejudice that every action motivated by private gain must be antisocial by virtue of this fact alone was widely current in the 18th century. Even today, man-in-the-street socialism takes comfort in the idea that a free market economy cannot possibly promote public interests because it is a system motivated by private profit rather than by consciously designed social ends. It was Smith's task to shift the burden of proof and to create the presumption that decentralized atomistic competition does in some sense produce 'maximum satisfactions'. No doubt, his demonstration of this proposition was incomplete and unsatisfactory. It seems at times to rest upon nothing else than the notion of the arithmetic addibility of individual satisfactions: since everyone maximizes his own satisfactions when freely permitted to do so, laissez-faire will maximize the satisfactions of the whole community. But in fact Smith's demonstration of the doctrine of 'maximum satisfactions' went much deeper. In Book I, chapter 7, he had shown that free competition tends to equate prices to costs of production, tending to optimize the allocation of resources *within* industries. In Book I, chapter 10, he showed that free competition in factor markets tends to equalize the 'net advantages' of factors in all industries and thus to establish an optimum allocation of resources *between* industries. He did not show that the different factors would be combined in optimal proportions in production or that the product sold would be optimally distributed among individual consumers. Nor did he demonstrate that economies of scale and external effects in production and consumption frequently impede the achievement of competitive optima, although his discussion of public works contains the core of the argument. But he did take the first step toward the theory of the optimum allocation of *given* resources under conditions of perfect competition.

It is true to say, however, that his own faith in the benefits of 'the invisible hand' rested very little upon static considerations of allocative efficiency in circumstances where competition is perfect. A decentralized price system was held to be desirable because of its dynamic effects in widening the scope of the market and extending the advantages of the division of labour – in short, because it was a powerful engine for promoting the accumulation of capital and the growth of income. That economic development is in fact the principal subject of Smith's book is evident from its full title, *An Inquiry into the Nature and Causes of the Wealth of Nations*. It is evident also from his distinction between productive and unproductive labour, from his admittedly confused analysis of what we have called the 'hierarchy of productivity of industries', from his emphasis on saving, from his treatment of the role of capital, from his strange approach to the theory of value – emphasizing the measurement of value over time and not the determination of relative prices at any one time – and most of all, from his discussion of economic policies in terms of their impact upon economic growth in the past as well as upon economic development in different countries in his own day and age. However, what distinguishes Smith's 'theory of economic development', if one can use such a phrase, from later and even from more recent efforts in the subject is a continuous harking back to the framework of social institutions that harness and channel pecuniary motives. So frequently accused of *Harmonielehre*, the vulgar doctrine of the spontaneous harmony of interests, Smith instead seems to be forever emphasizing that the powerful motive of self-interest is only enlisted in the cause of the general welfare under definite institutional arrangements.

A few examples from his discussion of the public services and his analysis of educational institutions must suffice, although one could illustrate the argument just as readily from his treatment of mercantilist policies, land tenure systems, and joint-stock companies. He limits the proper functions of government, as we know, to the safeguarding of property rights, the provision of national defense and the maintenance of certain public works. He realized that the remuneration of government officials raises special problems, insulated as they are from ordinary market pressures or from other institutionalized arrangements that compel individuals to pursue their economic activity in a manner conducive to the national welfare. The guiding principle which he lays down is that 'public services are never better performed than when their reward comes only in consequence of their being performed, and is proportioned to the diligence employed in performing them'. He goes on to show, however, that in some fields, such as law, education, and the church, to define the measure 'diligence' in a strictly quantitative sense may create more difficulties than it solves. Furthermore, generosity may be as damaging to efficient public services as niggardliness: 'if any [public] service is very much under-paid, it is very apt to suffer by the meanness and incapacity of the greater part of those who are employed in it. If it is very much over-paid, it is apt to suffer, perhaps, still more by their negligence and idleness'. Virtually the whole of Book V, chapter 1, 'Of the Expenses of the Sovereign or Commonwealth', is taken up with the problem of devising techniques for rewarding lawyers, clerks, judges, clergymen and teachers in such a way that the pursuit of their own interests will advance the interests of society as a whole.

His devastating criticism of English university education, for example, centered on the absence of anything like 'payments by results' in Oxford and Cambridge: the colleges were heavily endowed, the governing body of the colleges consisted of the teachers themselves, most teachers derived their income entirely from these endowments, and class attendance was largely compulsory, the result of being that the income of teachers bore no relationship to their proficiency either as pedagogues or as scholars. The situation in the public schools was much better, principally because 'the reward of the schoolmaster in most cases depends principally, in some cases almost entirely, upon the fees or honoraries of his scholars'. He favoured state aid in providing school buildings but, drawing on his knowledge of the Scottish system of parish schools, preferred to see teachers rewarded on a private fee basis supplemented by a small fixed stipend; the notion was that a fixed salary would never give a teacher the incentive to exert himself to the utmost.

Similarly, he argued that the greater part of the expense of public works, such as highways, bridges, canals and harbors, should be met out of appropriate tolls on the users of these services, with the remainder coming out of local revenue when the benefits were local and only otherwise out of general revenue. But the case for public highways, he contended, is much stronger than for public canals: the self-interest of a canal owner requires him to maintain the canal, or it will become impassable through neglect and cease to be a source of income, but 'a high road, though entirely neglected, does not become altogether impassable ... The proprietors of the tolls upon a high road, therefore, might neglect altogether the repair of the road, and yet continue to levy very nearly the same tolls. It is proper, therefore, that the tolls for the maintenance of such work should be put under the management of [public] commissioners or trustees.' This subtle distinction serves to illustrate Smith's shrewd perception of the incentive effects of different organizational arrangements.

Adam Smith was not satisfied to argue that a free-market economy secures the best of all possible worlds. He was very much preoccupied with the specification of the exact institutional structure that would guarantee the beneficent operation of market forces. His cynical references to class interests and the weapons of 'ideology' which the various social classes wield in the struggle for economic and political supremacy demonstrate his awareness that self-interest is just as likely to thwart as to promote the public welfare; the market mechanism would foster harmony but not unless it was surrounded by an appropriate legal and institutional framework. Until recently, this was entirely taken for granted by economists, but not that the growth of the public sector has raised such problems anew – hence the burgeoning of interest in the economics of bureaucracy and economics of property rights – the *Wealth of Nations* should remind us that the benefits of competition call for more than laissez-faire. It was not for nothing that Adam Smith spoke of *political* economy.

In appraising Adam Smith, or any other economist, we ought always to remember that brilliance in handling purely analytical concepts is a very different thing from a firm grasp of the essential logic of economic relationships. Superior technique does not necessarily imply superior economic insight, and vice versa. Judged by standards of analytical competence, Smith is not the greatest of 18th-century economists. But for acute insight into the nature of the economic process, for economic wisdom rather than theoretical elegance, Smith had no equal in the 18th or even in the 19th century.

NOTES ON FURTHER READING

The definitive edition of the *Wealth of Nations* is by E. Cannan (1904, reprinted 1937), and the unedited original is easily available in paperback. Cannan's introduction to his edition is a masterpiece, which requires little or no revision in the light of subsequent findings. Nevertheless, it is capped by the introduction to the new Glasgow edition of the *Wealth of Nations*, eds. R. H. Campbell, A. S. Skinner, and W. B. Todd (1976). The Penguin paperback edition of the *Wealth of Nations*, ed. A. S. Skinner (1970) – actually only Books I–III – contains a superb 100-page introduction by the editor, which is almost a book by itself. The standard biography by J. Rae, *Life of Adam Smith* (1895) is now superseded by R. H. Campbell and A. S. Skinner, *Adam Smith* (1982), although it must be said that so little is known about Smith's life and personality that both books are intellectual rather than personal biographies.

There has been a remarkable recent revival of interest in Smith connected in part with the rise of 'libertarianism', which hails Smith as a forerunner, but for the rest sparked off by the new University of Glasgow edition of the complete *Works and Correspondence of Adam Smith*. All that has survived of Smith's writings are here edited afresh: *The Theory of Moral Sentiments*, the *Lectures on Rhetoric and Belles Lettres*, several essays on philosophical subjects, the correspondence, a recently discovered set of student notes on the *Lectures on Jurisprudence*, as well as the so-called 'Early Draft of Part of the *Wealth of Nations*'. The edition is accompanied by two volumes of critical essays edited by T. Wilson and A. S. Skinner (1976); the first volume contains fourteen papers on Smith's moral and political philosophy; the second volume is made up of sixteen papers on virtually every aspect of Smith's economic doctrines, making it perhaps the best, single secondary source on the *Wealth of Nations* – special attention is drawn to the essays of G. J. Stigler, A. I. Bloomfield, and A. T. Peacock, which manage to be original on topics which by this time virtually defy originality. See also the symposium on the *Wealth of Nations* in *SJPE*, June, 1976, particularly D. P. O'Brien, 'The Longevity of Adam Smith's Vision: Paradigms, Research Programmes and Falsifiability in the History of Economic Thought', the entire Winter, 1976 issue of *HOPE*, and the delightful appraisal by G. J. Stigler, 'The Successes and Failures of Professor Smith', *JPE*, December, 1976. On the effect created by the Glasgow edition, see H. C. Recktenwald, 'An Adam Smith Rennaisance *anno* 1976. The Bicentenary Output – A Reappraisal of his Scholarship', *JEL*, March, 1978, and E. G. West, 'Scotland's Resurgent Economist: A Survey of the New Literature on Adam Smith', *SEJ*, October, 1978.

For a provocative discussion of Smith's attitude toward the innovators of his day, see R. Koebner, 'Adam Smith and the Industrial Revolution', *EHR*, April 1959, in which it is argued that Smith failed to anticipate the Industrial Revolution. S. Hollander, *The Economics of Adam Smith* (1973), chaps. 3, 7, vigorously denies this thesis but I remain persuaded by Koebner's case. The remainder of Hollander's book provides something like a wholesale reinterpretation of the significance of Adam Smith as a policy-oriented economist. Hollander's style – meticulous exegesis of the original text with running commentaries on all the major secondary sources – requires great patience from readers. L. S. Moss provides an assessment of Hollander's new look at Smith: 'The Economics of Adam Smith: Professor Hollander's Reappraisal', *HOPE*, Winter, 1976.

E. Cannan, *History of the Theories of Production and Distribution* (1917, reprinted 1953), chap. 1, sects. 5–7; chap. 3; chap. 4, sects. 1–3; chap. 6, sects. 1–3, calls for special notice as the classic discussion of Smith's confused treatment of the concepts of capital and income. P. H. Douglas in another classic treatment analyzes 'Smith's Theory of Value and Distribution', *Adam Smith, 1776–1926* (1928, reprinted in *DET*). The Marxist interpretation of Smith's value theory is that Smith had two labour theories of value: I deny this interpretation but the reader should consult what is perhaps its best exposition, R. L. Meek, *Studies in the Labour Theory of Value* (1956), chap. 2. For counter-arguments to the Marxist interpretation, see Schumpeter, *History of Economic Analysis*, pp. 181–94, which, incidentally, ranks Smith below Petty, Cantillon, Quesnay, and Turgot in an effort to reverse the standard ranking of 18th-century economists; see also H. M. Robertson and W. L. Taylor, 'Adam Smith's Approach to the Theory of Value', *EJ* 1957, reprinted in *EET*, *RHET*, and *ASCA*, III; and D. F. Gordon, 'What Was the Labour Theory of Value?' *AER*, May, 1959. My interpretation of the troublesome chap. 5 in Book I of the *Wealth of Nations* draws heavily on my earlier article, 'Welfare Indices in the *Wealth of Nations*', *SEJ*, 1959, reprinted in *ASCA*, II.

Smith's doctrine of productive labour, and what his followers made of it, is sympathetically discussed by M. H. Myint in a stimulating book, *Theories of Welfare Economics* (1948), chap. 5, supplemented by V. W. Bladen, 'Adam Smith on Productive and Unproductive Labour: A Theory of Full Development', *CJEPS*, 1960, reprinted in *ASCA*, III. Myint's entire book is invaluable for its emphasis on the classical preoccupation with problems of economic development. For Adam Smith's 'model' of economic growth, see J. J. Spengler's copiously documented article in two parts, 'Adam Smith's Theory of Economic Growth', *SEJ*, 1959, reprinted in *ASCA*, III. H. Barkai, 'A Formal Outline of a Smithian Growth Model', *QJE*, August, 1969, provides another attempt at formalizing Smith's argument and succeeds better than most. But Eltis, *The Classical Theory of Economic Growth*, chap. 3 is the only mathematical model of Smith which succeeds in capturing the Smithian notion of increasing returns to scale in manufacturing. N. Rosenberg, 'Adam Smith, Consumer Tastes, and Economic Growth', *JPE*, 1968, reprinted in *ASCA*, III, shows that while Smith may have neglected demand in his theory of value, he emphasized demand forces in his account of the process of economic growth in Europe. I re-examine Smith's contributions to the economics of education in a paper included in the second volume of *Essays on Adam Smith*, eds. T. Wilson, A. S. Skinner. For a different view of how Adam Smith fits into the history of human capital theory, see B. F. Kiker's definitive history, appropriately entitled, *Human Capital: In Retrospect* (1968 in paperback).

J. Viner, 'Adam Smith and Laissez Faire', *SJPE*, 1927, reprinted in his *The Long View and the Short* (1959) and in *ASCA*, II, is an article no one can afford to neglect. It concludes that 'the modern advocate of laissez faire who objects to government participation in business on the ground that it is an encroachment upon a field reserved by nature for private enterprise cannot find support for this argument in the Wealth of Nations'. This reading may be accompanied by J. Viner's lecture, 'The Intellectual History of Laissez Faire', *JLE*, October, 1960, which traces the history of the doctrine from Aristotle through Adam Smith to modern times. Viner draws on both of these papers in his masterful, brief account, 'Smith, Adam', *IESS*, 14, reprinted in *ASCA*, I. The contrast between the rationalism of natural-law doctrine and Smith's own historical method is discussed by H. J. Bitterman, 'Adam Smith's Empiricism and the Law of Nature', *JPE*, 1940, reprinted in *ASCA*, II. Those who see an obvious and rather simple ideological bias in Smith's book should read A. H. Cole, 'Puzzles of the *Wealth of Nations*', *CJEPS*, February, 1958. Smith's concern with the appropriate institutional framework for an efficiently functioning competitive market economy is clearly brought out by N. Rosenberg, 'Some Institutional Aspects of the *Wealth of Nations*', *JPE*, 1960. For a brilliant exposition of Smith's treatment of the concept of competition, see P. J. McNulty, 'A Note on the History of Perfect Competition', *JPE*, August, 1967, Part I. W. J. Samuels, *The Classical Theory of Economic Policy* (1966) emphasizes the non-deliberative forces of social control, in the form of moral values, religion, custom and education, which figure heavily in the policy prescriptions of Adam Smith and all the classical economists that followed him. D. Winch, *Adam Smith's Politics: An Essay in Historiographic Revision* (1978) objects to the current tendency to treat Smith as a forerunner of modern libertarianism and insists on treating him as an 18th-century thinker in his own right, who worked with the concepts and language of that century: Smith's values were pre-capitalist, pre-industrial and pre-democratic.

The old question whether Smith's *Theory of Moral Sentiments*, in which ethical rules of conduct are explained as the result of the socially acquired capacity for empathy, clashes with or complements Smith's *Wealth of Nations*, in which economic behaviour is explained as the result of restrained selfishness, a question that has now been debated for almost a century, comes up again in an exchange between E. G. West, 'Adam Smith's Two Views on the Division of Labour', *Ec.*, 1964, and N. Rosenberg, 'Adam Smith on the Division of Labour: Two Views or One?' *ibid.*, 1965, reprinted in *RHET* and *ASCA*, III. Several papers by A. L. Macfie in his *Individual in Society* (1967) and R. L. Heilbroner, 'The Socialization of the Individual in Adam Smith', *HOPE*, Fall, 1982, also take up this theme.

J. Cropsey, *Polity and Economy: An Interpretation of the Principles of Adam Smith* (1957) and J. R. Lindgren, *The Social Philosophy of Adam Smith* (1973) make a strong case for the argument that knowledge of Smith's entire social and political philosophy is necessary for an understanding of the *Wealth of Nations*. Likewise, A. S. Skinner, *A System of Social Science. Papers Relating to Adam Smith* (1979) ties together a series of papers by means of the argument that Smith conceived a unified theory of social science, to which every one of his writings makes a contribution; although one is reluctant to disagree with one of the greatest living authorities on Adam Smith, this thesis of the essential unity of all of Smith's writings may be doubted – in particular, Smith's failure ever to relate the arguments of his two major works, *Theory of Moral Sentiments* and *Wealth of Nations*, remains an enigma.

On the distinct theory of history which commanded wide support in 18th-century Scotland and which permeated every page of the *Wealth of Nations*, see G. Bryson, *Man and Society: The Scottish Inquiry of the Eighteenth Century* (1968); and A. S. Skinner, 'Economics and History – The Scottish Enlightenment', *SJPE*, February, 1965. P. Mirowsky, 'Adam Smith, Empiricism, and the Rate of Profit in Eighteenth-Century England', *HOPE*, Summer, 1982, shows how careless Smith was with facts even though his book is peppered with empirical observations. H. Myint, 'Adam Smith's Theory of International Trade in the Perspective of Economic Development', *Ec*, August, 1977, D. E. W. Laidler, 'Adam Smith as a Monetary Economist', *CJE*, May, 1981, and G. M. Anderson, R. D. Tollison, 'Adam Smith's Analysis of Joint-Stock Companies', *JPE*, December, 1982, take up particular topics in the *Wealth of Nations*. E. G. West, 'Adam Smith's Economics and Politics', *HOPE*, 1976, reprinted in *Adam Smith and Modern Political Economy*, ed. G. P. O'Driscoll, Jr. (1979) and *ASCA*, II, and D. Winch, 'Science and the Legislator: Adam Smith and After', *EJ*, September, 1983, each argue in their own way that Adam Smith conceived of *political* economy as embracing what we would nowadays call political science and the economics of bureaucracy. Finally, D. Willis, 'The Role in Parliament of the Economic Ideas of Adam Smith, 1976–1800', *HOPE*, 1979, reprinted in *ASCA*, I, and S. Rashid, 'Adam Smith's Rise to Fame: A Reexamination of the Evidence', *TEC*, Winter, 1982, show that Smith did not immediately become the oracle of economic wisdom that popular opinion has sometimes supposed. H. F. Thompson, 'Adam Smith's Philosophy of Science', *QJE*, 1965, reprinted in *ASCA*, I, offers a highly original but somewhat controversial analysis of Smith's youthful essay on the history of astronomy; see also L. J. Ralph, 'Adam Smith's Theory of Inquiry', *JPE*, 1969, reprinted in *ASCA*, I.

Reading Adam Smith, or Ricardo and Mill for that matter, is a good deal more interesting when one is acquainted with the contemporary institutions that are being criticized, such as the Poor Laws, the Corn Laws, the Sinking Fund, and the like. The reader who knows little of British economic history of the period is urged to repair the deficiency by perusing A. Redford, *An Economic History of England, 1760–1860* (2nd edn., 1960), a little book that manages to cram an unbelievable amount of information into 200 pages; lacking Redford, he or she ought to consult T. S. Ashton, *The Industrial Revolution 1760–1830* (1948), another marvel of compression.

3

Population, diminishing returns, and rent

THE THEORY OF POPULATION

Although Malthus was by no means the first writer to speculate on demographic problems, he was the first to succeed in devising a theory of population growth. Ever since, his views have been the point of departure in every discussion of population problems. In his own day, however, the theory attracted attention, not so much as a scientific contribution to the study of demography, but as a refutation of the optimism of Godwin, Condorcet and Owen regarding the perfectibility of human society by means of social legislation. More important for our purposes, Malthus' theory had definite analytical consequences that made it an integral part of classical economics long after the 'vision' that prompted Malthus had receded into the background. By emphasizing the rigid dependence of population growth on the food supply, the Malthusian theory lent support to the subsistence theory of wages and prepared the way for the Ricardian preoccupation with the land-using bias of economic progress; by explaining poverty in terms of a simple race between population and the means of subsistence, it provided the touchstone for all classical thinking about economic policy. Any one of these features would have been enough to make its influence significant. Putting them all together, they fully account for Malthus' astonishing success which, indeed, has few parallels in the history of social science.

Malthus rapidly gained adherents, but he also made bitter enemies. It is hardly surprising, of course, that his doctrines met with violent resistance from social reformers and men of letters. Malthus always went out of his way to antagonize all those who believed in the amelioration of social conditions. Every effort at the deliberate improvement of conditions was said to come to grief upon the irrepressible tide of human numbers. To relieve poverty directly by state subsidies or private charity, he liked to argue, was to remove the principal check against an increase in population, namely, the necessity for each person to fend for himself and to bear the full burden of his own improvidence. These implications were driven home in one purple passage after another, almost as if to irritate the sensitive reader. Nevertheless, with hindsight, it is plain to see that these were merely the ideological trappings of the theory, not its rigorous consequences. With a minor adjustment in outlook, and admitting the moral propriety of birth control, men like Francis Place and John Stuart Mill were later to make use of the Malthusian doctrine as a banner in a program of social reform.

1. The Population Explosion

The first edition of Malthus' *Essay on Population* was published in 1798. The first decennial census was taken three years later and suggested, contrary to the prevailing belief, that the population of England was rapidly increasing. We now know that the last decades of the 18th century did witness a population explosion, and we have become accustomed to crediting Malthus with prophetic foresight in drawing attention to the dangers of such population spurts. But as a matter of fact, history was kind to Malthus for he shared the general belief of contemporaries that the population of England had increased little, if at all, since the revolution of 1680. In the second edition of the *Essay* in 1803 he took notice of the census of 1801 but barely examined its findings and he showed no awareness that he was living in a time of population growth without precedent in European history. His argument was never meant simply to reflect the prevailing situation in Great Britain; it was couched instead in universal terms. Modern authorities are still not agreed on whether the Industrial Revolution in Britain largely created its own labour force by a demand pull on births or whether improvements in sanitation, nutrition and housing produced the additional numbers by a supply push on the death rate. It is certain, however, that the 1780s and 1790s saw a significant decline in mortality, acompanied by a more or less significant increase in the birth rate. Malthus himself emphasized birth and marriage rates and even in the later editions of the *Essay* he seriously under-estimated the fall in the death rate that had taken place. It is not so much that he got the facts wrong, for even now we cannot agree what the facts were, but rather that he never clearly grasped, or even took much interest in, the nature of the population explosion that gave such prominence to his views.

2. Malthus' Analytical Schema

Malthus' frame of reference was confined to a dualistic opposition between a biological capacity for procreation, attributed to natural instincts that man shares with animals, and a set of checks that limit this capacity (see Table 3–1).

Table 3–1

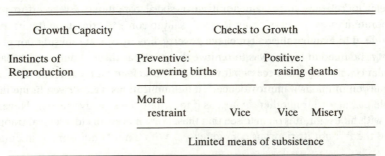

Growth Capacity	Checks to Growth	
Instincts of Reproduction	Preventive: lowering births	Positive: raising deaths
	Moral restraint Vice	Vice Misery
	Limited means of subsistence	

The checks themselves are classified into positive and preventive checks, separating the forces that affect the death rate and the birth rate. Upon this 'positive' dichotomous classification, he superimposed a 'normative' tripartite division of the checks into misery, vice and moral restraint. As a master check behind all the others is the 'means of subsistence', defined sometimes as a biological, sometimes as a cultural, minimum supply of provisions required for existence.

These are the categories Malthus employed to construct his theory. The theory itself consisted in essence of three propositions; (1) man's biological capacity to reproduce exceeds his physical capacity to increase the food supply, (2) either the preventive or the positive checks are always in operation and (3) the ultimate check to reproductive capacity lies in limitations of the food supply. The first proposition is obviously the crucial primitive axiom; the second and third propositions are really deductive corollaries of the first. Lack of subsistence is an ultimate check, not in the sense that it comes later in time but in that all the other checks are analyzed as ways in which the scarcity of food manifests itself; this is true even of the preventive checks because Malthus found it difficult to conceive of any motive for voluntary limitation of numbers other than fear of hunger.

The utter simplicity of the ideas involved, calling for no new analytical concept or factual discovery, was the essence of Malthus' immediate appeal. All he seemed to be doing was bringing together a few familiar facts of life and deducing the necessary consequences of these facts. Surely, population always multiplies up to the limits of the available food supply? And, surely, an unchecked multiplication of human beings must quickly lead to an impossible situation, whatever the plausible rates of increase that can be imagined for the means of subsistence? The famous contrast that Malthus drew between the two kinds of progressions, the geometrical increase in numbers and the arithmetical increase in food, carried the hypnotic, persuasive power of an advertising slogan. It was easy to see – 'a slight acquaintance with numbers will show', as Malthus said – that even the smallest finite sum growing at the smallest *compound* rate must eventually overwhelm the largest possible finite sum growing at the highest *simple* rate (consider $2 + 4 + 8 + 16 + 32 + \ldots$ in contrast to $1,000 + 1,003 + 1,006 + 1,009 + \ldots$). Additional people could reproduce themselves, hence the compounding factor, whereas additional food could not. It followed that whatever the initial situation, there would soon be 'standing room only'. The reader was likely to forget at such moments that unchecked populations growing at the maximum biological rate do not exist in the real world and hence that all such hair-raising comparisons still leave the fundamental hypothesis unverified.[1]

3. The Empirical Content of the Theory

Malthus defended his theory partly by logic, partly by facts, but not rigorously by either. He had no doubt that what we have called his primitive axiom was factually true. From dubious American data that did not distinguish between fecundity and

[1] If Malthus were writing today he would no doubt have cited a recent calculation showing that if the human race had sprung from a couple living in 10,000 B.C. and had grown since then, not at the maximum biological rate but only at a modest 1 percent per annum, the earth would now be a sphere of flesh several thousand light-years in diameter with a surface advancing into space at a rate many times faster than the rate at which light travels.

immigration, he inferred that an unchecked population will double itself every 25 years, implying a growth rate of just under 3 percent per annum (actually, rates of 5 percent per annum seem to be biologically possible). At a Malthusian rate of 3 percent per annum, the present world population of 4.5 billion would reach 9 billion by the year 2008; on the other hand, at the actual growth rate nowadays of 1.6 percent, world population will amount to about 6 billion in the year 2008. This shows the effect that fairly small differences in the rate of compounding can have in so short a period as 24 years. In view of the universal rule of declining population growth in advanced civilizations, a rule which dates back long before the present era, it was a little rash of Malthus to generalize a rate of 3 percent. However, the more important point is that he admitted that the standard of living had not declined in the American colonies, from which it follows that subsistence there must also have grown at a compound rate of 3 percent. But this he denied: there are 'no cases on record', he insisted, of subsistence growing at any steady compound rate. But if subsistence only increases arithmetically, how is it that population increases geometrically without producing starvation?

Identifying 'means of subsistence' with foodstuffs, he tried to show, by logic this time, that a rapid increase of food crops is out of the question since the supply of land is limited and technical improvements in agriculture do not come fast enough. The magic phrase that was subsequently used to sanction this assertion is the Law of Diminishing Returns. But Malthus argued, not that land was only augmentable at increased cost, but that capital accumulation and technical change could never offset limitations in natural resources. But there is no *law* of diminishing returns to technical progress. The law of diminishing returns, properly understood, is a static proposition about returns to varying factor proportions under given technical knowledge, having nothing to do with the dynamic problem of an actually growing population working a given land area under conditions of constantly improving technology. To confuse the two is tantamount to confusing Galileo's precisely specified law of falling bodies in a perfect vacuum with a casual generalization about the effects of dropping a lead ball and a feather from a tower.

Malthus did not mention a tendency to diminishing returns in agriculture until the second edition of the *Essay*, and throughout the six editions and even in the last published statement of his theory, the *Summary View on Population*, he showed a decided preference for a direct appeal to the reader's intuition at the expense of a careful formulation of the law. The confusion as to which version of the law of diminishing returns is relevant to the comparative growth of population and subsistence is present in everything Malthus wrote. In the *Summary View* we are told, first that the power to produce food is 'obviously limited by the scarcity of land . . . by the decreasing proportion of the produce which must necessarily be obtained by the continual additions of capital applied to the land already in cultivation' – an incomplete statement of the static law framed characteristically in average rather than marginal terms. Then a dozen pages later we are asked to believe that 'although the saving of labour and an improved system of husbandry may be the means of pushing cultivation upon much poorer lands than could otherwise be worked; yet the increased quantity of the necessities of life so obtained can never be such as to supersede, for any length of time, the operation of the preventive and positive checks to population' – the questionable dynamic notion of diminishing returns to technical progress so typical of all classical reasoning about secular changes in agriculture.

In the nature of the case, Malthus was contrasting a *hypothetical* capacity of population to grow at a certain rate with an *actual* incapacity of food to grow at the same rate. At first glance there would seem to be no way of verifying such an assertion. But it was central to his argument that population is never restrained for motives other than the fear of hunger, so the pressure of population on the available food supply is ever present. As he said in his correspondence with Nassau Senior, 'except in new colonies, favourably circumstanced, population was always pressing against food, and was always ready to start off at a faster rate than that at which the food was actually increasing'. This has the clear falsifiable implication that a steady rise of living standards can never be associated in 'old' countries with a growing population. And, indeed, this is just what Malthus asserted in the first edition of the *Essay*. But by the second edition, he added a new check to his argument: 'the [moral] restraint from marriage which is not followed by irregular gratification'; by this he means simply the postponement of marriage, accompanied by strict continence before marriage – he condemned contraception under all circumstances as 'improper'. This new proviso rendered the theory perfectly general and perfectly empty: rising living standards prove that moral restraint is checking population growth; falling living standards prove that the absence of prudential restraint results in misery or vice.

Any critic who produced evidence of subsistence increasing faster than population, without signs of 'misery and vice', was silenced by drawing the logical implication that the working class was practising 'moral restraint'. This left the critic with no reply other than to show that the average age of marriage had not in fact increased or that the rate of illegitimate births had not in fact fallen. Since contemporary population statistics were not adequate to verify such assertions, Malthus had furnished himself with an impregnable defense. There were a few critics who attacked the theory by questioning the notion that birth control constitutes 'misery and vice'. Malthus' argument here was simply that man, being naturally indolent, could hardly be expected to work or save if it were made so easy for him to escape the consequences of his 'natural passions'. He could rely on the weight of contemporary opinion to lightly dismiss all so-called neo-Malthusian checks 'both on account of their immorality and their tendency to remove a necessary stimulus to industry'.

In consequence, the Malthusian theory of population comes dangerously close to a tautology masquerading as a theory. So long as we hold with Malthus that birth control is morally reprehensible, the history of population growth in the last two centuries proves him right: nothing has stemmed the tide of human numbers but 'misery and vice'. If, on the other hand, we consider birth control morally defensible, Malthus is vindicated again: 'moral restraint' in the larger sense is one of the checks that has limited the tendency of population to outstrip the food supply. The

Malthusian theory cannot be refuted because it cannot be applied to any actual or any conceivable population change: it purports to say something about the real world but what it says is true by definition of its own terms.

Malthus' own statistical investigations were inconclusive, not so much because good statistics were lacking, but because his theory was incapable of being confronted by empirical evidence. Keynes once praised Malthus' facts and figures as 'inductive verification', and even Marshall paid tribute to what he regarded as 'the first thorough application of the inductive method to social science'. But Malthus himself was nearer the mark when he observed in the Preface to the second edition of the *Essay* that 'any errors in the facts and calculations which have been produced in the course of the work ... will not materially affect the general scope of the reasoning'.

4. Automatic checks

Critics sometimes suggest that Malthus misled his readers by entertaining the biological possibility of a rate of population growth far in excess of rates usually observed in the real world. But there is no methodological bar to hypotheses that postulate the existence of abstract 'tendencies' that in reality are never observed unaccompanied by disturbing influences. What is required is that the hypothesis entails predictable consequences; in practice, this usually means showing that the 'pure tendency' is in some sense independent of the counteracting factors, so that the deviation caused by 'frictions' can be quantified. Consider again of the role of a perfect vacuum in Galileo's law of falling bodies: Galileo specified the exact conditions for his law to hold and he also specified the precise effects of such 'frictions' as air resistance that would cause deviations from the law in practical circumstances outside the laboratory. In the case of Malthus, however, the checks were themselves the product of population pressures and moral restraint in particular was admitted to be an automatic check induced by population growth. It is not often realized that in the later sections of the *Essay*, Malthus did in fact concede everything his contemporary critics from Godwin to Senior held out against him; yet, he could not afford it prominence at the center of his system without destroying it.

It was Senior who first divided consumer goods into 'necessaries, decencies, and luxuries'; as the economy develops, the luxuries of one generation become the decencies of the next and, eventually, the necessaries of subsequent generations. The desire to preserve one's standard, the hope of rising in the world, Senior stressed, are motives as strong as those leading to marriage and procreation. Thus, a rise in living standards provides automatic preventive checks to the growth of population. Malthus denied the practical importance of 'the desire to better one's condition' among the working class and in particular denied Senior's claim that this principle supplied an automatic check. For Malthus, only an improvement of moral and religious habits could alleviate the problem. Yet in many places in the *Essay*, he spoke of the prevalence in England of 'a decided taste for the conveniences and comforts of life, a strong desire of bettering their condition (that master-spring of public prosperity)', in consequence of which 'a most laudable spirit of industry and foresight are observed to prevail . . . throughout a very large class of people'. And in the last chapter of the book, entitled 'Of Our Rational Expectations respecting the Future Improvement of Society', he pinned all his hopes on the 'apparently narrow principle of self-interest which prompts each individual to exert himself in bettering his condition'. After a volume dedicated to showing that only prodigious efforts will stave off famine and disease, he concluded in the last few pages that the powerful check of competitive emulation was operative and would be increasingly operative in all 'civilised and populous' countries.

Some will argue that it is too much to ask that theories about historical tendencies should demonstrate the independence of the counteracting factors from the dominant tendency itself. Such a requirement is suitable to the physical sciences but it is a counsel of perfection in the social sciences. At a minimum, however, it may be agreed that even social scientists are obliged to specify the time period over which the preponderant tendency is supposed to achieve its result. Obviously, if we are given a prediction which is not falsifiable within a specified period of time, we can never falsify the theory because at every future moment of time we will be told to 'wait and see'. In this way, many theories in the social sciences that appear to be scientific because they make concrete predictions are in fact rendered devoid of empirical meaning. Malthus' theory of population is one of the best examples in the history of western thought of such metaphysical theorizing. He invented a game that we will meet again and again: it might be labeled 'the apocalyptic fallacy', denoting the habit of making predictions with open-ended time horizons. The reader will come to see that the greatest practitioner of 'the apocalyptic fallacy' in the history of economic thought was not Malthus, but Karl Marx.

In the light of these remarks it is easy to see why Malthus displayed such a startling lack of interest in the laws of population growth: he neglected to consider the time lag necessary for population to respond to changes in the means of subsistence and said nothing about the age and sex distribution of the population, particularly the proportion of women of childbearing age, as affecting a population's growth capacity. In all his writings he seemed to regard the birth rate as independent of the death rate and the checks to population growth as independent of the size of the population itself. He was aware, having read Adam Smith, of the finding that the size of the family in almost all societies is inversely related to the height of the income class; yet, he drew no important conclusions from this fact. Indeed, it is largely because of Malthus' own treatment that the growth of population came later to be regarded as peculiarly subject to nonpecuniary considerations lying outside the domain of economics.

5. The Optimum Theory of Population and Subsistence Wages

One of the difficulties in interpreting Malthus is to give definite meaning to the concept of overpopulation. If we suppose that Malthus means a population too large to be fed with domestic resources, then the possibility of foreign trade is enough to banish the Malthusian specter. But sometimes Malthus, and certainly Nassau Senior and John Stuart Mill, suggested a more meaningful definition: a population too large for maximum efficiency of production, so that a reduction in numbers would raise income per head. In the 1920s, this suggestion was crystallized into the so-called 'optimum theory of population': if the population of a particular area may be too small for maximum efficiency – 'the division of labour is limited by the extent of the market' – as well as too large, it is obvious that there must be some point in between at which it is of optimum size. In other words, a population of optimum size is one that maximizes income per head. This concept of optimum population implies that the tendency of wages to sink toward subsistence levels is proof of overpopulation. Consider Figure 3–1: if wages per man are equal to the subsistence rate, equilibrium requires that population be of size B. For any smaller population, extra numbers produce more income than they cost to maintain and hence population will increase; any increase beyond B, however, is choked off through the positive check. An improvement of technology or an expansion of foreign trade will raise the income curve (see dotted curve in Figure 3–1) and generate population growth until wages are once again equal to subsistence.

Figure 3–1

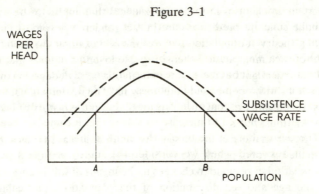

This interpretation rests on a fairly mechanical conception of the connection between wages and population. In fact, the wage rate might be at subsistence with population $= A$, the country being underpopulated rather than overpopulated simply because technical progress is so rapid that population never has the chance to catch up. During the adjustment process, workers get accustomed to higher living standards; the subsistence wage rate shifts up and population growth slows down until technical change gives it a new jolt. If subsistence is a function of 'habit and custom', as Ricardo was to emphasize, and not just a biological minimum, the statement that wages are at subsistence has no specific implications for the desired level of population.

This should dispel the notion, which is the small coin of popular social histories, that the classical economists were 'pessimists' simply because they believed that wages tend to be held at subsistence. They might have been pessimists on other grounds, but without exception they did believe that it was possible to raise the standard of living of workers. The wages-population mechanism was used to demonstrate the perfect elasticity of the long-run supply curve of labour, yielding the result that wages were supply determined independently of demand. In practice, however, it was admitted that the adjustment to rising wages might require a generation or more. In his *Principles* (1820), Malthus noted that 'a sudden increase of capital cannot effect a proportionate supply of labour in less than sixteen or eighteen years', giving expression for the first time to a specific time lag between an increase in wages and an increase of population. This lag permits real wages to rise, which in turn alters the equilibrium subsistence wage rate. In this way, even without belief in moral restraint or birth control, it was possible to look forward to a rosy future while continuing to operate analytically with a subsistence theory of wages.

It is evident that the subsistence *theory* of wages is not a theory at all: it amounts to taking subsistence as a datum, given by the workers' attitude to procreation and, possibly, the prevailing level of medical knowledge. It is only another example of the classical tendency to simplify analysis by reducing the number of variables to be determined. In any concrete case of wage determination, the subsistence theory is hopelessly ambiguous because we never know what time period is relevant to the particular problem. For instance, a subsistence wage rate implies that workers rear a replacement labour force: ignoring infant mortalities, each family has two children. Since population growth is normally positive with the labour force increasing all the time, the 'market' rate of wages must always be in excess of the 'natural' subsistence rate at any moment. What is the actual nature of the adjustment mechanism by which wages fall: will some children who would otherwise have died young reach working age, or will the extra income be spent on having more children? Or will mortalities be unaffected and births be allowed to increase so slowly that income per head rises permanently? There is nothing in the theory that helps us here, but these are the questions we want answered when we consider the future prospects of living standards.

6. Malthusianism Today

The concept of an optimum population is intellectually clarifying, but it is only fair to say that it is of little assistance in social action. In practice, the problem of overpopulation is not that of closing a gap between a population's actual size and its optimum size but that of confining the growth of a country's population to an optimum moving path through time. Even if it is possible to discover that a country is overpopulated at any moment of time, the process of moving to the optimum level may affect the very location of that optimum; the theory has nothing to say about the nature of an optimum path of growth and does not even insure that the optimum, once reached, can be maintained. This is the familiar problem of dynamic stability in price theory, but it is particularly relevant here because a positive rate of population growth is probably one of the preconditions of maximizing income per head and in this sense, an optimum population is necessarily a moving rather than a stationary plateau.

The merit of the optimum population theory is that it provides an analytical framework that makes it possible to consider under- as well as overpopulation. But it is like the Malthusian theory in being silent on the crucial question of the determinants of population growth. That mortality trends are affected by sanitary measures and medical improvements is reasonably well understood. It is fertility trends that are problematic. The Malthusian theory, however, does suggest the possibility of dealing with fertility rates in terms of conventional economic theory and, at first glance, it is difficult to understand why later economists did not pursue the classical type of explanation of changes in the birth rate. The outstanding feature of classical population theory is that it treats the production of children not as a means of spending income on 'consumer goods' for the sake of psychic satisfaction in the present but as a means of investing in 'capital goods' for the sake of a future return. In the Malthusian theory, children were thought to be produced at constant costs: an increase in the demand for labour necessarily generated a stream of expected returns in excess of costs and, therefore, resulted in an increase in the birth rate. But it is more realistic to assume that children are produced at increasing costs in the sense of the current expenses of rearing a child as well as the opportunities forgone by the mother. The growth of population is typically associated with urban crowding, a rise in the mother's earning potential and a rise in the school leaving age, all of which contribute to an increased cost of having children. At the same time, the lessening of family ties associated with the process of industrialization reduces the expected returns from children in the form of old-age security. Given the steady rise in the cost of rearing children relative to the decline in expected returns, it is hardly surprising that fertility is a declining function of national income in industrialized societies. Elements such as these might have been used to construct an economic theory of population growth in the spirit of classical economics.

This line of thought was never pursued by economists after Malthus, not at any rate until very recently. The decline of fertility in the last half of the 19th century was explained by exogenous changes in the 'taste for procreation'. In practice, economists simply abandoned the field of population studies. The result was to leave the profession unprepared to tackle the problem of overpopulation in the underdeveloped countries that came to the fore after World War II. The difficulty of most underdeveloped countries today is that of having, on the one hand, the high birth rates typical of agrarian economies and, on the other, the low death rates characteristic of industrialized economies. Economic development will in time cure these difficulties as they were cured in industrial Europe, but for the next few generations these countries face the alternatives of suffering the Malthusian checks of famine and disease or somehow promoting the voluntary limitation of families in conflict with prevailing religious mores. As always, there are lucid extremists on both sides of this question: neo-Malthusians hold that all efforts at economic improvement in the backward countries must be subordinated to, and in fact come after, the successful introduction of birth control; some Marxists and most Catholics, on the other side, dismiss all efforts to spread birth control techniques, contending that population control without industrialization will not work or else that birth control is immoral in itself. The name of Malthus is still bandied about in the debate, but it is difficult to believe that the Malthusian theory of population has much relevance to the discussion of modern population problems: it sheds no light on the causes of declining fertility in developing societies; it tells us little about the demographic relationship between fertility and mortality; it is silent on the economic consequences of shifts in the age distribution of a population; and it is of no help in framing policies for areas of heavy population pressure.

If Malthus' theory were indeed a theory, we would want to ask: What would happen if the theory were not true? The answer is, or ought to be, that income per head would rise, not fall, with increasing population. The history of Western countries, therefore, disproves Malthus' theory. The defenders of Malthus reply: But what of India today? No one denies that India is overpopulated and poor. It is overpopulated because the death rate was lowered by the introduction of Western medicine, thus divorcing population growth from the current level of income. It follows that India would be better off if she could also 'Westernize' her birth rate. But what has this piece of advice to do with the Malthusian theory of population?

DIMINISHING RETURNS AND THE THEORY OF RENT

The Malthusian theory of population focused attention on the limited supply of land. Among its by-products was the concept of diminishing returns and, more surprisingly, a theory of the nature of ground rent. These two ideas are so intimately connected that they emerged simultaneously as part of the reaction to the publication of Malthus' *Essay*.

The year 1815 saw the appearance in Britain of four publications by West, Torrens, Malthus and Ricardo, each of which independently formulated the theory of differential rent. Each tract was in its own way a reaction to committees appointed by Parliament to report on the recent fall in grain prices, and each took as its starting point the relationship between high grain prices and the extension of cultivation to less fertile and less accessible land during the years of the Napoleonic Wars. The underlying explanation, the four authors agreed, lay in the phenomenon of diminishing returns, 'the principle', as West put it, 'that in the progress of the improvement of cultivation the raising of rude produce becomes progressively more expensive'. 'Each equal additional quantity of work bestowed on agriculture', West went on to explain, 'yields an actually diminished return ... Whereas it is obvious that an equal quantity of work will always fabricate the same quantity of manufacturers'. One would think from West's formulation that 'the principle' only holds true for a given state of technology; but in fact West thought, as did Torrens, Malthus and Ricardo, that returns to agricultural activity do actually diminish in the course of time despite technical change. Of the four authors, he was the most explicit on this point: 'the necessity of having recourse to land inferior to that already in tillage, or of cultivating the same land more expensively, tends to make labour in agriculture less productive in the progress of improvement ... [which] more than counteracts the effect of machinery and the division of labour in agriculture'.

It was only later in the 1830s that Ricardo's followers began to substitute what Cannan once called 'the roughly general rule of diminishing returns rashly deduced from experience during the great war' by 'a pseudoscientific law of a tendency to diminishing returns'. Pseudoscientific or not, it is important to keep in mind that most of the classical economists regarded the law of diminishing returns as a simple generalization of everyday experience, whereas modern economists define it to be a statement about what would happen if one were to increase the amount of one input while holding all the others constant; the modern definition cannot be verified simply by glancing at the real world.

7. The Law of Diminishing Returns

The vague reference to 'an equal quantity of work' in West's statement of the 'law' of diminishing returns is characteristic of rent theory in this period. As Ricardo was to make clear, West was really thinking of a single homogeneous dose of capital and labour combined in fixed proportions and applied to land in equal successive increments: despite references to three factors of production, land, labour and capital, the argument is really developed in terms of a two-factor model. Moreover, it is always the average rather than the marginal product of capital and labour that is said to be diminishing. For most purposes, however, this confusion between the proportional and the incremental law of diminishing returns is not very serious: a monotonically declining average product always implies a declining marginal product, although the converse does not necessarily hold true.[2] With each of the four authors, the law of diminishing returns is supposed to be applicable only to agriculture and the proof of its validity is either by way of an appeal to history to show that the growth of population forces recourse to inferior soil, or through a logical

---

[2] Holding one factor fixed and varying the other (see Figure 3–2), we obtain a typical curve of the total product (*TP*); the average product (*AP)* is equal to the slope of a line drawn from the origin to each point on the *TP* curve, or tan θ, and the marginal product (*MP*) is equal to the slope of a tangent drawn to each point on the *TP* curve: these two slopes are only equal at the point where the *AP* curve reaches a maximum. Rational factor-hire eliminates regions I and IV from consideration. Since *MP* reaches a maximum before *AP*, *AP* is still increasing in region II, whereas *MP* is already declining; only in region III do both decline together. Thus, declining *AP* always implies declining *MP* but not vice versa.

Figure 3–2

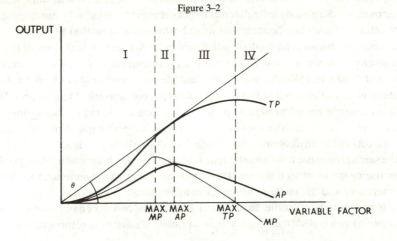

deduction from the fact that different grades of soil are at any moment of time simultaneously cultivated. If it were possible to raise additional product at constant or diminishing expense from soil of given fertility, why resort to inferior soil? But the extension of cultivation to inferior soil is no proof of universally diminishing returns to equal amounts of labour applied to equal quantities of land at a constant state of technique: some plots of land may show increasing returns as long as these do not rise as fast as returns diminish on other plots. Furthermore, the extension of cultivation is a temporal process with techniques altering all the time; in that case, even when the fertility of all uncultivated land is known and correctly estimated, an improvement in technology may make land profitable for cultivation that had hitherto been regarded as unprofitable. At the new level of technical knowledge the acres last taken into cultivation might be more productive than previous acres.

Some minor writers in subsequent decades tried to prove diminishing returns by a *reductio ad absurdum*. If proportional increments of labour and land produced proportional or increasing increments of output, the country's wheat supply could be grown in a flowerpot: the extension of cultivation, therefore, proves the existence of diminishing returns. But even with increasing returns, the country's wheat supply can not be grown in a flowerpot if returns in the flowerpot do not increase as rapidly as returns in actual production: the extension of cultivation *is* compatible with increasing returns.

Similarly, some of the later classical writers thought that the fixed supply of land guaranteed eventually diminishing returns. But this is only true if we are working with a two-factor model. Once a third factor is admitted, capital may increase relative to labour sufficiently to offset the effects of the increasing ratio of labour to land even in the absence of technical change: the fact that the supply of land is fixed proves nothing about the law of diminishing returns. The problem is one of defining exactly what we mean by diminishing returns and very little progress was made on this question until the beginning of the 20th century; even in Marshall's *Principles*, the treatment of this question left much to be desired [see chapter 10, section 16].

Assuming for the moment that the law of diminishing returns does at any rate pertain to intensive if not to extensive cultivation, it follows that price is regulated by the least favourable circumstance under which production is carried on. All four authors of the pamphlets of 1815 shared this insight and inferred from it that rent is the excess of the product over the outlays of the marginal farmer for capital and labour. In modern language, price is determined by marginal cost, but the marginal costs of the intramarginal farmer exceed his average costs and it is this excess which goes to the landlord as rent.

8. Differential Rent

Let us be more specific. The theory of differential rent is formally identical with the marginal productivity theory, though the marginal increments considered were enormously large instead of being negligibly small as marginal analysis requires. Suppose we are given the schedule of the grain produced on five grades of land of equal acreage shown in Table 3–2. From it we derive the table of incremental products resulting from the application of successive doses of 'capital-and-labour' (Figure 3–2).[3] We will suppose that the price per bushel of corn is $1 so that the schedule of physical quantities can be translated into money values by writing dollar signs in front of each number. The price of one homogeneous dose of 'men-with-shovels' is given at $140. Each farmer on each grade of land will apply doses of the variable factor so long as it adds more to revenue than to cost. Since the composite doses of 'capital-and-labour' are indivisible, farmer E will find it profitable to apply one unit but no more. Competition will insure equalization of the marginal value productivity of capital-and-labour in all locations; hence, two units of capital-and-labour will be applied to land D, three to land C, and so forth. Grade A land will produce a product worth $800 with five units of capital-and-labour – the sum of their marginal products – whose total cost is $700. Thus, rent on A will be $100; rent on B, $60; rent on C $30; rent on D $10; and rent on E, zero. Reading horizontally, E is the extensive margin of cultivation, being that quality of land which yields a total product ($140) just equal to the cost of the capital and labour expended upon it ($140). But if it pays at all to apply resources to E, it pays to apply them more intensively to $A, B, C,$ and D until an intensive margin equal to the extensive margin is reached; reading vertically, the intensive margin is the last increment of the variable agent on superior land that adds only as much to receipts as to costs ($140).

Table 3–2

Capital-and-labour	Total Product from Land					Marginal Product from Land				
	A	B	C	D	E	A	B	C	D	E
0	0	0	0	0	0					
						180	170	160	150	140
1	180	170	160	150	140					
						170	160	150	140	
2	350	330	310	290						
						160	150	140		
3	510	480	450							
						150	140			
4	660	620								
						140				
5	800									

The fact that rent so determined is equal to the marginal productivity of land is easy to demonstrate. In Ricardian theory, the variable factor receives a reward equal to its marginal product, while the fixed factor earns the intramarginal residual. Holding capital-and-labour constant and varying the amount of land until the value product of a marginal acre is equal to its cost should yield a rental per acre identical to

---

[3] Throughout this text, hyphens are used in the term 'capital-and-labour' when we are referring to a single homogeneous dose of both capital and labour.

Figure 3–3

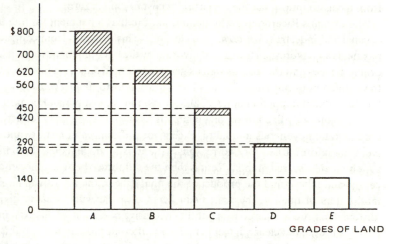

rents calculated as an intramarginal surplus to a varying amount of capital-and-labour applied to a fixed amount of land. Suppose we withdraw a unit of land from use, say grade *B*. The total product now falls by $620. The four units of capital-and-labour released are now employed at the intensive margins on *A, C, D,* and *E* where – ignoring the inappropriately large numbers in our example – they would produce $560 worth of product. Hence, the marginal value product of *B* is equal to $60, which is the same figure given above for rent calculated as a residual.

9. The Alternative Cost of Land

The Ricardian theory, however, has one feature not shared by modern productivity analysis. The only kind of rent considered in the Ricardian theory is agricultural rent; moreover, it is rent for the 'raw produce' of agriculture as a whole, not rent for land devoted to a particular product. Land used for tillage is thought to have no competing uses for grazing; labour and capital shift from one unit of land to another, but land itself never shifts between alternative uses. This explains the presence of the extensive margin in classical rent theory: land is supposed to be taken up freely when needed, not from some other rent-paying alternative, but from nonpaying idleness. And since land is completely specialized and fixed in supply, it follows that rent is price determined, not price determining: as Ricardo has it, 'corn is not high because a rent is paid, but a rent is paid because corn is high'. But as Adam Smith pointed out in the *Wealth of Nations* (Book I, chapter 5), when the market price of a commodity sinks below its natural price, 'the interest of the landlords will immediately prompt them to withdraw a part of their land' into better rental uses than this low-price commodity affords. Here rent is a cost to the individual producer that enters into the determination of price. In his formal chapter on rent (Book I, chapter 11), however,

Smith lost sight of the plurality of uses of land and slipped imperceptibly into considering rent for land as a whole. His followers emphasized the latter half of Smith's reasoning and without further explanation deduced bold practical maxims from the assumption that the opportunity cost of land is zero.

This explains Ricardo's careful definition of rent as a payment for 'the use of the original and indestructible powers of the soil'. This excludes from contractual rent payments any interest on the capital invested by the landlord in the form of buildings, drains, hedges and the like, as well as gains resulting from the removal of timber or the extraction of minerals. What is left is pure rent to 'land', considered as virgin territory, and untapped mineral wealth; it is an inexhaustible and nonreproducible agent, unalterably fixed in supply, completely specialized in the production of one crop, and homogeneous in quality, except for differences in fertility and location. Rent, therefore, arises for two reasons. If land is homogeneous, the limitation of supply creates 'scarcity rents'. Rent is then the difference between the product of all capital-and-labour and the product of the final dose at the intensive margin. When land differs in quality, the scarcity of acres of a particular quality gives rise to 'differential rents'. Ricardo thought that extensive no-rent land did exist in contemporary Europe, but clearly it would make no difference to the theory if this were not true. Rent would no longer constitute a pure differential, but scarcity rents would still exist.

From the notion that 'rent does not enter into price', that rent is not payment for the using up of resources, the classical economists drew the practical corollary that it would make no difference if landlords were thrown to the wolves. The expropriation of rents by the state would not affect production provided, of course, it were only pure economic rents that were being confiscated. Similarly, if rents were remitted from landlords to tenants, the price of agricultural products and the average rate of profit in agriculture would be exactly the same because the transfer of income would not affect the marginal cost of producing corn. But, of course, the remission of rents would probably alter the spending pattern of landlords and tenants and hence the demand for agricultural product. Since the location of the margin of cultivation is itself a function of the level of demand for corn, the marginal cost of producing corn would alter. In principle, Ricardo closed this gap in the theory by assuming that the demand for corn was perfectly inelastic – 'the desire of food', as Adam Smith had said, 'is limited in every man by the narrow capacity of the human stomach' – so that whatever determines the size of population determines the volume of demand for 'raw produce'. But, in practice, the problem of explaining the location of the margin was simply ignored.

10. Land as a Factor of Production

The core of the Ricardian doctrine of rent is still with us, though in attenuated form. John Stuart Mill was the first clearly to admit that the rent that land could earn in one use forms a cost that must be paid when it is used for some other purpose. Jevons seized upon this statement to show that land does have a supply price like any other economic input and that, contrariwise, all inputs when completely specialized earn a differential rent. The cost of any input cannot be less than what the input can earn in the most remunerative alternative use. In recent times this has been called the 'transfer earnings' of an input. The earnings of any input in excess of its transfer price constitute rent; from the viewpoint of the firm hiring the productive agent, rents are part of the costs of production; but from the point of view of the industry or of society as a whole, they are price determined and may be taxed away without affecting the supply of the agent. If the supply of an agent is fixed and if its services are specific to one use, transfer earnings are zero and the whole of its reward is rent, both from the individual and from the social point of view. But no agent is ever completely nonreproducible or incapable of being adapted to other uses; it all depends on the time period relevant to the case. In the short run, for example, fixed capital earns quasi-rents, not interest, for the supply of machines is nonaugmentable and non-adaptable. But in the long run, new machines can be built and old machines put to new purposes, so quasi-rents are always in the process of being eroded. In practice, therefore, the distinction between transfer earnings and rents leaves considerable room for doubt, which is to say that it is difficult accurately to estimate the price elasticity of supply of a factor of production.

The classical authors treated land as a 'free gift of Nature', a special factor of production distinct from man-made means of production and reproducible human labour. But in reality, natural resources do not differ from the general run of capital goods in requiring initial development and subsequent maintenance charges. If by 'land' we mean resources given by nature and available for use without cost, a very large part of the territorial resources of a society are not 'land' at all: fields that have been drained, cleared, and manured are as much the product of past labour as are machines. If 'land' is a factor of production, it must be said to consist of the heritage of equipment and improvements of the past given to the present generation as free goods. The classical predisposition to regard land as not producible is largely the result of thinking in physical rather than economic terms. Marshall argued, however, that territory does have some claim to be considered as a special factor of production. For one thing, it has the characteristic of certain long-lived goods – such as railway embankments, bridges, and some buildings – of being maintainable by relatively small expenditures on running repairs. In addition, it is expensive and sometimes it is impossible in a settled country to augment the supply of land by draining swamps or irrigating deserts. Consequently, the supply of economic space is typically much less elastic than the supply of capital goods. In this sense, Marshall thought that the classical analysis of rent, particularly with reference to the circumstances of a country like Great Britain, was not in essence misleading. Some British economists share Marshall's sympathy with the Ricardian approach to rent but, for the most part, modern economics has abandoned the notion that there is any need for a special theory of ground rent. In long-run stationary equilibrium, the total product is resolvable into wages and interest as payments to labour and capital – there is no third factor of production – and the theory of differential rent is interesting only because it marks the first appearance of the marginal principle in economic theory.

11. Site Value Taxation

Ricardian theory showed that ground rent, being a return to a nonreproducible natural agent, was eminently suitable for taxation. His mentor and disciple, James Mill, was the first to draw the obvious corollary that all future increments in rent from some current base year could be taxed away without serious harm. Ricardo himself was not happy with the proposal, but it remained an academic question in his lifetime. But with the publication of John Stuart Mill's *Principles* in 1848, a section of which reproduced his father's arguments, and the subsequent formation of the Land Tenure Reform Association under Mill's aegis, the idea caught on. John Stuart Mill proposed totally to exempt present rents and to tax 'the future increment of unearned rent' by taxing the capital gains of increases in the price of land. Henry George in *Progress and Poverty* (1879) went a little further and proposed to confiscate all rents in the manner of the physiocrats, a measure that he claimed would abolish poverty and economic crises, the latter being simply the result of speculation in land values. This would be a 'single tax' because he thought that its proceeds would be sufficient to defray the entire expenses of the state. His proposal was widely misunderstood, partly because of his own clumsy exposition, as advocating nationalization of land. In point of fact, he only proposed to tax pure ground rent, exempting the returns from site improvements. In short, 'the single tax' was designed to reduce the price of land as mere space to zero, leaving untouched the rentals of property located on the land; it was intended to put all property on the same basis irrespective of its location.

The Marshallian objection to the 'single tax' is obvious: all economic agents, not simply land, may earn 'rents' in the short run; and even Ricardian differential rents are incentive payments in the long run, encouraging the economical use of fertile and therefore scarcer land. George might have replied that no quasi-rent has either the persistence or the generality of ground rent, and Marshall would probably have agreed with that. Furthermore, if it were administratively feasible to distinguish pure economic rent for land as a distance-input from rent for site improvements of all kinds, the Marshallian argument would lose some of its force: the elasticity of supply of space is indeed very low (notice, however, it is not zero because land has depth as well as length and width). What George was after was to destroy land speculation, and he should have devoted all his energies to clarifying the distinction between a tax on 'site values' and a tax on 'betterment'. But this aspect of his argument was little developed in *Progress and Poverty*. Instead, George directed all his fire at the suggestion that landlords should be compensated once and for all for the rents that the state would tax away; he realized that this would reduce his proposal to that of taxing merely future increments of the rental values.

The administrative difficulties of putting a Georgian tax scheme into action are no greater than those involved in distinguishing income and capital under the progressive income tax. Provided there is no deception that such a tax would raise much revenue except in rapidly growing cities, there would seem to be nothing wrong with the principle of site value taxation, that is, the taxation of land values with full or partial exemption of the improvements made on the land. Ultimately, of course, the issue rests on the violability of property rights: the property rights of landowners must be weighed against the stimulus which a Georgian tax would give to improvements of existing sites. Still, if we want to stimulate investment in slum property, there are many easier ways of doing it than that of taxing site values. On the other hand, if it is land speculation and 'unearned income' from land that we dislike, a change in the treatment of capital gains under the income tax and a surtax on absentee landlords might be the answer. If all this should be deemed to raise too many administrative difficulties, we might advocate nationalization of land. We must realize, however, that land speculation performs an economic function: people differ in their expectations of the future economic development of particular locations, and the profits of those who have forecast correctly are, of course, matched by the losses of those who have not. If we nationalize land, the community will have to bear the costs of mistaken forecasts; the existence of ghost towns and declining neighborhoods shows that such mistakes are not uncommon: land values do not always rise everywhere.

Be that as it may, *Progress and Poverty*, a wonderful example of old-style classical economics, was thirty years out of date the day it was published and the idea of confiscating the income of a leading social class was deeply shocking to a generation bred on Victorian pieties. In consesquence, the concept of site value taxation was never seriously discussed, and to this day the only examples of it are to be found among local governments in the United States, Australia, and New Zealand. The milder Mill proposal, however, was eventually adopted in the British Budget of 1909 for urban lands not used for building purposes, and the British Town and Country Planning Act of 1947 finally applied the principle of taxing future rental increments to all plots of land.

The idea that Ricardo had planted proved to be as irresistible to the early exponents of marginal utility as to Ricardo's immediate followers. Walras and Wicksteed were both advocates of land nationalization, albeit with full compensation. Walras' scheme was to compensate the proprietors with bonds, using future rents to pay interest and to redeem the loan. But as the price of land is nothing but the future stream of expected rents discounted at the going rate of interest, full compensation would mean that rental receipts would be entirely swallowed up by meeting annual interest payments, and the state would never be able to redeem the bonds. Walras solved this problem by believing with Ricardo that rents tend to rise in a growing economy: he proposed to pay the proprietors a price on the basis of 99 years' purchase – the equivalent of perpetuity as far as the individual is concerned – and thereafter all rents would accrue to the state. Here, as elsewhere, the failure of Ricardo's prognosis to be borne out by the course of events doomed this proposal almost as soon as it was announced.

NOTES ON FURTHER READING

The reader should peruse Malthus' final statement of his theory, *A Summary View of the Principle of Population*, an article of some fifty pages written for the 1830 edition of the *Encyclopaedia Britannica*, reprinted either in *Introduction to Malthus*, ed. D. V. Glass (1953) –

together with some fine background articles by H. L. Beales and D. V. Glass – or the American paperback, T. R. Malthus, *On Population* (1960), or the British Penguin version of the first 1798 edition of Malthus' *Essay*, ed. A. Flew (1970). The second edition of Malthus' *Essay*, quadrupled in length and significantly revised, appeared in 1803, after which the main text was not substantially altered until the sixth and last edition in 1826 (but the appendices to the third and fifth editions of 1806 and 1817 contain important defenses against contemporary criticism). This final sixth edition is available in hardback with a biography and critical introduction by G. T. Bettamy (1890), or in paperback without the appendices. The first two chapters of the *Essay*, embracing less than 3 percent of the total work, state the whole of the theory; the bulk of the book is devoted to rather tedious descriptive accounts of population in various societies that illustrate the thesis laid down in the first two chapters. There is some typical Smithian economic theory in the chapters on the Poor Laws, the Corn Laws, and the proper mixture of industry and agriculture in an economic system: Book III, chaps. 6–12; the first few chapters of Book IV and, particularly, the last few pages of the book throw light on Malthus' vision of the good society. The reader should also consult the highly revealing published correspondence between Senior and Malthus, reprinted in G. F. McCleary's *The Malthusian Population Theory* (1953).

A recent modern biography of Malthus by P. Thomas, *Population Malthus: His Life and Times* (1979), contains much new material on Malthus the academic but little fresh material on Malthus the demographer. The logical structure of Malthus' theory is brilliantly exposed in K. Davis, 'Malthus and the Theory of Population', *The Language of Social Research*, eds. P. F. Lazarsfeld, M. Rosenberg (1955). J. Stassart, *Malthus et la population* (1957), provides a reliable French guide to 'what Malthus really said'. Cannan's incisive critique of Malthus has stood the test of time wonderfully well: *Theories of Production and Distribution*, chap. 5, and *Review of Economic Theory* (1929), chap. 4. Schumpeter's *History of Economic Analysis*, pp. 250–8, 578–84, covers the same ground and from nearly the same viewpoint; G. J. Stigler, 'The Ricardian Theory of Value and Distribution', *JPE*, 1952, reprinted in his *Essays in the History of Economics* (1965) and in *EET*, adds emphasis to Cannan. McCleary's *Malthusian Theory of Population* offers a spirited defense of the theory; the hostile reader should test his critical faculties on this book. J. J. Spengler attempts to reconcile Malthus' *Essay* with Malthus' *Principle of Political Economy* in 'Malthus's Total Population Theory: A Restatement and Reappraisal', *CJEPS*, 1945, reprinted in *EET*. See also J. J. Spengler, 'Was Malthus Right?', *SEJ*, July, 1966, which question appears to be answered by 'not quite but . . .'. Readers who are still unconvinced that the Malthusian doctrine had relevance to the contemporary world should consult K. Smith, 'Some Observations on Modern Malthusianism', *PS*, July, 1952.

The controversy over the nature of the population explosion in the 1780s is brilliantly canvassed in a collection of recent papers, *Population in Industrialization*, ed. M. Drake (1969), which includes a comprehensive bibliography. For a fascinating review of the great 19th-century debate in England on the Malthusian theory, see K. Smith, *The Malthusian Controversy* (1951). D. E. C. Eversley, *Social Theories of Fertility and the Malthusian Debate* (1959), supplements this account by emphasizing the development of the standard-of-living theory. M. Blaug, *Ricardian Economics* (1958), chap. 6, sketches the virtual abandonment of the Malthusian theory by Ricardo's early followers. *Marx and Engels on Malthus*, ed. R. L. Meek (1953), is rich in invective but surprisingly thin in substance.

The history of population theory before and after Malthus is succinctly covered in the United Nations volume, *The Determinants and Consequences of Population Trends* (1953), chap. 3, reprinted in *Population Theory and Policy*, eds. J. J. Spengler, O. D. Duncan (1956), a collection which contains many other useful papers. P. H. Douglas, *The Theory of Wages* (1934), chap. 13, surveys the work done on the long-run supply curve of labour since Malthus.

Most of the great economists in the latter half of the 19th century commented extensively on the Ricardian theory of rent and, among these, Marshall and Wicksteed are the most illuminating. There is an outstanding discussion of the mixed static-dynamic character of Ricardo's rent theory in H. Sidgwick, *Principles of Political Economy* (1883), Book II, chap. 7. The crucial distinction between the alternative cost of land to an individual producer and the social cost of land to the whole community is brought out by D. H. Buchanan in a review of the history of rent theory from Smith to Marshall: 'The Historical Approach to Rent and Price Theory', *Ec*, 1929, reprinted in *Readings in the Theory of Income Distribution*, eds. W. J. Fellner, B. F. Haley (1946). For a good statement of modern rent theory, see D. A. Worcester, Jr, 'A Reconsideration of the Theory of Rent', *AER*, 1946, reprinted in *Readings in Microeconomics*, ed. D. R. Kamerschen (1967). H. J. Barnett and C. Morse, *Scarcity and Growth, The Economics of Natural Resource Availability* (1963, and in paperback), chap. 3, contains an interesting review of the concept of natural resource scarcities from Malthus to John Stuart Mill.

Henry George is still with us: there are Henry George Schools of Social Science in all the major cities of America and there are even a few outside America; the *American Journal of Economics and Sociology* is a Georgist publication and its pages will demonstrate that site value taxation is far from being a dead issue. S. B. Cord, *Henry George: Dreamer or Realist?* (1965), despite its jejune tone and some theoretical fuzziness, gives a fascinating account of the reactions of four generations of economists to *Progress and Poverty*. All the leading British and American economists of the day – Alfred Marshall, Francis Walker, Edwin Seligman, Thomas Carver, and Richard Ely – wrote extensive critiques of George. As R. V. Andelson, *Critics of Henry George. A Centenary Appraisal of Their Strictures on Progress and Poverty* (1979), makes clear, the story is one of persistent misunderstanding, misrepresentation and downright evasion of the issues by the leading members of the economics profession. For a concise presentation of George's proposals in his own words, see 'A Single Tax on Land Values' (1890), reprinted in *ETHA*. For a useful modern appraisal of his work, see E. Teilhac, *Pioneers of American Economic Thought* (1936), chap. 3. On the economics of George's proposals in a current context, see *The Assessment of Land Value*, ed. D. M. Holland (1970), particularly the essay by U. K. Hicks, 'Can Land Be Assessed for Purposes of Site Value Taxation?'

4

Ricardo's system

At the heart of the Ricardian system is the notion that economic growth must sooner or later peter out owing to scarcity of natural resources. The bare outline of the system can be grasped by supposing that the whole economy consists of a giant farm engaged in producing wheat by applying homogeneous doses of 'capital-and-labour' to a fixed supply of land, subject to diminishing returns. We have already seen how Ricardo avoids the necessity of handling three variables by reducing capital and labour to one variable input. The argument contains one further simplifying assumption: the demand for wheat is perfectly inelastic, being a simple function of the size of the population; the moment we posit a certain population, the output of wheat is determined. At this point we apply the marginal productivity theory to show that the variable input will obtain its marginal product and the fixed factor, land, will earn a 'surplus', determined by the gap between the average and the marginal product of the variable input for both extensive and intensive cultivation (Figure 4–1). Rent is

Figure 4–1

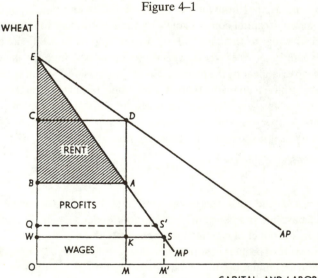

equal to the total product ($OCDM$) minus the marginal product of capital-and-labour (AM) multiplied by the number of doses applied (OM). Since the total product is given either by the rectangle under the average product curve ($OCDM$) or by the area under the marginal product curve ($OEAM$), rent can be read off the diagram as the shaded triangle or as the rectangular rent box so labeled. The magnitude of rent is determined solely by the gap between the average and the marginal product, by the strength of the forces making for diminishing returns. The curves are drawn as straight lines in the diagram for convenience only, although, as we shall see, Ricardo's arithmetical examples do assume straight-line average and marginal productivity functions.

1. The Theory of Wheat Profits or the Corn Model

So much for the straightforward marginal-productivity part of the theory. Now for the strictly classical part of the argument: since capital and labour are combined in fixed proportions, the marginal productivity theory cannot determine the division of the product-less-rent between capital and labour. The subsistence theory of wages is now introduced to determine the wage rate by the constant supply price of labour in terms of wheat (OW). The supply curve of labour (WS) is infinitely elastic at the subsistence wage rate. Total profits are a residual equal to the total product-less-rent minus the wage bill ($OWKM$); per unit of capital-and-labour, profits are equal to the marginal product of the composite dose (AM) minus the wage rate (KM). This composite dose is, strictly speaking, a dose of fixed-and-working-capital-and-labour, with the proportions between the two types of capital kept constant. In physical terms, the rate of growth of tools and implements is always equal to the rate of growth of the labour force and the proportions in which they are combined, together with the postulated subsistence wage rate, determine the amount of working capital required. So long as the turnover period of capital is one year – think of the agricultural harvest – capital consists solely of annual advances to labour. In other words, capital is equal to the wage bill or 'wages fund' ($OWKM$), the aggregate demand for labour in terms of wheat. This is the third 'trick' in the argument: fixed capital is made to disappear by the proviso that implements wear out in one year. The annual rate of profit is given by the ratio of total profits to capital invested and, since annual capital consists solely of circulating or working capital, it follows that the ratio of total profits to the wage bill determines the giant farm's rate of profit as a percentage rate on capital employed. Thus, the rate of profit is

$$r = \frac{\text{Profits}}{\text{Wages}} = \left(\frac{AM - KM}{KM} \right) 100\% = \left(\frac{AM}{KM} - 1 \right) 100\%.$$

Now, if $OW = KM$, the subsistence wage rate may be regarded for all practical purposes as a constant, and hence the rate of profit depends on and varies directly with the marginal product of capital-and-labour (AM).

As long as the rate of profit is positive, capitalists are induced to accumulate. In the course of capital accumulation, the labour force will grow proportionately, AM will move to the right and both marginal product of capital-and-labour and the rate of profit will fall until at last the stationary state is reached with $AM = KM = SM'$ and $r = 0$. We may qualify the argument by supposing that there is a minimum rate of profit (say, QW) below which capitalists will not be willing to incur the risk of investment: the simplest assumption consonant with Ricardo's *obiter dicta* is that this minimum-of-existence reward for capital is some small but positive constant. This does not affect the argument in the slightest; all that happens is that the stationary state comes sooner. Furthermore, technical progress must be admitted to shift the productivity functions upward, which serves to stave off the stationary state. This is partially offset by the fact that the long-run-supply curve of labour WS is drifting upward through time as workers become accustomed to a higher standard of living. The subsistence rate of wages is, after all, that rate at which population growth would cease, but this does not happen until the economy has attained the stationary state. The accumulation of capital is continually raising the 'market price' of labour above its 'natural price'; this induces population growth, whereupon the market wage is bid down again to the natural wage. The process comes to a halt only when wages have eaten up the whole of the product-less-rent, that is, when profits have fallen to minimum acceptable levels.

To illustrate what will happen, we plot the curve of total product-less-rent as the size of the labour force: for 'labour force' read 'population' because the labour force participation rate in classical economics is always treated as a given constant (Figure 4–2). When population = OM, the wage bill = RM (equal to our previous rectangle $OWKM$) and total profits = PR (equal to our previous rectangle $WBAK$). The wage rate is equal to the wage bill divided by the number of workers, $RM/OM = \tan \alpha$, and is assumed to be a given constant. The existence of positive profits induces investment and pulls the market wage above RM; this tends to choke off investment, but at the same time the induced growth of population forces the market wage back to the natural wage; profits are now $P'R'$, which gives rise to further investment, and so on, until the stationary state S is reached. If capital accumulation is taking place all the time, the market wage may never have time to fall back to the natural wage; the demand for labour is continually outrunning the supply. The result of this is that workers come to expect a higher minimum-of-existence level, defined as that rate at which they have no incentive to 'produce' more labour. The wage line in our diagram therefore would rotate counterclockwise, and the stationary state consequently would be reached sooner. All this is ignored for the purpose of the argument: the subsistence wage rate is simply a datum, given by 'habit and custom'. Capital accumulation is what propels the system toward the stable equilibrium of the stationary state; population growth is merely a by-product of this adjustment. Thus, in the Ricardian system, economic growth is frequently viewed as if all demographic adjustments depend on the fact that the stock of capital is not yet optimally adjusted to the labour force and the supply of available land. It is precisely this feature of the Ricardian model which makes it so hard to grasp for the modern reader: it is a mixture of comparative statics and comparative dynamics within one and the same framework.

To return to our central conclusion: the rate of profit in the economy varies directly

Figure 4–2

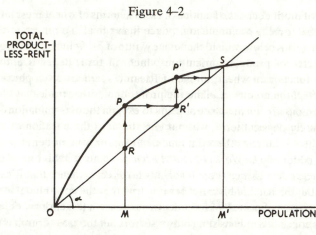

with the strength of diminishing returns. The Malthusian tendency of population to increase up to the limits set by the means of subsistence provides a virtually unlimited supply of labour that can be employed at a constant real wage fixed in terms of wheat or 'corn'. There is no fixed capital of any kind and all capital is working capital. In other words, wheat is the only output of the giant farm and it is also the only input. As the labour force increases, extra wheat to feed extra mouths can only be produced by extending cultivation to less fertile land, or by applying additional capital-and-labour to land already cultivated with diminishing results. The difference between the net wheat product per worker on the least fertile land and the constant wheat wage per worker goes to the tenant farmer as profit. Owing to the action of competition, the advantages of working superior land go entirely to the landowner in the form of ever increasing rents. As more land is taken up, the net produce per worker falls, whereas the real wage remains the same. Obviously, profits per worker decline. At the same time, the wheat value of the capital per worker increases because wheat is continually becoming more expensive to produce in terms of real resources used up. Divide the falling profits per worker by the rising capital per worker and it follows that the rate of profit on capital, which supplies the motive for investment, declines. Eventually, capital accumulation must come to an end.

What happens, however, if the economy consists of two sectors, a wage goods industry, like agriculture, producing 'corn' and a manufacturing industry producing 'cloth' for consumption out of profits and rents? This does not affect the point, argued Ricardo in his early pamphlet, *Essay on The Influence of a Low Price of Corn on the Profits of Stock* (1815). The money rate of profit earned on capital must be equal in equilibrium between the two industries. In agriculture, wheat is the only input as well as the only output; hence, the money rate of profit in agriculture cannot diverge from the wheat rate of profit; any change in the price of wheat affects inputs and output in the same degree. Manufacturing uses wheat only as a capital input to produce cloth, and therefore equality in the rate of profit throughout the economy implies a definite relationship between the price of cloth and the price of wheat. If the wheat rate of profit declines, the price of cloth in terms of wheat must fall to prevent cloth from being more profitable to produce than wheat. To reiterate: all prices are measured in terms of wheat, and the 'money' rate of profit in industry is governed by the wheat rate of profit in agriculture which, in turn, depends entirely on the production function of wheat; in one of Ricardo's famous catch-phrases: 'it is the profits of the farmer which regulate the profits of all other trades'.

This ingenious argument, which appears to explain the determination of the rate of profit in purely physical terms without entering into the question of valuation, is known in the literature as the 'corn model'. It was only in modern times that Piero Sraffa, the editor of *The Works of David Ricardo*, detected this line of reasoning as implicit in Ricardo's *Essay*. There is actually no direct evidence that Ricardo had the corn model in the back of his mind but it is true that the corn-model interpretation neatly rationalizes almost all of Ricardo's arguments in this early work, in which the economy is conceived as consisting of two sectors but the rate of profit is determined exactly as it would be in a one-sector economy. Nevertheless, on balance one must conclude that the corn-model interpretation of Ricardo's *Essay* is a modern 'rational reconstruction' and that Ricardo himself never went so far as simply to assume that wages are entirely spent on wheat, that all agricultural products are wage goods and that all manufactured products are luxuries which are never consumed by workers, for these are the assumptions necessary to deduce the average rate of profit in the economy merely from the wheat rate of profit in agriculture.

In the *Essay*, Ricardo did use corn as a measure for aggregating the heterogeneous inputs of agriculture on the assumption that all prices rise and fall with corn prices, and he also employed arithmetical examples in which all inputs and outputs of both agriculture and manufacturing are expressed in terms of corn, but that is still a far cry from the corn-model version, which simply attributes far more rigor and consistency to Ricardo's analysis than is warranted. Suffice it to say that, in normal circumstances, a change in the terms of trade between 'corn' and 'cloth' will alter real wages and hence will upset the proposition that 'the profits of the farmer regulate the profits of all other trades'. The terms of trade between corn and cloth involves a change in relative prices and the analysis of such a phenomenon requires a theory of value. It was only in the *Principles*, published two years after the 1815 *Essay*, that Ricardo first took up the question of value theory.

2. The Labour Theory of Value

Adam Smith confined the application of a labour theory of relative prices to a conjectural 'rude and original state of society'. Ricardo went a step further and argued that a one-factor theory of value is capable, however imperfectly, of explaining price determination in the real world. But Ricardo's misgivings on this question have more significance in the history of the labour theory of value than do his positive assertions. He was the first to show just why a labour-cost theory cannot fully account for the relative prices of reproducible commodities under perfect competition. If he adhered to the labour theory at all, he did so only as a rough approximation and because it served as a convenient device for expounding his model. His central purpose, he tells us, is not to explain relative prices, but 'to determine the laws which regulate the distribution of the produce of industry'. Nevertheless, let us consider for a moment why any one-factor theory of value fails to explain the relative prices we observe about us.

When we are faced with only one factor of production, the price of a product is equal to the average input requirement of that factor per unit of output multiplied by its money rate of reward. Let there be two goods X_1 and X_2. Let each require a_i labour inputs per unit of output, rewarded at the rate w_i. Then the cost of production equations for long-run prices are

$$p_1 = w_1 a_1 \qquad p_2 = w_2 a_2 .$$

If labour is homogeneous, perfect competition will ensure $w_1 = w_2$. Thus relative prices are entirely determined by relative labour-input requirements, irrespective of the pattern of demand:

$$\frac{p_1}{p_2} = \frac{a_1}{a_2} .$$

Even when two or three factors are employed, a pure labour-cost theory of value will still more or less acccurately predict all *significant* changes in relative prices simply because labour costs usually bulk large in total costs. As Samuelson has expressed it: 'the operational significance of a one-factor hypothesis lies in the powerful predictive value that it gives to technology alone'.

But the presence of capital, even if it is only working capital, does imply that a simple labour theory can never *exactly* predict changes in relative price. Production is time-consuming and workers need finished consumer goods today; they cannot wait to be paid out of the finished product of today's labour when it is actually sold sometime in the future. So the employer 'advances' finished goods to the worker, the sum of which constitutes the so-called 'wages fund' or circulating capital. The capitalist must earn interest on the money value of the goods in process that he has 'advanced' to workers. The money flow of the final product, made up of finished consumer goods and unfinished capital goods, exceeds the sum of wages paid out by the interest returns of the capitalists. That interest exists is due simply to the lapse of time that always occurs between the application of inputs and the appearance of output. Who receives it is a matter of who can afford to do the requisite 'waiting'. In the language of the Austrian theory of capital, workers are forced to pay a premium on present goods because they cannot wait for the completion of the productive process; the present value of future output discounted at the ruling rate of interest equals the present value of wages but output normally exceeds its present value precisely because the rate of interest is positive. Whether 'waiting' is a factor of production that requires a minimum rate of reward to be forthcoming at all is a question that we can leave open for the moment – in any case, this aspect of the problem never troubled Ricardo in the slightest. All we need for the purpose of the present argument is that the market rate of interest, or to use classical language, the rate of profit, is normally positive.

To digress for a moment, it ought to be pointed out that the classical theory of business profits refers to what we would now call the 'pure' rate of interest, the rate on riskless perpetual bonds. This does not mean that the classical economists failed to distinguish between the rate of return on real capital and the market rate of interest. But in long-run equilibrium and with perfect certainty, the two rates are equal and therefore in their theory of value and distribution they ignored the distinction. Nowadays we draw a distinction between the capitalist earning interest and the entrepreneur earning profit. This distinction goes back to Adam Smith, who spoke of 'the monied interests' of inactive investors in contrast to businessmen who actively employ capital. But, for the most part, the classical writers had in mind the owner-manager of a firm, earning both implicit interest and profit. In the modern sense of the term, profits as such consist partly of monopoly gains due to imperfect competition, partly of 'rents' to factors in inelastic supply and partly of returns to uncertainty-bearing [see chapter 11, section 21]. In the classical period, theorems about profit do not touch upon any of these three considerations, being in fact theorems about interest rather than profit. If we nevertheless continue to talk about the classical theory of profit, it is only because of customary usage; it would be much better if we spoke of the classical theory of interest.

To continue the argument: when the rate of profit is positive, the price of a commodity is influenced not merely by the amount of labour required to produce it but also by the length of time for which that labour is embodied in production. The price of a product in the long run is equal to its wage cost plus a profit margin on the capital advanced. If one worker produces one bushel of wheat in *one* year and two workers one yard of cloth in *one* year, the relative price of the two goods is equal to the ratio of the amounts of labour required to produce each of them: cloth will be twice as expensive as wheat. At any given rate of profit, the amount of profits earned on cloth are always just twice the amount earned on wheat and no change in the rate of profit will alter this result. But if one worker can produce a bushel of wheat in *one* year while it required two workers *two* years to produce a yard of cloth, the profits earned on the wages of the first year will themselves have to earn profits for the second year; instead of cloth now being four times as expensive as wheat (two workers for two years as against one worker for one year), its relative price in terms of wheat will in fact be greater than four. And a change in the rate of profit will now affect relative prices even though the relative quantities of labour required to produce the two goods remain the same as before. To put it more tersely, if X_1 and X_2 are produced in unequal periods of time t_1 and t_2 with $t_1 > t_2$, then if r is the rate of profit per period, the cost-of-production equations for long-run prices are

$$p_1 = wa_1(1 + r)^{t_1}, \qquad p_2 = wa_2(1 + r)^{t_2},$$

with

$$\frac{p_1}{p_2} = \left(\frac{a_1}{a_2}\right)(1 + r)^{t_1 - t_2}.$$

It follows that we can no longer predict relative prices from the labour coefficients alone unless $t_1 = t_2$. In short, the labour theory of value cannot account for relative prices when capital as well as labour is involved in the productive process. And note that this is true even if capital is only working capital. The presence of fixed capital could of course create further deviations from an explanation in terms of labour time.

3. Capital Costs and Labour Values

The whole of the first chapter in Ricardo's *Principles* is devoted to the point we have just been making. Instead of speaking of unequal production periods, Ricardo prefers to group the objections to the pure labour-cost theory under the headings of 'The different proportions of fixed and circulating capital', 'The unequal durability of fixed capital', 'The time which must elapse before it (the product) can be brought to market', and 'The rapidity which it (the capital) is returned to the employer'; but all of these, as he himself explained, 'come under one of time', an observation that makes Ricardo the 'father' of the Austrian theory of capital. And it makes no difference whether we speak of different periods of production of commodities or of its reciprocal, different turnover rates of capital. The latter expression has the advantage of translating Ricardo's insight into the common parlance of business. Commodities produced at equal unit costs sell at equal prices when the profits on turnover are also equal. The rate of profit on the turnover of capital tends to equality in a competitive system for the same time period, not for different time periods. If a capital sum yields $10 every year, it must yield more than $20 every two years, otherwise it will not be invested in a two-year period. Equality in the *annual* rate of profit will in fact insure that the shorter process is no more profitable than the longer one.

Actually, the problem is a little more complicated than Ricardo made out. By confining capital to working capital, the problem is indeed reduced to one of 'time'. But fixed capital cannot be distinguished from working capital merely on grounds of its greater durability, as Ricardo thought. Labour working with fixed capital in the shape of a machine produces as a by-product a slightly older machine, which gets embodied in subsequent production. The used machine has a price determined by its initial cost, by the wage and interest rates that ruled during its period of operation, and by the method that was employed to charge depreciation. This creates difficulties of a kind that are even now not completely resolved. The history of capital theory after Ricardo, through Böhm-Bawerk and up to Wicksell, was confined for that reason to the examination of working capital, not fixed capital [see chapter 12, section 8]. Still, for our purposes, the use of fixed capital does not alter the point being made. Goods are produced at different ratios of fixed capital to labour and capital sunk in durable machines must have earned the going rate of profit each year over the whole length of life of the machines. The more machines per worker, the greater the weight of nonlabour income in the cost price and the lower the ratio of wage costs to sales price. Hence, goods produced with equal amounts of direct labour, but with unequal amounts of machinery of unequal durability, cannot sell at the same price. It is useless to reply that machines are only embodied labour, for the whole point is that the present value of a machine exceeds the value of all the wages expended on its production in the past by the amount of annual interest charges. It is not necessary to argue that capital goods cannot be reduced solely to labour, that yesterday's labour, which produced today's capital goods, was itself working with capital goods and land existing yesterday, and so on back to the Garden of Eden in an infinite regress. Even if it were true that the first machine was produced by labour alone eons ago, the fact remains that from that point onward the labour theory of value consistently neglects at least one element determining current prices. Notice that this kind of difficulty has nothing to do with the neglect of demand; it is a difficulty that remains even when the supply curve of every product in the economy is perfectly elastic, so that all prices are supply determined.

No labour theory of value is analytically satisfactory that does not address itself to this fatal objection. Peculiarly enough, after having discovered the exception to the rule, Ricardo shrugged his shoulders at it, saying in effect that the magnitude of the deviations that it caused was of minor significance next to changes in the quantities of labour required to produce goods. This statement will not do if we are trying to explain how relative prices are determined at any moment of time. But if, like Ricardo, we are not basically concerned with this question, then it is true that a knowledge of the respective labour coefficients alone can explain most price variations, particularly if r is small. Under certain circumstances, the labour theory of value may serve as a useful first approximation to the problem of price determination, but never more than as a first approximation.

4. The Ricardo Effect

The way Ricardo approached the problem of value theory is characteristic of his preoccupation with distribution. He assumed at the outset that the purchasing power of money over all goods and services, as measured by the average level of prices in the economy, is constant and hence that distribution is a matter of dividing a given real national product among landlords, capitalists, and labourers. Rent, being an intramarginal surplus, does not enter into the determination of prices. The value of a commodity, therefore, is determined by the variable inputs applied on no-rent land and distribution is, in the first instance, a problem of dividing a product-less-rent between capital and labour. The fact that capital-labour ratios differ among industries means that any change in money wage rates or the rate of profit necessarily alters the structure of prices and therefore the value of the product-less-rent. A change in the *level* of prices owing to a change in money wages has already been ruled out by the assumption of the constant purchasing power of money. A truly general rise of wages in all industries including the gold-mining industry, cannot, Ricardo argued, raise prices: it is impossible to raise both the gold price of commodities and the commodity price of gold because one is the reciprocal of the other. Even if gold is not domestically mined, the argument holds good if the country in question is on a gold-exchange standard with paper notes fully convertible into gold; all we need to do in such a case is apply Hume's specie-flow mechanism [see chapter 1, section 2]. This leaves only the effect of a change in money wages on the *structure* of prices.

As Sraffa has said: 'The effects on value of different proportions or durabilities of capital can be looked upon from two distinct aspects. First, that of occasioning a *difference* in the relative values of two commodities which are produced by equal quantities of labour. Second, that of the effect which a rise of wages has in producing a *change* in their relative value.' We have been emphasizing the first, but it was the second that really interested Ricardo. He was struck by the fact that measured in money of constant purchasing power, a rise in wages would raise the price of labour-intensive goods relative to the price of capital-intensive goods or, to put it differently, lower the relative price of capital-intensive goods. Since average prices are being held constant, it is true by definition of an arithmetical average that a commodity produced with an average ratio of capital to labour, and so *ad infinitum*, will not alter in price as a consequence of an increase in wage rates. Measured in terms of such a commodity, a labour-intensive good like wheat rises, while a capital-intensive good like cloth falls in price. We need a name for this effect, for it will come up frequently in our story. Fortunately, it already has a name. It is what Hayek has called the 'Ricardo Effect' [see chapter 12, section 27].

5. The Invariable Measure of Value

A commodity produced with a period of production that is an arithmetic mean for the economy as a whole will, Ricardo realized, provide an 'invariable measure of value': a standard of measurement invariant to changes in relative factor rewards. If the total product-less-rent is measured in terms of this yardstick, its value will not alter with every change in the distribution of the product between capital and labour. For a given quantity of capital and labour, that total product will always have the same value. Ricardo decided that 'gold' is the commodity that most closely approaches the requirement of an invariable measuring rod and, in places, he ventured to suggest that a period of twelve months is both the period of production of gold and the 'average period of production' of the economy as a whole, but it is difficult to know whether such assertions were meant to be taken seriously as statements of fact. The principle, however, remains the same, whatever commodity is said to be representative of the general degree of 'roundaboutness' in the economy.

So far, so good. Instead of deflating national income with a weighted index of prices in general, we deflate it with the hypothetical price of 'gold'. This solution to the index-number problem seems, however, to have got mixed up in Ricardo's mind with the problem of locating the source of variations in the ratios of exchange between goods. Normally, a change in the money price of wheat will tell us nothing about conditions of production in agriculture. Under a gold standard, the money price of wheat may rise because wheat is more costly to produce, but equally well because of a technical improvement in the gold mining industry. Or it may be that a rise in the demand for labour is pushing up money wage rates and wheat happens to be a more labour-intensive good than gold. But Ricardo wanted to be able to speak unambiguously about a rise in the price of wheat caused by rising input requirements in agriculture. To do so, he took a further step and stipulated that the invariable yardstick must be conceived as being produced at all times by a constant quantity of capital and labour.

By itself this is still not enough. A change in the rate of wages or the rate of profit will alter the price of wheat, measured in terms of the invariable standard, if the capital intensity of wheat production departs from the social average. Suppose that the relative price of wheat increases owing to the pressure of diminishing returns. Money wages must now rise to keep real wages constant and, in consequence, the price of wheat in terms of the invariable standard alters once again for reasons having nothing to do this time with the inputs embodied in the production of wheat. If workers consume manufactured products, which have fallen in price measured in terms of the yardstick, the problem gets even more complicated. It is clear that the invariable standard does not really help to solve this problem even though it succeeds in valuing the national product independently of its distribution among the participating factors of production.

It is apparent that Ricardo realized this, and he got round it by collapsing the two problems into one. The invariable yardstick is not only produced with an 'average period of production' for the economy as a whole, as well as with a constant amount of capital and labour, but this average period is taken to be equal to the annual production cycle of agriculture. Thus, when wheat sells at $1 in terms of the measure of value, this means that the production of a bushel of wheat requires the same quantity of capital and labour as the production of gold designated as $1. The price of wheat is not affected by the wage rate and is determined solely by two labour coefficients, its own and the fixed coefficient of the 'ideal money'. After a long journey we have come right back to the original 'corn model' that may be read into the 1815 *Essay on the Low Price of Corn*.

The whole of the famous chapter on value in the *Principles*, as well as the last paper Ricardo wrote, is concerned with justifying this procedure. It is a muddle because Ricardo is trying to resolve two different problems at one and the same time: on the one hand, to find an appropriate unit of social accounting to add up the real net national product and, on the other hand, to attach an absolute number to every economic good expressing its 'difficulty or facility of production'. Underlying both problems is the fatal objection to the labour theory of value: the value either of a single good or of the total national product is influenced by the division of outlays between capital and labour. Ricardo cut this Gordian Knot by actually ignoring capital. Instead of simply neglecting it outright, he confines himself to comparing goods produced by the same ratio of capital to labour. To get to the value of the total product, we blow up the average as found in agriculture and gold mining and arrive at the total with the same proportion of capital to labour. There will be goods more capital intensive than the average but they are matched by an equal number that are less capital intensive, by definition of the problem. Changes in the ratio of wages to profits will alter this distribution of goods around the average but cannot affect the average itself and, therefore, cannot affect the value of the total product, which is a function only of the amounts of capital and labour employed in the economy. Capital turns over once a year and hence consists solely of the wage bill; the wage bill is spent entirely on wage goods; all wage goods consist entirely of wheat; and wheat (as well as gold) is the yardstick for valuing the national product. It follows that the value of the total product is determined by labour requirements and by nothing else. Now, obviously, this is a sleight of hand that resolves problems by defining them away. But so tortuous is Ricardo's exposition that we are likely to deceive ourselves that he has actually substantiated the labour-cost theory of value.

Indeed, if Ricardo had not encountered so much criticism, he might have retained the definition of the invariable standard advanced in the first edition of the *Principles*, to wit, a commodity that would require at any time the same amount of labour unassisted in any way by capital. Wheat was then said to be produced by labour alone and thereafter the whole argument ran on exactly as in the third edition. What Ricardo wanted to do in the chapter on value was to show that the labour theory, despite its flaws, provides a convenient shortcut for expounding the 'real' nature of distribution in a growing economy. The chapter is virtually impossible to follow because it still shows marks of the process of thinking through assumptions without facing up to the fact that assumptions have meaning only in terms of their implications; if only Ricardo had clarified his intentions, the chapter might have been cut in half and perhaps assigned to a later stage in the argument.

6. The Fundamental Theorem of Distribution

We saw earlier that in a one-sector wheat economy, the rate of profit varies directly with the marginal product of capital-and-labour applied to land; that is,

$$r = \left(\frac{AM}{KM} - 1 \right) 100\%$$

But AM/KM is the ratio of the total product-less rent to total wages, whose reciprocal is labour's share of the final product minus rent. Thus, the rate of profit varies inversely to wages if by 'wages' we mean the relative share of labour in the final product (less rent) of a one-year investment. This is Ricardo's 'fundamental theorem'. When we introduce money into the system, this theorem must be assumed to apply to the rate of money profit and the rate of money wages. It is not merely a matter of relative shares, as is sometimes alleged. Ricardo would hardly have gone to the length of emphasizing such a truism over and over again. Moreover, it is a truism only if we deduct the rental share. It is *not* a truism with respect to the total national product, however, since the rental share has yet to be determined. Be that as it may, let us now spell out the fundamental theorem for a money economy whose output consists of more than wheat. This will prove to be a good exercise in manipulating a fairly simple model. It looks difficult, but it is only simple algebra plus a little elementary calculus. The particular formulation of Ricardo that we adopt here is due to Pasinetti and it is only one of the many attempts in recent years to spell out Ricardo's meaning in mathematical terms.

If the price of wheat is determined at the margins of cultivation, rent must be spent on some good other than wheat. Let us introduce 'gold', consumed by landlords, which we use at the same time as a *numéraire* or yardstick in which to express all prices. There are two production functions in our two-sector economy:

Wheat: $X_1 = f(N_1)$,
Gold: $X_2 = f(N_2)$,

with $N_1 + N_2 = N$ being the total number of workers in the economy; since capital is always combined in fixed proportions with labour, N_1, and N_2 are in fact the doses of capital-and-labour required to produce wheat and gold. We assume $t_1 = t_2$, that is, gold and wheat are produced in equal periods of time (thus getting rid of the entire problem of an 'invariable measure of value'), and hence

$$\frac{p_1}{p_2} = \frac{a_1}{a_2} \, .$$

But a_2, the capital-and-labour required to produce one unit of gold, is assumed constant by definition of the *numéraire*. So the relative price of wheat is entirely determined by a_1, the capital-and-labour required to produce one unit of wheat on no-rent land.

To standardize our notation:

The production function of wheat: $X_1 = f(N_1)$, subject to $f'(N) > 0$ and $f''(N) < 0$, in other words, a positive marginal product and diminishing marginal productivity. (1)

The production function of gold: $X_2 = \dfrac{N_2}{a_2}$, where a_2 is a constant. (2)

The total number of workers: $N = N_1 + N_2$. (3)

The real wages bill: $\bar{W} = \bar{w}N$, with $\bar{w} = $ the constant real wage rate in terms of wheat. (4)

The physical stock of capital: $K = \bar{W}$. (5)

The real annual rental $\bar{R} = X_1 - N_1 f'(N_1) = f(N_1) - N_1 f'(N_1)$, that is, the total product minus the product at the no-rent margin. (6)

Real annual profits in agriculture: $\bar{\pi}_1 = X_1 - \bar{R} - \bar{w}N_1$. (7)

Real annual profits in the gold industry: $\bar{\pi}_2 = X_2 - \bar{w} N_2$. (8)

The money price of gold: $p_2 = a_2 = \dfrac{N_2}{X_2} = 1$. (9)

This is a vital step in the argument: in a two-commodity economy, where relative prices are determined solely by relative labour requirements per unit of output, the choice of one commodity as the *numéraire* in which to express money prices is equivalent to setting its labour-input coefficient equal to unity.

The money price of wheat

$$p_1 = \left(\frac{a_1}{a_2} \right) p_2 = a_1 = \frac{N_1}{(X_1 - \bar{R})} \, . \tag{10}$$

After substituting from equation (6), equation (10) may also be written:

$$p_1 = \frac{N_1}{X_1 - X_1 + N_1 f'(N_1)} = \frac{N_1}{N_1 f'(N_1)} = \frac{1}{f'(N_1)} \, . \tag{10a}$$

In other words, the price of wheat is an inverse function of the marginal productivity of labour in agriculture.

Money profits in agriculture: $p_1\bar{\pi}_1 = p_1(X_1 - \bar{R} - \bar{w}N_1)$. (11)

Money profits in the gold industry: $p_2\bar{\pi}_2 = p_2X_2 - p_1\bar{w}N_2$. (12)

Money profits in the whole economy:

$$\pi = p_1\bar{\pi}_1 + p_2\bar{\pi}_2 = p_1X_1 - p_1\bar{R} + p_2X_2 - p_1\bar{W}.$$ (13)

The expression $(p_1X_1 - p_1\bar{R})$ in equation (13) is the money value of the wheat product minus rent. Substituting equation (10), it turns out this is equal to N_1, that is, if

$$p_1 = \frac{N_1}{(X_1 - \bar{R})}, \quad \text{then} \quad p_1(X_1 - \bar{R}) = N_1.$$

From equation (9), the value of the total gold product, p_2x_2, is equal to N_2. This result appears dimensionally impossible since a money value cannot be equal to a certain number of workers. But we must remember that by a money value in this model we mean its value in terms of the amount of labour required to produce a unit of gold, (N_2/X_2). Thus, the first three terms in equation (13) $= N_1 + N_2$. Furthermore, the fourth term, $p_1\bar{W}$, is the total wage bill which is itself equal to $(N_1 + N_2)\bar{w}p_1$. Hence, total money profits can also be written:

$$\pi = (N_1 + N_2)(1 - \bar{w}p_1).$$ (13a)

Total money rent: $p_1\bar{R} = p_2X_2 = N_2$. (14)

The money wage rate: $w = p_1\bar{w} = \dfrac{\bar{w}}{f'(N_1)} = \bar{w}a_1$. (15)

Finally, the money rate of profit:

$$r = \frac{\pi}{p_1K} = \frac{(N_1 + N_2)(1 - \bar{w}p_1)}{\bar{w}p_1(N_1 + N_2)}$$

$$= \frac{1 - \bar{w}p_1}{\bar{w}p_1} = \frac{1}{\bar{w}p_1} - 1 = \frac{f'(N_1)}{\bar{w}} - 1.$$ (16)

The conclusion we reach is identical to the simple 'corn model' interpretation of Ricardo's 1815 pamphlet: given the real wage rate, the rate of profit varies directly with the marginal product of N_1, and – we can now add – inversely to the price of wheat as well as to the money wage rate. Despite the fact that there are nonwage goods, the rate of profit is completely independent of the conditions of production outside the wage-goods industry. It is true, of course, that this conclusion depends on the fact that workers spend all their wages on wheat and on the way we eliminated rent by looking at the margins of cultivation. And it should be noted that the Ricardian method of 'getting rid of rent' in determining relative prices is not really legitimate, since the location of the margin is itself a function of demand and hence of wage and profit rates; the lower the rate of profit, for example, the greater the pressure to cultivate land hitherto regarded as uncultivatable. But substitution in consumption is ruled out in the Ricardian model for, as we recall, the output of wheat, and hence the classification of land in order of its fertility, is determined by the size of population and the technical conditions of production in agriculture. We can get rid of rent because land is fixed in supply *and* because final demand for the product of land is fixed.

7. The Effect of Capital Accumulation

The system is now subject to three possible dynamic adjustments: the population adjustment when the market wage differs from the natural wage, the capital accumulation adjustment when r exceeds the minimum rate necessary to induce investment; and technical progress, which shifts the production function X_1. The first is frequently put aside by Ricardo for purposes of establishing 'strong conclusions'. The third is dealt with parenthetically but the core of the argument abstracts from technical change. It is the second mechanism alone that largely produces the Ricardian conclusions for a growing economy. His effort is confined to describing what happens to product prices, factor prices and factor shares in the process of capital accumulation. His results are simply expressed by taking the derivatives of all the crucial variables with respect to capital and inspecting the signs of the derivatives, a simple problem as all the functions are one-variable functions. Rewriting equation (5), $K = \bar{W} = \bar{w}N$ or $N = K/\bar{w}$, we obtain:

$$\frac{dN}{dK} = \frac{1}{\bar{w}} > 0, \text{ that is, total employment increases.} \tag{17}$$

From the original form of (5) we have

$$\frac{d\bar{W}}{dK} = 1 > 0, \text{ that is, the real wage bill increases.} \tag{18}$$

From $(N_1 + N_2) = K/\bar{w}$ and (6) we have

$$\frac{d\bar{R}}{dK} = f'(N) - N_1 f''(N_1) \frac{dN_1}{dK} - f'(N) = -N_1 f''(N_1) \frac{dN_1}{dK} > 0, \tag{19}$$

that is, total real rents rise.

This follows from the fact that $f''(N_1) < 0$, so that $-N_1 f''(N_1) > 0$ and $dN_1/dK > 0$.

From (10a) we have

$$\frac{dp_1}{dK_1} = \left\{ \frac{-f''(N_1)}{[f'(N_1)]^2} \right\} \frac{dN_1}{dK} > 0, \text{ that is, the price of corn rises.} \tag{20}$$

From (15) we have

$$\frac{dw}{dK} = \bar{w} \left(\frac{dp_1}{dK} \right) > 0, \text{ that is, the money wage rate increases.} \tag{21}$$

Finally, from (16) we have

$$\frac{dr}{dK} = \left[\frac{f''(N_1)}{\overline{w}}\right]\frac{dN_1}{dK} < 0, \text{ that is, the rate of profit falls.} \tag{22}$$

Noticing that the value of total output is $(p_1X_1 - p_1\overline{R}) + p_2X_1 = N$, we could go on to define the relative shares of wages, profits and rents in total income and, taking derivatives with respect to capital, we could examine what will happen to relative shares in the course of capital accumulation. But the expressions we would get would be extremely messy to interpret. It is simpler, and will serve the same purpose, to revert to a one-sector wheat model, keeping the same notation but dropping the numbered subscripts. Ricardo argued not only that the profit rate would fall in a growing economy but also that the relative share of profits in total income would fall and that both labour's and land's relative share would rise. The proof of these propositions takes three chapters in the *Principles* but turns out to be dependent upon the particular production function of wheat that Ricardo selected for his arithmetical examples. The reader who does not like calculus and is willing to take things on trust may skip the next section: its purpose is to show that Ricardo failed to demonstrate that the rental share will rise in the course of economic progress, a surprising result considering that it was precisely this prediction that made him famous; along the way we learn a few elementary propositions in the modern theory of production.

8. The Trend of Relative Shares

We begin with a given production function for the economy, $X = f(N)$, subject to $f'(N) > 0$ and $f''(N) < 0$. What happens to relative shares as N, the number of doses of capital-and-labour, increases? Take first labour's relative share. As all output is homogeneous, we do not have to worry about prices: output equals income and real values equal money values. It is clear without any mathematics that the share of wages in total income must rise as income increases: at a given real wage rate, the wage bill grows proportionately to the number of workers; output or income, however, grows less than proportionately owing to the postulate of diminishing returns. Spelling it out, labour's relative share is

$$\frac{\overline{W}}{X} = \frac{\overline{w}N}{f(N)}.$$

Taking the derivative with respect to N, we obtain

$$\frac{d}{dN}\left(\frac{\overline{W}}{X}\right) = \frac{\overline{w}}{[f(N)]^2}[f(N) - Nf'(N)] > 0, \tag{23}$$

that is, labour's relative share rises.

The bracketed expression $[f(N) - Nf'(N)] = \overline{R}$, and therefore, so long as land commands a rental, the whole expression is positive: the share of wages in total income rises with every increase in N.

Now for the rental share. It is defined as

$$\frac{\bar{R}}{X} = \frac{f(N) - Nf'(N)}{f(N)} = 1 - \frac{Nf'(N)}{f(N)} .$$

Rather than taking the derivative with respect to N, let us convert this expression. Dividing both numerator and denominator by N, we get

$$\frac{\bar{R}}{X} = 1 - \frac{f'(N)}{f(N)/N} .$$

But $f'(N)$ is the marginal product (MP) and $f(N)/N$ is the average produce (AP) of the variable input N. Thus,

$$\frac{\bar{R}}{X} = 1 - \frac{MP}{AP} .$$

The ratio MP/AP is nowadays defined as the 'elasticity' of a production function: the proportional change in the total product associated with the proportional change in the variable input. Using the standard notation for elasticity, we have

$$\varepsilon = \frac{dX}{X} \bigg/ \frac{dN}{N} = \frac{N}{X}\frac{dX}{dN} = \frac{N}{f(N)}f'(N) = \frac{f'(N)}{f(N)/N} = \frac{MP}{AP} .$$

So $\bar{R}/X = 1 - \varepsilon$, in which case $\varepsilon = (X - \bar{R})/X$. Thus the share of the total product which capital and labour together receive, $(X - \bar{R})/X$, is exactly equal to the ratio $MP/AP = \varepsilon$. (This result is not confined to the one-factor argument before us: the relative share of a variable input in a multi-factor production function is always equal to the ratio of its marginal and average product.) It follows that $\bar{R}/X$ will rise only if the *absolute* value of ε falls in the course of capital accumulation. It is hard to visualize ε, so we shall translate it into the elasticity of the average product curve η. Defining η in a straightforward fashion as the proportional change in the average product associated with a proportional change in the variable input, we have

$$\eta = \frac{d(X/N)}{X/N} \bigg/ \frac{d/N}{N} = \frac{N}{X/N}\frac{d(X/N)}{dN} = \frac{N^2}{X}\frac{d}{dN}\left(\frac{X}{N}\right) = \frac{N^2}{X}\frac{1}{N^2}\left(N\frac{dX}{dN} - X\right)$$

$$= \frac{N}{X}\frac{dX}{dN} - 1 = \varepsilon - 1 = \frac{MP - AP}{AP} .$$

Accordingly, η varies in the same direction as ε and can be read visually off a diagram as the size of the gap between the AP and the MP curves. The translation of ε into η reads: the rental share accruing to the fixed factor will rise along a given invariable production function if the *absolute* value of the elasticity of the average product curve falls as we apply additional units of the variable input, that is, if the gap between the AP and MP curves increases.

In general, η does not necessarily fall along a production function showing diminishing returns to the variable input. Diminishing returns is a necessary but not sufficient condition for an increase in the rental share of the fixed factor. It is possible

Figure 4–3

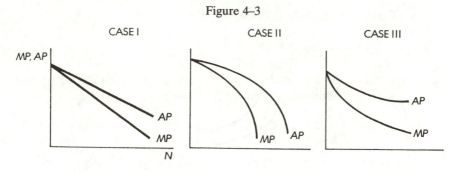

that the increment of output on no-rent land increases total output by a proportion greater than the percentage increment in rental payments on intramarginal land. Rents rise as a share of output if returns diminish at a constant or at an increasing rate: it depends, not on the sign of the slope of either the MP or the AP curve, but on the rate of change of the slope of the MP curve compared to the rate of change of the slope of the AP curve. In other words, Ricardo was right in thinking that the rental share would rise in the course of economic progress if it were true that the proportionate rate of change of MP is always greater than that of AP, that is, if η falls. However, we cannot in general exclude the possibility that η rises over certain ranges of output despite diminishing returns.

To illustrate, consider the productivity curves of three different production functions shown in Figure 4–3, all obeying the condition of diminishing returns to the variable input as well as the Ricardian prediction of a rising rental share. Productivity curves I are derived from a parabolic total product curve that continues to increase at a constantly diminishing rate; η falls continuously along this AP curve no matter how far they are extended and this is the simplest example of the Ricardian prediction of a rising rental share. Productivity curves II are concave from below, in which case the Ricardian prediction holds with double force as the total product increases at a diminishing rate, which is itself accelerating [see chapter 3, figure 3–2]. Productivity curves III, however, are convex from below; they show diminishing returns but at a declining rate; nevertheless, η is falling continuously along the AP curve and the gap between AP and MP is continually widening as in the previous examples; the Ricardian prediction of a rising rental share continues to hold good because the proportionate rate of change of MP is still greater than that of AP.

Let us now take a case where the productivity curves are likewise convex from below but where η is rising because the proportionate rate of change of MP is less than that of AP (Figure 4–4). In that case, we reverse the Ricardian prediction. As we shall see, the arithmetical examples on which Ricado based his arguments implicitly assume linear productivity functions (case I), so it is no wonder that he concluded that the rental share will increase.

Unless we are going to commit ourselves to a particular form of the production function, we must conclude that the rental share is indeterminate. If the rental share

Figure 4-4

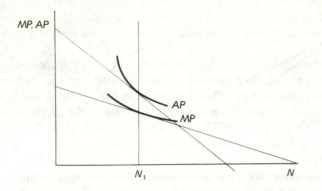

Note – The principle of constructing this diagram is very simple: for any given N, say, N_1, make sure that the horizontal-intercept of the tangent to the MP curve exceeds the horizontal-intercept of the tangent to the AP curve.

is indeterminate, so is the share of wages plus profits in total income: we know that labour's share will rise but the share of residual profits may go either way simply because the total share of wages and profits may go either way. Thus contrary to what Ricardo thought he had demonstrated, the postulate of diminishing returns is insufficient to derive his general theorems about the pattern of income shares in a growing economy. Commentators ever since Ricardo's time have tried to simplify his fundamental theorem that 'profits vary inversely with wages' by saying it refers to the relative shares of capital and labour, rather than to wages per man and profits percent on capital invested. But, surprisingly enough, the very opposite is true: the theorem holds true on his own assumptions for money wages and the rate of profit but it does not hold true for the relative shares of labour and capital.

9. Technical Change

A growing economy is likely to experience technological progress, which will shift the MP and AP curves upward. What will happen to factor rewards and relative shares in that case? On this question the Ricardian system is not very informative. There are some general remarks in the *Principles* about the effect of improved methods in manufacturing on real wages and in the chapter on rent there is a formal discussion of the effect of 'improvements' in agriculture on rents. Let us look briefly at Ricardo's theory of agricultural improvements for what it is worth. His argument is that the short-run effect of such improvements is to lower rents and therefore that landlords will have no incentive to introduce them. He divides the changes in techniques into two types: (1) landsaving innovations that increase the output from a given amount of land by 'more skilful rotation of crops, or the better choice of manure'; and (2) capital-and-labour saving innovations that reduce the doses of capital-and-labour required to produce a given output on a given amount of land, such as 'improvements in agricultural implements, . . . economies in the use of horses employed in husbandry, and better knowledge of the veterinary arts'. The first of the two types, he concludes, lowers rents per acre as well as the rental share, while the second lowers total money rents but not necessarily total rents expressed in terms of wheat.

Let us consider first a landsaving innovation. Obviously, its immediate effect is to lower rents per acre, but is it necessarily true that total rents and the rental share will fall? Ricardo assumes that the productivity of each grade of soil is raised equi-proportionately. Raising the productivity of each grade of soil by an equal percentage amount necessarily means that the innovation raises output per unit of cost less on the margins of cultivation than on the intramargins. Referring back to our numerical example in chapter 3 (Table 3–2), a 10 percent increase in output on land E constitutes a smaller absolute cost-reducing improvement than a 10 percent increase in output on land A. To illustrate the argument graphically, we need to draw the productivity functions of land, holding capital-and-labour constant, in such a way as to raise the new curves above the old while tilting them downwards (Figure 4–5). The demand for wheat is perfectly inelastic, so the total product remains unchanged $(ORDS = OR'D'S')$. As long as the curves are straight lines, it is indeed true that total rents as well as the rental share will fall. But the conclusion is dependent in the first place upon the assumption that the marginal and average products of land are linear functions – convex productivity functions would produce precisely the opposite effect – and in the second place upon the notion that the improvement raises output per unit of land by a constant percentage amount. If, instead, Ricardo had assumed that output is raised by equal absolute amounts per unit of land – an isoelastic upward shift in the productivity curves – the result would have been to increase rents. The reader can prove these propositions for himself by using the rule that η, the elasticity of the average product curve of a variable factor, in a two-factor production function varies in the same direction as the relative share of that factor; and as we move back on a straight line from right to left we can translate every statement about relative shares into statements about absolute shares.

Ricardo's analysis of capital-and-labour saving innovations is no more conclusive. Here he begins by assuming that innovations raise the productivity of capital-and-labour by equal absolute amounts – in which case, rents fall – and then passes on to an example in which productivity is raised by equal percentage amounts – in which case rents rise. Even in the latter case, it is only wheat rents that rise, not money rents, for the innovation causes the price of wheat to fall. Ricardo does not consider what will happen to the now displaced capital-and-labour. Presumably, wage and profit rates will fall again, inducing the cultivation of new land and, hence, rents will rise whatever the immediate effect of the innovation.

In general, the striking feature of Ricardo's analysis of technical change in agriculture is his emphasis upon the short run, while elsewhere he concentrates upon long-run effects. He frankly admitted that the fall in rents due to innovations is really temporary: the fall in the price of corn stimulates population by raising real wages, and so rents per acre will eventually rise again. This curious reversal in the method of

Figure 4–5

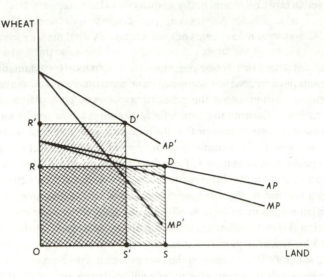

analysis may have something to do with Ricardo's ideological bias against landlords. But we must not forget that in spite of the numerous references to the accumulation of capital and the growth of population, Ricardo's model is not actually concerned with economic growth in the long run. The purpose of the model was to demonstrate the inexpediency of the Corn Laws, which protected British wheat farmers by prohibiting foreign wheat except in years of famine prices. Restrictions on the importation of cheap wheat *tend* to reduce the rate of profit by forcing the rapid extension of cultivation to successively less fertile areas of land at home. The summary treatment given to technical change may be due to the fact that Ricardo really had his eye on the effects that a Corn Law imposes in a comparatively short period of time. Certainly he shows very little interest in the structural changes of an economy over long periods, a subject to which Adam Smith had given some of his best analysis. Even Ricardo's so-called 'pessimism' is entirely contingent upon the maintenance of the Corn Laws. There is no indication whatever that he regarded the stationary state as something that would actually come about in the near future. After all, in the *Principles* the fundamental theorem of distribution is coupled with the Law of Comparative Cost to show that social welfare is increased by free trade and that repeal of the Corn Laws would permit a country like Britain to reap the benefit of her comparative advantage in manufacturing presumably for centuries to come.

We have reviewed the analytical skeleton of Ricardo's system. The qualifications that he made, his frequent recognition of the restrictive assumptions of his model, are best examined in a reader's guide to the *Principles*, to which we now turn. A guide is certainly needed as this is undoubtedly the most difficult to read and the most difficult to grasp of all the great treatises of economics.

READER'S GUIDE TO 'PRINCIPLES OF POLITICAL
ECONOMY'

10. Value

The first chapter of the book consists of seven sections, the first of which states
without compromise that relative prices are determined by the relative amounts of
labour required to produce commodities, independently of the rate of reward to
labour. Adam Smith's water-diamond paradox is quoted and Ricardo immediately
alters the implicit meaning of Smith's 'use value', defining it as 'utility', the capacity
of a product to 'contribute to our gratification'. The theory of exchange value is
restricted to reproducible goods under conditions of perfect competition. Nonreproducible goods are called 'scarce', meaning goods fixed in supply. In chapter
17 such goods are described as selling at a 'monopoly price' entirely determined by
demand. The rest of **chapter 1, section 1**, is devoted to attacking the doctrine that
outlays on wages determine relative prices, a doctrine that Ricardo attributes to
Adam Smith. The problem of value, Ricardo notes, is this: 'two commodities vary
in relative value, and we wish to know in which the variation has really taken place'
(this is not how most economists would state the problem of value; it is a
characteristically Ricardian way of conceiving the issue). Smith's measuring rod,
the purchasing power of a commodity over labour, Ricardo tells us, will not
illuminate this problem: Smith identified a labour-embodied with a labour-
commanded theory. This criticism makes sense only if we assume that Smith was
trying to *explain* relative prices with a labour-commanded theory. Actually,
Ricardo's quarrel with Smith is that the amount of labour that a product can
command in exchange constitutes a poor *measure* of value.

Table 4–1

	Wages in Corn	Corn Price per Bushel	Money Wages	Expenditure on Corn	Expenditure on Other Things
I	1 bu.	80s.	80s.	40s.	40s.
II	1¼ bu.	40s.	50s.	20s.	30s.

Note: s. = shillings

Ricardo now constructs a numerical example (see Table 4–1) to show that Smith's
yardstick cannot distinguish between 'a rise in the value of labour' and 'a fall in the
value of things . . . on which wages are expended'. Suppose that labour is paid in corn
and consumes a half-bushel of corn per week, trading the rest for 'other things'. Corn
now falls in price for any reason whatever, and labour receives more corn but not
enough to maintain a constant market basket of the same goods (despite changes in
relative prices, the composition of the market basket remains unchanged; Ricardo

always ignores the possibility of commodity substitution). In this case, Ricardo alleges, Smith would have to say that labour had risen in value because 'his standard is corn', whereas he should have said that the value of labour had fallen because labour's real wages have decreased; labour has less purchasing power over all goods. Obviously, this criticism is unfair because it ignores the fact that Smith's standard is designed for long-run comparisons, and a huge long run at that. Naturally, if the price elasticity of demand for corn is zero and the cross-elasticity of demand for all goods is also zero, a fall in money wages leaves the labourer worse off. But what of the subsequent repercussions of the fall in money wages? Population growth would slacken, Smith might have argued, the demand for corn would fall off, corn prices would rise, followed by money wages and, ultimately, real wages must rise back to previous levels. What irritated Ricardo was Smith's assumption that the wages of labour can be measured in corn because the price of corn stays constant through time. It would have been a simple matter, however, to have shown that Smith's belief in the stability of corn prices 'from century to century' is irrelevant to the effects of such policy measures as the Corn Law of 1815. Instead, Ricardo chose to attack Smith on Ricardian grounds, completely ignoring the underlying rationale of Smith's measure, the idea that the disutility of labour is invariant at all times and all places [see chapter 2, section 10].

11. Relative Wages

It is becoming clear that Ricardo is not in fact concerned with explaining why relative prices are what they are. Throughout this chapter he is really discussing the choice of a proper standard of value for the purpose of explaining shifts in the structure of prices through time. When he states that 'the inquiry to which I wish to draw the reader's attention relates to the effect of the variations in the relative value of commodities, and not in their absolute value', he means *temporal* variations in relative value. This impression is confirmed by **chapter 1, section 2**, which dismisses the problem of wage differentials between labour of different skills with the argument that the occupational structure does not vary significantly over periods of moderate lengths: the scale of wages continues 'nearly the same from one generation to another; or at least the variation is very inconsiderable from year to year, and therefore, can have little effect, for short periods, on the relative value of commodities'. This fact, if it is a fact, has relevance only within the context of intertemporal comparisons of value – notice, also, Ricardo's careless and undecided attitude about the exact time span to which his argument applies.

Ricardo's chapter on value, therefore, is not subject to the usual charge that a labour theory of value involves circular reasoning. The alleged circular argument is this: relative values are explained on the basis of the labour hours embodied in goods, and then the higher price of goods produced by skilled labour is explained by the higher wage rates of skilled over unskilled labour; but why is the value of skilled labour greater than the value of unskilled labour?; because the product it produces is more valuable. Smith, Ricardo and Marx have been ridiculed for relying on 'the higgling and bargaining of the market' to establish a quantitative relation of equivalence between skilled and unskilled labour. But criticism of the labour theory of value on this score is at best superficial. Differences in the productivity of different types of labour are due either to differences in ability, whether natural or acquired, or to superior schooling and training. Unless the subject under investigation is relative wages, it is perfectly legitimate to assume that all labour is homogeneous, ignoring specialized talents and treating skilled labour as a common multiple of unskilled labour. When relative wages come to the forefront, we may resort to Adam Smith's demonstration that perfect competition yields a wage scale in which an hour of labour, no matter how priced, corresponds to the same disutility of labour for everyone. This does, however, imply that the common unit of labour time, which is said to determine value, is itself a subjective phenomenon, a product of occupational choice. But that is a different argument against the labour theory of value than that of circular reasoning.

12. The Invariable Measure of Value

The **third section** of **chapter 1** reduces the value of capital goods to that of labour expended in the past. By 'embodied labour' then is meant both the direct and the indirect labour applied via the use of machines. We are told that only a commodity produced with a constant quantity of direct and indirect labour furnishes an invariable standard for locating the source of a change in the relative prices of any two commodities. In **section 4 and 5** we meet with the difficulties created by the different proportions in which fixed and circulating capital are combined in different industries, compounded by the difficulty that the two kinds of capital might differ in their durability. The distinction between fixed and working capital is said to be a matter solely of degrees of durability; this reduces the whole problem to the different time periods for which working capital is locked up in the productive process.

Since production cycles differ widely in the length of time required for their completion, relative prices are never strictly determined by relative labour time. This fundamental finding is brought out with the aid of four numerical examples – three in section 4 and a fourth in section 5. In each example a comparison is drawn between the value of 'corn' produced by labour alone for one year and the value of 'cloth' requiring exactly the same amount of labour in year 1 to build a machine, or an inventory of semifinished goods, by means of which cloth is produced in year 2. In the first case the value of cloth at the end of year 2 is greater than twice the value of a year's corn crop because the profit on cloth production at the end of year 1 is reinvested in year 2 – the capital of the clothier earns interest for two years. The second example is identical to the first except that labour is now expressed in money terms and a rate of profit is stipulated. The machine considered so far does not depreciate at all. In the third example an inventory of goods rather than a machine is produced, but in the fourth example the rate of annual depreciation is supposed to be 100 percent, so the machine is fully used up in' year 2. The conclusions drawn from the third and fourth examples are, of course, the same as that drawn from the first.

Thus, goods embodying equal quantities of direct and indirect labour will differ in exchange value when the time required for their production differs, and a uniform change in money wages will alter their exchange ratios even though there has been no change in the labour expended upon them. A rise in money wages will raise the value of goods made with short-lived capital or with little machinery relative to goods made with long-lived capital or much machinery: this is the only way that the rate of profit can be kept at equality between all trades, irrespective of differences in cost outlays. This Ricardo Effect, however, is dismissed as slight in magnitude: even if money wages rose enough to cause the rate of profit to fall by 6 or 7 percent – 'for profits could not, probably, under any circumstances, admit of a greater general and permanent depression than to that amount' – relative prices would not vary more than 6 or 7 percent, a conclusion based on the second of the four examples (hence, Stigler's famous joke that Ricardo held a '93% labour theory of value'). Ricardo is satisfied that the labour-cost theory provides a good first approximation to secular shifts in relative prices.

Early in **chapter 1, section 5**, Ricardo indicates his method of treating depreciation. It is supposed that a quantity of labour is employed to maintain capital intact; depreciation costs are thus shared as direct wage costs by each manufacturer in proportion to the durability of his equipment. This explains why Ricardo rarely mentions depreciation as a separate business expense. The rest of section 5 examines a case in which a rise in money wages raises the price of most goods relative to that of machines because of the fact that the 'machine' is not produced entirely by direct labour. 'Machines', he concludes, 'would not rise in (relative) price, in consequence of a rise of wages.' The result, he agrees, is to induce the substitution of machines for labour. In **section 6** we are at last provided with an invariable measure of value. Ricardo postulates that 'gold' is produced with an average ratio of labour to capital of average durability. All values are to be expressed in terms of this invariant yardstick. It follows now that any change in wages can affect prices only in terms of 'gold'. Since gold is produced with a capital structure that is an average for the economy as a whole, its value never varies when wages rise or fall, being strictly determined by the labour required to produce it. This makes it 'a perfect measure of value for all things produced under the same conditions precisely as itself, but for no other'. The operative assumption for Ricardo's system, which is nowhere stated in so many words in the *Principles*, is that wheat is to be produced under the same circumstances as the invariable yardstick. Thereby, the relative price of wheat in terms of 'gold' is made a function solely of the man-hours embodied in its production.

Section 7 briefly relaxes the general assumption throughout the book of a constant value of money. The last pages of the chapter explain with marvelous confusion what is meant by 'a rise or fall in wages, profits and rent'. A fall in wages means a fall in the labour inputs required to produce wage goods. Upon Ricardo's assumptions, this is tantamount to a fall in labour's share but not to a fall in money wages. In his example, however, money wages do fall and, in general, the money wage rate in Ricardo's model does vary directly with the labour inputs required to produce wheat. In the third edition of the *Principles*, Ricardo altered this section to make the product that is being divided refer to the product of a single farm rather than that of the whole economy. Apparently, Ricardo had realized that all his conclusions depended upon wheat being produced with the same production period as the invariable yardstick.

13. Demand and Supply

To round off the subject of value, the reader should turn now to **chapter 4**, on natural and market price, which is intended to justify concentration upon long-period prices, and then to **chapter 30** on demand and supply. Ricardo had no patience for mere demand-and-supply explanations of price for, with the exception of wheat, all goods are supposed to be produced under conditions of constant costs. Unfortunately, this chapter fosters the impression that cost of production is something separate and apart from demand and supply, although in his unpublished *Notes on Malthus* Ricardo does say that 'market price will depend on supply and demand – the supply will be finally determined by the natural price – that is to say by the cost of production'. Throughout chapter 30 Ricardo speaks of demand and supply not as schedules but as quantities actually bought and sold. To prove that price cannot be explained merely by demand and supply, he postulates the case in which a perfectly inelastic demand curve intersects a perfectly elastic supply curve (Figure 4–6); the supply curve shifts down, the price falls, but the quantity bought and sold remains the same. 'Here, then, we have a case where the supply and demand has scarcely varied', he says, 'and yet the price of bread will have fallen 50 per cent.'

14. Social Accounting

From chapter 30 we turn back to **chapter 20** on 'value and riches', which employs man-hours per unit of output as a standard to evaluate net national product. By 'riches' Ricardo means the magnitude of physical output; more riches mean more real income. Value, however, varies inversely as the labour time required per unit of product. For Ricardo, 'value' is an inverse index of the average productivity of labour and therefore of economic welfare; welfare is a matter of minimizing human effort per unit of output. For Adam Smith, 'value' is also an inverse index of economic welfare: as output per man rises, the amount of labour commanded by the total product falls because welfare is a matter of maximizing labour's purchasing power over real income. At face value, Ricardo's standard should give the same answer as Smith's standard, but Smith's standard, it is true, becomes ambiguous when real wages are themselves rising or falling. On the other hand, Smith's standard digs deeper than does Ricardo's. Why should a reduction in efforts per unit of product constitute an improvement in welfare unless labour is painful, or at least not becoming any less painful over time?

This chapter contains Ricardo's only explicit reference to Smith's distinction between productive and unproductive labour, though it is obvious elsewhere that he accepts it without question. In the last paragraph of the chapter, having criticized

Figure 4–6

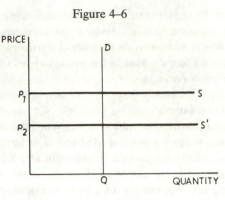

Say's identification of value, riches and utility, Ricardo implicitly denies the principle of diminishing marginal utility.

15. Did Ricardo Hold a Labour Theory?

Before proceeding to other topics, we should pause for a moment to ask ourselves just what kind of value theory Ricardo advances. Certainly, he does not adhere to what Stigler has called an *analytical* labour theory of value, the theory that labour inputs are the sole determinant of relative prices. A consistent analytical labour theory must face the problem of explaining the nature of nonlabour income, a subject to which Ricardo gives no attention. Indeed, Ricardo must be credited with the decisive argument against a pure labour-cost theory: the so-called Ricardo Effect. He did advance an *empirical* labour theory, emphasizing the quantitative importance of labour inputs and in particular their strategic role in bringing about changes in relative prices over time. This involves nothing more than the belief that the approximate ratios in which goods exchanged are quantitatively influenced more by relative labour costs than by, say, relative interest charges. This type of theory is perfectly compatible with a Marshallian short-run theory, in which the existence of scarce factors in fixed supply will cause relative prices to vary with the rate of output of goods and hence with the pattern of demand. The difference is simply one of emphasis.

The great advantage of a one-factor theory is its tractability for purposes of popular exposition. But why a *labour* theory? The most obvious reason is that labour costs do dominate total costs in almost all industries. Land was of course regarded in Ricardo's day as a free 'gift of Nature', while capital goods were neither hired nor bought in terms of homogeneous physical units (such as horse power or weight per ton of iron). This left physical man-hours as a rough-and-ready yardstick for explaining changes in relative prices.

Adam Smith, we have seen, could not swallow even an empirical labour theory but, like Ricardo, he was in search of an appropriate unit of social accounting and found it in the number of wage units that the product can command in exchange. The common element in the labour theories of Smith and Ricardo was that both proposed what has been called a 'labour theory of absolute value': 'the notion that an absolute number may be attached to any economic good, independently of any other economic good'. This is welfare economics, not value theory. Whether we should use money wages, man-hours, or relative prices as the weights to add up to real national product is a question, not of empirical fact, nor of logical deduction, but of normative judgment. Normative judgments are open to discussion but not to scientific proof or disproof. In the course of a particular normative judgment, however, writers are likely to claim analytical virtue for their position. When Ricardo in the last months of his life sat down to write a paper on 'Absolute and Exchange Value', he used language as emotive as anything written by Marx: labour is the best measure of value, labour is the 'cause' and 'substance' of value, labour is the original purchase price of everything, and the like. For the first time Ricardo referred to 'what I mean by the word value' and he explained that it meant not labour and 'waiting' but labour alone. But, unconnected with the problem of explaining relative prices, such assertions should not be taken seriously. When Keynes came to justify his choice of a wage unit to measure output in the *General Theory*, he spoke with sympathy of the classical doctrine that the expenditure of human labour constitutes a unique social cost in terms of which all other productive contributions can be expressed. He categorically denied that capital is 'productive'. But obviously Keynes did not hold an analytical labour theory of value. No more did Ricardo.

16. Rent

Chapters 2 and 3 distinguish rent from profit on capital as return to an indestructible, nonaugmentable factor of production. At the end of chapter 28, however, Ricardo observes that returns to capital sunk in the exploration and preparation of land for cultivation partake of the nature of rent, since the yield of such capital is not an incentive reward. Enough has been said about Ricardo's rent theory [see chapter 3, sections 8, 9] to make a *précis* of his argument unnecessary. The upshot of the chapter, of course, is that rent can be eliminated as an element in the pricing of goods.

For a moment in chapter 2, Ricardo generalizes the concept of marginal cost to all industry but later, in chapter 17, he asserts definitely that manufacturing operates under constant returns to scale, marginal cost therefore being equal to average cost. Rent is said to be due to the niggardliness of nature – the scarcity of land – and not, as the physiocrats would have it, to the bounty of nature, that is, the physical productivity of land. If land were not physically productive, capable of producing a surplus over the maintenance needs to the cultivators, no rent would arise. But unless land is also scarce in relation to demand, physical productivity will not result in value productivity. In a footnote, Adam Smith's preference for agriculture as the most productive sector in the economy is soundly condemned. The fact that a like amount of labour and capital yields wages, profits *and* rent in agriculture but only wages and profits in manufacturing is no evidence that land is more productive, Ricardo observes: on the margins of cultivation the value of wheat is in fact exhausted by the returns to labour and capital.

17. Agricultural Improvements

The effects of improvements in agriculture are discussed in **chapter 2**. We have seen that improvements need not reduce total rents, even in the short run. In the course of examining the second type of improvement, a capital-and-labour-saving innovation, Ricardo commits an interesting mistake, so easy to overlook that even Marshall missed it in his comments. Ricardo assumes that four portions of capital (and labour) are employed, 50, 60, 70, 80, each of which produces the same output. Any improvement that permits the same output with 45, 55, 65, 75 units of capital will not affect wheat rents but will lower money rents, Ricardo asserts. We might think that this is one of those improvements that raises productivity by equal absolute amounts; the productivity curves shift upward isoelastically and wheat rents fall. But Ricardo says that wheat rents are not affected. The trouble is that he has lowered costs per unit of output, not raised output per unit of cost, by equal absolute amounts. This makes all the difference. Rent in Ricardian theory is determined by output per unit of cost, and to lower costs per unit of output by equal absolute amounts, leaving cost differentials unaffected, is tantamount to raising output per unit of cost more on the intramarginal applications of capital than on the marginal application. This will *raise* wheat rents and leave money rents constant rather than lower them as Ricardo predicted. As a matter of fact, Ricardo himself gives the right answer to his problem in chapter 9, 'Taxes on Raw Produce'.

To show that wheat rents will rise in Ricardo's example, we translate from cost per unit of output to its reciprocal, output per unit of cost. At the margin, rents are zero, so 80 units of capital must receive 80 quarters of wheat. If x is the constant amount of wheat produced by the successively larger portions of capital applied to different plots of land, wheat rents summed over the four plots in the two cases are:

$$\tfrac{30}{80}x + \tfrac{20}{80}x + \tfrac{10}{80}x + 0 = \tfrac{3}{4}x. \tag{1}$$

$$\tfrac{30}{75}x + \tfrac{20}{75}x + \tfrac{10}{75}x + 0 = \tfrac{4}{5}x. \tag{2}$$

Wheat rents rise because $\tfrac{4}{5} > \tfrac{3}{4}$. It is assumed that the initial price of corn is £4 per quarter. Since corn is produced with $\tfrac{5}{80}$ less capital, the price of corn falls $\tfrac{1}{16}$, from £4 to £3.75. Total money rents, therefore, remain the same:

$$\tfrac{3}{4} \cdot £4 \quad = £3 \tag{3}$$

$$\tfrac{4}{5} \cdot £3.75 = £3 \tag{4}$$

To complete the topic of rent we go to **chapter 24**, in which the theory of differential rent is employed to point out contradictions in the *Wealth of Nations*. Noteworthy is Ricardo's insistence upon the fact that no-rent land does exist in England. In one place, Ricardo considers the repercussions of an autonomous shift to a potato diet on the part of the working class; the analysis reveals the full sweep of Ricardo's macroeconomic generalizations – these pages bear rereading after chapters 5 and 6. A rising price of corn is shown to involve a fatal conflict of interests. Last, there is **chapter 32**, which attacks Malthus' belief that rent is a genuine addition to wealth, not merely a transfer of purchasing power from wheat-consumers to landlords. Actually, Ricardo is attacking the political rather than the theoretical implications of Malthus' rent theory. In the middle of the chapter, he considers the possibility of permanently raising the standard of living in workers; Ricardo's conclusion is somewhat ambiguous here – as in chapter 5, on wages, where the same topic is discussed at greater length. The distinction between gross and net revenue, taken up in **chapter 26**, is briefly touched upon. The last passage in chapter 32 denies that utility is measurable.

18. Wages

Chapter 5 on wages and **chapter 6** on profits together contain the heart of Ricardo's system. At the outset of **chapter 5**, Ricardo defines 'natural wages' as those wages which will keep population stationary in contrast to short-run 'market wages' which permit the growth of population if they exceed 'natural wages'. While money wages rise through time because of the rising price of wheat, the wages-population mechanism will keep real wages constant. But the subsistence minimum is held to be a matter of 'habit and custom', which takes the sting out of the alleged constancy of real wages. Since manufactured goods tend to fall in price, Ricardo observes, a rising price of wheat need not prevent a gradual rise in real wages. Some comments in the middle of the chapter about young countries like Ireland and Poland with an abundance of fertile land show that Ricardo regarded overpopulation in underdeveloped countries as the result, not the cause, of backwardness and poverty. Reducing population in such cases, he points out, would merely cause wages to rise and the supply of effort to fall.

There follows a discussion of the relation between the rate of capital accumulation and the trend of market wages. Labourers spend half their income on wheat. When the price of wheat rises, money wages rise only half as fast: the composition of labour's market basket is never affected by changes in the price of wheat relative to other things. This means that wages in terms of wheat – money wages divided by the respective price of wheat – fall. This leads Ricardo to draw a contrast between workers whose money wages rise but whose wheat wages fall and landlords for whom both money and wheat rents rise. The closing portion of the chapter, dealing with the Poor Laws, was written by James Mill. In the manner of Malthus, it holds out for total abolition of public relief.

We may wonder why Ricardo is so careful in this fifth chapter, and again in chapter 22, to avoid assuming that money wages rise proportionately with the price of wheat. It is not merely because he realized that workers in fact consume other things than wheat. The assumption that money wages rise at the same rate as wheat prices, that workers, as it were, are being paid a constant amount of wheat, produces the paradox that the worker's welfare improves with a higher cost of living. Malthus actually advanced this paradox in his 1815 pamphlet on rent: suppose workers do consume cloth as well as bread but that money wages rise proportionately with the price of bread; then every increase in the price of bread relative to cloth raises the worker's money income in the same proportion as the bread part of his diet and hence increases his real income or command over both bread and cloth; presumably, he will substitute cheap cloth for dear bread, but even if his demand for bread is perfectly inelastic, the relative price of cloth has fallen and hence his real income is improved. Contrariwise, a fall in the price of bread is actually harmful to workers. To avoid such anomalies, Ricardo makes money wages rise less than proportionately to the price of wheat. This did not stop Ricardo, however, from talking about 'deterioration' in living standards when wages constant in terms of the whole basket of goods have fallen measured in terms of wheat alone.

19. Profits

Chapter 6, on profits, is undoubtedly the most difficult chapter in the whole book. It expounds the fundamental theorem that 'profits depend on high or low wages' with the aid of a single example whose implications are not as obvious as Ricardo makes out. Before discussing the example, let us reiterate the logic of the fundamental theorem. The problem is to show that despite the fact that capital and labour grow at the same rate, the rate of profit on capital tends to fall solely because wage goods are more costly to produce (obviously if capital grows faster than labour, there are additional reasons why the rate of profit falls). With the extension of cultivation, given amounts of newly employed capital-and-labour produce only diminishing increments of output. The price of wheat must now increase so that the amount of value produced by equal, successive inputs of capital-and-labour remains the same; that is, the price of wheat rises to the extent of the diminution in the marginal physical product of capital-and-labour in order to keep profits in agriculture at a level with those in industry. Owing to the fact that wheat is measured in terms of the invariable standard, the product of a given quantity of capital and labour always has the same value, regardless of its productivity. Therefore, the larger the value of labour, the smaller the value of capital, and the rise in the price of wheat has raised the value of labour by raising money wages. Thus, wages as a proportion of the product of marginal investment have risen, and with it the rate of profit has fallen in all sectors. This is not equivalent to the fall in capital's relative share because Ricardo has no determinate theory of the share going to rent.

In Ricardo's numerical example (shown in Table 4–2), columns 1–7 incorporate Ricardo's own example in chapter 5 on wages and the last footnote to chapter 2 on rent. Columns 9 and 11 appear in the chapter on profits. Columns 8, 10, and 12 have been added and are not given by Ricardo. A word on column 3, which alone is not self-explanatory: the initial price of wheat is £4 per quarter. When two doses of variable inputs are applied, the price of wheat must rise $\frac{18}{17}$ because the quantity of capital-and-labour per quarter has risen in this proportion: $\frac{18}{17} \cdot £4 = £4.23$. Thus, column 3 is obtained by multiplying the ratio of the initial marginal product to the subsequent marginal products by the initial price of wheat.

We notice that, expressed in terms of wheat, both the share of wages and the share of profits fall and the share of rents rises. Ricardo now expresses his results in terms of money and calculates the money rate of profit percent on an assumed

Table 4-2 Ricardo's numerical example

1	2	3	4	5	6	7	8	9	10	11	12
						Wheat Wages		Wheat Profits		Wheat Rents	
Inputs (10 Workers per Dose)	MP in X Units of Wheat	Price of Wheat per X (£.s.d.)	Wheat Wages = 3X (£.s.d.)	Cloth Wages of Constant Value (£.s.d.)	Money Wage Rate (4) + (5) (£.s.d.)	$10 \cdot \frac{(6)}{(3)}$	Wage Share (7)/180	(2) − (7)	Profit Share (9)/180	Sum of First Differences of (2)	Rental Share (11)/180
1	180	4. 0.0	12. 0.0	12.0.0	24. 0.0	60	0.333	120	0.666	–	–
2	170	4. 4.8	12.14.0	12.0.0	24.14.0	58.3	0.323	111.7	0.621	10	0.555
3	160	4.10.0	13.10.0	12.0.0	25.10.0	56.6	0.314	103.4	0.574	20	0.111
4	150	4.16.0	14. 8.0	12.0.0	26. 8.0	55	0.301	95	0.528	30	0.166
5	140	5. 2.10	15. 8.6	12.0.0	27. 8.6	53.3	0.296	86.7	0.481	40	0.222

Table 4–3

1	13	14	15	16
Inputs	Money Rents (11)(3) (£.s.d.)	Money Profits (9)(3) (£.s.d.)	Money Wages 10(6) (£.s.d.)	Rate of Profit on K = £3,000 (percent)
1	–	480. 0.0	240.0.0	16
2	42. 7.6	473. 0.0	247.0.0	15.7
3	90. 0.0	465. 0.0	255.0.0	15.5
4	144. 0.0	456. 0.0	264.0.0	15.2
5	205.13.4	445.15.0	274.5.0	14.8

amount of capital fixed at £3,000 (see Table 4–3). The rate of profit falls even as money wages per man rise. This assumes that the amount of capital invested remains the same. But as Ricardo observes, rising wheat prices will call for an increase in the amount of capital, which further depresses the rate of profit. Notice that columns 14 and 15 summed across the rows always add up to £720. The product-less-rent is measured in terms of the invariable standard, which has the property of keeping the total value of the product – or, as Ricardo says, 'the real value' of the product – constant.

This demonstration of the fundamental theorem, however, has a fatal flaw, as Cannan pointed out long ago. The share of the factors is computed not as a percentage of what the total product would be as more inputs are applied but as a percentage of 180X, the marginal product of the first dose, which is equal to the total product when one dose is applied. The value of the total product-less-rent (£720) is always the same as the value of the product of the first dose, and the rate of profit falls only because the value increments of the subsequent doses are not added to total money profits. Ricardo purports to explain the pattern of factor rewards and income distribution in an economy whose total income is growing and proves his case by explaining the distribution of the product of a fixed margin when inputs increase.

Column 8, Table 4–2, showing a falling share of wages, is subject to another criticism. We know that if real wages are constant the share of wages in total income ought to rise, for the total product is rising less than proportionately to the doses of labour applied. But real wages are constant in terms of a market basket of wheat plus cloth, while in columns 7 and 8 we are looking at real wages in terms of wheat alone. Real wages, even when expressed in wheat alone, rise as a share of output when output is defined as the actually growing product of successive inputs, not as the output of the first dose of capital-and-labour (see Table 4–4).

Nevertheless, Ricardo is right in spite of himself. For his table of marginal products (see column 2, Table 4–2) assumes that if $X = f(N)$, then

$$f'(N) = 190 - 10N, \qquad (0 < N < 19).$$

Table 4–4

N	X	W at w = 6x	W/X
1	180	60	0.333
2	350	120	0.343
3	510	180	0.353
4	660	240	0.364
5	800	300	0.374

When we integrate this expression, we obtain

$$X = \int(190 - 10N)dN = 190N - 5N^2$$

with $f''(N) = -10 < 0$ and $f'''(N) = 0$. This is a quadratic production function with linear average and marginal product curves (see Figure 4–3, case 1). The average product is $X/N = 190 - 5N$. By the definition adopted above, the elasticity of this curve is

$$\eta = \frac{N}{X/N}\frac{d(X/N)}{dN} = \frac{190}{5N} - 1.$$

Since $d(\eta)/dN = -5(190)/5N^2 < 0$, the rental share rises as N increases. Since the wage share also rises, the share of profits π/X does fall with every increase in N. The amount of capital grows at the same rate as labour, and the average product of capital X/K declines at the same rate as that of labour. If π/X falls and X/K falls, the rate of profit also falls because $r = (\pi/X)(X/K)$. Q.E.D.

20. Foreign Trade

Chapter 7, on foreign trade, attempts to prove two propositions: (1) the 'value' of the national product is the same for a closed economy as for an open one: foreign trade as such will not affect wage rates or the rate of profit; (2) foreign trade does increase a country's 'riches', and real income will always be higher with free trade than without. The first proposition is directed against Smith's view that a high rate of profit in foreign trade pulls up the rate of profit at home. Smith ignores the shift in demand to foreign goods, argues Ricardo. Ricardo now distinguishes between three kinds of goods, analyzing each in turn: (1) home-produced goods for home consumption, such as cloth, shoes, corn, and hats; (2) home-produced goods for export; and (3) imported luxuries, such as wine – the demand for wine is assumed to be elastic. The gist of the argument is that the rate of profit will not be raised unless imports consist of wage goods, a simple deduction from the fundamental theorem. But at one point Ricardo does admit that the importation of cheaper luxury goods enables capitalists as consumers to save more; this stimulates capital accumulation, and in this way foreign trade, even when it does not involve the import of wheat, would seem capable of affecting the rate of profit.

21. Law of Comparative Cost

This brings us to the Law of Comparative Cost, which demonstrates the benefits of what Torrens aptly called the 'territorial division of labour'. Ricardo was virtually the first economist to advocate a separate theory of international as distinct from intranational trade. The basis of this separate theory is the relative immobility of capital between nations. The labour theory of value cannot pertain to goods traded across national boundaries because the rate of profit does not tend to equality between countries. But in that case, what determines the movement of goods between countries and on what basis will the barter terms of trade be determined? The answer to both questions is comparative cost advantages.

One can conceive of three kinds of cost ratios for pairs of goods between countries: equal differences, absolute differences and comparative differences. Suppose that both cloth and wine are produced by labour alone in two countries, England and Portugal, so that relative prices are simply the reciprocals of unit labour requirements. (It did not trouble Ricardo that his example was deliberately artificial since England produced no wine in his day – it did in earlier times and it does so today.) The distinction between the three cost ratios is set out in Table 4–5.

Table 4–5 *Labour Hours Required to Produce a Unit of Cloth and Wine*

	Equal Differences: I			Absolute Differences: II			Comparative Differences: III		
	Cloth	Wine	Pw/Pc	Cloth	Wine	Pw/Pc	Cloth	Wine	Pw/Pc
England	100	88	0.88	100	60	0.6	100	120	1.2
Portugal	99	80	0.88	90	80	0.88	90	80	0.88

Even Adam Smith knew that no foreign trade could arise when the cost ratios for two goods between two countries are equal; in case I, despite the fact that Portugal can produce both goods more cheaply, there is no incentive for trade. He thought that trade took place only when both countries had an absolute cost advantage in one good, that is, case II, where England has an absolute advantage in wine and Portugal has an absolute advantage in cloth. In the 18th century, a few authors began to advance the rule that each country would find it profitable to import those goods which could be obtained in exchange for exports at less cost than their home production would entail. But almost no one, not even Adam Smith, realized that this meant that under free trade all goods are not necessarily produced in countries where their real costs of production are lowest: it might pay a country to import a product even though it could be produced at less cost at home than abroad. The doctrine of comparative cost is simply a rigorous statement of the informal 18th-century rule.

In Ricardo's example (case III), Portugal has a comparative advantage in wine since the cost difference for wine is relatively greater than that for cloth: $\frac{120}{80} >$

$\frac{100}{90}$. What has to be compared is not costs but ratios of costs and it does not matter whether we compare the cost ratios of producing the same good in different countries or of producing different goods within the same country. An obscure pamphlet published in 1818 gave a simple algebraic statement of the necessary conditions. Let W and C denote the number of labour hours required to produce one unit of wine and cloth, the subscripts p and e identifying the respective countries. Then:

$$\text{Equal cost-differences:} \qquad \frac{W_p}{W_e} = \frac{C_p}{C_e}. \qquad\qquad (1)$$

$$\text{Absolute cost-differences:} \qquad \frac{W_p}{W_e} > 1 > \frac{C_p}{C_e}. \qquad\qquad (2)$$

$$\text{Comparative cost-differences:} \qquad \frac{W_p}{W_e} < \frac{C_p}{C_e} < 1. \qquad\qquad (3)$$

To return to Ricardo's example: it is clearly to Portugal's advantage to send wine to England, where a unit of it commands 1.2 units of cloth, as long as 1 unit of wine can be traded with England for more than 0.88 units of cloth; it is to England's advantage to specialize in cloth if less than 1.2 units of cloth must be given for 1 unit of wine. Hence, the comparative cost doctrine states the upper and lower limits within which exchange can take place between countries to their mutual benefit. If 1 unit of British cloth were exchanged for 1.2 units of Portuguese wine, all gains from trade would go to Portugal. If instead the ratio were $1 : \frac{8}{9} = 1 : 0.88$, all gains would go to England. Ricardo assumes a $1 : 1$ ratio: England produces cloth with 100 man-hours and receives 1 unit of wine, which would have cost her 120 man-hours to produce at home, and Portugal obtains cloth for 80 manhours, which would have cost her 90 man-hours to produce at home. Clearly, the comparative cost case is much subtler than the absolute-cost case. In the latter it is self-evident that an international division of labour leads to an increase in total output. The 'gains of trade' in the comparative cost example show up as an overall saving in cost per unit of product; before trade, it took 390 labour hours for England and Portugal each to produce one unit of cloth and wine; after trade, these 4 units require only 360 labour hours. The point of Ricardo's analysis is to show that the conditions that make international trade possible are quite different from the conditions under which domestic trade will arise. If England and Portugal were two regions in the same country, all capital and labour would migrate to Portugal and both goods would be produced there. Within a nation, trade between two places requires an absolute difference in costs, but a comparative difference is a sufficient condition for the existence of international trade.

Ricardo's doctrine is incomplete: it shows how nations may gain by trade, but it fails to tell us how the gain from trade is divided among the trading countries. The actual barter terms of trade, as John Stuart Mill was soon to show, depend not only on the cost conditions but also on the pattern of demand. Since Ricardo's theory requires that all goods are produced at constant costs – there is only one factor of production – one may wonder why demand has anything to do with international

Figure 4–7

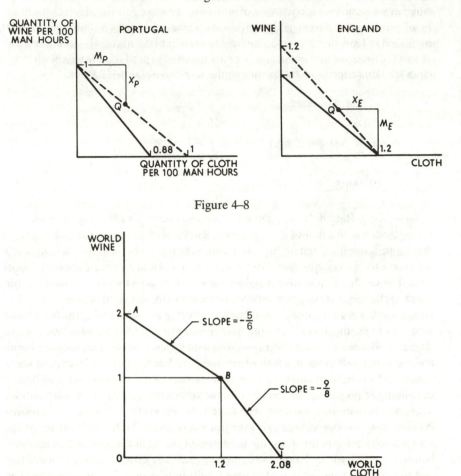

Figure 4–8

prices when, under the same constant cost conditions, domestic prices are entirely determined by supply. The reason lies in the fact that goods produced at constant costs *within* countries will not in effect be produced at constant costs when they are traded *between* countries.

This is easy to show if we render Ricardo's argument in strictly modern terms (Figure 4–7; ignore the broken lines for the moment). Portugal can convert 1 unit of wine into 0.88 units of cloth. England can convert 1 unit of wine into 1.2 units of cloth. The barter terms will lie somewhere between 1 cloth : 1.2 wine and 1 cloth : 0.88 wine. We can now construct the production-transformation curve for the two-country world (Figure 4–8) by simply adding the values along the axes of the diagrams of Figure 4–7. The segmented line *ABC* is the world's transformation curve, giving the maximum possible world output of wine for each given level of cloth, and the converse holds. The pattern of world *demand* for wine and cloth will be shown by an indifference curve (not drawn) that must be tangent either to the line segment AB, the point B, or to the line segment BC, as Ricardo assumed, where each maximizes her comparative advantage by complete specialization in one good. The exact slope of the barter-price line, however, can vary between $-\frac{5}{6}$ and $-\frac{9}{8}$, depending upon the location of the particular tangency point. Despite the fact that constant costs pertain within each country, the world production-possibility frontier between cloth and wine is concave from below and the cost of converting one good into another for the world as a whole increases in both directions, although not continuously. International prices are governed by supply *and* demand even in the long run despite the fact that relative prices within countries are assumed to be determined by labour costs alone. This, by the way, is a really decisive objection to the labour theory of value: it fails altogether to explain the determination of international prices.

The same apparatus can be employed to demonstrate the advantages of an international division of labour, that is, the gains of free trade. Assume, for example, that the barter terms of trade settle at point B in a ratio of $1:1$. England can now convert 1.2 units of cloth into 1.2 units instead of 1 unit of wine: her production-possibility frontier moves out to the right (see broken line in Figure 4–7). By importing wine and exporting cloth, she can reach a point like Q and thus consume more of both goods. But the same thing is true for Portugal, where England's imports (M_E) and exports (X_E) equal Portugal's exports (X_P) and imports (M_P) respectively. Thus, international trade is a way of enlarging the production possibilities of both countries. Reverting to a world production-transformation curve (Figure 4–9), the two countries might end up on the broken line at points like Q outside the old production-transformation curve, with England's imports (M_E) = Portugal's exports (X_P) and England's exports (X_E) = Portugal's imports (M_P). However, if there is an intense world demand for cloth, the indifference curve (not drawn) will be steeper than the one tangent at B and the barter-price line will rotate clockwise, favouring England, the cloth-exporter, and forcing Portugal to export more wine to obtain a unit of cloth. Contrariwise, a rise in the world demand for wine relative to cloth will cause the barter terms of trade to move from $1:1$ in the direction of $1:\frac{5}{6}$, favouring Portugal. Nevertheless, so long as the terms of trade stay within the upper and lower limits, both countries are better off with free trade than without.

It is clear that the doctrine of comparative cost would hold even if the production-possibility frontier were smoothly concave to the origin, in which case specialization would rarely be carried to the limit. A smooth concave curve, with the marginal cost of converting one good into another rising continuously in either direction, implies that goods are produced at increasing cost within countries. In other words, abandoning the labour theory of value, and with it the assumption of constant costs, would in no way affect the validity of Ricardo's doctrine. The Law of Comparative Cost can be expressed succinctly as stating that each country will produce those

Figure 4–9

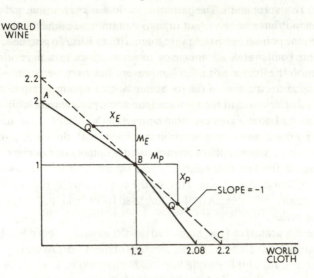

goods whose alternative costs are relatively lowest, alternative costs being the number of units of one good that must be forgone to produce a unit of another good. This way of stating the doctrine covers every possible cost situation.

22. The Natural Distribution of Specie

Ricardo did much more than state the Law of Comparative Cost. He also saw its implications for international wage and price levels, although it was Nassau Senior who ten years later developed Ricardo's hints into a fully fashioned theory of international prices. Ricardo realized that if Portugal had an absolute advantage in both wine and cloth but a greater relative advantage in wine, foreign trade with England is only possible if money wage rates in Portugal are higher than in England. If the hourly wage rate in terms of gold is the same, Portugal will not import cloth since every Portuguese consumer can then get cloth more cheaply from domestic suppliers. England would have to ship gold to Portugal to pay for wine imports until hourly gold wages in Portugal rose enough to make it profitable for Portuguese consumers to import English cloth. In general, then, the low-cost country has the higher hourly gold wage and, hence, a higher money price for similar goods. Hume's 'natural distribution of specie' therefore not only works to balance each country's exports and imports but also results in such relative price levels between countries as to induce each country to produce those goods in which it has a comparative advantage. In Senior's memorable phrase, relative price levels between countries are determined by differences in 'the cost of obtaining gold': the greater the efficiency of labour in the export industries of a country possessing no gold mines and the less the expense of conveying gold, the lower will be the cost of obtaining precious metals and the higher will be the level of average wages and prices relative to countries exporting gold bullion. This argument has an important practical implication: a high level of wages in a country may be the result of higher efficiency in which case it does not prevent that country from competing with foreign producers. To put the same thing a little differently, an overall disadvantage in productivity in a particular country relative to the rest of the world need not prevent her from participating in international trade; there is always a rate of exchange that would permit her to export those goods in which she had the least comparative disadvantage, while importing those in which she had the greatest disadvantage.

To drive the point home, consider the following example, as Ricardo himself might have given it. Suppose that one man-hour in both countries can produce the following amounts of cloth and wine.

> In England, 16 units of cloth and 8 units of wine.
> In Portugal, 20 units of cloth and 15 units of wine.

Comparative cost ratios are as follows:

> Cloth, Portugal to England, as 10:8.
> Wine, Portugal to England, as 10:5.33.

From the cost differences it follows immediately that average hourly money wages in England must be between 53.3 and 80 percent of money wages in Portugal.

Let us suppose that the wage rate in Portugal is $5 per man-hour. We know that the price ratio between cloth and wine in Portugal is 4 : 3. Then, in Portugal, if

> the money price per unit of cloth is, say, $3,
> the money price per unit of wine is $4.

If England's wages were equal to wages in Portugal, then in England, at the existing exchange rate,

> the money price per unit of cloth is $3.75;
> the money price per unit of wine is $7.50.

The prices are fixed by the given domestic cost ratios of cloth and wine in England (2 : 1) and by the given cost ratios for the two goods between the two countries (for cloth 10 : 8 or $3.75 : $3 and for wine 10 : 5.33 or $7.50 : $4). But at these prices it would pay England to import both goods from Portugal. Her balance of payments would become unfavourable and gold would flow out of the country, thus deflating British wages and prices. If wages fell 20 percent to $4 per man-hour, then in England

> the money price per unit of cloth would be $3,
> the money price per unit of wine would be $6,

and now it would be possible for her to reap the benefits of her comparative advantage in cloth. Likewise, if England paid still lower wages, $2.66 per man-hour or 53.3 percent of hourly wages in Portugal, then in England

the price per unit of cloth would be $2,
the price per unit of wine would be $4,

and both countries would still find it to their advantage to specialize completely in one product.

It may be noted that when England's wage level reaches its upper limit (80 percent of Portuguese wages), the barter terms of trade are exclusively in her favour (4 cloth : 3 wine). When it reaches its lower limit (53.3 percent of Portuguese wages), the barter terms are exclusively in Portugal's favour (2 cloth : 1 wine). It seems, therefore, that the relative efficiency of labour in the two countries influences the relations of wage and price levels between them in two ways: (1) the country with the more generally efficient labour will have a higher wage and price level than the other country; and (2) the difference so established takes place within definite limits determined by comparative cost ratios. This is the gist of the classical theory of international prices.

23. The Purchasing Power Parity Theory

To conclude our discussion of **chapter 7**, it is noteworthy that Ricardo denies what has since been called the 'purchasing power parity theory' of exchange rates. It was standard classical doctrine that 'the value of money is everywhere the same': with free trade and a metallic standard, the rate of exchange between two currencies depends solely on their relative purchasing power over identical exportable goods. But, of course, the prices of nonexportable goods differ between countries. Hence, the doctrine that an equilibrium rate of exchange is to be found as the quotient between the price levels of different countries – the so called 'purchasing power parity theory' – ignores everything that creates discrepancies in the average prices of all goods between two countries. The last few pages of chapter 7 relate to the difficulty of proving the depreciation of an inconvertible currency such as England experienced between 1797 and 1819. This topic is best considered later when we look at Ricardo's monetary theory. **Chapter 25** on colonial trade should be read after chapter 7; it is largely devoted to showing that any tax or bounty upon exports or imports alters the international distribution of specie and therefore the comparative cost ratios between countries expressed in money terms.

24. Say's Law

The Ricardian theory of profits is contrasted with the Smithian theory in **chapter 21**, on the effects of accumulation upon profits and interest. Smith's theory of declining profits, Ricardo correctly observes, assumes a definite limit to the stock of investment opportunities available at any time. But in the absence of rising costs in the wage-goods industry, Ricardo insists, full capacity use of any amount of capital is possible: there are no inherent barriers to production on the side of demand. This leads to a statement of Say's Law of Markets and a denial that hoarding – an excess demand for money to hold – can be a permanent problem in a growing economy. In a footnote on Say, Ricardo even denies the need for price-interest adjustments to ensure full investment of savings, but this is an overzealous comment because the mechanism of interest variations, acting upon the demand for loanable funds, is explained later in the same chapter. In general, 'gluts' are impossible because demand is insatiable: although the demand for corn is inelastic, the demand for most consumer goods is highly elastic and will expand with every increase in the productivity of labour. Ricardo admits that a sudden upward shift in the propensity to save might produce a temporary 'general glut': but as capital would then be growing faster than population, market wages would rise above natural wages and purchasing power would increase once again. With Ricardo, therefore, the economy is conceived as descending smoothly into the stationary state without any hitch from a failure of effective demand.

It is evident from the context in which Say's Law first arises in the *Principles* that Ricardo believed that Smith and Malthus had already been answered by the fundamental theorem on distribution that he had presented in the earlier chapters of his book without any mention of the Law of Markets. Say's Law now appears, not as a basic premise in the Ricardian system, but merely to confirm the theory that 'the increased difficulty of obtaining food' is the only permanently operative cause of a fall in the rate of profit.

In the latter part of chapter 21, Ricardo points out that the ruling rate of profit cannot in practice be estimated from the market rate of interest as Adam Smith believed, not only because of the intrinsic difficulty of calculating the trend value of the rate of interest, but also because of the disturbing effect of the Usury Laws, which then prohibited a rate of interest in excess of 5 percent. In a classic passage, Ricardo presents the germ of Wicksell's theory of the divergence between the natural and the market rate of interest [see chapter 15, section 3], an argument that Ricardo repeats in **chapter 28**, 'On Currency and Banks'. In a trade depression, when prices fall, the market rate of interest will rise temporarily owing to the involuntary accumulation of inventories. Likewise, an increase in the quantity of money will temporarily depress interest rates, but as soon as the new money has acted on prices, the interest rate will rise back to its 'natural rate', the rate of profit on capital. This is the classical doctrine of the 'real' nature of the interest rate, about which we will have more to say below; its central idea is that monetary forces act upon the rate of interest only when the money market is disequilibrium.

25. Pessimism?

Turning back to **chapter 19** on sudden changes in the channels of trade, we meet with Ricardo's views on Britain's long-term growth prospects. Writing in the difficult years of postwar conversion, Ricardo is anxious to discourage the belief that the current 'revulsion of trade' marks the onset of secular stagnation. If the Corn Laws are repealed, he argues, Britain's prospects for growth are actually very favourable. Ricardo does not insist upon immediate total repeal of the Corn Laws, as Cobden and Bright were to do twenty years later. Since the poor rates fall heaviest on land, landlords are entitled to some relief for their special tax burdens. Hence, Ricardo calls for gradual reductions in import duties on grain over a ten-year period, coupled with a small bounty on exportation in years of bumper crops. Gradual repeal would have the additional advantage of cushioning the blow of disinvestment in agriculture. Nevertheless, rents would fall and landlords would sustain losses in consequence of repeal. But the loss of landlords from free trade, Ricardo observed, would be more than offset by the welfare gains of other classes; this argument reminds one immediately of the Hicks-Kaldor 'compensation principle' in modern welfare economics [see chapter 13, section 9].

26. Monetary Theory

Chapter 27, 'On Currency and Banks', seems to stand apart from the rest of the book and, unfortunately, gives an entirely inadequate impression of Ricardo's theory of money. Ricardo is a 'metallist' and naturally expounds a labour theory of the value of the monetary metal. This is by no means contradictory to the quantity theory of money. Given unhampered coinage and the possibility of melting coins, the quantity of money in the long run is governed by the cost of production of gold. If the value of money in circulation exceeds its cost of production, mining is stimulated and more metal is presented for coinage and, when the reverse holds true, mining is contracted and money is melted down for nonmonetary uses. In this way the value of money is controlled by its cost of production and the price level reflects the exchange value of the monetary commodity itself. Owing to the large stock of gold and silver in existence, however, the rate of current output of gold and silver mines actually has a negligible effect upon the value of money. In that sense, the metallist theory of the value of money has very little significance for monetary problems. In the years 1797–1819, Britain was off the gold standard and on an inconvertible paper standard. Since the cost of manufacturing paper currency is too small to exercise any effective control over its quantity, the value of the currency in such circumstances is almost entirely determined by its quantity, which in turn depends on banking policy. Thus, the classical theory of the value of money in the short run is the quantity theory for both specie and paper, while the cost-of-production theory was reserved for the long run and for specie money only.

27. The Bullionist Controversy

It is very difficult to follow Ricardo's attack on the Bank of England in this chapter without some knowledge of the issues that animated the so-called 'Bullionist Controversy' during the Napoleonic wars. A brief statement of the debate must suffice for present purposes. In 1797, war with France had brought a suspension of specie payments: the Bank of England was authorized to refuse payments for its notes in gold. Inconvertibility of notes coincided with a state of war involving heavy remittances by the United Kingdom to its allies and large-scale borrowing by the government. In addition, an unusual series of bad harvests led to abnormal imports of wheat, with consequent disturbing effects on the balance of payments. Prices rose gradually, and gold commanded a premium in the market over the quoted mint price.

Under a convertible paper currency, a premium on gold or a discount on paper cannot arise. Under a gold standard, the exchange rate between two currencies is determined by the ratio of the gold prices of the two currencies plus or minus the cost of handling and shipping gold. When a country promises to sell gold freely in unlimited amounts at a fixed price, the supply of currencies of other gold standard countries becomes perfectly elastic at the gold export or upper gold points. In Figure 4–10, the supply of dollars on foreign exchange markets becomes perfectly elastic at $2 = £1. At $4 = £1, the demand for dollars also becomes perfectly elastic because the Bank of England stands ready to buy any amount of gold offered at the gold-dollar parity. Within the narrow range between the gold points, the exchange rate is flexible: an export surplus *raises* exchange rates in favour of England – *lowers* the price of dollars per pound sterling – thus stimulating imports; similarly, an import surplus leads automatically to *falling* exchange rates for England – *raises* the price of dollars in terms of pounds.

Thus, so long as paper is freely convertible into gold, the exchange rate with any other country cannot fall below the gold-export point, that is, below the mint-parity by more than the cost of shipping gold. If an overissue of notes depresses the value of paper below gold bullion, causes the exchange rate to fall below the gold-export point, it would be more profitable to ship gold than to buy foreign bills to pay for imports. Notes would then be presented to banks for payment in gold and the banks would be obliged to protect their reserves by contracting the volume of the note issue. This would tend to raise the value of money, putting an end to the outflow of gold and restoring the exchange rate to par. Convertibility of a paper currency therefore provides an automatic check to overissue of the currency or paper inflation. When a paper currency is made inconvertible, however, the paper price of gold bullion is still governed by the exchange rates with countries on a metallic standard, but there is no longer any automatic check to a fall in exchange rates below the metallic parity, that is, to a permanent premium on bullion over paper. This does not mean, however, that a 'premium on bullion' is just shorthand for domestic inflation under inconvertibility. The title of one of Ricardo's famous tracts, *The High Price of Bullion: A Proof of the Depreciation of Bank Notes*, is quite misleading. Even without inflation, heavy foreign lending and grain imports can produce an unfavourable balance of payments, a fall in the foreign exchange value of the pound below the current gold-export point and a rise in the market price of gold beyond its mint-price. The central issue in the debate was just this: Is the premium on gold over paper evidence of inflation and, if so, is inflation due to the reckless monetary policy of the Bank of England?

Ricardo led the Bullionists with the argument that the Bank had overissued and that this was the cause of inflation or, to use the language of the day, the cause of 'the depreciation of bank notes'. In the absence of any confidence in the then little-used tool of an index number of prices, the first problem was to prove that British prices had risen relative to other trading countries. Ricardo's test was the premium actually quoted on bullion. The cause of the inflation was the excess issue of notes by the Bank of England; the country banks were exonerated because they had to maintain a fixed percentage of reserves against their own notes in the form of Bank of England

Figure 4–10

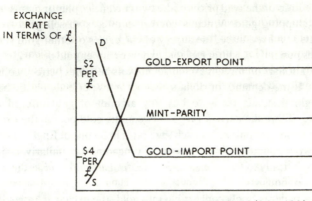

AMOUNT OF FOREIGN EXCHANGE (DOLLARS)

notes, while the Bank itself was not subject to any such limitation. The Directors of
the Bank and the antibullionists argued that it was impossible to overissue paper
money even when it was inconvertible as long as new notes were issued only on
discount of sound, short-term commercial paper. This is the real-bills doctrine,
which we have already encountered in the *Wealth of Nations*; it had little relevance
here because the Bank got its notes into circulation, not only by commercial
discounting, but also by purchasing public bonds. The antibullionists argued, in the
main, that the terms of trade had moved against England, not because of monetary
inflation, but because of the state of the balance of payments. But if home prices were
not rising, Ricardo retorted, an adverse balance of payments with the exchanges
turning against England would stimulate exports and cause the foreign remittances
to be transferred in goods. Therefore, the fall in the exchanges and the premium on
bullion had nothing to do with heavy foreign lending.

This touches on a difference in approach to the corrective mechanism for
disturbances in the balance of payments, which we will consider subsequently [see
chapter 6, section 23]. In a sense, both sides avoided the real issues. The premium on
gold over paper was caused in part, and perhaps in large part, not by an excess
currency, or an unfavourable balance of payments, but by a speculative flight to
bullion and foreign currency. It is obvious, however, that at bottom, government
expenditures were behind the inflation and the Bank of England was simply refusing
to acknowledge its responsibility as a central bank, clinging to the notion that it was
no more than *primus inter pares*, passively serving 'the needs of trade'. Ricardo's
plan to nationalize the Bank, therefore, was a recognition on his part of the necessity
for a clearly defined monetary policy by a central monetary authority.

28. The Machinery Question

In **chapter 31**, 'On Machinery', added in the third edition of the *Principles*, Ricardo
broke new ground and shocked his contemporaries by maintaining that the

introduction of new machinery might be injurious to workers. The basic argument is that if the installation of new machines involves the diversion of labour previously required to produce wage goods, if instead of new machines being financed out of retained earnings they are financed by drawing down the wages fund, then output may fall for a time and produce unemployment. Ricardo's proof is by way of a single example, that of a farmer who diverts half his annual labour force, hitherto employed to make finished goods, to the construction of a machine (see Table 4–6).

Table 4–6

Year	Gross Product (£)	Net Product (£)	Wages Fund (£)	Value of Machine (£)
1	15,000	2,000	13,000	0
2	15,000	2,000	5,500	7,500
3	7,500	2,000	?	?

It is immediately conceded that the fall in price consequent upon the actual utilization of the new machine would expand output, so that some workers would be reabsorbed. Whether wage cuts would also stimulate the reemployment of displaced labour, Ricardo does not say. In fact, his analysis is so severely short run that he does not trouble to spell out any of the adjustments that would be bound to follow the employment of new machinery. The argument is peculiar because it supposes a contraction of output and claims at best that the demand for labour is lessened for 'a considerable interval'. In the closing pages of the chapter, Ricardo scuttles his own argument by pointing out that when machinery is financed out of previous earnings it involves none of these dire effects, and indeed only rapid technical advance ensures continuous economic growth. A warning against state intervention to discourage technical progress brings the chapter to a close.

The significance of this chapter is that it relaxes the two-factor assumption maintained elsewhere in the book and analyzes, not the effect of process innovations, but the substitution of capital for labour along given production functions. Ricardo seems to have realized by this time that the rise in money wages and the fall in the rate of profit implied by his model must lead to a constantly rising ratio of machinery to labour. This contradicts his usual assumption that capital and labour grow at equal rates and creates new complications. No wonder that this chapter seems glued on to the rest of the book as an afterthought.

Toward the end of the chapter Ricardo introduces the notion that labourers have an interest in the pattern of luxury spending by the rich because spending on 'menial servants' increases the demand for labour by more than an equivalent amount of spending on luxury goods, assuming that luxury goods are not produced entirely by labour. This is a proposition that, transmuted by John Stuart Mill, became the maxim: 'Demand for commodities is not demand for labour' [see chapter 6, section 3].

29. Taxation

The tax chapters in Ricardo's book contain much additional insight into his system. They represent a rigorous working out of his theory of factor shares with a notable emphasis upon the short run. First, there is **chapter 26**, 'On Gross and Net Revenue', which defines taxable capacity as depending exclusively upon net revenue. Ricardo takes the concept of subsistence wages seriously and deducts from gross revenue all output necessary to maintain human as well as physical capital intact, leaving the sum of profits and rents as net revenue. But a footnote early in the chapter mentions a difficulty in this concept of the net returns to economic activity: market wages often exceed the minimum wages necessary to maintain labour. **Chapter 8**, 'On Taxes', lays down the tautological rule that all taxes hamper capital accumulation unless met by 'an increased production, or by a diminished unproductive consumption'. It is not conceded that taxes ever stimulate effort. **Chapter 9** deals with specific taxes on the raw produce of agriculture. Two numerical examples are used to show that a specific tax will raise the price of grain by the amount of the tax: the money expenditures of consumers rise, but total money rents are unaffected. An unchanged aggregate money rent means a fall in wheat rents, however, since the tax falls heavier on the superior acres where the total wheat produced is larger. Since the supply curve of labour is perfectly elastic, real wages net of tax remain the same and if landlords do not themselves consume grain, the whole burden of the tax falls on profits. Ricardo goes on to consider possible causes for a rise in the price of wage goods. In the course of the analysis he commits himself to the notion of a predetermined wages fund and admits that the supply of labour is actually relatively inelastic: labour is singularly slow to respond to a change in its own price. At the close of the chapter, Ricardo points out that taxes distort the structure of prices, hence the ratios of comparative costs, which in turn alter the level of prices by altering the international distribution of specie.

Chapter 10 develops the theory that a tax on rent cannot be shifted simply because it is a tax on a factor in fixed supply. It is only by varying the supply that the incidence of a tax is made to fall on the buyer. A tax on rent would tax all contractual rent and, since not all contractual rent is 'pure economic rent', some part of the tax would fall on profits.

Chapters 11 and **12**, on tithes and land taxes, raise no new issues. **Chapters 13** and **14** provide an interesting discussion of the movement in the price of a taxed commodity toward its equilibrium level: the adjustment takes longer, the more durable the commodity in question, the more inelastic its supply and the more elastic its demand. Of course, this is modern language and the term 'elasticity' does not appear in Ricardo. Nevertheless, there is simply no doubt that Ricardo in these chapters is perfectly aware of the fact that there are systematic differences in the price-responsiveness of demand for and supply of different categories of goods.

Moreover, he arrives by intuition at exactly the same answers that we would reach today using the modern apparatus created by Marshall.

The next chapter, 'Taxes on Profits', contains an important discussion of the effect of a uniform profit tax upon the supply prices of products. Although the tax will be shifted forward, it will have an unequal effect on the selling prices of different products because of differences in the composition and turnover rates of capital. Owing to the differential effect of taxes, an increase in the quantity of money will affect the structure as well as the level of prices; the level of prices, however, will ultimately return to its pretax level because of the specie-flow mechanism. **Chapter 29** covers much the same points as **chapter 15** but from a different viewpoint.

The thesis of chapter 9, that real wages cannot be taxed, is revised in **chapter 16**, 'Taxes on Wages'. Tax revenues spent by the government raise the demand for labour and hence money wages. Money wages rise by less than the tax and therefore real wages fall. This rather odd argument rests on the idea that the private demand for labour is unaffected by government spending: the wage bill net of tax remains unchanged. If the wage bill net of tax is to remain unchanged, money wages must rise. As some modern commentators have pointed out, the only way that insertion of the circuit of taxes and public expenditures could raise total spending on labour is that it somehow increases the velocity of circulation; Ricardo's argument is an early and peculiar version of the 'balanced-budget multiplier'. The views of Adam Smith and several other writers on the question of taxes on wages are then examined. Ricardo employs the standard 18th-century view that the demand for 'necessaries' displays little price-elasticity compared to the demand for 'luxuries'.

Chapter 17 is perhaps the most interesting of the tax chapters; it contains the famous defense of taxation as opposed to borrowing as a method of financing a war. The classical case against public debts is developed at length: a public debt invites flight of capital and deficit financing cuts into private thrift; the burden of the debt is not so much the annual interest charges as the squandering of resources that the debt represents.

30. The Lasting Influence of Ricardo

As a rigorous theorist, Ricardo is obviously Adam Smith's superior. On the other hand, the *Wealth of Nations* contains more in the way of substantive generalizations on the workings of economic systems than does Ricardo's *Principles*, more perhaps than any other 18th- or 19th-century treatise on economics. If *the* problem of economics is the allocation of limited means among competing ends, as we are often told, then Adam Smith contributed more to economics than did Ricardo – the only place where Ricardo addressed himself specifically to the allocation problems is in the chapter on foreign trade and here, at any rate, he saw further and deeper than did Adam Smith. If *the* problem of economics is growth and development, as we are also told, there is again more in Smith than in Ricardo. But if economics is essentially an engine of analysis, a method of thinking rather than a body of substantive results,

Ricardo literally invented the technique of economics. We may have replaced his clumsy numerical proofs by more elegant geometrical demonstrations, but most of the time we still employ a mode of reasoning that Ricardo made familiar. His gift for heroic abstractions produced one of the most impressive models, judged by its scope and practical import, in the entire history of economic theory: seizing hold of a wide range of significant problems with a simple analytical model involving only a few strategic variables, he produced dramatic conclusions oriented to policy action. In short, he was the first to master that art that brought success to Keynes in our own day. Not everyone will consider this praiseworthy. Even Schumpeter calls Ricardo's habit of applying severely simplified abstractions to the solution of practical problems 'the Ricardian Vice'. And to the Historical School and the American Institutionalists, Ricardo has always stood for everything they detest in orthodox economics.

The influence of Ricardo's treatise made itself felt almost as soon as it was published and for over half a century it dominated economic thinking in Britain. The leading periodicals and even the *Encyclopaedia Britannica* itself fell into the hands of Ricardo's disciples; popular literature echoed Ricardian ideas and Parliament increasingly succumbed to Ricardian policy proposals. Although the Corn Laws were not in fact repealed until 1846, Ricardo's writings helped to make free trade a popular objective of British policy. Indeed, Ricardo had unwittingly provided the theoretical justification for the long-range solution to the growth problem which Britain actually adopted in the 19th century: she became 'the workshop of the world' and bought most of her food abroad.

Even those contemporary economists who turned against him on particular questions – Bailey, Scrope, Read, Jones, Longfield, Senior, Whately – succumbed to the leading Ricardian doctrine that the productivity of labour in agriculture governs the rate of return on capital as well as secular changes in the distributive shares. As long as the Corn Laws remained on the statute books, the issue of free trade gave practical significance to the Ricardian system. And when repeal came in 1846, Mill's *Principles*, published two years later, brought new authority to Ricardo's ideas suitably amended. After 1870, however, most economists turned their backs on what they understood to be the Ricardian theory of value and distribution and agreed with Jevons that Ricardo had 'shunted the car of economic science on the wrong track'. Marx's warm praise of Ricardo did not enhance Ricardo's reputation with academic economists, though Ricardo could hardly have been more innocent than he was of the role of mentor of Marx. But the last decade of the 19th century saw another change in attitude to Ricardo as a number of writers were suddenly struck by the idea that the old-fashioned Ricardian theory of rent was really a special case of a much more general theory. Ricardo had shown that the final dose of labour-and-capital on an intensively used rent-yielding piece of land adds nothing to rent but consists solely of wages and interest, rent being due to the superior productivity of the intramarginal units. Wicksteed, Wicksell and John Bates Clark now realized that there is nothing unique about a no-rent margin; when land is the variable factor and labour-and-capital is the fixed factor, the margin will be a no-wage, no interest margin. With that insight, the general marginal productivity theory of distribution was born and to Ricardo's other accomplishments must now be added that of having invented marginal analysis. For some years, Ricardo came back into vogue and Marshall even went so far as to argue that the foundation of Ricardo's theory of 'cost of production in relation to value' remained intact. In the 1930s, the pendulum swung back again: concern over the problem of aggregate effective demand caused many economists to agree with Keynes that 'the complete domination of Ricardo's approach for a period of 100 years has been a disaster to the progress of economics'. But this is a harsh judgment which supposes that but for Ricardo, economics would have addressed itself in the past to the macroeconomic problem of unemployment. Ricardo's avowal of the famous 'Law of Markets', asserting a tendency toward full-employment equilibrium, was poorly thought out and remained little more than a dogma. As a monetary theorist, Ricardo was not even representative of the best work of his own day. Still, what has survived is the Law of Comparative Cost and the method of comparative static analysis that Ricardo invented. And the central problem that Ricardo posed, namely, how the changes in the relative shares of land, labour, and capital are connected with the rate of capital accumulation, remains one of the abiding concerns of modern economists. In that sense, Ricardian economics is still alive.

31. Sraffa: Ricardo in Modern Dress

Ricardian economics is alive in yet another sense. Ricardo's search for an 'invariable measure of value' – a yardstick that is itself invariant to changes in either the wage rate or the profit rate – came to be regarded after his death as one of those conceptual aberrations to which great economists are sometimes prone. Almost no one besides John Stuart Mill and Karl Marx even understood what Ricardo was driving at and for almost the whole of the 19th century, commentaries on Ricardo hardly so much as mentioned his quest for an invariable measure. Then in 1960 Piero Sraffa, the modern editor of Ricardo's works, published a puzzling book entitled *Production of Commodities by Means of Commodities: Prelude to a Critique of Economic Theory*. This book purported to show that Ricardo's problem can in fact be solved and, furthermore, that the solution is fraught with profound implications for modern economic theory. Let us spend a few pages trying to explain what Sraffa is all about, thus illustrating one of the maxims laid down in the introduction of this book: there is a mutual interaction between past and present economic thinking which illuminates both. Without first struggling through Ricardo, one might find Sraffa incomprehensible, particularly as his book contains neither an introduction nor a conclusion. But after reading Ricardo, Sraffa is almost plain sailing.

Sraffa's book would have been better understood if its title had been longer: instead of *Production of Commodities by Means of Commodities*, it should have been called 'Production of Commodities by Means of Commodities and Labour', or, for short, 'Production of Commodities Without Anything Called Capital'. On the first page of the book we find ourselves in a Ricardian long-run equilibrium and no words are wasted in telling us how we got there, or what would happen if we departed from it; labour is homogeneous and it is the only 'primary', nonreproducible input in the system, whose amount is given at the outset of the analysis; fixed input-coefficients prevail in all industries (firms are never mentioned) and, hence, production would obey the condition of constant returns to scale if output ever varied, a possibility that Sraffa never considers; every industry produces a single commodity by a single technique, a 'technique' being initially defined as some combination of homogeneous labour and working capital (later in the book, when we are introduced to fixed capital and the general problem of joint production of two or more commodities by a single industry, this gives way to the condition that each industry uses a unique combination of homogeneous labor and intermediate products in order to produce a final commodity); producers are implicitly assumed to maximize profits and to minimize unit costs of production, in consequence of which the rate of profit is equalized between industries; the economy is closed and the pattern of demand is said to play no role in determining prices, although it does of course affect the scale of output in each industry.

Sraffa's mode of exposition is entirely Walrasian and by page 5 of his book we are already counting equations and unknowns to see if they match as a means of ensuring ourselves that we have a determinate solution [see chapter 13, section 3]. He begins with a simple system of simultaneous input-output equations expressed in physical terms (one for each commodity in the economy) and shows that if such a system is in stationary equilibrium with wages fixed at subsistence levels, relative prices as well as the rate of profit will be simultaneously determined. But if wages are variable and rise above subsistence, the system of $k - 1$ independent linear equations can no longer determine the $k + 1$ unknowns ($k - 1$ relative prices, the rate of profit, and the rate of wages). By varying wages from 0 to 1 as fractions of national income, Sraffa proceeds to demonstrate the so-called Ricardo Effect which had so troubled Ricardo himself. We recall that Ricardo was struck by the fact that, measured in money of constant purchasing power, a rise in wages (or fall in the rate of profit) would raise the price of labour-intensive goods and lower the price of capital-intensive goods, labour-intensity and capital-intensity being interpreted with reference to the average capital-labour ratio observed in the economy. Similarly, in Sraffa's system, an arbitrary change in the share of wages alters the entire structure of relative prices, creating 'deficit' and 'surplus' industries with reference to the 'critical proportions' between 'labour' and 'means of production' that mark the medium between the two extremes. To get around this problem, Sraffa devises a 'standard commodity', capable of expressing relative prices irrespective of the level of wages or the rate of profit, to take the place of the previous yardstick. To determine relative prices, we must assume that either the rate of profit or the rate of wages is given at the outset, because we still have no more than k independent equations to determine the $k + 1$ unknowns. Nevertheless, taking either wages or profits as given, we will have achieved a theory of price determination in which it is always possible 'to tell of any particular price fluctuation whether it arises from the peculiarities of the commodity which is being measured or from those of the measuring standard', which is something we certainly cannot say about fluctuations of money prices in the real world.

How is the trick accomplished? The easiest way to see what is involved is to recall Ricardo's 'corn-model', which Sraffa read into Ricardo's early *Essay*, according to which corn is both the only output of agriculture and the only input into agriculture and industry (in the form of seeds and food 'advanced' to workers); this makes corn a perfect 'measure of value' because whatever happens to wages and profits must affect both inputs and outputs of corn simultaneously, leaving the relative price of corn unaffected. Indeed, the price of corn can only change if the technology of producing it is improved. Similarly, Sraffa requires a 'standard commodity' that consists only of outputs combined in the same proportions as the reproducible non-labour inputs that enter into all the successive layers of its manufacture, in which case it will have the same properties as Ricardo's 'corn'. He provides us with the numerical example, showing that we can take fractions of inputs and outputs in the total system of equations to construct a 'reduced-scale system' whose industries do produce outputs in the same proportion as they use non-labour inputs. This system is the 'standard system' and its mixed output bundle is the 'standard composite commodity'. It has the property that the 'multipliers', or ratios of net output to inputs by commodity groups, equal the ratio of the net output of the actual system to its 'means of production', which ratio is now labeled the 'standard ratio' (we may sum it up crudely by saying that the output-capital ratio of the subsystem equals that of the actual system). Sraffa then goes on to show, in one of the book's many elegant demonstrations, that there is one and only one such 'standard system' embedded in any actual economic system: the ratio of net outputs to inputs in the 'standard system' and the proportions of net output going to wages in that system determine the rate of profit in the economy as a whole.

Along the way, Sraffa draws a fundamental distinction between a 'basic' commodity, which enters directly or indirectly into the production of every other commodity in the economy, including itself, and a 'nonbasic' commodity, which enters only into final consumption. If we treated labour itself as a produced 'means of production' then 'wage goods' would constitute examples of such 'basic' commodities, on the assumption that they are technically required to cause households to produce the flow of labour services. Ricardo clearly believed that wheaten bread was 'basic' in this sense but, as Sraffa rejects any and all versions of the subsistence theory of wages, it is not immediately evident what actual commodities he would label as 'basics'. However, there appear to be enough basics in an actual economy since basics are simply means of production which are themselves produced, that is, capital goods. Similarly, workers are nonbasics in Sraffa's system and so are acres of land. The upshot of the distinction is that the 'standard commodity' consists only of basics and indeed of all the basics in the economy. These basics enter into the production of the invariant yardstick in a 'standard ratio', that is, in the same proportion as they enter into their own production. It is in this sense that we can think of the 'standard commodity' as representing the interconnected, undecomposable core of an economy, made up as it is entirely of basics, which is surrounded by a decomposable belt of nonbasics.

It turns out, and this is the punch of the argument, that both relative prices and either the rate of profit or the rate of wages (depending on which one is given exogenously) depend only on the technical conditions of producing the 'standard commodity' and are in no way affected by what happens to nonbasic commodities. In a way this is obvious: a change in the cost of producing a nonbasic no doubt alters its own price but, by definition of a nonbasic commodity, the effect stops there since the product in question never becomes an input into any other technical process. It is also obvious, at least intuitively, that an exogeneous change in wages or in any other input price unconnected with a change in productive techniques has no effect on relative prices measured in terms of the 'standard commodity' for the simple reason that the change alters the measuring rod in the same way as it alters the pattern of output prices being measured. The 'standard commodity' therefore provides an 'invariable measure of value' and Ricardo's old problem is at long last solved.

All this applies only to the simplified case in which all the intermediate inputs consist of working capital; joint products are ruled out by assumption. Every technique which employs durable capital goods, however, affords an example of joint production, in the sense that a commodity is produced together with a somewhat older but still usable machine. It is of course possible to get around this problem by treating the same machine at different ages as so many different products, each with its own price, but that procedure will not work with jointly-produced consumer goods, as in the famous wool-mutton example. In any case, as soon as we have joint products, the whole argument becomes infinitely more complicated. The 'multipliers' which are used to form the 'standard system' now have to be negative rather than positive, at which point, Sraffa concedes, 'it becomes impossible to visualise the standard system as a conceivable re-arrangement of the actual processes', but only as a 'system of abstract equations', having no 'bodily existence'. Even the fundamental distinction between basics and nonbasics breaks down and the definition of basics is now only capable of being stated in the language of matrix algebra.[1] Nevertheless, it is shown that, despite joint production, the basic thesis of the book is preserved. In Sraffa's own words: 'the chief economic impli-cation of the distinction [between basics and nonbasics] was that basics have an essential part to play in the determination of prices and the rate of profits, while non-basics have none', and this implication is not reversed by the phenomenon of joint production.

What are we to make of these conclusions? It is one of the peculiar features of Sraffa's analysis that it is entirely independent of and perfectly compatible with any special theory of the distribution process. It provides no theory of the determination of the rate of profit other than that nonbasics play no role whatever, and indeed Sraffa's principal thesis is that national output, whether expressed in physical or in value terms, will be entirely unaffected by how the net output is shared out between wages and profits. The notion that the functional distribution of income is indetermi-

---

[1] Joint production also destroys the notion, mooted earlier in Sraffa's book, of reducing all inputs to 'dated labour', that is, to labour inputs weighted by given rates of profits and compounded over the time they are embodied in each technique in the process of production. In that sense, Sraffa repudiates the labour theory of value, even if we suppose that the concept of 'dated labour' is compatible with that theory.

nate, depending rather on the 'class struggle', has now become an article of faith among certain neo-Keynesian economists (such as Kaldor, Robinson, and Pasinetti), and it is precisely for that reason that Sraffa's work is regarded in some quarters as the *locus classicus* of all anti-orthodox distribution theories.

It is difficult to see, however, why anyone would be persuaded by Sraffa's treatise to believe in the theoretical indeterminacy of income distribution and hence in the importance of power bargaining over wages and profits. There is hardly a sentence in Sraffa's book which refers to the real world and it is perfectly obvious that the author is only too keen to exchange practical relevance for logical rigor. For example, Sraffa gets rid of demand in the explanation of prices by the steady-state assumption of long-run equilibrium plus the assumption that all commodities are produced under conditions of constant costs, in which case the scale of output of a commodity makes no difference to input proportions. In the preface to his book, Sraffa actually denies that he is making any assumption about returns to scale: 'The investigation is concerned exclusively with such properties of an economic system that do not depend on changes in the scale of production or in the proportion of "factors".' It is true, of course, that when we assume fixed proportions between inputs in every industry (and presumably uniform fixed proportions between firms in an industry), nothing does depend on the scale at which output is produced.

Sraffa's rigid view of technical possibilities may not matter for the characterization of the balanced, steady-state growth path, but it certainly matters for problems of comparative statics. For one thing, profit maximization and equality of the rate of profit between different industries is inconsistent with the existence of increasing returns to scale in some industries. The moment we have increasing returns to scale ('natural monopolies'), the pattern of demand is vital to the explanation of relative prices [see chapter 10, section 3]. We get no help from Sraffa on this question because he provides no theory whatsoever of the behavior of decision-making units. Profits are equalized between industries but we are not told why. As soon as we consider alternative stationary states which differ in the scale of output, the structure of the 'standard commodity' itself will change unless constant-returns-to-scale conditions obtain. This is apart from the question of what would happen if the production functions of individual enterprises were not of the strictly fixed-coefficient type; in that case, the choice of different techniques would depend as much on relative prices as relative prices do on the techniques actually adopted and, once again, the invariance of the measuring rod would break down.

The neglect of demand and change in Sraffa's system threatens the very practical conclusions which his advocates wish to draw from it, namely, that the wage-profit relationship in an economy can be whatever we would like it to be: economic forces do not limit the possibilities of a prices and incomes policy! Actually, Sraffa's model is so restrictive as to rule out any meaningful discussion of its empirical implications for the real world. Be that as it may, a final assessment of Sraffa's achievement must involve consideration of the Rip-van-Winkle phenomenon, whereby Sraffa solves a technical problem that Ricardo posed 150 years ago *as if its solution still has substantive significance*! For Ricardo, the theory that wages tend to fall to subsistence levels and the deduction that the rate of profit is determined only by the technical conditions of producing wage goods did have substantive significance. The economy in which he lived made it plausible to identify wage goods with basics and basics with agricultural commodities, leading straight to the practical dictum that the rate of profit in agriculture largely determines or, at any rate, significantly influences the general rate of profit. But in a modern economy, where basics are not the output of any unique collection of industries, the demonstration that relative prices and either wage rates or the rate of profit are determined solely by the technology employed in the production of basics has no particular significance for an understanding of how the functional distribution of income is actually determined. In Ricardo, 'corn' is both an 'invariable measure of value' and the prime wage good consumed by workers. In Sraffa, the 'standard commodity' is an 'invariable measure of value' but workers do not consume it.

Worse still is the suspicion that all commodities in a modern economy are basics, in which case Sraffa's Fundamental Theorem – relative prices and either the wage rate or the profit rate depend only on the production of basics – is not worth arguing about. Consider the meaning of nonbasics in Sraffa's system: these are products which enter only into final consumption and not into the production of other products. You may think that certain service industries, like hotels, restaurants, and laundries, constitute perfect examples of nonbasics. But suppose that hotels cater to business lunches, the expenses of which are written off as part of the costs of carrying on business, or suppose that laundries serve business firms (like hotels) as well as private customers; in all such cases, these industries are basics, not nonbasics. Or are they? We talk of hotels, restaurants, and laundries as producing different products because consumers do not treat the outputs of these industries as identical services even if they are sold at the same price. But Sraffa's distinction between basics and non-basics refers to 'commodities', defined as we recall by their *technical* character-istics of production. If a hotel restaurant produces meals with the same technology as a self-service cafeteria, they are the same 'commodity' for Sraffa. Thus, to discover whether there are any nonbasics in a modern economy, we would first have to translate Sraffa's definitions into the definitions of the industrial census and that might prove to be a formidable task. Suffice it to say that power-bargaining theories of distribution must get along without Sraffa's support, or else we must be told how so abstract a theory can be brought down to earth.

There is even a lingering doubt that Sraffa's book, whatever else we may say about it, has finally vindicated Ricardo's old quest for an 'invariable measure of value', capable of separating and measuring those changes in relative prices due to changes in technology from those due to changes in the rate of wages and profits. Such a divining rod, Ricardo kept saying, would have to be invariant, not just to changes in wages and profits, but also to changes in its own methods of production. Now, Sraffa's 'standard commodity' fills the bill on the first score but fails on the second score: it is not invariant to changes in its own technology of manufacture and, therefore, falls short of solving Ricardo's problem, which was how to link the determination of the rate of profit directly and unambiguously to the action of diminishing returns in agriculture. The truth of the matter is that there is no such thing as an 'invariable' yardstick that will satisfy all the requirements that Ricardo placed upon it. All of which is to say that, despite the fact that Ricardo was the first truly rigorous analytical economist, it is impossible to exonerate him from all analytical errors: he was at times inclined to square a circle using only a ruler and compass (which is, of course, impossible).

32. Ricardo in Still More Modern Dress

This is not the only bone of contention in modern interpretations of Ricardo. At one time, as we remarked before, Ricardo was regarded as the virtual inventor of the method of comparative statics and certainly the prime example of the age-old tendency of economists to emphasize long-run equilibrium values at the expense of any consideration of short-run, disequilibrium adjustments. But developments in modern growth theory have reminded us that Ricardo frequently expressed himself in language that is deeply evocative of steady-state growth theory. Thus, our earlier mathematical formulation of Ricardo's two-sector model based on work by Pasinetti interprets the Ricardian system as a half-way house to a steady-state growth model. Ricardo writes as if a long-term steady state had been achieved in the labour market via population growth, while at the same time the capital accumulation process is still characterized by disequilibrium adjustments, which will only achieve stationariness at some future time; in other words, the 'market price' of labour is at its 'natural price', determined by the minimum cost of subsistence, but the rate of profit is still above its 'natural' equilibrium level.

At first glance, this constant-wage interpretation is an attractive one, which squares with many of Ricardo's observations and particularly with his theorems on the incidence of taxes. On the other hand, it leaves unexplained many passages in the *Principles*, for example, in chapter 5 on wages, in which Ricardo declares that population is growing because the 'market wage' of labour in fact exceeds its 'natural wage'. Some modern commentators have therefore produced variable-wage versions of the Ricardian system in which as much attention is given to the short-run disequilibrium adjustments in both labour and capital markets as to the long-run equilibrium solutions of the stationary state. Others have gone even further in modernising Ricardo, arguing that Ricardo was aware of a definite interaction between the wages-population mechanism and the investment-profits mechanism, such that the economy is studied in terms of the properties of a dynamic, moving equilibrium in which the rate of growth of population is kept equal to the rate of growth of capital.

All these commentators are concerned to express Ricardo's frequently reiterated dictum that 'profits vary inversely with wages' and his equally frequently reiterated belief that the rate of profit only falls 'in the last instance' because of diminishing returns to agriculture. The old, constant-wage interpretation, however, is unable to account for those passages in which Ricardo clearly says that real wages – wages expressed in terms of a basket of physical commodities – can actually fall alongside of the falling rate of profit well before the economy has reached the stationary state.

The great merit of the 'new', variable-wage interpretations is that they can neatly accommodate those remarks of Ricardo which the 'old' view had to put down as *obiter dicta*.

At the same time, even the new view has difficulty in making sense of passages in which Ricardo insists that the rate of profit depends only on the cost of producing wage goods and on nothing else – won't the rate of profit fall if capital, for whatever reason, grows faster than labour? Thus, it may be that Ricardo really operated with three models – (1) a Pasinetti-type, constant-wage model; (2) a disequilibrium, variable-wage model; and (3) a genuine, dynamic equilibrium growth model – adopting one or the other at different stages in his argument. Indeed, that seems to me to be the inescapable conclusion of all the swapping of quotations. Once again, we need to remind ourselves that it is simply not possible to square *everything* that Ricardo said with *one* totally consistent formulation of the Ricardian system.

NOTES ON FURTHER READING

Ricardo's *Principles of Political Economy and Taxation* is available in paperback but the hardback version, edited by P. Sraffa, *The Works of David Ricardo*, Vol. I (1951), is well worth the extra cost if only because of the editor's magnificent introduction. The Penguin paperback edition by R.M. Hartwell (1971) also contains an excellent introduction. Ricardo's own 'Essay on the Influence of a Low Price of Corn on the Profits of Stock', *Works*, Vol. IV, is a good way of starting before reading the *Principles*. Nothing that Ricardo wrote is without interest and a perusal of his 'Notes on Malthus', *Works*, Vol. II, the Parliamentary speeches, *Works*, Vol. V, and the fascinating letters, *Works*, Vols. VI–X, will convey the flavor of Ricardian economics in a way that all the commentaries in the world never can do.

There is no standard biography of Ricardo. The first part of J.H. Hollander, *David Ricardo: A Centenary Estimate* (1910), supplies an old but still valuable sketch and D. Weatherall, *David Ricardo. A Biography* (1976) embodies the more recent researches of Sraffa and others. The second half of Hollander's book is also recommended as the best nontechnical account of Ricardo's general views and opinions.

The failure to distinguish between a positive theory of relative prices and a normative theory of social accounting has been the source of infinite confusion in commentaries upon Ricardo's theory of value. Like Adam Smith, Ricardo did not hold an 'analytical' labour theory of value, as G.J. Stigler shows: 'Ricardo and the 93% Labour Theory of Value', *AER*, 1958, reprinted in his *Essays in the History of Economics*: see also my *Ricardian Economics*, chap. 2, and D.F. Gordon, 'Value, Labour Theory Of', *IESS*, 16. Commenting on Stigler's article, H. Barkai argues that Ricardo actually held an 80 percent labour theory of value, at least on the strength of his own assumptions: 'The Empirical Assumptions of Ricardo's 93 per cent Labour Theory of Value', *Ec*, November, 1967. G.W. Wilson and J.L. Pate, 'Ricardo's 93 per cent Labour Theory of Value: A Final Comment', *JPE*, January/February, 1968, confirm Barkai's findings by a somewhat different route and, incidentally, shows convincingly that Ricardo strengthened rather than weakened the labour-mainly theory of value in the third edition of his *Principles*. Ricardo's value theory is really concerned with intertemporal variations in the normal prices of broad groups of commodities. This was pointed out long ago by J.M. Cassels, 'A Re-interpretation of Ricardo on Value', *QJE*, 1935, reprinted in *EET* and *RHET*, and it is reemphasized by Sraffa in his Introduction to Ricardo's *Principles, Works*, Vol. I, sects. IV–V.

There is hardly an economist of note in the 19th century who did not criticize Ricardo's writings on the problem of value; the reader should at least look at Marshall's 'Notes on Ricardo's Theory of Value', *Principles of Economics*, Appendix I. G. Myrdal, *The Political Element in the Development of Economic Theory* (1953), chap. 3, argues that the classical labour theory of value and the notion of an invariable measure of value stem from natural law doctrine. W.C. Mitchell, 'The Postulates and Preconceptions of Ricardian Economics', *The Backward Art of Spending Money* (1937), has something to contribute to this question. See also a provocative essay by S. Moore, 'Ricardo and the State of Nature', *SJPE*, November, 1966, where 'state of nature' refers to precapitalist pricing conditions.

In a brilliant article, V. Edelberg defends Ricardo's dictum that profits vary inversely to wages: 'The Ricardian Theory of Profits', *Ec*, February, 1933; this article is, unfortunately, couched in the language of the Austrian theory of capital and may mean little to the reader unacquainted with Böhm-Bawerk. Tucker gives a lucid exposition of Ricardo's theory of profits in *Progress and Profits in British Economic Thought*, chap. 6. For a general treatment of Ricardo's system, see Cannan's *Production and Distribution Theories*, chaps. 7 and 8, particularly pp. 193–202, 220–8, 253–62, and 268–78. Cannan was the first to show that there is something wrong with Ricardo's arithmetical examples of the effects of capital accumulation on relative shares but it was not until H. Barkai, 'Ricardo on Factor Prices and Income Distribution in a Growing Economy', *Ec*, August, 1959, that it was realized that Ricardo was implicitly assuming linear average and marginal productivity functions. See also Schumpeter's unsympathetic and occasionally misleading comments in his *History of Economic Analysis*, pp. 471–5, 590–6, 636–7, 671–6, and 680–5.

Sraffa alleged that Ricardo's early theory of profits depends on an unstated 'corn-model' and, hence, that Ricardo's lifelong obsession with the 'invariable measure of value' must be seen as an attempt to preserve the simple logic of the corn-model. This is an issue that has been hotly debated, most recently by P. Garegnani, 'On Hollander's Interpretation of Ricardo's Early Theory of Profits', *CAMJE*, March, 1982, and S. Hollander, 'Professor Garegnani's Defence of Sraffa on the Material Rate of Profit', *ibid.*, June, 1983. The debate is adjudicated, and hopefully laid to rest, by T. Peach, 'David Ricardo's Early Treatment of Profitability: A New Interpretation', *EJ*, December, 1984.

Five years after Ricardo's death, William Whewell, a logician and historian of science, translated some of Ricardo's propositions into mathematics: see J.L. Cochrane, 'The First Mathematical Ricardian Model', *HOPE*, Fall, 1970. In more recent times, mathematical formulations of Ricardo's system have multiplied in large numbers. Almost the first to venture into this territory was H. Barkai who treated a one-sector version of the Ricardian theory in 'Ricardo on Factor Prices and Income Distribution in a Growing Economy', *Ec*, August, 1959, and 'Ricardo's Static Equilibrium', *ibid.*, February, 1965. The latter article by Barkai argued that Ricardo did not assume a zero-elasticity demand for wheat, a failure which renders his model indeterminate; this contention was denied by G.J. Stigler in 'Textual Exegesis as a Scientific Problem', *ibid.*, November, 1965, which also raised the general question whether we can ever decide what an author assumes merely by enumerating quotations. P.A. Samuelson presents a Ricardo-like linear programming model to show that one cannot 'get rid of rent' by going to the margins of cultivation once commodity substitution is allowed for: 'A Modern Treatment of the Ricardian Economy: I and II', *QJE*, 1959, reprinted in *The Collected Scientific Papers of Paul A. Samuelson*, ed. J.E. Stiglitz (1966), Vol. 1 L.L. Pasinetti focuses on the determinacy and stability of Ricardo's system, conceived as a simplified two-sector model: 'A Mathematical Formulation of the Ricardian System', *REStud*, 1960, reprinted in his *Growth and Income Distribution* (1974). I have borrowed heavily in the text from Pasinetti's formulation. For a brilliant commentary on and critique of Pasinetti, see R. Findlay, 'Relative Prices, Growth and Trade in a Single Ricardian System', *Ec*, February, 1974. H. Brems, 'An Attempt at a Rigorous Restatement of Ricardo's Long-Run Equilibrium', *HOPE*, Fall, 1970, takes up Pasinetti's approach from a slightly different angle. M.A. Akhtar, 'The "Classical Dichotomy" in Ricardian Economics', *HOPE*, Fall, 1975, and Eltis *The Classical Theory of Economic Growth*, chap. 6, manage to include fixed capital in a mathematical restatement of Ricardo, a difficulty which had defeated all earlier contributors to the discussion. Each of these mathematical models throws light in its own way on Ricardo's arguments and yet all of them leave something out as, for example, the 'invariable measure of value'. It is worth adding that, with the exception of Akhtar and the appendices to the articles by Samuelson and Pasinetti, none of the seven authors employs mathematics more advanced than calculus.

In the first edition of this book, I argued that the rental share in Ricardo's model falls rather than rises whenever the average product curve of capital-and-labour is convex from below. That was a bad slip and several critics have taught me better: K.V. Sastri, 'The Ricardian Theory of Factor-Shares', *EEH*, Summer, 1971; and G. Chiodi, 'Nota sull'andamento delle quote distributive nel sistema Ricardiano', *RPE*, 62, 1972. The reader is warned that my definition of the elasticity of the average product curve is Walrasian, whereas Sastri's definition is Marshallian, that is, mine is the multiplicative inverse of his and when I say 'falling', he says 'rising'.

Did Ricardo hold the 'iron law of wages' or did he contemplate a permanent excess of money wages over the real subsistence wage rate? Did he assume that capital grew independently of labour or did he believe in the 'balanced growth' of capital and labour? J.R. Hicks and S. Hollander, 'Mr. Ricardo and the Moderns', *QJE*, August, 1977, present one view; C. Casarosa, 'A New Formulation of the Ricardian System', *OEP*, March, 1978, and G. Caravale and D. Tosato, *Ricardo and the Theory of Value, Distribution and Growth* (1980), present another; and P.A. Samuelson, 'The Classical Canonical Model of Political Economy', *JEL*, December, 1978, presents yet a third view. Samuelson's canonical model embraces both Smith and Ricardo, dissolving the differences between them. S. Hollander, 'Of Professor Samuelson's Canonical Classical Model of Political Economy', *ibid.*, June, 1980, protests that the differences between Smith and Ricardo are substantive, not just semantic as Samuelson has claimed. Samuelson grants the point in 'Noise and Signal in Debates Among Classical Economists: A Reply', *ibid.*, but insists that the canonical model is in Smith and that Ricardo exaggerated his own departures from Smith.

O. St Clair, *A Key to Ricardo* (1957), is an excellent guide to 'what Ricardo actually said': it is virtually a collation of Ricardo's opinions on every economic topic. Some useful pieces on special topics are: R.O. Roberts, 'Ricardo's Theory of Public Debts', *Ec*, August, 1942; A. Marshall, 'Ricardo's Doctrine As to Taxes and Improvements in Agriculture', *Principles of Economics*, Appendix L, as amended by H.G. Johnson, 'An Error in Ricardo's Exposition of His Theory of Rent', *QJE*, November, 1948; W.D. Grampp, 'Malthus on Money Wages and Welfare', *AER*, 1956, reprinted in *RHET*, which must be supplemented by L.A. Dow, 'Malthus on Sticky Wages, the Upper Turning Point, and General Glut', *HOPE*, Fall, 1977; H. Barkai, 'Ricardo's Second Thoughts on Rent as a Relative Share', *SEJ*, January, 1966; and E.F. Beach, 'Hicks on Ricardo and Machinery', *EJ*, December, 1971; J.R. Hicks, 'A Reply to Professor Beach', *ibid*; and S. Maital, P. Haswell, 'Why Did Ricardo (Not) Change His Mind? On Money and Machinery', *Ec*, November, 1977.

The definitive treatment of the classical theory of international trade is by Viner, *Theory of International Trade*; chap. 8, sects. 1 and 2, and chap. 9, sect. 1, deal specifically with Ricardo. Wu, *International Price Theories*, chaps. 3 and 4, supplements Viner's analysis. There is also the breathtaking survey by J.S. Chipman, 'A Survey of the Theory of International Trade: Part 1, The Classical Theory', *Ecom*, July, 1965. R. Dorfman, P.A. Samuelson, and R.M. Solow, *Linear Programming and Economic Analysis* (1958), chaps. 2 and 3, present the classical theory of international trade in linear programming terms. There is a remarkable essay by W.O. Thweatt, 'James Mill and the Early Development of Comparative Advantage', *HOPE*, Summer, 1976, which, apart from crediting James Mill with the first clear statement of the principle of comparative advantage, argues that Ricardo's conception of foreign trade never effectively went beyond the idea of absolute advantage. On the 'evil' influence generally of James Mill on Ricardo, see Hutchison, *On Revolutions and Progress in Economic Knowledge*, chap. 2. The tax chapters in Ricardo's *Principles* are carefully analyzed and evaluated by C.S. Shoup, *Ricardo on Taxation* (1960), but even the general reader will learn much from watching Ricardo at work, as it were, on specific problems. The same ground is covered with extraordinary succinctness by R.A. Musgrave, *The Theory of Public Finance* (1959), pp. 385–92.

A great deal has been written on the background of the Bank Restriction Period. For a convenient brief account, see E.V. Morgan, *The Theory and Practice of Central Banking, 1797–1913* (1943), chap. 2. The most authoritative account of the bullionist controversy is by Viner, *Theory of International Trade*, chap. 3, supplemented by F.W. Fetter's more recent treatment, *Development of British Monetary Orthodoxy 1797–1875* (1965), chaps. 1, 2, and 3. See also R.S. Sayers, 'Ricardo's Views on Monetary Questions', *QJE*, 1953, reprinted in *Papers in English Monetary History*, eds. T.S. Ashton and R.S. Sayers (1953), and in *The Classical Economists and Economic Policy*, ed. A.W. Coats (1971 and in paperback).

Ricardo was a Member of Parliament and his Parliamentary speeches provide a wonderful opportunity to examine his involvement in the issues of his day. B. Gordon, *Political Economy in Parliament 1819–1823* (1976) and F.W. Fetter, *The Economist in Parliament: 1780–1868* (1980) cover the ground but they are not books for beginners, requiring as they do a thorough knowledge of the economic and political history of the period.

I have left to the last the most recent and the most exhaustive study of the Ricardian model and Ricardo's views on just about everything: S. Hollander, *The Economics of David Ricardo* (1979). This massive book is nothing less than a full-scale frontal attack on the entire body of Ricardian scholarship, arguing that absolutely everybody else has more or less misinterpreted Ricardo. Consider just some of the iconoclastic themes of Hollander's opus: (1) Ricardo's method of analysis was identical to that of Adam Smith; (2) Ricardo's work was basically in the tradition of general equilibrium analysis that runs from Smith to Walras to modern days and, in particular, Ricardo treated pricing and distribution as interdependent; (3) Ricardo's profit theory did not originate in a concern over the Corn Laws and Ricardo never believed, even in his earlier writings, that profits in agriculture determine the general rate of profit in the economy; (4) Ricardo's value theory was essentially the same as that of Marshall in that it paid as much attention to demand as to supply, and Ricardo never regarded the invariable measure of value as an important element in his theory; (5) Ricardo could have established his fundamental theorem that 'profits vary inversely with wages' without his invariable yardstick and frequently took the short-cut of assuming identical capital-labour ratios in all industries to give him the answers he looked for; (6) wages in Ricardo are never conceived as constant or fixed at subsistence levels; (7) Ricardo never assumed a zero price-elasticity of demand for corn, in effect making the demand for agricultural produce a simple function of the size of the population; (8) Ricardo was not a quantity theorist in the conventional sense, nor a rigid Bullionist, nor did he hold a monetary theory that was very different from that of Adam Smith; (9) Ricardo did not predict a rising rental share, nor did he ever commit himself to any clear-cut predictions about any economic variable, least of all the rate of profit; and (10) Ricardo was never seriously concerned about the possibility of class conflict between landowners, on the one hand, and workers and capitalists, on the other. I believe that every one of these ten assertions is false but readers will have to consult the book and to make up their own minds. Ample ammunition for this nail-biting exercise is provided by D.P. O'Brien: 'Ricardian Economics and the Economics of David Ricardo', *OEP*, November, 1981; S. Hollander, 'A Response to Professor O'Brien', *ibid.*, March, 1982; D.P. O'Brien, 'Ricardian Economics', *ibid.*

The discussion of Sraffa's book is taken from my *Cambridge Revolution. Success or Failure?* (1974), which contains references to other attempts to explain Sraffa's meaning. A simple exposition of Sraffa in the language of Marx by M.C. Howard and J.E. King, *The Political Economy of Marx* (1975), pp. 149–60, may be helpful to some readers. For doubts that Sraffa's 'standard commodity' is indeed the solution of Ricardo's puzzle about the 'invariable measure of value', see Caravale and Tosato, *Ricardo and the Theory of Value, Distribution, and Growth*, chap. 3; N-P. Ong, 'Ricardo's Invariable Measure of Value and Sraffa's "Standard Commodity"', *HOPE*, Summer, 1983; and M.C. Howard, 'Ricardo's Analysis of Profit: An Evaluation in Terms of Piero Sraffa's Production of Commodities By Means of Commodities', *MeEc*, September, 1981.

Sraffa's *Production of Commodities By Means of Commodities* has become in recent years the basis of a far-reaching reinterpretation of the entire history of economic thought. The economic thinking of the last 200 years, we are told, reveals two great branches, a general equilibrium branch leading down from Jevons, Walras and Marshall to the Arrows, Debreus and Samuelsons of today, in which all the relevant economic variables are mutually and simultaneously determined, and a Ricardo–Marx–Sraffa branch in which distribution takes priority over pricing because economic variables are causally determined in a sequential chain starting from a pre-determined real wage. Books like M. Dobb, *Theories of Value and Distribution Since Adam Smith* (1973, and in paperback), J.T. Young, *Classical Theories of Value: From Smith to Sraffa* (1978), A. Roncaglia, *Sraffa and the Theory of Prices* (1978), and V. Walsh and H. Gram, *Classical and Neo-Classical Theories of General Equilibrium* (1980), all represent variations of this theme, which, I must say, is an exaggeration so gross as to be positively misleading. For some antidotes to this way of interpreting the history of economic thought, see Hutchison, *On Revolutions and Progress in Economic Knowledge*, chap. 9, and S. Hollander, 'On the Substantive Identity of the Ricardian and Neo-Classical Conceptions of Economic Organizations: the French Connection in British Classicism', *CJE*, November, 1982.

5

Say's law and classical monetary theory

SAY'S LAW OF MARKETS

In an economy with an advanced division of labour, the means normally available to anyone for acquiring goods and services are the power to produce equivalent goods and services. Production increases not only the supply of goods but, by virtue of the requisite cost payments to the factors of production, also creates the demand to purchase these goods. 'Products are paid for by products' in domestic as much as in foreign trade; this is the gist of Say's Law of Markets. From such an innocent notion has come the furore that has not quite died out even now.

The assertion that 'products are paid for by products' is by no means trivial. In one sense, it is the beginning of sound thinking in macroeconomics. It is one thing to speak of one industry producing 'too little' or 'too much' in terms of its independently given demand and supply curves: the demand curves for an industry is derived from the incomes generated by all other industries and is given independently of its own supply. But we cannot speak in the same sense of an entire economy producing too little or too much because aggregate demand and aggregate supply are not independent of each other. The demand for the output of any one industry must increase in real terms when the supplies of all industries increase, since these are precisely what generate demand for that industry's products. Say's Law, therefore, warns us not to apply to macroeconomic variables propositions derived from microeconomic analysis. While it is possible for a particular good to be produced in excess relative to all other goods, it is impossible for all goods to be produced in relative excess.

We seem to be talking about words: one must not *say* 'general overproduction' or 'general underproduction' for that is a logical impossibility. But, of course, it is only a logical impossibility in a barter economy. Overproduction must be relative to something and, by talking of all goods in an economy without mentioning money, we have excluded anything relative to which goods can be produced in excess. An oversupply of one particular product means an under-demand for it in terms of all other products, for the supply of other products given in exchange for it represents the demand for this product; excess supply of one good necessarily means excess demand for at least one other good. Hence, in a barter economy there can be no such thing as an excess of supply over demand for all goods. But in a monetary economy a general excess supply of *commodities* is a logical possibility, for it simply implies that there is an excess demand for money. If Say's Law is meant to be applicable to the real world, therefore, it states the impossibility of an excess demand for money. 'Impossibility' in this case cannot mean logical impossibility. It must mean that the demand for money cannot be permanently in excess because this is a situation of disequilibrium. Before deciding just what Jean Baptiste Say himself did mean, we have to nail down the notion of equilibrium in the money market. Having done this, the role of Say's Law in classical theory becomes much simpler to explain.

1. Say's Identity

Assume that there are n goods in a closed economy. If we select any one of the n goods to be a *numéraire* by setting its price identically equal to unity and expressing all other prices in terms of it, there will be $n-1$ exchange ratios or relative prices to be determined. For example, imagine that x_1 is wheat, x_2 apples, and x_3 oranges, and that 2 apples exchange for 1 unit of wheat $(x_2/x_1 = 2)$ and 1 orange for 2 units of wheat $(x_3/x_1 = 1/2)$. Relative prices will be the reciprocals of these exchange ratios, so that $p_2/p_1 = \frac{1}{2}$ and $p_3/p_1 = 2$. In that case, it must be true that 4 apples will exchange for 1 orange $(p_3/p_2 = p_3/p_1 \cdot p_1/p_2 = 4)$. The complete set of exchange ratios for our 3-commodity system is given directly by 2 exchange ratios and the identity of the *numéraire*, which in this case is wheat. The *numéraire* may be set equal to unity or to any other specified number, say, a specified number of dollars. The fact remains that this kind of money serves only as an abstract unit of account; it may exist in a physical sense, but it need not, and trade has all the characteristics of barter. No one holds this sort of money as money and no one desires to hold it. This kind of accounting money is quite different from circulating money, which people do want to hold in an actual monetary economy because it serves as a store of value as well as a unit of account.

In an economy in which only accounting money is used – the medium of exchange being an arbitrary commodity like any other – the total value of all goods demanded is always identically equal to the total value of all goods supplied. Summing over all the n goods (commodities plus money) demanded and supplied, this identity can be written as

$$\sum_{i=1}^{n} p_i D_i \equiv \sum_{i=1}^{n} p_i S_i.$$

This identity (conventionally called Walras' Law) simply states the *logical* impossibility of oversupply of all goods in a 'barter' economy where money is only accounting money. However, as soon as we have one good acting not only as a medium of exchange but also as a store of value, the amount demanded of the $n-1$ commodities will be equal to the total value of the $n-1$ commodities supplied only if the demand for money (D_n) is equal to the supply of money (S_n). We substitute an equality sign for the identity sign and write

$$\sum_{i=1}^{n-1} p_i D_i = \sum_{i=1}^{n-1} p_i S_i$$

if and only if $D_n = S_n$. This follows from the fact that the total demand for money is equal to the value of all the commodities offered in exchange for money:

$$D_n = p_1 S_1 + p_2 S_2 + \ldots + p_{n-1} S_{n-1} = \sum_{i=1}^{n-1} p_i S_i.$$

And the total supply of money is equal to the value of all the commodities demanded with money:

$$S_n = p_1 D_1 + p_2 D_2 + \ldots + p_{n-1} D_{n-1} = \sum_{i=1}^{n-1} p_i D_i.$$

During a specified time period, therefore, any difference between the demand and the supply of commodities must reveal itself as a positive or negative excess flow demand for money – either $D_n > S_n$ or $D_n < S_n$. An excess supply of all commodities *means* an excess demand for money. If ED_i stands for excess demand for commodities, ES_i for excess supply of commodities, and ED_n for excess demand for money then,

$$\sum_{i=1}^{n-1} p_i D_i - \sum_{i=1}^{n-1} p_i S_i \equiv \sum_{i=1}^{n-1} ED_i \equiv \sum_{i=1}^{n-1} ES_i \equiv ED_n.$$

What meaning has the phrase 'excess demand for money'? It means that people want to add to their stock of cash balances in the current period and this they can do only by demanding fewer goods than are being supplied. We now see that to assert the *logical* impossibility of general overproduction in a monetary economy is tantamount to asserting that the vector $ED_n \equiv 0$: people hold the amount of money in existence in the form of cash balances and never want to alter these balances by financing a purchase out of them or by using the proceeds from a sale to add to them. Following current practice, we will call this strong version of Say's Law 'Say's Identity'.

Say's Identity states that the money market is always in equilibrium because, regardless of prices, people supply commodities only to use the money received to demand other commodities 'immediately'. It may not be apparent at first glance how strong an assumption this is. It implies that a change in the level of prices in no way disturbs the relations between commodity markets and the money market – the marginal rate of substitution of commodities for money is by definition equal to zero. This, in turn, implies that commodity markets themselves are undisturbed: a change in the price level never leads to intercommodity substitution.

Say's Identity can be translated into the so-called 'homogeneity postulate': the excess demand functions for commodities depend only on relative prices and not on the absolute price level, or, in mathematical jargon, the demand functions for commodities are 'homogeneous of degree zero in money prices'. Homogeneous functions have the property that if each of the variables in the function is multiplied by a constant, the total function is increased by some power of that constant. The degree of a homogeneous function denotes the value of the power by which the constant is raised. For example, for a homogeneous function $f(xy)$ and a constant = 2,

zero degree: $f(2x,2y) = 2^0 f(x,y) = f(x,y)$

first degree: $f(2x,2y) = 2^1 f(x,y) = 2f(x,y)$

second degree: $f(2x,2y) = 2^2 f(x,y) = 4f(x,y)$,

or, in general, $f(\lambda x,\lambda y) = \lambda^m f(x,y)$, where λ is any arbitrary positive constant and m is the degree of the homogeneous function. We have already encountered, without saying so, first-degree homogeneous functions in the form of production functions obeying the condition of constant returns to scale: double the inputs x and y, and output is just doubled. Here, however, $f(x,y)$ is a demand function of a commodity whose price is x, the prices of all other goods being represented by y. If this demand function is homogeneous of degree zero, the doubling of prices leaves the amount demanded of that commodity unchanged. This is easy to show. Given a homogeneous zero-degree demand function for x, and letting $y, \ldots z$ represent the prices of all goods other than x, we have $D_x = f(\lambda x,\lambda y, \ldots \lambda z)$. Putting $\lambda = (1/x)$, we have $D_x = f(1, y/x, \ldots z/x)$. The function of z independent variables has been replaced by an equivalent function in which the dependent variables are ratios, of which there are $z - 1$. These ratios are relative prices and the demand function for x varies only with the $z - 1$ relative prices, not with the z absolute prices. Notice that in effect we are right back to accounting money, with x playing the role of the *numéraire*. Obviously, if there is only accounting money in the system, all demand functions are homogeneous of degree zero in absolute money prices because there are really no such things as absolute money prices.

In a world in which Say's Identity holds, money is a 'veil' which can be lifted without affecting the analysis of relative prices. But, surely, this is true only because we have created a money economy and then imposed upon it a condition that equates it in operation to a barter economy? In a barter economy, people would never change their money balances because there are none. To introduce money but to abstract from its store-of-value function does not get us any further. Why then all the rigmarole about Say's Identity? The classical economists frequently asserted the impossibility of general over-production in a monetary economy; Say's Identity spells out the meaning of such assertions. But before we ask whether Say, Ricardo, and John Stuart Mill actually held Say's Identity, we need to consider the role of monetary theory in an economy where $ED_n \equiv 0$.

2. Dichotomization of the Pricing Process

To say that the market for a product is always in equilibrium, that excess demand for it is identically equal to zero, is to imply that the price of the product is indeterminate. Whatever the forces that determine that price, they are nonmarket forces. Therefore, Say's Identity, which asserts that the money market is always in equilibrium, leaves the value of money indeterminate. Mathematically, this indeterminacy is the result of not having enough economically meaningful equations to solve for the given unknowns. With n goods, we have n known demand and supply functions. Actually, only $n-1$ of these functions are independent. Given $n-1$ of these functions, the nth function is completely determined: any set of prices that satisfies the $n-1$ functions necessarily satisfies the nth: by Walras' Law, we can always eliminate one equation. So we have $n-1$ unknown goods prices, or $n-2$ unknown relative prices of commodities plus an unknown value of money, and $n-2$ known excess demand functions for commodities plus a known excess demand function for money. But the latter is not a genuine equation for by Say's Identity $ED_n \equiv 0$. And so we have only $n-2$ equations to determine $n-1$ unknowns; the system is indeterminate.

This is the basis of Patinkin's famous charge in modern times that both the classical and the neoclassical economists 'dichotomized the pricing process': they determined relative prices in commodity markets and absolute prices in the money market, which necessarily assumes that the money stock in the hands of the public remains invariant regardless of prices. But if people do have a demand for nominal money holdings because receipts and payments cannot be perfectly synchronized – the transactions motive for holding cash – or because of uncertainty about the future – the precautionary and speculative motives – it is a demand that will vary with every change in the value of money or the price level; it is a demand for *real* balances. The 'missing equation' we spoke of above is something like the Cambridge equation:

$$D_n = \kappa \sum_{i-1}^{n-1} p_i S_i = M,$$

where κ is the proportion of the total supply of goods measured in money that people will want to hold as cash balances and M is the supply of money.

The Cambridge κ is formally identical to Fisher's $1/V$ [but see chapter 15, section 2]: we can say that people, on the average, want to hold a certain proportion, say, $\kappa = \frac{1}{12}$ of their total transactions T, or we can say that M turns over 12 times a year, $V = 12$. The former expresses the 'rest theory', while the latter expresses the 'motion theory' of the velocity of money. In either case, the idea is that if prices rise, people will seek to add to their cash balances to compensate them for the reduction that has taken place in the real value of these balances. This means that they increase the quantities of the commodities or services they supply and reduce the quantities they demand. The demand functions for commodities alter because of the increase in absolute prices and 'the homogeneity postulate' ceases to hold.

3. Say's Identity and the Quantity Theory of Money

We now take the last step in the long story of spelling out the implications of Say's Identity. The pure Lockean version of the quantity theory of money – the value of money is determined by the quantity of money in circulation and by nothing else – implies Say's Identity, and vice versa. Indeed, the quantity theory was the chief element making for a 'dichotomization of the pricing process'. The merit of the quantity theory had been to demonstrate that money as such does not constitute wealth; in focusing exclusive attention on the medium-of-exchange function of money, however, it led to a neglect of the interdependence between commodity and money markets deriving from the function of money as a store of value.

The theory may be taken to mean that in *equilibrium* $MV = PT$ or $M/P = T/V$. With Locke, the constancy of the ratio M/P, implying the strictly proportional variations in the stock of money and the level of prices, demoted this equality to an identity. People were said to demand a given amount of real balances for transaction purposes, that is, M/P: 'Every man must have at least so much money, or so much timely recruits, as may in hand, or in a short distance of time, satisfy his creditor who supplies him with the necessaries of life, or of his trade', wrote Locke in 1691. This would seem to say that a stable demand for active money balances preserves a certain proportion of the quantity of money to the volume of trade. But the unwillingness to admit that M and P could vary independently implied that every increase in the volume of transactions was simply absorbed by a change in the velocity of circulation. Similarly, an increase in the stock of money was apparently always absorbed by a change in the level of prices without any relation to transactions in commodity markets. In other words, assertions to the effect that the price level is entirely determined by the stock of money, that M and P always vary proportionately, and that T is determined solely by real forces are tantamount to denying any motive for holding cash balances, even the transactions motive, and end up by treating money as if it were accounting money. It is only when money has no function other than serving as a medium of exchange that absolute prices have nothing whatever to do with what happens in commodity markets.

Since the value of money is a relationship between the stock of money on the one hand and the supply of all commodities on the other, one of them cannot be described as *the* determinant of the relationship. All factors influencing MV/T determine the price level. However, in the anxiety to deny any monetary influences on the volume of trade, many early quantity theorists sought comfort in the doctrine that the level of prices is determined by M alone and, in so doing, they effectively dichotomized the pricing process, denied any reason for holding money as a store of value and committed themselves in effect to Say's Identity.

4. Say's Equality

We have now amassed all the pieces with which to categorize classical monetary theory. Is it true that the classical economists held Say's Identity? We have seen that statements denying that there are any reasons for holding money – that money is only a medium of exchange, that money is a veil because relative prices are exclusively determined by real forces, that supply automatically creates its own demand irrespective of the price level, that absolute prices always vary in proportion to the quantity of money – are all expressions of Say's Identity. Many classical economists did in fact say such things: we would have no difficulty in culling numerous assertions of this kind from the writings of Ricardo, McCulloch, Senior, Torrens, James Mill, and John Stuart Mill. But before we leap to the conclusion that they were guilty of dichotomizing the pricing process, we must distinguish between blanket assertions about the unimportance of money as such, when an author is not aware of the logical implications of such a statement, and explicit analyses of the problem of falling or rising prices in a monetary economy.

We know that every one of the classical economists was aware of the occurrence of business depressions. Ricardo wrote a special chapter on the setbacks to trade in the postwar period and contemplated the possibility that technical change might give rise to unemployment. His followers lived through the slumps of 1825, 1836, and 1847, and each one of them recognized that a free market economy is subject to periodic fluctuations in business activity. Whatever Say's Law meant to them, it was not that the level of prices in the real world cannot fall for reasons other than a change in the quantity of money. Moreover, they were all acquainted with the Cantillon Effect, which denies 'the homogeneity postulate' by asserting that changes in prices produced by cash injections vary with the nature of the injection and, moreover, that changes in absolute prices are almost always associated with alterations in relative prices [see chapter 1, section 8]. Unless they were merely talking nonsense, they could not have meant that aggregate demand is always equal to aggregate supply regardless of variations in prices and that departures from full employment cannot possibly take place. Rather, they were driving at the idea that a perfectly competitive economy always *tends* to full employment.

Depressions cannot be permanent because supply creates its own demand on a micro- and a macroeconomic level through automatic price and interest variations. This proposition has been called 'Say's Equality', asserting in effect that an excess supply of goods or an excess demand for money tends to be self-correcting. If demand proves insufficient to sell all goods at cost-covering prices, including the going rate of profit, prices must fall. The purchasing power of nominal cash holdings will rise, and everyone will find himself holding excess real balances; there is an excess demand for money. In the effort to reduce the level of individual cash holdings, the demand for commodities increases until the excess supply in commodity markets is eliminated. A zero excess demand for money is an equilibrium condition because prices, along with the rate of interest, will continue to fall as long as there is an excess demand for cash. The same argument holds in reverse for a rise in prices owing to a positive excess demand for commodities. 'Supply creates its own demand', therefore, not despite the behavior of prices, but because of them. According to this argument, absolute prices are determined by the same set of forces that determine relative prices: for every set of relative prices there is a corresponding unique absolute price level at which the money market will be in equilibrium. This is true for a closed economy as much as for an open economy, except that for an open economy the price level has the additional task of bringing exports and imports into balance. It is clear, therefore, that Say's Equality does not dichotomize the pricing process.

5. Say's Equality in Classical Writings

The classical economists never spelled out Say's Equality but their writings are replete with references to a vaguely stated process of adjustment by which deviations from full employment tend to be self-correcting. We have already witnessed Ricardo defending Say's Law as valid irrespective of price-interest variations in the very same chapter in which he explains how variations in the rate of interest govern the demand for investment funds [see chapter 4, section 24]. Surprisingly enough, Jean Baptiste Say criticized Ricardo for stating Say's Identity and emphasized the function of the interest mechanism in equilibrating saving and investment. Elsewhere he himself was satisfied with the almost Keynesian assertion the production cannot be increased without generating new income with which additional output can be bought. By the way, he never used the phrase 'supply creates its own demand' to denote his Law of Markets; those words were Keynes's invention and were apparently never used by anyone before Keynes. James Mill and McCulloch discussed the question at various places in their writings, sometimes expressing Say's Identity, sometimes Say's Equality. But the one classical author who gave a really lucid presentation of the problem was John Stuart Mill. In the second essay of his *Unsettled Questions of Political Economy*, published in 1844 but written as early as 1830, he showed, first of all, complete awareness that Say's Identity holds only for accounting money in a barter-type economy:

> In order to render the argument for the impossibility of an excess of all commodities applicable to the case in which a circulating medium is employed, money must itself be considered as a commodity. It must undoubtedly be admitted that there cannot be an excess of all other commodities and an excess of money at the same time.

The 'utility of money', however, consists in the possibility of being able to sell without having to buy and

> ... it may very well occur, that there may be, at some given time, a very general inclination to sell with as little delay as possible, accompanied with a general inclination to defer all purchases as long as possible [an excess demand for money]. This is always actually the case in those periods which are described as periods of general excess. And no one, after sufficient explanation, will contest the possibility of general excess, in this sense of the word.

There follows a detailed explanation of why 'under-supply of money' must be temporary and, while the argument is somewhat loose, the distinction between Say's Identity and Say's Equality could hardly be drawn in clearer terms. Mill does not state the real-balance effect in so many words: for him a fall in absolute prices decreases the public's demand for cash, not because of its effect in raising the real value of cash balances, but because of the expectation that the fall in prices will soon come to an end. Still, an automatic equilibrating mechanism is contemplated. The discussion in Mill's *Principles* on this point is identical in content to the *Essays*. It is true that very early in the *Principles* he argues that 'money, as money, satisfies no want'. This occurs in a section deprecating the mercantilist identification of wealth with money, and Mill immediately proceeds to say that money derives its 'utility' from the fact that it permits a seller to buy 'at the times which suit him best'. The first three sections of the chapter 'Of Excess Supply' restate Say's Identity. It is here that Mill says that 'all sellers are inevitably, and by the meaning of the word, buyers', a statement that Keynes quoted to show that Mill's exposition of Say's Law in no way differed from Ricardo's. But in the fourth section of the chapter, Mill speaks once again of the 'under-supply of money' during a commercial crisis and, elsewhere in the book, he provides a vivid description (but not a theory) of the onset of a slump and the restoration of equilibrium [see chapter 6, section 19].

6. Keynes and Say's Law

When a classical economist asserted the impossibility of 'gluts', he had in mind not periodic crises but secular stagnation. Could the capitalist system absorb the constant increases in productive capacity without breakdown from limits inherent in the system? Say's Equality supplied an affirmative answer to this question: with flexible prices the system does tend to full-capacity equilibrium. The classical economists never established this proposition with any rigor, but they appealed to what is at any rate a perfectly valid comparative static argument.

It was Keynes's contention that a perfectly competitive, 'mature' economy does not in fact tend automatically toward full employment. The inflexibility of wages and prices, the low interest-elasticity of investment demand, the 'liquidity trap', any or all of these might suffice to prevent attainment of full-employment equilibrium. In addition, he might have said, even if Say's Equality is a valid comparative static argument, it fails to demonstrate that a full-employment equilibrium is dynamically attainable: the process of moving toward equilibrium *through time* may displace the equilibrium point itself, so that equilibrium is forever pursued but never attained. But instead of granting the theoretical validity of Say's Equality as far as it goes – and it goes far enough to refute dire predictions of permanent overproduction – and then pointing to the qualifications that deprive it of practical significance in a developed economy, Keynes chose instead to attack Say's Identity, which he ascribed to every economist before him.[1] As a result of Keynes's criticism, Say's Law has been given an importance out of all proportion to its actual role in classical and neoclassical theory.

It must have struck many readers of the *General Theory* as odd that a proposition such as Say's Law that was said to be basic to Marshallian reasoning is covered in Marshall's *Principles* in one paragraph. The Keynesian explanation is that Say's Law was so much orthodox doctrine that Marshall did not bother to explain it. But a much more convincing explanation is that the possibility or impossibility of permanent overproduction was a dead issue by 1890. Instead of asserting that 'if people do not spend their money in one way they will spend it in another', which is one of Keynes's versions of Say's Identity, Marshall declared that 'though men have the power to purchase they may not choose to use it', and left it at that. The failure to pursue the argument may have been misleading but certainly there is no suggestion here that excess demand for money is always and necessarily zero.

---

[1] This explains Keynes's term 'classical economics' as denoting the broad stream of orthodox economics from Smith to Pigou that fell victim to Say's Law. We have been using 'classical economics' in the standard sense to mean all the followers of Adam Smith through J. S. Mill and J. E. Cairnes. The term 'classical economics' was first used by Marx in a peculiar sense to mean the school of political economy, from Petty to Ricardo in England and from Boisguilbert to Sismondi in France, that 'investigated the real relations of production in bourgeois society'.

7. The Direct Mechanism

We must now look a little more closely at the classical conception of Say's Equality. Just what is the mechanism that brings markets once disturbed back to equilibrium? We have already seen that Say's Identity would preclude the need for any monetary theory. Contrariwise, belief in Say's Equality implies concern with the operation of money markets. It is in the realm of classical monetary theory that we must look for the reasoning behind Say's Equality.

Classical monetary theory consists essentially of two strands of thought, both of which relate the quantity of money to the price level: the 'direct mechanism' expounded by Cantillon and Hume and the 'indirect mechanism' first stated by Thornton and then reiterated by Ricardo. It was a commonplace of classical analysis that an increase in the quantity of money affects prices directly through its prior effect on demand: the increase in money receipts generates an increase in the outflow of expenditures because people are satisfied with their existing holdings of cash balances. The 18th-century doctrine that the quantity of money is determined by the 'needs of trade' was based on the recognition that there is a stable demand for working balances. As we have seen, both Hume and Cantillon paid attention to the manner in which a cash injection is disbursed and to the various lags involved in the process. They showed in effect that an increase of money raises prices equiproportionately only if the extra cash is neutrally distributed, that is if everyone's initial money holdings are increased equiproportionately. As Hume put it, imagine everyone's money holdings doubled overnight; prices would begin rising and in this special case would rise until prices had exactly doubled.

This special case has a particular significance in the history of monetary theory and we must establish it with some care. Let us begin by building up the demand curve for nominal money holdings as a function of the level of prices. This demand is made up of a transactions demand for active money balances (M_1) and a demand for inactive money balances or 'hoards' for speculative motives (M_2). We can assume with Locke that the transactions demand curve for money is a rectangular hyperbola (see Figure 5–1). Being a rectangular hyperbola, the product of the abscissa and the ordinate values of every point on the curve is a given constant. But since the ordinate shows the relative price of money – the amount of real income that must be surrendered to acquire one unit of money – and the abscissa the quantity of money demanded, the area of any subtended rectangle shows the real value of the amount of cash balances demanded. In assuming that the transactions demand for cash balances is a rectangular hyperbola, we are saying that people do demand more nominal balances when prices rise, but only in order to preserve the real value of working balances. We now add the demand for inactive balances as functions of the rate of interest. In true Keynesian fashion [see chapter 16, section 1], M_2 is shown as independent of the level of prices (see Figure 5–1). When we sum the two demand curves horizontally, we get D_n, the demand curve for *all* money to hold, which is necessarily steeper than a rectangular hyperbola (if we shift a rectangular hyperbola rightward by a constant amount, it ceases to be a rectangular hyperbola – try it and see).

Thus, the demand curve for nominal money has a steeper slope than a rectangular

Figure 5–1

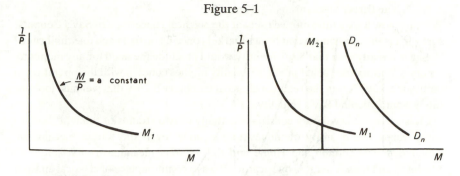

hyperbola: it does not show money and prices varying proportionately. It shows the change in the demand for *nominal* money balances as prices change: each individual demand curve for nominal balances is downward sloping because at higher prices the typical individual will want to hold more nominal *money* balances, but the slope is greater than that of a rectangular hyperbola because at higher prices the typical individual will want to hold less *real* money balances. The precise shape of the curve depends on how the desire to hold real balances competes with the desire to consume commodities. In the normal case, when neither real balances nor commodities are 'inferior goods' – the kind of goods one wants less of, the higher one's income – the individual and therefore the market demand curves for nominal money holdings will slope downward at an elasticity less than unity. A demand curve of unitary elasticity, a rectangular hyperbola, would mean that an individual would want to hold the same amount of real balances when prices fall despite the fact that he is better off. But the typical individual will reduce his nominal balances to buy more goods when prices fall at given levels of real income.

We now superimpose a supply curve of money determined by exogenous forces. Under a gold standard, the money supply would itself be a function of prices but, for the purposes of the present argument, it is convenient to assume modern conditions with the supply of money governed by banking policy. Starting from an equilibrium relationship between money and prices, an intersection point of D_n and S_n at A, let us now double the supply of money and distribute the new money equiproportionately to the initial money endowments of individuals, a so-called 'neutral' increase in M (see Figure 5–2). The demand curve for money will shift to the right (DD'_n), because with more money but the same absolute prices, people will want to buy more commodities and therefore will want to hold more nominal balances to finance their increased transactions. There is now an excess supply of money xy which is identically equal to the excess demand for commodities. The excess demand for commodities drives up prices until prices have doubled at $1/2P$ (notice that if D_n had shifted so far that $xy = 0$, the increase in the quantity of money could not have affected prices). Prices must rise in the same proportion as money, for otherwise someone is holding idle balances he does not want to hold. These would act to drive up prices still further. If A was an equilibrium point, people must have been satisfied

Figure 5–2

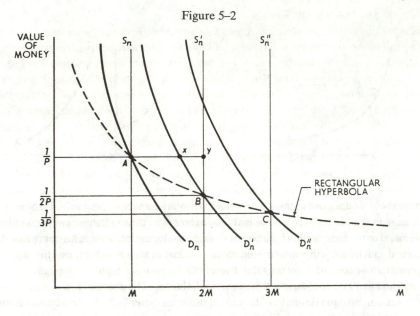

with their real-balance holdings. The supply of money having doubled, prices must double, no more no less, if the value of real balances in the new equilibrium is to be equal to that in the old equilibrium. Thus at intersection B, $2M/P = M/P$, and similarly for intersection C.

Consider now a curve connecting ABC, the locus of demand-supply equilibria. This turns out to be a rectangular hyperbola, showing the effect, *ceteris paribus*, of a neutral increase in the quantity of money on absolute prices. It shows that individuals have no incentive to change their demand for real balances if both the money supply and the price level vary in the same proportion. In equilibrium, the money supply exerts no influence on consumption and investment decisions because all 'real' magnitudes do not change. But that is only true in equilibrium.

To reiterate: we start from an equilibrium relationship between money and prices, introduce a change in one of the independent variables – in this case, the quantity of everyone's nominal money holdings – and show that the system returns to equilibrium with prices rising proportionately to the increase in money. This is typical comparative static reasoning and demonstrates that there is nothing wrong with the quantity theory of money when it is correctly expounded. Our demonstration of the theorem that a proportionate increase in the money holdings of every individual causes prices to rise in the same proportion is borrowed from Patinkin. The theorem was never rigorously stated by the classical economists but it was asserted again and again by Hume, Ricardo, John Stuart Mill, and many others [see chapter 6, section 15], who may be said to have grasped the essence of the argument, including the essence of the assumptions that are required to make it true.

8. The Indirect Mechanism

Now for the indirect mechanism connecting money and prices, the second strand in classical monetary theory. It has been said that the quantity theory of money assigns no explicit role to the rate of interest and that no monetary theory is worth very much if it neglects the interest rate. Now it is true that the Equation of Exchange does not refer to the interest rate, but then the quantity *theory* of money is a far cry from the identity $MV \equiv PT$. In any case, the classical theory of the indirect mechanism connecting M to P refers specifically to the money rate of interest. The indirect mechanism was first stated by Henry Thornton in his *Nature of the Paper Credit of Great Britain* (1802), the greatest single work on monetary theory produced in the classical period, and was then taken over verbatim by Ricardo and Mill. The argument is that monetary equilibrium in an economy with nonmonetary assets exists only when the money rate in the loan market equals the rate of return on capital in commodity markets. A cash injection must come into the loan market via the banking system; the increased supply of loanable funds causes the market rate of interest to fall below the yield of capital; the volume of borrowing rises as the price of investment goods increases and the demand for loans is stimulated. Eventually, the increased demand for loans will catch up with the supply of loans. However, as long as the bank rate remains below the rate of profit on capital, the demand for loans is insatiable. Soon the demand for loans overtakes the supply and the bank rate will begin to rise again. If the real rate of return on capital has remained invariant, equilibrium is restored only when the bank rate has returned to its previous level. Prices are higher, but the rate of interest is as before. Ergo, in equilibrium, the rate of interest is independent of the quantity of money in circulation.

This theory of the two rates – the natural and the market rate of interest– was independently rediscovered a century later by Wicksell, who was surprised to find that it was an old idea [see chapter 15, section 3]. Ricardo had used it to show that the note issue of the Bank of England can expand beyond all assignable limits provided the bank rate is kept low enough; convertibility of the note issue under gold-standard conditions would deprive the Bank of power to regulate the discount rate, at least below the 5 percent limit of the Usury Laws; inconvertibility, however, in effect gave the Bank the capacity to maintain inflation by artificially depressing the discount rate [see chapter 4, section 27]. Quite apart from that, Thornton's argument emphasizes the connection between money and commodity markets and hence shows that classical theory, fairly interpreted, does not dichotomize the pricing process.

9. Saving, Investment, and Hoarding

In the standard interpretation, the rate of interest in classical economics is determined in the loan market, or what Keynes calls the 'bond market'. The money rate of interest depends on the demand and supply of loanable funds, identified with investment and saving respectively. It was rarely pointed out that investment may be financed out of hoards or out of inflationary bank credit. Ricardo, for one, strenuously denied that 'credit can create capital'. We will examine the notion that inflationary credit expansion cannot foster growth in a moment: it is nothing less than the controversial 'forced saving' doctrine. The idea that investment is never financed out of hoards is much easier to deal with. By 'hoarding' we mean withdrawing money income from current expenditure without diverting it to nonconsumption purposes; in other words, the building up of cash balances. In the classical period, the term was always used in a pejorative sense: only a 'miser' would want to increase his monetary holdings above the minimum required for transactions purposes. Taken strictly, the typical classical comment to the effect that hoarding is 'abnormal' would imply that people never add their savings to cash balances and never finance investment out of cash balances. The excess demand for money is identically equal to zero, and we are back to Say's Identity and the indeterminacy of absolute prices.

In a monetary economy, therefore, savings and investment cannot be always and necessarily equal to the supply and demand for loans. But in equilibrium this will be true because equilibrium is given by the condition that people are satisfied with their cash holdings. It is evident, then, that a consistent interpretation of classical economics implies the denial of the proposition that planned saving is identically equal to planned investment. This kind of statement is simply a Keynesian translation of the language of loanable funds. Since the classical economists held Say's Equality rather than Say's Identity, they must have allowed for the Keynesian possibility that intended saving may not be realized. The 'indirect mechanism' has the virtue of focusing attention on the demand side of the loan market as a function of the rate of interest. For every supply of real saving and bank credit there is a price level that will keep the rate of interest equal to a given rate of return on capital, thus insuring equilibrium in the loan market. Clearly, if intended saving exceeds intended investment, the rate of interest will fall and the price level will rise, working to restore equilibrium. The only difference between this kind of argument and the Keynesian one is that saving according to Keynes is a function of income, whereas in classical analysis saving is a complicated function of the interest rate and the level of prices via the character of investment opportunities. Income variations produce equilibrium in Keynes; price and interest variations produce equilibrium in classical theory. All this is disguised by the fact that the classical economists almost never used the word 'investment' and spoke of 'saving' to denote, not the process, but rather the result of saving, that is, the actual resources saved: with them 'saving' already implies the conversion by way of investment into additional capital equipment. This suggests that saving is actually identified with investment, but this cannot be what they had in mind. It is perfectly true, however, that the failure to spell out equilibrium adjustments often led classical writers to assume the comparative static result at the outset and to argue about relations between variables as if these were always in equilibrium.

Although most classical writers did not explicitly distinguish between saving and lending, on the one hand, and investment and borrowing, on the other, they did not argue that saving and investment alone determine the rate of interest. The loanable-funds theory, with its implication that the rate of interest is influenced by the state of the money market, is contained in Thornton and Ricardo and it is ably expounded in Book III, chapter 23, of J. S. Mill's *Principles* [see chapter 6, section 15]. When John

Stuart Mill defined saving as income 'not consumed by the person who saves it' and hoarding as income 'not consumed at all', we can only infer that 'intended saving' in the modern sense is equivalent to classical saving plus hoarding, for the excess of intended saving over intended investment in modern analysis produces the same economic effects as an increase of hoarding in classical economies.

10. The Real Interest Rate

The market rate of interest in classical theory is not determined by the quantity of money in circulation: the classical economists held a real theory of interest. The interest rate is ultimately determined by the same real forces that govern the rate of profit on capital, for in equilibrium the two rates are equal. This result is really a corollary of the previous argument that a neutral doubling of M will double P. If $2M = 2P$, then people will supply and demand exactly double the value of loanable funds upon which the rate of interest depends. It is the initial excess supply of loans that depresses the rate of interest. When the price level has finally doubled, the *real* quantity of money in the economy is the same, and so the demand and supply of loans interesect at the same interest rate. With costs twice as high, any given investment requires twice as much borrowing to finance it. The rate of return on investment is not affected, for with the doubling of cost goes a doubling of anticipated money returns. When the additional cash has been absorbed into circulation by the price increase, people increase their demand for loans to the same extent that the banks originally increased their supply, and the equilibrium rate is ultimately unchanged.

Figure 5–3

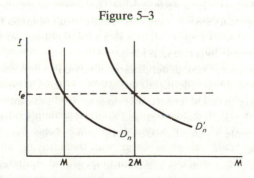

This is the pure logic of the real theory of interest held by the classical school. The market demand curve of money with respect to the interest rate is negatively inclined, but the market-equilibrium curve, the locus of all demand-supply equilibria, is always horizontal (see Figure 5–3). An individual will demand more money when the rate of interest falls, everything else including absolute prices remaining the same. But if he holds money simply to enable him to conduct a certain *real* value of transactions, he will want to hold exactly twice as much money at a given rate of interest when prices have doubled. Aggregate this result for all individuals and we reach the classical conclusion of the invariance of interest rates to the money supply.

11. Forced Saving

In Keynesian theory, doubling the money stock does not double the price level and does affect the rate of interest. This is because Keynes's demand function for money, in particular his speculative demand, contains a 'money illusion', a tendency to react to changes in money balances, even when they are not associated with changes in real balances. Whenever there is money illusion in either the money market, the loan market, or commodity markets, the classical theorems do not hold.

Likewise, if the monetary increase is not distributed equiproportionately to the initial money holdings, the argument loses all semblance of precision. Suppose the extra cash flows into the hands of capitalists with relatively low propensities to consume. This rise in prices will then alter the composition of total output in favour of investment and cause the rate of interest to decline permanently. This, of course, is the Cantillon Effect. The classical economists were, therefore, perfectly aware that certain kinds of cash injection can 'create capital' and thus permanently lower the rate of interest. All such exceptions come under the heading of 'forced saving', a possibility generally admitted, though with various degrees of emphasis, by all the classical writers.

The doctrine of forced saving was one of the many theoretical contributions of the Bullionist Controversy. The central idea is very simple: suppose there is an excess supply of loans in a fully employed economy resulting either from a cash injection or the drawing-down of idle balances, so that investment is no longer limited by voluntary saving decisions of income recipients; the market rate of interest falls and the demand for investment funds rises. But if the capital stock is already utilized at capacity, where do the real resources required for investment come from? If they do not come from voluntary saving, they must be the result of involuntary saving. And this is exactly what does happen. The extra capital formation is 'forced' out of fixed-income recipients by a rise in prices.

Thornton called forced saving 'defalcation of revenue'. Bentham called it 'forced frugality'. Malthus dubbed it 'fictitious capital'. Mill labeled it 'forced accumulation'. Since Mill, it has been called 'enforced saving' by Wicksell, 'automatic stinting' or 'imposed lacking' by D. H. Robertson, and 'real levies' or 'doctoring of contracts' by Pigou. All these writers agreed about the meaning of the doctrine, at least in its monetary aspects.

The only major writer who was reluctant to accept the thesis was Ricardo. After attacking the Bank for issuing notes in excess, he was not likely to be sympathetic to the notion that inflation is sometimes capable of increasing investment in real terms. Still, he admitted that an increase in paper money may redistribute income to entrepreneurs by means of wages lagging behind prices; this is not quite the same thing as 'forced saving' because here the increase in saving is perfectly voluntary. Ricardo relegated forced saving proper to the short run, arguing that the squeeze on consumption causes consumer goods prices to rise, thus limiting the degree to which the excess supply of funds actually materializes in additional real investment. Moreover, as money incomes rise in the process of inflation, increased consumption demand will eventually transfer resources back again to the consumer goods sector.

Whether Ricardo was justified in his skepticism it would be difficult to say. It is apparent that the forced-saving doctrine is the more convincing, the more elastic the supply of goods, the more elastic the supply of productive services, the more gradual the cash injection, and the greater the number of fixed-income recipients. Generally, inflation promotes growth in real output by absorbing hitherto idle resources into employment. The forced-saving doctrine, restricted as it is to the case of full employment, is probably of very little significance. The fact remains, however, that all the classical economists, including Ricardo, granted the possibility of an effect, however small, upon the long-run rate of interest and hence upon the rate of return to real capital from monetary expansion alone. There was disagreement over the significance of the Cantillon Effect, Ricardo and James Mill minimizing its importance. But there was no dogmatic denial of the partial validity of a monetary theory of interest properly stated.

12. Conclusion

In retrospect it is all too obvious that the confusion about classical monetary theory is solely due to the superficial resemblance between the valid comparative statics assertion that in equilibrium relative prices are unaffected by the quantity of money, when money is injected into the system in an appropriately neutral manner, and statements denying that an influx of money can ever have beneficial effects on output. Even an unqualified statement that the quantity of money has no effect on relative prices did not necessarily mean that the author subscribed to Say's Identity. Both Ricardo and Mill made such assertions in places where they were concerned with relative price determination; elsewhere, sometimes a few pages later, they are found discussing the time path between two equilibria in which relative prices, including the interest rate, *are* disturbed by an injection of cash. It is true that they were not aware, with the possible exception of Mill, of the entire logical structure of the problem and frequently expressed themselves in a misleading manner. But whenever the problem of Say's Equality arose explicitly, it was analyzed in a manner that is at least formally valid, though incomplete.

The Mercantilists held a monetary theory of interest. The classical school held a real theory of interest. Who was right? It is easy to see now that this is really a false issue because the question implies dichotomization of the pricing process. Nevertheless, if the interest rate in question is an equilibrium interest rate, then there can be no doubt that it is largely determined in 'real' markets, not in the money market. Furthermore, the classical theory of interest is more general because it encompasses all the elements of both a real and a monetary theory, while a monetary theory, particularly under a gold standard, leaves the quantity of money itself undetermined and unrelated to commodity markets. It is for good reason that we spoke earlier of the theoretical advance brought about by 'real' analysis [see chapter 1, section 9].

MALTHUS' THEORY OF GLUTS

It has been said that just as free traders give the best arguments for protection, defenders of Say's Law give the best arguments for the possibility of a general glut. Malthus himself never produced a logical refutation of the Law of Markets, probably because he did not really understand the theory at the back of it. If he had merely wanted to argue that gluts are possible and very likely to occur, he had any number of arguments to appeal to. He could have argued that investors are very sensitive to future profit expectations and that a loss of confidence resulting from a bad harvest or an external gold drain is enough to cause them to retain income in the form of idle balances; no doubt, falling prices will eventually restore equilibrium but the process of deflation itself might sap confidence and, in this way, the adjustment could be a long and painful one. Or he could have argued that a sticky bank rate causes the stock of money to lag behind the growing volume of output; this leads to a falling price level – after all, prices did fall steadily in the British economy after 1821 – and since wages are rigid downward or have a floor at the subsistence level, this leads to losses throughout the economy. But Malthus had no truck with any of these explanations for the simple reason that he wanted to demonstrate, not the possibility of *temporary* overproduction, but the possibility of *permanent* overproduction of all commodities. Without exogenous spending by 'unproductive consumers', the process of capital accumulation leads inherently to secular stagnation; this is Malthus' basic argument.

13. Malthus' Case

Malthus made things difficult for himself by rejecting all purely monetary explanations of gluts. Nor did he resort to inflexibility of wages and prices to justify his argument. Worst of all, he assumed, as did all his contemporaries, that saving means 'the conversion of revenue into capital'; saving is a synonym for accumulation. 'No political economist of the present day', he remarked, 'can by saving mean mere hoarding'. An excess supply of loanable funds created by bank credit is presumably absorbed by a fall in the market rate of interest and a rise in the price level; at any rate, Malthus did not dispute the Thornton-Ricardo argument of the 'indirect mechanism'. There is no hint whatever in his writings of the decisive Keynesian break with orthodox analysis, making saving a function of income rather than the rate of interest, so that oversaving is eliminated by a fall in the level of income. Malthus consistently adhered to the Smithian saving-is-spending theorem [see chapter 2, section 14]. Within such a model it would have been difficult to deduce even a temporary lack of effective demand caused by oversaving. As it was, Malthus' aim was more ambitious. At the root of his thinking is a typical underconsumptionist fallacy, and his writings at best represent an important chapter in the long history of this 'underworld' doctrine. To show what is meant, let us digress for a moment to consider the standard arguments of underconsumptionists.

14. The Doctrine of Underconsumption

The underconsumptionist position is that aggregate demand in the private sector of a closed economy is *always* insufficient, or forever threatening to become insufficient, to buy all goods at cost-covering prices. This position has crude and sophisticated versions. The crudest version simply ignores the fact that aggregate demand equals consumption plus investment. It appeals to the fact that most consumers are workers who can never buy back the products they produce because the value of output necessarily exceeds the value of wages paid out. Hence, a certain volume of spending on luxury articles and labour services out of profits and rents is necessary to ensure continued reproduction. Malthus actually used this argument in a few places, but he did not rest his case on it. It is easy to show, of course, that the consumption of capitalists and landlords and the investment of capitalists is precisely what causes consumer goods to be so priced that workers alone can never buy them back. Nevertheless, this does not prevent the total value of output from being exactly equal to total income.

Table 5–1 gives a simple example for a two-sector economy in which workers save nothing and the propertied classes have an average propensity to consume of 0.6. The sales value of consumer goods (80) equals to the consumption expenditures of workers (50) plus the consumption expenditures of capitalists and landlords (30). Since nonlabour income is 50, saving equals investment (20). Consumption (80) + investment (20) = total output (100) = total income. This conclusion holds for a stationary economy in which investment is merely replacement demand for capital goods used up, as much as for a growing economy in which net investment is positive. It holds, among other reasons, because the propertied classes do spend all their receipts; but if they did not, output and income would merely be proportionately lower. Malthus was no doubt influenced by the argument of Cantillon that the spending of rental receipts depends upon the disposition of landlords because rent, unlike wages and profit, is not a necessary expense of production. But as long as landlord spending habits are stable, the failure to spend all rentals causes no deadlock. By itself, instability of spending patterns can explain cyclical fluctuations but not secular stagnation, and it is the latter that concerns us here.

The more sophisticated versions of the underconsumptionist thesis agree that total income is equal to total cost payments in an economy for any given period and as long as investment in every period fills the gap between income and consumption, any given income level can be maintained indefinitely. However, investment not only creates income but also adds to capacity in subsequent periods. If next year's consumption and investment are identical to this year's, excess capacity must appear. The existence of excess capacity discourages investment because it makes it possible for producers to meet existing demand with smaller outlays of capital. As soon as

Table 5–1

	Output of Consumer Goods $	Output of Capital Goods $	Total $
Wages	40	10	50
Profits and rents	40	10	50
Value of output	80	20	100

investment falls, incomes fall, and the slump is on. Now it is true that the fall in income cures the difficulty in time by absorbing capacity. As soon as the economy swings up again, however, the problem reappears. It is clear that what is needed to absorb constantly increasing capacity is constantly increasing incomes. It is not enough for consumption and investment to repeat themselves period after period; they must increase exponentially. Now comes the clinching argument that produces underconsumptionist conclusions. Surely, it is absurd to expect either consumption or investment to rise by a constant percentage amount year after year? For notice that every act of saving tends to cut down the demand for consumer goods, and when these savings are invested, the supply of goods is simultaneously augmented. Paradoxically, it is just when saving and investment are interdependent that the problem seems most intractable. Now we are at the heart of Malthus' position: an underconsumption theory of the oversaving type.

The paradox that saving as such creates trouble is easy to resolve. For one thing it proves too much: it suggests that purchasing power is *always* insufficient to absorb available output and hence would shift the problem to explaining why there are booms at all. Initially, the gap caused by saving is filled by equivalent investment; in the next period the supply of consumer goods rises, but costs usually fall precisely because of the previous investment; this frees purchasing power and permits the absorption of additional output. Still, costs may not fall sufficiently, and hence investment must rise to generate additional purchasing power. We are back to the incredible notion of investment rising by increasing absolute amounts year after year.

The Malthusian oversaving argument is only one version of the underconsumptionist theory. The socialist version holds that stagnation sets in because the share of wages in total income tends to fall as income increases. The Hansen-Keynes version holds that stagnation is the result of declining rates of return on investment. But the core of all these versions is the idea that consumption and investment cannot be expected to increase indefinitely at constant proportional rates of growth.

15. Exponential Growth

The impossibility of exponential growth is so intuitively appealing that most people are surprised that consumption, saving, investment and income have grown at an exponential rate over long periods of time. The saving-income or consumption-income ratio has remained practically constant in advanced economies since 1870 – there is no reliable data, unfortunately, for the earlier period. Since real income has been growing at about 2 percent per annum, investment and consumption must also have grown at 2 percent per annum. Along the trend line, investment and consumption have increased in absolute amounts year after year.

This proves that it can happen but it does not prove that it has to happen. However, we are not trying to prove the impossibility of secular stagnation but rather to disprove the thesis that secular stagnation is inevitable. Investment is indeed capacity-adding but this does not necessarily spell breakdown at some future point. There is always some rate of investment sufficiently high to create demand for the additional output of a previous period's investment. This can be shown by the now familiar Harrod-Domar growth equation. Macroeconomic equilibrium requires that planned saving S equals planned investment I. Dividing by Y = income, we have

$$\frac{S}{Y} = \frac{I}{Y} \equiv \frac{\Delta K}{Y}.$$

Let Δ stand for the increment of income in a period. Then

$$\frac{S}{Y} = \frac{\Delta K}{Y} \frac{\Delta Y}{\Delta Y} \equiv \frac{\Delta Y}{\Delta Y} \frac{\Delta K}{\Delta Y}$$

or, $G = s'/z$, where G is the rate of growth of income, $\Delta Y/Y$, s' is the average propensity to save, S/Y, which is taken to be equal to $\Delta S/\Delta Y$, the marginal propensity to save, and z is the incremental capital-output ratio, $\Delta K/\Delta Y$. So long as all the variables relate to a single time period, z stands for 'the accelerator', ΔY being the independent variable and ΔK the dependent variable, showing the amount of this year's investment induced by a *change* in this year's income. However, if we think of two periods of time, it is possible to treat z as a productivity coefficient, ΔK being the independent and ΔY the dependent variable, showing the increment of next year's income that is produced by this year's increment of capital. Clearly, there is no reason why $I_t = f(\Delta Y_t)$ should be the reciprocal of $\Delta Y_{t+1} = f(I_t)$. In most formulations of the Harrod-Domar model, z is defined as 'the accelerator' but, in Domar's original formulation, z is defined as a productivity coefficient. We will employ both meanings of the incremental capital-output ratio z.

   Now, smooth growth requires that planned saving shall equal planned investment, which in turn requires that additions to productive capacity are fully utilized: if realized investment in any one year is equal to I, capacity in the next year will rise by I/z and income must now grow at the same rate as capacity if investment intentions are to be sustained; so, if there is sufficient demand to maintain full capacity use of the capital stock in any one year, it can be maintained by increasing the rate of investment by I/zY or s'/z percent the next year.

   The argument can be illustrated graphically by a slight elaboration of the ordinary short-run income-determination diagram found in elementary textbooks (Figure 5–4). Assuming that the average and marginal propensities to save are equal, we draw the saving function through the origin. The investment function is drawn in the usual manner to show that $I = f(Y)$ – notice this is not the same thing as the accelerator $I = f(\Delta Y)$ – and the intersection of the two functions determines the equilibrium level of income. Now we superimpose a third function P' depicting the relationship $\Delta Y_{t+1} = f(I_t)$. The slope of P' is $\Delta K/\Delta Y = z =$ a constant. With respect to the saving function, Y is the independent variable; with respect to the P' function, it is the dependent variable; therefore, z is given the meaning of a productivity coefficient.

   Assume that OY_1 is the initial full-capacity income in year 1. This level of income generates a flow of investment $S_1 Y_1 = \Delta K$. In consequence of this investment, productive capacity has increased by an amount $S_1 P_1 = Y_1 Y_2 = \Delta Y$. The incremental

Figure 5–4

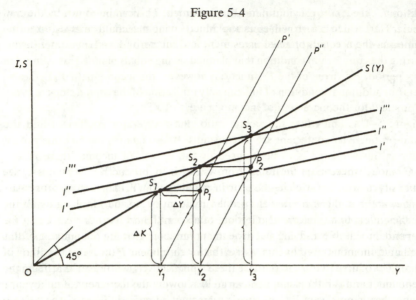

capital-output ratio is given by $S_1Y_1/Y_1Y_2 = z$. Full-capacity income has now increased from OY_1 in year 1 to OY_2 in year 2. Unless income grows to OY_2, excess capacity will develop. With a given saving function, income will grow only if investment raises from I' to I'': here is the accelerator effect. If Y_1Y_2 does induce the shift to I'', we arrive at a new full-capacity income OY_2 at the end of year 2, which generates investment to the amount of S_2Y_2. Drawing a new function P'' parallel to P', because the incremental capital-output ratio is a constant, we find productive capacity has increased by amount $S_2P_2 = Y_2Y_3$, the new full-capacity income being OY_3. It is evident by inspection that $Y_3 - Y_2 > Y_2 - Y_1$, that is, full capacity is growing by increasing absolute amounts, which requires the investment schedule to rise by increasing absolute amounts in order to prevent excess capacity. Income, investment, saving and consumption will all have to grow by increasing absolute amounts, which is precisely what would happen if they grew exponentially. And they have grown exponentially in many countries for over a century.

It will be noticed that the accelerator is not simply the reciprocal of the productivity coefficient, the reason being that one refers to this year's income while the other refers to next year's income. The productivity coefficient, as we have seen, is given by the slope of $P' = S_1Y_1/Y_1Y_2 = S_2Y_2/Y_2Y_3$. The accelerator however, is given by $S_2Y_2/Y_1Y_2 = S_3Y_3/Y_2Y_3$, which is clearly not the reciprocal of the slope of P'. In the usual interpretation of the Harrod-Domar model, z is the accelerator and the P' function is simply ignored. What produces smooth growth in the usual formulation is the interaction of the accelerator and the multiplier. The Keynesian multiplier, the reciprocal of the marginal propensity to save, is present in Figure 5–4: it is simply the reciprocal of the $S(Y)$ line. The multiplier is defined as the value of the ratio $\Delta Y/\Delta I$, that is, the change in income generated by an *increase* in investment. Thus, when I'

shifts to I'', the multiplier multiplies this increment of investment into additional income Y_2Y_3, which in turn generates unplanned saving that could be invested; at the same time, the accelerator accelerates Y_2Y_3 into further induced investment, thus ensuring the equilibrium condition that planned saving equals planned investment in every period. By virtue of the P' function, however, the income-path $Y_1Y_2Y_3$ also meets our additional condition of full-capacity utilization of the capital stock in every period.

Figure 5–4 assumes that the saving ratio, the accelerator coefficient and the capital-productivity coefficient are all constants. It also ignores the fact that not all additional investment has to be induced by the growth of income: there is also 'autonomous' investment resulting from changes in productive techniques, the growth of scientific knowledge, the growth of population, in short, all reasons other than income that might increase the propensity to invest; furthermore, autonomous government expenditures are also left out of account. But Figure 5–4 can easily be generalized to allow for saving and investment functions that are not linear and that contain autonomous components, as well as for curvilinear P functions that show a declining productivity of capital. All these qualifications will mean that income, investment, saving and consumption can grow at lower rates to preserve equilibrium: it makes exponential growth look even easier than it looks in Figure 5–4.

The upshot of this digression into modern growth theory is not to deny the very possibility of secular stagnation but simply to show that it is not necessarily inevitable: nothing whatever excludes either consumption or investment or both from growing by equal percentage amounts for ever and ever.

Furthermore, recalling the earlier distinction between Keynesian and Marxian unemployment [see chapter 1, section 4], it is clear that stagnation in Malthus' day was a rather different matter from stagnation in the 20th century. The problem then was not oversaving but undersaving. When secular saving rates are deficient relative to the capital requirements that would absorb a growing population into employment, and that was the situation facing the British economy after Waterloo, saving is indeed a virtue and not a vice. It was an inappropriate time in history to decry oversaving and to advocate a lower rate of capital accumulation. Thus, whatever we may conclude about the real dangers of stagnation in the 20th century, it hardly induces a more sympathetic attitude to Malthus' theory.

The development of the British economy between the death of Malthus (1834) and the publication of John Stuart Mill's *Principles* (1848) threw up many new economic problems that could not be analyzed by a mere extension of the traditional Ricardian tools. Among these were the growth of foreign investments, accompanied by increasing speculation in foreign securities and the rise of emigration to the New World in sufficient numbers to affect domestic labour markets. Ricardo had attacked the fear of excess capital at home with the aid of Say's Law of Markets and had never seriously considered the possibility that emigration might be required to relieve the Malthusian pressure of population upon the means of subsistence: free trade and free trade alone would suffice to prevent the rate of profit from declining and, thereby, create the conditions for further economic advance. By the 1840s, however, a number of economists began to moot the doctrine that Britain was suffering from a chronic tendency to oversave and that a policy of capital exports and emigration might eliminate the recurrent slumps to which she has been subjected ever since Waterloo. In short, something not unlike the modern Keynes-Hansen thesis of 'the mature economy' made its appearance in the second quarter of the 19th century. Surprisingly enough, Mill's authoritative restatement of the Ricardian orthodoxies in 1848 included support for Edward Gibbon Wakefield's elaborate scheme of State-supported emigration. In defending planned colonization, however, Mill minimized the stagnationist line of thought implicit in Wakefield's arguments and carefully expounded Say's Law so as to deny, not the possibility of alternating booms and slumps, but rather the possibility of breakdown and permanent deficiency of aggregate demand from causes inherent in a market economy. In so doing, he popularized the prescriptions of the colonizers, while glossing over the theory on which they were based. The mass migrations of the seventies and early eighties were largely unaided by the State, and far more people went to America than to the underpopulated British colonies. In consequence public interest in colonization faded away and with it concern over the problem of redundant capital and labour.

16. What Malthus Actually Said

Book I of Malthus' *Principles*, which is devoted to value and distribution theory, makes much more difficult reading than Book II, which deals specifically with the question of general overproduction. Ostensibly, it is a typical Ricardian treatment, with an emphasis on the perfect measure of value, the theory of differential rent and the relation between profits and wages sharing a total product-less-rent. At various points, however, Malthus takes issue with Ricardo so as to bring out the pivotal role of effective demand. He distinguishes between Ricardo's 'extent of demand' as the quantity actually bought on the market at a given price and the 'intensity of demand' as 'the will and power to make a greater sacrifice in order to obtain the object wanted'. The purpose of this distinction was to clarify the meaning of 'gluts', denoting an excess of supply relative to the intensity of demand, which causes price to fall below cost. The implied distinction between a shift and a movement along a demand curve, however, is not pushed further. Malthus shows no interest in demand theory as such and made no substantive use of his terminological clarification. He likewise rejected Ricardo's measure of value and went back to Smith's standard, the number of wage units that a product can command in exchange. His defense of this standard of value is extremely confusing, and his preference for it seems based on little else than that it permitted him to define a 'general glut' as a case in which the number of wage units currently commanded by present output falls short of the quantity of the direct and indirect labour embodied in its production. Throughout Book I, Malthus seems to be trying to break away from the Ricardian postulates, while in fact remaining thoroughly imprisoned in them.

Very early in the *Principles*, and again in the concluding chapter of the work, we meet one of Malthus' favourite subsidiary arguments, to the effect that spending on productive labour (*read*: investment) necessarily creates a deficiency of effective demand. Since workers receive less than the value of the product they produce, 'no power of consumption on the part of the labouring classes can ever alone furnish an encouragement to the employment of capital'. Nor can the gap be filled by the demand of capitalists for 'they have, by the supposition, agreed to be parsimonious, and by depriving themselves of their usual conveniences and luxuries to save from their revenue and add to their luxuries'. It followed that there would be a general glut of commodities unless purchasing power were sustained by additional 'unproductive consumption' on the part of some group other than capitalists and workers. This is the saving-defeats-itself fallacy mentioned earlier.

But the argument that Malthus seems to have in mind most of the time is the case of an increase of saving and investment, with profits at a minimum and the supply of labour given in the short run. We will recall that the Ricardian theory of the falling rate of profit is essentially based on the notion of capital and labour growing at the same rate in relation to a limited supply of land, with result that the costs of producing wage goods rises. At one point in his book [see chapter 4, section 24], Ricardo speculated briefly on the effects of a sudden increase in capital accumulation with population lagging behind; this, he admitted, would produce a fall in the rate of profit unconnected with a rising cost of producing wheat and, in the short run, this situation would correspond to a 'universal glut'. In Ricardo's argument, the glut is temporary because the increase in wages elicits population growth, which raises short-run profits once again. Malthus, however, stresses the inelastic supply of labour in the short run: 'an increase of labourers cannot be brought into the market, in consequence of a particular demand, till after a lapse of sixteen or eighteen years'. The argument is then immediately generalized: 'a country is always liable to an increase in the quantity of the funds for the maintenance of labour faster than the increase of population'. Whenever this happens, increased wage rates put capitalists in a price-cost squeeze and investment falls off. On the other hand the increased wages do not add to effective demand because workers prefer leisure to increased consumption. In this way, Malthus thought he had shown that 'an inordinate passion for accumulation must inevitably lead to a supply of commodities beyond what the structure and habits of such a society will permit to be profitably consumed'.

It is perfectly true that if the propensity to save in an economy is such that the realization of saving and investment plans requires a rate of growth of income in excess of the rate of growth of the labour force that growth path cannot be long sustained. But Malthus seems to be pleading a short-run version of this kind of secular oversaving. It is a curious argument indeed for the author of the *Essay on the Principle of Population* but, quite apart from that, it made little sense in an economy in which as much as 6–10 percent of the population was on public relief. The one factor that was not in short supply at the time was labour.

The central idea to which Malthus returns again and again is that 'saving, pushed to excess, would destroy the motive to production'. Even if he meant that too much planned saving as distinct from planned investment would destroy 'the motive to production', his argument would be suspect under the circumstances then prevailing. But 'the principle of saving' for Malthus always means 'saving from the stock which might have been destined for immediate consumption, and adding it to that which is to yield a profit; or in other words, . . . the conversion of revenue into capital'. And so his conclusion is that too high a propensity to save *and* to invest causes trouble by encroaching upon consumption. This fallacious argument is summed up in a nutshell in the last pages of his book, where he decries the tendency 'to recommend saving' while 'under-stocked employments' are 'glutting the markets of Europe'. 'As soon as the capitalists can begin to save from steady and improving profits, instead of from diminished expenditure', he observes, 'we may then begin safely and effectively to recover our lost capital by the usual process of saving a portion of our increased revenue to add to it'.

Malthus does occasionally affirm, like Ricardo, that there are no secular limits to the expansion of aggregate output. 'The question of a glut', Malthus noted, 'is exclusively whether it may be general, as well as particular, and not whether it may be permanent as well as temporary'. In short, general gluts are possible but all gluts, whether general or partial, are temporary in nature. If we take such occasional remarks seriously, and interpret Malthus charitably as attempting to develop a dynamic theory of the optimum rate of saving, we may interpret his attacks on Say's Law as an attack on the Smithian doctrine that increased quantities of savings necessarily promote the growth rate of an economy. In so doing, we can make sense of Malthus but only at the expense of making nonsense of the vehement Ricardian dismissal of the Malthusian theory of general gluts. In the thousands of words that Malthus wrote on the question of general gluts, there are not more than a dozen that clearly express a theory of oversaving where saving is not identical to investment. The bulk of Malthus' words instead point directly to permanent and not just temporary disequilibrium. In that sense, John Stuart Mill was perfectly right to depict Malthus and Sismondi in his *Principles* as believing in the possibility of secular stagnation [see chapter 6, section 16].

Malthus' policy recommendations are designed to slow down the rate of capital accumulation and to encourage 'unproductive consumption' on the part of landlords. His earlier defense of the Corn Laws, therefore, fitted in very nicely with the reasoning of his general treatise. He suggested public work schemes to alleviate unemployment, but on grounds that bear no resemblance to Keynes's proposals. In private correspondence, Ricardo and Malthus had discussed the advisability of putting idle labour to work on public projects like road building. Ricardo, of course, did not think that public roads would remedy the postwar depression: if capital were being used to capacity, spending on public works would simply raise the demand for consumer goods; inflation would then transfer resources from the private to the public sector without affecting the total volume of employment. Though this sounds like the discredited 'Treasury View' of the 1930s, it had some merit in the kind of economy in which Ricardo lived. Malthus, at any rate, agreed with Ricardo, adding that public projects created no additional spending. In his *Principles*, Malthus swung over to public works spending as a temporary measure of relief for unemployment. The proposal had two objections, he noted. It might prevent labour from 'gradually accommodating itself to a reduced demand'. This he thought could be corrected by giving low wages. Second, it would require an increase of taxation to finance the project, and this could well have the effect of reducing private investment. This objection, however, was precisely the virtue of public works for Malthus: 'The objection to employing a large sum in this way, raised by taxes, would not be its tendency to diminish the capital employed by productive labour; because this, to a certain extent, is exactly what is wanted.'

17. Ricardo and Malthus
The debate between Ricardo and Malthus on the possibility of general gluts would never have caused the confusion it did if both participants had made up their minds as to what Say's Law really implied. Ricardo did not regard the postwar depression as a harbinger of secular stagnation, as Malthus most certainly did. 'You often appear to me to contend', wrote Ricardo to Malthus, 'not only that production can go on so far without an adequate motive, but that it has actually done so lately, and that we are now suffering the consequences of it in stagnation.' As a result, Ricardo was driven to insist on Say's Law as fully operative at every moment in time; this in itself suggests that he thought of Say's Law, not as denying the possibility of depression, but as affirming the long-run tendency of the economy to full employment equilibrium. But instead of spelling out the process that would lead to automatic absorption of a constantly expanding output, Ricardo took refuge in the dogmatic assertion of Say's Identity. Malthus failed to challenge Say's Law effectively and provided no incentive to put the case correctly. Moreover, rarely mentioned, but always immediately below the surface of discussion, was the question of political bias. In Malthus, so far from the interests of landlords being always opposed to the rest of the community, economic prosperity is made to depend upon a prosperous landlord class. There is no doubt that Ricardo's advocacy of a rigid version of Say's Law, quite as much as his doctrine of the effect of improvements in agriculture, was motivated by a strong bias against landowners. The Law of Comparative Cost demonstrated the advantages of repeal of the Corn Laws; observation of the political scene strongly suggested that repeal was impossible without weakening the influence of the landowning interests; in that sense, Malthus' opinions were politically dangerous and had to be opposed.

Such considerations, while they serve to explain the vehemence with which the problem of Say's Law was discussed, should not influence our judgment of the analytical issues. Malthus saw a problem, the problem of stagnation resulting from inadequate demand. He did not conceive the problem accurately and in analyzing it committed one logical blunder after another. Ricardo's defense of Say's Law was dogmatic and hardly impeccable, but it was logical, given his premises and assumptions. Robert Torrens, a contemporary economist, summed it up when he said: 'As presented by Mr. Ricardo, Political Economy possesses a regularity and simplicity beyond what exists in nature; as exhibited by Mr. Malthus, it is a chaos of original and unconnected elements.' It is fortunate for the history of economics that good logic triumphed over bad. A victory for Malthus would have made economics the happy hunting-ground of every quack ready with panaceas to cure the allegedly inherent defects of the market economy. One can only marvel at Keynes's astounding assertion that 'if only Malthus, instead of Ricardo, had been the parent stem from which 19th-century economics proceeded, what a much wiser and richer place the world would be today'. No doubt, economic theory would have benefited from a continuing discussion over the meaning of Say's Law; the flaws in Malthus' argument, its unpalatable political overtones, and the anxiety to give 'scientific' status to the case for a free market economy unfortunately made such a constructive debate impossible. It took many years to realize that, as Hansen put it in his *Business Cycles* (1927): 'The Say-Ricardo school, while fundamentally sound, left the problem [of business cycles] unsolved. As has so frequently been true of economic generalizations, it tackled the problem in terms of long-run tendencies, which in effect meant that it refused to recognize the problem at all. On the other hand, the Lauderdale-Malthus-Sismondi solution is logically untenable to anyone who will take the pains to think the problem through to the end'.

NOTES ON FURTHER READING

Apart from the relevant chapters in Ricardo's *Principles* and in Mill's *Principles*, the outstanding primary sources on the Law of Markets are J. B. Say's *Letters to Malthus* (1820, reprinted 1936) and the essay by J. S. Mill, 'Of the Influence of Production on Consumption', *Essays on Some Unsettled Questions of Political Economy* (1844, reprinted 1948). There is also the famous exchange of letters between Malthus and Ricardo, which has to be read to be believed. There has always been some question whether it was Say himself or whether it was James Mill who first codified the Law of Markets. W. J. Baumol, 'Say's (At Least) Eight Laws, or What Say and James Mill May Really Have Meant', *Ec*, May, 1977, argues for Say as having priority, while W. O. Thweatt, 'Baumol and James Mill on "Say's Law of Markets"', *ibid.*, November, 1980, insists that priority must go to Mill.

Schumpeter wrote what is probably the most brilliant single commentary on the role of Say's Law in classical economics: *History of Economic Analysis*, pp. 615–25. G. S. Becker and W. J. Baumol, 'The Classical Monetary Theory: The Outcome of the Discussion', *Ec*, 1952, reprinted with revisions in *EET*, is an important article in which the distinction between Say's Identity and Say's Equality was first drawn explicitly, although the distinction was broached by Lange in 1942. The Becker-Baumol article constitutes a prolegomenon to D. Patinkin, *Money, Interest, and Prices* (2nd edn, 1965), a book that ranks with Hicks' *Value and Capital* as a significant contribution to modern microeconomics; with reference to our theme, see chaps. 3, 8, 14, 15, and Notes A, F, G, and L, particularly Note L. Patinkin objects to Say's Equality as a misleading term because no classical economist specified the equilibrating mechanism that would validate Say's Equality. This is perfectly true but the same purist insistence on rigor would lead one to deny that there is such a thing as a classical theory of long-run prices, since no classical economist really demonstrated the existence, determinacy and stability of equilibrium in a *single* commodity market.

A. W. Marget, *The Theory of Prices* (1942), Vol. II, chap. 1, subjects Keynes's allegation that all economists before him divorced value and monetary theory to an exhaustive examination. One of the 'lessons of doctrinal history', Marget concludes, is that monetary theory in fact never lagged far behind developments in general theory. This is additional material in the rest of Vol. II that pertains to this theme (see, in particular, pp. 606–20 on Keynes's Law) but it must be read in its entirety. Whatever the ultimate verdict on Marget's attempt to resuscitate the quantity theory of money, no student should miss this supreme example of polemical scholarship, so amply documented that the footnotes virtually swallow the text. Patinkin accepts Keynes's allegation, but not for Keynes's reason: he argues that both the classical and the neoclassical economists 'dichotomized' the pricing process by failing to integrate the explanation of relative prices with that of absolute prices. On this great and never ending debate, see the review article by L. J. Mauer, 'The Patinkin Controversy: A Review', *KYK*, 19, 2, 1966, and for a modern textbook version, see J. Ascheim and C.-Y. Hsieh, *Macroeconomics: Income and Monetary Theory* (1969), chaps. 2 and 7.

For an excellent account of Thornton's work in particular and classical monetary theory in general, see Schumpeter, *History of Economic Analysis*, pp. 276–99, 314–34 and 688–738; see also F. A. Hayek's masterly introduction to the 1939 reprint of Thornton's *Nature of the Paper Credit* (1802), pp. 36–58; D. A. Reisman, 'Henry Thornton and Classical Monetary Economics', *OEP*, March, 1971; T. W. Hutchison, 'Thornton, Henry', *IESS*, 16; C. F. Peake, 'Henry Thornton and the Development of Ricardo's Economic Thought', *HOPE*, Summer, 1977; and P. Beaugrand, J. C. W. Ahiakpor, and C. F. Peake, *ibid.*, Spring, 1982, who continue the argument about Thornton's precise influence on Ricardo. On the history of the forced-saving doctrine, see F. A. Hayek, 'A Note on the Development of the Doctrine of "Forced Saving"', *QJE*, 1932, reprinted in his *Profits, Interest and Investment* (1939), chap. 7; Viner, *Theory of International Trade*, chap. 4, sect. 3; M. A. Hudson, 'Ricardo on Forced Saving', *ER*, June, 1965; B. A. Corry, *Money, Saving and Investment in English Economics 1800–1850* (1962), chap. 3; and F. Machlup, 'Forced or Induced Savings: An Exploration into Its Synonyms and Homonyms', *REStat*, 1943, reprinted in his *Essays in Economic Semantics* (1963).

J. S. Mill's position is analyzed in some detail by B. A. Balassa, 'John Stuart Mill and the Law of Markets', *QJE*, May, 1959; this article uses the terms 'commodity money' and 'credit money' for what we have called 'accounting money' and 'circulating money'. L. C. Hunter in a 'Comment', *ibid.*, May, 1960, delves deeper into the classical theory of saving and investment. In an article on 'Mill and Cairnes on the Rate of Interest', *OEP*, February, 1959, the same author examines a set of unpublished notes that Cairnes sent to Mill as the latter was preparing the sixth edition of *Principles* dealing with the question of short-run monetary influences on the rate of interest.

Regarding Malthus' attack on Say's Law, Malthus' *Principles of Political Economy* (2nd edn., 1836, reprinted 1951) is the chief primary source. Additional material is found in Malthus' *Definitions of Political Economy* (1827), reprinted with an introduction by M. Paglin (1963), and also available in *Five Papers on Political Economy by T. R. Malthus*, ed. C. Renwick (1953) and *Occasional Papers of T. R. Malthus*, ed. B. Semmel (1963). Malthus' use of a particular standard of value to establish the possibility of general gluts is explained by Myint, *Theories of Welfare Economics*, chap. 3. Malthus' contributions to demand theory are analyzed in two valuable articles by V. E. Smith: 'The Classicists' Use of "Demand"', *JPE*, 1951, reprinted in *EMDT*; and 'Malthus' Theory of Demand and Its Influence on Value Theory', *SJPE*, October, 1956. The first of these two pieces is particularly useful for a review of all the leading classical writers on demand.

Keynes's famous eulogy on Malthus is to be found in his *Essays in Biography* (1933). Hutchison, following in Keynes's footsteps, traces a line of 18th-century underconsumptionists who were driven underground by Smith's theory of saving that culminated in Say's Law: *A Review of Economic Doctrines, 1870–1929* (1953), pp. 346–56. See also T. W. Hutchison, 'Bentham as an Economist', *EJ*, 1956, reprinted in *EET*: Bentham did most of his work on economics in the last two decades of the 18th century and carried on the kind of macroeconomic monetary analysis that Cantillon and his contemporaires had developed.

For the historical and intellectual context in which the controversy on gluts was fought out after Ricardo's death, see my *Ricardian Economics*, chap. 5. G. J. Stigler, 'Sraffa's Ricardo', *AER*, September, 1953, offers some cogent comments on the inconclusive debate between Ricardo and Malthus. Malthus' arguments are examined afresh and with great clarity by R. G. Link, *English Theories of Economic Fluctuations, 1814–1848* (1959), chap. 2. See also Schumpeter, *History of Economic Analysis*, pp. 480–3. Several commentators claim to have found many of the building blocks of *The General Theory* in Malthus. B. A. Corry, however, demonstrates succinctly that Malthus cannot be regarded as a precursor of Keynes: 'Malthus and Keynes – A Reconsideration', *EJ*, December, 1959; see also my *Ricardian Economics*, Appendix B; and R. D. C. Black, 'Parson Malthus, the General and the Captain', *EJ*, March, 1967. For the contrary view, see S. Hollander, 'Malthus and Keynes: A Note', *EJ*, June, 1962; and P. Lambert, *L'oeuvre de John Maynard Keynes. Exposé – Analyse critique – Prolongements* (1963), chap. 3. Nor was Malthus a strong advocate of government spending – his views on this question were perfectly in keeping with majority opinion in his day: Corry, *Money, Saving and Investment in English Economics*, chaps. 7–9. See also a brief but controversial piece by H. G. Vatter, 'The Malthusian Model of Income Determination and Its Contemporary Relevance', *CJEPS*, February, 1959. B. J. Gordon, 'Say's Law, Effective Demand, and the Contemporary British Periodicals, 1820–1850', *Ec*, November, 1965, shows that Malthus did not lack allies in his day. But as F. W. Fetter makes clear in 'Economic Controversy in the British Reviews, 1802–1850', *ibid.*, these allies were almost always drawn from one end of the political spectrum; this fact was not unconnected with their failure to gain a hearing with the Ricardian economists. In a further article on the same subject, F. W. Fetter, 'The Rise and Decline of Ricardian Economics', *HOPE*, Spring, 1969, argues quite rightly how false the Keynesian picture of a doctrinal battle between Ricardo and Malthus on the question of aggregate demand would have seemed to Ricardo's contemporaries.

T. Sowell's recent book, *Say's Law. An Historical Analysis* (1972), summarized in his *Classical Economics Reconsidered* (1974), chap. 2, adds a new emphasis on the role of Sismondi in the debate; it was Sismondi and not Malthus who was regarded at the time as the great opponent of *Pax Ricardiana*. Sowell also denies that Say's Law in the classical period had anything to do with secular stagnation, insisting instead that it was a debate about short-run frictional problems. With the best will in the world, I remain unconvinced by Sowell's interpretation. The same must be said for S. Rashid, 'Malthus' Model of General Gluts', *Hope*, Fall, 1977, which argues that the satiation of wants was Malthus' central point, and Eltis, *The Classical Theory of Economic Growth*, chap. 5, which insists that Malthus did not equate saving to investment and clearly distinguished *ex ante* from *ex post* saving and investment. If the reader is now persuaded that he understands the meaning of Say's Law, at least in modern terms, he should take a look at W. H. Hutt, *A Rehabilitation of Say's Law* (1974), which argues that Say's Law is true then and now and, paradox of paradoxes, that it offers a complete and satisfactory explanation of the inherent tendency to depression in modern industrial society!

On the discussion in the 1830s and 1840s about emigration as a solution for population growth, connected with the case for colonization as a remedy for domestic economic stagnation, see D. N. Winch, *Classical Political Economy and Colonies* (1965), chaps. 5, 6, and 9; and E. R. Kittrell, 'The Development of the Theory of Colonization in English Classical Political Economy', *SEJ*, 1965, reprinted in *Great Britain and the Colonies, 1815–1865*, ed. A. G. L. Shaw (1970 and in paperback).

The real antisaver of the age was not Malthus but the Earl of Lauderdale whose oft-mentioned but little read *Inquiry* was published in 1804. F. A. Fetter gives an excellent critique of Lauderdale's attack on Smith's doctrine of thrift: 'Lauderdale's Oversaving Theory', *AER*, June, 1945. For a lighter article considering the causes of Lauderdale's neglect, see A. V. Cole, 'Lord Lauderdale and his "Inquiry"', *SJPE*, June, 1956; and M. Paglin, *Malthus and Lauderdale: The Anti-Ricardian Tradition* (1961). Another significant but neglected Keynesian forerunner was Thomas Joplin, a contemporary writer on currency questions who, unlike Malthus, did treat saving as a function of income. On Joplin, see R. L. Meek, 'Thomas Joplin and the Theory of Interest', *REStud*, 18, 3, 1951; and R. G. Link, *Theories of Economic Fluctuations*, chap. 3.

Expositions of the Harrod-Domar one-sector growth model can now be found in any one of the numerous recent textbooks on growth theory. For an excellent but advanced discussion of Harrodian dynamics, with references to the literature, see R. G. D. Allen, *Mathematical Economics* (2nd edn., 1965), chap. 3.

6

John Stuart Mill

All through the second half of the 19th century, Mill's *Principles of Political Economy* (1848) was the undisputed bible of economists. In the 1890s Marshall's treatise began to dislodge Mill in the English-speaking countries but as late as 1900 Mill's work was still the basic textbook in elementary courses in both British and American universities. The extraordinary durability of the book was due in large part to its blending of classical and anticlassical elements. It represented the final synthesis of Ricardian doctrine with many of the qualifications and refinements introduced by Ricardo's critics, hinting just enough at the 'real cost' of capital and the role of demand in determining prices to reconcile Ricardian notions with the new utility theory of value. Its comprehensive treatment of almost all branches of the subject gave it a unique place in economic literature and its loftiness of tone and elegance of style further enhanced its authority.

It is an easy book to read. Indeed, it is too readable. The argument flows along so smoothly that the reader is simply lulled into agreement. The whole book exudes immense confidence and even when Mill is uncertain about a particular question – as we now know he was from his private correspondence with Cairnes – he does not permit the text to be affected by theoretical doubt. Disparate ideas drawn from divergent lines of approach are allowed to coexist without any attempt at unification. Mill studiously avoided any claim to analytical originality, although such claims, as we shall see, would have been justified. The aim was simply, as he says in the Preface, to write an up-to-date *Wealth of Nations* 'adapted to the more extended knowledge and improved ideas of the present age'. The subtitle of the book reveals his intention to treat abstract principles in relation to 'their applications to social philosophy' and while he does not slight theoretical problems, the tone of the book subtly suggests the unimportance of rigorous analysis for its own sake.

But for all its theoretical eclecticism, or perhaps just because of it, Mill's *Principles* affords the best opportunity for a review of classical economics as a whole. Bailey's *Critical Dissertation on the Nature of Value* (1825), Longfield's *Lectures on Political Economy* (1834), and Senior's *Outline of the Science of Political Economy* (1836) are more exciting to read. They cover only part of the ground, however, and do not adequately convey the flavor of classical economics applied to practical problems, without which the postponement of 'the marginal revolution' to the 1870s becomes

179

difficult to understand. For better or for worse, it was primarily in Mill's formulation that the ideas of the writers in the first half of the 19th century reached the founders of the 'new economics' in the second half.

READER'S GUIDE TO THE 'PRINCIPLES OF POLITICAL ECONOMY'

1. Laws of Production and Distribution

The 'Preliminary Remarks' that open the book launch straightway into a condemnation of mercantilism, concluding in a passage that emphasizes the 'realness' of economic relations: 'money, as money, satisfies no want'. In his anxiety to discredit monetary panaceas, Mill forgets the store-of-value function of money, although he is perfectly aware of it elsewhere in the book. Wealth (*read*: income) is defined as the sum of all goods bought and sold in the market; the question as to whether services are to be included is postponed to Book 1, chapter 3. There follows a brief sketch of economic development since ancient times, issuing in the famous distinction between the Laws of Production, given by technical conditions, and the Laws of Distribution, governed by 'human institutions' and 'the laws and customs of society'. By this distinction Mill means not that the pricing of productive factors – functional distribution – is independent of the technical conditions of production, but that the personal distribution of income among 'the three main classes of society' is influenced by the distribution of property, itself the product of historical change. Nothing can be done about the Laws of Production for they partake of 'the character of physical truths'. But the Laws of Distribution are subject to human decision and are capable of being altered even under a regime of private property. This distinction became one of the chief props of Mill's thinking, reconciling the ideas of Ricardo and Malthus with his own comprehensive reform proposals.

Strictly interpreted, the distinction between the two kinds of laws is untenable for it implies independence of the forces determining the size of the cake from those governing its slices. But, taken loosely, it says nothing more than that propositions about productive efficiency hold true in a way that propositions about distributive equity do not. Is it perhaps an old-fashioned way of distinguishing between positive and normative economics, separating questions of 'what is' from 'what ought to be'? Everything depends on how such a distinction is actually applied in a particular case. Mill's division of the subject matter into 'production' and 'distribution', treated respectively in Books I and II, is open to question even when the distinction between the two kinds of laws is accepted. By treating the problem of value in Book III *after* discussing production and distribution, he more or less suggests that distribution has nothing to do with valuation, being a product of historical accident.

This is the sort of trap economists writing before the development of general equilibrium theory were always falling into: we cannot analyze the determination of relative prices in product markets on the assumption of a given distribution of income, property and personal services and then turn to factor markets to discuss the pricing of land, labour and capital because product and factor prices are simultaneously determined; nor can we begin instead with factor prices because nothing can be said about them until one has demonstrated how product prices are determined. Did Mill arbitrarily decide to reverse the usual order of treatment to minimize the more abstract parts of the subject? Or was he genuinely confused about the relationship between production and distribution, between the technical characteristics of the production function and the valuation of the inputs that are applied to production? There is evidence for both interpretations in the *Principles* itself. A charitable view is that he saw the problem but lacked the analytical apparatus to solve it. Like many classical economists, he failed to distinguish the pricing problem with *given* material and human resources from the feedback effect of the growth of these resources on prices: there was no explicit awareness of the difference between short run and long run in the Marshallian sense. This aggravated Mill's difficulty of presenting value and distribution theory in an orderly sequence. At bottom, however, the difficulty has no solution except in a general equilibrium framework of analysis.

2. The Doctrine of Productive Labour

Book I, chapter 1, considers the relationship between land and labour as the two 'original' factors of production. **Chapter 2** deals with labour alone, and **section 2** gives an excellent statement of the classical notion of a wages fund: the time-consuming, discontinuous character of the productive process requires 'food produced in advance'. From this it follows that profit or interest must be a reward for the sacrifice or 'abstinence' of those who can afford to wait for the final product. No passage in the entire book shows more clearly that the wages fund doctrine, based as it is on the idea that capital is nothing but a series of 'advances', logically implies a waiting theory of interest.

Book I, chapter 2, sections 7–8, and the whole of **chapter 3** are devoted to a defense of Smith's concept of productive labour. At the outset Mill dismisses the controversy over what constitutes productive labour as semantic and taxonomic, involving no question of substance. Productive labour is productive of 'wealth' and 'it is essential to the idea of wealth to be susceptible of accumulation'. Wealth, he notes, consists in essence of tools, machines and the skill of the labour force, the stock of what we would now call nonhuman plus human capital. Although it is 'permanence' not 'materiality' that is decisive, Mill feels that no great harm is done by following traditional usage, defining productive labour as productive of 'material objects'. He adds, however, that labour services expended in acquiring skills or in protecting property are to be considered productive. Mill leaves no doubt about the purpose of the distinction. It is to show that the rate of capital accumulation is a function of the proportion of the labour force employed 'productively'. Profits earned by employing unproductive labour are merely transfers of income; unproductive labour does not generate net value added.

The distinction between the two kinds of labour is applied to consumption in

section 5 of **chapter 3**. The only productive consumers are productive labourers, but not all consumption by productive labourers is productive consumption: 'that alone is productive consumption, which goes to maintain and increase the productive powers of the community'. This idea goes back to the physiocrats; it is the notion that a certain quantity of the consumer goods produced in an economy, namely, wage goods, must be fed back into the production of manpower itself in the household sector. Productive consumption is simply an input necessary to maintain human capital intact. If wages are at subsistence, the whole of the wages bill is required for productive consumption. Mill concedes, however, that workers do consume some 'luxuries' and, in that sense, a portion of wages is consumed unproductively. The fact remains that consistent classical income accounting implies deducting all productive consumption from the gross national product to arrive at the true net national product, which consists simply of profits plus rents; the net product is entirely created by productive labour and is spent entirely on investment goods and *true* consumption goods, that is, non-wage goods. The logic of this argument is impeccable, although the statistical problem of segregating wages into its productive and unproductive components might be daunting. The point is, however, that only a society bent on maximizing capital accumulation, come what may to current living standards, would want to adopt this kind of accounting. And Mill was not at all sure, as Smith was, that a higher growth rate is really desirable. The closing passage of chapter 3 conveys Mill's characteristic emphasis on distribution.

3. Theory of Capital

The next three chapters contain Mill's theory of capital, 'a stock, previously accumulated, of the products of former labour'. **Book I, chapter 4, section 1**, develops Ricardo's proposition that the demand for labour is greater, the greater the capitalist's reinvestment of earnings and the smaller his expenditure on goods for personal consumption [see chapter 4, section 28]. **Section 2** notes that wages generally exceed the physiological minimum and continues to drive home the idea that wages are 'paid out of capital', that capital consists essentially of advances to workers. This chapter is a preliminary to the celebrated **chapter 5**, which contains the four 'fundamental propositions respecting capital'.

The first of these propositions is that 'industry is limited by capital', which seems to mean that employment cannot be augmented except by capital formation. In the course of expounding this position, Mill assumes that capital is fully employed, but he immediately goes on to discuss the possibility of excess capacity (**chapter 5, section 2**). When there is excess capacity, governments can 'create' capital, an idea that Ricardo had strenuously denied. Capital formation as such never produces unemployment (**chapter 5, section 3**). Here we have the first of a series of barbs at 'authours of the highest name' who have held out the prospect of investment running into the barrier of limited demand, arguing that therefore 'the unproductive expenditure of the rich is necessary to the employment of the poor'.

The second fundamental proposition states that 'capital is the result of saving', which links up with the third proposition that 'capital, although the result of saving, is nevertheless consumed'. This is of course Adam Smith's saving-is-spending theorem, or the indestructibility of purchasing power, which underlies Say's Law of Markets. Taken strictly, it implies Say's Identity [see chapter 5, section 3]. But Say's Identity denies the possibility of excess capacity, which has already been admitted under the first proposition. It should be evident now that, however much the saving-is-spending theorem encouraged the classical thinkers to ignore 'hoarding', its essential meaning was that saving and investment create effective aggregate demand just as surely as do consumption expenditures.

In **sections 6** and **7** of **chapter 5**, Mill notes that 'the great part' of the income of the current year is currently produced: the average durability of capital goods is only about ten years. This accounts for the fact that countries recover so quickly after destructive wars; skills, technical knowledge and the more durable buildings usually remain unimpaired and make possible a rapid recovery. This obviously valid argument has never received the attention it deserves; it could be elaborated into a complete theory of the causes of economic growth.

Mill turns now to the surprising growth of wealth during the Napoleonic Wars, surprising because classical theory suggests that wartime spending by the state on armaments reduces capital investment in the private sector. The war, Mill declares, gave rise to 'unfounded theories ... tending to exalt unproductive expenditure, at the expense of productive' – another jibe at Malthus. In his youth Mill had joined Ricardo in denying the stimulating effects of war expenditures. Now, however, he was prepared to admit the income-generating effects of public spending. Suppose, for the sake of argument, he begins, we assume that capital is fully employed during a war. Then, why prosperity? Because government loans for war purposes reduce wages and the workers in this way really pay for the war. The only reason given for this peculiar conclusion is that 'the loan cannot have been taken from that portion of the capital of the country which consists of tools, machinery and buildings', a dogmatic assertion that contradicts the fact, stated a few pages earlier, that the maintenance of capital involves annual charges on production. Mill then goes on to show that, in rich countries, government loans do not in fact siphon off funds that would have been invested in the private sector – there is no 'crowding out' – but rather absorb excess capital that would have flowed abroad or that would have been spent on luxury goods. In a footnote, he grants that a war can divert labour as well as capital from productive employment and, hence, that wages need not fall in wartime. This possibility is dismissed in the case of England, which had a comparatively small standing army: government revenues during the Napoleonic Wars were derived from taxes on circulating capital at the expense of the civilian labour force.

The most controversial proposition in the chapter on capital is the fourth: 'demand for commodities is not demand for labour' (**chapter 5, section 3**). Leslie Stephen once described it as 'a doctrine so rarely understood, that its complete apprehension, is perhaps, the best test of an economist'. But Cannan called it 'the biggest blunder made in economic theory in modern times', and Jevons, Sidgwick and Nicholson all commented adversely on it. Even Marshall, always partial to Mill, agreed that it 'expresses his meaning badly'. What Mill was driving at was the idea that the total volume of employment is a direct function of the rate of capital accumulation and that consumers' demand, while it determines the allocation of labour between different industries, influences total employment only at one remove. Since the decision whether the proceeds of sales will be used to reconstitute the wages fund rests with employers, demand for commodities is not *necessarily* demand for labour. Having made the decision to save a certain portion of his income, the only way in which an individual can *directly* influence the demand for labour is by substituting labour services for commodities in his own consumption. This is Ricardo's old argument, laid down in the chapter on machinery, that the interest of labour is best served by the most labour-intensive kind of spending on personal consumption.

All this is unobjectionable, when properly interpreted, but the dozen pages explaining this proposition in Mill's book are among the most tortuous in the whole literature of economics. Among other things, it is never made clear whether this proposition is supposed to hold regardless of the existence of unemployed resources. Mill seems to be assuming full employment by affirming that an increased demand for labour in one industry must draw labour out of another. In that case it seems to follow tautologically that an increased demand for consumer goods cannot increase the demand for labour. But Mill's object is to show that the demand for labour will in fact fall off under full employment conditions when resources are shifted into the manufacture of additional consumer goods: an increase in consumption means a decrease of investment, and investment under the wages fund doctrine can only mean 'advancing' more wage goods to labour in subsequent periods.

Given the rigid discontinuity of production implied in the wages fund doctrine, it is perfectly true that an increase in aggregate consumption demand under full employment impairs the wages fund and so leads to a decline in the amount of employment demanded at any given wage rate. This can be demonstrated by translating Mill's argument into mathematics. If $\bar{W}$ = the output of wheat available as a wages fund, N = the amount of labour employed combined in fixed proportions with capital, a = the labour-input coefficient, and $\bar{w}$ = the real wage rate, then this year's employment depends only on last year's wheat harvest and on this year's real wage rate.

$$N_t = \frac{\bar{W}_{t-1}}{\bar{w}} \tag{1}$$

This year's harvest, the wages fund, is determined by the fixed labour-input coefficient and the size of the labour force.

$$\bar{W}_t = N_t a. \tag{2}$$

Substituting equation (1) into equation (2), we have

$$\bar{W}_t = \bar{W}_{t-1} \frac{a}{\bar{w}}.$$ (3)

Rewriting equation (3) as $\bar{W}_t - \bar{W}_{t-1} \left(\dfrac{a}{\bar{w}} \right) = 0$, we recognize it as a very simple homogeneous first-order difference equation, whose solution (say, by the iterative method) is

$$\bar{W}_t = \bar{W}_o \left(\frac{a}{\bar{w}} \right)^t,$$ (4)

which may be read as saying that if $\bar{W} = \bar{W}_o$ in the base year, then by year t it will equal $\bar{W}_t$. But in fact a certain proportion u of $\bar{W}$ is spent on luxury goods and personal labour services. Equation (1) should be rewritten as

$$N_t = \frac{\bar{W}_{t-1}}{\bar{w}} - u \left(\frac{\bar{W}_{t-1}}{\bar{w}} \right) = \bar{W}_{t-1} \left(\frac{1-u}{\bar{w}} \right).$$ (5)

That is, the amount of labour producing wage goods equals the total amount of labour supported out of $\bar{W}$ minus the amount of unproductive labour. Substituting equation (5) into equation (2) and writing it in reduced form, we have

$$\bar{W} = \bar{W}_o \left[\frac{a(1-u)}{\bar{w}} \right]^t.$$ (6)

With sample values of $\bar{w} = 2$, $a = 4$, $u = \frac{1}{3}$, the expression in the squared brackets equals $(1.33)^t$: $\bar{W}$ and therefore N grow at a compound rate of 33 percent per year and any increase in u lowers the rate of growth of both the wages fund and the volume of employment. But on the same grounds, the Ricardian redistribtuion of 'unproductive consumption' from consumer goods to personal services leaves u unaffected and so cannot add to the production of wage goods. But Ricardo, of course, applied the argument to a situation in which some labour is unemployed, from which it follows that demand for commodities *is* demand for labour. Mill's proposition would have seemed less paradoxical if he had carefully distinguished between the cases of full employment and underemployment.

4. The Wages Fund Doctrine

Before proceeding further we must consider the wages fund doctrine in a little more detail. This doctrine has been so frequently ridiculed that it is difficult nowadays to appreciate its partial validity and, in particular, to realize that it marks the beginning of an appreciation of the nature of capital as a factor of production. Usually we think of capital as a sum of money, the total value of the assets of a business firm. But if we lift the 'veil' of money, what are the characteristics of the real capital stock that the sum of money represents? Production is time-consuming but workers must be hired and equipment installed before there are final products ready for sale. The capital fund of a firm, therefore, is nothing but the power to purchase labour and the products of other firms over the period during which the firm has no output to sell. Since labour itself spends its wages on finished goods, the firm's capital in real terms consists simply of other firms' products. If we add together the capital of all the firms in the economy, we arrive at society's real capital stock as the sum of all intermediate products on the way to final consumption.

The real meaning of capital emerges even more clearly if we think of the whole economy as a giant firm. This giant firm, like any other firm, must pay workers for their services as they are rendered before the services have ripened into consumers' goods. To tide itself over this period, the firm must be in possession of a stock of finished consumer goods as well as semifinished producer goods capable of being added to inventories as they are depleted. All these goods, whether finished or unfinished, represent produced 'means of production' in the sense that they are all in the process of being converted into final output. In other words, the real capital fund of a society can be defined as the sum total of all produced goods-in-process in the hands of producers, wholesalers and retailers; in practice, this amounts to an inventory of consumer goods and raw materials as well as plant and equipment.

What the classical economists did was to seize on a part of the total stock of produced inputs, namely, wage goods consumed by workers, identifying the part with the whole. On the notion that a worker's staple article of consumption is wheat, they treated agriculture as the wage goods industry *par excellence*. The fact that wheat becomes available in the form of annual harvests, which must be willy-nilly stored as a 'fund' for future consumption if its actual use is to be more or less continuous throughout the year, made it possible to define capital simply as 'advances' to workers to support them from seedtime to harvest time. In practice, the employer does not 'advance' anything; he merely buys labour services. But in real terms, he does exchange past output for current labour before current labour has produced anything: wages are paid out of 'capital', and capital is nothing but 'inchoate wealth' entering into the production of current goods and services. Marx objected to the wages fund doctrine on the grounds that capitalists do not really 'advance' wages to workers; on the contrary, since wages are usually paid after they are earned – at the end of the week – workers are really the creditors of their employers. But the question is whether workers get paid before the output that they have produced has been sold. In some cases, only a few days are required to produce an article, in which case the employer benefits from the convention of paying workers every seven days. But on average, the period of fabrication greatly exceeds a week, even in manufacturing, and the employer does in fact advance wages to workers.

The idea that capital is to be understood in terms of a time interval between production and consumption is implicit in the wages fund doctrine and it is from this idea that all later work on capital stems. But the proposition that this time interval can be identified with the annual period of production in agriculture invested the whole analysis with artificiality. At best, the theory emphasizes the complementarity of capital and labour, insisting that, in the absence of an increase in the rate of capital accumulation, aggregate wages cannot be permanently raised. The wage rate, it implies, is not subject to an arbitrary bargaining decision but depends upon the growth of previous investment. But at worst, it suggest that the whole of the wages fund is necessarily exhausted in any period and that the fund is rigidly predetermined by technical conditions; it denies the impossibility of increasing payrolls by curtailing the 'unproductive consumption' of capitalists and seems to depict the aggregate demand for labour as perfectly inelastic at any moment in time.

In point of fact, however, the wages fund doctrine was rarely employed by the leading economists to deprecate trade union action to raise wages. The more common practice was to exploit the doctrine to emphasize the necessity for family limitation. The wages fund as the 'demand' for labour was set against the existing 'supply' of labour; the wage rate was said to be determined by dividing the number of workers into the total sum of money available for wage payments; it followed that to raise wages it was necessary either to raise the dividend or to lessen the divisor, to produce more or to procreate less. Although the theory was frequently presented as an ordinary case of the working of the law of demand and supply, no notion of a schedule of demand and supply prices was presented and no attempt was made to define a true equilibrium wage rate. Nor was it made clear how the wages fund theory was related to the subsistence theory of wages. It is tempting to argue that the wages fund doctrine accounts for the demand side, while the subsistence theory is concerned with the supply side. But since the latter holds in the long run, while the former pertains to the short run, this raises as many questions as it settles. It is true to say, however, that the wages fund doctrine contains whatever theory of the demand for labour was developed by the classical economists.

A good example of how a wages fund theorist might combine classical doctrine with sympathy for trade unions is Mill's own treatment of the Combination Laws in one of the last chapters of the *Principles* (Book V, chapter 10, section 5). 'It is a great error', he remarks, 'to condemn *per se* and absolutely either trade unions or the collective action of strikes'. In the absence of unions, the monopsony power of the employer – shades of Adam Smith's 'tacit and universal combination not to raise wages' – frequently results in wages below the competitive level. Unions, therefore, are to be welcomed as a countervailing force: 'Far from a hindrance to a free market for labour, [they] are the necessary instrumentality of that free market'. When Mill in 1869 retracted the wages fund doctrine in a famous article in the *Fortnightly Review*, he interpreted it as denying that unions could raise wages, or at least 'limited their operations in that respect to the somewhat earlier attainment of a rise which the competition of the market would have produced without them'. But his discussion in the *Principles* belies this interpretation. And lest it be thought that Mill is unique, it is worth mentioning that the so-called founder of the wages fund doctrine, John Ramsay McCulloch, advanced the same argument about monopsony in the labour market in his influential *Essay on Wages* (1826).

5. Advance Economics and Synchronization Economics

What, if anything, remains of the wages fund doctrine? In a developed economy, goods that can be produced only at comparatively long intervals do not form a very large part of society's consumable output; most goods can be produced fairly continuously throughout the year. It would be unrealistic to think that 'roundabout production' depends on the prior existence of a stock of such goods. But the fact remains that such accumulated stocks of consumer goods are constituents of capital, and that the amount payable in wages during any slice of time is limited by the quantity of wage goods that can be produced during its course with the aid of equipment inherited from the past. In a stationary state, this consideration would have no significance. Although production is time consuming, a stationary economy functions *as if* output in every period is consumed in the same period: the stock of consumer goods available at the beginning of each year is used up through the year, but it is always exactly replaced at the end. In a stationary state, the flow of consumption and the flow of productive services are perfectly synchronized. In this kind of economy it is strictly true that wages are paid out of current product. But in a growing economy, wages are in part paid out of past product and the stock of goods-in-the-pipelines has real significance for the functioning of the system. This assertion is sometimes denied and it is useful to categorize the denial as involving 'synchronization economics'. The opposite view, which insists on the importance of the time structure of production, we will call 'advance economics'. The coinage is Schumpeter's and it will serve us in good stead when we come to consider the controversies that raged over the Austrian theory of capital at the end of the century. Suffice it to say that the Austrian theory rests upon 'advance economics' and in this way links up with the wages fund doctrine. To throw out the wages fund theory *in toto* is to cut oneself off from the key to the meaning of real capital that it furnishes. It was a bad theory of wages but it had all the ingredients of a good theory of capital.

6. The Machinery Question

Book I, chapter 6, section 1, distinguishes between fixed and circulating capital in the traditional manner with special emphasis, however, on fixed capital sunk in land. **Section 2** takes up Ricardo's doctrine about the adverse effect on employment of increasing the ratio of fixed to working capital [see chapter 4, section 28]. Ricardo's argument is dismissed as being inapplicable to cases other than the conversion of arable land to pasture. But the thesis that the introduction of machinery leads automatically to the reabsorption of displaced labour through price reductions that stimulate demand is also rejected. Lower prices, Mill points out, do not by themselves foster additional investment because 'demand for commodities is not demand for labour': the increased demand consequent upon lower prices must be set against the loss in purchasing power of displaced workers. Still, in the end, Mill does deny that the substitution of machinery for labour injures the working class even in the short run (**section 3**). Moreover, he concludes that 'there is probably no country whose fixed capital increases in a ratio more than proportional to its circulating' – a surprising statement from someone living through the Railway Age. And while Ricardo had frowned on state interference with the rate of technical advance, Mill does not hesitate to recommend public measures to moderate its rapidity.

Notice that the closing page of this chapter makes the ratio of fixed to circulating capital a technical matter, not a function of relative factor prices. This implies that the portion of the accumulated capital stock actually used as a counterpart of wage payments is not a function of the wage rate, and hence that there is no such thing as a demand curve for labour. The rate of growth of total capital is a function of the rate of profit; it is only by affecting the rate of profit that changes in wage rates influence the demand for labour. Apparently, once the capital stock is given, purely technical conditions determine the proportion devoted to 'supporting' labour.

There is a certain confusion in Mill's presentation of the machinery question because, like Ricardo, he seems at one point to be analyzing the substitution of capital for labour at a given state of technical knowledge, and then suddenly to address himself to genuine cost-reducing improvements in techniques. The theory that technological unemployment automatically generates compensatory adjustments, clearly stated for the first time by McCulloch in the 1820s, is certainly intended to apply to laboursaving innovations. This theory, incidentally, was more than the naive argument that all technically displaced labour will necessarily be absorbed in the making of the machines themselves. The argument rested on the idea that innovations must under perfect competition result in price reductions and the expansion of output. If demand is at all elastic, total receipts rise and the employer will increase his expenditures on either consumption or investment. On the other hand, if demand is unresponsive to lower prices, purchasing power in the hands of consumers is freed for spending on other goods. Directly or indirectly, laboursaving machinery entails the increase of output and the consequent re-absorption of displaced labour. The adjustment is a slow one and may leave pockets of unemployment for long periods of time. For this reason, most classical economists, including McCulloch, recommended government assistance to the victims of technological unemployment. No one went as far as Mill did, however, in suggesting direct interference with private decisions to introduce new machinery.

7. The Rate of Growth of the Factors of Production

Book I, chapter 7, section 1, contains the offhand remark that 'by far the largest portion' of total capital consists of working capital, although in the previous chapter Mill remarks upon 'the enormous fixed capital now embarked in the cotton manufacture'. This chapter is devoted to a consideration of the forces determining the general productivity of resources in different countries. It is full of good sense, though the subject does not easily lend itself to rigorous treatment. What is emphasized throughout is the crucial element of people's attitudes to pecuniary goals. In **section 4**, Mill implicitly classifies innovations into laboursaving, land-saving and capitalsaving, although the terminology used is different. **Book I, chapter 8**, on the division of labour, adds little to Adam Smith's treatment and may be passed over without loss. The next chapter contains one of the first discussions in economic literature of the forces making for increasing returns to scale. It is heavily indebted to a remarkable book, *Economy of Machinery and Manufactures* (1833) by Charles Babbage, which is quoted without stint. Mill predicts an increase in the scale of business firms in the course of economic progress, a prediction that is often attributed to Marx as one of his accurate forecasts. The advantages of scale, Mill suggests, must be set off against the dangers of monopoly and agreements to restrict entry and to keep up prices: 'where competitors are so few, they always end up by agreeing not to compete. They may run a race of cheapness to ruin a new candidate, but as soon as he has established his footing they come to terms with him' (**section 3**). 'Natural monopolies', meaning industries whose technology favours large firms, should be nationalized, Mill concludes. The last section of **chapter 9** lays the groundwork for the case in favour of small-scale peasant farming, which Mill develops at greater length in Book II.

Book I, chapter 10, takes up the Malthusian theory of population, laid down as an axiomatic truth (**sections 2–3**). Mill denies that the desire to 'keep up with the Joneses' is an effective force for family limitation among the working class in England – this assertion is retracted in **Book IV, chapter 7, section 3**. The elasticity of supply of labour in response to a rise in wages is said to be very high. Nevertheless, the rate of population growth has been slackening since the census of 1821 and 'subsistence and employment in England have never increased more rapidly than in the last forty years [1862]' (**section 3**).

Book I, chapter 11, deals with the theory of saving: 'abstinence from present consumption for the sake of future goods'. The rate of saving is made a function of the rate of interest (**section 2**) but the parameters of the function are discussed in detail under the heading of 'the effective desire of accumulation' (**section 3**). This chapter, together with the earlier chapter 7 and section 1 of chapter 13, contains the essence of the classical contribution to the theory of economic development.

In **chapter 12** we meet at last with the law of diminishing returns to labour in the cultivation of a given amount of land, stated in terms of a 'given state of agricultural skill and knowledge' – an improvement in presentation due to Senior – and verified by the extension of cultivation to inferior soil. Mill leaves no doubt that he is a disciple of Ricardo when he declares this general law of agricultural industry to be 'the most important proposition in political economy'. **Section 3** takes up the cudgel against the American economist, Henry Carey, for holding that land in a young country is actually taken up in inverse order of its fertility. Mill goes on to reiterate Ricardo's analysis of improvements in agriculture but he goes much deeper in tracing the forces offsetting diminishing returns. Indeed, his list of offsetting factors is so impressive as to throw doubt on the existence of any tendency towards historically diminishing returns in agriculture. **Chapter 13** reviews the previous three chapters and concludes that economic progress must be essentially conceived as a race between technical change and diminishing returns in agriculture. In **section 2** of **chapter 13**, Mill concedes that since the 1820s, technical change in England has outstripped the forces making for rising wheat prices; capital has increased faster than population and the standard of living has risen.

8. Socialism

We come now to **Book II**, dealing with the laws of distribution. **Chapter 1**, 'Of Property', defies a *précis*. It is deservedly the most famous chapter in the book and marks the first appearance of the subject of socialism in a major treatise of economics. In many ways it is less dated than other parts of Mill's book. No doubt, the ideas of Saint-Simon and Fourier, which Mill discusses, bear little resemblance to the more familiar doctrines of Marx. And Mill's critique of contemporary objections to socialism has little relevance today. Likewise, the dismissal of the problem of central planning strikes the modern reader as superficial. But now that many economists believe that economic theory as such can say little of general validity about the respective merits of capitalism and socialism, the final passage of **section 3** on the importance of respect for individual differences in tastes has all the more bearing on the great debate. Mill's treatment of socialist theory is extremely sympathetic but he really differs from socialists on the fundamental question: the social ills experienced under capitalism are not traced by Mill to the private ownership of property, but rather to rampant individualism and inadequate safeguards against the abuse of property rights. Notice too the distinction that Mill draws between communism – a society in which income is equalized regardless of the productivity of individuals – and socialism, which retains the incentives of differential pecuniary rewards. This distinction is identical to the one Marx drew between rewarding 'each according to his ability' under socialism and rewarding 'each according to his need' under communism.

9. Custom and the Laws of Distribution

Book II, chapter 2, continues the theme and argues that labour does not have a 'right to the whole product' because the supply price of abstinence is in fact positive (**section 1**). **Section 3** opens Mill's attack on the institution of inheritance with a plea for progressive inheritance duties to reduce inequalities in the distribution of property income. The supply price of land is zero and hence property rights in land are sanctioned only by expediency; but landlords are in fact poor improvers (**sections 5–6**). **Chapter 3** notes briefly that few land tenure systems in the world, other than the English and Scottish, duplicate the tripartite class structure of society as a whole in agriculture alone. This is precisely why the Ricardian system proved difficult to export and never won general acceptance on the Continent. **Book II, chapter 4**, on competition and custom, is a characteristic Millian warning against the hasty application of competitive models to the real world. Mill's distinction between 'custom' and 'competition' as stages in world history was very probably the source of inspiration for Maine's well-known contrast between 'status' and 'contract' and Tönnies' equally famous distinction between *Gemeinschaft* and *Gesellschaft*. It is a deep chapter and it makes a further contribution to Mill's general theory of economic development (if only modern development economists read Mill!). **Book II, chapter 5**, deals with slavery but says very little about the economics of a slave state. **Chapters 6** and **7** take up the issue of peasant proprietorship, a cause that Mill made his own. The topic has no contemporary interest and may be skipped. The same holds true of the next three chapters, which discuss other systems of land tenure.

10. The Distributive Shares

Book II, chapters 11–16, are concerned with the theory of class income distribution. In **chapter 11** Mill defines that 'elliptical' expression, the wages fund, as that part of working capital used to pay wages plus all expenditures on unproductive labour (**section 1**). The wages bill, being a flow, is equal to the wages fund multiplied by its turnover rate. Mill concedes that the entire wages fund need not be used up in any period but he does not deduce the practical implications of this admission (**section 2**). He proceeds to deny what German writers have called the *Paralleltheorie*, namely, that money wages always vary in the same direction as the price of food. But wages do follow the price of food 'after an interval of almost a generation'. Ricardo, Mill observes, assumed that wages are at long-run equilibrium, an assumption which 'contains sufficient truth to render it permissible for the purposes of abstract science'. Surprisingly enough for a Ricardian economist, Mill minimizes the benefits of repealing the Corn Laws on the living standards of the working class: unless workers restrict their numbers, real wages will rise only as long as it takes to 'people down to their old scale of living'. **Sections 3–6** come back to the Malthusian theory of population. In the last pages of the chapter, Mill reduces the whole debate over the Malthusian theory to the question whether a slackening in the growth of population in a country like Britain would or would not raise wages. He thinks it obvious that it would and rests his argument on that. He assumed, as a matter of course, that England is overpopulated but fails to distinguish between the advantages of *being* a smaller population and the advantages of *reducing the rate of growth* of population [see chapter 3, section 5].

Book II, **chapters 12–13**, spell out the practical implications of the Malthusian theory. In Mill's hands, the Malthusian theory becomes a relentless argument in favour of family limitation and every conceivable policy measure is judged in the light of its effects upon the birth rate. 'Little improvement in morality can be expected until the producing [of] large families is regarded with the same feeling as drunkenness or any other physical excess'. Mill never wrote more eloquently than in these chapters. He joins the hope of voluntary family limitation with the demand for female emancipation, and in **chapter 13, section 1**, comes close to hinting at the necessity for the introduction of birth control devices, an idea regarded at the time as so outrageous that it simply could not be stated openly.

Chapter 14 is a series of glosses on Book I, chapter 10 of the *Wealth of Nations*. But a new idea is now added to Smith's theory of the structure of wages, the concept of noncompeting groups. Mill seems to have arrived at this distinction by considering Smith's jewelers in whom 'great trust' is placed. Generalizing from this case, he concludes that there is a 'hereditary distinction of caste' between different grades of labour, 'a class of considerations which Adam Smith, and other political economists, have taken into far too little account' (**section 2**).

Book II, **chapter 15**, rounds off the subject of distribution by analyzing profits as the 'remuneration of abstinence', measured by 'the current rate of interest on the best security', and expressing 'the comparative value placed in the given society upon the present and the future' (**section 1**) – a good illustration of our earlier contention that the classical theory of profit is really a theory of interest [see chapter 4, section 2]. **Section 5** states that 'the cause of profit is, that labour produces more than is required for its support'. This is no Marxian exploitation theory different from the abstinence theory. The fact that labour is *physically* productive does not, in the absence of other considerations, prove that it is productive of *value* and profit is a difference between two values. The whole of capital is now said to consist of working capital; fixed capital itself is broken down to wages advanced in the past (**section 6**). In this sense, following Ricardo, the rate of profit is made dependent on the ratio of profits to wages on no-rent land. Mill suggests amending Ricardo's dictum that 'profits depend on wages' to read: profits depend upon the cost of labour. The cost of labour to the employer – by which Mill seems to mean wage costs per unit of output – is in turn explained as being a function of money wages and the average productivity of labour. This reformulation of Ricardo's fundamental theorem is grossly misleading: the rate of profit depends upon wage costs per unit of output only when the average productivity of capital is constant. **Book II, chapter 16**, provides an excellent review of Ricardian rent theory with a rebuttal of some of the more popular contemporary objections to it.

11. The Abstinence Theory of Interest

While we are in no position as yet to do justice to different theories of interest, it would be a pity to pass by the abstinence theory without further comment. The abstinence theory is not a complete theory of interest. It is merely a theory of the supply of savings and does not explicitly relate thriftiness to the demand for investment. Mill took the idea of the abstinence theory from Nassau Senior but improved its formulation. Senior talked of saving as if it were carried out under conditions of constant subjective cost; he completely ignored individual differences in the disutility of saving. This opened the theory to ridicule on the grounds that abstaining from the present enjoyment of income is hardly painful to the average saver in the upper income brackets. The very phrase 'reward for abstinence' suggested a glib justification for rentier income and many modern Marxist writers still interpret the abstinence theory as meaning precisely that. But the supply schedule of savings is positively sloped, not perfectly horizontal, and the rate of interest is governed by the *marginal* supply price of abstinence. In a rich economy, this marginal sacrifice may well be small and will certainly exceed the rate necessary to induce saving on the part of most individuals. The bulk of rentier income, as Mill makes clear, consists of intramarginal surpluses, pure Ricardian 'rents', which accrue to the saver through no effort of his own. And, of course, there is nothing in the theory that justifies the private ownership of property as such. If abstinence is required for capital accumulation, society as a whole can bear the burden just as well.

Abstinence has two possible meanings. It may refer to a sacrifice incurred in *creating* capital: by saving we add to the value of our property, which we can do only by abstaining from consuming the current income of property. This is the meaning that Senior gave to 'abstinence'. But the present owner of property may have inherited his wealth, thus enjoying income from someone else's abstinence. Hence, Senior had to argue that return on inherited property is of the nature of rent, not interest. In Senior's version, abstinence would disappear in the stationary economy where net saving is zero by definition. Not until Mill do we get the Casselian notion of abstinence: a reward for forbearing to *consume* one's capital. Property confers on the owner the right of consuming his property; if he fails to do so, he is abstaining from exercising that power. But why should it be necessary to reward an owner for not consuming his wealth? Because everyone prefers consumption now to consumption later, partly on the rational ground that he may be dead before the later date comes and partly from a weak-minded failure to value future consumption at its true worth. The reasons for 'time preference' are not very clearly indicated either by Senior or by Mill but the essential idea is there [see chapter 12, section 3]. People will not refrain from using purchasing power they command unless they are assured of more consumption in the future for every amount given up in the present. They will insist on earning interest and we can say that the rate of interest measures, as Mill put it, 'the comparative value placed, in the given society, upon the present and the future'.

It is sometimes said that the only reason the rate of *interest* is normally positive in a capitalist society is that the rate of *profit* is expected to be positive. When the productive advantage of utilizing capital is positive, present purchasing power is necessarily more valuable than an equal future amount because it permits its owner to invest in production and to earn a net surplus of receipts over costs. Hence, in a growing economy it is hardly surprising that people have positive time preference; the fact that the rate of interest is positive does not prove that people would consume their capital in the absence of a reward for holding it intact. But this argument is misleading, for it amounts to saying that the rate of interest is determined solely by productivity considerations, by the demand side in the loan market. The rate of interest is determined by both productivity *and* thrift. The role of abstinence is to act as a brake on the investment process; if saving involved no sacrifice whatever, its supply presumably could be augmented indefinitely. Hence, the mere fact that investment yields a net return should produce a flow of savings large enough to permit investment to depress the net yield of capital to zero. The productivity of investment alone cannot account for a positive rate of interest.

Moreover, interest created by pure time preference could exist in Adam Smith's 'rude' society, where there is no property in capital and hence no profit income. Suppose that some of the hunters were to consume more than their catch of deer, while others are willing to postpone consumption of their present catch. Then the latter could lend to the former out of today's catch against the promise of a larger repayment from the future catch. If the number of 'improvident' hunters exceeded the number of 'provident' ones, the rate of interest would be positive: a deer today would be more expensive than a deer tomorrow and, hence, the price of deer would no longer be determined solely by the quantity of labour required to catch them.

The abstinence theory of interest, like any theory of interest, attempts to explain the scarcity of capital. Why does the possession of capital yield an income? To say that capital is scarce is to imply that saving does involve some kind of social cost. The social cost of adding to the stock of capital is that of diverting current consumption to investment. It is always possible to increase future output indefinitely by investing more and consuming less in the present. But the results of present investment become available only after a lapse of time: 'waiting' is involved in every act of investment. It is because the supply of 'waiting' is limited that capital is scarce.

'Waiting', no doubt, is merely a neutral synonym for 'abstinence' when abstinence is given its Seniorian meaning of 'the conduct of a person who abstains from the unproductive use of what he can command'. But the waiting theory avoids the weaknesses of the abstinence theory strictly interpreted. The abstinence theory assumes that saving is a function of the interest rate and stands or falls upon that ground. But it has always been recognized that the bulk of saving in a capitalist economy is business saving out of previously earned profits that may be little influenced by the rate of interest. Even Senior conceded that 'capitals are generally formed from small beginnings by acts of accumulation, which become in time habitual. The capitalist soon regards the increase of his capital as the great business of his life; and considers the greater part of his profit more a means to an end than as a subject of enjoyment'. Moreover, personal saving in the upper income brackets is largely involuntary, the result of income exceeding customary levels of expenditure. The effect of social taboos on the squandering of capital and the halo that surrounds the practice of saving is such as to leave little scope for interest-induced saving. Mill observed that 'the savings by which an addition is made to the national capital usually emanate from the desire of persons to improve what is termed their conditions of life, or to make a provision for children or others'. Still, this argument can be pressed too far. Saving is, no doubt, a function of the level of income and of its distribution but it is also dependent upon the rate of interest. The advantage of speaking of 'waiting' rather than of 'abstinence' is that we do not commit ourselves in advance to the nature of the supply curve of savings and, in addition, lay appropriate stress on the fundamental element of time, which alone creates the need for a social sacrifice if the stock of capital is to be increased.

The abstinence theory of interest is more than a piece of crude apologetics. In essence, it is simply a logical deduction of the view of capital contained in the classical wages fund doctrine. If capital consists principally of 'advances' to workers, the rate of interest is the reward for those who can afford to lend present wage goods in return for future wage and non-wage goods.

12. The Theory of Value

Owing to the peculiar construction of Mill's book, and possibly because of a desire to answer the big questions before turning to the little ones, factor pricing has already been discussed before anything has yet been said about the principles determining product prices. **Book III, chapter 1**, at last plunges into the subject of value, beginning with a clarification of the meaning of such terms as 'use value', 'exchange value', 'general exchange value', 'price', and the like. Mill suggests that it is convenient to consider the value of a commodity in relation to its purchasing power over all other goods whose relative prices do not vary among themselves. In other words, the price of wheat is compared to the fixed price of a composite commodity bundle. This will permit one to speak of a cost-reducing improvement in agriculture lowering the relative value of wheat without having to specify all its attendant effects on other commodities (**section 2**). This is nothing but Marshall's method of partial equilibrium analysis. Mill goes on to point out that value is essentially a relative concept: 'there cannot be a general rise of values' (**section 4**). He confines his discussion to goods produced under competitive conditions (**section 5**).

Book III, chapter 2, introduces the concepts of demand and supply. Manufacturing is carried on at constant costs, while agriculture is carried on at increasing costs (**section 2**). Demand is defined as 'effectual demand', not in Adam Smith's sense of the term as the demand which realizes the 'natural price' of a commodity, but in the ordinary sense of desire backed up by purchasing power. Supply being the quantity offered for sale and demand being the desire to purchase on the part of those who have the power, he raises the question as to how can there be a ratio between a quantity and a desire, 'two things not of the same denomination'? (**section 3**). Without drawing a demand curve, Mill is clearly cognizant of the fact that demand determines price because it is essentially a schedule of quantities, itself a function of price. And, indeed, he shows quite clearly that an equilibrium price is one that equates demand and supply; it is not a ratio between demand and supply that determines prices: 'the proper mathematical analogy is that of an *equation*' (**section 4**). Does this make Mill the inventor of the Marshallian cross? Alas, no, for Cournot had already drawn demand and the supply curves ten years earlier and Mill, after all, did not go that far.

For the purpose of explaining relative prices, Mill classifies goods into three groups: (1) perfectly inelastic supply or 'absolutely limited in supply'; (2) perfectly elastic supply or 'susceptible of indefinite multiplication without increase of cost'; and (3) relatively elastic supply or 'susceptible of indefinite multiplication but not without increase of cost' (**chapter 2, sections 3, 5,** and **chapter 3**). (See Figure 6–1.) The value of goods in the first class, he notes is determined solely by demand; in the second class, by 'another law', namely, cost of production; and in the third class, by cost of production 'in the most unfavourable existing circumstances'. He has in mind the distinction between demand-determined prices (case I) and supply-determined prices (case II) but fails to point out that the law of demand and supply is perfectly general and embraces both cases (case III). Moreover, he leaves no doubt that zero elasticity of supply is a phenomenon of the short run – all reproducible goods may be augmented in quantity, given sufficient time – while constant costs typically occur in the long run. But Mill perpetuates Ricardo's misleading distinction between long-run prices determined by costs and short-run prices determined by demand and supply. This seems to be a mistake in terminology, however, not in substance. Although Mill spoke awkwardly of the law of demand and supply as a 'law of value anterior to cost of production', in chapter 9 of Book III he observed that 'cost of production would have no effect on value if it could have none on supply'.

Figure 6–1

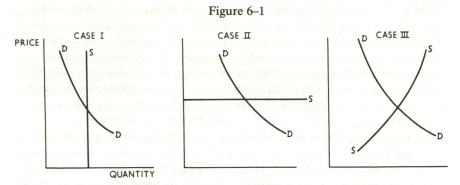

Toward the end of **Book III, chapter 3, section 1**, Mill mistakenly defines the long-run price as an average trend value of a series of short-run market prices. The distinction between the short and the long run is not in principle a distinction between a brief and a long period of time [see chapter 10, section 1]. And the least-square trend of a time series of prices does not represent the price in stationary long-run equilibrium.

Book III, chapter 4, lays down the doctrine that value depends principally on the quantity of labour required to produce goods (**section 1**). With equal ratios of capital to labour in all industries, relative prices are not affected by changes in wage rates (**section 2**). The prices of commodities produced by labour of different skills are affected by differences in relative wages but in considering 'the causes of *variations* in value, quantity of labour is the thing of chief importance' (**section 3**). However, wine and cloth produced by equal amounts of homogeneous labour will not sell at equal prices because wine is 'called upon to yield profit during a longer period of time than the other' and 'all commodities made by machinery are assimilated, at least approximately, to the wine in the preceding example' (**section 5**). The whole of section 5 is, in fact, an excellent review of Ricardo's first chapter on value – it takes Mill three pages to say what Ricardo said in thirty.

Book III, chapter 4, section 6, and **chapter 5** generalize the concept of rent to all goods and factors in inelastic supply. In such cases, prices are always determined by marginal costs, and 'the price paid for a differential advantage in producing a commodity cannot enter into the general cost of production of the commodity'. On the other hand, rent *is* an expense of production that affects price when the factor in question is subject to alternative uses. **Chapter 6** summarizes the previous five chapters and calls for no special comments.

To round off the topic, the reader should now turn to **Book III, chapters 15** and **16**. Chapter 15 is a brief but interesting review of the old problem of Ricardo's quest for the philosopher's stone: an invariant unit of measurement with which to pinpoint the source of a change in relative prices. 'The desideratum sought by political economists', Mill remarks 'is not a measure of the value of things at the same time and place, but a measure of the value of the same thing at different times and places'. This 'desideratum' is impossible to attain, Mill contends. It is significant that he did not even contemplate the idea that the difficulty could be solved by a price index. He was perfectly well acquainted with the concept of index numbers but, like most of his contemporaries, did not believe it feasible to construct a price index of all goods. A 'general measure of exchange value' being out of the question, Mill goes on to say, 'writers have formed a notion, under the name of a measure of value which could be more properly termed a measure of cost of production', that is, 'some means of ascertaining the value of a commodity by merely comparing it with the measure, without referring it specially to any other given commodity'. This is an excellent statement of the meaning of Ricardo's 'invariable measure of value'. Mill does not explain, however, how such an invariable 'measure of cost of production' can be constructed. And that is where the problem was put to rest for the next 112 years [see chapter 4, section 31].

Book III, chapter 16, 'Some Peculiar Cases of Value', marks the first appearance in economic literature of the problem of joint costs (**section 1**). Mill considers the case in which two goods are produced in fixed proportions and he shows that the price of each product must be such as to clear its market, subject to the condition that the sum of the two prices equals their joint cost. The case of joint costs presents a new qualification to the labour theory of value. Even in a one-factor economy, the relative prices of joint products – say, venison and deer skins – are determined by demand as well as by supply.

13. The Quantity Theory of Money

Book III, chapter 7, is a standard 19th-century textbook treatment of the advantages of the precious metals as a medium of exchange. The closing page of this chapter states the 'neutrality' of money in the most uncompromising fashion but in **Book III, chapter 8, section 2**, we are told that people normally hold cash balances as 'a reserve for future contingencies'. An increase in the supply of money raises the level of prices proportionately *if* there are 'no alterations of the proportions in the demand for different commodities'. This is a perfect statement of what we earlier called a 'neutral' distribution of extra cash in exact proportion to the size of individual holdings [see chapter 5, section 7]. Like Cantillon, Mill realized that the process of increasing the quantity of money may alter relative prices. Barring that possibility, and provided that the only means of payment are coins and redeemable paper, the value of money varies inversely with the quantity of money in circulation. Velocity is discussed in **chapter 8, section 3**, and the distinction between the 'motion theory' and the 'rest theory' of velocity is drawn. The equation of exchange, $MV = PT$, is clearly expressed in words. Bank credit, which Mill excludes from M, complicates matters and he is not willing simply to add bank credit to currency in circulation because he denies that bank reserves consisting of legal tender always bear a constant ratio to deposits (**section 4**). He points out that a mere increase in M does not raise prices if the money is hoarded and likewise for an increase of M that keeps pace with a rising T.

All this is said to be a straightforward application of the law of demand and supply but, in the next chapter, the long-run value of gold and silver is made dependent upon cost of production. We have already noted [see chapter 4, section 26] that the quantity theory of money is not incompatible with 'metallism', that is, the labour theory of value applied to the monetary metal. If gold rises above its 'natural' price, the level of prices falls and gold producers can purchase all inputs for less gold; the output of gold then rises until gold is once again at its natural value. But, as Mill himself observes, gold being extremely durable and the gold stock large relative to the annual output of gold mines, such an adjustment takes place only slowly. Hence, the cost of production of gold has little influence on prices, which are largely governed by the quantity of money actually in circulation (**chapter 9, section 3**).

Book III, chapter 10, on bimetallism, contains nothing of importance. In the eagerness to refute the popular fallacy that capital can be created simply by turning the money crank. Mill denies that bank credit can do more than divert capital from one field to another – the full-capacity assumption he had earlier discarded in Book I, chapter 11, section 1. In his 1844 *Essays*, Mill had accepted the forced saving doctrine. In the first edition of the *Principles* he made no mention of it. But in the sixth edition, published in 1865, he added a footnote admitting that inflation can 'create capital', even if the capital stock is already utilized at capacity, by drawing resources from the luxury sector to the sector producing capital goods.

The rest of **Book III, chapter 11**, describes the nature of contemporary credit instruments with copious quotations from Thornton. **Chapter 12** shows that bank credit would act on prices just as would an increase in the supply of metals if the supply of credit is tied to the gold supply. Under a convertible paper standard, prices cannot rise for long without inducing a compensatory outflow of gold. But when paper is inconvertible, an elastic currency may promote a speculative boom such as took place in 1824, leading to collapse in the following years: 'this is the ideal extreme case of what is called a commercial crisis' (**section 2**). The crisis of 1847, however, was the result of a sharp rise in interest rates owing to a heavy draft on the money market produced by the railway boom and the unprecedented importation of corn. From **section 4** onward, **chapter 12** contains little of importance, except for **section 8**, which denies the doctrine of the Currency School that a control of bank notes would in effect control checkbook credit.

14. Inflation

Book III, chapter 13, deals at length with inconvertible paper currencies. A convertible currency cannot be issued to excess because the advantage of turning coins and notes into bullion keeps it in check (**section 1**). An inconvertible currency can be issued to excess, however, the test being whether the market price of bullion has risen above the mint price fixed prior to suspension of specie payments (**section 2**). This is merely a reproduction of Ricardo's argument and a very uncritical reproduction at that. **Sections 3** and **4** attack inflationary papermoney schemes on comparative static grounds. The Hume-Cantillon argument that the process of increasing M may stimulate T is paraphrased but dogmatically rejected on the grounds that the gains of some are matched by the losses of others: 'there is no way in which a general and permanent rise of prices . . . can benefit anybody, except at the expense of somebody else' **(section 5)**. Without making any reference to the existence or nonexistence of idle resources, Mill suddenly introduces a new pro-inflationary argument never contemplated by 18th-century economists: a rise in prices lowers the real value of debt and hence favours debtors against creditors; now 'the productive class . . . generally owe large debts to the unproductive . . . especially if the national debt be included'. We recognize this as an argument that has since become the stock-in-trade of the doctrine of the benefits of 'creeping inflation'. But Mill has no sooner presented it than he dismisses it on grounds of equity. The denial of the doctrine that 'money stimulates trade' is therefore allowed to stand side by side with the footnote admission of forced saving and the debtor-creditor argument without any effort at reconciliation. This is all the more remarkable since the fourth edition of the *Principles* came out in 1857, by which time 'The Currency Extension Act of Nature' – the gold discoveries of 1848 in California and Australia – had added about 30 percent to the gold coinage of the United Kingdom. These eight years were extremely prosperous and the boom was widely attributed to the beneficial effects of the gold inflow.

15. The Loanable Funds Theory

We pass on to **Book III, chapter 23**, which deals with the determination of the rate of interest. Gross profits on capital, Mill observes, consist of wages of management, a risk premium and interest **(section 1)**. He distinguishes in so many words between the capitalist earning interest for abstinence and the 'employer' – we would say 'entrepreneur' – earning a compensation for risk. The rate of interest is determined by the demand and supply of loanable funds. The demand for loans consists of investment demand plus government demand plus landlord demand for unproductive consumption; the supply of funds is made up of savings plus bank notes plus bank deposits **(section 2)**. The rate of interest is subject to alteration owing to changes in the demand and supply of funds independently of the rate of profit **(sections 3–4)**. This section should dispel the notion that the classical economists never distinguished between the market rate of interest and the yield of capital. The quantity of money as such has no influence on the rate of interest, Mill goes on to observe, but a change in the quantity of money necessarily alters the interest rate **(section 4)**. Inflation 'while in process' *raises* the interest rate when the inflation is due to government expenditure financed by the issue of inconvertible paper, but additional bank credit or an inflow of gold tends to *lower* the rate of interest. In equilibrium, the market rate of interest must equal the rate of return on capital; the rate of interest is therefore ultimately determined by real forces.

16. Say's Law

We turn back to **Book III, chapter 14**, which refutes the thesis that oversaving is possible. The doctrine of Malthus, Chalmers and Sismondi, Mill confesses, 'involves so much inconsistency in its very conception, that I feel considerable difficulty in giving any statement of it'. The essence of the argument, he goes on to show, is that all producers may fail to sell at cost-covering prices owing to the failure of purchasing power to absorb the extra capacity created by rapid capital accumulation. Note the statement in **section 4**, which observes that during a commercial crisis 'there is really an excess of all commodities above the money-demand: in other words, there is an undersupply of money', a clear statement of Walras' Law [see chapter 5, section 1]. Mill expresses the fear that the theory of oversaving may give comfort to restrictionist policies: Chalmers, says Mill, 'inculcates on capitalists the practice of moral restraint in the pursuit of gain; while Sismondi deprecates machinery'.

17. The Currency-Banking Controversy

Book III, chapters 22 and **24**, should be read consecutively, dealing as they do with the question of how to assure price stability under a mixed paper currency.

For an appreciation of Mill's position, it is necessary to sketch the background of the great controversy that divided his generation on the issue of currency regulation. Ricardo had laid down *the* currency principle: a mixed gold-paper currency should be made to vary in the same way as a purely metallic currency, so that it responds automatically to any inflow or outflow of gold. In his day, the fact that the note issue was inconvertible made some kind of regulation of the currency mandatory. With the resumption of specie payments in 1821, the question arose whether convertibility as such provided an automatic mechanism to stabilize the currency. Ricardo's writings suggested that this was not so and the so-called Currency School, led by Overstone, Norman and Torrens, took its stand on a regulated note issue that would tie the currency to the movement of the foreign exchanges. The Bank of England leaned toward the views of the Currency School and, under the guidance of one of its great governors, Horsley Palmer, it followed the rule of maintaining a constant ratio of security holdings – loans, investments and discounted paper – to total liabilities. This rule seemed to make regulation an automatic matter, for it tended to maintain a constant internal circulation unless acted upon by external gold movements. The Bank Charter Act of 1844 achieved the same effect by centralizing the note issue in the hands of the Bank and at the same time limiting its power to issue notes against securities up to a fixed amount, above which they could be issued only in exchange for gold and silver. Moreover, the Act formally separated the Issue Department from the Banking Department and left the function of discounting entirely unregulated on the strength of the notion that changes in deposits would follow changes in the note issue.

In contrast to the Currency School, the Banking School, numbering Tooke and Fullarton among its most prominent advocates, denied that it was possible to overissue a convertible paper currency inasmuch as 'the needs of trade' automatically controlled the volume of notes issued. There was no need for statutory control of the currency as long as convertibility was maintained. In addition, it was argued that the use of bank deposits, bills of exchange and other forms of credit as substitutes for Bank Notes would defeat the Currency School's efforts to control the money supply through the control of Bank Notes only. The emphasis of the Banking School on the overall structure of credit is very reminiscent of the stress on 'liquidity' in the British Radcliffe Report of 1959.

It is clear that at bottom neither school recognized the necessity for discretionary management of the currency. The Currency School wanted to regulate the note issue in order to leave central banking free, while the Banking School balked at the idea of any monetary management whatever. Neither side recognized the essential functions of a central bank as a 'lender of last resort', a fact which gives the entire controversy a somewhat dated appearance. But underlying the debate were important differences of opinion about the definition of money that persist to this day. The Currency School has been characterized as asserting that only gold and redeemable notes are money and that their total circulation should be made to reflect the changes in gold supply. But, in effect, their argument was more subtle. Just as Thornton and the Bullion Report had argued earlier that the issues of country banks were substantially governed by Bank of England Notes, so the protagonists of the currency principle argued that, while credit could influence prices just as much as coins and paper money, the superstructure of credit could not for long get out of line with the supply of gold and Bank Notes; the latter were the basic monetary instruments because they were always demanded for final payments in a crisis. Moreover, they held that the low velocity of circulation of bank deposits and bills of exchange rendered these credit instruments a quantitatively unimportant part of the money supply. On the other hand, the Banking School's stress on the variety of sources of credit, and their insistence that it was necessary to control near-money as well as money proper, is relevant once again in view of the current debate over the role of financial intermediaries in monetary policy.

18. The Real Bills Doctrine

The Banking School based its contention that a mixed currency will expand and contract with the needs of business on the fact that a bank's assets will normally consist of 'real bills'. If banks restrict their loans to self-liquidating commercial paper, that is, to discounting short-term notes based on goods in process, the means of payment in an economy will necessarily expand in pace with the volume of goods produced. This doctrine is stated quite plainly in the *Wealth of Nations* [see chapter 2, section 13] and was attacked by Thornton, Ricardo and the Bullion Committee as being the standard view of the Directors of the Bank of England. The Banking School held the real bills doctrine in the form of a Law of Reflux: if banks should ignore the policy of real-bills-only and lend on long terms or for speculative purposes, the rise in prices would cause the 'excess issue' to flow back to the banks through repayment of loans or conversion into specie. The Law of Reflux thus assures the impossibility of inflation produced by an overexpansion of bank credit. Some exponents of the real bills doctrine conceded that loans to the government by the central bank might be inflationary. Barring the last contingency, however, it followed that a rise in prices is not typically preceded but, on the contrary, is followed by an increase in the circulating media. It is easy to see why the Banking School and

Thomas Tooke in particular are associated with the contra-quantity theory of money.

In opposition to the Law of Reflux stands the Thornton-Ricardo doctrine of the market rate of interest as the connecting link between money and prices: at any bank rate below the long-term equilibrium interest rate, the demand for loans and discounts is insatiable. Confining loans or discounts to bona fide commercial paper does not furnish a check to overissue, even when the currency is convertible. Most of the good arguments against the real bills doctrine are already found in Thornton's *Nature of the Paper Credit* (1802). First of all, the same product may be sold a number of times, each sale giving rise to a new real bill. In this way the money supply may expand far beyond the needs of business, even though each loan is made on short-term commercial paper. Second, bankers may have difficulty in distinguishing real from speculative bills, and anyway tend to regard customers' loans as the least liquid of their assets. Most important of all, the current volume of bills is a function not merely of the volume of transactions but also of the length of time for which bills must run, that is, the velocity of circulation. Since commercial bills are near-money, a bill may be spent several times during its life and each time it is spent, it acts on prices. Inasmuch as velocity tends to rise in a boom, banking in terms of real bills will not prevent the ratio of bills to currency from rising at the very time when the money supply ought to be contracted. The expansion of loans increases money incomes, raises demand, and so justifies additional borrowing. Stability either in the quantity of money or in the volume of credit cannot be achieved by the restriction of discounts to real bills. The real bills doctrine entirely ignores the rate at which bills, real or not, are discounted. An expansion of loans can always be induced by a reduction in the bank rate or by a failure to raise the bank rate when profits are rising. But despite Thornton's impressive rebuttal of the Law of Reflux, the real bills doctrine lived on into the 20th century to be written into the Federal Reserve Act of 1913.

19. Mill's Position on Monetary Management

Mill starts out by endorsing the real bills doctrine: the Law of Reflux is 'far nearer to being the expression of the whole truth than any form whatever of the currency theory' (**Book III, chapter 24, section 2**). In Book III, chapter 13, and again in Book III, chapter 22, Mill had pointed out that the overissue of a convertible currency leads to either an outflow of gold via a deficit in the balance of payments or the melting down of coin for conversion to industrial use, induced by the rising price of industrial gold relative to the fixed money value of gold coin. This contention is qualified in **chapter 24, section 2**, by the distinction between the two states of markets: 'the quiescent' and 'the speculative' – this is as near as Mill ever came to a statement of turning points in the business cycle. In the quiescent state, the Law of Reflux would provide an automatic check to overissue. But in the speculative state, when everyone expects prices to rise, bank credit may indeed rise without limit even if the banks obey the rule of real-bills-only. He takes note of the Tooke-Fullarton objection that speculative purchases are typically financed by checks and that the note issue begins to expand only *after* prices have risen. When speculation has spread from dealers to producers, however, Mill declares, the volume of Bank Notes begins to rise and it is only then that the inflationary upsurge takes hold. In this way, Mill appears to effect a compromise between the views of the Banking School – valid for quiescent states – and the Currency School – valid for speculative states. His own leanings are clearly toward the Banking School however – with Adam Smith and against Thornton and Ricardo – as is made clear in his negative evaluation of the Charter Act of 1844 (**Book III, chapter 24, sections 3–6**). The comments on the speculative state, nevertheless, grant the gist of the Currency School's criticism of the real bills doctrine.

20. Theory of International Values

Book III, chapter 17, provides a good review of the Law of Comparative Costs [see chapter 4, section 21]. In **chapter 18** it is shown that the barter terms of trade depend not only on cost conditions but also on 'reciprocal demand'. The 'equation of international demand' stipulates that the value of one country's exports must equal the value of the other country's imports, and the terms of trade are therefore determined 'by the amount and extensibility of demand', or what we would now call the level and elasticity of demand for imports in each country (**section 2**). The greater and more elastic the foreign demand, the more favourable are the terms of trade to the home country. In **section 3**, Mill introduces the cost of carriage and notes that every increase of transport costs means a lessening of the gains from trade; once we allow for transport costs, the ratios of exchange between two products are no longer the same in the two countries; finally, transport costs give rise to goods of domestic trade that are never exported or imported. The argument is generalized to more than two commodities and two countries in **section 4**.

In **section 5** it is argued that a cost-reducing improvement in the linen industry of 'Germany' may turn the barter terms of trade in favour of 'England' by more than the fall in linen's relative price. In the last paragraph of section 5, where this argument is considered, Mill comes close to expressing the concept of price elasticity of demand (ω), so close, indeed, that only the substitution of the word 'proportion' for his 'ratio' suffices to yield the modern Marshallian definition. He divides all exports into three classes: (1) those in which 'the demand is increased in greater ratio than the fall in price' – $\omega > 1$; (2) those in which total receipts remain constant when the price falls because the quantity demanded increases in 'the same proportion with the cheapness' – $\omega = 1$; and (3) those in which receipts fall because the quantity demanded increases in a smaller 'ratio' than the fall in price – $\omega < 1$. Edgeworth dismissed **sections 6–9** of this chapter as 'laborious and confusing'; it was added in later additions in response to the criticism that multiple equilibria are possible when either country has an inelastic demand for the other country's product.

Later neoclassical writers added little to Mill's pure theory of international values except to allow for varying costs in either country. The only real point of substance concerned the relative size of the two countries and the relative importance of the two traded commodities: a small country producing an item important in inter-

Figure 6–2

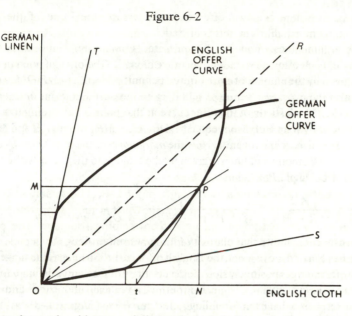

national trade may be able to specialize exclusively in its production and so turn the terms of trade in its favour; or, if one country is large relative to another, it can force exchange at the limit of the range of comparative costs. The formal presentation of Mill's argument, however, was considerably improved. In the late 1870s, Marshall devised an elegant geometrical illustration of the action of reciprocal demand. He measured all export goods in terms of a common unit – 'the representative bale' – and constructed each country's offer curve for the other country's exports.

Offer curves or 'reciprocal demand' curves are peculiar demand curves because they express demand not in terms of the price per unit of the other good but in terms of the total supply of the other good; they are analogous to a total instead of an average revenue curve. The English offer curve (Figure 6–2) shows that on exchange for *OM* amount of linen, England is willing to *offer ON* amount of cloth; in other words, in exchange for *ON* cloth, England *demands OM* linen; likewise, Germany is offering *OM* linen for *ON* English cloth. The price lines *OS* and *OT* represent the terms on which England could obtain linen at home and Germany could obtain cloth at home in the absence of trade, denoting the respective comparative-cost ratios of linen to cloth in the two countries. They are straight lines because of the assumption of constant costs. The offer curves follow the price line in the absence of trade and then move away from the price line, showing each country's willingness to offer less exports for every increment in imports. The price lines set the outer limits for the offer curves because no country will offer more exports for imports than it can produce in import-competing industries at home. Equilibrium in trade requires the value of imports to equal the value of exports simultaneously for each party to the trade. The equilibrium quantities of cloth and linen that will be traded are thus given by the point where the two offer curves intersect, the slope of the ray OR representing the equilibrium 'terms of trade'.

Mill's argument can now be demonstrated graphically. Notice first that the elasticity of each offer curve falls as we move along it. The price of linen in terms of cloth is given by the amount of cloth offered per unit of linen, say $MP/OM = ON/PN$. This is also the average revenue of selling cloth measured in terms of linen, or cot angle PON. The elasticity of the offer curve at that point is, according to a formula made famous by Joan Robinson, equal to $AR/(AR - MR)$, where AR and MR stand for average and marginal revenue. Now the *marginal* revenue on selling ON amounts of cloth for PN amounts of linen is given by the tangent to the English offer curve at point P, or cot angle PtN. Thus,

$$\omega = \frac{AR}{AR - MR} = \frac{ON/PN}{(ON/PN) - (tN/PN)} = \frac{ON}{ON - tN} = \frac{ON}{Ot} > 1.$$

Casual inspection shows that elasticity falls as we move along the curves; that is, t approaches N as we move along the English offer curve. So long as the tangent to the English offer curve is positively sloped, the elasticity of England's demand for linen is > 1. Unitary elasticity would mean a perfectly vertical offer curve and inelastic demand implies a backward-bending offer curve (see Figure 6–3). A technical improvement in Germany's linen-export industry would alter the conditions of supply as shown by the displaced curve OG': whereas Germany was willing initially to offer NQ linen for ON cloth, she is now prepared to offer as much as NQ' linen. The effect of the cost reduction on the terms of trade clearly depends on the shape of the English offer curve. If it is a straight vertical line beyond the old intersection point, that is Or_2 – the case of unitary elasticity where the English demand for linen increases in 'the same proportion with the cheapness' – the terms of trade do not turn in England's favour as much as when her demand for linen is inelastic (Or_1). If her demand is highly elastic, Or_3, we have the case in which the terms of trade move in her favour by *less* than the initial fall in linen's relative price. Since England is trading cloth on the horizontal axis for linen on the vertical axis, England gets better terms of trade with a counterclockwise rotation of the price lines OP, OP', OP'', etcetera, whereas Germany's position would improve with a clockwise rotation of the price line.

Later, in **Book V, chapter 4, section 6**, Mill takes up the question of the effect of a tax on exports and imports. The same diagram will do duty for that problem. If OG' represents the initial untaxed offer curve, the OG is the displaced offer curve net of tax when Germany taxes English imports and/or Germany's exports. According to the position of the original intersection, we have the three cases Mill distinguishes in his discussion.

It is also evident from Marshall's diagram that when England's or Germany's offer curve bends backward because of inelasticity of demand, multiple equilibria are perfectly possible and the terms of trade become indeterminate, as Mill realized (**Book III, chapter 18, section 6**).

Figure 6–3

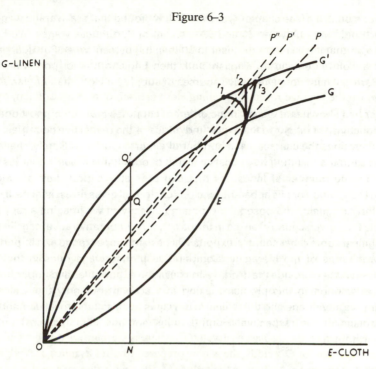

21. International Wage and Price Levels

In **Book III, chapter 19,** and **chapter 25, section 2,** Mill elaborates upon the Seniorian doctrine of the relative value of money in open economies: the price level will be highest in countries whose export industries are the most efficient [see chapter 4, section 22]. But Mill goes further than Senior in demonstrating that a country's relative 'cost of obtaining gold' varies also with the cost of transportation: if the cost of carrying linen to England is increased, the price of linen in Germany and hence the general price level in Germany will fall relative to the price level in England via the operation of the specie-flow mechanism. Moreover, those countries whose exportable goods are most in demand abroad and who have the least home demand for foreign goods will have the relatively higher price level.

Senior's doctrine in respect of relative wage levels between countries also needs amendment in the light of reciprocal demand. First, when demand and supply conditions promote favourable barter terms of trade for a country, the level of wages in that country will be high relative to other trading nations. Second, the greater the importance of cloth in international trade relative to linen, the higher the level of wages in Britain relative to the German wage level. And lastly, the less elastic the English demand for German linen, or the more elastic Germany's demand for English cloth, the higher the English wage level relative to that of Germany. Recalling the numerical example employed in our previous exposition of Senior's doctrine [see chapter 4, section 22], we found that the average wage in England could vary between 80 and $53\frac{1}{3}$ percent of Portuguese wages. We have now shown that it is likely to be closer to 80 than $53\frac{1}{3}$ percent when Portugal has a greater absolute demand for English cloth than England has for port wine and when Portugal has more alternative sources of supply for cloth than England has for port.

Senior had shown that wages in the different countries must be proportional to the productivity of labour in the export industries of the respective countries. But what determines the character and number of export industries? Surely, the level of wages and the resulting wage costs per unit of output in various industries will determine the number of industries that can profitably export their products? Toward the solution of this apparently vicious circle, Mill gives no assistance. It was Mountfort Longfield who posed the problem correctly: if we imagine a range of products for a given country ranked in terms of their comparative advantage in real costs against some other country, exports will be in the upper range and imports in the lower range of the hierarchy. Comparative money wage rates in the two countries will then provide the dividing line between exportables and importables. The final solution to this problem, taking into account not only the scales of comparative advantage and the structure of wages but also reciprocal demand for the products of the respective countries, was not given until much later by Edgeworth.

22. Hume's Law

Book III, chapter 20, deals with the elementary principles of foreign exchange adjustments under a gold standard, emphasizing the role of prices in bringing about equilibrium in the balance of payments. **Book III, chapter 21**, discusses the international distribution of specie. Mill's version of Hume's Law is much broader than that of any previous author. He shows that an inflow of gold lowers interest rates even as it raises prices (see also chapter 24, section 4). As the interest rate falls, short-term capital will flow abroad, thus promising an adjustment of the exchange rate. Mill was one of the first authors to emphasize the fact that the central bank can protect its reserves during an external drain by raising the bank rate, thus assisting the rise in the market rate of interest that is already taking place as a result of the gold outflow. The rise in interest rates attracts capital from abroad; the demand for British bills of exchange rises and, as the price of bills increases, it becomes profitable to ship bullion instead; thus, the exchange rate turns in favour of England. This mechanism, linking the bank rate to international movements of specie, was stated systematically by George Goschen's *Theory of the Foreign Exchanges* (1861). The essence of it, however, is in Mill and to some extent even in Thornton.

Section 2 of **chapter 21** takes up the effect of technical improvements in the production of exports on the gains of trade shared between countries: the whole of the gain of a reduction in the cost of making English cloth goes to Germany if German demand for English cloth is of unitary elasticity. If the German demand is price-inelastic, the price to German buyers will be greater than to English buyers. The gains to England exceed the gains to Germany only if the German demand is relatively elastic. If 'gain' is measured by the fall in the price of cloth relative to a given amount of linen, the result is obvious and can be read off the Marshall offer curves.

23. Transfer Payments

Chapter 21, section 4, is concerned with the question of unilateral transfers. It is significant that Mill does not select the export of capital as an example of transfer payments possibly because of the fundamental classical assumption of the immobility of capital between countries. Instead, he cites government remittances abroad and interest payments to foreign creditors as examples of capital transfers. Mill treats the whole question very briefly and solely in terms of price adjustments, although later in the book he gives a clear statement of the role of income changes as a corrective force to a disturbance in the balance of payments (**Book III, chapter 24, section 4**). Under a gold standard, the attempt to transfer capital to another country leads, in the first place, to a rise in the price of bills drawn on the borrowing country. There follows a flow of gold from lender to borrower – the rate of exchange being at the lending country's gold-export point – followed in turn by a rise in prices in the borrowing country relative to the lending country. The lender acquires a favourable balance and the borrower an unfavourable balance of trade, which tends to become equal to the rate of borrowing, at which point the exchanges return to parity and relative prices stabilize at new levels. Here price changes and gold flows bring about all the adjustments on the assumption that international demand in the trading countries remains unaffected by the capital transfer – *the* classical theory of transfer payments. This theory is to be contrasted with the modern Keynesian theory of transfers, which emphasizes changes in incomes and shifts in demand.

In the classical theory, the change in imports and exports is accompanied by movements in their prices along given demand curves. The transfer of capital, therefore, leads to a change in the barter terms of trade in favour of the receiving country. According to Keynesian theory, this change in the barter terms of trade is not a necessary consequence of the transfer. When a payment is made to foreigners unaccompanied by an equivalent receipt, the aggregate expenditure of the home country exceeds its income. The tendency to contract outlays at home, while foreigners are spending more, causes the demand for imports in both paying and receiving countries to shift and necessarily to shift in the direction of restoring equilibrium in the balance of payments. This shift in the demand curves may be sufficient to permit the transfer to be made in the form of goods without any change in prices.

24. The Vent-for-Surplus Doctrine

In **Book III, chapter 17, sections 4** and **5,** Mill dismisses Smith's 'vent-for-surplus' argument in favour of foreign trade as 'a surviving relic of the Mercantile theory'. Comparative cost analysis regards the territorial division of labour as a matter of moving along a static world production-transformation curve, constructed on the basis of the given resources and given techniques of the trading countries; specialization is conceived as a fully reversible process of reallocating resources. In the vent-for-surplus theory of international trade, however, emphasis is put upon the indirect gains of foreign trade conceived as a dynamic force widening the extent of the market and generating new wants. It is a consideration, as Mill says, 'principally applicable to an early stage of industrial advancement'; the opening up of a backward country to foreign trade 'sometimes works a sort of industrial revolution'. These remarks touch upon the whole question of secular changes in comparative advantage to which none of the classical economists gave very much attention. It is curious that classical theory, generally oriented as it was to problems of long-run development, should have developed an almost wholly static theory of international trade. But here, as elsewhere, it must be recognized that much of what appears to be development economics in this period is nothing but a special form of comparative static analysis in which the passage of time is conceived as being irrelevant to the outcome of the adjustment process.

25. The Basis of a Theory of International Trade

Before passing on to other questions, we must raise the question whether there is in fact any basis for a separate theory of international trade. The classical economists advocated a special theory of international as distinct from intranational trade because of the relative immobility of resources between nations. This meets with the objection that the difference is one of degree, not of kind: there is much immobility within an economy – recall Smith's remark that 'men are of all luggage the most difficult to transport' – and capital and labour do at times move across national boundaries. Either, it is said, we assume for theoretical purposes perfect mobility in domestic as well as in foreign trade, or, if we must be realistic, we should assume imperfect mobility in all cases. Cairnes, following Mill's own suggestion, argued that labour within a country is in fact immobile between certain noncompeting occupations. Exchange between such groups is therefore exactly like exchange between countries, that is, wages and profits are not equalized by the movement of labour and capital. Hence, it is not true that domestic trade takes place on the basis of cost of production, while international trade is governed by reciprocal demand; between noncompeting groups of domestic industries, value is also regulated by reciprocal demand. Cairnes thus took the first step toward a general theory of value in which domestic trade and international trade are merely special cases depending upon the prevailing degree of factor mobility.

It would probably avoid misunderstanding if we followed Bastable and spoke of a classical theory of 'interregional' trade rather than of 'international' trade. The classical economists never claimed that their definition of 'nation' coincided with the political boundaries of countries. Mill advisedly used the term 'distant places' and pointed out that trade with the colonies is really internal trade, not subject to the law of international values (Book III, chapter 25, section 5). At all events, we can agree that nations are conspicuous examples of noncompeting groups and the case for a separate theory of international trade rests on that claim. There is nothing to prevent one from applying the doctrine to regions within a country when the relevant conditions hold. Even the classical economists applied the specie-flow mechanism to trade between London and the provinces, arguing that the country banks could not overissue without losing gold to London.

As we have already observed, the neoclassical economists added little of substance to Mill's pure theory of international trade. By the pure theory of international trade we mean the theory that asks: assuming that balance-of-payments equilibrium is maintained, what are the gains of trade and how are these gains distributed between countries via the terms of trade? In modern times, however, the pure theory has been reformulated by two Swedish economists, Heckscher and Ohlin. The Heckscher-Ohlin theory explains the pattern of trade in terms of the relative factor endowments of countries: a country will tend to have a comparative advantage in those products which use intensively the country's relatively abundant factor of production, and will therefore import products which use intensively the country's scarce factor. This theory absorbs Ricardo's Law of Comparative Cost, supplemented by Mill's concept of reciprocal demand, but goes beyond it by linking the pattern of trade to the economic structure of trading nations. In this way, the Heckscher-Ohlin theory provides a model for analyzing the effects of a change in trade on domestic economic structures and, in particular, on the domestic distribution of income. It throws into relief the old classical proposition that trade is a substitute for international factor movements and thus raises the question whether, in the absence of complete international factor mobility, trade alone could work to equalize the prices of all factors of production in all trading countries. Suffice it to say that, although the Ricardo-Mill theory of international trade has stood up much better than many other parts of classical political economy, even this theory has now been so thoroughly transformed that it is sometimes difficult to recognize the old wine in the new bottles.

26. Statics and Dynamics

The last chapter of Book III of Mill's *Principles* lays down the Ricardian view of economic development as a race between 'population and agricultural skill', repeating the gist of Book I, chapter 13. Ostensibly, its purpose is to show that the 'laws of distribution' are not affected by the presence of money in the economy, being the result of 'real' forces. The whole of Book IV is devoted to analyzing the nature of these forces determining the secular changes in factor prices and distributive shares. In chapter 1, Mill announces the distinction between 'statics' and 'dynamics', which he had borrowed from Comte. So far, he declares, we have examined 'the economical laws of a stationary and unchanging society', a rather surprising assertion in view of the discussion of the Malthusian theory of population, the laws of returns, and the question of socialism in Book I. Now, he goes on to say, we add the 'dynamics of political economy to the statics'. It is hardly necessary to say that the terms 'statics' and 'dynamics' have undergone considerable changes of meaning since Mill's day. 'Dynamics' now denotes analysis that takes explicit account of temporal leads and lags in economic relationships – witness current models employing difference equations – as against 'statics' in which all the variables refer to the same point of time. Quesnay's *Tableau Economique*, though it employs the concept of the stationary state as an expository device, is primitive 'dynamics' in the modern sense of the word because of the assumption of a one-year income-spending lag. The wages fund doctrine represents another example of elementary economic dynamics. For Mill, however, 'dynamics' means analysis of historical change, whereas 'statics' seems to denote what we now call comparative static analysis: the comparison of an initial equilibrium situation that is disturbed by an exogenous 'shock' with the subsequent equilibrium situation after the disturbance has worked itself out. But Mill is by no means consistent in this: we have already seen examples of his 'dynamics' and numerous examples of static reasoning occur in Books IV and V.

27. The Falling Rate of Profit

Chapter 2 of **Book IV** treats the Smithian problem of secular changes in the structure of prices from a Ricardian viewpoint. As in Book I, chapter 13, Mill concedes that a strong 'impulse' toward agricultural improvements has shown itself since 1830 or thereabouts, such that the tendency to diminishing returns has been more than offset. He suggests that a time series of agricultural prices, adjusted for seasonal variation and changes in the value of money, will reveal which of the two opposing forces, diminishing returns or technical change, has in fact predominated (**section 3**). This is a new note in the literature: the Ricardian system predicted rising wheat prices in the absence of free trade and no one before Mill had proposed submitting this proposition to an empirical test.

The rest of chapter 2 (**sections 4** and **5**) defends commodity speculation as a method of ironing out fluctuations in prices. **Book IV, chapter 3**, looks at the possible changes in the distributive shares under four conditions: (1) when population increases faster than capital (**section 1**); (2) when capital increases faster than population (**section 2**); (3) the typical Ricardian case in which capital and population increase proportionately (**section 3**); and (4) when capital and population do not grow at all but technical change is reducing the inputs required to produce output (**section 4**). Section 4 contains an analysis of the effects of laboursaving innovations in agriculture on the value of rent. It adds nothing to Ricardo's presentation except an emphasis on the short-run nature of his argument.

Book IV, chapter 4, provides an original treatment of 'the tendency of profits to a minimum'. Mill notes that there is a minimum supply price of capital, namely 'a rate which the average person will deem an equivalent for abstinence'. This rate tends to fall with economic progress because 'mankind becomes more willing to sacrifice present indulgence for future objects': the larger the annual output, the less anxious people are to supplement current consumption by drawing on accumulated savings. In addition, the growth of capital depresses its productivity. As Mill points out, riskless consols stand at 3 percent in England. *In the absence of technical change*, the present rate of capital accumulation must reduce this 'in a small number of years' to 1 percent, which he takes to be the minimum supply price of capital. The rate of profit is, therefore, habitually within 'a hand's breadth of the minimum' and the country is forever on the verge of stationariness (**section 4**). The counteracting forces to this tendency are examined in **section 5**. They consist of (1) capital losses during a crisis (**sections 5–8**); (2) technical improvements, particularly in the production of wage goods (**section 6**); (3) the extension of foreign trade, insofar as it lowers the real cost of obtaining wage goods (**section 7**); and (4) the export of capital (**section 8**). Capital exports offset the declining rate of profit, not because they provide a 'vent-for-surplus', but because they are typically sent to the colonies to produce primary goods for export to the home country, the ultimate effect of which is to lower the real cost of obtaining wage goods. In section 5, Mill links the periodicity of crises to the very tendency of the rate of profit to fall, the waste of capital in the slump preparing the way for a recovery of profit expectations. This chapter, as we shall see, was read and carefully noted by Marx. In the following chapter (**chapter 5**), Mill concludes that the tendency of the rate of profit to fall weakens the case against government spending in such countries, a point which he had already made in Book I, chapter 4, section 8.

All through Books IV and V there is a continuous repetition of material discussed at earlier stages in the *Principles*. This is partly the result of Mill's haste in composition – the whole of the *Principles* was said to have been written in eighteen months – but probably more the result of his double distinction between Production versus Distribution and Statics versus Dynamics, which imposed a peculiar structure on the order of presentation of his arguments.

28. The Stationary State

Book IV, chapter 6, on the stationary state, is strongly colored by Mill's social views. He divorces himself at the outset from 'political economists of the old school' citing Smith, Malthus and McCulloch, who identify all that is 'economically desirable' with 'the progressive state' and regard the approach of stationary conditions as the coming of the day of judgment. 'I am not charmed', Mill remarks, 'with the idea of life held out by those who think that the normal state of human beings is that of struggling to get on'. American readers will note the comments on America in the first edition, which Mill later struck out (**section 2**). The whole of this chapter is nothing so much as a prolegomenon to Galbraith's *The Affluent Society*. Witness the Galbraithian assertion that 'it is only in the backward countries of the world that increased production is still an important object: in those most advanced, what is economically needed is better distribution'.

Book IV, chapter 7, on the 'Probable Futurity of the Labouring Class', starts out by rejecting Carlyle's theory of the élite, the rich guiding the poor in paternal obligation: 'The poor have come out of leading-strings, and cannot any longer be governed or treated like children' (**section 1**). Mill's favourite schemes are discussed in **sections 4–6**: peasant proprietorship, profit sharing, and consumer cooperatives. His detailed illustrations of profit-sharing schemes and early cooperative ventures make tedious reading. The last section (**section 7**) criticizes socialists for declaiming against competition; it is not competition but the structure of property rights, Mill declares, which produces the evils socialists deplore.

29. Taxation

Book V, on the scope of government, launches into the question of taxation. **Chapter 2,** on Smith's canons of taxation, defends the ability-to-pay theory on the grounds that the sacrifices involved in paying taxes ought to be equalized. It is not made clear whether the sacrifices in question are total, average, or marginal sacrifices [see chapter 9, section 5]. Mill rejects the benefit theory of taxation grounded upon the *quid pro quo* principle (**section 2**). Equality of sacrifices, Mill notes, means a progressive tax on incomes above subsistence levels because of the law of diminishing marginal utility of income; the law is clearly suggested in **section 3**. He condemns progressive taxation on incentive grounds, however, although he favours progressive inheritance duties because they represent a tax on 'unearned income'. If it were possible to separate consumption from investment spending, a tax on expenditures would be preferable to an income tax (**section 4**). In **section 5** we come at last to the famous proposal to tax the 'unearned increment' of rental values.

30. The Incidence of Taxes

Book IV, chapter 3, concerned with direct taxes on income, continues in the vein of chapter 2. **Chapter 4,** on excise taxes, is full of interesting asides. In **section 2,** Mill asserts that a specific or *ad valorem* tax will raise the price of a good by at least the amount of the tax and usually by more. In the short run, this is impossible: even if demand is perfectly inelastic, the tax can raise price only by the amount of the tax. But it soon becomes clear that demand is not taken to be typically inelastic. Mill has in mind the case of a long-run downward-sloping supply curve of an industry operating under increasing returns to scale. For such an industry a tax that shifts the supply curve to the left will indeed raise the price of the product by more than the amount of the tax. **Section 3** discusses a tax on wheat and shows that any tax that does not affect intramarginal differentials will leave corn rents the same. A 'tithe' would lower corn rents because it would fall more heavily on intramarginal land. A specific tax per unit of wheat produces lower corn rents but not money rents because corn prices rise to the extent that output is reduced. All this is straightforward Ricardian tax analysis [see chapter 4, section 29].

Section 4 of **chapter 4** discusses the effect of commuting tithes to money payments, a subject of interest to Mill's generation because of the Commutation of Tithes Act of 1834. **Section 5** contains yet another deprecatory remark on the benefits of repealing the Corn Laws – recall Book I, chapter 11, section 4. Mill denies that the Corn Laws have kept up rents and wheat prices but he concedes that they have retarded growth. **Section 6**, on export and import taxes, we have already discussed in connection with the theory of international trade.

Book IV, chapter 5, on taxes on contracts, is uninteresting. The next chapter is an early contribution to the much-vexed question, which has flared up again in the 'new' welfare economics, of the burden of direct versus indirect taxes. Mill's comments hardly come to grips with the issues but he does minimize the so-called 'optional' argument in favour of indirect taxes on which both Smith and Ricardo had relied: indirect taxes are less burdensome than direct taxes because they can be avoided by not purchasing the taxed commodity.

31. The Public Debt

Book IV, chapter 7, represents Mill's final summing up of the case against government spending considered in the context of capital abundance in wealthy countries: the subject had been touched upon in Book I, chapter 4, section 8, and again in Book IV, chapter 5. The test of whether government spending is hampering private capital formation is the rate of interest – notice again Mill's inclination to subject theoretical arguments to an operational test. If the government is actually siphoning off funds from the private sector, the rate of interest will rise (**section 1**). Ricardo's recommendation of a capital levy to redeem the public debt is discussed inconclusively in **section 2**. Budgetary surpluses should be applied to redeeming taxes, not to paying off the public debt, because all taxes are objectionable in principle (**section 3**).

32. The Scope of Government

Chapters 8 and **9** consider the efficiency with which the British government has executed its indisputably legitimate functions; the verdict is negative. **Chapter 8, section 3**, on the need for law reform is in the best manner of Bentham. **Chapter 9, section 1**, reiterates the proposal to revise the inheritance laws, sketched earlier in Book II, chapter 2. Mill's friend Alexander Bain recalled subsequently that Mill anticipated a 'tremendous outcry' over his legislative recommendations on inherited wealth: 'He frequently spoke of his proposals as to inheritance and Bequest, which, if carried out, would pull down all large fortunes in two generations. To his surprise, however, this part of the book made no sensation'. **Sections 2** and **3** of **chapter 9** attack primogeniture and entails; **section 6** gives reluctant approval to the Limited Liabilities Act of 1855, which Mill had opposed before its introduction.

With **chapter 10** we pass over to the disputable sphere of government action. **Section 1** dismisses protectionism but allows the infant-industry argument, a concession that Mill came to regret as it was seized on in America and Australia to justify protective tariffs. **Section 2** deals with the Usury Laws, **section 4** with the Patent Laws, and **section 5** with the Combination Laws, which we have already discussed. The last chapter in the book, **chapter 11**, provides an excellent exercise in political theory: **sections 1–6** review virtually every cogent argument ever advanced against the extension of government intervention in economic affairs. In Book V, chapter 1, section 2, Mill had rejected any rule that limited the interference of government save 'the simple and vague one' of expediency. Now he concludes that '*laissez faire*, in short, should be the general practice; every departure from it, unless required by some greater good, is a certain evil'. And to show what he meant, he proceeded to recommend compulsory education and a state system of examinations because the consumer of education is not a 'competent judge of the commodity', and to approve the regulation of hours of work on the ground that public action is sometimes necessary to give effect to the self-interests of individuals. Since his views on both questions are rather different from those of other classical economists, we pause a moment to place them in perspective.

33. Education in Classical Economics

The classical economists did not conceive a mass education as an investment in economic growth but they recognized that it might contribute indirectly to growth by promoting civic peace and population control. In Adam Smith, the division of labour is said to have certain deleterious consequences on the working population which public education can counteract. He favoured education more for purposes of moral improvement than for the development of productive skills and in this he was followed by almost all writers in the classical tradition. The spread of Malthusian ideas further encouraged approval of popular instruction as a means of fostering the prudential virtues. Nevertheless, the notion was that the state would assist private schools with financial grants, and almost no one entertained the idea of entirely free public education before the late 1860s.

Adam Smith favoured 'payment by results' in higher education but state-aided lower schools on the model of the Scottish system of parish schools. Scottish parish schools rewarded teachers on a fee basis, supplemented by a small fixed stipend, the fee varying with the subjects taught. In England, on the other hand, teachers were licensed by the Church, religious dissenters were excluded, and many schools and colleges were financed by endowments with strict limitations laid down by the testators. It was the endowment system which Smith singled out for criticism when writing about education. His proposals for public education called for state aid in providing the buildings, leaving the teachers largely dependent on fees to give them an incentive to exert themselves.

It was in the light of this climate of opinion that Mill wrote about education. He was the first to cite education as a case of 'market failure', that is, a case where the market mechanism will not function efficiently. Long experience of education is necessary to appreciate education, he argued, and hence the buyer of education is typically incompetent to judge its quality: 'the uncultivated cannot be competent judges of cultivation' (Book V, chapter 11, section 8). With this argument he created the first of the three economic justifications that have ever since been put forward for a system of public education – the other two being that of 'natural monopoly', the necessity for a school to be of a certain minimum size for efficient operation, and that of the 'externalities' generated by educated individuals. Surprisingly enough, however, Mill refused to sanction free public education because he was convinced that 'a government which can mould the opinions and sentiments of people from their youth upwards, can do with them whatever it pleases'. And so he advocated compulsory education at home or a private school until a certain age, accompanied by a state examination system: if a child failed to pass such an examination, his parents would be taxed and the proceeds would be devoted to continuing his education. In addition, there would be special financial dispensations to the children of the poor. Public schools might have to be set up in certain outlying districts but, in general, the presumption was that schooling could be efficiently provided on a private basis once the community had decided on the minimum educational standards that it expected each child to meet.

Mill left no doubt that he regarded both the quantity and quality of private education in England as seriously inadequate: 'I hold it therefore the duty of the government to supply the defect, by giving pecuniary support to elementary schools' (Book V, chapter 11, section 8). Nevertheless, he went on to say, 'the government must claim no monopoly for its education, either in the lower or in the higher branches; must exert neither authority nor influence to induce the people to resort to its teachers in preference to others, and must confer no peculiar advantages on those who have been instructed by them'. Apparently, Mill would not approve, were he alive today, of the now universal principle of free public education.

34. The Classical Economists and the Factory Acts

The history of factory legislation in England begins with an Act of 1802. All through the first half of the 19th century, the succeeding Factory Acts had been heatedly controverted, often by the classical economists themselves. Only a year before the publication of Mill's *Principles*, the passage of the Ten Hours Bill of 1847, which finally secured a 58-hour week for all boys below eighteen years of age and for girls and women of all ages, had set off another round of debate. The classical analysis of the Factory Acts had always consisted of two quite different strands of thought. On the one hand, factory legislation was criticized in terms of the doctrine of 'freedom of contract' between enlightened economic agents. On the other hand, it was held that continuous reductions in hours of work could spell the ruin of British industry if unaccompanied by falling money wages.

Insofar as the problem was treated as a matter of enlightened individualism, the attitude of the classical economists was unambiguous: where self-interest was plainly unenlightened, as in the case of children, they recommended intervention by the state, differing only about the proper age of consent and the parents' right of supervision. Unfortunately, while they supported the principle of granting protection to children, they were aware that the unavoidable consequence of that was a shorter working day for adult operatives simply because children were employed in cotton factories solely as assistants to adults; rather than countenance restrictions on the employment of adults, they preferred to dispense with the benefits of regulated child labour. Thus, what we have is, on the one hand, differences of opinion among various classical economists as to the desirability of further restrictions on the employment of children and, on the other hand, a general tendency towards rearguard action designed to prevent the effective regulation of adult labour. In practice, this meant that they acquiesced in just so much legislation as had already been achieved; at each stage of the controversy, they warned against further limitations of hours; moreover, notions about the age at which a worker becomes a 'free agent' invariably changed in the wake of legislation, at each turn approving a *fait accompli*.

Insofar as the problem was conceived in terms of the effects of lower hours on output, the typical assumption of the day was that the productivity of labour had little to do with the length of the working day. The level of formal analysis barely rose above the commonplace, however, and no effect was made to distinguish the short-run and long-run effects of a change in hours. Here too, the classical economists were inclined to argue that shorter hours in the past had not had much effect on output; nevertheless, any further limitation of hours would probably reduce output per man. All in all, the friends of factory legislation were not far wrong in regarding 'political economy' as a major obstacle to factory reform.

We turn now to Mill's treatment of the question in the closing pages of the *Principles* (**Book V, chapter XI, sections 9** and **12**). First of all, he dealt with the specifically economic objections to the Factory Acts. Whether a reduction of hours without a cut in wages would inevitably depress output and generate unemployment was, he noted 'in every particular instance a question of fact, not of principle' (**section 12**), a point no one else had made so forcibly before. As for the theory of free agents, he drew attention to what is now known as the 'free-rider problem' in welfare economics: 'There are matters in which the interference of law is required, not to overrule the judgments of individuals respecting their own interest, but to give effect to that judgment: they being unable to give effect to it except by concert, which concert again cannot be effectual unless it receives validity and sanction from the law' (**section 12**). 'Even if a nine-hour day were in the collective interest of the working class', he wrote in *Principles*, 'state action would be required to give it effect because the immediate interest of every individual would be in violating it'. He hastened to add that he did not approve of the Ten Hours Bill: this Bill excluded working women from factories, although women were 'free agents' as much as men. Here Mill the feminist came into conflict with Mill the humanitarian. Still, he concluded, whatever one thinks of Ten Hours legislation, 'it serves to exemplify the manner in which classes of persons may need the assistance of law, to give effect to their deliberate collective opinion of their own interest, by affording every individual a guarantee that his competitors will pursue the same course, without which he cannot safely adopt it himself'.

Unwittingly, Mill had stumbled upon a fundamental insight in welfare economics, namely, the concept of 'public goods' whose benefits are indivisible, with the result that the market mechanism fails utterly to induce consumers to reveal their preferences for such goods [see chapter 13, section 15]. Strangely enough, however, the consumption of leisure, for that is the 'public good' in question, is an atypical example of the general case. It would have been much easier to argue that lack of perfect foresight on the part of businessmen leads them to act myopically. In general, it is true to say that pecuniary motives alone can be relied upon to lead to the adoption of a workday that optimizes output per man hour. But entrepreneurs may have little incentive to reduce hours since the immediate effect, if wages are kept constant, is to increase costs and to decrease output; on the other hand, a simultaneous reduction in wages under these circumstances is likely to affect efficiency adversely. In the long run, output per man might actually rise with shorter hours but lack of perfect foresight renders this a risky decision that no entrepreneur acting in isolation is willing to take. Thus, state interference might be required to force all entrepreneurs to act in their own long-run interest. Needless to say, Mill did not reason like this simply because he had no theory of the firm from which he might have drawn this argument. Instead he chose the more difficult ground of arguing from the desire of the working class for more leisure to the conclusion that sometimes only a universal compact can secure the identity of private and public interests. When the concept of 'public goods' was rediscovered by Italian writers on finance in the 1890s, no one thought of Mill in this connection, and indeed, the debate on the Factory Acts continued for another fifty years without any detectable reference to Mill's remarkable analysis.

35. John Stuart Mill as an Economist

Is the economics of Mill's *Principles* Ricardian economics? Mill himself thought that he was only qualifying Ricardo. He once said in a letter, 'I doubt if there be a single opinion in the book, which may not be exhibited as a corollary from his [Ricardo's] doctrines.' But his qualifications at times affect essentials of Ricardo's theory and, in the sphere of policy, he carried Ricardo's system to lengths undreamt of by Ricardo. Schumpeter argued that, despite Mill's reverence for Ricardo, he cannot be considered a disciple of Ricardo. Nevertheless, the fact remains that on all important questions, such as the determination of factor prices and their variations in the course of economic progress, Mill adhered to Ricardo's postulates: everything is traced back to the cost of producing wage goods as the crucial element in the determination of the rate of profit; under the portmanteau of 'corn', wage goods are identified as the product of agriculture; and the law of diminishing returns to scale as well as to technical progress is held to be uniquely applicable to agricultural production. This is the framework of Ricardo's system and, once present, no admissions of the 'real cost' of capital or of the role of demand – so important to later generations preoccupied with the determination of relative prices under static conditions – can prevent the emergence of typically Ricardian conclusions. Nassau Senior, one of Ricardo's leading critics, was surely right when he remarked in a review of Mill's book that 'Mr Mill's exposition of the theory of Profit and of Rent ... does not differ materially from that of Ricardo'.

Mill's *Principles* is more than an *oeuvre d'assemblage*, a mere restatement of what has gone before. Even on a purely theoretical plane it is full of genuine novelties. The equation of International Demand is an obvious example but, in addition, there is the concept of noncompeting groups in labour markets; the correct statement of the law of supply and demand as an equation rather than an identity; the three-fold classification of price-elasticities of demand in terms of the total revenue effect of a change in price; the treatment of economies of scale; the analysis of the problem of joint products; and, finally, the concept of opportunity costs. Moreover, Mill's theory of interest is nearly forty years ahead of his time. Even when he draws specific ideas from his predecessors he almost always improves upon their presentation: this shows up in his statement of the abstinence theory of profit and the generalization of the Ricardian rent concept, borrowed from Bailey and Senior, and again in his emphasis on the role of 'custom', particularly with respect to land tenure, derived from Richard Jones. The quality of theoretical eclecticism, which so irritates the modern reader, worked in the final analysis to Mill's advantage. For a period of two generations he taught England its economics, and the multiplicity of analytical ideas, often running in opposite directions, opened the way to subsequent refinement and development.

The essential Mill, however, is to be found in his proposals for economic reform and in his pervasive moral tone, at once sentimental and austere, with the flourishes of abstract theory kept in check by a desire to preach social amelioration. It is exactly the same flavor that imbues Marshall's *Principles*. And, just as Marshall, with his genius for pure theory and his competence in mathematics, spoke disparagingly of abstract analysis and mathematical economics, so Mill, with all his flair for theoretical work, told a friend: 'I regard the purely abstract investigation of political economy . . . as of very minor importance compared to the great practical questions which the progress of democracy and the spread of socialist opinion are pressing on.' Despite his sympathetic treatment of socialist arguments, however, he was no socialist. Indeed, he is a perfect example of what we mean when we call someone a 'classical liberal'. He attributed the social ills he saw around him, not to private ownership of the means of production as a socialist would, but to the untrammeled exercise of private property rights. He did say that 'laissez-faire should be the general practice; every departure from it, unless required by some greater good, is a certain evil', but he was perfectly willing to advocate piecemeal collective action in the interest of 'some greater good'. It might be added that in this he was not alone; the notion that a noninterventionist bias kept classical economists from proposing social and economic reform is a widely held myth, kept alive by the failure to read the works of the leading classical economists. Mill's attitude to capitalism as an economic system was free from any sort of dogmatism: he simply thought it premature to dispense with the profit motive while there were still ample prospects of improvement under the present economic order. This was an enlightened attitude to adopt in 1848. It is today the typical attitude of most Western economists.

In one important respect, however, Mill's *Principles* is hopelessly dated, namely, the relentless insistence that every conceivable policy measure must be judged in terms of its effects upon the birth rate. He was an ardent defender of the Malthusian theory of population. But it is interesting to notice that he escapes almost all the gloomy implications of the Malthusian doctrine by an optimistic belief, so different from Malthus's own, in the capacity of the working class to practice voluntary family limitation. He never says how it is to come about but we know that he favoured birth control, although he did not dare to advocate it publicly. And so he could write in his *Autobiography*, describing the views held by the younger utilitarians like himself: 'Malthus's population principle was quite as much a banner and point of union among us, as any opinion specially belonging to Bentham. This great doctrine, originally brought forward as an argument against the indefinite improvability of human affairs, we took up with ardent zeal in the contrary sense, as indicating the sole means of realizing that improvability by securing full employment at high wages to the whole labouring population through a voluntary restriction of the increase of their numbers'.

NOTES ON FURTHER READING

There is no cheap paperback edition of the whole of Mill's *Principles*: the Penguin paperback, with a splendid introduction by D. Winch (1970), contains only Books IV and V plus the chapters on Property from Book II. Until recently, the most useful edition of Mill's *Principles* was the *variorum* edition by W. J. Ashley, with an introduction describing Mill's intellectual development and several appendixes containing excerpts from his other writings. While this edition is very scarce, the sixth *People's Edition* (1865) and the seventh edition (1871), the last to be revised by Mill himself, are easy to come by in secondhand book shops – there is little point in reading any edition earlier than the third (1852) because he made significant alterations in the second and third editions. However, the Ashley edition has now been superseded by Vols. II and III of the *Collected Works of John Stuart Mill* (1965), ed. J. M. Robson, with an excellent introduction by V. W. Bladen and a hundred pages of Mill's correspondence relevant to the book. There is also Mill's *Essay on Economy and Society*, being Vols. III and IV of the *Collected Works* (1967), with a useful introduction by L. Robbins.

Of all the classical economists, none had so varied and rich a career as Mill. We are fortunate in having an authoritative modern biography of him: *The Life of John Stuart Mill* by M. St J. Packe (1954); Packe's treatment of Mill's philosophical, political and economic ideas, however, leaves something to be desired. For a general account of Mill's intellectual position, see *The Improvement of Mankind: The Social and Political Thoughts of J. S. Mill* (1968) by J. M. Robson, the editor of the *Collected Works*. Mill's relation to Bentham is explored in a brilliant article by J. Viner, 'Bentham and J. S. Mill: the Utilitarian Background', *AER*, 1949, reprinted in Viner's *The Long View and the Short*. The same terrain is covered from a wider angle by P. Streeten, 'Keynes and the Classical Tradition', *Post-Keynesian Economics*, ed. K. K. Kurihara (1954).

Anyone who still believes that the classical conception of the proper scope of government was wholly negative must read L. Robbins, *The Theory of Economic Policy in English Classical Political Economy* (1952), particularly the concluding lecture 'The Classical Theory in General Perspective'. Samuels, *The Classical Theory of Economic Policy* is an important extension of Robbins' argument stressing the role of nonlegal social controls in classical thought. See also the balanced perspective of Coats's introduction to his valuable collection of essays, *The Classical Economists and Economic Policy*. My *Ricardian Economics*, chap. 10, discusses the position of the leading Ricardian economists on such prominent issues of public policy as the Poor Laws, the Corn Laws, and the Factory Acts. W. D. Grampp, *The Manchester School of Economics* (1960), analyzes the relationship between the free trade doctrines of the classical school and the Anti-Corn Law League of Cobden and Bright. D. P. O'Brien, *The Classical Economists* (1975), chap. 10, reviews the policy prescriptions of the classical economists in respect of the Factory Acts, technological unemployment, pauperism, education, trade unions, Ireland and colonial policy. In fact, this book should be read straight through since it is the best, single reference in the literature on the entire sweep of classical economic doctrines: it combines a firm historical grasp with a thorough command of modern analysis and, as a bonus, contains an excellent annotated bibliography. One of its unique features is a chapter on classical public finance, a topic scarcely covered at all in other sources.

While we are on the subject of classical economics as a whole, let me also recommend D. Winch, *The Fontana Economic History of Europe, Vol. III, chap. 9, The Emergence of Economics as a Science, 1750–1870* (1971 in paperback), which is particularly strong on the spread of English political economy in Europe.

In view of the current interest in problems of growth and development, most readers will benefit from E. McKinley, 'The Problem of "Underdevelopment" in the English Classical School', *QJE*, May, 1955, a veritable compendium of classical ideas on development, revised and shortened in an essay contributed to *Theories of Economic Growth*, ed. B. F. Hoselitz (1963). For the construction of a classical model of growth, see A. Lowe, 'The Classical Theory of Economic Growth', *SR*, 1954, reprinted in *RHET*. A masterly book by R. D. C. Black, *The Classical Economists and the Irish Problem* (1960), examines classical policy proposals for an unique backward country, illuminating both the strengths and the weaknesses of Ricardian economics conceived as a theory of economic development.

P. S. Schwartz, *The New Political Economy of J. S. Mill* (1972), is a full-length treatment of Mill's views on economic policy. Chap. 6 on laissez-faire and chap. 7 on socialism demonstrate that Mill did have a *new* political economy: instead of first circumscribing the role of government and then consigning the remainder to the market mechanism, as his predecessors had done, he began by codifying various types of 'market failure' and then specified government action to repair these defects; in short, he invented the approach to economic policy which we customarily credit to Pigou. R. B. Ekelund, Jr. and R. D. Tollison, 'The New Political Economy of J. S. Mill: The Means to Social Justice', *CJE*, May, 1976, agree with this view but E. G. West, 'J. S. Mill's Redistribution Policy: New Political Economy or Old?', *EQ*, October, 1978, takes the view that Mill was still steeped in the old pre-Victorian tradition. On more specific topics in Mill, see Taussig's classic study of the wages fund doctrine, which covers everyone from Adam Smith through Mill to Amasa Walker: *Wages and Capital* (1896, reprinted 1932), in particular pp. 181–2, 214–15, 235–6, 263–5, and 319–25. Taussig shows that, contrary to popular belief, the wages fund doctrine was employed primarily to analyze problems of population control rather than to discourage trade union action to raise wages. See also Schumpeter, *History of Economic Analysis*, pp. 662–71. W. Breit, 'The Wages Fund Controversy Revisited', *CJE*, 1967, reprinted in *RHET*; R. B. Ekelund, Jr., 'A Short-Run Classical Model of Capital and Wages: Mill's Recantation of the Wages Fund', *OEP*, March, 1976; E. G. West and R. W. Hafer, 'J. S. Mill, Unions, and the Wages Fund Recantation: A Reinterpretation', *QJE*, November, 1978; R. B. Ekelund, Jr. and W. F. Kordsmeier, 'J. S. Mill, Unions, and the Wages Fund Recantation: A Reinterpretation – Comment', *ibid.*, August, 1981; and J. Vint, 'A Two Sector Model of the Wages Fund; Mill's Recantation Revisited', *BREI*, Autumn, 1981, are more recent analyses of Mill's 1869 recantation of the wages fund doctrine.

There is a vast body of commentary on what Edgeworth called the *locus vexatissimus* of classical economics, Mill's fourth proposition on capital. For a history of this commentary, see J. H. Thompson, 'Mill's Fourth Fundamental Proposition: A Paradox Revisited', *HOPE*, Summer, 1975. For an ingenious resolution of the dispute between Carey and Mill on the order in which different types of land will be cultivated under the assumptions of Ricardian rent theory – the question that Mill raised in Book I, chap. 3, sect. 3, of the *Principles* – see R. Turvey, 'A Finnish Contribution to Rent Theory', *EJ*, June 1955. W. L. Miller, 'Richard Jones's Contribution to the Theory of Rent', *HOPE*, Fall, 1977, discusses a contemporary anti-Ricardian economist who deeply influenced Mill's discussion of rent theory. C. J. Dewey, 'The Rehabilitation of the Peasant Proprietor in Nineteenth-Century Economic Thought', *ibid.*, Spring 1974; W. L. Miller, 'Primogeniture, Entails, and Endowments in English Classical Economics', *ibid.*, Winter, 1980; and M. E. Bradley, 'Mill on Proprietorship, Productivity, and Population', *ibid.*, Fall, 1983, throw light on the problem of land reform in classical economic thought, an issue near and dear to J. S. Mill. In a provocative article on 'The Nature and Role of Originality in Scientific Progress', *Ec*, 1955, reprinted in his *Essays in the History of Economics*, Stigler shows that, in terms of identifiable theories, Mill must rank as one of the most original writers in the history of economics. N. B. de Marchi, 'The Success of Mill's *Principles*', *HOPE*, Summer, 1974, is a far-ranging scholarly account of the reception of Mill's treatise.

Schumpeter's comments on Mill are scattered throughout Part III, chaps. 6 and 7, of his *History of Economic Analysis*: see pp. 527–34, 541–50, 603–5 and 640–5. But the reader should really *study* the whole of chap. 6, running well over a hundred pages, which contains the bulk of Schumpeter's discussion of classical economics. Similarly, F. H. Knight ranges over the whole of classical economic theory in a long article: 'The Ricardian Theory of Production and Distribution', *CJEPS*, 1935, reprinted in his *The History and Method of Economics* (1956, and in paperback). While this is not an essay for the tyro as it presumes a thorough acquaintance with modern economics, it is a brilliant review of the subject from the standpoint of uncompromising 'absolutism'.

The most authoritative commentary on the classical theory of international trade, as summed up by Mill, is Viner, *Theory of International Trade*, chap. 6. See also Schumpeter, *History of Economic Analysis*, pp. 605–15; and O'Brien, *The Classical Economists*, chap. 7. Comparative cost theory is contrasted with Smith's dynamic approach to international trade, echoes of which found their way into Mill's *Principles*, by M. H. Myint, 'The "Classical Theory" of International Trade and the Underdeveloped Countries', *EJ*, June, 1958. D. P. O'Brien, 'Customs Unions: Trade Creation and Trade Diversion in Historical Perspective', *HOPE*, Winter, 1976; A. I. Bloomfield, 'The Impact of Growth and Technology on Trade in Nineteenth-Century Economic Thought', *ibid.*, Winter, 1978, and 'British Thought on the Influence of Foreign Trade and Investment on Growth, 1800–1880', *ibid.*, Spring, 1981, show that the classical economists, including Mill, had plenty to say about secular changes in comparative advantage even though they failed to treat the topic systematically in their treatises. D. R. Appleyard, J. C. Ingram, 'A Reconsideration of the Addition to Mill's "Great Chapter"', *ibid.*, Winter, 1979, battle with the formidable J. S. Chipman, 'Mill's Superstructure: How Well Does it Stand Up?', *ibid.*, over the sections which Mill added to his famous chapter 18, 'Of International Values', in the third edition of the *Principles* in which he wrestled for the first time with the problem of multiple equilibria. M. C. Kemp, 'The Mill-Bastable Infant Industry Dogma', *JPE*, February, 1960, discusses Mill's reluctant endorsement of the infant-industry argument. There are some excellent surveys of modern developments in the pure theory of international trade, all of which start from Ricardo and Mill and then proceed to take the reader through the Heckscher-Ohlin theory to more recent developments: in ascending order of difficulty, see L. A. Metzler, 'The Theory of International Trade', *A Survey of Contemporary Economics*, ed. H. S. Ellis (1949); G. Haberler, 'A Survey of International Trade Theory', *Special Papers in International Economics*, No. 1 (2nd ed., 1961); W. M. Corden, 'Recent Developments in the Theory of International Trade', *Special Papers in International Economics*, No. 7 (1965); R. Caves, *Trade and Economic Structure* (1960), particularly chap. 2; and J. Bhagwati, 'The Pure Theory of International Trade: A Survey', *EJ*, 1964, reprinted in *Surveys of Economic Theories* (1965), II.

There is useful background information on a variety of topics in W. D. Grampp, 'The Economists and the Combination Laws', *QJE*, November, 1979; C. E. Amsler, R. L. Bartlett, C. J. Bolton, 'Thoughts of Some British Economists on Early Limited Liability and Corporate Legislation', *HOPE*, Winter, 1981; and R. B. Ekelund, Jr., O. E. Price, 'Sir Edwin Chadwick on Competition and the Social Control of Industry: Railroads', *ibid.*, Summer, 1979, extended in R. B. Ekelund, Jr. and R. F. Hébert, *A History of Economic Theory and Method* (2nd ed. 1983), chap. 9.

On the much-discussed controversy between the Currency School and the Banking School, see Viner, *Theory of International Trade*, chap. 5; and the lucid and comprehensive discussion by M. R. Daugherty, 'The Currency-Banking Controversy', *SEJ*, October, 1942, January, 1943. Among the leading exponents of the Banking School was Thomas Tooke, whose *History of Prices* left a profound impression on all writing in this period. In a brilliant *Introduction to Tooke and Newmarch's History of Prices* (1928, reprinted 1962), T. E. Gregory reviews monetary controversy in the whole period from the Suspension of Cash Payments in 1797 to the passage of the Bank Charter Act in 1844, analyzing Tooke's position on all the leading topics under debate. On the history of the real bills doctrine, see the ponderous but painstaking study by L. W. Mints, *A History of Banking Theory* (1954), particularly chaps. 4, 6, and 7. For an excellent article-length account of the history of the real bills doctrine, specifically relating it to the modern proposal that the monetary authorities should abandon money growth targets and instead adopt a target for the rate of interest, see T. M. Humphrey, 'The Real Bills Doctrine', *ERV*, September/October, 1982. Indeed, Humphrey has published a whole series of historical articles in the Federal Bank of Richmond's *ERV*, bound together in his *Essays on Inflation* (2nd edn., 1980 in paperback), of which 'The Quantity Theory of Money: Its Historical Evolution and Role in Policy Debates', *ERV*, 1974, 'Two Views of Monetary Policy: The Attwood-Mill Debate Revisited', *ERV*, 1977, 'The Monetary Approach to Exchange Rates: Its Historical Evolution and Role in Policy Debates', *ERV*, 1978, and 'The Purchasing Power Parity Doctrine', *ERV*, 1979, speak directly to the issues in the Currency-Banking controversy. One might be forgiven for thinking that work on 19th-century monetary history had begun to yield diminishing returns but Fetter, *The Development of British Monetary Orthodoxy, 1797–1875*, surpasses even the comparable chapters in Viner; written as a continuous historical narrative, in which the key concepts recur again and again, it is not easy to recommend anything less than the whole of it; but for a representative sample, see the pages on the gold standard as an article of faith, pp. 139–43, the currency-banking controversies, pp. 187–94, and opinion on the specie-flow mechanism, pp. 226–31, 242–9.

The name of Nassau William Senior has come up frequently in the course of the text. There is a comprehensive study of Senior's many incisive but fragmented contributions to classical theory: M. Bowley, *Nassau Senior and Classical Economics* (1937). The book suffers, however, from a certain tendency to modernize Senior's presentation and to exaggerate his emancipation from Ricardian assumptions. Senior had a checkered career as a civil servant and S. L. Levy's biography, despite its absurd title, makes absorbing reading: *Nassau Senior: The Prophet of Modern Capitalism* (1949). G. J. Stigler, 'The Classical Economists: An Alternative View', *Lectures on Economic Problems* (1949), analyzes the famous Handloom Weavers' Report, written under Senior's direction, and shows that it displays analytical insights not found in the formal treatises of the period.

Senior was only one of the many able economists writing in this period. L. Robbins has published a full-length study of *Robert Torrens and the Evolution of Classical Economics* (1958). Chaps. 4 and 5 and pp. 251–4 of Robbins' book, dealing with Torrens' banking theory, present the currency-banking controversy with great clarity. Torrens is best remembered for the terms-of-trade argument in favor of protective tariffs: his argument is taken apart and put back together in chap. 7 of Robbins' study. D. P. O'Brien, *J. R. McCulloch – A Study in Classical Economics* (1970), is another full-length study of a major contributor to classical economics. O'Brien revises the standard view of McCulloch as a dogmatic disciple of Ricardo, showing that his work was on the whole more influenced by the 18th-century Scottish tradition. L. S. Moss, *Mountfort Longfield. Ireland's First Professor of Political Economy* (1976) provides a comprehensive study of one of the most original minor anti-Ricardian economists of the period. See also R. M. Romano, 'William Forster Lloyd – A Non-Ricardian', *HOPE*, Fall, 1977; and R. M. Romano, 'The Economic Ideas of Charles Babbage', *ibid.*, Fall, 1982.

Bowley, *Nassau Senior*, chap. 1; Schumpeter, *History of Economic Analysis*, pp. 534–41; and my *Methodology of Economics* (1980), chap. 3, discuss classical views on methodology, a subject on which little has been said in this text. On factual work in this classical period, for this is the era in which fact finding became popular, see Schumpeter, *History of Economic Analysis*, pp. 519–26. For the bearing of empirical findings on the development of Ricardian doctrine, see M. Blaug, 'The Empirical Content of Ricardian Economics', *JPE*, February, 1956, and *Ricardian Economics*, chap. 9. N. B. de Marchi, 'The Empirical Content and Longevity of Ricardian Economics', *Ec*, August, 1970, takes issue with my interpretation and, in the course of so doing, re-examines both Ricardo's and Mill's attitudes to the relation between theories and facts. Mill's methodological position is particularly interesting because he wrote a major work on the philosophy of both the natural and the social sciences. On Mill's *System of Logic*, see the perceptive essay by J. C. Whitaker, 'John Stuart Mill's Methodology', *JPE*, October, 1975; and my *Methodology of Economics*, chap. 3. Also relevant here is W. L. Miller, 'Richard Jones: A Case Study in Methodology', *HOPE*, Spring, 1971.

7

Marxian economics

Marx the economist is alive and relevant today in a way none of the writers are that we have thus far considered. Marx has been reassessed, revised, refuted and buried a thousand times but he refuses to be relegated to intellectual history. For better or for worse, his ideas have become part of the climate of opinion within which we all think. No one now does battle for Adam Smith or Ricardo but blood pressures still go up when Marx is under examination. This poses problems of interpretation not previously encountered in this book. The difficulty will be to keep Marx from being drowned by neo-Marxian reformulations and to separate Marx the classical economist from the Leninized Marx who crops up so frequently in popular debates. There is the further handicap that Marx created a system that embraced all the social sciences and we can only consider his economics on its own by doing an injustice to his philosophical, sociological and historical ideas. To some extent, the same problem arose in discussing Adam Smith, but only to some extent. There is a consistency in all aspects of Marxism that goes far beyond Adam Smith's efforts at comprehensive political economy. Nevertheless, to keep this chapter from turning into a book, we shall have to carve out Marxian economics from Marxism. Even so, what we are left with is an enormous canvas, conceived on more grandiose lines than anything that had ever gone before.

The 20th century has witnessed a strong revolt against great philosophical systems such as Marxism, which purport to explain society in all its aspects. We live in an age of specialization, no less in social science than in technology. But this is precisely why we should study Marx. Whatever one may think of the ultimate validity of Marxism, it is a dull mind that fails to be inspired by Marx's heroic attempt to project a systematic general account of 'the laws of motion' of capitalism.

1. Terminology

Our first task is to explain Marx's use of the labour theory of value to determine both relative prices and the rate of profit on capital; in other words, to explain how 'surplus value' is determined in his system. This is admittedly a dull exercise and we cannot promise to make these pages entertaining reading. But once the theory of surplus value has been cleared out of the way, the story turns to 'the laws of motion' of capitalism and this is fascinating stuff from almost every point of view. The reader is urged to persevere.

Since most of the Marxian economics thrives in a cloud of terminological confusion, the first step is to agree on a set of definitions. In this chapter we will consistently use capital letters for stocks and lowercase letters for flows. Marx's 'constant capital', c, is defined as the sum of depreciation charges on fixed capital and inputs of raw materials. Adding the wages of production workers v, Marx's 'variable capital', we get the flow of total capital outlays, k. In other words, Adam Smith's 'fixed capital' plus raw materials equals Marx's 'constant capital', while Smith's 'circulating capital' minus raw materials equals Marx's 'variable capital'. Dividing the components of the flow of k by the appropriate annual rates of turnover t_c and t_v, or multiplying by the appropriate durabilities measured in years, d_c and d_v, we get the stock of capital invested, K. $K \equiv C + V$, where C stands for the value of the stock of durable equipment and inventories of raw materials and V stands for the stock of working capital required to meet weekly payrolls. Following Marx, surplus value, s, is defined on a flow basis as the excess of gross receipts over fixed and variable costs. For the economy as a whole, this amounts to the excess of net national product over the wages bill. The *gross* national product $\equiv c + v + s$, but the *net* national product $\equiv v + s$. The 'rate of surplus value' $\sigma \equiv s/v$. The rate of profit, r, as Marx defined it, is equal to s/k; on a stock basis it is equal to s/K.

Apart from σ and r, another fundamental ratio in the Marxian system is the 'organic composition of capital', q. Marx never explicitly defines this concept, sometimes writing $c/(c + v)$ and once or twice $v/(c + v)$, both of which are ratios of two flows. What he had in mind, however, was clearly the ratio of machine costs to labour costs, C/v. When multiplied by the wage rate, v/N – the total wage bill divided by the number of workers – and ignoring V as negligibly small so that $C \equiv K$, this becomes the familiar concept of the amount of capital per man, a ratio of two stocks:

$$\frac{K}{v} \cdot \frac{v}{N} \equiv \frac{K}{N} \equiv Q.$$

At all times Marx shuffles freely between stocks and flows without warning the reader. His expression for r is actually the share of profits in the turnover of capital; it is only equal to the rate of profit on capital invested on the assumption that the whole of the capital stock turns over once a year. Thus,

$$r \equiv \frac{s}{c/t_c + v/t_v} = \frac{s}{c + v} \text{ if } t_c = t_v = 1.$$

Marx discusses the different turnover rates of c and v at great length in Volume II of *Capital* – writing n for our t_c – but elsewhere he loses sight of the distinction between stocks and flows. For the time being we shall follow Marx's procedure in Volume I and set $t_c = t_v = 1$: society's capital stock, therefore, is entirely consumed and reconstituted each year and, given a constant wage rate, $q = Q$

2. Value and Surplus Value

The first volume of *Capital* is so constructed as to bring out the essential nature of profit as surplus value produced by labour. It is convenient to assume at the beginning that the capital-labour ratio is identical in every industry, although it is important to notice that Marx never made such an assumption, either explicitly or implicitly. If we do make that assumption, it follows that the ratio of profits to wage charges is the same for every product and hence commodity prices will differ only because some employ more direct plus indirect labour – more labour and more capital – than others. In short, all products exchange in proportion to the labour embodied in their production. Now, if all prices correspond to labour values, how is it that surplus value emerges when employers are only willing to pay workers enough to live on and no more? Competition will compel employers to pay the economic value of the labour services employed; whatever the source of surplus value, it comes about because of, not in spite of, competition.

The answer that Marx gives runs in terms of the historical dispossession of a large group in society that is impelled to live by the sale of personal services as a result of the concentration of property in the hands of a few. Labour power becomes a commodity, traded on the market like any other commodity at a normal price governed by the labour time necessary to produce it, that is by the labour time necessary to produce the wage goods which go to maintain workers. The commodity labour power is bought and sold at its full value but the value of the products of labour power exceeds its own value. As Marx would say, 'the exchange-value of labour power' is bought and paid for, but what is actually acquired is 'the use-value of labour'. In Marxian imagery, only a part of the worker's working day is spent in replacing the equivalent of his own value, namely, the subsistence goods that go to maintain him; during the remainder of the day, the worker works for the capitalist. Surplus value is nothing but 'unpaid labour'.

Marx concluded, as did Ricardo, that profits or total surplus value depend on the cost of wage goods. Surplus value can be increased either by lengthening the working day – 'absolute surplus-value' – or by raising the productivity of labour, thus lessening the time required to produce wage goods – 'relative surplus-value'. The 'rate of exploitation' or 'rate of surplus-value' is solely a function of the direct labour employed. Constant capital in the form of machinery and raw materials only transmits its own value to the product; it does not create additional value. It differs from variable capital because it is bought by capitalists and sold by capitalists, whereas variable capital is sold by workers and bought by capitalists, and it seemed obvious to Marx that the origin of surplus value cannot lie in an exchange between capitalists. It is true that machinery enhances the productivity of labour and that, insofar as depreciation charges and raw material costs enter into the total value of the final product, they *add* to the value produced by labour. But the value that machines and raw materials add to labour is no more than the value at which they were purchased. This is why the value of the total net national product consists entirely of wages plus a markup proportional to labour time: $v + \sigma(v)$. In the language of social accounting, raw materials as well as the current services of machines constitute intermediate products that are netted out of gross income. Interest on fixed capital, however, is present in the Marxian schema but it is subsumed under surplus value on the premise – which is yet to be proved – that it is really a function of the employment of direct labour.

3. The Great Contradiction

So far, we have faithfully followed Marx's own exposition. It is evident that as matters stand, something is wrong with the argument. In a system in which relative prices correspond to relative labour values, the net product of equal quantities of labour would be sold for equal quantities of money; given uniform money wage rates between industries, the rate of surplus value would be everywhere the same. But the organic composition of capital, q, is not the same in different industries. If profits per man, σ, are everywhere the same, while capital per man, q, varies from industry to industry, the rate of profit per unit of capital, r, will vary inversely with capital per man. This implies that the higher the degree of mechanization, the lower the rate of profit, which flies in the face of the fact that capitalists are motivated to substitute capital for labour by the prospect of earning higher profits. In other words, if s/v is uniform between industries but c/v is not, $s/(c + v)$ will also differ between industries. But competition between capitalists does in fact establish a uniform rate of profit on capital regardless of its composition. We are now caught in a contradiction: with a uniform r and with different values of q, we cannot logically have a uniform σ. Recall that $r \equiv s/(c + v) \equiv \sigma/(q + 1)$: if one ratio is equal between industries, the other two ratios must be equal between industries. Since q in fact differs between industries, so must σ. This implies, however, that the net product of equal quantities of labour cannot sell for equal quantities of money: relative prices cannot correspond to relative labour values.

On Marx's own grounds the labour theory of value is only formally correct if we assume that there are no differences in the ratio of capital to labour between industries. Anyone who has read Ricardo will hardly be surprised by this conclusion.

In view of the fact that widely different capital-labour ratios are observed in the real world, it would seem that we must abandon the labour theory of value as a theory of relative prices: the pressures that equalize the rate of profit necessarily produce different rates of surplus value between industries. This is just what we would expect: profits per man employed are, surely?, a function of output per man employed, which in turn is greater where capital per man is greater. But if labour values do not correspond to prices owing to variations in σ between different products, the theory of surplus value will also have to be abandoned. The amount of surplus value that a worker produces is apparently influenced by the amount of capital with which he is furnished: surplus value is not simply 'expropriated labour'. But Marx, of course, does not give up the assumption that profits depend only upon the amount of human labour employed; σ *must* be equal in all industries, irrespective of the observed variations in the ratio of capital to labour and irrespective of the fact that profits per unit of total capital tend to equality. The solution to the problem is given in the third volume of *Capital*, in which Marx transforms 'values' into 'prices'. The so-called

Transformation Problem is worth careful consideration, not perhaps for its own sake but because it marks the first and only attempt in the history of economic thought to carry the labour theory of value to its logical conclusions. This section is heavy-going: it is a jigsaw puzzle. But no one can grasp the *tour de force* that is the theory of surplus value without taking the trouble to separate the pieces of the puzzle.

4. The Transformation Problem

Marx's solution to the 'great contradiction' is best approached by looking at his own numerical example (see Table 7–1). The economy consists of five industries and none of the products of the five industries enters into the production of any other. The capital invested in every industry is the same and is equal to 100 units. The turnover rate of variable capital is everywhere equal to unity, but the turnover rates of constant capital differ considerably from industry to industry. Adding the value of the fixed capital actually used up to the wages paid out, we arrive at the 'cost price' of a commodity. With $\sigma = 1$, the labour value of each commodity is equal to the cost price plus a markup proportional to the outlays on wages. So far the argument is that of Volume 1. At this point we take account of the fact that capitalists actually sell products at 'prices of production': to the 'cost price' they add a uniform markup proportional to the total capital invested, regardless of the share of the wages in total costs. Thus, while 'values' are equal to $c + v + \sigma(v)$, 'prices of production' are equal to $c + v + r(C + V)$.

Table 7–1

	Capital	c	v	Cost Price	s at $\sigma = 1$	Value	Profit at $r = 0.22$	'Price of Prod'.	Price > Value
I.	$80C + 20V$	50	20	70	20	90	22	92	+ 2
II.	$70C + 30V$	51	30	81	30	111	22	103	− 8
III.	$60C + 40V$	51	40	91	40	131	22	113	− 18
IV.	$85C +. 15V$	40	15	55	15	70	22	77	+ 7
V.	$95C + 5V$	10	5	15	5	20	22	37	+ 17
Σ	$390C + 110V$	202	110	312	110	422	110	422	0

We find that in no case does 'value' correspond to 'price of production'. However, lo and behold, the sum total of deviations of prices from values is equal to zero. Moreover, the deviations are uniquely related to the organic composition of capital in each industry. The average composition of capital in the whole economy $q_0 = 390/110 = 3.55$. When the composition of capital in an industry exceeds this average, as with q_1, q_4 and q_5, the product sells at a price in excess of its value; contrariwise, when the composition of capital is below the social average, price is less than value. Apparently, if we had an industry whose composition equalled the social

Table 7–2

	Capital	Cost Price	s at $\sigma = 1$	Value	Profit at $r = 0.33$	'Price of Prod'.	Price > Value	q
I.	$250C + 75V$	325	75	400	108.3	433.3	+ 33.3	3.3
II.	$100C + 50V$	150	50	200	50	200	0	2.0
III.	$50C + 75V$	125	75	200	41.6	166.6	− 33.3	0.7
Σ	$400C + 200V$	600	200	800	200	800	0	

average, q_0, prices would actually correspond to values. Let us bring this out by constructing a simple three-sector model on Marx's own assumptions, setting both t_c and t_v equal to unity for convenience so that $(c + v) = (C + V)$ (see Table 7–2).

How is it that in Department II the price of the product is exactly equal to its labour value? Obviously, because $q_2 = q_0$, which means that the share of labour in the cost price of Department II is identical to the share of labour in the cost price of output as a whole, namely one third. The trick in Marx's argument is very simple: first, we derive the total amount of surplus value from the amount of variable capital employed; next, we calculate the average rate of profit on total capital invested by dividing the total surplus value by the amount of capital in the economy; and then we add profits at the going rate to the cost price to arrive at prices $\equiv C + V + r(C + V) \equiv (1 + r)(C + V)$. Obviously, the deviations of price from value must now cancel out in the aggregate because we have defined total profits, π, to be equal to the total surplus value, Σs. Different industries share in a pool of surplus value, not in proportion to their variable capital, but in proportion to their quotient of the total capital invested in the economy. By setting $\Sigma s = \pi$, however, we insure that the industry whose $q_i = q_0$ will sell its product at a price equal to its value simply because it earns profits exactly equal to its surplus value. To reiterate: the total surplus is derived by applying a given σ to v; total profits are derived by applying the given r to $v/(c + v)$. An industry in which $q = c/v = q_0$ is a scalar model of the whole economy. But how do we know that profits in the aggregate are determined by applying a coefficient σ to variable capital alone? We do not know. This is precisely what is to be proved. Instead of proving it, Marx assumes it at the outset.

To make certain that we have grasped the logic of the argument, let us restate it in a different way. Price will be higher or lower than value depending on whether $q \gtrless q_0$. Since value $\equiv c + v + s$ and $\Sigma s \equiv \pi$, it follows that with a given σ, any industry whose $q < q_0$ will earn a higher rate of profit. As it can earn only the average rate, the profits it does obtain are less than the surplus value generated in the industry; this is what causes the price of its product to be less than its value. Conversely, industries with a high degree of mechanization sell at prices in excess of value by appropriating surplus value from other industries. Interindustry equality in the rate of profit causes surplus value to be redistributed from labour-intensive industries to capital-intensive industries. The industry with an average degree of mechanization is unaffected by this process. And so Marx concludes that 'the sum of prices equals the sum of values', that is, GNP measured in prices equals GNP measured in labour values.

5. Solutions of the Transformation Problem

Quite apart from the actual meaning of Marx's argument, it remains to be shown that the problem admits of a uniquely determined solution when both output and input values are transformed into prices. In Marx's solution just outlined, the equal rate of profit is calculated in relation to the *value* of invested capital, and then outputs are expressed in terms of prices instead of values. But, obviously, the price calculation ought to transform inputs as well as outputs. Marx himself did not give the general solution, but it is easy to show that it is in fact possible to transform *all* values into prices. Reading across the rows of Table 7–3 we have each industry's cost input according to its origin, including the surplus accruing to it; reading down the columns, we have the allocation of each department's output according to its destination. Under stationary conditions, Marx's 'simple reproduction', in which all surplus value is spent by capitalists on luxury goods, the sum of each row would equal the sum of the corresponding column. But under conditions of 'expanded reproduction', this will not be true. Department I produces capital goods used for further processing. Department II produces wage goods consumed by workers, and Department III produces luxury goods consumed by capitalists. Now, $\pi_i = r(c_i p_1 + v_i p_2)$, and the principle of equal profitability says that $r = \pi_1/(c_1 p_1 + v_1 p_2) = \pi_2/(c_2 p_1 + v_2 p_2)$, etcetera. Since $o_1 = (1 + r)(c_1 p_1 + v_1 p_2)$ and $o_2 p_2 = (1 + r)(c_2 p_1 + v_2 p_2)$, whereas luxury goods do not function as cost inputs, we can write

$$1 + r = \frac{o_1 p_1}{c_1 p_1 + v_1 p_2} = \frac{o_2 p_2}{c_2 p_1 + v_2 p_2}. \tag{1}$$

Cross-multiplying the right-hand side, thus implies that

$$(o_1 c_2)p_1^2 + (o_1 v_2 - o_2 c_1)p_1 p_2 - (o_2 v_1)p_2^2 = 0 \tag{2}$$

or, dividing through by p_2^2, that

$$\frac{p_1^2}{p_2^2}(o_1 c_2) + \frac{p_1}{p_2}(o_1 v_2 - o_2 c_1) - (o_2 v_1) = 0. \tag{3}$$

Table 7–3

Values		Prices	
I.	$c_1 + v_1 + s_1 = o_1$	I.	$c_1 p_1 + v_1 p_2 + \pi_1 = o_1 p_1$
II.	$c_2 + v_2 + s_2 = o_2$	II.	$c_2 p_1 + v_2 p_2 + \pi_2 = o_2 p_2$
III.	$c_3 + v_3 + s_3 = o_3$	III.	$c_3 p_1 + v_3 p_2 + \pi_3 = o_3 p_3$
Σ	$o_1 + o_2 + o_3 = \Sigma o$	Σ	$cp_1 + vp_2 + \pi p_3 = \Sigma op$

If we define $x \equiv p_1/p_2$, we recognize this as a familiar quadratic equation of the general form $ax^2 + bx + c$, whose solution is $x = (-b \pm \sqrt{b^2 - 4ac})/2a$. Rejecting the negative root of x as economically irrelevant, it follows that the positive root of $x \equiv p_1/p_2$ is one solution of equation (3). Without going through the tedious algebra, we may conclude that there must be a set of relative prices, p_1/p_2, which satisfies equation (1), which in turn implies that the rate of profit, r, as well as p_3 can be determined. Thus, the original set of price equations will uniquely determine r plus the three prices in terms of any one commodity.

The three-industry model is unnecessarily restrictive: it assumes that the ultimate use of any product is predetermined by its department of origin. But it has been shown that the transformation of values into prices based upon the principle of equal profitability can be carried out even for an n-fold subdivision of the economy with all possible uses for each product. As long as we stay with relative prices, there is no problem. To determine absolute prices, however, we need an invariant characteristic of the value system, and unless we analyze the nature of money, the selection of such a characteristic will be entirely arbitrary. Marx himself suggests two definite aggregate characteristics of the value system that are said to remain invariant to the transformation process: (1) 'total values equals total prices', which is tantamount to selecting the weighted average of all prices as the *numéraire*; and (2) the total surplus in value terms is equal to profits in price terms. Unless we make some very strong assumptions, however, it is not possible to satisfy both invariance conditions simultaneously for the simple reason that we have four unknowns, namely, r, p_1, p_2, and p_3, but five equations, that is, three department equations and two identities in the form of invariance conditions. The problem is overdetermined. What are these strong assumptions? Brushing aside the trivial case where $r = 0$, they are either that the organic composition of capital is equal in all three departments, or that there is an actual real-life median department of economic activity whose organic composition is equal to the aggregate organic composition of capital in the economy as a whole, so that labour-intensive departments neatly cancel out capital-intensive departments (as in Table 7–2). We may conclude that Marx was mistaken: when both input and output values are appropriately transformed into prices, we may retain either the aggregate version of the labour theory of prices ('total values equals total prices') or the aggregate version of the labour theory of profits ('total surplus value equals total profits'), but we cannot in general retain both.

But so what? Why not make do with one invariance condition? If we choose one of the two invariance conditions, but not both, we will obtain a labour theory of relative prices but only by giving up the labour theory of profits. When we talk of an equal rate of profit in all industries, we are talking of r in price terms. But according to the theory of surplus value, r is determined in labour value terms and there is absolutely no reason why r in value terms should be equalized between industries: with an equal σ but different q's between industries, r in value terms must also be different between different industries. Thus, if only one invariance condition holds, r in value terms may well diverge from r in price terms. If we are going to apply the labour theory of value to both prices and profits, as Marx clearly wanted us to do, we need both invariance postulates and that, as we have seen, is only possible in special cases. In short, it *is* technically possible to solve the Transformation Problem but it is not possible to do so while retaining both the labour theory of relative prices and the labour theory of profits.

Since Marx's day other invariance postulates have been proposed. The first author to treat the transformation problem after Marx was Bortkiewicz, a German statistician and mathematical economist, writing in the first decade of this century. Bortkiewicz claimed invariance for the unit value of luxury goods, the products of Department III in the traditional three-sector breakdown of the economy; that is, he set $p_3 = 1$. Taking a leaf out of Ricardo's book, Bortkiewicz identified luxury goods with gold and thus ensured that money prices are expressed in terms of the labour value of gold. On applying Bortkiewicz's solutions to the given value system, it appears that total surplus values are equal to total profits but that 'total values' necessarily diverge from 'total prices'. This is a consequence of the fact that $q_3 < q_0$. If Bortkiewicz had followed Ricardo the whole way, he would have made wage goods the 'invariable measure of value' by setting $p_2 = 1$ and assuming $q_2 = q_0$. And, indeed, this is one of the strong assumptions required to make the sum of values come out equal to the sum of prices.

We could give other examples of invariance postulates but to little purpose. The Marxian quest for the appropriate transformation of values into prices is nothing else than the Ricardian hunt for a perfect 'invariable measure of value'. The whole problem is derived from Ricardo, a fact that emerges more clearly in Bortkiewicz's solution than in Marx's own. The divergence of values from prices does not appear as such in Ricardo: in Ricardo it is a matter of prices altering when wages and profits change with given labour values. It was Ricardo who in effect was the first to ask: Will propositions about the rate of profit laid down in a world in which commodities sell at labour values hold in the real world in which commodities sell at 'normal prices'? We can now see that when Ricardo measured all values in terms of gold and assumed that gold was produced with an average ratio of capital to labour, he was in fact assuming $q_3 = q_0$ and $p_3 = 1$. At times he made things even simpler for himself by simultaneously assuming that $q_2 = q_0$ and $p_2 = 1$ [see chapter 4, section 12]. The logic of Ricardo's procedure, its formal validity, but also its incredibly restrictive character, emerges very clearly in the light of the Marxist transformation problem. That is why we have taken some care to spell it out.

6. Historical Transformation

By now the reader has surely grown weary of juggling to and fro with averages and ratios. It is time to ask what all this is supposed to prove. It was Marx's intention to show that the average rate of profit, calculated as it is on total capital invested, hides the true nature of profit, namely, its sole dependence on capital expended to purchase direct labour services. In the first volume of *Capital* we get an analysis of σ stripped of all disguises: surplus value accrues to each capitalist in accordance with his outlays on labour. But since capital-labour ratios differ between industries while r is everywhere uniform, it cannot be true that profits in each industry depend solely on wage capital. So let us translate to the price calculus of capitalists and show that, despite all appearance to the contrary, the average rate of profit depends in fact on an average rate of surplus value as a function of the size of the labour force. It is quite clear that Marx thought he had actually demonstrated that total profits must equal total surplus value. Where this not so, he argued, the average rate of profit would be indeterminate: producers add a markup to the cost price of a commodity, but how is this markup itself determined? 'The sum of the profits of all spheres of production must be equal to the sum of surplus-values'; to deny this, Marx declared, is to leave 'political economy . . . without a rational basis'.

And yet nowhere does Marx give any reason for believing that the rate of surplus value is in fact uniform between industries. What we actually observe is that profit per man varies with capital per man in each industry. The implausible assumption that each worker generates a constant surplus no matter where he is employed requires proof to become credible. And the proof is never forthcoming. The whole of *Capital* is in fact a long drawn-out *petitio principii*. The rate of surplus value is not observable in the market. There is of course nothing wrong with a theory that involves unobservable variables – witness 'ego' in psychology or 'utility' in neoclassical economics. But s and v are not only unobservable variables; they are also nonbehavioral variables. No economic agent acts in response to the rate of surplus value: workers are interested in maximizing real wages and capitalists are motivated by the rate of profit. Since s and v and, indeed, all labour values are neither observable nor behavioral variables, we simply do not know what to assume about the rate of surplus value and we have no more reason to assume that it is equal than that it is unequal between industries. For example, how do we know in Table 7–2 that price exceeds 'value' in capital-intensive industries but falls below 'value' in labour-intensive industries? If we did not ascribe a uniform σ to all industries, the more natural assumption to make is that different rates of surplus value fill the gap between cost price and the 'price of production', in which case capital-intensive industries would generate more surplus per worker than labour-intensive industries. Once we had gone that far, the temptation to conclude that capital generates as much surplus value as labour would be irresistible. Be that as it may, the point is that the Marxist formulation of the Transformation Problem neatly stands reality on its head: it is observable prices that have to be transformed into unobservable values, not *vice versa*.

We shall see that Marx flirted with the idea that competition itself guarantees the equalization of the rate of surplus value across industries, an idea which has been echoed by a number of recent commentators on Marx. The argument goes like this: competition secures both a uniform rate of wages for homogeneous labour and a working day of uniform length across all lines of employment; with everybody working the same number of hours a day and paid the same rate of wages measured in labour hours, the ratio of 'unpaid' to 'paid' labour must be the same in all industries, and the ratio of unpaid to paid labour is simply another way of measuring the rate of surplus value. The fallacy in this argument is simply the identity that is tacitly assumed between labour values and money prices, applied in this case to the price of wage goods. Just because workers are observed receiving the same money wage, it hardly follows that the labour time required in different industries to produce the goods that will command an equivalent bundle of wage goods is everywhere the same, regardless of whether the industry in question is labour-intensive or capital-intensive. If only goods did exchange according to ratios of embodied labour, then an equal wage rate and a working day of equal length would guarantee an equal rate of surplus value. But since goods do not exchange in accordance with the labour theory of value, we cannot infer an equal σ from an equal w and an equal working day.

What makes Marx so deceptive to read is his tacit assumption that the total direct and indirect labour embodied in commodities can be determined quite simply by 'looking and counting'. But this is by no means true because the input of indirect labour via the application of machines can only be observed as a value compounded over time at the ruling rate of profit. It is perfectly true that the series converges fairly rapidly so that the most of the total labour embodied in the production of a commodity is captured by going back two or three years. After all, the problem of determining the total labour value of, say, steel is simply the reciprocal of the problem of discovering how much direct and indirect employment would be generated by the production of more steel. Both problems can be solved if we are willing to be *almost* right. But the point is that we cannot be precisely right. The value of a commodity can never be totally reduced to direct labour inputs applied in the past if only because of the existence of 'joint products' [see chapter 4, section 31]. It follows that the assumption of an uniform rate of surplus value among industries, which is so vital to Marx's argument, can be neither inferred from direct observation nor deduced from the economic behavior of workers and capitalists.

Marx merely *attributes* all income to labour and so presumes the existence of a purely fictitious ratio s/v, arbitrarily set equal across all industries. If instead he had operated with a capital theory of value, attributing the whole of the surplus solely to machinery and implements, and defined the rate of surplus value as s/c, he could have carried on transforming values into prices in exactly the same way as he did. It is not always appreciated that the assumption that will make s/v equal between all industries, namely an equal organic composition of capital everywhere, will also make s/c equal everywhere. With a capital theory of value we can say that all capitalists share in a pool of surplus value, a pool created solely by the nonhuman factors of production; in the process of equating profit margins per unit of capital invested in both labour and machines, capitalists necessarily cause prices to fall below value in capital-intensive industries and to rise above value in labour-intensive industries. But this argument would no more prove that surplus value is created only by machines than Marx's argument proves that surplus value is created only by labour.

The only place in which Marx approaches something like a substantive argument about surplus value is in his suggestion that 'value' exists not only theoretically, but also historically, prior to 'price of production'. Prices were at one time in accordance with the labour theory of value, says Marx. Just as ontogeny repeats phylogeny in biology, so the capitalist system grew in the same way as Volume III of *Capital* succeeds Volume I. Under 'simple commodity production', in which each worker owns his own tools, everyone earns the same income for equal working time. Here unequal capital-labour ratios do not come in to plague us because there is no tendency toward equal profitability and the movement of workers between occupations merely establishes an equal rate of surplus value. Marx supposes that this condition actually prevailed in ancient and medieval economies. Engels went so far as to say that 'the law of value has prevailed during a period of from 5 to 7,000 years'. Soviet writers have pointed out that this accounts for the fact that the process of industrialization in capitalist countries always begins with the development of light industry. At early stages of capitalist development when the transformation into prices has not yet been effected and the rate of profit is still unequal between industries, capital will be attracted to labour-intensive consumer goods industries where the rate of profit is higher than in capital-intensive industries producing machinery.

This extraordinary argument is not without significance for an understanding of Marx's preconceptions. Taken at its face value, it is untenable: all societies that have ever approximated the conditions of 'simple commodity production' have been custom ridden. Competition was never allowed to equate skilled labour to so many units of unskilled labour, and hence the ratios at which products exchanged could not have corresponded to the quantities of 'socially necessary simple labour' required to produce them. Moreover, what has happened to what Marx called 'primitive accumulation'? Instead of capitalism arising out of colonial plunder, piracy, the slave trade, debasement of the currency and enclosures, we suddenly have an orderly historical process of the transformation of values into prices. The interesting implication of the argument, however, is that it admits that the labour theory of value can be operative even when the sociological spectrum of capitalism is missing. All that is really necessary is the presence of competition. 'Simple commodity production' is nothing else than Adam Smith's 'early and rude state of society' in which commodities exchange at ratios proportional to embodied labour because there is no capital. Adam Smith conjectured the existence of such a society only to illustrate the action of competition under simplified assumptions. But Marx, in a thoroughly un-Marxist fashion, actually supposes that a precapitalist economy functions in the same way as a Smithian society of beaver and deer hunters.

7. What Price Value?

It should now be obvious that the labour theory of value is not a theory of value at all in the now accepted use of the term. It does not claim that the price of a commodity is equal to the labour embodied in its production or that competition enforces such a distribution of productive resources between various industries that relative prices in the long run tend to be proportional to labour inputs. Long-run prices in Marx are determined in the same way as in orthodox theory, that is, by long-run costs of production, including profit at the ruling rate. But an adequate theory of value must explain how market forces produce such an equilibrium 'normal price'. This involves an explanation of how the values of the factors of production are determined and how the level of prices, including factor prices, results from the supply of factors and the pattern of demand for finished goods. On all these counts, we get no assistance from *Capital*. What Marx means by the value of a commodity is its price in terms of labour time if the share of wages in total costs for this commodity is equal to that of output as a whole. Moreover, the commodity in question must be reproducible at constant cost and sold within a perfectly competitive, closed economy. It is clear, therefore, that for any practical pricing problems, the Marxist theory of value will prove worse than useless.

It has been argued that it was not Marx's intention to supply a detailed theory of relative prices. The Marxian system is fundamentally concerned with macro-economic relationships and, in particular, with the distribution of income between property owners and wage earners. Some Marxists have expressed their discomfort at this face-saving argument. A theory of class-income distribution that is economic and not ethical in content must have *some* reference to actual prices. The whole point of Volume 1 of *Capital* is to show how the existence of surplus value is consistent with a state of affairs in which commodities exchange in accordance with the quantities of labour embodied in them. The theory of surplus value is essentially a statement about the relationship of the value of labour power to the value of the final product. Surely, this is a statement about relative prices.

Nevertheless, it would seem that Marx's constant harking back to the basic division between 'paid' and 'unpaid' labour refers to the aggregate output of the entire economy: in any developed economy, workers do not spend part of their time producing their own consumption goods. What Marx seems to be saying, therefore, is something like this: if a given net national product requires 100 man hours to produce and if 60 percent of output goes to wages, then the value of the surplus is 40 man hours; in a particular capital-intensive industry in which wages absorb only half of net output, the extra 10 man hours of profit are to be attributed to the fact that the price of the product exceeds its value. Put this way, it is seen that total profits in the system are limited by the amount of unpaid labour that can be squeezed from the working class. Marx's 'value', therefore, is not a ratio at which products exchange but purely an abstraction that is posited, not observed, by crediting each worker with an average rate σ. When the total surplus formed from this average is broken up and redistributed among industries, it is possible to *say* that prices diverge from value and that profits are, in the last analysis, simply unpaid labour.

It has also been argued that the theory of surplus value is merely an expression of the particular ethical or political viewpoint that property income *ought* to accrue to workers rather than to capitalists, landlords and rentiers. The labour theory of value, according to this interpretation, is a theory of natural rights rather than a theory of prices. But however much every sentence of *Capital* radiates moral zeal, Marx did not write three volumes to furnish a *positive* demonstration of a *normative* propo-sition. The labour theory of value may be associated with definite moral sentiments, but it does not rest on them. At bottom, its appeal is to science, not to ethics. Marx did, after all, criticize and reject the so-called Ricardian Socialists who put forward in the 1830's and 1840's the doctrine of 'labour's right to the whole produce of labour'.

Besides, Marx knew perfectly well that workers cannot stake a claim to the whole product even under communism, much less under capitalism: even a communist society will have to reinvest some part of the total product to maintain the capital stock and will have to support the non-working part of the population out of the net product.

8. The Marxist Case for the Labour Theory

We have seen that the labour theory of value can in some fashion explain all observed price phenomena in a capitalist economy. The skeptic would say that any schema can be made to work at the cost of theoretical complexity: given enough epicycles, even the Ptolemaic hypothesis can be upheld. But Marxists retort that economics is replete with theories that require substantial qualification before they can be applied to real-world situations: it is all a matter of the degree of appropriate abstraction about which no rules can be laid down. But economy of logic does have its virtue: the fewer the epicycles, the better. Should we not apply Occam's Razor to the troublesome assumption that only labour adds value to the product, the value of raw materials and machinery being merely passed on? By dropping this notion we remove the arbitrary assumption that the ratio of value added by labour to wages tends to equality between industries and so dispense with the formalistic transformation problem. After all, a good many economists have used the labour theory of value as a rough approximation to the secular trend in the 'real costs' of producing commodities, without all the rigmarole of transforming value into price. Even Keynes expressed 'sympathy' with the labour theory of value in the *General Theory* on the grounds that relative prices are determined in the short run by prime or variable costs and that, over the economy as a whole, prime costs are all wage costs. It is clear, however, that Marxists mean more than this by the labour theory of value. Why do they cling to it?

When pressed, Marxist writers concede the limited importance of the labour theory as a theory of relative prices. But they insist that this theory throws into sharp relief in a way no other does the fundamental division of income between wage earners and property owners. The point is that the labour theory, and the labour theory alone, leads to the theory of surplus value, and it is the latter that is appealing. Only the labour theory of value, they declare, is based on the fact that labour is a unique social cost, it alone starts from the firm bedrock of *objective* costs, it alone emphasizes that production and exchange involve social relations between men and not just technical relations between things, and so on. In part, such arguments seem to be a reaction against the colorless neutrality of modern economics with its rigid divorce of price theory from welfare economics. But, on a deeper level, what Marxists are saying is that, unless we begin with a labour theory of value, we cannot argue that capitalists get a part of the total product without working. But what reasons do we have for thinking that profit is 'unearned income'? This question, which seems to be at the bottom of the debate between Marxists and non-Marxists, is almost never raised explicitly in the literature.

9. Profit as Unearned Income

The first point to note is that the concept of surplus value in Marx is not formally derived from the labour theory of value at all. In order for labour power to sell at its value, there must be an equilibrating mechanism in the labour market that causes the 'market price' to conform to the 'natural price' of labour services. The classical economists found such a mechanism in the theory of population but Marx rejected the Malthusian theory and denied that labour is produced in accordance with rational cost calculations. What he put into its place is 'the reserve army' of the unemployed, which, however, has no necessary tendency to preserve wages at the 'value' of labour power, however effective it may be in holding wages down. In short, without being aware of it, Marx denies the applicability of the labour theory of value to wages because the equilibrating mechanism that is the foundation of this theory does not work in the labour market. This is all to the good, for it permits us to discuss the theory of surplus value on its own grounds without any connection with the difficulties of the labour theory of value.

Marx's problem is to show how surplus value, a costless gain to the capitalist, is preserved in an economy in which prices are determined by impersonal forces and the relation between employer and worker is based on contract rather than status. Under perfect competition one might think that capitalists – whose individual contributions to total output are too small to influence price – would expand output in the effort to reap more surplus value, until wages are bid up so as to reduce the surplus to zero. Having discarded the Malthusian wages-population mechanism, Marx had to invoke something else to keep wages down. He found it in the concept of a chronic excess supply of labour. Excess supply of labour implies that the ruling wage rate lies above the equilibrium wage. It is easy to see how this situation might be maintained in an underdeveloped economy in which the equilibrium wage rate that would clear the labour market is well below the subsistence wage rate. In that case the wage rate will be kept artificially high by all kinds of social conventions favouring a 'fair wage' and the result is hidden as well as open unemployment. This is what we have earlier described as Marxian unemployment: full-capacity use of the capital stock is nevertheless insufficient to absorb the available labour supply [see chapter 1, section 4].

But, surely, this kind of structural unemployment must disappear in an advanced economy? No, not necessarily. At any rate, Marx argued that unemployment is required even in an advanced economy to keep wages from eating into profits, thus undermining the incentive to accumulate capital. Hence, booms deplete the reserve army and slumps replenish it but secular growth at full employment is a contradiction in terms to Marx. In other words, there is in Marx something very much like the Keynesian idea of 'unemployment equilibrium' but it is not a static equilibrium as in Keynes but a dynamic, moving equilibrium, involving positive growth rates of capital and labour.

For the moment, let us accept this theory of the dynamic process that keeps capitalism going. In what sense can we now say that surplus value or profit is an unearned income? In describing surplus value as 'expropriated labour time', Marx apparently means to imply that surplus value does not remunerate a productive effort; it is not a payment that is technically necessary to enable production to go on; it is merely the result of the fact that the means of production are privately owned under capitalism. Does this contradict the teachings of 'bourgeois' economics? Let us take the most apologetic of all interest theories, the abstinence theory of interest espoused by Nassau Senior [see chapter 6, section 11]. The capitalist has practised abstinence from present consumption and may therefore demand interest or profit as a 'just reward' for his pains. He may demand all he will but why does competition allow him to earn interest? Obviously, because workers do not possess the where-withal to wait until the goods they are currently producing are ready for sale; it is only because capitalists can advance wages that they receive interest as their personal income. Does this theory 'justify' the payment of interest? In one sense, yes: positive net investment cannot take place unless some people are willing to postpone present consumption; since no one is apparently willing to do so without a reward, elimi-nation of interest would mean the drying up of investment. But this in no way justifies *private* ownership of the means of production. If postponement of the present enjoyment of income is really a sacrifice, the abstinence theory of interest will justify a positive interest rate on money loans just as well under socialism as under capitalism. In general, all theories of interest, whether a marginal productivity theory or a time-preference theory or what have you, must explain the receipt of surplus value by capitalists, landlords and rentiers in terms of the fundamental institutional fact that workers do not own the means of production.

The issue is not how to justify interest or profit but how to justify private property of capital equipment and the concomitant power to hire labour. Acceptance of one or another bourgeois theory of interest implies nothing about the institutional structure of a society. To rationalize private ownership of the means of production, we need an additional argument designed to show that private decentralized decision-making is more efficient or more productive than central planning. Contra-riwise, arguments in favour of socialism require demonstration that public ownership and central direction are more efficient or better in some well-defined way than is decentralized decision-making.

It is curious that Marx, the prophet of socialism, gave the whole dispute about the respective merits of capitalism and socialism a wrong slant by conflating the economic and the social implications of a theory of interest. The debate about capitalism versus socialism revolves around the question of how certain functions can be most efficiently performed, functions bound up with the ownership of property. Instead, Marx is caught up in the purely metaphysical problem of whether capital is barren or productive, whether interest or profit is a payment for services rendered or merely income stolen from workers. Marx admits that though all value is produced by labour, labour's capacity to create value is enhanced by working with capital equipment. But to say that the output of labour is greater with than without capital is to say that capital is productive. This proves nothing about the merits of capitalism. One may believe that capital is productive, and even that capitalists are productive – another proposition altogether – and yet believe that the price we pay for free enterprise in the form of recurrent slumps and gross inequalities in the distribution of income is too great to warrant its perpetuation. In other words, it is not necessary to be a Marxist to believe in socialism, nor does approval of capitalism imply denial of the facts from which Marx drew the unwarranted conclusion that profit is a type of legalized plunder.[1]

The difficulty is that there is an unbridgeable divide between pragmatic socialists who object to capitalism because it is inefficient and inherently inegalitarian and Marxist-type socialists who condemn it because it exploits workers and makes a fetish of material production and acquisition. If we say that 'socialism is about equality', we can consider the merits of collective ownership of the means of production in terms of its effects on the distribution of income, the concentration of economic power, the pace of technical change, the influence of both workers and consumers on management decisions, the maintenance of full employment and the rate of economic growth. In other words, we can reach a decision on state ownership, at least in principle, on the strength of factual evidence. But if instead the fundamental objection to capitalism is not merely that it fosters inequalities, nor that it is inefficient, nor that it is doomed to collapse, but that it constitutes a jungle in which capitalist tigers roam at will to prey upon helpless workers, then only a consensus on certain value judgments can resolve the great debate on nationalization. We have to agree, as it were, on a conception of 'the good society' before we can claim to be socialists. It is perfectly clear that what makes Marxism so difficult to discuss is that Marx attacked capitalism both on positive and on normative grounds. He was not satisfied merely to argue that capitalism produces undesirable economic results; quite apart from these results, he argued that profit or interest as a distributive share lacked an economic *raison d'être*: it is not a necessary cost payment and it would disappear if we nationalized the means of production.

10. Marx and Böhm-Bawerk
The distinction between interest as a distributive share and interest as a necessary cost payment is well brought out by contrasting Marx's theory of interest with Böhm-Bawerk's. The 'dean of bourgeois economists' regarded labour and land as

---

[1] The same facts can be made to look quite different when seen through different lenses. Here is Keynes describing the flourishing capitalism of the 19th century in *Economic Consequences of the Peace* (1919): 'Europe was so organized socially and economically as to secure the maximum accumulation of capital. While there was some continuous improvement in the daily conditions of the life of the mass of the population, Society was so framed as to throw a great part of the increased income into the control of the class least likely to consume it. The new rich of the 19th century were not brought up to large expenditures, and preferred the power which investment gave them to the pleasures of immediate consumption. In fact, it was precisely the *inequality* of the distribution of wealth which made possible those vast accumulations of fixed wealth and of capital improvements which distinguished that age from all others. Herein lay, in fact, the main justification of the Capitalist System. If the rich had spent their new wealth on their own enjoyment, the world would long ago have found such a régime intolerable. But like bees they saved and accumulated, not less to the advantage of the whole community because they themselves had narrower ends in prospect.

'The immense accumulations of fixed capital which, to the great benefit of mankind, were built up during the half-century before the war, could never have come about in a Society where wealth was divided equally. The railways of the world, which that age built as a monument to posterity, were, not less than the Pyramids of Egypt, the work of "labour" which was not free to consume in immediate enjoyment the full equivalent of its efforts' (pp. 18–19).

the only primary factors of production and, like Marx, treated capital as produced means of production that merely transmit value to the product; he denied that 'abstinence' is an independent factor of production and he also denied that that interest owes its existence to the personal activity of capitalists [see chapter 12, section 4]. According to Böhm-Bawerk, 'surplus value' is produced by labour and land alone but it accrues only after the passage of time. Workers actually do receive the entire *present* value of their future output, properly discounted at the going rate of interest, but the *future* value of that output will necessarily exceed its present value. The central task of the theory of interest is to show why there is such a difference in the value of labour's product over time. But, whatever the reason, this discounting of the future value of goods is possible only because workers' lack of financial reserves forces them to pay a premium on present goods. Insofar as interest is a distributive share, therefore, Marx's and Böhm-Bawerk's explanations do not differ significantly.

But interest is also a price that governs the distribution of the income stream of a community over time. It acts to allocate resources between current and future consumption. And it is one of Böhm-Bawerk's contentions that interest is a general economic category not peculiar to capitalism but obtaining whenever present and future goods are exchanged. By way of contrast, Marx completely neglects the problem of resource allocation over time under socialism. It is not merely that Marx is reluctant, as he puts it, to write 'recipes for the cook-shops of the future' but rather that Marxian economics falls down just where it is most needed, namely, to provide an economic rationale for a socialist economy.

11. Surplus Value and Economic Surplus

Marx's 'proof' of the exploitative nature of profits runs in terms of the endlessly reiterated assertion that workers produce more than the cost of their own maintenance and replacement. But all that this proves is that capitalism produces a surplus product over and above the biosocial minimum standard of life of the population. Again and again Marx thinks he is showing us that the surplus is attributable to labour alone, when all he is demonstrating is that the productive process generates a surplus. On Marx's definition, 'exploitation' can cease only when the whole current net output of labour accrues to labour as current consumption: 'exploitation' means positive net investment. Similarly, some modern Marxists make things easy for themselves by defining capitalist exploitation as occurring whenever capitalists claim a share of the net product. However, to base a theory of exploitation on the mere fact of private property in the means of production is cheating: it means that the nature of profits is explained by the simple casual observation that machines and factories are not freely available to everyone. This wins the argument by ruling out any argument.

In one of his early works, *The German Ideology*, Marx defined 'exploitation' as 'the harmful use of another person for one's own benefit'. Capitalists certainly employ workers for their own benefit but how do we demonstrate that their profits are necessarily derived at the expense of workers? How do we 'prove' that profits are the results of 'exploitation'? Not by invoking labour's 'right' to the whole product because that is a claim that cannot be justified under any social system. Not by pointing to the fact that workers produce more than the cost of their own maintenance and replacement because that proves that the economy generates a surplus, not that the surplus is due solely to living labour. Not by saying over and over again with Marx that the worker works part of the day for himself ('necessary labour') and part of the day for the capitalist ('surplus labour') because such a division of the working day for each and every worker is a fiction: workers in wage goods industries work all day to produce their own and other workers' wage goods, whereas workers in capital goods industries never produce their own wage goods, much less anyone else's. But perhaps by emphasizing the fact that workers under capitalism are only 'free agents' in the legal sense and that they lack any control over their own working conditions.

Labour under capitalism is ostensibly free but it is actually forced labour to secure a product by means which subordinate the desires and interests of workers to those of the capitalist. The capitalist maintains a 'despotism of the work place' and it is in this sense that profits are the fruits of 'exploitation'.

Now, this view of the essence of the labour contract and the true nature of what Marx called 'the labour process' suggests an explanation of the nature of profits as surplus value, which is entirely divorced from any and all aspects of the labour theory of value. It is a sociological rather than an economic explanation, which is indeed to be found in Marx tucked away between the basic argument in terms of the labour theory of value. Many modern Marxists, inclined to abandon the labour theory of value as untenable, have opted for this line of reasoning as the more promising way of defining 'exploitation'. And it must be said that Marx once again had a remarkable insight even if he failed to make the most of it: the employment contract under capitalism is in fact 'incomplete' in the sense that it stipulates the rate of pay for labour, and the hours of work of labour, but fails to lay down the intensity or quality of the labour that is to be performed. Given the character of productive processes, it is only rarely that it is possible to attribute output to individual workers; hence, time-wages are much more common than piece-wages. That implies, however, that capitalists must somehow maintain the quality of labour by constant monitoring of job performance, backed up by the threat of dismissal. In short, there *is* something like a 'despotism of the work place' and profits only accrue to capitalists who are effective despots.

Of course, one may argue whether the same is not just as true under socialism, except that the profits now go to the state. But if socialism means labour-managed enterprises, as Marx appears to have thought, the workers now become their own despots and 'exploitation' disappears. Whether an economy of labour-managed enterprises could function effectively is not a question we can take up here. All we are suggesting is that here at last is a consistent way of defining 'exploitation' so as to limit it to capitalism. Unfortunately, as we suggested, it was not the principal line of argument which Marx employed: he was too deeply influenced by Ricardo to give up an 'economic' explanation of profits as surplus value in the contemporary sense of 'economic', that is, an argument resting on the labour theory of value.

Nowadays we have a somewhat different sense of what is meant by an 'economic' explanation of profits. If there is any economic sense in giving the name of 'surplus value' to the incomes of capitalists and landlords, it must be because such payments, unlike the wages of workers, are not necessary to call forth the services of capital and land. A 'surplus' in economic theory can only mean an excess of the receipts of an agent over its supply price. The classic example of such a surplus is Ricardo's rental payments to landlords in possession of superior land. The question of what constitutes a Ricardian rent depends entirely upon the point of view we take [see chapter 3, section 10]. As long as an agent has alternative uses, its earnings are necessary from the viewpoint of the firm – the narrowest point of view. But if an agent is committed to the industry, or if the 'net disadvantages' of transferring to other industries are prohibitively high, payments to the agent may be higher than is necessary to keep the services of the agent in the industry: since competition between firms in the industry will assure equalization in the price of every unit of the productive service, marginal and intramarginal units alike, the agent may well earn a surplus from the viewpoint of the industry. As we take a wider and wider view, from the firm to the industry to the economy as a whole, the alternatives available to a productive agent become more restricted in scope, and the payment necessary to keep a unit of the productive service within the economic arena considered becomes smaller. For the economy as a whole, there are no alternative opportunities in the short run and the whole of an agent's reward is a surplus: payments for services yielded by property in the short run are economically unnecessary because the property is already in existence and 'bygones are forever bygones'. In the short run, as Marshall would say, all interest is in the nature of a quasi-rent [see chapter 10, section 2]. The same is true of the bulk of wages in the short run except that labour needs some daily maintenance payments.

But if we now give our attention to the long run, we 'narrow' our point of view by considering the possibility of new alternative earnings for the factors of production. Payments for the use of property do now appear to be economically necessary, even from the point of view of society as a whole. Payments to the owner of a requisite productive service to compensate him for the loss of an alternative use constitute the supply price of the service. The sacrifice of a future use for a present one is just as real and necessary as the payments that go to workers to enable them to rear a new generation of workers. Surpluses may and do exist, but they may exist just as much in a society that has abolished private property in the means of production.

With this lesson in Marshallian economics in mind, we can now restate the Marxist theory of profit as 'surplus value'. The only condition under which the supply price of capital is always zero, no matter how narrow or wide our point of view, is when neither saving nor investment is in any way connected with the interest rate or the profit rate – let us agree to speak of these as synonyms from now on. If a fall in the rate of profit depresses saving or investment, then the supply price of capital is in fact positive, meaning by 'supply price' simply the payment that induces capital to be supplied.

The reader may be tempted to think that this proves our point: profit is not merely surplus value. But as a matter of fact, Marx seems to have foreseen the Marshallian objection, for he argues that all saving is carried out by capitalists for the purpose of reinvestment and that capitalists automatically reinvest all profits regardless of prospective returns. There is no problem of inducement to invest in Marx and if the theory of surplus value is really taken seriously, there cannot logically be any problem of investment incentives. Unfortunately, this view destroys Marx's theory of business cycles and, indeed, his whole conception of the 'breakdown' of capitalism.

We have reached an intriguing result that we must pursue further: either the theory of surplus value is untenable or Marx's prediction of the increasing instability of a capitalist economy must be abandoned.

12. The Laws of Motion of Capitalism

It is clear that Marx's attack on capitalism has actually nothing to do with the essence of property income as 'unpaid labour'. Labour does not receive the whole product under capitalism but it would not receive the whole product under socialism. Capitalism has to be abolished, argues Marx, not because of any inherent injustice in the prevailing class distribution of income, not because workers' consumption might conceivably be raised by the 20 or 30 percent of the national income now consumed by capitalists, but because the system results in wars, in colonial exploitation and, above all, in a waste of human resources through unemployment. Similarly, he sees socialism as bringing full employment, increased control of workers over their working conditions, emancipation of the individual, release of new cultural energies and international peace. This means that we can examine Marx's analysis of the 'laws of motion' of capitalism without regard to the logical subtleties of the Transformation Problem. In fact, Marx's analysis of the structural development of capitalism at no point hinges on acceptance or rejection of the labour theory of value.

But here we encounter a difficulty not experienced before. For no matter which of Marx's predictions we examine – absolute or relative impoverishment, increasing severity of business cycles, absolute growth of unemployment, gradual elimination of small and medium-sized enterprises, falling rate of profit – we find no complete analysis of the phenomenon in question. In some cases all we have to go by is a series of vague and even contradictory statements. If we leave Marx, we find a mass of literature by his disciples, who offer a bewildering variety of interpretation of the basic historical drives of capitalism. In the end, we must conclude that some of the predictions have been refuted by the course of events, while others remain suggestive and debatable; but none of them can be regarded as even theoretically established. Nevertheless, this part of Marx's writings is in many ways the most fecund, abounding as it does in provocative hypotheses.

13. The Law of the Falling Rate of Profit

We begin with the famous law of the declining rate of profit by recalling that the rate of profit, r, varies inversely with 'the organic composition of capital', q, and directly with the rate of surplus value, σ:

$$r = \frac{s}{c + v} \equiv \frac{\sigma}{q + 1}.$$

At this point we drop the assumption that the whole of the capital stock is consumed each year and explicitly introduce variations in the turnover rate or durability of capital:

$$r = \frac{s}{K} \equiv \frac{s}{c/t_c + v/t_v} \equiv \left(\frac{s}{c + v}\right) t \equiv \left(\frac{\sigma}{q + 1}\right) t \equiv \frac{\sigma}{Q}.$$

t_c and t_v are the respective turnover rates of constant and variable capital; t is a weighted average of these two turnover rates; $Q = (q + 1)d$, where d is a weighted average of the durabilities of c and v and $t = 1/d$. This formulation has the advantage of emphasizing what every businessman knows: any increase in the turnover rate of capital, or, what is the same thing, any reduction in its durability, increases the rate of profit.[2]

The expression $r = \sigma/Q$ is equivalent to the more familiar expression that makes the rate of profit a function of the amount of surplus per man – a flow per unit of stock – and the ratio of capital to labour – a ratio of two stocks. We simply start with Marx's expression and multiply through by wages per man:

$$r = \frac{s/v \cdot v/N}{K/v \cdot v/N} = \frac{s/N}{K/N}.$$

As far as Marx was concerned, the very expression $r = \sigma/Q$ establishes the law that the rate of return on capital must fall with the increased mechanization of industry. Having concluded that the wage rate rises little, if at all, in the course of capital accumulation, while technical change constantly raises the stock of equipment per worker, he thought it obvious that Q must show a steady upward trend. It is true that this will not lower r if the rate at which σ is rising exceeds that of Q. And since mechanization raises the productivity of labour, it can hardly fail to raise σ. Marx realized that there is some functional connection between Q and σ, but after satisfying himself that σ could rise only within 'certain impassable limits', he assumed it to be a constant. He did recognize the influence of *autonomous* increases in σ, which he handled under the label of 'absolute and relative surplus value', but these too he dismissed, with more justification, as having definite physical limits.

[2] An example may clarify the problem. Let $K \equiv 500$, consisting of $C \equiv 400$, $V \equiv 100$. C consists of fixed assets plus a stock of raw materials and V consists of a sum of money or a stock of wage goods to make wage payments until the product is sold. Suppose it takes six months to manufacture the finished product. The stocks of raw materials and wage goods turn over twice a year: $t_c \equiv t_v \equiv 2$. Suppose, in addition, that fixed assets have an average durability of 10 years: $t_f \equiv \frac{1}{10}$. If the total value of fixed assets is 300, outlays on depreciation per cycle of production lasting 6 months will equal 15. Outlays on raw materials and wages over the same period will both equal 100. Therefore, $c \equiv 115$ and $v \equiv 100$. Assume that σ for one turnover of c is 100 percent. Then the value of the finished product $c + v + s \equiv 315$. For one turnover of c, we have $s/(c + v) \equiv 100/215 \equiv 46.5$ percent. The annual rate $s/(c + v)$ will be twice this, or 93 percent. Since s per annum $\equiv 200$, the rate of profit, however, is $r \equiv s/K = 200/500 = 40$ percent. This may also be expressed in terms of the average turnover rate t calculated as the weighted average of t_f, t_r, and t_v. We have $t = 300 t_f + 100 t_r + 100 t_v/500 = 0.86$. Then r is given by $s/(c + v)$ for one turnover of c multiplied by t: $(46.5)(0.86) = 40$ percent as before.

The constancy of σ was only a simplifying assumption but, as has been frequently pointed out, it was a particularly clumsy simplification for the Marxian system. Since wages and profits exhaust total income, a constant σ implies constant relative shares. This means that real wages rise as fast as the average productivity of labour. Writing σ for net output and o/N for the average productivity of labour, we have

$$\sigma = \frac{s}{v} \equiv \frac{s/o}{v/N \cdot N/o} .$$

When wages, v/N, rise as fast as the productivity of labour, o/N, the denominator remains unaffected and, therefore, so does σ. However, not only did Marx state in so many words that labour's share would decline, but such a decline is implied by the very notion of 'the reserve army.' However interpreted, chronic unemployment presumably means that wages do *not* rise as fast as the average productivity of labour. And as long as this is true, every increase in output per man raises σ. *A fortiori*, if real wages are constant, σ will rise sharply as K/N increases. Thus, the tendency for r to fall is indeterminate: it all depends on the nature of the explicit function $\sigma = f(Q)$.

Marx's attempt to demonstrate the existence of an upper bound to this function is hopelessly muddled, reflecting the difficulty of measuring prices with a yardstick that is itself changing through time. As time goes by, the average productivity of labour rises and the 'value' of products measured in embodied labour falls. This rise in productivity, however, is the result of a rising organic composition of capital. With a constant rate of profit, a rising Q entails prices falling but not falling as fast as labour values – just as the price for a particular commodity exceeds its value when it is produced with a Q in excess of the national average. It is quite clear, therefore, why Marx operates with a constant σ in his numerical examples: it ensures prices moving proportionately to labour values. Notice that he had no right to write $r = s/(c + v)$ because r is expressed in price terms, whereas s is expressed in (labour) value terms. He should have written $r = \pi/(c + v)$, where π equals total money profits, in which case he would have revealed that the connection between r and σ is by no means straightforward, particularly when considered through time. For example, our earlier statement that a constant σ implies constant relative shares of wages and profits is strictly speaking untrue: the ratio of direct and indirect man hours required to produce investment and luxury goods consumed by capitalists to the man hours required to produce wage goods consumed by workers may remain constant, while the ratio of money profits to money wages varies considerably in response to changes in the consumption patterns of capitalists and workers, and hence changes in the price of wage goods and non-wage goods. Relative prices are *roughly* proportionate to relative labour costs, which is to say that s/v is by no means identical to the ratio of total profits to total wages. Waiving that point, Marx is bound in principle to agree that a rising σ is an integral part of the general process of rising productivity engendered by the steady increase of Q. The only question is: are there any limits to the rising rate of surplus value?

Most of us would be prepared to say that profits per man cannot rise without limits. As productivity increases, workers will certainly enforce a rise in money wages through trade union action. This is an argument Marx does not use because the assumption of perfect competition eliminates the possibility of trade unions. But even in a perfectly competitive economy, real wages must rise as more complex machinery requires more highly trained workers to operate it, while the increased intensity of labour required more or better food and clothing to maintain workers' energies. More complex machinery, however, also works to raise the gap between output and wages upon which σ depends. The fact that the increased productivity of labour also reduces the money value of output is irrelevant because at the same time it is also cheapening the goods bought by workers. We end up with the proposition that σ will rise if productivity increases faster in the wage goods industries than in other sectors; it will fall if productivity increases are confined to the making of machines and luxury goods.

Marx should have claimed that the value of wage goods lags behind the fall in the (labour) value of the total product. But on logical and on empirical grounds this would be a weak argument. The best argument he comes up with is this: the 24-hour limit to the working day makes it impossible to raise σ beyond a definite amount; at the same time, the rise in Q involves a reduction in the amount of employment associated with each unit of capital, so a rise in σ may not raise the total surplus associated with that capital. These two arguments are apparently additive: there will eventually come a point at which no conceivable rise in σ can possibly prevent the total quantity of surplus produced by a given capital from falling below its original level; at that point r will fall. What Marx is forgetting here is that 'value' is constant only when the productivity of labour is constant. At any moment in time, $s + v$ is a given amount for a given amount of labour; hence, the 24-hour limit to the working day prevents σ from rising to infinity (assuming $v > 0$). But with a rising productivity of labour there is nothing to stop σ from increasing indefinitely. With constant real wages, both the 'value' of s and the 'value' of v are falling, but by definition of rising output per man, s/v is always increasing. It may be true that c/v is also rising, but an infinitely high σ is always capable of offsetting the increase in q. Marx's law of the falling rate of profit, therefore, even when accepted on its own grounds, is caught up in a bewildering mesh of opposing forces whose resolution is not deducible from elements supplied by the theory. At bottom, his problem was that of inferring trends in the price system from unobservable trends in the arbitrary (labour) value system.

It is possible, however, to make out a case for Marx's law on highly simplified neoclassical grounds. First, we must rigidly distinguish movements along a production function at a given state of technical knowledge from shifts in the production function caused by technical change. In Marx these two are considered together, implying that capital is not normally increased without altering 'the state of the arts' and, likewise, that innovations are typically embodied in new investment. Assuming that we can in principle distinguish capital investment at a constant state of technique, we boldly define an aggregate production function obeying constant returns to scale – constant costs or constant returns to scale is the natural assumption for a labour theory of value. By the properties of this function, output rises for every increase in capital per man along the given function but less than proportionately to the increase in capital. As the capital-output ratio rises, the increase in capital will entail a fall in r and a rise in w. Innovations may offset this tendency, but not all innovations will necessarily do so. If technical change does not work to reduce capital per unit of output, r will nevertheless fall. This is because the capital-absorbing effects of the innovational process govern the degree to which wages rise as capital increases. If wages rise as fast as output per man, relative shares are unaffected and the rising capital-output ratio alone leads directly to a fall in r. In the Marxian system, labour's share is alleged to fall through time; therefore, a rising capital-output ratio here does not necessarily imply a falling r. But this is only to say that the Marxian law of the falling rate of profit is predicated upon a very rapidly rising capital-output ratio, which implies in turn that technical change is heavily slanted toward labour-saving improvements. For the claim that capital per man rises faster than profits per man, or in Marxian terms that Q rises faster than σ, is tantamount to claiming that the capital-output ratio rises faster than the profit share of output:

$$r = \frac{\sigma}{Q} \equiv \frac{s/N}{K/N} \ .$$

Multiplying through by N/o, we get

$$r = \frac{s/o}{K/o} \ .$$

The fact that the aggregate capital-output ratio has remained practically unchanged in advanced economies over the last seventy-five years is fairly damaging to the Marxist schema. Together with the slow, downward drift in the profit share of output, it suggests the conclusion that profits per man may have risen almost as fast as capital per man and hence that r has declined little, if at all.

14. A Glance at the Data

Is it in fact true that r has not fallen in the history of capitalism? This is not the place for a thorough discussion of the evidence, but let us glance briefly at a recent effort by an American Marxist, J. Gillman, to submit the falling rate of profit to a statistical test. Using census data for American manufacturing over the period 1849–1939, the author starts out by accepting Marx's categories on a flow basis. The results are very disquieting: although q showed a fairly strong tendency to rise until the turn of the century, the trend value through 1919–39 was constant. Since σ rose persistently (as measured by the ratio of profits to wages!), the trend in s/k was decidedly upward over the whole of the ninety-year period.

When the ratios are converted to a stock basis, however, the data breaks clearly into two historical phases. Until 1919 capitalism in manufacturing behaved very nearly as Marx had predicted: Q rose significantly, and σ did not increase sufficiently to prevent r from falling. Then something went wrong. The organic composition of capital stabilized in the 1920s at levels reached in 1919 and fluctuated countercyclically in the 1930s; it fell all through World War II and then rose a little up to 1950. If the decade of the 1930s is excluded, there is in fact some indication of a secular decline in Q. In addition, neither σ nor r showed any definite trend over the years 1919–50. These findings are complemented by evidence with respect to the capital-output ratio in American manufacturing: estimated in 1929 prices, the ratio rose through 1880–1919 and has fallen continuously since that time.

15. Capitalsaving Innovations

The reasons Marxists themselves give for the decline in Q since 1919 is the increasing importance of capitalsaving innovations. There is a certain tendency to regard these innovations as novel manifestations of a complex technology that Marx could not possibly have foreseen: laboursaving improvements are *induced* by rising wages eating into profit margins, but capitalsaving improvements just happen, for technical reasons, to occur only in late-stage capitalism.

Such was not Marx's own attitude, however. In Volume III of *Capital*, he gives great prominence to 'cheapening the elements of constant capital' as one of the 'counteracting causes' to the falling rate of profit. And to show what he means, he devotes two chapters to the tendency of certain inventions to shorten the time of production, thus raising profits by reducing the stock of goods that must be carried for a given output. 'Cheapening the elements of constant capital', that is, raising t_c, evidently refers to innovations that release fixed capital. Apart from better quality machines, any improvement that widens the scope of auxiliary instruments, reduces the need for floor space, or lengthens the physical life of a plant belongs to this class of innovations. Under the same heading, Marx also discusses innovations that save working capital by lowering freight charges, by reducing delivery time and by effecting fuel savings through recovery and use of waste products. Marx is not only aware of the importance of capitalsaving changes but regards them as the product of automatic market forces. 'Capitalist production', he writes, 'enforces economies in the employment of constant capital' which tend 'to check the fall in the rate of profit'. But the decline in the value of 'the elements of constant capital' is not a 'counteracting cause' at all: it is a necessary element of the rising productivity of labour in all sectors, and, particularly, in the capital goods sector. The steady tendency of the capital-labour ratio to rise through time not only automatically increases s/v but also automatically reduces c/v, all variables being measured in terms of labour. There is nothing in Marx that would stop us from assuming that technical progress is neutral on balance, the productivity of labour rising just as fast in the capital goods industries as in the consumer goods industries. And this would mean that economic progress constantly raises productivity and hence σ but leaves the 'value' of Q unchanged.

16. The Reproduction Schema

The law of the falling rate of profit is fundamental to Marx's analysis of the cyclical character of economic growth under capitalism. But before we turn to his theory of business cycles, we must pause a moment to consider the famous reproduction schema of Volume II. These have a particular historical interest, not only because they have never ceased to fascinate Marx's followers, but because they represent the first example of a type of analysis associated with the names of Harrod and Domar in our own times [see chapter 5, section 15]. The problem is to state the macroeconomic conditions for balanced growth of the system, so as to raise the question whether hitchless expansion is actually possible.

Marx begins by dividing the economy into two departments producing capital goods and consumer goods respectively. He then distinguishes between simple and expanded reproduction. 'Simple reproduction' denotes a condition of stationariness in which net investment is zero. What conditions are required to keep a stationary economy stationary? The answer is seen by noting that the whole output of Department I must be devoted to capital replacement in both departments: $c_1 + v_1 + s_1 = c_1 + c_2$. Simultaneously, the whole output of Department II must match the wages bill plus property income: $c_2 + v_2 + s_2 = (v_1 + v_2) + (s_1 + s_2) =$ the net national product. Both of these equations reduce on cancellation to the condition: $v_1 + s_1 = c_2$, that is, the net output of Department I must be matched by the replacement demand of Department II. If $v_1 + s_1 > c_2$, it signifies that outlays on replacement of fixed capital exceed depreciation allowances, that is, net investment is positive. On the other hand, the failure to use depreciation accruals for replacement of worn-out capital must cause output to shrink. This argument emphasizes some basic macroeconomic relationships: it shows, for example, that while total outlays must equal total income for the economy as a whole, income may exceed outlays in some industries without causing any difficulty; or, similarly, the fact that workers cannot buy back the total product does not by itself cause disequilibrium.

Unfortunately, Marx does not explicitly state the conditions for smooth 'expanded reproduction'. Moreover, he only examines growth at a constant rate, the case in which growth does not involve a change in Q. With respect to an increasing rate of growth, he merely suggests that if savings increase without concurrent investment, this need not spell deadlock if credit money is being introduced into the system, or if capital is being exported. Formally, however, the equations for expanded reproduction at a constant rate are similar to those for simple reproduction. Breaking up surplus value into its constituent parts, we have s_v spent on hiring labour, s_c spent on consumer goods, and s_k spent on capital goods. Hence, the output of Department I must be equal to the total demand for capital goods:

$$c_1 + v_1 + s_{k_1} + s_{c_1} + s_{v_1} = (c_1 + s_{k_1}) + (c_2 + s_{k_2}).$$

Also, the output of Department II must be equal to the total demand for consumer goods:

$$c_2 + v_2 + s_{k_2} + s_{c_2} + s_{v_2} = (v_1 + s_{c_1} + s_{c_1}) + (v_2 + s_{c_2} + s_{v_2}).$$

Cancelling out, both equations yield

$$v_1 + s_{c_1} + s_{v_1} = c_2 + s_{k_2}. \tag{1}$$

The demand for consumer goods emanating from Department I must equal the demand for capital goods on the part of Department II; or, the net output of Department I must grow *pari passu* with gross investment expenditures in Department II, a conclusion identical to that reached earlier for 'simple reproduction'. Equation (1) can be further manipulated to show that balanced growth depends upon a definite distribution of the labour force between the two sectors as a function of the rate of surplus value, the propensity to invest in the two sectors and the capital intensity of production in the consumer goods industries.

This construction can be made to yield a few insights but on the whole it is based on assumptions so restrictive as to deprive the argument of much value. The economy is closed; all products sell at long-run 'normal prices'; the rates of turnover of capital are identical in the two departments; only capitalists save; savings in each department are always fully invested in the same department; there is no technical change; real wages are constant; real surplus per man is constant, and so on. Moreover, a two-sector model is a treacherous instrument for analyzing a real economy in motion. Many industries do not fall neatly into either category, producing both capital and consumer goods – think of coal, transport and chemicals. Moreover, the division within such industries between the categories of capital and consumer goods varies through time as a result of changes in the pattern of demand. This works havoc with the Marxian conditions for expanded reproduction. Nevertheless, equation (1) plays a definite role in the Marxian system by suggesting the improbability of smooth expansion: most of what Marx had to say about business cycles arose out of considering the reasons why equation (1) might not hold.

At one time, economists used to sneer at the Marxian equations of 'expanded reproduction': they were regarded as curios in the museum of economic thought. Then in an article in 1939, and later in a book published in 1948, Harrod startled the economic profession with his equation for 'warranted growth'. Marx's equation (1) may be oversimplified but it does refer to a two-sector economy. Harrod's equation pertains to a one-sector closed economy: the average equals the marginal propensity to save; the average equals the marginal capital-output ratio; both saving ratios and capital-output ratios are constants; both saving and investment are functions of income only; there is no factor substitution; there is no technical change, and so on. In short, Harrod's equation is more restrictive and less illuminating than Marx's. Moreover, it shares the major shortcoming of Marx's equation (1), namely, the failure to indicate what would happen if the stated conditions for smooth expansion were violated. Both Marx's and Harrod's equilibrium growth paths are unstable, simply because any growth path so narrowly defined can be nothing more than 'a knife-edge equilibrium'. On these grounds, there is little to choose between Marx and Harrod. This sort of growth theory is essentially uninteresting because no economy could function if it did not contain definite stabilizing features that permitted the system to absorb the 'shocks' that it regularly receives from the outside. What we want to know is how much we can rely on these stability properties and for that purpose we need more flexible models of the growth process than either Marx or Harrod provided. This explains why all the recent developments in growth theory have gone far beyond Harrod's original formulation. It is only now that we can say that Marx's equations for expanded reproduction are old-fashioned. It is salutary to remember that we must say as much for Harrod's *Towards a Dynamic Economics* (1948).

17. Business Cycles

Marx does not have a special theory of business cycles and in fact specifically disavows any attempt to provide such a theory. His view seems to be that crises are merely expressions of the 'fundamental contradiction of capitalism', namely, that production is carried on for profit rather than for use and that the very drive for increased profits destroys investment opportunities. Marx's theory of the business cycle is coextensive with his general analysis of capital accumulation.

His picture of the cyclical process, however, runs something like this: in a boom, the demand for labour resulting from accumulation will run ahead of the available supply; the reserve army is depleted and the relative scarcity of labour causes wages to rise; hence, profits fall and accumulation slows down. A reduction in the rate of capital accumulation leads to a fall in aggregate demand and hence to a downturn. In the slump, capital values are written off and the reserve army is replenished, thus driving wages down. This restores the profitability of production and sets the stage for a resumption of accumulation: the slump is both a retribution and a catharsis.

This cyclical reserve army theory is joined to the secular tendency of the rate of profit to fall and the possibility of disproportionate rates of growth of capital goods and consumer goods industries. The maldistribution of income under capitalism owing to the failure of real wages to rise as fast as output per man is, as Marx said, 'the last cause of all crisis.' This does not mean that Marx held an underconsumption theory, either in the sense that the saving-and-investment process eventually causes overproduction unless some new source of consumption demand appears, or in the sense that a deficiency of consumption demand is always the initiating cause of a slump [see chapter 5, section 14]. The first version, held by Malthus is refuted by the reproduction schema, which shows that expanded reproduction at a constant rate is theoretically possible. The second version is refuted by Marx's penetrating observation that wages are never higher than right before the crash; to raise wages will not of itself perpetuate the boom, because it merely creates a situation in which capitalists are dissatisfied with the relationship between wages and prices. What Marx had in mind was the notion that capitalism tends continually to expand production without any reference to the effective demand that alone can give it meaning. The expansion of production does not automatically generate a proportionate increase in effective demand because the excessive rate of capital formation lowers the rate of profit, even while the innovations embodied in the increments of capital hold down wage rates by being largely laboursaving.

18. The Investment Function

The first thing to notice by way of criticism of Marx's conception of the business cycle is that it assumes too glibly that money wages vary inversely with the rate of profit in the short run. In the boom, a rise in money wages caused by falling unemployment raises money costs of production. Before we conclude, however, that this implies a reduction in profit margins, we must take account of the effect of higher money wages upon effective demand. The rise in demand for consumers' goods is bound to raise prices in the short run, particularly because Marx supposes that the marginal propensity to consume of workers is always equal to unity. In the short run, all variable costs of production over the economy as a whole consist of wage costs. Hence, on the average we would expect that rising money wages would raise prices as much as average costs, leaving profits per unit of output as well as real wages unaffected. Likewise, in the slump, cutting wages will not raise profit margins if workers habitually spend all their income. Realistically, the workers' marginal propensity to consume is less than unity, but, on the other hand, wage costs are only a fraction of total costs in the long run; given time to adjust the size of plant, it is not at all clear that cutting wages in the slump works to restore profits.

Be that as it may, the profit margin is not the same thing as the rate of profit on capital. Suppose an increase of money wages in the boom does reduce gross and net profit margins; as long as capitalists are the only savers and invest without fail, there is no reason why the increase in money wages should affect the rate of profit. Likewise, the fall in money wages in the slump may act to increase profit margins, but if effective demand falls off in proportion to the reduction in payrolls, investment will not be encouraged.

Capitalists, Keynes has taught us, can pull themselves up by their own bootstraps via the multiplier. The crucial question is the inducement to invest. This brings us at last to the deepest problem in the Marxian system. Precisely what does govern the willingness to invest? We have seen that Marx pictures capitalists as reducing investment at the peak of the boom in response to the falling rate of profit. Apparently, then, capitalists do not always invest the whole of non-labour income; if they did, crises could never take place. Yet elsewhere Marx views capitalists as caught up in a dynamic race that forces them to accumulate on pain of elimination. And as we know, the theory of surplus values implies as much: investment is not a function of the rate of return to capital. How do we resolve this contradiction?

What Marx is saying is that the pursuit of wealth in a capitalist society is regarded as an end in itself. Capitalists save and invest for reasons of prestige and social status, a way of 'keeping up with the Rockefellers'. Hence, changes in the rate of profit will have little effect on investment, except insofar as low profit rates leave the wealthy with less income to save. Investment demand will be maintained and the capital stock will be used to capacity as long as investment yields any positive return, however small. This is not incompatible with periodic shrinking of investment due to the shock effect of a fall in the rate of profit. In other words, whereas we usually think of factor demand and supply curves as being *more* elastic in the long run than in the short run, Marx suggests that the demand for investment and the supply of business saving is actually *less* elastic in the long run. As Keynes once observed: 'It is not necessary . . . that the game should be played for such high stakes as at present. Much lower stakes will serve the purpose equally well, as soon as the players are accustomed to them'.

The Marxist view of the mainsprings of capital accumulation makes excellent sociological sense. The typical businessman in the heyday of 19th-century capitalism was not interested in pecuniary profit for what it would buy in the way of personal consumption. The motive that produced economic development under capitalism was 'conspicuous accumulation' for its own sake, not maximum profits to increase personal spending power. In this sense, and taking the widest view, it is indeed true that the supply price of capital was effectively zero. But this does not mean the 'real cost' of saving was zero, that society effortlessly converted present income into future income at will. It is simply that the institutions and social climate of 19th-century capitalism in effect shifted this burden to wage earners by producing sharp inequalities in the distribution of income. The reduction of these sharp inequalities by means of redistributive taxation and social welfare legislation has not reduced the rate of interest to zero. Nor would socialism tomorrow do so. Nothing can reduce the rate of interest to zero except capital saturation: a state of affairs in which real incomes are so high that postponement of present consumption is painless. To test the theory of surplus value, we must ask: is the failure to pay workers the whole national product in the form of wages and collective consumption *merely* a matter of institutional considerations? The institutions of capitalism actually disguise the nature of interest as an index of the cost of 'waiting', and it would seem that a satisfactory theory of the rate of interest must begin by abstracting from the specific sociological characteristics of capitalism.

19. The Myth of a Laboursaving Bias

Accepting Marx's picture of the investment process, however, implies abandonment of his dire predictions about the imminent breakdown of capitalism, predictions based upon a belief in the predominantly laboursaving slant of technical change grinding down rates of reward to both capital and labour. In orthodox theory, an increase in capital per man along a given aggregate production function cannot lower both profit and wage rates. Technical progress, however, may produce this perverse result under special circumstances, particularly because technical progress is irreversible. In Marx, technical change is indissolubly connected with increases in capital per man and hence the issue is even more complicated than it is in orthodox theory. In Marx, 'the passion for accumulation' expresses itself in innovations that are predominantly of the laboursaving type; the wage rate *must* be kept down in order to keep profits up, but the scramble for more profits defeats its own purpose.

This 'paradox of accumulation' colors the whole of Marx's analysis of the laws of motion of capitalism. It is indeed the contradiction to end all contradictions. The easy retort is to say that it has not actually happened. But suppose that it could happen. What would the world have to be like to have it happen? Consider the arguments which suggest that capital accumulation cannot for long lower both profit and wage rates. First of all, the fall in the rate of profit depresses saving, not necessarily because it affects the willingness to save but because it affects the ability to do so. Since all savings come out of profits in the Marxian system, as business saving falls, so does investment, and the system settles down to a slower rate of growth, which brings the rate of profit back to previous levels. Secondly, if capital is being incessantly invested in laboursaving improvements, the capital-output ratio must be rising. This means a higher share of depreciation and interest charges in total costs, with consequent pressures to effect economies in the use of capital: innovations become less and less laboursaving and wages start rising. Similarly, 'the passion for accumulation' entails a chronic excess demand for capital; consequent difficulties in obtaining finance, expressing themselves in an upward sloping supply curve of funds available to the firm, should make capitalists alert to every possibility to save capital. Finally, laboursaving technical change implies that the rise in man hour productivity is concentrated in the finishing stages of production. All cost reducing changes in the capital goods industries release capital for the economy as a whole: they lower machine prices and bring about substitution of capital for labour. Therefore, if technical change in the economy as a whole is slanted in the labour-saving direction, it must be concentrated in the consumer goods industries. Hence, prices of consumer goods fall faster than machine prices and this induces substitution of cheap labour for dear capital all round. The rate at which labour is being displaced in the economy falls off, the reserve army stops growing and wages rise. It is possible that the scope for factor substitution is so limited that the mechanism just outlined would not work. But in a highly developed multi-industry economy, it is difficult to believe that factor endowments could long continue to be grossly inappropriate to available technology.

The idea that the innovational process as a whole is the outcome of responses to market pressures should have been congenial to Marx, who may be said to have discovered it. We may sum up by noting that if technical progress is plentiful and yet produces a fall in the rate of return to capital, it suggests that the factorsaving slant of innovations is out of line with relative factor scarcities. In an economy in which capital is the scarcer factor, a persistent bias toward laboursaving improvements must erode the profits that each individual producer expects to reap from an improvement – this is the Marxian case. When labour is the scarcer factor, as in advanced Western economies, a bias toward capitalsaving improvements likewise works to reduce the yield of capital. Perhaps the reason that technical change has not exhibited either bias to any marked degree is that the long-term pattern of innova-tions is the outcome of successive adjustments to differential rates of growth in the factor supplies as reflected in relative prices. Producers in a perfectly competitive market face infinitely elastic factor supply curves, that is, factor prices are given to them. It would seem, therefore, that the perfectly competitive market provided no signal to induce the 'appropriate' factorsaving innovation. But factor supply curves do shift through time, and there is nothing in the static theory of the competitive firm that leads us to deny that firms will learn to adapt themselves to a persistent trend in the shifting of factor supply curves. In other words, producers simply become conditioned by experience to avoid disappointment by choosing improvements that save the relatively scarcer factor.

This response mechanism is not likely to operate very smoothly, as the existence of business cycles will testify. At the crude, aggregative level adopted here, one can think of many objections [see chapter 11, section 25]. Nevertheless, the notion that rational, optimizing behavior precludes the possibility of any pronounced bias in technical change over long periods of time is plausible in itself and is supported by historical evidence. The idea, as we have been showing, really goes back to Marx. But Marxian economics provides only a truncated theory of factorsaving innovations. Changes in factor prices are said to affect the choice of new techniques, but capitalsaving innovations are not treated on the same footing as laboursaving innovations. Yet Marx recognized that a falling rate of profit will induce entrepreneurs to economize upon fixed and working capital. The failure to consider the consequences of such tendencies is the fatal weakness of the Marxian theory of capital accumulation. It results in a theory of economic growth in which investment improvements dry up, not because there have been too few laboursaving improvements, but because there have been too many. This conclusion is hard to justify in any competitive economy and has certainly proved to be irrelevant to the experiences of developed capitalist countries. Marx erred in not envisaging the possibility that labour might become the relatively scarcer factor. It is for this reason, and not because of any serious logical errors, that he failed correctly to depict the historical evolution of capitalism.

20. Impoverishment of the Working Class
Having banished the bogey of simultaneously falling profit and wage rates, we can make short shrift of most of Marx's other secular predictions, such as the increasing amplitude of business cycles, the growing volume of chronic unemployment, the decline in domestic investment outlets, and the law of the absolute and relative 'immiseration of the proletariat'.

The last prediction, however, is worth consideration on its own merits. Marx never denied that real wages might rise under capitalism. He strongly implied that labour's relative share would fall but in fact never used the phrase 'relative impoverishment'. The notion that he pronounced a theory of the growing poverty of the working class is just folklore Marxism. The doctrine of absolute impoverishment is actually an argument about quality, not quantity. Marx spoke, not of material poverty, but of 'pauperization' and the growing 'misery' and 'mental degradation' of the working class: as he put it, 'in proportion as capital accumulates, the lot of the labourer, be his payment high or low, must grow worse'. Presumably, Marx was thinking of the Smithian notion that mechanization destroys the demand for skills and reduces workers to mechanical ciphers. Nevertheless, the failure of wages to rise with the productivity of labour is an element in the doctrine of absolute impoverishment. The fact that labour's relative share under capitalism has steadily risen for a century or more would, surely, have surprised Marx.

Marx's followers have advanced a number of explanations of the tendency for living standards to rise under capitalism, two of which we will examine in some detail. First, there is the popular contention that Marx's mistake was political, not economic, best represented by a book like J. Strachey, *Contemporary Capitalism* (1956). This starts from the alleged constancy of relative shares and then asks how this can be squared with the conscious action that has been taken over the last century to redistribute income in favour of labour: factory acts, minimum wage legislation, the growth of the social services, the progressive income tax, the rise of inheritance taxation, the voluntary redistribution of great fortunes through public foundations and, lastly, the growth of trade unions. And all that this has done, Strachey observes, is to leave relative shares constant and to slightly equalize the distribution of personal income. Does this not show that Marx's analysis of the basic tendencies of capitalism was sound? To be sure, Marx underestimated the economic consequences of trade unions and the rise of the labour vote. But if we switched off the heavy counter pressures of state action and labour organizations, who would doubt that the basic tendency of wages to hover about subsistence levels would reassert itself?

Apart from the fact that this argument explains the facts only by the miracle of two equally opposing forces, there is something about this way of looking at things that is essentially alien to the spirit of Marxism. It implies that the division of the product between capital and labour is fundamentally a matter of the political wage bargain, that competitive pressures in the labour market exert no influence on wage rates, and that the 'rate of exploitation' is not subject to any general rule. If this is so, a theory purporting to describe capitalism's laws of motion should provide an analysis of the bargaining process that on this view is as fundamental to the system as the economic tendency toward subsistence wages. It is Marx, more than any other writer, who claims to have shown that trade unions can never do more than ameliorate the fundamental contradictions of capitalism. In the context of Marxism it is not legitimate to drag in trade unions as a *deus ex machina* to rescue Marx's falsified predictions. One could understand a bourgeois economist drawing a rigid line of division between economic and political forces; but if Marxism is all it claims to be, a science of society, we cannot accept the idea that wages are determined by economic forces, which unions can 'offset' or 'counteract'. Unions are not fortuitous institutions. They are generated by forces inherent in capitalism. A mature capitalist economy without unions is almost as difficult to imagine as capitalism with a negative rate of interest. In general, Marxists in the wake of Marx himself have carried the game of shifting levels of discourse in the middle of an argument to a fine science: one moment something is an 'absolute law', the next it is a 'counteracting cause'; it is an 'inherent economic tendency' for one purpose and a political accident for another. The Marxist theory of trade unions and government intervention under capitalism remains to be written.

The second and equally popular argument suggests that the high standard of living of workers in advanced countries is somehow due to the exploitation of the colonial masses. This notion is almost impossible to get hold of because its meaning is not at all clear. Lenin talked vaguely of the 'aristocracy of labour' in the home country sharing in the superprofits of imperialism but the extra yield of foreign over domestic investment has not been such as to reasonably account for the tripling of real wages over the last century. Moreover, taken at face value, it would mean that the rise in living standards in the advanced countries has been matched by a deterioration of standards in the colonies. J. Kuczynski, a German Marxist, did argue that the law of absolute impoverishment holds strictly not for individual countries but for the whole labour force employed within a given capitalist society both at home and abroad. He carried out a series of statistical studies designed to verify the thesis but after a number of inconclusive volumes he abandoned the project.

Nevertheless, the general argument cannot be so easily dismissed. It might be interpreted to mean that unemployment in the major capitalist countries would have been much worse in the absence of imperialism. After all, Great Britain in the years 1870–1914 did invest abroad something like half her domestic savings, whose interests and dividends amounted to one tenth of her national income. Surely, the transfer of so much saving must have reduced potential domestic deflationary pressures and stabilized national income? But it is a mistake to assume that savings that went overseas would have existed at all in the absence of capital exports: foreign investment, by stimulating exports, generates income and hence saving just as much as domestic investment does. Without foreign investment, British income would no doubt have grown less rapidly, but so would have domestic savings. Moreover, most overseas investment in the heyday of Edwardian imperialism did not offset domestic saving in any sense whatever; the bulk of it was due to the reinvestment of undistributed profits on previous investment. We may conclude by rejecting the idea that the British worker was made better off at the expense of the Indian peasant or African miner.

21. Economic Imperialism

If Marxism is alive today, it is so more by virtue of the Marxist theory of imperialism than of any other aspect of Marxian economics. The Marxist theory of imperialism is much more than a theory that attempts to account for the rising living standards of workers under capitalism. It is a theory of the nature of the foreign policy of capitalist governments and, indeed, a theory of economic development that accounts for the gap between poor and rich countries in terms of the dynamics of foreign investment in capitalist countries. It was Lenin rather than Marx who developed all the implications of the argument, but nevertheless no discussion of Marx's predictions is complete without some attention to the theory of imperialism.

We must begin by conceding that the history of colonialism does not make edifying reading: the story of the imposition of foreign rule rarely does. But this is not what is at issue. By 'imperialism' is meant a foreign policy that seeks political and economic control over backward areas to guarantee the home country an outlet for idle savings and surplus manufactured goods in exchange for strategic raw materials. Marxist theory supposes that a closed capitalist economy must suffer from a chronic insufficiency of effective demand, from a basic imbalance that can only be corrected by the opening of foreign markets. Imperialism, the direct or indirect exploitation of backward areas, is therefore an inherent feature of advanced capitalist economies. Thus, the question we must ask is: can a closed capitalist economy in principle expand indefinitely on its own resources? If so, the elimination of imperialism would not mean the end of the capitalist system. And if the Marxist argument stands up, it follows that only a socialist society can break away from the imperialist pattern. The question is not whether, say, British rule in Africa was ruinous or beneficent but whether the Dark Continent was plundered to sustain capitalism in England; not whether the United States did or did not practise dollar diplomacy in Latin America with the aid of the Marines but whether a free enterprise economy can help to raise incomes in the Caribbean or Southeast Asia without committing economic suicide.

The brute facts marshalled by Lenin and his disciples are all too frequently beyond dispute, but what we are concerned with here is with the inferences they have drawn from them.

The core of the thesis is Marx's vision of capitalism, subject to chronic underconsumptionist tendencies. Marx himself talked of colonies as a thing of the past – in his day Britain was said to have acquired her colonies 'in a fit of absence of mind' – and abstracted from foreign trade in his central analysis. Still, Marx, and for that matter John Stuart Mill, did argue that the export of capital counteracts the decline of the rate of profit in a country by draining off excess savings. It was not difficult to stretch this into the proposition that the inability to dispose profitably of goods and capital at home leads inevitably to imperialist ventures. The entire theory of imperialism was ready made for Lenin by the German followers of Marx and Lenin took it over without further examination, neatly combining in his emphasis on foreign investment the high-profit pull of backward areas with the low-profit push of late-stage capitalism:

> In backward countries profits are usually high, for capital is scarce, the price of land is relatively low, raw materials are cheap. The possibility of exporting capital is created by the entry of numerous backward countries into international capitalist intercourse; main railways have either been built or are being built there; the elementary conditions for industrial developments have been created. The necessity of exporting capital arises from the fact that in a few countries capitalism has become 'over-ripe' and (owing to the backward state of agriculture and the impoverished state of the masses) capital cannot find 'profitable' investment [*Imperialism. The Highest Stage of Capitalism*, 1917, chap. 4].

How can domestic markets expand indefinitely, Lenin seems to be asking, when incessant laboursaving technical change holds down wages even as the eagerness to mechanize and to accumulate capital chokes of investment opportunities? This is the kind of underconsumptionist argument that is as implicit in Lenin as in Marx. But as we saw earlier, it is possible for a closed capitalist economy to expand indefinitely; even Marx himself had conceded that smooth 'expanded reproduction' is conceivable. Granted that a closed capitalist economy can theoretically grow along an equilibrium path, we have not yet disposed of the high-profit pull thesis. Surely, the prospect of supernormal profits in the poorer countries will induce an outflow of capital from the richer nations? This kind of argument had considerable *a priori* appeal in days when foreign investment was a significant fraction of total investment, but it fails to explain, as we shall see, why foreign investment took the pattern it did and why the flow of funds to the backward areas was so limited even in the 19th century. Nor can it account for the common observation that domestic savings in underdeveloped countries are often hoarded or exported to the advanced countries: if the rate of return is really as high there as it is claimed, what prevents local capitalists from emerging?

Contrary to popular belief, however, the yield of capital is generally higher in a capital-rich economy than in an underdeveloped country because capital in advanced countries is invested in a complementary fashion in basic industry, transport and power. Without the presence of social overhead facilities, such as roads, railways, harbors, docks, dams and power plants, the potentially high yield of capital in poor countries cannot be exploited. Lenin made his case by simply assuming that social overhead capital, what he called 'the elementary conditions for industrial development', was already in existence in the backward countries. But when this was the case, as in Canada and Argentina, these countries did not long remain underdeveloped.

Other things being equal, investors prefer to place their capital at home rather than abroad. The fact that capital was nevertheless exported does indicate that foreign investment offered higher rates of return than domestic investment. But taking into account the riskiness of foreign investment and the distinct possibility of default, the realized differential yield was usually more modest than might be expected. Supernormal profits and huge windfalls did occur but losses were not uncommon, and on average it is doubtful whether profits on overseas investment in the 19th century exceeded earnings at home by more than 2 or 3 percent.

Neither the push nor the pull version of economic imperialism stands up under analysis. Although weak in theory, Lenin's book has nevertheless been praised as giving a succinct review of the facts of imperialism. Lenin's version of the facts, however, is even more suspect than his theoretical reasoning, and has given rise to what can only be described as a total misconception of the typical pattern of foreign investment in the heyday of imperialism. We may pass over Lenin's belief that modern imperialism is characterized by the growth of monopoly and the participation of investment banks in the conduct of business enterprises. Finance capitalism, as Lenin defines it, never did establish itself in Great Britain, which had the largest empire of all, and even in Germany and America it largely disappeared after World War I. Nor is there strong evidence of a long-run trend towards the increased concentration of industry since about 1914. These issues do not touch the heart of the matter. The picture of foreign investment which Lenin projects in his book is that of capital exported to staple-producing, backward countries under the direct political control of the major powers, concentrating almost exclusively on the extractive industries and earning enormous rates of return for a narrow class of investors at home; an accompanying feature is the deliberate dumping of excess supplies upon restricted colonial markets. It is not too much to say that the whole of this is an elegant fiction. Lenin granted, for example, that the bulk of French capital held abroad was invested in Russia, not in the French colonies, while German capital was mostly invested outside her own negligible holdings in Africa. He insisted that 'the principal sphere of investment of British capital is the British colonies', while in fact over half of Britain's foreign assets in the decades before 1914 were held outside the Empire. Even within the Empire, Canada, Australia, and New Zealand – hardly outstanding examples of the ruinous effect of imperialism – accounted for one half of British investment and more was invested in Australia and New Zealand alone than in India and the whole of Africa. Outside the Empire, the United States and Argentina took the lion's share of British capital. Instead of capital flowing to densely populated China or India, where capital was scarce and labour cheap, two thirds of Britain's overseas investment in the years 1870–1914 went to the so-called 'regions of recent settlement', stimulated and complemented by the migration of something like 60 million people. The unique element of capital movements in the classic era of imperialism was just this: capital and labour flowed together from the Old World to the New, a striking fact completely ignored in the Marxist literature. Instead of the backward areas with their 'teeming millions' providing the dumping ground for surplus goods, the greater part of British manufactured exports likewise flowed to the regions of recent settlement in the wake of capital and labour.

The preoccupation with the extraction of mineral and plantation products for export to the industrial countries, so often thought to be the typical imperialist pattern of international investment, played a minor role in the period before 1914. The demand for foreign capital came to a large degree from public development schemes. At the outbreak of World War I, only 25 percent of Britain's overseas investment consisted of the strictly 'colonial' type of investment in agriculture, industry and mining. The proportion of government loans and other public investment was even higher in French and German than in British foreign investment, and in each case over half of the capital invested abroad was placed in other European countries, with less than 10 percent of the total invested within the respective colonies.

The fact that very little capital went to the densely populated countries and that most of it was put into fixed interest bearing government bonds or securities directly guaranteed by some branch of government is surprising only to those held in the grip of the Leninist conception of foreign capital ruthlessly exploiting native labour. Even today, developed countries like Canada, Great Britain, France, Germany and Australia together account for about one half of all direct American foreign investment. The preference of American investors for relatively developed and culturally familiar economies is a fact difficult to fit into the Leninist theory. Yet it is clear that safety motives and risk aversion have always loomed large in determining the flow of international capital. By stressing the prospect of super profits from the exploitation of colonial labour, the Marxist theory of imperialism provides no guide to the pattern which foreign investment took in the 19th century, or which it is taking today.

The case of the United States has always proved particularly troublesome to Marxist doctrine. America's colonies in the Pacific had little significance from an economic standpoint, and even Latin America, her principal sphere of influence, never attracted as much American capital or commodity trade as the Dominions. American foreign investment is now an even smaller fraction of total domestic capital formation than in the past. Since World War II, the net outflow of private long-term American capital, including reinvested profits, has amounted on the average to no more than 5 percent of total gross private domestic investment in the U.S.A., with earnings from overseas investment accounting for only about 1–2 percent of America's national income. It has been estimated that if the United States were exporting capital today on a scale equivalent in terms of real income per head to that of the United Kingdom at the turn of the century, the total value of American foreign investment would have to be twenty times larger than what it is; each year the United States would have to lend abroad a sum equal to twice the aid given under the entire Marshall Plan. Even if we add to direct plus portfolio investment abroad all public loans and grants abroad, as well as outlays on military establishments overseas, we reach an average annual sum for most of the postwar years of about 10 percent of the national income of the United States. Is it possible that these relatively minor expenditures provide a vital outlet for idle funds without which American capitalism would not be maintained, as Marxists are wont to claim? These sums at best bear no comparison to overseas spending in the Edwardian imperial heyday, which suggests the paradoxical conclusion that the more advanced capitalism is, the less it requires foreign outlets.

Taking a wider view, it is obvious that the world of nation-states has long been characterized by the relation of dominance and dependence among unequal political sovereignties. The point of a *theory* of imperialism is to explain the observed patterns of dominance and dependence around the world in terms of a finite set of variables, so as to predict and retrodict changes in that pattern resulting from changes in one or more of the explanatory variables. The Marxist theory of imperialism is a reductionist theory, inasmuch as it claims to reduce all the relevant variables to economic ones, and in particular, to the profit-maximising drives of national corporations seeking raw materials, new investment outlets and additional markets for final products. This theory is rich in predictions: foreign investment flows predominantly to poor countries in inverse proportion to the level of effective demand at home; foreign investment in poor countries is typically concentrated in the mineral extraction industries; overseas dependencies constitute the principal export markets for the products of the major imperialist powers; the richest capitalist countries are those that have enjoyed the largest empires and the poorest countries are those that were once colonies; and, lastly, the demise of imperialism means the demise of capitalism and *vice versa*.

The theory is rich in predictions but the real world is rich in refutations of that theory. Indeed, there must be few theories in social science that have been so frequently falsified by experience as the Marxist-Leninist theory of imperialism. Its advocates put Ptolemy to shame in the number of epicycles they can generate to account for every anomalous event in the field of international relations; the war in Vietnam when the U.S.A. had in fact few investments in Southeast Asia; the Russian invasion of Czechoslovakia for no conceivable economic reason; the prosperity of Sweden and Switzerland, who lack and always have lacked colonies; the increase in the rate of economic growth in Japan, Germany and the Netherlands after they were deprived of their colonies; and so forth. The fact that the Marxist theory of imperialism was never fully worked out by Marx himself, that the Leninist version is patently specific to the context of World War I, and that indeed there exists no single, rigorously formulated version of that theory makes it all too easy to weave endless complications around the basic theme that are capable of saving it in the face of any and all facts.

The difficulty is that Marxists cannot conceive of an alternative explanation.

Power politics? Surely, there is more to it than that? There must be a deeper explanation. But a theory of power politics among nation-states, striving for security in an international political system characterized by the absence of a supranational authority, is just as deep, just as complex, just as much the unintended social outcome of individual actions as the Marxist scenario of economic imperialism. Indeed, if we are going to think clearly about the very real problems of national dominance and dependence around the world, we must begin by discarding the hoary Leninist myth that colonies are indispensable to advanced capitalist countries and that the developed economies are rich only because they plundered Asia and Africa.

22. The Role of Institutional Assumptions

We conclude our discussion by raising a difficult question provoked by the study of Marxian economics. What is the appropriate level of abstraction for an economic theory? Debates between Marxist and orthodox economists invariably break down over the nature of the questions that economics ought to answer. When both schools of thought turn to the same questions, they do not really reach different results. As a theory of relative prices, for example, the labour theory of value is nothing but a static theory of general equilibrium, applicable to any closed exchange economy regardless of the character of property ownership, provided the input coefficients of production are given by purely technical considerations and perfect competition prevails. The labour theory of value is a special case of the more general Walrasian theory. Marxists themselves do not argue that orthodox price theory is wrong but merely that its findings are not very interesting. Similarly, when a Marxist and a bourgeois economist turn to the question of long-run economic development under capitalism, their disagreements are not traceable to matters of fact and logic but to specific sociological assumptions that each regards as appropriate to a meaningful analysis of the problem.

Let us take a typical example: the theory of profit. The orthodox economist starts with certain data, such as the preference scales of households, production functions, factor endowments, forms and distributions of property, all of which he regards as outside the scope of economic theory. On the basis of such data he develops a theory of factor prices according to which a hiring agent, the entrepreneur, purchases the services of hired agents, workers and capital owners. In a stationary economy, this gives rise to equilibrium wage and interest rates. In a growing economy, it may leave a residual as profits to the entrepreneur. Imperfect competition in product markets or monopsony in the labour market may enhance this residual and distort factor prices. Changes in the data themselves must now be introduced to analyze the effects of advertising, technical change, saving propensities and population growth. Finally, to explain the wages, interest and profits that are actually received by flesh-and-blood workers and capitalists, one must take into account inheritance laws, the tax structure, monetary institutions and so forth. The process, therefore, of moving from functional to personal income distribution takes the form of progressively relaxing more and more of the data given at the outset of the analysis.

Marxists, on the other hand, introduce the distinction between the haves and the have-nots at the outset of the argument, operating straightway with personal income aggregated by social class. It is illegitimate, they argue, to regard the distribution of property as a datum, for it is not given independently of the determination of wages and profits. It is only by specifying the property relations that distinguish a capitalist economy from an ordinary exchange economy, and making this distinction the cornerstone of the analysis, that we can explain the historical performance of the capitalist system, the utter dependence of profits upon continuous technical progress, the relentless pressure to increase capital equipment per worker, the evident tendency toward concentration of production, the economic function of unemployment, and the general role of business cycles in governing the form which long-run development takes. But Marxian economics pays a price for this sort of hardheaded realism. Oscar Lange made this point very strikingly:

> Let us imagine two persons: one who has learned his economics only from the Austrian School, Pareto and Marshall, without ever having seen or even heard a sentence of Marx or his disciples; the other one who, on the contrary, knows his economics exclusively from Marx and the Marxists and does not even suspect that there may have been economists outside the Marxist School. Which of the two will be able to account better for the fundamental tendencies of the evolution to Capitalism? To put the question is to answer it.
>
> But this superiority of Marxian economics is only a partial one. There are some problems before which Marxian economics is quite powerless, while 'bourgeois' economics solves them easily. What can Marxian economics say about monopoly prices? What has it to say on the fundamental problems of monetary and credit theory? What apparatus has it to offer for analysing the incidence of a tax, or the effect of a certain technical innovation on wages? And (irony of Fate!) what can Marxian economics contribute to the problem of the optimum distribution of productive resources in a socialist economy?
>
> Clearly the relative merits of Marxian economics and of modern 'bourgeois' economic theory belong to different 'ranges'. Marxian economics can work the economic evolution of capitalist society in to a consistent theory from which its necessity is deduced, while 'bourgeois' economists get no further than mere historical description. On the other hand, 'bourgeois' economics is able to grasp the phenomena of the every-day life of a capitalist economy in a manner that is far superior to anything the Marxists can produce. Further, the anticipations which can be deduced from the two types of economic theory refer to a different range of time. If people want to anticipate the development of capitalism over a long period a knowledge of Marx is a much more effective starting point than a knowledge of Wieser, Böhm-Bawerk, Pareto or even Marshall (though the last-named is in this respect much superior). But Marxian economics would be a poor basis for running a central bank or anticipating the effects of a change in the rate of discount ['Marxian Economics and Modern Economics', *REStud*, June, 1935, pp. 191–2].

The formal principles of the theory of economic equilibrium are the same for any exchange economy, and the economic problems of a capitalist system have characteristics shared by a socialist economy. In refusing to abstract at any point from the institutional framework in which the economic process is embedded in a capitalist society, Marxists have cut themselves off from the task of clarifying the pure logic of economic relationships. Their strength has lain in providing a systematic account of the evolutionary process of capitalism. In recent years their monopoly has been challenged. Orthodox economics has come to devote more attention to explaining the hitherto successful performance of the capitalist system, so as to discover what light past trends may shed on future prospects. For the first time there is the real possibility that the cold war between the two schools of thought may be drawing to a close.

READER'S GUIDE TO 'CAPITAL'

To read *Capital* is a major undertaking. It is a badly arranged work, excessively repetitious, and replete with special terminology. Every page bears testimony to the author's obsession with analytical riddles and Hegelian 'contradictions'. When the reader is not driven to despair by the lengths to which a chain of arguments is pursued, he is irritated by the author's condescending tone toward his adversaries or put off by the fervor with which even the most abstract propositions are expounded. Nevertheless, *Capital* should hold no terrors for anyone who has managed to get through Ricardo's *Principles*. The method of reasoning is the same and the entire analysis is steeped in Ricardian assumptions. Moreover, Marx's style, at least in the first volume that he completed and finished for the press, is a great deal more animated than Ricardo's. There is the difficulty of Marx's Hegelian jargon, but too much has been made of that. One soon grows used to it and it is no more than window dressing: Marx himself speaks of 'coquetting' with 'the modes of expression' peculiar to Hegel. Furthermore, the flow of argument is relieved, as it never is in Ricardo, by the frequent incursion of historical material. The reader might indeed follow Marx's own advice to a friend and begin, not with the difficult first chapter of Volume I, but with the historical chapters 10, 13–15, and 25–33.

23. Value

Volume I, chapter 1, begins with the distinction between use value and exchange value and immediately lays down the unqualified proposition that goods exchange at ratios that are reciprocals of the ratios of labour required to produce them. Marx approaches the question in an Aristotelian fashion by asking: what have commodities in common by virtue of which they can be equated to one another for purposes of exchange? This common element must be quantifiable and, at the same time, it cannot itself have exchange value, for then it would explain nothing; it must be, as Marx says, something 'contained in ... yet distinguishable from' the exchange value of commodities and representing 'a greater or less quantity'. A modern reader might be tempted to infer that the common property is the marginal utility of goods. But this entails the concept of measurable utility. For Marx, 'the exchange of commodities is evidently an act characterized by a total abstraction from use-value', and in his sense of the term 'use-value', namely, total utility, it undoubtedly is. Like Ricardo, he assumes as a matter of course that a product's 'worth' to an individual bears no relationship to the price that the individual is willing to pay and that, furthermore, 'worth' cannot be quantified.

24. Socially Necessary Labour

Nowhere in the first chapter does Marx state the necessary conditions under which competitive rates of exchange tend to reflect the labour embodied in the production of commodities: equal capital-labour ratios in all industries and constant costs of production. The absence of any qualifications in the initial statement of the labour theory of value in this chapter is precisely what puzzles the reader. The assumption of constant costs, however, is already tucked inside the concept of 'socially necessary labour', which Marx introduces immediately after his 'proof' of the labour theory of value. Value is determined by the man hours required to produce commodities; the intensity of effort, however, is not constant per unit of time, either for one individual or between individuals. Shall we choose the labour effort of the best man or the worst man, the first or the last hour in the day, as our common unit of labour time? Marx selects the 'labour-time socially necessary', that is, 'with the average degree of skill and intensity prevalent at the time'. He takes it for granted, however, that each employer attempts to use labour at its maximum intensity. In marginal terms, this amounts to taking the least intensive man-hours as the common unit of labour time. The only condition under which the least intensity is equal to the average intensity of labour is that of constant costs: each plant is operated at optimum capacity where average and marginal costs are equal, and the average costs of all plants within an industry are identical. It follows that the long-run supply curve of the industry is horizontal and that demand, and hence utility, has no influence on price.

Apart from differences in the intensity of effort, there is the quite different problem of labour of different skills. In **section 2** of **chapter 1** Marx decides to treat unskilled common labour as the fundamental value-creating unit, regarding skilled labour as a simple multiple of unskilled labour. Later, in chapter 7, he defends this procedure by the argument that the 'production' of skilled labour involves the expenditure of labour time in the form of training; skilled labour is more valuable than unskilled labour because these 'commodities' also exchange for one another according to the man hours required to produce them. This ignores the fact that training takes time and that the outlay on training must earn interest for the training period. The difference between the wages of skilled and unskilled workers is a function of the man hours required to produce the two types of labour *and* of the time for which they are produced; in other words, the problem of what determines the rate of profit rears its ugly head even in respect of wages. Furthermore, there are other reasons for differences in wages than differences in training costs. Some skills, for example, are entirely or largely due to natural abilities. In the whole of *Capital* there is only one reference to Smith's equalization of 'net advantages' in the labour market [see chapter 2, section 8]. In Volume III, chapter 8, Marx points out that 'the surplus labour of the goldsmith produces correspondingly more surplus-value than that of the day-labourer'. The study of such 'frictions', Marx goes on to say, 'may be dispensed with as being accidental and unessential in a general analysis of capitalist production'. It is easy to see why Marx ignored Smith's argument, for it implies that workers are not indifferent to the nature of their work and that the exercise of choice among occupations has something to do with the determination of the average wage rate. Moreover, it would mean that the standard unit of labour is a unit of disutility, not an objective 'expenditure of human brains, nerves and muscles'.

However, the assumptions of homogeneous labour and a given wage structure – for this is all that Marx's argument amounts to – are perfectly legitimate as first approximations in the explanation of relative prices. The proper criticism of Marx is not that he made these assumptions, but that he never relaxed them anywhere to ask how relative wages themselves are determined. Marx simply posits a situation in which the conditions of equilibrium have been reached, without explaining how they are reached, how the amount of labour 'socially necessary' is determined.

25. Commodity Fetishism

The reader will miss little by skipping the pedantic third section of chapter 1 on which the hands of Hegel lie all too heavily. **Chapter 1, section 4**, on 'the fetishism of commodities', however, is crucial to an understanding of the Marxist attitude to 'bourgeois' economics. Commodity 'fetishism' refers to the tendency to reify commodities, to treat what are in fact social relations between men as if they were relations between things. In a footnote Marx attacks 'vulgar economy', as distinguished from 'classical Political Economy'. Instead of penetrating below the surface to 'real' or 'ultimate' determinants, as did Adam Smith and Ricardo, the 'vulgar economist' operates with the superficial concepts of demand and supply, with the subjective attitudes of economic agents toward money costs. In the minds of individuals, the mental connections between goods acquire the quality of independent forces that dominate market reactions. Yet actually they are nothing but the product of the independent actions of all individuals in a market that hold sway despite the deliberate intent of each economic agent.

If this is what Marx meant by his doctrine of 'commodity fetishism', it would seem to indict modern economics even more than the theories of such 'vulgar economists' as Malthus, Senior and Mill. And yet the indictment, while ostensibly profound, rests on a simple confusion between price-determined behaviour as seen by individuals and behavior-determined prices as they appear in the market. Price theory begins with entrepreneurs and households facing given prices and adjusting the quantity supplied and demanded in accordance with their own 'maximand'. The summation of the resulting individual supply and demand schedules constitutes the market schedules that determine prices. Individuals do in fact act in terms of their own mental beliefs and fetishes but prices are nevertheless determined by the objective outcome of individual actions. If the agents in the process were aware of the consequencs of their actions, economics would be a branch of psychoanalysis. The whole point of the theory of perfect competition is to analyze the wholly objective outcome of purely subjective actions and reactions. There is nothing 'superficial' about lifting the veil of objective determination to penetrate to the 'ultimate' subjective motivations and beliefs from which the whole process stems. In comparison with orthodox economics, it is Marxian economics that seem prone to the sin of 'vulgarity'. No doubt, Marx's retort would be that class relationships do not appear in orthodox economics and that these constitute the 'real' elements of an economic situation. But that is a different charge: whether we group economic agents together as entrepreneurs and households, or as workers, capitalists and landlords has nothing to do with the phenomenon of 'commodity fetishism'. The reader should now turn to the Preface to the second German edition of Volume I in which Marx explains why 'scientific' bourgeois economics came to an end in 1830: 'Political Economy can remain a science only so long as the class-struggle is latent or manifests itself only in isolated and sporadic phenomena'. In point of fact, however, the decade of the 1830s is the high point of classical economics in terms of vigor of debate and appearance of new ideas: among the outstanding works of this decade are Lloyd's *Lecture on the Notion of Value* (1833) and Longfield's *Lectures* (1834) – neither of which is cited by Marx – as well as Scrope's *Principles* (1833), Jones' *Essay on the Distribution of Wealth* (1831) and Senior's *Outline* (1836).

26. Theory of Money

Volume I, chapters 2 and **3**, contain Marx's theory of money, a subject that he dealt with at greater length in *Critique of Political Economy* (1859). There is nothing in these chapters not found in Ricardo or Mill. The Equation of Exchange is very clearly stated in verbal terms but the quantity *theory* of money is rejected on the grounds that V and T are variables (**chapter 3, section 2b**). The store-of-value function of money is discussed under the heading of 'hoarding' (**chapter 3, section 3a**). Say's identity is repudiated (**chapter 3, section 2a**) and Marx gives a vivid description of the liquidity panic that marks the onset of a depression (**chapter 3, section 3b**). A footnote in **chapter 3, section 2c,** contains one of Marx's many derogatory comments on J. S. Mill.

27. Surplus Value

Part II, chapters 4 and **5**, set the stage for the solution of the riddle of surplus value. The exchange of goods begins with a sale of a commodity (C) for money (M) and ends with a purchase of a commodity (C) with money (M), that is, ($C - M - C$), but the process of production begins with a purchase and ends with a sale, ($M - C - M$). How is it that a surplus value is produced in the act of turning money capital into commodities and commodities back again into money? It cannot be because goods are bought below their value and sold above their value, for in that case the sum of all individual gains would be zero. Surplus value has to be explained in terms of 'an exchange of equivalents', everything being bought and sold at its value. Having posed the problem, Marx proceeds to the answer in **chapter 6** and **7** – there is real art of presentation in these chapters. Labour itself cannot be bought and sold in a nonslave economy. What is in fact bought is the services of labour or labour power, 'a commodity, whose use-value possesses the peculiar property of being a source of value'. The rental value of these services, 'as in the case of every other commodity', is determined by the labour required to produce it, that is, the labour required to produce the means of subsistence that will sustain the supply of labour services. Since labour is *physically* productive, it follows, Marx suggests, that the value of labour's output will exceed the value of labour's services. Hence, the existence of surplus value is compatible with 'the exchange of equivalents'. In other words capitalists will hire labour power but obtain something more than that, namely, the product of labour itself.

Marx was very proud of the distinction between labour and labour power, which he thought cleared up Smith's confusion between embodied and commanded labour [see chapter 2, section 3]. But what he had really discovered was the Walrasian distinction between the service flow of labour and the stock of labour resources, and it is perfectly true that this distinction is peculiar to a nonslave economy. Whether it proves anything about the nature of profits as surplus value is of course another question.

Moreover, if workers really sell their labour power and not their labour, the favourite phrase 'unpaid labour' is subtly misleading, assuming as fact something that is supposed to be proved: there may be unpaid labour but there is no unpaid labour power. Marx notes that 'a historical and moral element' enters into the determination of the value of labour power, something that is not true of other commodities (**chapter 6**). But he fails to point out that competition provides no mechanism to reduce the 'market price' of labour power to its 'natural price'. The labour theory of value as such does not guarantee that labour power will sell at its (labour) value.

Volume I, chapter 8, defines constant and variable capital; **chapter 9** defines the rate of surplus value. Notice the footnote at the close of chapter 9, section 1, as well as the last footnote to chapter 5, both of which point out that prices are assumed to be equal to values: 'we shall, however, see, in Book III, that even in the case of average prices the assumption cannot be made in this very simple manner'. This, apart from any other evidence, shows clearly that Marx was aware from the outset of the so-called 'great contradiction' [see below].

Volume I, chapter 9, section 3, contains Marx's famous attack on Senior's last-hour theory, a superb example of Marx's polemical powers. But for Marx's criticism, Senior's pamphlet would long ago have passed into oblivion. It met with the unanimous condemnation of all Senior's fellow economists: they objected to the unrealistic numerical example upon which his conclusions were grounded. Ironically enough, Senior's calculations do not in fact show that all net profits are produced in the 'last hour': on his own assumptions, he merely showed that a shortening of the work day by one hour, given constant output per man hour, will reduce the rate of profit from 10 to 8 percent. Marx discusses Senior's figures but fails to make this point.

28. The Factory Acts

The long tenth chapter, entirely historical in character, contains Marx's indictment of contemporary factory conditions and tells the story of the political struggle to regulate hours and to eliminate the employment of children. The purpose of this chapter is to suggest that capitalists resist the passage of Factory Acts because they strive to maximize the rate and amount of surplus value. It is only in **Volume I, chapter 11**, that Marx admits that individual capitalists do not care a fig about surplus value *per se*: if their object was to maximize the rate of surplus value, it would be hard to explain why they ever substitute capital for labour. The fact is that they want to maximize *r* and lengthening the working day does not necessarily raise *r*. Although it always pays, *ceteris paribus*, to work machines as intensively as possible, extra hours do involve extra overhead costs and may involve a reduction in output per man hour. The resistance of capitalists to hours legislation is not due to a 'were-wolf's hunger for surplus-labour'. It is the result of the divergence between private and social costs and the failure of atomistic competition to put a price on the social cost of overutilizing labour. As Marx himself points out: *'Après moi le déluge!* is the watchword of every capitalist . . . . Hence Capital is reckless of the health or length of life of the labourer, unless under compulsion from society'; and again, 'the English Factory Acts ... curb the passion of capital for a limitless draining of labour-power by forcibly limiting the working-day by state regulations, made by a state that is ruled by capitalists and landlords. Apart from the working-class movement that daily grew more threatening, the limiting of factory labour was dictated by the same necessity which spread guano over the English fields'. This is a striking observation for it is not always realized that there is nothing in the Marxist theory of the state – the state is simply the executive committee of the ruling class – that precludes social legislation in the public interest.

29. Marx's Use of Historical Material

Although Marx was much more aware of methodological issues than, say, Ricardo, he made no serious effort in his writings to verify his conclusions or to check his predictions against the available body of data. This may seem a strange statement in view of the wealth of empirical material in *Capital*. But the statistical and historical data in *Capital* is used, not to test the conclusions of theory, but to build up a graphic picture of capitalist society. Marx is never ashamed to admit that the data is selective; it is meant to illustrate a thesis, not to establish it. By virtue of its style of presentation, however, it has a powerful effect upon the reader. The suggestion is that the conditions depicted are a necessary product of capitalism, generated by the peculiar nature of that system, and that similar conditions will be found wherever such a system is in force. But chapter 10 on 'The Working Day' demonstrates the need to ask in every case what conclusions can be legitimately drawn from the material presented. For example, it would be absurd to believe that the conditions described in the historical chapters reflect 'exploitation' of labour rather than the low output per head of the working population in the early years of the 19th century. The living standards of the British working class during the Industrial Revolution could not have been raised significantly even by a perfectly egalitarian distribution of income. A glance at modern national income statistics shows that if we now confiscated all rents and profits, dividends and interest payments in countries like Great Britain and the United States and handed them over to the working class, wages and salaries would rise by about 20–25 percent, assuming that output would be unaffected by such a redistribution. If we accept the Marxist tenet that the rich have been getting richer and the poor poorer, the argument applies with double force to the 19th century. In the final analysis, the deplorable material standards of most working people in the heyday of the Industrial Revolution had more to do with the birth pangs of industrialization than with capitalist methods of organizing production. Similarly, 'alienation' of workers under capitalism, namely, a sense of isolation, self-estrangement and powerlessness, has surely more to do with the hierarchical organization of the division of labour in factories than with the private ownership of the means of production? Marx is a past master of the fallacy of misplaced concreteness: all the ills of industrialization and urbanization are blamed on capitalism and the question whether socialism would really avoid these ills is brushed aside as Utopian futorology.

30. Division of Labour and Machinery

Volume I, chapter 12, distinguishes between 'absolute surplus value' obtained by lengthening the working day and 'relative surplus value' obtained by increasing the productivity of labour, which in turns cheapens wage goods. There follows what is in effect a digression from the main theme: **chapters 13** and **14** deal with the advantages of the division of labour. Marx's treatment is much more erudite than Smith's but, on the whole, it adds detail rather than new insights. **Chapter 13** provides a striking illustration of Marx's tendency to hypostatize the rate of surplus value. 'The directing motive, the end and aim of capitalist production', he remarks, 'is to extract the greatest possible amount of surplus-value'. However, on Marx's own showing, the motive of the capitalist is to maximize, not the sum of profits, or the total amount of surplus value, or even the rate of surplus value, but rather the rate of profit on total capital invested. **Chapter 13** also contains one of Marx's rare remarks on the nature of entrepreneurship.

Volume I, chapter 15, the longest in the book, is again largely historical in character, treating of the effects of machinery on working conditions, on the composition of the labour force, and on the total volume of employment. **Section 6**, on the theory of 'compensation', however, is of theoretical interest. Marx alleges that Mill, McCulloch, Senior and Torrens held the view that all technically displaced labour must necessarily be reabsorbed in the making of laboursaving machines. This is a travesty of the classical theory of technological unemployment. Nowhere does Marx mention the effect of lower prices upon the demand for goods, a consideration that is an essential element in the classical theory [see chapter 6, section 6]. The last footnote in chapter 15 deals with Mill's statement of the law of diminishing returns and affords a representative example of Marx's style of criticism. In chapter 24, however, Marx concedes that Mill should not be classed with 'the herd of vulgar economic apologists'.

31. Surplus Value and Labour Productivity

Volume I, Part V, is devoted to the effect of changes in absolute and relative surplus value. The opening pages of **chapter 16** define 'productive labour' as labour that produces surplus value; this question is dealt with at greater length in Volume II of *Capital* and in the so-called fourth volume of *Capital*, entitled *Theories of Surplus Value*. The last few pages of the chapter ridicule Mill's theory of profit; while Mill's language is hardly felicitous, his views are not as absurd as Marx makes out. **Chapter 17** considers the combined effect of a change in hours and a change in the productivity of labour. Notice the proposition that 'a working-day of given length always creates the same amount of value, no matter how the productiveness of labour, and, with it, the mass of the product, and the price of each single commodity produced, may vary'. Value per unit of output falls as productivity rises, but the total value of output remains unchanged. This would be true if we could assume that the ratio of capital to labour is equal in all industries for then a given rise in the productivity of labour entails an equal rise in the productivity of capital.

Chapter 19 plays fast and loose with the distinction between labour and labour power. 'Labour is the substance, and the immanent measure of value, but *has itself no value*', meaning that the worker as such has no value; it is only his services that are valuable. Ricardo expressed the same thing by saying that the price of labour depends on the quantity of labour required to produce wage goods. This chapter also contains one of Marx's characteristic assertions about the law of demand and supply: 'If demand and supply balance, ... then demand and supply cease to explain anything. The price of labour, at the moment when demand and supply are in equilibrium, is its natural price, determined independently of the relation of demand and supply' (see also Volume III, chapter 10). This marks a retrogression from Ricardo who at least adhered to the implicit notion of market schedules; given Mill's exposition in his *Principles* [see chapter 6, section 12], Marx's misunderstanding is really unpardonable. It is difficult to say, however, how much it led him astray: he operated throughout with the case of constant costs, completely ignored short-run pricing, and seemed totally unaware of the restricted scope of his theory. **Chapter 20** is uninteresting, but **chapter 21**, on 'Piece-Wages', is worthy of mention. **Chapter 22** provides a superficial and very much watered-down version of Senior's doctrine of international wage levels [see chapter 4, section 22].

32. The Accumulation of Capital

After the rather slack fifth and sixth parts of Volume I, the argument moves into higher gear in Part VII. **Chapter 23** takes up the stationary state, 'simple reproduction' Marx calls it. Notice that surplus value is said to be positive even under stationary conditions. **Chapter 24** is full of interesting material, criticizing in turn the saving-is-spending theorem (**section 2**), the abstinence theory of interest (**section 3**), and the wages fund doctrine (**section 5**). Marx's criticism of the abstinence theory falls below all acceptable standards: the notion of time preference, without which the theory is meaningless, is not even mentioned. Saving for the purpose of productive investment, Marx explains, is virtually automatic under capitalism, the result of the competitive race to take advantage of the latest improvements in technique: 'Accumulate, accumulate! That is Moses and the prophets!' Oddly enough, he does admit what he calls 'a Faustian conflict between the passion for accumulation, and the desire for enjoyment', that is, the concept of abstinence in disguise [see chapter 6, section 11].

The only point that Marx makes against the wages fund doctrine, which he attributes for no apparent reason to Bentham, is that the wages fund is not fixed or predetermined at the beginning of a production period. The classical doctrine that 'what is saved is spent' or 'consumed by productive labourers' is denied on the grounds that savings are invested in constant as well as variable capital.

Volume I, chapter 25, introduces the concept of organic composition of capital, distinguishing between the ratio of capital to labour in physical and in value terms. This chapter lays down Marx's conception of the determination of real wages (**section 1**). He takes pains to point out that both money wages and real wages can rise and rise indefinitely as long as it does not 'threaten the system itself'. Marx's hesitation about the nature of the investment function comes out clearly when he supposes at one point that a rise in wages results in a slackening of accumulation 'because the stimulus to gain is blunted'. This implies that investment is a function of the going rate of profit but immediately thereafter he goes on to advance the more typical view that there is no problem about the inducement to invest: 'The rate of accumulation is the independent, not the dependent variable; the rate of wages, the dependent, not the independent, variable'. This is followed once again by the notion that wages rise in the boom, choking off investment, whereupon wages fall again: 'the rise of wages is therefore confined within limits that not only leave intact the foundations of the capitalist system, but also secure its reproduction on a progressive scale'. A curious footnote in this section remarks on the monopoly of the theory of population by 'Reverends of Protestant Theology'. Malthus perhaps?

33. Absolute and Relative Impoverishment

Section 2 of **chapter 25** discusses the increasing organic composition of capital as a fundamental law of capitalist development. Accompanying this process is the 'concentration and centralization' of capital, that is, the growth in the size of firms and the reduction in the number of firms in an industry – notice that his 'centralization' of capital is what we nowadays call 'concentration' of industry. **Section 3** of **chapter 25** is devoted to the concept of the 'industrial reserve army'. Marx cites Malthus on the slow adjustment of population to changes in wages and on this ground rejects the classical wages-population mechanism. In several places Marx suggests that the absolute amount of unemployment grows in the course of capital accumulation. The greater the industrial reserve army, the greater is 'official pauperism'; 'this is the absolute general law of capitalist accumulation'. Marx adds cautiously: 'Like all other laws it is modified in its working by many circumstances, the analysis of which does not concern us here'. He proceeds, two paragraphs later, to enumerate the action of the law in bringing about 'misery, agony of toil, slavery, ignorance, brutality, mental degradation'. It is evident that the so-called doctrine of 'absolute impoverishment' – a phrase that Marx does not use – does not mean, or even necessarily entail, a fall in real wages. Marx did believe, however, that labour's share would fall – he remarks casually in chapter 24, section 4, that 'real wages ... never rise proportionally to the productive power of labour'. **Chapter 25, section 5**, is designed to supply illustrative material of 'the absolute general law', but, shocking as are the conditions Marx reveals, the working of the law is not really clarified by the selective evidence he presents (see also Volume II, chapters 4 and 5).

34. Primitive Accumulation

Instead of capitalism growing naturally out of feudalism by the gradual emergence of a 'spirit of rational calculation', it comes into the world 'dripping from head to foot, from every pore, with blood and dirt'. By means of the slave trade, piracy and colonial plunder, wealth is concentrated in the hands of the few, while forcible enclosures of arable land create a propertyless proletariat. The whole of **Part VIII** of **Volume I** (see also Volume III, chapters 20, 36, and 47) is given over to a description of this historical process of 'primitive accumulation' in the 14th and 15th centuries: 'the capitalistic era dates from the 16th century'. It is doubtful whether Marx's account of the slave trade and colonial booty bears the weight he puts upon it. Moreover, his treatment of the role of enclosures indiscriminately identifies enclosures of arable land with the enclosures of wasteland – by the 18th century, however, most enclosures served to raise the total acreage under cultivation. **Volume I, chapter 32**, contains the most frequently quoted passage in *Capital* on the eventual 'expropriation of the expropriators'.

35. The Costs of Distribution

One of the problems left over for solution from Volume I is the question whether the distribution, as distinct from the production, of commodities creates surplus value. This problem is discussed in **Volume II, Part I,** and again in **Volume III, chapters 16–19**. The reader should pass over Volume II, chapters 1–5, which are immensely tedious and add little to an understanding of Marx's system; it is **chapter 6** in **Volume II** and the four chapters in Volume III that are relevant for our purpose.

On the face of it, the 'circulation' as well as the production of commodities enhances their value, since there is a visible difference between 'the purchase price' paid by the wholesaler and the realized 'sale price' to consumers. Nevertheless, Marx contends, the labour expended in distributing commodities does not add value to the product: clerks, typists, bookkeepers, and salesmen are 'unproductive' workers. Commercial capital merely appropriates part of the surplus value produced in the industrial sphere: the middleman buys commodities below their labour value and sells them at their value, and the difference constitutes his gross profit margin. It does not matter whether distribution is actually handled by independent middlemen; an office staff and a sales force attached to the factory are just as 'unproductive' as the workers employed by wholesalers and retailers. However, the transportation, shipping, warehousing and packing of goods are part of the productive process and, hence, do create value. But true selling costs in the

Marxian sense, that is, office and clerical overheads, promotional expenses and the financing of goods in transit are all 'dead expenses' (Volume II, chapter 6, sections 2 and 3).

Like Smith, Marx disavows any connection between 'productive' labour and 'useful' labour. There is no questioning the usefulness of the unproductive function of merchandizing in a highly specialized economy where buyers and sellers must be brought together. Also any reduction in the 'time of circulation' raises the average rate of profit in the economy (Volume III, chapter 16). Marx clearly adopts the 'value version' of Smith's doctrine of productive labour [see chapter 2, section 14] but the concept plays a role in *Capital* different from that in the *Wealth of Nations*. The proposition that the rate of capital accumulation is a function of the ratio of productive to unproductive labour, which is in the foreground in Smith's treatment, hardly appears in *Capital*. In Marx the problem is a purely formal one: is the 'value' of a commodity proportional to all the labour expended on its production and distribution, in which case the denominator of σ refers to the total wage bill in the economy, or is it merely a function of the labour expended in manufacturing and transportation, so that a portion of the total capital of a society 'must be set aside for secondary operations, which are no part of the process of creating value' (Volume III, chapter 17)? Marx's distinction between productive and unproductive labour, therefore, stands or falls with the labour theory of value and has no interest apart from it. Hence, we need not trouble ourselves with Marx's occasional inconsistencies when he speaks of wage workers in service industries as productive workers, merely because they are hired to create marketable services (Volume I, chapter 16, Volume III, chapter 17). If this line of thought were pursued, only the government sector would prove to be unproductive. After all, if the rate of profit in an economy can be raised just as much by technical improvements in marketing and distribution as by technical improvements in agriculture and manufacturing, as Marx himself admits, most of us would conclude that there is no sense in which a salesman or a typist can be said to be 'unproductive'.

The import of Marx's doctrine of productive labour is that the rate of profit is not actually equal to s/K, but rather to $\bar{s}/K$, where $\bar{s}$ stands for disposable surplus value after meeting administrative overhead, sales and advertising expenses, rents and indirect business taxes. Likewise, $\sigma \neq s/v$, but $\sigma \equiv \bar{s}/\bar{v}$, where $\bar{v}$ excludes what we may roughly call salaried personnel. The national income of the economy is now equal to $(\bar{v} + \bar{s})$, the wage bill of productive workers plus the disposable surplus value generated by them. The Soviet system of national accounts attempts in fact to measure national income in accordance with this Marxian notion.

36. The Turnover of Capital

In **Volume II, chapter 8,** Marx defends his distinction between constant and variable capital against the orthodox distinction between fixed and circulating capital, the former transferring only part of its value to the product during each turnover, while the latter has to be renewed after each turnover. The only difference between the two distinctions lies in the treatment of raw materials. **Chapter 8, section 2,** provides an excellent 'bourgeois' account of the subject of capital depreciation, separating user's cost from depreciation proper. To this is added the problem of obsolescence (**chapter 9**). Marx explains in chapter 9 how to calculate the average period of turnover of all capital when its various components turn over at different rates. Adam Smith's and Ricardo's theories of capital are criticized in **chapters 10** and **11**. **Volume II, chapter 12,** considers differences in the turnover rate or durability of capital invested in different industries, irrespective of the organic composition of capital in these industries. What Marx calls 'the working period' is what Böhm-Bawerk later called 'the period of fabrication' of goods. Marx goes on in the next chapter to treat 'the time of production' with reference to such goods as wine and timber, which require ageing or finishing after their manufacture; **chapter 14** introduces the further consideration of 'the time of selling', the time interval between the completion of the product and the receipt of sales proceeds. These three chapters (12–14) are remarkable for their clarity and adroit use of historical examples.

The *facts* of the time-consuming character of the productive process have never been better described, not even by Böhm-Bawerk. But what is striking about the treatment is Marx's failure to relate the fact of differences in the durability of capital in different industries to the problem of price determination, getting sidetracked instead by the spurious problem of the periodic 'release' of money capital – Engels' refreshing postscript to chapter 15, section 4, is warning enough to pass over Marx's calculations in the preceding sections. **Volume II, chapter 16,** shows Marx's awareness of the necessity to redefine all the ratios in Volume I to take account of differences in the turnover rate of capital: 'the annual rate of surplus-value coincides only in one single case with the current rate of surplus-value ... in the case that the advanced capital is turned over only once a year' (section 1). Chapter 16, sections 2 and 3, contain nothing of interest. **Chapter 17** turns to the questions raised at length in Part III of Volume II: the realization of surplus value under conditions of simple and of expanded reproduction.

37. The Reproduction Schema

After some initial procrastination in Volume II, chapters 18 and 19, Marx gets down to the task in **chapter 20**. No part of *Capital* is as difficult to follow as this chapter. The essence of the matter is stated in sections 2 and 3, but the remaining sections are full of interesting hints. Unfortunately, **chapter 21** on expanded reproduction is even less finished than chapter 20 on simple reproduction. Marx's refutation of the vulgar underconsumptionist theory of crisis occurs in chapter 20, section 4, but an earlier footnote in chapter 16, section 3, nevertheless gives credence to some versions of underconsumption.

38. The Great Contradiction Again

If surplus value is proportional to variable capital employed, why is it that the more mechanized processes earn the same rate of profit on total capital invested as do the less mechanized ones? Profits per cent of capital tend toward equality regardless of the technique in which capital is invested. This implies that surplus value is not a function of v alone, in which case commodities apparently do not exchange according to the total labour embodied in their production. This is the so-called 'Great Contradiction', whose resolution Marx had promised for Volume III. His occasional remarks in Volume I show that he had worked out the solution before 1867. We have Engels' word that the draft of Volume III was in fact completed in 1865, two years before Volume I was published; in addition, we have a letter from Marx to Engels, written in 1862, outlining the solution. In Preface to Volume II (1885), Engels dared Marx's critics to show how 'an equal average rate of profit can and must come about, not only without a violation of the law of value, but by means of it'. In the decade that intervened between the publication of Volumes II and III (1885 to 1894), this 'prize essay competition' drew several contributions from leading German economists, vying with one another to solve the puzzle posed by Marx. According to Engels, who reviewed some of the essays in the Preface to Volume III, no one succeeded in carrying off the prize. But Engels' protests notwithstanding, it is evident that Schmidt and Fireman each gave a possible solution and that Lexis solved the problem in the same way as Marx did. This is hardly surprising: anyone who knew his Ricardo should have had no trouble in resolving the Marxian dilemma.

Midway through the Preface, Engels refers parenthetically to 'Jevons' and Menger's theory of use-value and marginal profits' on which George Bernard Shaw is erecting 'the Fabian church of the future'. The *Fabian Essays*, in which Sidney Webb and G. B. Shaw fused Ricardo's theory of rent as reworked by Henry George and the Jevons-Wicksteed theory of utility into a new brand of English socialist theory, had appeared in 1888. This remark of Engels is the only public notice that either Marx or Engels ever took of the new departure in economic thought, despite the fact that Marx died nine years after the publication of Jevons' *Political Economy* (1874). By the time Engels edited Volume II of *Capital*, Böhm-Bawerk's attack on Marx in *Capital and Interest* (1884) was already attracting attention on the Continent. Volume III of *Capital* was published in 1894, five years after Böhm-Bawerk's *Positive Theory of Capital* (1889) and Wieser's *Natural Value* (1889) with their frequent attacks on the labour theory of value, and four years after Marshall's *Principles* (1890). But Engels had long before lost interest in economic theory and made no mention of the new currents of thought.

39. The Transformation Problem

Chapters 1–3 of **Volume III** marks the transition from the labour theory of value to the theory of 'prices of production'. The unqualified term 'price of production' always refers to the 'purchase price' at which the middleman buys the good. **Chapters 4–6** digress from this theme and should be read in conjunction with chapters 13–15, which discuss the law of the declining rate of profit. **Chapters 8–12** show how values can be transformed into prices without violating the labour theory of value applied to output as a whole. Throughout the early chapters of the third volume, Marx displays a lively sense of the paradoxical character of the theory of surplus value. 'It is immaterial for the capitalist', he notes in chapter 2, 'whether he is supposed to advance constant capital in order to make a profit out of his variable capital, or whether he advances variable capital in order to make a profit out of the constant capital.... Although it is only the variable portion of capital which creates surplus-value, it does so only on condition that the other portions, the material requirements of production, are likewise advanced'. And again, in the last pages of chapter 9, he declares that 'in its disguise of profit, the surplus-value had actually concealed its origin, lost its character, and become unrecognizable'; 'the capitalist had a practical interest only in the rate of profit'; 'by the transformation of value into prices of production, the basis of the determination of value is itself removed from direct observation'; and so on. Marx is proud of the paradox. The bourgeois economist is a 'vulgar' economist because he refuses 'to penetrate through the outward disguise into the internal essence and the inner form of the capitalist process of production', meaning he refused to see that equality of the rate of profit on total capital invested is really predicated upon a uniform rate of surplus on variable capital. The total surplus is determined by the size of the labour force and this surplus is then shared out among each capitalist in proportion to his share of the total capital stock of the community, 'a process which takes place behind his back, which he does not see, nor understand, and which indeed does not interest him at all'.

Marx steadily ignores the fact that he has not yet given any reason to believe that the rate of surplus value is in fact uniform between industries. There is a paragraph in Volume III, chapter 10, in which he admits that a uniform rate of surplus value 'has been assumed by us', presupposing 'a competition among the labourers and an equilibration by means of their continual emigration from one sphere of production to another'. He proceeds to make 'the essential point ... visible' by examining production in a noncapitalist society in which 'the labourers themselves are in possession of their respective means of production'. This is the only place in the 2,000 pages of *Capital* where Marx recognizes that the concept of a uniform rate of surplus per man requires defense. But the idea that the mobility of labour between industries establishes such a rate is a fallacy of the first order: mobility of labour produces a uniform rate of reward for labour, but no more equalizes the rate of surplus per man than it equalizes total output per man between industries; indeed, as we argued above, if it does not equalize total output per man between industries, even a uniform wage rate and an equal working day will not equalize the rate of surplus per man between industries.

In the short **chapter 7** Marx comments briefly on differences in managerial ability within an industry, suggesting that the going rate of profit is earned by the marginal firm, while firms with superior management earn what we now call 'rents of management'. The technical as distinct from the organic composition of capital, Marx declares, is governed by strictly technical conditions (**chapter 8** and opening sentence of **chapter 9**). Marx's assumption, therefore, is that of fixed coefficients of production. But, elsewhere, he speaks of laboursaving technical change induced by a rise of wages (Volume III, chapter 14, section 4). Thus, the ratios of capital to labour observed in different industries are, as a matter of fact, functions of relative factor prices.

The transformation of labour values into normal prices in **chapter 9** is carried out only in terms of output. Marx was aware of the necessity of transforming input as well as output values, but he apparently found the task beyond him: 'it is necessary ... to bear in mind that there is always the possibility of an error, if we assume that the cost price of commodities of any particular sphere is equal to the value of the means of production consumed by it. Our present analysis does not necessitate a closer examination of this point'. The transformation is carried out on the *assumption* that 'the sum of the profits of all spheres of production must be equal to the sum of surplus-values, and the sum of the prices of production of the total social product equal to the sum of its values' (**chapter 10**). Without this assumption, Marx contends, 'political economy would be without a rational basis'; we would be back with Adam Smith, for whom prices are determined by 'adding a more or less arbitrary amount of profit to the actual value of commodities' (**chapter 13**).

In **Volume III, chapter 10,** Marx suggests that 'it is quite appropriate ... to regard the value of commodities not only theoretically, but also historically, as existing prior to prices of production'. In societies in which 'the labourer owns his means of production' – 'and this is the condition of the landowning farmer and of the craftsman in the old world as well as the new' – 'prices are indeed governed solely by the 'law of value'. In a developed capitalist economy this is true only for 'capitals of average composition' (**chapter 9**).

The last half of chapter 10 is concerned with deviations of the actual price from long-run normal levels. 'Price of production' is what 'Adam Smith calls *natural price,* Ricardo *price of production,* or *cost of production*, and the Physiocrats, *prix nécessaire*, because it is in the long run a prerequisite of supply'. Nevertheless, Marx heaps ridicule on Malthus' suggestion that 'the great principle of demand and supply is called into action to determine what A. Smith calls natural price as well as market price' because 'if demand and supply balance, then they cease to have any effect'.

Volume III, chapters 11 and **12**, criticize Ricardo's dictum that 'profits vary inversely as wages' but come to the same conclusion as Ricardo: a rise in money wages leaves the price of goods produced with the average technique unaffected but changes other prices inversely to the degree of mechanization.

40. The Law of the Falling Rate of Profit

The whole of Volume III, Part III, chapters 13–15, as well as chapters 4–6 of Part I, are concerned with the 'mystery' of the falling rate of profit, 'whose solution has been the goal of the entire political economy since Adam Smith'. **Chapter 14** on the 'Counteracting Causes' is particularly interesting. Marx lists five offsetting forces to the falling profit rate, and, in four of the five cases, he emphasizes that 'the same causes which produce a falling tendency in the rate of profit, also call forth counter-effects'. This is a very peculiar use of the term 'tendency to fall'. We would be inclined to say that there is a tendency for the rate of profit to be constant when some forces act to reduce the rate while other forces act automatically to raise it, unless of course we have reasons to believe that one set of forces tends to predominate over the other. Marx thought he had created a presumption that the rate of profit would fall by stressing the case in which the rising organic composition of capital increases the rate of surplus value by raising the productivity of labour but not proportionately to the rise in q. However, he does admit, in Volume III, chapter 14, that σ tends to rise with q. In **chapter 15, section 2,** he gives the argument that σ will not rise as rapidly as q, an argument that he had already stated in Volume I, chapter 11: 'to the extent that the development of the productive power reduces the paid portion of the employed labour, it raises the surplus-value by raising its rate; but to the extent that it reduces the total mass of labour employed by a certain capital, it reduces the factor of numbers with which the rate of surplus-value is multiplied in order to calculate its mass. Two labourers, each working 12 hours daily, cannot produce the same mass of surplus-value as 24 labourers each working only 2 hours, even if they could live on air.... In this respect, then, the compensation of the reduction in the number of labourers by means of intensification of exploitation has certain impassable limits'. In the first case, total surplus value equals forty-eight man-hours; in the second case, it equals at best twenty-four man-hours. Hence, an increase in q cannot be compensated beyond a certain point by an increase in σ.

This argument is not only far fetched but it is also fallacious. First, the total size of the labour force does increase in the course of development despite the rise in q; as Marx points out toward the end of the chapter, 'it is but a requirement of the capitalist mode of production that the number of wage workers should increase absolutely'. Moreover, at constant real wages, σ rises at the same rate as the productivity of labour in the wage-goods industries. If the average product of labour can in principle rise to infinity, so can σ. A rising rate of σ applied to a rising quantity of v, owing to the growth of the labour force at constant real wages, is perfectly capable of offsetting an ever rising q.

It is worth noting that Marx never links the process of a rising q specifically to the rise in σ and certainly does not emphasize the functional relationship between them. In Volume I, chapter 12, Marx noted that relative surplus value is 'directly proportional' to the productivity of labour. But this point is not mentioned in Volume I, chapter 25, which introduces the concept of the organic composition of capital. In Volume III, chapter 2, Marx remarks that 'we shall see that alterations affecting the factors c, v, and s imply also changes in the productivity of labour', but although this chapter considers almost every possible combination of changes in the fundamental ratios r, σ, and q, the promise is never fulfilled. Again, in Volume III, chapter 14, the tendency of σ to rise is not related functionally in any way to the increase in q. This leaves only the passage in Volume III, chapter 15, which we have just considered. It is difficult to escape the conviction that Marx was deliberately misleading the reader in order to cover up a loose end in the argument. The Hegelian proposition that 'the same causes which produce a falling tendency ... also call forth countereffects' was heavensent to later Marxists: it allowed them to indulge in the game of finding counteracting tendencies to Marxist 'laws of motion', which prove these laws by – counteracting them!

41. Capitalsaving Innovations

The third counteracting cause, 'cheapening of the elements of the constant capital', is nothing else but capitalsaving innovations. We turn back to **Volume III, chapters 4** and **5,** which deal at length with 'economies in the employment of constant capital', marking the first explicit discussion of capitalsaving innovations in the literature of economics. **Chapter 4**, contributed by Engels, refers both to the release of working capital by improved means of communication and transportation, which have 'in the last fifty years doubled or trebled ... the productive capacity' of the capital engaged in world commerce, and to economies of fixed capital in 'the recently discovered methods of making iron and steel, such as the process of Bessemer, Siemens, Gilchrist-Thomas etc.'. At the close of the chapter, Engels illustrates the importance of turnover rates of capital on the rate of profit by data drawn from an actual cotton-spinning firm. With a profit rate of 33.3 percent, the annual rate of σ equals 1307 percent, due to the fact that payrolls turn over eight-and-a-half times in one year. Notice too the negligible portion of the stock of working capital required: $2\frac{1}{2}$ percent of total capital. **Chapter 5** begins by noting that double work shifts save capital. It quotes a Report of the Factory Inspectors that neatly distinguishes fixed and variable costs of operation – could Marshall have learned his theory of the firm by reading Blue Books? Marx also comments upon the tendency to increasing returns of scale: expenses of fuel, power, light and buildings do not rise proportionately with output. Capitalsaving innovations take the form of (1) 'progressive improvements of machinery' (see in particular Volume III, chapter 3 on steam engines); (2) the use of waste products previously discarded (section 4); and (3) the reduction in annual repair and maintenance charges owing to the greater durability of machines. Marx even makes the point that all cost-reducing improvements in the machinery industries release capital in all industries using machinery. This leads him to say, although he obviously did not realize what he was conceding, that the capital-output ratio tends to decline through time; 'While the circulating part of constant capital, such as raw material, etc., continually increases in mass to the extent that the productivity of labour grows, it is not so with the fixed capital, such as buildings, machinery, apparatus for lighting, heating etc. Although a machine becomes absolutely dearer with the growth of its body mass, it becomes relatively cheaper. If five labourers produce ten times as many commodities as formerly, this does not increase the outlay for fixed capital tenfold; although the value of this part of constant capital increases with the development of the productive forces, it does not increase by any means in the same proportion with them' (chapter 15). Marx also makes the interesting observation in the last paragraph of the chapter that 'the first leaders in a new enterprise are generally bankrupted' owing to bottlenecks in new inventions that need time to be ironed out.

42. Foreign Trade

One of the counteracting causes is foreign trade, insofar as it cheapens wage goods and raw materials. Capital invested in foreign trade may yield a higher rate of profit because 'an advanced country is able to sell its goods above their value even when it sells them cheaper than the competing countries'. It is not clear what this means inasmuch as the labour theory of value is not applicable to trade between countries. Moreover, capital invested in colonies may yield a higher rate of profit 'for the simple reason that the rate of profit is higher there on account of the backward development, and for the added reason, that slaves, coolies, etc., permit a better exploitation of labour'. This it the foundation of Lenin's theory of imperialism, but as it stands, it is singularly unconvincing. As Marx had shown elsewhere, it is not low real wages but low wage costs per unit of output that govern profits; backward countries have low wages, but owing to the low productivity of labour, their costs of production may well be prohibitively high. And there is no 'simple reason' why the rate of profit should be higher in backward than in advanced countries.

43. Business Cycles

Volume III, chapter 15, section 3, contains the bulk of Marx's comments on business cycles in *Capital* (see also Volume I, chapter 25, and Volume III, chapter 30), a subject which he discussed more fully in *Theories of Surplus Value*. Here we get further hints of the 'the narrow basis on which the conditions of consumption rests', which is made 'the cause of crises' in the ultimate paragraph of chapter 15. And again, in chapter 30: 'the last cause of all real crises always remains the poverty and restricted consumption of the masses as compared with the tendency of capitalist production to develop the productive forces in such a way, that only the absolute power of consumption of the entire society would be their limit'. The incidence of crises is linked to the falling rate of profit à la Mill. Marx points out in several places that innovators reap surplus profits until the innovation is adopted by others. Capitalists innovate 'for the sake of self-preservation and on penalty of failure'. There are some typical Malthusian remarks in this chapter as well as in chapter 13: 'the time of prosperity would have promoted marriages among the labourers and reduced the decimation of the offspring'. At the beginning of the chapter, Marx remarks that 'the rate of accumulation falls with the rate of profit', but at the end he declares: 'in spite of the falling rate of profit the inducements and facilities to accumulate are augmented'. His hazy conception of the inducement to invest is never more strikingly revealed than here.

There is a useful review of the history of booms and slumps in the cotton industry through 1845–60 (chapter 6, section 3); see also Engels' description of the crash of 1847 (chapter 25).

Say's Law of Markets is briefly discussed in chapter 15 and Marx attacks Ricardo's followers for admitting 'periodic overabundance of capital' while denying 'general overproduction of commodities'. But there is no contradiction between the recognition of recurring crises and the assertion of Say's Equality, namely, the possibility of full employment equilibrium at all levels of output and the unlimited development of an inherently adaptive economy. Marx supposes that a 'general glut' refers to business depressions instead of to secular stagnation. Despite Mill's treatment of the question, Marx interprets the Law of Markets as an identity, and hence his criticism of Say's Law, both in *Capital* and in *Theories of Surplus Value*, never gets beyond an attack on the fallacy of abstracting from money.

44. Money and Interest

Part V of **Volume III** is extremely uneven, consisting for the most part of disconnected observations on monetary disturbances and the rate of interest as well as a running, logic-chopping commentary on parliamentary testimony about currency management. The only chapters worth reading with any attention in this section are **chapters 21–3** and **25**; chapter 30 has already been referred to as containing some of Marx's important observations on the business cycle.

For Marx, the rate of interest is essentially a monetary phenomenon; although interest is a derived income from profit – the average rate of profit in Marx always means profit inclusive of interest – it is only tenuously connected with the rate of return on capital. Marx holds that 'the rate of interest in capitalist countries is overwhelmingly determined by conditions (loans granted by usurers to owners of large estates who draw ground rent) which have nothing to do with profit' (Volume III, chapter 13). The demand for loanable funds is dominated by consumption loans, and since most profits are automatically plowed back into the industry in which they are earned, even the supply of loans is little influenced by business savings. Hence, the loan market is affected by business activity only in the last stages of the boom and at the onset of a slump when the rising preference for liquidity leaves the loan market glutted with idle funds. Moreover, 'there is no such thing as a natural rate of interest', that is, the interest rate is a short-run phenomenon and there is no tendency toward long-run equilibrium. Marx's remarks on the determination of the rate of interest are made incidentally in chapter 22, for he disavows any concern with what he describes as 'minor fluctuations of the money-market'. The rate of interest, however, does exhibit a secular tendency to decline, not only because of the tendency of the rate of profit to fall, but also because of the development of credit institutions and the efficient concentration of 'the money savings of all classes of society' into the hands of bankers.

Chapters 25–35 touch in one way or another upon all issues dividing the Currency from the Banking School. Marx's symphathies lie with the Banking School. As early as 1859 he had taken his stand against the quantity theory of money, probably because he believed it to be at variance with the labour theory of value applied to money. Like Tooke, Marx argued that the quantity of money in circulation was governed by the flow of money expenditures; although he does not commit himself explicitly, Marx gives credence to the Law of Reflux based on the real bills doctrine: 'the quantity of circulating notes is regulated by the requirements of commerce, and every superfluous note wanders back immediately to the issuing party' (**chapter 33**).

In the absence of details, there is nothing to choose between a quantity theory and a contraquantity theory of money. Under a convertible paper standard and a passive monetary policy, the quantity of money in circulation is indeed the result, not the cause, of the level of prices; acting through the volume of trade and the demand for money-to-hold, 'real' forces generate a flow of money demands that determines absolute prices; the elasticity of the money supply is no doubt an element in the price-setting process but it is a purely passive element. This kind of formulation has its advantages over a simple quantity theory because it is more likely to avoid 'dichotomization' of the pricing process. But when the quantity of monetary metals is increasing sharply, owing to the discovery of new gold mines, the quantity theory comes into its own. Furthermore, as soon as the monetary authorities practice an active monetary policy, the contraquantity theory is bound to lead to misunderstanding. At the time Marx was writing, the Bank of England was in fact practising monetary management. The practice of using the Bank's discount rate as an instrument of credit regulation may be said to start from the Bank Charter Act of 1844, which repealed the Usury Laws. After 1844 the Bank also practiced something like an 'open market policy' by the device of 'borrowing on Consols'. The theory of monetary management by means of the bank rate had been advanced a half-century earlier by Thornton. It is noteworthy that Marx nowhere refers to Thornton's analysis of the two rates, which decisively refutes the theory of the Banking School (see in particular chapter 24, in which Marx summarizes Ricardo's theory of money). The Thornton-Ricardo argument would have supplied a definition of the long-run equilibrium rate of interest, whose existence Marx denied. In long-run equilibrium, the rate of interest is equal to the yield on real capital; at any lower rate, the demand for loanable funds for investment purposes is insatiable and, at any higher rate, the supply of loanable funds increases indefinitely. If the money market is dominated by investment loans, the money rate of interest will tend to be governed by the rate of return on real capital, despite the autonomous influence of monetary policy. We must conclude, therefore, that Marx's theory of money, even on its own reading, fares badly next to the best work of his predecessors.

45. Theory of Rent

Marx's theory of rent, developed in loving detail through **Volume III, chapters 37–43**, is simplicity itself. First, there is 'differential rent', as in Ricardo, resulting from differences in the fertility and location of different grades of land. If the price of production of an individual capitalist is lower than the average price of production of the product – Marx uses the example of a power-driven mill enjoying the advantage of a waterfall – he will earn a surplus over and above the average rate, assuming that demand is high enough to allow him to participate in the market. Competition for the use of the waterfall will permit its owner to charge a rent, thus equalizing the rate of profit earned by capitalists. The rate of profit is now given by $r = (s - e)/(c + v)$, and the 'rate of rent' by $e' = e/(c + v)$. Thus, $r = [\sigma/(q + 1)] - e'$. Differences in σ owing to differences in the site value of fertility of land will be compensated by differences in e', so as to leave r uniform between industries. Second, there may be 'absolute rent', something not found in Ricardo, owing to the fact that agriculture operates with an organic composition of capital below the social average. As a result the 'value' of agricultural products is in excess of its 'price of production'. Normally, the flow of capital would reduce the rate of profit in agriculture to the average rate but, owing to the existence of landed property, the landowner is able to charge the tenant an extra rental equal to the abnormal surplus earned in agriculture. Marx is careful to avoid commitment to the view that the organic composition of capital in agriculture is in fact below the average: this is 'a question which can be decided only by statistics' (**Volume III, chapter 45**). If this is not so, absolute rent disappears and all rent is differential rent.

Marx's theory of absolute rent has no validity except in terms of his theory of surplus value and the resulting necessity of transforming value into prices. We will therefore pass it by except to note that it has the strange implication that absolute rent is negative if the agricultural sector is more capital-intensive than the rest of the economy which has in fact been the case in the U.S.A. and the U.K. ever since 1930. Marx's discussion of differential rent is more detailed than Ricardo's but it is also less comprehensive. Marx misunderstood Ricardo's theory as implying that there must exist cultivated land on which no rent is paid – see the closing pages of Volume III, chapter 43. In other words, he did not understand that there is an intensive as well as an extensive margin of cultivation; this is a serious misunderstanding when we realize that Ricardo's intensive margin is the origin of all later marginal thinking [see chapter 11, section 1].

Two other points are worthy of mention in these rent chapters. In chapter 39, Marx denies that the demand for wheat is perfectly inelastic, as Ricardo had assumed. The Ricardian view, Marx asserts, is due to observing the impact effect of drought or bumper crops in which 'the sudden and short cheapness does not get time to exert its full effect upon the extension of consumption'. Moreover, the amount of wheat used to produce whisky or beer varies with the price of wheat, and the falling price of wheat brings about the substitution of wheaten bread for bread made out of rye and oats. One hardly expects such comments from Marx. Equally surprising are the remarks made in **Volume III, chapter 45**, on the opportunity cost of using land for pasture instead of for tillage, drawn from the *Wealth of Nations*. **Volume III, Part VII**, contains discursive notes on the classical concept of the productive triad, land, labour and capital. **Chapter 48** clarifies Marx's attack on vulgar political economy. The other three chapters merely repeat earlier material.

46. Marx as an Economist

All doubts that Marx was a great classical economist should have vanished by now. For sheer capacity to drive an economic argument to its logical conclusion, Marx was without equal in his own century. But it takes more than power to pursue abstract deductive reasoning to be a great economist. However, Marx possessed the other attributes as well: a feel for the interrelationships between different facets of economic activity, a sense of the constant interaction between historically conditioned institutions and the built-in structural characteristics of an economic system, and a flair for empirical generalizations based on close observation of economic life. Nevertheless, we have witnessed Marx committing logical errors, twisting the facts, drawing unwarranted inferences from the historical record, and almost deliberately closing his eyes to the weaknesses in his own analysis. The explanation is simply that he set for himself an impossible task. The *leitmotif* of Marxian economics is the theory of surplus value. But this theory is untenable. Nothing in the three volumes of *Capital* persuades us to believe that every worker of equal skill generates an identical amount of surplus value, no matter what equipment he works with or what kind of output he produces. The proposition is in any case a statement about the division of the working day between a portion that is paid and a portion that is unpaid. But we cannot observe this division. What we observe are money wage rates and the money prices of goods and services produced. Even when all workers are paid the same, they do not produce goods and services of equal money value. If we take it for granted that these differences in the money value of products correspond roughly to differences in the direct and indirect labour costs of producing them, and that the same rule applies to the money value of wage goods, there is still no reason to believe that a worker in the toothpick industry works the same number of hours in the day to earn the equivalence of his wages as a worker in the steel industry. And when we drop the assumption of an equal rate of surplus value throughout all lines of employment, the entire house that Marx built comes tumbling down.

The ploy that makes Marxian economics so appealing when read uncritically is the ploy of the two-tier argument: now-you-see-it-now-you-don't. There is a first floor to the house, the visible world of prices, wage rates and profit rates, and a basement to the house, the invisible world of labour values and surplus value. It is not only that the first floor is visible, while the basement is not; the economic actors that reside on the first floor are ignorant of the nether world of the basement. The subterfuge that Marx perpetrates is to move the basement to the first floor and the first floor to the second floor, subtly suggesting that the first floor is in some sense more real than the second one and that, indeed, the hallmark of science is to get underneath the apparent motivation of workers and capitalists on the second floor to the 'essence' of the matter on the first floor. It is a cunning sleight-of-hand and it has fooled generations of readers.

When we discard this totally arbitrary assumption of an equal rate of surplus value per worker, is there anything left to Marxian economics? What is left, I think, is a 'vision' or a conception of economics as a brand of 'magnificent dynamics' concerned with the long-run evolution of economic systems, that and a host of disconnected but nevertheless remarkable insights into the nature of technical change, the business cycle, and the volume of employment. For a theory of socialism, however, we must go elsewhere. *Je ne suis pas marxiste*, Marx once said. If only it had been true!

NOTES ON FURTHER READING

There is nothing much to choose between any of the English editions of *Capital*: Vols. I, II and III, however, are now available in new translations as Penguin paperbacks (1976, 1978) with

long, tendentious introductions by E. Mandel. There is no point in reading just Vol. I of
Capital. Vols. II and III are not addenda; they are vital to the story. Rather than reading
only the first volume, it would be better to read Borchardt's adroitly arranged selections
from all three volumes in the Modern Library edition of *Capital and Other Writings*, ed.
M. Eastman (1932), or the similarly arranged, *Marx on Economics*, ed. R. Freeman (1961
in paperback). Those who find my Reader's Guide to *Capital* too brief or too carping must
look at A. Brewer, *A Guide to Marx's Capital* (1984), which keeps its critical comments to a
minimum. A revealing supplement to *Capital* is Marx's *Theories of Surplus Value*, planned
as a fourth volume to *Capital* but actually the first to be written, and only published after
Engels' death, in 1905–10. The whole of it in three volumes is now available in a remarkably
cheap English edition from Moscow, ed. E. Burns (1963); the preface by the Institute of
Marxism-Leninism in Moscow is a good example of how Soviet economic commentators
write about economics in the West (see particularly pp. 33–4). Nor is this all there is to read
of Marx, even if we stick to economic doctrines. Some of Marx's unpublished *Economic and
Philosophical Manuscripts of 1844* first appeared in German in 1932 and then in English in
1960. The young Marx in these writings is obsessed with 'alienation' rather than 'exploitation' under capitalism and a huge literature has sprung up in the last ten years debating the
issue whether the young Marx contradicts or complements the old Marx. Since this young
Marx was a Marx who had not yet learned classical economics, we can pass the question by.
But for those readers who want to get their feet wet in these waters, see a Marxist treatment
of the controversy by E. Mandel, *The Formation of the Economic Thought of Karl Marx.
1843 to Capital* (1971), chaps. 10–11, and a non-Marxist treatment by J. Plamenatz, *Karl
Marx's Philosophy of Man* (1975). Likewise, Marx's unpublished manuscripts in economics
from the years 1857–8 have also recently seen the light of day: *Grundrisse. Foundations of
the Critique of Political Economy*, ed. M. Nicolaus (1973 in paperback). Apart from the historical passages in the book, extracted by E. Hobsbawm under the title *Pre-Capitalist
Economic Formations* (1965), the *Grundrisse* adds little to our knowledge of the Marxian
system. However, it does pinpoint the moment of the discovery of the concept of surplus
value and with it the birth of a specifically Marxian economics: all of Marx's previous
economic writings lack this feature. Nevertheless, most of the *Grundrisse* is virtually
unintelligible, being written in a sort of Hegelian shorthand. This is a book for exuberant
Marxologists and for them only.

There are as many as ten biographies of Marx, starting with F. Mehring's classic *Karl
Marx, The Story of His Life* (1935) and ending with the more recent study by D. McLellan,
Karl Marx, His Life and Thought (1973 in paperback). McLellan's book is reliable and stu-
diously fair but, in consequence, rather dull. I personally prefer J. Seigel, *Marx's Fate: The
Shape of a Life* (1978), which combines a psychological biography with a detailed account of
Marx's intellectual development against the background of the changing pattern of historical
circumstances that helped to shape his ideas.

And now for the secondary material. There is a vast literature on Marxian economics and
we shall be even more selective here than elsewhere in the book. Nevertheless, the list is a
long one. We begin with textbooks. P. M. Sweezy, *The Theory of Capitalist Development*
(1942), and J. Robinson, *An Essay on Marxian Economics* (1942, 2nd edn, 1967, with a new
preface), still provide the most satisfactory accounts of Marxian economics. Sweezy's invaluable book has shortcomings, which its author has since acknowledged: it improves Marx by
Keynesian embellishments and contains an untenable 'proof' of underconsumptionist tendencies. Chap. 7 of Sweezy's book reintroduced the Transformation Problem in the Marxist
literature; since then the subject has been worked on by others and Sweezy's treatment is
now somewhat outdated. The core of Sweezy's book is Parts I and II; Part III on business
cycles is much less satisfactory. Part III, chap. 11, however, is about the only account in
English of the important 'breakdown controversy' among German Marxists – see also the
introduction by J. Robinson to the English edition of R. Luxemburg, *The Accumulation of
Capital* (1951), reprinted in Robinson's *Collected Economic Papers* (1960), II; and

N. Georgescu-Roegen, 'Mathematical Proofs of the Breakdown of Capitalism', *Ecom*, 1960, reprinted in his *Analytical Economics* (1966).

J. Robinson's *Essay*, written in a mood of bitter dissatisfaction with modern economics, is lucid and penetrating. The chapter on 'Real and Money Wages', however, suffers from a failure to appreciate the Ricardian basis of Marx's argument about wages and prices. Nevertheless, if the reader has only a limited interest in Marx, this is the one book to read. J. A. Schumpeter has written a keen appreciation of Marxian economics in *Capitalism, Socialism, and Democracy* (1942), chap. 3, reprinted in his *Ten Great Economists* (1951 in paperback). Marx is also discussed in various places in Schumpeter's *History of Economic Analysis*, in particular, pp. 383–92, 438–42, 596–8, 647–52, 661–2, 681–7, 747–50, 877–80, and 1131–2. An excellent exposition of Marx's ideas, and a virtual *précis* of the difficult opening chapters of Vol. I of *Capital*, will be found in E. Roll, *A History of Economic Thought* (4th edn, 1973 in paperback). Rogin, *The Meaning and Validity of Economic Theory*, chap. 9, ranges far and wide through Marxian economics and, despite its turgid style, is particularly useful on Marx's theory of business cycles and on the Marxian conception of the role of the state in capitalist development.

A. Balinsky, *Marx's Economics* (1970) is a sound, nonpolemical treatment. Even better is M. Desai, *Marxian Economics* (2nd edn, 1979 in paperback), which takes up the Transformation Problem where Sweezy left it in 1942, and which is noteworthy for emphasizing the nonobservability of value relations in Marx. Along similar lines, see also G. Hodgson, 'Marxian Epistemology and the Transformation Problem', *ES*, November, 1974. Howard and King, *The Political Economy of Marx*, particularly the last half, chaps. 5–8, is another example of an undogmatic but sympathetic modern textbook treatment. The attempt to modernize Marx is taken one step further in M. Morishima, *Marx's Economics. A Dual Theory of Value and Growth* (1973). Here Marx is reinterpreted as a latterday von Neumann who founded dynamic general equilibrium theory. But the last chapter of this strangely ahistorical book takes away with one hand much of what has been given with the other hand in previous chapters. This is no way to learn Marx but it may be a very good way for a Marxist to learn modern growth theory (see the revealing exchange between C.C. von Weizsäcker and Morishima in *EJ*, December, 1973, June, 1974). It is worth noting that much of Morishima's book is devoted to establishing the validity of what he calls the 'fundamental Marxian theorem', according to which the rate of profit expressed in price terms is positive in a capitalist economy if and only if the rate of surplus value expressed in terms of labour time is positive; this, according to Morishima, is a correct mathematical statement of what Marx was really driving at. Unfortunately, he fails to point out that this celebrated theorem has no causal significance; that is, it can just as well be read the other way round. To finish off the subject of textbooks, I do *not* recommend E. Mandel, *Marxist Economic Theory* (1968 in paperback), a typical example of traditional, dogmatic Marxism, utterly ignorant of the advances in Marxism economic theory made by modern techniques, and enlivened only by Trotskyite digs at Soviet planning (for a much too kind article-review, see I. Guelfat, *JEL*, December, 1970).

The classic critique of Marx is by E. Böhm-Bawerk, *Karl Marx and the Close of His System* (1898). P.M. Sweezy has republished Böhm-Bawerk's tract together with the equally famous reply by R. Hilferding and L. von Bortkiewicz's first classic 1896 paper on the Transformation Problem (1949). Böhm-Bawerk criticized Marxian economics as a theory of relative prices and made heavy weather of the 'great contradiction' between Vols. I and III of *Capital*. In some ways the chapter on Marx in Böhm-Bawerk's *Capital and Interest* (1884, reprinted 1950), Book IV, chap. 3, is more to the point. P.H. Wicksteed, 'The Marxian Theory of Value' (1884), reprinted in *The Common Sense of Political Economy* (1933), II, confronts the labour theory of value as an explanation of relative prices with the marginal utility theory. The Lausanne version of Böhm-Bawerk's critique is by V. Pareto, *Les systèmes socialistes* (1926); on the whole, it is surprisingly ineffectual. For a review of these and other criticisms from a Marxist standpoint, see R.L. Meek, *Studies in the Labour Theory of Value*, chap. 6, and W.J. Blake, *An American Looks at Karl Marx*, also published under the title *Elements of Marxian*

Economic Theory and Its Criticism (1939). Blake's study contains an excellent annotated bibliography of the pre-war Continental literature covering all phases of Marxist thought.

The debate between Marxist and orthodox economics flared up again in the 1930s, led by O. Lange's brilliant essay, 'Marxian Economics and Modern Economic Theory', *REStud*, 1935, reprinted in *MME*. Lange argued that the superiority of Marxian economics in analyzing capitalist evolution is due not to the labour theory of value but to the exact specification of the institutional framework of capitalism. M.H. Dobb drives this point home in a forceful Marxist attack on modern economics: *Political Economy and Capitalism* (1937), chap. 5, supplemented by his essay, 'On Some Tendencies in Modern Economic Theory', *Economic Theory and Socialism* (1955). No student should fail to read this chapter and to ask himself whether he is prepared to meet the charges. For an instructive exchange of opinions occasioned by the publication of Dobb's book, see A.P. Lerner and M. Dobb, *JPE*, August, 1939, April, 1940.

On recent discussions in Marxist circles concerning the Transformation Problem, see R.L. Meek, 'Some Notes on the Transformation Problem', *EJ*, 1956, reprinted in *EET*, and the literature cited there. J. Robinson supplies a skeptical note on the significance of the problem: 'The Labour Theory of Value', *SS*, 1954, reprinted in her *Collected Economic Papers* (1951), I. For another article on the same theme, full of flashes and insights, see J.S. Chipman, 'The Consistency of the Marxian Economic System', *EI*, August, 1952. Of direct relevance is Marx's inadequate mathematical expertise, on which see L. Smolinski's fascinating 'Karl Marx and Mathematical Economics', *JPE*, September/October, 1973. The three-sector solution of the transformation problem sketched in the text above is due to J. Winternitz' 'Values and Prices: A Solution of the So-Called Transformation Problem', *EJ*, June, 1948. The general *n*-industry solution is given by F. Seton, 'The "Transformation Problem"', *REStud*, 1957, reprinted in *Penguin Modern Economic Readings: The Economics of Marx*, eds. M.C. Howard and J.E. King (1967 in paperback), an essay which might be said to be the last word on the problem. But no, there followed P.A. Samuelson, 'Understanding the Marxian Notion of Exploitation: A Summary of the So-Called Transformation Problem Between Marxian Values and Competitive Prices', *JEL*, 1971, reprinted in *Collected Scientific Papers of Paul A. Samuelson*, II, (1972) which provoked a reply by A.P. Lerner and a further exchange with M. Bronfenbrenner, *ibid.*, March, 1972, March, 1973. At this point, W.J. Baumol saw the need to go back to fundamentals: 'The Transformation of Values: What Marx "Really" Meant (An Interpretation)', *ibid.*, March, 1974, to which we must add M. Morishima and G. Catephores, 'Is There an "Historical Transformation Problem"?', *EJ*, June, 1975, and R.L. Meek, M. Morishima, and G. Catephores, 'An Interchange', *ibid.*, June, 1976, which finally lays the ghost to the suggestion that 'simple commodity production' actually existed in the 15th and 16th centuries.

Both Sweezy and Robinson agreed in 1942 that Marx's 'law' of the declining rate of profit was no law at all. Nevertheless, there have been endless unsuccessful attempts since 1942 to reinstate the Marxian law as an inexorable tendency under capitalism. On balance, however, most Marxists are now willing to concede that the trend line of the rate of profit is indeterminate. P. Van Parijs, 'The Falling-Rate-of-Profit Theory of Crisis: A Rational Reconstruction by Way of Obituary', *RRPE*, Spring, 1980, provides a useful survey of the debate over the last 40 years. The Marxian law is submitted to a statistical test with negative results by J.M. Gillman, *The Falling Rate of Profit* (1956).

Marx's view of the process of capital accumulation is analyzed by J. Steindl, *Maturity and Stagnation in American Capitalism* (1952), chap. 14, reprinted in *MME*. W.J. Fellner, 'Marxian Hypotheses and Observable Trends under Capitalism: A "Modernised" Interpretation', *EJ*, March 1957, shows under what conditions it is possible to have both the rate of profit and the rate of wages falling through time. This theoretical possibility is denied by P.A. Samuelson, 'Wages and Interest: A Modern Dissection of Marxian Economic Models', *AER*, 1957, reprinted in *Collected Scientific Papers of Paul A. Samuelson*, I; with 'Comment' by F.M. Gottheil and 'Reply' by Samuelson, *ibid.*, September, 1960. Samuelson's article is primarily an exercise in thinking through a Marx-like model but it abounds in incisive comments on the Marxian system. See also the illuminating paper by J.E. Elliott, 'Marx and Schumpeter on Capitalism's Creative Destruction: A Comparative Restatement', *QJE*, August, 1980.

An old article that still bears careful rereading is L. von Bortkiewicz, 'Value and Price in the Marxian System' (1907), reprinted in *IEP*, No. 2, 1952. The first part of the article deals with the Transformation Problem; the second with the theory of the declining rate of profit. It also contains a scathing review of Marx's tendentious criticism of Ricardo. Ricardo was perhaps the only bourgeois economist whom Marx admired, and yet Marx's comments on Ricardo are not only petty but grossly unfair. Marx regarded himself as Ricardo's intellectual heir and all too many commentators have taken him at his word: see G.S.L. Tucker, 'Ricardo and Marx', *Ec*, August, 1961, and A. Walker, 'Karl Marx, the Declining Rate of Profit and British Political Economy', *ibid.*, November, 1971. Marx's treatment of J.S. Mill is even worse and disguises his debt to Mill's *Principles* on several counts: see B.A. Balassa, 'Karl Marx and John Stuart Mill', *WA*, 83, 2, 1959; and B. Shoul, 'Karl Marx and Say's Law', *QJE*, November, 1957. J.E. King, 'Marx as a Historian of Economic Thought', *HOPE*, Fall, 1979, and 'Utopian or Scientific? A Reconsideration of the Ricardian Socialists', *ibid.*, Fall, 1983, does his best to defend Marx as a reputable historian of economic thought but does little to alter the conclusion that, despite Marx's voluminous writings on the history of economic thought, the ratio of sense to nonsense, of insights to invectives, in his commentaries is too low for comfort. As a striking example, see the devastating analysis of Marx's critique of Senior's last-hour theory in O. Johnson, 'The "Last Hour" of Senior and Marx', *ibid.*, Fall, 1969.

On the Marxian theory of the business cycles, see, in addition to Sweezy and Robinson, Dobb's *Political Economy and Capitalism*, chap. 4, which disposes of the allegation that Marx held a simple underconsumptionist theory; H. Smith, 'Marx and the Trade Cycle', *REStud*, June 1937; J.D. Wilson, 'A Note on Marx and the Trade Cycle', *ibid.*, February, 1938; and 'A Reply' by Smith, *ibid.*, October, 1938. Wilson stresses the fallacy of looking for a monocausal explanation of business cycles in the writings of Marx. For a masterly exposition of Marxian macroeconomics, see M. Bronfenbrenner, '*Das Kapital* for the Modern Man', *SS*, 1965, reprinted in *MME*, and his 'The Marxian Macro-Economic Model: Extension From Two Departments', *KYK*, June 1966. See also H.J. Sherman, 'Marxist Models of Cyclical Growth', *HOPE*, Spring, 1971; S. Maital, 'Is Marxian Growth Crisis-Ridden?', *ibid.*, Spring, 1972; and D.J. Harris, 'On Marx's Scheme of Reproduction and Accumulation', *JPE*, 1972, reprinted in the Howard-King readings, *The Economics of Marx*, all of which pay tribute to Marx's writings on the business cycle.

On the relationship between Marx and Keynes, see E.E. Ward, 'Marx and Keynes' *General Theory*', *ER*, April, 1939; S.S. Alexander, 'Mr. Keynes and Mr. Marx', *REStud*, 1940, reprinted in *RHET*; L.R. Klein, 'Theories of Effective Demand and Employment', *JPE*, 1947, reprinted in *REA*, II and *MME*; S. Tsuru, 'Keynes versus Marx: the Methodology of Aggregates', *Post-Keynesian Economics*, ed. Kurihara, reprinted in *MME*; and J. Robinson, 'Marx and Keynes', *Economica Critica*, 1948, reprinted in *Collected Economic Papers*, I, and *MME*. Most authors are impressed by the similarities between the two thinkers: two-way disaggregation on the product side of the social accounts; a monetary theory of the rate of interest; the rejection of Say's Law; emphasis on the declining marginal efficiency of capital; and a chronic tendency toward oversaving in a mature economy. But the differences are more profound than the similarities, as Robinson and Tsuru point out. Klein's essay is particularly valuable for its attempt to recast the Marxian system into an econometric model with specific behavioral assumptions.

J.M. Letiche, 'Soviet Views on Keynes: A Review Article Surveying the Literature', *JEL*, June, 1971, provides a view of Keynes as seen from behind the Iron Curtain. On the subject of Soviet Marxism, V.G. Treml, 'Interaction of Economic Thought and Economic Policy in the Soviet Union', *HOPE*, Spring, 1969, gives a devastating picture of the destruction of economic thought, Marxian or otherwise, in the U.S.S.R. under Stalin and its gradual, guarded revival in recent years. The traditional Marxist arguments about the distinction between 'value' and 'price' are being increasingly challenged in the Soviet Union: I. Guelfat, *Economic Thought in the Soviet Union* (1969). In this connection, see also J.S. Dreyer, 'The Evolution of Marxist Attitudes Towards Marginalist Techniques', *HOPE*, Spring 1974. Marx's doctrine of productive labour, excluding all services from national income as being 'transfer payments', is to this day the basis of Soviet social accounting: see V. Holesovsky, 'Marx and Soviet National Income Theory', *AER*, June, 1961.

Much has been written on the validity of Marx's predictions, but most of this literature is worthless because it fails to consider the exact nature of the prognosis. See, for example, A.L. Harris, 'Pure Capitalism and the Disappearance of the Middle Class', *JPE*, June, 1939, and P.L. Williams, 'Monopoly and Centralisation in Marx', *HOPE*, Summer, 1982. J. Kuczynski's interpretation of Marx's doctrine of absolute impoverishment, as applicable not to individual countries but to the world as a whole, is to be found in his introduction to *Labour Conditions in Great Britain* (2nd edn. 1946). For some recent French attempts to verify Marx's law of absolute impoverishment, see J. Marchal and J. Lecaillon, *Le répartition du revenu national* (1959), III, pp. 340–71; the whole of this third volume is full of useful summaries of various examples of French and English marxmanship. See also T. Sowell, 'Marx's "Increasing Misery" Doctrine', *AER*, 1960, reprinted in *RHET*; and F.M. Gottheil, 'Increasing Misery of the Proletariat: An Analysis of Marx's Wage and Employment Theory', *CJEPS*, February, 1962, or his *Marx's Economic Predictions* (1966), chap. 11 – the whole of Gottheil's book in fact provides a compendium of Marx's predictions,, distinguishing *ad hoc* predictions from those that logically emanate from the Marxian system. B. Gottlieb, on the other hand argues that Marx's system should be understood as a sociological bargaining theory of wages, and in that sense his predictions do not have the force of economic laws: 'Marx's Mehrwert Concept and the Theory of Pure Capitalism', *REStud*, 18, 3, 1950–1; and 'A Comment' by R.L. Meek, *ibid.*, 19, 2, 1951–2. See also '*Das Kapital*: A Centenary Appreciation', *AER*, May 1967, with articles by A. Erlich, M. Bronfenbrenner, and P.A. Samuelson, the first two of which are full of compliments but the last of which is damning. Every reader ought in the end to draw up his own score card!

Recent years have seen a definite revival of Marxian economics, as some of the above citations may have already revealed. An early example of the revival was P. Baran and P.M. Sweezy, *Monopoly Capitalism* (1966), which substituted a law of the rising 'economic surplus' as a proportion of total output for the old Marxist law of the falling rate of profit. For a discussion of this and other Marxist works of recent vintage, see M. Bronfenbrenner's two articles, 'Radical Economics in America: A 1970 Survey', *JEL*, September, 1970, and 'The Vicissitudes of Marxian Economics', *HOPE*, Fall, 1970. Some papers in *A Critique of Economic Theory*, ed. E.K. Hunt and J.G. Schwartz (1972 in paperback), a book by A. Bose, *Marxian and Post-Marxian Political Economy* (1975 in paperback), and particularly I. Steedman's brilliant study *Marx After Sraffa* (1977 in paperback), reveal the impact of Sraffa on Marxian writers: Sraffian Marxists entirely abandon the labour theory of value and totally repudiate the Transformation Problem as meaningless and irrelevant. I have examined this 'new wave' in Marxian economics elsewhere: *A Methodological Appraisal of Marxian Economics* (1980), chap. 1, and 'Another Look at the Labour Reduction Problem in Marx', *Classical and Marxian Political Economy: Essays in Honour of Ronald L. Meek*, eds. I. Bradley and M. Howard (1982). Since then J. Roemer, *Analytical Foundations of Marxian Economic Theory* (1982) and *A General Theory of Exploitation and Class* (1983) has made a valiant attempt to rework the micro-foundations of Marxian economics in a totally fresh and original way with the aid of game theory, heralding perhaps the coming of another 'new wave' in Marxian economics. This new brand of Marxian economics revels in linear algebra and is as technical as most of 'bourgeois' economics.

Unfortunately, there is no single critical account of Marx's contributions to economic history and, particularly, his treatment of 'primitive accumulation' in Vol. I of *Capital*. The reader will benefit from comparing a modern Marxist account by M. Dobb, *Studies in the Development of Capitalism* (1946), chap. 5, with a deliberately anti-Marxist treatment by J. Baechler, *The Origins of Capitalism* (1975); A. Gerschenkron attacks Marx's and similar modern arguments in 'Reflections on the Concept of "Prerequisites" of Modern Industrialization', *L'Industria*, 1957, reprinted in his *Economic Backwardness in Historical Perspective* (1962 in paperback). F. Pryor, 'The Classification and Analysis of Pre-capitalist Economic Systems by Marx and Engels', *HOPE*, Winter, 1982, suggests that the Marxist theory of feudalism and the transition from feudalism to capitalism is much less securely thought out than is sometimes supposed. R. Nordahl, 'Marx on the Use of History in the Analysis of Capitalism', *ibid.*, Fall, 1982, demonstrates that Marx practiced a kind of 'conjectural history' of his own, according to which historical categories correspond not to actual history but to a simplified abstraction of historical developments. For a striking illustration of Marx's questionable use of historical material, see E.G. West, 'Marx's Hypothesis on the Length of the Working Day', *JPE*, April, 1983.

This text of this chapter has borrowed heavily from two earlier papers of mine: 'Marxian Economics and Technical Change', *KYK*, 1960, reprinted in *MME*, and 'Economic Imperialism Revisited', *Yale Review*, 1961, reprinted in K.E. Boulding and T. Mukerjee, *Economic Imperialism. A Book of Readings* (1972), an anthology which also includes two excellent papers by D.K. Fieldhouse and D.S. Landes on the Hobson-Leninist theory of imperialism. There is a further book of readings, *The Theory of Capitalist Imperialism*, ed. D.K. Fieldhouse (1967 in paperback), with a trenchant conclusion by the editor. There is an important paper by M.B. Brown, 'A Critique of Marxist Theories of Imperialism' in *Studies in the Theory of Imperialism*, eds. R. Owen and R. Sutcliffe (1972), an uneven but nevertheless refreshing volume. A. Nove provides a fascinating essay on 'Lenin as an Economist' in *Lenin: The Man, The Theorist, The Leader*, ed. L. Shapiro and P. Reddaway (1967). L. Robbins, *The Economic Causes of War* (1939) has never been equalled as a profound assessment of the Leninist theory of imperialism. For a book-length treatment, taking account of both pre-war Marxist theories of imperialism as well as the newer postwar theories of colonialism, see B.J. Cohen, *The Question of Imperialism. The Political Economy of Dominance and Dependence* (1974). Lastly, there is S.J. Rosen and J.R. Kurth, *Testing Theories of Economic Imperialism* (1974). A reading of this book provides a valuable methodological lesson about all such heroic theorizing of the sociopolitical kind.

A. Emmanuel, *Unequal Exchange. A Study of the Imperialism of Trade* (1972 in paperback), is a recent example of the attempt to go back to Marx to build a non-Leninist theory of imperialism. Emmanuel turns Ricardo's theory of international trade on its head by assuming that capital is perfectly immobile between countries; since the international mobility of capital equalizes the rate of profit around the world, the labour theory of value is as applicable to world prices as it is to domestic prices, except that the inequality of wage rates creates a systematic tendency toward 'unequal exchange', in the sense that the exports of rich countries always command more labour and hence more surplus value than the equivalent imports from poor countries. Even without questioning the basic thesis, the book is worth reading for another example of how Marxist economists reify labour values, treating them as if they were perfectly measurable magnitudes that can in fact be exported and imported. For a devastating critique, see P. A. Samuelson, 'Illogic of Neo-Marxian Doctrines of Unequal Exchange', *Inflation, Trade and Taxes*, eds. D.A. Belsley, and others (1976).

There is, as we know, more to Marx than his economics, although it is only fair to say that Marx himself would have been the first to stress the priority of Marxian economics over the Marxian philosophy of history, Marxian sociology, Marxian political science, and so on. There are so many good books on Marxism in general that references would be otiose. The serious student can consult R.N. Carew-Hunt's annotated bibliography, *Books on Communism* (1959). Since 1959, five more excellent new entries on the list are H.B. Mayo, *Introduction to Marxist Theory* (1960 in paperback), G. Lichtheim, *Marxism* (1961 in paperback); A. Walker, *Marx: His Theory and Its Context* (1978 in paperback) R. L. Heilbroner, *Marxism: For and Against* (1980 in paperback) and the stupendous three volumes of L. Kolakowski, *Main Currents of Marxism* (1978 in paperback), which were it stronger in economics than it is would be the only book on Marxism one would need to read. M. M. Bober, *Karl Marx's Interpretation of History* (2nd edn, 1948), is an older book that is particularly important in giving the student of economics a rounded view of Marx's contribution.

8

The marginal revolution

THE EMERGENCE OF MARGINAL UTILITY: AN ABSOLUTIST OR RELATIVIST INTERPRETATION?

The term 'marginal revolution' is usually taken to refer to the nearly simultaneous but completely independent discovery in the early 1870s by Jevons, Menger and Walras of the principle of diminishing marginal utility as the fundamental building block of a new kind of static microeconomics. It constitutes, so the argument goes, one of the best examples of multiple discoveries in the history of economic thought, which simply cries out for some sort of historical explanation: it is too much to believe that three men working at nearly the same time in such vastly different intellectual climates as those of Manchester, Vienna and Lausanne could have hit by accident on the same idea. The trouble is that none of the standard explanations is convincing. The levels of economic development in England, Austria and Switzerland were so different in the 1860s that all crypto-Marxist explanations in terms of changes in the structure of production or the relationship between social classes strain our sense of credulity. Likewise, the utilitarian-empiricist tradition of British philosophy, the neo-Kantian philosophical climate of Austria and the Cartesian philosophical climate of Switzerland simply had no elements in common that could have provoked a utility revolution in economics. In matters of economic policy, there was in fact continuity with classical thinking and when Jevons and Walras wrote on policy questions, as they often did, there was little or no connection between their practical recommendations and their views on value theory. As for an alleged 'need' to defend the capitalist system, there was hardly anything more suitable than the old wages-population mechanism of classical economics, or the writings of Bastiat which owe nothing to marginal utility. Lastly, there was no real sense of intellectual crisis in the 1860s either in England or on the Continent which might have encouraged a search for alternative economic models; besides, historicism offered such an alternative model which continued to gain new adherents after 1860, not only in Germany but also in England. In short, the simultaneous discovery of marginal utility may call for an explanation but none of the available explanations is satisfactory.

Perhaps the difficulty is that the idea of a 'marginal revolution' is the sort of rational reconstruction of the history of economic thought, like the concepts of 'mercantilism' and 'classical economics' as defined by Keynes, that is bound to generate spurious historical puzzles. This is a large part of the problem but it is not the whole of it. The debate over the so-called marginal revolution has in fact confused two quite different things: the explanation of the origins of the revolution, if revolution it was, and the explanation of its eventual triumph.

1. The New Departure

Let us recall the main lines of classical economics. Whether we look at Smith, Ricardo or John Stuart Mill, the economic problem is seen in essence as a contrast between nonaugmentable land and augmentable labour, with capital subsumed under the latter as stored-up intermediate goods. The function of economic analysis was to reveal the effects of changes in the quantity and quality of the labour force on the rate of growth of aggregate output. Since the rate of growth of output was held to be a function of the rate of profit on capital, secular trends in factor prices and in distributive shares naturally came to the fore as key elements in the economic process. The accent was on capital accumulation and economic growth in the context of a private enterprise economy. In classical economics, free competition was thought to be desirable because it tended to expand the area of the market by bringing about an improved division of labour: economic welfare was conceived in physical terms and taken to be roughly proportional to the volume of output.

After 1870, however, economists typically posited some given supply of productive factors, determined independently by elements outside the purview of analysis. The essence of the economic problem was to search for the conditions under which given productive services were allocated with optimal results among competing uses, optimal in the sense of maximizing consumers' satisfactions. This ruled out consideration of the effects of both increases in the quantity and quality of resources and the dynamic expansion of wants, effects that the classical economists had regarded as the *sine qua non* of improvements in economic welfare. For the first time, economics truly became the science that studies the relationship between *given* ends and *given* scarce means that have alternative uses. The classical theory of economic development was replaced by the concept of general equilibrium within an essentially static framework.

All this is nicely exhibited in the attitude of the 'new economics' to the Malthusian theory of population. With the advent of marginal analysis, the Malthusian theory disappeared from economics but not because economists ceased to believe in it. Most of the great figures of this period – Jevons, Marshall, Wicksteed, Walras, Wicksell and Clark – regarded the Malthusian theory as valid in the main. But the growth of population was treated as an exogenous variable in the new economics. As Jevons said, the 'problem of economics' is: 'Given, a certain population, with various needs and powers of production, in possession of certain lands and other sources of material: required, the mode of employing their labour which will maximize the utility of the produce'.

The emphasis on allocation of given means with maximum effect is much stronger in the Lausanne and Austrian traditions than in the English School dominated by

Marshall. Marshall learned his economics from Mill and retained a link with classical thought via the 'real cost' theory of value. Moreover, he never entirely abandoned the deep-rooted classical belief that economic welfare depends as much on capital accumulation and population growth as on efficiency in resource allocation. He shied away from the heroic abstractions of general equilibrium, stationary conditions and perfect competition in favour of partial analysis of particular sectors with special emphasis on the long-run adjustments of industries expanding under loosely competitive conditions. But even Marshall devoted more attention to the action of competition in tightening up the allocation of resources within a given market environment than to the expansion of the market area itself. His long-run theorizing is essentially static, as he himself would have been the first to admit.

The dominant role of the concept of substitution at the margin in the new economics accounts for the sudden appearance of explicitly mathematical reasoning. Again, it is not utility theory but rather marginalism as such that gave mathematics a prominent role in economics after 1870. It is no accident that the Austrians, who were always insistent on the primary role of utility, were wholly innocent of any mathematics: neither Menger nor Wieser nor Böhm-Bawerk ever employed a genuine algebraic equation or geometric formulation in any of their writings. More than that: they were opposed on methodological grounds to mathematics as a tool of economic analysis. In a letter to Walras in 1884, Menger insisted that mathematics was of no use in helping the economist to get at the qualitative 'essence' of phenomena like value, rent and profit. This attitude remained characteristic of the Austrian writers who went so far as to eschew all emphasis on the mutual and simultaneous determination of all economic variables.

With this exception, however, all the great economic theorists of this period had at least an intermediate training in mathematics. Jevons, Marshall, Wicksteed, Wicksell and Cassel are examples among the so-called literary economists, although among these only Marshall and Wicksell can be said to have been technically competent mathematicians. Economists like Cournot, Walras, Edgeworth and Pareto were, of course, avowedly mathematical economists, although here again it is worth noting that Walras had only the instincts and none of the techniques of a mathematician. Nevertheless, it is a striking fact that, among the great economists of the latter half of the 19th century, only J. B. Clark and Böhm-Bawerk managed to make fundamental contributions to economic theory without use or knowledge of mathematics.

2. The Maximization Principle

The kind of mathematics that economists employed in this period was confined to calculus. Economic functions were invariably assumed to be differentiable continuous functions. The underlying principle of maximization, however, is equally applicable to discontinuous functions. The general principle is that of ordering a series of attainable positions in terms of the respective associated values of a relevant maximand, the optimum position being one that assigns the greatest possible value to the maximand. Whether the maximand is utility or profits or physical product, the analysis remains formally identical. Marginal analysis proper applies only when the maximand function is continuous at the maximand. But discontinuities present only a formal, not a substantive, difficulty in the analysis. In that sense, marginal analysis as such takes second place; what takes first place is the principle that economic behavior is maximizing behaviour subject to constraints.

To become somewhat more explicit, the principle at issue is that of equalizing marginal values: in dividing a fixed quantity of anything among a number of competing uses, 'efficient' allocation implies that each unit of the dividend is apportioned in such a way that the gain of transferring it to one use will just equal the loss involved in withdrawing it from another. Whether we refer to allocating a fixed income among a number of consumer goods or a fixed outlay among a number of productive factors or a given amount of time between work and leisure, the principle always remains the same. Moreover, in each case the allocation problem has a maximum solution if and only if the process of transferring a unit of the dividend to a single use among all the possible uses is subject to diminishing results. In the theory of the household, an optimum situation obtains when the consumer has distributed his given income in such a way that the marginal utility of each dollar or purchase is equal; the 'law' of diminishing marginal utility insures that such an optimum exists. In the theory of the firm, an optimum result is obtained when the marginal physical product of each dollar's worth of factor purchases is equalized: the 'law' of diminishing marginal productivity plays the same role here as diminishing marginal utility in the theory of demand. Both examples are merely particular applications of the 'equimarginal principle'. The whole of neoclassical economics is nothing more than the spelling out of this principle in ever wider contexts, coupled with the demonstration that perfect competition does under certain conditions produce equimarginal allocations of expenditures and resources.

It is easy to see that the equimarginal principle refers only to definite quantities of money, resources or time to be distributed, and has only as much significance as the initial assumption of a fixed dividend. In our own time, we have become acquainted with a kind of economics that does not rest on maximization principles. In modern macroeconomics we may posit an aggregate outcome of individual choices in accordance with a definite global rule without necessarily being able to show why the global rule works: Keynes's consumption function, for example, is not built up from individual maximizing behavior. In classical economics, analysis does ultimately hark back to the maximizing actions of individuals but, instead of investigating resource allocation at a moment of time, what is emphasized is the time paths of successive equilibria. For better or for worse, however, economic theory in the period 1870–1914 consisted almost wholly of static microeconomics based squarely on the equimarginal rule.

3. Value and Distribution

Classical economics derived the prices of products from the so-called 'natural' rates of reward of the three factors of production. These were in turn explained by separate theories: land rentals were determined as a differential surplus over the marginal costs of cultivation, wages of labour were governed by the long-run costs of producing the means of subsistence and the rate of profit on capital was treated as a residual. Only in the case of labour was the problem of distribution solved by a straightforward application of value theory. The value of land and of capital had to be explained by principles quite different from those used to account for the relative prices of products.

In the 'new economics', distribution theory was treated as nothing more than an aspect of general value theory. Factors were rewarded because they were scarce relative to consumers' wants for the products that the factors could produce. The process of production and distribution had significance only insofar as it modified the possibility of consumers' choice. The demand for factors was a derived demand; given the supply of factors and their technical rates of transformation, the prices of productive services and the prices of consumer goods alike were determined by consumers' wants. Hence, there was no room for a special analysis of the value of each factor of production. That the classical authors provided a special theory of distribution is precisely the criticism leveled against them by the writers of the present period.

The classical economists frequently wrote as if distribution preceded the valuation of products in a causative sense. The early marginalists, and particularly the members of the Austrian School, on the other hand, seemed to argue that the causal order should be reversed, the income of productive factors being the resultant of prices in product markets. In point of fact, of course, both product and factor prices are mutually and simultaneously determined. The real claim of the new economics was that it broke down the departmentalized approach of Ricardian economics. Ricardo, Mill and Marx treated all commodities as if they were produced under conditions of constant costs with fixed technical coefficients. Ricardo admitted the variability of factor proportions in the chapter on 'Machinery' but this concession was never incorporated into the mainstream of classical theory. Even so, generality was sacrificed in the case of agricultural goods where marginal costs of production diverged from average costs. Classical economics, therefore, was forced to operate with two theories of value: the price of industrial goods depended solely upon conditions of supply, while the price of agricultural goods varied with the scale of output and hence the pattern of demand. This implied a fatal indeterminacy in classical distribution theory: since wage goods consisted largely of the products of agriculture, real wages depended on the position of the 'margin of cultivation' and hence on the length to which investment was carried in agriculture.

Thus, long-run wages in the classical system depended on the rate at which capital accumulation proceeded, which in turn depended on the state of demand. But Ricardo and even Marx were inclined to treat the supply of capital as being governed by a minimum-of-existence rate of profit on lines analogous to the wages-population mechanism. Above this minimum rate, the supply of capital was stimulated by a rise and checked by a fall in the rate of profit, via its effects on the power to invest. Mill suggested instead that the supply of capital was a function of the rate of profit through the incentive effect but this left the notion of a long-run supply price of capital hanging in the air. Ultimately, classical economics provided no determinate analysis of the conditions governing the supply of capital and never gave the state of demand a position coordinate with the conditions of supply. In this sense, the Ricardian theory of distribution not only lacked generality but also stopped short of fulfilling its own promise.

Neoclassical theory achieved greater generality and economy of argument by explaining both factor and product prices on the basis of a single principle. The new theory encompassed both reproducible and nonreproducible goods, both constant and varying costs. Ricardo's differential rent theory was generalized to all nontransferable resources, while the postulate that value is determined by production under 'the least favourable circumstances' was made the basis for the determination of all prices. Greater generality, however, is rarely an unambiguous achievement. Unless a new theory encompasses all the variables of the old, the order of generality will vary with the question under analysis. Neoclassical economics was in some ways more restrictive than was classical theory: for example, it took the supply of labor as given. Moreover, its boast for greater economy of argument was largely whittled away in subsequent decades. Böhm-Bawerk's contribution to the theory of interest can be boiled down to the proposition that the capital market presents unique problems because of the omnipresence of the time-discount factor. The 'peculiarities of labour' are noted and discussed by Marshall. In each case, special elements, missing in most product markets, are adduced to account for the characteristics of factor markets. When the supply of resources is given at the outset of the analysis, these difficulties largely disappear. But as soon as we leave the realm of short-run analysis and take up classical questions about capital accumulation and population growth, the claim of the new economics that distribution theory is nothing more than a particular aspect of value theory seems to have only formal significance. An unkind critic might say that neoclassical economics indeed achieved greater generality, but only by asking easier questions.

4. The Genesis of Marginal Utility Theory

Having delineated the leading features of the new economics, we are now in a position to speculate briefly on the origins of the marginal revolution. The explanations that have been advanced fall roughly into four classes: (1) an autonomous intellectual development within the discipline of economics; (2) the product of philosophical currents; (3) the product of definite institutional changes in the economy; and (4) a counterblast to socialism, particularly to Marxism.

Let us examine these in turn. The first is the most plausible single explanation and is indeed the most widely held of the four listed above. It points to the bankruptcy and disintegration of classical economics in the 1850s and 1860s, to the virtual abandonment of the labour theory of value in Mill's *Principles* and, in particular, to Mill's recantation of the wages fund doctrine in the late 1860s. In the process of attacking the wages fund doctrine, Thornton and Longe drew attention to the possibility of perverse demand and supply functions in the labour market; inspired by this controversy, Fleeming Jenkin drew demand and supply curves in a paper published in 1870 – Cournot had done so as early as 1838, but he was almost unknown in England. Jevons had been working on his book since 1860 and had already published a 'Brief Account of a General Mathematical Theory of Political Economy', which outlined the marginal utility theory of value. The 1850s had seen a revival of interest in the writings of Bentham: following in Bentham's footsteps, Richard Jennings stated the principle of diminishing marginal utility in 1855 in the form of a 'law of the variation of sensations', and McLeod foreshadowed Jevons' concept of discommodity and disutility in his discussion in 1858 of zero and negative value. These were the writers from which, as Jevons said, 'my system was, more or less consciously, developed'.

So far as England is concerned, then, we can detect something like a pure filiation of ideas under the impulse of a growing sense of dissatisfaction with older views. The fact that Jevons' book was poorly received lends support to this interpretation. Marginal utility doctrine made its way slowly against persistent opposition; the new and the old continued to exist side by side. Marshall's *Economics of Industry* (1879) shows the influence of the 'revolution' and Edgeworth's *Mathematical Psycics* (1881) is a speculative excursion into the higher realms of the new theory. But Cairnes' *Leading Principles* (1874) and Sidgwick's *Principles* (1883) were entirely cast in the old mold. The dominant view among English economists in the 1870s and 1880s was that of the Historical School. English historicism was an indigenous growth, whose roots go back to Carlyle's and Ruskin's protests against the narrow scope of clasical political economy. It represented a reaction not only to classical economics but to all abstract economic theory of any variety. This English *Methodenstreit* was put to rest by John Neville Keynes's *Scope and Method of Political Economy* (1890) and by Marshall's conciliatory attitude in the *Principles* (1890), by which time the new movement had successfully vanquished all vestiges of classical economics.

The difficulty with this 'absolutist' explanation of the marginal revolution is that of applying it to the Continent. Neither Menger nor Walras was stimulated, as was Jevons, by writers who hinted at the idea of *marginal* utility; nor were they reacting to a well-entrenched school of ideas such as dominated the British universities in the 1850s and 1860s. Walras was building on the ideas of his father, Auguste Walras, in the light of the inspiration he received from studying Cournot and Dupuit. Menger credited a long list of 18th- and 19th-century writers with the utility theory of value, but none of the authors he mentioned had connected the idea of diminishing marginal utility with the problem of price determination. Gossen's remarkable book *Entwicklung der Gesetze des menschlichen Verkehrs* (1854), which clearly formulated the law of diminishing marginal utility and applied it to individual acts of consumption, escaped his attention. Nevertheless, despite the diversity of background and tradition, Menger and Walras hit upon the idea of marginal utility almost at the same time. It is difficult to believe that this was entirely due to adventitious intellectual forces.

This leads one to look for some general movement in philosophy or social science that might have promoted an emphasis on introspection as an instrument of forming hypotheses about economic behavior. Some authors have been struck by the renaissance of Kantian philosophy somewhere around the middle of the century, beginning in Germany and spreading out over the Continent. 'Back to introspection and sense-impression' was the watchword of this philosophical trend. There is no evidence, however, that Menger himself was motivated by any such philosophical leanings – he remained steeped in Aristotelian modes of thinking all his life – and in the case of Walras there is every suggestion of a studious disinterest in contemporary philosophical debates. Once again, it is the British scene that alone lends support to the argument: hedonism enjoyed considerable vogue in England in the 1850s and must be put down as one of the germinal influences on Jevons' thinking.

A different argument along the same lines explains the delayed acceptance of utility theory in England on the grounds that subjective value theory is the product of a Catholic culture, whereas the labour theory of value naturally emanates from a Protestant outlook on the world. Protestantism places work and labour at the center of theology, while Catholic philosophy is supposed to exalt moderate pleasure-seeking instead of work and money making. Since Catholicism dominated the Continent, we have here an explanation of the prevalence of utility theory in 18th-century French and Italian economics and the long delay in the acceptance of that theory in Great Britain and Germany. It is not obvious, however, how this helps to explain the rise of *marginal* utility theory on the Continent and in England. Moreover, many of the 19th-century forerunners of the new theory of value do not fit the pattern: Lloyd, Longfield and Senior were Protestants, and Gossen was notoriously anti-Catholic.

This leaves the possibility of accounting for the rise of marginal utility theory by changes in the economic environment. A bold effort along these lines was attempted by one of the most brilliant of all Bolshevik thinkers, Nikolai Bukharin. In a book entitled *Economic Theory of the Leisure Class* (1927), Bukharin explained the marginal revolution in 'relativist' terms on the basis of two very questionable assumptions: (1) 'the psychology of the consumer is characteristic of the *rentier*', and (2) marginal utility theory is 'the ideology of the bourgeoisie who has already been eliminated from the process of production'. Any amateur historian can see the flaw in this argument. Nevertheless, it has a certain force: the consumer and not the capitalist is the dominant figure in neoclassical economics; the employer of labour is no longer identified with the investor of capital; the manager, the entrepreneur and the rentier have become separate economic agents, and personal saving rather than business saving is regarded as the typical source of investment funds. All this involves a conception of economic institutions different from that found in the writings of Smith and Ricardo. Economic growth is now taken for granted and problems of secular stagnation or technological unemployment disappear in the economic literature. It is not farfetched to see a connection between changes in the economic structure of society around the middle of the century and the theoretical innovations of the subjective value trio. The difficulty here is of making the connection concrete in terms of the personal intellectual awareness of institutional changes – something that Bukharin failed to do – and at the same time of taking account of differences in the economic structure of Austria, France and England.

Finally, there is the argument that marginal utility theory was nothing but the bourgeois answer to Marxism. Here, at any rate, it is possible to be quite definite. The first volume of *Capital* appeared in 1867; it was not translated into English until 1887. Jevons' 'Notice' was written in 1862 and published in 1863; it shows him in full possession of the theory of marginal utility and even of the marginal productivity theory of capital. Marshall began his work in 1867 and the outline of his system is already discernible in his review of Jevons' book in 1872. In their formative years, neither Jevons, nor Marshall, nor Menger, nor Walras had ever heard of Marx, who died obscurely in 1883. Later in the 1880s, when Marxism spread through the European labour movement, Böhm-Bawerk, Wicksteed, Pareto and Wieser employed the new theory to attack Marxian economics [see chapter 7, section 38]. But there is nothing unusual about the attempt to fortify a promising line of thought by turning it against contemporary rivals. Böhm-Bawerk may be said to have set out more or less deliberately in his work on interest theory to provide an alternative solution to the Marxist concept of exploitation. But this concerns the development of marginal economics, not its genesis. The first generation of economists in the new tradition had no knowledge of socialist thought, much less of Marxism.

Marginal utility theory was ideologically neutral in the sense that it emerged without any direct reference to practical questions and was compatible with almost any position on social and political issues. But Marxists do not claim that the subjective value trio was actuated by a sinister desire to come to the defense of capitalism but rather that marginal utitlity theory naturally supports a faith in things as they are, being readily employable to defend the status quo. Actually, classical economics is a far better instrument for defending private property. It would be difficult to think of an argument more agreeable to business interests than the classical wages fund doctrine. The nomenclature of utility and disutility, on the other hand, leads one immediately to ask whether a free enterprise system represents such a use of resources in satisfying wants as to insure society the greatest surplus of utility over disutility. It is true that both Jevons and Walras thought they had demonstrated that perfect competition does maximize the satisfactions of all the members of society. But this piece of apologetics was roundly condemned by the second generation of economists in the utility tradition. Indeed, one of the uncomfortable aspects of utility theory seemed to be the implication that only an egalitarian distribution of income maximizes satisfactions. Most writers after 1870 were extremely critical of the existing inequalities in income distribution and did not hesitate to use utility theory to fortify their critical outlook.

In general, we find great differences in the political attitudes of economists within the mainstream of neoclassical economics. The Marshallian tradition culminated in Pigou's *Wealth and Welfare* (1912), which is virtually a blueprint for the welfare state. The Fabians adopted the utility theory in *Fabian Essays* (1889) to display the systematic inequities of the market mechanism. The reformist element was equally strong in the Lausanne School: Walras was a land reformer and Pareto grew increasingly sympathetic to the idea of a corporate state. It was the Austrian School that was markedly conservative and given over to attacks on socialism and the espousal of laissez-faire. The aversion to radical politics was a characteristic note of economists trained in Vienna seminars, just as interventionism and a bored attitude to Marxism were characteristic of Cambridge economists. If the argument is that politics entered into the development of modern economics, one can only concur. But the idea that modern economics has no other *raison d'être* than to provide an apologetic for capitalism is too farfetched to be entertained.

5. A Multiple Discovery?

Let us now raise the question whether the discovery of marginal utility by Jevons, Menger and Walras was in fact a 'multiple' in Robert Merton's sense of the term. After an intensive investigation of hundreds of multiple discoveries in the history of science, Merton concluded that 'all scientific discoveries are in principle multiples, including those that on the surface appear to be singletons'. Once a science has become professionalized, Merton argued, the same discoveries will be made independently by several investigators and for that reason even the breakthroughs that appear in retrospect to be 'singletons' are in fact 'forestalled multiples'. Although a 'multiple' will typically occur over a period of ten years or less, there may be cases where a so-called 'simultaneous' discovery involves longer periods; even these are 'multiples' if the successive discoveries are really similar. Enough has now been said to indicate that the concept of 'multiples' is by no means easy to interpret, particularly in fields less professionalized than the natural sciences. The gist of the argument, however, seems to be that 'mature science' is characterized by cumulative, continuous progress such as to make the next leap forward, if not absolutely inevitable, at least highly predictable.

We may now rephrase our question about Jevons, Menger and Walras: was the state of economic science in the 1860s such as to make the eventual emergence of the marginal utility principle a perfectly predictable phenomenon, in which case it is hardly surprising that three men discovered it independently and concurrently? The answer to that question must surely be negative.

First of all, it is highly doubtful that we can speak of *one* economic science in the 1860s as if it were a common heritage shared among economists around the world, studying the same treatises, reading the same journals, and employing a common set of tools in the analysis of a similar range of problems. A glance at the authorities cited in Jevons' *Theory* (1871), Menger's *Grundsätze* (1871) and Walras' *Elements* (1874) will show that there were at least two, if not three or four models of economic science extant at that time. Although Jevons struggled against the tyranny of Mill's influence, German economists had long since rejected *Smithianismus* and all Ricardian varieties thereof, while Swiss or French economists for their part never exhibited much interest in either the analytical features of English classical political economy or the rallying cries of the German historical school. The lack of communication between economists in different countries right up to the 1890s and, in particular, the insularity of British economics is perfectly exemplified by the fact that Jevons, a leading economic bibliophile, died in 1882 without realizing that a man called Menger had written a book on economics which would one day be likened to his own

Theory of Political Economy. Secondly, the notion that economic science as such was inexorably moving towards the discovery of marginal utility somewhere around the middle of the century is simply a rationalization after the fact. Surely, the much more likely next step in English classical economics of the 1860s was either the generalization of the marginal concept in Ricardian rent theory to all factors of production, that is, the breakthrough to a marginal productivity theory of factor pricing, or perhaps the further refinement of Ricardian value theory into something like linear input-output analysis? But the former came only belatedly in the 1890s among the generation that succeeded our marginal utility trio, and the latter has only emerged in the 20th century.

What of the counterargument, however, that marginal utility was not discovered but only rediscovered in the 1870s? Lloyd and Longfield had developed the distinction between total and marginal utility in 1834, followed soon after by Senior – we may ignore Bernoulli in the 18th century as an 'outlier'. If Jevons, Menger and Walras do not constitute a 'multiple', perhaps Lloyd, Longfield and Senior deserve the title. But Lloyd, Longfield and Senior made little substantive use of marginal utility and thus only illustrate Whitehead's adage that 'everything of importance has been said before by somebody who did not discover it'. The same objection does not apply to Dupuit (1844), Gossen (1854) and Jennings (1855), all of whom not only rediscovered marginal utility but employed it to analyze consumer behavior; moreover, Gossen did so with all the confidence and revolutionary ardor of Jevons and Walras. Nevertheless, the same argument that applied to Jevons, Menger and Walras applies now to Dupuit, Gossen and Jennings: they struck on the law of diminishing marginal utility at about the same time but in response to totally different intellectual pressures and without the benefit of an inherited corpus of similar economic ideas.

We have now collected three trios of economists, nine names in all, who between 1834 and 1874 seized on the idea of marginal utility, four of whom saw it indeed as the stock from which a new economics could be evolved. If we deny that this constitutes a Mertonian 'multiple', are we not splitting hairs?

It is clear how we might escape from the dilemma. Recall Merton's own warning that even discoveries far removed from one another in time ought to be construed as 'simultaneous' if they really involve the same phenomenon. Thus, from the fact that marginal utility was independently discovered over and over again in different countries between 1834 and 1874, we might argue that there must have been a core of economic ideas which was held in common by economists all over the world, whose inner logic would eventually dictate the exploration of consumers' demand with the tools of utility theory. In other words, we can infer the state of science from the existence of a multiple, instead of the other way around. But that is to deprive the theory of multiples of its most attractive feature, namely, the idea that the development of a science is to some extent predictable. So long as we take Merton's argument seriously as providing something more than an inductive generalization with many exceptions, we must deny that even nine names necessarily make a 'multiple'. The point is very simple: if communications between scientists were perfect, all multiples would be forestalled and we would only observe singletons; at the other end of the spectrum, if there were no communication whatsoever between scientists, multiples would have no more significance than the fact that lightning does occasionally strike twice in the same place. Multiples are only interesting phenomena insofar as there is a high but nevertheless imperfect degree of communication between the practitioners of a discipline.

It is true that classical economics had no theory of demand and that its theory of price determination would sooner or later strike someone as peculiarly asymmetrical. But as the example of Cournot will show, it would have been perfectly possible to repair this deficiency without introducing utility considerations. It is also true that marginal utility was 'in the air' throughout the 19th century and kept turning up afresh every ten years or so: Lloyd and Longfield, 1834; Dupuit, 1844; Gossen, 1854; Jennings, 1855; Jevons, 1862; Menger, 1871; and Walras, 1874. But that is a far cry from saying that marginal-utility economics was, in some sense, inevitable. We might as well say that the emergence of macroeconomics in the 1930s was inevitable because certain Swedish economists were thinking along the same lines in the 1920s as Robertson and Keynes. *Post hoc ergo propter hoc* is a perennial temptation in intellectual history.

6. When is a Revolution a Revolution?
The 'marginal revolution', like the Industrial Revolution, went unrecognized by those who lived through it. The now standard version, which dates the revolution near 1871 and links together the names of Jevons, Menger and Walras as having written essentially about the same thing, was first announced by Walras in 1886 but for some time the Austrian accounts of the history of marginal-utility theory did not recognize Walras' own claim as a pioneer. Most of the histories of economic thought published between the years 1870 and 1890 did not even mention marginal utility and no complete account of the theory appeared in any history of economic thought until after the turn of the century. Here was a revolution that was not generally admitted to have taken place until more than a generation after the event.

The long-delayed acceptance of the marginal utility theory of value, which went hand in hand with the delayed acceptance of a rational account of its history, is perhaps the best indication we can have that it was indeed an anomaly which did not emanate logically from classical economics. This suggests, in other words, that the last quarter of the 19th century was one of those revolutionary phases in the history of economics when, in the language of Thomas Kuhn, economists adopted a new 'paradigm' to guide their work.

Unfortunately, there appears to be no firm agreement as to just what the new paradigm was that Jevons, Menger and Walras put forward. Was it a new emphasis on demand rather than supply, on consumer utility rather than on production costs? Was it something as ambitious as a subjective theory of value, which was to supplant the objective labour-cost theories of the past? Was it rather the extension of the principle of maximization from business firms to households, making the consumer and not the entrepreneur the epitome of rational action? Was it perhaps the equimarginal principle, enshrined in the proportionality of marginal utilities to prices as the condition of consumer equilibrium? Was it instead, as Schumpeter liked to say, the explicit or implicit discovery of general equilibrium analysis? Or lastly, was it simply the first conscious recognition of constrained maximization as the archetype of all economic reasoning? Whichever version we adopt, it is difficult to sustain the thesis that Jevons, Menger and Walras were really preoccupied with the same paradigm.

Menger is in any case the odd man out: he was not self-consciously aware, as Jevons and Walras were, of being a revolutionary; he eschewed mathematical formulations and hence the pure logic of extremum problems; he only formulated 'Gossen's second law' in words and certainly did not emphasize it (see below); he rejected cost theories of value but, on the other hand, was deeply suspicious of all determinate theories of pricing and underlined discontinuities, uncertainties and bargaining around the market price. In other words, there is a great deal more to be said for coupling Jevons and Walras with Gossen rather than with Menger, and the only reason for the standard version is that Menger's name was continually invoked by his disciples Wieser and Böhm-Bawerk, both of whom were determined to persuade the profession that Austrian economics was a differentiated product. Similarly, it takes hindsight to see much in common between Jevons – a precisely formulated theory of barter exchange, an explicit mathematical statement of 'Gossen's second law', a theory of the short-run supply schedule of labour, and some grandiose but unfulfilled promises of a new kind of utility economics (see below) – and Walras, who really did derive demand curves from utility schedules, struggled likewise to derive supply curves from marginal productivity considerations, worked out a theory of market pricing, and wove all the elements together within a general equilibrium framework.

The whole question is made more difficult by the ironic fate which history visited on the founders. In the end, as Hutchison has said, what was important in marginal utility was the adjective rather than the noun. Utility theory was gradually deprived of all its bite and reduced from cardinal to ordinal utility and from ordinal utility to 'revealed preferences'; cost theories of value were shown, not to be wrong, but only valid in special cases; and general equilibrium virtually disappeared, only to be revived in the 1930s by Hicks and Samuelson as 'everybody's economics'. Could anyone have foreseen in 1871 the tortuous path by which marginal utility economics led via Paretian welfare economics to cost-benefit analysis and dynamic programming? Not for nothing do we speak of a 'marginal revolution' and not a 'marginal utility revolution' but marginalism as a paradigm of economic reasoning is a 20th-century invention; there is as much marginalism in Ricardo as in Jevons or Walras but it is applied to different things.

If we are going to describe the last quarter of the 19th century as a period when economists developed a new 'paradigm', the only defensible definition of that paradigm is the proposition that pricing and resource allocation with fixed supplies of the factors of production is *the* economic problem, largely or entirely dismissing all questions about changes in the quantity and quality of productive resources through time. Whether we label this shift to a new paradigm as a 'revolution', given the fact that it took at least twenty to thirty years to complete and in some sense is still going on, is a matter of words. Jevons, Menger and Walras are not the founders of this new way of looking at economic problems but they are important landmarks in the early stages of the shift of emphasis. That they published nearly simultaneously is a pure coincidence, because their reflections on the problem are actually separated by more than a decade. Only biographical data can tell us why Jevons and Walras (and Gossen) each insisted on the novelty of his ideas, whereas Menger (and Lloyd and Longfield and Jennings) did not. Therefore, to try to explain the origins of the Marginal Revolution in the 1870s is doomed to failure: it was not a marginal *utility* revolution; it was not an abrupt change but only a gradual transformation of old ideas; and it did not happen in the 1870s.

7. The Slow Uphill Struggle

The fact that Jevons, Menger and Walras all published their works within the span of three years, while a coincidence, was not an insignificant coincidence; it encouraged the acceptance of marginal utility economics, or at any rate greatly increased the probability of its early acceptance. Nevertheless, the new economics still failed to make much headway for at least a generation despite the fact that all three founders were academic economists with established reputations, who argued their case persuasively and spared no efforts to push their ideas. The historical problem, therefore, is to explain, not the point in time at which the marginal concept was applied to utility, but rather the delayed victory of marginal utility economics.

This is not a difficult problem provided we do not insist that historians 'retrodict' in essentially the same way that scientists predict. What historians do is to make past events intelligible – they illuminate rather than explain – and in the nature of the case, therefore, there can be no hard and fast rules on whether *A* caused *B* or was merely associated with *B*. It is, therefore, fruitless to argue whether the diffusion of marginal utility economics, as distinct from its genesis, was largely the result of endogenous or exogenous influences. It is precisely in this period that economics began to emerge as a professional discipline with its own network of associations and journals, the dilettante amateur of the past giving way for the first time to the specialist earning his livelihood under the title of 'economist'. A professionalized science necessarily develops its own momentum, the impact of external events being confined to the 'shell' and not reaching the 'core' of the subject. But in 1870, or 1880, or even 1890, shell and core were still deeply intertwined. Economics was becoming professionalized in the last quarter of the 19th century but it still had a long way to go to become a thoroughly professionalized subject.

It seems clear, therefore, that no monocausal explanation can do justice to the long uphill struggle of the marginal revolution. One is struck in reading the treatises of the 1870s and 1880s by the bewildering variety of attitudes adopted toward the principal tenets of classical economics, such as the labour theory of value, the quantity theory of money, the Ricardian theory of differential rent, etc. Jevons, Menger and Walras each in his own way emphasized the methodological advantages of abstracting from historical and institutional considerations in the interest of obtaining perfectly general results from the minimum number of assumptions. But such considerations had little appeal to most contemporary economists, who still cared more about relevance than about rigor. As far as applied problems were concerned, marginal utility was, as we have said earlier, largely irrelevant and the methodological problem that troubled most economists in the critical decade of the 1880s was the issue of induction versus deduction, the conflict between fact gathering and model building. Wherever there was a historicist bias – a pervasive bias in Germany and a widespread one in England – marginal utility economics was dismissed together with English classical political economy as excessively abstract and permeated with implausible assumptions about human behavior. The fact that Jevons and Walras chose to express themselves in mathematical terms was undoubtedly responsible for further resistance to their ideas; the notion of reducing social phenomena to mathematical equations was still new and profoundly disturbing to 19th-century readers. It was the rise of Marxism and Fabianism in the 1880s and 1890s that finally made subjective value theory socially and politically relevant; as the new economics began to furnish effective intellectual ammunition against Marx and Henry George, the view that value theory really did not matter became more difficult to sustain. Furthermore, the addition of marginal productivity to marginal utility in the 1890s related the new economics to the problem of distribution, making it virtually impossible to deny a logical conflict between the ideas of Jevons, Menger and Walras and those of Smith, Ricardo and Mill. In 1891 Marshall provided a reconciliation between marginal utility economics and classical economics which made the new ideas palatable by showing that they could be fitted together into a wider context. But even at this late stage, the Marshallian integration was not immediately accepted on the Continent, and the three interlocking 'revolutions' that had characterized the last two decades of the 19th century – the marginal utility revolution in England and America, the subjectivist revolution in Austria and the general equilibrium revolution in Switzerland and Italy – continued well into the 20th century.

JEVONS

Space is lacking for a detailed treatment of the individual contributions of the subjective value trio. We will deal with Walras in some detail later [see chapter 13]. He is not on the same footing as Menger and Jevons, both of whose works were soon superseded by the second generation of marginal utility theorists. But to convey something of the flavor of the pioneers, we will spend a moment on Jevons' writing simply to demonstrate how much there was still left to do for someone like Marshall in fulfilling Jevons' promise of a new economics.

Jevons was indebted to a host of forerunners but he did not learn as much from them as he might have. For example, he never drew a demand curve, despite the fact that Jenkin's paper on trade unions, published in 1870, made use of the graphic device of demand and supply curves. Similarly, he never developed a theory of the firm although he declared that he owed the idea of investigating economics mathe-matically to Lardner's *Railway Economy* (1850), a book containing the first expo-sition in English of what approximates to the modern theory of the firm. Lardner drew total cost and total revenue functions and showed that profits are maximized at a level of output at which tangents to the two functions become parallel, that is, at the output level for which marginal cost and marginal revenue are equal. Jevons apparently failed to see the full significance of this argument for his reference to it in the first edition of the *Theory of Political Economy* was dropped by the third edition.

It is not merely that Jevons overlooked some of Lardner's ideas. He showed no awareness of the need for a theory of the firm. Cost is a bygone by the time an article comes on the market and its relationship to revenue is only of interest to the producer of the article. Jevons concentrated instead on the willingness of the holder of the article to sell out of a given stock, the case in which costs are indeed irrelevant. Hence, it never occurred to Jevons to use cost curves to build up a supply curve. Jevons was not alone in this. Menger also failed to apply marginalism to production, and like Jevons, he did not draw demand and supply curves despite the fact that the fourth edition of Rau's *Grundsätze* (1844) and Mangoldt's *Grundrisse* (1863) both used demand and supply curves to demonstrate the formation of price.

8. The Theory of Exchange

Jevons approached value theory by looking at two individuals engaging in exchange. Exchange cannot take place unless the relative marginal significance of the com-modity received exceeds that of the commodity given up for each party in exchange. This marginal significance is not a constant magnitude but changes with different persons and under different circumstances. What the classical writers called value in use or total utility is an abstraction. All we know is the relative significance of an increment of one commodity to a decrement of another. In modern parlance, we can obtain the *total* utility of a commodity for an individual only by integrating a differential coefficient, the *marginal* utility of the stock of the commodity.

At this point Jevons formulated the Law of Diminishing Marginal Utility. He appealed to a physiological generalization, citing Richard Jennings as his authority, that the strength of the response to a stimulus diminishes with each repetition of that stimulus within some specified time period. With the publication of Fechner's *Elemente der Psychophysik* (1860), this kind of statement came to be known as the Weber-Fechner Law. Jevons was the only economist in this period to base the law of diminishing marginal utility on a physiological principle. Edgeworth, Pareto and Wicksell noticed the Weber-Fechner Law but made no real use of it. The standard practice of the new economics was to establish the law of diminishing marginal utility on purely introspective grounds.

With the aid of the law of diminishing marginal utility, Jevons proceeded to the 'equation of exchange': the ratios of increments of commodities consumed must, in equilibrium, be equal to the corresponding ratios of the intensities of last wants satisfied, or, as Jevons put it, to the 'final degrees of utility'; and the ratios at which the two goods exchange must be inversely proportional to the final degrees of utility.

With a slight change in nomenclature, the 'equation of exchange' turns into the familiar modern textbook condition of consumer equilibrium: the proportionality of marginal utilities to relative prices.

As Jevons expressed it: let a and b represent the quantities of two goods held initially by two individuals; let x and y be the actual quantities exchanged and ϕ and ψ the final degrees of utility to the respective parties. Then

$$\frac{\phi_1(a-x)}{\psi_1(y)} = \frac{y}{x} = \frac{\phi_2(x)}{\psi_2(b-y)}.$$

For the first individual, for example, the marginal utility of $(a-x)$ goods left over after exchange – or the marginal utility of x goods given up – to the marginal utility of y goods acquired in exchange is inversely proportional to the ratios at which the goods have been exchanged. The higher the importance ascribed to a good, the less of that good anyone is willing to offer in exchange for something else; marginal utility is inversely related to the quantity of goods possessed and therefore to the goods given up in exchange. To convert Jevons' expression to the modern consumer's allocation formula, we look at either individual and observe that an equilibrium allocation of expenditures implies that

$$\frac{MU_x}{MU_y} = \frac{y}{x} = \frac{p_x}{p_y} \quad \text{or} \quad \frac{MU_x}{p_x} = \frac{MU_y}{p_y} = \frac{y}{x}.^1$$

9. Bilateral and Competitive Exchange

Jevons seized upon the case of isolated exchange in the belief that it permitted a simple demonstration of the pure logic of price determination, which might then be carried over to the more complicated case of competitive exchange. But in point of fact, isolated exchange has properties not found in competitive exchange. Exactly ten years after the publication of Jevons' book, Edgeworth showed that isolated exchange, or what he called 'bilateral monopoly', does not yield unique and determinate relative prices. His demonstration of the indeterminacy of bilateral

---

[1] A terminological note for the mathematically sophisticated reader: Jevons' 'final degree of utility' was written du/dx; it is the same thing as Menger's 'lowest importance of satisfactions' or Walras' *rareté*, 'the intensity of the last want satisfied by any given quantity consumed of a commodity'. It indicates the rate of increase of total utility per unit of the commodity acquired. The Austrians later spoke of *Grenznutzen*, the modern equivalent of 'marginal utility'. But marginal utility is not strictly speaking the derivative of utility with respect to quantity but the differential increment of utility. As Marshall points out in the first mathematical note to his *Principles*, marginal utility is not du/dx but $(du/dx)\Delta x$ where $u = f(x)$ is the total utility function of commodity x and Δx is the increment of x consumed; it can be represented by a 'thick straight line', of which the breadth measures the unit affording marginal utility divided by the size of the marginal increment. Present-day textbooks still sometimes speak of marginal utility as the utility of the last unit. This is likely to be misunderstood; the marginal utility of the last unit is the utility of every unit because any unit can be last; to say that marginal utility is the utility of the marginal unit implies that we can obtain total utility by multiplying marginal utility by the number of units consumed, which is incorrect. Marginal utility is the utility of the last unit minus the change in utility of the preceding unit, and so on for every unit, when the last unit is added. Thus, marginal utility $= (du/dx)\Delta x$ and total utility is the integral

$$\int_o^x \frac{du}{dx}\Delta x.$$

monopoly in *Mathematical Psychics*, apart from its intrinsic interest, has an important place in our story, for it marks the first introduction of indifference curves into economics. Edgeworth defined an indifference curve as denoting a combination of two goods, x_1 and x_2, such that they yield equal utility. Instead of the now conventional box diagram introduced by Pareto, in which the different quantities of both goods that each individual holds appear on four axes, Edgeworth turns the axes around and lets the abscissa represent the money offered by Crusoe for Friday's labour – the quantity of x_1 obtained by the individual – and the ordinate the labour offered by Friday – the quantity of x_2 given up (see Figure 8–1). Since the individual will insist upon additional x_1 to offset the loss of an amount of x_2, the slope of the indifference curves will be positive. Since $dx_1 MU_1$ will be the gain of utility from an increment dx_1 and $dx_2 MU_2$ will be the loss of utility from a decrement dx_2, the slope of the indifference curves with respect to x_1 axis will be

$$\frac{dx_2}{dx_1} = \frac{MU_1}{MU_2},$$

as given by the condition that $dx_1 MU_1 = dx_2 MU_2$ for movements along an indifference curve. Although Edgeworth drew only one curve for each trader, a family of indifference curves fills the plane.

Figure 8–1

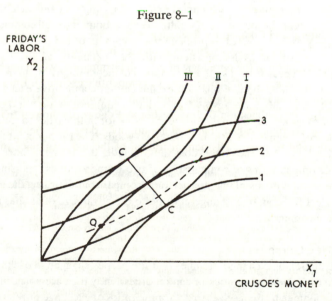

The 'curves of indifference' 1, 2, 3 are those of Friday possessing x_2 but no x_1; curves I, II, III are those of Crusoe possessing x_1 but no x_2. Edgeworth provided some arguments to show that these curves are convex with respect to their own axes. The loci of tangency points of the two sets of indifference curves form what Edgeworth called 'the contract curve', *CC*. The final contract between the two traders must take place on *CC* because any other point is such that one party may improve his situation without worsening the situation of the other by moving back to the contract curve. Thus from point *Q*, Crusoe can move to a higher indifference curve II while Friday remains on the same indifference curve 2. However, any point on the *CC* curve is possible equilibrium and the precise position along *C* depends on bargaining and strategy. This problem of indeterminacy does not arise under competitive exchange because all traders then face the same given prices for all goods.

Coming back to Jevons, having analyzed two-party, two-commodity barter trade, Jevons tried to generalize the equation of exchange by introducing the concept of 'trading bodies', letting ϕ and ψ stand for the collective marginal utilities of buyers and sellers. This is, of course, completely unsatisfactory, as Edgeworth soon pointed out. First of all, we are not told how the utility functions are aggregated. Second, the marginal utility of a product for a trading body is the average of the individual marginal utilities of its members; but competitive exchange cannot be considered a simple function of the size of the initial supply of goods as with bilateral exchange. The average marginal utility also depends on the distribution of this supply before and after the exchange. Be that as it may, from the rule that both parties maximize satisfaction in bilateral exchange when each person 'procures such quantities of commodities that the final degrees of utility of any pair of commodities are inversely as the ratios of exchange of the commodities', Jevons quickly concluded that 'so far as is consistent with the inequality of wealth in every community, all commodities are distributed by exchange so as to produce the maximum of benefit'. The operative clause here is 'so far as is consistent with the inequality of wealth in every community'. But even if we take the distribution of income as given, it is not possible to assume from an analysis of bilateral exchange that competitive exchange maximizes satisfactions all round. Jevons forgot that in equilibrium it is not the marginal utility of each good by itself that must be the same for both parties to the exchange but the *ratio* of the marginal utilities of the two goods. The former condition would include the latter but the latter does not include the former. Since utility is measurable only in terms of comparisons of two or more goods, and since Jevons denied the possibility of making interpersonal comparisons of utility, the conclusion that 'a perfect freedom of exchange must be to the advantage of all' has no clearly assignable meaning.

10. The Catena

Jevons' 'equation of exchange' assumes that the parties engaged in exchange are in possession of a given initial stock of commodities. Only then are unspecified utility functions adequate by themselves to determine ratios of exchange or relative prices. When output is known, we might paraphrase, marginal utility determines value. What determines output? Jevons' answer is given in the wellknown catena:

> Cost of production determines supply;
> Supply determines final degree of utility;
> Final degree of utility determines value.

This chain of causation is not only naive but conflicts with the claim that value is determined by utility. The first two steps are merely suggestions, since Jevons supplied no theory of production. His only explanation of the connection between costs of production and utility is that the marginal utility of the product obtained in equilibrium must equal the marginal disutility of producing it. This hardly depicts equilibrium for the entrepreneur because it depicts 'feelings' as one of the coordinates. Even the last step in the argument is not quite right. Those engaged in exchange compare final degrees of utility of both goods traded, and from these comparisons every individual arrives at a set of demand prices. It is these scales of demand that determine prices. But Jevons expressed utility schedules in pecuniary terms without explicitly introducing demand curves and reasoned directly from the equivalence of marginal utilities to the equivalence of price offers. When money is one of the two goods being traded, it is possible to construct a demand curve for the commodity in question by assuming that the marginal utility of money remains constant. Jevons realized that this assumption is legitimate only when additional expenditures on the commodity do not 'appreciably affect the possessions of the purchaser'. But he made no effort to show how market demand curves are built up from individual demand curves constructed on such *ceteris paribus* assumptions.

11. Disutility of Labour

Jevons' theory of labour supply is his most important contribution to the main stream of neoclassical economics. If human effort has a positive value on account of its irksomeness, he argued, labour will be supplied as long as the individual contemplates a preponderance of satisfaction over dissatisfaction. On the assumption that the disutility of labour first decreases and then increases with the duration of effort, while the marginal utility of the product that labour produces falls monotonically, Jevons illustrated the argument graphically (see Figure 8–2). The upper curve expresses the decreasing marginal utility of the product on the supposition that the product increment is due solely to additional labour. The lower curve shows the disutility of labour per units of product. When $ab = bc$, the utility of the product equals the disutility of labour required to produce it; hence, the amount of labour that will be supplied in equilibrium is that implied by $0b$ units of product.

Jevons' statement of the theory requires that units of painful effort remain of the same efficiency throughout the working day. Moreover, it assumes a nonexisting symmetry between the factors governing the demand for and supply of labour. The argument could be restated, however, to overcome these objections. The more serious criticism is that Jevons' theory does not seem to be in accord with typical methods of hiring labour in a modern economy. The idea that workers can balance efforts against rewards is realistic enough for piecework, where the worker faces given rates of pay and adjusts his supply of effort so as to maximize income and minimize subjective sacrifice. But under modern factory conditions, labour services are generally sold in lumpy amounts on a take-it-or-leave-it basis; the labourer may have to work far in excess of the point at which the marginal utility of income equals the marginal disutility of effort. The indivisibility of labour may be overcome by

Figure 8–2

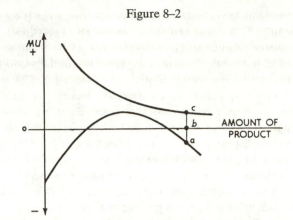

absenteeism and lateness but this may not be enough to equate irksomeness to the rate of reward. Furthermore, the disutility of work is a function not only of duration and intensity but also of environment and the quality of work to be done. Almost all of these are in some degree beyond the control of workers. Jevons' notion of workers freely determining the hours they will work simply does not fit the facts of the labour market.

Despite these objections, Marshall and Edgeworth accepted Jevons' analysis of the short-run supply curve of labour. They insisted that the possibility of varying the intensity of work, the existence of piece-rate wages, the flexibility of overtime hours and the possibility of choosing different occupations with different working hours were important enough to endow the Jevonian conception with general applicability. The Austrian writers, insisting that the utility of the product is the sole determinant of value, refused to admit that the individual workman can effectively vary the daily amounts of his physical labour and so influence product prices. Böhm-Bawerk went so far as to deny the fact that disutility can influence the allocation of labour services between various uses, arguing that skilled labour is better rewarded than unskilled labour, although it is no more irksome. But this comes down to the assertion that competition fails to equalize the money incomes of alternative occupations; it should have been clear from Book I, chapter 10 of the *Wealth of Nations* that even if the disutility of labour does not directly affect the quantity of effort supplied, its influence on the choice of occupations does affect wage rates and therefore relative prices. The upshot of this debate was that the English School at least attempted to discuss the supply curve of labour, whereas the Austrians effectively closed the door to the subject.

12. Negatively or Positively Sloped Labour Supply Curves

All through this period economists could not make up their minds whether the short-run supply curve of labour was positively or negatively inclined. In *Risk, Uncertainty, and Profit* (1921), Knight contended that it is always negatively inclined.

At the margin of indifference, he said, the rational worker will equate the marginal disutility of labour and the marginal utility of income (see Figure 8–3). If wages are raised, the marginal utility of income will be reduced. Thus, the added disutility of the last unit of labour time will now exceed the added utility of the last unit of money wage. Hence, the worker will want to shorten his working day when wages rise.

Figure 8–3

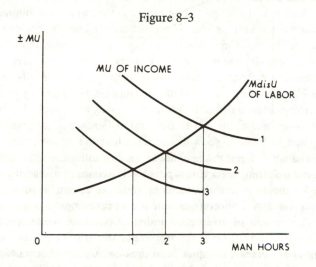

Knight's argument is that a rise in wage rates lowers the worker's schedule of the marginal utility of money, which is therefore cut by the curve of marginal disutility at a point indicating fewer hours. The negative supply curve of labour is then deduced by correlating hours and wage rates. In a now classic article, published in 1930, Robbins showed that the labour supply curve may be backward bending, that is, positively sloped over a range and then becoming negatively sloped. It all depends on the elasticity of the supply of effort, or as he put it, the 'elasticity of demand for income in terms of effort'. Probably, for the mass of workers, this elasticity is greater than unity, meaning that a unit of extra effort will be expended only if income rises thereby more than proportionately. In that case, the supply curve of labour will be positively sloped. If the elasticity coefficient is less than unity, however, the supply curve will be negatively sloped.

Since the advent of the indifference-curve technique, the matter can be put even more simply: it all depends on the relative weight of the substitution effect versus the income effect of a rise in wage rates. If labour is specific to an occupation and perfectly immobile, the supply curve of labour may be negatively sloped; having no alternatives, the worker is likely to relax his efforts when returns to labour increase. There being no substitution effect, the income effect is supreme – Knight's case. But whenever it is possible to switch employment or freely to substitute work for leisure, the supply curve *may* be positively sloped. Needless to say, all this concerns the supply curve of individual workers. Even if all the individual supply curves are negatively inclined, the aggregate short-run supply of labour may and usually will vary positively with the wage rate, owing to variations in the participation rate of women and first entrants into the labour force.

13. Capital Theory

Little need be said about Jevons' other contributions. His essay on 'A Serious Fall in the Value of Gold' would have given him a place in the history of economic thought even if he had written nothing else: it probed deeply into the problem of index numbers and for the first time constructed a price index weighted by base-year quantities for a period as long as a half-century. Among his other pioneering inductive studies was that of the connection between cycles in sunspots and business activity. The idea that there are rhythms of temperature caused by solar activity which affect crop yields and thereafter economic activity in general is by no means as silly as it has been made out to be. But Jevons' statistical case was singularly unconvincing and he failed to show theoretically how this or any other exogenous disturbance is capable of generating endogenous fluctuations.

Finally, there is Jevons' theory of capital, which contains all the ingredients of Böhm-Bawerk's theory except the stress on time preference. Jevons treated the productivity of capital as a function of time alone; investment is a quantity of two dimensions, the amount of investment and the period for which the amount is invested. Jevons in effect laid down the proposition that is at the core of the Austrian theory of capital: an increase of capital is tantamount to a lengthening of the period of investment [see chapter 12, section 8]. As Jevons showed, the rate of interest depends on the ratio of the product increment to the increment of capital. Let $F(t)$ be the production function, giving the product of a certain amount of labour as a monotonically increasing function of t. For $t + \Delta t$, the total product equals $F(t + \Delta t)$, and the marginal product equals $F(t + \Delta t) - F(t)$. When we extend the time of production by Δt, Jevons argued, we allow the product $F(t)$ which we could have received at end of time t to remain invested for the extra period Δt. Hence, the increase of capital in this case $= \Delta t \cdot F(t)$. Dividing the increment of output by the amount of additional investment, we have the marginal product of capital:

$$\frac{F(f + \Delta t) - F(t)}{\Delta t F(t)} .$$

In the continuous case, the limit of this ratio determines the instantaneous rate of interest

$$\frac{dF(t)}{dt} \frac{1}{F(t)} = \frac{F'()}{F(t)} .$$

The rate of interest, therefore, is equal to 'the rate of increase of the produce divided by the whole produce'.

This is clearly a marginal productivity theory of interest, though of an oversimplified kind. Jevons never applied this kind of argument to wages and rents. He seems to have been aware of the general application of marginal productivity analysis to all the factors of production but he never worked it out. There is reason to think, however, that if he had not died prematurely in 1882 at the age of forty-six he would have joined Wicksteed and Marshall in England, John Bates Clark in America, Wicksell in Sweden, and Walras in Lausanne in formulating the general marginal productivity theory of distribution.

OTHER FORERUNNERS

Marshall's early works are all of a later date than the treatises of Jevons, Menger and Walras but we have Marshall's own authority for the assertion that his theory of value and distribution was 'practically completed in the years 1867 to 1870'. It was not to Jevons but to Cournot and Thünen that Marshall was indebted for his leading ideas. 'Under the guidance of Cournot, and in a less degree of von Thünen, I was led to attach great importance to the fact that . . . the demand for a thing is a continuous function, of which the "marginal" increment is, in stable equilibrium, balanced against the corresponding increment of its cost'. In the same way that we discussed Jevons simply to indicate the unfinished character of much of his work, we will now touch lightly on some of the forerunners of the Marginal Revolution merely to show that even if Jevons, Menger and Walras had never lived, all the ingredients of marginalism were available in the writings of these lesser known figures. Once we add Cournot, Thünen, Dupuit and Gossen, to mention only a few, we arrive at Marshall almost without benefit of the three founding fathers of the Marginal Revolution.

14. Cournot on Profit Maximization

Cournot, in a book that for sheer originality and boldness of conception has no equal in the history of economic theory, was the first writer to define and to draw a demand function. He took no interest in utility theory but assumed as a matter of course that the market demand curve was negatively inclined: this market demand curve did not express the quantities which the sum of consumers in a market *would* purchase at different prices, holding constant 'population, and the distribution of wealth, tastes, the habits of the consuming population', but rather the actual quantities they did purchase annually at an average of annual prices – Cournot's demand curve is an empirical relationship between sales and prices. He treated monopoly as the pure case and defined a demand function, $D = F(p)$, a total revenue function, $R = pF(p)$, and a marginal revenue function, $M = F(p) + pF'(p)$ where $F'(p) < 0$, objectively given to the monopolist. The given revenue functions are then confronted with total and marginal cost functions in order to show that instantaneous gains will be maximized if the monopolist produces an output at which marginal cost equals marginal revenue. To prove the existence and uniqueness of this maximum, Cournot employed the familiar tests of calculus: the first derivative of the total profit function, $\pi = pF(p) - \phi(D)$, must vanish and the second derivative must be negative. All this in 1838!

In Book V, chapter 13, of his *Principles*, Marshall adopted Cournot's analysis of profit maximization but expressed the equilibrium conditions in terms of the monopolist's total cost and total revenue rather than in terms of the marginal values of these variables. And so the concept of *marginal* revenue had to be rediscovered in the 1920s when the case of imperfect competition drew theorists' attention to the possibility of a downward-sloping demand curve confronting the individual firm.

15. Duopoly Theory

Cournot not only founded the theory of pure monopoly but also the theory of duopoly. His theory of duopoly is based on the competitive assumption that buyers name prices and that sellers merely adjust their output to given prices. Each duopolist estimates the demand function for the product and then sets the quantity sold on the assumption that his rival's output remains fixed. Although each duopolist adjusts his output simultaneously to the output of the other, each assuming at every point that the rival's output is constant, a determinate solution nevertheless emerges. Cournot demonstrated this result graphically by means of reaction curves (Figure 8–4). Each reaction curve shows the optimum output of one duopolist as a function of the output of its rival, assuming that either can supply the entire output in question (mineral water) and that the cost of producing mineral water is zero. Assume that A is producing A_1; then duopolist B will maximize profits by producing B_1; once B produces B_1, however, A will maximize profits by a lower volume of sales, say A_2; given A_2, however, B is motivated to incease output to B_2, and so forth. Equilibrium is reached when the two ouput levels are compatible with each other at $\bar{A} = \bar{B}$; moreover, as Cournot points out, this equilibrium is 'stable' under the conditions specified in the sense that any deviation from it leads to reactions, that bring the quantities supplied back to the levels $\bar{A}$ and $\bar{B}$.

Figure 8–4

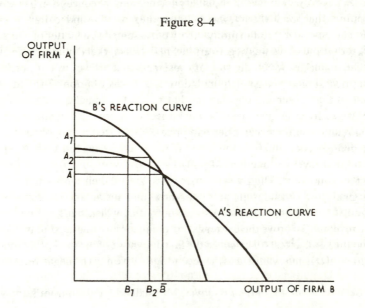

In the 1880s, the French mathematician Bertrand criticized Cournot's solution and suggested instead that sellers set prices and that each seller determines his price on the assumption that his rival's price, rather than his output, remains constant. Edgeworth, in the 'Theory of Monopoly' (1897), carried the argument one step further and introduced uncertainty of mutual reactions, concluding that this rendered the solution indeterminate. In the 1920s, the reaction patterns were made to include sales, costs, quality of product and service competition. Cournot's symmetry assumption about the intentions and policies of the two firms, grounded on the arbitrary notion that firms never test each other's reactions, was discarded once and for all. But as soon as it is admitted that the two parties will indeed try to test each other's reactions, we have a whole catalog of cases, depending upon what we assume about their behavior. They may go to the 'Cournot point', the case of noncooperative equilibrium in which each party maximizes profits subject to some notion about the other party's reaction; they may go to the 'minimax point' and maximize profits subject to the assumption that the rival will adopt the most damaging policy; or they may go to the point of cooperative equilibrium and maximize joint profits. Each of these assumptions entails different price-quantity outcomes, and on *a priori* grounds there is no reason for believing that one outcome is more likely than another.

Cournot did more than invent the theory of pure monopoly and the theory of duopoly: he also planted the idea that perfect competition is the limiting case of the entire spectrum of market structures defined in terms of the number of sellers. He showed that his duopolists would end up with a common price for mineral water that would be lower than the price that would obtain under simple monopoly but higher than the one generated by free competition with many sellers; similarly, monopoly produced the lowest output and competition with many sellers produced the highest output, the duopoly case falling in between the two. Indeed, he entertained the curious notion that the homogeneous output of any set of n firms would precisely equal $n/n + 1$ times the output of a competitive industry: as the numbers of sellers increase, the output of the industry converges in the limit on the output of a perfectly competitive industry. Here, in embryo, is the later popular notion of perfect competition as the standard for judging the outcome of non-competitive market structures.

16. Dupuit and the French Engineering Tradition
Since its establishment in 1747, the Ecole des Ponts et Chaussées (School of Civil Engineering) in Paris had gradually established a tradition among its teachers and graduates of concern with the economic evaluation of public works. One of these graduates was Jules Dupuit who published a series of papers between 1844 and 1853 on the problem of measuring the social benefits of publicly provided goods and services, in the course of which he developed the distinction between total and marginal utility in relation to demand prices. Although Dupuit wrote after Cournot, and although at one point both lived and worked in Paris at the same time, there is no evidence that Dupuit had ever read Cournot (or *vice versa*). Nevertheless, there are striking similarities in their treatment of demand. Like Cournot, Dupuit believed

that the inverse relationship between price and quantity was an obvious fact of experience that required no theoretical justification but, unlike Cournot, Dupuit interpreted the demand function as simply a function of marginal utilities: the demand function is negatively inclined because the additional utility derived from the purchase of additional units of the same commodity normally declines.

Analyzing the social benefits of publicly provided goods, such as drinking water, roads, canals and bridges, Dupuit realized that the value of these benefits may be greater than that indicated by the price actually paid for the service, inasmuch as most people would be willing to pay more for the service than they actually do pay. Assuming that production costs are zero, he constructed a marginal utility curve for a collective good by supposing that the State charges the maximum toll for each additional unit of service, lowering the toll by small steps as it offers additional units. In this way total receipts from the service are equal to the whole area under the demand curve; in utility terms, the total benefit from the existence of the facility is likewise measured by the whole area under the marginal utility curve. The 'relative utility', or what Marshall was later to call the 'consumers' surplus', is equal to the excess of total utility over marginal utility, multiplied by the number of units of the service. It is measured by the roughly triangular area under the demand curve above the price-quantity rectangle.

Dupuit's own diagram, with the axes transposed, is shown in Figure 8–5.[2] NP is the marginal utility or demand curve for the services of a bridge. Op is the toll, Or is the quantity demanded, $Ornp$ is the total utility obtained from the bridge, and pPn is the consumers' surplus. A reduction in the toll by pp' results in a net gain of consumers' surplus of qnn' (the shaded triangle): the total gain to consumers of $p'pnn'$ minus the loss in receipts of $p'pnq$.

Without drawing a supply curve, Dupuit went on to consider the producers' surplus from selling the services of a bridge at a uniform price per unit. If the supply curve represents the marginal cost curve of the industry, the 'producers' surplus' is equal to the excess of the money received in the industry over the aggregate marginal costs, namely, the shaded triangle spn (see Figure 8–6). The total benefit of the bridge to the community is the sum of consumers' and producers' surplus represented by the large curvilinear triangle sPn. With the aid of some such implicit construction, Dupuit proceeded to develop some elementary theorems about the net social loss of a rise in tolls on public services.

When we compare Dupuit's original paper 'On the Measurement of the Utility of Public Works' (1844), with Marshall's refinement of the same concept [see chapter 9, section 13] we are struck by the inadequacy of Dupuit's discussion. Dupuit never realized that the argument hinges on the measurability of utility. A consumers' surplus from one particular public service may be dependent on surpluses arising from other services consumed. Moreover, the surpluses of different persons may not be additive: the placing of the apostrophe in 'consumers' surplus' tacitly assumes

---

[2] Like Cournot and other mathematical economists of the day, Dupuit placed the independent variable, price, on the x axis and the dependent variable, quantity, on the y axis. It was Marshall who first reversed this standard procedure so as to maintain the same axis labels for both individual demand functions, $q = f(p)$, and market demand functions, $p = f(q)$ [see chapter 10, section 14].

Figure 8–5

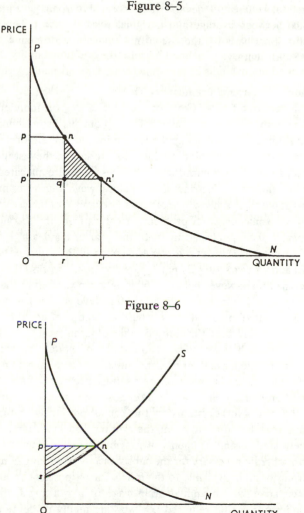

Figure 8–6

interpersonal comparisons of utility. There are further problems connected with the measurement of producers' surpluses. Nevertheless, Dupuit's paper, primitive as it is, is a remarkable performance.

Moreover, Dupuit went on in other papers to consider the factors that give rise to monopoly pricing, analyzing the output and welfare effects of discriminatory pricing on the part of monopolists, whether public or private. The preoccupation with the theory of pure monopoly is in fact a common theme among all the nineteenth-century engineer-economists: Dupuit in France, Dionysius Lardner in England, Charles Ellett Jr. in America, and many others. The 1840s and 1850s saw the coming of railways and the Railway Era naturally directed attention to the economics of public utilities. The regulated pricing of railroads threw up the contrast between marginal and total welfare and the heavy fixed costs of railroads gave prominence to the divergence between average and marginal costs. In short, here at last is a concrete institutional basis for the rise of marginalism in economics in the third quarter of the 19th century.

17. Thünen's Marginal Productivity Theory

Despite the pioneering efforts of Cournot and Dupuit, the true founder of marginal analysis in the 19th century is Thünen. Throughout his astonishing book, *The Isolated State*, Thünen relentlessly applied the principle that all forms of expenditure should be carried to the point at which the product of the last unit equals its cost: the total product is maximized only when resources are allocated equimarginally. A presentation of his doctrine of the 'natural wage' illustrates his procedure and affords us at the same time with another early example of the use of differential calculus to solve a maximization problem. It comes from the second volume of Thünen's *Isolated State*, published in 1850, the year of his death, that is, twelve years after Cournot's *Researches into the Mathematical Principles of the Theory of Wealth* (1838) and six years after Dupuit's paper on public works (1844), neither of which Thünen had read. Nevertheless, 1850 is only two years after the appearance of Mill's *Principles* and more than a decade before Jevons' 'Brief Account' (1862).

Consider an 'isolated' or 'ideal' state where all land is of equal fertility. At its outer edge land rent is zero, so the entire product of farms located in this outer ring of cultivation is divided between workers and owners of capital. Workers cultivating existing plots are free to leave their present employments to take up new land; the wages of such workers are in excess of their subsistence needs; and wages are the only expense of production. Since any worker possessing sufficient capital is free to move from the hired-worker status to the capital-producing status, wages on existing farms must be equal to what the worker and his capital can earn by cultivating new land. Using Thünen's own symbols, let a represent the known annual amount of grain necessary for the subsistence of a working family and y the unknown surplus of grain available to the family for purposes of accumulation, so that $(a + y)$ is the unknown annual grain-wage of a working family; q is the unknown quantity of capital required per working family to develop new land, measured in $(a + y)$ units of grain; z is the unknown rate of profit in the economy; and p is the known average annual product of a working family when assisted by q units of capital. Thus,

$$p = (a + y) + q(a + y)z.$$

Under perfect competition,

$$z = [p - (a + y)] / q(a + y).$$

Thünen assumes that each working family converts its annual surplus, y, into capital, q, and that each wishes to maximize the annual returns to the capital, expressed as:

$$zy = [p - (a + y)]y / q(a + y).$$

This is maximized when

$$\frac{d}{dy}\left\{ [p - (a + y)]y / q(a + y) \right\} = 0.$$

Thünen solves this equation for $(a + y)$, which yields $\sqrt{ap}$, the geometric mean between the necessary subsistence level, a, and the average product, p, of a working family.[3] He now turns the problem around to find the amount of capital per family, q, which maximizes zy and solves for the wage as the remainder of the product after profit has been paid, showing that the wage that would emerge as the marginal product of labour in such circumstances is, once again, $\sqrt{ap}$.

Most of Thünen's later critics seized on the fact that his reasoning really takes the rate of profit, z, as given instead of treating it as an unknown to be determined. In addition, Thünen reduced capital to units of grain and ultimately to quantities of labour, which suggests that he was really thinking of capital as circulating capital, more or less ignoring fixed capital. In this he was simply the child of his times. Finally, Thünen treated the concept of subsistence wages, a, as if it were subject to precise quantitative measurement; here for once he was behind the times because even Ricardo had warned his readers that the subsistence wage is a cultural and not a biological minimum, being influenced by workers' expectations and aspirations.

But perhaps none of these criticisms go as deep as the objection to Thünen's implicit assumption that working families should aim at maximizing yz, the surplus of *one* year's wages, rather than the whole income from this year's labour and all the invested capital they own; or, to express it another way, that they should aim at maximizing their short-run income from capital alone rather than their joint lifetime income of wages and profits. On deeper reflection, it appears that Thünen supposed that workers would divide themselves into two mutually exclusive groups: (1) a first group that would produce capital goods, that is, seeds and foodstuffs, and (2) a second group that would produce grain for final demand with the physical capital produced by the first group. In consequence, what Thünen ultimately provides is the analysis of a peculiar two-sector model in which one sector maximizes income from capital and the other maximizes income from work.

Thünen's magic formula for the wage rate, $\sqrt{ap}$, was ridiculed almost as soon as it was announced, in part because it was misinterpreted as depicting the long-run equilibrium wage rate that would prevail under normal conditions in a capitalist economy, whereas it was designed deliberately to reform the real world by means of

[3] $\dfrac{d}{dy}\left\{ [p - (a + y)]y/q(a + y) \right\} = \dfrac{d}{dy}\,(py - ay - y^2)/q(a + y) = 0$

$$= \frac{(a+y)(p - a - 2y) - (py - ay - y^2)}{(a + y)^2} = 0.$$

Therefore
$$(a + y)(p - a - 2y) = (py - ay - y^2)$$
$$ap - a^2 - 2ay - 2y^2 = -y^2$$
$$a^2 + y^2 + 2ay = ap$$
$$(a + y)^2 = ap$$
$$(a + y) = \sqrt{ap}.$$

profit-sharing in what would nowadays be called a 'labour-managed market economy'. Perhaps if he had called it the 'just wage', he might have been better understood. He had become convinced in the closing years of his life that the low wages and poverty of large sections of the working class in much of Europe was principally due to the absence of free land; America was less troubled by poverty, he thought, because of free land available on the frontier. It was thoughts such as these that gave rise to the notion of a 'natural wage' that emerges, not spontaneously from a competitive process under a regime of private ownership of capital, but by the self-determination of voluntary agents on the frontiers of the 'isolated state' where land is free. Thünen claimed that his formula for the natural wage was approximated under frontier conditions in the U.S.A. but he nevertheless put it forward as an abstract theorem that held strictly true only under the special assumptions of his model of the 'isolated state'.

Be that as it may, his treatment of distribution anticipated the whole of what later came to be known as the marginal productivity theory of distribution [see chapter 11] and in some respects he improved even on the presentation of John Bates Clark, which came almost fifty years later. Thünen varied the inputs of labour, while holding capital and land constant, the inputs of capital, while holding labour and land constant, and of course the inputs of land while holding capital and labour constant, and he even emphasized the impact of variations in factor and product prices on the optimum input mix. His analysis culminated in the perfectly modern statement that net revenue is maximized when each factor is employed to the point at which its marginal value product (*Wert des Mehrertrags*) is equalized to its marginal factor cost (*Mehraufwand*). Although the discussion proceeds in verbal terms, illustrated by numerical examples, Thünen correctly points out that the marginal product of a factor is a partial differential coefficient of a multi-variable production function. Moreover, apart from clearly recognising the distinction between fixed and variable factors and between average and marginal returns of a factor, Thünen took great care to define the input of capital, labour and land in strictly homogeneous units, observing that this condition was rarely obtained in practice – this too was literally sixty years ahead of his time.

Even all this does not exhaust Thünen's contributions to economics [see chapter 14]. His sophisticated treatment of the concept of marginal productivity, his use of differential calculus and marginal reasoning to provide equilibrium solutions of economic problems, and his perfectly general statement of the 'law' of variable proportions make Thünen the first truly modern economist.

18. Gossen's Second Law

Our fourth and last pioneer is Hermann Heinrich Gossen, whose *Entwicklung*, published in Germany in 1854, went completely unnoticed at the time. Bitterly disappointed with the poor reception of his work – which, he had claimed, would do for economics what Copernicus had done for astronomy – Gossen recalled all the unsold copies of the book and destroyed them. In consequence, when Jevons rediscovered the book in 1878, he and Walras only managed to find a few copies still remaining. Walras was amazed to see that Gossen had not only formulated the principle of diminishing marginal utility and graphed it but had also grasped the distinction, which Dupuit never did, between a negatively inclined marginal utility curve and a negatively inclined demand curve. Similarly, Jevons was astonished to find that Gossen had formulated a theory of the marginal disutility of labour strikingly similar to his own, including a virtual replica of his own diagram of the equalization of the marginal utility of the product and the marginal disutility of work (see above Figure 8–2). Both of them were particularly struck by what soon came to be called Gossen's 'second law': 'A person maximizes his utility when he distributes his available money among the various goods so that he obtains the same amount of satisfaction from the last unit of money spent upon each commodity'.

NOTES ON FURTHER READING

The causes of the 'marginal revolution' is a subject that has been intensively investigated in recent years. A whole issue of *HOPE*, Fall, 1972, reprinted as *The Marginal Revolution in Economics*, eds. R. D. C. Black, A. W. Coats and C. D. W. Goodwin (1973), is devoted to it. A. W. Coats' 'Retrospect and Prospect', the closing piece in that volume, gives an excellent overview of current thinking about the marginal revolution as a historical problem. I have borrowed in the text from my own opening paper to the symposium. This issue of *HOPE* complements another indispensable source book for the debate on the marginal revolution: R. S. Howey, *The Rise of the Marginal Utility School, 1870–1889* (1960). Howey analyzes in loving detail the similar and dissimilar themes of the 'triumvirate', their sources and inspirations, the reviews that their books received and the slow spread and subsequent refinements of marginal utility thinking.

For a quick survey of the state of economic thought around 1870 in England, Germany, Austria, France and the United States, see Hutchison, *Review of Economic Doctrines*, chaps. 1, 8, 12, and 16. Hutchison denies any institutional basis for the rise of marginal economics other than the pricing problems of public utilities: 'Insularity and Cosmopolitanism in Economic Ideas, 1870–1914', *AER*, May, 1955. On this question, see also G. J. Stigler, 'The Influence of Events and Policies on Economic Theory', *AER*, 1960, reprinted in his *Essays in the History of Economics* and in *RHET*. The policy views of Jevons, Marshall and other first-generation members of the marginalist school are canvassed in T. W. Hutchison, 'Economists and Economic Policy in Britain After 1870', *HOPE*, Fall, 1969. The rise of the English Historical School is traced by A. W. Coats, 'The Historicist Reaction in English Political Economy, 1870–1890', *Ec*, May, 1954. G. M. Koot, 'T. E. Cliffe Leslie, Irish Social Reform and the Origins of the English Historical School of Economics', *HOPE*, Fall, 1975, shows that English historicism was a home-grown product, not imported from Germany. While we are on the subject of the German Historical School, there is one and only one indispensable book: G. Eisermann, *Die Grundlagen des Historismus in der deutschen Nationalökonomie* (1956). For a good textbook treatment, however, distinguishing between the English and German Historical Schools, see H. W. Spiegel, *The Growth of Economic Thought* (2nd edn., 1982), chaps. 17 and 18.

S. G. Checkland attributes the intellectual stagnation in British economics in the 1860s to the hegemony of Mill and the academic authority of Fawcett and Cairnes: 'Economic Opinion in England as Jevons Found It', *MS*, May, 1951. But N. B. de Marchi, 'The "Noxious" Influence of Authority: A Correction of Jevons' Charge', *JLE*, August 1973, shows that there was no 'Mill faction' which discriminated against original thinkers. E. Kauder argues that the delayed acceptance of utility theory in England was due to its predominantly Protestant culture: 'The Retarded Acceptance of the Marginal Utility Theory', *QJE*, 1953, reprinted in *RHET* and with slight alterations in his book, _A History of Marginal Utility Theory_ (1965), chap. 1; for a cogent criticism of this thesis, see 'Comment' by J. P. Henderson, _QJE_, August, 1955.

On Menger and the background of German economics before 1870, see G. J. Stigler's generous tribute in his _Production and Distribution Theories_ (1941), chap. 6, in contrast to F. H. Knight's negative judgment in his introduction to the English translation of Menger's _Principles_ (1950). A recent centenary volume, _Carl Menger and the Austrian School of Economics_, eds. J. R. Hicks and W. Weber (1973), contains a number of useful articles, particularly those by F. A. Hayek, T. W. Hutchison, K. Menger, W. Weber, E. Streissler and K. W. Rothschild. See also S. Bostaph, 'The Methodological Debate Between Carl Menger and the German Historicists', _AEJ_, September, 1978; and M. Alter, 'Carl Menger and Homo Œconomicus: Some Thoughts on Austrian Theory and Methodology', _JEI_, March, 1982. W. Jaffé, 'Menger, Jevons and Walras De-Homogenized', _EQ_, 1976, reprinted in _William Jaffé's Essays on Walras_, ed. D. A. Walker (1983), stresses the differences between the three cofounders of the marginal utility tradition.

R. K. Merton's theory of multiple discoveries is developed in a number of papers included in his _Sociology of Science: Theory and Empirical Investigations_, ed. N. W. Storer (1973).

W. S. Jevons' _Theory of Political Economy_ is available in a paperback edition with a useful introduction by R. D. C. Black (1970). Any further reading on Jevons must begin with Keynes's sparkling essay in _Essays in Biography_, chap. 4, reprinted in _DET_. L. Robbins discusses 'The Place of Jevons in the History of Economic Thought', _MS_, 1936, reprinted in his _Evolution of Modern Economic Theory_ (1970) and in _ETHA_; B. H. Higgins stresses Jevons' views on utility theory in 'W. S. Jevons – A Centenary Estimate', _MS_, 6, 2, 1935. Stigler, _Production and Distribution Theories_, chap. 2, is particularly useful on Jevons' theory of labour. Several articles in _MS_, March, 1972, and December, 1982, reassesses Jevons' contributions to economic thought. See, in particular, three papers by R. D. C. Black, the editor of the _Papers and Correspondence of William Stanley Jevons_ in seven volumes (1972–9): 'Jevons, Marginalism and Manchester' _MS_, March, 1972; 'Jevons, Bentham and De Morgan', _Ec_, May, 1972; and 'W. S. Jevons and the Foundation of Modern Economics', _HOPE_, Fall, 1972. See also his grand summing-up in 'W. S. Jevons, 1835–82', _Pioneers of Modern Economics in Britain_, eds. D. P. O'Brien and J. R. Presnell (1981).

Marshall's 1872 review of Jevons' _Theory_, reprinted in _Memorials of Alfred Marshall_, ed. A. C. Pigou (1925), makes an interesting contrast with the later treatment in his _Principles_, Appendix I. See also P. H. Wicksteed, 'On Certain Passages in Jevons' _Theory of Political Economy_', _QJE_, 1889, reprinted in his _Commonsense of Political Economy_, II. Jevons' early paper, 'Brief Account of a General Mathematical Theory of Political Economy' (1862), is reprinted in _ETHA_. On the Knight-Robbins controversy over the supply curve of labour, see Douglas, _Theory of Wages_, chap. 12.

R. M. Robertson discusses Jevons' English forerunners in a brilliant essay: 'Jevons and his Precursors', _Ecom_, July, 1951. D. L. Hooks, 'Monopoly Price Discrimination in 1850: Dionysius Lardner', _HOPE_, Spring, 1973, reexamines the views of one of the most original minor economists of the 1850s who directly influenced Jevons. Fleeming Jenkin's paper on trade unions (1870), which stimulated Jevons to publish his _Theory_ prematurely, is reprinted in _Readings in Economics of Taxation_, eds. R. A. Musgrave and C.S. Shoup (1959). A. D. Brownlie and F. F. Lloyd Prichard, 'Professor Fleeming Jenkin, 1833–1885: Pioneer in Engineering and Political Economy', _OEP_, November, 1963, provide the first complete account and assessment of Jenkin's contributions to economics.

On the history of mathematical economics before Cournot, an esoteric subject at best, see R. M. Robertson, 'Mathematical Economics before Cournot', _JPE_, December, 1949; C. D. Calsoyas, 'The Mathematical Theory of Monopoly in 1839: Charles Ellet, Jr.', _JPE_, April, 1950; and the monograph of R. D. Theocharis, _Early Developments in Mathematical Economics_ (2nd edn, 1983), which sets out the essentials of some thirty contributions including a superb full-length treatment of Cournot, covering not just his contributions to mathematical economics but also his views on economic policy. This is as good a place as any to mention _Precursors in Mathematical Economics: An Anthology_, eds. W. J. Baumol and S. M. Goldfeld

(1968), a collection of thirty-four classical pieces in mathematical economics that span a period of two centuries, each selection being introduced and masterfully placed in context by the editors.

Cournot's *Researches into the Mathematical Principles of the Theory of Wealth* (1960) was translated into English in 1898. I. Fisher supplies a *précis* of the book in *QJE*, 1898, reprinted in *DET* and *ETHA*. Much has been written on Cournot's duopoly theory. For a review of the Cournot-Bertrand-Edgeworth debate, see A. J. Nichol, 'A Re-appraisal of Cournot's Theory of Duopoly Price', *JPE*, 1934, reprinted in *EET*, and 'Edgeworth's Theory of Duopoly Price', *EJ*, March, 1935; see also Schumpeter, *History of Economic Analysis*, pp. 954–63, 976–85. The entirely empirical character of Cournot's demand theory is documented in C. L. Fry and R. B. Ekelund, Jr., 'Cournot's Demand Theory: A Reassessment', *HOPE*, Spring, 1971.

R. W. Houghton, 'A Note on the Early History of Consumer's Surplus', *Ec*, February, 1958, discusses Dupuit, Jenkin and the development of Dupuit's work by Auspitz and Lieben in the 1880s. Dupuit's remarkable essay, 'On the Measurement of the Utility of Public Works' (1844), is reprinted in *IEP*, No. 2, 1952, and *Penguin Modern Economics Readings, Transport*, ed. D. Munby (1968 in paperback); it is matched by an equally remarkable essay five years later, 'On Toll and Transport Charges' (1849), reprinted in *IEP*, No. 11, 1962. Dupuit has been frequently hailed as an early advocate of marginal cost pricing in public utilities, which ignores the fact that his proposals for charges for public services had nothing whatever to do with cost considerations: see R. B. Ekelund, Jr., 'Jules Dupuit and the Early Theory of Marginal Cost Pricing', *JPE*, May-June, 1968, and 'Professor Stigler on Dupuit and the Development of Utility Theory: Comment', *ibid.*, September-October, 1972; also see A. Abouchar, 'A Note on Dupuit's Bridges and the Theory of Marginal Cost Pricing', *HOPE*, Summer, 1976.

In a series of superb papers in *EMDT*, R. B. Ekelund, Jr. and company have been reassessing the contributions of Cournot and Dupuit to the theory of demand, consumers' surplus and price discrimination. R. B. Ekelund, Jr. and R. F. Hébert, 'Public Economics at the École des Ponts et Chaussées: 1830–1850', *JPUE*, 2, 1973, 'French Engineers, Welfare Economics, and Public Finance in the Nineteenth Century', *HOPE*, Winter, 1978, and their textbook, *A History of Economic Theory and Method* (2nd edn., 1983), chap. 12, demonstrate that Dupuit was not an isolated figure, as earlier historians of economic thought (including myself) had believed, but came out of an older tradition among French engineers concerned with the welfare aspects of public finance, which developed outside the corpus of professional economics and which indeed has continued to develop largely outside the French economic mainstream to this day (see Notes on Further Reading, chap. 13 below).

The first two parts of Thünen's *Isolated State* is available in English in two separate volumes: *Von Thünen's Isolated State*', ed. P. Hall (1966), which reproduces the whole of the first part, published in 1826, dealing with location theory [see chapter 14], and excerpts from the second part, published in 1850, concerned with the doctrine of the 'natural wage'; this second part is also available in its entirety in B. W. Dempsey, *The Frontier Wage* (1960). A. H. Leigh gives a coherent account of Thünen's contributions to marginal productivity theory in 'Von Thünen's Theory of Distribution and the Advent of Marginal Analysis', *JPE*, 1946, reprinted in *EET*; see also Schumpeter, *History of Economic Analysis*, pp. 465–8. H. D. Dickinson, 'Von Thünen's Economics', *EJ*, December, 1969, provides some incisive comments on the doctrine of the 'natural wage'.

Gossen's *Entwicklung* or *Development of the Laws of Human Relations* (1984) has finally been translated into English by R. C. Blitz – 129 years after its first appearance! F. Y. Edgeworth's essay on Gossen in *PDPE* is still worth reading. See also the valuable introduction by F. A. Hayek to the German reprint of Gossen's *Entwicklung* (1927) and W. Stark, *The Ideal Foundations of Economic Thought* (1943), chap. 3. Another German pioneer of marginal utility economics, of whom we have said nothing, is Mangoldt, whose *Outline of Economics* (1863) stood with one foot in the old and one foot in the new economics but which, nevertheless, contained a number of original contributions to the subjective theory of value: see K. H. Hennings, 'The Transition from Classical to Neoclassical Economic Theory: Hans von Mangoldt', *KYK*, 33, 4, 1980.

9

Marshallian economics: utility and demand

UTILITY THEORY

The founders of marginal utility theory treated the existence of a yardstick for measuring utility as something that was unproblematical. Menger and Walras never seriously raised the question of the measurability of utility. Jevons first denied that utility was measurable but then suggested a way of measuring it via the approximate constancy of the marginal utility of money, a procedure that Marshall later adopted and refined. Jevons also denied the possibility of making interpersonal comparisons of utility, pointing out that price theory did not require such comparisons, but then went on to make statements about welfare that involved both cardinal measurement and interpersonal comparisons. Menger and Walras, on the other hand, saw no difficulty in comparing the utility of different individuals. All the three founders of utility theory worked with a so-called 'additive utility' function, treating the utility of a commodity as a function of the quantity of that commodity independently of the quantities of other commodities consumed. They paid very little attention to the precise shape of the utility function and assumed a law of diminishing marginal utility as a matter of common experience. Walras drew linear marginal utility functions in his book. Menger's tabular representations implied linear functions. Most of Jevons' curves were drawn convex from below. None of them admitted any exception to the fundamental law of diminishing marginal utility and Jevons went out of his way to deny that there were any exceptions.,

Furthermore, Walras alone succeeded in linking actual utility to demand, although even he did not rigorously derive the implications of diminishing marginal utility for demand behavior: he began his analysis with given demand curves and obtained his equilibrium market conditions before he ever said a word about utility. Jevons, on the other hand, bridged utility and demand by the illegitimate concept of Trading Bodies and Menger simply postulated certain demand prices that were somehow representative of marginal utilities. None of these technical issues in utility theory was cleared up until the 1890s, and indeed some were not elucidated until well past the turn of the century. Marshall's statement of utility theory is superior to that of either Jevons or Walras but succeeding editions of Marshall's *Principles* were marked by increasing caution and reticence as the work of Edgeworth, Fisher and

Pareto began to undermine the earlier notions of measurability, additivity and comparability. Before examining Marshall's resolution of some of the technical difficulties in utility theory, we must review the theoretical issues that plagued analytical progress in this area.

1. The Measurability of Utility

Suppose a consumer chooses goods *A*, *B*, *C* and *D* according to his preferences. Given consistent ranking for the four goods, we can construct the consumer's utility index by attaching arbitrary numbers of ascending order to the various outcomes: an indefinite number of such indices will rank the four outcomes in the same way (see Tables 9–1 and 9–2). If order alone is the same among all these possible indices, we have ordinal utility, a function 'unique up to a monotonic transformation'. Suppose we construct a new series indicating the same order of preference among *A*, *B*, *C* and *D*. But now we ask something more restrictive of these indices: they must all be the same but for an additive and multiplicative constant. That is, if *x* is one index and *y* another, *y* satisfies the linear equation $y = ax + b$, where *a* and *b* are constants. The only difference, then, between two indices related in this way is the point of origin and the arbitrary units of the scale. Such cardinal indices are for obvious reasons called 'unique up to a linear transformation'.

Table 9–1 *Ordinal utility. Monotonic transformations*

	I	II	III
A	16	5	...
B	8	4	...
C	4	3	...
D	2	2	...

Table 9–2 *Cardinal utility. Linear transformations*

	I	II	III
A	16	33	...
B	8	17	...
C	4	9	...
D	2	5	...

These two types of utility scales differ strikingly in one respect. Scales that are monotone transformations of each other vary together in the same direction: this is the only property that they have in common. But scales that are linear transformations of each other assert something much stronger: when the interval differences of one scale increase or decrease successively, the interval differences of the others also increase or decrease successively to the same extent. When we have picked one of the infinite number of utility functions that will satisfy $A > B > C > D$ up to a linear transformation, we can compare *differences* between the successive intervals so as to conclude, say, that the utility of *A*, U_A, exceeds the utility of *B*, U_B, by more than U_B exceeds U_C. In our example, we can say that $U_A > U_B$ twice as much as $U_B > U_C$, a statement that is meaningless when applied to utility functions unique up to a monotone transformation.

Measurability up to a linear transformation involves knowledge not only of the signs of the first differences of the utility scales but also of the signs of the second differences: the first differences tell us about the *direction* of preference; the second differences tell us about the *intensity* of preference. If we can do no more than rank utilities *ordinally* up to a monotonic transformation, marginal utility has meaning only in being positive or negative but diminishing or increasing marginal utility has no meaning. But if utility is *cardinally* measurable up to a linear transformation, the first and second derivatives of the utility function do have meaning: the value of the first derivative is an index of marginal utility and the negative sign of the second derivative defines the law of diminishing marginal utility. Utility measured in this way is analogous to heat registered by a Centigrade or Fahrenheit thermometer: since a Fahrenheit scale is related to a Centigrade scale by the linear equation $\frac{9}{5}C° + 32 = F°$, it is possible to make statements about variations in the intensity of heat regardless of the type of thermometer employed.

2. Operational Measurement of Utility

The operational construction of an *ordinal* utility scale would seem to be a simple matter: we simply let the individual choose between goods and write down a series of numbers preserving the order in which he ranks them. But in order to construct a *cardinal* utility scale, we have to ask the individual to perform a *Gedankenexperiment*, projecting himself into two different situations: having chosen *A* over *B*, we must give him *B* again and ask him to choose between *B* and *C*, comparing the intensity of preference in the two situations. This is a purely subjective procedure but, as long as the utility of one good is entirely independent of all other goods, it is in fact possible in principle to construct a cardinal utility scale.

This was first demonstrated by Irving Fisher in his essay, 'A Statistical Method of Measuring "Marginal Utility" and Testing the Justice of a Progressive Income Tax' (1927). Fisher's method runs as follows: endow an individual with an arbitrary quantity of any commodity, say, 100 loaves of bread. Let the marginal utility of the 100 loaves be equal to one 'util', the units of the utility scale. Now, starting from a position of not having any milk, find the minimum amount of milk the individual will accept in exchange for the hundredth loaf of bread worth 1 util. Given the possession of the first increment of milk, say, 3 cubic inches, repeat the experiment for a second increment, and so forth, showing of course that the typical individual will insist on ever larger increments of milk as he surrenders additional loaves of bread. We thus obtain a schedule giving the amounts of milk necessary to obtain equal increments of utility, from which we derive a corresponding schedule of the total utility of milk consumed (see Table 9–3). By summing the increments of milk (3, 4, 5, 6, 7), we can also obtain a schedule of the total utility yielded by the successive quantities of milk consumed (3, 7, 12, 18, 25). By interpolating, we can thus find the amount of utility obtained from equal increments of milk (see Table 9–4).

Granting the ability of the individual to choose consistently between specified amounts of two goods, this utility function is determined up to a linear transformation. But if the marginal utility of milk depends not only on the quantity of milk but also on the quantities of other foodstuffs consumed, Fisher showed, we will get a new utility function not linearly related to the old whenever we change the commodity in terms of which the utility of milk is measured. If we drop the notion of one-variable 'additive utility' functions, namely, $U_A = f(A)$, $U_B = f(B)$, and so on, and adopt 'generalized utility' functions, namely, $U_A = f(A,B,C,...)$, $U_B = f(B,A,C,...)$, we can no longer measure utility cardinally by the method of pairwise choices.

Table 9–3

Increments of Milk (cu. in.)	Utility of Increments of Milk	Total Utility of Milk
3	1	1
4	1	2
5	1	3
6	1	4
7	1	5

Table 9–4

Quantity of Milk (cu. in.)	Total Utility of Milk	Marginal Utility of Milk (per 3 cu. in.)
3	1.0000*	.....
6	1.7667	0.7667
9	2.4333	0.6667
12	3.0000*	0.5667
15	3.4667	0.4667

*From Table 9.3

The idea of generalized utility functions was introduced by Edgeworth in *Mathematical Psychics* (1881) and emphasized by Fisher in his remarkable doctoral dissertation, *Mathematical Investigations in the Theory of Value and Prices* (1892). But although most economists conceded the interdependence and, hence, the nonadditivity of utility functions, the additive utility function was only slowly and very reluctantly abandoned. The hypothesis of universal 'independence' of commodities has, as we shall see, the implication that no commodity is an 'inferior' good – the kind of good of which less is bought as income is increased. This implication is contradicted by evidence showing that many goods, if narrowly enough defined, are 'inferior' for some ranges of income. The hypothesis of universal 'independence', therefore, must be rejected. A generalized utility function, however, makes it impossible to devise a *simple* operational procedure for measuring cardinal utility. Even if the measurability of utility is taken for granted, it makes it impossible rigorously to deduce upward-sloping income curves and downward-sloping demand curves from the law of diminishing marginal utility; a more complicated and a more ambiguous theory of demand is the result. It is not difficult to understand, therefore, why most writers in this period, and particularly the nonmathematical writers, preferred to work with additive utility functions.

So much for measurement of utility for purposes of the theory of demand. But what of utility measurement in welfare economics? Here even measurement unique up to a linear transformation may not be sufficient. Although we can devise such a measurement if the utility functions are additive, it does not follow that we can integrate the marginal utility curves and so obtain the corresponding total utilities. Sums obtained by adding interval differences based on two indices identical up to a linear transformation do not yield equal totals, owing to the fact that both the zero point of the scale and the unit of measurement are arbitrary. We can say that the temperature rose twice as much from Sunday to Monday as from Monday to Tuesday, and this statement holds true whether we use a Fahrenheit or a Centigrade thermometer. But we cannot say that the temperature was twice as high on Monday as on Sunday for this statement depends on which thermometer we use: for example, 20°C = 68°F but 40°C = 104°F. *Sums* of measurement of temperature make no sense because the results differ according to the scale chosen. With reference to utility, measurability up to a linear transformation gives us the sign of marginal utility as well as its rate of change but does not allow us to find the total utility of a bundle of goods by a process of summing the marginal utilities.

To obtain the absolute value of the individual's total utility from a bundle of goods, we would have to be able to calculate ratios, not merely between the interval differences among the numbers assigned to the utility scale, but between the numbers themselves. This implies measurement 'unique up to a proportionate transformation', which is possible if the indices differ only by a multiplicative constant. If utility were measurable in this sense, it would belong to the field of weights and lengths, where the zero point of measurement is well defined, instead of to the field of temperature measurement where the zero point depends on which scale we adopt. To put the same point somewhat differently, in *ordinal* utility theory we know only the successive contour lines on the map of an individual's utility mountain without being able to judge whether the mountain in question is Mount Everest or a molehill. In *cardinal* utility theory we can at least compare the distances between the contour lines to get a picture of the shape of the mountain. We still do not know, however, how high it is because we do not know where the mountain begins or how steeply it rises: the unit and the origin of measurement are entirely arbitrary. However, under certain restricted conditions, Marshall argued, we can determine the absolute height of the mountain. By assuming constancy in the marginal utility of money, Marshallian welfare economics did achieve the strongest possible measurement of utility, namely, measurement unique up to a multiplicative constant.

3. The Bernoulli Hypothesis

Up to this point we have been concerned with utility theory as a means of predicting how consumers choose among a number of 'sure prospects', or, at any rate, how they evaluate a bundle of 'sure prospects'. But how do we explain consumers' behavior in the presence of uncertainty? People buy insurance, thus choosing certainty over uncertainty, but they also engage in gambling, choosing uncertainty over certainty. Is it possible to rationalize this kind of behavior by assuming that people act so as to maximize the 'mathematical expectation' of their income?

All attempts to define a utility function by observing the reaction of individuals to probability situations go back to Bernoulli's memoir on the St Petersburg Paradox (1738). The nature of the paradox is this: a coin is tossed until heads appears; if heads appears on the first toss, A pays B $1; if heads appears for the first time on the second toss, A pays B \$2; if heads appears on the third toss, A pays B \$4; and so on, always paying 2^{n-1} for each nth toss if heads appears. What fee should B be willing to pay for the privilege of playing this game if it is to be a 'fair game'? A 'fair game' is one in which the player is never asked to pay more than the total mathematical expectation of success, that is, the actuarial value of the gamble, at each stage of the game. The expected gain or loss of income from a 'fair bet', therefore, always equals zero. The mathematical expectation of success on the first toss is $p \cdot \$1 = (\frac{1}{2}) \cdot \$1 = \$0.50$; on the second toss it is $(\frac{1}{2})(\frac{1}{2}) \cdot \$2 = \$0.50$; on the nth toss it is $(\frac{1}{2})^n \cdot \$2^{n-1} = (2)^{-n}$. $\$2^{n-1} = \$2^{-1} = \$0.50$. Since the total expectation E is the sum of the expectations at each stage of the game, $E = \$0.50 + \$0.50 + \ldots$. The sum of this infinite series is infinitely large and so B must pay A an infinite sum of money for the privilege of playing this 'fair game'. Since people are clearly not willing to pay an infinitely large stake for a 'fair gamble', the assumption that people act as if they were maximizing the mathematical expection of their income produces a contradiction.

Figure 9–1

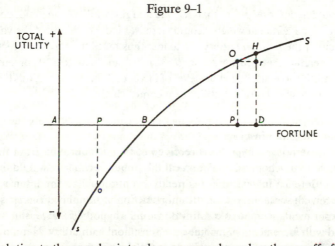

One solution to the paradox is to place an upper bound on the payoff of the game. Bernoulli's solution, however, was to argue that people are guided not by the 'mathematical expectation' but by the 'moral expectation' of success, the probabilities being weighted by the utility of income. Moreover, the marginal utility of income declines with every increment of income. Given diminishing marginal utility of money income, people will insist on a larger gain to compensate them for the risk of a given loss: no one will pay as much as \$1 for the 50–50 chance of winning \$2. Bernoulli illustrated the argument graphically (see Figure 9–1). The individual's wealth at the outset is AB and the chance of winning BP is 50 percent. The total utility of a gain and the total disutility of the fee paid for the privilege of playing the game are measured along the ordinate. If sBS were a straight line, an individual would pay a fee pB precisely equal to the expected gain BP. Since the utility-of-income curve is concave from below, pB is the largest amount that should be paid for a 50 percent change of winning BP, being the point where the utility of gain PO is equal to the disutility of the fee *po*. Bernoulli then went on to assume that the curve is a logarithmic one. If *rH* is the utility of an infinitely small gain *PD* to an individual who possesses *AP*, Bernoulli conjectured that *rH* is directly proportional to *PD* and inversely proportional to *AP*. That is, letting *P* be the amount of an individual's 'fortune' and *dP* the increment to his fortune, then

$$dU = k\,\frac{dP}{P} \quad \text{or} \quad \frac{dU}{dP} = \frac{k}{P}\,, \text{ where } k \text{ is a constant.}$$

Assuming with Bernoulli that *c* is the amount of 'fortune' necessary for existence, the total utility derived from income *P* may be represented by the definite integral

$$\int_{c}^{P} k\frac{dP}{P} = k(\log P - \log c) = k \log \frac{P}{c}\,,$$

where *c* is the constant of integration.

The 'Bernoulli hypothesis' states that *dU*, the marginal utility of income, declines at the same percentage rate at which income increases independently of the value of *k*. The schedule of the *marginal* utility of income thus takes the form of a rectangular hyperbola, meaning that a 10 percent increase in income leads to a 10 percent decline in marginal utility no matter what the level of income. As we shall see, this is only one of a family of possible marginal-utility-of-income schedules.

4. Gambling and Insurance
In the 1860s, Bernoulli's hypothesis received some corroboration from the newly emerging field of psychophysics. The so-called Weber-Fechner Law held that a just noticeable difference in sensation is directly proportional to the intensity of the stimulus received: sensation is a logarithmic function of stimulus. Fechner's psychophysical experiments seemed to confirm Bernoulli's hypothesis, at least if 'stimulus' is identified with increments of income and 'sensation' with utility. Neither Menger nor Walras, however, paid any attention to the Weber-Fechner Law. But Jevons was acquainted with Fechner's work and accepted the implication of Bernoulli's hypothesis that 'gaming is, in the long run, a sure way to lose utility'. Marshall followed him in this and agreed that utility maximization must be rejected as an explanation of choices involving uncertainty. If the utility of a given sum gained is always less than the utility of the same sum lost, the rational individual will take out 'fair' or slightly 'unfair' insurance but will never gamble at 'fair' odds: he will be willing to pay more than $1 as a premium to protect himself against the 1 percent probability of losing $100 but he will not be willing to pay $1 for the 1 percent chance of winning $100. The widespread phenomenon of buying lottery tickets at less than fair odds must be explained by the 'love of gambling'. In other words, people do not seem to behave as if they were maximizing the expected utility of income.

The Marshallian ban on the utility analysis of choice under uncertainty lasted until recent times, when Neumann and Morgenstern showed that this is precisely the case in which it is possible to devise an operational procedure for measuring utility up to a linear transformation.[1] This is of little help in the theory of consumption in which individuals typically choose among sure alternatives. But it does imply that we may some day be able to measure the income-utility curve in cardinal terms. Empirical work along the lines of Neumann and Morgenstern has yielded ambiguous results and so investigators have turned back to the problem of rationalizing the seemingly contradictory behavior of individuals who hedge against large losses and at the same time gamble at 'fair' odds. One such hypothesis, the Friedman-Savage hypothesis, is that the income-utility curve is only concave from below in the lower and upper ranges but convex from below – increasing marginal utility of income – in the middle range. Both the Bernoulli hypothesis and the Friedman-Savage hypothesis imply that utility is dependent on the absolute level of income: once the curve is constructed, individuals choose among alternative situations by moving along the curve. The utility of income, however, may be related to changes in the level of income, in which case a much simpler rationalization of the fact that most individuals gamble and also take out insurance suggests itself. The Markowitz hypothesis explains this phenomenon by assuming that the income-utility curve contains three and not two inflection points with present income at the middle inflection point, whatever the absolute level of present income (see Figure 9–3). Small increments in income yield increasing marginal utility, but large gains in income yield diminishing marginal utility; this accounts for people's reluctance to accept large but their eagerness to accept small 'fair bets'. On the other hand, small decrements in income yield increasing marginal disutility; hence, the eagerness to hedge against small losses but a devil-may-care attitude to very large losses.

---

[1] The essence of the Neumann-Morgenstern procedure is this: suppose an individual finds $U_A > U_B > U_C$; form a lottery ticket of A and C and offer him a choice between the certainty of B and either A with probability p or C with probability $(1 - p)$; find that p which would make $pU_A + (1 - p)U_C = U_B$. For example, the individual is given a one-fifth chance of winning nothing and a four-fifths chance of winning \$10. The 'mathematical expectation' of the lottery ticket is $(1/5 \cdot \$0) + (4/5 \cdot \$10) = \$8$; the 'moral expectation', however, is $(1/5 \cdot 0) + (4/5 \cdot 1) = 4/5$, where U, the utility of winning \$10, is arbitrarily set equal to unity. Suppose we find the individual is indifferent between \$6 and the lottery ticket – apparently, when $B = \$6$, $U_B = 4/5$ of U_A. By varying the probabilities in the gamble and setting the average utility of the outcomes equal to different Bs, we can elicit the entire utility curve with zero and unity arbitrarily defined (see Figure 9–2).

Figure 9–2

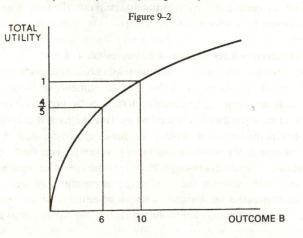

Figure 9–3

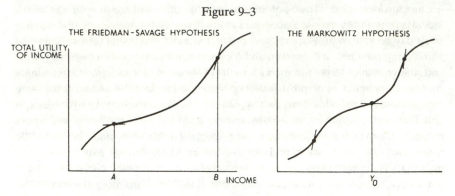

THE FRIEDMAN-SAVAGE HYPOTHESIS   THE MARKOWITZ HYPOTHESIS

TOTAL UTILITY
OF INCOME

A   B   INCOME Y_0

The point of these recent developments is to indicate that diminishing marginal utility of money income is a very different thing from diminishing marginal utility of a specific commodity. Even if all the things money income can buy are subject to a law of diminishing marginal utility, it does not follow that money income itself is. It is possible to rationalize people's behavior by a particular income-utility curve and it may even be possible some day to measure the utility of income cardinally. When an individual is willing to pay a fee of $10 for the 50–50 chance of winning $20, we can conclude that the marginal utility of money is constant to him in the relevant income range. If he insists on better-than-fair odds, we can conclude that he values the loss of $10 more than the gain of $10, from which it follows that the marginal utility of money to him declines with the relevant range, and contrariwise if he is willing to accept less-than-fair odds. But the theory of demand does not require cardinal measurement of utility and no one has yet found an operational procedure that would permit us to measure people's choices among sure alternatives in a way that would be 'unique up to a linear transformation'. In Marshallian theory this problem is neatly circumvented by confining the analysis to goods that absorb a small portion of the consumer's total expenditure. For such goods, the marginal utility of money income may be considered approximately constant, clearing the way for a simple transition from utility to demand.

5. The Bernoulli Hypothesis and Progressive Taxation

Before passing on to the theory of demand, let us briefly consider one of the popular uses of Bernoulli's hypothesis in this period, namely, to justify the progressive income tax. It may seem, at first glance, that the notion of declining marginal utility of income always justifies tax progression. But this is not so. Assuming that all individuals with the same income have the same capacity for want satisfaction so that the same income-utility schedule may be applied to all taxpayers, and assuming that we want to distribute the tax bill so as to inflict 'equal sacrifice on everyone' measured in terms of income surrendered, it is nevertheless true that we arrive at different conclusions depending on whether we seek to equalize absolute, proportional or marginal sacrifice. With equal *absolute* sacrifice, the tax bill is so distributed as to extract the same absolute amount of total income-utility from each individual. With equal *proportional* sacrifice, we try to extract the same proportion of total income-utility from each individual; hence, the 'rich' pay more and the 'poor' pay less under this scheme than under the former. With equal *marginal* sacrifice, we minimize aggregate sacrifice by inflicting the same loss of marginal utility on all individuals. On *a priori* grounds, it is not clear which concept of equal sacrifice should be applied: Sidgwick and Marshall favored the first; Cohen-Stuart, an important Dutch writer on public finance, preferred the second; and Edgeworth and Pigou held out for the third. Whichever concept is chosen, the actual rate structure required to implement 'equal sacrifice' still depends on the precise shape of the income-utility curve.

If all that is known is that the marginal utility of income declines at some undetermined rate over its entire range, progression is only clearly justified by the concept of equal *marginal* sacrifice. Whatever the negative slope of the curve, this theory would proceed by levelling the highest income down to the next highest, and so on, until the necessary revenue had been raised. To get progression from equal absolute and equal proportional sacrifice requires that the marginal utility-of-income curve be steeper than a Bernoulli curve, that is, steeper than a rectangular hyperbola. The Bernoulli hypothesis implies that a given percentage increase of income results in the same increase in total utility, whatever the level of income. It follows that in this case the principle of equal *absolute* sacrifice calls for a proportionate tax: an individual with twice as much income as another should pay twice the number of dollars in tax. Even with equal *proportional* sacrifice, declining marginal utility of income as such does not necessarily lead to progression, as Cohen-Stuart and Edgeworth showed.

Moreover, although the marginal utility of income may decline at a given income level, an increase in income may cause the schedule to shift upward owing to a rise in aspiration levels. If the long-run schedule connecting the points on the upward shifting short-run schedules is constant, none of the three concepts will justify a progressive tax, and the notion of equal absolute sacrifice will now require a regressive tax. Further complications result if the individual utility schedules are interdependent so that the satisfactions derived from income depend not only on one's own income but also on one's place in the income distribution scale. And, lastly, differences in tastes, and hence differences in the income-utility schedules, preclude *any* deduction about rate structure from *any* concept of equal sacrifice without interpersonal comparisons of utility. As soon as we admit that people differ in their capacities for want satisfaction, we are driven to the conclusion that an optimal income distribution would award larger incomes to the efficient utility 'engines', the only problem being to discover who these are.

It has been argued that in the absence of specific knowledge, we should assume that 'all men are equal'. But this is the fallacy of equiprobabilities. In the face of ignorance, it is no more plausible to assume that the income-utility curves are the same than that they are different, for each has a 50 percent chance of happening. And once we admit that they may be different, we can justify almost any income distribution by inferring the capacity to enjoy income from observed income itself.

For example, take Edgeworth's infamous observation in *Mathematical Psychics:* 'if we suppose that capacity for pleasure is an attribute of skill and talent . . . we may see a reason deeper than Economics may afford for the larger pay, though often more agreeable work, of the aristocracy of skill and talent. The aristocracy of sex is similarly grounded upon the supposed superior capacity of the man for happiness. . . . Altogether . . . there appears a nice conciliance between the deductions from the utilitarian principle and the disabilities and privileges which hedge round modern womanhood.'

Perhaps the only way to rescue the assumption that men and women are alike in their capacity for enjoying income is to adopt the one-man-one-vote principle upon which our political institutions are based. Taxation is a matter of political consensus and here we may legitimately take refuge in truths that are said to be self-evident. This disposes of the problem of interpersonal comparisons but still leaves us with the problem of which concept of equal sacrifice to apply.

The problem was never resolved in the neoclassical period, and in some sense it is still unresolved, although as time passed the idea of equal marginal sacrifice gained more and more adherents simply because it justified progressive income taxation without having to specify the precise shape of the utility-of-income curve. It is characteristic of the Anglo-Saxon tradition in public finance that the entire question was discussed solely in terms of taxation, totally ignoring the expenditure side. Obviously, even if one believes that the marginal utility of income declines monotonically with income, one may nevertheless favor a proportionate or even a regressive income tax provided one knows that government expenditures will be wholly devoted to social services from which the poor alone benefit. In recent years, largely as a result of the influence of Italian writers on public finance, the tendency to discuss tax progression solely from the side of revenue has more or less disappeared and, in consequence, there has been a sharp decline of interest in the Law of Diminishing Marginal Utility of Income.

6. Derivation of Demand Curves

We return now to the theory of demand. Marshall was virtually the first author after Walras clearly and explicitly to derive demand curves from utility functions. In Mathematical Appendix II of his *Principles*, Marshall gives the equilibrium condition for the consumption of commodity x as $MU_x = p_x MU_n$. Taken across all goods this gives the familiar equimarginal rule:

$$\frac{MU_x}{p_x} = \frac{MU_y}{p_y} = \frac{MU_z}{p_z} = MU_n,$$

MU_n being what Marshall calls the marginal utility of money. The 'marginal utility of money' is a confusing phrase because what Marshall had in mind was not the marginal utility of an individual's *stock* of money holdings but the marginal utility of his money income *flow* per limit of time, say, a day or a week. In equilibrium, an individual will want to hold a stock of money that gives him ready command over a certain desired proportion κ of his real income, such that

$$\frac{M}{P} = \kappa\frac{Y}{P},$$

where P is a general price index. Formally, therefore, we should write a separate fraction in the consumer allocation formula, representing the marginal utility of a dollar held in idle money balances at given market prices. If the individual saves, we have another fraction giving the present marginal utility of the future yield of earning assets over their current prices. For convenience, however, we may assume that all expenditure is on current consumption goods. A rise in money income flows initially into an individual's money stock holdings, lowers the marginal utility of these holdings, and then raises expenditures until the marginal utility of money *held* is once again equal to the marginal utility of money *spent*. In other words, in disequilibrium, the marginal utility of money holdings regulates expenditures and the marginal utility of money spent gives the equilibrium level to which the marginal utility of money holdings tends to move. To avoid confusion on this issue in the future, we will replace MU_n by MU_e, the marginal utility of money expenditures in general. It is not necessary to divide this marginal utility by a general price index because the price of money in terms of dollars is unity. MU_e is thus the common value of the ratios of the marginal utility of commodities to their prices, the uniform utility of a dollar on the margin of expenditure in all directions.

We can now restate the equimarginal rule for consumer equilibrium in three equivalent forms: the consumer maximizes satisfactions when (1) he equalizes weighted marginal utilities over all goods, that is, the marginal utility of each good weighted by its price; (2) he equalizes the ratio of marginal utilities with the ratio of the corresponding prices for every pair of goods consumed; and (3) he equalizes the marginal utility of a dollar's worth of each commodity purchased at given market prices, that is, he equalizes the marginal utility of dollars spent in all markets.

Suppose the consumer has achieved equilibrium and p_x falls. Immediately, the equality $MU_x = p_x MU_e$ becomes an inequality. To restore equilibrium, more of x must be bought to reduce MU_x. There is no doubt that the consumer will buy more of x when the price falls because at lower p_x, he obtains a larger marginal utility per dollar from x than from any other commodity. The 'law' of diminishing marginal utility guarantees that MU_x falls as more x is bought to restore equilibrium. The substitution effect of the fall in price, therefore, yields a negatively inclined demand curve on the assumption that the consumer always acts so as to maximize his satisfactions within the constraints of his given income and given prices. This argument assumes, however, that the individual is deprived of the increase in real income owing to the fall in p_x, so that MU_e remains constant through the adjustment process. Once the individual has again equalized the marginal utility of expenditures in all directions, we restore the nominal increment of real income: this lowers the marginal utility of money holdings and thereby leads to an increase in the purchase of every commodity, including x. The income effect in this case is positive, and we obtain a negatively inclined demand curve as well as a positively sloped income curve for x.

The typical Marshallian method of deriving demand curves from the underlying utility curves is based on the notion of additive utility functions: the utility function of each commodity purchased by the individual is independent of every other. An additive utility function does not permit consideration of substitutability and complementarity between commodities; all commodities are treated as if they were 'independent goods'. But Marshall realized that some commodities are rivals in consumption while others are jointly consumed: x and y are substitutes when MU_x decreases as the quantity of y increases; they are complements when MU_x increases as the quantity of y increases. Recognition of such interrelations among commodities leads straightway to a generalized utility function, the utility of x being a function of $x, y, z, \ldots n$. With a generalized utility function, however, diminishing marginal utility no longer has the necessary corollary that all demand curves have negative and all income curves positive slopes. When we restore the increment in real income resulting from a reduction in p_x, we cannot be sure that *all* commodities will be consumed in larger quantities. Suppose an increase in y purchased not only reduced MU_y but also MU_x because x and y are substitutes. Then when a portion of the increment of real income is spent on y, MU_x may fall by so much that the amount of x must be reduced below its original quantity to fulfill the conditions for maximum satisfaction: the income effect is negative and the demand curve for x *may* then be positively sloped; x is an 'inferior good'.

7. The Constancy of the Marginal Utility of Money

One way of resolving this problem is to eliminate the income effect by assumption. This is exactly what Marshall did when he argued that the marginal utility of money – our MU_e – is approximately constant in most cases. Of course, absolute constancy in MU_e would be a very rare case as can easily be demonstrated. A price change that would leave MU_e strictly unaffected could result only from a marginal-utility function with an elasticity equal to unity in the relevant range. If a 1 percent drop in p_x increases the quantity demanded of x by 1 percent, total expenditure on x is unaffected by the fall in price; hence, real income is the same at the old price as at the new. If the elasticity of the utility function over the relevant range is less than unity, a fall in p_x reduces total expenditure on x, everything else being the same; the increase in real income lowers the marginal utility of money holdings and results in larger purchases of every commodity – all demand curves shift to the right. As a result, the new equilibrium MU_e is other than it was before. Contrariwise, if the elasticity of the marginal-utility curve is greater than unity, a fall in p_x, given MU_e raises total expenditure. The marginal utility of money balances will now rise, thus shifting all demand curves to the left and altering the final equilibrium value of MU_e. The strict assumption of a constant MU_e, therefore, entails unitary price elasticity of the marginal utility curves over the relevant range of price variations.

Unable to contend that MU_e is really constant, Marshall was satisfied to argue that MU_e is approximately constant for small changes in the price of 'unimportant' commodities, that is, commodities absorbing a negligible portion of an individual's total expenditures. For all practical purposes, MU_e remains constant and may be employed as the unit of measurement of utility to the individual, representing the increase in total utility that results from adding one dollar to the consumer's total expenditure. Given the basic formula $p_x = MU_x/MU_e$, knowledge of MU_e and knowledge of the individual's demand curve for commodity x permit us to infer the underlying marginal utility function of x. In this way, without postulating that the marginal utility of money income can in fact be measured cardinally, Marshall achieved something tantamount to cardinal measurement of the marginal untility functions of 'unimportant' commodities.

The method is perfectly analogous to the way we usually derive the demand schedule for a factor. Marginal utility plays the same role in the theory of consumption as the marginal physical product of a factor in the theory of production. We convert marginal physical product into dollar terms by multiplying it by the marginal revenue of the product – with firms facing given prices, marginal revenue under perfect competition is equal to average revenue, which in turn is equal to the price of the product. The analogous concept in the theory of consumption is the reciprocal of MU_e: is might be called 'the marginal revenue of utility'. If MU_e is the increase in total utility resulting from the addition of one dollar to the consumer's total expenditure, then MR_u is the dollar value of adding one util to total utility. Suppose $MU = 20$ utils per dollar. Then MR_u is 5 cents; adding a util to total utility is equivalent to adding 5 cents to total expenditures: $p_x = MU_x MR_u$ and the right-hand side of this expression gives us the marginal rate of substitution between money and the commodity in question. MR_u is therefore related to MU as the marginal revenue product of a factor is related to its marginal physical product. The demand schedule for a factor is identical with its marginal revenue product schedule; in the same way, the demand schedule of the consumer *is* the marginal rate of substitution schedule. The analogy, however, is purely formal. The price of the product does indeed remain constant when the firm changes its purchases of factor inputs in response to a change in factor prices. But MR_u almost always alters somewhat when the price of a particular commodity changes – the only case in which this does not happen is when the marginal-utility schedule, and hence the demand curve, for a specific commodity is a rectangular hyperbola over the relevant range.

8. Restatement

Given a fall in price, the demand curve for x is derived from the marginal utility curve for x in two stages. We draw straight-line functions in Figure 9–4 purely for convenience. In equilibrium, the consumer equates MU_x to $p_x MU_e$. When $p_x = p_{x_1}$, he buys q_1 amount of x. At a lower price p_{x_2}, he moves down the marginal utility curve because of the substitution effect. If the elasticity of the MU_x curve is less than unity, the drop in price releases income for spending on other goods, that is, the rectangle $O(MU_{x_1})(O_{q_1})$ exceeds the rectangle $O(MU_{x_2})(P_{q_2})$; more is bought of all goods including x and MU_e falls to MU'_e. In consequence of the income effect that is now added to the substitution effect, the consumer buys q_3 of x at the lower price. In this way, we can derive the demand curve of every 'superior' good.

Instead of confronting a given marginal utility function with various prices, we can adopt one of Jevons' diagrams and graph the moving ratio MU_x/p_x directly (Figure 9–5). The rational consumer equates the weighted marginal utilities of all goods, making each equal to the common MU_e, so that his entire income is exhausted. A fall in p_x leads to an upward shift in the weighted marginal utility function of x. If we deprive the consumer of the nominal increase in real income owing to the fall in p_x, he buys more of x and less of y. Restoring the increment of real income, he will buy still more of x as well as of y as MU_e falls.

Figure 9–4

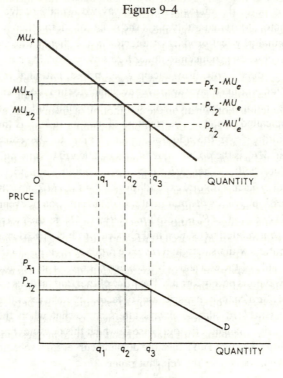

Figure 9–5

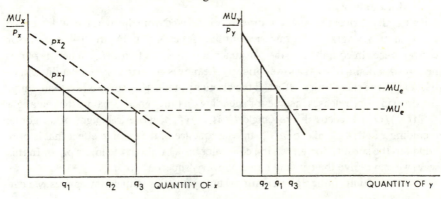

In principle MU_e may either rise, fall or remain the same. If the elasticity of demand in the range $p_{x_1} - p_{x_2}$ is equal to unity, the individual will spend as much on x at the new price as at the old; hence, MU_y/p_y and MU_e will not be affected; the income effect is zero and the individual will end up buying q_2 of x and q_1 of y. If demand is inelastic, the individual buys more of x at the lower price but still has income left for spending on other goods. In consequence, MU_e falls. Contrariwise, an elastic demand for x raises MU_e by pulling expenditure away from other goods. At given prices, MU_e is inversely related to the amount of real income. But every reduction in price raises the potential purchasing power of money income. The fact that an individual has more real income when he spends a marginal dollar lowers MU_e but the fact that he can buy more goods for a marginal dollar when some prices have fallen raises MU_e. The balance of forces may go either way.

All this assumes that x and y are independent goods. If x and y are either substitutes or complements, the problem is complicated by a new consideration. Each weighted marginal utility function is drawn up on the assumption of given tastes, a given money income and a given set of prices of all goods, including the price of the good in question. If x and y are substitutes, MU_y and hence MU_y/p_y shift down as more x is acquired; if they are complements, MU_y and hence MU_y/p_y shift up as more x is acquired. Unless x and y are independent goods, therefore, every change in p_x involves a shift in *all* the weighted marginal utility functions. It is easy to see now how the so-called 'Giffen Paradox' might arise (see below). The price of x falls and more of x is purchased owing to the substitution effect. The income effect of the price fall, however, leads to an increase in y purchased: x and y are strong rivals and the increase in consumption of y sharply depresses MU_x. It is possible that the curve MU_x/p_{x_2} will fall so sharply that in equilibrium less of x is actually purchased than before (see Figure 9–6). We conclude, therefore, that a positively inclined demand curve is the outcome of a significant perverse income effect owing to extreme rivalry between goods.

'Inferior goods' are goods whose income elasticity of demand is negative. If we hold MU_e constant by assuming with Marshall that the item in question is 'unimpor-

Figure 9–6

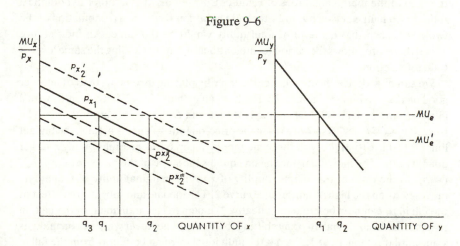

tant', we eliminate the possibility of any income effect from a change in price and thus eliminate inferior goods by definition. Without adopting this approach in the strict sense, we can take comfort in the fact that we will rarely encounter inferior goods, provided we define commodities broadly enough. On the other hand, when goods are narrowly enough defined, they are almost all inferior for some ranges of income. Food as a whole is certainly not an inferior good: food is complementary to other broadly defined commodities, such as 'clothing' and 'housing', and the income effect of a change in the price of all foodstuffs is therefore bound to be positive. But margarine or any other cheap brand of a particular food might be inferior because preferred substitutes are readily available. Nevertheless, it is worth noting that despite the vast empirical evidence on price and income elasticities of demand, there are few clear cases on record of 'inferior goods'.

9. The Indifference-Curve Approach

So far the exposition of the theory of consumer behavior has been Marshallian in spirit, implying cardinal measurement of utility. It is possible, however, to approach these problems from the viewpoint of ordinal utility theory by employing indifference curves. The technique of indifference curves was invented by Edgeworth [see chapter 8, section 9] and refined by Pareto and Fisher. But it never became popular and subsequently fell into disuse. It was revived by A. L. Bowley in his *Mathematical Groundwork* (1924); Bowley did not, however, explore its implications for the measurability of utility. In 1934 Hicks and Allen showed that indifference curves can be employed to reconstruct the theory of consumer behavior on the basis of ordinal utility, only to discover that Johnson and Slutsky had independently demonstrated the same results as early as 1913 and 1915.

The indifference-curve technique assumes that the individual can consistently rank his preferences and, moreover, that he can discern 'indifference' between two given alternatives at a given time. What we actually observe is one point on the indifference curve, a point at which the slope of the price line between x and y equals the ratio of the marginal utilities of x and y. But we *infer* that at other hypothetical ratios of exchange between x and y the individual could choose a combination of the two goods such that his level of total utility would be the same. An indifference curve, therefore, shows the various combinations of x and y yielding the same level of total satisfaction.

We can now derive the demand curve for x by placing income instead of another good on the y-axis (see Figure 9–7). The individual finds himself initially at R_1 with a given income equal to OM, spending NM on x and ON on goods other than x. The price of $x = OM/OQ'$ is shown as p_1 in the price-quantity plane. If p_x falls, the budget line MQ' shifts to MQ'': with the same money income it is possible to buy a larger quantity of x. The individual once again equates the slope of the price line OM/OQ'' ($= p_2$) to the ratio of the marginal utility of x to the marginal utility of money: he moves to R_2 on the higher indifference curve 2. The income and substitution effect of the fall in p_x can now be broken up neatly. We deprive the individual of the gain in real income from the fall in p_x by shifting the budget line down without changing its slope until it is tangent to 1. Even if the individual were no better off from the fall in

p_x, he would move to S and thus buy more of x. When we restore his income gain, he moves to R_2. Consequently, the fact that he buys more of x when the price falls is due to the combined impact of the substitution and the income effect. Graphic inspection will show that a positively sloped demand curve implies successively flatter indifference curves, so that the price-consumption line bends back on itself (see Figure 9–8). This must mean that increments of money income are being spent on some substitute y, which makes the individual increasingly reluctant to acquire additional units of x at the same price.

The slope of an indifference curve expresses the marginal rate of substitution, MRS, of two goods. In our case, $MRS = MU_x/MU_e$. We have drawn the indifference curves as convex from below, showing diminishing MRS as smaller and smaller amounts of money are offered for unit increments of x. It is sometimes asserted that convexity of indifference curves is tantamount to assuming the law of diminishing marginal utility. This is a misunderstanding. If the consumer could compare the magnitude of the utility gained by moving from indifference curve 1 to curve 2 relative to the utility gained in moving from 2 to 3, utility would be measurable in

Figure 9–7

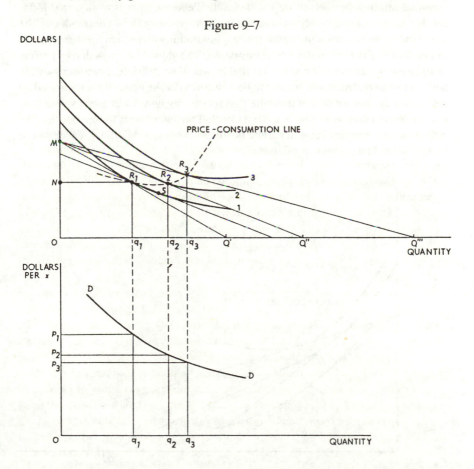

cardinal terms. Diminishing marginal utility would then be shown by successively closer indifference curves. But the indifference-curve approach assumes only that the individual can rank total utilities in orders of magnitude: he knows that curve 2 is higher than curve 1 but he does not know how much higher. But what of the shape of a single indifference curve? For any bundle made up of two goods, more of at least one good raises the total utility of the bundle – on anybody's definition of utility – and moves the individual on to a higher indifference curve. But what happens if we move along an indifference curve by having more of one good but less of the other? Is it necessarily true that *MRS* diminishes?

The notion of 'indifference' itself is not subject to direct measurement. Although choices between what we might call 'unambiguously separate' bundles of goods – bundles that differ only by having more of at least one of the goods – can be rationalized by an ordinal utility scale, no operational method for deriving the exact shape of indifference curves has ever been devised. The indifference-curve technique requires us to compare *signs* of marginal utility: as we move along the curve toward the y-axis, MU_x is negative and MU_y is positive, but the relative value of the marginal utilities themselves are not defined. We know, that is to say, that indifference curves are negatively inclined but their precise shape is not determined. The use of indifference curves by themselves implies nothing more than measurability of utility unique up to a monotone transformation. The individual states that he prefers $4x$ to $1y$ but not $2x$ to $1y$. We may infer that he would be indifferent between, say, $3x$ and $1y$. Furthermore, it follows that to be reduced to $2x$, he must be compensated by more than $1y$, but we do not presume that he can say how much more y would be equivalent to a unit reduction in x. To make that presumption is to suppose that the individual can compare increments and decrements of marginal utility, which would imply cardinal measurement of utility.

Figure 9–8

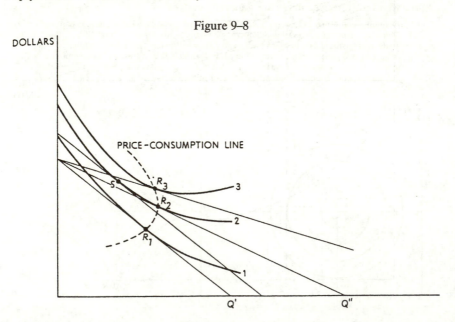

DOLLARS

PRICE-CONSUMPTION LINE

S

R_3

R_2

R_1

3

2

1

Q'   Q"

Figure 9–9

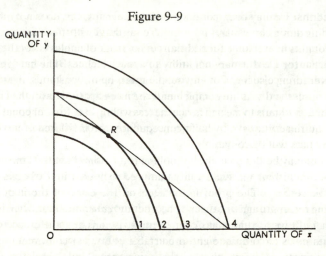

Since indifference maps are not directly observable, convexity can be inferred only from observations of people's behavior. Concave indifference curves have the implication that the individual will succumb to monomania. If the budget line is given in Figure 9–8, *R* would not be a stable equilibrium point for the individual could get on a higher indifference curve by moving along his budget line. Maximizing utility, the individual would end up consuming only *x* and no *y*; if the budget line met the extremities of the *same* indifference curve, the individual could spend his income either entirely on *y* or entirely on *x*. Concave indifference maps seem to be equivalent to a distaste for variety, which cannot be ruled out on *a priori* grounds. Nevertheless, distaste for variety cannot characterize modal behavior and so we may *assume* that indifference curves are generally convex.[2]

---

[2] Assuming that utility mountains have no dips in their surfaces, what we have is contour lines to which we cannot attach absolute numbers (see Figure 9–10). Only quadrant III is relevant for the analysis of the usual case in which both *x* and *y* are what Jevons called 'commodities': having more of at least one good increases total utility. If *y* were income and *x* were a 'discommodity' such as man hours, we would be in quadrant IV; when the reverse is true, we are in quadrant II. In quadrant I, both goods are 'discommodities' or nuisances.

Figure 9–10

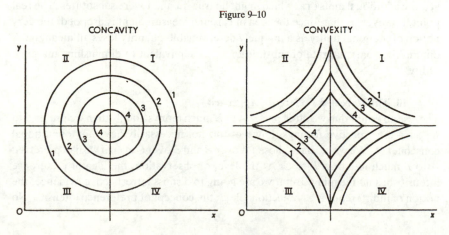

Granted that we may draw convex indifference maps, this does not mean that we are assuming diminishing marginal utility. To say that I will offer successively smaller amounts of nuts in exchange for additions to my stock of apples is not the same thing as saying that for me the marginal utility of apples declines. The marginal utility of apples, everything else including my stock of nuts being constant, might be increasing but as apples and nuts are complements the more apples I have, the greater is the marginal utility of nuts to me and hence the less willing I am to offer equal amounts of nuts to acquire additional apples. In consequence, the indifference curves between apples and nuts will be convex.

This point may be driven home by looking for a moment at the kind of 'proof' of the law of diminishing marginal utility that used to appear in textbooks around the turn of the century. The proof is modeled on the classical proof of the law of diminishing returns in agriculture and proceeds by *reductio ad absurdum* [see chapter 3, section 7]. If we assume that marginal utility is constant, the effort to maximize utility does not yield a unique and predictable pattern of consumer's expenditure among a variety of goods; that is, the equimarginal rule does not produce an equilibrium pattern of allocation. If we assume rising marginal utility, the consumer will buy the product with the highest or most rapidly rising marginal utility and thus succumb to monomania. Since people do in fact consume a large variety of goods, rising marginal utility must be rejected along with constant marginal utility. This proof shows at best that the marginal utility of some goods falls, not that it falls for every good. But what is worse is that the proof depends on the implicit assumption of independence among the utility functions. If additive utility are replaced by generalized utility functions, even rising marginal utility in all directions may lead consumers to seek variety because of complementarities between goods.

The advantage of the indifference-curve technique is that it forces us by virtue of the concept of 'indifference' itself to pay attention to the interrelationships between goods. Increasing marginal utility and concave indifference maps seem vaguely similar, since both lead to monomania. But increasing marginal utility produces monomania only if we ignore complementarities between goods, whereas concave indifference curves imply that one is willing to offer ever larger amounts of y to acquire additional units of x, which might be true if x and y were substitutes. The real point, however, is that, once the idea of cardinal measurement is dropped, the very notion of marginal utility as a uniquely determinable quantity loses all meaning. A diminishing marginal rate of substitution is *not* equivalent to diminishing marginal utility.

10. The Revealed Preference Approach

There is no doubt that we often prefer A to B much more strongly than we prefer B to C. Such introspective feelings, however, do not necessarily have any operational consequence. We would have chosen A over B and B over C even if we had preferred A to B much less than B to C. At the level of observation, the idea of preference intensity has no meaning. But if we are going to dismiss introspective evidence, the notion of indifference is as objectionable as the concept of preference intensity. No *single* act of choice on the part of the consumer can prove his indifference between two situations. Unless we are going to give indifference a statistical meaning – the individual does not choose *B* over *A* more frequently than he chooses *A* over *B* in a large number of observations – we must dismiss the concept of indifference with the same behaviorist argument that we used against the notion of preference intensity. In recent times, Samuelson has shown that it is possible to derive demand curves solely from an individual's 'revealed preferences' without the use either of the concept of preference intensity or the concept of indifference. The only assumption we must make is that of 'transitivity': if the individual is found to have chosen *A* over *B* in a particular instance, then he cannot choose *B* over *A* in any other instance. The assumption may be stated more simply: no two observations of choice behavior can provide conflicting evidence of an individual's preferences. The consumer behaves 'rationally' but only in this minimum sense of consistency of choices.

The 'Fundamental Theorem of Consumption Theory', according to Samuelson, states that the demand for a commodity always changes in the same direction as that of a change of the income of the consumer; positively sloped income curves always imply negatively inclined demand curves. To demonstrate this theorem, let us suppose that the consumer devotes his entire income to the purchase of only two goods. The original price-income situation is represented in Figure 9–11 by *AB* and the consumer is observed to have chosen the combination *x* and *y* represented by the Point *R*. *R* is 'revealed' to have been preferred to all other combinations of *x* and *y* within the area *OAB* attainable by him. Suppose that the price of *x* falls and that the new price-income line is *AC*. Let us now deprive the consumer of an amount of money income that would leave him with exactly enough to buy the same quantities of everything at the lower price of *x*. The new price-income line *DE* is parallel to the old line *AC* and passes through *R*. It is evident that the consumer cannot choose any point above *R* on *DE* for the simple reason that *R* was revealed to be preferred to any such point in the original price-income situation. To choose a point that was previously available but was revealed by his choice of *R* to have been worse than *R* is tantamount to inconsistent behavior. We rule out this possibility by assumption. Hence, the consumer must either choose *R* or a point in the newly available shaded area; he must choose to buy either the same amount of *x* or more. If we now grant him back that amount of money originally taken away from him, he will buy more of *x* if the income elasticity of demand for *x* is positive. We have, therefore, proved that the demand curve for *x* is negatively inclined if the income curve for *x* is positively inclined. On the same grounds, if the income effect is negative, the change in demand owing to a change in price is indeterminate.

Since the substitution effect cannot be isolated from the income effect on the level of observation, the 'revealed preference' approach cannot distinguish between the Giffen Paradox – a negative income effect combined with a weak substitution effect – and a negative income effect combined with a strong substitution effect. On the other hand, the revealed-preference approach yields the same results as the Hicksian indifference-curve approach without resorting to the nonoperational concept of 'indifference'. Furthermore, the distinction between substitution and income effects

Figure 9–11

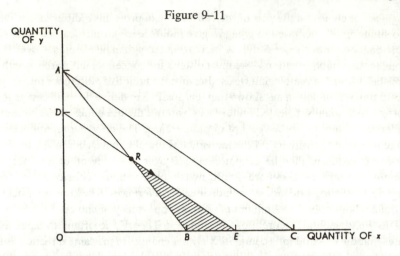

in the indifference-curve approach is purely taxonomic: it provides us with boxes for classificatory purposes but does not tell us how to fill them. Clearly, if we cannot measure utility in cardinal terms and so feel impelled to abandon the old marginal utility theory, there is little point in not going the whole way to the outright behaviorism of the revealed-preference approach.

11. Marshallian Demand Curves

It is possible, as we have seen, to rationalize the negative slope of the demand curve for 'unimportant' goods by means of utility theory, invoking either cardinal or ordinal utility. But why not deduce the demand curve directly from recorded data? After all, the fact that quantity and price are generally inversely related had been known long before utility was ever thought of. Price-quantity data, however, refer to successive observations through time, whereas a demand curve refers to alternative intentions to purchase at one and the same time. To construct a Marshallian demand curve, we have to ask consumers how much they would purchase if prices were other than they are but other things are exactly the same. From casual observation we feel quite sure that most demand curves are negatively inclined. But this is hardly a satisfactory foundation for so important a concept. In the absence of elaborate econometric techniques that have only recently become available, we have little alternative but to deduce the negative inclination of the demand curve from fundamental psychological postulates.

The effort to link utility to demand in the Marshallian manner via the 'law of satiable wants' is beset by two difficulties. When we replace additive by generalized utility functions, the law of diminishing marginal utility does not furnish 'one general Law of Demand'. Moreover, a generalized utility function robs us of any operational procedure for the cardinal measurement of utility. With the elimination of cardinal measurement, the very notion of deriving *diminishing* increments of utility from additional units of a good loses all meaning and it is no longer possible to make statements about the welfare effects of a change in price.

No wonder then that Marshall tried to simplify his argument by the device of holding MU_e approximately constant. Although he spoke of one general Law of Demand, he inferred from some data on bread consumption supplied by a contemporary statistician named Robert Giffen that the whole aggregate demand curve for bread, and particularly the demand curve for bread among the poorer classes, was positively inclined – hence 'Giffen's Paradox'. By abstracting from the income effect, he eliminated all the practical consequences of intercommodity relationships and in this way rescued the additive utility function. If the utility functions for individual goods are additive, goods are necessarily independent of each other. And if they are, utility can be cardinally measured along the lines proposed by Fisher.[3] It is true that we can 'explain' consumer behavior just as well with ordinal as with cardinal measurement of utility. Consumers are only expected to equate ratios of marginal utilities to ratios of prices and the theory of price determination never requires either interpersonal comparisons of utility or intrapersonal comparisons of the utility differences between pairwise choices. But Marshall was reluctant to abandon the use of the demand curve to measure the consumer's surplus from a change in price and for that reason, despite all submissions to the contrary, he retained both the additive utility function and the concept of an approximately constant MU_e.

Marshall's uneasiness about the assumption of a constant MU_e may account for his failure to draw up an explicit list of the restrictions placed upon the demand curve for an individual commodity x. The traditional description of *ceteris paribus*, a description derived from Edgeworth and never repudiated by Marshall, includes such items as: (1) tastes; (2) money income; (3) the prices of closely related goods; (4) the prices of unrelated goods; and (5) expectations about future prices. The logical corollary of ignoring income effects is to hold real income, not money income, constant along the demand curve. In the foregoing list, however, (2), (3) and (4) together imply that real income varies with every change in the price of x. Moreover, (3) and (4) violate the general assumption of the *Principles* that the purchasing power of money is to be kept constant; every change in the price of x unaccompanied by an opposite change in some other price alters the value of money.

There are two ways of resolving this dilemma. One is to argue that the real-income effect of a change in the price of an 'unimportant' commodity, and the corresponding change of the purchasing power of money, is so small as to be negligible. This was Marshall's own way out of the dilemma. The other, advocated by Friedman, is to

---

[3] It must be kept in mind that we are concerned at this point with the derivation of *individual* demand curves from individual utility curves. A generalized utility function may also contain as one of its variables the effect of other people's utility functions. This poses a new additivity problem. Since each individual demand curve is drawn up on the assumption of given demand functions of other consumers in the same market, the market demand curve for the product can no longer be constructed by simply summing horizontally over the individual demand functions; this would be like explaining fashions by the summation of individual ideas about dress. Interdependence between the individual preference functions often referred to as the 'snob effect', 'bandwagon effect', or simply Veblenesque Effect, raises special problems in the interpretation of market demand curves.

replace (4) by the condition that the prices of all related goods move inversely to the price of x so as to keep real income constant along the demand curve for x. The latter definition would indeed avoid most of the pitfalls in the usual Marshallian treatment. A Friedman-Marshall demand curve *must* be negatively inclined under the conditions implied by its very construction. Moreover, by freezing only the prices of obvious substitutes and complements and by treating only the behavior of an average of all other prices, it claims to provide a more practical and useful concept of the demand curve. But however impractical may be the usual injunction to keep each individual price except one constant, it is no less impractical to be told to keep *some* prices constant. Any specified set of price changes must be arbitrary since the changes imposed are not necessarily those that would occur in the real world in association with a change in the price of x. The traditional approach is also arbitrary in specifying no change in any price except the one under examination, but at least it is not ambiguous. Moreover, it is not clear what starting price is to be considered for drawing up the Friedman-Marshall demand curve of a commodity: keeping the level of an individual's real income constant implies a different offsetting price variation for each different starting price.

In reality, the income effect is as integral a part of consumer behavior as the substitution effect. It is true that a demand curve drawn up so as to allow for income effects may be either negatively or positively inclined; the usual Marshallian demand curve has no empirical implications that are capable of being contradicted by single observations. It is also true that Marshall himself occasionally entertained the idea of interpreting demand curves as constant real-income curves. Nevertheless, the traditional method of drawing demand curves has the advantage of focusing attention on the fact that price changes in the real world do invariably affect the real income of buyers in the market and so shift their demand curves in all other markets. Conceptually, the traditional demand curve is simpler to grasp and closer to the spirit of approximation that characterizes partial equilibrium analysis. Econometrically, the overwhelming difficulties in the way of actually drawing up a demand curve constructed on the traditional interpretation are no greater than those involved in drawing it up on the Friedman interpretation.

The real world contains no objective entity corresponding to *the* demand curve. For some purposes it is conceivable that a constant real-income curve might prove more useful. For most purposes, however, the traditional interpretation provides a superior instrument for grasping the inverse price-quantity relationship asserted by the Law of Demand. The concept of a demand curve has, after all, only a limited practical applicability. A demand curve, like a supply curve, is an aid to straight thinking. It is nothing but a device for distinguishing the various forces that influence price. The Marshallian 'cross' of demand and supply helps us understand why a free market tends to clear itself, why an equilibrium price once reached may be stable, and how prices act as signals transmitting relevant information to buyers and sellers. They permit us to indicate without quantitative precision what would happen to price and quantity if income or technology underwent specified changes. They help us to grasp the consequences of taxes and subsidies, price floors and price ceilings. It is not too much to say that almost everything we know about the behavior of the economic system can be illuminated by way of reference to the fundamental cross of demand and supply. Looked at in this way, there is nothing to choose between the two interpretations of the demand curve. The method of holding money income and all other individual prices constant yields a richer but also a more complicated theory of demand. That is all.

12. The Status of the Subjective Theory of Value

By making utility the 'explanation' of consumer behavior, the founders of the subjective theory of value ran into a double-barrelled opposition: it was argued, on the one hand, that the utility theory of value rests on bad or at least questionable psychology and that, on the other hand, the psychological aspects of consumer behavior are irrelevant to the objective facts of the economic process, which runs its course irrespective of individual feelings. Much of this opposition was based on a confusion between the two meanings given to the word 'utility'. In the theory of consumer behavior, utility is a quantity that it is useful to regard an individual as maximizing in the interpretation and prediction of behavior. A utility function is nothing more than a way of describing an individual's preferences between various real and hypothetical alternatives. Such a function no more 'explains' an individual's choices than a production-transformation curve 'explains' the state of technology. In welfare economics, however, utility is a quantity that an individual 'should' maximize or that society 'should' help him to maximize. Here utility is indeed a quantitative concept, whereas in the theory of consumer behavior utility is strictly speaking no quantity at all but simply a choice indicator.

As soon as this distinction is firmly grasped, most of the criticism that was at one time levelled against utility theory as a theory of consumer behavior falls to the ground. The most common objection found in the critical literature is the objection to the so-called 'hedonistic premise', the tendency to identify the desire that prompts an individual to purchase with the underlying utility or satisfaction that he derives from the purchase. According to the critics, marginal utility theory, ignoring as it does the habitual and conventional forces that shape desires and wants, constitutes an inadequate explanation of consumer behavior. Now it is clear that if price measures any subjective quantity, it measures 'desires' and not 'satisfactions': it is a measure of satisfactions only to the degree to which desire is an accurate reflection of satisfaction. The effect of ignorance on the part of buyers of the quality of the product, the effect of fraud or misrepresentation on the part of sellers, and possibly the effect of aggressive advertising is to increase the disparity between desire and satisfaction. These constitute important problems in welfare economics, not in the theory of demand. The law of diminishing marginal utility may be replaced by the law of the diminishing marginal rate of substitution; this would not alter by one jot the effort to deduce the Law of Demand from fundamental postulates about consumer behavior. The theory of price determination does not require the 'hedonistic premise'.

The defenders of the subjective theory of value were almost as confused on this point as the critics. After citing impulse, habit, self-denial, mistaken expectation, and other causes of disparities between desire and satisfaction, Marshall concluded that, given the absence of direct measurement of either desire or satisfaction, we must fall back on price and make it serve 'with all its faults, *both* for desires which prompt activities, and for the satisfactions that result from them'. This is a footnote to the first page of a chapter devoted to the theory of demand! The tendency to draw facile welfare conclusions from utility theory, ignoring inequalities of the distribution of income and the difficulties in making meaningful interpersonal comparisons – the chief offender being Marshall himself – were largely responsible for producing a skeptical attitude toward the achievements of marginal utility analysis.

When the misconceptions of the nature of utility theory are cleared away, what is left of most of the criticisms of received utility theory is a profound distaste of economic analysis that proceeds by drawing up demand and supply curves on the basis of *given* wants and *given* techniques. The theory of consumption, it was argued, should throw light on the inherent tendency of wants to expand and change instead of being concerned with the mechanical process by which given wants are satisfied. With the growth of advertising and other forms of nonprice competition, business firms not only set out to create new wants but to foster 'pecuniary canons of taste'. Once consumers have developed the habit of judging quality by price, every change in price affects their tastes. There is no point in drawing up demand curves for homogeneous products on the basis of given tastes when every change in price alters the nature of the product in consumers' minds and so shifts the demand curves. The traditional theory of consumer behavior, based as it is on the belief that consumers' tastes are stable and independent of prices, must be abandoned in favor of a broad socioeconomic theory of consumption. With various degrees of vehemence, this kind of criticism was voiced over and over again by members of the American Institutionalist School, not to mention Marxists.

In its extreme form, an emphasis upon the inherent instability of wants is destructive not only of the theory of demand but also of traditional welfare economics grounded upon the doctrine of 'consumers' sovereignty'. It is an objection that cannot be lightly dismissed. Insofar as demand theory is concerned, it is perfectly true that it cannot get along without the assumption of stable tastes. The fundamental principle of utility theory is that consumers act 'as if' they were maximizing utility and this principle can be translated into the 'consistency postulate': if an individual prefers A to B in one situation, he will not be found to choose B in preference to A in another situation. It is clear that consistency means constant tastes and that inconsistency can be interpreted as a change in tastes. Indeed, the 'consistency postulate' amounts to the proposition that a utility function exists, a question that has been discussed by mathematical economists since the days of Fisher and Pareto under the heading of 'the integrability problem'. If it were really true that tastes are always in a process of flux, consumer behavior would be utterly unpredictable – at least in the absence of the broad theory of consumption that critics ask for – and none of the familiar propositions of the theory of demand would stand scientific scrutiny.

It is not clear how far the critics want to carry this argument. Even an Institutionalist may occasionally permit himself the luxury of drawing demand and supply curves to illustrate the workings of the market mechanism. If the pattern of wants is never stable even for a short period of time, it is difficult to see why businessmen spend so much money creating new wants; why generate new wants if their inherent instability makes it impossible to guarantee that they can be exploited for a definite period of time? Without denying that tastes are continuously being molded by the action of producers, it is still possible to investigate the pattern of consumers' demand on the provisional assumption of given wants. No doubt the formal theory of demand cannot be applied to the real world of imperfect competition without serious qualification. But that is hardly an argument for placing a ban on demand curves.

Acceptance of the concept of a demand function as a useful tool of analysis does not, of course, constitute an endorsement of traditional utility theory. We could follow Cournot's and Cassel's approach, employing demand functions directly without a utility substructure. The reason why most economists have rejected this approach is that it seems tantamount to throwing away information. Since demand curves cannot be simply observed, it is hoped that the specification of behavioral assumptions – and that is all utility theory is – will add information on the nature of demand functions. And yet the long and tortuous history of utility theory presents a disheartening picture. Few of the sponsors of utility bothered to test the implications of the theory; and, indeed, utility theory did not prove to be a fruitful source of hypotheses about demand. The attitude of the utility theorists was that utility theory was merely a matter of common sense. The inadequacy of this criterion is demonstrated, as Stigler said in his review of the history of utility theory, by the slow intellectual progress of utility theory: 'The additive utility function was popularized in the 1870's; it was 1909 before the implication of positively sloped income curves was derived. The generalized utility function was proposed in 1881; it was 1915 before its implications were derived. The chief of these implications is that, if consumers do not buy less of a commodity when their incomes rise, they will surely buy less when the price of a commodity rises. This was the chief product – so far as hypotheses on economic behavior go – of the long labors of a very large number of able economists. These very able economists, and their predecessors, however, had known all along that demand curves have negative slopes, quite independently of their utility theorizing.'

WELFARE ECONOMICS

13. Consumer's Surplus

If it were possible to measure the marginal utility of money income by some such method as that suggested by Neumann and Morgenstern it would be possible to trace the consumer's marginal utility function for a particular good from his demand schedule by the equilibrium formula $MU_x = p_x MU_e$. But even without cardinal measurement of MU_e, we can say that the marginal utility of an 'unimportant' commodity is equal to its price measured in terms of MU_e, treated as a constant. For small variations in real income, we can assume that the addition of one dollar to the consumer's total expenditure increases his total utility by a constant amount. Thus, the price that a consumer is willing to pay for a particular quantity of x directly expresses the marginal utility of x to him. Likewise, the *total* utility of acquiring a certain quantity of x, given the fact that x is 'unimportant' in the budget of the consumer, may be derived by summing the marginal utilities associated with the successive increments of x from O to C (Figure 9–12). With each thin parallelogram expressing the marginal utility of a finite increment of x, the total utility of the quantity $OC = OABC$. The consumer would be willing to pay the sum $OABC$ but he actually pays $OEBC$ for quantity OC. Hence, EAB equals the consumer's surplus from buying amount OC of x; this triangle measures the loss in the consumer's welfare if he were prevented from buying any quantity of x. The surplus is really a utility surplus but it is expressible in pecuniary terms because of our invariable unit of measurement, namely, the marginal utility of expenditures in general.[4]

Marshall defined this kind of consumer's surplus as 'the excess of the price which he would be willing to pay rather than go without the thing, over that which he actually does pay'. We can think of it, in the manner of Dupuit [see chapter 8, section 16], as the amount that can be extracted from the consumer by discriminatory pricing. If a monopolist could shade his price along the consumer's demand curve, his marginal revenue would be equal to the price charged for the last unit sold, for he could always sell an extra unit at a lower price without lowering the price of every other unit. The maximum possible gain from this kind of quantity discrimination is Dupuit's 'price surplus', being a money measure of the utility surplus to a consumer from being able to buy each unit of the commodity at the same price. Mathematically, the price surplus is *estimated* as the area under the demand curve from zero to the given quantity minus the price-quantity rectangle.

We do have to assume that the demand curve crosses the price axis. If the individual's offer for the first unit is not defined so that the demand curve does not touch the y-axis, the integral under the demand curve is infinite. But this objection is easily overcome by measuring consumer's surplus from some positive value of the x-axis. There is a more fatal objection to the estimate of the price surplus as the triangle under the demand curve. If we start with a given income for the individual and let him buy successive units of x at the maximum price he will pay for each unit, we trace out a constant real-income curve, that is, a Friedman-Marshall demand curve, or a 'marginal valuation curve' as Hicks called it, which always lies below the Marshallian demand curve at lower prices and above it at higher prices. This is due to the fact that real income increases along a Marshallian demand curve as the price

---

[4] The marginal utility of money income is not the only invariable measure we might use. In his *Alphabet of Economic Science* (1889), Wicksteed suggested the use of 'a given amount of work as the standard unit by which to estimate the magnitude of satisfaction. For example, one might express the utility of numbers of tons of coal by the lifting work one is willing to do to acquire another hundred weight.' 'In academical circles', Wicksteed remarked, 'it is not unusual to take an hour of correcting exam papers as the standard measure of pleasure and pain'. Despite this clinching piece of evidence, however, there is no reason to believe that it is possible to put welfare economics on a sound basis by defining an invariant unit of disutility of labour in the manner of Adam Smith [see chapter 2, section 10].

Figure 9–12

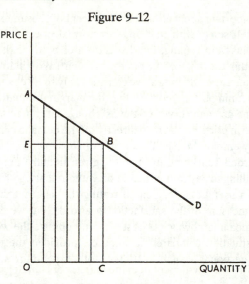

falls; at lower prices, the constant real income curve shifts, as it were, to the right; the loci of intersections of the shifting constant real-income curve with the successive horizontal price lines trace out a Marshallian demand curve (see Figure 9–13). If the starting price is p_2, the marginal valuation curve is m_2; if the starting price is p_1, the marginal valuation curve is m_1, and so on. An unambiguous measure of consumer's surplus can be derived only from something like a marginal valuation curve, which holds real income constant by showing all units purchased separately at their full marginal prices. For a given quantity of x purchase, the Marshallian demand curve overstates the amount of consumer's surplus.

It was partly in recognition of this objection that Marshall confined himself for all practical purposes to the measurement of the consumer's surplus from a given *change*

Figure 9–13

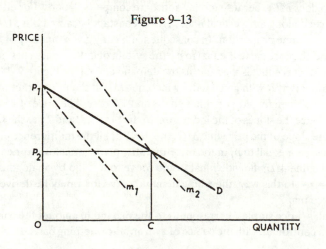

in price. In all important applications of the concept of consumer's surplus, Marshall concerned himself solely with the range of normal price variations, defining the consumer's surplus from a change in price as the area between the demand curve and the price axis within the range of the price movement. We will follow Hicks in calling this 'Marshall's measure'. So long as we consider only small changes in the quantities consumed of an 'unimportant' commodity, the marginal valuation curve practically coincides with the demand curve and the psychological gain or loss to the consumer of a small change in price may be read directly off the demand curve. This means that we cannot really employ Marshall's concept of consumer's surplus to measure the satisfaction afforded from being able to buy a given amount of x at a price below what one would be willing to pay rather than to do without it altogether. It is true that the notion remains a useful one for demonstrating the fact that the price paid for an article is not a measure of the satisfaction it affords, but we cannot measure this surplus in any meaningful way. At best we can appraise the welfare effect of one price-quantity situation compared to another, provided the expenditure on the commodity in question is a small fraction of total expenditures.

14. Restatement

The difficulties in measuring consumer's surplus from a demand curve can be illustrated by means of indifference curves. Placing money on the vertical axis and the commodity x on the horizontal axis (see Figure 9–14), Marshall's assumption of a constant marginal utility of money corresponds to indifference curves that are vertically parallel: at any given quantity of x the slope of the curves, expressing the marginal rate of substitution between money and x or MU_x/MU_e, is the same no matter how large the quantity of money on the ordinate; MRS depends only on the quantity consumed and not on the amount of money spent on goods in general. The individual's money spending is so large that small changes in the volume of his spending do not affect his willingness to part with it; or to put it differently, even when the quantity of x is constant, as MU_e falls with increases in the quantity of money, so does MU_x, because money and x are competing goods. For either reason, as we proceed along any vertical line, MRS is constant because both MU_x and MU_e change in the same proportion. In consequence, at any given quantity of x, the MRS of every indifference curve is equal to p_x: the system of indifference curves reduces to a single MRS curve that is the same as the demand curve (see Figure 9–14). Suppose the individual is at R with given money income OM; at the price structure MOQ he buys Oq_1 of x, spending Rq_1 on other goods and TR on x. The price of $x = TR/MT = OM/OQ$. Since the slopes of the indifference curves at S, R and T are the same, being equal to the slope of the price line MQ, the MRS of all the indifference curves at the quantity Oq_1 are equal to p_1 in the price-quantity plane. At a lower price of x, given by the price line ML, the individual would move to R', and by analogous reasoning $OM/OL = p_2$. In this way, the whole demand curve for x may be derived from the indifference map.

Marshall's 'price surplus' corresponds to the maximum amount the consumer will offer when confronted with the choice of x on an all-or-nothing basis. If the consumer

Figure 9–14

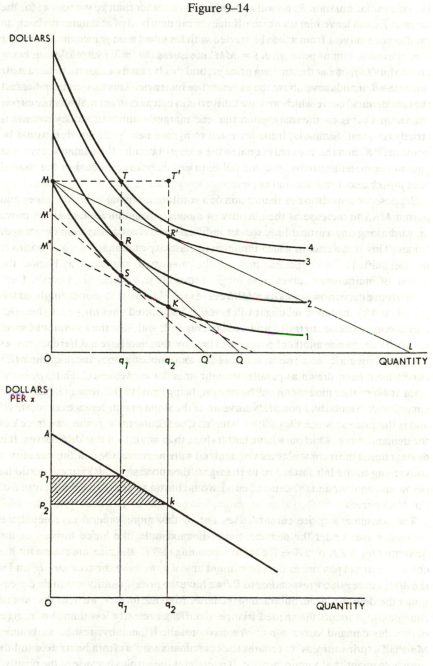

is at the initial situation R, he will at most offer TS rather than go without x, for the offer of TS will leave him no worse off than being deprived of x: it puts him back on indifference curve 1 from which he started with his given money income M before x was offered to him at price p_1. $RS = MM'$ measures the 'price surplus' from being able to buy Oq_1 of x at the uniform price p_1, and this is exactly equal to the area p_1Ar under the demand curve above the expenditure rectangle. This follows from the fact that the demand curve which we have derived is in fact a constant real-income curve, drawn up as it is on the assumption that the marginal utility of money income is strictly constant. Similarly, if the price fell to p_2, the new 'price surplus' would be equal to $R'K$, and this is exactly equal to the area p_2Ak under the demand curve; the gain in consumer's surplus from the fall in price, therefore, is equal to the shaded area p_2p_1rk under the demand curve.

Suppose we now drop the assumption of a constant marginal utility of money and permit MRS to increase as the quantity of money income increases. As we move upward along any vertical line, we cut indifference curves at successively steeper slopes. This is the case in which the income elasticity of demand for x is positive: parallel shifts in the budget line increase the quantity demanded of x. Hence, the system of indifference curves is no longer reducible to a single MRS curve. Each indifference curve now has its own MRS curve (see Figure 9–15). For example, at the price line MQ the amount bought will be Oq_1. The dotted lines $m_{1,2\ 3}$ are the MRS curves corresponding to the indifference curves 1, 2, and 3 for the amount of Oq_1 of x: they lie above one another because the slopes of the successive indifference curves for a given quantity of x rise with increasing amounts of money income; the MRS curves have been drawn as parallel straight lines for convenience. Thus, p_2 is the price at which the amount Oq_1 will be bought, being equal to the slope of indifference curve 2 at R. Similarly, p_1 on MRS curve m_3 is the slope of indifference curve 3 at R' and is the price at which Oq_2 will be bought. Connecting these points, we trace out the demand curve, which now has a flatter slope than any one of the MRS curves. It is evident that if the income elasticity of demand were negative, the indifference curves converging to the left instead of to the right, the successive MRS curves would lie below one another and the demand curve would have a steeper slope than any one of the MRS curves.

The consumer's 'price surplus' does not in this more general case equal the triangular area under the demand curve. For example, the 'price surplus' at the quantity Oq_1 is RK or $TK - RT$. Corresponding to TK, the maximum amount the consumer would pay rather than go without any of x, we have the area Op_3sq_1 under the MRS curve m_1; corresponding to RT we have the price-quantity rectangle Op_2rq_1 under the demand curve. Subtracting the latter from the former, we have the shaded triangle p_2p_3d *minus* the shaded triangle drs. This is clearly less than the triangle under the demand curve p_2p_3r. We have reached the same results as before: Marshall's 'price surplus' overstates the consumer's surplus from being able to buy the whole quantity at a uniform price. It overstates the surplus because of the positive real income effect. Once again, it is apparent that if the income elasticity of demand for x were negative – if MRS became smaller as the quantity of money income

Figure 9–15

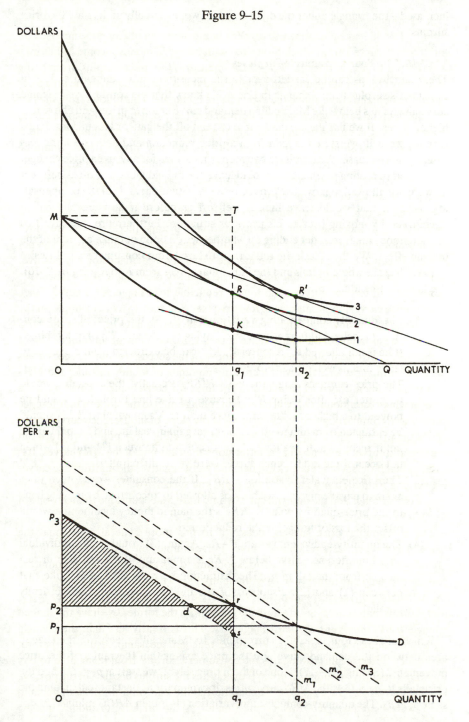

increased – the triangle under the demand curve would actually understate the price surplus.

15. The Four Consumer's Surpluses

These conclusions can be carried over to the measurement of the gain or loss in consumer's surplus from a change in price. We know that the constant real-income curve always lies below the Marshallian demand curve at lower prices and above it at higher prices. If we use the demand curve to read off the gain or loss in consumer's surplus, we will overstate the gain from a price reduction and understate the loss from a price increase. We thus have two money measures for any given price change: (1) the compensating payment that would leave the individual as well off as before if he were not allowed to move back to the previous situation; and (2) the compensating payment that would leave him as well off as before if he were allowed to 'recontract' by moving back to his previous situation. Furthermore, we have two further money measures, depending on whether we do or do not take account of the income effect. We thus reach the full array of Hicks' 'four consumer's surpluses'.

Take the case where p_x falls and the individual moves from R to R' (Figure 9–16). We have in ascending order:

(1) The quantity-compensating variation – $R'r'$. As the price falls, the consumer reaches indifference curve 2, buying Oq of x and $R'q$ of other things. If he is not allowed to 'recontract', $R'r'$ can be extracted from him so as to leave him as well off as before.

(2) The price-compensating variation – $R'R'_1$. Actually, the consumer would be better off after losing $R'r'$ because a price line through r' would be tangent to a higher indifference curve than 1. A sum equal to $R'R'_1$ should be extracted from him to offset the initial gain in real income from the price fall if recontracting is allowed. The distinction between (1) and (2) would not occur if the indifference curves were vertically parallel.

(3) The price-equivalent variation – RR_1. If the consumer were forced once again to pay the higher price but was allowed to 'recontract' by moving back to the price-quantity point R, RR_1 is the gain in money income that would offset the loss of foregoing the reduction in p_x.

(4) The quantity-equivalent variation – Rr. Again, (3) would put the individual on an indifference curve below 2. Rr is a measure of the full gain in real income from the fall in p_x. The distinction between (3) and (4), like that between (1) and (2), disappears if the indifference curves are vertically parallel.

Which of these four measures corresponds to 'Marshall's measure': the shaded area between the demand curve and the price axis within the range of the price movement? (See figure 9–17). None of them precisely. If we start at $p_2 = OB$ and the price falls to $p_1 = OA$, the MRS curve m_1 is drawn up for a constant real income the same as at p_2. The quantity-compensating variation (1) is then $ABCG$ minus GFL, or

Figure 9–16

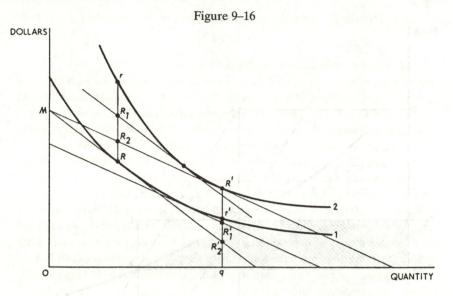

the amount $OBCLq_2$ that the individual would be willing to pay for q_2 to be as well off as before minus the amount $OAFq_2$, which he actually does pay. The individual would not be better off than if he had been compelled to purchase the extra quantity of q_1q_2 at p_2 but worse off than if he had been allowed to purchase the whole of q_2 at p_1. The price-compensating variation (2), therefore, is $ABCG$. Thus, the two compensating payments (1) and (2) fall short of 'Marshall's measure'. On the other hand, the two equivalent variations (3) and (4) exceed 'Marshall's measure'. If m_2 is drawn up for a constant real income the same as at p_1, the price-equivalent variation (3) evaluated at the lower quantity q_1 is $ABDF$ on analogy with the price-compensating variation. Likewise, the quantity-equivalent variation (4) is $ABDF$ plus CKD: to stay on m_2 and to buy q_1, the price would have to rise to S, in which case the total loss of consumer's surplus would have been $ABSKDF$; in fact, the amount $BSKC$ was not paid, so that we are left with $ABDF$ plus CKD. Thus the two equivalent variations are greater than 'Marshall's measure' shown by the shaded area.

It should be noted that for a rise in price the gains and losses in terms of utility are the same as for an equivalent fall in price, but consumer's surplus measured in terms of money is not because the value of money in terms of goods is different in the two cases. In effect, for a rise in price the compensating variations (1) and (2) become equivalent variations (3) and (4), and *vice versa*.

16. Tax-Bounty Analysis

Having exhausted our patience on the subtleties of *estimating* the consumer's surplus from a demand curve, we must now observe that if the fraction of expenditures devoted to the commodity in question is small and if the demand curve over the range between the two prices is highly elastic, the four consumer's surpluses merge and become equal to 'Marshall's measure'. Assuming this is so, we have not yet shown

Figure 9–17

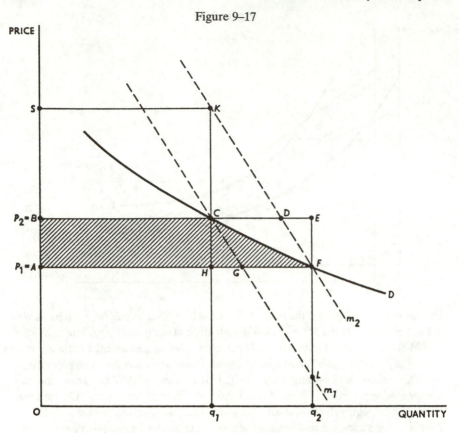

how we can add the individual consumers' surpluses in a market to obtain a measure
of the aggregate consumers' surplus from a change in price. In Marshall's practical
use of the tool, the apostrophe in 'consumers' surplus' always comes after the *s*: it is
the collective gain of all the buyers in a market that interests him. He begins with the
individual's surplus and then employs the argument that most markets are homogeneous with respect to the income class of buyers to justify the idea that the
individual is a modal representative of the group. In this way he achieves additivity
without raising the question of how the aggregate surplus is distributed among
individual buyers. It is clear that Veblenesque Effects – other people's utilities or
incomes appearing in each individual's utility function – destroy the possibility of
aggregating consumer's surpluses. Even with additive utility functions, the notion of
consumers' surplus involves us in interpersonal comparisons.

   Marshall's principal use of the concept in tax-bounty analysis affords a beautiful
example of the careless way in which most neoclassical economists arrived at welfare
conclusions. Marshall begins by showing that a tax imposed on a commodity obeying
the law of constant returns or constant costs results in a loss of consumers' surplus
that exceeds the amount of the tax receipts, and, conversely, a subsidy to such a
commodity exceeds the gain in consumers' surplus. We couple a demand curve with a

Figure 9–18

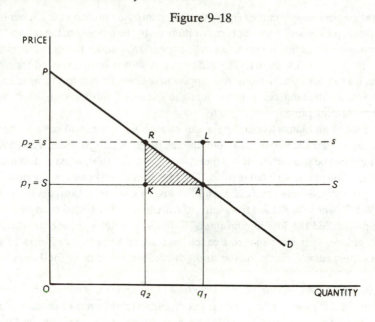

Figure 9–19

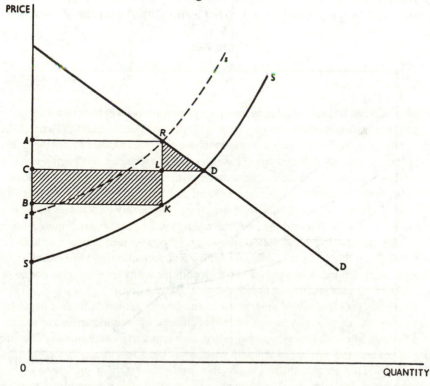

horizontal long-run supply curve (Figure 9–18) and impose a uniform tax *LA* per unit of the product purchased. The supply curve shifts up by the amount of the tax and the loss of consumers' surplus is expressed by the area *SsRA* under the demand curve. Tax receipts are equal to *SsRK*. The difference is shown by the shaded triangle. Likewise, if a subsidy shifts the long-run supply curve down from *ss* to *SS*, the triangle *RAL* above the demand curve represents the excess of subsidies paid out over consumers' surplus gained.

In the case of an industry operating under diminishing returns to scale a bounty gives the same results as above. To overcome the forces making for increasing costs, the subsidy must be proportionately larger; once again, the subsidy exceeds the gain in consumers' surplus from a fall in price. The effects of a tax, however, are now less certain. Tax receipts here are *BARK* and the loss in consumers' surplus is *CARD* (Figure 9–19). Since the shaded rectangle *BCLK* exceeds the shaded triangle *RDL*, tax receipts exceed the loss in consumers' surplus, a result opposite to what we obtained before. It is clear that this conclusion depends on the steepness of the long-run supply curves, that is, on the strength of the forces making for diminishing returns.

With increasing returns or decreasing costs, the long-run supply curve slopes downward. In this case, the loss in consumers' surplus must once again exceed tax receipts. Taxing a decreasing cost industry raises prices and thus raises the loss in consumers' surplus above tax receipts. The effect of a subsidy, however, depends entirely on the slope of the supply curve (see Figure 9–20). The amount of the subsidy

Figure 9–20

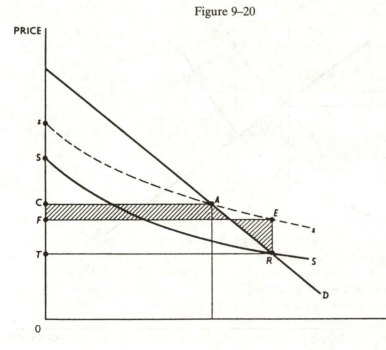

is *TFER*, and the gain in consumers' surplus is *TCAR*. As shown, the shaded trapezoid is greater than the shaded triangle; therefore, the gain in consumers' surplus exceeds the subsidy payment. But if the supply curve were more elastic, we would approach the constant cost case: subsidy payments would exceed consumers' surplus.

The argument may be summed up by supposing that an increasing cost industry and a decreasing cost industry both face the same demand curve (see Figure 9–21). Initially, the increasing cost industry produces Oq_2 and the decreasing cost industry produces Oq_1. A tax is placed on the first industry and the tax receipts are then used up to subsidize the second industry, that is, rectangle $KAFG$ = rectangle $CLHD$. The *net* gain in consumers' surplus is shown by the shaded area $CBED$. The increasing cost industry now produces Oq_1, and the decreasing cost industry now produces Oq_3; the *net* gain in physical output is q_2q_3.

Figure 9–21

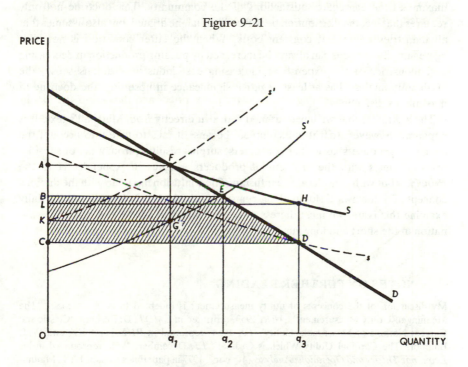

What may we conclude from all this? Apparently, it is possible for the state to increase aggregate economic welfare by taxing increasing cost industries where tax receipts *may* exceed the resulting loss in consumers' surplus, and using the proceeds to subsidize decreasing cost industries, where subsidy payments *may* be less than the resulting gain in consumers' surplus. The argument depends on the possibility of distinguishing increasing from decreasing cost industries, a formidable problem, as we shall see. Moreover, the forces making for increasing or decreasing costs must make themselves sharply felt in each group of industries. Marshall's proof is purely geometrical but the underlying reasoning is perfectly simple. A tax on increasing cost industries raises their supply price and reduces the amount they supply; this makes it possible to produce the supply at lower costs, at a margin that represents a superior use of resources. The supply price rises but by less than the tax, owing to the savings effected by producing a superior marginal unit at lower cost. Tax proceeds are now used to subsidize decreasing cost industries; their prices fall as the quantity supplied increases because the increased amount is supplied at lower costs per unit. Total satisfactions have increased all round because resources have been shifted from goods produced at rising supply prices to goods produced at falling supply prices.

Marshall expressed some caution about the practical applicability of this piece of reasoning. He warned of the administrative problems of collecting the tax and determining the level of the subsidy. It plays an important part, however, in his refutation of vulgar *Harmonielehre*: the doctrine that perfect competition necessarily maximizes the aggregate satisfactions of the community. This doctrine not only requires that income distribution be perfectly equal, he argued, but also assumes that all industries operate at constant costs. When the latter condition is not met, aggregate satisfactions can always be increased by pushing production in decreasing cost industries at the expense of increasing cost industries. In this sense, the tax-bounty analysis has at least negative significance in upsetting 'the doctrine of maximum satisfactions'.

The argument that we have outlined is drawn directly from Marshall's text. It is apparent, however, that it is incomplete because it fails to take into account the change in producers' as well as consumers' surplus resulting from a tax or subsidy. Marshall deals with the problem of producers' surplus in Appendix H to the *Principles* but with considerable confusion. The confusion has to do with the dubious concept of a downward sloping long-run supply curve. But before we can fruitfully examine this issue, we must digress to review Marshall's theory of price determination in the short and long run.

NOTES ON FURTHER READING

My discussion of the concepts of utility measurement is indebted to A. A. Alchain, 'The Meaning of Utility Measurement', *AER*, 1953, reprinted in *EMDT*; D. Ellsberg, 'Classic and Current Notions of Measurable Utility', *EJ*, 1954, reprinted in *RHET* and *UT*; and W. J. Baumol, 'The Cardinal Utility Which is Ordinal', *EJ*, December, 1958, reproduced in his *Economic Theory and Operations Analysis* (4th edn., 1977 in paperback), chap. 17. T. Majumdar's lively monograph, *The Measurement of Utility* (1958), provides additional insights.

On the history of utility theory, there is G. J. Stigler, 'The Development of Utility Theory', *JPE*, 1950, reprinted in *EET* and *UT* as well as in his *Essays in the History of Economics*, a breath-taking two-part article that surveys the whole literature down to 1914, concluding with some interesting comments on the characteristics of 'successful' theories. D. N. Rosenstein-Rodan, 'Marginal Utility' (1927), reprinted in *IEP*, No. 10, 1960, gives an excellent picture of European marginal utility doctrine around World War I, proliferating in subtle distinctions and metaphysical classifications. Reading this essay, one is made to realize how much has been swept away by the Hicks-Allen Revolution – all to the good, we would say. A. R. Sweezy, 'The Interpretation of Subjective Value Theory in the Writings of the Austrian Economists',

REStud, June, 1934, suggests that the younger Austrian writers of the 1920s were moving independently toward the notion of ordinal utility.

Bernoulli's 1738 paper on the St Petersburg Paradox is reprinted in *UT* and *Precursors in Mathematical Economics*, eds. Baumol and Goldfeld. The latter also reprint W. E. Johnson's remarkably prescient paper 'The Pure Theory of Utility Curves' (1913). The much better known paper by Slutsky (1915), the first to really separate the substitution from the income effect of a price change, is available in *Readings in Price Theory*, eds. G. J. Stigler and K. E. Boulding (1953). P. A. Samuelson, 'St. Petersburg Paradoxes: Defanged, Dissected, and Historically Described', *JEL*, March, 1977, places the St Petersburg Paradox in its historical context. E. D. Fagan, 'Recent and Contemporary Theories of Progressive Taxation', *JPE*, 1938, reprinted in *Readings in the Economics of Taxation*, eds. Musgrave and Shoup, surveys the history of the theory of progressive taxation in the tradition of utility theory. On the same topic, see also the lucid review in Musgrave, *Theory of Public Finance*, chap. 5.

J. Viner, 'The Utility Concept in Value Theory and Its Critics', *JPE*, 1925, reprinted in *UT* and in his *The Long View and the Short*, analyzes the traditional criticisms that have been leveled at utility theory; the first of these articles, concerning the role of utility in demand theory, is still as relevant as it was in 1925; the second, dealing with welfare economics, is now somewhat dated. F. H. Knight, 'Realism and Relevance in the Theory of Demand', *JPE*, 1944, reprinted in *EMDT*, argues that the indifference-curve approach does in fact imply diminishing marginal utility and represents no substantial advance over the older utility theory. He is correctly taken to task for this assertion by R. L. Bishop, 'Professor Knight and the Theory of Demand', *JPE*, April, 1946. See also Schumpeter, *History of Economic Analysis*, pp. 1054–73.

G. J. Stigler, 'The Early History of Empirical Studies of Consumer Behavior', *JPE*, 1954, reprinted in his *Essays in the History of Economics*, reviews the early empirical work on income curves and demand curves; the latter did not begin in earnest until just before World War I. K. A. Fox, 'Demand and Supply: Econometric Studies', *IESS*, 4, provides a quick history of empirical work on demand after 1900. In 'Notes on the History of the Giffen Paradox', *JPE*, April, 1947 ('Comment' by A. R. Prest, *ibid.*, February, 1948), Stigler shows that Marshall read a positively sloped demand curve for bread into Giffen's 'hint'; Giffen's data on bread consumption do not positively establish the Paradox. For a reassessment of Stigler's arguments, see W. P. Gramm, 'Giffen's Paradox and the Marshallian Demand Curve', *MS*, March, 1970, and S. Rashid, 'The Beeke Good: A Note on the Origins of the "Giffen Good"', *HOPE*, Winter, 1979.

M. Friedman, 'The Marshallian Demand Curve', *JPE*, 1949, reprinted in *EMDT*, *AMCA*, III, and his *Essays in Positive Economics* (1953 in paperback), argues that demand curves should be defined as constant real-income curves and that this interpretation comes closer to what Marshall really intended: the appendix to Friedman's essay contains a thorough exegesis of the relevant sections of the *Principles*. R. F. G. Alford, 'Marshall's Demand Curve', *Ec.*, 1956, reprinted in *AMCA*, III, rejects Friedman's interpretation and restates the traditional position; as a piece of pedagogy, this article has much to recommend it. Along the same lines, see also W. J. Fellner, *Emergence and Content of Modern Economic Analysis* (1960), chaps. 14 and 15. L. Yeager, '*Methodenstreit* over Demand Curves', *JPE*, 1960, reprinted in *EMDT*, raises the methodological issue inherent in the Friedman interpretation. E. J. Mishan, 'Theories of Consumer's Behaviour: A Cynical View', *Ec.*, 1963, reprinted in *EMDT*, seeks to persuade the reader that all current theories of consumer's behavior are not worth the trouble required to understand them and that the budding economist would be just as well off if he accepted the 'law of demand' on trust.

J. P. Henderson, 'William Whewell's Mathematical Statements of Price Flexibility, Demand Elasticity and the Giffen Paradox', *MS*, September, 1973, shows that, forty-five years before Marshall and nine years before Cournot, Whewell invented and wrote down the inverse of the price-elasticity of demand and sought ways to identify Giffen goods. D. A. Walker, 'Marshall's Theory of Competitive Exchange', *CJE*, 1969, reprinted in *AMCA*, III, explains how the assumption of a constant MU_e for each trader in a market allowed Marshall to circumvent the problem of disequilibrium transactions.

Whether Marshall meant to hold constant the marginal utility of money *stocks* or money *flows* continues to be a bone of contention among Marshall commentators: see H. H. Lieb-hafsky, 'Marshall and Slutsky on the Theory of Demand', *CJE*, 1961; R. A. Bilas, 'Liebhafsky and the Constant Marginal Utility of the Numeraire: A Comment', *ibid.*, 1965; G. Higgins and H. H. Liebhafsky, 'Pareto and the Marshallian Constancy Assumption', *SEJ*, 1968; and N. Georgescu-Roegen, 'Revisiting Marshall's Constancy of Marginal Utility of Money', *ibid.*, 1968, all reprinted in *AMCA*, III. R. B. Ekelund, Jr., E. G. Furubotn, and W. P. Gramm, *EMDT*, a book of readings that we have frequently referred to, also includes a 100-page monograph on the evolution of demand theory, chap. 2 of which covers demand theory in the Marshallian tradition. The history of interpretations of Marshallian demand theory seems to have no end: for a recent startling re-interpretation, see T. Biswas, 'The Marshallian Consumer', *Ec.*, February, 1977.

R. L. Bishop, 'Consumer's Surplus and Cardinal Utility', *QJE*, May, 1943, contains an excellent discussion of the difficulties in Marshall's concept, including some of the older objections thrown out by Nicholson and Cannan. Marshallian surplus analysis is examined by Myint, *Theories of Welfare Economics*, chap. 9; see also chap. 8 of his book on the 'Characteristic of Neo-Classical Welfare Economics'. For a translation of the problem in terms of indifference curves, see J. R. Hicks, 'The Four Consumer's Surpluses', *REStud*, Winter, 1943, and K. E. Boulding, 'The Concept of Economic Surplus', *AER*, 1945, reprinted in *Readings in the Theory of Income Distribution*, eds. W. Fellner and B. F. Haley (1946). J. N. Morgan, 'The Measurement of Gains and Losses', *QJE*, February, 1948, cites and reviews all the recent literature on consumer's surplus and suggests practical methods for measuring it. A. P. Lerner, 'Consumer's Surplus and Micro-Macro', *JPE*, February, 1963, discusses the treatment of the four consumer's surpluses in Hick's *Revision of Demand Theory* (1956) and defends the practical importance of the notion in welfare economics. For an interesting diagrammatic presentation of four producer's surpluses on the same footing as four consumer's surpluses, see E. J. Mishan, 'Rent as a Measure of Welfare Change', *AER*, 1959, reprinted in his *Welfare Economics. Five Introductory Essays* (1964 in paperback).

10

Marshallian economics: cost and supply

Marshall's theory of price determination revolves around the distinction between (1) a 'market period' in which supplies are absolutely fixed in amount; (2) a 'short period' in which the quantities supplied can be augmented but productive capacity is fixed; and (3) a 'long period' in which productive capacity is variable but the resources potentially available to the industry are fixed in amount. It would be useful to add a fourth period, 'the very long run', in which techniques of production as well as productivity capacity can be altered. Indeed, Marshall himself seems to have had such a fourth period in mind.

The time dimension that pervades Marshall's analysis has been aptly described as 'operational time'. Although the terminology employed conveys an air of clock time, the impression is deceiving; periods are short or long, not according to the revolving hands of a clock, but according to the partial or complete adaptations of producers and consumers to changing circumstances. The actual clock-time periods to which the supply curve applies are left undefined and must be separately specified for each particular industry.[1] To be sure, the short run normally does involve a shorter period of clock time than the long run but this is not necessarily and always true. It is conceivable, for example, that the time needed to increase output from existing facilities exceeds the time required to install new equipment. We would then have a long run preceding a short run. Since time is conceived operationally, Marshallian analysis does not preclude such oddities.

1. The Short Run
Between the instantaneous market period and the long period lies the indefinite morass of the short run. This is a period too short to permit changes in capacity – the size of plant and amount of equipment of firms – but long enough to allow for changes in the degree of utilization of capacity. It is in the short run that the problem of time is most troublesome. In long-run equilibrium all adjustments are complete and therefore independent of particular time periods. In the short run, however, the dynamic problems that characterize temporary adjustments are the heart of the matter. In the

[1] Modern economics abounds in definitions that conceive of time in operational terms: there is D. H. Robertson's 'day', a period too short to dispose of earned income; there is Hicks' 'week', a period during which variations in prices can be ignored; and so on. But the 'stationary state' of classical economics is still the supreme example of a functional-time definition.

371

first place, we cannot just select any definite clock-time period and call it short run for the simple reason that expansion of capacity and changes in the degree of utilization of existing capacity are likely to proceed simultaneously. Second, adjustments that are made in the short run may depend on whether the change in price is expected to be temporary or permanent; expectations of the future do affect the adjustment process, perhaps decisively so. Third, the responses of producers in a given time period are asymmetrical with respect to a rise and a fall in price. Because of the durability of existing equipment, the short run may be much longer when the adjustment is a contraction than when it is an expansion, and this lack of symmetry is the greater, the longer lived is the equipment relative to its period of construction.

Provided these kinds of difficulties are kept in mind, we can now proceed to analyze the adjustment of an industry toward short-period equilibrium. All costs can be classified into prime and supplementary costs, or, to use current terminology, variable and fixed costs. In the short run, each firm is burdened with certain unalterable commitments in the form of existing facilities. Variations in the level of output will be accompanied by variations in certain prime costs such as wages of production workers, expenses for raw materials and maintenance costs of machinery. But as long as plant and equipment themselves cannot be altered, some costs will remain fixed in amount regardless of the rate of output: the usual list of fixed costs contains such things as obsolescence charges on machinery, ground rent, property taxes and possibly the salaries of supervisory personnel. Facing given prices, entrepreneurs maximize profits by producing that level of output at which total costs increase at the same rate as total receipts, or marginal costs are equal to marginal revenues. Under perfect competition, price is not affected by the individual firm's decision to produce; hence, price or average revenue is always equal to marginal revenue. Profit-maximizing behavior under perfect competition may, therefore, be expressed succinctly as marginal cost pricing. Moreover, in the short-period situation, marginal cost is in no way influenced by fixed costs. The rate at which total costs increase as a function of output is not affected by the addition of a lump sum to total costs at all levels of output. The economic sense of this is that the alternative costs of fixed investments in the short run are zero: bygones are forever bygones.

From data on total costs of production within a given plant, we obtain the corresponding figures for average and marginal costs. The now familiar graphic illustration, not found in Marshall's *Principles*, shows the firm maximizing profits at $\bar{q}_3$ (see Figure 10–1). The total revenue curve *TR* is a straight line coming out of the origin because the slope of this line, which is price or average revenue *AR*, is constant at all levels of output. The total cost curve *TC* is given the usual plausible sigmoid shape, based on the idea that the plant is designed to be operated under normal circumstances at something like 50–80 percent of capacity. Drawing successive vectors from the origin to different points along the total cost curve, we obtain average total costs *ATC* as the slope of the various vectors. Marginal cost *MC* is the slope of the total cost curve itself. *A* is an inflection point in the total cost curve where marginal costs are at a minimum. Average total costs reach a minimum at *B* where

Figure 10–1

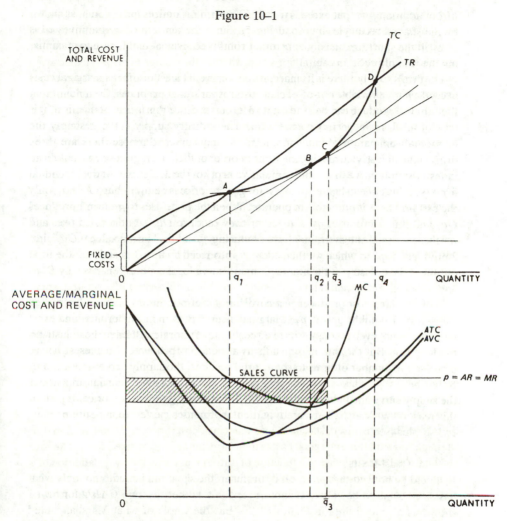

$ATC = MC$. As long as an average value declines, the corresponding marginal value must be below the average; the average can only decline because the marginal additions to the total are smaller than the average. Similarly, when an average value increases, the corresponding marginal value must lie above it. Hence, when the average has reached its minimum point, neither declining nor increasing, the marginal must equal to average value. The ATC curve must cut the AR curve at q_1 and q_4 because $TC = TR$ at these points. The average variable cost curve AVC is obtained by a parallel downward shift in the TC curve to eliminate the presence of fixed costs; it follows that the minimum point of the AVC curve is reached earlier than the minimum point of the ATC curve. Profit *per unit of output* is maximized at q_2 where the gap between ATC and AR is at a maximum. At this point, however, the

MR of additional output exceeds its *MC*. The firm maximizes *total* profits, as shown by the shaded rectangle, by producing $\bar{q}_3$. Since the amount of capital invested is given in the short run, maximizing total profits is equivalent in this case to maximizing the rate of profit on capital.

The firm's supply curve is its marginal cost curve, at least insofar as marginal costs exceed average variable out-of-pocket costs: at various given prices, the amount that the firm will produce can be read off its *MC* curve. Since this is true of one firm, it is true of all firms in perfect competition. The industry supply curve is simply the horizontal summation of individual firms' supply curves. Suppose there are three firms in the industry; arranging the firms in order of their average costs, we obtain an industry supply curve that is the cumulative array of the *MC* curves of the individual firms (see thick line in figure 10–2). As long as the price is below p_2 but above p_1, only the first firm finds it profitable to operate. When the price rises to p_2, firm 1 produces Oq_2 and firm 2 produces q_2q_4; together they produce Oq_4. As the price rises and reaches p_3, firm 3 enters the industry, producing q_6q_7; firm 1 now produces Oq_3, firm 2 produces q_3q_6, to which we then add q_6q_7 produced by firm 3 to arrive at the total output of the industry. If the market demand curve for the industry is given by D, p_3 and q_7 will clear the market.

With the high-cost producer just covering out-of-pocket costs, the industry is in short-period equilibrium at p_3. Marginal firm 3 is earning no profits whatever; indeed, it is not even recouping its fixed costs and at this rate will leave the industry in the long run. But the intramarginal firms are earning producers' surpluses. As we increase the number of firms to some large number, the supply curve smooths out. Nevertheless, producers' surplus always exceeds the roughly triangular area above the supply curve and below the horizontal line indicating the market price. It was for this reason that Marshall invented 'particular expenses curves' to measure producers' surplus (see below).

2. Quasi-Rents

It should be noticed that producers' surplus in the short run includes not only what has since come to be called 'economic rent' – total net revenue *CABD* for firm 1 shown as a shaded area in Figure 10–2 – but the whole of what Marshall called 'quasi-rent' – the shaded area *CABD* plus the cross-hatched area *ECDF*, which is the difference between *AVC* and *ATC* multiplied by the quantity produced. Actually, Marshall gave no explicit formal definition of the term 'quasi-rent' and some statements in the *Principles* suggest that he meant to confine the term to an area like *ECDF* rather than the entire shaded area *EABF*. Still, most commentators take the wider definition of the term and we will follow them in this practice.

Why *quasi*-rents? Marshall reserves the term 'rent' for the so-called 'free gifts of nature'. Like Ricardo, Marshall singles out land as a unique resource because its supply is virtually unresponsive to higher rates of reward. But income derived from man-made assets which are temporarily fixed in supply partakes of the nature of rent. The term 'interest' is applicable to new prospective investment only. Sunk capital yields a value product net of maintenance and replacement and this net value product

Figure 10–2

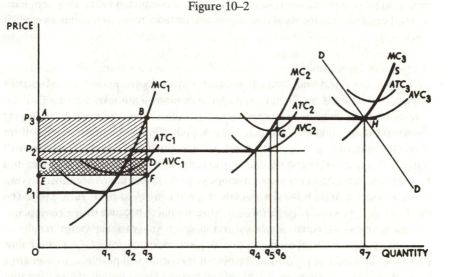

on fixed investment is called 'quasi-rents'. But quasi-rents include more than this. They comprise all the returns to the firm in excess of the returns of the marginal firm.

Like rents on superior grades of land, quasi-rents are price determined and not price determining. In other words, in the short run, the price paid for the services of capital goods is analogous to the price paid for the services of natural agents because in each case the return is not necessary to call forth the corresponding service. The analogy to Ricardian rents is, however, somewhat misleading. Ricardian rents are only price determined for the economy as a whole. If land has competing uses, as it usually has, Ricardian rents do enter into the costs of production of an individual farmer: the alternative costs of using a tract of land to an individual farmer are measured by the rental payments required to bid that land away from competing uses. But Marshall's quasi-rents are price determined both for society as a whole and for the individual entrepreneur; they are the result of the failure to achieve complete adjustment in any given slice of time and will disappear in the long run as all costs become variable.

It is clear that quasi-rents must accrue to the individual entrepreneur if they deserve to be called 'quasi-rents' rather than cost outlays. A firm may be a low-cost producer because a favourable site either reduces its freight charges on raw materials or the cost of shipping the product to market. If so, the period of time must be too short to allow this unimputed income or 'profits' to be swallowed up by rental payments to landlords as other firms compete for the favourable site. Similarly, if the favourable cost position is due to superior management, the recipient of 'economic rent' must be the entrepreneur, not the manager. That is, the 'short period' must be too short to prevent the entrepreneur from adding to capacity and also too short to prevent him from overcoming the resource immobilities that alone permit him to collect the intramarginal surplus. Be that as it may, in the long run the cost ladder must straighten out and when all adjustments are completed in the long run, each firm will produce long identical cost curves that include 'rents' as imputed or explicit costs.

3. The Long Run

So far we have traveled through familiar terrain because most of Marshall's short-period analysis has found its way into modern textbooks. Marshall's long-period analysis, however, is not quite such smooth sailing and it has been largely discarded without anything else taking its place. Our first problem is to show how we obtain the long-run average cost curve of an individual firm, a subject that Marshall completely neglected to analyze. As was first shown by Viner in 1931, the long-run average cost curve of a firm is the envelope of all its short-run average cost curves.

Suppose the firm finds itself with plant 1, producing q_1 at p_1 (Figure 10–3). The short-run marginal cost curve $SRMC_1$ is upward sloping because with a *given* plant, the employment of equal additional amounts of any variable factor results in diminishing increments of output. Since long-run marginal costs $LRMC$ are below short-run marginal costs $SRMC$ at the output level q_1, it will pay the firm to enlarge its plant or to build a new one capable of producing a larger output at lower per unit costs. Since *all* factors are now variable, the law of diminishing marginal productivity is not applicable to this case. What we have is a movement from one plant curve to another such that when we increase all the factors by a given amount, output increases more than proportionately. As long as we are moving along the downward-sloping portion of the long-run average cost curve, $LRAC$, we are in the phase of increasing returns to scale. With a plant larger than plant 1, however, $SRMC$ may still exceed $LRMC$ and so the firm is induced to build a still larger plant. This process will continue until the firm reaches plant 2, producing output q_2. Beyond this point it incurs decreasing returns to scale. We will consider the reasons for decreasing returns to scale in the next chapter but for the moment let us insist that returns to scale do not decrease because of rising input prices; long-run cost curves, like short-run cost curves, are drawn up on the assumption of given factor prices. If the price rises sufficiently, the firm is willing to enter the phase of decreasing returns to scale because the $SRMC_3$ of producing q_3 in plant 3 is still lower than it would be in plant 2, assuming that q_3 could be produced at all in plant 2. But as soon as the price falls again, the firm is motivated to scrap plant 3 and to build a smaller plant that can produce a smaller quantity more efficiently. If the price is equal to p_2, the firm will settle down at plant 2, equating $SRMC$ with $LRMC$, earning zero profits and experiencing constant returns to scale.

The firm's long-run supply curve is given by that portion of its $LRMC$ curve where $LRMC \geqslant LRAC$. With respect to the long run, the firm tries to equate $LRMC$ to price. If the price exceeds $LRMC$, the firm expands its scale of operations. When, with a given plant, short-run profit maximization causes the price to be less than $LRMC$, the firm contracts its scale and moves down to a smaller plant. Therefore, its long-run output response to a changing price can be read off its $LRMC$ curve. Nevertheless, the lower portion of its $LRMC$ curve, where $LRMC < LRAC$, is not

Figure 10–3

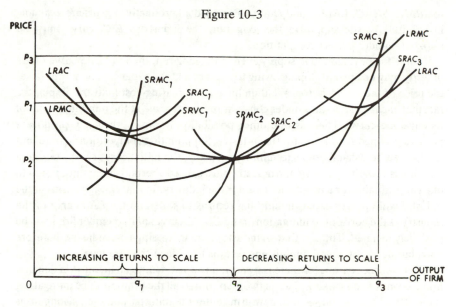

part of the firm's long-run supply curve for the simple reason that average costs are not being covered.

Notice that the minimum point of each *SRAC* curve always lies above the *LRAC* curve except at the output level at which the *LRAC* curve itself reaches a minimum. This is precisely what is meant by saying that the *LRAC* curve is an envelope curve: it is the locus of all the lowest possible average costs of producing any output when the entrepreneur is able to make all desired adjustments. If the *LRAC* curve went through the minimum point of each and every *SRAC* curve, it would have to lie above some portion of the *SRAC* curve. This is economically absurd for it would mean that cost per unit when capacity cannot be varied is less than when it can be varied. Surely, it cannot be to a firm's advantage *not* to be able to vary all the elements in total costs?[2]

When we draw upward-sloping long-run supply curves for an *industry*, we do not necessarily assume that the *firms* are operating under decreasing returns to scale. If a firm were operating along the rising portion of its *LRAC* curve, it would be earning quasi-rents or positive profits. In the long run, returns owing to differential advantages are capitalized and imputed to costs. Hence, if one firm were earning positive profits, all firms would be earning positive profits, which is incompatible with long-run industry equilibrium under perfect competition. So long as entry into the industry is free, all firms must be operating at constant returns to scale equating price

---

[2] Viner in his classic 1931 article on the envelope curve instructed his draftsman to draw a U-shaped *LRAC* as a curve passing through the minimum points of all the *SRAC* curves and not lying above any one of them; his draftsman told him that this was mathematically impossible but Viner insisted that he should try. In subsequent reprints of the article, Viner deliberately left this error uncorrected so as to provide 'pleasure' to 'future teachers and students'. The error is now patently obvious. Such are the benefits of hindsight!

to *SRMC*, *SRAC*, *LRMC*, and *LRAC*. Provided all productive agents are available in infinitely elastic supply in the long run, the industry's *LRS* curve must be horizontal under perfect competition.

If some factor is limited in supply even in the long run, then the *LRS* curve of the *industry* may be upward sloping owing to the fact that the expansion of output raises the price of the scarce factor. We then have an increasing-cost industry despite the fact that each firm operates under constant returns to scale at the minimum point of its envelope curve. There is one other possibility, however, that may produce a positively sloped *LRS* curve for the industry. Suppose that competition is 'pure' but not 'perfect' in Chamberlin's terminology, that is, the initial cost of operation to a new firm is such that profits in the industry must exceed a certain minimum amount to make it profitable for a newcomer to enter the industry. In that case, the firms in the industry will operate under diminishing returns to scale and the *LRS* curve of the industry as the horizontal summation of the *LRMC* curves of its member firms will be positively inclined. The fact that an industry is an increasing-cost industry therefore may, but need not, entail diminishing returns to scale at the firm level.

Whatever the reasons for increasing cost, an adjustment to an increase in demand may be conceived as taking place in two steps. First, all the firms produce more along their *SRMC* curves and second, new firms enter the industry and the existing firms build larger plants to accommodate the increase in demand. As the demand curve shifts, price rises from p_1 to p_2 and output increases from q_1 to q_2 (see Figure 10–4). Now the long-run adjustment shifts the short-run supply curve; output increases to q_3 and price falls to p_3. If competition is 'perfect', the larger quantity requires a higher price because new firms have bid up the price of the scarce factor. If competition is 'pure', the larger quantity requires a higher price because each firm is subject to diseconomies of scale. In either case, the increasing-cost industry is in long-run

Figure 10–4

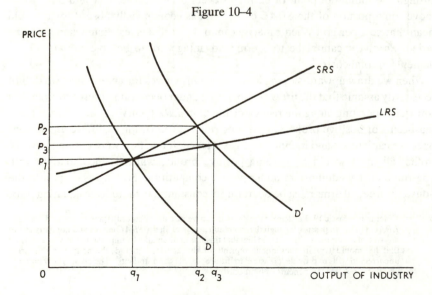

equilibrium at p_3 and q_3 in the sense that no firms are induced to enter or leave the industry.

But suppose the industry is a decreasing-cost industry. Can the long-run supply curve be downward as well as upward sloping, as Marshall believed? First, it is clear that the *short*-run supply curve for the industry cannot be downward sloping. Since the industry supply curve is the sum of the firms' supply curves, the industry supply curve cannot be negatively inclined unless at least some of the firms have negatively inclined supply curves. But this is impossible, since a necessary condition for internal equilibrium of the firm is that the firm's *MC* curve be rising at the point of equilibrium, that is, the *MC* curve must cut the *MR* curve from below. If net revenue π is equal to total cost minus total revenue, the condition for a maximum extremum value is that the first derivative of the net revenue function with respect to output q is zero and that the second derivative is negative. That is, if $\pi = f(R - C)$, then the conditions for maximizing profits are

$$\frac{d\pi}{dq} = f'(R - C) = 0,$$

$$\frac{d^2\pi}{dq^2} = f''(R - C) = <0.$$

But $f'(R - C) = 0$ if $f'(R) = f'(C)$, that is, if marginal revenue equals marginal cost. And if $f''(R - C)<0$, then $f''(R)<f''(C)$, that is, marginal revenue increases less rapidly than marginal cost.[3] Therefore, profits are only maximized in diagrams 1 and 2, not in diagrams 3, 4 and 5 (Figure 10–5).

Figure 10–5

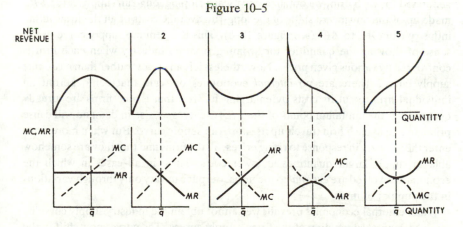

Hence, the competitive industry's short-run supply curve must be positively inclined. But as Cournot showed in 1838, the same argument holds for the long-run supply curve. If the industry supply curve is declining in the long run, at least some of

[3] Remember that the slope of a negatively inclined function, $f'(\ )$, is negative. Hence, the condition that $f''(\ )<0$ for such a function means that it turns down at an increasing rate. In diagram 1 of Figure 10–5, $f''(R) = -\infty$ and $f''(C) = 0$; in diagram 2 of Figure 10–5, $f''(R)<0$ and $f''(C)>0$; etc.

the firms must have negatively inclined $LRMC$ curves. But this implies that the firms are not in equilibrium because declining $LRMC$ means that $LRMC<LRAC$. In trying to equate price with $LRMC$, the firms will expand their scale of operations. Indeed, they will go on expanding even if their $LRMC$ curves eventually turn up as long as $LRMC<LRAC$. In other words, as long as there are economies of scale, the $LRMC$ curve is *not* a true supply curve in the sense of the schedule that traces out the quantities forthcoming from a firm when it is confronted with various given prices. No firm can possibly be in long-run equilibrium unless $LRMC \geqslant LRAC$, unless it operates in the phase of constant or diminishing returns to scale. If this is true for each firm, it follows that it is also true for the industry supply curve in the long run. *Competitive equilibrium is incompatible with downward-sloping long-run supply curves.*

4. External Economies

The conclusion that decreasing-cost industries cannot exist under perfect competition depends on the assumption that the supply curves of the individual firms are independent of one another. But as Marshall first pointed out, competitive equilibrium may be compatible with falling supply curves if 'external economies' produce interdependence between supply curves. External economies are present whenever an increase in the output of an entire industry increases the amount any individual firm in the industry is willing to supply at each price, that is, if it shifts any firm's short-run supply curve or MC curve to the right. Suppose all the firms are all exactly alike, earning zero profits and producing quantity $Q = \Sigma q$. If an increase in demand causes all firms to produce more, in the course of which external economies are generated for each firm, we obtain a downward-sloping long-run supply curve LRS made up of the downward shifts of the long-run average costs of all the firms in the industry from AC to AC' (see Figure 10–6). This is a genuine supply curve in the sense of showing the quantities forthcoming from an industry when each firm is confronted by various given prices. Nevertheless it is an *ex post* rather than an *ex ante* supply curve. There are no *internal* economies of scale that could permit an individual firm to cut its costs by enlarging its size, that is, the firms are already operating at the minimum points of the $LRAC$ curves. A rise in demand will cause prices to rise as each firm travels up its short-run supply curve. But when more firms enter the industry in response to rising prices, all the firms find that they are somehow able to supply larger quantities at lower costs. Thus, in all cases in which the economies involved are *external* to the firms, output can vary only through variations in the number of firms.

When external economies prevail, we cannot obtain the industry supply curve by mere horizontal summation of the firms' supply curves. The curves now shift in the process of summation: the output of each and every firm depends on the output of the industry, and yet the industry's output is nothing more than the sum of the output of the firms. Theoretically, the problem requires the solution of a system of simultaneous equations; in practice, each firm assumes some value for total output and the mutual adjustment of all the firms *may* then lead to convergence toward the true

Figure 10–6

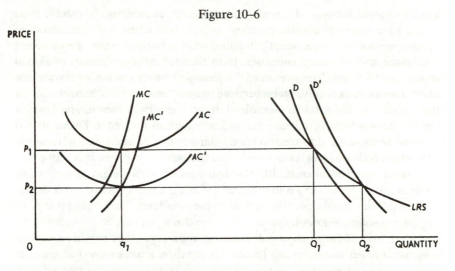

value. At any rate, the downward-sloping long-run supply curve depicts average costs *after* the industry has reaped all the external benefits appropriate to a particular output. This is the sense in which it is an *ex post* supply curve.

Assuming then that external economies alone can account for downward-sloping industry supply curves, what are external economies and how frequently are they encountered? This question has different answers depending on the scope of the inquiry. According to Marshall, external economies are dependent on (1) 'the general development of the industry', and (2) the 'general progress of the industrial environment'. But if we are dealing with competitive output from the standpoint of partial equilibrium analysis, we must ignore (2), which involves dynamic consider-ations that have no place in a static frame of reference. The economies appropriate to our analysis are reflected in the downward-shifting cost curves of individual firms as the industry's output expands. Lower costs may be due to the increased efficiency of each firm and/or lower factor prices. Lower factor prices imply external or internal economies in the supplying industry. If lower factor prices are due to internal economies in the supplying industry, that industry cannot be a competitive industry. This condition is ruled out by the assumption that all industries operate under perfect competition, which we have seen is incompatible with *internal* economies of scale. Therefore, lower factor prices must be due to external economies in the supplying industry, which involves the same problem as the one we are trying to explain. Thus, what has to be explained is why each firm should become more efficient as the industry's output expands. The industry's output expands only if the output of at least one firm expands or if new firms enter the industry. By definition, the existing firms have no incentive to expand. So the question is: Why do the costs of other firms fall when the output of a new firm is added to the existing firms?

It is clear that the external economies we are after involve economies that are external to the firm but internal to the industry, involving a particular kind of interdependence between the firms that make up an industry. Marshall's own examples are unconvincing because they are not confined to single industries: he mentions economies arising from the localization of industry, from the development of auxiliary and subsidiary industries, from the increasing availability of skilled labour, and from the development of the means of transportation and communication. This list does not distinguish between ordinary reversible movements along a static curve and historical irreversible shifts in the curves themselves. Now, a long-run 'forward-falling' industry supply curve such as the one in Figure 10–6 is reversible because it is drawn up on the assumption of a constant state of technical knowledge. Technical progress is irreversible and hence is depicted by a shift of the curve, not a movement along it.[4] But Marshall argued that the long-run supply curve in a decreasing-cost industry is irreversible because the economies of larger output will be retained when output falls back to its previous level. This implies that firms add to their technical knowledge as they move down the supply curve, for if the economies were already a matter of common knowledge, they should have been exploited at lower output levels. To be consistent, we must assume that external economies are lost as the industry's output contracts and this means that we must exclude all dynamic irreversible changes.

5. What Are External Economies?

External economies or external diseconomies exist whenever the production function of one firm contains variables that are not physical inputs but rather the effects of the activities of other firms. In other words, some firm is rendering a service to other firms without being able to appropriate to itself all of the value of these services, or else is inflicting a loss on other firms without having to pay a fee for its nuisance value. External economies or diseconomies therefore always involve some kind of non-market interdependence. Such 'technological economies', as they are called, are few and far between in a static context. Two examples of such economies satisfying the strict Marshallian condition of being fully reversible are (1) the labour force case and (2) the trade journal case. With the growth and localization of an industry in a particular area, all firms eventually benefit from the development of a steady supply of skilled labour and a well-informed labour market. Thus, as new firms arrive in the area and draw in still more skilled labour, all the existing firms find that the cost of labour turnover and labour training declines. The trade journal case, on the other hand, exemplifies external economies arising from improved communication about market conditions. When the industry reaches a certain size, it becomes feasible to publish information and to make it cheaply available to all. Once again, the existing firms reap the benefits of cheaper information in the form of lower average costs of production. A third possible example, although it is not clear that it is always fully reversible, is that of the vertical disintegration that comes with a widened market.

---

[4] For a downward-sloping, forward-falling supply curve, an increase of supply due to technical progress is portrayed by a shift of the curve to the *left*, implying a reduction in average costs per unit at which various scales of output can be produced. If the negatively inclined supply curve was not forward falling but instead backward rising – typified by workers who work longer hours when the wage rate falls – an increase of supply will be correctly portrayed by shifting the curve to the *right*.

Since 'the division of labour is limited by the extent of the market', the growth of industry brings into being a host of specialized auxiliary industries to service the needs of the parent industry and the effect is to lower costs as a function of the output of the entire industry. Contrariwise, the classic example of a technological external *dis*economy, causing the long-run supply curve to be upward sloping, is the case in which the firms in an industry use a resource that is free but nevertheless scarce, such as a publicly owned road or a common oil field.

All such phenomena reflect hidden inputs or outputs, the benefits or costs of which are not appropriated by the agents in the market. As long as we confine ourselves to particular industries and to cases in which the effects are reversible, we do have considerable difficulties in coming up with convincing examples. But if we include irreversible dynamic phenomena, we have no difficulty whatever in finding examples of technological external economies. The leading case is a change in technological knowledge itself; the full benefits of most changes in knowledge are not easily captured by the originator even with strong patents and copyrights. There is no doubt, therefore, of the importance of technological external economies but one may well question their significance from the point of view of partial equilibrium analysis. It is possible to rescue the concept of a downward-sloping industry supply curve with the aid of reversible external economies but their exceptional occurrence explains why most modern economists are reluctant to endorse Marshall's belief in the existence of decreasing-cost industries.

'Real' or technological external economies must be kept distinct from 'pecuniary' external economies – a vital point made by Viner. An industry that expands along a downward-sloping long-run supply curve can sell its products at lower and lower prices, even though the prices of the factor services that it buys are rising as more factor services are purchased. This kind of effect may benefit other industries but, unlike 'real' external economies, these pecuniary external economies reflect an interdependence among producers that *is* transmitted through the price system. 'Pecuniary' external economies are ubiquitous in any integrated economic system but they present no problem for price theory because they will necessarily be fully exploited by the beneficiaries and therefore eliminated in the long run. In development economics, however, pecuniary external economies represent *the* problem.

Once again, we see that the kind of external economies admitted into the purview of our analysis depends entirely upon the level of discourse we adopt. The common tendency in the interwar literature to regard external economies as economic curiosa reflected the limited scope and assumptions of partial equilibrium analysis. In recent years, however, the concept of external economies has emerged in a variety of disguises in discussions of the industrialization of backward areas. The meaning that the concept has now acquired in the 'doctrine of balanced growth' is a very wide one, covering a number of quite distinct mechanisms by which investment in one field may give rise to nonappropriable benefits and hence new investment opportunities elsewhere. In partial equilibrium analysis, however, it is perfectly legitimate to regard downward-sloping long-run industry supply curves as very rare birds indeed.

6. Producers' Surplus

Having established what is meant by the notion of a falling supply curve for an industry, we can now return to the tax-bounty analysis. We recall that Marshall's text discusses only the gain or loss in *consumers'* surplus from a change in price [see chapter 9, section 16]. We must now take account of producers' surplus. Marshall defines a worker's surplus, a saver's surplus, and a producer's surplus, each being defined as the excess of actual earnings from a given quantity of work, saving or sale of output over the amount that the individual would accept rather than refuse to offer his services altogether. It is, in this sense, perfectly analogous to the consumer's price surplus. Having introduced producers' surplus in a footnote, Marshall does not take it up in detail until Appendix H, where it turns out to be something very different, namely, the 'producers' surplus triangle'. In Appendix H it has nothing to do with the increasing marginal disutility of effort, or indeed with any money measure of surplus satisfactions or dissatisfactions. It is simply the excess earnings obtained by low-cost firms over the earnings of the marginal firm in an industry, a pure Ricardian differential rent.

Marshall defines this intramarginal surplus in the short run by means of a 'particular expenses curve'. This is not a supply curve, that is, a cumulative array of the *marginal* costs of different firms in an industry, but rather a cumulative array of the *average* costs of different firms. For any short-period equilibrium, price is equal to the marginal costs of the individual producers as well as to the average cost of the marginal firm (see Figure 10–2 above). The *PE* curve shows the firms' average costs for that equilibrium price-output combination arranged in ascending order from left to right. Since at any other price, each firm would produce a different output and incur a different average cost, it follows that there is a definable *PE* curve for each point on the short-period supply curve of an industry. The end point of each *PE* curve shows the marginal cost which is equal to the average cost of producing that output for the marginal firm. The industry supply curve is, thus, the locus of end points of the *PE* curves (Figure 10–7).

The *PE* curves always lie below the short-period supply curve for the simple reason that each intramarginal firm's average cost curve lies below its marginal cost curve at the profit-maximizing output level. Since this is the short run, we might ask: what is the relevant average cost curve for measuring the producer's surplus – the average total cost curve or the average variable cost curve? The difference between *ATC* and *AVC* is average fixed cost, that portion of quasi-rents retained by the entrepreneur in the short run. Quasi-rents are scarcity rents, being the earnings of productive resources temporarily fixed in supply. What we are after, however, is a measure of differential rent. In the short run, however, even differential rents are scarcity rents inasmuch as the entrepreneur only earns these differential rents due, say, to a favourable site or a better-than-average manager, because competition has not yet been able to convert these quasi-rents into necessary factor payments. Thus, there is no difference in principle between quasi-rents in excess of average total costs and quasi-rents in excess of average variable costs. Still, average fixed costs may be paid out even in the short run and so the *PE* curve is best defined as a cumulative array of

Figure 10–7

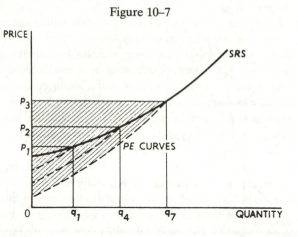

the average *total* costs of the firms in an industry – the reader may construct his own *PE* curve in Figure 10–2 by joining points *D*, *G*, and *H*. Thus, the shaded area in Figure 10–7 shows the excess earnings of the low-cost producers over the high-cost marginal producer for output q_7.

Marshall applied the *PE* curve not only to short-run but also to long-run supply curves. Indeed, it was the latter application that really interested him. We know that the superior services to which the producers' surplus is due in the short run will tend to be capitalized in the long run and become permanently embodied in the supply curve. In the long run, therefore, all the firms will have identical cost curves inclusive of rent and the *PE* curve must coincide with the long-run industry supply curve. But what if the long-run supply curves are horizontal so that producers' surplus disappears?

Given perfect competition, there are two reasons why the long-run supply curve may be upward sloping and one reason why it may be downward-sloping. Take first an increasing-cost industry. Suppose some factor like land is nonreproducible, or at any rate less than infinitely elastic in supply. As the industry expands in response to rising demand, the average cost curves of each firm shift up owing to pecuniary external diseconomies in the form of rising scarcity rents (see left-hand side of Figure 10–8). The short-run supply curve of the firm, its *MC* curve, does not change when scarcity rents rise because the total cost of producing all levels of output rises by a constant amount. Assuming that there are *n* firms in the industry, we show on the left-hand side the short-run cost curves of one firm in long-run equilibrium with its accompanying envelope curve, and on the right-hand side the resulting supply curve of the industry as a whole blown up *n* times. The long-run supply curve is upward sloping owing to the existence of pecuniary external diseconomies.

The same result, however, may be due not to pecuniary but to 'real' external diseconomies. As the output of the industry expands, the supply curve of each firm shifts to the left, and hence the supply price of the industry as a whole rises (see Figure 10–9). It is clear that in this case, as in all others involving 'real' economies or

Figure 10–8

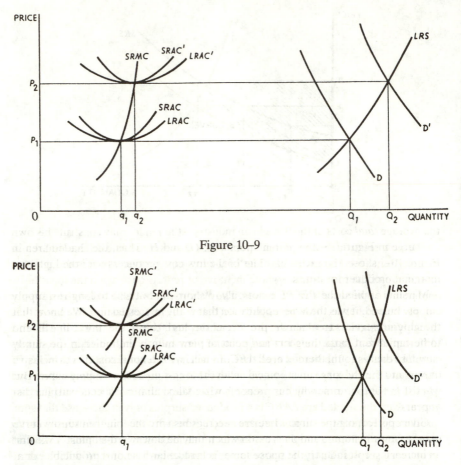

Figure 10–9

diseconomies, the increase in output of the industry as a whole results in variations in the number of firms.

Finally, the presence of 'real' external economies will cause the supply curve of each firm to shift to the right as the output of the industry increases and so yield a decreasing-cost industry (see Figure 10–6 above). There is no need to go on to consider pecuniary external economies because these must be due to 'real' economies somewhere in the system. Pecuniary diseconomies, however, need not have any technological counterpart and therefore had to be treated separately.

Real external economies or diseconomies do not create 'rent' and hence our discussion of producers' surplus in the long run is confined to the case of pecuniary external diseconomies (see Figure 10–8). As long as entry is free – competition is 'perfect' and not just 'pure' – the presence of scarcity rents in such an increasing-cost industry can be read off as the roughly triangular area above the long-run supply curve.

Figure 10–10

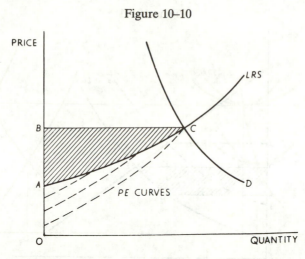

We now reintroduce the particular expenses curves by adding differential rent to scarcity rent (see Figure 10–10). The long-run supply curve, which is the marginal cost curve of the industry as a whole inclusive of rent, is once again the locus of the end points of the successive *PE* curves. The *PE* curves always lie below the short-run supply curve; hence, they necessarily lie below the more elastic *LRS* curve. The roughly triangular area above the *PE* curve and below the price line is thus differential rent from the short-run point of view but, in the long run, producers' surplus reduces to the shaded area *ABC*. In fact, we are not justified in drawing *PE* curves at all in the long run unless we believe that cost differences between firms will persist in the long run, which is precisely what Marshall himself believed. Furthermore, even the shaded area *ABC* is a producers' surplus only in the sense that some producer is earning the surplus but this need not be a producer in the industry. If the scarce factor in limited supply is management, all managers in the industry will earn producers' surplus. But if the scarce factor is land, the whole of *ABC* will be earned outside the industry. Similarly, if the supply price is falling because of real external economies, producers' surplus does not even have a well-defined meaning: we cannot say that it is the excess over the minimum amount that producers would accept to supply output because it is wholly dependent on an increase in everyone's output.

Be that as it may, we can now complete the tax-bounty analysis by coupling producers' with consumers' surplus. Suppose we levy an excise tax on an increasing-cost industry. The loss in producers' surplus is given by *ADEB* (Figure 10–11). This is derived in the following way: before the tax, producers' surplus was equal to *DEC*; after the tax it is equal to *abs* = *ABC*. *DEC* minus *ABC* = *ADEB*. We know [see chapter 9, section 16] that the loss in consumers' surplus from the rise in price, ignoring real-income effects, is equal to *DabE*. Hence, the combined loss in producers' and consumers' surplus is *AabEB*. Tax receipts are equal to *AabB*. We reach the anti-Marshallian conclusion that the combined loss in consumers' and

Figure 10–11

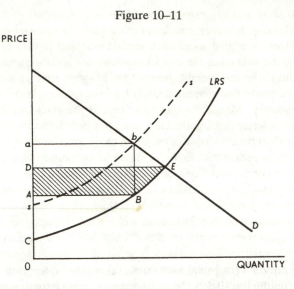

producers' surplus from a tax actually exceeds the amount of tax receipts. Even if all the revenue from the tax were returned as a lump sum to the buyers and sellers in the market, they would be worse off than before. If we use the tax receipts instead to subsidize a decreasing-cost industry, we will certainly generate an increase in consumers' surplus and we *may* increase the producers' surplus in that industry. If we recall, however, that the reason the industry is a decreasing-cost industry is that it generates external economies to the firms then in long-run equilibrium these unexpected benefits from expansion must be passed on to consumers in the form of lower prices; therefore, there is no gain in producers' surplus from subsidizing a decreasing-cost industry. This means that the net effect of the entire operation is highly uncertain.

All this does not even take into account the four consumers' surpluses! Suffice it to say that, as a piece of deductive reasoning, we have little reason for confidence in the Marshallian theorem that the state can increase economic welfare by taxing increasing-cost industries and subsidizing decreasing-cost industries.

7. The Asymmetrical Welfare Effect

The skeptical reader may have wondered whether, all technicalities aside, it really made sense to add a money measure of consumers' satisfactions to an actual sum of producers' money. Surely, these two things are not on the same footing? And, indeed, there was something wrong here, which became apparent only when Pigou, in *Wealth and Welfare* (1912), translated Marshall's tax-bounty analysis into his own terminology of private and social costs. It is perfectly obvious from Pigou's comprehensive survey of the doctrine of consumers' and producers' surplus, published in the *Economic Journal* in 1910, that he was aware of the very ambiguous outcome of Marshall's line of argument. Possibly for that reason he discarded the doctrine in

Wealth and Welfare and in its successor, *Economics of Welfare* (1919). The same essential conclusions, however, emerge in a new garb. In an increasing-cost industry, argued Pigou, marginal social costs exceed marginal private costs. Marginal social cost may be defined as the sum of the marginal private cost of producing a commodity plus the nonrecoverable positive and negative effects associated with an increment of output of that commodity, which accrue to or are borne by individuals outside the industry. Marginal social costs exceed marginal private costs in an increasing-cost industry because the latter does not include the increase in costs to buyers as a result of the expansion of output of the industry in question. Production is carried too far in such industries in the sense that economic welfare is maximized only when the marginal social cost of producing a commodity equals its marginal private cost. Marginal social cost is a measure of the alternative output forgone from the production of a particular commodity. Only when prices are everywhere reflective of social as well as private costs will a dollar expenditure by consumers purchase the same value worth of factor units irrespective of the commodity acquired. If an increasing-cost industry is taxed, its marginal private cost can be raised until it equals its marginal social cost. Likewise, a decreasing-cost industry operates at an output level below the social optimum, since its marginal social cost of production falls short of its marginal private cost. Hence, its output must be expanded by a subsidy.

It took the better part of thirty years to unravel the thread of truth that runs through the Marshall-Pigou argument. The basic flaw, however, was pointed out as early as 1913 by Allyn Young and was forcibly restated by Frank Knight in 1924: the causes of changes in long-run supply prices are not symmetrical in the two types of industries. In an increasing-cost industry, social costs exceed private costs because the expansion of the industry raises its own costs as well as the cost of all other goods in which this factor is used. The effect is to transfer purchasing power from other industries to the industry in question. What is involved is a pecuniary external diseconomy: the expansion of the increasing cost industry does not represent a using up of resources and hence does not result in a genuine social cost. But in the case of a decreasing-cost industry, the expansion of output does involve a saving of resources because, Young and Knight might have added, such an industry only expands along a falling supply curve because of the presence of real external economies.

This argument is impeccable and requires only one addendum. A rising long-run supply price may be the result of pecuniary external diseconomies but it may also be the result of real external diseconomies. In the latter case, forcing the industry to contract does represent a saving of resources. But, in general, it remains true that pecuniary external economies or diseconomies cannot create a divergence between private and social costs. Given the exceptional nature of genuine technological diseconomies and retaining the assumption of perfect competition, we may conclude that the proposal to contract increasing-cost industries by taxes has no significance for aggregate welfare; all it does is to redistribute purchasing power. To be sure, if we can find any decreasing-cost industries, subsidizing their expansion will certainly raise aggregate economic welfare. But it is not possible to advocate subsidization on this score alone because we must necessarily reduce someone's welfare when we raise the required funds for the subsidy program.

To reiterate: the existence of producers' surplus in the sense of 'rent' does not indicate a failure to achieve an optimum allocation of resources. On the contrary, competition will insure that the money costs to all producers in the industry will be equalized by imputing rent to scarce factors in inelastic supply. These Ricardian rents, or transfer costs, or producers' surplus, serve the social function of limiting the use of the scarce facor to the point at which its marginal value product is equal in all uses in the industry. In the case of land, for example, the exploitation of superior land is restricted by the landlord's rent to the point at which its marginal cost is equal to cost on rentless inferior land. In consequence, equal additions of investment on superior or inferior land will make equal additions to output and equal units of output will incur the same costs. The creation of differential as much as of scarcity rents, therefore, is one of the optimizing characteristics of a competitive market.

8. The Representative Firm

Marshall's 'restless quest for realism', his refusal to be bound by static assumptions, is perfectly symbolized by his invention of the concept of the 'representative firm'. Despite the recourse to external economies to reconcile decreasing costs with competitive equilibrium, Marshall seems to have believed that business firms in most manufacturing industries are in fact able to take advantage of internal economies of scale. He gave numerous examples of such internal economies and almost none of diseconomies that could not be overcome in time. The implication was that firms expand slowly but without any apparent limit. This creates a dilemma in stating the conditions of long-run equilibrium for an industry. The supply price of an industry in the long run is determined by the minimum average costs of the marginal firm, including 'normal profits'. 'Normal profits', which Marshall defined as 'the supply price of average business ability and energy', might be thought of as that level of profits which if expected to continue in the future would lead to zero net investment. If firms enjoy internal economies, they must necessarily grow in size with the growth of the industry itself. Expansion by *external* economies will now favour the larger firms and so alter the size distribution of firms in the industry. The fact that all the firms earn only 'normal profits' has no significance now in limiting entry, since a still larger newcomer to the industry could always do better than the marginal firm. Marshall rescued himself from this difficulty, however, by a biological analogy. He claimed that firms go through cycles of energy and business initiative and are thus unable to take constant advantage of decreasing costs. Although he conceded later that the growth of joint stock companies mitigated the effect of the high mortality of unusual entrepreneurial ability, he never abandoned the conviction that the history of firms is characterized by a biological life cycle.

Marshall's belief in the eventual senility of growing firms won very few adherents even in his own time. It is difficult to see what any assertion about the returns-to-age schedule of a firm – Marshall seems to be saying the the curve relating a firm's average costs to its age is U-shaped – has to do with static returns to scale. Once we accept Marshall's idea, however, we must reconstruct the usual formulation of long-period equilibrium and replace the idea of a marginal firm by a representative firm. The final equilibrium situation must now be defined as one in which a representative firm earns just 'normal profits' and no more. The industry is in equilibrium and its output is constant through time because the increase in output from firms that are growing and being 'born' is matched by the loss in output from firms that are declining and 'dying'. The representative firm provides us with a miniature illustration of the supply curve of the industry; its unit costs represent the average unit costs of the firms in the industry and its unit cost curve depicts the reactions of supply via the number and size of firms in the process of long-period adjustment. Here, as elsewhere, it is not clear whether Marshall is referring to a one-plant firm or a multiplant business unit. On the whole, however, it appears that the representative firm is a representative business organization, not a representative production unit. Marshall describes it as neither a newcomer nor a well-established firm but one with an average access to internal and external economies. This has the danger of suggesting that it has a real existence. The representative firm, however, is an abstraction; it is neither an arithmetic average, nor a median, nor even a modal firm. It is representative, not with respect to size, but with respect to average costs. Marshall likens it to a typical tree of a virgin forest, for it always remains representative of the average life cycle of the firms in industry, growing as does the industry itself.

The concept of a representative firm is one of Marshall's many concessions to brute facts. Much as he was preoccupied with supplying a purely formal body of analysis, he was, at the same time, attempting to account for the experience of his age. The growth in the size of firms, he thought, made it necessary to concede the existence of economies of scale. On the other hand, he was unwilling to accept the implication that this entailed the destruction of competition. Hence, the resort to biological analogies. It is obvious, however, that static theory has almost nothing of significance to say about the temporal process of growth in the size of firms: *being* large, yes, but not *growing* large. Marshall's device of the representative firm allowed him to state the conditions for equilibrium of total output of an industry without requiring at the same time that all the member firms of the industry be in equilibrium. The trouble with the notion is that it is a purely *ex post* construction: it describes the features of an equilibrium situation but contains no analysis of the path toward equilibrium and fails in any way to demonstrate that the process will in fact converge to equilibrium. It yields a conception of long-run equilibrium that does not conform to stationary conditions but constitutes, in Guillebaud's words, a 'sort of conceptual halfway house between the real dynamic world and the stationary hypothesis'.

9. Monopolistic Competition

The concept of the representative firm retained its place in economic theory until an alternative reconciliation of increasing returns with competitive equilibrium suggested itself. Taking a hint from Marshall's suggestion of 'the difficulties of marketing', the entire Marshallian theory of value was reconstructed by Sraffa, Harrod,

Chamberlin and Robinson on the basis of the individual firm as a monopolist of its own particular market. Marshall had toyed with this solution as a reinforcement for his other two explanations of increasing returns under competition, but he apparently regarded it as a special case. The heated debate in the 1920s over 'empty economic boxes' in Marshallian theory culminated in the triumphant generalization of Marshall's hint of the existence of product differentiation. The almost total rejection of long-period analysis that this entailed banished the concept of the representative firm and the associated problem of falling supply price from economic literature. Price theory ever since has been a theory of the firm in the short run, supplemented by an analysis of entry conditions into collections of producers of fairly close substitutes. The gain in rigor from this piece of surgery has been immense but the price in terms of a lopsided theory of competition has been equally great. In distribution theory or in welfare economics, the argument is invariably carried through to the full long-period adjustment before being dropped, but in the theory of supply, the long run is fuzzed over or entirely confined to the individual firm floating uneasily in a situation in which it can exclude rivals from duplicating its product – hence, the downward-sloping demand curve of monopolistic competition – but cannot prevent them from eroding its profit – hence, Chamberlin's tangency solution.

This is not the place for a full-scale rehearsal of the theory of imperfect or monopolistic competition but the chapter would be incomplete without a brief consideration of the outstanding modern attack on the standard Marshallian view that the theory of competition supplemented by the theory of monopoly completes the economist's 'box of tools' for analyzing the structure of modern industry. We will concentrate on Chamberlin's *Theory of Monopolistic Competition* (1933) rather than Robinson's *Economics of Imperfect Competition* (1933) because the latter merely refined Marshall's theory of monopoly without claiming that a new instrument of analysis was required to deal with market structures characterized by product differentiation and advertising expenditures. Despite superficial similarities between the two books, it is now perfectly obvious that Chamberlin was the true revolutionary.

Chamberlin's case of 'monopolistic competition' is a market structure in which (1) the number of sellers is sufficiently large so that each firm can act independently, without regard to the effect of its actions on those of its rivals – notice, oligopoly does not fulfill the conditions of monopolistic competition; (2) there is a heterogeneous product, buyers having preferences for the branded products of particular sellers; and (3) entry into 'industries' – groups of products that are close substitutes for each other – is unrestricted, new sellers being able to commence production of very close substitutes for existing brands of the product. In those circumstances, each seller has a determinate demand schedule for his product, given the prices of the other firms, and these demand schedules confronting each seller are less than perfectly elastic. Chamberlin analyzes price determination under monopolistic competition by means of two types of demand curves *dd* and *DD* (see Figure 10–12). Take one particular seller producing its own brand of a certain product. Demand curve *DD* represents the demand schedule confronting this firm when all the other firms in the 'group' charge the same price for the product. Since the product of our firm is differentiated by means of packaging, labelling and service guarantees, it can sell more of its own brand by lowering its price, provided the other sellers in the group do not match the price reduction. With each fixed price assumed for the other firms, the firm in question faces a particular *dd* curve whose elasticity varies inversely with the strength of brand preferences; whenever its price cuts are matched by the other firms, the *dd* curve shifts down. If the situation were one of perfect competition, the horizontal demand curve facing each individual firm would be the *dd* type, since no seller would take account of the reactions of other sellers to his price change. For the single-firm monopolist, on the other hand, *dd* would coincide with *DD* because he would have no effective rivals. In monopolistic competition, however, both curves are relevant: each firm keeps on lowering its price in the expectation that its demand curve is like *dd*. The effect of this behavior, when all firms are considered together, is to bring about a curve like *DD* facing the entire 'group'.

Figure 10–12

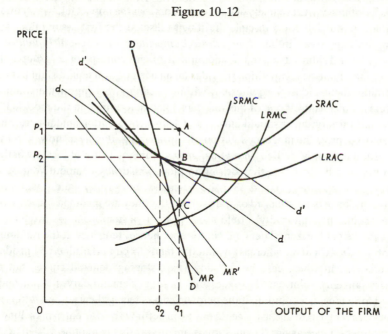

When the demand curve facing the firm is in fact $d'd'$, the firm in question maximizes profits by producing q_1 at p_1, earning supernormal profits $AB \cdot Oq_1$. This induces its rivals to cut their prices on competing brands or to produce new competing brands, each firm counting on the others not to react to its actions. The result is that the demand schedule for our firm shifts down to *dd* and this continues until *dd* is tangent with both the short-run and long-run average cost curve at q_2 and p_2; profits are maximized because marginal cost equals marginal revenue but the profits that are earned are merely normal profits. This long-run tangency solution is the major empirical implication of monopolistic competition: we have short-run excess capacity, defined as the difference between equilibrium average costs and minimum average costs, and unexploited economies of scale in the long run; there are too many firms in the industry compared with the situation under perfect competition, and each charges a higher price because it is too small for maximum efficiency. It is apparent, however, that the price of eliminating underutilization in monopolistic competition is that of forgoing consumers' preferences for variety in styles and brands. That is, whether the tangency solution is 'good' or 'bad' is a matter of welfare economics, not positive economics.

Chamberlin's reasoning proceeds by way of three simplifying assumptions: (1) despite product heterogeneity there are sufficiently large gaps in the chain of substitutes as to make it possible to demarcate 'groups' of firms and to talk about entry into a group; (2) 'both demand and cost curves for all the "products" are uniform throughout the group', an assumption which Chamberlin himself describes as 'heroic'; and (3) 'any adjustment of price or of "product" by a single producer spreads its influence over so many of his competitors that the impact felt by any one is negligible'. It was left for a disciple, Triffin, to discard the first assumption with Chamberlin's approval. In his *Monopolistic Competition and General Equilibrium Theory* (1940), Triffin advocated abandonment of the concept of a 'group': the theory of monopolistic competition provides an analysis of firm equilibrium but can say nothing about industry equilibrium without defining the gap in the chain of substitutes, which is itself one of the variables to be determined in the model. It is strange that this argument should have won Chamberlin's endorsement because it threatens to deprive the tangency solution of any meaning. It is clear, however, that this question cannot be settled on *a priori* grounds: the question of fact is whether certain firms do behave as if they belong to monopolistically competitive groups. Similarly, assumptions (2) and (3), the so-called 'uniformity' and 'symmetry' assumptions, have been attacked on the grounds that they are incompatible with the tangency solution: 'uniformity' would seem to imply a homogeneous product, in which case we get horizontal demand curves and, hence, tangency at the minimum point of the *SRAC* curve, whereas 'symmetry' tends to be undermined by product differentiation, in which case we get downward-sloping demand curves but no necessary tangency solution. However, uniformity of demand curves is not really required for a tangency solution: if the demand curves facing the firms are different, tangency of average cost and average revenue can occur with different firms selling at different prices. Once again, the question is one of fact that cannot be settled at the outset by examining assumptions.

Likewise the assumption of symmetry amounts to the assertion that the large-number case with product differentiation but without oligopolistic interdependence is an important market structure in modern economies. The most damaging criticism that can be made against the theory of monopolistic competition is not that some of its assumptions are unrealistic but that most of the product markets that appear at first glance to conform to the requirements of the Chamberlinian tangency solution turn out on closer examination to involve the 'conjectural interdependence' characteristic of oligopoly: product differentiation takes place typically in a market environment of 'competition among the few'. While it is perfectly true that the twelve pages in the *Theory of Monopolistic Competition* on 'mutual dependence recognized' constituted a then original contribution to the theory of oligopoly, this was not the core of Chamberlin's book. That is to say, there appears to be a misplaced emphasis in Chamberlin's work: monopolistic competition may be as rare as perfect competition.

The original appeal of Chamberlin's book was that its predicted consequences were directly contrary to the implications of the perfectly competitive model. For example, it can be rigorously demonstrated that profit maximizers in perfectly competitive markets have no incentive to advertise. However, advertising expenditures in an increasing number of product markets are a well-attested phenomenon and the theory of monopolistic competition implies that firms selling a heterogeneous product will indeed resort to advertising. Such conformities of the implications of monopolistic competition with even the most casual impressions of the real world supported the claim that here was a genuine advance over Marshallian theory. Unfortunately, Chamberlin's promise to provide a theory of selling costs as a type of interfirm competition has proved to be largely unfulfilled: in the absence of a specified relationship between changes in DD and changes in dd, which the theory of monopolistic competition does not provide, it is impossible to predict the effect of a change in cost or demand either on the price, the size of plant, or the number of firms in the group. Indeed, given the presence of selling costs, even the tangency solution is robbed of its dramatic import. The average cost curve which Chamberlin shows to be downward sloping at the equilibrium point is an aggregation of production and advertising outlays. The level and slope of every dd curve is produced by a given level of advertising expenditures. The curve of advertising expenditure per unit of output is a rectangular hyperbola and we construct the $SRAC$ curve by adding it vertically to the U-shaped curve of average production costs. It follows from this construction that the minimum point of Chamberlin's average production-plus-selling-cost curve occurs at a larger volume of output than the minimum point on the curve that takes account only of production costs. Thus, the tangency solution is perfectly compatible with rising unit production costs provided only that unit selling costs are falling fast enough to offset any rise in unit production costs. Even on Chamberlin's own grounds, therefore, it cannot be demonstrated that unrestricted entry into a monopolistically competitive industry leads to excess capacity and unexploited economies of scale.

It is one of the ironies of intellectual history that the case that Chamberlin seized upon – large numbers with free entry and product differentiation but without recognition of interdependence – is now regarded as being only trivially different from perfect competition. The revolution in price theory engendered by the *Theory of Monopolistic Competition* was to multiply the number of market structures that economics must analyze, to show that the test of satisfactory market performance is not simply the automatic consequence of the form of competition, and that welfare pronouncements and policy prescriptions in a world of monopolistic competition and oligopoly cannot be based merely on the degree to which a particular market structure departs from the norms of perfect competition. Price theory has ever since been more complicated and less satisfying, and it is hardly surprising that some critics should now complain that we are left with little more than *ad hoc* theorizing. We can never go back to the bold generalities of Marshallian price theory. It is precisely for that reason that we are justified in speaking of a Chamberlinian Revolution in modern microeconomics in the same way that we speak of a Keynesian Revolution in macroeconomics.

READER'S GUIDE TO THE 'PRINCIPLES OF ECONOMICS'

The preface to the first edition pays tribute to the principle of continuity, exemplified in the motto *Natura non facit saltum*, as the unifying element in the treatment of the book. Running through the *Principles* is 'one Fundamental Idea', namely, that of 'the general theory of equilibrium of demand and supply'. The final paragraph of the Preface contains one of Marshall's typical skeptical comments on mathematical economics: mathematics is at best a useful piece of scaffolding, which should be removed in the presentation of final arguments (see also Book III, chapter 1; Appendix D, section 1; Mathematical Appendix XIV).

The preface to the eighth edition carries an apologetic note about the largely statical character of the analysis in the *Principles*. Despite the frequent use of the device of *ceteris paribus*, Marshall insists that the keynote of the book is dynamics rather than statics. Even so, statics and dynamics are not the whole of economics: 'The Mecca of the economist lies in economic biology rather than in economic dynamics'. The notion of a price-determining margin, Marshall observes, has received increasing stress in successive editions of the *Principles*, and with it has come increasing emphasis on the fact that the relevant margin 'varies with the conditions of the problem in hand, and in particular with the period of time to which reference is being made'.

10. Introduction

It is characteristic of Marshall's approach to economics that the book begins with a statement of 'the pains of poverty and the stagnating influences of excessive mechanical toil', whose elimination 'gives to economic studies their chief and their highest interest' (**Book I, chapter 1, section 2**). The fundamental feature of modern industrial life, Marshall continues, is not competition but self-reliance, deliberate choice making and rational forethought (**section 4**). Appendices A and B complement the introductory chapter: the first gives a sketch of the growth of the free enterprise system and the second provides a capsule history of economic thought, which is notable for its conciliatory comments on the German Historical School.

11. Scope, Substance, and Method

Economics owes its progress to the fact that 'money affords a fairly good measure of the moving force of a great part of the motives by which men's lives are fashioned'. This thesis forms the burden of **Book I, chapters 2–4**. Marshall admits that the 'desires' that prompt to action sometimes bear little relationship to the realized 'satisfactions' from that action (**section 1**; see also Book III, chapter 3, note 1). Price theory, however, can get along merely on the basis of 'revealed desires'. The divergence between desires and satisfactions raises no special problems until we get to welfare economics. But Marshall is reluctant to cede any ground whatever. After noting the real difficulties connected with intertemporal and interpersonal comparisons of utilities, he nevertheless concludes that 'the money which people of equal incomes will give to obtain a benefit or avoid an injury is a good measure of the benefit or injury' (**section 2**). Similarly, after stating Bernoulli's hypothesis of diminishing marginal utility of income, he avoids applying it directly to whole income classes, not because of the impossibility of aggregating individual utilities, but on the strength of the astonishing assertion that 'by far the greater number of the events with which economics deals affect in about equal proportions all the different classes of society' (**section 2**).

Sections 3–7 defend the economist's concern with the sphere of rational action, that part of men's conduct that is dominated by deliberate choice. **Appendices C and D** pursue the theme of the proper scope and method of economics. **Book I, chapter 3**, defines the concept of an economic law. **Chapter 4** touches on the relationship between pure economic theory and applied economics; section 3 contains an interesting list of the chief practical questions to which economists ought to address themselves. The four brief chapters which make up **Book II** deal with the definition of fundamental terms. **Book III, chapter 3, section 2**, provides some very sensible comments on Smith's doctrine of productive labour. **Book III, chapter 4,** and **Appendix E** introduce the reader to the much discussed question of the appropriate definition of capital.

12. Wants and Activities

Book III, chapter 1, introduces the theory of demand, a subject that 'until recently . . . has been somewhat neglected'. It is typical of Marshall's apologetic attitude to his English predecessors that he criticizes Ricardo and his followers merely for 'laying disproportionate stress on the side of cost of production': they 'were aware that the conditions of demand played as important a part as those of supply in determining value, yet they did not express their meaning with sufficient clearness' (see also Book III, chapter 3, section 6; Book V, chapter 5, section 5; Book VI, chapter 2, section 1; and Appendix 1). Equally characteristic is the closing comment of the chapter to the effect that 'the reaction against the comparative neglect of the study of wants by Ricardo and his followers shows signs of being carried to the opposite extreme'.

Marshall's insistence on the importance of the supply side is central to his belief developed in **chapter 2** of **Book III** that 'activities' – questions involving the energy, efforts, and quality of human agents in the economic process – in some sense dominate and mold those very 'wants' that are taken as data in static equilibrium analysis. Here and elsewhere in the *Principles*, Marshall displays a reluctance to take wants as given. He inquires into the formation of consumers' preferences (**Book III, chapter 2**) before proceeding to develop the theory of value based on given tastes (**chapter 3**). Changes in the mode of production and their influence on human character, he seems to be saying in chapter 2, are more important determinants of economic welfare than the mechanical efficiency with which given resources are allocated to satisfy given wants. Despite his belief that a decentralized economy does within limits tend to produce optimum results, his faith in free enterprise is in fact grounded on the notion that certain superior qualities of human character – initiative, industry, frugality and rationality – are invariably associated with such a system. He was firmly opposed to socialism, although sympathetic to some of the views of socialists, because he did not think that socialism would conduce to the development of that 'firmness of character' that feeds the springs of enterprise under a private property system. No doubt, this kind of thinking reflects what Schumpeter called 'mid-Victorian morality, seasoned by Benthamism'.

13. Marginal Utility

Book III, chapter 3, opens with a statement of 'the law of satiable wants or of diminishing utility' as a 'familiar and fundamental tendency of human nature'. Marshall gives no proof for the existence of such a law but he does defend it against possible misinterpretations. Suppose it be argued that the marginal utility of the last necessary yard of wallpaper to cover a wall is greater than that of earlier yards; in that case, Marshall suggests, we must make the entire wall the unit of utility analysis. What of the case of the desire for music growing with the more music a man hears, or the virtue of cleanliness and the vice of drunkenness, which grow by what they feed on? Here we must perforce conclude, according to Marshall, that the utility function has shifted. In the end we are left with a completely tautological definition of the law of diminishing marginal utility, referring to given tastes at an instantaneous moment of time, so stated as to include any and all eventualities.

14. Consumer's Demand

Having stated the law of diminishing marginal utility in section 1, Marshall proceeds immediately to deduce from it that demand schedules are negatively inclined (**section 2**). Employing an 'additive' utility function and assuming that the marginal utility of money is 'a fixed quantity', he shows that an individual's demand price for a commodity will fall with every addition to the amount of the commodity possessed or consumed. The underlying rationale of this procedure is given by the equation

$$\frac{MU_x}{p_x} = \frac{MU_y}{p_y} = MU_e,$$

stated in Mathematical Appendix II. Marshall writes the marginal utility of money 'or general purchasing power at a person's disposal at any time' as $d\mu/dm$, or MU_e [see chapter 9, section 6]. His du/dx and du'/dx' is our MU_x and MU_y. Defining p as 'the price which he is just willing to pay for an amount x of the commodity which gives him a total pleasure μ', dp/dx is the price paid for an additional unit of x. And so we have in equilibrium

$$\frac{d\mu}{dm}\frac{dp}{dx} = \frac{du}{dx},$$

which is equvalent to our $MU_e p_x = MU_x$, and likewise for every other commodity. Jevons' equation for isolated exchange, namely that $MU_x/p_x = MU_y/p_y$, becomes

$$\frac{du}{dx}\frac{dx}{dp} = \frac{du'}{dx'}\frac{dx'}{dp'}.$$

A constant MU_e and a declining MU_x gives a negatively declining demand curve; similarly, Marshall remarks, a constant MU_x and Bernoulli's hypothesis of a declining MU_e, $d^2\mu/dm^2 < 0$, give a positive income curve: 'the marginal utility to him of an amount x of a commodity remaining unchanged, an increase in his means increases ... the rate at which he is willing to pay for further supplies of it' (Mathematical Appendix II and chapter 3, section 3).

Marshall draws a demand curve in **section 4**. Cournot, following standard mathematical practice, had placed price as the independent variable on the abscissa and quantities demanded as the dependent variable on the ordinate. Marshall established the now familiar arrangement showing price on the y-axis and quantity on the x-axis. His reason for violating common mathematical usage was to permit graphic derivation of market demand curves as the sum of individual demand curves (**section 5**); using the same coordinate system throughout, market demand curves could then be coupled with market supply curves, quantity now being the independent variable and price the dependent variable to be determined. Nevertheless, the Marshallian procedure is somewhat clumsy: in computing the price elasticity of demand of an individual demand curve, we have to accustom ourselves to inverting the first derivative of the demand function.

A demand curve for a commodity is drawn up on the basis 'other things remaining equal'. Marshall never furnished an explicit list of the content of *ceteris paribus* but he comes closer to doing this in **section 6** than anywhere else in the book. A footnote touches upon the associated difficulty of defining a commodity.

Book III, chapter 4, defines the concept of price elasticity algebraically as well as geometrically. **Mathematical Appendix III** introduces the notion of a constant-outlay curve, a demand curve whose elasticity is everywhere equal to unity. The demand for 'necessaries' is said to be typically inelastic, while the demand for 'luxuries' is said to be highly elastic – an old idea in the history of economic thought (**section 3**). Elasticity of demand is governed by the ease of substitution in consumption (**section 4**); elasticity of demand for a commodity, therefore, has no meaning except in connection with a particular definition of the scope of the commodity in question (first footnote, **section 3**). The conceptual and statistical difficulties in measuring elasticity are discussed in **sections 5–8**.

The equimarginal principle with reference to consumption is stated in **Book III, chapter 5, sections 1–2**. It is then applied to the distribution of purchases through time. Given a subjective preference for present over future consumption, the marginal utility of a commodity will differ depending upon the date at which it is expected to be consumed (**section 3**). Although in principle intertemporal comparisons of utility, even for the same individual, have no scientific validity, it is possible to deduce the existence and shape of an individual's intertemporal utility curve from his willingness to pay interest for a money loan, assuming that his tastes and money income remain the same between two dates and ignoring the uncertainty that attaches to future events (**section 4**). The economy and care with which Marshall sets out the notion of time preference makes a striking contrast with Böhm-Bawerk's prolix and confusing exposition of the same idea (see also Book IV, chapter 7, section 8).

15. Consumer's Surplus

Consumer's surplus is defined in **Book III, chapter 6, section 1**, as the excess of what the consumer would pay for a commodity rather than to go without it over what he does pay – in other words, the roughly triangular area under a demand curve above the price-quantity rectangle (see **Mathematical Appendix VI**). A similar utility surplus can be defined for the marginal utility curve that underlies the demand curve. Consumer's surplus becomes consumers' surplus in **section 3**, provided we 'neglect for the moment the fact that the same sum of money represents different amounts of pleasure to different people'. The first footnote in section 3 announces Marshall's intention 'henceforward' to measure price per unit of the commodity demanded, that is, to multiply Jevons' 'final utility', du/dx, by Δx; see also Mathematical Appendix 1 [see chapter 8, section 8].

The chief difficulty in aggregating individual consumer's surpluses is the existence of different income-utility curves (**section 3**). Marshall brushes this objection aside on the grounds, encountered earlier, that important economic events affect different income classes in about equal proportions. This paves the way for the application of consumer-surplus analysis in Book V, chapter 13, involving intergroup comparisons of utility. At this point, Marshall encounters two further difficulties. First of all, the individual's utility function for a particular commodity varies with the amounts of other commodities consumed: consumer's surplus, therefore, can be estimated only on the static assumption that other commodities do not vary in price (**section 3**). Furthermore, it must be supposed that MU_e is constant along the demand curve (**section 4**), which is approximately true when the expenditure on the commodity in question involves only a small part of the total outlays of individuals (see **Mathematical Appendix VI**). For both these reasons, Marshall now abandons the previous concept of consumers' surplus and adopts instead a definition that limits the calculation of the surplus to 'the neighbourhood of the customary price' (**section 4**). Summing up, we conclude that consumer's surplus is approximately measurable when the commodity in question constitutes an insignificant item in the individual's budget and when the change in price is small. No particular reason has been given to lead one to believe that individual surpluses can be satisfactorily aggregated to form a consumers' surplus.

Having stated 'one general law of demand' in Book III, chapter 3, Marshall now allows for the possibility of positively sloping demand curves, the so-called Giffen Paradox – **Book III, chapter 6, section 4**. Giffen's Paradox, however, implies a 'generalized' utility function, a conception that Marshall dismisses as 'less adapted to express the every-day fact of economic life' than an 'additive' utility function (see **Mathematical Appendix XII**). The closing section of this chapter once again postulates Bernoulli's hypothesis (see also **Mathematical Appendix VIII**). In a footnote Marshall draws attention to its implications with respect to gambling and insurance.

16. The Law of Diminishing Returns

Book IV, chapter 1, introduces the productive triad and the notion of the increasing marginal disutility of labour as one of the 'fundamental principles of human nature', yielding a positively sloped supply curve of human efforts in the short run. 'Land' is defined in **chapter 2, section 1**, as consisting of those resources given without cost or effort: 'the fundamental attribute of land is its extension'. This definition is, however, immediately fuzzed over and by the end of the chapter we are back to agricultural land for which the farmer pays a contractual rent to the landlord. This leads straightway to a statement of the law of diminishing returns à la Mill: not only is the law confined to the case in which capital and labour are jointly applied to land but, given a constant level of technical knowledge, it is proportional rather than incremental returns that are said to be diminishing (**Book IV, chapter 3, section 1**). An unambiguous incremental definition of the law is found later in the same chapter (sections 3 and 8), but the proportional definition occurs again in Book V, chapter 2, section 1, and Book VI, chapter 10, section 8. Marshall's proof of the law is again perfectly classical in character: unless the law were in operation, cultivation would never have been extended to new land (section 1).

Marshall leaves no doubt that he regards the law of diminishing returns in this context as a historical law, for 'whatever may be the future developments of the arts of agriculture, a continued increase in the application of labour to land must ultimately result in a diminution of the extra produce which can be obtained by a given extra amount of capital and labour' (**Book IV, chapter 3, section 2**). The intramarginal surplus over and above the marginal cost of cultivation is only part of 'the full rent of a farm in an old country' (**section 2**). The large variety of return schedules that are compatible with diminishing returns are illustrated in **section 3**. Ricardo's assertions about the order of cultivation in a growing economy are defended against Carey's attack (**section 5**). Ricardo spoke carelessly 'as though there were an absolute standard of fertility', ignoring the fact that 'a mere increase in demand may invert the order in which two adjacent pieces of land rank as regards fertility' (**section 3**) and that 'the order of fertility of different soils is liable to be changed by changes in the methods of cultivation and the relative values of different crops' (**section 4**). It is not to be doubted that there does exist something like a Malthusian pressure of population upon the means of subsistence; still, 'Ricardo, and the economists of his time . . . did not allow enough for the increase of strength that comes from organization' (**section 6**; see also Book IV, chapter 7, section 3).

So far, the whole of this third chapter in Book IV is entirely classical in tone, a somewhat improved version of J. S. Mill's treatment of the same subject. Near the end of the chapter, however, Marshall at last generalizes the law of diminishing returns to all the agents of production, making it applicable to manufacture as well as to agriculture (**section 7**). Nevertheless, 'the fixedness of the whole stock of cultivable land in an old country' implies that 'from the social point of view, land is not on exactly the same footing as those implements of production which a man can increase without limits' (**section 8**). In the final analysis, therefore, Marshall retains the classical notion that the 'free gifts of Nature', which comprise land as a factor of production, are coterminous with the soil for which farmers pay rent.

17. The Growth of Population

As in Mill, the exposition of the law of historically diminishing returns leads on to a discussion of the dynamics of population growth (**Book IV, chapter 4**). The Malthusian theory of population is set out with admirable succinctness, and its essential validity is boldly proclaimed: 'there will probably be great improvements in the arts of agriculture; and, if so, the pressure of population on the means of subsistence may be held in check for about two hundred years, but not longer' (**section 3**). **Sections 4–5** discuss the inverse relationship between fertility and income. **Sections 6–7** provide a fairly pedestrian history of the growth of population in England since the Middle Ages. The whole of **Book IV, chapters 5** and **6**, may be passed over, although the concluding sections at the end of both chapters give further evidence of Marshall's orthodox classical attitude to population problems.

18. The Growth of Capital

Book IV, chapter 7, pursues the subject of time preference and the supply of savings, broached earlier in Book III, chapter 5. Marshall notes that the classical economists regarded savings as made almost exclusively from business profits (**section 7**). But 'in modern England rent and the earnings of professional men and hired workers are an important source of accumulation', particularly since 'human faculties are as important a means of production as any other kind of capital'. From the point of view of capital as it is conventionally defined, however, it would seem that Marshall, like most of the economists of his generation, exaggerated the significance of personal saving; his theory of saving completely neglects business saving, which probably accounted in his day for about half of all new funds.

'Human nature being what it is, we are justified in speaking of the interest on capital as the reward of the sacrifices involved in the waiting for the enjoyment of material resources' (**section 8**). The neutral term 'waiting' is chosen in preference to 'abstinence', though Marshall does not explain why Senior's term is likely to be misunderstood: it was not merely that the term 'abstinence' carried an honorific connotation but that it was difficult to break away from Senior's practice of speaking of average rather than marginal abstinence [see chapter 6, section 11]. The short-run supply curve of saving is said to be positively sloped (**section 9**). It may be backward bending, however, because of the Sargant Effect: individuals who are saving to provide a certain income for old age will find that they must save more if the rate of interest falls. Nevertheless, 'while human nature remains as it is every fall in the rate is likely to cause many more people to save less than to save more than they otherwise would have done' (**section 9**). Moreover, the long-run supply curve of saving is also positively sloped, not so much because 'a rise in the rate increase the *desire* to save' as because 'it often increases the *power* to save, or rather it is often an indication of the increased efficiency of our productive resources'.

19. The Division of Labour or Industrial Organization

Book IV, chapters 8–9, treat of a conventional subject in a conventional way. **Chapter 8**, however, contains some incisive comments on Social Darwinism, the working philosophy of businessmen everywhere at the turn of the century. At the close of chapter 9, economies of scale are divided into two classes: (1) external economies, dependent on 'the general development of the industry', and (2) internal economies, 'dependent on the resources of the individual houses of business engaged in it'. **Book IV, chapter 10**, analyzes the localization of industry as a chief source of external economies (see in particular section 3). The growth of tertiary industries in England is discussed in **section 4. Chapter 11** turns to internal economies as a source of the advantages of production on a large scale. Marshall's list of these economies indiscriminately mixes perfectly and imperfectly competitive conditions: (1) superior use of specialized machinery; (2) improved facilities for developing new machines and products; (3) discounts on bulk purchases; (4) greater opportunities for selecting managers and foremen with specialized skills; (5) favourable credit rating with bankers and, hence, ability to borrow on easier terms; and (6) ability to overcome marketing difficulties by spending on advertising (**sections 1–3** and **5**). This raises the question whether the growth of firms reaping the benefits of internal economies will destroy competition. Marshall's answer is that small firms do in fact survive because of the short-lived nature of dynamic entrepreneurship as well as the marketing difficulties that growing firms encounter (**section 5**).

The character of entrepreneurial ability and the context in which energetic innovators will come to the fore is further discussed in **Book IV, chapter 12**. Marshall's explanation of the unique functions performed by the entrepreneur as distinct from the business manager is far from precise (**sections 2** and **5**). Unusual business talents are rarely inherited; this accounts for the fact that firms in the hands of partners will rarely grow rapidly for more than a generation (**section 6**). But 'since the joint-stock companies in the United Kingdom do a very great part of the business of all kinds that is done in the country', offering 'very large opportunities to men with natural talents for business management, who have not inherited any material capital, or any business connection' (**section 9**), it is difficult to see how this chapter is supposed to live up to its promise of showing why large firms do not in fact drive their smaller rivals out of business. The famous 'trees in the forest' paragraph in the following chapter (**chapter 13, section 1**) does little to clear up the difficulty. Despite 'the great recent development of vast joint-stock companies, which often stagnate, but do not readily die .... Nature still presses on private business by limiting the length of the life of its original founders, and by limiting even more narrowly that part of their lives in which their faculties retain full vigour.' By some process of arithmetic addition, we are led to the conclusion that 'in almost every trade there is a constant rise and fall of large businesses, some firms being in the ascending phase and others in the descending'.

In the last paragraph of this chapter, Marshall distinguishes between interest as 'the supply price of capital', the net earnings of management as 'the supply price of business ability and energy', and the gross earnings of management as the sum of the net earnings plus 'the supply price of that organization by which the appropriate business ability and the requisite capital are brought together'. Marshall's net earnings of management correspond to what other authors have called 'wages of management'. Marshall's gross earnings seems to correspond to the common definition of 'profits' when it is calculated inclusive of wages of management.

So far we have met only one kind of external economy, that caused by the localization of industry. **Book IV, chapter 11, section 4**, briefly mentions another: the growth of trade knowledge as the result of more newspapers and technical publications. The summary in chapter 14, however, mentions a more comprehensive kind of external economy stemming from 'the modern facilities for communication offered by steam transport, by the telegraph and by the printing press' that accrues to an industry independently of its own growth. **Section 2** defines the 'representative firm' of an industry as 'in a sense an average firm', whose expenses govern the supply price of the industry's product. This leads up to a statement of the Law of Increasing Returns as a counterfoil to the Law of Diminishing Returns. Marshall gives credence to the classical idea that agriculture is dominated by the latter, while manufacturing is largely subject to the former; in a footnote, however, he concedes that 'the forces which make for Increasing Return are not of the same order as those that make for Diminishing Return'. **Section 3** virtually amounts to a statement of the optimum theory of population. 'The accumulated wealth of civilized countries', Marshall concludes, 'is at present growing faster than population.'

20. Equilibrium of Demand and Supply

The bulk of Marshall's contributions to the theory of value and distribution are to be found in **Book V. Chapter 1** gives a short account of the concept of a 'market'. **Chapter 2** examines the simple case in which supply is perfectly inelastic and all sales are made out of fixed stocks. The proviso that the marginal utility of money must be supposed approximately constant is mentioned once again (section 3). The last paragraph of chapter 2 draws attention to an important 'peculiarity' of the labour market. Low wages, stemming from initial monopsony in the labour market, may cause workers to attach a high marginal utility to money, which then perpetuates low wages by affecting workers' willingness to supply labour. Moreover, workers sell labour in a lump sum and are thus prevented from making marginal calculations of efforts and rewards. 'These are two among many facts in which we shall find, as we go on, the explanation of much of that instinctive objection which the working classes have felt to the habit of some economists ... of regarding the labour market as like every other market.'

The efforts and sacrifices of labour and waiting together make up the 'real cost of production' of a commodity (**Book V, chapter 3, section 2**). When the real wage rate and the interest rate are constant, 'the money measure of costs corresponds to the real cost' (**chapter 3, section 7**). The normal supply price of a commodity may be taken to be the 'normal expenses of production (including *gross* earnings of management)' of the 'representative firm'; it is a price that will preserve constancy in the aggregate output of an industry (**section 5**). Marshall defines equilibrium in terms, not of the equality of quantity demanded and supplied, but in terms of the equality of the demand and supply price (**section 6**). Market and normal prices are identified with Smith's market and natural price (**section 6**). There follows the famous 'blade of a pair of scissors' paragraph, concluding with an equally famous assertion that 'as a general rule, the shorter the period which we are considering, the greater must be the share of our attention which is given to the influence of demand on value; and the longer the period, the more important will be the influence of cost of production on value'.

21. Stability Conditions

Stability conditions in the market are touched on in a footnote to **Book V, chapter 3, section 6**, and again in Appendix H, section 2.

Marshall insisted that his formulation of the problem was identical to that of Walras. Walras, however, insisted that his approach did not yield the same results as Marshall's. And as a matter of fact, Walras was right. The now standard Walrasian approach treats supply and demand curves as end points of horizontal lines corresponding to the quantity demanded or supplied at a given price. But Marshall viewed the schedules as end points of a set of vertical lines, each corresponding to the price at which a given quantity is produced or consumed; instead of price being the independent and quantity the dependent variable, Marshall regarded quantity as the independent and price as the dependent variable. Marshall talks about the supply price of a quantity; the individual is asked, not how much he would demand or supply at a given hypothetical price, but what is the highest price he would be willing to pay or accept for a certain amount of a commodity. Marshall's demand schedules should really be called sales functions, not demand functions, since they depict the price at which a certain quantity can be sold.

The quantity-dependent Walrasian approach relies on movements of price to reach equilibrium, while the Marshallian price-dependent approach relies on movements of quantity; that is, Walras provides what has been called a 'price-adjuster model' of the market, while Marshall provides an 'output-adjuster model'. Of course, both price and quantity vary in disequilibrium and for simple problems there is no difference between the two approaches. But the dynamic assumptions of the two systems are quite different.

Take the case of a normal demand curve and a forward-falling or backward-bending supply curve. In Marshallian analysis (see Figure 10–13), a shift to the right of the demand curve, given the supply curve, always increases the quantity supplied if the supply curve is positively inclined. But if the supply curve is negatively inclined, this result occurs only if the algebraic slope of the supply curve is less than that of the demand curve. For Marshall, Figure 10–13a is stable: the moment the demand curve shifts, the demand price d_1 exceeds the supply price s_1 for q_1, causing the quantity supplied to rise, which steadily narrows the gap between demand and supply price until a position of stable equilibrium is reached at q_2. It is stable by the Marshallian criterion of stability; a positive excess demand price, EP, causes a rise in the quantity produced per unit of time, and vice versa.

Figure 10–13

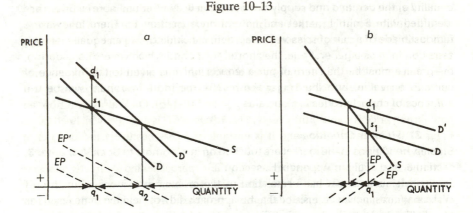

Figure 10–13b is unstable on Marshallian grounds. As soon as demand shifts, the demand price d_1 exceeds the supply price s_1, which increases the quantity produced per unit of time, so that output moves away rather than towards the equilibrium value. Any position to the right of q_1 increases output, any position to the left of q_1 decreases output: q_1 is not a stable level of output.

Walras' stability condition is that excess demand quantity, ED, equals zero at the equilibrium level and that a positive excess demand always leads to a rise in price, and *vice versa*. When the supply curve is positively sloped, an upward shift of the demand curve generates positive excess demand which makes the price rise to a new stable equilibrium. This is also true for negatively inclined supply curves but only if the algebraic slope for the supply curve is greater than that of the demand curve. For Walras Figure 10–14b is stable. As demand shifts, excess demand e_1e_2 is positive, the

Figure 10–14

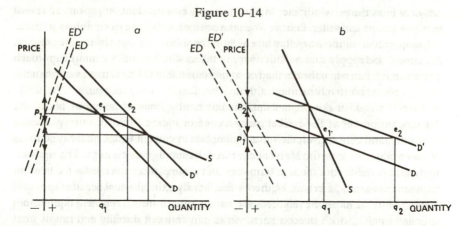

price rises, and this reduces supply, squeezing excess demand down to zero. The final price p_2 is stable because at greater output, excess demand is positive: a positive rate of price change causes the supply to fall by more than demand, thus eliminating excess demand. However, Figure 10–14a is unstable. As demand shifts, excess demand e_1e_2 is positive, the price rises, but the new equilibrium price is lower than the old equilibrium price; as the price moves away from the equilibrium value, supply falls faster than demand, increasing excess demand, which makes the price rise even faster.

To sum up: on Marshall's criterion, an equilibrium price is stable if the excess *price* curve *EP* is negatively inclined (as in Figures 10–13a and 10–14a) and it is unstable if *EP* is positively inclined (as in Figures 10–13b and 10–14b). On Walras' criterion, an equilibrium price is stable if the excess *demand* curve *ED* is negatively inclined (as in Figures 10–13b and 10–14b) and it is unstable if *ED* is positively inclined (as in Figures 10–13a and 10–14a).

Neither Marshall nor Walras realized why their approaches led to directly opposite results. Marshall usually had in mind the case of a long-run forward-falling supply curve manifesting the existence of external economies. In the context of the long-run theory of production, it seemed only reasonable to think of sellers adjusting output in response to a change in demand. Walras, on the other hand, was thinking of a backward-rising supply curve in a market period when stocks of goods are given; he found it reasonable to assume that buyers adjust prices in response to changes in demand. Actually, when Marshall in Book V, chapter 2 of the *Principles* discussed the determination of the price of corn in a market period, he employed the language of Walras' price-adjuster model, and similarly there are occasions in the *Elements of Pure Economics* when Walras uses output adjustment to show that the price will be stable in long-run equilibrium. Nevertheless, neither Marshall nor Walras realized that the question whether buyers or sellers adjust output or prices in disequilibrium cannot be decided on *a priori* grounds: these are simply different behavioral assumptions. In the short run, when stocks of goods are not given and output can be varied from given plants and equipment, the output-adjuster model is just as reasonable as the price-adjuster model, and only empirical investigation can reveal just how buyers and sellers behave when the price departs from its equilibrium value.

Comparative statics shows that an equilibrium point is denoted by the intersection of demand and supply curves. This does not tell us whether the system will approach a new equilibrium when the demand or supply curve shifts. This is true even when the supply curve is positively inclined, although we do not usually recognize it. Actually, of course, we do make certain implicit but nonrigorous assumptions about the dynamic properties of the market process even in static theory. But the Walrasian excess demand concept, which is usually implied in current textbook treatments, is no more plausible than the Marshallian excess demand-price concept. The rigorous analysis of stability conditions in terms of observable market behavior is the heart of economic dynamics, a branch of theory that hardly existed a few decades ago.

By stability we mean the requirement that the system should return to equilibrium after any small 'shock'. In economics, we usually think of stability in terms of what mathematicians call 'asymptotic stability': every path starting sufficiently near equilibrium converges to equilibrium as time elapses. This suggests a weaker definition useful for some purpose, namely, 'quasi-stability': every path starting near equilibrium remains confined close to equilibrium, without necessarily converging on it. Both the stronger and weaker definitions refer only to small perturbations that are local in character. A system may be locally stable in theory but unstable in practice because it is always subject to larger perturbations. For example, a bicycle in motion is usually stable for small shocks but not for large ones; similarly, the human body is stable for mild bacterial infections but not for heavy infections. It is easy to see that even when we have proved that a market price is locally stable, it does not follow that it is also *globally* stable, that is, equilibrium is approached by all possible motions of the system, whether starting from points near equilibrium or not. Enough has now been said to show that the task of the economist is far from completed when he has shown that the 'blades of a pair of scissors' combine to produce a unique price and quantity in a market.

22. Short Run and Long Run

Book V, chapter 4, shows that all investment is carried to the point at which the discounted future returns just equal accumulated cost outlays (**section 2**). The distribution of investment among alternative uses provides an illustration of the equimarginal principle (**section 4**). Prime and supplementary costs, or variable and fixed costs, are distinguished in **section 5** of **chapter 4**. The complex problem of value must be broken down by means of the *ceteris paribus* method (**Book V, chapter 5, section 2**). The 'famous fiction of the "Stationary State"' has proved a convenient first step toward a solution of the problem of value. In a stationary state 'the plain rule would be the cost of production governs value' because constant returns to scale obtain (**section 2**). The assumption of a stationary state is 'unconsciously implied in many popular renderings of Ricardo's theory of value, if not in his own versions of it' (footnote, section 8). The case of capital's growing at the same rate as labour, with land available in abundance and no technical change, exhibits all the distinctive features of a stationary state (section 3). Marshall then proceeds to define what he calls 'the statical method'; it has since been called 'partial equilibrium analysis' (**section 3**). The influence of the element of time on the relations between cost of production and value is illustrated with reference to the fishing industry.

In summarizing the nature of short-period adjustments, Marshall points out that producers often practice a 'restrictive strategy' when the going price fails to cover fixed costs. Instead of 'spoiling the market' by supplying the amount called for by their marginal cost curves, they supply less so as to cause the price to rise (see Figure 10–15). 'In fact however they seldom pursue this policy constantly and without moderation.' Comments such as these shows how Marshall allows for the phenomena of imperfect competition even as he is expounding the theory of perfect competition.

Figure 10–15

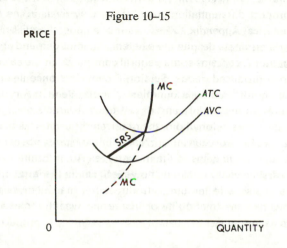

Reasons for employing the concept of a 'representative firm' are reviewed in **Book V, chapter 5, section 7. Section 8** classifies the problems of value by the periods to which they refer: market price, short-period normal price, long-period normal price, and secular changes in normal price. 'The remainder of the volume is chiefly concerned with the third of the above classes: that is, with the normal relations of wages, profits, prices, etc., for rather long periods.' The use of partial equilibrium analysis in problems relating to very long periods is 'dangerous' (footnote, section 8). 'In the opinion of the present writer the problem of normal value belongs to economic Dynamics' (footnote, section 2).

23. Joint and Composite Demand and Supply

When two or more productive factors are in joint demand, the demand schedule for any one factor can be derived from the demand curve and the final product by the vertical subtraction of the supply curves of the factors other than the one in question (**Book V, chapter 6, section 1**). The graphic illustration in the footnote assumes that the technical coefficients of production are fixed. The four laws of the elasticity of derived demand state that the elasticity of demand for a factor will be the lower (1) the less easily this factor can be replaced by other factors in the production of the final product; (2) the more inelastic is the final demand for the product; (3) the smaller is the share of this factor in total costs – the importance of being unimportant; and (4) the more inelastic is the supply of cooperating factors (**section 2**, and **Mathematical Note XV**). The aggregate demand curve of a factor is the sum of its composite demands in various uses (**section 3**). The well-known difficulty, first discussed by J. S. Mill [see chapter 6 of section 12], of the impossibility of assigning separate supply prices to two or more joint products is mentioned in **section 4**. The last footnote in **section 5** shows how to derive the composite supply curve of a factor and then goes on to comment on the instability of competitive equilibrium in cases in which some industries operate under increasing returns. Foreshadowing the modern solution of the problem, Marshall notes that 'product differentiation' may 'keep many rivals in the field for a long time'. **Mathematical Appendix XXI** shows that a general equilibrium of prices is theoretically determinate despite the existence of joint demand and supply.

   Book V, chapter 7, contains some general comments on the calculation of fixed costs for jointly produced goods. **Section 2** considers once again the tendency toward oligopoly fostered by economies of scale. **Section 3** broaches Knight's distinction between uncertainty and risk. If the individuals engaged in a certain industry are 'gamblers' – for whom 'the deterrent force of risks of loss in it is less than the attractive force of chances of great gain' – the presence of uncertainty may actually reduce average gains in the industry, as Adam Smith had once argued (**section 4**). Marshall ventures to say, however, that 'in the large majority of cases the influence of risk is in the opposite direction', that is, most people are risk averters for whom 'the total utility of increasing wealth increases less than in proportion to its amount'.

24. Marginal Net Product

Book V, chapter 8, opens with a statement of the concept of general equilibrium (**section 1**) and moves on to an exposition of the principle of substitution at the margin (**section 2**). The marginal product of a factor is defined as the marginal *net* product in an effort to overcome Hobson's objection that a single factor cannot be varied in amount without altering the amounts employed of all other factors; in mathematical terms, this reduces to the argument that a change in any one of the first partial derivatives of the production function involves significant changes in all the other first-order differentials. Marshall points out correctly that the marginal product of a variable factor is defined on the basis of an optimum combination of all factors, in which case the change in the productivity of the fixed factors consequent on a change in the variable factor involves only negligible variations in higher-order differentials. However, in that case the marginal net product of a factor will equal its marginal gross product, and the terminological concession to Hobson becomes pointless and even misleading.

In **section 4** Marshall for the first time distinguishes clearly between the static law of variable proportions and the historical law of diminishing returns. He takes the edge off the distinction, however, by confining his examples to agriculture. Marginal productivity theory, he insists, is not a complete theory of distribution but rather a theory of the forces governing the demand for factors (**section 5**).

25. Rent and Quasi-Rent

The famous distinction between interest on new capital and quasi-rent on sunk capital, ground rent being merely 'the leading species of a large genus', is developed in **Book V, chapter 9**. In a footnote, Marshall refers to Fetter's attack on 'extension as the fundamental attribute of land, and the basis of rent'. Marshall's reply is that the prominent role of ground rent in the development of rent theory is a historical accident: rent is a payment for *any* nonaugmentable resource. Scarcity rents are distinguished from differential rents in the concluding section of the chapter. Marshall warns, however, that 'in a sense all rents are scarcity rents, and all rents are differential rent'.

The final footnote of **Book V, chapter 9**, and the first few pages of **chapter 10** are devoted to clearing up misconceptions with respect to the nature of quasi-rent: quasi-rents are once again defined as the total returns to temporarily specialized agents minus their cost of replacement. **Chapter 10, section 5**, touches on the concept of opportunity or alternative costs, a phrase that Marshall never used. The footnote to this section, attacking Jevons' formulation of the rent problem, with its pointed comment that it is 'inexpedient' to say that 'rent does not enter into cost of production' but 'it is worse than inexpedient' to say that is does, has been the subject of endless discussion. Marshall fails to point out that the problem can be looked at not only from the short- and long-run point of view but also from the individual and the social point of view. If 'land in an old country is approximately (and in some senses absolutely) a *permanent and fixed stock*', as Marshall claims (**chapter 10, section 3**), rent is price determined even in the long run. As long as land has alternative uses, however, rent is nevertheless price determining to the individual farmer.

Book V, chapter 11, completes the discussion of rent with an analysis of urban site values. The footnote to section 1 states a simple theorem in location economics, one of 'a great many fanciful, but not uninstructive, problems which readily suggest themselves' [see chapter 14].

26. Increasing Returns

Chapter 12 returns to a subject raised earlier in chapters 3 and 5 of Book V: the special difficulties connected with the idea of decreasing-cost industries. Marshall notes that, on the face of it, 'the elasticity of supply of a commodity which conforms to the Law of Increasing Return ... is theoretically infinite for long periods' (**section 1**). This implies that there are no limits to growth in the size of firms but this is incompatible with the maintenance of competition in the industry. The resolution of this dilemma lies in some combination of: (1) 'real' external economies; (2) the life cycle of firms; and (3) 'the difficulties of marketing'. **Section 2** of this **chapter 12** mentions all three theories in rapid succession. This first paragraph clearly implies the existence of 'real' economies external to firms but internal to the industry. In **section 3**, Marshall observes that 'we expect the short-period supply price to increase with increasing output' but 'we also expect a gradual increase in demand ... to increase the economies both internal and external' at the disposal of most firms. The long-run supply curve will 'exclude from view any economies that may result from substantive new inventions', but it will 'include those that may be expected to arise naturally out of adaptations of existing ideas'. In this sense, the curve is not fully reversible. The second paragraph of section 2 sketches the reasons for 'the rise and fall of individual firms'. The third paragraph resorts to market imperfections to explain why firms cannot constantly take advantage of internal economies. A footnote provides the starting point for the theory of monopolistic competition; 'when we are considering an individual producer, we must couple his supply curve – not with the general demand curve for his commodity in a wide market, but – with the particular demand curve of his own special market. And this particular demand curve will generally be very steep.' The last footnote to this section seems to accuse Cournot of overlooking the incompatibility of internal economies and the maintenance of competition. But it was Cournot who first posed the problem explicitly.

The device of a representative firm is discussed once again in **Book V, chapter 12, section 3**. The chapter closes with the admission that the problem is one of 'organic growth' not 'statical equilibrium'. 'The Statical theory of equilibrium is only an introduction to economic studies, and it is barely even an introduction to the study of the progress and development of industries which show a tendency to increasing return.' We pass on to **Appendix H** where the problem is further discussed. In section 3 of this appendix, Marshall argues that *neither long-run demand nor long-run supply curves are really reversible*, and this is so whether the industry in question is a decreasing- or increasing-cost industry. In a famous sentence he sums up the crucial difficulty in the concepts of short and long run, involving as they do 'operational time' rather than clock time: 'We should have made a great advance if we could represent the normal demand price and supply price as functions both of the amount normally produced and of the time at which the amount became normal'.

27. The Particular Expenses Curve

Book V, chapter 12, section 4, introduces the concept of a particular expenses curve. Marshall's exposition of this tool is confusing in the extreme. He applies it to the short run only in the final paragraph of Appendix H. His Figure 39 (Figure 10–16) shows a demand curve and a *PE* curve for an industry in long-run equilibrium. The long-run supply curve for the industry is not drawn at all, but it is made quite clear that it would lie above the *PE* curve. 'The difference between the particular expenses curve and a normal supply curve lies in this, that in the former we do, and in the latter we do not, take the general economies of production as fixed and

Figure 10–16

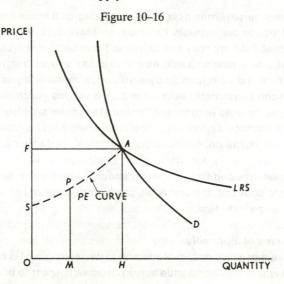

uniform throughout' – that is, we must draw a different *PE* curve for each point on the supply curve. The reason Marshall makes use of a *PE* curve to show the producer's surplus or the 'differential advantages' accruing to an industry in the long run is his belief that differences in average costs between firms will persist in the long run. If he had in fact drawn the supply curve of an industry, it would represent the unit costs of the representative firm. But this implies that 'strong' or 'mature' low-cost firms are earning a positive producer's surplus, while 'weak' or 'senile' high-cost firms are earning negative producer's surplus. The firm that is representative of the industry as a whole should earn no producer's surplus whatever in the long run. Marshall concedes that 'the producer of the *OH*th unit is supposed to have no differential advantage'. In that case, the producer of the *OH*th unit is a marginal firm and the supply curve of the industry is the usual marginal cost curve of the industry as a whole. We can then interpret Marshall's Figure 39 in a straightforward fashion without assuming that the 'producer's surplus' – notice the place of the apostrophe – accrues to the representative firm.

28. Tax-Bounty Analysis

Marshall opens **Book V, chapter 13**, with a discussion of the various reasons that may cause demand and supply curves to shift (sections 1 and 2). The effects of such shifts depend upon the elasticity of the curve that remains unchanged (section 3). In **section 4** it is shown that a specific tax levied on increasing-cost industries combined with a subsidy paid to decreasing-cost industries increases aggregate consumers' surplus. The doctrine that 'maximum satisfaction is *generally* to be attained by encouraging each individual to spend his own resources in that way which suits him best' is thus qualified even if we ignore inequalities of income by assuming that 'a shilling's worth of happiness is of equal importance to whomsoever it comes' (**section 7**). Marshall notes that the combined loss in producers' and consumers' surplus from a tax on an increasing-cost industry actually exceeds the amount of the tax receipts (footnote to section 6), while a subsidy to a decreasing-cost industry may not increase producers' surplus, though it must increase consumers' surplus (**section 5**). He argues that the latter difficulty could be overcome by a 'compensating payment': 'if a general agreement could be obtained among consumers, terms might be arranged which would make such action amply remunerative to the producers, at the same time that they left a large balance of advantage to the consumers' (**section 5**). The conclusions of this chapter, he warns, 'do not by themselves afford a valid ground for government interference'.

To avoid misunderstanding, the reader should turn now to **Appendix K** where it is shown that consumers' surplus or producers' surplus cannot be added to workers' or savers' surpluses.

29. Theory of Monopoly

The net revenue of a monopolist producing at decreasing cost is maximized at the output level where the net revenue curve becomes tangent to a 'constant outlay' curve (**Book V, chapter 14, section 3**). We may suppose that the monopolist has already exploited all the internal economies available to him and is producing a plant of optimum size. The falling supply price is due to external economies and hence the supply curve in Marshall's Figure 34 is the monopolist's long-run average cost curve. As Marshall remarks in **Mathematical Appendix XXII**, if $y = f_1(x)$ is the demand function and $y = f_2(x)$ is the supply function, the maximum net revenue is found by maximizing $[xf_1(x) - xf_2(x)]$. Since $xf_1(x)$ is total revenue and $xf_2(x)$ is total cost, this amounts to equating marginal revenue and marginal cost.

A lump-sum tax, such as a license duty on gross or net revenue, will not alter the optimum output level (**section 4** and **Mathematical Appendix XXIII**). But a tax proportional to output will induce the monopolist to raise his price and restrict output (**section 4**). Marshall is careful to discourage the idea that output is always less and price always higher under monopoly than under competition (**section 5**). One of the difficulties is that a monopolist may choose to suffer losses in the short run in order to maximize long-run profits (**section 6**).

Marshall adds the monopolist's net revenue to the consumers' surplus to form the 'total benefit' accruing to producers and consumers together from the sale of the product. In a footnote he shows how to obtain a total benefit curve. The decision on the part of a nationalized industry to maximize total benefit always results in a larger output and lower price than the decision to maximize net revenue alone (**section 7** and **Mathematical Appendix XXIII**).

These results are used in **section 8** to produce the interesting conclusion that it may be worthwhile to operate a government enterprise at a loss if the total benefit or at least the 'compromise benefit' – consumers' surplus being discounted by the necessity to levy taxes to make up the deficiency – is positive. Marshall goes on to express the naive hope that the future will produce statistical 'demand schedules sufficiently trustworthy to show in diagrams that will appeal to the eye, the quantities of consumers' surplus that will result from different courses of public and private action', thus dispelling the suspicion that falls on all public projects that do not show a balance of pecuniary profit (**section 9**). The chapter closes with a brief note on the indeterminacy of duopoly and the pervasiveness of competitive forces even in industries that are technically 'natural monopolies' (section 9).

Book V, **chapter 15** provides a serviceable summary of the whole of Book V but adds nothing new.

30. The Marginal Productivity Theory of Distribution

'The Keynote' of **Book VI**, Marshall remarks, 'is in the fact that free human beings are not brought up to their work on the same principles as a machine, a horse, or a slave. If they were there would be very little difference between the distribution and exchange side of value.' The first chapter of Book VI abstracts from this difficulty as well as from all other aspects of factor supplies. After a brief history of wage theory (**chapter 1, section 2**) and a sketch of a simple Ricardian theory of distribution (**sections 3–6**), we are given a succinct statement of marginal productivity theory as a theory of the demand for productive agents. The wage of a 'marginal shepherd' is governed by his marginal product (**chapter 1, section 7**); this result is applied to the capital market in **section 8** to show that the pure rate of interest is likewise regulated by the marginal productivity of capital. Marshall asserts that marginal productivity theory 'cannot be made into a theory of interest, any more than into a theory of wages, without reasoning into a circle'. His objection is based, presumably, on the fact that the theory has nothing to say about the forces governing the supply of factors. But this is not how he expresses it at this point. On the contrary, he seems now to lend support to Hobson's criticism, which he had earlier rejected (see Book V, chapter 8, section 4): 'The doctrine that the earnings of a worker tend to be equal to the net product of his work, has by itself no real meaning; since in order to estimate the net product, we have to take for granted all the expenses of production of the commodity on which he works, other than his own wages' (**section 7**). This statement is open to various interpretations but it seems to deny the mutual and simultaneous determination of factor prices. The chapter closes with a brief comment on the calculation of national income (**section 10**).

31. The Supply of Productive Agents

Book VI, **chapter 2**, introduces 'the reflex influence of remuneration on the supply of different agents of production'. Marshall insists on the importance of Jevons' disutility of labour as governing the supply of productive effort in the short run [see chapter 8, section 11]. 'There seems ... to be no good foundation for the suggestion made by Böhm-Bawerk ... that value must be determined generally by demand, without direct reference to cost, because the effective supply is a fixed quantity: for even if the number of hours of work in the year were rigidly fixed, which it is not, the intensity of work would remain elastic' (footnote, section 2). The short-run supply curve of labour is generally positively sloped, though it may be backward bending (**section 2**). The long-run supply curve of labour is also positively sloped (**section 3**).

Every increase in earnings increases the supply of labour, yet the 'iron law of wages' does not hold for 'the modern western world'. Wages have risen because wants have become adjusted to a higher level of 'activities', meaning an increase in the energy and initiative of human agents and an increase in expenditures on rearing and training. Similarly, the supply of saving generally responds positively to the rate of interest, not because of the static principle of substitution, but because saving habits become increasingly rational as the future is more vividly regarded (**section 4**). Marshall's interest in 'the high theme of economic progress' is never more evident than in this chapter. His final attitude to the marginal productivity theory of distribution is summed up in section 3; 'Wages tend to equal the net product of labour; its marginal productivity rules the demand-price for it; and, on the other side, wages tend to retain a close though indirect and intricate relation with the cost of rearing, training, and sustaining the energy of efficient labour.'

The special character of land as a productive agent is stressed once again in **chapter 2, section 5. Section 9** touches on the relations between wages and interest in an economy in which the capital stock is growing faster than the labour force: 'the rate of interst will constantly fall, unless indeed invention opens new advantageous uses of roundabout methods of production'. For all the crudities of the classical wages fund doctrine, 'there is ... a rather forced sense in which we may perhaps be justified in saying that the earnings of labour depend upon advances made to labour by capital'. At any rate, 'the modern doctrine of the relations between labour and capital is the outcome to which all the earlier doctrines on the subject were working their way; and differs only in its greater exactness, completeness and homogeneity, from that given by Mill in the third chapter of his fourth book; the only place in which he collects together all the various elements of the problem' (**section 10**).

32. The Peculiarities of Labour

Book VI, chapter 3, deals with the problem of relative wages and, apart from the clarifying distinction between time earnings, piecework earnings and efficiency earnings, adds nothing to Adam Smith's famous discussion. **Chapters 4** and **5**, on the other hand, represent what is perhaps the most penetrating contribution to labour economics since the *Wealth of Nations*. In these chapters Marshall is concerned with those forces acting on the supply of labour that lead to cumulative disadvantages in labour's bargaining position. He distinguishes five 'peculiarities'. The first two have to do with the special role of nonpecuniary considerations in the supply of labour: (1) the absence of a 'capital market for labour' (**sections 2–4**), and (2) the inseparability of the worker himself from his labour services (**section 5**). Education and labour training are not merely a function of prospective earnings: since 'the worker ... retains his own property: those who bear the expenses of rearing and educating him receive but very little of the price that is paid for his services in later years'. Children of the working class generally receive inadequate education and labour training and 'this evil is cumulative' (**section 2**). Moreover, labour training initiated by employers results in benefits which cannot be fully appropriated by the employer (section 4); labour training constitutes an important example of irreversible 'real' external economies. The second 'peculiarity of labour' refers to the fact that the sale of labour always involves the 'purchase' of working conditions. Sweated trades paying less than efficiency wages, therefore, may justify themselves in time by depressing the efficiency of labour.

It will be noticed that Marshall was reluctant to give an unqualified endorsement to the Smithian doctrine that education and training can be regarded as a type of investment in 'human capital' [see chapter 2, section 8]. Now it is perfectly true that modern economies lack a 'capital market for labour' and in this sense human capital formation is not exactly analogous to physical capital formation. Nevertheless, the recent appearance of student loan schemes in a number of countries shows that the absence of a capital market for labour is more a matter of a difference of degree than of kind. Even so, the absence of a capital market for labour only suggests that human capital formation need not be carried to the point where its prospective returns, discounted at the prevailing rate of interest, equals its costs but it does not refute the idea that a general tendency toward such an equilibrium at the margin nevertheless makes itself felt. That is to say, it *may* be fruitful to look at the demand for education as an investment decision geared to prospective lifetime earnings. At any rate, in recent years a number of economists have come round to the view that Marshall, in overemphasizing the first two 'peculiarities of labour', cut himself off from a line of analysis that can throw much light on the complicated relationship between education and economic growth.

Furthermore, Marshall may have been wrong in regarding on-the-job training as an example of real external economies that cannot be appropriated by the firm providing that training. Becker has recently distinguished 'general training' from 'specific training', the former raising the marginal productivity of workers equally to any firm, the latter raising it more in the firm providing the training than in other firms. The idea of general training is self-explanatory: formal education is a leading example; specific training may take the form of orientation programs, rotation among departments, and so forth. Now, under competitive conditions, wage rates are determined by the marginal productivity of workers in any firm whatever. Hence, firms will have no incentive to pay the costs of 'perfectly general training'. This does not mean that it will not be provided but simply that, if provided, the cost of such training is passed on to trainees in the form of reduced earnings during the training period. Only to the extent that on-the-job training is 'specific' will the firm have an incentive to bear the burden of training expenses; however, by definition, 'specific training' does not generate real external economies. This distinction breaks down if on-the-job training is a joint input with machinery in a particular investment project; in that case, there are no identifiable training costs that can be shifted to trainees. The issue is an empirical question that awaits further study. Be that as it may, it indicates that we must be cautious about assuming with Marshall that training in industry necessarily involves real external economies.

The next two 'peculiarities' of labour are very much matters of degree and their significance is debatable: (3) the perishability of labour; and (4) the lack of a 'reserve fund' (**section 6**). Marshall concludes, however, that 'it is certain that manual labourers as a class are at a disadvantage in bargaining; and that the disadvantage wherever it exists is likely to be cumulative in its effect . . . . It lowers his wages; and as we have seen, this lowers his efficiency as a worker, and thereby lowers the normal value of his labour.'

The fifth and most important of the peculiarities consists of the long period of time required to vary the supply of specialized labour: 'Not much less than a generation elapses between the choice by parents of a skilled trade for one of their children, and his reaping the full results of their choice' (**chapter 5, section 2**). Furthermore, 'the birth-rate in every grade of society is determined by many causes among which deliberate calculations of the future hold but a secondary place' (**section 3**). But whatever the importance of this fifth peculiarity in limiting the action of competition in the labour market, it is difficult to see in what way it constitutes a cumulative force tending to increase labour's disadvantage in bargaining. Possibly this explains why Marshall held it over for separate discussion to chapter 5.

33. The Theory of Interest

The real rate of interest is governed on the supply side by 'prospectiveness' or time preference and on the demand side by 'productiveness' (**Book VI, chapter 6, section 1**). Marshall minimizes Böhm-Bawerk's contributions to the theory of interest and in a footnote takes issue with the proposition that 'every lengthening of a roundabout process is accompanied by a further increase in the technical result'. On the contrary, Marshall argues, it is because the rate of interest is positive that technical processes are exploited in order of their roundaboutness. This point, however, was eventually conceded by Böhm-Bawerk himself and does not vitally affect his theory. A brief description of scholastic doctrine on interest (**section 2**) is followed by Marshall's only extended reference to Marx (**section 3**). Every attempt to establish the premise that interest is 'unpaid labour', Marshall observes, 'has necessarily assumed implicitly that the service performed by capital is a "free" good, rendered without sacrifice, . . . and this is the very conclusion which the premise is wanted to prove'. If one is going to devote only one sentence to Marxian economics, it is difficult to imagine how one could say anything more penetrating!

Gross and net interest are distinguished in **sections 4** and **5**. Fisher's distinction between the money and the real rate of interest is explained in **section 7**: a money rate of 5 percent per annum corresponds to a real rate of 15.5 percent when prices are falling 10 percent per annum, that is, the purchasing power of $105 at the beginning of the year is equivalent to that of $115.50 at the end of the year. Similarly, a money rate of 5 percent corresponds to a negative real rate of 5.5 percent when the annual rate at which prices are rising is 10 percent [see chapter 12, section 24].

34. The Theory of Profit

The next two chapters on business profits are extremely diffuse and difficult to summarize. A great many salient points are made but the discussion lacks terminological clarity. Notice Marshall's doubt as to whether joint stock companies have 'the enterprise, the energy, the unity of purpose and the quickness of action of a private business' (**Book VI, chapter 7, section 6**); the importance of trusts and cartels, despite their recent growth, 'is apt to be exaggerated' (**chapter 8, section 10**). The views of 'some American writers' who regard profits as 'remuneration of risk simply' are attacked on the ground that many risks can be insured against; Marshall comes close here to stating Knight's uncertainty theory of profits (**chapter 8, section 2**). Marshall attributes profits to a fourth factor of production, namely 'organization', the institutional arrangements of modern business. In addition, he visualizes conjuncture or opportunity earnings, resulting from the fact that agents are more productive when combined in a going enterprise than when used separately (**chapter 8, section 10**). We will have occasion to examine the validity of these assertions in the next chapter. A footnote in **chapter 8, section 3**, concerning 'fishmongers and greengrocers in working-class quarters' deserves special mention. It contains a hint at the structure of Chamberlin's theory of monopolistic competition: despite geographical product differentiation and finite demand elasticities, profits are normal – the so-called tangency solution [see chapter 10, section 9].

35. The Theory of Rent

Book VI, chapters 9 and **10**, may be passed over, concerned as they are with the familiar problem of different land tenure systems. Marshall observes that the distinctive features of English land tenure largely account for Ricardo's discovery of 'the deepest and most important line of cleavage in economic theory': 'the distinction between the quasi-rents which do not, and the profits which do, directly enter into the normal supply prices of produce for periods of moderate length' (chapter 9, section 5).

Chapter 11 provides an excellent summary of the whole of Book VI.

36. The Course of Economic Progress

The last two chapters of the book provide Marshall with the opportunity of looking both backward and forward, touching on the springs of secular growth and projecting the future. **Book VI, chapter 12, sections 2–4**, contains an interesting account of England's industrial development in the 18th and 19th centuries. 'Probably more than three-fourths of the whole benefit she has derived from the progress of manufacturers during the nineteenth century has been through its indirect influences in lowering the cost of transport of men and goods, of water and light, of electricity and news: for the dominant economic fact of our own age is the development not of the manufacturing, but of the transport industries' (**section 4**). Economic growth has brought an increase in the ' "telescopic" faculty' (**chapter 12**, section 8), a gradual narrowing of wage differentials (section 9), a discernible tendency toward income equalization in England if not in America, and a decline in the 'inconstancy of employment' (section 12).

Population prospects are reviewed once again in sections 1 and 2 of chapter 13. Some support is given to the shorter-hours movement (section 3). The lump-of-labour fallacy is attacked in section 4, followed by an agnostic discussion of the effects of trade unions (sections 7–10). Mill's formulation of Say's Law of Markets is cited in section 10; 'though men have the power to purchase', Marshall observes, 'they may not choose to use it'. The general characteristics of a boom and slump involving a multiplier process are then described. Section 11 states the case against socialism; but 'this cautious attitude does not imply acquiescence in the present inequalities of wealth'. Bernoulli's hypothesis suggests that every move toward income equalization raises economic welfare (section 13). The closing pages of the book contain some suggestions for extending the scope of government control over 'medical and sanitary matters' and for increasing government aid to education.

37. The Greatness of Marshall's Contribution

Judged by the exacting standards of present-day theory, Marshall's *Principles* is an unsatisfactory book. In the hope of being read by men of affairs, Marshall hid his diagrams and mathematics in footnotes and appendices and covered up every knotty point in the analysis. Moreover, an ambivalent attitude on the part of the author toward his own subject matter pervades the entire book. Ostensibly, the *Principles* is a study of static microeconomic theory but time after time the reader is told that the conclusions of static analysis are unreliable and that microeconomics fails to come to grips with the vital issues of economic policy. The 'Mecca of the economist', says Marshall, lies not in comparative statics, nor even in dynamic analysis, but rather in 'economic biology'. By 'economic biology', Marshall apparently means the study of the economic system as an organism evolving in historical time. This sounds very much like the methodological program of American Institutionalism. And yet Marshall's efforts throughout his life were devoted to teaching, expounding and refining the very kind of theory that he deprecated repeatedly in his book.

More than one commentator has puzzled over Marshall's 'schizoid' attitude toward partial equilibrium analysis. And yet there is nothing very mysterious in it: it is the typical attitude of the modern economist. The value of the neoclassical contribution to economics in providing a rigorous explanation of the determination of prices in long-run stationary equilibrium is rarely denied. But the limited scope of this kind of analysis and its ultimate remoteness from practical problems is now well understood, not least of all by those who continue to devote themselves to improving it. Marshall's greatness lies in possessing this type of perspective at a time when most of his contemporaries had almost completely lost sight of the age-old 'inquiry into the causes of the wealth of nations'.

This is not to deny, however, that Marshall's peculiar integration of static microeconomics with bits and pieces of the classical theory of economic development made it more difficult for subsequent writers to grasp the true significance of partial equilibrium analysis. On the positive side, the Marshallian distinction between the market period, the short period and the long period provided a general framework in which all previous theories of value found a place. His repeated emphasis on the 'two blades' of demand and supply brought home as nothing else had the action of both techniques of production and consumers' preferences in determining relative prices. His analysis of the Laws of Returns brought order and meaning to the theories of Smith, Ricardo and Marx. But his reconciliation of decreasing costs and competitive equilibrium via the notions of external economies, monopolistic competition and the representative firm, fruitful as were all but the last, raised false problems that took the best efforts of a generation of economists to sort out. And his total neglect of monetary forces in a work on the principles of economics, however much he warned his readers of this failing, did much to persuade economists that monetary theory belonged to the periphery of the science.

Nevertheless, if a man's contribution is to be judged on the basis of his solution of old problems as well as the posing of new problems to subsequent generations, Marshall's *Principles* must be considered one of the most durable and viable books in the history of economics: it is the only 19th-century treatise on economic theory that still sells in the hundreds every year and that can still be read with great profit by the modern reader.

NOTES ON FURTHER READING

The long-awaited variorum edition of Marshall's *Principles*, prepared by C. W. Guillebaud, finally appeared in two volumes in 1961, tracing the subtle changes that Marshall made to the eight editions of his book and clearly revealing the points at which he was uneasy. See especially Guillebaud's 'Editorial Introduction' to Vol. II of this edition and G. J. Stigler, 'Marshall's *Principles* After Guillebaud', *JPE*, 1962, reprinted in *AMCA*, II. The introduction to *The Early Economic Writings of Alfred Marshall, 1867–1890*, ed. J. K. Whitaker (1975), gives an account of the evolution of Marshall's economic theory in the two decades before the publication of his *Principles*, decisively rejecting Marshall's own claim (always expressed in private correspondence and never made public) that he was an independent discoverer of marginal doctrines on a par with Jevons and Walras. The classic biographical account of Marshall by Keynes, *Essays in Biography*, and reprinted in *AMCA*, I, is probably the most brilliant biographical essay that Keynes ever wrote. Both Hutchison, *Review of Economic Doctrines*, chap. 4, and B. A. Corry, 'Marshall, Alfred', *IESS*, 10, provide brief introductions to Marshall's life and works. For an excellent and detailed overview of the whole of Marshall's contributions to analysis, see the recent essay by D. P. O'Brien, 'Alfred Marshall, 1842–1924', *Pioneers of Modern Economics in Britain*, eds. O'Brien and Presnell. The pathbreaking study of Marshall's philosophical preconceptions and their influence on his economic views is by T. Parsons, 'Wants and Activities in Marshall', *QJE*, 1931, reprinted in his *Structure of Social Action* (1937), and *AMCA*, I, and 'Economics and Sociology: Marshall in Relation to the Thought of His Time', *ibid.*, 1932, reprinted in *AMCA*, I.

The centenary of Marshall's birth produced a number of reassessments, the most important of which was G. F. Shove's long essay, 'The Place of Marshall's *Principles* in the Development of Economic Theory', *EJ*, 1942, reprinted in *EET*, *ETHA*, and *AMCA*, II. One of the aims of this essay was to dispel the popular notion that Marshallian economics represents a compromise between Ricardian and marginal-utility economics, instead of a generalization of Ricardo's theory of value and distribution as expounded by J. S. Mill; Marshall's *Principles*, argues

Shove, is of the 'true Ricardian stock, neither a cross-bred nor a sport'. Shove also defended Marshall's political attitudes as the attitudes of a 'liberal' in the Victorian sense of the word in his 'Mrs. Robinson on Marxian Economics', *EJ*, April, 1944. J. Viner, 'Marshall's Economics, in Relation to the Man and to His Times', *AER*, 1941, reprinted in *DET* and *AMCA*, I, is written with characteristic charm and wit, emphasizing the profound influence of J. S. Mill on Marshall's social views. Schumpeter writes of Marshall with a certain degree of revulsion: see 'Alfred Marshall's *Principles*: A Semi-Centennial Appraisal', *AER*, 1941, reprinted in his *Ten Great Economists* and *AMCA*, II, and reproduced in his *History of Economic Analysis*, pp. 833–40, 920–4, 932–8, 990–8, 1045–53, 1060–2, 1083–4. D. H. Macgregor, 'Marshall and His Book', *Ec*, 1942, and C. W. Guillebaud, 'Marshall's *Principles of Economics* in the Light of Contemporary Economic Thought', *ibid.*, 1952, both reprinted in *AMCA*, II, each contribute to the task of 'explaining' Marshall to a generation bred on macroeconomics and the theory of the firm in the short run. A. C. Pigou, *Alfred Marshall and Current Thought* (1953), conjectures what Marshall might have said, were he still alive, on such topics as mathematical economics, elasticity of demand, the rate of interest, measurability of utility and socialism. L. E. Fouraker, 'The Cambridge Didactic Style', *JPE*, 1958, reprinted in *AMCA*, I, holds that the difficulties in grasping Marshall's meaning are mainly a matter of his style of presentation, but G. Pursell, 'Unity in the Thought of Alfred Marshall', *QJE*, 1958, reprinted in *AMCA*, I, contends that Marshall's striving for a unified approach led him to minimize theoretical complications, with the result that difficulties are hidden away instead of being brought to the surface.

R. Opie, 'Marshall's Time Analysis', *EJ*, 1931, reprinted in *AMCA*, I, emphasizes Marshall's operational conception of time and discusses some of the problems created for his analysis by clock-time considerations. H. M. Robertson, 'Alfred Marshall's Aims and Methods Illustrated from His Treatment of Distribution', *HOPE*, 1970, reprinted in *AMCA*, I, illustrates the working out of Marshall's time period method in his treatment of distribution. R. Frisch reconstructs Marshall's theory of short-run and long-run supply price with the aid of current graphical techniques: 'Alfred Marshall's Theory of Value', *QJE*, 1950, reprinted in *Penguin Modern Economics Readings: Price Theory*, ed. H. Townsend (1968 in paperback) and *AMCA*, III. Frisch's rendition seems entirely faithful to Marshall's intention but see some objections by D. H. Robertson, *Economic Commentaries* (1951), chap. 1. All the relevant articles in the Great Debate on increasing returns and falling supply price are included in *Readings in Price Theory*, eds. Stigler and Boulding: see especially J. Viner, 'Cost Curves and Supply Curves', and H. S. Ellis and W. J. Fellner, 'External Economies and Diseconomies'; the latter article should be read after perusal of chap. 10 on the 'Four Cost Curves' in J. Robinson, *The Economics of Imperfect Competition* (1953). The Appendix to Robinson's book provides an authoritative restatement of the issue of 'Increasing and Diminishing Returns'.

Stigler, *Production and Distribution Theory*, chap. 4, covers a number of topics in Marshall's *Principles* and is particularly useful on Marshall's treatment of internal and external economies; see also *ibid.*, pp. 112–25 for Edgeworth's pathbreaking clarification of the distinction between proportional and incremental returns as late as 1911! Stigler's article 'The Division of Labour is Limited by the Extent of the Market', *JPE*, June, 1951, analyzes the effects of vertical disintegration, the earliest recognized source of increasing returns in the broad sense. The recent flowering of external economies in writings on 'balanced growth' and their relationship to strict Marshallian external economies is lucidly discussed by H. W. Arndt, 'External Economies in Economic Growth', *ER*, November, 1955.

L. Robbins' critique of 'The Representative Firm', *EJ*, 1928, reprinted in *AMCA*, III, succeeded in virtually eliminating the concept from the literature. In recent years, however, some Cambridge enthusiasts have attempted to revive the doctrine: see P. Newman, 'The Erosion of Marshall's Theory of Value', *QJE*, 1960, reprinted in *AMCA*, III, and the literature cited there. 'Nobody knows Marshall who knows only the *Principles*', remarked Schumpeter. And, indeed, Marshall's *Industry and Trade* (1919) and *Money, Credit and Commerce* (1923) are indispensable to an understanding of his entire system. *Industry and Trade* is something of a prolegomena to Chamberlin's and Robinson's works, as H. H. Liebhafsky shows: 'A Curious

Case of Neglect: Marshall's *Industry and Trade'*, *CJEPS*, 1955, reprinted in *AMCA*, IV; see also S. Stykolt, 'A Curious Case of Neglect: Marshall on the "Tangency Solution"', *CJE*, 1956, reprinted in *AMCA*, IV. But even the *Principles* shows awareness of product differentiation and market imperfections: see D. C. Hague, 'Alfred Marshall and the Competitive Firm', *EJ*, 1958, reprinted in *AMCA*, III; S. Hollander, 'The Representative Firm and Imperfect Competition', *CJEPS*, May, 1961; and B. J. Loasby, 'Whatever Happened to Marshall's Theory of Value', *SJPE*, 1978, reprinted in *AMCA*, III. The modern theory of 'workable competition' is actually a natural outgrowth of the thinking fifty years ago of Marshall, Clark, and their contemporaries, as G. S. Peterson explains: 'Antitrust and the Classic Model', *AER*, 1957, reprinted in *Readings in Industrial Organization*, eds. R. B. Heflebower and G. W. Stocking (1958). In this connection, consult G. J. Stigler, 'Perfect Competition, Historically Contemplated', *JPE*, 1957, reprinted in *RHET* and his *Essays in the History of Economics*, which examines the vast changes that came over the concept of perfect competition in the course of the 19th century.

F. W. Ogilvie's hypercritical essay, 'Marshall on Rent', *EJ*, 1930, provoked a sympathetic restatement by M. T. Holland, *ibid.*, 1930; both essays are reprinted in *AMCA*, III. C. W. Guillebaud, 'Davenport on the Economics of Alfred Marshall', *EJ*, 1937, reprinted in *AMCA*, II, provides an excellent exposition of Marshall's concept of long-run equilibrium. Marshall's views on 'the peculiarities of labour' are critically dissected by W. H. Hutt, *The Theory of Collective Bargaining 1930–1975* (1975 in paperback). This book consists of three essays: the first traces the history of the concept of 'Labour's Disadvantage' in bargaining, and the second metes out the same treatment to 'Indeterminateness' resulting from bilateral monopoly in the labour market. The latter problem was the subject of a famous article by J. R. Hicks, 'Edgeworth, Marshall and the Indeterminateness of Wages', *EJ*, 1930, followed by a controversy with M.H. Dobb, *ibid.*, 1931, both reprinted in *AMCA*, III. Of Marshall's four laws of the elasticity of derived demand, the third, the so-called 'importance of being unimportant', has caused endless argument. On this, see M. Bronfenbrenner, *Income Distribution Theory* (1971), pp. 147–50, and S. C. Maurice, 'On the Importance of Being Unimportant: An Analysis of the Paradox of Marshall's Third Rule of Derived Demand', *Ec*, 1975, reprinted in *AMCA*, III. See also A. Petridis, 'Alfred Marshall's Attitudes to and Economic Analysis of Trade Unions: A Case of Anomalies in a Competitive System', *HOPE*, 1973, reprinted in *AMCA*, III, dealing with Marshall's lifelong interest in the problem created for competitive theory by the existence of trade unions.

J. J. Spengler, 'Marshall on the Population Question', *PS*, March and June, 1955, provides a good survey of the state of population theory between Mill and Marshall and furnishes a detailed *précis* of Marshall's views on demographic change, B. Glassburner, 'Alfred Marshall on Economic History and Historical Development', *QJE*, 1955, reprinted in *AMCA*, I, and A. J. Youngson, 'Marshall on Economic Growth', *SPJE*, 1956, reprinted in *AMCA*, IV, discuss Marshall's work in economic history. R. McWilliams Tullberg analyzes 'Marshall's "Tendency to Socialism"', *HOPE*, 1975, reprinted in *AMCA*, I. T. Levitt, 'Alfred Marshall: Victorian Relevance to Modern Economics', *QJE*, 1976, and J. K. Whitaker, 'Some Neglected Aspects of Alfred Marshall's Economic and Social Thought', *HOPE*, 1977, both reprinted in *AMCA*, I, reminds us that Marshall refused to keep 'ought' strictly separate from 'is' and harbored policy ideas that would even now put him left of center in the political spectrum. J. N. Wolfe, 'Marshall and the Trade Cycle', *OEP*, 1956, reprinted in *RHET* and *AMCA*, IV, supplemented by Hansen, *Business Cycles and National Income*, pp. 270–6, contrasts Marshall's emphasis on price and credit fluctuations with Keynes's emphasis on variations in income.

The contrast between Marshallian and Walrasian stability analysis is exemplified by Walras' first paper in English, 'Geometrical Theory of the Determination of Prices', *AAPSS*, 1892, reprinted in *ETHA*. D. G. Davies provides an illuminating 'Note on Marshallian *Versus* Walrasian Stability Conditions', *CJEPS*, November, 1963. Marshall's complex attitude to the theory of human capital is further discussed in my *Introduction to the Economics of Education* (1970), pp. 2–6. For a wider view of the theory, see Kiker's history, *Human Capital: In Retrospect*.

The theory of monopolistic competition has acquired a vast literature that only the specialist can command. The student must, of course, begin with E. H. Chamberlin's own book, *The Theory of Monopolistic Competition* (8th edn., 1962), which includes a bibliography on monopolistic competition up to 1956 of some 1500 items. The origin of the theory of monopolistic competition was different from the theory of imperfect competition: it stemmed from a debate between Taussig and Pigou on the reasons for the observed pattern of multiple railway rates, whereas Robinson's theory derived from the empty-economic-boxes debate among the English disciples of Marshall: see E. H. Chamberlin, 'The Origins and Early Development of Monopolistic Competition Theory', *QJE*, November, 1961; T. P. Reinwald, 'The Genesis of Chamberlinian Monopolistic Competition Theory', *HOPE*, Winter, 1977; Ekelund and Hébert, *History of Economic Theory and Method*, chap. 20; and G. L. S. Shackle, *The Years of High Theory. Invention and Tradition in Economic Thought 1926–1939* (1967), chaps. 3–6. D. P. O'Brien, 'Research Programmes in Competitive Structures', *Journal of Economic Studies*, 10, 4, 1983, provides an excellent comparison of the respective impacts of Robinson's *Imperfect Competition* and Chamberlin's *Monopolistic Competition*. Among the most brilliant of Chamberlin's early critics was N. Kaldor, whose essays on the subject are still pertinent: see particularly 'Professor Chamberlin on Monopolistic and Imperfect Competition', *QJE*, 1938, reprinted in his *Essays on Value and Distribution* (1960). Recent years have seen the destructive critique of G. J. Stigler, 'Monopolistic Competition in Retrospect' *Five Lectures on Economic Problems* (1949), reprinted in *Readings in Microeconimics*, ed. D. R. Kamerschen (1967 in paperback), followed by M. Friedman, 'The Methodology of Positive Economics', *Essays in Positive Economics*. Chamberlin replied in *Towards a More General Theory of Value* (1957), chaps. 1, 15, and 16. G. C. Archibald reexamined the entire debate in a scintillating essay on 'Chamberlin versus Chicago', *REStud*, 1961, reprinted in *Readings in Industrial Economics*, ed. C. K. Rowley (1972), which argued that the Chicago critics were, paradoxically enough, rejecting the assumptions of the theory of monopolistic competition, instead of testing its empirical implications; see also Friedman's comment on Archibald and Archibald's reply to Friedman, likewise reprinted in the Rowley readings.

There is a useful symposium on 'The Theory of Monopolistic Competition after Thirty Years', in *AER*, May, 1964, with papers by J. S. Bain, R. L. Bishop, and W. J. Baumol, the last two being reprinted in *RHET. Monopolistic Competition Theory: Studies in Impact*, ed. R. E. Kuenne (1967), consists of seventeen essays on the Chamberlinian Revolution, of which those by W. Fellner and J. S. Bain are particularly valuable as exercises in historical perspectives. Nevertheless, those who would read one commentary on Chamberlin are better advised to consult R. Robinson, *Edward H. Chamberlin*, Columbia Essays on Great Economists, No. 1 (1971 in paperback), which, among other things, contains a brief Reader's Guide to Chamberlin's book.

11

Marginal productivity and factor prices

THE DEMAND FOR FACTORS OF PRODUCTION

In the first edition of the *Principles*, Marshall used the term 'consumer's rent' instead of consumer's surplus to emphasize the fact that the triangle under the demand curve is in some ways analogous to Ricardian rents earned by producers. Following this train of thought, we might go so far as to say that the marginal-utility theory of value is in some sense a simple application of Ricardian rent theory to consumption demand. It was not until the 1880s, however, that it first dawned on economists that the Ricardian theory of differential rent is indeed a special case of a much more general theory. Ricardo had demonstrated that, land being a fixed factor with a specific use, rent accrues only to intramarginal farmers. Writers like J.B. Clark, Wicksteed and Wicksell now realized that when land has alternative uses there is nothing unique about a no-rent margin. It is equally possible to picture a no-interest margin where the total product is exhausted by wages and rent or a no-wage margin where the entire price is resolvable into interest and rent.

But whereas Ricardo had used the marginal principle to show that the fixed factor earns a residual surplus, determined by the gap between the average and marginal product of the variable factor, Clark, Wicksteed and Wicksell emphasized the other side of the coin: any variable factor must obtain a reward equal to its marginal product. If we measure the quantities employed of a factor of production along the abscissa, the quantities of the other factors being fixed, the demand price per unit of the factor literally is its marginal productivity curve and the corresponding rectangle under that marginal productivity curve represents its share of the total product (see Figure 11–1). If this is so, the remaining triangle under the marginal productivity curve or equivalently the remaining (shaded) rectangle under the average productivity curve must be sufficient to reward the fixed factors on the basis of their respective marginal productivities. Since this is true of one variable factor, it must be true of all, each considered in turn. Is this generally true? Will the total product be exhausted when each factor is awarded its marginal product? The answer to the last question is affirmative, argued Wicksteed in *Essay on the Coordination of the Laws of Distribution* (1894), provided the production function is of a special kind. Whether

Figure 11–1

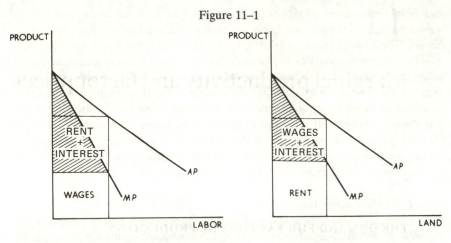

production functions necessarily conform to type or whether market forces can be expected to lead to product exhaustion were among the most keenly debated questions in economics around the turn of the century. But before we examine this debate, we must consider the marginal productivity theory of distribution in its own right.

1. Marginal Productivity Theory

Marginal productivity theory contends that in equilibrium each productive agent will be rewarded in accordance with its marginal productivity as measured by the effect on the total product of the addition or withdrawal of a unit of that agent, the quantity of the other agents being held constant. With reference to labour, for example, the wage rate cannot in equilibrium exceed the marginal value product of labour: since any unit of labour may be the marginal unit, the rate of pay necessary to bring the marginal unit of labour into production marks the maximum the entrepreneur will pay to retain any other unit in employment. On the other hand, wages cannot in equilibrium be less than the marginal value product of labour: so long as additional labour adds more to revenue than to costs, it will pay to hire more labour; competition among employers, therefore, will bid up wages to the marginal value product of labour. *Ergo*, labour will be rewarded in accordance with its marginal productivity.

Marginal productivity theory is often described as a theory of distribution but that statement is misleading on two counts. A theory of *distribution* might be expected to tell us something about personal income distribution or at any rate the distribution of incomes between wages, profits and rents. But marginal productivity theory is a theory of factor pricing, not a theory of the distribution of relative shares: it is, as Cannan said long ago, a theory of pseudodistribution. Moreover, it is not even a complete theory of factor pricing because it has nothing to say about the supply side of factor markets. Strictly speaking, it is only a theory of the demand for a factor. This is why Marshall objected to statements implying that the marginal productivity of a factor 'determines' its rate of reward. One might think that in the short run, it would be legitimate to assume that the supply of a productive agent was given. Surely, the supply of labour is fixed in the short run and hence wages are effectively governed by the demand price of labour? But if we define a unit of labour, not as an individual worker, but as an hour's work at the standard level of intensity, the labour supply curve is by no means perfectly inelastic. If so, marginal productivity theory is unable alone to specify the hourly rate of wages in the labour market. In the long run it is obvious, of course, that the rate of growth of the labour force is an independent element acting on wages. Indeed, in the extreme case of the subsistence theory of wages, the long-run supply curve of labour is infinitely elastic and labour's marginal product has no influence whatever upon the rate of wages.

2. The Normative Implications

J. B. Clark, the American founder of marginal productivity theory, regarded the theory as providing a normative principle of distributive justice: market forces secure a set of returns to productive agents which are not only 'efficient' but are also 'fair'. Although he developed the theory in the context of a stationary state with perfect competition, perfect foresight and perfect mobility of factors, fully realizing that the perfectly competitive stationary state merely provides long-period equilibrium values toward which the actual values in the real world are continually tending, his formulation invited profound misunderstanding. It would be less misleading to say the very opposite: marginal productivity theory shows us that market results are by no means 'fair' or 'equitable'. If a factor is relatively scarce, it will command a high price and there is no reason to think that a high efficiency-price for a productive agent will also accord with our ethical notions of justice between persons. Besides, marginal productivity theory also tells us that the returns to productive agents are perfectly susceptible to human action. It shows that, say, wages may be raised by reducing the numbers available for hire, by raising the efficiency of workers, by increasing the quantity of capital they work with, and so forth, quite apart from the naked exercise of bargaining power. If wages can be raised by human action, why should the wages generated by spontaneous market forces by regarded as 'the best of all possible outcomes'?

Böhm-Bawerk once posed the following objection to the marginal productivity theory of wages: if the product of the marginal unit of labour governs the wage rate and labour works subject to diminishing returns, the intramarginal worker will receive less than the amount that he contributes to the total product; to the extent that labour fails to receive this intramarginal surplus, marginal productivity theory pictures the worker as subject to 'exploitation'. Clark replied to this objection in the *Distribution of Wealth* (1899) by pointing out that the theory assumes each factor to be homogeneous, all units of the factor being equally efficient; the marginal productivity of labour falls as more labour is added to a given amount of capital because capital per unit of labour is falling. In the same way, the greater marginal productivity of fewer workers is solely the result of the fact that they have more capital to work with; the greater productivity of fewer workers may just as well be attributed to the productivity of capital. Clark did not realize the full consequences of this reply for it destroys the idea that a wage in accordance with the marginal productivity of labour is a 'just wage'. There is no such thing as a specific marginal product of a factor considered in isolation: the factors of production are essentially complements and the marginal product of one factor is a consequence of the marginal product of the other factors.

Payment in accordance with marginal productivity does have a normative function, however, but only in a restricted sense of the term. It furnishes, as Aristotle might have said, a principle of 'commutative justice' rather than 'distributive justice'. A straightforward application of the equimarginal principle tells us that, but for nonpecuniary considerations, the whole of the labour force should be so distributed among alternative employments as to equalize the marginal value product of labour in all uses. In other words, the normative function of rewarding factors in accordance with marginal productivity is to achieve efficiency in resource allocation. To attack the theory by showing that it assumes perfect mobility of labour, perfect knowledge on the part of buyers and sellers, perfect competition and full employment – assumptions that are patently unrealistic – is to miss the point. If there is immobility of labour and hence inequalities of wages for the same type of labour under identical working conditions in the same labour market, the total product is not being maximized; the total product is not maximized because labour is not being rewarded according to its marginal product. In each case, the removal of 'frictions' will improve the allocation of resources and thus leave more product to be distributed among the participating factors of production.

3. Exploitation

Pigou characterized a situation in which a factor receives less than the marginal increment it adds to the total product as 'exploitation'. Pigovian exploitation is due to 'monopsony' in the labour market, resulting in a divergence between average and marginal factor costs; that is, marginal factor costs MFC exceeds average factor costs AFC. Instead of facing a given wage rate that it cannot affect by its own hiring policy, the firm necessarily bids up the wage rate when it expands its labour force: it is too large an employer not to affect the wage rate by its own action. If perfect competition prevails in the *product* market, we have the situation depicted in Figure 11–2a. The firm multiplies labour's marginal physical product by the price per unit of final product to obtain the marginal value product of labour MVP; it buys ON amount of labour by equating MVP to MFC, paying a wage rate equal to AFC. The difference between AFC and MFC represents the excess of labour's MVP to the firm over labour's *average* rate of reward: it is purely an intramarginal surplus. When there is both monopolistic competition in the product market and monopsony in factor markets, we have the situation depicted in Figure 11–2b. Additional output can be sold only at lower prices; the firm faces a downward-sloping demand curve for its product and the marginal revenue product curve MRP – labour's marginal physical product multiplied by marginal revenue – lies below the average revenue product curve ARP – the average physical product of labour multiplied by average revenue.

Figure 11–2

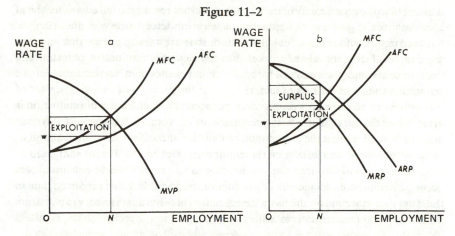

The firm still determines the employment it will offer by equating *MRP* to *MFC* but now it earns an additional surplus on the employment of each unit of labour, including the marginal unit.

The term 'exploitation' to describe a situation in which labour receives less than its marginal value or marginal revenue product conveys the unfortunate suggestion that labour's *MVP* or *MRP* constitutes its 'just' reward. But Pigou's point has nothing to do with equity. Pigovian exploitation differs from Marxian 'exploitation' because it is due to imperfect competition in the labour market; Marxian exploitation, on the other hand, prevails even in perfectly competitive labour markets, where *MFC* = *AFC*, exploitation being depicted as the entire triangular area under the *MVP* curve and above the horizontal wage line. Pigou's argument is designed to show that maximum efficiency in production is incompatible with a difference between the wage rate and the *MVP* or *MRP* of labour to the firm. It is the community and not the workers in question who are being exploited. Monopsony profits, like all other departures from perfect competition in factor markets, represent a failure to maximize output from given resources.

To avoid misunderstanding, we must remember that marginal productivity theory addresses itself only to static welfare considerations. The wage rate necessary to achieve optimum efficiency from the static point of view may fail to provide dynamic efficiency, say, an income adequate to educate children so as to provide labour of better quality in the future. But in the absence of knowledge of a specific divergence between static and dynamic efficiency, payment in accordance with marginal productivity must be assumed *prima facie* to contribute to the attainment of the optimum welfare conditions [see chapter 13, section 8].

4. Is Continuous Substitution Possible?
Almost at the outset, the marginal productivity theory met with the formal objection that factor inputs are not usually capable of being combined in infinitely variable quantities. In the early versions of his general equilibrium model, Walras assumed

that the input-output coefficients in each industry are rigidly fixed by technical considerations. This does not imply that wages are indeterminate because as long as the fixed input coefficients differ between industries, it will still be true that only one wage rate will clear the labour market. Nevertheless, the assumption of technically fixed input coefficients is extremely restrictive: it not only eliminates the problem of optimizing the combinations of factors but also the problem of choosing a plant of optimum size: no price or cost accounting is needed and efficiency in production is achieved by the purely engineering requirement of avoiding outright waste. Walras eventually realized that the assumption of fixed input coefficients is not required to demonstrate the existence of general equilibrium. But he and Pareto continued to insist that technical conditions approximating to fixed input coefficients do in fact occur: although some coefficients of production are variable, others are fixed, and in the latter case marginal productivity theory fails to provide a satisfactory explanation of how factor prices are determined.

5. The Theory of Imputation

The assumption of fixed input coefficients also appears in Wieser's theory of imputation, outlined in his *Ursprung des Wirtschaftlichen Wertes* (1884), one of the earliest nonmathematical solutions to the problem of factor pricing. The germ of this theory is to be found in Menger's distinction between 'first-order' consumer goods and 'high-order' intermediate goods, and the dependence of the demand for the latter on the want-satisfying power of the former. Although Wieser recognized the possibility of varying the proportions of the factors employed in the production of a particular good, he based his imputation theory on the postulate that the factors combine in fixed proportions in each industry but in different proportions in different industries. Following Wieser, let us suppose that there are three factors employed in the following proportions in three industries:

$$x + y\ \ = 100$$
$$2x + 3z = 290$$
$$4y + 5z = 590.$$

The numbers on the right-hand side of the equations are the given prices per unit of the three final products: x, y and z stand for the prices of the respective factor units. It is assumed that the value of the final product is equal to the value of the factors that enter into its production; that is, the final product is exhausted by the respective factor payments, which, as we will see, means that constant returns to scale prevail. Since we have three linearly independent equations in three unknowns, the system has a unique solution for x, y and z: solving by Cramer's Rule, we obtain $x = 40$, $y = 60$ and $z = 70$. Since the input coefficients are fixed, the marginal product of a factor in an industry has no meaning. Nevertheless, it is possible to 'impute' a price to each factor and in this way to determine the allocation of factors between the industries.

The assumption of perfect complementarity between productive factors remained a favourite Austrian premise. Long after the 'law of variable proportions' had become a standard feature of Marshallian and Walrasian economics, the Austrians retained the cumbersome doctrine of imputation. Even in the later editions of the *Positive Theory of Capital*, Böhm-Bawerk went no further than to admit partial factor substitutability. Some craven scruple of thinking too precisely about discontinuities and indivisibilities prevented him from accepting a perfectly general 'law of variable proportions'. In its mature version, the Austrian theory of imputation might be characterized as a marginal productivity theory with a difference: the marginal value product of a factor is construed as the gain in consumers' satisfaction resulting from the output produced by a *finite* increment of that factor; in other words, it is the factor's marginal physical product, inexactly defined, multiplied by the consumers' marginal utility from the extra product. Quite apart from the unnecessary concession to realism implied in making the increment of the factor a finite unit, the argument implies the existence of something like 'social marginal utility' and suggests that entrepreneurs impute consumers' satisfactions to the means of production. This clumsy formulation can be avoided by the simple recognition of the mutual and reciprocal determination of factor and product prices.

6. Linear Programming

The objection to the assumption of complete variability in factor proportions is nothing more than the objection to the notion of perfectly smooth, perfectly continuous production functions. Until recently, the vested interest of economics in continuous differentiable functions has stood in the way of a fair appraisal of this objection. It is clear, however, that the general assumption of smooth, continuous factor substitution renders marginal analysis inappropriate for most short-run situations in which a limited time horizon makes for rigidities in the productive process. In recent years, however, a type of analysis called linear programming has sprung up to deal in operational terms with the case of discontinuous factor substitution. This approach consists essentially of applying Wieser's theory of imputation to a single firm. Without realizing it, Wieser had in fact stated a typical linear programming problem defined as that of maximizing a linear relationship subject to a number of linear constraints.

Figure 11–3

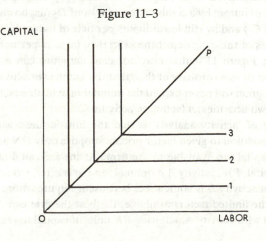

The case of a firm faced with rigid technical coefficients of production is exemplified by a series of L-shaped isoquants whose vertices lie on a given ray OP (Figure 11–3). An isoquant is analogous to an indifference curve except that a constant total product produced by various combinations of two productive factors replaces the constant total utility yielded by various combinations of two consumption goods. The distances between the isoquants along any ray from the origin show the returns in the form of total physical output to equiproportionate increases in *both* factors. If returns to scale are constant, every increase in labour and capital in the ratio t raises output by the ratio t; thus, the vertices of the L-shaped isoquants are equidistant from each other. Similarly, increasing returns to scale are depicted by smaller and smaller distances between the isoquants and contrariwise for diminishing returns to scale. Suppose now that the firm is faced, not with one given technical combination of factors, but with a number of such combinations, each characterized by fixed input coefficients. Every one of these 'activities' so-called is characterized by a separate input vector and each activity can be carried on at any level, fractional or otherwise, with output proportional to the quantity of the factors required; in short, constant returns to scale prevail. Moreover, production can proceed by using two or more activities simultaneously and adding the results. For example, the final product can be produced by four different machines, each with a rigidly determined labour per machine ratio; the firm can choose between them or can elect to use them in combination. This idea of a set of additive activities is the basis of the linear programming analysis of production. The firm is now faced with the same problem that Wieser posed for the total economy, namely, that of maximizing its total product subject to a set of linear constraints.

An output of, say, 1 unit is obtained by the combination of inputs represented by A_1, B_1, C_1 and D_1 (Figure 11–4), an output of 2 units by A_2, B_2, C_2 and D_2, and so on. By the property of constant returns to scale, A_1 and A_2 lie on the vector OA such that $A_1A_2 = A_2A_3 = A_3A_4$, and so forth for the other activities. If the four activities are truly independent such that they could be chosen alone, the corners always form a 'convex' cone. Any point within the cone is a possible combination of inputs. Thus, C_2' is a possible activity. But the output generated by C_2' can be produced with fewer inputs per unit of output by a combination of B_2 and D_2 (as shown by a straight line joining B_2 and C_2) and by still fewer inputs per unit of output by activity C_2. In the short, the edges of the cone depict the efficiency frontier per units of output. It is apparent from Figure 11–4 that only adjacent activities can enter into efficient combinations and, as a corollary of this, that the number of activities in an optimal production program will never exceed the number of available factors of production (two factors, two activities, n factors, n activities).

The essence of 'activity analysis' is that the firm is faced with given physical constraints in addition to given factor prices. Suppose only ON units of labour and OK units of capital are available to the firm. At the indicated price line between labour and capital, PW, activity A is optimal, and so is activity B or any combination of the two. But activity B is not feasible because it requires more than ON units of labour. With the limited factors available, the best the firm can do is to produce 2 units of output with activity A, allowing RK units of capital to remain idle. Despite

Figure 11-4

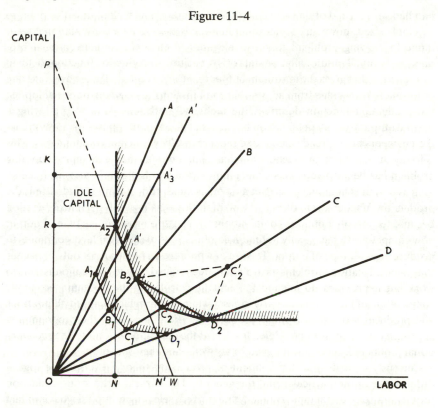

the positive price of capital, the marginal productivity of capital to the firm is zero. Thus, the maximum isorevenue contour in this case is L-shaped with a vertex at A_2; more generally, the maximum isorevenue contour coincides with the maximum efficiency frontier (as shown by the thick, shaded line in Figure 11-4). Similarly, if the quantity of labour and capital available to the firm is ON' and OK, all of the stock of limited factors can be employed by using two activities together in the proportions indicated by the slope of vector A': the isorevenue contour would then move out from the origin towards the vertex point A'_3.

It is easy to see from Figure 11-4 that when the factor price line is tangent to the isorevenue contour, factor proportions are indeterminate within a range. Moreover, if relative factor prices cause the firm to operate at a corner point like activity B_2, relatively large changes in factor prices may leave the optimal factor proportions unaffected; the more acute the angle at B_2, the greater the change in relative factor prices which can occur without altering the optimal factor proportions. Thus, factor substitution is discontinuous, taking place only when the factor price line rotates around the 'corners' of the convex cone. Needless to say, as new activities are introduced which render combinations of previous activities inefficient, the range of discontinuity in factor substitution is reduced; in the limit, we approach the continuous convex isoquants of neoclassical economics.

These brief remarks do not begin to do justice to the range of problems that can be handled with the aid of linear and nonlinear programming techniques. The point to be emphasized, however, is that programming is essentially a computational technique for solving problems that are relegated to engineers in conventional production theory. Traditionally, we start off by positing a production function, defined as a function that gives the maximum output that can be obtained at the existing state of technical knowledge from all possible combinations of *given* quantities of inputs; the production function describes the technically efficient ways of producing a desired output from all possible combinations of given inputs on the assumption that the engineers have already eliminated the technically inefficient combinations. This is to say that standard production function cannot be specified until a programming problem has been solved. This programming problem is a purely technical one so long as output is homogeneous. But as soon as multiproduct firms are admitted, the production functions cannot even be written down as a purely technical function because technically optimum combinations of inputs to produce one type of output now compete with technically optimum combinations of identical levels of inputs to produce another type of output. The use of a production function not only presumes that some allocation problems have already been solved before the economist sets to work but it provides no method for actually calculating the optimum economic combination of factors, particularly in cases where the firm faces capacity limitations and produces more than a single product. On the other hand, the programming approach can, at least in principle, answer all the allocation questions that conventional production theory is designed to answer – and then some.

Curiously enough, the development of production theory reversed the logical order between the particular and the general. The earliest writers on production problems assumed that input coefficients are fixed, selecting as typical what is in fact a special case. This was succeeded by the view that factor substitution may generally be assumed to be continuous. More recently, it has come to be recognized that the optimizing approach of marginal analysis can only be applied to the concrete production problems of business enterprises by recognizing that factor proportions are not in fact fully variable in the short run. The so-called general case – convex isoquants and smooth and continuous substitution – brushes too many allocation problems under the carpet, and the intermediate case – discontinuous factor substitution in the presence of bottlenecks – is surprisingly enough the more powerful tool for analyzing the firm's maximization problems.

We return now to Wieser's theory of the imputation of factor prices from product prices. The graphical analysis of production in Figure 11–4 could have been written down algebraically as a typical programming problem:

Maximize revenue $= aA + bB + cC + dD$

subject to the linear constraints

$eA + fB + gC + hD \leq OK$ *capital*

$iA + jB + kC + lD \leq ON$ *labour*

and

$A \geq 0, \qquad B \geq 0, \qquad C \geq 0, \qquad D \geq 0,$

where A, B, C and D are the unit-activity levels as before: a, b, c and d are the known revenue coefficients given by the market prices for output; and e, f, g, ... l are constant physical input coefficients determined from production data. The problem is to calculate the profit-maximizing output level for the firm subject to two input constraints. Graphically, we found the highest possible isorevenue line which had any point in common with the feasible input region and the resulting set of optimal activities was in fact the solution of the mathematical problem stated above. Associated with this linear programming maximization problem is a dual minimization problem which may be written:

$$\text{Minimize costs} = p_K\, OK + p_N\, ON$$

subject to the constraints

$$p_K e + p_N i \geqslant a$$
$$p_K f + p_N j \geqslant b$$
$$p_K g + p_N k \geqslant c$$
$$p_K h + p_N l \geqslant d$$

and

$$p_K \geqslant 0,\, p_N \geqslant 0,$$

where p_K and p_N are the unknown prices of units of capital and labour. The revenue coefficients in the 'primal' problem now replace the input constraints in the 'dual' problem; the inequality signs are reversed; the rows of coefficients in the 'primal' problem become columns in the 'dual' problem; and two new variables, p_K and p_N, appear in the 'dual' problem. Now, suppose we impute artificial accounting values or 'shadow prices' to these variables p_K and p_N, such that the net profit from a unit-activity level is zero when each input is costed at its shadow price per unit. Then the dual linear programming problem is that of finding the very smallest valuation of the firm's stock of inputs which completely accounts for all the profits of a unit of output.

Lo and behold, the solution of this dual problem gives exactly the same answer as the solution to the primal problem! When we have solved the profit-maximizing primal problem, we have also solved a cost-minimization dual problem, in the course of which we necessarily 'impute' prices to the factors of production. The argument has been confined to a single firm but it holds just as well for any number of firms: provided the factors of production combine in different proportions in different firms or industries, the fact that they combine in fixed proportions in each firm or industry does not prevent a supercomputer from assigning determinate values to the factors. But competition itself is such a supercomputer: by destroying all supernormal profits, it forces firms to assign such accounting values to the inputs as to minimize average costs of production.

7. The Hobson Objection

After this digression to modern economics, we come back to the history of marginal productivity theory. The marginal productivity theory of wages assumes a constant amount of capital as the quantity of labour is varied. But if the *quantity* of labour is increased, the *quality* of capital will almost always undergo some change: more workers require, not just more, but different machines. If every change in the quantity of labour is accompanied by changes in the organization of capital, how can variations in output be attributed to labour alone? Is there a discernible and specific marginal product of labour?

This criticism was most vigorously stated by John Hobson in *The Industrial System* (1909) and has since been echoed by many other gifted amateurs in economic theory. It is probably the oldest and most persistent objection advanced against marginal productivity theory. In a long unsatisfactory footnote in the *Principles*, Marshall replied to Hobson with a lesson in differential calculus. A factor's marginal product is not a finite amount of output: it is the rate of change of the total product with respect to the variable agent in question; the units are the infinitesimal ones of the calculus. If the production function is given by $X = f(K, N)$, an increase in the quantity of labour will cause the marginal productivity of labour to fall, that is,

$$\frac{\delta X}{\delta N} > 0 \quad \text{and} \quad \frac{\delta^2 X}{\delta N^2} < 0,$$

and will usually increase the marginal productivity of the other factor, that is,

$$\frac{\delta^2 X}{\delta N \delta K} > 0.$$

But the slight change in the productivity of the fixed factor when the amount of the variable factor is increased, as shown by the nonzero value of the cross-partial derivative, involves a higher order differential of 'the second order of small' and hence may be neglected. This is particularly so since all marginal variations in comparative static analysis are assumed to take place around a previously established optimum, in this case an optimum combination of factors.

Despite this reply, Marshall in fact capitulated to Hobson by introducing the concept of the marginal *net* product of a factor [see chapter 10, section 24]. In his well-known example of the marginal shepherd, he showed that the employer has a joint demand for labour and capital. Substitutability being limited in the short run, he recommended measuring the marginal product of joint additions of capital and labour and then subtracting the cost of one factor to determine the marginal net product of the other. This notion makes sense, however, only in the case of *strict* jointness – the case of fixed input coefficients – and even then is illegitimate because we are assuming that we already know the cost of the cooperating factor to the industry as a whole. Since no separate productivity can be imputed when the two factors are combined in strictly fixed proportions, to talk of marginal product, net or gross, is misleading. Either factor substitution is possible and a factor's marginal product can be defined or factor substitution is ruled out and the concept of a marginal product has no meaning.

8. The High-Wage Economy Theory

The chief critics of marginal productivity theory in its early days were the trade-union leaders and their spokesmen. Books like *Industrial Democracy* (1897) by Sidney and

Beatrice Webb emphasized the influence of custom on wage determination and attacked the notion that unions cannot secure an increase in wages in excess of labour's marginal product in one industry except at the expense of workers in some other industry. The Webbs argued that an artificial wage rate, secured by union action, might justify itself by affecting the efficiency of the work force, stimulating entrepreneurs to rearrange their plant and equipment and so altering the equilibrium wage rate. This has ever since been known as the 'high-wage economy theory' and to this day constitutes an important element in the creed of labour unions.

This is not the place to consider the argument in detail. Obviously, it proves too much. It is revealing, however, to strip this proposition down to its fundamentals. Marginal productivity theory is a theory of wages on the industry level, the supply of labour to the industry being given; for the firm, it is an employment theory, the rate of wages being given. The high-wage economy theory alleges that an artificial increase in wages increases efficiency and leads to an expansion of output; the rise in demand for labour then justifies the rise in wages. Marginal productivity theory says that $w = f(MP_N)$; the high-wage economy theory says that on the contrary, $MP_N = f(w)$. These are two possible situations in which both the first function and its inverse may hold. One is the case of a backward economy in which wages are at physical subsistence levels, so that an increase of wages may raise the standard level of effort of workers by overcoming dietary deficiencies. Traditional marginal productivity theory cannot handle this case: once workers' efficiency varies with wages, the supply curve of labour varies with the demand for labour, and demand and supply analysis breaks down. The other possibility is that of an advanced economy in which one function is relevant to static analysis and its inverse pertains to dynamic changes; that is, $w = f(MP_N)$ and $MP_N = f(\dot{w})$, where $\dot{w}$ indicates the derivative of w with respect to time. There is certainly nothing implausible about the latter case but the marginal productivity theory of wages has had little to say about it. The Webbs had a point, as has always been conceded, but it was not clear even to them what it was. Recognition of the dynamic effects of wage changes, however, serves to remind us that traditional marginal productivity theory, when properly understood, does not yield flat pronouncements on trade union action.

9. The Present Status of Marginal Productivity Theory

When economics turned back in the 1890s to the classical problems of factor pricing, it took some time to realize that the new marginal productivity theory dealt with a much more restricted range of questions than those posed by Smith, Ricardo and Mill. The relative shares of land, labour and capital, which had been at the heart of classical distribution theory, disappear as a problem in marginal productivity theory: the microeconomic focus of the new theory precludes conclusions about the tripartite division of national revenues à la Adam Smith. With the demise of the wages fund theory, not only that theory but all the macroeconomic problems of distribution with which it was concerned were abandoned. It took a long time, however, before economists became fully aware of the limited content of marginal productivity theory. Right up to the 1920s it was not uncommon for economists to discuss such issues as the level of wages and employment as a whole in terms of the operation of the entire economy conceived as a giant firm. The interdependence of aggregate demand and supply, however, renders the theory inapplicable to such problems. Indeed, it is easy to show that marginal productivity analysis is necessarily based on the assumption of a given level of income in the economy as a whole.

The individual firm under perfect competition hires factors according to the equimarginal principle. An optimum combination of factors implies equalization of the weighted marginal physical products taken over all the factors, the weights being factor prices:

$$\frac{MP_N}{p_N} = \frac{MP_K}{p_K} = \ldots = \frac{1}{MC}.$$

The common ratio is the reciprocal of marginal cost, an analogue to the marginal revenue of utility in the theory of consumer behavior. We already know that the competitive firm maximizes profits by equating marginal cost to price. Profit maximization implies cost minimization and the latter is a synonym for payment to factors in accordance with marginal productivity. If a competitive firm obeys the equimarginal rule, it will hire labour up to the point at which the weighted marginal physical product of labour is the reciprocal of marginal cost or the price of final product, or, equivalently expressed, up to the point at which the marginal value product of labour equals the given money wage rate: $MP_N/w = 1/p = 1/MC$, and $MP_N \, p = w$.

The firm's demand curve for labour is given by its MP_N curve. Summing horizontally over all firms in an industry, we obtain the industry's demand curve for labour. But we cannot obtain the *market* demand curve for labour simply by way of the horizontal summation of industry demand curves. That would imply that the product demand curves and hence the derived labour demand curves of each industry are independent of each other. But the product demand curve of each industry is drawn up on the basis of given incomes and given price configurations throughout the economy. Changes in the level of wages necessarily affect incomes and hence the pattern of consumer demand. And every change in the product demand curves alters the industry demand curves for labour.

The crucial hypothesis of traditional marginal productivity theory, therefore, is the assumption that consumer demand curves are invariant to the prices paid for the factors of production. Since the product demand curves are drawn up on the basis of fixed money incomes, marginal productivity analysis proceeds by treating the level of income as a datum. This is the essence of Keynes's objection to wage cutting as a remedy for unemployment. On marginal productivity grounds, an excess supply of labour would seem to denote wage payments in excess of labour's marginal product somewhere in the economy. Cutting real wages, therefore, appears to be the appropriate remedy. But wages are incomes as well as costs and a general decline in real wages must lower the aggregate demand for final goods and services. There is no guarantee, therefore, that wage cutting will succeed in eliminating unemployment.

The failure of the marginal productivity theory to throw light on the determination of relative shares is not solely due to its microeconomic bias. Variations in factor prices and hence relative shares are the result of both movements along given production functions and shifts in the production function themselves. Marginal productivity theory, however, has traditionally neglected the problem of technical change as falling outside the purview of economic analysis. Schumpeter in his *Theory of Economic Development* (1912) tried to fill the gap, insisting on the importance of 'innovations' for the understanding of economic progress. But Schumpeter failed to provide a systematic theory of innovations and, besides, economic progress was not the subject on the agenda of marginal productivity theorists. And so economists continued by and large to abstract from technical progress.

Recent decades have seen progress in classifying technical innovations in terms of their effects on relative shares. We will examine these developments stemming from Hicks' *Theory of Wages* (1932) in a later section of this chapter. Suffice it to say, however, that no determinate theory of relative shares in the presence of technical progress has yet emerged. Macroeconomic distribution theory is now in a state of limbo with most members of the profession claiming that marginal productivity considerations constitute a sound basis for such a theory, although the theory itself awaits future development, while a minority contends that a perfectly satisfactory post-Keynesian theory of relative shares is already at hand, devoid of the very concept of marginal productivity. To these questions we will return anon.

LINEARLY HOMOGENEOUS PRODUCTION FUNCTIONS

In his brilliant *Essay on the Coordination of the Laws of Distribution* (1894), Wicksteed tried unsuccessfully to prove that the total product is precisely exhausted when each factor is rewarded its marginal product. In a review of Wicksteed's book that appeared shortly thereafter, A.W. Flux gave an elementary but elegant proof of Wicksteed's contention.

If the production function is given by $X = f(x, y, z)$, then by assumption of constant returns to scale

$$\frac{dX}{X} = \frac{dx}{x} = \frac{dy}{y} = \frac{dz}{z} = \text{a constant } \lambda. \tag{1}$$

By the theorem of ratios, if

$$\lambda = \frac{a}{b} = \frac{c}{d} = \frac{e}{f} \text{ then } \lambda = \frac{la + mc + ne}{lb + md + nf}$$

where $a, \ldots f$ and $l, \ldots n$ are any real numbers.

Applying this theorem to equation (1) by multiplying each ratio by the appropriate first partial derivative of X, we have

$$\frac{dX}{X} = \frac{\dfrac{\delta X}{\delta x} dx + \dfrac{\delta X}{\delta y} dy + \dfrac{\delta X}{\delta z} dz}{\dfrac{\delta X}{\delta x} x + \dfrac{\delta X}{\delta y} y + \dfrac{\delta X}{\delta z} z} = \frac{dX}{x \dfrac{\delta X}{\delta x} + y \dfrac{\delta X}{\delta y} + z \dfrac{\delta X}{\delta z}} = \text{a constant } \lambda, \tag{2}$$

where dX is the total differential of X. Therefore,

$$x\,\frac{\delta X}{\delta x} + y\,\frac{\delta X}{\delta y} + z\,\frac{\delta X}{\delta z} = X \tag{3}$$

for all values of x, y, and z. But the first partial derivatives of X, $\delta X/\delta x$, $\delta X/\delta y$ and $\delta X/\delta z$ are the marginal products of infinitely small increments of x, y and z. Hence, given constant returns to scale, the total product will be exhausted by factor payments in accordance with marginal productivity.

To illustrate: let X be of the form $Ax^l y^m z^n$, where A is a constant and l, m and n obey no law. In this case

$$\frac{\delta X}{\delta x} = lAx^{l-1}y^m z^n$$

$$x\,\frac{\delta X}{\delta x} = lAx^l y^m z^n = lX$$

and, likewise,

$$y\,\frac{\delta X}{\delta y} = mX \text{ and } z\,\frac{\delta X}{\delta z} = nX.$$

Hence equation (3) takes the form

$$(l + m + n)\,X = X$$

for all values of x, y and z. But that implies $(l + m + n) = 1$. X is a homogeneous function of the first degree because the exponents of the expression $Ax^l y^m z^n$ sum to unity.

10. Product Exhaustion

It was Flux, not Wicksteed, who first related the problem of product exhaustion explicitly to Euler's mathematical theorem of homogeneous functions. Euler's Theorem states that if $f(x, y, \ldots z)$ is a homogeneous function of the mth degree, it is true that

$$x\left(\frac{\delta f}{\delta x}\right) + y\left(\frac{\delta f}{\delta y}\right) + \ldots z\left(\frac{\delta f}{\delta z}\right) = mf$$

or, more generally, that if $f(x, y, \ldots z)$ is a homogeneous function then and only then will $f(\lambda x, \lambda y, \ldots \lambda z) = \lambda^m f$, where λ is an arbitrary positive constant and m is the degree of the function [see chapter 5, section 3]. A function is homogeneous if all its terms are of the same dimension, that is, if the sums of the exponents of the variables in all its *separate* terms are equal; it is homogeneous of the first degree if these sums are equal to unity. Now, it is apparent that production functions will usually be homogeneous. Nonhomogeneous functions typically involve additive variables, the variables in one term of the equation being raised to one power while the variables in another term are raised to a different power – a special case of this is a function with additive constants. A nonhomogeneous production function would therefore imply some output with one of more zero inputs or even without any inputs at all, which seems economically meaningless. However, there is no guarantee that homogeneous production functions will be linearly homogeneous, that is, of the first degree (note that it is not the function itself that need be linear; a nonlinear function may be homogeneous of the first degree). The value of m determines the returns to scale that obtain for a particular homogeneous production function. If we double all the inputs ($\lambda = 2$), will we double output? If so, $m = 1$, and output is a linear function of the rates of input of all the factors taken together. If output more than doubles, $m > 1$, and we have increasing returns to scale. If output less than doubles, $m < 1$, and we have diminishing returns to scale.

We now verify Flux's argument that $X = Ax^l y^m z^n$ is a linearly homogeneous function if $(l + m + n) = 1$ with the aid of more familiar notation. Let $X = AN^\alpha K^\beta$, the so-called Cobb-Douglas production function, where A is a parameter expressing shifts of the production function, which are unrelated to changes in the quantity of the factors employed; it is often taken to be a function of time and has been called, among other things, 'technical change', 'total factor productivity', 'the residual' and 'the measure of our ignorance'. Then the *marginal* physical product of labour is

$$\frac{\delta X}{\delta N} = \alpha A N^{\alpha-1} K^\beta > 0 \text{ if } \alpha > 0 \text{ and } \beta > 0$$

and

$$\frac{\delta^2 X}{\delta N^2} = \alpha(\alpha - 1) A N^{\alpha-2} K^\beta = \alpha(\alpha - 1) \frac{X}{N^2} < 0 \text{ if } \alpha < 1.$$

The *average* product of labour is

$$\frac{X}{N} = A N^{\alpha-1} K^\beta = \frac{1}{\alpha}\left(\frac{\delta X}{\delta N}\right),$$

which is to say that the marginal productivity of labour is proportional to its average productivity, the factor of proportionality being α:

$$\frac{\delta X}{\delta N} = \alpha\left(\frac{X}{N}\right). \tag{4}$$

Similarly, the marginal physical product of capital is

$$\frac{\delta X}{\delta K} = \beta A N^\alpha K^{\beta-1} = \beta\left(\frac{X}{K}\right) > 0 \text{ if } \alpha > 0 \text{ and } \beta > 0 \tag{5}$$

and

$$\frac{\delta^2 X}{\delta K^2} = \beta(\beta - 1) \frac{X}{K^2} < 0 \text{ if } \beta < 1.$$

By Euler's Theorem

$$N\frac{\delta X}{\delta N} + K\frac{\delta X}{\delta K} = mX. \tag{6}$$

Substituting (4) and (5) into (6), we have

$$N\alpha\left(\frac{X}{N}\right) + K\beta\left(\frac{X}{K}\right) = \alpha X + \beta X = (\alpha + \beta)X = mX,$$

or

$$(\alpha + \beta) = m.$$

If $(\alpha + \beta) = 1$, X is necessarily a first-degree homogeneous function.

But what does all this have to do with the proposition that factor payments in accordance with marginal productivity will exactly exhaust the total product if and only if the production function is linearly homogeneous? It will be useful to prove this proposition for any linearly homogeneous production function, whatever its particular form. We prove first that the marginal product of each factor in the linearly homogeneous case depends only on the *ratio* etween the amounts of the factors employed. If $X = f(x, y)$ is a linearly homogeneous function, then

$$f(\lambda x, \lambda y) = \lambda^m f(x, y) = \lambda X.$$

We choose $\lambda = 1/x$, so that

$$f(1, y/x) = F\left(\frac{y}{x}\right) = \lambda X = \frac{X}{x}.$$

From which we get

$$X = xF\left(\frac{y}{x}\right).$$

The function $f(\ )$ in two variables has been replaced by the function $F(\ )$ in one variable.

Differentiating partially with respect to x, we find that neither x nor y appears alone in the expression for the marginal product of x:

$$\frac{\delta X}{\delta x} = F\left(\frac{y}{x}\right) + xF'\left(\frac{y}{x}\right)\frac{\delta}{\delta x}\left(\frac{y}{x}\right)$$

$$= F\left(\frac{y}{x}\right) + xF'\left(\frac{y}{x}\right)\left(-\frac{y}{x^2}\right)$$

$$= F\left(\frac{y}{x}\right) - \frac{y}{x}F'\left(\frac{y}{x}\right),$$

where

$$F'\left(\frac{y}{x}\right) = \frac{\delta F(y/x)}{\delta(y/x)}.$$

Thus, $\delta X/\delta x$, the marginal product of x, is equal to the difference between two terms, both of which are a function of the ratio y/x. The distributive share of x is

$$x \frac{\delta X}{\delta x} = xF\left(\frac{y}{x}\right) - yF'\left(\frac{y}{x}\right).$$

But we already know that $X = xF\left(\frac{y}{x}\right)$. Hence,

$$x \frac{\delta X}{\delta x} = X - yF'\left(\frac{y}{x}\right).$$

On the other hand, for y we have

$$\frac{\delta X}{\delta y} = xF'\left(\frac{y}{x}\right) \frac{\delta}{\delta y}\left(\frac{y}{x}\right)$$

$$= xF'\left(\frac{y}{x}\right)\left(\frac{1}{x}\right) = F'\left(\frac{y}{x}\right).$$

and y's distributive share is

$$y \frac{\delta X}{\delta y} = yF'\left(\frac{y}{x}\right).$$

Thus, if both x and y are paid their marginal products, the sum of the two distributive shares will be exhausted by the total product:

$$x \frac{\delta X}{\delta x} + y \frac{\delta X}{\delta y} = X.$$

All this is in real terms. In money terms, we have to multiply through by the price of the product but as long as competition is perfect this does not alter the result:

$$x \left(\frac{\delta X}{\delta x} p\right) + y \left(\frac{\delta X}{\delta y} p\right) = pX.$$

In words, x multiplied by the marginal value product of x plus y multiplied by the marginal value product of y exactly equals the money value of output if the underlying production function is linearly homogeneous. What happens if the production function is linearly homogeneous but competition is not perfect? Under monopolistic competition, we can only sell more output by lowering the price. Therefore, the last equation becomes

$$x \left(p \frac{\delta X}{\delta x} + X \frac{\delta p}{\delta x}\right) + y \left(p \frac{\delta X}{\delta y} + X \frac{\delta p}{\delta y}\right) = pX.$$

The product is exhausted when the factors are rewarded their marginal *revenue* products but the homogeneous production function is now necessarily of degree greater than one. This result is not surprising: it is a translation of the results of Chamberlin's tangency solution [see chapter 10, section 9], which has the monopolistically competitive firm operating in equilibrium under increasing returns to scale.

11. The Formal Properties of Linear Homogeneous Production Functions

Economists have long been fond of linearly homogeneous production functions. Indeed, so frequently is this particular homogeneous production function assumed at the outset of economic arguments that students have almost come to believe that higher or lower than first-degree homogeneity is economically impossible. But this is far from being true. The reasons for the appeal of first-degree homogeneity as the general case will become evident as we proceed to examine the economic meaning of a linearly homogeneous production function. We must begin, however, by reviewing the formal properties of such functions.

The reader who does not care for mathematical reasoning may skip this section but he is warned that in so doing he is bypassing the hard core of neoclassical economics. The first point to notice about first-degree homogeneous production functions is that, as shown above, the marginal products of the factors are invariant to the absolute amount of the factors employed: proportionate changes in the amounts of all the factors employed leave their marginal productivity unaffected. It follows from this that the composite marginal product of an extra amount of all the factors taken together, leaving their proportions unchanged, equals the sum of the marginal products of the factors added separately. That is to say, when the production function obeys constant returns to scale and there are at least two factors, the factors are always complements: increasing the amount of one factor in isolation lowers its own marginal product but necessarily raises the marginal product of the other factors. The term 'complements' is a bit vague. What is implied is the second of the four possible relationships between two factors of production. Drawing unit iso-quants, we have Figure 11–5. Case I of fixed input coefficients is ruled out because we are talking about increasing the amount of one factor in isolation – we are assuming that it is possible to define the marginal product of a factor. Case III is similarly ruled out by assumption because we have at least two factors: if factors are perfect substitutes for each other, they are the same factor for economic purposes. Case IV, however, is perfectly possible, particularly between two factors in a three-factor production function [see below].

We now take up Case II, expressing the theorem that the factors in a constant-returns-to-scale production function that permits factor substitution are always 'imperfect complements'. Notice first of all that if $X = f(K, N)$ is a linearly homogeneous production function, the assumption that MP_N and MP_K are positive *ipso facto* ensures that each is a declining function of the amounts of labour and capital employed. From Euler's Theorem, we have that

$$X = N \frac{\delta X}{\delta N} + K \frac{\delta X}{\delta K}.$$

Dividing both sides by K and transposing terms, we have

$$\frac{X}{K} - \frac{\delta X}{\delta K} = \left(\frac{\delta X}{\delta N} \right) \frac{N}{K}$$

Since X, K and N are positive in the relevant range, X/K and N/K are always positive. By assumption, $\delta X/\delta K$ and $\delta X/\delta N$ are always positive. But $\delta X/\delta N$ will be

Figure 11–5

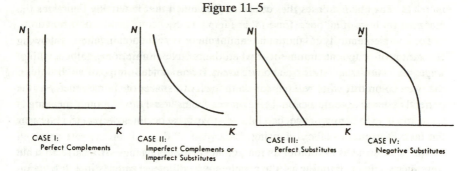

CASE I:
Perfect Complements

CASE II:
Imperfect Complements or
Imperfect Substitutes

CASE III:
Perfect Substitutes

CASE IV:
Negative Substitutes

positive only if $\delta X/\delta K < X/K$, that is, if the marginal product of capital is less than its average product, which immediately implies that the marginal product of capital is declining, or $\delta^2 X/\delta K^2 < 0$. A similar argument holds for labour's marginal physical product if instead of dividing both sides by K, we had divided through by N.

Furthermore, applying Euler's Theorem once again, and remembering that the marginal product of capital is a function, not just of the amount of capital, but also of the amount of labour employed,

$$\frac{\delta X}{\delta N} = \frac{\delta}{\delta N}X = \frac{\delta}{\delta N}\left(N\frac{\delta X}{\delta N} + K\frac{\delta X}{\delta K}\right) = \frac{\delta X}{\delta N} + N\frac{\delta^2 X}{\delta N^2} + K\frac{\delta^2 X}{\delta N\delta K}.$$

Hence,

$$N\frac{\delta^2 X}{\delta N^2} = -K\frac{\delta^2 X}{\delta N\delta K}$$

or

$$\frac{\delta^2 X}{\delta N^2} = -\frac{K}{N}\frac{\delta^2 X}{\delta N\delta K}. \tag{7}$$

A similar calculation for the marginal product of capital shows that

$$\frac{\delta^2 X}{\delta K^2} = -\frac{N}{K}\frac{\delta^2 X}{\delta K\delta N}. \tag{8}$$

Now, $\delta^2 X/\delta N^2$ and $\delta^2 X/\delta K^2$, the second-order partial derivatives, are always less than zero for a linearly homogeneous production function. Because of the negative sign appearing in the right-hand expressions of (7) and (8), $\delta^2 X/\delta N\delta K$ and $\delta^2 X/\delta K\delta N$, the cross second-order partial derivatives, must be positive if N and K are positive. This proves the contention of complementarity between K and N because the cross second-order partial derivatives show the effect on the marginal product of a fixed factor when the amount of the variable factor is altered.

As soon as we have increasing or diminishing returns to scale, however, it is no longer necessarily true that all the cross-derivatives are positive. If $\delta^2 X/\delta K\delta S$ is large enough – where S is some third factor accounting for varying returns to scale – $\delta^2 X/\delta K\delta N$ *may* be negative: labour and capital are then rival factors because an increase in capital increases the reward of S so much that it actually depresses the marginal product of labour. (Case IV in Figure 11–5).

The complementarity of labour and capital along any production function showing constant returns to scale implies that when the rental per unit of capital $\bar{n}$ is falling, wages per man $\bar{w}$ must be rising, and *vice versa*. It does not follow from this, however, that we can predict what will happen to the relative shares of the two factors. It is perfectly conceivable that capital rentals are falling gently, while the wage rate is rising rapidly. In consequence, capital's relative share declines despite the fact that the ratio of capital to labour is rising. Clearly, it all depends on the rate at which capital is substituted for labour as relative factor prices change. If returns to scale were increasing or diminishing, the problem would be even more difficult because then we could not even be sure that an increase in the capital-labour ratio would cause capital rentals to fall and wage rates to rise.

The rate at which capital can be substituted for labour or *vice versa* along a given production function is summarized by Hicks' 'elasticity of substitution', ϕ. It is defined as the percentage change in the relative amount of the factors employed resulting from a given percentage change in their relative marginal products or relative prices:

$$\phi_{K,N} = \left. \frac{K}{N} d\left(\frac{N}{K}\right) \middle/ \frac{\bar{w}}{\bar{n}} d\left(\frac{\bar{n}}{\bar{w}}\right) \right.,$$

where the denominator refers to the ratio of the marginal products of the two factors or the marginal rate of substitution MRS, which under perfect competition comes to the same thing as the ratio of factor prices. Consider an ordinary unit isoquant: the absolute value of the tangent to the isoquant at A expresses the ratio $\bar{w}/\bar{n}$ or MRS; the slope of a ray drawn from the origin to A will then give us the ratio K/N (see Figure 11–6). Suppose that the ratio $\bar{w}/\bar{n}$ increases so that we move upwards to B, a higher K/N ratio. What is now the relationship between these two ratios? This is a question about ϕ. In short, ϕ is simply the ratio of the relative change in the slope of a ray drawn from the origin to a point on the isoquant to the relative change in the absolute value of the tangent gradient of the isoquant at that point.

An easy rule about ϕ is that it is inversely proportional to the curvature of the isoquant: the flatter the isoquant, the lower is MRS and the larger is ϕ. To read off ϕ in Figure 11–6, consider that the change in N/K in going from point A to point B is given by the absolute change $AE/OE - CE/OE = AC/OE$ divided by the original position AE/OE, that is, AC/AE. Likewise, the ratio $\bar{w}/\bar{n}$ was originally FE/AE. The absolute change in $\bar{w}/\bar{n}$ is $FE/AE - FE/ED = FE/AD$. Therefore, the relative change in $\bar{w}/\bar{n}$ is the absolute change FE/AD, divided by the original position FE/AE, which is AE/AD. But what we are after is the relative change in $\bar{n}/\bar{w}$, which is its reciprocal AD/AE. Thus

$$\phi_{K,N} = \left. \frac{K}{N} d\left(\frac{N}{K}\right) \middle/ \frac{\bar{w}}{\bar{n}} d\left(\frac{\bar{n}}{\bar{w}}\right) \right. = \frac{AC}{AE} \middle/ \frac{AD}{AE} = \frac{AC}{AD}.$$

Figure 11–6

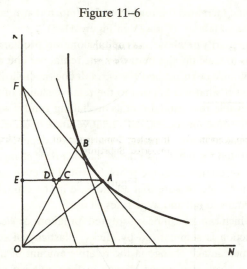

Since $AC < AD$, $\phi < 1$ for the isoquant in question over the relevant range, meaning that a 1 percent fall in $\bar{n}/\bar{w}$ leads to a less than 1 percent fall in N/K, so that labour's relative share rises.

Thus, a very simple way of discovering whether a certain range of an isoquant shows $\phi \gtreqless 1$ is to start at one end of the range and then to see where a line parallel to the tangent gradient of the isoquant at the other end of the range intersects the corresponding K/N ray. If the line intersects a point like C, $\phi = 1$, meaning that a 1 percent rise or fall in $\bar{n}/\bar{w}$ leads to a 1 percent rise or fall in N/K, leaving relative shares the same. The nearer the point of intersection to the original isoquant, the larger ϕ; in the extreme case, a linear isoquant expressing perfect substitution between the factors gives $\phi = \infty$. It is easy to see that we can now distinguish between the Marshallian short and long run, not just in terms of the elasticity of supply as Marshall did, but in terms of the tendency of ϕ to approach its technically determined maximum value. In the short run with given plant and equipment, the scope of substitutability between capital and labour is limited to variations in machine time and possibly variations in the labour intensity of handling materials. In the long run, however, new plant and equipment can be installed and the elasticity of substitution approaches its maximum feasible value, determined by the whole range of technical alternatives available to the firm at any moment of time. Thus, the value of ϕ in the long run always exceeds its value in the short run.

Summing up, for a family of unit isoquants, see Figure 11–7.

A few caveats about ϕ are in order. ϕ refers only to the same isoquant, not to changes both in the ratio of factors employed and in the scale of operations. So long as the production function is linearly homogeneous, this does not destroy the value of the ϕ-index. Under constant returns to scale, a move from A to D gives the same value for ϕ as a move from A to B since $\phi = 0$ for the change from B to D (see Figure 11–8). But the moment a homogeneous production function is not linearly homo-

Figure 11–7

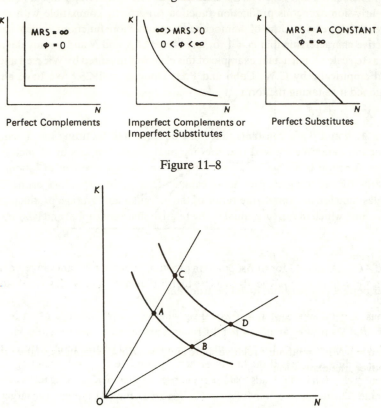

Perfect Complements   Imperfect Complements or   Perfect Substitutes
                             Imperfect Substitutes

Figure 11–8

geneous, the isoquants are no longer parallel in the sense of having the same slope along any straight line from the origin; when the production function is not of the first degree, the firm's optimal factor combinations for given relative factor prices, and hence the value of ϕ, varies with the level of output. To make the same point somewhat differently: under constant returns to scale, *MRS* is determined solely by changes in the ratios of the factors employed and $\phi_{K,N} = \phi_{N,K}$: the ease with which capital can be substituted for labour is identical to the ease with which labour can be substituted for capital. This is never true under diminishing or increasing 'returns to scale. Moreover, the definition of ϕ breaks down when we have monopolistic competition and the factors are no longer paid in accordance with their marginal value products. If the reward of each factor were proportional to its marginal physical product, no great harm would be done. But if the gap between marginal cost and price varies with output, as it must under monopolistic competition, the formula for ϕ can no longer be applied. Lastly, if nonneutral technical change is defined as the pivoting of inward-shifting isoquants – more of this below – then ϕ is only well defined for linearly homogeneous production functions under conditions of perfect competition and neutral technical change.

So much for the digression on the concept of ϕ. The upshot of the discussion is that a linearly homogeneous production function is perfectly compatible with $\phi \gtrless 1$. However, there is a class of homogeneous production functions which has the attractive characteristic that $\phi = 1$ for any values of K and N and for any degree of returns to scale. A particular example of this class was invented by Wicksell and first tested empirically by C.W. Cobb and P.H. Douglas in 1928.[1] We have already mentioned it as taking the form

$$X = AN^{\alpha}K^{\beta}$$

where A, α and β are constants that must be estimated by fitting the function to production data. We showed that the marginal product of labour of such a production function is always equal to α times the average product of labour and, similarly, for the marginal product of capital. That is, the exponents of the Cobb-Douglas function are simply the ratios of the marginal and average products of the two factors, which in turn are equal to the relative shares of capital and labour. That is,

$$\alpha = \frac{\delta X}{\delta N}\frac{N}{X} \quad \text{and} \quad \beta = \frac{\delta X}{\delta K}\frac{K}{X}.$$

Under perfect competition, it will be true that

$$\bar{w} = \frac{w}{p} = \frac{\delta X}{\delta N} \quad \text{and} \quad \bar{n} = \frac{n}{p} = \frac{\delta X}{\delta K}.$$

Thus, $\alpha = wN/pX = $ labour's relative share and $\beta = nK/pX = $ capital's relative share. Moreover, the expression

$$\frac{\delta X}{\delta N}\frac{N}{X}$$

is simply the proportionate change in output resulting from a proportionate change in labour, which is to say that α is also the elasticity of the production function with respect to labour. A similar interpretation holds for β with respect to capital. Lastly, *MRS*, the marginal rate of substitution of capital for labour, along a Cobb-Douglas production function takes the simplest form possible:

$$MRS = \frac{\bar{w}}{\bar{n}} = \frac{\alpha}{\beta}\frac{K}{N} \quad \text{or} \quad \frac{K}{N} = \frac{\beta}{\alpha}\left(\frac{\bar{w}}{\bar{n}}\right).$$

Douglas's procedure, first in association with Cobb and then with a number of other co-workers, was to estimate A, α and β from production data and then to

---

[1] In the second part of the second volume of *The Isolated State*, written in the late 1840s but published posthumously in 1863, Thünen states that the empirically estimated production function of his own agricultural estate takes the general form of
$$p = h(g + k)^n$$
where p is the product per unit of labour, h is a given shift parameter, which depends on the fertility of the soil and the intensity of human effort, g is a positive constant, k is the quantity of capital per unit of labour, and n is a positive parameter less than unity. Multiplying both sides by N, the number of labour units, we get:
$$X = pN = hN(g + k)^n = hN^{1-n}(gN + kN)^n,$$
which is identical in form to the Cobb-Douglas production function.

compare the estimated value of α and β with the relative shares of labour and capital; if the shares agreed with the respective values of α and β, he concluded that the factors were receiving their marginal products. At first, he *assumed* $\alpha + \beta = 1$, estimated α from the relative share of labour and then deduced $\beta = 1 - \alpha$. But in later work, he tested an unrestricted form of the function, allowing $\beta \gtrless 1 - \alpha$. As we noted earlier, $\alpha + \beta$ governs the degree of homogeneity of the Cobb-Douglas production function. Suppose that labour and capital increase by 10 percent. Then

$$X = A(1.10N)^\alpha(1.10K)^\beta = A(1.10)^{\alpha+\beta}N^\alpha K^\beta.$$

Output will now increase by $(1.10)^{\alpha+\beta}$ and the question whether it will increase by more or less than 10 percent depends on the value of $\alpha + \beta$. Summarizing:

$\alpha + \beta = 1$: constant returns to scale
$\alpha + \beta > 1$: increasing returns to scale
$\alpha + \beta < 1$: diminishing returns to scale

Cobb-Douglas functions can characterize any degree of returns to scale and this partly accounts for their popularity with econometricians. However, the feature that has made Cobb-Douglas functions famous is that the elasticity of substitution is always unity over the entire range of the function, a feature that is not affected by what is being assumed about the sum of α and β. It is this which guarantees that the relative shares of labour and capital will not be affected by the relative supplies of the two factors, providing a simple rationale for the alleged 'relative constancy' of factor shares over long periods in developed countries. The long-run constancy of factor shares is a fact that is now being increasingly questioned as a fact. Nevertheless, the belief that the elasticity of substitution in the real world appeared to be unity gave an immediate appeal to the Cobb-Douglas form or its latest relative the 'constant elasticity of substitution' (CES) production function. It also explains the interest of economists in neutral technical change: once the isoquants shift *and* pivot, A in the Cobb-Douglas function is no longer merely a shift-parameter whose value does not affect ϕ. With nonneutral technical change, variations in A necessarily affect *MRS* and hence ϕ.

A proof of the property that $\phi = 1$ for any Cobb-Douglas function is easy. As we saw above

$$\frac{K}{N} = \frac{\beta}{\alpha}\left(\frac{\overline{w}}{\overline{n}}\right), \quad \text{so that} \quad \frac{d\,(K/N)}{d\,(\overline{w}/\overline{n})} = \frac{\beta}{\alpha}.$$

Also

$$\frac{K}{N}\left(\frac{\overline{n}}{\overline{w}}\right) = \frac{\beta}{\alpha}.$$

Substituting into the definition of ϕ given earlier, we get

$$\phi = \frac{K}{N}\left(\frac{\overline{n}}{\overline{w}}\right)\bigg/\frac{d(K/N)}{d\,(\overline{n}/\overline{w})} = \frac{\beta}{\alpha}\bigg/\frac{\beta}{\alpha} = 1.$$

Notice that this result does not rely on the condition that $\alpha + \beta = 1$. It holds for any Cobb-Douglas function, whatever the value of the sum of α and β.

The peculiarity of the Cobb-Douglas form is precisely that the constant parameters of the production function that have to be estimated are themselves the elasticities α and β that are also the relative shares of the participating factors. There are very few production functions in which this is the case. The student can try his hand at the following examples of linearly homogeneous production functions:

$$X = aN + bK \tag{1}$$

$$X = \sqrt{N^2 + K^2} \tag{2}$$

$$X = \sqrt[3]{N^2 K} \tag{3}$$

$$X = \sqrt{aN^2 + 2cNK + bK^2} \tag{4}$$

$$X = \frac{aN^2 + 2cNK + bk^2}{dN + eK} \tag{5}$$

where $a, b, \ldots e$ are constants. It is easy to see that these are *homogeneous* functions – all the separate terms in each equation are in the same dimension – and also that they are *linearly* homogeneous – the exponents in all the separate terms sum to unity. Nevertheless, the constants in equations (1), (4) and (5) are not equal to the elasticities of the production function with respect to labour and capital and $\phi \neq 1$ for any of them. If this is true for many homogeneous production functions of the first degree, then how much more true is it for the still wider class of lower and higher order homogeneous production functions.

Summing up, linearly homogeneous production functions imply that: (1) the marginal product of a factor varies only with changes in the *relative* amounts of the factor employed; (2) the participating factors are complements, such that an increase in a variable factor depresses its own marginal productivity but increases the marginal productivity of the fixed factor; and (3) the total product is exactly exhausted by payments to the participating factors in accordance with their marginal productivity. However, first-degree homogeneity does not itself insure constancy of the relative shares. That is only true of special production functions such as the Cobb-Douglas type. It follows that if the elasticities of a production function are estimated from the relative shares of the factors and these are assumed to sum up total income, it implies *ipso facto* that the production function is Cobb-Douglas.

12. The Economic Meaning of Linearly Homogeneous Production Functions

Marginal productivity factor payments exhaust the product if and only if the production function is linearly homogeneous. But what happens when the homogeneous production function is not of the first degree?

Competition in factor markets will always ensure that factors are rewarded their marginal value or marginal revenue product irrespective of the character of the production function. If the production function is not of the first degree, however, the total product will either exceed or fall short of the sum of the distributive shares.

In the case of diminishing returns to scale, the sum of market-imputed factor payments will fall short of the value of output, leaving a residual to be earned by some 'fixed' factor. In the case of increasing returns, the total product is insufficient to reward all the contributing factors according to their marginal productivity and some factor must be earning less than its marginal productivity. The explanation of these propositions lies in the relationship between average and marginal costs. A production function that is linearly homogeneous generates a horizontal long-run average cost curve. In the case of increasing returns or decreasing costs, the long-run marginal cost curve lies below the long-run average cost curve [see Figure 10–3]. Since payment according to the marginal product of a factor is simply a corollary of marginal-cost pricing, it is hardly surprising that the competitive firm would suffer losses in this phase of its operation. This is the basis of the Hotelling-Lerner proposition that marginal-cost pricing in all industries would require subsidies to any industry operating with a falling supply price [see chapter 13, section 18]. The point is, however, that the phenomenon of increasing returns to scale destroys competition and hence the basis of marginal productivity factor payments. Similarly, a price that would cover long-run marginal costs, when long-run marginal exceed long-run average costs, would necessarily leave a residual. But when long-run marginal and average costs are equal, the product will be exhausted by the sum of all factor payments.

This is nicely brought out by the Walras-Wicksell proof of the product-exhaustion theorem, which combines short-run cost minimization conditions with the long-run equilibrium condition that unit costs must equal the sales price per unit of output. If $X = f(K, N, \ldots)$, then the equilibrium condition is that

$$pX = Kp_K + Np_N + \ldots, \tag{1}$$

where p is the price output and p_K and p_N are the prices of the factors. Costs are minimized by maximizing net revenue:

$$\pi = TR - TC$$

$$= pX - (Kp_K + Np_N + \ldots).$$

Therefore

$$\frac{\delta \pi}{\delta K} = p \frac{\delta X}{\delta K} - p_K = 0, \qquad \frac{\delta p}{\delta N} = p \frac{\delta X}{\delta N} - p_N = 0.$$

Whence, in equilibrium,

$$p \frac{\delta X}{\delta K} = p_K, \qquad p \frac{\delta X}{\delta N} = p_N, \ldots \tag{2}$$

Substituting equation (2) into equation (1) we have

$$pX = Kp \frac{\delta X}{\delta K} + Np \frac{\delta X}{\delta N} + \ldots$$

or

$$X = K \frac{\delta X}{\delta K} + N \frac{\delta X}{\delta N} + \ldots.$$

As a final check on the argument, we can define an elasticity of total costs TC as a function of output so that the product is exhausted when each factor is paid its marginal product:

$$\psi = \frac{X}{TC}\frac{dTC}{dX} = \frac{MC}{AC}.$$

Likewise, the elasticity of average costs AC can be expressed as

$$\tau = \frac{X}{TC/X}\frac{d(TC/X)}{dX} = \frac{X^2}{TC}\frac{d}{dX}\left(\frac{TC}{X}\right) = \frac{X^2}{TC}\frac{1}{X^2}\left(X\frac{dTC}{dX} - TC\right)$$

$$= \frac{X}{TC}\frac{dTC}{dX} - 1 = \psi - 1 = \frac{MC - AC}{AC}.$$

If $\psi = 1$, $\tau = 0$, and we have the case of constant returns to scale with average equal to marginal costs. If $\psi < 1$, $\tau < 0$, average cost exceeds marginal cost and we have increasing returns to scale. If $\psi > 1$, $\tau > 0$, and we have diminishing returns to scale with average costs increasing as output increases.

THE OPTIMUM SIZE OF THE FIRM

When Wicksteed first discovered the product-exhaustion theorem, he argued that it was universally valid. It was not really, he said, 'a law of distribution, but an analytical and synthetical law of composition and resolution of industrial factors and products which holds equally in Robinson Crusoe's island, in an Indian village ruled by custom, and in the competitive centres of the typical modern industries'. Part of the explanation for Wicksteed's curious conclusion is that, like most of his contemporaries, he treated the conditions of increasing, constant and diminishing returns to scale as mutually exclusive alternatives instead of different phases of the long-run cost curve of an industry. But this is not the whole explanation of his extraordinary assertion. As Joan Robinson has said: 'For most of the contemporaries of Wicksteed (though not, I think, for Marshall), the "theory of marginal productivity" was a formulation of a somewhat mysterious law of nature. For the modern economist it is merely a series of self-evident propositions displaying the implications of the initial assumption that the individual employer acts in such a way as to maximize his profits. It is this fundamental difference in point of view which gives what appears to the modern reader such a perverse and fantastic character to the controversies surrounding the "adding-up problem".'

13. Wicksell's Proof of Product Exhaustion

It was Knut Wicksell who first realized that product exhaustion is not usefully defined as holding under any and all circumstances: exhaustion of the product is a condition of equilibrium corresponding to the point at which the production function becomes tangent to a linearly homogeneous function.[2] Wicksell's argument was that the

---

[2] Wicksell was the first to state this clearly in print. Actually, it had been said as early as 1895 by Enrico Barone in an unpublished review article of Wicksteed's *Essay on the Coordination of the Laws of Distribution*. Barone submitted the article to *The Economic Journal*, claiming that

market mechanism will automatically produce this condition in the long run. If a hiring agent pays all the hired agents their marginal products, he may be left with something over and above the marginal product of his own productive services. If so, this induces the hired agents themselves to become the hiring agent, which tends to eliminate the residual. On the other hand, if the residual should prove to be negative, the hiring agent would cease to be a residual income recipient and would rent the use of his services at the value of its marginal product. The hiring agent, of course, is the entrepreneur but Wicksell assumed that entrepreneurship is not itself a factor of production; its function can be carried on by any factor, say, the salaried manager. Whether this is true or not, the result of the process just described is that, under perfect competition and the free hire of factors, firms tend to operate at the lowest point of their long-run average cost curves, at an output level and with a combination of resources such as to yield a linearly homogeneous production function. Indeed, perfect competition *means* that production is carried on with constant returns to scale because nonconstant returns to scale are incompatible with perfect competition.

Wicksell's argument assumes that there is an optimum size of the firm. At this point we must raise the question, which we have so far ducked: are there in fact genuine economies or diseconomies of scale? If the long-run cost curves of the firms in an industry are horizontal, the size of each firm is indeterminate. If the size of each firm is indeterminate, so are the number of firms in the industry, casting doubt on the large-numbers property of perfect competition. This explains why economists have been loath to abandon the notion of U-shaped $LRAC$ curves but it does not tell us whether there are any good grounds for that idea.

14. The Indivisibility Thesis

If two productive agents are perfect substitutes for each other when used in combination to produce a given output, they are necessarily infinitely divisible: the isoquants in this case are straight lines, meaning that the marginal rate of substitution of the two factors is a constant. To illustrate, we construct a production table (Figure 11–9) such that a given total amount of capital and labour produces the same total output irrespective of the proportions in which the two factors are combined. MP_N is defined for any given amount of K and may be read off the table as the first interval difference along any row. Similarly, MP_K can be found by looking at the first interval difference along any column. In all cases, MP_N and MP_K are constant. Since $MRS =$

product-exhaustion was implicit in Walras' cost-minimization equations and hence that Walras, without ever mentioning marginal productivity, had nevertheless a prior claim over Wicksteed as the discoverer of the 'law of marginal productivity'. Edgeworth, the editor of *The Economic Journal*, rejected Barone's article. When Walras published the third edition of his *Elements* in 1896, he added an appendix on Wicksteed, essentially repeating Barone's argument and virtually accusing Wicksteed of plagiarism. This appendix irritated many contemporary economists and caused anguish even among Walras' supporters. Walras finally withdrew it in the fourth edition of the *Elements* (1900), the first explicitly to incorporate the marginal productivity theory of distribution, but the priority dispute raged on for many years. Ironically enough, it turns out that Walras had been handed the entire marginal productivity theory, together with the product-exhaustion theorem, by a mathematician friend in a letter written in 1877, seventeen years before the appearance of Wicksteed's *Essay*, but was unable to make use of it because he did not know enough mathematics at the time to understand the letter.

Figure 11–9

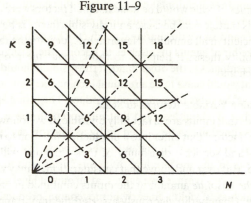

MP_N/MP_K, MRS is constant. Perfect substitutability leads, not only to constancy in the marginal products, but also to constancy in returns to scale: if the marginal product of an additional unit of capital is equal to the marginal product of an additional unit of labour, surely the two added together will raise output by twice the constant marginal product of capital and labour?

It is clear, on the other hand, that convex isoquants reflecting diminishing marginal productivity imply that the factors are not perfect substitutes for each other. The obvious explanation of this phenomenon is that infinite divisibility of all the participating factors cannot be obtained in the short run. Some factors, such as capital equipment for instance, are available only in discrete amounts in the short run. Similarly, if constant returns to scale do not prevail in the long run, it must be because less than perfect divisibility of all the factors prevents them from being perfect substitutes for each other. *Ergo*, varying returns to scale are explained by indivisibilities: this is the so-called 'indivisibility thesis'.

Let us paraphrase the argument: there is a certain optimum proportion of factors; because the factors are available only in discrete lumpy units, this optimum proportion cannot be attained unless the aggregate amount of the factors employed is large; the inefficiency of small-scale production is due to the failure to obtain the lumpy factor in fractional units having proportionate efficiency; with perfect divisibility, the optimum could be achieved for any aggregate; hence, economies of scale are due to indivisibilities. The same argument will account for diseconomies of scale by the existence of some indivisible agent, such as that of managerial coordination. It follows that all the phenomena that characterize nonconstant returns to scale are reducible to indivisibilities.

The proposition that the production function must be linearly homogeneous and that, when it is not, lumpiness of some factor is the explanation is not one that could be controverted by empirical evidence. After all, a perfectly divisible and perfectly homogeneous factor of production is defined as a class of different units of a productive service that are perfect substitutes for one another. From this it follows immediately that increments in the amounts of a homogeneous factor are of the same unit efficiency and, hence, that their efficiency is invariant with respect to scale. To say that economies of scale would be nonexistent if factors were available in infinitely divisible units is tautological because an indivisible factor is *defined* as one which is not equally efficient in all amounts. Nevertheless, despite the tautological character of the indivisibility thesis, it helps us to think about the problem by providing a classificatory scheme.

15. Genuine Variable Returns to Scale

No one contends that inputs are in fact fully divisible: if we follow Samuelson's advice and restrict the 'factors' that enter into a production function to inputs of measurable physical goods and services, divisibility of these 'factors' will not imply constant returns to scale. But over and above that consideration, it may well be that efficiency is affected by the *absolute* amount of the inputs combined in production. In the last years of his life, Chamberlin vigorously asserted the importance of genuine economies and diseconomies of scale. Biology furnishes many examples of genuine nonproportionalities and it may be that physical production is characterized by similar properties[3].

Moreover, even if the factors themselves are perfectly divisible, the activities they perform may be nonproportional to output. Such activities as record keeping, credit and finance administration and production planning need not be proportional to output even with fully divisible factors of production: doubling the size of orders and sales may not double the paperwork required because of the use of carbons. Furthermore, the existence of random variables in the production function may create economies of scale via the principle of pooled reserves. Seventy years ago Edgeworth argued that, owing to the law of large numbers, commercial banks' holdings of cash reserves for purposes of liquidity vary less than proportionately to the volume of deposits. Since then it has been shown that optimal inventory safety margins as protection against random variations in demand vary with the square root of demand; similarly, auditing costs and quality controls tend to vary with the square root of the items to be audited or checked. The implications of such economies of scale are disturbing to the marginal productivity theory of factor pricing. If factors are awarded their marginal products, the product is more-than-exhausted under increasing returns to scale: thus, competition cannot survive and there is no mechanism that forces monopolists to pay the factors they hire their marginal products. If economies of scale characterize much of modern manufacturing, marginal productivity theory is simply irrelevant.

16. Diseconomies of Management

On the side of the technical *dis*economies, however, it seems difficult to come up with any very convincing examples of genuine nonproportionalities. There are no financial diseconomies of scale and selling costs are not necessarily subject to diminishing

---

[3] An oft-cited biological example is that of the flea, which can jump over a man if the man is scaled down to the size of a flea, but which cannot jump at all if it is scaled up to the size of a man. The strength of the flea's wings and muscles is proportional to their cross-section, which is an area. His weight is proportional to volume, which is a cube. Hence, if we increase the scale of a flea by a thousand, we increase his strength by a million but his weight by a billion.

returns. It is true that when a firm has saturated its market, selling difficulties may appear. This is a limitation on the side of demand, however, not on the side of costs. The chief factor making for diseconomies of scale appears to be diseconomies of management, reflecting the indivisibility of managerial functions. But why should it not be possible to overcome managerial diseconomies by decentralization of decision making? However, this will usually entail a change in the quality and type of managerial services, which is ruled out by definition in static analysis. Similarly, the assumption of a given level of technical knowledge rules out the possibility of learning to overcome administrative bottlenecks by the progressive subdivision of functions. But managerial services defined to be unalterable by experience take on the character of a fixed factor. Hence, managerial diseconomies may be said with justice to be due entirely to indivisibilities.

17. The Growth of Firms

Managerial diseconomies will ensure a limit to the amount of expansion that a firm can undertake in a given period. But the fact that there is a size of firm that is optimal from the point of view of static efficiency does not mean that growing firms are bound eventually to become inefficient. Technical and even managerial diseconomies of scale need not limit the size of the firm in contrast to the size of the plant: processes can always be duplicated when they become inefficiently large. Even if there is an optimum output for each of the firm's plants and product lines, there may not exist an optimum output for the firm as a whole. Moreover, even if a multiplant firm is too big to maximize efficiency with given resources, it may not be able to achieve efficiency via decentralization without some positive rate of growth. Once again, it is apparent how remote is the traditional theory of the firm from the actual laws that govern the growth of firms in the real world.

It is interesting to see what happens to the concept of an optimum size of the firm when the problem is viewed dynamically. Suppose that the long-run optimum size of a firm is at least as large as that of the whole industry, so that long-run stable equilibrium of the industry is impossible under perfect competition from the viewpoint of static theory. Assume now that the average and marginal cost of producing a given output at a given moment of time is a decreasing function of output, indicating that expansion is profitable, but an increasing function of the *rate of change* of output at that moment, indicating that contraction is profitable if output has been increasing. Then, given the rate of output at t, average and marginal costs will be increasing with the rate of output at $t + 1$ if the rate of growth of output has accelerated between the two periods. Each firm will now have an equilibrium output at each moment of time, equating the marginal cost of producing a given rate of output at that moment to the price of the product, and yet output will increase from one moment to the next. What we have is a moving equilibrium and stability now consists of a tendency to approach a rate of change of output rather than a given level of output. Provided the industry's demand curve continues to shift to the right, attainment of long-run equilibrium may in this way be permanently delayed and pure if not perfect competition might exist indefinitely.

THE THEORY OF PROFIT

In long-run competitive equilibrium the reward of each factor, including the hiring factor, equals its marginal value product; there is no residual for the entrepreneur and profits are zero. But what of those theories that speak of profit as the returns to a distinct fourth factor of production called 'organization' or 'entrepreneurship', comprising the services of ultimate coordination and decision making, as well as risk taking and uncertainty bearing? It would seem that in this case we can simply apply standard marginal productivity theory and define 'normal profits' as the marginal product of the entrepreneur. Thus, we could say with Marshall that, in long-run equilibrium, profits are 'normal' because pure, residual profits are zero. Is this a tenable point of view?

18. The Meaning of Pure Profit

First of all, we have to make it clear what we mean by 'pure profits'. However confused in their terminology, economists since the days of Adam Smith have always meant to exclude all necessary cost outlays from the definition of pure profit. Pure profit is a return over and above opportunity cost payments, the payments necessary to draw forth productive services from their most remunerative alternative employments. At the same time, pure profit is also a return in excess of 'real' costs, since it is not required to maintain any productive agent in existence. Pure profits are therefore perfectly analogous to Ricardian rents in cases where land has no alternative uses whatever. If land does have alternative uses, ground rent must be paid by the firm in order to secure land on which to operate. Similarly, if the transfer cost or opportunity cost of the ultimate decision maker is positive, pure profit must be defined net of the wages of management. Likewise, the fact that some businessmen earn consistently more than others might lead us to define pure profit as a 'rent of ability', an intramarginal surplus accruing to superior business talent. But in long-run equilibrium, such intramarginal rents are imputed to costs in the form of wages of superior management; the rent-of-ability theory of profit is really a theory of differential wages travelling in disguise.

Sticking to our definition of pure profit as being neither an opportunity cost nor a real cost, we can define it as a residual left over after all contractual costs have been met, including the transfer costs of management, insurable risks, depreciation and payments to shareholders sufficient to maintain investment at current levels.

19. The Entrepreneur as a Factor of Production

If we treat the entrepreneur as a distinct factor of production, receiving his marginal product, we cannot logically equate this marginal product to pure profit. Pure profit is either the marginal product of some factor or it is a non-imputed residual. We have just concluded that it is a residual. Hence, the marginal product of entrepreneurship cannot be pure profit.

But the concept of the entrepreneur as a factor of production, separate from and in addition to the conventional triad of land, labour and capital, is itself inconsistent, as

Edgeworth never tired of pointing out. We cannot precisely define the marginal product of a factor unless the factor is both infinitely divisible and strictly homogeneous. If it is not infinitely divisible, the *marginal* product can only be calculated approximately. If it is not strictly homogeneous, we are not talking about one and the same factor. In practice, the definition of a factor always represents some compromise between the twin claims of divisibility and homogeneity. All too frequently, if a factor is rigorously defined as being finely divisible, the resulting factor class has little economic significance: think of minutes or even seconds of labour. And, on the other hand, if it is defined as satisfying homogeneity in the strict sense, it turns out to be indivisible: think of men of the same age, native ability, work experience and educational attainment.[4] But in the case of entrepreneurship the usual practical compromises have to be carried to excessive lengths. If the entrepreneur is a person, a firm has room for only so many entrepreneurs, and it is straining language to speak of entrepreneurs as members of a homogeneous group; if entrepreneurship is a function, it cannot be finely divided in terms of something like entrepreneurial man hours as the fundamental unit of supply. In short, entrepreneurship is a function that fails to satisfy the conditions required to define a 'factor of production'.

What then is it? On the one hand, it appears to be a vital function in an economic system characterized by private ownership of capital and, on the other hand, it is ruled out by marginal productivity theory as playing any role in long-run equilibrium. Here is a puzzle that requires some sorting out. To understand the strange disappearance of the entrepreneur from the center of the stage of economic theory, we must jog back a little.

20. The History of the Concept of Entrepreneurship
Adam Smith in the *Wealth of Nations* clearly separated the functions of the capitalist from those of the manager and emphasized the fact that the 'profits' of the capitalist exclude the 'wages' of management as a payment for 'the labour of inspection and direction'. However, Smith did not distinguish in any way between the capitalist as the provider of the 'stock' of the enterprise and the entrepreneur as the ultimate decision maker. He did use the terms 'projector' and 'undertaker' as English equivalents of the French word 'entrepreneur' but only as synonyms for the business proprietor. This failure to isolate the entrepreneurial function from that of pure ownership of capital became the standard practice of all the English classical economists. Thus, the term 'entrepreneur' or any of its English equivalents is totally

---

[4] In *the Essay on Coordination of the Laws of Distribution*, Wicksteed tried to reduce constant returns to scale to a tautology by defining all inputs as being strictly homogeneous. Instead of accepting the crude productive triad of classical economics, he decided that 'we must regard every kind and quality of labour that can be distinguished from other kinds and qualities as a separate factor . . . instead of speaking of so many £ worth of capital we shall speak of so many ploughs, so many tons of manure, and so many horses, or footpounds of power'. It follows that a proportionate increase in all these strictly homogeneous but also strictly indivisible inputs must increase output equiproportionately. But Wicksteed failed to realize that he had tacitly banished the concept of a marginal product. If one input is indivisible, the smallest increase in output that will leave input proportions unaffected is a 100 percent increase. In that case, however, the marginal productivity principle cannot be applied. To calculate the marginal product of an input it is necessary to define an input as being finely divisible as well as homogeneous.

absent in the writings of Ricardo and so is the concept of the businessman as the principal agent of economic change.

Some would argue that the English classical economists may be forgiven for having amalgamated the functions of the capitalist and the entrepreneur. Of course, the corporate form of business organization, in which the capitalist role of stockholders is sharply distinguished from the decision-making role of managers and entrepreneurs, had been invented centuries before. Nevertheless, until the 'railway mania' of the 1840s, trading on the British stock exchange was largely confined to government bonds and public utility stocks and the prevalent form of business ownership in the heyday of the Industrial Revolution was the small to medium-sized family firm, the capital funds being provided by the owner, his relatives or his friends. No wonder then that the classical economists failed to highlight the distinctive character of the entrepreneurial function.

On further reflection, however, this historical explanation of the neglect of entrepreneurship in English classical political economy appears somewhat unconvincing. The fact of the matter is that the concept of the entrepreneur as having a function quite distinct from that of both the capitalist and the manager had already been formalized by Richard Cantillon, writing some twenty years before Adam Smith.

Cantillon observed that discrepancies between demand and supply in a market create opportunities for someone to buy cheap and sell dear and that it is precisely this sort of arbitrage that brings competitive markets into equilibrium. He named people who take advantage of these unrealized profit opportunities 'entrepreneurs', that is, individuals who are willing 'to buy at a certain price and sell at an uncertain price'. Moreover, he noted that action of this kind need not involve production and need not absorb the personal funds of the entrepreneur, although it frequently did. In short, entrepreneurship for Cantillon is a matter of foresight and willingness to assume risk, which is not necessarily connected with the employment of labour in some productive process. Cantillon therefore left no doubt of the difference between the functions of the entrepreneur and those of the capitalist.

Adam Smith read Cantillon but took no notice of his analysis of entrepreneurship. Similarly, Ricardo had the benefit of Jean Baptiste Say's writings, which leaned heavily on Cantillon in distinguishing between the provision of capital to a business enterprise, on the one hand, and the multiple functions of superintendence, direction, control and judgment, on the other. Nevertheless, there is not so much as a hint of the special role of entrepreneurship in Ricardo. It is evident that Ricardo, and for that matter virtually all the other leading English classical economists, regarded production and the investment of capital as a more or less automatic process, involving no critical decision making and certainly no risky judgment or imagination of any kind. Ricardo recognized that the first capitalist to introduce a novel improvement such as a new machine is liable to reap extra returns but this did not lead him to single out the capacity to innovate as the feature which distinguished one capitalist from another.

And exactly the same thing is true of Marx. Despite his emphasis on the constant accumulation of capital, on the remorseless pressure to innovate or to perish, Marx too treated the business process as virtually automatic once the required capital is forthcoming. According to Marx, squeezing the work force to make greater efforts is one of the two principal sources of extra profits for capitalists, the other being the introduction of new machinery. But there is never any problem in Marx about which new machines the capitalist is to introduce; likewise in Marx, there appear to be no choices to make about the size of the business, or the number of products to manufacture, or the type of markets to penetrate. In other words, Marx, like all economists before him and since him, realized that the action of competition requires differences in behavior among economic agents – after all, if they all acted exactly the same in the face of the same circumstances, economic change and progress would be impossible to explain. Nevertheless, Marx took no interest in these individual differences among capitalists that alone account for the dynamic evolution of the capitalist system.

Marx knew perfectly well that capitalists can borrow all their capital from banks, which is why he regarded 'interest' on capital as a deduction from the 'profits' of enterprise. He also knew that the special skills of managers, including the skills of monitoring and supervising the labour force, can be hired on the labour market. But he never considered whether the residual income left over after paying the interest on borrowed capital and the wages of management corresponded to any particular economic function, for example, the function of buying inputs at certain prices and selling output at uncertain prices, as a result of which there may be losses instead of profits. He must have thought either that capitalists bear no risks, or that if they do bear risks, there is an apparently limitless supply of people in a capitalist economy willing to bear such risks. At any rate, Marx, like Smith and Ricardo, simply conflated the functions of the capitalist and the entrepreneur.

For the first entirely adequate statement of the entrepreneurial role, we must go not to Marx, not to Say or even Cantillon, but to Thünen. In the second volume of *The Isolated State* (1850), Thünen defined the gains of the entrepreneur as the income which is left over from the gross profits of a business operation after payment of (1) interest on invested capital, (2) the wages of management, and (3) an insurance premium against the calculable risk of losses. The rewards of the entrepreneur, Thünen went on to say, are therefore the returns for incurring those risks which no insurance company will cover because they are unpredictable. Since novel action is precisely the condition under which it is impossible to predict the probability of gain or loss, the entrepreneur is necessarily an 'inventor and explorer in his field'. Notice: this masterful grasp of the entrepreneur as the residual income claimant of a risky, unpredictable income, typified by but not confined to the innovative entrepreneur, predates the publication of Marx's *Capital* by 17 years! Moreover, Marx had read Thünen's *Isolated State*. In short, let us not say that Marx identified the entrepreneur as the capitalist because he could not have known better.

Mill's *Principles* (1848) popularized the term 'entrepreneur' among English economists but failed to break the hold of the Smith-Ricardo tradition of the entrepreneur as simply a multifaceted capitalist. Soon, thereafter, the 'marginal revolution' shifted attention away from the internal organization of a business enterprise, thus eliminating the role of both the capitalist and the entrepreneur. When perfect competition has done its work, when we have reached long-run equilibrium, the total product is exactly exhausted by marginal productivity factor payments; 'profits' are eliminated and the entrepreneur, as Walras said, 'neither benefits, nor loses'.

We are now at the heart of the question with which we began. So long as economic analysis is preoccupied with the nature of static equilibrium under conditions of perfect competition, there is simply no room either for a theory of entrepreneurship or a theory of profit as the residual income claims of persons who assume the risks associated with uncertainty. What the older classical economists had called 'profits', or what Marx calls 'surplus value', is now said to be 'interest' and of course perfect competition produces a positive rate of interest even in stationary equilibrium. But a permanent, positive residual over and above wages and interest can only be the result of constant technical progress disrupting the stationary state and the new economics had little to say about the circumstances governing technical progress.

The growing popularity of general equilibrium theory set the seal on the possibility of theorizing about entrepreneurship. As a matter of fact, static equilibrium analysis came increasingly to typify the study of economics as the 19th century gave way to the 20th. And even in the 1930s when Keynesian macroeconomics arrived on the scene, Walrasian static equilibrium analysis was refurbished, a process which reached even greater stages of refinement in the 1950s and 1960s. Despite valiant attempts to dynamize microeconomics, large parts of modern economics remain steeped in a static general equilibrium framework. No wonder then that the elementary textbook of today is rich in the treatment of consumer behavior, the profit-maximizing decisions of business firms (in short-run equilibrium), the theory of wages, the theory of interest, the theory of international trade, etcetera, but poor in the analysis of technical change, the growth of big business, the causes of the wealth and poverty of nations – and the theory of entrepreneurship.

This is the more remarkable in that this virtual consensus about the unimportance of entrepreneurship has been seriously questioned on at least two notable occasions in the 20th century. The first occasion came with the publication of Frank Knight's *Risk, Uncertainty and Profit* (1921), an acknowledged but little read classic of modern economics.

21. Profit as a Return to Uncertainty Bearing

Knight began by elaborating on Thünen's distinction between 'risk' and 'uncertainty'. Many uncertainties of economic life are like the chances of dying at a particular age: their objective probability can be calculated and to that extent they can be shifted via insurance to the shoulders of others. Such risks thus become an element in the costs of production, a deduction from and not a cause of profits or losses. There are other uncertainties, however, which can never be reduced to objective measurement because they involve unprecedented situations. 'The only "risk" which leads to profit', Knight remarked, 'is a unique uncertainty resulting from an exercise of ultimate responsibility which in its very nature cannot be insured nor capitalized nor salaried'.

The beauty of Knight's argument was to show that the presence of true 'uncertainty' about the future may allow entrepreneurs to earn positive profits despite perfect competition, long-run equilibrium and product exhaustion. Production takes place in anticipation of consumption, and since the demand for factors of production is derived from the expected demand of consumers for output, the entrepreneur is forced to speculate on the price of his final product. But it is impossible to determine the price of the final product without knowing what payments are being made to the factors of production. The entrepreneur resolves this dilemma by guessing the price at which output will sell, thereby translating the *known* marginal physical products of the factors of production into their *anticipated* marginal value products. Although the factors are hired on a contractual basis and therefore must be paid their anticipated marginal value product, the entrepreneur as a residual, noncontractual income claimant may make a windfall gain if actual receipts prove greater than forecasted receipts.

We cannot describe this noncontractual, windfall gain as a necessary price that must be paid for the performance of a specific service, the cost of bearing uncertainty, for that would imply a definite connection between the level of profit and the burden of bearing uncertainty. But no such connection exists. If it did exist, uncertainty-bearing would have all the characteristics of a productive factor and marginal productivity theory would apply to it: profits would equal the marginal product of entrepreneurship and would therefore constitute a standard charge on production. But profits are the windfall difference between the expected and realized returns of an enterprise and as such would cease to exist in a stationary economy in which all future events can be perfectly foreseen. Profits are not a distinctive distributive share but are an element found in the payments to all types of productive agents. When most entrepreneurs take a bearish view of the future – expecting prices to fall – the contractually hired agents may receive less than the realized value of their marginal products and profits in this case are really drawn from the productive factors themselves. Similarly, when entrepreneurs are bullish in their outlook – expecting prices to rise – there may be losses instead of profits because the hired factors are rewarded on the basis of their anticipated marginal products and these may now exceed the value of the marginal products that are ultimately realized when output is sold.

Knight's book, although published over sixty years ago, has withstood criticism remarkably well. There was little problem about assimilating his contributions to orthodox economic ideas because Knight did not question static economic analysis so far as it went. Unfortunately, he failed to persuade orthodox economists that the uncertainty theory of profit was anything more than a footnote to mainstream analysis, tying together some loose ends that had been left lying around ever since Adam Smith. Economics was now provided with a satisfactory explanation of profits and entrepreneurship but, of course, the main focus of analysis continued to be the pricing of factors of production in accordance with marginal productivity principles under stationary conditions.

22. Profit as a Return to Innovation

Ten years before the appearance of Knight's book, the young Schumpeter had contributed a wholly different view of *the* economic problem in *The Theory of Economic Development* (1912). In this book, entrepreneurship and its connection with dynamic uncertainty is placed at the centre of economic inquiry. Schumpeter developed his argument by constructing a model of an economy in which technical change of any kind is absent. Such an economy, he contended, would settle down to a repetitive and perfectly routine economic process in which there is no uncertainty about the future. Hence, there would be no profits in such an economy and, moreover, even the rate of interest would fall to zero. In short, competitive long-run stationary equilibrium as visualized in traditional theory rules out both profit and interest. Schumpeter's claim that only technical innovations and dynamic change can produce a positive rate of interest has been hotly disputed [see chapter 12, section 13] but at the expense of considering his associated views on innovation and enterprise. Distinguishing between 'invention' and 'innovation' – the discovery of new technical knowledge and its practical application to industry – and defining 'innovation' broadly as the introduction of new technical methods, new products, new sources of supply and new forms of industrial organization, Schumpeter traced all disrupting economic change to innovations and identified the innovator with the entrepreneur. The entrepreneur is the source of all dynamic change in an economy and the capitalist system for Schumpeter cannot be understood except in terms of the conditions giving rise to entrepreneurship.

As in all previous theories of entrepreneurship, the entrepreneur in Schumpeter is a functional role which is not necessarily embodied in a single physical person and certainly not in a well-defined group of people. The entrepreneur may be the capitalist or even a corporate manager but whether all these different functions are combined in one or more persons depends on the nature of capital markets and on the forms of industrial organization. But Schumpeter went even further than his predecessors in recognising that the same person may be an entrepreneur when he is an innovating businessman, only to lose that character as soon as he has built up his business and settled down to running it along routine lines. Thus, the actual population of entrepreneurs in a capitalist economy is constantly changing because the function of entrepreneurship is typically mixed up with other kinds of activity.

23. Profit as a Return to Arbitrage

Schumpeter's influence on entrepreneurial theory has been overwhelming and subsequent writers on entrepreneurship have usually defined their own position by contrasting it with his. In the meanwhile, however, mainstream economic theory has continued to neglect Schumpeter's writings on entrepreneurship as it continues to neglect Knight's theory of profits because neither fits in with static equilibrium analysis. The theory of entrepreneurship has however been given a new lease of life by the modern Austrian School, descending from Ludwig Mises and Friedrich Hayek. Thus, a student of Mises, Israel Kirzner, has recently sought once again to persuade his fellow economists that the properties of disequilibrium states deserve as much attention as those of equilibrium states. Disequilibria are due to intertemporal and interspatial differences in demand and supply and hence give rise to unrealised profit opportunities. The essence of entrepreneurship, for Kirzner as much as for Cantillon, consists in the personal alertness to such potential sources of gain. There is a subtle change of emphasis in Kirzner's discussion of entrepreneurship from that of Schumpeter's: Schumpeter always portrayed the entrepreneur-innovator as a disequilibrating force disturbing a previous equilibrium, whereas Kirzner depicts him as seizing upon a disequilibrium situation and working to restore equilibrium. But not too much should be made of this change of emphasis, which is no doubt a reflection of the state of contemporary economic theory in 1912 and 1973: in the days before World War I, economists needed convincing that an achieved state of general equilibrium is the exception and not the rule, whereas nowadays economists need convincing that the process of arriving at general equilibrium has never been satisfactorily explained.

Unfortunately, the new Austrian theory of entrepreneurship reduces entrepreneurship to any kind of arbitrage and in so doing wipes out most of the crucial questions that have been traditionally posed about entrepreneurship. The popular stereotype of the entrepreneur as a swashbuckling business tycoon may take too narrow a view of entrepreneurship but, on the other hand, the Austrian conception of the entrepreneur as anyone who buys cheap and sells dear perhaps errs on the side of being too general. But perhaps we have now said enough to show that the theory of entrepreneurship begins where marginal productivity theory leaves off: there is more to distribution than is dreamed of in the static analysis of factor pricing.

AGGREGATE PRODUCTION FUNCTIONS

What nowadays passes under the label of the 'neoclassical theory of production and distribution' is more an invention of the 20th century than of the 19th. The notion that the functional distribution of income may be explained simply by invoking the principles of marginal productivity as enshrined in an aggregate production function for the economy as a whole was broached for the first time in Hicks' *Theory of Wages* (1932). Until Hicks there was in fact no theory of the shares of wages and profits in total income that commanded universal assent and 19th-century writers like Wicksteed, Wicksell, Walras and Marshall analyzed the problem of factor pricing without appealing to the concept of an *aggregate* production function, making homogeneous output a function of homogeneous capital and labour, much less an aggregate production function of the Cobb-Douglas variety with its unitary elasticity of substitution. So strong has been the hold of Hicksian thinking on recent writings about income distribution that it comes as something of a shock to realize that only J.B. Clark and possibly Böhm-Bawerk among the great 19th-century economists ever operated with a simplistic marginal productivity theory of distribution applied to the economy as a whole, conceived as it were as one giant firm. Thus, the view that the rate of wages and the rate of interest in neoclassical theory are determined by *the* marginal productivities of labour and capital is a vulgar simplification of the ideas of

19th-century economists. Nor is it an adequate characterization of the best ideas of 20th-century economists. Let me explain.

In 1954 Joan Robinson published a famous article in which she produced a now familiar argument against what she called 'neo-classical economics teaching': the stock of capital in an economy cannot be measured without knowing the rate of interest and hence 'the production function' cannot be used to determine the rate of interest as the marginal product of that capital. Robert Solow replied to this charge by admitting that the conditions for meaningful measurement of capital in a production function were so stringent as to make it unlikely that they would be encountered in any but special circumstances. However, he failed to mention the fact that Robinson's unqualified phrase, 'the production function', referred solely to *aggregate* production functions and that the *stock* of capital really had no business to appear as an argument in any production function except as a crude proxy for the *flow* of capital services, measurement of which does not require knowledge of the rate of interest in an economy.

Members of the so-called Cambridge School (Cambridge, U.K.) have gone on ever since equating neoclassical economics with the aggregate-John-Bates-Clark version of marginal productivity theory, virtually ignoring the Walrasian tradition of general equilibrium analysis which neither invokes nor implies *aggregate* production functions, or, for that matter, the existence of the aggregate capital stocks as an economic variable. It can hardly be doubted, however, that the aggregate two-inputs-one-output version of the neoclassical theory of factor pricing has been much in evidence in recent years. Ever since Solow's own seminal work in the late 1950s, estimation of aggregate production functions for purposes of measuring the sources of economic growth and drawing inferences about the nature of technical change has become a widespread practice in economic research. There is also little doubt that this type of empirical work is frequently employed as classroom illustrations of the practical power of apparently abstract theory. Such illustrations may mislead more than they inform: the concept of an aggregate production function is fraught with enormous difficulties and it is not too much to say that empirical work on production functions has come dangerously close on occasion to 'measurement without theory'. This is only to say that the Cambridge School is right but for the wrong reasons. The problems are not those of valuing capital but of achieving consistent aggregation of micro-production functions.

24. The Concept of Micro-Production Functions

Let us spend a moment reexamining the concept of micro-production functions. The traditional approach to the theory of the firm makes the strong assumption that it is always possible to specify a function which expresses the maximum volume of physical output obtainable from all technically feasible combinations of physical inputs, given the prevailing level of technical knowledge about input-output relationships. Notice that the arguments of this function by no means include all the forces that affect output, a well-known point, and that both output and inputs must be measured in flow terms. Notice also that technical knowledge is assumed to be freely available, a point rarely emphasized. It is customary for purposes of exposition to classify the inputs into more or less homogeneous classes which ought to carry the labels 'man-hours' 'machine-hours', and 'acres-per-year', and not of course 'labour', 'capital' and 'land'. On the further convenient assumption that the production function so defined is smoothly differentiable, and the strictly necessary assumption that the firm is profit-maximizing, the theory then proceeds by deriving the input demand functions as inverse forms of the marginal product equations. If factor and product markets are perfectly competitive, firms will hire workers, machines and space until wage rates, machine rentals and land rentals are equal to their respective marginal value or marginal revenue products.

Not a word has yet been said about the rate of interest and deliberately so: the marginal value or marginal revenue product of machines is equated in equilibrium with the money rentals per hour of machines; it cannot be equated to the rate of interest for the simple reason that it is not expressed in the same dimensions as the rate of interest, which is a pure number, being a rate per cent per year. To obtain a theory of interest, we need more flesh on the bones of our simplistic theory of the firm, not to mention a theory of the supply of finance.

To put it somewhat differently, we live in a nonslave economy and therefore the price of workers as distinct from the price of their services is economically irrelevant. But many firms prefer to buy their machines rather than to rent them and we have not yet said anything about machine prices for outright purchase. Since machines like men last a long time, firms will somehow have to discount the future flow of machine services to arrive at a present value of machines for purposes of deciding whether it would be worthwhile to buy rather than to hire them. Facing given machine prices, they will know the cost of purchasing a given number of machines; after estimating the projected future returns from the use of these machines, they can calculate the 'internal rate of return' on the project in question. Facing a going rate of interest in the capital market, they can then decide whether or not to undertake the investment, and whether to finance it by borrowing or by drawing on internal funds. To the profit-maximizing entrepreneur, therefore, the analogue to the real wage bill as the total cost of labour services is the real interest bill as the total cost of machine services.

The price of machines is, of course, determined in market equilibrium in exactly the same manner as the price of a final product produced with the aid of these machines, but what determines the going rate of interest in the capital market? For the moment we need say no more than that it is the total demand for and supply of loanable funds, the demand being made up of loans for purposes of both production and consumption, and the supply being made up of personal savings, business savings, net credit creation and government budgetary deficits [chapter 15, section 7]. If we are talking about the real rather than the money rate of interest, thus ignoring the rate of change of prices, we may collapse our explanation into the shorthand phrase 'the productiveness of industry on the one hand and the thrift of firms and individuals on the other'; this will suffice us for the present. What needs to be emphasized, however, is that the rate of interest is simultaneously determined with the hourly rentals of all machines in the economy, not to mention the hourly wage rates of all types of labour, the yearly rentals of acres of land and of course the prices of all final products.

The determination of the rate of interest is therefore intimately related to the micro-production functions of goods and services but the relationship is not a simple one, and an aggregate demand for loanable funds in an economy in no way presupposes an actual or nominal aggregation of individual production functions. In order for this economy to operate at all, it is unnecessary for anyone to calculate the value of the aggregate stock of capital, just as it is unnecessary for anyone to know the size of the labour force. The famous or rather infamous theorem that the rate of interest is in equilibrium equated to *the* marginal product of capital only applies to one-sector models of the economy, a world in which we steadfastly ignore the heterogeneity of output. In that world, *the* rate of wages is also equated to *the* marginal product of labour, which, for some strange reason, is a proposition that wins assent even if the equivalent proposition about capital is denied. In the real world in which we live, capital like labour is as heterogeneous as output and there is no such thing as *the* marginal product of the total stock of capital in the economy, just as there is no such thing as *the* marginal product of the labour force.

Thus, so long as we stay firmly within the microeconomic tradition of Walrasian general equilibrium theory, we avoid every one of the endlessly reiterated dilemmas of the Cambridge critics: that capital, as a collection of machines rather than a fund of purchasing power, cannot be valued in its own technical units, although apparently labour and land can be so measured; that the valuation of capital presupposes a particular rate of interest, although the interest rate is in fact determined in orthodox theory with the aid of the value of capital; and hence that the so-called 'marginal productivity theory of distribution' cannot actually explain how the rate of interest is determined.

It is quite extraordinary that the notion of measuring 'labour' simply in terms of the number of man-hours is generally accepted as a reasonable assumption, whereas the notion of measuring 'capital' in terms of, say, horsepower or tons of steel is dismissed as nonsense. In other words, all factors of production can somehow be measured in their own technical units but such measurements have no obvious economic meaning. When 'labour' is measured, not in terms of man-hours, but in terms of economically meaningful 'efficiency units', wage weights are required for aggregating labour both within a single firm and across industries, in which case the problem of measuring 'labour' is on all fours with the problem of measuring 'capital'. Fortunately, the aggregation of either labour or capital, even at the level of the firm, is unnecessary for a logically rigorous theory of price determination.

All this does not imply that the concept of a microeconomic production function is unimpeachable. It is on the contrary a very strong assumption and one which should not be swallowed, as it usually is, as if it were a fact of life. The essence of the concept is rigidly to divorce costly factor substitution from costless technical progress, so as to concentrate analytical attention on movements along, as opposed to shifts of, the production function. But suppose that technical progress is dynamically induced by trends in relative factor prices, an idea which has been around for a long time, and suppose in addition that it is frequently embodied in new machines – the so-called 'embodied-investment hypothesis'. In that case, factor substitution becomes increasingly difficult to distinguish from technical progress and the concept of a production function may have to be abandoned as being misleading.

There are further difficulties associated with the idea that the technical knowledge required to specify a production function is freely available to production engineers. If it is costly to explore alternative input combinations, as it surely is, we have to define a meta-production function for the individual firm, which relates maximum output to all possible combinations of inputs, given the gain in output of purchasing more engineering information about these input mixes. If we do this, the production function is no longer defined independently of prices and therefore cannot be used in the traditional manner to derive input demand functions to explain the determination of prices. In other words, we cannot simply include R & D in production functions without undermining the very concept of the production function.

All this is not to say that we should discard production functions altogether in order to reconstruct microeconomics on different foundations, assuming that we knew how to do that, but simply that orthodox price theory is far from being true *a priori*.

25. The Problem of Aggregation
The problems just outlined about micro-production functions are as nothing compared to the difficulties inherent in the concept of an aggregate production function, whether for the economy as a whole, or for leading sectors and industries of the economy. The standard practice since the pioneering work of Cobb and Douglas in the late 1920s has been to regress a multiplicative function of the money value of nonfarm output, suitably deflated, on (1) the size of the labour force, (2) the money value of durable equipment plus inventory holdings, likewise suitably deflated, and (3) a total-factor-productivity term, usually expressed as a function of time, while constraining the unknown exponents of the labour and capital terms to sum to unity. Having estimated the exponents in this way, we can then take advantage of the simple but elegant theorem that the labour exponent of a Cobb-Douglas production function will equal the share of the wages in national income (as explained above). When the estimated exponent in question agrees closely with labour's relative share, which it usually does, we announce triumphantly that the real world apparently does reward factor services in accordance with marginal productivity theory; despite monopolies, taxes, nationalized industries and labour unions, the whole economy works as if all production functions are linearly homogeneous of the Cobb-Douglas variety, the total product being exactly exhausted when all factors are paid their marginal value products.

Actually, such beautiful results raise more questions than they answer. Even if all micro-production functions in the economy are of the Cobb-Douglas form, obeying conditions of constant returns to scale, the aggregate production function of that economy would not necessarily provide a clue either to the rate of wages in different labour markets or to the share of labour in any particular industry, and hence would not necessarily provide a convincing test of the presence or absence of competitive factor pricing in terms of marginal products. A whole class of well-behaved micro-economic production functions, having all the properties economists favour – homogeneity, positive substitutability, positive but less than infinite complementarity between factors, etc. – simply will not aggregate into a well-behaved macro-economic production function. This is easy to demonstrate, although the demonstration involves some elementary mathematical reasoning.

Certain rules for the valid aggregation of utility and production functions were developed in an extensive debate on aggregation in the pages of *Econometrica* in the 1940s. These rules lean heavily on Leontief's so-called 'theorem on separable functions': a twice differentiable function of three variables can be written if and only if the ratio of first derivatives of *MRS* between any two variables is independent of the third. Thus, a valid aggregate production function must be 'additively separable' in labour and machines. This condition is met by a Cobb-Douglas production function when it is expressed in logarithms: the log of the labour term is then added to, and is separable from, the log of the capital term. But even if every micro-function is Cobb-Douglas, being additively separable in log form, the macro-production function cannot arise from arithmetical addition of the micro-functions for the simple reason that the operation of addition cannot be performed logarithmically: adding the logs of natural numbers is like multiplying the numbers themselves. It follows that an aggregate Cobb-Douglas production function cannot be given a straightforward economic interpretation in terms of micro-production functions. Indeed, for an aggregate Cobb-Douglas production function to provide marginal productivity conditions analogous to microeconomic Cobb-Douglas production functions, we must interpret the exponents of the macro-function as weighted geometric rather than arithmetic means of the constituent micro-functions, the weights being proportional to the corresponding exponents of the production function of each firm.[5] It is obvious that if there is a change in the distribution of the individual exponents among firms, the exponents of the aggregate production function must necessarily change. Since we learn nothing about the distribution of exponents among firms from estimating an aggregate production function, it is easy to see that a close match between the labour-exponent of an estimated macro-production function and the observed share of wages in national income is no test whatsoever of the existence of competitive factor pricing in individual labour markets. Since a geometric mean is

---

[5] This aggregation theorem, which is due to L.R. Klein, is almost obvious. In general, if all the micro-functions take the form

$X_1 = N_1^\alpha K_1^\beta$ where $\alpha + \beta = 1$
$X_2 = N_2^a K_2^b$ where $a + b = 1$
$X_n = N_n^A K_n^B$ where $A + B = 1$

and $\alpha = a = A$ and $\beta = b = B$, the exponents being different between the n firms although the marginal products of N and K are everywhere the same, the aggregate production function is $X = (N_1^\alpha K_1^\beta) + (N_2^a K_2^b) + \ldots + (N_n^A K_n^B)$, which is linearly homogeneous but not Cobb-Douglas. Since we cannot add Cobb-Douglas microfunctions arithmetically into a macro-function which is Cobb-Douglas, we had better multiply the micro-function. This gives $X_n = (N_1^\alpha K_1^\beta) (N_2^a K_2^b) \ldots (N_n^A K_n^B)$. Taking the nth root of X, the right-hand side becomes a geometric mean of all the individual micro-functions, thus preserving the multiplicative form of the Cobb-Douglas production function.

relatively insensitive to the addition of extreme values to a series, a situation in which most firms pay labour less than its marginal value product, while a few large ones pay labour more, might well yield a geometric mean of the labour-exponents of individual firms that corresponds very nearly to the relative share of labour in the economy as a whole.

To clinch the argument about the inadmissibility of inferring unobserved micro-production functions from an observed macro-production function, we need only refer to some remarkable recent results by F.M. Fisher. Fisher has shown that the capital of firms can be aggregated if and only if the micro-production functions differ from each other by a 'capital augmenting technical difference', such that different capital goods in different firms can be represented as more or less of the same thing. Even if all firms used exactly the same equipment, however, aggregation problems would arise with respect to labour and output, which are almost as serious as those arising with respect to 'capital': the ratios of labour types and the mix of output within firms would have to remain roughly constant over time. Fisher then delivered the *coup de grâce* to this entire line of thinking by estimating an aggregate Cobb-Douglas production function for a simulated economy in which differences between the techniques employed by different firms are deliberately constructed so as to deny the rule of 'capital augmenting technical differences', in consequence of which meaningful aggregation of the micro-functions is ruled out by definition. Nevertheless, he discovered that an aggregate Cobb-Douglas production function predicts labour's share quite successfully, provided that the share is held roughly constant over the time-period of the simulation exercise. It appears, therefore, that the splendid fits of the aggregate Cobb-Douglas production function, which have always been obtained in the past by applying the method of least squares, are due to the relative constancy of labour's share over considerable stretches of historical time, although the actual mechanism generating output and wages may be quite different from that implied by the existence of microeconomic Cobb-Douglas production functions interacting with factor supplies in competitive markets.

26. Measurement of Capital

It is time to draw the argument to a close. The concept of an economically meaningful aggregate production function requires very strong and highly implausible conditions. If this is what the Cambridge critics have been attacking, one can only applaud their critical acumen. But aggregation of production functions is a problem that is rarely mentioned by members of the Cambridge School. Instead, it is the measurement of capital to which they return again and again. But meaningful aggregation of capital is no more difficult than meaningful aggregation of labour; that is to say, it is just as difficult. Even if capital were physically homogeneous, aggregation of labour and indeed aggregation of output for purposes of estimating aggregate production functions would still require stringent and patently unrealistic conditions at the economy level. The notion propagated by the Cambridge writers that the aggregate version of the neoclassical theory of income distribution would be plain sailing if only capital could be aggregated in physical terms actually flatters the theory more than it deserves.

We have seen reasons to question the view that an estimate of a Cobb-Douglas aggregate production function provides a reliable test of the presence of competitive price imputation. Aggregate production functions, however, are frequently estimated in order to separate and measure the contribution of technical progress to economic growth on the assumption that factor prices are competitively determined, a procedure which takes for granted what for other purposes has to be proved. If we refuse to aggregate in any way, we get the Walrasian general equilibrium theory, which is sterile for empirical research. Some aggregation is necessary for empirical work and the usual device is to utilize equilibrium prices as weights of aggregation, which is to say that the results are not themselves an explanation of prices or a test of any theory of how equilibrium prices are determined except under carefully specified conditions.

One may reject the idea of an aggregate function and remain an adamant neoclassical economist. At any rate, one need not rely on estimates of aggregate production functions to prove that competition works, nor on standard measurements of technical progress without independent evidence that the price weights are competitively determined prices. These are the basic issues and the insistence of the Cambridge critics on the difficulties of measuring the stock of capital without assuming the existence of a predetermined rate of interest is simply a red herring.

TECHNICAL CHANGE AND PROCESS INNOVATIONS

So far in this chapter, it has been assumed that firms move along given production functions in response to changing prices, with the nature of the response depending on the form of the production function. We now introduce technical change, defined graphically as an upward shift in the production function or an inward shift of each and every isoquant towards the origin. The question before us is: What if anything does the marginal productivity theory of distribution tell us about technical change?

The first point to notice is that economic theories of technical change have been confined traditionally to 'innovations' rather than 'inventions': the entrepreneur is viewed as facing a list of known but as yet unexploited inventions from which he may select. How this list is itself drawn up and continuously augmented is an issue that was always handed over to economic historians and industrial sociologists. But an analysis of the rate at which techniques improve in an economy cannot really ignore the pace and scope of inventive activity. Economists, however, have rarely addressed themselves to the analysis of what Kaldor has aptly called 'the degree of technical dynamism' in an economy. Instead, they have been almost exclusively concerned with the actual pattern of technical change in economies that are known to be technically dynamic. Received economic doctrine is not very useful in answering questions like: Is technical change slowing down in advanced economies? Are we about to enter an era of 'automation' that will throw up entirely new problems? Will all the underdeveloped countries in time show the same creative capacity to adopt Western innovations as Japan displayed in the 19th century? The range of questions that it has tried to answer have to do with the factorsaving bias of technical change over time and, hence, the effect of technical progress on relative factor prices and relative factor shares.

Innovations fall into two classes: process innovations and product innovations. The terms are self-explanatory. The distinction is to some extent an artificial one: the introduction of a cost-reducing process is sometimes accompanied by a change in the product mix, while new products frequently require the development of new equipment. In practice the two are usually so interwoven that any distinction between them is arbitrary. Nevertheless, in principle, novel ways of making old goods can be distinguished from old ways of making novelties. Since the index-number problem has so far doomed all theoretical analysis of innovations which alter the quality of final output, the refusal to discriminate between product innovations and process innovations would close the subject of technical progress to further analysis.

A process innovation is defined as any adopted improvement in technique which reduces average costs per unit of output at given input prices. The new technique may involve drastic alterations in equipment but this is not a necessary feature of the definition: the mere reorganization of a plant may be as factorsaving as the introduction of new machines. We have to guard ourselves against a widespread misunderstanding at this point. An innovation represents an addition to existing technical knowledge. Since the production function already takes account of the entire spectrum of known technical possibilities – known, in the sense of being practised somewhere in the system – innovating activity ought to denote the adoption of hitherto untried methods. But few indeed are the successfully adopted innovations which do not have a long history of unsuccessful trials, and even the imitation of previously tried techniques almost always involves a 'creative response'. This difficulty has caused some authors to define technical progress as any change in the production methods of an enterprise, regardless of whether the new method has been tried before. But this compromise blurs the distinction between a movement along and a shift of the production function. In the interest of theoretical clarity, we will adhere for the time being to the traditional definition.

Process innovations as defined above have been under serious discussion for a generation or more, although older contributions go back to Pigou, Schumpeter, Wicksell, Marx and Ricardo. In the 1930s attention was chiefly focused on the problem of classifying innovations into mutually exclusive boxes such as labour-saving, capitalsaving and neutral. Some attempt was made to interpret the history of technical change in terms of these classifications. This aspect of the discussion has come to dominate the stage in the postwar period. Recently, interest has centered on the mechanism which accounts for systematic bias or lack of it in the factorsaving slant of technical change. Nothing like a consensus has yet developed with respect to any of these questions. Indeed, it is fair to say that contemporary economics lacks a systematic theory accounting for the rate and slant of innovations over time, and this failure to provide an explanation of the origin and nature of technical change probably constitutes the most important deficiency in current theorizing on economic growth.

27. Taxonomy

Assuming there are only two factors of production, it seems natural to classify an innovation as laboursaving when it raises, and capitalsaving when it lowers, the capital-labour ratio. The factor-proportions criterion, however, remains ambiguous unless a level of output or a time period is specified. The introduction of an innovation cannot fail to affect a firm's output decision and, unless the firm operates at constant returns to scale, a larger output will in the long run imply a different capital-labour ratio even at constant factor prices. Furthermore, innovations take time to install and the results of newly installed equipment do not accrue immediately: this is the basis of Lange's distinction between the gestation period and the operation period of an innovation. An innovation which is capitalsaving once in operation may nevertheless absorb capital relative to labour during its gestation period of construction. Conversely, an innovation which reduces initial capital costs may ultimately prove to be capital-using if it accelerates the rate of replacement of equipment.

It would seem that the way out of these difficulties is to classify innovations with reference to their effect on the capital-labour ratio utilized in the production of a *given* volume of output. Technical change is represented graphically by a movement toward the origin of an isoquant like I in Figure 11–10a. Since factor prices are given to the individual firm, as depicted by parallel factor-price lines, this leads to a straightforward interpretation of different innovations: I_a is a laboursaving innovation (I_b is a capitalsaving innovation) because the tangency of I_a with the factor-price line occurs at a higher (lower) capital-labour ratio.

The classificatory scheme which has gained the widest adherence is that associated with the works of Hicks and Robinson. Their definition of innovations differs from that just laid down. They define a laboursaving innovation as one which raises the marginal product of capital relative to that of labour *at a given capital-labour ratio* employed in producing a given output, and conversely for a capitalsaving innovation (see Figure 11–11b). Thus, along a ray from the origin denoting a given capital-labour ratio, I_a is a laboursaving innovation (I_b is a capitalsaving innovation) because I_a lowers (raises) the marginal rate of substitution of capital for labour.

On the face of it, the Hicks-Robinson definition does not conflict with our earlier definition: an innovation which is laboursaving at constant factor prices in terms of the capital-labour ratio will certainly be laboursaving at constant factor-proportions in terms of relative marginal products. The earlier definition, however, is applicable to individual firms or industries facing given factor prices, while the Hicks-Robinson definition is geared to the economy as a whole, thus assuming the existence of an aggregate production function. In aggregative analysis we are interested in the effect of innovations on relative factor prices. Changing factor prices induce factor substitution and the Hicks-Robinson definition is designed to distinguish the latter

Figure 11–10

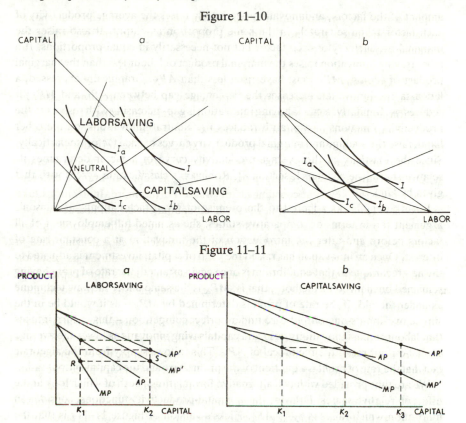

Figure 11–11

from technical change proper. For the economy as a whole, the capital-labour ratio by itself is obviously an inadequate criterion for classifying innovations. An innovation which is laboursaving on the industry level may, if it is widely adopted in other industries, lower wage rates relative to interest rates, thus inducing substitution of labour for capital. The net result may be that the capital-labour ratio in each and every industry is no greater than it was before.

For a given capital-labour ratio, a laboursaving innovation reduces labour's share of total income while a capitalsaving innovation increases it. The ultimate effect on relative shares depends of course on the ease of substitution between capital and labour in response to changing factor prices. With the aid of Hicks's concept of the elasticity of substitution, we can add that, say, a laboursaving innovation will only tend to raise labour's relative share if $\phi > 1$: it will lower the wage rate relative to the interest rate at a given capital-labour ratio but if it increases the scope of factor substitution, it may raise the ratio of labour to capital enough to offset the fall in the relative wage rate.

Joan Robinson both extended and simplified Hicks's argument by showing that ϕ varies with the elasticity of the average productivity of a factor, η. For any given amount of the factors, an innovation necessarily raises the average productivity of each factor taken separately in the same proportion as output. It also raises the marginal productivity of each factor but not necessarily in equal proportions. If a laboursaving innovation raises the marginal product of labour less than the marginal product of capital, MP_N must have risen less than AP_N. Graphically expressed, a laboursaving innovation increases the percentage gap between AP_N and MP_N; it reduces η_N. Similarly, a capitalsaving innovation is gap-increasing with respect to the productivity functions of capital: it reduces η_K. Neutral innovations, on the other hand, raise the average and marginal productivity curves of each factor isoelastically. Since the elasticity of the average-productivity curve of a factor determines its relative share [see chapter 4, section 8], Robinson's classification agrees with that given by Hicks.

But whereas Hicks adhered to the premise of given factor inputs, Robinson's argument ran in terms of comparative statics: she assumed full employment of all factors before and after the introduction of the innovation at a constant rate of interest. Once an innovation has raised the yield of capital, investment is adjusted to the new technique so that equilibrium is once again attained, the rate of profit having remained unchanged throughout; that is, MP_K is the same under the new technique as under the old. If the rate of profit is determined by MP_K – as it would be in the simple two-inputs-one-output case under perfect competition – this in turn implies that laboursaving innovations raise and capitalsaving innovations lower the average capital-output ratio, the reciprocal of AP_K. This follows simply from the algebraic fact that the rate of profit is a quotient of the profit share and the capital-output ratio.

We are thus provided with two alternative formulations, both of which look at the effect on relative shares. Drawing linear capital-productivity functions, consider an innovation which raises AP_K to AP_K'. Hicks's version of Figure 11–11*a* is that the innovation is laboursaving because capital's relative share for K_1 amounts of capital has increased in consequence of the innovation owing to the fact that $\phi < 1$. Robinson's version is that the innovation is laboursaving because the elasticity of AP' at K_2 – determined by the condition $K_1R = K_1S$ – is greater than the elasticity of AP at K_1; since the percentage gap between the two curves had decreased, capital's relative share as well as the capital-output ratio have risen. The argument for capital-saving innovations is, of course, perfectly symmetrical (see Figure 11–11*b* and ignore K_3 for the moment).

The Hicks-Robinson classification came in for considerable criticism. Firstly, it was argued that the scheme breaks down when the underlying production functions do not obey constant returns to scale: it is only for linearly homogeneous production functions that the marginal productivity of a factor is determined solely by the ratios of the factors employed and not by their absolute amounts. We can always apply Hicks's definition to a given amount of the factors but nothing much can be said about the new equilibrium level of inputs without knowledge of the shape of the production function. A backward rising supply curve for labour and imperfect competition further complicate matters. But the fatal objection to Hicks's criterion, and Robinson's extension of it, is that it takes no account of commodity substitution. The effect of an innovation cannot be inferred solely from the physical characteristics of the production function. Capitalsaving innovations, for example, produce commodity substitution toward capital-intensive goods, which fall in relative price as a consequence of the improvement in technique. If final demand for capital-intensive goods is generally more elastic than final demand for labour-intensive goods – a plausible proposition – capitalsaving improvements might well have the ultimate effect of raising capital's relative share despite the fact that $\phi < 1$. Even on an industry level, we emerge with different answers depending upon the elasticity of demand facing the industry adopting the innovation and the ratio of capital to labour in that industry relative to the average for the economy as a whole.

In the light of these objections, Harrod in *Towards a Dynamic Economics* (1948) discarded Hicks's emphasis on given factor proportions and once-over innovations which completely displace the older techniques. He devised a classification explicitly designed to apply to a steady stream of technical improvements: laboursaving technical change raises and capitalsaving technical change lowers the capital coefficient or capital-output ratio, while neutral progress leaves the coefficient undisturbed, all at 'a constant rate of interest'. Harrod's criterion has met with the objection that all technical change, insofar as it prevents MP_K from falling as capital accumulates through time, tends to reduce the average capital-output ratio. The capital coefficient appears to be an index of the rate of innovating activity rather than of its factorsaving bias; a non-increasing capital-output ratio suggests that diminishing returns to capital along given production functions are being adequately offset by innovations. Harrod replied, however, that laboursaving innovations, because they are gap-reducing, are capable of raising MP_K without raising AP_K or lowering the capital-output ratio. A steady stream of laboursaving innovations, therefore, is not likely to produce a perversely falling capital-output ratio. Thus the trend in the capital coefficient can be made to yield rough insights about the direction of technical change.

It remains true, however, that Harrod's definition is rigorous only if the rate of interest ($= MP_K$) stays constant, in which case it is Robinson's definition traveling in disguise. Harrod accepted the test of relative shares but rejected Hicks' and Robinson's comparative static analysis as 'inappropriate'. But if it is indeed inappropriate, keeping the rate of interest constant does not tell us what will actually happen to MP_K. Hence, the capital-coefficient criterion cannot be precise: an innovation which is capitalsaving in terms of relative shares may be laboursaving in the technical-coefficient sense if it fails to prevent a fall in MP_K – see for example K_3 in Figure 11–11b.

For purposes of explaining the history of technical change, the capital coefficient suffers from the same shortcomings as the capital-labour ratio. The capital stock has been growing faster than the labour supply in all developed economies for a century or more. How much of this change in relative factor supplies has been induced by the rate and direction of technical change, and how much has been due to autonomous influences on saving propensities and birth and death rates? If we knew that the impulse to change came from the side of factor supplies, that autonomous forces were raising the ratio of capital to labour, we could infer from the observed long-run stability of the capital-output ratio and from the failure of returns to capital to fall significantly through time that innovating activity had been plentiful and not seriously biased in a laboursaving direction. For if the aggregate production function obeys nonincreasing returns to scale, an increase of capital per man must in the absence of innovations raise capital requirements per unit of output and lower interest rates relative to wage rates. But we have no way of separating autonomous from induced capital formation and we have no direct knowledge of the shape of the aggregate production function. Not knowing which is cause and which is effect, we cannot discriminate between arguments that account for the changes in the capital-labour and capital-output ratios by the character of technical change and those that explain the nature of technical change by the fact that capital for whatever reason grew faster than labour. As soon as we leave the abstract world of given factor proportions, classifications of innovations in terms of capital-labour ratios, capital-output ratios, or relative shares are all equally arbitrary.

28. The Automation Bias in Technical Change

No one has ever been hard pressed to find examples of laboursaving innovations, or to describe in general what we have in mind when we talk about them. Capitalsaving improvements, however, are often said to be difficult to exemplify because they represent exceptions to the general trend of technical change. And, indeed, if we confine ourselves to spectacular inventions it is difficult to find examples other than those usually mentioned such as radio telegraphy, airplanes and explosives for mining. But *any* change in the production function involves technical change. In this sense examples of capital-saving innovations are perfectly easy to come by, and some excellent examples were given by Marx 100 years ago [see chapter 7, section 15]: better quality machines, smaller machines, more durable plants, reductions in delivery times, fuel savings, and so forth. On the face of it, there is no reason to believe that such improvements are any less frequent or pervasive than laboursaving improvements, or that they become important only when an economy is already richly endowed with capital. Some of the crucial innovations of the Industrial Revolution released rather than absorbed capital, and improvements in production layout and in machine design were as important then as now.

Until quite recently, however, the prevailing view among economists was that technological progress has always been dominated by labour-displacing inventions, by a relentless tendency towards total automation of production. The usual rationalization for this viewpoint is that given by Hicks in *The Theory of Wages*. Drawing a distinction between innovations induced by changes in relative factor prices and innovations dependent upon autonomous progress in scientific and technical knowledge, he argued that the more rapid increase of capital relative to labour over the last century had caused induced innovations to be largely laboursaving. Autonomous innovations, however, could be assumed to have been randomly dispersed without bias in either direction. Hence, the two types taken together yielded a preponderance of laboursaving improvements; this, he noted, seemed to be in conformity with observed facts. Apart from the troublesome notion of innovations induced by changes in factor prices – this would seem to involve factor substitution, not technical change – it is clear from the reference to random dispersion that Hicks treated each innovation as having equal weight. But particular innovations differ radically in economic significance. What does the frequency distribution of the *number* of innovations of one kind or another have to do with the factorsaving slant of a continuous stream of improvements? Hicks's entire discussion begs the question whether technical progress has in fact been biased in any economically meaningful sense.

It is difficult nowadays to appreciate how quickly and how recently economists have changed their minds on this question. In 1937 Joan Robinson declared: 'It appears obvious that the development of human methods of production, from the purely hand-to-mouth technique of the ape, has been mainly in the direction of increasing "roundaboutness", and that the discovery of short cuts, such as wireless, are exceptions to the general line of advance'. But in 1956 she concluded: 'There is no reason to expect technical progress to be exactly neutral in any one economy, but equally there is no reason to expect a systematic bias one way or the other'.

The notion of a steady automation bias in technical change derived its appeal from knowledge of the familiar facts of industrial history, strengthened by the tendency to discuss technical progress as if it consisted solely of the introduction of new machines. Since most capitalsaving innovations consist of relatively minor improvements in the utilization of machinery, they tend to escape recognition. Indeed, awareness of the very existence of capitalsaving improvements came late in the history of economic thought. The classical economists realized that timesaving improvements raise the rate of profit by increasing the turnover of money capital, but such ideas were not systematized and economies of fixed capital were never seriously contemplated.

Sidgwick in *The Principles of Political Economy* (1883) seems to have been the first to question the traditional idea that technical change is necessarily capital-using. Taussig in *Wages and Capital* (1896) suggested that the inventions of the future might save capital by 'shortening the period of production' and J.B. Clark, a decade later, made the point that many capital-using innovations do ultimately release capital after their gestation period is over. As Jevons put it: 'The first cost of a steam collier is greater than for sailing colliers of equal tonnage. But then capital invested in the steam vessel is many times as efficient as the sailing vessel'. But none of them doubted that technical change had been overwhelmingly laboursaving in the past. The growing influence of the Austrian theory of capital around the turn of the century, emphasizing as it did capital formation which increases the durability of plant and equipment, further encouraged the belief that economic development, even when technical change is allowed for, typically entails not only an increase in capital per man but also a steady rise in capital requirements per unit of output [chapter 12, section 14].

The break with the concept of the automation bias can be traced to the stagnation thesis of the 1930s: the increasing importance of capitalsaving innovations was said to be one of the factors that contributed to the existence of a chronic deflationary gap in advanced economies. In the 1940s, the empirical finding of the long-run stability of the aggregate capital-output ratio made economists more receptive to the idea of neutral technical change. Neutrality came to be assumed in model building, the earliest and most notable example being Harrod's growth model. Harrod employed a two-sector breakdown of the economy and it is a peculiarity of two-sector models that overall neutral technical progress need not imply neutral innovations in each sector. All technical advance, whatever its factor-saving bias, in the sector making investment goods is capitalsaving inasmuch as it reduces the capital cost of real investment in every sector even at a constant rate of interest. But cheaper machines in turn induce the substitution of capital for labour. In the same way, all technical advance in the consumption goods sector cheapens labour and so encourages the substitution of labour for capital. Hence, overall neutrality for Harrod means either unbiased technical change proceeding at a uniform rate at all 'stages of production', an interpretation that seems to be one favoured by Harrod himself, or else a situation in which technical change in the investment goods sector is just offset by a laboursaving bias in the consumption goods sector, leaving the average capital-output ratio constant at an unchanged rate of interest.

Whatever interpretation we accept, it remains that the trend in the aggregate capital-output ratio, even when calculated at a constant rate of interest, furnishes only presumptive evidence of neutrality. Leaving aside the consideration that only strongly biased technical change will show up clearly, the aggregate capital-output ratio is influenced not only by the direction of technical change but also by saving propensities, interindustry shifts in investment, expectations about the future rate of technical advance, and the cumulative influence of the rate of growth of output. Moreover, the denominator of the ratio includes the end-product of spending on education, health and training, while the numerator refers solely to nonhuman capital. It is always possible to argue that technical change has shown no tendency toward 'capital deepening' because of the rise in the ratio of human to nonhuman capital over the last century. The fact that capital has grown faster than labour may itself be a statistical illusion, the result of measuring labour in man hours instead of efficiency units. Furthermore, it is not at all clear how capital is to be measured for purposes of verifying the neutrality hypothesis. And what is still more serious is that there appears to be no agreement as to whether the average capital-output ratio has exhibited surprising stability for long periods of time, while others declare that the ratio has shown considerable variability considering the forces that act on it in both directions.

The argument for neutrality gains something when facts about the capital coeficient are combined with other empirical findings. The sharp rise that has been witnessed in the capital-labour ratio should have led, in the absence of innovations, to a falling yield on capital as well as a falling share of profits in total income. In the last 100 years the rate of technical change has in fact been very high, judged by the upward trend in the average productivity of labour. Yet the rate of return on capital in the U.K. and the U.S.A. has shown only a mild downward trend. This suggests that innovations, however plentiful, were not sufficiently laboursaving. The shift in the distribution of income from property to labour that took place over the same period likewise suggests that technical progress was not strongly biased in a laboursaving direction. A somewhat stronger version of this impressionistic argument relies upon the Hicksian proposition that the elasticity of substitution between machinery and labour must eventually fall below unity in an economy where the capital stock is always growing faster than the labour supply; without innovations, the fact that $\phi < 1$ implies that the profit rate and the profit share will fall as the capital-labour ratio increases. Economic growth in the advanced economies has, therefore, depended upon sufficient laboursaving technical change to prevent the chronic excess of saving over investment that would be produced by the falling yield on capital. In the light of the Great Depression of the 1930s, it would seem that technology has not been sufficiently laboursaving; neutral technical change or even a mild capitalsaving bias in the last three or four decades best accounts for the course of events.

If the data are compatible with the assumption of neutral but also with that of somewhat biased technical change, why the eagerness to uphold neutrality? In good part, no doubt, for model-building conveniences but also because the idea of a persistent bias in the stream of innovations is itself difficult to swallow. It supposes the absence of any market mechanism that would counteract the bias. The standard view, however, best represented by Schumpeter's *Theory of Economic Development*, is that there is indeed no reason to believe that technical change is directly responsive to market pressures. The proof of this assertion is tautological: any market mechanism involves reactions to changing prices and technical change is defined as consisting of cost-reducing improvements at constant factor prices; by definition, a market response is excluded. The traditional attitude, however, has recently been challenged.

29. The Inducement Mechanism

An individual firm under perfect competition, facing given wage and interest rates over which it has no control, is not concerned with the factorsaving character of improvements. Its aim is to reduce total costs irrespective of whether the saving is made in the operating costs of labour or in the total cost of capital, provided they are of equal magnitude. However, the activities of all producers taken together may not be consonant with relative factor scarcities in the economy, with the result that future factor prices diverge from current ones. But no individual firm can take account of these macroeconomic repercussions. Hence, the competitive market seems to provide no signals to induce appropriate factorsaving innovations.

Given the orthodox view of the competitive firm, therefore, something like the relative constancy of the aggregate capital coefficient can only be explained in terms of a technically determined 'life-cycle' of capital-output ratios: major changes in productive technique are laboursaving and capital-using but these occur only sporadically in most countries; once the new methods are in use, routine day-to-day modifications raise the capacity of equipment without additional expenditures; as a consequence, the capital-output ratio tends after a time to return to its technically determined normal level; since spurts of investment do not occur simultaneously in all industries, the net effect is to maintain a roughly constant trend in the aggregate capital coefficient.

In opposition to this viewpoint, W.J. Fellner in *Trends and Cycles in Economic Activity* (1956) has reasserted Hicks's concept of induced innovations, notwithstanding the textbook theory of the competitive firm. The argument runs as follows. Firstly, strong biased technical change even under perfect competition creates conditions akin to monopsony in factor markets and a monopsonist is made directly aware of relative factor scarcities in the economy by the gap between average and marginal factor costs. For example, persistent 'over-shooting' in the laboursaving direction is bound in the short run to raise annual capital costs per unit of real investment and in the long run to reduce the elasticity of the supply of capital to a firm to below infinity; some form of capital rationing is instituted and firms are now induced to find capitalsaving improvements. On the other hand 'overshooting' in the capitalsaving direction leads to tightness in the labour market reflected in 'wage drift'; once again, a situation of quasi-monopsony provides incentives to introduce laboursaving innovations. Secondly, although producers may face perfectly elastic supply curves in all factor markets, they become conditioned by experience to avoid disappointment by choosing improvements which save the relatively scarcer factor. Even a perfectly competitive firm 'learns' to adapt itself to a persistent and hence discernible trend in the shifting of factor-supply curves. In this way, sharp cumulative changes in factor rewards, relative shares and the capital coefficient are offset by appropriately slanted technical change.

In effect, Fellner's two arguments come to the same thing: because of a 'learning process', firms behave *as if* they were monopsonists. The idea that firms learn from experience may strike one as alien to the static theory of competitive price. But in fact, the competitive firm cannot rationally decide upon a particular level of output without some estimate of future product and factor prices. To determine the profitability of investment, firms must obtain information which permits them to form expectations of future sales and prices. Thus, the competitive firm is by necessity forward looking and driven to adjust behavior in the light of expected events. But even if individual firms lack foresight and act simply on the expectation that prices will remain unchanged, a Darwinian selection process will produce an automatic adjustment mechanism. Firms which persist in adopting capitalsaving devices when wage rates are rising and interest rates falling will not prove viable. The successful innovator, alert to the signals transmitted by the price system, will be saving labour and absorbing capital, and the economist looking on will find the system as a whole adapting technical change to relative factor scarcities.

The theory of market-induced innovations is not required to explain why every individual firm adopts certain inventions rather than others. There is almost always a large gap between the average and the best-practice technique in an industry because machines are not scrapped until their operating costs equal the total cost including capital charges of a new machine. The delay in the adoption of the best-practice technique is itself conditioned by relative factor prices: when real investment is cheap relative to labour, standards of obsolescence are stringent and the spread between the best and the average-practice technique is narrow. A fall in the interest rate or equipment prices lowers the capital costs of adopting the best-practice techniques; both tend to induce scrapping of old machines. On the other hand, when real investment is dear relative to labour, the capital structure of an industry consists largely of outmoded equipment. Thus, as soon as one firm in an industry has established the best-practice technique by introducing an innovation, the problem of the speed with which the new technique is diffused throughout the industry falls outside the domain of the theory of technical change.

Whatever the validity of the theory of market-induced innovations, it is subject to important qualifications. There is, first of all, the problem of indivisibilities of capital in certain industries, restricting the scope of adjustments to relative factor prices. Then there is the fact that improvements which save working capital are frequently the result of external economies generated by the growth of social overhead facilities, which accrue to firms independently of their own actions and in no direct relationship to relative factor scarcities in the economy. Next, there is considerable evidence that inventive activity, as distinct from innovative activity, is itself responsive to perceived profit opportunities but this does not imply that inventions nowadays can be simply 'manufactured' in research laboratories to suit economic needs. Although we have no reason to believe that the available pool of inventions is itself systematically biased, this is a possibility which should not be overlooked. On the other hand, the presence of monopoly may not prove to be as serious an objection to the thesis as appears at first glance. No clear picture has emerged of the relationship between market structure and innovations; the rate of growth of firms as related to their age seems to be a more important influence than size or power to set the price. Lastly, there is the possibility that wage-price rigidities will permit 'overshooting' in the short run. And if overshooting of a capitalsaving type occurs in an economy in which capital is already the relatively abundant factor, the resulting fall in the yield of capital may lead to Keynesian 'unemployment equilibrium'. Instead of increasing labour scarcity inducing corrective laboursaving technical change, there is an excess supply of labour encouraging further 'overshooting'. Thus, the presence of a deflationary gap can put the adjustment mechanism out of commission. On the other hand, market-induced innovation is one of the forces preventing Keynesian unemployment. Without flexible wages and prices, however, it is powerless to act.

It is evident from casual impression that industrialized countries have not suffered over the last 100 years from excessively biased technical change. If technical progress is not something that happens wholly by chance, this suggests that some kind of adjustment mechanism has been at work. But proof by way of *post hoc, ergo propter hoc* is inherently unsatisfactory. The theory of market-induced innovations, however, could be verified directly. Unfortunately, most of the available empirical material on technical change is useless for this purpose: it has not been gathered systematically to test any hypothesis and is rarely available in a suitably disaggregated form. What we need to test the notion of the 'learning firm' is to make detailed case studies of innovating activity in particular industries. Until then we shall not be able to choose decisively between the concept of a technically determined 'life-cycle of capital-output ratios' and the theory of market-induced innovations.

30. The Neglect of Technical Change

The *rate* of technical advance influences the *direction* of technical change via changing standards of obsolescence. In this way, the flow of *inventions* plays a role in determining the pattern of *innovations*. New machines represent *product innovations* for the machine goods industries but *process innovations* for the consumer goods industries. *Technical change* by producing cheaper machines or cheaper workers generates its own pressures to bring about *factor substitution*. None of these watertight distinctions is realistic. Nevertheless, all fruitful theoretical analysis of changing technology has to this date proceeded upon the basis of these distinctions. The neoclassical conception of technical change as involving shifts in the production function is full of difficulties, and the very notion of a production function as something that is purely technically determined, showing no traces of the influence of factor prices, tends to break down once we accept the idea that current output decisions are influenced by expectations of the future. The case for the neoclassical approach is that it provides a meaningful framework for organizing our knowledge of technical progress and, to provide a more decisive consideration, that we have nothing else that is really convincing to put in its place.

Judging from recent economic studies, the real-world importance of technical change in contrast to factor substitution is the inverse of the attention their respective analysis now receives in economic textbooks. It is for this reason that we have taken so much space to consider the theory of technical change. On the whole, the results to date are not very impressive: in the presence of technical change, the marginal productivity theory of distribution hardly warrants the title of theory, consisting for the most part of boxes into which evidence can be put with little assurance that another box would not do equally well. The simple explanation of this theoretical lacuna is that technical change is a very difficult problem. But difficult or not, decades of neglect of the problem have left economists ill-prepared to deal with it.

31. Marginal Productivity Once Again

We have by now collected an extensive list of the shortcomings of marginal productivity theory: it is static, it is of little practical use in production problems, it neglects the supply side in factor markets, it cannot be applied to factor markets as a whole because of the interdependence of demand and supply, it sheds no direct light on the problem of relative shares because the conditions for valid aggregation of micro-production functions are rarely encountered, and it fails to integrate the phenomenon of technical change. Nevertheless, in the eyes of most economists, contemporary distribution theory is marginal productivity theory properly qualified to make allowances for these objections. And, of course, so long as no satisfactory alternative theory is in sight, it will remain secure from attack.

A *simpliste* marginal productivity theory of distribution explains the rate of wages and the rate of interest or profit simply by technology and consumer's preferences, factor supplies being taken as given. Hence, the theory has few practical implications. Radical critics are quite right to argue that it relegates to 'sociology' such forces as unions, the corporate power structure, the monetary system, the state of aggregate demand and government policies toward incomes and prices, all of which seem to be very relevant to problems of income distribution. Even here there is a confusion of language because by a 'theory of distribution' the critics mean a theory of distributive shares, whereas in the neoclassical tradition, the theory of income distribution is a theory of factor pricing. Even so, there is nothing in the so-called 'marginal productivity theory of distribution' that would deny that the 'class struggle' has a lot to do with the determination of distributive shares, or even with the rate of wages and profit.

Actually, the great mystery of the modern theory of distribution is why anyone regards the *share* of wages and profits in total income as an interesting problem. It has, after all, little practical relevance. The standard of living of workers is reflected in the real wage rate and the relative position of workers is better measured by the ratio of the average wage per worker to the average income per head of the population than by labour's relative share. Labour's share actually rose in the first half of the 1930s during a period when unemployment worsened; it fell in the late 1930 but even in 1939 was much worse than in 1920. Moreover, depending on how we allocate the income of the self-employed between wages and profits, we can make the figures on shares come out almost as we like. It makes an enormous difference whether we define labour's share as (1) wages and salaries over national income, or (2) wages and salaries minus the wage bill in the public sector over national income minus the public sector wage bill, or (3) wages and salaries plus the *pro rata* wage share of the income of the self-employed over national income. The universal view before World War II that labour's share has long been constant in advanced countries has now been replaced by the view that the trend in labour's share has been steadily upward ever since 1900. Besides, from the point of view of profit receivers, there is clearly no simple relationship between the profit share and the after-tax rate of return on capital, which is presumably what investors care about. As for collective bargaining, it is conducted in terms of the money wage rate, or at any rate money earnings, working conditions, grievance procedure, etc., and rarely in terms of the share of net sales going to labour rather than management.

Nor is it self-evident that the distributive shares are an interesting theoretical problem. It is of course definitionally true that labour's relative share of total income is equal to the average rate of wages and salaries divided by the average product of labour in the entire economy. Likewise, the profit share is by definition equal to the average rate of profit on capital invested either divided by the average product of capital or multiplied by the capital-output ratio. But the 'average product of labour' or the 'capital-output ratio' are not behavioral entities in standard theory: economic agents do not maximize or minimize them; no producers or consumers, no workers or capitalists respond to them; they are just *ex post* magnitudes that can be measured but which nevertheless have no theoretical status. It is perfectly possible, therefore, to have a theory of wages or a theory of the rate of profit without having a theory of the share of wages and profits, and vice versa. The fact of the matter is that distributive shares are the outcome of a wide variety of forces and any theory which attempts to tackle the problem finds itself making so many heroic, simplifying assumptions that the results are simply *curiosa*.

If we stick to the general equilibrium theory of functional income distribution, however, we are unlikely to come up with answers which will shake the world. In general equilibrium theory, the functional distribution of income may be said to be 'determined' by the initial distribution of resources among households, the preferences of households, the production function of firms and the behavioral assumptions of economic agents, such as utility and profit maximization. But the theory does not 'explain' the functional distribution of incomes. In short, the neoclassical theory of functional income distribution, call it the marginal productivity theory or what you will, is a much more modest theory than many of its enemies would have us believe.

READER'S GUIDE TO THE 'COMMON SENSE OF POLITICAL ECONOMY'

'Never was a work of this kind more unfortunately named', writes Robbins in his introduction to the 1932 reprint of Wicksteed's *Common Sense of Political Economy* (1910). 'It is not "common sense" in the ordinary sense of the term, and it is not *political* economy. It is, on the contrary, the most exhaustive non-mathematical exposition of the technical and philosophical complications of the so-called *marginal* theory of pure Economics, which has appeared in any language'.

Wicksteed's brief introduction to the book is a lucid summary of all its salient features: (1) the equimarginal principle of resource administration as the master theme of economic theory; (2) the attack upon the concept of the Economic Man as an unnecessary vestige of older analysis; (3) the rigorous demonstration that Ricardo's residual rent theory is a marginal productivity theory when properly stated; (4) the idea of the supply curve as a reverse demand curve; (5) the attempt to revise the doctrine of the laws of return; and (6) the constant reminder, in opposition to Marshall, of the revolutionary character of marginal utility economics and its decisive break with the classical mode of economic reasoning.

32. Consumer Behavior

The first chapter of *Common Sense* discusses the economics of household behavior, introducing the notion of a 'scale of preferences', or as we would say, a generalized utility function, after disposing of the objection that 'a great part of our conduct is impulsive and a great part unreflecting' (pages 28–33). Wicksteed does not claim that transitivity, or 'the consistency postulate', is always satisfied but argues that it is legitimate to assume transitivity (pages 33–4; also pages 122–4). It must be said that he dismisses this question too easily. This is followed by a long chapter that provides an exhaustive explanation of the meaning of Gossen's second law: satisfaction is maximized when resources are so distributed among different uses as to secure equal want satisfactions in all uses. Few writers have ever taken such pains to explain to the nonmathematical reader why marginal significance can be expressed in terms of either increments or decrements, and why discontinuities and indivisibilities do not constitute decisive obstacles to marginal analysis. The law of 'diminishing psychic returns' is carefully expounded to avoid the misconception that the marginal utility of a good must decline monotonically throughout the whole range of consumption (pages 82–3; see also pages 435–8). Wicksteed reminds us of the necessity of assuming constant tastes (pages 84–6; see also pages 491–2) but his illustrations of the workings of the law, charming as they are – see the parable of 'the indolent young man' and the case of Caesar 'that day he overcame the Nervii' (pages 78–9) – tend to degenerate into 'dinner-table demonstrations'. Notice the mention of backward-bending labour supply curves (page 77) and the Jevonsian emphasis upon prospective costs (pages 88–9).

Chapter 3 is concerned with indivisible durable goods whose services accrue over a period of time, making it impossible to 'keep margins trimmed'. The notion of positive time preference, as distinct from irrational underestimation of the future, is skilfully woven into the discussion (pages 112–4). Interdependence between the individual utility functions – Veblenesque Effects – are briefly considered (pages 115–16). By the time we have reached the end of chapter 3, every possible objection that critics have raised against the concept of the rational calculating consumer has in one way or another been touched upon. Yet Wicksteed never raises the basic methodological question: what is the appropriate level of abstraction in the analysis of consumer behavior? Why assume that the individual can in principle bring about 'the ideal coincidence between marginal significances and market prices' when this is admittedly an unrealistic assumption?

In **chapter 4** we make 'the momentous transition from personal to communal economies' and begin to study 'the forces which regulate the terms on which alternatives are offered'. Isolated exchange may not yield a determinate equilibrium (pages 141–3) but 'in an exchanging community ... there is a perpetual tendency to establish an equilibrium', such that 'the relative marginal estimates formed by all the individuals, of all the exchangeable commodities of which they severally possess a store, are identical' (page 143). This does not mean that aggregate welfare is maximized in equilibrium for 'there is no theoretical means of constituting a comparison between the sensations and experiences of two different minds' (pages 145–50; see also page 170). The reader should now turn to **Book II, chapters 1–4,** which show how to construct curves of total and marginal utility as well as individual and market demand curves. The treatment of consumer's surplus is excellent and avoids most of the pitfalls in the concept: the marginal utility of money must be approximately constant, the individual surpluses are not additive because each marginal utility curve is drawn up on the basis of other things being equal, and consumers' surplus has no meaning whatever because 'communal curves of price-and-quantity saleable cannot be interpreted psychically, though they rest on a psychic basis' (pages 467–90). Wicksteed stresses the ubiquity of commodity interdependence (pages 478–9); inferior goods are briefly discussed in the appendix to chapters 2 and 3 (pages 490–1).

33. The Content of the Maximand
Turning back to **Book I, chapter 5,** we find a detailed analysis of the concept of *homo oeconomicus.* In a famous passage, Wicksteed poses the conflict between the introspective and behaviorist approach to economics: 'We may either ignore motives altogether, or may recognise all motives that are at work, but in no case may we pick and choose between the motives we will and the motives we will not recognise as affecting economic conditions' (page 165). 'Economic forces and relations', he points out, 'have no inherent tendency to redress social wrongs or ally themselves with any ideal system of redistributive justice' (page 169). Vulgar harmony doctrine is dismissed with great force and eloquence (pages 189–92) and the whole of this chapter, in its insistence on the impossibility of isolating 'economic motives' and its emphasis on the means-end-character of rational action, reads nowadays as an introduction to Robbins' *Nature and Significance of Economic Science* (1932).

34. Price Formation
After this digression we return to the problem of price formation in **chapter 6.** The individual scales of preferences have been summoned to yield collective scales, market demand curves in fact. Given the stock of goods in the market, the price depends on the market demand curve, which registers not only the intentions of buyers but also those of sellers at their 'reserve prices' (pages 229–34). Notice the brief discussion of the problem first analyzed by Walras: final equilibrium in a market is not independent of the path that the market takes toward the equilibrium point (pages 226–7). The chapter closes with an interesting description of the whole range of possible markets from the oriental bazaar dependent upon bilateral bargaining, to competitive retail trade at quoted prices to monopolized markets (pages 248–61).

35. Supply as Reverse Demand
We must pause here and examine Wicksteed's concept of 'reserve prices'. The prospective sellers have a reservation price below which they have an own-demand for the good being traded. Thus, the demand curve in the market shows the monetary evaluation of marginal satisfactions that will be derived from various quantities of a stock of goods by *everyone* in the market. In a moment of enthusiasm, Wicksteed even went so far as to deny the existence of supply curves: 'what about the "supply curve" that usually figures as a determinant of price, co-ordinate with the demand curve? I say it boldly and baldly: There is no such thing'. But then he adds that 'what is usually called the supply curve is in reality the demand curve of those who possess the commodity' (page 785; see also 506–7, 516, 823–4).

Wicksteed's argument is perfectly straightforward if we think of supply as a rate sold in the market out of a given stock *OR* by 'producers' who are themselves

Figure 11–12

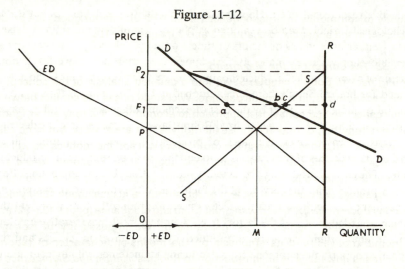

'consumers' of the particular product. We are in a Marshallian market period, except that the buyers and sellers are not well-defined separate groups of individuals. Wicksteed assumes that sellers have an own-demand for their product if prices fall below the reservation price p_2 (see Figure 11–12). A Marshallian supply curve SS could now be built up out of the quantities sellers want to dispose of at each price. But Wicksteed suggests instead that we add to the buyers' demand curve the own-demand of sellers: this is always the vertical difference between the total stock OR and the quantity offered by sellers along a Marshallian supply curve. At the price p_1, for example, we add $cd = ab$ to the buyers' demand curve, we obtain the total market demand curve DD, intersecting RR at p, OM being sold to buyers and MR retained by sellers. Whether we draw a supply curve or not, the equilibrium price is therefore one where new demand plus reservation demand is equal to the total stock available. Notice also that Wicksteed's total demand curve is identical to the excess demand curve ED centered on the price axis.

36. The Doctrine of Alternative Costs
Since Wicksteed's construction yields the same price and quantity as that of Marshall's, we may wonder why Wicksteed was so insistent on the notion of 'supply as reverse demand'. It is true that reversibility of supply curves is an everyday occurrence in markets where dealers sell out of stock. But in most consumer markets, producers do not themselves consume what they produce and the product in question does not change hands more than once. For agricultural commodity markets, the stock exchange and the money market, the Wicksteed construction can be clarifying. But in most markets of continuous production for a well-defined group of consumers, the Marshallian cross is more useful and less likely to be misunderstood. The source of Wicksteed's vehemence about reversible supply curves lies in the central Austrian assumption that he made his own, namely, that the supply of all

productive resources is fixed. He wanted to show that, as Robbins has put it, '*all* psychological variables can be exhibited as phenomena of demand acting on fixed stocks – either of products or factors or time – or human capacity'. The concept of reversible supply curves made its first appearance in Böhm-Bawerk's famous example of a horse market in which the suppliers are themselves farmers who have a demand for horses. Supply here is conditioned not by the 'real cost' of calling a commodity into existence but by the cost of excluding other uses, including that of the supplier himself. Wieser generalized Böhm-Bawerk's example into the doctrine of alternative costs: given the stock of productive agents, competition will so distribute the services of these agents as to equalize their marginal value product in all uses. The costs of producing a commodity reflect nothing but the competing offers of other producers for the services of the factors used to produce it; they represent the payments needed to attract the factors used to produce it; they represent the payments needed to attract the factors from their next most remunerative employment. In equilibrium, the marginal productivity of resources in all uses and the alternative opportunities forgone from producing an increment of any commodity will be equalized. Thus, as Wicksteed liked to say, cost of production is simply and solely 'the marginal significance of something else'.

The importance of the alternative cost doctrine to those who espoused it was that it demonstrated the fallacy of all 'real cost' theories of value. The Austrians spoke with disdain of Marshall's two-sided theory, in which supply prices call forth the services of productive agents by overcoming physical limitations and subjective resistance, as a concession to classical economics. Alternative cost theory made both demand and supply dependent upon utility by tracing all costs back to utilities forgone. 'The only sense, then, in which cost of production can affect the value of one thing', Wicksteed remarked, 'is the sense in which it is itself the value of another thing. Thus, what has been variously termed "utility", "ophelimity", or "desiredness", is the sole and ultimate determinant of all exchange values' (page 391). And again, after showing how the pricing of a fixed stock can be analyzed without drawing a supply curve, he generalized the argument to the case of continuous production: 'cost of production is merely the form in which the desiredness a thing possesses for some one else presents itself to me. When we take the collective curve of demand for any factor of production we see again that it is entirely composed of demands, and my adjustment of my own demands to the conditions imposed by the demands of others is of exactly the same nature whether I am buying cabbages or factors for the production of steel plates . . . It is not until we have perfectly grasped the truth that costs of production of one thing are nothing whatever but an *alias* of efficiencies in production of other things that we shall be finally emancipated from the ancient fallacy [of real costs] we have so often thrust out at the door, while always having the window open for its return' (page 788). Significantly enough, he added a footnote in which he conceded that 'as we recede from the market and deal with long periods . . . cases may arise in which something like a "supply curve" seems legitimate. The terms on which nature yields increasing supplies of some raw material, for instance, cannot be legitimately regarded as the reserve prices in which she expresses her own demand!'

37. Alternative Costs and Factor Prices

Before resolving this conflict between the Austrian and Marshallian approach, let us see how Wicksteed actually applies the doctrine of alternative cost to the earnings of productive agents. In chapter 7 he presents the capital market as 'the market in advances' in which present income is exchanged against future income; the rate of interest expresses the terms on which these alternatives are available to individuals. The rate of interest is positive because claims against future income will somehow exceed claims against present income; an incisive discussion of the *raison d'être* of consumption loans (pages 268–80) is followed by an eclectic and far-ranging discussion of the 'grounds for interest' (pages 280–310; see also pages 748–53). It is strongly suggested that saving is not a function of the rate of interest, certainly not in the long run (pages 294–8).

Similarly, it cannot be assumed that labour is supplied according to the principles of rational cost accounting, that is, according to the discounted value of the prospective returns net of construction and maintenance charges – recall Marshall's similar remarks [see chapter 10, section 32]: 'The production of undifferentiated human capacity . . . must in the main be regarded as "consumption" technically, not production . . . The whole question of the ultimate supply of human effort, therefore, carries us far beyond the limits of economic inquiry' (pages 336–7). For nonhuman resources, there is a constant tendency for allocation at equilibrium to produce an equalization of the marginal significance of all uses of each resource. As applied to labour, Wicksteed admits, this doctrine has certain limitations. Owing to the division of labour, the reserve price of labour is effectively zero in the short run (page 324). Moreover, labour is notoriously immobile between occupations and labour training is frequently more influenced by the financial status of parents than by prospective rates of reward (pages 332–6). Nevertheless, every worker substitutes leisure for wage income at the margin and 'remuneration for human effort, so far as it is determined by economic forces, follows the law of the market, just as the price of commodities does' (page 338). Presumably, this means that labour will be supplied at a given wage rate so as to equate the marginal rate of substitution between leisure and effort to the wage rate (see pages 522–6), while at the same time the supply so forthcoming will be allocated between occupations so as to equalize the marginal cost of one commodity in terms of any other.

But the limitations of alternative cost theory when applied to labour go further than Wicksteed seemed to realize. As Adam Smith had shown, competition tends to equalize, not the monetary returns, but the 'net advantages' of different occupations to individuals. And if differences in the psychic costs of two occupations result in differences in total earnings of homogeneous units of labour, then the cost of labour to one industry is not equal to the alternative product that labour could have produced in another industry. What this means is that 'real costs' in the form of the relative irksomeness of different occupations do have an effect on the allocation of human resources between competing lines of production. The problem goes even deeper than that. In order for the market to equalize alternative costs, however interpreted, the resource in question must be capable of variation at the margin. But labour cannot, as a rule, sell its services in varying proportions to different buyers: the choice between different occupations is essentially an either-or decision. The worker's decision to enter an occupation is not a marginal choice and for that reason there seems to be a fundamental nonparallelism between the allocation of human and nonhuman resources.

The conflict between alternative cost theory and real cost theory can be formally resolved by treating leisure and 'agreeableness of work' as displaced goods. Either we say that the optimum distribution of labour services between different industries and occupations is one which equates differences in the marginal value product of the services to differences in the marginal disutility of labour, or we say that it is one which equalizes opportunity costs, interpreted as including the nonpecuniary returns attached to producing a given product. The choice of an occupation with a smaller money income and a lower disutility must now be regarded as the worker's joint purchase of leisure and agreeableness. Thus, differences in monetary returns to units of homogeneous labour represent prices paid by workers for different conditions of work. By this verbal sleight-of-hand we can rescue the proposition that equilibrium prices will be equal to opportunity costs. Nevertheless, the fact remains that unless workers are indifferent among occupations and unless the factors of production are perfectly inelastic in supply, the production-possibility curve defining all optimum feasible outputs from a given amount of productive factors is not uniquely defined. We may *say* that equilibrium prices will be equal to the slope of the production-possibility curve but we cannot draw a unique production-transformation curve on the basis of a given amount of labour, capital and land.

Alternative cost theory has the advantage, by its very terminology, of focusing attention on the question of static allocative efficiency., But ignoring short-period variations in the supply of effort leaves us with a range of indeterminacy. One may quarrel about the empirical significance of this range – most of the arguments between Marshall and Edgeworth, on the one hand, and Wieser and Böhm-Bawerk, on the other, over Jevons' theory of the disutility of labour took this form [see chapter 8, section II] – but it cannot be denied that it exists. Real cost theory emphasizes the variability of factor supplies even in the short run and goes beyond alternative cost theory by remaining in touch with the problem of dynamic allocative efficiency involving the growth of population and the accumulation of capital.

38. Distribution

Wicksteed rejects not only the classical triad but any attempt definitively to enumerate the factors of production: 'We know already that the same principle determines the claims of them all so that the division, could we accomplish it, would have no theoretic importance' (page 367). Every factor receives a share determined by its marginal product, including the entrepreneur who is regarded as a separate quantifiable factor (pages 367–72). He renounces the notion of product exhaustion via marginal productivity payments (page 373n) but does not in fact abandon the idea. 'Within limits, the most apparently unlike of these factors of production can be substituted for each other at the margins, and so brought to a common measure of marginal serviceableness-in-production' (page 361; also pages 779, 789); given complete substitutability between the factors, no distributive share can really be a residual (see page 792). Interestingly enough, Wicksteed is perfectly aware of the fact that the entrepreneur is really engaged in 'a series of speculative transactions based on estimates made in advance'. He comes very close to saying that the presence of uncertainty creates the possibility of 'profit' from a divergence between anticipated and realized marginal products (pages 372–3; also page 798).

39. The Laws of Return

We pass on to **Book II, chapter 5,** dealing with the laws of return. In contrast to Marshall, Wicksteed draws a clear distinction at the outset between diminishing returns from increments of one productive agent and diminishing returns from increases in the scale of the plant (pages 527–8). The law of diminishing returns in the former sense is said to be 'an axiomatic statement of a universal principle'. But this is only strictly true if the production function is linearly homogeneous, which Wicksteed denies to be the general case (pages 529, 534). The classical generalization that diminishing returns apply to agriculture, while increasing returns apply to manufacturing, is soundly condemned (page 533). Nevertheless, 'whether in agriculture or manufactures, it seems to be a fairly general rule that when an increased demand causes an increased production that presses against the existing limits, at first cost of production will rise, but ultimately it will fall' (page 534). Part of the confusion in Wicksteed's treatment of the laws of return is that he does not appear to regard increasing returns as an instance of economies of scale to a *firm*. When he draws a downward-sloping supply curve, it is the *LRAC* curve of an *industry* (page 353). Thus, he concludes that all reversible short-run and long-run industry supply curves are upward sloping but that historical cost curves fall to the right (pages 537–9). This may explain his failure to see the incompatibility of increasing returns to scale with perfect competition (pages 529–30). At any rate, though this chapter marks a great advance on Marshall's discussion of the laws of return, it is far from dealing adequately with the subject. Twenty years were to pass before the problem of decreasing-cost industries was satisfactorily resolved by Viner and others.

Wicksteed's refutation of the theory that 'rent does not enter into cost' fails to point out that the Ricardian assumption of a fixed amount of land does imply that rent is not a cost from a social point of view (pages 540–2). It is odd that Wicksteed, believing as he did in land nationalization (see pages 686–90), should fail to discuss the social implications of relative fixity in the supply of land. Here as elsewhere in the *Common Sense*, however, he reiterates his belief that land is not ultimately limited in quantity, even in Great Britain (pages 365, 533). The chapter closes with an attempt to contribute to 'the gaiety of nations' by vanquishing the Malthusian specter of imminent diminishing returns to further increases in the labour supply (pages 546–9).

40. The Law of Rent

Chapter 6 is the most deservedly famous chapter in the whole book. With characteristic thoroughness, Wicksteed demonstrates that rent determined as the mixtilinear area under the marginal product curve of labour and capital is identical to rent determined as the rectilinear area under the marginal product curve of land. Once again, Wicksteed fails to point out that this is true only if the production function is homogeneous and of the first degree. His numerical examples, however, clearly assume constant returns to scale (see page 555) and indeed product exhaustion is now categorically affirmed to hold universally (page 573). The practice of labelling as 'rent' any and all intermarginal surpluses is sharply condemned on the ground that it promotes the use of unscientific residual-claimant theories (pages 568–73). The habit of defining land à la Ricardo as a 'free gift of nature', Wicksteed suggests, should be abandoned once and for all (pages 573–40).

41. Applied Economics

Chapter 7 on banking and currency contains very few surprises. The power of banks to create credit is completely misunderstood (pages 587–7) but this is what we might expect in a pre-war treatment of the subject. It is true that the deposit multiplier had been explained long ago by Robert Torrens and more recently by Marshall but it was still far from common knowledge among economists [see chapter 15, section 11]. The quantity theory of money is attacked as a tautology, with the result that Wicksteed has difficulty in explaining how inconvertible paper currencies maintained their value (pages 610–22). **Book III** contains some 'samples of analysis' of applied economics. The discussion of gambling (pages 628–34) is perfectly Marshallian in tone. The housing problem is touched upon but not really explored (pages 634–6). A brief note on voluntary unemployment is followed by a discussion of 'recurrent general depressions' that might have been written by J.S. Mill a half-century earlier (pages 637–40). The problems of social accounting are mentioned: 'The "services" for which the wages of shame are paid constitute a part of the national revenue as much as any other; but if Portia is Brutus' wife and not his harlot her companionship ceases to count in the national revenue' (page 651).

The notion that current income per head affords an indication of what equal distribution would yield to everyone is effectively scotched; the point of Wicksteed's argument is to show the valuation of national income is not independent of its distribution, an obvious point that is nevertheless frequently overlooked (pages 652–6). Wicksteed proceeds to show that redistribution would render 'the realisation of the usual middle-class ideal impossible'; nevertheless, the weight of his argument comes down in favour of income equalization (pages 656–62). Protectionist sentiments grounded upon beggar-my-neighbor policies are neatly confuted (pages 666–75). The advantages of extending the scope of state enterprises and other forms of collective action are sympathetically considered (pages 675–83; see also pages 341–2). Owing to fewness on the buying side in a labour market, 'workmen, taken severally, are at a disadvantage in bargaining with the employer' (page 690) – one of Marshall's 'peculiarities of labour'. When marginal labour costs exceed average labour costs, competition among employers will fail to bid wage rates up to the marginal value product of labour (pages 691–2). This is particularly true if entry into the industry is limited (pages 692). But 'while discovering the economic justification of collective bargaining we have also unveiled the theoretical possibility of its being an economically destructive force' (page 692). The book closes with a review of the methods that might be adopted to alleviate the economic problem of poverty.

NOTES ON FURTHER READING

For a useful review of the history of marginal productivity theory with special reference to labour, see Douglas, *Theory of Wages*, chap. 2; and P.A. Samuelson, 'Economic Theory and Wages', *The Impact of the Union*, ed. D. McCord Wright (1951 in paperback). On the historical struggles between the second-generation marginalists and latter-day advocates of the wages fund doctrine, see S. Gordon's illuminating essay, 'The Wage-Fund Controversy: The Second Round', *HOPE*, Spring, 1973. D.H. Robertson, 'Wage Grumbles', *Economic Fragments* (1931), reprinted in the Fellner-Haley *Readings in the Theory of Income Distribution*, discusses virtually all the criticisms that have been directed in the past against the marginal productivity theory of wages. See also a clarifying survey by F. Machlup of 'The Meaning of the Marginal Product', reprinted in the *Readings* just cited and in his *Essays in Economic Semantics*. G.F. Bloom, 'A Reconsideration of the Theory of Exploitation', *QJE*, 1941, also reprinted in the same *Readings*, subjects the Pigovian concept of exploitation to a thorough reexamination. The instructive debate between R.A. Lester and F. Machlup on the empirical content of marginal productivity theory in labour markets, conducted in the pages of *AER* in 1946–7, is reprinted in *REA* II. For a brief but penetrating discussion, see Schumpeter, *History of Economic Analysis*, pp. 939–44; and Hutchison, *Review of Economic Doctrines*, pp. 315–19. W.J. Fellner weighs the 'Significance and Limitations of Contemporary Distribution Theory', *AER*, May, 1953, made up as it is of marginal productivity theory on the demand side.

The indispensable reference on the role of product exhaustion in the genesis of marginal productivity theory is Stigler, *Production and Distribution Theory*, chap. 12; see also chap. 7 on Wieser's imputation theory and chap. 11 pp. 296–308, on Clark's marginal productivity theory. A.W. Flux's 1894 review of Wicksteed's *Essay* is reprinted in Baumol-Goldfeld's *Precursors in Mathematical Economics*. J. Robinson, 'Euler's Theorem and the Problem of Distribution', *EJ*, 1934, reprinted in her *Collected Economic Papers, I*, provides a brilliant analysis of the economic meaning of product exhaustion; her concept of the marginal productivity of the entrepreneur to the industry, however, is open to question. Schumpeter, *History of Economic Analysis*, pp. 1026–52, reviews the general concept of the production function, citing recent literature.

On linear programming, see the brief expositions by R. Dorfman, 'Mathematical, or "Linear" Programming', *AER*, 1953, reprinted in *Readings in Microeconomics*, ed. D.R. Kamerschen (1967 in paperback), and W.J. Baumol, 'Activity Analysis in One Lesson', *AER*, December, 1958; also the extended treatment by Dorfman, Samuelson, and Solow, *Linear Programming and Economic Analysis*, particularly chaps. 6, 7, and 8, and Baumol, *Economic Theory and Operations Analysis*, chaps. 5, 6, 7, and 12.

The *locus classicus* for the notion of the optimum firm is E.A.G. Robinson, *The Structure of Competitive Industry* (1932), chaps. 2–7. See also an influential essay by N. Kaldor, 'Equilibrium of the Firm', *EJ*, 1934, reprinted in his *Essays on Value and Distribution*. Chamberlin's assault on the indivisibility thesis was launched in the essay, 'Proportionality, Divisibility and Economies of Scale', *QJE*, 1948, reprinted in his *Theory of Monopolistic Competition*,

Appendix B: quite apart from its central thesis, this article is a valuable pedagogic exercise. See also T.M. Whitin and M.H. Peston, 'Random Variations, Risk and Returns to Scale', *QJE*, November, 1954; and H. Leibenstein, 'The Proportionality Controversy and the Theory of Production', *QJE*, November 1955, reprinted in Kamerschen's *Readings in Microeconomics*. An important article on the relationship between the static theory of the firm and empirical evidence about firm sizes is E. Penrose, 'Limits to the Growth and Size of Firms', *AER*, May, 1955, amplified in her book, *The Theory of the Growth of the Firm* (1959, reprinted 1980). Some of the implications of economic dynamics for the theory of the firm are discussed by M.W. Reder, *Studies in the Theory of Welfare Economics* (1947), chaps. 9–10.

For a review of the mathematics of linearly homogeneous production functions, see R.G.D. Allen, *Mathematical Analysis for Economists* (1938 in paperback), pp. 269–4, 284–9, 315–22, 340–3, and 369–74, and Baumol, *Economic Theory and Operations Analysis*, chap. 11. P.J. Lloyd, 'Elementary Geometric/Arithmetic Series and Early Production Theory', *JPE*, January/February, 1969, given an account of Thünen's contributions to the concept of production functions. J.R. Hicks, 'Marginal Productivity and the Principle of Variation', *Ec*, February, 1932, discusses Pareto's reluctance to assume variable instead of fixed input coefficients. W. Jaffé throws 'New Light on an Old Quarrel: Barone's Unpublished Review of Wicksteed's "Essay on the Coordination of the Laws of Distribution" and Related Documents', *Cahiers Vilfredo Pareto*, 1964, reprinted in *William Jaffé's Essays on Walras*, ed. Walker. P.H. Douglas gives a brief account of the origins of the Cobb-Douglas production function in *The Theory and Empirical Analysis of Production*, ed. M. Brown (1967). P.A. Samuelson devotes another of his brilliant historical essays to 'Paul Douglas's Measurement of Production Functions and Marginal Productivities', *JPE*, October, 1979.

On the various meanings that have been historically assigned to the term 'entrepreneur', see L.M. Fraser, *Economic Thought and Language* (1937), chap. 15. Edgeworth's criticisms of the received doctrine on entrepreneurship are canvassed by Stigler, *Production and Distribution Theory*, chap. 5, pp. 125–9. Schumpeter, *History of Economic Analysis*, pp. 893–8, discusses the concept of entrepreneurial functions and explains why one should avoid drawing supply curves of entrepreneurial services. S.M. Kanbur, 'A Note on Risk Taking, Entrepreneurship, and Economic Theory', *HOPE*, Winter, 1980, takes up Schumpeter's peculiar notion that entrepreneurial action in the face of noninsurable uncertainty in no sense involves a burden that requires a reward. For an excellent, detailed history of the theory of entrepreneurship, see R.F. Hébert and A.N. Link, *The Entrepreneur. Mainstream Views and Radical Critiques* (1982). For the modern Austrian theory of entrepreneurship, see I. Kirzner, *Competition and Entrepreneurship* (1973) and *Perception, Opportunity and Profit. Studies in the Theory of Entrepreneurship* (1979), and for an attempt to revitalize the neoclassical theory of entrepreneurship, see M. Casson, *The Entrepreneur. An Economic Theory* (1982).

F.H. Knight, *Risk, Uncertainty and Profit* (1921), covers the history of profit theory up to the publication of his own landmark. J.F. Weston, 'The Profit Concept and Theory: A Restatement', *JPE*, 1954, reprinted in *RHET* and Kamershen's *Readings in Microeconomics*, sketches the history of the discussion since that time and defends the uncertainty theory. B. Bret, *Théories contemporaines du profit* (1956), chap. 3, contains an excellent critical discussion of Knight's uncertainty theory. See also W.J. Fellner, *Probability and Profit* (1965), chap. 1, for the most recent developments in the uncertainty theory of profits.

The section on technical change draws on my 'Survey of the Theory of Process-Innovations', *Ec*, 1963, reprinted in *Penguin Modern Economic Readings: The Economics of Technical Change*, ed. N. Rosenberg (1971 in paperback), which contains detailed references to the Hicks-Robinson-Harrod classification of innovations. The diagrammatic derivation of the elasticity of substitution stems from R.W. Jones, '"Neutral" Technological Change and the Isoquant Map', *AER*, September, 1965. On the inducement mechanism, see W.J. Fellner's 'Two Propositions in the Theory of Induced Innovations', *EJ*, 1961, reprinted in Rosenberg's *Penguin Modern Economics Readings: The Economics of Technical Change*, and 'Does the Market Direct the Relative Factor-Saving Effects of Technological Progress?', NBER, *The*

Rate and Direction of Inventive Activity (1962). W.D. Nordhaus, 'Some Skeptical Thoughts on the Theory of Induced Innovations', *QJE*, May, 1973, reviews still more recent developments in that area.

The current status of macrodistribution theory is well conveyed by R.M. Solow, 'A Skeptical Note on the Constancy of Relative Shares', *AER*, September 1958; and M.W. Reder, 'Alternative Theories of Labour's share', *Allocation of Economic Resources*, ed. M. Abramovitz and others (1959 in paperback). N. Kaldor, 'Alternative Theories of Distribution', *REStud*, 1957, reprinted in *RHET* and his *Essays on Value and Distribution*, provides a useful contrast between classical and neoclassical theories of distribution, on the one hand, and his own post-Keynesian theory, on the other. The criticisms of the Cambridge School directed against marginal productivity theory, as well as the Kaldorian theory of distribution, are more fully discussed in my *Cambridge Revolution: Success or Failure?* (1974 in paperback).

On Wicksteed's *Common Sense*, see Stigler, *Production and Distribution Theories*, chap. 3; Hutchison, *Review of Economic Doctrines*, chap. 5; and L. Robbins' introduction to the *Common Sense*, reprinted in his *Evolution of Modern Economic Theory*. For an interesting portrait of the Unitarian minister, classical scholar and economist, see C.H. Herford, *Philip Henry Wicksteed; His Life and Work* (1931). The reader may gain an accurate impression of the conflict between real cost and alternative cost theory by perusing Edgeworth's reviews of some Austrian publications of the 1890s, reprinted in F.Y. Edgeworth's *Papers Relating to Political Economy, III*, pp. 31–2, 50–64. In a classic essay, 'On a Certain Ambiguity in the Conception of Stationary Equilibrium', *EJ*, 1930, reprinted in *REA* I, L. Robbins showed that the battle between the English and the Austrian school stemmed from 'a failure on the part of the participants to perceive that each was adopting a different assumption with regard to the conditions of equilibrium . . . . Marshall and Edgeworth were assuming the fluidity of supply of capital and labour which was characteristic of the classical conception of equilibrium, Böhm-Bawerk and Wieser were assuming the fixity of supply which is the assumption of Clarkian statics'. Böhm-Bawerk's concessions to the disutility theory are reviewed by Stigler, *Production and Distribution Theories*, pp. 182–92.

On the shortcomings of alternative cost doctrine in dealing with the allocation of labour between employments, see F.H. Knight, 'The Common Sense of Political Economy', *JPE*, October, 1934. The conflict between the Austrian and the English approach to the nature of costs flared up again in the 1930s in the theory of international trade: see Viner, *Theory of International Trade*, pp. 489–93 and 516–26; G. Haberler, 'Real Costs and Opportunity Costs', *ISSB*, Spring, 1951; and J. Vanek, 'An Afterthought on the "Real Cost-Opportunity Cost" Dispute and Some Aspects of General Equilibrium Conditions of Variable Factor Supplies', *REStud*, June, 1959, reproduced in part in his *International Trade: Theory and Economic Policy* (1926), chap. 12.

12

The Austrian theory of capital and interest

BÖHM-BAWERK'S THEORY OF INTEREST

Both land and labour are 'original' or primary factors of production whose supply is either fixed or a function of noneconomic decisions but capital is a 'produced' or intermediate factor whose supply is dependent on the land and labour expended on its production in the past. This distinction between original and produced factors of production is fundamental to Böhm-Bawerk's theory of interest. It leads straightway to a formulation of the problem of 'the origin of interest'. In long-run competitive equilibrium, the value of the total product will be exhausted by factor payments in accordance with marginal productivity. Since capital goods are themselves the product of previous applications of land and labour, their value should be equal to the cost of wages and ground rents incurred in producing them. In other words, the entire *net* value added to final goods should be precisely equal to the payments made to the 'original' factors. If the rate of interest is positive, it must be due to the fact that there are, not two, but three 'original' factors, say, land, labour and 'waiting'. But this Böhm-Bawerk denied.

The role of capital in production is to permit adoption of more productive but also more time-consuming 'roundabout' methods of production. Robinson Crusoe can catch fish directly by a hand-to-mouth technique or indirectly by the round-about method of constructing a net. With the aid of the net he can catch more fish than he could catch with his bare hands, even after allowing for the cost of constructing and maintaining the net. This is what we mean when we say that capital goods like fishing nets are physically productive. But physical productivity is not the same thing as value productivity. If physical capital is to yield a net *value* product, something must prevent it from being produced in such abundance that its value is reduced down to the cost of construction and maintenance. This 'brake' on the production of capital goods, Böhm-Bawerk proceeds to show, lies in the nature of roundabout methods themselves. It is complemented by the phenomenon of 'time preference'. The ultimate limitation on investment is a limitation of the time we are willing to wait for a return. As a result, the value of all finished goods will not even in long-run equilibrium be completely swept back to the 'original' factors.

1. The Productivity of Greater Roundaboutness

'That roundabout methods lead to greater results than direct methods', Böhm-Bawerk declares, 'is one of the most important and fundamental propositions in the whole theory of production'. This is a statement few would deny. But Böhm-Bawerk goes further: roundabout methods are always more time consuming than direct methods and every increase in the length of time for which the 'original' factors are invested in production increases the total product at a diminishing rate. This proposition, like the previous one, is defended on the basis of 'the experience of practical life' but is actually far from being a matter of common experience. Is it never possible at a given state of technical knowledge to increase the total product by investing in less time-consuming methods of production? Is it really true that capital can be expended only in lengthening the period of production?

It is obvious that, if the rate of interest is positive, no one will adopt a more roundabout method, yielding its results at a later date, unless it is more productive. But this proposition cannot be reversed to prove that capital can be invested only by increasing the degree of roundaboutness. Given the level of investment, a reduction in the rate of interest does encourage the adoption of longer processes insofar as it reduces the opportunity cost of waiting for returns that accrue later in time, but it also renders hitherto unprofitable projects feasible by reducing initial capital costs; these projects may well require less time to complete than the range of previously adopted methods. Be that as it may, it is not really legitimate to establish Böhm-Bawerk's propositions about the nature of roundaboutness on the basis of a positive rate of interest when the purpose of these propositions is to prove that the interest rate will be positive.

Böhm-Bawerk's assumptions are very strong: it is not simply that more roundabout methods are generally more productive but that, as he said, every 'wisely chosen' lengthening of the period of production increases the total product at a rate that diminishes with the time of the lengthening; furthermore, the production period cannot be extended without additional capital and conversely, capital can only be invested to lengthen the production period. Böhm-Bawerk's proof of these assumptions, gradually elaborated in reply to criticisms, either takes the form of assuming that the rate of interest is positive and then ignoring the effect of a lower interest rate on installation costs, as well as the possibility of investing capital in new products rather than in new methods, or else falls back on the premise that capital is previously applied labour, land being neglected for the sake of simplicity; since capital is stored-up labour, the more capital there is, the older is the average age of the capital stock. The latter proof is based on the original-factors doctrine and hence carries little conviction. But it helps to shed light on the major shortcoming of Böhm-Bawerk's capital theory. Most of his reasoning makes much better sense when it is realized that his 'capital' is only circulating capital, that is, funds tied up in the form of goods in process. The function of working capital is, not to cooperate with labour in production, but as it were to support labour during the interval between the application of inputs and the emergence of output. Assuming the amount of labour to remain fixed, longer production periods obviously require more working capital per man and, conversely, more working capital per man is required only when it is found that the period of production can be profitably extended. Indeed, we shall see that in the end Böhm-Bawerk produces a theory of interest that is identical to the classical wages fund doctrine, except that the length of the period of production is now a variable instead of a technically given constant.

2. The Three Reasons for Interest

Before proceeding to the demonstration that the most profitable lengthening of the period of production is a function of the interest rate, Böhm-Bawerk raises the question of 'the origin of interest'. Interest arises out of a process of lending present income against the promise of future income: some individuals in the community are apparently willing to pay a premium on present income for the privilege of disposing of it as they see fit over some future period of time. The question: Why is the rate of interest positive? may be expressed in Böhm-Bawerk's language as: Why are people only willing to deliver a certain quantity of goods in the present if they can be sure of being repaid with a greater quantity of goods of the same kind and quality in the future? In modern terminology this might be translated into the question: Why is it that the price of a bond is invariably less than the sum of the total future payments confidently expected from it? What stops people from being so eager to buy bonds that their prices are bid up to the point where net interest disappears?

Böhm-Bawerk's answer is that there are three independent 'reasons' or 'grounds' why people on the average prefer present to future goods, in effect discounting the future by paying a premium on present goods. The first two 'reasons' operate to create an aggregate excess demand for consumption loans: (1) 'different circumstances of want and provision' in the present and in the future; and (2) 'underestimation of the future'. The third 'reason' creates an excess demand for production loans: (3) 'the technical superiority of present over future goods'.

3. The First Reason

The argument for the first reason for interest is that some people are living below subsistence levels while others expect to be better off in the future; both groups will prefer present over future goods. To make sense of this argument, we have to distinguish between a stationary and a dynamic economy. The appropriate assumption for a static theory of interest such as Böhm-Bawerk's is that the income stream is constant through time. As Wicksell pointed out, this immediately disposes of the first reason: the young who are acquiring their skills have a high discount on the future but the old who have passed their peak earnings probably discount the present in favour of the future. A stationary economy would have a population of uniform age distribution. Hence, there is no reason to think that 'spenders' will predominate over 'savers'.

On the other hand, if we assume that the income stream is rising through time and that everyone expects it with perfect certainty to continue to rise then the law of diminishing marginal utility of income necessarily implies positive time preference [see chapter 9, section 3]. This proposition was established for the first time by

Michel Landry in *L'intérêt du capital* (1904): if individuals act so as to maximize the sum of utilities over all future time, they are willing to pay a premium on present goods when income is rising through time. The reason for this is that increments of present consumption will add more utility than the increments of consumption that will have to be sacrificed in the future when the loan is repaid simply because future income will be higher. This is true even if present consumption can be substituted for future consumption on identical terms, that is, if the interest rate is zero. A rising income stream leads via a buoyant demand for consumption loans to a positive rate of interest. As soon as the rate of interest is positive, however, we no longer need the law of diminishing income utility to account for positive 'time preference'. Ordinary rational optimizing behavior will now produce the same result.

All we have to do is apply the equimarginal principle, which must hold for intertemporal consumption planning as much as for the distribution of expenditure within any given time period [see chapter 8, section 2]. The rational individual will so distribute his expected future income among different years as to insure that the marginal dollar received in any year makes the same contribution to total utility as any other. He will convert the expected flow of income into a planned flow of consumption expenditures in such a way as to equalize the weighted marginal utility of planned consumption over all future periods. That is to say, Y dollars spent this year can earn rY dollars in interest next year and hence are equivalent to $Y + rY = (1 + r)Y$ dollars available next year, $(1 + r)^2 Y$ dollars available two years from now, and so on. Thus Y in year t is equivalent to the *discounted* value of Y in year $t + 1 = Y_{t+1}/(1+r)$, the discounted value of Y in year $t + 2 = Y_{t+2}/(1+r)^2$, and so on. Similarly, if MU is the marginal utility of goods consumed this year and MU/p is the corresponding weighted marginal utility, then MU_t/p_t is equivalent to the *discounted* value $MU_{t+1}(1+r)/p_{t+1}$, $MU_{t+2}(1+r)^2/p_{t+2}$, etcetera. Therefore the formula for consumer equilibrium reads:

$$\frac{MU_t}{p_t} = \frac{MU_{t+1}(1 + r)}{p_{t+1}} = \frac{MU_{t+2}(1 + r)^2}{p_{t+2}} = \ldots \frac{MU_{t+n}(1 + r)^n}{p_{t+n}}.$$

Assuming that prices and the rate of interest do not vary though time, this means that the marginal intertemporal rate of substitution between the consumption of the good in the current year and all future years must be equal to the corresponding discounted price ratios, or the common discount factor, $(1 + r)$.

$$\frac{MU_t}{MU_{t+1}} = \frac{p_t}{p_{t+1}}\frac{MU_{t+1}}{MU_{t+2}} = \frac{p_{t+1}}{p_{t+2}} = \ldots \frac{(1 + r)^2}{(1 + r)} = \ldots \frac{(1 + r)^n}{(1 + r)^{n-1}} = 1 + r$$

Provided the rate of interest is positive, the marginal utility of current consumption will exceed that of consumption next year in the ratio $(1 + r)$, indicating the existence of 'time preference'. An increase in r will cause consumers to postpone consumption so as to raise MU_t and to lower MU_{t+1}; in other words, provided the rise in the rate of interest does not affect the marginal utility of expenditures in general [see chapter 9, section 6], an increase in r will promote saving; this is why the neoclassical supply curve of saving as a function of the interest rate is normally taken to be positively sloped. Also, the more distant the time period, the smaller is the marginal utility of future consumption relative to present consumption and the more the individual must get additional units of consumption now to compensate him for a unit less in the future. If consumers were really indifferent between different time periods, they would always postpone consumption to the future because consumption in the future will always be larger than consumption in the present at a positive rate of interest. As *t* approached infinity, future consumption would approach satiety and present saving-income ratios would rise close to unity. Casual empiricism, therefore, suggests that individuals do attach a time discount to the marginal utility of future income streams. Since a positive interest rate *means* that goods are estimated as less valuable the later they are available, this observation is not very surprising. However, it illustrates the difficulty of establishing the notion of intrinsic 'time preference' on the basis of people's behavior in an economy in which interest already exists.

To avoid fatal ambiguity of language, we must define 'time preference' in terms of a zero rate of interest. Positive time preference means that individuals prefer present income over the same amount of future income despite the fact that these are available on the same terms: $MU_t > MU_{t+1}$ even if $(1 + r) = 1$; in Fisherian terminology, the indifference curves between present and future consumption have a slope greater than unity (see below). It is clear that this definition adheres to Böhm-Bawerk's meaning and intent; failure to observe it renders discussion of the three 'reasons' meaningless.

We can summarize our conclusions with reference to the first ground by saying that it fails to show why a stationary economy should exhibit a definite pattern of time preference; furthermore, it must rely on a dubious law of the constantly diminishing marginal utility of income to demonstrate that a dynamic economy will exhibit positive time preference.

4. The Second Reason

The second independent reason for positive time preference is prospective under-estimation of the future, that is, a tendency toward myopia on the part of economic agents, which Böhm-Bawerk attributed to: (*a*) deficiency of imagination, (*b*) limited will power, and (*c*) the shortness and uncertainty of life. This second reason was criticized by Menger, Wieser and many others because it implies irrationality of behavior. Menger had himself proposed the second ground in his *Grundsätze* but deleted it in a later edition, lest it be construed as giving support to Böhm-Bawerk's theory. Wieser went out of his way in *Natural Value* (1889) to observe: 'One may thus say that it is a sound maxim among all peoples of normal development to appraise alike the present and the future'. Even Wicksteed thought that 'ordinary prudence estimates the significance of a unit in the future just as that of a unit in the present'. Indeed, it is rather peculiar that all the fundamental criticisms of this second reason have come from members of the Austrian School.[1]

---

[1] What is even more surprising is that Böhm-Bawerk himself denied that abstaining from present consumption constitutes a 'real' cost even though it is irksome. In *Capital and Interest* (1884), he

The argument that the assumption of inherent myopia must be rejected because it implies irrational behavior is methodologically unsound; all motives, rational or otherwise, that are shown to be significantly related to economic behavior ought to count in economics. This is nothing more than traditional practice. J. S. Mill was fond of pointing out that economics studies man as a creature motivated by pecuniary self-interest; however, Malthus had shown that sexual instincts are so strong that men rear large families despite the fact that self-interest dictates family limitation. Hence, the motive to procreate without limit, Mill concluded, is an aspect of human behavior that economics cannot afford to neglect.

Apart from moralizing about time preference, there are a number of valid arguments that have been advanced against 'deficiency of the telescopic faculty' as a general assumption. Deficiency of imagination and limited will power are offset by the desire to bequeath fortunes to heirs and, particularly, by the widespread social approval of 'rainy day' saving, which Marshall argued was increasingly the characteristic feature of industrialized countries. If we take the evangelical overtones out of Marshall's language, it comes down to the proposition that the rate of time preference declines as income per head rises; the larger the income per head, the less anxious anyone is to supplement present consumption by borrowing or drawing down on accumulated savings. Certainly, the possibility of not being able to enjoy future income through death or physical incapacity suggests that individuals do frequently discount the future, but loss of future enjoyment is feared quite as much as loss of earning power and leads to a discount on the present; a bird in the hand is worth two in the bush, because the individual anticipates that he will not live to catch the birds in the bush, but it is worth less than one bird in the bush if he fears that he will soon be unable to catch birds and, even if he does, unable to eat them!

Prodigality and improvidence on the one hand, saving and abstemiousness on the other – can one strike a balance? The modern view is that there is no more reason for thinking that most people discount the future than that they discount the present, always remembering that these are subjective discount rates independent of the rate of interest. As we shall see, Irving Fisher expresses Böhm-Bawerk's second reason by saying that the time preference of each individual depends on the size, certainty and time shape of his income stream; it is not assumed that people are typically 'patient' or 'impatient'. As Fisher uses the term, 'the impatience principle' does not denote a psychic discount of the 'true' future value but simply the fact that people will

attacked the abstinence theory of interest on the grounds that interest is often paid without any corresponding 'pain' and that the theory involves double counting. The first objection simply confuses average and marginal abstinence; in equilibrium the rate of interest is equal to the marginal supply price of abstinence and all intramarginal savers will earn a saver's surplus [see chapter 6]. The second objection is difficult to grasp but appears no less fallacious. What Böhm-Bawerk seems to have meant is that true abstinence involves the renunciation of present consumption to build up the capital stock: to add (1) the pain cost of abstaining *permanently* from a present enjoyment to (2) the alternative cost of choosing future in preference to present goods is to engage in double counting. This argument ignores the fact that the choice between present and future goods is not like the choice between two goods available in the present precisely because of the second reason for interest. Böhm-Bawerk would not have rejected the abstinence theory, which is really implied by his second reason, if it had not been for the fact that adherence to the original-factors doctrine prevented him from admitting that abstinence or waiting is an independent 'real' cost of production.

not defer the enjoyment of income except for sufficient reasons (see below). A sufficient reason in the real world, of course, is the existence of a positive rate of interest. It is perfectly possible, although unlikely, that aggregate time preference is now zero or even negative in wealthy countries, meaning that personal savings would still be forthcoming even at a zero rate of interest.

5. The Third Reason

Every investment of goods in productive processes increases the resulting product, albeit at a decreasing rate. Present goods can be invested now and reinvested as they accrue tomorrow but goods available tomorrow can only be invested tomorrow. This 'technical superiority of present over future goods' is not a matter merely of a larger physical product but also of a larger value product. Present goods applied today to *roundabout* production yield a larger physical output in the future than an equal quantity of goods applied at a future date to *direct* production; furthermore, they yield a larger physical output than an equal quantity of goods applied at a future date to *roundabout* production because of diminishing returns from lengthening the period of production. Since the larger of two quantities of the same good available to an individual at the same time is the more valuable, a quantity of present goods always has a greater value than the same quantity of future goods. This is Böhm-Bawerk's formulation of the meaning of 'productivity' theories of interest: the net physical productivity of capital by itself creates a value discount on the future, independently of the factors of needs, provisions and deficient perspective.

Despite repeated attacks, Böhm-Bawerk insisted all his life that the third reason constitutes an independent ground for a positive rate of interest. But as Fisher and others argued, the first two reasons operate both on the demand and the supply side in the loan market, while the third reason affects only the demand for production loans. Without the aid of one of the two other reasons, the admittedly greater physical productivity of more roundabout methods will not by itself create a premium on present goods. The 'technical superiority of present over future goods' makes it possible to supply more goods in the future than at present with the same resources; thus provisions in the future will come to exceed provisions in the present but this only causes people to discount the future because of the first reason for interest.

6. The Interaction of the Three Reasons

Fisher's argument about the interaction of the three reasons is fundamental. Assume that myopia is absent, so that we are interested only in maximizing the product, regardless of when it is maximized. The fact that capital is physically productive would not cause anyone to prefer income today over tomorrow since by definition we are indifferent about the date at which the final product emerges. The productivity of capital, however, will influence the relative abundance of goods today and tomorrow; with real income rising through time, people are willing to pay a premium for goods available today instead of tomorrow because of the law of diminishing utility of income and hence a positive rate of interest emerges. In the absence of something like the law of diminishing utility of income, only undervaluation of the future can account for the fact that the productivity of capital leads to a positive rate of interest.

Böhm-Bawerk's three grounds together provide an exhaustive explanation of the existence of interest in a stationary as well as in a dynamic economy. In a stationary state, the presence of the second reason constitutes a necessary but not sufficient condition for a positive rate of interest. It is not sufficient because the presence of the third reason might generate enough extra output to satisfy the demand for present goods; similarly, the third reason is neither a necessary nor a sufficient condition to cause the interest rate to rise above zero. In a dynamic economy, on the other hand, the first reason is not a necessary but it is a sufficient condition for a positive rate of interest. Summing up, the rate of interest can only be zero when (1) the flow of income is constant through time; (2) time preference is neutral; and (3) the net product cannot be increased by postponing consumption for the sake of future production.

The interaction of the three reasons not only explains the existence of interest but also fixes the length of the average period of production that will yield the highest present value. Since any further roundaboutness always promises a further increase in the value of the total product, a zero rate of interest would encourage an unlimited increase in the period of production.[2] This would mean a scarcity of present goods, leading via the first or second reason to the reemergence of interest and the reversal to direct methods of production. The true function of a positive rate of interest then is to act as a brake on the tendency to neglect present wants by overextending the period of production. The interest rate rations the limited supply of present goods among industries in accordance with the community's estimation of the relative value of present and future goods. If an economy is highly 'capitalistic', the stock of consumer goods will be large, the degree of roundaboutness will be great, and the increment of product yielded by further extensions of the average period of production will be small. Hence the rate of interest will be low. This is Böhm-Bawerk's explanation of the tendency of the rate of interest to fall as the capital-labour ratio rises, reflecting the twofold diminution of the advantages of greater roundaboutness and the disappearance of the premium on present goods.

7. The Determination of Interest

In the last part of the *Positive Theory of Capital* (1889), Böhm-Bawerk finally moves beyond the question why the rate of interest should be positive to ask how the rate is actually determined. At this point the argument shifts ground radically: no more is heard of consumption loans, personal saving and discounting of the future. The

---

[2] This is not quite right, as Wicksell showed. The fact that increasing roundaboutness is subject to diminishing returns, if it is a fact, will make lengthening profitable to only a limited extent. If by investing $50 I can receive $100 of final product from a one-year process or $150 from a two-year process, it will pay me to choose the shorter process in both years: at the end of the first year I can then reinvest $100 at double the scale, ending up with $200 instead of $150. On the other hand, if I had to invest $75 to get $100 from a one-year process or $150 from a two-year process, the longer process would be more profitable: $100 reinvested in the second year would bring only $133.33. Thus, if indefinite lengthening is to be profitable, the final product must increase at more than a geometric rate as time increases at an arithmetic rate. Diminishing returns from lengthening the period of production precludes this possibility.

economy consists of capitalists and workers. Capitalists are conceived in the classical manner as active entrepreneurs in possession of capital. The demand for funds emanates solely from capitalists and the supply come primarily from retained earnings. Moreover, all capital in effect consists of means of subsistence advanced to workers. Hence, the determination of the rate of interest is a matter of the exchange of labour for consumer goods. Workers do, but capitalists typically do not, undervalue the future because of the good old classical reason that workers cannot afford to wait for the fruits of their labour.

With a fixed supply of the subsistence fund, a datum in Böhm-Bawerk's model, the rate of interest is determined by the marginal productivity of lengthening the average period of production. The point at which greater roundaboutness ceases to yield a positive addition to the total product is outside the horizon of even the wealthiest societies. At a zero rate of interest, capitalists would have an infinite demand for present goods to advance to their workers. Thus, the rate of interest rises until the entire subsistence fund is used in lengthening the average period of production. The lower the interest rate, the longer the profitable period of production, because at a lower rate of interest the present value of a stream of future goods is greater and hence the premium on present goods is smaller. And so the equilibrium rate of interest is determined by 'the productiveness of the last extension of production economically permissible', that is, by the marginal productivity of extending the period of production. The wage rate will then be equal to the marginal productivity of labour discounted to the present.

Despite Böhm-Bawerk's ceaseless criticism of productivity theories of interest, his own theory in the last section of the book clearly attributes interest to the productivity of capitalistic methods of production. Indeed, it is nothing more than a marginal productivity theory of interest so stated as to bring out the fact that capital is a two-dimensional quantity of time and physical amount. It bears an obvious similarity to the wages fund doctrine: instead of assuming a given labour supply and a fixed period of production of one year to determine the wage rate as a function of the variable subsistence fund, Böhm-Bawerk assumes the supply of labour and the subsistence fund to be given and then determines the wage rate and the interest rate as a function of the variable period of production. The theory remains static: we are not examining economic behavior *through* time but the allocation of resources between different methods of production available at one *point* in time, each of which requires different periods of time for its completion.

THE AVERAGE PERIOD OF PRODUCTION

Most modern versions of the theory of production assume either that production is timeless or that the investment period is determined by technical conditions. All the inputs are applied at a single moment of time and output emerges at some later single moment. Capital theory begins by taking this simple case and treating the investment period as an independent variable in the production function. We will adopt Ragnar Frisch's terminology and call this (1) the *point input-point output* case. The analyses of wines laid up for storage and trees planted for timber production, which figure so prominently in neoclassical capital theory, are examples of the point input-point output case. Next we have the situation in which the inputs are applied continuously in variable patterns over time: (2) the *flow input-point output* case. So far, capital is merely circulating capital or goods in process. Then we have investment in durable capital goods, where the input of a single date yields output at various future dates: (3) the *point input-flow output* case. Lastly, we reach full generality with the really typical case of (4) *flow input-flow output*.

One would imagine that capital theory was largely interested in (3) and (4), involving investment in fixed capital. However, all Böhm-Bawerk's work and most of Wicksell's was concerned with the optimum investment period of continuously applied circulating capital, that is, with case (2), the flow input-point output case. Cases (3) and (4) raise intractable difficulties resulting from the fact that there is no way of linking particular units of input embodied in fixed equipment with particular units of finished output: all the inputs embodied in durable equipment are jointly responsible for the whole stream of future output. By neglecting fixed capital, Austrian capital theory avoided such problems as the optimum rate of depreciation and replacement of old equipment that are always linked up with the decision to invest in new equipment. No doubt, the major explanation for this neglect was an inability to handle these complications with the analytical tools that were available. But there was more to it than that. In some sense, the concentration on working capital as the representative case was deliberate: what Böhm-Bawerk and Wicksell wanted to emphasize was that capital is an input whose use necessarily involves the passage of time and, conversely, that any output whose production takes time must necessarily employ capital as an input as a direct consequence of the time-consuming character of the production process. For that reason, the amount of capital that is employed in a production process cannot be measured by a single number such as its pecuniary value. Measurement of capital must always involve at least two dimensions, magnitude and duration, since capital can be increased either by using more of it or by leaving it invested in an existing process for a longer period of time.

8. Böhm-Bawerk's Model

Böhm-Bawerk's treatment of the determination of the interest rate deals with the case of two inputs and one homogeneous output: all output is made up of consumption goods and inputs, consisting solely of labour-years and working capital in the form of consumer goods to feed and clothe workers, are applied continuously at a uniform rate. The amount of labour and the amount of working capital are fixed. Workers are indifferent between occupations and uniform wage rates prevail throughout the economy; all firms have identical production functions. Our first problem is to define a metric for capital in this one-sector economy. It will not do to express capital in money values because that presumes knowledge of the rate at which to discount the future services of capital: the purpose of the model, however, is to determine the unknown rate of discount. Nor can we express capital even in this case simply as a physical stock of consumer goods because that would ignore the two-dimensional quality that characterizes capital as a factor of production. A given physical amount of capital need not have a homogeneous age structure; indeed, it never has except in the point input-point output case. The heterogeneous structure of the real capital stock makes it necessary to measure capital by the average 'period of production' utilized in the economy: the average time that elapses between the instant a factor input is applied to production and the instant its fruits become available for consumption.

The process of investing working capital to support labour during the cycle of production may be likened to a flow of water into a reservoir. The average length of time that each drop of water remains in the reservoir obviously depends on the rate of flow of water per hour and the size of the reservoir. The Bathtub Theorem, as Dorfman has called it, says that in a reservoir of given volume the average number of hours of retention of water equals the stock of gallons of water in the reservoir divided by the rate of inflow or outflow in gallons per hour. Thus, when the tank holds ten gallons and the rate of flow is two gallons per hour, the average period of retention of a drop of water is five hours. Similarly, inputs remain frozen in an enterprise for an average period of time that depends on the rate of flow of inputs and output and the total amount of capital available. If the flow of inputs equals the flow of output, the average period of production of the enterprise for a given size of plant is equal to the dollar value of the capital funds invested in the plant divided by the dollar flow of inputs or output per year. The quotient of the average period of production is neither a pure number nor a period of clock time; thus, this period is lengthened either when more capital is invested for the same clock time or when the same capital is 'frozen' in production for a longer clock time.

The average period of production of a one-sector economy may be written as

$$\theta = (K/I),$$

where K stands for the stock of real capital and I for the flow of inputs or the rate of investment. In a stationary economy, however, net investment is zero and the application of inputs corresponds to capital consumption: workers continuously consume the stock of food and clothing, which is at the same time being continually replenished. Ignoring the consumption of capitalists as negligibly small, capital consumption is going on at the rate $N\bar{w} = I$, where N stands for the given number of workers in the economy and $\bar{w}$ for the wage rate. Thus,

$$\theta = (K/N\bar{w}).$$

The next step is to show that the average period θ for which labour is tied up when it is applied continuously throughout the fabrication period of the economy is $\frac{1}{2}t$, where t equals the absolute length of the period of production. This proposition goes back to Jevons and is easy to verify. Suppose one unit of labour costing $1 is applied every day for a 5-day fabrication period (see Figure 12–1). The total amount of working capital required to complete one cycle of production is then $5. However, this is only true if labour is applied discretely in whole numbers. If we apply labour continuously from $t = 0$ to $t = 5$, the amount of working capital that is tied up in one

Figure 12–1

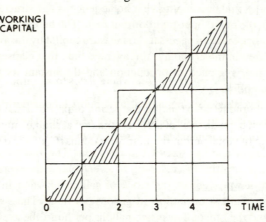

cycle of production is, not \$5, but \$2½ (as shown by the sum of the shaded triangles in Figure 12–1). In the continuous case, therefore, if we invest 5 units of labour in a production cycle whose absolute length t is 5 days, the average period θ for which labour is tied up is $2\frac{1}{2}$.

We can now write the basic equation of the Böhm-Bawerk's model as set forth by Wicksell: $\theta = \frac{1}{2}t = K/N\bar{w}$ or $K = \frac{1}{2}N\bar{w}t$. As a physical stock, capital is the accumulated result of $\frac{1}{2}Nt$ man-years of labour. The total value of labour tied up in the capital stock is precisely half the value invested in the total output of a period of production.

Now for the technical relations. Output per year is $X = Nf(t) = Nf(2K/N\bar{w})$; the production function exhibits diminishing returns: $f'(t) > 0$ and $f''(t) < 0$. Facing given wage rates, capitalists will maximize the annual rate of profit or interest with respect to t, the parameter under their control, which is defined as

$$r = \frac{X - N\bar{w}}{K} = \frac{Nf(t) - N\bar{w}}{\frac{1}{2}N\bar{w}t} = \frac{f(t) - \bar{w}}{\frac{1}{2}\bar{w}t}.$$

To maximize r,

$$\frac{dr}{dt} = 2\,\frac{\bar{w}t[f'(t)] - \bar{w}[f(t)] + \bar{w}^2}{\bar{w}^2t^2}$$

$$= 2\,\frac{tf'(t) - f(t) + \bar{w}}{\bar{w}t^2} = 0.$$

Therefore

$$f(t) - tf'(t) = \bar{w}.$$

The wage rate so determined is equal to the marginal product of labour:

$$X = Nf(t) = Nf\left(\frac{2K}{N\bar{w}}\right),$$

$$w = \frac{\delta X}{\delta N} = f\left(\frac{2K}{N\overline{w}}\right) + Nf'\left(\frac{2K}{N\overline{w}}\right)\left(-\frac{2K}{N^2\overline{w}}\right)$$

$$= f\left(\frac{2K}{N\overline{w}}\right) + f'\left(\frac{2K}{N\overline{w}}\right)\left(-\frac{2K}{N\overline{w}}\right),$$

and since $-t = \left(-\dfrac{2K}{N\overline{w}}\right)$, $\overline{w} = f(t) - tf'(t)$, where $f(t)$ is total output per man-year, $f'(t)$ is the marginal product of extending the period of production, and $tf'(t)$ is the total imputed interest per man-year of labour estimated at simple interest. Thus, the wage rate is equal to the total output per man-year minus $tf'(t)$. We defined the rate of interest earlier as

$$r = \frac{f(t) - \overline{w}}{K/N} = \frac{f(t) - \overline{w}}{\frac{1}{2}\overline{w}t}.$$

When labour is paid its marginal product, this reduces to

$$r = \frac{tf'(t)}{\frac{1}{2}\overline{w}t} = 2\frac{f'(t)}{\overline{w}}.$$

We could have found this directly by taking the marginal product of capital:

$$\frac{\delta X}{\delta K} = \frac{\delta[Nf(\frac{2K}{N\overline{w}})]}{\delta K} = Nf'(t)\left(\frac{2}{N\overline{w}}\right) = 2\frac{f'(t)}{\overline{w}}.$$

Figure 12–2

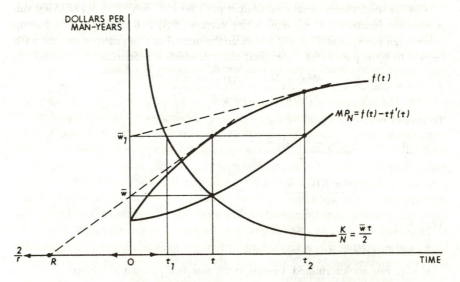

The gist of Böhm-Bawerk's elaborate arithmetical argument can now be illus-trated in one diagram (Figure 12–2). First, we draw the production function, $f(t)$, which does not start at the origin but at a subsistence wage rate: if the wage rate is equal to or less than the subsistence wage rate, only direct 'immediate' methods of production will be adopted. Next, we draw the curve $K/N = \bar{w}t/2$ as a rectangular hyperbola, showing an inverse relationship between $\bar{w}$ and t when the given amount of K provides full employment: if $\bar{w}$ rises, the flow of consumables provided by K will be drawn down at a greater rate and the period for which the stock of capital suffices will fall; with a given K and N, $\bar{w}$ varies inversely with t. The schedule of the marginal product of labour MP_N is traced by starting, say, at t_2 and finding the corresponding value of the production function $f(t)$, then moving along the tangent to $f(t)$ at that point to find $\bar{w}_1$ and marking the corresponding point on the MP_N curve for t_2, and so forth. But what determines $\bar{w}$? At $\bar{w}_1$ producers must adopt t_1 as shown by the rectangular hyperbola K/N; however, the marginal product of labour at t_1 is less than the wage rate $\bar{w}_1$, causing producers to discharge labour, and the excess supply of labour now causes wages to fall. The same consideration will show that a wage rate that would lead producers to adopt t_2 would lead to an excess demand for labour, driving wages up. The only length of the production period that is compatible with $\bar{w} = MP_N$ and full employment of labour is t. At t, the gap between $f(t)$ and MP_N is $t f'(t)$, which is equal to total imputed interest per man-year; since the interest rate is equal in equilibrium to MP_K, total imputed interest per man-year at t is

$$\frac{K}{N}(MP_K) = \frac{\bar{w}t}{2}\, 2\frac{f'(t)}{\bar{w}} = tf'(t).$$

We can depict MP_K on the same graph by extending the horizontal axis in the westward direction. Since $MP_K = 2f'(t)/\bar{w}$, $f'(t) = r\bar{w}/2 = O\bar{w}/OR$. It is then easy to see by graphic inspection that the higher is the wage rate, the longer is the period of production, the greater is $2/r$, that is, the lower is the rate of profit or interest.

Therefore, with a given size of labour force and a given capital stock, Böhm-Bawerk's model determines the equilibrium wage rate, the equilibrium interest rate and the optimum period of production for the economy as a whole.

9. The Definition of the Average Period.

By treating the whole economy as a single consumption-good sector, Böhm-Bawerk managed to reduce capital to a stock of unripened consumables on the way to completion. The model fails, however, to come to grips with many of the fundamental problems of capital theory. For example, the rate of interest cannot fall to zero for, by definition, $f'(t) > 0$ no matter how large the capital stock. As soon as we take up a two-sector economy, however, the fact that machines are used to make machines as well as consumer goods makes it possible to depress the rate of interest to zero even if $f'(t) > 0$. Although every increment of capital yields a positive increment of output, it is a diminishing increment; the cost of maintaining capital, however, remains constant. A time must come when the gross product of capital is just equal to depreciation charges. At that point, the net productivity of capital has fallen to zero and, in the absence of positive time preference, the rate of interest will be equal to zero.

The period of production, which is a simple enough concept when capital consists solely of working capital, becomes much more difficult to handle when the economy consists of two or more sectors that use each other's output as well as their own output as inputs, particularly when one or more of the sectors produce durable machines that become inputs at one instant of time but then yield their output slowly over a stretch of time. Indeed, it has been argued repeatedly, for instance by Clark in the 1890s and by Knight in the 1930s, that the average period of production of fixed plus working capital cannot be calculated except under special conditions and that, when it is calculated, it turns out to be of infinite length. To this problem we now turn.

It must be said at the outset that the term 'period of production' has been used in a bewildering variety of senses. First, there is the distinction which we have already encountered between the absolute and the average period of production. Either of these, however, may be interpreted as applying to a single product, a single factor or the economy as a whole. As applied to the final product, we are 'looking back' from the end result to the beginning of a process. As applied to a factor of production, we are 'looking forward' from the application of inputs to the completion of a process.

The absolute period of production can be defined as the time interval elapsing between the first application of primary factors and the emergence of the final consumer good for which these factors were responsible. For the economy as a whole, the looking-backward version of the absolute period refers to the interval of time between present consumption and the application of the first 'original' factor that contributed to *any* output at this moment passing into consumption. In the looking-forward version, it refers to the time interval between the present and the emergence of the last product attributable to *any* factor now employed. Obviously, in either case, the absolute period is infinite in length. But the absolute period has almost always been applied, not to all output or all factor inputs, but to a particular finished product or a particular primary factor. This is true of Böhm-Bawerk, who adopted the looking-backward-from-the-product version, and of Wicksell and Hayek, who worked with the looking-foward-from-the-factor version. And the absolute period of production of particular products or particular factors is *not* infinite if we accept the doctrine of 'original' factors.

Similarly, the average as distinct from the absolute period can be applied to a particular product or to the whole economy. It is usually expressed in the looking-forward sense and asks the question: How much time on the average will elapse between the investment of primary factors at this moment and the emergence of the output that will someday be imputed to their activity at this moment? In the looking-forward sense, the average period cannot refer to a particular factor applied at a moment of time or it would not be an average period. Hence, it should be understood as referring only to the economy as a whole, which is exactly how Austrian writers always employed it.

10. The Calculation of the Average Period

Böhm-Bawerk's practical suggestions for measuring the average period of production involve astonishing terminological and conceptual confusions. Although the rigorous closing section of the *Positive Theory* deals only with working capital, earlier sections of the book suggest how to measure the average period when durable machines are used or when the primary factors are not invested at a uniform rate. In the flow input-point output case, in which all capital consists of consumer goods in process, the average period of production is as we have said before, the sum of the investment periods of all the continuously applied labour inputs weighted by the number of inputs, or $\frac{1}{2}t$ where t is the absolute length of the production period. Böhm-Bawerk typically assumes that the individual investment periods are 'staggered' – applied discontinuously at the beginning of each year. If labour is applied at a nonuniform rate in the successive years, the inputs will have to be dated and weighted accordingly. Nevertheless, the average period of production remains a weighted arithmetic mean of labour-days per year, weighted by the duration of labour services up to the moment of final sale, divided by the total number of labour-days applied. If the labour inputs are of different types so that their rates of reward are different, the investment periods must be weighted not by the number of inputs but by their total quantity-times-price values. Böhm-Bawerk always assumes labour to be a homogeneous input, so this problem does not arise.

Now for the flow input-flow output case. In calculating the time elapsing between the investment of primary factors in the production of machines of given durability and the moment when the machine-made product reaches the consumer, we have to add the following time periods: (1) the construction period of the machine; (2) half the life time of the machine, on the assumption that it continuously releases the value of the primary factors that have produced it; and (3) the time from the instant the machine is used to the instant at which its output reaches the final consumer. We then add these time intervals and divide by the number of primary factors applied. Böhm-Bawerk gives the following oversimplified example to bring out the nature of the calculation. Suppose the production of a consumer good requires 100 labour-days at the rate of one labour-day per year applied on the first day of 10 successive years and 90 labour-days applied at the last minute during the 10th year to finish the good with a time of finishing practically equal to zero. Then if a is the input in labour-days per year and t is the years for which they are invested, the weighted average period of production

$$\theta = \frac{(1_a \cdot 10_t) + (1_a \cdot 9_t) + \ldots + (1_a \cdot 1_t) + (90_a \cdot 0_t)}{10_a + 90_a}$$

$$= \frac{55 \text{ labour-days per year}}{100 \text{ labour-days}} = 0.55 \text{ year.}$$

Another good also requires 100 labour-days over a 10-year period but now the rate of applying labour is 20 labour-days applied on the first day of 2 successive years, 5 labour-days applied for the remaining 8 successive years, culminating in 20 labour-days to finish the article with a zero finishing time. In that case

$$\theta = \frac{(20_a \cdot 10_t) + (20_a \cdot 9_t) + (5_a \cdot 8_t) + (5_a \cdot 7_t) + \ldots + (5_a \cdot 1_t) + (20_a \cdot 0_t)}{80_a + 20_a}$$

$$= \frac{560 \text{ labour-days per year}}{100 \text{ labour-days}} = 5.6 \text{ years.}$$

Since the elements making up the average period of production differ greatly in magnitude, the average is affected by the kind of mean selected. Why calculate the average period as an *arithmetic* mean? Why not calculate a geometric or a harmonic mean? In general, there is no reason to prefer the arithmetic to the geometric mean, and yet the two will always give different results. This is a point that Fisher brought up repeatedly against Böhm-Bawerk and which the latter steadfastly ignored. The fact is, however, that it does not matter which mean we use provided we keep using the same one. The average period of production is only intended to provide an ordinal index of capital intensity for purposes of comparing different equilibrium situations characterized by differences in the amount and structure of capital. This purpose is served just as well by one mean as by another so long as we do not switch means in the middle of the comparison.

There is, however, a more serious failing in Böhm-Bawerk's calculations. As Wicksell pointed out, Böhm-Bawerk always implies that the accumulated inputs earn simple interest and very different results are obtained if the inputs in fact earn compound interest. The fact that inputs earn interest does not appear explicitly in Böhm-Bawerk's examples but that is because the interest factor always cancels out when the inputs earn only simple interest. For instant, if 1 man-year is invested for 2 years and 1 man-year is invested for 1 year, the average period of production by Böhm-Bawerk's formula is:

$$\theta = \frac{(1_a \cdot 2_t) + (1_a \cdot 1_t)}{2_a} = \frac{3_{at}}{2_a} = 1\tfrac{1}{2} \text{ years.}$$

This should have been written as:

$$\theta = \frac{1_a(1 + 2_r) + 1_a(1 + r)}{2_a} = \frac{2_a(1 + \theta r)}{2_a}$$

$$= \frac{2_a + 3_a r}{2_a} = \frac{2_a + 2_a \theta r}{2_a}$$

$$= 4_a + 6_a r = 4_a + 4_a \theta r$$

so that

$$\theta = \frac{6_a}{4_a} = 1\tfrac{1}{2} \text{ years.}$$

With compound interest, however, the formula becomes:

$$\theta = \frac{1_a(1 + r)^2 + 1_a(1 + r)}{2_a} = \frac{2_a(1 + r)^{\theta}}{2_a}.$$

Solving for θ, we have

$$\theta = \frac{\log(2 + 3r + r^2) - \log 2_a}{\log(1 + r)}.$$

At, say, $r = 0.10$, $\theta = 1.55$ instead of 1.5. The difference is small because the number of years involved are few. But if the absolute period were longer, the difference would become more pronounced. In Wicksell's formula, the earlier inputs are more heavily weighted by the compound interest factor and hence the average period of production is longer. What this means is that the calculation of the average period of production is not invariant with respect to the interest rate. A lower rate of interest immediately shortens the measured average period of production, even if production processes have not changed, because it lowers the weights attached to earlier inputs. To put the problem another way, the fact that the inputs earn compound interest over the length of the production cycle means that the period of production is not properly described by the arithmetic mean θ; together with the mean or first moment of the time distribution of input, we must also calculate the higher moments, such as the variance, the skewness and the kurtosis.

11. Is the Average Period Infinitely Long?

We asserted earlier that the absolute period of production of particular primary inputs, and hence the average of all such absolute periods, will not be infinite in length. This has been denied, however, particularly by J. B. Clark, on the ground that it is impossible to trace back all capital to labour and land expended in the past: there was no time in the past, however distant, when the primary factors alone were combined to produce a machine. Even if for the moment we accept the original-factors doctrine, it is still true that it may be impossible to discover any moment of time when the primary factors alone were employed to produce 'intermediate means of production'. The reason lies in the whirlpool structure of production. Böhm-Bawerk always assumes that the 'stages of production' form a linear hierarchy in which the output of 'higher' stages is always used exclusively as inputs by 'lower' stages nearer to final consumption. But this ignores the circularity that characterizes much of production: some of the output of the coal industry may be used to generate electricity in a factory that makes coal-cutting machinery or, more to the point, coal itself may be utilized in the coal industry to generate electricity to drive ventilating machinery in coal shafts. Production may take the form of a linear sequence like raw cotton → yarn → grey cloth → dyed cloth but it also may take the form of circular relations like iron ore → steel → mining equipment → iron ore. In input-output studies, circular interdependence of this kind has been found to characterize a significant portion of interindustry relations in advanced economies. Hence, the absolute period of production, even when defined with reference to particular products or particular factors, may be infinite in a large number of cases.

While the absolute period may be infinite, however, the average of such absolute periods nevertheless can be finite. It is well known that an infinite series of successively diminishing values can converge to a finite limit under certain circumstances. This is essentially what is true of the average period of production. An economy's capital stock is, in Samuelson's words, 'a perpetual stew, to which something is always being added and from which something is always being taken out. . . . Some part of what is now being added will never come out of the stew, just as some part of what is in the stew is of infinite age. But it is a simple exercise in infinite processes to show that the average age of the stew is finite, and the average expectancy of a particle staying in the stew is also finite'. Whirlpool structures, while presenting difficulties for the calculation of an average period of production, do not make it impossible to define an average period of finite value. 'The schoolboy's penknife may contain iron from a mine opened up in the time of Caesar', to quote Stigler's homely example, but the iron applied in the first century is so small as to have a negligible influence on the period of production of current iron-using processes. It is true that past investments are weighted by time but this is offset by the small amount of inputs invested in earlier periods: the bulk of labour and of labour expended on producing machines has been expended in the recent past.

All this supposes, however, that there is some sense in which 'original' factors can be defined. One of the arguments that the opponents of Böhm-Bawerk have employed against his theory is that labour is really a produced factor via expenditures on labour training and education, and that even the so-called free gifts of nature need maintenance expenditures if they are to be forthcoming. Since the average period of production is defined in terms of 'original' factors, any denial of that concept involves a denial of the average period of production. Now, it is perfectly true that the original-factors doctrine has been the source of much confusion and sterile metaphysical arguments: we only have to think of Marx's theory of surplus value or the endless discussion of rent as a price-determined income. Nevertheless, there is a real meaning to the assertion that some resources are *economically* nonaugmentable, even if this assertion is only a matter of degree and point of view. The rate at which entrepreneurs will invest working capital is clearly an economic problem, and machines do have their supply prices. But the supply of 'land', meaning all permanent income-yielding goods, whether natural or man-made, is virtually fixed and the long-run supply of labour is not simply a matter of rational cost accounting. In this sense, and only in this sense, land and labour may be considered 'original' factors. But this is quite enough, or almost quite enough, to give definite meaning to the average period of production.

12. Waiting as an Original Factor

Nevertheless, it remains to be seen how we define the average period of production in the general flow input-flow output case; that is, how do we tackle the task which Böhm-Bawerk never faced up to? To do so, we have to borrow a leaf from Cassel and admit the presence of a primary factor other than labour or land related specifically to investment in fixed capital. It was Böhm-Bawerk's failure to do this that prevented him from extending the argument to durable capital goods. Let us follow Dorfman and suppose that the economy consists of two sectors, one of which produces homogeneous consumer goods called 'foodstuffs' and another of which produces homogeneous 'machines' of a given technical durability. It is assumed that the machines are productive in the sense that a given amount of resources devoted to maintaining old machines and producing new machines will always result in a greater flow of output, although only after a lapse of time, than will the application of the same amount of resources to the immediate production of foodstuffs. There are two primary factors: labour and 'waiting'. Waiting represents the social cost of forgoing the production of food in order to use the resources thus released to maintain and build up the stock of machines; it is a genuine factor service performed at a specific place and time and it is measured in terms of the goods in which it is embodied – one unit of food deferred for one unit of time. The owner of a machine can sell the machine at any time for its current, depreciated value and consume the proceeds in the form of food: by not doing so, he is performing the scarce service of 'waiting' as measured by the current value of the machines estimated in terms of foodstuffs multiplied by the length of the waiting time. Thus, the 'total rate of waiting' in the economy equals the total value of machines in the economy measured in terms of foodstuffs, and the 'stock of waiting' equals the amount of waiting performed in the past that is congealed in the existing stock of machines.

The average period of production of the economy as a whole is the appropriately weighted average of the looking-forward periods of investment of all the 'original' factors used in the economy. We have designated labour and waiting as the only original factors. All we need do to get the overall period of production is to define the average periods of investment of labour and of waiting and to find appropriate weights to add these together. The period of investment of labour, θ_N, depends on the flow of labour services performed per year and the stock of unrealized labour services embodied in the stock of new and old machines in the economy. θ_N, measured in man-years, is equal to the stock of embodied labour divided by the value of labour services performed in a year. The period of investment of waiting, θ_W, is likewise a function of the flow of waiting performed per year plus the stock of waiting congealed in the existing stock of machines. But the dimensions of waiting are foodstuffs forgone per year and the quantity of waiting so defined depends on the units in which foodstuffs are measured. A period of investment, however, has the dimensions of time and must not be influenced by the choice of units of measurement other than that of time. It looks as if we cannot measure the quantity of waiting performed in a year in natural units. We can measure it in value or price-times-quantity units, however, for prices will cancel out in the averaging process.

Having decided to use value weights, we now derive the average period of production for the economy as a whole. The labour term of the overall average period is equal to θ_N times the flow of labour N in the economy. Since θ_N equals the stock of embodied labour services divided by N, $\theta_N N$ is the value of unrealized labour services congealed in the current stock of machines. In the same way, the waiting term of the overall period is equal to the unrealized waiting services in the stock of machines, $\theta_W W$. Since there are no other 'original' factors, the labour term and the waiting term add up to the total value of the stock of machines in the economy. These must now be weighted, however, by the units in which labour and waiting are measured. When value weights are used, the sum of the weights will be the value of labour performed in the economy in a year plus the value of the waiting performed. Since labour and waiting are the only primary factors in the economy, the sum of these weights will add up to national income. Thus, the weighted average period of production for the economy as a whole is the value of the stock of machines divided by the national income; in short, the capital-output ratio, one of the Great Ratios of modern economics! But this is exactly what we might have expected from the 'Bathtub Theorem': the average period of retention of a drop of water is equal to the content of the reservoir divided by the rate of flow of water; the average period of production in an economy employing capital is equal to the stock of capital divided by the rate of flow of the primary inputs.

We will recall that our two-sector economy produces machines of a given technical life. How then is the average period of production lengthened? Not by producing more durable machines but by producing more machines of the same durability. In the one-sector model that Böhm-Bawerk analyzed in detail, the period of investment is lengthened by lengthening the time period for which each consumer good remains in the pipelines. In the two-sector model, increased roundaboutness is brought about by investing more capital in machines of the same or even of lesser durability. Thus, the durability of machines in an economy is no indication of the length of the average period of production.

Suppose we now take one further step toward the real world and permit the period of production to be lengthened by the introduction of longer-lived machines, whose higher initial cost is offset by their lower annual maintenance and depreciation charges. This brings up a new problem discussed by Wicksell in his review of Ackerman's book (see below): what is the optimal durability of a machine? Insofar as the average period of production is concerned, it is still possible in principle to calculate a finite period of production but a single figure for the period of production can now reflect radically different capital structures corresponding to different capital-labour ratios, thus depriving the concept of significance as a summary statistic of the degree of capital intensity in the economy. This structure, however, is just as applicable to a global measure like the capital-output ratio as it is to the average period of production. As Solow has recently put it: 'There is no reason to suppose that any single object called "capital" can be defined to sum up in one number a whole range of facts about time lags, gestation periods, inventories of materials, goods in process, finished commodities, old and new machines, buildings of varying durability, and more or less permanent improvements to land. Only someone who is naively identifying all the many aspects of capitalistic production with one of them, it does not matter which, would believe that the theory can be summed up by defining something called "capital" and calling the interest rate the marginal productivity of "it".'

Thus, it would be nice to have 'one number' to sum up something called 'capital' but alas it is not to be. Because it is not to be, growth economics is a harder subject but microeconomics gets along very well without it. The decisive objection to the concept of the period of production in capital theory is that what we really want to know for purposes of analyzing intertemporal allocation problems is the rate of return on capital; the period of production may be a useful expository device but it is perfectly possible to calculate the rate of return on an individual capital project or a combination of capital projects without being able to measure the stock of capital assets. After all, we are not usually worried in the theory of wages about the fact that units of labour cannot be easily measured in efficiency units or that the stock of human capital cannot be satisfactorily measured in value terms.

13. Synchronization of Production and Consumption

Agreeing that the average period of production is neither a necessary nor a useful measure of the capital intensity of an economy, we must nevertheless spend a moment on certain traditional objections to the Austrian theory of capital, namely, the Clarkian view that the time-dimension is not essential to an understanding of the phenomenon of capital. If we confine ourselves to stationary conditions, Clark argued, the length of time for which a stock of capital is embodied in production turns out to be economically irrelevant. In stationary equilibrium, with net investment equal to zero, the number of production periods that are coming to a close at any instant of time are exactly equal to the number of production periods just beginning. Hence, stratification of the economy into production periods of different lengths can be only an arbitrary procedure, having no economic significance. A stationary state involves automatic synchronization of inputs and outputs; capital is necessarily maintained intact and the only demand for capital is for replacement purposes; there is no waiting whatever for output because every application of inputs that bears their fruit some time hence is matched by the simultaneous emergence of output from past outlays of productive effort.

To reinforce his point, Clark distinguished between specific capital goods and 'capital' viewed as abstract productive power. Pure 'capital' he described as a permanent homogeneous fund of *value* – a perpetual income stream – invested in an ever-changing series of concrete capital goods but distinct from them in the same way in which a reservoir is distinct from the drops of water of which it is at any given moment composed; since the capitalized yield of equipment is a yield calculated net of depreciation, pure 'capital' is also an indestructible fund of automatically replaceable values.

It is difficult to see the force of this argument. Clark did not pretend to show that synchronization is a condition of equilibrium in the stationary state; on the contrary, synchronization is laid down as an axiom and since this is tantamount to postulating that capital is maintained intact, we are then told that capital maintains itself automatically. But there is nothing automatic about capital replacement even under stationary conditions. It is true that to maintain an equilibrium stock of capital requires no further net investment but only reinvestment of funds regularly recovered from sales. But it is also true that when a community succeeds in maintaining a stock of machines, the members of the community have fewer goods available for consumption in the present than they would have if they failed to replace worn-out machines. By definition, in a stationary state no one can refrain from present consumption in order to augment future consumption but they can increase present income by depleting future income. Their refusal to do so expresses the social cost of 'waiting'. The general principle remains the same in either a stationary or a dynamic economy: there is a time lag between capital formation and the increased supply of consumer goods that capital formation makes possible. Even with zero net investment and perfect synchronization of production and consumption, the time structure of the capital stock is not a matter of indifference. Everything else being the same, the members of a stationary economy are always better off, the longer the average period of production. Clark's definition of pure 'capital' simply eliminates the problem of time by definition: obviously, capital as a fund of abstract purchasing power cannot possibly have a time structure.

The gist of the conflict between 'synchronization economics' and 'advance economics' [see chapter 6, section 5] can be seen by resorting to that copy-book example of capital theory, the planting of trees for timber production. Suppose we have a forest with 50 rows of trees from 1 to 50 years old: every year, the oldest row will be cut down while a new row is simultaneously planted. In other words, timber production and timber consumption are perfectly synchronized. The fact that the average period of production of the forest is 25 years is irrelevant, according to Clark: once the process is synchronized, it does not matter whether the oldest row is 50 or 10,000 years old. But as Cassel or Hayek would argue, even in this case there is a definite limit to the possibility of investing available inputs in the production of timber, subsumed under the rubric of 'waiting'. First, we have to abstain from increasing the present supply of timber by cutting down trees less than 50 years of age. Second, more waiting would allow the trees to grow older and so lead to an increase in the future supply of timber. The last case is excluded by the assumption of stationary equilibrium and zero net productivity of 'capital' but the first case remains valid in a stationary state and expresses the social cost of waiting.

Clark's argument clearly implies that the rate of interest in a stationary state will be zero. Waiting-theorists have always argued that the rate of interest cannot be zero in a stationary economy. A zero interest rate would mean that there would be no reason to refrain from consuming capital: if capital has a zero net yield, why devote resources to maintain it? A positive rate of interest is needed to keep the stationary state stationary. As Cassel used to say, interest is 'the price paid for waiting' and in a stationary state it is the bait that keeps people from consuming their capital.

It is clear that this argument is valid only if people have positive time preference.[3] It is not necessary to prevent anyone from depleting capital if everyone regards a dollar tomorrow on the same terms as a dollar today. If everyone acts so as to maximize the sum of utilities over all future time, the law of diminishing marginal

---

[3] Cassel produced an argument having nothing to do with time preference to show why the rate of interest must be positive in a stationary state. Sargant had argued that the supply curve of 'rainy day' saving is negatively sloped because individuals who save to provide a definite annual income from their capital for old age will have to save more if the rate of interest falls [see chapter 10, section 18]. Cassel pointed out that inasmuch as rainy-day savers can save only a certain amount out of present income, a fall in the rate of interest does not increase the supply of saving but merely increases the length of time they will have to save. Take the example of someone who saves $1,000 a year towards an annuity that will pay $1,000. At 6 percent compound interest, it take 12 years to accumulate the required capital fund of $16,000; at 3 percent it takes 24 years, and at 1 percent it takes 70 years. At near zero rates of interest, Cassel concluded, the shortness of the earning period of the average individual will alone cause people to deplete their capital, and this will maintain a positive premium on present income. Although this has little to do with time preference, it may have been in Böhm-Bawerk's mind when he cited the shortness of life as one of the factors in the second reason for time preference.

utility of income at a zero rate of interest gives us as an even distribution of income over time. This is really obvious: the first and second reasons for a positive rate of interest are absent by definition under stationary conditions; if the third reason is also inoperative, the rate of interest will be zero. We conclude that the average period of production in an economy is indeed irrelevant if time preference is neutral and capital yields no output net of maintenance and replacement. So long as time preference is positive, however, zero net productivity of capital or synchronization of production and consumption will not reduce the rate of interest to zero. Hence, it will not deprive the time structure of production of economic significance.

The controversy reached its culmination in the first chapter of Schumpeter's *Theory of Economic Development*. Schumpeter's purpose was to construct a model of an economy in which technical change is missing and then to demonstrate that, under these circumstances, the rate of interest would be necessarily zero. Without technical change, he argued, the economy must settle down to a 'circular flow', a stationary and synchronized economic process in which there is no uncertainty about the future. This implies that the net yield of capital has fallen to zero and, assuming that there is no intrinsic rate of time preference, this implies that the rate of interest will be zero. Thus, interest would not exist in competitive long-run stationary equilibrium as visualized in traditional theory. Only innovations and dynamic change can produce a positive interest rate. There is nothing surprising about this conclusion. The whole argument proceeds by spelling out definitions but it fails to establish the basic thesis that an economy without innovations must settle down to a 'circular flow'. A capitalist economy minus technical innovations does not necessarily yield a stationary state for there is still the possibility of increasing the total product through the routine investment of land and labour in the construction of capital goods.

14. The Average Period and the Capital-Output Ratio

It has not been fashionable in recent years to talk about periods of production. 'Nearly every one who comes to the study of capital falls a victim to Böhm-Bawerk's theory at some stage or other', wrote Hicks in *Value and Capital*. 'The theory stands up very well to the most obvious objections which can be made against it; yet, as one goes on, difficulties mount up. The definition of the "time taken in production" gets harder and harder; and so most people find themselves driven, in the end, to abandon the theory, even if they have nothing much to put in its place'. The capital-output ratio, however, is a standard item in every modern economist's toolchest. But the capital-output ratio, we have argued, comes down to the same thing as the average period of production: they both attempt to measure the average amount of 'waiting' that is incurred in investing more capital to increase the flow of output. The Austrian proposition that in static equilibrium a fall in the rate of interest lengthens the average period of production and that an increase in capital, for a given quantity of labour and a given production function, lengthens the average period has its counterpart in the modern proposition that every increase in the quantity of capital in consequence of a fall in the rate of interest will raise the capital-output ratio. Unfortunately, it is not true in general that a lower rate of interest means a higher capital-output ratio. The Switching Theorem (see below) shows that 'the degree of roundaboutness' in an economy can no more be represented by a single dimension such as the capital-output ratio than by the average period of production.

The problem gets more complicated when we allow for technical change. Where Böhm-Bawerk really went wrong was in thinking that the average period of production would lengthen even with technical change. In the first edition of the *Positive Theory*, the distinction between capital accumulation along given production functions and capital accumulation along different production functions altered by technical change was not clearly drawn. Böhm-Bawerk admitted that some innovations do reduce roundaboutness but the capital so released, he insisted, tended to be applied to lengthening the period of production elsewhere. Only if innovations are both capitalsaving and product-replacing will the average period of production be shortened. This he dismissed as an exceptional occurrence, citing the secular increase in physical capital per head as presumptive evidence of the greater frequency of time-increasing innovations: 'industrial experience will verify two propositions . . . first, that with the larger capitalistic equipment, the product per unit of labour increases; and second, that this increase in product does not go on *pari passu* with the addition of capitalistic equipment'. But 'industrial experience' has not verified the belief that the capital-output ratio tends to rise through time. Although capital per man has been rising, technical change has increased output per man sufficiently to prevent the capital-output ratio from rising. On the basis of the available evidence, it appears that developed economies have not experienced any appreciable increase in the average degree of 'roundaboutness' over the last fifty to seventy years.

The fact is, however, that Böhm-Bawerk was not justified in appealing to new and better machines as evidence of 'the law of roundaboutness': the theory was designed to deal with capital formation in the absence of technical change. After all, it is easy to show that the rate of interest will be positive when capital formation embodies new technical knowledge. If this is all we mean by productivity of capital, we do need Böhm-Bawerk's elaborate third reason to prove the technical superiority of round-about capital-using production. What has to be demonstrated is that, within the context of the static state where technology is given, the longest periods of production are the most costly, so that any new capital will be invested in a still longer period of production.

The problem is similar to that of establishing the existence of time preference when the rate of interest is already positive: casual observation in the real world will always reveal that more time-consuming methods of production are more productive because no one will select a longer method of production at a positive rate of interest unless it is more productive; shorter but less productive methods are never observed because rational investment behavior weeds them out. Here, as elsewhere, Böhm-Bawerk seems to be arguing in circles.

THE SWITCHING THEOREM

And now for the final nail in the coffin of the Austrian theory of capital: the Switching Theorem. The simplest illustration of the theorem is the one chosen by Samuelson in his 1966 declaration of unconditional surrender after an acrimonious debate about its general validity.

15. Double Switching

Consider the case of two techniques A and B that can produce the same good in three years by the application of either 7 man-years in the second year for technique A or 2 man-years in the first year followed by 6 man-years in the third for technique B.

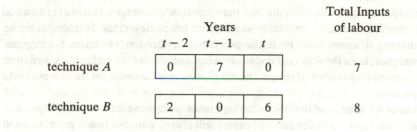

	Years			Total Inputs of labour
	$t-2$	$t-1$	t	
technique A	0	7	0	7
technique B	2	0	6	8

At what interest rate would these two techniques be equally profitable? Since the quadratic equation $7(1+r) = 2(1+r)^2 + 6$ has two roots, $r = 0.5$ and $r = 1$, the fact is that an interest rate of either 50 or 100 percent would equate the returns to both techniques. At a rate of interest above 100 percent, A is the more profitable technique because 2 units of labour compounded for 2 years added to 6 uncompounded units of labour in the final year will overwhelm 7 units of labour compounded for one year. As the rate of interest falls below 100 percent, however, B becomes the more profitable technique because its larger wage bill is now accumulating less interest. As the rate of interest continues to fall, however, it becomes profitable to switch back to A at some interest rate below 50 percent at which point the lower labour requirements of A begin to outweigh all other considerations. This is the phenomenon of 'reswitching'.

We can spell out the comparison between A and B by calculating the present discounted values of the costs of the two techniques at various interest rates [see below, section 20] as viewed by a capitalist in year $t-2$, using the formulas:

$$PV_A = 0 + 7/(1+r) + 0 = 7/(1+r)$$

$$PV_B = 2 + 0 + 6/(1+r)^2 = 2 + 6/(1+r)^2$$

It is evident that for $r > 1$, A is the less costly and hence more profitable technique. For $0.5 < r < 1$, B is the less costly and hence more profitable technique but for $r < 0.5$, A is once again more profitable. Furthermore, the switch points occur precisely at $r = 0.5$ and $r = 1$ at which $PV_A = PV_B$ (see Table 12–1).

Table 12–1: *Costs of A and B at Various Interest Rates*

r	0	0.25	0.5	0.75	1.0	1.25	1.5	2.0
PV_A	7	5.6	4.67	4	3.5	3.1	2.8	2.33
PV_B	8	5.84	4.67	3.96	3.5	3.19	2.96	2.66

In this simple example, 'reswitching' arises from the compound-interest effect of changes in the interest rate on the comparative costs of inputs applied at different dates in identical technical processes producing the same good; alternatively expressed, it arises from the fact that many production processes characterized by the uneven application of inputs over time yield multiple internal rates of return and are, therefore, equally profitable at different borrowing rates. In more complex examples, it arises both from the staggered application of inputs to identical techniques, from the different gestation periods of alternative techniques, and from the fact that the output of such technical processes sometimes enters as inputs into other processes.

The phenomenon of double switching makes it impossible to say unambiguously either that (1) a fall in the rate of interest will always alter the rankings of the most profitable of all available techniques in a unidirectional manner, or that (2) it will always increase the capital-intensity of the economy by promoting a greater degree of 'roundaboutness'. The latter, known as 'capital reversing', is a generalization of the former and it implies that there is no strictly monotonic relationship between a change in the rate of interest and either the capital-labour or the capital-output ratio. But if it is not possible to find an index of the value of the capital stock of an economy that is uniquely associated with one and only one rate of interest, we can never speak unambiguously of 'an increase in capital-intensity'. As a consequence, it appears that we have to give up the idea of a demand curve for capital as a function of the interest rate.

16. The Many-Products-One-Technique Simplification

To motivate the last point we must digress briefly to explain the simply enormous difference between one-sector and two-sector models of the economy – the difference is much larger than twice! The simplifying assumption that an economy produces only one product – the one-sector model – has ancient roots in the history of economic thought. Its purpose is simply to get rid of all differences between physical and value relationships, insuring, for example, that a rise in the capital-output ratio really does mean that more physical capital is used to produce a unit of output, or that a rise in the rate of investment really does mean that a higher fraction of output will be accumulated for future use. So much of Böhm-Bawerk's exposition of the theory of capital is, as we have seen, confined to this simple one-sector case. But the same simplification is produced by the assumption that, while there are many goods, they are all produced by the same technology; when this is the case, values and physical quantities will always move proportionately in response to a change in any basic economic variable. When there are many goods produced by the same technique (the many-products-one-technique simplification), or one good produced by different techniques (the one-product-many-techniques assumption), switching is ruled out and the capital-labour ratio is always uniquely associated with a particular rate of interest.

The trouble starts when we have at least two products and at least two different techniques, that is, when we have a genuine two-sector model. There is a famous article by Samuelson on the Surrogate Production Function, published in 1962, which more or less unwittingly fell into the trap of the many-products-one-technique simplification. Samuelson wanted to show that actual statistics of capital, labour and output, derived as they are from a world of heterogeneous capital goods which cannot be aggregated in any simple way, nevertheless can be interpreted 'as if' they derive from a world where capital is perfectly and instantly malleable, a stock whose heterogeneous structure is therefore irrelevant. Defining the 'MIT School' as actually holding the view that 'capital theory can be rigorously developed without any Clark-like concept of aggregate "capital", instead of relying upon a complete analysis of a great variety of heterogeneous physical capital goods and processes through time', he nevertheless offered the Surrogate Production Function as '*some* rationalisation for the validity of the simple J. B. Clark parables which pretend there is a single thing called capital'.

Samuelson assumed a two-sector economy in which both a consumer good and a capital good are produced by means of nonproducible labour and a single produced capital good, combined in each case in rigidly fixed proportions. There are a large number of such fixed-proportions techniques available and the problem is to choose among them. The system is in stationary equilibrium, such that for a given wage rate there is always one technique for each sector which is the most profitable, or for a given interest rate there is always one technique that pays the highest wage rate. This is expressed by drawing trade-off curves for each sector between the real wage rate and the real interest rate. These turn out to be straight lines intersecting at a single 'switch-point' on the assumption that there are fixed input proportions and, indeed, the same proportions in both sectors. He then shows that it does not matter how many capital goods there are: we will have as many straight lines as there are capital goods, the slopes declining as the same proportion of labour to machines produces more and more output in the sectors in question. The envelope of all these straight lines is the so-called 'factor-price-frontier' and the slope of its straight-line segments may be used as a simple index of capital per man in the economy, the elasticity of the envelope at each point being a measure of the relative shares of labour and capital in national income. Unfortunately, this is only a one-sector model travelling in the disguise of an *n*-sector model by virtue of the critical assumption that the ratio of labour to machines is the same in all sectors.

In a footnote to his article, Samuelson pointed out that if, in the two-sector case, more of a given machine relative to labour were needed to produce itself than to produce a consumer good, the trade-off curves between the wage and interest rates would be convex to the origin, because a rise in interest costs would then affect one sector more than the other. Likewise, if the proportion between physical capital goods and labour were higher in the consumer goods sector than in the capital goods sector, the trade-off curves would be concave to the origin. In other words, as soon as the capital-labour ratios differ between sectors, the factor-price-frontier no longer consists of straight-line segments and, furthermore, may be convex for certain stretches, concave for other stretches, and then becoming convex again, depending on how many sectors we have in our model and on the differences in the capital-intensities of the different sectors. In short, the trade-off curves may intersect each other twice or more. Members of the Cambridge School (Cambridge, U.K.) immediately generalized the Samuelson footnote: it is perfectly possible in a many-products-many-techniques model to have several 'switchpoints', that is, several wage rates and interest rates at which two or more different techniques for producing two or more different goods are equally profitable, in consequence of which changes in the relative values of goods can occur without equivalent physical changes in the technical methods of producing goods. In that case, it is impossible to draw a demand function for 'capital' as an inverse function of the rate of interest because we literally do not know what to write on the horizontal axis of the diagram.

It is worth noting, however, that the source of the difficulty is just as much the heterogeneity of output as the heterogeneity of capital: when output is homogeneous, as in the one-sector model, the heterogeneity of capital gets no chance to bite. Furthermore, the heterogeneity of capital only matters because capital goods are purchased outright instead of merely being hired. It is not questioned that capital rentals and even the price of capital goods will be lower in a capital-rich as compared to a capital-poor economy. But if both decline equiproportionately, the rate of interest will not change; if capital rentals fall less than the price of machines, the rate of interest may even rise. This enforces the point that it is not heterogeneity as such that makes capital difficult and labour easy to measure; it is rather that labour is only hired and hence that the value of its stock never figures in theories involving one- or two-sector models.

17. Is Switching Likely?
Everyone is now agreed that reswitching and capital-reversing are possible. But how likely are they to occur? Samuelson, in conceding the validity of the Switching Theorem, expressed some doubts about its empirical importance. Cambridge economists, on the other hand, have insisted that both switching and capital-reversing are extremely likely and, indeed, the general rule. But they have neither attempted to measure the empirical significance of switching in actual economies, nor discussed the problem of how one might go about measuring it. It is clear that it would not be an easy task. Movement along factor-price-frontiers, whatever their shape, involves movement among alternative equilibrium stationary states, which is a far cry from a process of substituting capital for labour in historical time. And it is the latter we have in mind when confronted with the standard Austrian proposition that a fall in the rate of interest will encourage capital-deepening.

Faced with the well-known problem of testing comparative-static propositions, the Cambridge economists have instead taken refuge in theorems about the conditions that are required to rule out switching. The most famous of these shows that to preclude switching in an n-sector model of fixed-coefficient techniques, we need at least one capital good in our model that is exceptional in that it is produced by a smooth neoclassical production function, and we also need the property that all inputs in the economy enter into the production of that capital good. Similarly, it has been shown that the empirical significance of switching also depends on whether the rate of interest falls below a certain critical level, and whether product prices change as firms readopt some previously used techniques. The upshot of the literature so far – and we have by no means seen the end of it – seems to be that measurement of switching rests on measurement of the degree of input substitutability in an economy, an issue that is unlikely to be resolved in the near future.

The favourite models of the Cambridge School always involve linear Leontief technologies in the sense that each product in each sector is produced with only one technique, which throws the entire burden of substitutability on the consumers choosing one mix of output rather than another, the different mixes implying different techniques and hence input-substitution through the backdoor. In other words, even in the worst case, where input-substitution in production is excluded by assumption, some degree of input-substitution in the large is reintroduced by the pattern of final demand, including the demand of overseas buyers. This is even more true if instead we adopt 'activity analysis' as a mode of describing the production possibilities open to firms [see chapter 11, section 6], which is still a long way from the smoothly substitutable production functions of neoclassical theory. It is not obvious, therefore, that switching among techniques does in fact occur. It remains an open question. If reswitching does not occur, it is still possible to have capital-reversing, at least when there are more than two techniques under consideration. But it takes still more tortuous assumptions about technology– such as wide gaps in the input coefficients of different techniques – to get capital-reversing without switching. If we cannot persuade ourselves that switching is a common occurrence, we are not likely to believe that capital-reversing is bound to happen.

18. A Post-Mortem

It must be conceded that switching and capital-reversing are perfectly possible phenomena but until they are shown to be empirically important rather than just logically possible, economists are ill-advised to throw away their textbooks on price theory, capital theory, growth theory and development economics just because the models in them frequently imply that a fall in the rate of interest will raise the capital-labour ratio of an economy. Besides, the Cambridge critics lack the strength of their own convictions. Would they go as far as to deny that, in general, India and China are well advised to favour labor-intensive techniques? No doubt, in particular cases, we would still have to carry out detailed project appraisals but surely we would be surprised to find a labour-surplus economy adopting the same capital-intensive technology as the U.S.A. or the U.K., that is, the same machines and the same way of manning the machines. If so, are we not conceding the real-world insignificance of switching and capital-reversing, at least in gross economic comparisons?

The fact remains, however, that the Switching Theorem suffices to show that the Austrian theory of capital – meaning the theory which reduces the differences between capital goods to 'time' and which then measures 'capital' as an 'average period of production', the rate of interest being determined by the interaction of the average period and the three reasons for positive time-preference on the part of individuals – is untenable. This was of course realized long before the modern debate on the Switching Theorem. Irving Fisher's classic book, *The Rate of Interest* (1907), consists essentially of what might be described as 'Böhm-Bawerk improved by ageing minus the period of production'. Fisher wanted to attack anew the problem of the theory of interest by adhering consistently to the microeconomic, general equilibrium formulation of economic behavior, while insisting on the point that 'capital' as a fund of purchasing power is merely the present value of discounted future returns and therefore cannot stand in a one-to-one relationship to either the stock or the structure of physical capital goods. In general, there are as many own-rates of interest in an economy as there are products produced with the aid of capital goods, and only in stationary equilibrium will the many own-rates of interest of different products be reducible to a single rate of interest. It is true that for easier exposition in the *Theory of Interest*, Fisher applied the general equilibrium treatment of the rate of interest to a one-commodity world but that is only what he called the 'first approximation' to the theory. The modern Arrow-Debreu general equilibrium theory, which turns the theory of interest into a special case of the theory of price of 'dated commodities', so that interest is an element in the price ratio between dated commodities and capital is the present embodiment of future-dated consumption goods, is entirely in the spirit of Fisher. The Fisherian theory may be open to the criticism of empty formalism but it is at any rate safe against the charge of denying the possibility of capital-reversing. Fisher's theory is, in fact, very helpful in showing how a fall in the rate of interest might lead to a fall and not a rise in the average capital-labour ratio of an economy.

FISHER'S THEORY OF INTEREST

Fisher's *The Rate of Interest* was extensively revised in 1930 and published under the title of *The Theory of Interest*. The later version is now recognized in Schumpeter's words as 'the peak achievement, so far as perfection within its own frame is concerned, of the literature of interest'. Not least of its qualities is its superb pedagogical structure: 'It teaches us, as does no other work I know, how to satisfy the requirements of both the specialist and the general reader without banishing mathematics to footnotes or appendices, and how to lead on the layman from firmly laid foundations to the most important results by judicious summaries and telling illustrations.'

19. Willingness and Opportunity

Fisher saw no difference between explaining why there is interest and explaining how interest is determined. He was content to show that individuals in receipt of income try to alter the successive amounts of income available for consumption at various times by means of saving and borrowing. The resultant price that is paid for income now rather than for income later is the rate of interest. The determination of this rate depends on the interaction of 'willingness' and 'opportunity', which together exhaust the relevant subjective and objective forces. First, there is what Fisher had earlier called 'the impatience principle' and which he now pointedly renamed 'the willingness principle': given the level of prospective income, its distribution over time and its uncertainty, circumstances are easily envisioned that might cause 'patience' to dominate 'impatience'. Individuals redistribute their consumption over time in an optimal way but nothing is said about the forces that cause them to regard one particular kind of redistribution as better than another. Next, there is the 'investment opportunity principle'; the rate of investment opportunity is called 'the rate of return over cost'. The rate of return over cost is defined with reference to a least two investment options: by 'cost' is meant the loss of withdrawing one income stream; by 'return' is meant the gain that results from substituting a new income stream; the rate of return over cost is that discount rate at which the present net values of two investment options are equalized. Whenever this discount rate exceeds the market rate of interest, one of the two options must be rejected.

20. Rate of Return over Cost

This last point needs amplification, since Keynes has identified his own 'marginal efficiency of capital' with Fisher's 'rate of return over cost'. Keynes's marginal efficiency of capital or 'internal rate of return', however, refers to a single investment option. It is that rate of discount which maximizes the present net worth of an investment by equating the present value of the series of prospective receipts to the present value of the total replacement cost of the investment. In short, it is that discount rate which maximizes the present value of receipts net of costs. The present value of net receipts available t years hence, discounted at the market rate of interest, is

$$PV = \frac{\pi}{(1 + r)^t} .$$

This follows from the fact that $90.91 will grow to $100 at an interest rate of 10 percent; therefore, the present value of $100 next year will be $100/(1.10) = $90.91. Continuous compounding converts this formula to

$$PV = \pi e^{-rt},$$

where Euler's e is the limit of the expression $(1 + 1/n)^n$ as n, the number of times a year that interest is compounded, approaches infinity. The present value of a stream of net receipts over t years discounted at an unknown internal rate of return i is

$$PV = \int_0^t \pi e^{-ix} dx = \pi \int_0^t e^{-ix} dx$$

$$= \pi \left[-\frac{e^{-ix}}{i} \right]_{x=t} - \pi \left[-\frac{e^{-ix}}{i} \right]_{x=0}$$

$$= -\frac{\pi}{i} e^{-it} + \frac{\pi}{i}$$

$$= \frac{\pi}{i} (1 - e^{-it}),$$

which is the general form for a perpetual, constant stream of π dollars discounted continuously at the rate i per year. If we set this expression equal to zero, we can then solve for the internal rate of return i that equates the present value of receipts to the present value of costs. Thus, the marginal efficiency of capital is that discount rate i which sets net present worth equal to zero. If i exceeds the market rate of interest r, this means that further capital outlays on this investment project will increase present net worth: the marginal-efficiency criterion instructs management to undertake investments so long as $i > r$.

Fisher's rate of return over cost is that critical discount rate at which *two* or more investment options have the same present net worth:

$$\int_0^t (\pi_1 - \pi_2) e^{-ix} dx = 0.$$

The ranking of investment options, Fisher then showed, depends on the rate of interest. A particular option may have a higher present value at one rate of interest and not at another. In practice, we can determine the internal rate of return on an investment project by an iterative procedure: we simply calculate the present values of the entire expected stream of net receipts from the project at successively higher discount rates until we reach a present value of zero. If the stream of net receipts is 'well behaved', that is, monotonically increasing until a peak is reached and then monotonically decreasing, a curve of present values such as PV_1 will always have a negative slope, and the internal rate of return is then found at the point i' where PV_1 cuts the horizontal axis (see Figure 12–3). If we have to choose between two investment projects, Fisher's rate of return over cost is i'': if $r < i''$, the first option is to be preferred to the second; on the other hand, if $i' > r > i''$, the second option should be chosen.

Normally, the Keynesian marginal-efficiency criterion applied to both projects separately will give the same answer as Fisher's rate of return over cost applied to pairs of projects. The difficulty arises when the stream of net receipts is not well behaved: projects may generate losses at the beginning and end of the span of their existence, so that the curve of present values crosses the horizontal axis several times; projects may not be independent so that the present value of one is conditional on the adoption of the other; and worst of all, the projects may be indivisible and only

Figure 12–3

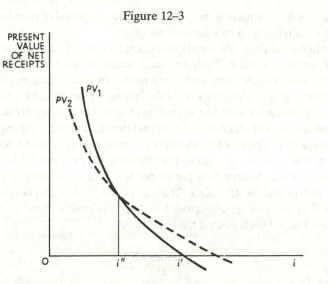

PRESENT
VALUE
OF NET
RECEIPTS

PV_2 PV_1

O i'' i' i

available on an all-or-nothing basis. In such cases, the marginal efficiency of capital or the rate of return over cost may not be definable at all in terms of real numbers, or if they are definable, there may be several internal rates of return that will equate to zero the present value of a single project or the difference between the present values of two projects. Furthermore, both criteria tell management to compare i to r. But the rate of interest in the market may not reflect the true opportunity value of cash to the firm. For example, if the amount of credit available to the firm is rationed, as it frequently is, the 'cost of capital' to the firm exceeds the market rate of interest and i should now be compared to the cost of capital, whatever it is, and not to the rate of interest. Suffice it to say that in general the only universally correct method of appraising investment projects is to follow the present-value rule and not the internal-rate-of-return criterion, that is, to discount the present value of expected net receipts at the cost of capital to the firm in question and to adopt those projects that have the highest present value. It must be realized, however, that when projects are interdependent and when the capital market is imperfect, even the present-value rule may fail. With this brief excursion into the very complicated subject of capital budgeting, we return to Fisher's model of interest rate determination.

21. Diagrammatic Exposition

By placing income today on the horizontal axis and income tomorrow on the vertical axis, we can express all possible conditions of 'willingness' and 'opportunity' by appropriate indifference curves between present and future income plus a transformation curve depicting the maximum amount of future income that can be obtained from a given amount of present income via production. We assume, of course, that we can speak of income as if it were a composite commodity always made up of exactly the same proportion of goods. Also tomorrow's income means next year's income; if there is more than one possible period of investment, we can not depict the result on a two-dimensional graph.

The 'willingness lines' are convex to the origin owing to the law of diminishing marginal utility of income. Their steepness expresses the community's aggregate time preference. Positive time preference means that the willingness lines have an absolute slope greater than unity *at the 45° income-stream line*. As we shall see in a moment, this income-stream line will not be observed in an economy unless the rate of interest is zero. This definition of time preference, therefore, corresponds to our earlier usage according to which individuals having positive time preference prefer present income over the same amount of future income even when they are available on the same terms. Neutral time preference is shown by willingness lines that are symmetrical around the 45° vector. Thus, in Figure 12–4, willingness line 1 reflects negative time preference, willingness line 2 reflects positive time preference, and willingness line 3 depicts neutral time preference.

Figure 12–4

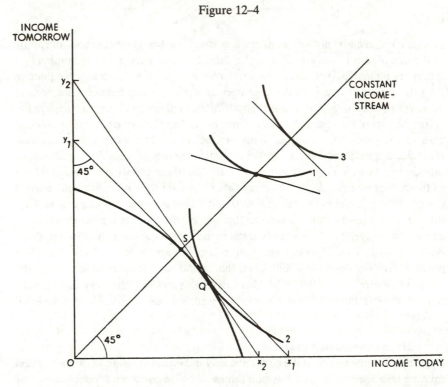

The 'opportunity line' or technical-transformation curve reveals the net productivity of capital. It is concave to the origin owing to diminishing returns from sacrificing present income to obtain future income; if a given amount of today's income could always be transformed into a larger amount of tomorrow's income, the opportunity line would be a straight line with an absolute slope greater than unity; if it were concave but symmetrical around the 45° vector, the marginal productivity of capital would decline at a constant rate; the less the rate of decline, the steeper the opportunity line.

The rate of interest is determined by the point of tangency between a willingness line and the opportunity line. A simple rule tells us that the rate of interest will be positive if the tangency point has an absolute slope greater than unity. This follows from the definition of present value. If x is income this year and $y = f(x)$ is income next year, then the present value of x now plus y next year:

$$PV = x + \frac{y}{(1+r)} = x + \frac{f(x)}{(1+r)} = \frac{x(1+r) + f(x)}{(1+r)}.$$

This present value will be maximized if

$$\frac{dPV}{dx} = 0 \quad \text{and} \quad \frac{d^2PV}{dx^2} < 0.$$

But

$$\frac{dPV}{dx} = \frac{(1+r) + f'(x)}{(1+r)} = 0 \quad \text{and} \quad \frac{d^2PV}{dx^2} = \frac{f''(x)}{(1+r)} < 0$$

if

$$(1+r) = -f'(x),$$

or

$$r = -[f'(x) + 1].$$

But $f'(x)$ is the slope of the opportunity line which is necessarily negative; $-f'(x)$ is the marginal rate of substitution of x for y, so that

$$MRS = \frac{MP_x}{MP_y} = (1+r),$$

where MP_x is the marginal product of capital in one-year processes and MP_y is the marginal product of capital in two-year processes. Hence, if we assume that all individuals have optimized their income streams by (1) equating the rate of return over cost i to the market rate of interest r for all possible investment options that convert x into y via production, and (2) by equating the marginal rate of substitution of x and y in consumption to $(1+r)$, we arrive at the result that the tangency point between a willingness line and the opportunity line will always have an absolute slope equal to the 'interest factor' $(1+r)$; if the absolute slope exceeds unity, the rate of interest must be positive.

Thus at Q in Figure 12–4 the rate of interest is equal to the slope of line y_2x_2; since the absolute value of the slope of y_2x_2 is greater than unity, the rate of interest is positive. It is easy to see that a zero rate of interest requires a tangency point such as S whose slope, like that of line y_1x_1, is exactly equal to minus unity; this can happen only if both the willingness line and the opportunity line are symmetrical around the 45° vector, meaning that time preference is neutral and that the *net* yield of capital is zero.

22. Some Uses of the Diagram

Any theory about the real rate of interest can be expressed in terms of Fisher's basic diagram. For instance, Frank Knight denied repeatedly that it is possible to generalize about time preference and, therefore, espoused a pure productivity theory of interest. He agreed that in equilibrium the rate of interest will be equal to the annual yield of an investment divided by the cost of investment. But the size of the capital stock at any time is so great, he contended, that new investment decisions have little effect on the rate of interest. The yield of capital goods at any moment is almost entirely determined by existing technology and the fixed supply of resources in the economy. In terms of our diagram (Figure 12–4), this contention amounts to asserting that the opportunity line lacks any curvature. Obviously, time preference will in this case affect the amount invested but not the rate of interest since the latter will be determined entirely by the constant slope of the opportunity line. This is simply another illustration of the Marshallian rule that demand has no influence on price if production is carried on at constant costs. The basic question here is an empirical one: Is it true that the size of the capital stock is such that no feasible additions from annual investment could appreciably influence the rate of interest? In recent years, gross private investment in the United States has run at 4–5 percent of the stock of reproducible wealth, including land. This hardly accords with the idea that new investment has a negligible effect on the rate of interest.

Schumpeter on the other hand, did not imply that the production-transformation curve in a stationary economy is a straight line throughout its entire length. By definition of stationariness, however, there is no demand for production loans because all gross investment is equal to depreciation accruals. He made consumer loans depend on time preference and he admitted, of course, that these are capable of causing interest to exist even in a stationary world. If the willingness lines are steep, however, the demand for consumer loans can only be brought into equality with supply at a positive rate of interest. This means that positive interest will also be earned in production even though the economy is stationary. Without imputed interest, depreciation accruals will be lent to consumers: positive interest is now the condition for maintaining capital intact. In short, Schumpeter cannot even determine the level of 'productive interest', as he calls it, without reference to time preference. To postulate neutral time preference as he does is really to beg the question he wants to put. It does not require innovations to produce positive time preference. A low level of income per head in a society experiencing no growth will by itself produce positive time preference.

23. The Theory of Investment Decisions

Facing a given interest rate, each person in the economy optimizes the size and time shape of his income stream by borrowing or lending, by investing or disinvesting. The sum total of these adjustments determines the rate of interest, subject to the market-clearing condition that desired lending equals desired borrowing or planned saving equals planned investment. This can be illustrated with the simple case of two individuals having expected claims to present and future income in amounts indicated by Q_1 and Q_2.

In Figure 12–5, the concave opportunity lines denote the ability to convert present income into future income by investing in capital goods; actually, each curve is an envelope of the most profitable investments for the individual, dividing the feasible from the nonfeasible region of income streams over time. Each individual faces a given interest rate, shown by the slope of the parallel 'market lines' and reaches an optimal position by altering the shape of his income stream until the concave opportunity curve is tangent to his convex willingness curve. Both individuals, starting from Q_1 and Q_2, will begin by investing until they attain positions S_1 and S_2. Then they will borrow or lend until they reach their highest attainable willingness curve, ending up at R_1 and R_2 respectively. This sequence is, of course, merely an expository device; in fact, individuals will make these decisions simultaneously.

Individual A starts with $35, invests $15 of income (the horizontal distance Q_1S_1), borrows $20 (the horizontal distance S_1R_1) and thus ends up with a larger present as

Figure 12–5

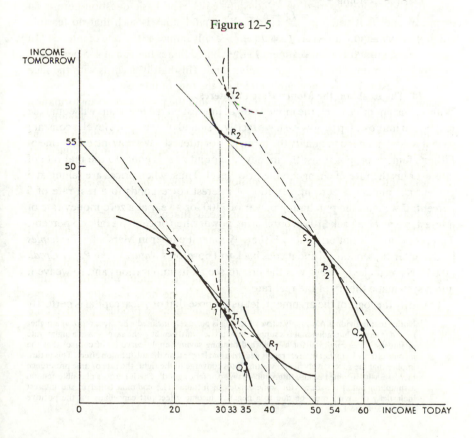

well as future income by dissaving \$5 (the horizontal distance Q_1R_1). Similarly, individual B begins with \$60, invests \$10 (Q_2S_2), lends \$20 (S_2R_2) and saves \$30 (Q_2R_2). Each individual maximizes utility subject to given tastes and income restraints and aggregate lending equals aggregate borrowing.

We have assumed an interest rate of 10 per cent: r is equal to the absolute slope of the market line minus 1, or $(55 - 50)/50 = 0.10$. If the rate of interest were higher, as shown by the dashed lines, the A would want to invest only \$5 (Q_1P_1), to borrow only \$3 (P_1T_1), but to save \$2 (Q_1T_1). At the same time, B would want to invest only \$6 (Q_2P_2), but to lend \$21 (P_2T_2) and to save \$27 (Q_2T_2). Since B wants to lend more than A wants to borrow, the rate of interest must fall back to 10 percent.[4] In equilibrium, the rate of interest must equal the marginal rate of transformation in production as well as each person's marginal rate of time preference in consumption. In addition, the rate of interest must equate aggregate desired lending to aggregate desired borrowing. But this is equivalent in this case to equating planned saving to planned investment. At $r = 0.10$, A's desired borrowing of \$20 is equal to his desired investment of \$15 plus his desired dissaving of \$5; and B's desired lending is equal to his desired saving of \$30 minus his desired investment of \$10. Therefore:

Desired Lending $\qquad$ Desired Borrowing

$$S_B - I_B = 30 - 10 \quad = I_A - S_A = 15 - (-5)$$

$$S_B + S_A = 30 + (-5) = \ I_A + I_B = 15 + 10$$
$$S = 25 \qquad = \qquad I = 25$$

24. The Real and the Money Rate of Interest

With a constant price level, the money rate of interest on riskless loans will equal the real rate of interest. Up to now we have tacitly assumed that the price level is constant so that we did not need to qualify the term 'rate of interest'. We now introduce one of Fisher's famous propositions: the money rate of interest is equal to the real rate of interest plus the rate of change in the price level. Thus, when prices are falling at 5 percent per annum, a zero money rate of interest corresponds to a real rate of 5 percent: if we lend the purchasing power of \$100 for a year at a zero money rate of interest, we receive back \$105 in purchasing power when prices have fallen 5 percent. This proposition is not original to Fisher. We met it earlier in Marshall's *Principles* [see chapter 10, section 33] and it goes back to Thornton's *Nature of the Paper Credit* (1803). Nevertheless, Fisher was the first to see all its implications and to weave it into a systematic theory of the real rate.

To clarify the logic of the argument, let us suppose that physical capital is perfectly

---

[4] Notice that individual A's supply curve of saving is positively inclined – he saves more at a higher rate of interest – but individual B's supply curve is backward bending – he saves less at a higher rate of interest. The condition for a backward-bending saving-supply curve is, of course, that the income effect of a higher interest rate is negative and larger than the substitution effect. This in turn implies that the successively higher waiting lines converge to the right: the rate of time preference increases with income because future income is an 'inferior good'. This is hardly a plausible general assumption but it can occur for some ranges of income. The common belief in the interest inelasticity of saving must be due to a negative income effect just cancelling out the positive substitution effect.

homogeneous and that a unit of it earns a rental of n dollars per period. To avoid an index-number problem, assume also a one-sector model: there exists only one physical good selling at a price of p dollars per unit and it is either consumed or used as capital in the production of more of itself. If the production function $X = f(K,N)$, the stock of capital under perfect competition will be used as an input until its marginal value product equals its money rental flow per period,

$$p \, \frac{\delta X}{\delta K} = n.$$

The money rental per year is simply the annual expected return – of which there may be a whole series over future years – minus the annual running expenses and depreciation charges: it is the net current product of the capital good. Dividing through by the price of a unit of final output, we obtain

$$\frac{\delta X}{\delta K} = \frac{n}{p}.$$

If this real rental were expected in perpetuity, its present value in dollars of constant purchasing power would be $(n/p)(1/r)$. Since capital can be sold as well as rented, competition ensures that the *price* of capital is equal to the present value of the expected stream of rental payments. Thus, in general $(n/p)(1/r) = p_K$. In this particular case, however, $p = p_K$ because output and capital are the same commodity. Therefore, $n/p_K = r$: the marginal physical product of capital is equal to the real capital rental per period, $\bar{n}$, or the money rental of a dollar's worth of capital.

This real capital rental is perfectly comparable to the real wage rate, both being measured in dollars of constant purchasing power over physical units per period of time, and the ratio of rentals per machine to wages per man is equal in equilibrium to the marginal rate of substitution of capital for labour, which in turn is measured entirely in physical units. The rate of interest, on the other hand, is a pure number because it is defined as dollars per dollars per unit of time; it is therefore in a different dimension from the wage rate – a fundamental point frequently overlooked.[5] The rate of interest enables us to determine the price of a machine from a knowledge of annual machine rentals, and *vice versa*. Thus, if the rent of a machine with an infinite life is $10 and the rate of interest is 10 percent, the machine will sell for $100. We have

[5] This shows that what Samuelson called the 'factor-price-frontier' is really a misnomer: the rate of interest is not the price of capital goods and to determine the returns to capital goods we ought to consult, not the theory of interest, but the theory of rent and quasi-rent. As we have just seen, the ratio of capital rentals to wage rates is wholly in physical terms because both numerator and denominator are money flows per physical unit per unit of time. However, the ratio of the wage rate to the interest rate, as depicted by the factor-price-frontier, is in value terms because we are dividing a money flow per physical unit per unit of time by a money flow per *money* amount per unit of time; in short, we are dividing a flow by a percentage rate. This ratio does not show the rate at which man-hours are substituted for machine-hours but rather the rate at which man-hours are substituted for money-per-unit-of-capital, implying, for example, that a proportional change in all prices will affect the slope of the factor-price-frontier. For that reason, the factor-price-frontier is better called a 'wage-interest-frontier'.

just shown that the marginal physical product of capital will be equal in equilibrium to the annual money rental of a representative capital good divided by its price; it might be called 'the real own-rate of interest' of the product in our one-sector economy. With a constant price level and perfect arbitrage, this own-rate will equal the money rate of interest. If prices are falling, however, the real rate will have to exceed the money rate to induce people to hold the product in question. When prices are falling at 5 percent per annum, a money rate of interest of 5 percent gives people no incentive to hold the product unless the own-rate of interest is higher than 5 percent. Conversely, if prices are rising, a given money rate will imply a lower real rate. Thus, the money rate of interest

$$r = n + \dot{p} \text{ or } n/p = r - \dot{p},$$

where $\dot{p} = 1/p \ (dp/dt)$, the time derivative of p expressed as a proportion of p or the rate of change of prices per unit of time. Thus, a change in the money rate of interest is equivalent to a change in the price level: a fall (rise) in the money rate of interest implies a rise (fall) in the price level because a change in the money rate of interest does not by itself affect the real rate of interest.

This proposition permits us to say something more about the economics of the stationary state. We saw that the real rate of interest in a stationary state would be zero if time preference was neutral. But even a stationary economy contains goods like wheat and timber that undergo percentage increases per unit of time in terms of themselves; this is why 18th-century authors like Turgot traced the productivity of capital to the inherent fecundity of nature. At a zero money rate of interest, there would be an infinite demand for money to buy and store goods that exhibit own-rates of growth. To prevent this from happening, prices would have to fall at a percentage rate equal to the physical productivity of such goods.

A zero or negative *money* rate of interest is almost impossible to maintain without some way of depreciating money. If money is not depreciating, the demand for money-to-hold at a zero or negative money rate of interest will always drive up the rate, since the cost of storing money is negligible. In the absence of inflation, a zero or negative money rate can be achieved by a tax per period of time on currency and deposit holdings. This, by the way, is the origin of Gesell's stamped-money scheme to encourage investment. In the absence of price changes, the money rate of interest cannot be zero or negative if the *real* rate of interest is positive: who would not be an entrepreneur if his creditors were willing to pay him for it? The excess demand for production loans would soon raise the money rate to a level above zero. The real rate of interest, however, could conceivably be zero but it could never be negative. While goods can be carried forward in time, they cannot be carried backward. When the real rate is positive, people are induced to convert present goods into future goods and this is always physically possible, at least if some goods are not perishable. But at a negative real rate, the incentive is to convert future goods into present goods. This can be carried out only insofar as it is possible to draw down on stocks of goods. Hence, a negative real rate results in an infinite demand for present goods of a perishable nature, which will tend to drive the real rate back to zero.

25. The Real Rate in a Dynamic Economy

We have shown that in static equilibrium the real rate of interest in a one-sector model will equal the marginal value productivity of a dollar's worth of capital goods – the demand price for capital – and the marginal rate of time preference – the supply price of capital. But this implies that both net saving and net investment are zero. If a dynamic economy is defined as one in which net investment is positive, it follows that the real rate of interest in such an economy is necessarily greater than the social cost of providing capital and less than the social advantage of using it. The individual's marginal supply price of 'waiting' is that interest rate which just causes him neither to add to nor to draw down his accumulated savings. The marginal supply price of 'waiting' to the community as a whole is that interest rate which just neutralizes the average rate of time preference in the community, causing net saving to be zero. Therefore, when the community is adding to its savings, the market rate of interest must exceed the average social rate of time preference. Similarly, positive net investment implies that the real rate of interest is less than the marginal physical product of a dollar's worth of capital, for otherwise the stock of capital would not be added to.

What governs the rate of investment in an economy is not the Keynesian 'marginal efficiency of capital' but what Lerner called the 'marginal efficiency of investment'. A firm compares the ratio of the marginal value product of a capital good to its price with the rate of interest on the money it would have to borrow to buy it. But when the economy as a whole increases its capital by investment, the concept of the marginal product of capital loses its definite meaning. The marginal product of capital is a static micro-concept, applicable if net investment is zero. When net investment is positive, the ratio of the marginal value product of capital to its price must exceed the money rate of interest and investment per unit of time will be such as to equate the marginal efficiency of investment to the interest rate. This is a perfect analogy to the marginal productivity theory of wages, which determines the optimum rate of employment of labour for a firm. A firm is in equilibrium when the marginal value product of labour is equal to the wage rate; its rate of hiring labour is then zero. Suppose the wage rate changes. We then have the question: How quickly will the firm alter its labour force? This is a question about the theory of the rate of hiring, which is analogous to the theory of investment. Similarly, if the entire employed labour force in an economy were increasing, the marginal product of labour at any moment of time would have to exceed the wage rate; otherwise, the rate of hiring of labour would not be positive.

26. Real versus Monetary Theories

The theories of interest that we have studied in this chapter focus their attention on the 'real' forces of productivity and thrift. The action of monetary authorities in recent decades and the presence of unemployment have seriously diluted the impact of the real forces contemplated in neoclassical theory. As a result, economists have largely ceased to be concerned with real theories of interest. The textbook theory of interest today is either a liquidity preference theory, in which the money rate of interest depends on the demand and supply of the stock of money and bonds, or a loanable-funds theory, in which the money rate of interest depends on the demand and supply of a flow of total borrowing and lending.

It is sometimes suggested that there is an inherent conflict between real and monetary theories of interest. According to real theories, interest is the yield of capital and a reward for abstaining from present consumption. According to monetary theories, interest is the price of money and a reward for parting with liquidity. These are supposed to be fundamentally conflicting explanations. Keynes himself seems to have fostered this interpretation when he stated dogmatically that interest is, not a reward for waiting, but a reward for not hoarding money. But general equilibrium considerations show that interest operates simultaneously, as D. H. Robertson has put it, on 'the three-fold margin' of consumption decisions, investment decisions and asset portfolio decisions. In other words, interest simultaneously rewards waiting, reflects the pure yield of capital, and compensates for the sacrifice of liquidity.

Given the enormous influence of the monetary authorities on the rate of interest nowadays, how much significance should we attach to real theories of interest? Patinkin offers a way of answering this question. A real theory determines the interest rate in the commodity market, while a monetary theory determines it either in the bond market or in the money market. We can say that interest is a real phenomenon if it behaves like a relative price and a monetary phenomenon if it behaves like an absolute price. As we saw in our earlier discussion of classical theory [see chapter 5, section 10], changes in the quantity of money and in liquidity preferences which leave relative prices invariant also leave the rate of interest invariant. On the other hand, technical change that affects the yield of capital and changes in time preference that affect saving decisions alter relative prices and also alter the rate of interest. The forces that have altered absolute prices over time have had little effect on the long-run rate of interest. In that sense, we can conclude that the long-run rate of interest is essentially a matter of real forces. There is scope, therefore, even in modern economies for real theories of interest.

THE RICARDO EFFECT

The rise of Keynesian economics in the 1930s was marked by fierce controversy over the saving-investment identity, the nature of the consumption function, the alleged superiority of the liquidity-preference over the loanable-funds approach, the efficacy of monetary and fiscal policy to induce recovery and many other hornets' nests that Keynes had uncovered in the *General Theory*. In the background, the old debate on capital theory, which had been reopened by Knight in 1933, raged on without showing any signs of being resolved. But even here the influence of Keynes made itself felt. In *Profits, Interest, and Investment* (1939), Hayek linked the Austrian theory of capital to the phenomena of the business cycle in an effort to show that, contrary to Keynes, a rising level of consumption must after a certain point reduce rather than increase the rate of investment. It is only fitting that we bring our discussion of capital and interest to a close by examining this favourite offspring of Böhm-Bawerk's last and greatest pupil.

27. The Concertina Effect

Hayek takes it for granted that commodity prices typically rise faster than money wages in the upswing of the business cycle: real wages fall in the boom. If entrepreneurs expect this higher price-wage ratio to persist, labour will be substituted for machinery. In Hayek's terminology, the fall in real wages leads to changes in the relative profitability of different methods of production in favour of shorter or less roundabout methods. At some point, investment demand for 'capital widening' in response to expanding consumer demand for current output – the demand for more machines of exactly the same type as before – is more than offset by this type of 'capital shallowing' and total investment demand in the economy falls off. Conversely, in a depression the rising level of real wages brings about a revival of investment as 'capital deepening' – the tendency to adopt more durable machines – begins to offset the decline in induced investment. The reasoning involved is familiar to any student of Böhm-Bawerk: the length of the period of production varies directly with real wages and inversely with the rate of interest. But whereas Böhm-Bawerk had applied this doctrine to long-run equilibrium conditions, Hayek adapted it to the circumstances of the business cycle. The length of the period of production falls in the upswing and increases in the downswing according to what has been aptly called 'the concertina effect'.

28. The Demonstration of the Effect

The 'concertina effect' is Kaldor's name. Hayek himself spoke of the Ricardo Effect. The Ricardo Effect takes its name from Ricardo's argument that a general rise in money wages leads to a substitution of machinery for labour [see chapter 4, section 4]. Ricardo assumed that labour costs in the machine goods industry are less than the average of labour costs in the economy as a whole, so that the rise in money wages does not produce a proportionate rise in the price of machines; hence, the money rate of interest or profit declines. We who are no longer so confident that the machine goods industry is especially capital intensive need firmer grounds for Ricardo's proposition.

If an increase in the level of wages raises machine prices in the same proportion as the price of labour, neither the real rate nor the money rate of interest will change. Suppose labour costs are on average 50 percent of total costs, then a 10 percent increase in money wages first of all raises the absolute price of finished goods by 5 percent. If the machine goods industry has the same capital structure as output in general, machine prices also rise by 5 percent. This then raises the price of output by 2.5 percent but, as machines are made by machines, we also have to take account of the effect of the 5 percent rise in machine prices on the price of machines, and so on. Thus, all prices will eventually rise by 10 percent, leaving the rate of interest unaffected. But if the rate of interest remains unchanged, the rise in wages will raise production costs of different methods and processes proportionately to the share of wages in total costs. Hence, it does not make it more profitable to invest in more capital-intensive methods. To get the Ricardo Effect, therefore, a rise in money wages must raise the price of machines less than proportionately.

The Ricardo Effect is really a misnomer because Hayek tries to show that even when Ricardo's assumption is not met, namely, that the machine goods industry is relatively capital-intensive, it will still be true that a rise in wages will induce substitution of capital for labour, and *vice versa*. In his initial essay on the problem, published in 1939, Hayek presented an example in which direct and indirect labour is applied at various dates to the production of a commodity. The rate of interest is 6 percent and is equal to the rate of profit per annum on capital. Now, while money wages remain constant, the price of the product rises by 2 percent, so that real wages fall 2 percent (see Table 12–2).

Table 12–2

	Labour Invested for				
	2 Yrs.	1 Yr.	6 Mos.	3 Mos.	1 Mo.
Initial amount of profit per turnover at 6% p.a.	12	6	3	1.5	0.5
Add extra 2% on profit margins due to the rise in product price	14	8	5	3.5	2.5
Final rate of profit p.a., neglecting compound interest	7	8	10	14	30

The initial amount of profit earned on each turnover of any amount of labour is simply the difference between the money wage rate and the undiscounted marginal value product of labour. A rise in the product price raises the amount of profit on each turnover proportionately, irrespective of the length of the period of turnover. But the annual rate of profit rises more for labour invested in short than in long periods. This leads to a substitution of short-period for long-period investments – a shift toward finishing goods at the expense of constructing machines – until the annual rate of profit is once again the same for all investment periods. *Ergo*, a rise in the ratio of output to input prices, a decline in real wages, leads to substitution of direct for indirect labour and shortens the average period of production.

It has been argued that firms do not normally confront a range of turnover periods of capital as great as Hayek supposes. Hence, the Ricardo Effect would not account for much investment reallocation. But this criticism ignores the fact that the argument applies not only between firms but also within firms, and within firms the turnover period does range from a few months for working capital to several years for equipment and building. Hayek's subsequent restatement of the Ricardo Effect explains the mechanism more convincingly in terms of money capital. A rise in the ratio of output to input prices increases the annual rate of profit on working capital

Figure 12–6

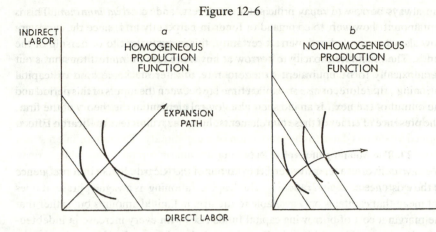

more than on fixed capital. This induces the firm to invest its liquid capital funds in processes with a high rate of turnover. When the fall in real wages is general, the result is that the average period of turnover of gross investment expenditures in the economy as a whole declines; in other words, the average period of production is shortened.

Notice that the Ricardo Effect does not depend on a falling rate of interest. On the contrary, the rate of interest, as well as the relative price of labour and of machines, is assumed to be constant. But what of our earlier contention that a change in real wages does not induce factor substitution when the rate of interest is constant? This conclusion still holds and more than one critic has argued that it disposes of Hayek's argument. Let us restate the criticism: the equimarginal rule states that the optimal combination of labour and capital is one where the ratio of the marginal physical products of any two factors is equal to the ratio of their marginal factor costs for the same period of time. In this case, the ratio of marginal factor costs is the ratio between the wage rate and the annual rentals of machines. Since neither the wage rate, the rental per machine, nor the rate of interest have altered in the case Hayek analyzes, the ratio of marginal factor costs remains the same as before. It is true that the rise in the product price tends to increase the scale of output but if the production function is linearly homogeneous, so that the marginal rate of substitution between labour and machines is independent of scale, this does not induce factor substitution.

To put teeth in the Ricardo Effect, we must assume either a nonhomogeneous production function, in which *MRS* alters in favour of direct labour as the scale of output expands (see Figure 12–6b) – any homogeneous production function, whatever its degree, generates a straight-line expansion path – or else an upward-sloping supply curve of credit to the firm. Hayek readily conceded this point, arguing that the traditional assumption of competitive theory of a perfectly elastic credit-supply curve to each firm leads to absurd results. If a firm is free to borrow funds without some absolute ceiling or expectation of a ceiling to the amount it can borrow at a finite rate of interest, it will borrow enough to push the marginal yield down to zero, knowing it can always borrow to repay principal and interest, and so on *ad infinitum*. This is tantamount, however, to command of funds in perpetuity and, since the funds are now also commanded with perfect certainty, this is equivalent to ownership of the funds. The indefinite capacity to borrow at any finite rate of interest thus turns out paradoxically to be equivalent to a zero rate of interest. Some kind of 'capital rationing', therefore, or else an explicit time lag between the inputs of this period and the output of the next, is an indispensable logical element in the theory of the firm. The presence of either of these two elements, however, validates the Ricardo Effect.

29. The Meaning of Capital Rationing

We have delivered a tentative verdict in favour of the Ricardo Effect in consequence of the existence of capital rationing. But 'capital rationing' is a vague phrase: it does not mean that capital is only available to the firm in limited amounts but rather that the marginal cost of borrowing capital funds rises with every increase in indebtedness. But even this is ambiguous. Does it mean that the marginal borrowing cost to the firm is an increasing function of the total capital invested K or that it is an increasing function of ΔK, the rate of investment per unit of time, irrespective of the total amount already invested? In the first case, credit is a limiting factor to the firm's scale of operations but not necessarily to its rate of investment in any time period. In the second case, credit restrictions would limit the firm's rate of expansion but not necessarily its scale of operations in the long run. If the second meaning is accepted, the Ricardo Effect falls to the ground because a fall in real wages will not now reduce capital intensity unless the rate of investment is rising, thus increasing the cost of capital to the firm. Presumably investment does increase in the upswing. We recall, however, that the Ricardo Effect is supposed to demonstrate that 'capital shallowing' will offset 'capital widening' at some stage in the boom, after which date total investment demand declines. We have just shown that the Ricardo Effect is operative only if net investment is positive. Hence, 'capital shallowing' can *never* offset investment demand for the purpose of 'capital widening' for the simple reason that it fails to operate when the rate of investment has ceased to be positive. As soon as the Ricardo Effect offsets capital widening, the rising marginal cost of borrowing levels off for firms which are investing and the effect of the fall in real wages on capital intensity dies away.

To rescue the Ricardo Effect, we have to interpret the upward-sloping supply curve of credit to firms under capital rationing as a relationship between the marginal borrowing cost and the total capital stock of the firm: the first of our two meanings of 'capital rationing'. Is there any evidence for such an interpretation? Yes, if the firm operates with some of its own funds. According to Kalecki's much-discussed 'principle of increasing risk', the subjective risk to the firm of increased indebtedness rises with every increase in the amount of borrowed capital relative to equity capital. Since loans take precedence over the claim of owners to the gross income of the firm, the riskiness of additional credit is an increasing function of the number of dollars borrowed. Moreover, lenders rely primarily on the value of the firm as a going concern for their security and hence a large loan is less attractive to lenders than a small loan. Therefore, given the fact that most firms own part of their own capital, the marginal cost of borrowing to firms will usually rise with the total amount of capital invested in the firm. This vindicates the Ricardo Effect.

But is it realistic to assume a given amount of the firm's own capital during the business cycle? What of the familiar fact that as much as 50–75 percent of corporate investment relies on internal sources in the form of retained profits and unused depreciation accruals? The firm's own capital is added to during the upswing by the ploughing-back of undistributed profits and hence the supply curve of credit as a function of the firm's capital stock is constantly shifted to the right. Thus, a fall in real wages need not reduce capital intensity because shifts in the marginal credit cost curve may be more than adequate to offset the limitation of credit.

The marginal cost of borrowing to individual firms, therefore, is not a simple unique function of its capital stock or, for that matter, its rate of investment. It seems to be a function of current planned investment over additions to the firm's own capital through retained profits and the new issue of shares in the preceding period. At any rate, shifts in this function will usually render the Ricardo Effect inoperative in the boom phase of the business cycle unless we introduce additional factors like restrictive monetary policy.

30. Conclusions

In hunting down the assumptions and postulates of the Ricardo Effect, we have arrived at the perhaps anticipated conclusion that it is only another instance of the vice of neoclassical economics: the hasty application of static theorems to the real world. A list of Hayek's basic assumptions will show that by relaxing any one of them we obtain a more useful explanation of the downturn than is afforded by the Ricardo Effect: (1) capital equipment is utilized to capacity but labour is not fully employed; (2) equipment is perfectly divisible; (3) there is no technical change and constant returns to scale prevail in all industries; (4) money wage rates and machine prices are constant; (5) the market rate of interest is constant but firms face less than perfectly elastic supply curves for borrowed funds; (6) elasticities of expectations are equal to unity, that is, everyone expects future prices to rise at the same rate as current prices.

Would it be possible to test 'the concertina effect' statistically? A rough-and-ready index of the average period of turnover of investment expenditures in the economy is the ratio of total investment in business inventories to the net total investment in both inventories and durable equipment. If Hayek is right, this ratio should rise in the boom and fall in the slump. It has been shown that this ratio is indeed positively correlated with the level of money income but, unfortunately, it is not positively correlated with the level of real wages. It is not clear, however, that this refutes the Ricardo Effect because of the special meaning which Hayek gives to the term 'real wages'.

31. Money and Real Wages

At the very outset of the discussion some readers may have wondered whether it is really true that real wages fall in the upswing and rise in the downswing. In the

General Theory, Keynes threw out the idea that money wages and real wages usually move in opposite directions. This sounds very much like Hayek's basic assumption but Keynes was forced in the end to retract his generalization and to accept the statistical finding that money and real wages usually rise together, although they do not always fall together. There is a certain confusion of terminology here. In neoclassical theory, 'real wages' do not denote the purchasing power of money wages over the cost-of-living basket of goods but rather money wages expressed in terms of the current output that labour produces. In Hayek's argument, it is evident that 'real wages' refer to the product-wage rate and, in fact, while real wages in terms of what workers buy with their money wages do not usually fall in a boom, the product-wage rate – money wages deflated by an index of wholesale prices – does typically decline in the upswing.

There is nothing amiss with the *a priori* argument that money wages do vary inversely with product-wages. Wage rates are determined by real demand and real supply functions. A fall in employment under perfect competition raises real wages by raising the marginal physical product of labour. Prices are determined by the condition that marginal cost equals marginal revenue. Marginal costs have now fallen; hence, prices fall and so do money wages. Or to put it the right way up, as incomes fall in a slump, money wages fall and accommodate themselves to the marginal physical product of labour, whatever it is. The level of real wages is entirely independent of the level of money wages because prices are always equated to marginal costs without any time lag. In a boom, money wages, marginal costs and sales prices rise, while real wages decline corresponding to the lower marginal physical product of labour at higher levels of employment. Thus, on neoclassical grounds it is perfectly true that real wages, properly defined as product-wages, fall in the upswing and rise in the downswing of the business cycle. It is simply that these real wages are not what we have in mind when we talk of 'real wages' rising in a boom and falling in a slump.

READER'S GUIDE TO THE 'LECTURES ON POLITICAL ECONOMY', VOLUME 1

If Wicksteed's *Common Sense* supplies a classic exposition of the subjective theory of value, the first volume of Wicksell's *Lectures* (1901) provides a masterly statement of the neoclassical theory of production and distribution.[6] From a technical point of view, it must be one of the most difficult books to read in the entire history of economic thought. Indeed, only Walras' *Elements* is more difficult. But 'no student of economics has completed his training', Schumpeter once said, 'who has not read the whole of this volume'. Wicksell thoroughly reworked Böhm-Bawerk's capital theory and transformed it into an explicit marginal productivity theory that made interest as the marginal productivity of waiting completely coordinate with wages

---

[6] We shall occasionally refer to Wicksell's *Value, Capital, and Rent* (1954), referred to hereafter as *Value*, which was published in 1893, eight years before the first volume of the *Lectures*. On some questions the two books provide an interesting contrast in treatment.

and rent as the marginal productivity of labour and land. By discarding Böhm-Bawerk's one-sector model in favour of a multi-sector treatment, Wicksell went far toward bridging the gap between the Austrian and Walrasian schools. The average period of production, as Böhm-Bawerk expounded it, comes near to being nonsense: whatever validity the concept may have rests on Wicksell's version of it. Wicksell has been justly called 'the economist's economist': few writers have commented with so much penetration on the ideas of their predecessors and contemporaries as he did.

32. Utility and Value

The introduction constitutes a defense of abstract economics. Note in particular the incisive critical comments on the German Historical School (pages xxii–xxiii, 11), the emphasis on the importance of population theory (page 6), and the declaration that modern economics, committed as it is to individual utility maximization, involves 'a thoroughly revolutionary programme' (page 4).

Part I, chapter 1, takes up the question of value theory by resolving Smith's water-diamond paradox (pages 18, 29–30). A money cost-of-production theory is shown to involve circular reasoning (pages 21–2). Ricardo's theory of value is briefly but sympathetically examined (pages 22–3; see also *Value*, pages 35–41). In Ricardo, cost of production depends on marginal costs but the location of the margin depends on demand and, hence, on the whole configuration of prices. Ricardo managed to ignore this because he treated demand as given by the size of population (pages 24–6). The case of joint supply creates independent difficulties for the classical theory of value (page 26).

Part 1, chapter 2, introduces marginal utility as a synthesis of utility and scarcity. Wicksell stresses the variability of the marginal utility of money. An exchange equilibrium involves only intrapersonal, not interpersonal comparisons of utility (pages 31–3, 43).

The question of measurability of utility is considered in **Part 1, chapter 3**. Wicksell concludes that utility is a cardinal magnitude because 'we can generally say' that differences between the successive intervals on a utility scale can be compared (pages 37–9; see also Appendix, pages 221–2). The simple case of a choice between the direct and the indirect use of a given stock of agricultural products, given a constant rate of production transformation, is treated graphically (pages 39–41). The possible interdependence of utility functions is emphasized at the outset (pages 41, 42, 45). Weak substitutability in consumption may produce the illusion of a positively sloped demand curve (pages 44–5). The supply curve of labour may be backward sloping (pages 45–6). The worker's marginal utility of earned income will equal in equilibrium his marginal disutility of effort; an increase in wages lowers the marginal utility of income and hence results in more work; but, on the other hand, his real income has risen, which tends to shift the income-utility curve upward, thus favouring less work and more leisure. This is nothing but the later distinction between a positive substitution and a negative income effect [see chapter 9, section 9]. An increase of pay for overtime, Wicksell observes correctly, will usually increase the supply of effort: since this affects the marginal rather than the average rate of remuneration, the substitution effect is likely to outweigh the income effect (page 46). Next, the proportionality rule for an exchange equilibrium is set out mathematically, both for additive and for generalized utility functions (pages 47–9).

Jevons' treatment of 'isolated exchange' does not yield to determinate solution because we have a single equation but two unknowns to be determined (pages 49–51). The case of barter exchange is then treated graphically: demand and supply curves for B are drawn, with reverse supply and demand curves for A, and the price of B in terms of A is chosen as the abscissa (pages 55–8). The reason the supply curve of B turns down eventually in Wicksell's diagram is that the rising price of B necessarily lowers MU_A faster than MU_B; this is a consequence of the assumption that every offer of B implies a demand for A (page 57; for a slightly different treatment of the same diagram, see *Value*, pages 83–92). This leads up to the problem of multiple equilibria and the possibility of unstable equilibria (pages 59–60). The 'admittedly artificial example' (on pages 60–2) may be passed over.

Exchange of three or more commodities requires the use of a medium of exchange to facilitate arbitrage (pages 63–5). There follows a simple but elegant statement of the Walrasian method of establishing the existence of a general equilibrium solution (pages 65–71); for a similar but more detailed exposition, see *Value*, pages 79–82). Money is assumed to be an abstract unit of account; hence, the Walrasian solution leaves absolute prices indeterminate (page 67). 'This is obvious', Wicksell remarks, 'so long as we regard the functions of money as purely formal.' In reality, he adds, the demand for money-to-hold is never a matter of indifference (page 68). This says everything [see chapter 5, section 2] that Patinkin tried to say with respect to the indeterminacy of absolute prices in some versions of the Walrasian system (see also Appendix, pages 223–5, where Cassel is criticized on this score).

Part 1, chapter 4, deals briefly with the objections to marginal utility theory based on discontinuities and the force of habit in consumer behavior (pages 68–72).

33. Welfare Economics

Part 1, chapter 5, examines the question: Does perfect competition maximize 'the gains from free exchange'? Walras, like Jevons, fell into the error of generalizing from the two-persons two-goods case (page 74). The first objection to this generalization is that competition does not preclude multiple equilibria. If each of these is a welfare optimum, the original proposition is shorn of its usual meaning (page 75). Moreover, state intervention can clearly increase the welfare of some individuals; since interpersonal comparisons of utility are by nature imprecise, it is not obvious that the general loss from, say, a protective duty exceeds the particular gains to some parties (pages 76–7). If we assume equal individual capacities for want satisfaction, the principle of diminishing marginal utility of income leads directly to the conclusion that greater equality of income distribution increases welfare (page 77). This assumes that total income is independent of its distribution. Wicksell is not unaware of this assumption (see pages 78–9, 82). The equimarginal rule in exchange implies a welfare optimum if and only if the utility functions are the same for all parties and if the final equilibrium is independent of the initial quantity of goods possessed (pages 79–81; the same argument is set out with illustrative arithmetical examples in *Value*, pages 64–76). This brilliant refutation of the harmony doctrine concludes with an irritable comment on Pareto's definition of a welfare optimum (pages 82–3).

34. Imperfect Competition

Wicksell's treatment of imperfect competition in **Part I, chapter 6**, follows Marshall closely. Some discursive remarks on joint supply lead into a brief discussion of retail pricing (pages 86–8). Because of site advantages, the product may be spatially differentiated; the result is a higher price and a larger number of retailers than would be the case if the market were perfectly competitive. When total cost is constant, so that marginal cost is zero and lies along the horizontal axis, the monopolist maximizes profits by setting price at the point where the elasticity of demand equals unity (pages 90–1). Wicksell is curiously reluctant to use the concept of elasticity, following Cournot rather than Marshall. When total costs are variable, instantaneous profits are maximized when the first derivative of the net revenue function vanishes (pages 92–3). Wicksell treats the case of a linear demand curve with constant marginal costs. (This produces the conclusion that when $MC = 2$, profits are maximized by raising the price $\frac{1}{2}MC$. This result has been generalized for nonlinear demand curves by Joan Robinson in *Economics of Imperfect Competition*. She shows that the monopoly price $= \frac{1}{2}(OA + MC)$. Her OA corresponds to $p = 24$ in Wicksell's Figure 5. If Wicksell's figure is redrawn so that g as well as p falls to zero, the formula reads: $MP = \frac{1}{2}(24 + 2) = 13$).

One of Edgeworth's theorems in the field of price discrimination is discussed in terms of a rather special graphic solution (pages 93–5). Any sharp distinction between monopoly and competition is explicitly disavowed (page 96) – shades of Chamberlin! A brief comment on Cournot's duopoly analysis closes the chapter. Curiously enough, Wicksell finds Cournot's symmetry assumption more 'reasonable' than those of Bertrand and Edgeworth (pages 96–7).

35. Production and Distribution

Part 1, chapter 7, criticizes the Walrasian assumption that the supply of productive agents and the technical input coefficients may be regarded as given, so that equilibrium in factor markets is simply a by-product of equilibrium in product markets (pages 97–6; see also the comments on Wieser's imputation theory in *Value*, pages 24–6). Notice the brief reference to Say's Law (pages 97–8). The problem of interest is that of allowing for the role of the time element in production (page 99).

We have finished the elementary and derivative section of the book and are beginning to touch on Wicksell's original contributions. The introductory section to **Part II** is given over to a general discussion of the role of production and distribution in a stationary state; various limitations on the analysis are laid down (pages 103–5) and a three-factor model is postulated (page 107). Marshall's fourth factor of production, namely, organization or enterprise, which earns profit just as capital earns interest is dismissed as lacking quantitative precision (page 107).

Part II, chapter 1, 'Non–Capitalistic Production', asks the reader to suppose an economy so primitive that the marginal productivity of capital is negligibly small. If, furthermore, we assume that the period of production is one year, we arrive at a pure wages fund doctrine. Under these circumstances, how will the product be divided (pages 108–10)? The law of diminishing returns is incorrectly defined in terms of proportional instead of incremental returns, that is, as a matter of diminishing average rather than marginal productivity (pages 110–11). Marshall is criticized for applying one law of return to agriculture and another to industry. The law of increasing return, so-called, is a matter of returns to scale, while the 'law of diminishing return' applies universally to increases in one factor, holding the rest constant (page 111).

The marginal productivity of labour determines the wage rate, subject to the condition that all labour is fully employed (pages 112–13). Rent is a surplus, determined by the gap between the average and marginal product of labour (page 113). Like Clark and Wicksteed, Wicksell does not draw an average product curve, which somewhat mitigates the error of defining diminishing returns in proportional terms.

The theory is restated in terms of a simple but very special production function: $X = k\sqrt{N}$, where k is 400 and there is a fixed amount of a second factor, 'land' (pages 114–16). $MP_N = \delta X/\delta N = k/2\sqrt{N}$; with 16 workers and the product selling at 10s., w = (400/8) · 10s. = 500s. Wicksell approximates the marginal product by adding a 17th worker. He concludes by showing that for any non-homogeneous production function of the form $X = kN^\alpha + B$, where B = land, and $\alpha < 1$, labour's share depends uniquely upon the value of α (page 116). In the special production function under analysis, $\alpha = \frac{1}{2}$. Since $\bar{w} = k/2\sqrt{N}$, $\bar{w}N = Nk/2\sqrt{N}$ and $\bar{w}N/X = Nk/2\sqrt{N}$ $(1/k\sqrt{N}) = \frac{1}{2}$; labour's share equals α and the fixed factor receives the residual.

There follows a lucid statement of Ricardian rent theory as a special case of the general marginal productivity theory (pages 116–18). Carey's objection to Ricardo's theory is briskly refuted (page 119). Rodbertus' rent theory is criticized (pages 119–20). Rodbertus' argument is simply that when all prices correspond to labour values and the rate of surplus per man is everywhere the same, the rate of profit is necessarily higher in a labour-intensive industry like agriculture. The landlord preempts this surplus, thus equalizing the rate of profit between agriculture and industry. The trouble with this argument is that products are not sold at their labour values. Wicksell passes over this point but goes to the heart of the matter by questioning the arbitrary assumption of an equal rate of surplus value per man. The intimate connection between Rodbertus' rent and Marx's 'absolute rent' should be obvious [see chapter 7, section 45].

Wicksell recognizes that when the law of diminishing returns is stated in terms of the average rather than the marginal product, we may get an apparent contradiction to the law (page 122). His denial of any phase of increasing marginal productivity, rather obscurely formulated, is clearly wrong (page 123; see also page 243n).

Ricardian rent theory is now generalized to any variable factor (pages 124–5). Wicksell is careful to point out that the margin in question is not Ricardo's extensive margin resulting from the application of labour and capital to inferior grades of soil, for here one of the necessary conditions of marginal analysis – constancy in one of the cooperating factors – is violated: the quality of land is varied, while the quantity of labour and capital is being increased.

Is the total product exhausted when each factor is rewarded its marginal product (pages 125–6)? In a famous passage, Wicksell argues that perfect competition will drive firms to operate at an output at which profits are zero and constant returns to scale prevail (pages 128–31). Wicksell notes some of the qualifications that must be made with respect to the universal validity of the product-exhaustion theorem (pages 131–3); he neglects the question of uncertainty, however.

Wicksell now turns to the influence of innovations on factor prices. The discussion lacks precision because of his failure to distinguish between laboursaving and landsaving innovations (pages 135–6). Ricardo's analysis of technological unemployment is neatly refuted: Ricardo failed to consider the reabsorption of labour due to falling wages (page 137). Wicksell now shows, arithmetically, graphically and algebraically that a laboursaving innovation must increase the total product, although it need not increase labour's absolute or relative share of income (pages 137–40). If the marginal product of labour falls short of the subsistence wage, welfare will be maximized by paying wages below subsistence and making up the difference by subsidies (pages 141, 143). This follows from the fact that the product is maximized when $\bar{w} = MP_N$, which in turn implies full employment of labour. Wicksell concludes that there exists no 'simple and intelligible criterion' for judging the effect of a factorsaving innovation on wages (page 143). Notice that he nowhere mentions the possibility of capitalsaving innovations.

36. Capital

With **chapter 2** of **Part II** we reach the subject of capital. Wicksell begins with some comments on the definition of the term 'capital' (pages 144–5). One central difficulty is that capital, as distinct from individual capital goods, is itself a quantity of value. Interest is nothing but a percentage rate of growth in the value of output. The present value of a capital asset is the flow of future income derived from the use of the asset discounted by this percentage rate of growth. As Fisher would have said, in this sense capital is not on the same footing with land and labour: capital is simply any stock, while every flow of income is analogous to interest, being a rate of growth per unit of time in the value of an asset. Wicksell does not express himself in this manner but this seems to be what he means (page 145). He goes on to remark that capital goods are man-made, while virgin soil and unskilled labour are 'original' factors (page 145).

Wicksell digresses briefly to show why marginal productivity theory cannot be simply applied to capital as it has been to labour and land (page 147–9). From the viewpoint of the individual entrepreneur, the price or value of capital is taken as given and so marginal productivity theory is fully applicable. But for the economy as a whole, every increment of capital necessarily alters wage and interest rates and hence changes the purchasing power of capital over goods in general: this is the so-called Wicksell Effect, of which more in a moment. This restates the point made above: capital cannot be treated on all fours with labour and land because capital cannot be measured in terms of its own technical units; particular capital goods yield quasi-rents, not interest. We can 'escape from this difficulty' by resolving all capital into the constituent amounts of 'original' factors that are embedded for a time interval in the productive process (pages 149–51).

The assumptions of the preliminary model are that capital produced in year t is invested, fully used up, and replaced in year $t + 1$. Stationary conditions prevail (pages 151–3). Interest is the difference between the marginal productivity of direct and indirect labour and land (page 154). Böhm-Bawerk's first two reasons for a premium on present goods are clearly irrelevant to investment decisions on the part of entrepreneurs, as Böhm-Bawerk himself admitted, but they are relevant to personal saving decisions, or, as Wicksell says, to the 'accumulation of capital' (page 154). But on 'the fundamental simplifying assumption of stationary economic conditions', these two grounds drop out (page 155). That leaves only the third ground, the technical superiority of present over future goods. Here Böhm-Bawerk claimed too much. All that it is necessary to assume is that 'waiting' is sufficiently scarce to raise interest above zero (page 155). It is shown that in equilibrium the rate of interest will equal the ratio of the marginal product of indirect labour $(l_1 - l)$ to its marginal cost (l) (page 156). This is a special case of the equimarginal principle. 'In given technical conditions', the increase of capital will cause the marginal product of capital to fall (page 157).

Now the analysis broadens out to consider investments for two or more years. Capital in real terms consists of goods in transit (page 158). A simple diagram is used to visualize the structure of capital in a stationary state (pages 159–60). The long-term interest rate is equal to the short-term rate when allowance is made for the greater risk but lesser liquidity of long-term paper (page 161). A fall in the rate of interest makes it profitable to use more inputs in two-year capital investments and fewer in one-year investments. This dependence of the 'average period of investment' on the rate of interest, 'already recognized by Ricardo', is the crux of the Austrian theory of capital (pages 162–3).

Increased roundaboutness will produce a scarcity of present labour and hence raise its marginal product. But an increase in the 'average period of investment' without a change in initial costs leaves a larger net income from a given annual outlay. For this reason, currently available inputs may become more abundant, thus lowering their marginal productivity. This seems to be the sense of Wicksell's distinction between the growth in 'height' as against the growth in 'breadth' of capital (page 163). The passage is obscured by Wicksell's failure to spell out the meaning of 'expansion in height' as against 'expansion in width'.

37. The Capital Structure

Wicksell speaks of the capital structure as having both a vertical and a horizontal dimension, being capable of expansion in both dimensions. The horizontal dimension or 'width' refers to the proportion of primary factors annually invested in the replacement of capital goods of various maturity dates. The vertical dimension or 'height' refers to the length of time for which the various capital goods are invested. If goods of different maturity dates are arrayed in descending order of the length of their investment periods, the result will be a triangular capital structure diagram (Figure 12–7).

Figure 12–7

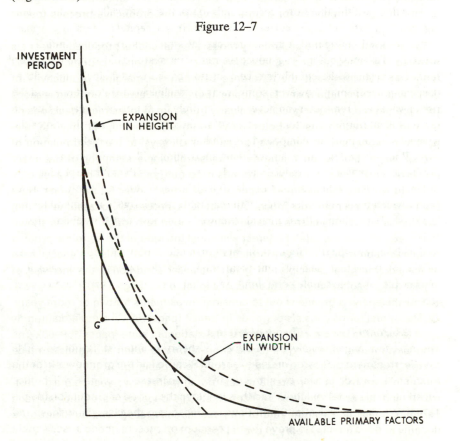

If we know the investment period of all capital goods and the interest rate, we can compute the weighted average investment period for this structure as the center of gravity of the capital structure triangle. The 'height' of the structure is then represented by the center of gravity G. 'Expansion in width' means a proportionate increase in all capital goods of different maturity dates: it rotates the convex compound growth curve to the right and hence increases the amount of invested primary factors. This would not change the 'height' dimension of capital; G would move laterally to the right. But 'expansion in height' raises the center of gravity of the capital structure by increasing the proportion of capital goods invested for long periods at the expense of those invested for short periods. This kind of 'forward tilting' of the capital structure will release primary factors and so shift G upward. The reason for this is that annual replacement requirements per unit of primary factors invested fall as the capital structure is stretched out. A mixed effect of both expansion in 'height' and in 'width' would represent net positive investment concentrated on the more time-consuming processes; hence, G would shift both upward and to the right.

Growth in 'width', therefore, corresponds to what Hawtrey called 'capital widening', while growth in 'height' corresponds to Hawtrey's 'capital deepening'. Apparently, Wicksell considered it typical for capital structures to expand initially by widening. This must before long reduce the rate of interest and bid up real wages and rent. This disturbs the equilibrium composition of the capital stock and induces deepening. Deepening, however, counteracts the decline in the interest rate and the rise in wages and rent but it can never do so entirely for the obvious reason that the more available primary factors are 'frozen' in the capital structure, the larger the triangular area under the compound growth line (pages 163–4; see also page 288).

As Wicksell points out, a laboursaving innovation will make deepening more profitable and may initially reduce wages. But since it raises the average productivity of labour as well as the marginal productivity of capital, it is very likely to lead to capital widening as well as deepening: 'the capitalist saver is thus, fundamentally, the friend of labour, though the technical inventor is not infrequently its enemy' (page 164).

Having completed the foundation of 'our static theory of capital', Wicksell mentions the fact that the flow input-point output case does not raise new 'questions of principle' over the simple point input-point output cases so far considered (pages 165–6).

38. Böhm-Bawerk's Theory of Interest

The next few pages review Böhm-Bawerk's theory of interest. Böhm-Bawerk's cavalier treatment of Ricardo draws a reproof. Ricardo laid the groundwork for the Austrian theory of capital by showing that an increase in wages will induce substitution of capital for labour and thus lengthen the period of production (pages 167–8). Wicksell is critical of Böhm-Bawerk's lapse into the classical wages fund doctrine and the attempt to prove that a premium on present goods arises simply out of the process of lending and borrowing consumption goods, independently of the productivity of investment (pages 160–70). The third reason for interest, which argues that the physical productivity of capital implies value productivity, is defective as an independent reason for a positive rate of interest (pages 170–1; see also *Value*, pages 106–15).

These are minor criticisms at best, for 'it may justly be said that the work [*The Positive Theory*] contains albeit in a somewhat imperfect form, the real and definite theory of capital' (page 171). Walras and Pareto, on the contrary, abstract completely from the time element and their theory of production is one that pertains under 'essentially noncapitalistic conditions, even though the existence of durable, but apparently indestructible instruments, is taken into account' (page 171). Wicksell apparently changed his mind about this criticism for in a review of Cassel's *Theory of Social Economy*, published in 1919, he remarked that we can either follow Walras and define real capital as consisting of only producers' goods or we can regard real capital as an aggregate of fixed and working capital having a time structure: 'We can *either* adopt Walras' method of taking a *cross-section* through social production at a moment of time ... *Or else* we can refer everything back to the original factors of production in conjunction with waiting (or preferably *time*). Here we take a *longitudinal section* instead' (pages 236–7; see also pages 226–7). Since Walras espoused the Clark-Knight synchronized view of capital, it is not clear whether Wicksell meant by this comment to endorse the Walrasian procedure as a perfectly satisfactory alternative explanation to the Austrian one.

39. The Optimum Storage Period

There follows Wicksell's classic analysis of the point input-point output case. The question is: What is the optimum storage period for wine produced in a given year at a fixed cost, the sales price W being an increasing function of time (page 172)? Some readers may be surprised by the choice of wine production as an example of a point input-point output process; it is simply not true that all the inputs for the making of wine are applied at one particular date, after which time alone adds value to the product; nor is it true that all output must be sold at another particular date. What Wicksell is thinking of, however, is the activity of wine merchants who have purchased new wine in barrels, 'grape juice' Wicksell called it, and must now decide the age of the bottled wine they will sell. At any rate, the example must not be taken seriously as an actual description of the wine industry; its purpose is purely illustrative of the case in which no physical inputs are applied over the period of investment.

We are given a definite quantity of circulating capital K, which is supposed to be sufficient for four years' storage of wine. The price of young bottled wine W_0 will vary directly with the price of inputs, that is, barrelled wine V_0, so as to employ the whole of K in storing wine for four years (pages 173–4). It is now assumed that the price of three- to five-year-old bottled wine, $W_3 - W_5$, is known. In order to determine the optimum selling time, we need to find the present value of new barrelled wine V_0, the internal rate of return i, and the *value* of K (page 174). Given $W_3 - W_5$, the choice of a four-year storage period implies a definite i. It is a simple matter, therefore, to calculate the discounted value V_0 (page 175). If interest is added discretely at the beginning of each year, the value of four-year-old bottled wine, K_4, must equal $V_0 - V_4$ (page 175). The amount of interest $= K_5 - K_4$, which is the value increment from extending the period of investment by one year. Therefore, the internal rate of return is $(K_5 - K_4)/K_4$. A further increase of K is then shown to lower i and to raise V_0 (page 176). The internal rate of return is thus the marginal productivity of 'waiting' (page 177).

The whole analysis is now presented again in mathematical form, allowing for the fact that interest is added continuously over the period concerned (pages 178–9). The final output of mature bottled wine W is a function of the period of investment t and is equal to the initial outlay on barrelled wine V_0 accumulated at compound interest. The present value of W therefore is Ve^{it} and, hence, $V_0 = We^{-it}$. In general, entrepreneurs will estimate the present value of gross expected receipts and future costs by discounting each stream at the market rate of interest r and investing until the difference between these values is zero. But in this case, as in Jevons' analysis, costs of production are constant. Hence, maximizing the net discounted money profit from wine activity is equivalent to maximizing the present value of revenue $V_0 = We^{-it}$. Facing a given interest rate r, the only variable at the entrepreneur's disposal is the length of storage t. Thus, differentiating $V_0 = We^{-rt}$ with respect to t, we obtain

$$d\,\frac{(We^{-rt})}{dt} = W'e^{-rt} - rWe^{-rt}.$$

Setting this equal to zero, we see that the implied rate of interest $r = W'/W$. Since $W = f(t)$ and $W' = f'(t)$, $r = f'(t)/f(t)$, which is identical to Jevons' formula [see chapter 8, section 13]: wine should be permitted to age up to the point where the marginal yield of storage equals the interest rate.

We have assumed above that r is given and that V_0 is maximized. But Wicksell, like Böhm-Bawerk, assumes that V_0 is given and that the entrepreneur maximizes i, the internal rate of return. That is, from $V_0 = We^{-it}$,

$$i = \frac{\log W - \log V_0}{t}.$$

i is at a maximum when

$$\frac{di}{dt} = \frac{1}{t^2}\left[t\left(\frac{W'}{W}\right) - (\log W - \log V_0) \right] = 0.$$

Hence

$$\frac{W'}{W} = \frac{\log W - \log V_0}{t}.$$

But we already know that the right-hand side is equal to i; therefore, $W'/W = i$, which is identical to our previous solution if $i = r$, as it will be in equilibrium.

The Wicksellian notion that entrepreneurs maximize an internal rate of return, rather than the present value of an investment calculated at the going rate of interest, is based on the assumption that the firm has no access to the market for borrowed funds and that its scale of operations is effectively limited by the amount of its own capital. The reason for this assumption, apparently, was to give substance to the idea of an optimum size of the firm. Unwilling to reply on the Marshallian diseconomy-of-management argument. Wicksell chose to argue that the firm can always reinvest its profits at a constant internal rate of return (see, e.g., page 244). If firms can borrow funds, maximizing the rate of return on capital invested will give the same result under perfect competition as equating the 'marginal efficiency of capital' or marginal internal rate of return to the market rate of interest: the firms will borrow so long as the internal rate earned on additional credit exceeds the market rate of interest. But even if firms have no access to the loan market, the market rate of interest cannot be less than the internal rate of return without inducing an increase in the number of firms such as to drive up the rate of interest.

40. The Value of Capital

Having determined the optimum storage period, Wicksell now considers the problem of the valuation of capital. V_0 now stands for the aggregate value of the annual grape harvest and W for the total sales value of matured wine. When production is continuous, K is the value of working capital needed to keep the process running, measured in terms of the product, that is, the unstored wine continuously invested in production and calculated at compound interest over period t. Naturally it is also equal to the capitalized value of total profits (page 179).

$$K = V_0 \int_0^t e^{ix} dx = V_0 \left[\frac{e^{ix}}{i} \right]_{x=t} - V_0 \left[\frac{e^{ix}}{i} \right]_{x=0}$$

$$= V_0 \left[\frac{e^{it}}{i} \right] - V_0 \left[\frac{1}{i} \right]$$

$$= \frac{V_0}{i} (e^{it} - 1) = \frac{W - V_0}{i}.$$

'By logarithmic differentiation of (1)' (page 179), we obtain

$$it = \log W - \log V_0,$$

$$idt + tdi = \frac{dW}{W} - \frac{dV_0}{V_0},$$

'and applying (2)',

$$i = \frac{W'}{W} = \frac{1}{W} \frac{dW}{dt},$$

'we obtain'

$$\frac{dW}{W} + tdi = \frac{dW}{w} - \frac{dV_0}{V_0}$$

$$- tdi = \frac{dV_0}{V_0}.$$

But

$$- tdi = - t \frac{di}{dt} dt = - \frac{d}{dt} \left(\frac{W'}{W} \right) tdt = \frac{WW'' - W'W'}{W^2} tdt,$$

which, written in determinant form, is

$$\frac{1}{W^2} \begin{vmatrix} W & W' \\ W' & W'' \end{vmatrix} t\,dt.$$

Thus we arrive at Wicksell's equation 5 (page 179), which makes it clear that the present value of the harvest V_0 will vary directly with the time of storage t but inversely with the internal rate of return i. The storage period in turn varies inversely with i but directly with K (page 180). This is shown by differentiating K with respect to t when V_0 is given.

$$\frac{dK}{dt} = \frac{1}{i^2}[i(W' - V_0) - i'(W - V_0)]$$

$$= \frac{1}{i^2}[i(W' + i'tV_0) - i'(W - V_0)]$$

$$= \frac{1}{i^2}[iW' - i'W + i'V_0 + i'itV_0]$$

$$= \frac{1}{i^2}\{iW' - i'[W - V_0(1 + it)]\}.$$

Since $i' < 0$, while the expression in square brackets is always positive, the whole expression will be > 0 so long as $W' > 0$. Similarly, from

$$K = \frac{W - V_0}{i}, \quad \text{or} \quad W = iK + V_0,$$

we get, holding V_0 constant,

$$\frac{dW}{dK} = i + K\frac{di}{dK} + \frac{dV_0}{dK}.$$

From formula 5 we have

$$\frac{dV_0}{V_0} = -t\,di.$$

Hence

$$\frac{dW}{dK} = i + (K - V_0 t)\frac{di}{dK} \quad \text{(p.180)}.$$

Since i falls for every increase in K and since K is always $> V_0 t$ when $i > 0$, the marginal product of capital dW/dK is always less than the rate of interest. Therefore, Thünen's formula that interest is determined by the 'yield of the last increment of capital' is in error (page 180; also page 177 and *Value*, pages 137–8). This is the now celebrated Wicksell Effect.

Now follows one of Wicksell's famous diagrams (page 180). (See Figure 12–8.)

Figure 12–8

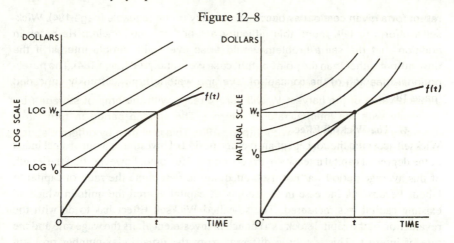

The same curve representing the function $W = f(t)$ is drawn on the left-hand side on semilog paper and on the right-hand side on ordinary paper. The initial cost of production is incurred at $t = 0$, that is, the vertical function starts at the price of unstored wine. Since $W_t = V_0 e^{it}$, $i = (\log W_t - \log V_0)/t$. For every i there is a family of parallel discount curves represented by the equation $W_t = V_0 e^{it}$, with gradient i and cutting the vertical axis at V_0. From the tangency condition, we can now read off the maximum t and the corresponding discounted value of the wine sold for a given i. As before, Wicksell instead assumes a given V_0 and reads off the maximum internal rate of return associated with the optimum t.

Up to now it has been assumed that labour and land were invested once and for all at $t = 0$, so that V_0 stood for the initial fixed cost outlay. Now it is observed that when inputs are invested continuously, the wage rate will equal the discounted marginal product of labour, or $w = We^{-it}$, and similarly for rent (page 181). Contradicting his previous discussion of Euler's theorem, Wicksell now speaks of product exhaustion as an 'identity' (page 182). Of the five equations that determine the rate of interest, Wicksell observes, one is actually missing. The amount of circulating capital, which is really unknown, has been assumed as given (page 182). That is to say, the annual grape harvest V_0 has been taken as a datum. This is a fatal admission, which points up the special character of the point input-point output case and shows in what sense it really fails to get beyond the wages fund doctrine. Notice the comment that when the inputs are invested at a uniform rate during t, the average period is just half the absolute period of investment; then and only then is Jevons' formula for the rate of interest correct (page 182 n.; also page 191 n.).

Böhm-Bawerk's method of calculating the average period of production implies that inputs earn only simple interest. When the inputs earn compound interest, the average period of production or investment is not independent of the rate of interest. In terms of the previous analysis, this means that W is not merely a simple function of t and that the notion of an optimum t that maximizes an internal rate of return for a given cost outlay becomes virtually unmanageable (page 184). Wicksell's efforts to talk round this difficulty are not very convincing. He notes in addition that the same problem would arise even with simple interest if the flow-output rather than the point-output case were analyzed (page 184). The purely notional meaning of the concept of 'average waiting time' is frankly conceded (page 184).

41. The Wicksell Effect

Wicksell accepted the concept of an average period of investment as an ordinal index of the degree of capital intensity in the economy. He noted, however, that the length of this average period was not itself adequate to determine the ratio of capital to labour because an increase in the supply of capital altered the units in which all existing capital was measured. The so-called Wicksell Effect has to do with the revaluation of the capital stock as a change in investment alters the wage rate and the rate of interest. This is a little different from the usual index-number problem because it would exist even if all output were homogeneous. While the marginal private product of each capital good tends to equal the rate of interest that would have to be paid on the capital invested in it, Wicksell discovered that the marginal social product of capital for the economy as a whole is usually less than the instantaneous rate of interest.

The Wicksell Effect constitutes, according to Joan Robinson, 'the key to the whole theory of capital accumulation'. As she puts it, the value of a given type of machine depends on the real wage rate: 'at a higher wage rate there is a higher value of a given type of machine'. As stated by Wicksell and Robinson, the *net* effect of a rise in wages and a fall in the rate of interest is always to raise the value of capital in terms of the product. Indeed, Wicksell nowhere mentions the fact that the tendency of a higher wage rate to absorb money capital in the form of wages is partly offset by the fall in the rate of interest, which releases some money capital hitherto used for interest payments and now available for the purchase of real capital. Obviously, whether wage absorption will outweigh the release of interest charges depends on the relative weight of labour and capital in the production of output. In general, there is no presumption either way. When capital is just goods in process, as in the Wicksellian analysis, it is hardly surprising that the value of capital in terms of the product rises when wages rise and the rate of interest falls. But when durable machines are employed, it is perfectly possible for an increase in wages to be accompanied by a downward revaluation of machines through the fall in the interest rate. In fact, when Wicksell came to deal with Ackerman's problem of investment in durable equipment, he discovered the Wicksell Effect in reverse: the marginal social product of capital may exceed the interest rate. He was puzzled and admitted that his previous discussion of wage absorption was not generally valid (pages 268–9, 292–3).

Wicksell's criticism of the Thünen formulation is misplaced because the latter is concerned with *real* capital and its yield to the individual firm. What the Wicksell Effect shows is that a fall in the rate of interest tends to increase the value of capital by more than the increase in its physical stock. leading as it does to a re-evaluation of the entire pre-existing stock. This does not concern the individual firm because under perfect competition prices of factors are taken as constants. A marginal increment of accumulation involves an error in measuring the capital stock in consequence of the Wicksell Effect, but since the change is a marginal variation around an equilibrium level, the error is of 'the second order of small'. We need to recall once again that all the capital theory that we have examined in this chapter is merely comparative statics, examining the effects on the equilibrium positions of firms and households of changes in the parameters that they face, such as prices, wages and the rate of interest. No attempt has been made to examine the dynamics of equilibrium adjustments, tracing the way individual agents or entire economies move from one equilibrium position to another. Firms and households are indifferent to the social valuation of capital. It is perfectly true that the economist who wants to make structural comparisons between different stationary states cannot ignore the Wicksell Effect: the purchasing power of the stock of capital over goods in general in equilibrium depends not only on the wage and interest rate but also on the way in which equilibrium is attained; the *value* of capital in two stationary states having the same real amount of capital may be different. Still, it is difficult to see how a Wicksell Effect in what must generally be regarded as an unpredictable direction can be 'the key to the whole theory of capital accumulation'. The Wicksell Effect may not be an ordinary index-number problem but it is merely a question of valuation, and it is difficult to see how a satisfactory solution to the problem of measuring capital would contribute much to the *theory* of capital formation.

What we have so far called the Wicksell Effect, some writers now label the Price Wicksell Effect to distinguish it from the Real Wicksell Effect. The Price Wicksell Effect involves a change in the value of the capital stock without any change in technology, whereas the Real Wicksell Effect involves a change in techniques induced by a change in the rate of interest. A negative Real Wicksell Effect is in fact what the Cambridge School calls 'capital-reversing', less capital-intensive technique being chosen at a lower rate of interest (see above). The negative Real Wicksell Effect never appears in Wicksell because his standard assumption of continuous factor substitution effectively rules it out. In other words, like Böhm-Bawerk, Wicksell certainly did believe that the demand for 'capital' is a well-behaved, negatively inclined function of the rate of interest; he was innocent of the Switching Theorem.

42. Definitions of Capital

Now we are out of the woods and come back to the age-old dispute over 'capital in the narrower sense' – intermediate products – or 'capital in the wider sense' – all sources of income of any kind (pages 185–6). Wicksell tries to justify his preoccupation with short-lived capital by arguing that most durable equipment is 'virtually' nonexhaustible and therefore earns rent, not interest. He goes so far as to suggest that disinvestment of fixed capital is 'usually impossible' (pages 186–7; see also page 237).

Böhm-Bawerk's decision to exclude the subsistence fund from 'social capital' is dismissed as a purely terminological confusion (page 187). Capitalists do not receive a discounted share of the product but rather an undiscounted residual after all factors have received their discounted marginal products (page 188). This is a truism when profits are zero, since the residual as a percentage of capital invested is itself the discount factor. Böhm-Bawerk's contrary assertion, which Wicksell attacks, probably refers to the profits of the entrepreneur, not the interest of the capitalist; and, of course, profits are not advanced out of capital.

The famous dispute as to whether wages are paid out of capital or out of the final product is nicely resolved (pages 188–90). The reader is reminded of the basic truth of the fourth of Mill's 'propositions respecting capital' (page 191). The point that rent is a discounted marginal product is brought home in an arithmetical example (page 192). The 'not yet defunct' wages fund theory is briefly discussed (pages 193–5; see also pages 245–6). The trouble with the theory is that it failed to treat the average turnover rate of capital – the reciprocal of the average period of production – as a function of the interest rate. Senior's last-hour theory, as well as Marx's unsatisfactory criticism of it, illustrate the dangers of ignoring the assumption of a fixed production period in the wages fund doctrine (pages 194–5).

Since little is heard nowadays of discounted marginal products, it is necessary to add that there is no difference in principle between an undiscounted and a discounted marginal productivity theory, provided we realize that the marginal product in question is not the same in the two theories. Productive agents receive the value of their marginal product in terms of immediate results, and this is necessarily equal to the discounted value of the finished consumer goods that their activity will eventually realize, that is, the discounted value of the future yield of their present contribution to output. Time theories of capital put emphasis, of course, on the fact that labour and labour alone receives a discounted share, while capital receives an undiscounted share. Followers of the Clark-Knight view of capital object to such terminology as being misleading, but no logical error is involved.

A final section on general equilibrium brings Part II to a close. Mill's theory of international values is briefly discussed (pages 198–200). The problem of general equilibrium is first stated verbally and then mathematically (pages 200–4). The analysis of the stationary state is incomplete without a theory of saving, despite the fact that net saving is zero under stationary conditions (pages 202–3).

43. The Accumulation of Capital

The opening remarks on the motives for savings and the possibility of backward-sloping supply curves of saving are strongly suggestive of Fisher's approach, in which the rate of interest depends on the interaction of 'willingness' and 'opportunity' (pages 207–9). Wicksell seems to believe that any positive rate of interest brings about net investment, which implies the anti-Austrian conclusion that the rate of interest will be zero under stationary conditions. Wicksell hedges by a value reference to 'approximately stationary conditions' (page 209).

He dismisses Cassel's argument designed to show that the rate of interest cannot fall to zero as having insufficient weight in the total picture. Cassel assumed (see above) that at near-zero rates, the shortness of the normal earning period of an individual would alone create a shortage of personal savings (pages 209–11). The reason for the apparent failure to satiate demand for capital is the presence of uncertainty about the future (page 211–12) – remarks such as this go to show to what extent Wicksell was a thoroughgoing radical. When the assumption of stationariness is abandoned, the problems of capital theory become 'essentially different' (page 213). Various possibilities are discussed rather awkwardly in terms of the principle of diminishing marginal utility of income (pages 213–14). A 'perfected capitalistic system' is one in which the marginal product of capital has fallen to zero (page 214). But in a private property system this might lead to an undesirable rise in rents (pages 214–15). Thünen's 'natural wage' is considered as an early example of a theorem about capital accumulation (pages 216–17).

44. Cassel's Theory of Social Economy
This review article by Wicksell contains a whole series of unusually incisive comments on a book that was at one time very highly regarded: on the subjective theory of value (pages 221–3); on the indeterminacy of absolute prices (pages 223–5); on general equilibrium (pages 225–7); on welfare economics (pages 227–8); on imperfect competition (pages 228–9); on the paradox of decreasing costs (pages 231–2); on the theory of capital and interest (pages 223–41); on population growth (pages 241–2); on the theory of rent (pages 242–5); on wage theory (pages 245–9); on monetary theory (pages 249–54); and, last, on business cycles (pages 254–7).

45. Durable Capital Goods
At the age of seventy-two Wicksell wrote a review article on Gustaf Ackerman's still untranslated book, *Real Kapital und Kapitalzins* (1923–4), dealing with the point input-flow output case. The analysis is exceedingly complicated despite the fact that the problem is artificially simplified by the assumption that the efficiency of the machines in question is constant over time until, for technical reasons, the life of the machine suddenly comes to an end: the case of the 'one hoss-shay'. There are no variable operating costs and there is no way of lengthening the output stream by making repairs; the machine, in other words, is very much like a light bulb. The problem that Ackerman and Wicksell analyze is how the entrepreneur chooses among a variety of constant-efficiency machines, the durability of each machine being a function of how much labour is invested in their manufacture. In the real world, machines are of the diminishing-efficiency type and require greater repair and maintenance charges the older they get. The economic life of such machines is usually shorter than the technical life, which can be extended almost indefinitely through adequate repairs. Here, even under static assumptions, there is the problem of how long it pays to go on extending the lifetime of a given machine, a problem that must be solved simultaneously with the problem of choosing between alternative machines of different technical durability. A cursory examin-

ation of Wicksell's article, however, will show that there is quite enough to worry about even when there are no economic problems connected with the utilization of chosen machines.

First, Wicksell presents a straightforward definition of the discounted capital value of all future income, $b per year, obtained continuously from a machine, an 'axe', during its life of n years (page 276). In equilibrium, this expression is equal to the cost of production of the axe measured in labour (formula 4, page 276). Costs increase but less than proportionately to the durability of the axe; hence, the cost function 5 on page 276. It is then shown that the optimal life of the axe depends uniquely on the particular cost function, whatever the size of income per year. The most profitable length of life of the axe varies inversely with the rate of interest (page 279). As long as the amount of labour invested is fixed, Jevons' formula for the rate of interest still applies (pages 279–81).

Suppose that the stock of axes has a uniform age distribution from 0 to t years (page 281). At any moment there are nt axes in use and M labourers out of the total labour force A are occupied in replacing the nth part of the stock worn out each year. The problem is to choose that t which will maximize profits. The derivation and solution of Wicksell's equation 15 (page 283) is reproduced in some modern textbooks of mathematical economics.

When the cost function is of constant elasticity – Wicksell's equation 5 on page 276 – equation 15 can be simplified as a function of M, b and w (page 284). A new model is then presented using a linearly homogeneous production function, with M a constant proportion of A (pages 284–91). The mathematics here is not really difficult but great patience is required to work out the results. The reader should press on, however, because the general drift of the argument is set out in words. The last section examines anew the crucial question whether a fall in the rate of interest, leading to an increase in capital, always lengthens the 'height' of capital or whether it may extend its 'breadth' (pages 293–9). Wicksell's conclusion is that the Austrian result holds even for fixed capital except where the second-order conditions for profit maximization fail to obtain (pages 295 n.).

46. Wicksell as an Economist

We will examine Volume II of Wicksell's *Lectures* in chapter 14: there we will meet Wicksell as a synthesizer of neoclassical monetary theory. In this chapter, we have witnessed his integration of Austrian capital theory and Walrasian general equilibrium analysis. In one sense, he was not an original thinker: he merely rebaked loaves kneaded by others. To be sure, there was the idea of capital structure measured in terms of 'height' and 'width', as well as the discovery of the Wicksell Effect, but these were at best glosses on previous theories, not major contributions to the corpus of economics. But there is a kind of synthesizing, refining and perfecting that by its outstanding quality is worth more than any number of theoretical novelties. It was this kind of integration and reconstruction that Wicksell supplied, and it was precisely what was so badly needed at the turn of the century. Marshall's *Principles* had banished general equilibrium to mathematical appendices and had swallowed the gist of Böhm-Bawerk without becoming involved in the morass of capital theory; in consequence, it was clear from reading Marshall that wages had something to do with the marginal productivity of labour but it was far from evident that the rate of interest had much connection with the marginal product of capital; the very concept of a perfectly general theory of factor prices is barely discernible in Marshall. In Wicksell, all the various strands of the neoclassical tradition are pulled together: Jevons' theory of utility and disutility; Cournot's theorem of profit maximization; Clark's marginal productivity theory; Wicksteed's notion of production functions; Marshall's laws of return; Böhm-Bawerk's theory of capital; and Walras' concept of multimarket equilibria. At the same time, the criticisms and interpretations of dozens of leading contemporary economists, such as Edgeworth, Barone and Pareto, not to mention the works of great economists of the past, such as Ricardo, J. S. Mill and Marx, are assimilated and woven into the total fabric. One might demur that Marshall did as much. True, but Marshall did it in a way that frequently succeeded in hiding gaps and shortcomings in received doctrine rather than displaying them openly as difficulties that remain to be tackled. Wicksell was not writing for businessmen or informed laymen. He was addressing the serious student of economics and was not afraid to admit that all was not well in the house that neoclassical economics had built. There is no hint in the pages of the *Lectures* of complacency, of a Marshallian air of surveying from the mountaintops, of a sense of swimming in halcyon seas of theoretical agreement. Better than any other book in this period, Wicksell's *Lectures* conveys the intellectual excitement of economic theory as an on-going inquiry, equipped with rules and procedures that are capable of weeding out error. One reads it not only to learn economics but also to realize that economics goes on learning.

NOTES ON FURTHER READING

The bulk of Böhm-Bawerk's writings on capital and interest have been newly translated by G. D. Huncke and H. F. Sennholz and published in a three-volume edition with the general title, *Capital and Interest* (1959). Vol. I contains *The History and Critique of Interest Theories* (1884) together with *Recent Literature on Interest* (1914). The *History and Critique* is one of the most extraordinary polemical works in the whole history of economics. Over a hundred authors are fitted into a Procrustean classificatory scheme of five types of interest theories. There has been much discussion, not only about the way the different writers are distributed among the five categories, but also about the categories themselves. With surprising regularity, Böhm-Bawerk's treatment is most unfair to those authors who come closest to his own approach: Ricardo, Senior, Jevons and Menger. *Recent Literature on Interest* contains a characteristically oversubtle attack on Marshall. Vol. II of the new edition comprises *The Positive Theory of Capital* (1889) in which Böhm-Bawerk developed his own theory of interest; the core of the argument is contained in Book II, chaps. 2–5, and Book IV, chaps. 1–3. He never properly revised or finished the first edition of his work and for fifteen years, while active as a Minister of Finance in the Austrian government, he had no opportunity to prepare a second edition. The second improved edition (1904) was followed by a third edition (1912) to which he added twelve 'exkursus' or elaborations to meet various criticisms that his ideas had received. These are reprinted in Vol. III of the new edition: the first and second 'exkursus', dealing with the effect of innovations on the average degree of roundaboutness, and the twelfth, dealing with Fisher's critique of the alleged independence of the third reason for interest, contain significant clarifications of the general argument.

Böhm-Bawerk, like Walras, was not just a pure theorist: he was also interested in the sociology of power and all the applied problems connected with the rise of trade unions, big business and collectivism. In this, as in so many other respects, he both influenced and was influenced by Wieser, Menger's other disciple. On this aspect of first-generation Austrian economics, see *Shorter Classics of Eugen von Böhm-Bawerk* (1962) and R. B. Ekelund, Jr., 'Power and Utility: The Normative Economics of Friedrich Wieser', *RSE*, September, 1970. Schumpeter's obituary article on Böhm-Bawerk, published originally in 1914 and reprinted in his *Ten Great Economists*, is perhaps the most readable general account of the theory ever given. It is an enthusiastic account, as befits an obituary notice, but it is valuable precisely because of its efforts to be wholly sympathetic. See also the brilliant account in Schumpeter, *History of Economic Analysis*, pp. 844–8, 898–909, and 924–32. By way of contrast, see Stigler's merciless critique from the Clark-Knight standpoint of the 'perpetual income stream' and 'indestructible capital fund': *Production and Distribution Theories*, chap. 8.

A good introduction to Böhm-Bawerk is V. Edelberg, 'The Ricardian Theory of Profits', *Ec*, February, 1933; Ricardo's insight that the problem of capital can be reduced to 'the relative time that must elapse before the results of labour can be brought to the market' supplies the key to the Austrian conception of capital. Rogin, *The Validity and Meaning of Economic Theory*, chap. 13, provides a superior textbook exposition of Böhm-Bawerk's theory, marred on occasion by some peculiar quasi-Marxian prejudices. R. E. Kuenne, *Eugen von Böhm-Bawerk, Columbia Essays on Great Economists* (1971 in paperback) is another useful introductory guide.

Our discussion of Böhm-Bawerk's model leans heavily on two articles by R. Dorfman: 'A Graphical Exposition of Böhm-Bawerk's Interest Theory', *REStud*, February, 1959, and 'Waiting and the Period of Production', *QJE*, August, 1959, with a 'Reply' by E. Neuberger, *ibid.*, February, 1960, and another reply by R. E. Kuenne under the title of 'The Stationary State and the Technological Superiority of Present Goods', *ibid.*, November, 1962. Böhm-Bawerk's famous arithmetical examples in the closing chapters of the *Positive Theory* are expounded graphically à la Dorfman by the editors of *EET*, pp. 542–8. J. Hirschleifer, 'A Note on the Böhm-Bawerk/Wicksell Theory of Interest', *REStud*, April, 1967, and D. E. R. Gay, 'The Aggregate Factor-Price Frontier in Böhm-Bawerk's Period of Production Capital Model: A Graphical Derivation', *EEJ*, July, 1975, take up where Dorfman left off. H. T. N. Gaitskell's belated attempt in the 1930s to salvage the concept of the average period of production is still eminently worth reading: 'Notes on the Period of Production', *ZN*, VII, No. 5, 1936; IX, No. 2, 1938.

Fraser, *Economic Thought and Language*, chap. 14, provides a valuable history of terminology in capital theory. The Knight-Hayek controversy of the 1930s reached a climax with N. Kaldor, 'The Recent Controversy on the Theory of Capital', *Ecom*, 1937, reprinted in his *Essays on Value and Distribution*; Kaldor defended the average period of production as 'meaningful' but 'irrelevant' to a dynamic economy. This article contains a complete bibliography of the debate. Subsequent echoes of the debate are reviewed by J. F. Weston, 'Some Perspectives on Capital Theory', *AER*, May 1951, which also gives a sketchy account of the final status of the controversy. The neoclassical 'Essentials of Capital Theory' are rehearsed by F. A. Lutz in *The Theory of Capital*, ed. F. A. Lutz, *et al.* (1960); see also the discussion of Lutz's paper, *ibid.*, pp. 489–509. *Theory of Interest* (1967) by F. A. Lutz is the best survey available of the history of interest theory since Böhm-Bawerk.

On Clark's concept of 'synchronization', see Stigler, *Production and Distribution Theories*, chap. 11, pp. 308–15. P. A. Samuelson, 'Dynamics, Statics, and the Stationary State', *REStat*, 1943, reprinted in *REA*, I, gives a sympathetic account of Schumpeter's theory of the 'circular flow' and shows that the prices of durable goods would not be infinite at a zero rate of interest. See also G. Haberler, 'Schumpeter's Theory of Interest', *REStat*, 1951, reprinted in *Schumpeter: Social Scientist*, ed. S. Harris (1951). H. S. Ellis and W. J. Fellner, 'Hicks and the

Time-Period Controversy', *JPE*, August, 1940, attacks Hicks' revival of the production-period concept in chap. 17 of *Value and Capital*; this article closes with an excellent brief statement of the Knightian view. Knightian objections and other treatments of time-preference-versus-productivity are carefully analyzed in R. E. Kuenne, *The Theory of General Equilibrium Economics* (1963), chap. 4, Parts 3–6, pp. 228–88, but the reader is warned that Kuenne's approach is heavy-going.

On the switching of techniques at different rates of interest in Austrian-type capital models, see P. A. Samuelson's fine expository article: 'Paradoxes in Capital Theory: A Symposium. A Summing Up', *QJE*, November, 1966; the whole issue of the journal is in fact given over to papers on the Switching Theorem. For further references, see my *Cambridge Revolution: Success or Failure?*. G. C. Harcourt, *Some Cambridge Controversies in the Theory of Capital* (1972 in paperback) provides a blow-by-blow account of the debate by a follower of the Cambridge School. For a more dispassionate analysis of the issues, see D. M. Hausman, *Capital, Profits and Prices* (1981).

For an illuminating presentation of Fisher's theory of interest, see J. W. Conard, *An Introduction to the Theory of Interest* (1959), chaps. 4 and 5. The best chapter in this somewhat uneven book, however, is chap. 15 on the neoclassical theory of the interest rate. *The* rate of interest in our discussion has not been specified as short or long term because the rate of interest as an effective rate of return for any given period of time will be the same on all securities regardless of term, provided net return is defined inclusive of capital gains and losses as well as interest income; this fundamental theorem of the neoclassical theory of the rate of structure is explained by Conard in chap. 15 of his book. For a splendid overview of Fisher's contributions to economics, including his theory of interest, see M. Allais, 'Fisher, Irving', *IESS*, 5. K. Velupillai, 'Irving Fisher on "Switches of Techniques"', *QJE*, November, 1975, shows that Fisher recognized the Switching Theorem, and even gave a numerical example of it, but failed to see its general significance. J. Hirschleifer, 'On the Theory of Optimal Investment Decision', *JPE*, 1958, reprinted in *The Management of Corporate Capital*, ed. E. Solomon (1959), demonstrates the general applicability of Fisher's theory to problems of capital budgeting. For a review of the theory of capital budgeting, see Baumol, *Economic Theory and Operations Analysis*, chap. 25; chaps. 26 of Baumol also furnishes a useful quasi-Austrian treatment of capital theory. See also R. M. Solow's lecture on 'Capital and the Rate of Return', *Capital Theory and the Rate of Return* (1963), which concludes that 'the central concept in capital theory should be *the rate of return on investment*'. D. Dewey, 'The Geometry of Capital and Interest', *AER*, March, 1963, elaborated in his *Modern Capital Theory* (1965), chaps. 4–6, employs the Fisher diagram to convey all the fundamentals of modern capital theory but sometimes includes, and sometimes excludes, the influence of technical change. W. Leontief, 'Theoretical Note on Time-Preference, Productivity of Capital, Stagnation, and Economic Growth', *AER*, March, 1958, and 'Comment' by F. M. Westfield, *ibid.*, December, 1959, use the basic Fisher diagram to illustrate the process of economic growth.

On the distinction between the marginal productivity of capital and the marginal efficiency of investment, see A. P. Lerner, *Economics of Control* (1944), chap. 25, supplemented by his paper 'On some Recent Developments in Capital Theory', *AER*, May, 1965; and T. Scitovsky, *Welfare and Competition* (1951), chap. 9, which contains much else besides. A. H. Hansen, *A Guide to Keynes* (1953), chaps. 5 and 8, is also useful on this question. Almost every possible type of supply curve of saving has been postulated by one neoclassical economist or another; for a review of the subject, see Douglas, *The Theory of Wages*, chap. 17, particularly the summary diagram on p. 457.

F. A. Hayek, 'The Ricardo Effect', *Ec*, 1942, reprinted in Hayek's *Individualism and Economic Order* (1948), chap. 2, gives references to the extensive discussion of the Ricardo Effect. The fundamental criticism of Hayek's thesis is given by N. Kaldor in 'Capital Intensity and the Trade Cycle', *Ec*, 1939, and 'Professor Hayek and the Concertina Effect', *ibid.*, 1942, both reprinted in his *Essays on Economic Stability and Growth* (1960). The last of these two pieces is an important contribution to *Dogmengeschichte*, attributing the Ricardo Effect to

Wicksell rather than to Ricardo. On the question of whether there is a Ricardo Effect in Ricardo, see C. E. Ferguson, 'The Specialization Gap: Barton, Ricardo, and Hollander', *HOPE*, Spring, 1973; and G. P. O. O'Driscoll, Jr., 'Comment on Ferguson', *ibid.*, Summer, 1975.[7] S. Tsiang, *The Variations of Real Wages and Profit Margins in Relation to the Trade Cycle* (1947), chap. 7, reviews the theory of the Ricardo Effect with great clarity and attempts to test it statistically. F. A. Hayek restated and defended the Ricardo Effect in conditions of full employment in 'Three Elucidations of the Ricardo Effect', *JPE*, March/April, 1969.

F. A. and V. Lutz, *The Theory of Investment of the Firm* (1951), chap. 2, discusses alternative criteria of profit maximization: chaps. 5 and 6 analyze the widening versus deepening effect of a fall in the rate of interest; this leads up to a careful discussion of the Ricardo Effect in chaps. 9–11. The reader is warned that this is a difficult but rewarding book on a difficult subject. A. Smithies, 'The Austrian Theory of Capital in Relation to Partial Equilibrium Theory', *QJE*, November, 1935, may be read as an introduction to the study by the Lutzs. The case against 'The Discounted Marginal Productivity Doctrine' is stated by E. Rolph, *JPE*, 1939, reprinted in the Fellner–Haley *Readings in the Theory of Income Distribution*.

The Austrian theory of capital survives today in E. R. Lindahl, *Studies in the Theory of Money and Capital* (1939), and F. A. Hayek, *The Pure Theory of Capital* (1941). Both authors reject the concept of an average period, however defined, and work with the notion of a multidimensional heterogeneous capital structure. Hayek's *Pure Theory* was poorly received (see A. Smithies, 'Professor Hayek on *The Pure Theory of Capital*', *AER*, December, 1941) and suffers from imprecision at critical turning points in the argument. But it contains many valuable features; see, in particular, chap. 4 on the characteristics of the Austrian as against the Anglo-American approach to capital; chap. 5 on the nature of the capital problem; chaps. 6, 11, and 14, rejecting the concept of the average period of production or investment; chaps. 17 and 18, and the very interesting Appendix I, on productivity versus thrift (Hayek reconsidered his conclusions on this score in *Ec*, February, 1945); chap. 13 on the distinction that Wicksell draws between the instantaneous rate or 'force of interest' r and the actual compound rate e^{rt}; and, finally, chaps. 20 and 21 on capital accumulation.

If Marshall is the typical example of an economist who lived the life of a scholarly recluse, Wicksell is the perfect example of an economist who was always embroiled in public controversies as the passionate advocate of one unpopular cause after another. In a magnificent biography, T. Gardlund, *The Life of Knut Wicksell* (1958), reveals Wicksell's complex character and recreates the Swedish intellectual atmosphere in the years before World War I. For a brief version of this book, see T. Gardlund, 'Wicksell, Knut', *IESS*, 16. Wicksell's *Selected Papers on Economic Theory*, ed. E. R. Lindahl (1958), makes available for the first time some of Wicksell's many untranslated journal articles; the most interesting of these are his reviews of V. Pareto's *Cours* (1899), Pareto's *Manuel* (1913), and A. L. Bowley's *Mathematical Groundwork* (1924); A. C. Darnell, 'Bowley, Wicksell and the Development of Mathematical Economics', *SJPE*, June, 1982, discusses the significance of the last of these three reviews. Another of Wicksell's papers in this volume on 'Böhm-Bawerk's Theory of Capital' (1911) gives a succinct summary of his final assessment of the ideas of his mentor.

Stigler, *Production and Distribution Theories*, chap. 10, and C. G. Uhr, 'Knut Wicksell: A

---

[7] The fact that the Ricardo Effect is hard to find in Ricardo exemplifies a general rule. According to R. K. Merton, 'eponymy' is 'the practice of affixing the name of the scientist to all or part of what he has found' but it is a striking fact that the outcome of eponymy is almost always to hang the right label on the wrong person. Thus, Thomas Gresham never stated Gresham's Law. Jean Baptiste Say only stated Say's Law after others had stated it for him. Robert Giffen never stated Giffen's Paradox. Francis Edgeworth never drew the Edgeworth Box. Ernst Engel never drew an Engel's curve. Walras never stated Walras' Law. Irving Fisher did not invent the Ideal Index Number and actually pleaded (in vain) that it should not be named after him. Arthur Bowley did not enunciate Bowley's Law. Arthur Pigou did not state the Pigou Effect – and so on. Indeed S. M. Stigler has advanced 'Stigler's Law of Eponymy': 'No scientific discovery is named after its original discover', a law which is confirmed as soon as it is stated (see *Transactions of the New York Academy of Sciences*, Series II, 39, 1980). Neverthless, there are also counter-examples in economics to Stigler's Law, such as Pareto-optimality and the Wicksell Effect.

Centennial Evaluation', *AER*, 1951, reprinted in *EET*, review Wicksell's contributions to theoretical economics. Uhr's article has since become a book: *Economic Doctrines of Knut Wicksell* (1960); chaps. 5–7 treat the problems of capital and interest; chap. 5 contains an excellent analysis of Wicksell's conception of the capital structure; and chap. 6 examines the Wicksell Effect with great thoroughness. On the Wicksell Effect, see J. Robinson, *The Accumulation of Capital* (1956), chap. 11, and the notes at the end of the book. See also E. Osborn, 'The Wicksell Effect', *REStud*, June, 1958. C. E. Ferguson and D. L. Hooks, 'The Wicksell Effect in Wicksell and in Modern Capital Theory', *HOPE*, Fall, 1971, relate the Wicksell Effect to the switching debate. B. Sandelin corrects some recent misinterpretations of the Wicksell Effect in 'The Wicksell Effect, Dewey and Others: A Note', *ibid.*, Spring, 1975, and goes on to explore the ramifications of the Wicksell Effect in 'Wicksell's Missing Equation, the Production Function and the Wicksell Effect', *ibid.*, Spring, 1980. See also L. W. Samuelson, 'Value and Physical Capital in Wicksell's Durable Goods Model', *ibid.*, Summer, 1982, and 'The Wicksell Effect in a Growing Economy', *ibid.*, Winter, 1982; and L. W. Samuelson, B. Sandelin, and T. Negishi, 'Wicksell's Missing Equation', *ibid.*, Fall, 1982.

On the mathematics of compound interest, see Allen, *Mathematical Analysis for Economists*, pp. 228–37 and 401–3; on Fisher's theory of interest, see pp. 376–8; on Wicksell's wine-storage problem, see pp. 248–50, 362–4, and problem 17, p. 265, and 13, p. 379; and on the Wicksell-Ackerman analysis of durable goods, see pp. 404–5 and problems 33–7, p. 411.

The reader who is still wondering 'what it is all about' is recommended to try his teeth on Dobb, *Political Economy and Capitalism*, chaps. 5 and 6, a powerful Marxist critique of any and all orthodox theories of interest grounded on time preference, productivity, or any other real cost of providing capital. The reader who cannot meet the attack has failed to learn the lessons of the Austrian theory of capital.

13

General equilibrium and welfare economics

WALRASIAN GENERAL EQUILIBRIUM

We have shown that consumers with given money incomes maximize utility relative to prices ruling in the market so as to obtain the same marginal utility per dollar from every product they purchase. At the same time, producers maximize profits relative to factor and product prices by employing the factors of production in such quantities and proportions as to obtain the same marginal value product per dollar of factor outlays; this leads them in the long run to build plants of optimal scale, producing levels of output at which average costs are minimized and marginal supply prices are equal to the given demand price for the final product. When we sum the demand prices of the consumers in a particular product market, the market demand price must in equilibrium equal the market supply price obtained by a similar process of summing the individual supply prices of the participating firms in the market. At the same time, however, the resulting demand prices of all industries in a particular factor market must equal the supply prices of the owners of factor services. The aggregate demand for all factors in any period must equal the incomes received by households from supplying factor services in the same period. This provides the household with the given incomes with which we started the analysis of consumer behavior, thus completing the circle. But what reason do we have for thinking that the whole process hangs together? Business firms enter product markets as suppliers but they enter factor markets as buyers; households, on the other hand, are buyers in product markets but suppliers in factor markets. Is equilibrium in product markets necessarily consistent with equilibrium in factor markets? Does the market mechanism guarantee convergence on a general equilibrium solution? If so, is this solution unique or are there several configurations of prices that will satisfy a solution? Even if a unique multimarket equilibrium exists, will it be stable in the sense that a departure from equilibrium sets up automatic forces that bring the system back to equilibrium?

1. The Concept of General Equilibrium

These are the questions that Walras attempted to answer in his *Elements of Pure Economics* (1874). As is so often true with searching questions, no one had realized how difficult it might be to answer them precisely. Indeed, it took some time before the questions themselves sank in. Many economists in the last decade of the 19th

570

century were still capable of asking: Are prices first determined in the market by demand and supply and then passed on to consumers to permit them to reach an optimum quantity adjustment, or do consumers first decide how much to purchase and do these decisions then result in market demand prices? Even if we start with given factor supplies and fixed input coefficients of production, factor prices are not determined until firms have decided to produce certain levels of output but this decision implies knowledge of product prices, and these are not determined until households have received income from the sales of factor services at certain prices. Obviously, product and factor prices are determined simultaneously. Many contemporaries of Walras found this proposition difficult to comprehend. They never quite overcame the suspicion that the argument constitutes a vicious circle. They could understand the validity of partial equilibrium analysis, based on the assumption that certain variables in the analysis are treated as parameters, but they could not grasp the idea that the existence of n partial equilibria does not in any way guarantee general equilibrium for the whole economy made up of n markets.

The analogy that immediately suggests itself is that of the consistency of a set of simultaneous equations. If each equation represents partial equilibrium in one market, then a set of such equations may well prove to be inconsistent, such that no values of the n variables simultaneously satisfies all n equations. For example, consider the following three linear equations in three variables:

$$2x + y = 10$$
$$x - 2z = 2$$
$$x + y + 2z = 1.$$

For $x = 3$, we have from the first two equations that $y = 4$ and $z = \frac{1}{2}$ but these values of y and z do not satisfy the third equation. The three equations are 'inconsistent' and hence the set of equations is 'overdetermined'. The problem of determining the existence of general equilibrium is thus analogous to the problem of finding a unique solution for a set of simultaneous equations.

Long before Walras, Cournot had realized that 'for a complete and precise solution of the partial problems of the economic system, it is inevitable that one must consider the system as a whole'. But Cournot thought that the problem of general equilibrium was beyond the resources of mathematical analysis. Walras' genius lay not only in seizing upon the problem that Cournot had recognized but in showing that it is capable of being solved, at least in principle. Oddly enough, Walras lacked the mathematical finesse of Cournot, or for that matter of Marshall or Wicksell, and his demonstration is not only mathematically clumsy but ambiguous and unfinished. Yet there is an architectonic quality to the whole performance that has led some commentators to credit Walras with the supreme achievement of theoretical economics. According to Schumpeter, Walras' *Elements* is nothing less than the 'Magna Carta of exact economics'.

2. The Walrasian System

In setting forth the Walrasian model, we will use Walras' own symbols to facilitate reference to the text, chiefly lesson 20 of the *Elements*. Far more elegant presentations of general equilibrium systems are now available in any number of textbooks. There is something to be said, however, for adopting Walras' own exposition: it is clumsy but it does effectively convey the peculiar flavor of his approach. We begin with the following parameters:

1. Technical coefficients of production, nm in number, being the fixed amounts of n productive services of land, labour, and capital, T,P,K, . . . required to produce m finished goods A,B,C, . . . That is, n columns of m rows:

$$(a_t, a_p, a_k \ldots)$$
$$(b_t, b_p, b_k \ldots)$$
$$(c_t, c_p, c_k \ldots)$$
$$\ldots\ldots\ldots$$

2. The 'scarcity' or marginal utility functions of each individual for n productive services and m consumer goods, nm in number, of the additive form:

$$MU_t = \phi_t(q_t), \ldots$$
$$MU_a = \phi_a(q_a), \ldots$$

Walras assumed that every individual has an own-demand for the services of the factor that he supplies. Although the *number* of workers, machines and acres of land are given in amount, the supplies of the services of labour, capital and land are variables even in the short run. To deny this, while at the same time keeping to the assumption of fixed coefficients of production, might mean that there is no set of prices for productive services that would clear all factor markets simultaneously. This explains the logical necessity of nm rather than n 'scarcity' functions. It leaves unanswered, however, the question of what it means to say that owners of machines have an own-demand for the services of machines. We shall return to this problem later. For the moment, we need merely note that it implies that the supply curve of production services will bend back at a certain price since this supply curve is nothing but the owners' aggregate demand curve for all other factor services. Walras did not neglect to notice this fact. Indeed, this is how he stumbled on the possibility of multiple equilibria.

Fixed input coefficients are, of course, an unnecessary assumption and, in later versions, Walras allowed these coefficients to vary as a function of relative factor prices. But he never abandoned the assumption of given marginal utility functions and, therefore, given initial quantities of goods and services possessed by the individuals trading in a market.

The reader may wonder why anything should be treated as given in a system purporting to provide a truly general equilibrium solution. But an equilibrium system must always be defined in terms of some given initial conditions. The difference between partial and general equilibrium analyses is not that one does and the other does not make *ceteris paribus* assumptions but that in general equilibrium analysis, as Samuelson has observed, 'the historical discipline of theoretical economics is practically exhausted. The things which are taken as data for that system happen to be matters which economists have traditionally chosen not to consider as within their province. Among these data may be mentioned tastes, technology, the governmental and institutional framework and many others.'

Individuals are in possession of given initial quantities of productive services $(q_t, q_p, q_k, \ldots)$ at given prices $(p_t, p_p, p_k, \ldots)$. They also face given prices of consumer goods $(p_a, p_b, p_c, \ldots)$. Hence, the budget equation of each individual stipulates that the quantities of the factor services offered $(o_t, o_p, o_k, \ldots)$ times their prices equals the quantities demanded of consumer goods $(d_a, d_b, d_c, \ldots)$ times their prices:

$$o_t p_t + o_p p_p + o_k p_k + \ldots = d_a p_a + d_b p_b + d_c p_c + \ldots.$$

All prices are 'normalized' by being arbitrarily defined in terms of one of the consumer goods, the *numéraire*. The equimarginal rule for utility maximization requires that the marginal utilities of the various goods purchased, as well as the marginal utilities of the productive services retained for direct consumption, are proportional to their prices. This provides n equations for productive services for each individual in which $p_a = 1$:

$$\phi_t (q_t - \phi_t) = p_t \phi_a(d_a)$$
$$\phi_p (q_p - \phi_p) = p_p \phi_a(d_a)$$
$$\ldots\ldots\ldots\ldots\ldots\ldots\ldots$$

and $m - 1$ demand equations for finished goods, because the equation for commodity A, the *numéraire*, drops out:

$$\phi_b(d_b) = p_b \phi_a(d_a)$$
$$\phi_c(d_c) = p_c \phi_a(d_a)$$
$$\ldots\ldots\ldots\ldots\ldots\ldots$$

There are thus $n + m - 1$ equations to solve for n unknown individual supply functions for productive services:

$$\phi_t = f_t(p_t, p_p, p_k, \ldots, p_b, p_c \ldots)$$
$$\phi_p = f_p(p_t, p_p, p_k, \ldots, p_b, p_c \ldots)$$
$$\ldots\ldots\ldots\ldots\ldots\ldots\ldots\ldots\ldots\ldots\ldots\ldots\ldots\ldots$$

and m unknown individual demand functions for consumer goods:

$$d_a = f_a(p_t, p_p, p_k, \ldots, p_b, p_c \ldots)$$
$$d_b = f_b(p_t, p_p, p_k, \ldots p_b, p_c \ldots)$$
$$\ldots\ldots\ldots\ldots\ldots\ldots\ldots\ldots\ldots\ldots\ldots\ldots\ldots\ldots$$

When we sum the individual supply and demand functions of firms and households, we obtain once more $n + m - 1$ equations, namely, the market supply equations for productive services, n in number:

$$O_t = \Sigma o_t = F_t(p_t, p_p, p_k, \ldots, p_b, p_c, \ldots)$$
$$O_p = \Sigma o_p = F_p(p_t, p_p, p_k, \ldots, p_b, p_c, \ldots)$$
$$\ldots\ldots\ldots\ldots\ldots\ldots\ldots\ldots\ldots\ldots\ldots\ldots$$

the market demand equations for finished goods, m in number:

$$D_b = \Sigma d_b = F_b(p_t, p_p, p_k, \ldots, p_b, p_c, \ldots)$$
$$D_c = \Sigma d_c = F_c(p_t, p_p, p_k, \ldots, p_b, p_c, \ldots)$$

. . . .

Furthermore, the quantity of factor services demanded must equal the quantity offered and the prices of finished goods must equal their average costs of production. This gives another equation $n + m$ namely, market-clearing conditions for n factor markets, where $a_t, b_t, c_t, a_p, b_p, \ldots$, are known:

$$a_t D_a + b_t D_b + c_t D_c + \ldots = O_t$$
$$a_p D_a + b_p D_b + c_p D_c + \ldots = O_p$$

. . . .

and equality of unit costs and prices for m final goods:

$$a_t p_t + a_p p_p + a_k p_k + \ldots = 1$$
$$b_t p_t + b_p p_p + b_k p_k + \ldots = p_b$$

. . . .

There are thus $2n + 2m - 1$ independent equations to solve and these are exactly equal to the number of unknowns to be determined: (1) n quantities of productive services supplied; (2) m quantities of finished goods demanded; (3) n prices of productive services; and (4) $m - 1$ prices of finished goods, since $p_a = 1$ by definition. For the moment we will assume that all exchange is carried on with accounting money, so that the demand and supply functions are all homogeneous of degree zero in absolute prices [see chapter 5, section 1]. This leaves the price level undetermined. But Walras himself dealt with this problem at a later stage by including the demand for money as circulating money in all the utility functions. Furthermore, up to this point it has been assumed that the technical coefficients of production are fixed. In the third edition of the *Elements* (1896), Walras dropped the assumption of fixed input coefficients and adopted the general marginal productivity theory of distribution. He retained the assumption of constant returns to scale, however, with the assumption that all firms have identical cost functions. Thus, we have to take account of nm additional unknown input coefficients but at the same time we acquire nm additional equations, namely, n equations stipulating the proportionality of the marginal products of factor services to their prices multiplied over m final goods in the economy. Thus we end up with $nm + 2n + 2m - 1$ independent equations to determine $nm + 2n + 2m - 1$ unknowns. General equilibrium is possible, as Walras would say.

3. The Existence of General Equilibrium

Walras thought that a proof of the existence of a general equilibrium solution involved nothing more than the counting of equations and unknowns to ensure that there are as many equations in the system as unknowns to be determined. Now, in general, it seems obvious that this condition must be satisfied for a complete and consistent solution. Geometrically speaking, the values of two variables in a set of linear equations cannot be determined unless we have at least two independent lines in two-dimensional space; the same argument holds for the values of n variables in a set of linear equations in n-dimensional space. If the equations are not 'independent' in the geometrical sense that the two lines actually coincide, the system is said to be 'undetermined'. Having two lines corresponding to two independent linear equations does not, however, guarantee the existence of a solution: the lines may fail to intersect. In that case, as we saw before, the equations are 'inconsistent' and the system is 'overdetermined'.

However, even if we have two independent and consistent equations, when the equations are non-linear there may be several solutions, that is, there are multiple equilibrium points because the curves intersect several times. Moreover, it is not enough that we obtain a unique solution for a general equilibrium system; we require that the system determine prices that are economically meaningful, that is, real non-negative and finite prices.

Suffice it to say that equality in the number of equations and unknowns is *not* a sufficient condition for the existence of a general equilibrium solution, let alone an unique solution. Indeed, it may not even be a necessary condition. This is a subtle point but it can be verified very simply. It is not a sufficient condition because it is possible to find a system of two equations in two unknowns that has no solution in the domain of real numbers, the only domain that has any economic meaning. For instance,

$$x^2 + y^2 = 0$$

$$x^2 - y^2 = 1$$

gives $x = \sqrt{\tfrac{1}{2}}$ and $y = i\sqrt{\tfrac{1}{2}}$, where the imaginary number i satisfies $i^2 = -1$. On the other hand, it is not a necessary condition because $x^2 + y^2 = 0$, a single equation in two unknowns, does have a unique solution for x and y in the domain of real numbers, namely $x = 0, y = 0$. Similarly, the following two independent equations in one unknown have an unique nonnegative solution, $x = 3$:

$$x^2 - 6x + 9 = 0$$

$$x^3 - 3x - 18 = 0.$$

The examples suggest that an unique general equilibrium solution may involve zero prices and indeed even negative prices, reflecting the positive cost of disposing of certain 'free goods'. Suppose the demand and supply of some good determines a zero or negative price (see Figure 13–1). It is therefore either a free good or a nuisance good. Even if it is merely a free good sold at a zero price, it cannot be excluded from the Walrasian system; it is the market that determines which goods shall be free and which scarce. Moreover, there may be a tendency, as Menger claimed, for the range of free goods to narrow in the course of economic development. The Walrasian equations, therefore, must include all goods and not merely

Figure 13–1

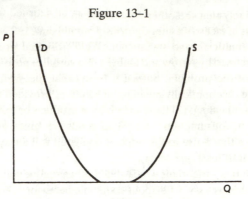

those that are normally economic goods. This is something that Walras never realized. Hence, his demonstration of the existence of a general equilibrium is unsatisfactory.

It is possible to restate the Walrasian model to allow for negative prices and negative quantities of goods. But negative factor prices and negative factor quantities present more serious difficulties. If the input coefficients are fixed and if the quantity of inputs is given, it is easy to see that it may not be possible to satisfy the market-clearing equations for productive services at nonnegative factor prices. Obviously, they can be satisfied mathematically at negative prices but the notion of workers paying firms to employ them makes no economic sense. If the supply of a factor still exceeds demand at zero prices, the factor has become 'redundant'; 'redundancy' not 'unemployment' is the right word because the economic value of the factor in question has fallen below zero. If the factor-supply schedules are actually elastic, as Walras supposed, the possibility of redundancy is reduced but not eliminated. Although the supply curves may be backward bending, they are very likely to be positively sloped at low rates of reward. Thus, as factor rewards fall to zero, the supply of productive services is reduced and the rise of 'voluntary unemployment' absorbs most or all of what would become redundancy. The abandonment of the assumption of fixed input coefficients likewise reduces the possibility of redundant factors. It does not guarantee its elimination because labour cannot be substituted for capital indefinitely even at a zero wage rate without reducing the marginal productivity of labour below zero. But so long as there exists any 'industry' in which labour without equipment can produce a desirable commodity, labour can never become redundant. A standard example of such an 'industry' is domestic service. In long-run equilibrium, the marginal productivity of labour in domestic and personal service will necessarily equal the biological or cultural subsistence wage; if the long-run supply of labour is not sufficiently elastic to produce this result, some institutional device of 'sharing' output between employers and workers will spring up. The fact remains that in the context of neoclassical theory, redundancy of factors is extremely unlikely.

If the market-clearing equations for factors can be satisfied at nonnegative prices, it suggests intuitively that the other equations can also be satisfied at nonnegative prices. That this is in fact so was not rigorously proved until 1933 by Abraham Wald, a German mathematician and statistician. Wald's original proof has since been generalized and refined by Arrow and Debreu. No verbal exposition can do justice to their treatment of the problem. Suffice it to say that the Walrasian system does possess an unique, economically meaningful solution, provided (1) returns to scale are constant or diminishing; (2) there are no joint products or external effects either in production or in consumption; and (3) all goods are 'gross substitutes' for each other, in the sense that a rise in the price of one good will always produce positive excess demand for at least one other.

Existence theorems – theorems which state that an unique solution exists for a set of equations – teach us very little about economic behavior. Obviously, in the real world unique price and quantities are somehow determined, and one might think that the economist's time is better spent discovering how the market produces an unique solution than in worrying whether a Walrasian system is solvable. Nevertheless, one could never confidently employ general equilibrium analysis unless one had first made sure that a general equilibrium model possessed a solution. Furthermore, the proof of an existence theorem will depend on certain restrictive conditions and these conditions may throw light on the way in which equilibrium is actually attained in the real world. This is a merely negative claim for existence theorems but it is enough to justify some attention to these purely technical questions.

4. Stability and Determinacy

The popular view that Walras merely counted equations and unknowns to demonstrate the existence of a general market equilibrium is not entirely justified. Walras also tried to show how the market will solve the equations by propelling the economy toward equilibrium. Moreover, he recognized the fact that it is not enough to show that an equilibrium solution exists. It must also be shown that that equilibrium is stable 'in the small' as well as 'in the large', and that it is 'determinate', meaning that the final position is independent of the path that is taken towards equilibrium.

In principle, determinacy raised problems different from those raised by stability and, as a matter of fact, stability conditions in a market and the theory of *tâtonnement* – Walras' solution to the problem of determinacy – are discussed separately from each other in his *Elements*. We saw earlier that Walras' stability analysis was based on the assumption that the rate of price change varies directly with the amount of excess demand [see chapter 10, section 21]. Walras, like Marshall, always treated instability in the context of multiple equilibria; the unstable position is invariably found between two stable positions. But unstable equilibria in Walras arise from the intersection of a backward-bending supply curve of a productive service with a more steeply falling demand curve. This implies the possibility but certainly not the necessity of multiple equilibria because the supply curve may never bend back again, no matter how high factor prices rise. Marshall, however, had in mind the case of instability arising out of the intersection of a forward-falling supply curve with a less steeply falling demand curve; here multiple equilibria are very likely in the sense that the external economies responsible for the falling supply price may be exhausted at still higher output levels.

Be that as it may, Walras went beyond Marshall in discussing not only stability in one market but also multimarket stability. Suppose that all prices except prices in the shoe market are in equilibrium. Applying the Walrasian criterion to the shoe market, we change the price so as to eliminate positive or negative excess demand. This must upset equilibrium in at least one other market because the equilibrium positions in all other markets were defined with reference to the initial disequilibrium price of shoes. We thus have to make further adjustments in all other markets, and then again in the shoe market, and so forth. Presumably, the successive adjustments in other markets cancel out or diminish in significance relative to the necessary adjustment in the shoe market. In this way, the whole system moves towards multimarket equilibria. This is as far as Walras carried the argument. In *Value and Capital*, Hicks tried to show that multimarket stability does exist provided that strong income effects are absent – this is in effect what is meant by the condition of 'gross substitutability' between all pairs of goods. Subsequent criticisms of Hicks' failure to make specific dynamic assumptions about the manner in which the system reacts to deviations from equilibrium may be said to have led to the emergence of economic dynamics as a new branch of economic theory. Here, as elsewhere, some of the problems that Walras seized upon were not taken seriously by economists until forty or fifty years later.

The problem of determinacy of equilibrium as well as stability of equilibrium is discussed in Marshall's *Principles*. Marshall's appendix on barter trade shows that equilibrium is indeterminate unless the marginal utility of one of the goods exchanged is constant. If this is not the case, the final rates of exchange will depend on the terms on which the earlier exchanges were made: in the process of trial and error, the respective offer curves will shift about with every act of exchange and a final equilibrium may never emerge. In the case of market exchange, this problem disappears in partial equilibrium analysis because the marginal utility of money for 'insignificant' goods may be considered as approximately constant and hence unaffected by initial purchases at disequilibrium prices. This assumption is inadequate for general equilibrium analysis. The gains and losses of exchanging at disequilibrium prices in one market will spill over into other markets and may thus prevent attainment of multimarket equilibrium.

Walras' solution to the problem of determinacy is the theory of *tâtonnement* or 'groping'. The problem, to restate it once again, is to show that the relative prices which emerge from the process of free competition are identically the same as the roots of the Walrasian system of equations in which the unknowns are the equilibrium prices and quantities exchanged. The market is represented as achieving this result *par tâtonnement*, that is, by blindly groping its way via a process of trial and error, which in no way depends on anyone knowing in advance the solution values of the equations. The difficulty in any such account is to allow for 'false prices' or disequilibrium transactions, which alter the distribution of assets among transactors (measured either in terms of the *numéraire* or in terms of any arbitrary set of prices) before equilibrium is reached, which in turn alter the excess demand prices of transactors, thus changing the final equilibrium solution itself to one that differs from that dictated by the set of equations.

Walras recognized this difficulty even in the first edition of the *Elements* but his ideas about the *tâtonnement* process altered over the years and, moreover, he described the process somewhat differently in his theories of exchange, production and capital formation. In his theory of exchange, he simply excluded disequilibrium transactions by assumption: trade taking place at 'false prices' is said to be 'suspended' until a new price is tried and actual exchange takes place only when the equilibrium price has been found. The popular notion that the Walrasian *tâtonnement* process involves a fictitious 'auctioneer', who announces price changes in accordance with the rule that prices in any particular market must change in the same direction as the excess quantity demanded in that market, only permitting final trade when the equilibrium price vector is arrived at, has actually no warrant in Walras' own writings.

Something very much like a fictitious auctioneer, however, is found in Walras' description of *tâtonnement* in production. Here he supposed that producers issue 'tickets' recording the quantities they would like to produce at each quoted price. These selling prices would then be varied according to whether they are greater or smaller than the average costs of production of each firm. Only when proposed selling prices equal unit costs of production are the equilibrium quantities actually produced. Similarly, prices are also 'cried at random' in markets for productive services and altered in accordance with the excess-demand-price rule until quantities on offer are found which reduce excess demands to zero. In both cases, the process described is designed to ensure that the final position of equilibrium is independent of the actual path followed in reaching it.

Walras hankered initially after a realistic description of the temporal sequence of price adjustments by which actual markets reach a final equilibrium solution. Indeed, he was persuaded by studies of the actual operation of the Paris Stock Exchange that disequilibrium transactions were not allowed to occur there, so that it became an example drawn from life of the mechanism of an ideal competitive market. But the changes in the formulation of the *tâtonnement* process in successive editions of his *Elements* show that Walras gradually abandoned this aim of realism. In the final analysis, he settled for the view that his description of the *tâtonnement* process was at best an abstract model of how actual markets move to equilibrium; moreover, it was by no means the only plausible model of that process.

Walras' theory of *tâtonnement* was criticized by Edgeworth, who offered instead the concept of 'recontracting'. Edgeworth assumed that buyers and sellers always enter into provisional contracts in order to take advantage of the possibility of recontracting at a later date. As long as quantities and prices are disequilibrating, someone will find it profitable to recontract a transaction. By this process, an equilibrium vector of prices is reached where no recontracts are to anyone's advantage; at this point all contracts are honoured and exchange takes place. Walras' theory of *tâtonnement* is often ridiculed. Edgeworth's theory of recontracting has by and large escaped calumny. But Edgeworth's theory of recontracting is only a little less artificial than Walras' conception of 'tickets' in his description of *tâtonnement* in production. Neither Edgeworth nor Walras provided a convincing account of how real-world competitive markets achieve multimarket equilibrium. In some sense, such an account has never been provided. Of course, modern mathematical economists establish the determinacy of general equilibrium by more elegant reasoning than that employed by Edgeworth and Walras – for example, the assumption that there are forward markets in all goods and services neatly disposes of the difficulty created by disequilibrium transactions – but that is not to be confused with the description in terms of actual behavior involving costly information of alternative trading opportunities and the irreversible lapse of time between successive transactions. All of which is to say that there is still much work to be done in disequilibrium economics.

5. Capital Theory

To conclude our discussion of Walras, we must comment briefly on his influential theory of capital. Walras was the first clearly to advance the fundamental distinction between stocks of resources and the service-income flows yielded by them. Walras defined all given resources as 'fixed capital, i.e. capital in general', namely 'all forms of social wealth which are not used up at all or are used up only after a lapse of time'. 'Circulating capital or income', he defined as 'all non-durable goods, all forms of social wealth which are used up immediately'. This peculiar identification of the income yielded by capital assets with 'circulating capital' illustrates the fact that Walras' theory of capital is solely concerned with durable producers' goods; raw materials and other goods in process are treated as if they are entirely consumed within the single production period of the goods into which they enter. Walras begins by noting that the prices of capital goods are rigidly proportional to their net yield at given interest rates. This is due to the fact that depreciation and maintenance charges, which are deducted from the annual gross yield, are said to be proportional to the price of capital goods, apparently irrespective of the magnitude of interest charges. If there are h capital goods, we thus have h present-value formulas that relate the unknown discounted value of capital goods to the known net annual capital rentals via the rate of interest. We have h equations but $h + 1$ unknowns because the discount factor is itself unknown. Hence, the rate of interest is indeterminate. The situation corresponds to stationary conditions; the stationary economy, according to Walras, has no market in which the values of capital goods can be determined for the simple reason that new capital goods are not produced in a stationary state.

This argument, which drew Wicksell's objections, is clearly based on the assumption that depreciation and replacement allowances are technically given constants. As Barone pointed out, however, it is a simple matter to render the value of capital determinate in a stationary economy by making the reinvestment of depreciation allowances a function of the rate of interest. But Walras' analysis is concentrated on a growing economy, in which the cost of producing new capital goods supplies additional equations to determine the interest rate. Entrepreneurs will demand new capital goods until their net yields equal the supply price of saving. With fixed coefficients of production for new capital goods, we obtain h equations stating the equality of the prices of capital goods and their current production costs. In addition, we have h further equations defining capital values as the present value of their perpetual net yields.

We now move over to the supply side. In the first three editions of the *Elements*, Walras simply postulated a given supply of savings. In the fourth edition of the *Elements* (1900), he introduced a utility theory of saving by carrying over the formal analysis previously applied to consumption. To establish a link between utility and capital goods that have no direct utility, he invented a homogeneous good E, representing a 'slab of perpetual income' per unit of time. Each household is said to have a normal demand function for E – in effect, a normal demand function for new capital assets – whose price is the reciprocal of the rate of interest: the greater the net yield of capital goods, the cheaper the price of E and the greater the demand for rights to 'perpetual net income'. The unknown prices of capital goods are now replaced by the single price of E. The demand for slabs of permanent income and the supply of savings must be distributed between industries in equilibrium according to the equimarginal rule that makes the net yield of capital goods proportional to their prices, the factor of proportionality being $1/E$, or the rate of interest. To the previous two h equations we can now add another equation, stating the equilibrium condition that the quantity of new capital goods demanded equal gross savings. In addition, we have an equation stating the total supply of gross savings – the quantity of E demanded times its price – as a function of all prices. These $2h + 2$ equations match the $2h + 2$ new unknowns to be determined: (1) the net yields of h capital goods: (2) the quantities demanded of h capital goods; (3) the price of E as the reciprocal of the rate of interest, that is, the uniform price of new capital goods; and (4) the supply of gross savings. With the rate of interest and the value of new capital goods thus determined, the value of old capital goods is also determined, namely, by discounting their yields by the rate of interest established in the market for new capital goods.

Walras began with a given distribution of the stock of capital goods among entrepreneurs. These capital goods generate known future capital rentals and, facing a given loan rate in the capital market, entrepreneurs can calculate whether to make use of the capital goods in production or to liquidate and to invest the proceeds in the loan market. But liquidation is only possible if there is a secondhand market for machines and, even so, liquidation will frequently involve capital losses. We face here the same old *tâtonnement* problem as in commodity markets; there is one and only one distribution of the stock of capital goods among entrepreneurs which will prove compatible with the final equilibrium rate of interest. The problem is to get to final equilibrium from the initial position and the reference to capital losses is enough to show that the path toward equilibrium may well inhibit its attainment. Once again, Walras fails to provide a truly dynamic analysis of the equilibrium conditions, in this case of the determination of the prices of existing capital goods.

The problem gets worse when new capital goods are produced. These must earn a uniform rate of return, or else their production fails to satisfy the equilibrium condition that capital funds are equally profitable wherever they are applied.

Combining the first problem with the second, we now require for equilibrium that capital funds earn a uniform rate of return whether they are applied to the production of new capital goods or to the purchase of old ones already in existence. Moreover, that rate of return will have to be equal to the rate of interest in the loan market because capitalists always have the option of becoming *rentiers*, living on the dividends from lending out their capital. In general, these triple equalities – the rate of return or rate of profit on capital = the internal rate of return on capital projects = the rate of interest in the loan market – have to be satisfied simultaneously but as soon as we consider uncertainty, depreciation and obsolescence as a result of technical progress, it is easy to see that there may well be no determinate and stable equilibrium that can be attained by *any* adjustments of the initial data. Walras certainly failed to solve this problem satisfactorily and he tended continuously to lapse into the assumption of identical capital goods, that is, either a homogeneous capital stock or an infinitely malleable one, in order to simplify the argument. Perhaps a better way of expressing it is to say with Jaffé that what Walras developed was a theory of capital formation, not capital accumulation, in the sense that there is saving and investing in his system and yet the quantities of capital goods in the hands of capitalists do not actually change; if they did change, it would create the old problem of determinacy, namely, that of proving that the equilibrium path of the system· arrives at the same terminal point as that indicated by the initial set of equations.

When we recall the prolix Austrian discussions over the definition of capital, the interdependence of the three reasons and the concept of an average period of production, Walras' theory of capital seems extraordinarily simple and elegant. In contrast to the thousands of pages that Böhm-Bawerk and Wicksell lavished on the subject, Walras takes exactly forty pages in the *Elements* to show how the rate of interest is determined. The Walrasian theory is formally impeccable but what is its substance? Walras went to a great deal of trouble in the fourth edition to introduce net saving as an integral part of the system and yet he said nothing about the shape or character of the offer curves of saving. To treat saving simply as a demand for a special kind of consumer good, namely E, is unsatisfactory because saving involves a comparison between present and future utilities. Judging from one of Walras' letters to Böhm-Bawerk, he did not deny the existence of time preference. Yet he never mentioned it in the *Elements*. Furthermore, he gave no reason why new capital goods should be demanded at all, and if they are, whether the durability of new machines will be different from the old as a function of relative factor prices. Indeed, he totally neglected the problem whether capital formation takes the form of widening, deepening or shallowing. Real capital in Walras has no time structure, which raises the question: How is capital to be measured? To measure it consistently, as Walras does, in money terms is to neglect the actual heterogeneity of the capital stock. On the other hand, the central point of a consistent general equilibrium approach to capital theory is indeed to deny the question of how to measure capital in the aggregate. The issue is how the rate of interest is determined in the loanable funds market and how that market gropes toward an equilibrium solution without knowledge of the value of the capital stock or even of the time structure of that stock. For that reason, Walras never committed himself, except in an occasional aside, to the famous proposition that a fall in the rate of interest will tend to raise the capital-labour ratio of the economy.

Walras' capital theory was adopted, as we have seen [see chapter 12, section 18], by Fisher who defined 'capital' as any stock that yields a flow of services over time – land, machines, buildings, raw materials, natural resources and human skills – and 'income' as the surplus of these services above those necessary to maintain and replace the stock of wealth. The logical outcome of this view is that capital is the only factor of production, that all distributive income consists of interest, wages being merely the interest payments on the stock of human capital, and that the national income consists entirely of consumption expenditures. Few economists since Fisher have been willing to go that far: to say that capital is the only factor of production is to imply that it is a homogeneous 'perpetual fund' of productive power, that one capital asset can always be transformed into another without any sacrifice of consumption, and that human capital is accumulated on identical principles as physical capital. Despite these objections, however, many modern writers on capital theory have found it useful, at least for purposes of exposition, to couple Fisher's notion that the quantity of capital in the economy is merely income in perpetuity divided by the rate of interest with the Walrasian concept of household demand prices for 'slabs of perpetual income'. This dispenses with all the murky Austrian *raisons d'être* of interest connected with the time-consuming character of production. In this sense, the age-old distinction between 'advance economics' and 'synchronization economics' is still with us, with the advance approach commanding the adherence of such writers as Lindahl and Hayek, while the synchronization approach descends through Walras, J.B. Clark and Fisher to F.H. Knight in modern times.

6. Monetary Theory

Walras preserves the symmetry of his system by introducing circulating capital along with the demand for money-to-hold. Consumers hold two kinds of 'circulating capital'; stocks of consumer goods and cash balances. Entrepreneurs, likewise, hold inventories of goods and cash balances. The quantities of inventories and cash balances demanded and supplied are now derived as functions of all prices and the usual market-clearing and zero-profit conditions are developed to show that the extended system has a solution.

In deciding how much money to hold to finance his transactions, the individual considers only the real purchasing power of money over goods and services. The total sum of the liquid real balances that society wishes to hold must in equilibrium equal the existing stock of money. The mechanism by which this equilibrium is achieved consists of variations in the interest rate. 'The effective demand for money is a decreasing function of the rate of interest', Walras declares, because interest is the price of forgoing the utility derived from holding assets in liquid form. Since the marginal utility of the services of a stock of money balances must stand in the same ratio to the rate of interest as the marginal utility of any other good or service, the 'price' of money must be the same in both its monetary and its nonmonetary uses; in other words, the money and the real rate of interest must be equal in equilibrium. In this way, Walras integrated the theory of money into his general equilibrium system.

7. Evaluation of Walras' Contribution

All too often, Walrasian economics is thin in substance, stressing form at the expense of content. We have already seen examples of this in his treatment of capital theory. Yet another is the famous Walrasian zero-profit rule of long-run equilibrium. This rule is not the result of a theory of the firm showing that zero profits are a tendency approached in stationary equilibrium. It is simply a postulate that entrepreneurship is a free service in a stationary economy. Indeed, it is not too much to say that Walras had no theory of supply. Even the supply of productive services by households is treated only in a purely formal sense. And although he adopted the marginal productivity theory in the third edition of the *Elements*, he made no contribution whatever to its development; in effect, he continued to emphasize the expansion of output without a change in factor proportions. His treatment of welfare economics and even his monetary theory would supply additional evidence of formalism but the point is already sufficiently clear. Walras' contributions to substantive economics are almost solely confined to the theory of consumer behavior, where he did see much further and more clearly than his contemporaries. How seriously we take this charge of formalism all depends of course on what we think Walras was doing. It is usually taken for granted that he was trying to investigate, at an admittedly abstract level, the workings of a perfectly competitive market economy. After a lifetime study of the Walrasian system, however, William Jaffé became convinced that it was never Walras' intention to construct anything like a realistic description of a competitive economy but rather to show that a rationally consistent economic system could be devised that would maximize social welfare by securing both commutative and distributive 'justice'. It was a vision of a peculiar sort of 'realistic utopia', not a positive analysis of perfect competition, or at any rate a formulation of a normative platform from which to launch policy changes designed to make the real world conform to the ideal world of general equilibrium. If Jaffé is right, the lack of substantive content in much of Walras' theorizing, the persistent tendency to fit the world to the model rather than the model to the world, takes on a wholly different meaning.

'The fox knows many things, but the hedgehog knows one big thing', said a Greek poet. Walras was a 'hedgehog' rather than a 'fox'. Whatever we think of his aims or the essential meaning of his work, we ought to be charitable in overlooking his weakness since the one big thing he did know, namely, the interdependence of all prices and quantities, was perhaps the first really novel big idea to emerge in economics since Ricardo. Of course, economists had always known that everything depends on everything else but the full implications of this generalization were not grasped before Walras. When we complain about Walras' formalism, we must also remember that nearly all economics nowadays *is* Walrasian economics. Certainly, modern theories of money, international trade, employment and economic growth are general equilibrium theories in a simplified form. Also, the 'new' welfare economics is an outgrowth of general equilibrium theory. Even Marshallian partial equilibrium analysis is nowadays handled in an explicit general equilibrium setting. In *Value and Capital*, a book which was largely responsible for the revival of Walras in modern economics, Hicks observed: 'It is clear that many economists (perhaps most, even of those who have studied Walras seriously) have felt in the end a certain sterility about his approach. It is true, they would say, that Walras does give one a picture of the whole system; but it is a very distant picture, and hardly amounts to more than an assurance that things will work themselves out somehow . . . Now the reason for this sterility of the Walrasian system is largely, I believe, that he did not go on to work out the laws of change for his system of General Equilibrium. He could tell what conditions must be satisfied by the prices established with given resources and given preferences; but he did not explain what would happen if tastes or resources changed.' This is only to say that comparative static analysis, as we know it, is almost wholly the result of the effort of three generations of economists to derive operational theorems about economic behavior within the general equilibrium framework. All of modern micro- and macroeconomics can be viewed as different ways of giving operational relevance to general equilibrium analysis: in Marshallian partial analysis, some variables are eliminated by treating them as data; in Keynesian income theory, some variables are eliminated by aggregating them with others; and in Leontief input-output analysis and activity analysis, the interrrelationships between variables are simplified by linear approximations. Every day it is becoming more apparent that Schumpeter was right: Walras' *Elements* was the prologomenon or Magna Carta of modern economics.

PARETIAN WELFARE ECONOMICS

The work of Pareto represents a decisive watershed in the history of subjective welfare economics. Earlier writers in the utility tradition had always treated 'welfare' as the sum of the cardinally measurable utilities of the individual households of a community; an optimum allocation of resources was one that maximized welfare in this sense. By the time of Marshall, it was recognized that this 'felicific calculus' rested on the assumption that all individuals have identical income-utility functions. In which case it followed, of course, that an optimum allocation of resources is achieved only when income is equally distributed.

The Benthamite postulate that aggregate welfare is simply the arithmetic sum of individual welfare evades the problem of interpersonal comparisons of utility by selecting the one case in which such comparisons raise no difficulty. Virtually all writers before Pareto in this way ignored the question of comparing different optima associated with different income distributions. Marshall worked with a concept of consumers' surplus without sufficient acknowledgment of the fact that this aggregate surplus is a function of individual variations in real income [chapter 10, section 13]. Edgeworth discarded the concept of equal capacities for want satisfaction but then defended the rule of equimarginal sacrifice in taxation on the assumption of uniform income-utility functions [chapter 9, section 5]. Wicksell criticized Jevons' and Walras' generalization of the optimum exchange conditions on the grounds that the optimum conditions of production and exchange depend on the initial factor endowments in the economy [chapter 12, section 33]. Wicksell faced the problem of interpersonal comparisons of utilities more candidly than did any contemporary writer but even he advocated specific economic policies whose benefits rest on the assumption that there are no significant individual differences in utility.

In the *Manual of Political Economy* (1906), Pareto broke away decisively from traditional practice, not only by rejecting cardinal utility and additive utility functions, but by restricting himself ruthlessly to welfare conclusions that do not depend on any interpersonal comparisons whatever. The restricted meaning of a Pareto optimum can be seen clearly by examining the marginal conditions of exchange in a perfectly competitive market. As all economists since Jevons have known, the optimum conditions of exchange depend only on intrapersonal, never on interpersonal comparisons of utility.

8. The Optimum Exchange Conditions

Suppose two individuals are in possession of OM amounts of good x and ON amounts of good y respectively. The indifference maps of the two individuals appear as shown in Figure 13–2. Following Pareto's procedure in the *Manual*, we now combine the two indifference maps in a box diagram by rotating Figure 13–2*b* 180° and imposing it on Figure 13–2*a* until M and N coincide (Figure 13–3). Every point within or on the boundaries of the shaded area represents possible acts of exchange to the mutual advantage of both parties because it leaves them at worst on indifference curves 1 and 1′ and possibly on higher indifference curves. However, the individual in possession of OM amounts of x will want to end up as far in the Northeast direction as possible, while the individual in possession of ON amounts of y will want to end up as far in the Southwest direction as possible; at the same time, they must agree on a ratio of exchange between x and y, represented by the slope of such price lines as $MP, MP′$,

Figure 13–2

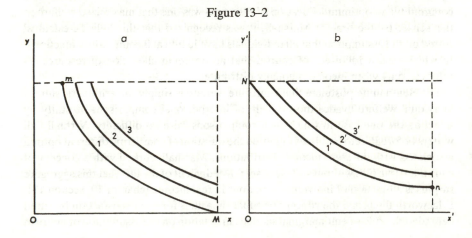

Figure 13–3

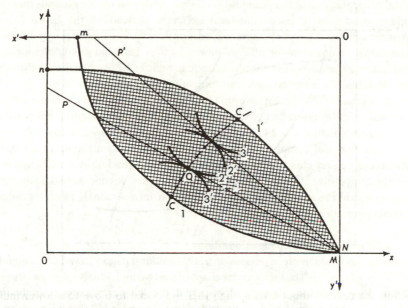

... ; hence trade can take place anywhere along the 'contract curve' *CC*, being the loci of tangency points of the two sets of indifference curves.

In the case of bilateral exchange, the assumption that each individual acts to maximize his satisfactions does not suffice to determine the equilibrium price at which the two goods will be traded [see chapter 8, section 9]. Exchange in a competitive market, however, will always land both individuals on the same point along the contract curve since both face the same set of given prices. If the relative price of *y* in terms of *x* is equal to the slope of the price line *MP*, each individual maximizes his satisfactions by acquiring additional amounts of *x* and *y* until their marginal utilities are proportional to their respective prices. Since both individuals react to the same set of prices, the ratios of marginal utilities or the marginal rate of substitution for any pair of goods must be the same for both individuals. Trade will take place at *Q* where the marginal rate of substitution between the two goods is the same. *Q* is an optimum exchange point for neither individual can move to a higher indifference curve without pushing the other individual to a lower indifference curve. *Q* is only an optimum, however, with reference to the given prices and initial quantities of *x* and *y* brought to the market. The sum of the satisfactions of the two individuals might well be higher at other points along the contract curve. Unless we are willing to make interpersonal comparisons of utility, we will have to be satisfied with the assertion that each point *on* the contract curve is superior only to other points *off* the contract curve.

For example (Figure 13–4), all points on the contract curve between *A* and *B* are superior to *D* because they permit one of the individuals to move to a higher

Figure 13–4

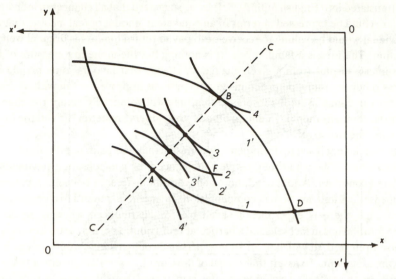

indifference curve without forcing the other individual to move to a lower indifference curve. But for that matter, F is also superior to D, although it is not itself an optimum point. But F is not comparable to either A or B, although all three are comparable to D: a movement from F to either A or B would increase the welfare of one individual, but it would necessarily decrease the welfare of the other individual. Thus, an unwillingness to make interpersonal comparisons of utility means that the only changes that can be evaluated are those that make everyone better or worse off, or that make at least one person better off without making anyone else worse off; an improvement in someone's welfare at someone else's expense cannot be judged in quantitative utility terms. A movement *toward* the contract curve always represents an unambiguous improvement of aggregate welfare but a movement *along* the contract curve alters the distribution of aggregate welfare among the participants in the market.

9. A Pareto Optimum

Pareto's formulation of a welfare maximum generalizes the results we have just achieved for an exchange economy. A Pareto optimum is defined as a position from which it is impossible to improve anyone's welfare, in the sense of moving him to a position that he prefers, by transforming goods and services through production or exchange without impairing someone else's welfare. To escape the necessity of making interpersonal comparisons of utility, Pareto refused to evaluate all other changes in welfare. In consequence, his definition gives up the notion of a unique social optimum and instead sets up an infinite number of noncomparable optima. The area of comparability is extended, however, by introducing the notion of a compensating payment. This was first pointed out by Enrico Barone in a famous article on 'The Ministry of Production of the Collectivist State', published in 1908 but not translated into English until 1935. Barone suggested that all changes in individual welfare could be expressed in terms of an equivalent amount of real income that the individual would be willing to receive or to pay to return him to his original welfare position. The idea is a familiar one: it is nothing but the monetary measure of the consumer's surplus from a given change. A change that favours some people but harms others can now be pronounced a unanimous improvement in welfare if the gainers can compensate the losers, so that they will voluntarily accept the change; after the compensation payments are made, the gainers are better off and the losers are none the worse off.

Barone did not insist that compensation must actually be paid, nor did Kaldor and Hicks in the 1930s when they revived the concept of compensation payments in welfare economics. And indeed there is a world of difference between a potential compensation and an actual compensation payment: a potential compensation claims that there is extra income available for distribution, whereas an actual compensation has in fact selected a particular redistribution of that extra income that is most preferred, at which point an interpersonal comparison of utility creeps back into the argument. To assert that repeal of the Corn Laws in 1846, to cite a frequent example in the history of welfare economics, increased the real income of consumers in Britain by more than it decreased the real income of British landlords is to claim that a compensation payment satisfactory to landlords could have been devised that would have induced them to accept repeal, while still leaving consumers better off with repeal than without it. Such an assertion is based on the private estimates of gainers and losers and does not involve any interpersonal comparisons. However, to recommend that landlords should actually be compensated for their losses from repeal implies approval of the initial distribution of resource endowments and associated incomes that generated the relative evaluations of gainers and losers; in so approving the *status quo ante*, we have committed ourselves willy-nilly to an interpersonal comparison of utility. Besides, once the compensation is paid, the final distribution of income will differ from the initial distribution, which in turn will generate a different set of estimates of potential compensation payments. What reasons are there for thinking that the second set will be the same as the first set of estimates?

10. The Scitovsky Double Criterion

This question leads naturally to the double criterion of an increase in social welfare introduced by Scitovsky. Before we can say that repeal of the Corn Laws increased the general welfare we must know, not only that income could have been redistributed *after* repeal, so as to make everyone better off than before, but also that it was not possible to improve welfare *before* repeal simply by redistributing income. Unless this last condition is satisfied, the effect of repeal involves, as it were, more than repeal itself. It is perfectly conceivable that repeal would have improved social welfare if landlords had been paid to accept the change voluntarily, while at the same time it would have paid landlords to bribe consumers not to push for repeal because the required bribe would have been less than the contemplated loss from repeal. This produces the contradiction that free trade is efficient from the viewpoint of the original distribution of income but inefficient from the viewpoint of the final distribution. This contradiction would not occur if free trade were a movement to super-efficiency, where everyone without exception is made better off. But normally an economic change involves losses to some people and then the double criterion must be met before we can say that welfare has increased.

Scitovsky thus attempts to separate efficiency from equity by defining an improvement in welfare as one that, for every possible distribution of income before the change, makes everyone better off after the change even if compensation payments are actually paid. This double criterion seems to rob us of most of the vantage ground gained by Barone's compensation principle. We are barred from comparing situations with different distributions of income that fail to meet the double criterion, which is to say, most situations we are likely to encounter in the real world.

The double criterion is reminiscent of the index-number problem that is met in the valuation of income when prices have changed. The question whether $\Sigma p_2 q_2 > \Sigma p_1 q_1$ has no simple meaning if both prices and quantities have changed. We can conclude only that real output has increased if a double criterion is satisfied: the value of total output must increase regardless of whether first-year or second-year prices are used as weights. In other words, we require both $\Sigma p_1 q_2 > \Sigma p_1 q_1$ and $\Sigma p_2 q_2 > \Sigma p_2 q_1$. Just as a change in prices forces us to check whether the value of output is a function of the weighting system used, so a change in the distribution of income makes it necessary to evaluate welfare in terms of the original as well as the final distribution of income. If the double criterion for an index number is satisfied, we can state unambiguously that real output has increased. This does not necessarily mean, however, that welfare has improved. Even if tastes are unchanged, each person's tastes are weighted by his total expenditure, which in turn depends on his income. Unless the quantity of all goods have increased equiproportionately, an increase in real output accompanied by differential price changes alters expenditure patterns and hence alters the community's valuation of income. If the double criterion for an increase in welfare is to be satisfied, we require that general welfare be invariant to changes in expenditure patterns and hence to changes in the distribution of income. Clearly, this is the strongest of all interpersonal comparisons of utility. Thus, the long discussion on welfare criteria – from Pareto through Barone to Hicks, Kaldor and Scitovsky – has brought us no further in evaluating policy changes which benefit some people but harm others on purely 'positive' grounds. Efficiency questions appears to be inseparable from equity questions.

11. Recent Welfare Economics

The effort of economists to defined a welfare optimum free from the necessity of weighting individual utilities has an ancient pedigree. A half-century before Pareto, J.S. Mill distinguished between the immutable 'laws of production' and the pliant 'laws of distribution' in an attempt to persuade his readers that questions about the size of the cake can be divorced from questions about its slices [see chapter 6, section

1]. The belief that 'efficiency' and 'equity' can somehow be separated represents one of the oldest dreams of economics. Virtually every economist before Pareto analyzed particular economic policies as if it were possible, first, to discuss the effects on allocative efficiency given the distribution of income and, second, to round off the analysis by adding a value judgment about the associated changes in income distribution. The two stages of the argument were never clearly distinguished, however, so it was often difficult to see just where interpersonal comparisons of utility entered in. The value of Pareto's definition of social welfare was to make the distinction between efficiency and equity crystally clear. But Pareto continued to believe that significant pronouncements about economic policy could be laid down solely on the basis of efficiency considerations. The development of the 'new' welfare economics, however, cast increasing doubt on that belief.

In recognition of the deadlock in the discussion, Bergson proposed that we evaluate welfare changes by means of a 'social welfare function', that is, a social indifference map ranking different combinations of individual utilities according to a set of explicit value judgments about the distribution of income. Unfortunately, it is not clear whether these are to be the value judgments of economists, the legislature, the electorate or any other specified group of persons, or how we are to resolve any differences in such judgments. And of course, it is these differences in the value judgments of different persons and groups that constitute the bugbear of welfare economics. The 'new' welfare economics descending from Pareto was an attempt to see how much can be said about general welfare without resort to interpersonal comparisons. The upshot of recent discussions is that very little survives once the taboo on interpersonal comparisons is rigidly imposed. This does not mean, of course, that a willingness to make such interpersonal comparisons would open up an impressive range of significant theorems regarding economic policies. Nevertheless, the true function of welfare economics is to invade the discipline of applied ethics rather than to avoid it. In any working social order, there is bound to be a good deal of consensus on social ends. Economic policies, however, are almost always means towards ends that are themselves imperfectly grasped; moreover, different ends may be in conflict with each other. The purpose of welfare economics should be to influence the social consensus by making explicit the goals and objectives of different policies and by demonstrating the consistency or inconsistency of particular means-ends relationships. This is no idle request for a reform in the content of welfare economics because the recent work of such economists as Arrow, Black, Downs, Buchanan, Tullock and Rothenberg on public choice and the 'calculus of consent' runs precisely along these lines. It raises the possibility of the emergence in the near future of some kind of interdisciplinary science of politics and economics that will rescue welfare economics from the theoretical blight to which it has fallen victim.

Having said this much, we ought to add a note of warning about the quaint notion of the 'new' welfare economics that propositions about 'efficiency' are somehow value-free, while propositions about 'equity' are necessarily value-laden. Interpersonal comparisons of utility are only one kind of value judgment and not perhaps even the most critical of the value judgments that inevitably enter into welfare economics.

Thus, the concept of a Pareto-optimal allocation of resources is predicted on three assumptions which are undeniably judgments of values: (1) that every individual is the best judge of his own welfare; (2) that the social welfare is defined only in terms of the welfare of individuals; and (3) that the welfare of individuals may not be compared. It is perfectly true that these value judgments command wide assent, at least among economists, but even a perfect consensus on value judgments does not render them 'objective': they nevertheless remain value judgments. In short, there is no such thing as 'value-free welfare economics' and, indeed, the phrase itself is a contradiction in terms. To say that something is an improvement in 'welfare' is to say that it is desirable and persuasive statements of this kind necessarily involve ethical considerations, that is, value judgments.

12. The Marginal Conditions

Once the question of income distribution has somehow been settled by a collective decision, a series of marginal conditions can be set out that must be satisfied if resources are to be optimally allocated. These marginal conditions are no more than the set of equations that must be solved to determine the unknown prices and quantities of all goods and services allocated to each and every use. Given a knowledge of the stocks of resources on hand and the technical coefficients of production, as well as a Bergsonian welfare function incorporating an ethics of distribution, it should be possible theoretically to solve the system of equations in terms of the unknown prices and quantities. In view of Walras' contributions to the theory of general equilibrium, it comes as something of a shock to realize that most of the marginal conditions of social optimum were never stated explicitly and in detail until very recently. Even Pareto and Barone did not go very far beyond a statement of the optimum conditions of exchange. The entire inventory of optimum conditions appeared for the first time in Lerner's articles on socialist economics in the mid–1930s, culminating in two classic articles by Bergson and Hicks in 1938 and 1939.

As a useful review of virtually the whole of neoclassical microeconomics, we will now list the more important optimum conditions. The reader can verify any of these himself by the usual equimarginal rule that defines an optimum as a situation in which no mutually profitable trade can be arranged.

1. *The optimum condition of exchange.* The ratio of the marginal utilities or the marginal rate of substitution for each pair of consumers' goods must be the same for all households that consume both; in other words, all households must end up somewhere along the exchange contract curve in a box diagram.

2. *The optimum condition of production.* Within the limits of technical constraints, the ratio of the marginal physical products or the marginal rate of substitution for each pair of productive factors must be the same for all firms in an industry producing a homogeneous product. With the productive factors measured along the axes of a box diagram, the isoquants of any pair of firms must be tangent to each other; all firms must end up

somewhere along the production contract curve. By extension, the marginal rate of transformation between any two products must be the same for any two firms that produce both.

3. *The optimum condition for the composition of output.* If the first and second conditions are satisfied, the marginal value product of each factor will be the same in each industry, and the prices that are used to arrive at these marginal value products will be equal to the common value for all households of the marginal rates of substitution in consumption. Summing up, the marginal rate of substitution between any pair of products for any household consuming both must be the same as the marginal rate of technical transformation between them in production.

4. *The optimum condition for intensity of factor use.* The marginal rate of substitution between work and leisure must be equal to the marginal technical rate of transformation between hours of work and the resulting product; in other words, it should not be possible to increase the *value* of output by paying a worker to work shorter or longer hours, or to shift to another occupation.

5. *The optimum intertemporal condition.* If we distinguish among inputs according to the moment of time at which they are applied and among outputs according to the moment of time they emerge, the first four marginal conditions can be applied to yield the optimum condition for allocation of factor inputs and product outputs through time. The marginal temporal rate of transformation between every pair of factors and products, as well as the marginal temporal rate of substitution between every pair of factors and between every pair of products, must be equal to the rate of interest on riskless securities. That is, the rate of interest must equate the marginal time preferences of all individuals with the rate of return over cost. When some assets are illiquid and their return uncertain, the marginal rates of substitution between every pair of assets of different degrees of liquidity and certainty must be equal for all households.

All these conditions may be summed up in one grand criterion: *Between any two goods (products and factors), the subjective and objective marginal rates of substitution must be equal for all households and all production units respectively and these subjective and objective ratios must be equal to each other.*

Together, the five conditions constitute a necessary basis for the attainment of maximum welfare. Since they are marginal or first-order conditions, they do not suffice to guarantee a welfare *maximum*. In addition, we require second-order 'diminishing returns' conditions to the effect that all indifference curves are convex and all transformation curves are concave from below in the neighborhood of the maximum welfare position. But even if both first-order and second-order conditions are satisfied, we cannot be sure that we have reached a *maximum maximorum*: 'There is nothing in the marginal conditions', as Boulding puts it, 'which can differentiate the top of a molehill from that of Mount Everest'. For welfare to be at a maximum, the 'total conditions', as Hicks calls them, must also be satisfied: it must be impossible to increase the sum of producers' and consumers' surpluses by introducing a new product or by withdrawing an old product. Provided the marginal, second-order and total conditions are all satisfied, economic welfare will be maximized. We stress again, however, that this maximum is merely one of an infinite number of Pareto optima among which we cannot choose without postulating a Bergsonian social welfare function, that is a set of scalars for the ranking of individual utilities.

Let us now imagine a capitalist economy in which we create a price system having the following characteristics: (1) all inputs and outputs have fixed prices which no buyer or seller can alter; (2) only products which can be sold at cost-covering prices will be brought to market; and (3) any firm can produce any product at these prices if it cares to do so. If every consumer now maximizes his utility and every firm now maximizes its profits, all the preceding first-order as well as the second-order optimum conditions are automatically satisfied by the market mechanism. At this stage, the reader should be able to demonstrate this Invisible Hand Theorem for himself. Notice that it states, not only that a long-run perfectly competitive equilibrium will yield an optimum allocation of resources, always subject to the proviso that the distribution of income is given, but also that every optimum allocation of resources is a long-run perfectly competitive equilibrium.

13. The Optimal Characteristics of Perfect Competition

'At least from the time of the physiocrats and Adam Smith', Samuelson has observed, 'there has never been absent from the main body of economic literature the feeling that in some sense perfect competition represented an optimal situation'. In precisely what sense is now apparent. This is not to say, of course, that Adam Smith or any other classical economist justified a competitive economy solely because it achieved the static efficiency conditions of general equilibrium. We know that they defended competition largely in terms of its dynamic effects on individual incentives [see chapter 2, section 19]. But the classical argument that the flow of capital and labour will level the rate of profit and wages between industries was a disguised way of stating that the marginal optimum conditions will be satisfied in equilibrium. Modern welfare economics, therefore, makes explicit one of the grounds on which perfect competition can be and has been justified.

It is sometimes thought that the less exacting requirements of *pure* competition would suffice to guarantee attainment of a social optimum: under pure competition, every household and firm buys or sells such a small part of the total amount of every commodity that prices cannot be influenced by individual actions and, furthermore, all prices of homogeneous products and factors are uniform throughout the economy. These two conditions are necessary but not sufficient, however. In addition, all factors must be perfectly mobile, so that supernormal profits are eliminated, returns to scale must be constant, and all economic agents must have perfect knowledge of available alternatives. Obviously, these conditions, defining the characteristics of *perfect* competition, are never attained in the real world. We may ask, however, whether appropriate government intervention might not enable us to approximate the requirements of perfect competition. In particular, public operation of large-scale enterprises operating under increasing returns to scale would remove one of the major threats to the maintenance of perfect competition. It may seem paradoxical to justify nationalization of industries on the grounds that it would buttress competition. But as Barone pointed out, Paretian welfare economics demonstrates that efficient resource allocation requires perfect competition and this is not the same thing as asserting the necessity of private ownership of the means of production. The price system as such is not a capitalist institution but simply a set of 'coefficients of transformation', which could serve the same functions in a centrally directed economy as in a capitalist economy. The state need only permit consumers and workers to maximize their own advantages and to order managers of enterprises to act *as if* they were private profit maximizers; even this element of coercion would not be necessary because profit maximizing could be made automatic simply by gearing managerial wages to profits. Once allocative efficiency is achieved by such a decentralized self-policing price system, supernormal profits can be redistributed in accordance with value judgments about the distribution of income. This is the gist of the Lange-Lerner version of market socialism. It is a remarkable fact that this is the only *theory* of socialism that has yet been forthcoming; it was the product not of Marxist or Soviet economists but of 'bourgeois economists' in the most pejorative sense of that term.

14. Nonmarket Interdependence

The notion of a social optimum enshrined in the marginal conditions assumes that an efficient allocation of resources can be determined simply by comparing the value of output in different uses: a transfer of any factor or product from one use to another alters welfare only insofar as it results in a change in the value of output. But suppose the transfer of factors to a particular firm gives rise to external diseconomies in the form of the production of smoke as by-product of the firm's operations? Or suppose a transfer of products to some consumers diminishes the satisfaction of other consumers because the latter are trying to 'keep up with the Joneses'? In all such cases, where the various production and preference functions are interdependent, we must replace the Pareto-optimum conditions by Pigou's golden rule of welfare maximization: equalization of marginal private and marginal social costs of all resources in all uses [see chapter 10, section 7]. Direct interactions between firms and households violate the efficiency conditions: a dollar's worth of a consumer's expenditure will no longer purchase the same value of factor units irrespective of the product acquired. Therefore, perfect competition is not a sufficient condition for allocative efficiency because perfect competition is compatible with external effects in production and consumption which violate efficiency; it is also compatible with a fixed workweek, which violates one of the marginal conditions, namely, the optimum intensity of factor use. However, perfect competition is a necessary condition for allocative efficiency because central planning only achieves the same results by duplicating the checks and balances of the competitive mechanism. We can now restate the Invisible

Hand Theorem to read: if production functions are linearly homogeneous and if all externalities of production and consumption are absent, then a perfectly competitive equilibrium satisfies Pareto optimality: no one can be made better off by state intervention except at someone else's expense. Alas, even this last formulation of the theorem does not do full justice to all the possibilities of 'market failure' for nothing has yet been said about public goods and second-best problems.

15. Public Goods

It is convenient to classify divergences between private and social costs or private and social benefits under two headings. First, we have nonappropriable 'real' external economies or nonchargeable external diseconomies. Second, we have the case which Pigou completely ignored, namely, that of 'public goods'. The peculiar nature of public goods is that their consumption is necessarily joint and equal: the more there is for one household, the *more* not the less there is for any other. This was first pointed out as early as 1890 by Ugo Mazzola, an Italian writer on public finance. The joint demand for public goods has the implication, as Wicksell emphasized in his *Finanztheoretische Untersuchungen* (1896), that the market mechanism will fail to induce consumers to reveal their preferences for such goods. Each individual left to his own devices will contribute nothing to the provision of public goods simply because the total supply of them remains unaffected by this decision; everyone benefits from public goods, whether he pays or not.

Despite the fact that both nonmarket interdependence and public goods create a divergence between private and social costs, their significance for welfare economics is by no means the same. Nonmarket interdependence can always be counteracted in principle by appropriate taxes and bounties designed to close the gap between marginal private and marginal social cost. For example, the marginal social product of a factory located in a residential neighborhood is much less than the marginal private product. No one household is motivated to bribe the factory to move into an industrial area, since the private cost would exceed the private benefit. However, all the relevant households are motivated to pool their resources in a voluntary association for purposes of bribing the factory to move away if the bribe plus the costs of such an association are less than the benefits of the change – the so-called Coase Theorem (see below). But if the number of households and hence the transaction costs of concerted action is large, a voluntary association of households is unlikely to develop. In that case, however, the state can levy a head tax on the residents of the area and use the funds to bribe the factory to move away. If the value of real estate rises in consequence, everyone is better off.

In the case of public goods, however, there is no question of balancing the taxes collected from the beneficiaries of a change against the compensating bounties paid to those harmed by the change. Public goods will not be provided at all in a purely competitive market because no one will agree to pay taxes to finance them: since everyone enjoys the indivisible benefits of such things as national defense, noise and smoke abatement, clearance of areas that produce infectious diseases and the like, no matter who pays for it, everyone is motivated to evade payment.

It is clear from this kind of reasoning that no market test can establish the 'proper' quantity of public goods. As Wicksell realized, only a political decision through the ballot box can determine the quantity of public goods that ought to be provided. It is true that there are very few examples of pure public goods: public roads really yield divisible, not indivisible, benefits in the sense that 'the more there is for you, the less there is for me'. The concept of public goods is indeed far more limited than might appear at first sight. It is not enough to have joint consumption; the condition of equal consumption must apply to all, whether they pay or not. Furthermore, there must be no rationing of the supply of a public good because a limitation on quantity is equivalent to a price, thus creating the possibility of a solution by a price system. It is doubtful, therefore, whether roads, police protection, parks, playgrounds, schools and hospitals are really instances of public goods. Nevertheless, as long as some activities have even a trace of public character, price calculations will fail to drive the economic system to the social optimum.

In fact, we seem to be faced by two rather different and overlapping definitions of a public good. A public good must be available to all if it is available to any – the characteristic of nonexcludability – and its consumption by one must not impede its consumption by others – the characteristic of nonrivalness. A congested road freely available to all is a public good insofar as it is nonexcludable but not to the extent that it is rival. Similarly, seats in a half-empty commercial theatre are public goods insofar as they are nonrival but not to the extent that they are excludable. In both cases, what appears to be a private good takes on a degree of publicness, in consequence of which a market mechanism may fail to secure a Pareto-optimal allocation of resources. Similarly, the economic benefits of education are largely personal and divisible and the inputs into the educational system such as teachers, buildings and equipment are bought and sold in private profit-maximizing markets. Nevertheless, not all the benefits of education are confined to those who have paid for it, nor is it possible entirely to exclude the less educated from the 'spillover benefits' generated by the more educated. Education, therefore, represents what might be called a 'quasi-public good' and the attempt to produce it by a market process might well result in social underinvestment in education. We reach the conclusion that the 'publicness' of certain goods severely qualifies the Invisible Hand Theorem in a way that Adam Smith never dreamed of.

16. Pigovian Welfare Economics

Before examining second-best problems, we take this opportunity to say a few more words about Pigovian in contrast to Paretian welfare economics. Pigou's analysis of the divergence between the marginal private and the marginal social product is confined to the problem of 'real' external economies or diseconomies associated with *marginal* increments of output. But most of the cases Pigou discussed involve what Hicks has called the 'total' rather than the marginal conditions. Examples in point are town planning and slum clearance, both of which contain degrees of 'publicness'. In these cases, no scheme of taxes or bounties can bring private and social cost-benefit calculations into harmony. The same thing is true of most irreversible external effects. Consider for instance, the following list of real external *diseconomies* of the dynamic type culled from the pages of the *Economics of Welfare*: industrial accidents, occupational diseases, employment of female and child labour, air and water pollution resulting from the disposal of untreated waste products, and unemployment resulting from technical change. All these cause social losses but their removal would almost certainly violate the marginal conditions. The determination of the *physical* magnitudes of these diseconomies would itself be a difficult task since they fall by definition outside the price system. Even if we could express them in physical terms, we could not value them subjectively without a scale of valuation, that is, without a social welfare function telling us how to compare the utilities of the different victims suffering losses. Pigou's own method is to calculate social costs by adding up the direct and indirect costs associated with a given unit of investment, all valued at market prices. But if market prices reflect only private not social costs, this method of valuation breaks down. It is only in partial analysis that we can employ Pigou's method. When the divergences between private and social costs are pervasive throughout the economy, we cannot use market prices as a measure of satisfactions.

Pigou used the size of the national dividend as an indicator of welfare: the national dividend is maximized only if the marginal social product, or, what comes to the same thing, the marginal social cost of all resources in all alternative uses, is the same. It is obvious that this definition of a welfare maximum is based on interpersonal comparisons. Moreover, the touchstone of Pigou's policy prescriptions is 'the transference of wealth from the rich to the poor': if such a transfer does not diminish national income, it must improve welfare. The dependence of this kind of reasoning upon the Benthamite assumption of arithmetically additive utility functions is self-evident. But to criticize Pigou's approach because it is based on normative assumptions is to miss the point. The purpose of the book was precisely to show that a real-world imperfectly competitive dynamic economy is riddled with direct nonmarket interactions, which can be eliminated, however, if we are willing to make certain 'reasonable' and broadly appealing interpersonal comparisons of utilities. Pigou was not writing a theoretical treatise but a tract for the times. The 'arithmetic of redistribution' – that favourite argument of Victorian conservatives against income redistribution – was the butt of his attack and his central message was that attempts to raise the income levels of the poor need not be eroded by automatic economic forces. It should be evident by now that value judgments cannot be avoided in practical welfare economics. The problem is that of making them explicit. It is on this score that Pigou's book is really open to criticism.

Pigou's *Economics of Welfare* seems to confirm one of the oldest of radical criticisms of competitive capitalism: consumers' choices as expressed in market values do not necessarily reflect the social significance of goods and services; there are utilities and not just desired ends that competition does not suitably produce. Indeed, no one can continue to believe in the spontaneous coordination of private and social interests who has digested Pigou's insistence on the possible interdependence of firms and households. Even the hallowed principle of consumers' sovereignty loses its force. Suppose an excise tax on alcohol would reduce the quantity of alcohol consumed. If consumers' satisfactions are interdependent, the adoption of such an excise tax cannot be construed as a denial of the general principle that the individual himself is the best judge of his own well-being: individuals would feel themselves better off if they were simultaneously induced to drink less; the proceeds of the tax can then be used to bribe the liquor interest to acquiesce.

The existence of Veblenesque Effects in consumption thus gives scope to government action to improve welfare. Consider now the case of the introduction of a new product. We already know that the market tests fail to indicate whether a new product should be produced. Once produced, however, it may be bought by each individual simply because others are buying it. But if wants are interdependent, its withdrawal would leave no one worse off. Hence, consumers' sovereignty does not provide a suitable standard to weed out undesired products. The startling implications of considerations such as these in a world in which most consumer goods are differentiated are obvious. With product differentiation, each firm is confronted with a downward-sloping demand curve. Even with the 'tangency solution', the number of firms will be larger, price higher and output lower than under perfect competition [see chapter 10, section 9]. But these disadvantages are counteracted by the variety of products available under monopolistic competition. If consumers' preference functions are independent, we must conclude that consumers are paying for the variety they desire. But with the presence of 'bandwagon' and 'snob' effects, we need some criterion of the socially desirable amounts of variety for the ordinary market test no longer has any meaning.

The trouble with Pigou's distinction between private and social costs is that it cannot be made rigorous. Paretian welfare economics, on the other hand, achieves a stringent and less ambitious definition of the social optimum inasmuch as Pareto optimality is defined with respect to an initial distribution of income. The practical relevance of this achievement for policy, however, is nil. A loose rule such as that entry into industries should be kept as free as is technically feasible has more relevance for public policy than the ideal principle of Pareto optimality. Pigovian welfare economics, on the other hand, is frankly normative and geared to practical applications: 'it is the promise of fruit and not of light that chiefly merits our regard'. It assumes a world of free not perfect competition, with degrees of immobility, indivisibility and imperfections of knowledge not found in the Paretian conception of perfect competition. Its shortcomings lie not so much in its dependence on normative assumptions as in its effort to depict what are really structural failures of the market mechanism as merely marginal divergences between the private and the social product.

In the last few years, Pigou's contention that state intervention in the form of taxes and subsidies is called for whenever the private and social product diverge has been challenged by R.H. Coase and others, who claim that the market mechanism can lead to a Pareto optimum despite externalities in production and consumption since it is usually possible to devise a private bargaining solution to eliminate the externalities; moreover, the administrative costs of taxes and bounties can easily absorb more resources than are lost through a deviation from a Pareto optimum. Take Pigou's own example of a railway damaging nearby fields; the argument is that if the railway could make a bargain with farmers having property adjoining the railway line, it would not matter that the railway cannot be charged for damage caused by fire and smoke; if the damage suffered by farmers were greater than the benefits reaped by the railway, the farmers could pay a sum sufficient to induce the railway to close down the line; if the damage were less than the benefit, aggregate welfare would be raised if the railway line were to bribe farmers to tolerate the damage. Thus, Pigou's general prescription of a tax to deal with external diseconomies assumes that the party imposing the diseconomies and the party suffering them cannot negotiate to their mutual advantage. Furthermore, it assumes that the administrative costs of achieving optimum resource allocation by means of a specific tax is always less than the external diseconomy itself.

Summing up, if property rights in all the relevant resources are clearly assigned and if all economic agents can get together to negotiate with one another – 'transaction costs are negligible' – the agents themselves will be motivated to enter into voluntary agreements to shift the costs of 'pollution' from the victims to the perpetrators. Secondly, under these circumstances it can be shown that value of national income is unaffected by the precise pattern of liability for pollution as determined by private negotiations; this second proposition has gone down in the literature as the Coase Theorem. Finally, it is argued that, even if transaction costs are so high as to make the Coase Theorem irrelevant, there is still no presumption that government intervention will improve matters; 'government failure' must be weighted against 'market failure'.

17. Second-Best Solutions

This brings us to the last and final objection to the Theorem of the Invisible Hand: the impossibility of piecemeal welfare economics as demonstrated by the theory of second-best. In an extraordinary article published in 1956, Lipsey and Lancaster proved that, if there are at least two markets in which the optimum conditions are not satisfied, a policy change designed to break down imperfections in one of these two markets cannot be justified on Paretian welfare grounds. Moving towards a Pareto optimality is not good enough: either we attain the first-best solution or there is nothing to choose between second-best, third-best and so forth. An oversimplified way of stating the Lipsey-Lancaster proof is this: assume we have a general equilibrium system with constraints in two equations and we solve the system for a second-best optimum by the usual technique of constrained maximization; assume now one of the two constraints is a policy parameter such as a tariff and the problem is to discover whether a reduction in the tariff would improve social welfare; it is impossible to demonstrate that this would necessarily happen and this is what they call 'the general theory of the second best'.

The implications of this argument for traditional welfare economics are devastating. The enforcement of contracts, to state only one of the minimal functions of government, is not costless. Unless such costs of policing competition are financed entirely by lump-sum head taxes or unpredictable capital levies [see below], the Pareto optimum conditions will not be satisfied in at least one market. That is only to say that all welfare economics of any possible relevance to the real world willy-nilly deals with second-best solutions. The case for perfect competition is that it constitutes a necessary though not sufficient condition for a Pareto optimum. But the existence of government virtually guarantees a second-best problem and hence when the optimum conditions are satisfied in all but one or two markets, there is no presumption in favour of satisfying Pareto optimality in the remaining markets. In general, therefore, there is no welfare presumption in favour of perfect competition.

18. Marginal Cost Pricing

Is there no scope then for piecemeal applied welfare economics? Is there nothing we can save from the wreckage of modern welfare economics? Must we abandon the old doctrine that efficiency in resource allocation is only achieved when prices equal marginal costs, which represented the essence of the Lange-Lerner rules for decentralized market socialism and its corollary that public enterprises must be required to set prices in accordance with marginal costs? A review of the history of the concept of marginal cost pricing (MCP) will place these questions in perspective and will serve, at the same time, as a way of drawing together the threads of our discussion of welfare economics.

The doctrine that the whole of the overhead costs of decreasing-cost industries or 'natural monopolies' must be financed out of general tax revenues and that the price of their output must depend only on marginal operating costs makes its first explicit appearance in the railway literature of the late nineteenth century, in particular the writings of such railway economists as Wilhelm Launhardt and Arthur Hadley, although hints of it are found in the much earlier work of Jules Dupuit and his disciples at the *Ecole des Ponts et Chaussées* in Paris [see chapter 8, section 16]. When Harold Hotelling resurrected the concept of MCP for public enterprises in a famous paper published in 1938, he advanced the general principle that the resulting deficits of decreasing-cost industries must be financed out of 'lump-sum taxes', that is, taxes that do not affect the behavior of economic agents at the margin because they leave the *pattern* of post-tax income the same as that of pre-tax income. His claim for the superiority of MCP and the exclusive reliance on neutral, lump-sum taxes was based on the 'new' welfare economics in the sense of Pareto. Hotelling's advocacy of MCP ran almost immediately into a barrage of criticisms, which have in fact continued to this very day. Nevertheless, these criticisms have failed to dislodge the Hotelling thesis, which indeed is the veritable credo of modern writers on transport economics.

In 1950 Ruggles provided a classic review of the early phases of the debate surrounding the Hotelling thesis, which included many of the great names of modern economics, such as Frisch, Lerner, Samuelson, Lewis, Meade, Coase and many others. It was a confusing discussion, which we can now see involved almost as many fallacies as valid objections. Some argued, incorrectly, that prices need only be proportional, not equal to marginal costs, in which case it might be possible to meet all the marginal conditions of Pareto-optimality and, at the same time, to cover total costs out of sales receipts. Some thought that MCP required identical tariffs for public utilities during peak and off-peak periods, whereas the exact opposite is true. Some said that perfect price discrimination would satisfy the marginal conditions, which is true, and that perfect price discrimination is preferable to MCP, which is not true since discriminatory charges are only one of many ways of pricing intramarginal units. In particular, a special form of price discrimination, namely multipart pricing, with a fixed, uniform 'admission' fee to all users or consumers to finance overhead costs plus a variable charge equal to marginal costs to recover operating costs, was held to be superior to MCP because it satisfied the benefit principle of taxation ('he who benefits ought to pay') and solved the deficit problem of decreasing-cost industries. Finally, it was argued that MCP failed to provide a profit-loss test of misconceived investment and that any change from average cost pricing to MCP without compensation payments by gainers (consumers of the public service) to losers (all taxpayers) necessarily leads to a change in income distribution, which is to say that the results of MCP are simply not comparable to those of average cost pricing.

After sorting out the sense from the nonsense in these criticisms, Ruggles nevertheless rejected the Hotelling thesis based on the 'new' welfare economics. At best, Hotelling had shown that a shift to MCP would entail a *potential* Pareto improvement (PPI), not an actual one. Hotelling believed that if deficits were financed by lump-sum taxes, the case for MCP rested on *actual* Pareto-improvements because lump-sum taxes fall only on the intramarginal consumers' and producers' surpluses. Ruggles argued that Hotelling was simply wrong because even lump-sum taxes are borne in part by those who make little or no use of a public service and hence involve a redistribution of income between users and non-users. We must either decide to ignore this effect by assuming that the utility of income is the same for all individuals, which takes us right back to the 'old' welfare economics of Marshall and Pigou, or we must deny that the associated redistribution is uniquely related to the incomes of users and non-users, which may or may not be true depending on the public service in question.

Ruggles' criticism of Hotelling has withstood the test of time and it is now a commonplace of writers on welfare economics to declare that the 'new' welfare economics can only approve a PPI: an actual Pareto-improvement requires the addition of a specific distributional judgment. This admission is sometimes regarded as marking the effective failure of the 'new' welfare economies, which had after all promised to provide important and significant statements on policy issues without invoking interpersonal comparisons of utility, thus separating questions of allocative efficiency from those of distributive equity. If the conclusions of welfare economics have to be confined to PPI rather than actual ones, the skeptics argue, the promised separation of efficiency and equity is only achieved at the cost of practical irrelevance. Hotelling himself believed that taxes on land rents, inherited income and current income all qualified as neutral, lump-sum taxes, from which it followed that PPI could always be realised in practice. The notion that taxes on land rents and inherited incomes are lump-sum taxes that do not affect the marginal conditions for maximising welfare must be put down as a piece of old-fashioned, nineteenth-century economics. Stranger still was Hotelling's notion that an inccome tax is a lump-sum tax when an income tax obviously alters the marginal rates of substitution between work and leisure.[1] That leaves us with a poll tax or head tax as the only candidate for a lump-sum tax. Unfortunately, such taxes appear to be politically impracticable. If so, there would seem to be no way in which we could ever realise a PPI in practice without committing ourselves to some interpersonal comparison of utility.

The late 1950s saw a number of major contributions to the debate, all of which endorsed Ruggles' central conclusion that the impracticability of lump-sum redistributions of income or wealth represented the Achilles Heel of the theory of MCP. Books like Little's *Critique of Welfare Economics* (1957) and Graaff's *Theoretical Welfare Economics* (1957) rejected MCP out of hand on second-best reasoning, that is, the impossibility in a mixed economy of achieving first-best conditions. Some authors, like Wiseman, went even further in claiming that the very notion of a general pricing rule for public utilities is an 'empty box'. As for MCP, Wiseman repeated the old argument that there exists no method for implementing the MCP rule for decreasing-cost industries, which does not entail a system of financing the resulting deficit, thus altering the distribution of income, which alteration however cannot be evaluated according to the 'new' welfare economics. Wiseman added the point, however, that the MCP rule gives no guidance in selecting the appropriate time-period for deciding on public utility prices and hence no guidance in selecting the length of the relevant planning period. Wiseman argued that the only practical planning period is one as long as the lowest common multiple of the life-periods of the assets involved, implying that MCP would always have to be supplemented by an exercise in investment planning.

Farrell wrote what is generally considered to be the definitive reply to Wiseman. It is noteworthy that he conceded all the standard, second-best arguments against MCP, avoided discussion of the special difficulties created by decreasing-cost industries, and ultimately rested his case for MCP on the still greater deficiencies of average cost pricing. In these and other defences of MCP, penned in the late 1950s, we have clearly travelled a long way from the dogmatic pronouncements of the early advocates of MCP in the golden halo created by the 1938 Hotelling paper. The new argument for MCP is, not that it is a perfect policy rule for public enterprises, but that it is a policy rule superior to average cost pricing.

The early 1960s witnessed a new twist to the MCP debate, which seemed at last to answer Wiseman's earlier criticism that MCP requires a decision on the length of the run over which marginal costs are defined, and yet provides no basis for such a decision. The answer takes its cue from the well-known theorem that short-run and

---

[1] Most of the early participants in the controversy over the Hotelling thesis agreed with Hotelling that an income tax is superior to an excise tax as a method of raising revenue to finance the MCP system. This thesis, soon to be known as the theory of the 'excess burden of indirect taxation', attracted almost as much debate in the 1940s and 1950s as the concept of MCP. It took almost two decades to arrive at the current view, namely, that there is no simple way of rating taxes according to their 'excess burden'.

long-run marginal costs coincide when capacity is optimally adjusted to demand, from which it follows that any difference between the short-run and long-run implications of MCP is a sure sign that capacity is not adjusted to its optimal level. If there is excess demand at a price determined by short-run marginal costs, MCP tells us that prices must be raised until demand equals capacity. At the same time, however, capacity should be raised to meet the demand that would be forthcoming at the price which is optimal on the basis of long-run marginal costs. In other words, if there is an optimal investment policy, there is no contradiction between short-run and long-run MCP and if there is such a contradiction, it constitutes a criticism, not of the MCP principle, but of the investment policy that is being pursued.

This argument is the gist of the contributions of a number of French economists, particularly Marcel Boiteux and Pierre Massé, who were connected with *Electricité de France* in the years that followed World War II. They noted that, in electricity pricing at any rate, there was little alternatative to pricing based on long-run marginal costs. Short-run marginal costs could either mean the cost of increasing output quickly or increasing it temporarily but, whatever the operational meaning of short-run marginal costs, administrative constraints on frequent tariff changes forced managers of electricity generating boards to focus on permanent output changes and hence long-run marginal costs. The theory of optimal capacity of the French engineers-cum-economists has been vigorously taken up by Ralph Turvey in his writings on the pricing problems of the British electricity industry. In his major study, *Optimal Pricing and Investment in Electricity Supply* (1968), he comes down firmly on the side of MCP as a second-best pricing rule, arguing that the prices of public enterprise products sold within the public sector should equal their long-run marginal costs, while those sold outside the public sector should be proportional to long-run marginal costs, the mark-up over marginal costs being determined by the prices of their private sector substitutes.

The striking feature of the French contributions to the MCP literature is the total failure to deal with the problem of deficits in decreasing-cost industries which, indeed, is hardly ever mentioned. If there really are 'natural monopolies', that is, public enterprises in which costs continue to decline monotonically for all foreseeable levels of output, it is of little help to be told that short-run marginal costs will be equal to long-run marginal costs when capacity is optimally adjusted because the optimum level of capacity of 'natural monopolies' is infinitely large. It is true that the evidence for increasing returns to scale in most public services is dubious and it has been argued that even decreasing costs in railways are really due to excess capacity and do not represent a true long-run equilibrium phenomenon. But even if we reject the notion of genuine decreasing-cost industries, the problem of deficits forms an integral part of the MCP principle.

Most British and American writers on MCP illustrate the problem of deficits with examples of nationalized industries like railway transport, the demand for which has been shrinking for long periods, so that financial deficits are really due to excess capacity. In that case, even prices equal to short-run marginal costs will not cover long-run marginal costs and will generate financial losses. We can, of course, raise prices to cover average costs, thus removing the deficit, but that only redistributes the social costs of carrying excess capacity from all tax-payers to users of the service. The French writers on MCP simply avoid discussing such issues of equity connected with pricing rules for public enterprises because they appear to be thinking of industries like electricity for which demand is growing and costs are almost certainly non-decreasing in the long run.

19. The Mislaid Maxim

We are now very close to the heart of the matter, which, in popular parlance, is the question: Should public enterprises always be expected to pay their own way? Those who advocate MCP, even with many ifs and buts, deny any presumption that public enterprises ought always to make a profit; they focus on current costs and treat historic costs as bygones that are forever bygones; and they insist on keeping questions of allocation and pricing analytically separate from questions of finance and equity. On the other hand, those who reject MCP in any and all of its varieties, arguing that only average-cost pricing provides an accounting check on management, and denying that efficiency and equity can ever be separated, end up insisting that every public enterprise must be expected to pay its own way, which paradoxically undermines the very case for public ownership that gave rise in the first place to the debate on public utility pricing. In other words, the opponents of MCP would appear to solve the pricing problem of public enterprises by dissolving it.

We come now to the last and most recent phase of the long controversy over the Hotelling thesis. The views of the early advocates of MCP, such as Hotelling and Lerner, that Pareto-optimality requires MCP in the public sector on the assumption that prices are equated to marginal costs in the private sector, is nowadays dismissed as extraordinarily naïve. Given imperfect competition, uncorrected externalities and non-lump-sum taxes, MCP in public enterprises can only be a second-best solution. But apart from all these considerations, there is the old problem of financing the deficit of decreasing-cost industries. Since the deficit must be financed by taxation, and since any tax other than a poll tax or an arbitrary head tax induces price distortions, MCP must involve the problem of maximizing output in the presence of an added constraint – the revenues of government must equal the algebraic sum of the deficits (or surpluses) of the individual firms in the economy – which is precisely the definition of a second-best problem. Even if there is no such thing as a 'natural monopoly', public enterprises or regulated private enterprises may be required by law to meet historic as well as current costs, in consequence of which MCP would once again involve the problem of maximizing output subject to an added revenue constraint. In either case, MCP is inherently a second-best problem, at least so long as lump-sum taxes are ruled out as impossible in practice. It can be shown, however, that the second-best case for MCP requires, not prices equal to marginal costs, but prices which deviate systematically from marginal costs. It is this theorem which Baumol and Bradford have labelled the 'Mislaid Maxim' in the sense that it goes back to the public finance literature of the

1920s, for example, Pigou's *Study of Public Finance* (1928), and even further back to the public utility pricing literature of the nineteenth century.

Far from setting prices equal to or even proportionate to marginal costs, second-best, quasi-optimal prices should deviate unequally from marginal costs throughout the economy, the deviation in any particular case being greater, the more price-inelastic the demand for the product in question. In the simple case where all cross-elasticities of demand are zero, the rule is that the deviation from marginal costs for any one product should be inversely proportionate to its own price-elasticity of demand. This idea of an optimal set of deviations from MCP in a second-best world is now a recognized feature of modern discussions of applied welfare economics, being the other side of the coin of the currently fashionable topic of 'optimal taxation'. These developments are clearly a far cry from the original Hotelling article. Nevertheless, they remain in the Hotelling tradition, not simply because long-run marginal costs remain the reference point to pronouncements on optimal resource allocation, but because the century-old separation of efficiency from equity characterized second-best as it did first-best welfare economics. Even in this literature, the First Commandment of the 'new' welfare economics – 'Thou Shalt Not Make Interpersonal Comparisons of Utility' – is scrupulously obeyed. But for this First Commandment, we could meet the revenue constraint that inhibits us from achieving a first-best solution by average-cost pricing rather than MCP. The case for MCP, or, as we should now say, the case for making MCP a point of departure for a set of optimal prices, stems basically from the fundamental conditions for Pareto-optimal efficiency and, of course, Pareto-optimality is only defined with reference to a particular distribution of income, or rather, resource endowments. If we are unwilling to divorce efficiency from equity, at least for the sake of argument, neither the concept of MCP nor that of optimal deviations from MCP makes any sense.

20. Cost-Benefit Analysis

In the final analysis, therefore, it is the willingness to analyse efficiency arguments apart from problems of income distribution that divides the advocates from the critics of MCP. The fundamental distinction between efficiency and equity is rarely defended in so many words by modern writers on MCP but is frequently and explicitly discussed in the literature on cost-benefit analysis. Cost-benefit analysis appraises economic projects in terms of their net total benefits over total costs on the assumption that it is desirable to maximize the sum of producers' and consumers' surpluses. But producers' surplus is simply the absolute value of the money amount by which the total costs of production of a particular output exceeds the revenue which that output yields under strict MCP, while the consumers' surplus is the money amount by which the consumers' total valuation of that output exceeds the revenue they have paid out again under strict MCP. Hence, cost-benefit analysis subsumes the MCP principle and is unthinkable without it.

Virtually all modern exponents of cost-benefit analysis are careful to point out that cost-benefit analysis can only show that a particular project is capable of generating a

PPI in which gainers could compensate losers and still themselves remain better off; it offers no opinion, however, on whether such compensation payment *should* be made; that is, it stops at the point at which it has enumerated the gains and losses to various individuals and ventures no judgment on how these gains and losses should be distributed. Since the actual adoption or rejection of a project by a public authority implies both a cost-benefit calculation and a distributional judgment, a number of writers have in recent years suggested that such distributional judgments should be integrated into cost-benefit analysis by means of weights attached to the net benefits which accrue to various income groups.

This proposal to use distributional weights in cost-benefit analysis has been vigorously opposed by Arnold Harberger on a number of different grounds. He argues, firstly, that economists are unlikely to agree on any particular set of weights. The view that distributional weights ought to decline with income, because of some notion of diminishing marginal utility of income, would no doubt command universal assent among economists. But the distributional weighting functions reflecting this viewpoint nevertheless can be shown to involve vastly different weights. Even the suggestion of a single premium magnifying the net benefits of beneficiaries below the poverty line is problematic. In general, the use of distributional weights would in most cases make project evaluation depend critically on how the project is actually financed. Hence, if we are concerned to reach a professional consensus in the area of applied welfare economics, we are well advised to ignore distributional effects in cost-benefit analysis.

Besides, even conventional valuations of social income, in which an increase in the size of the national income is regarded as 'good' and a decrease as 'bad', in effect assume that the size of the cake can be treated independently of the sharing out of its slices. In evaluating a change in national income, we typically accept base-year or final-year prices as if the choice involved no value judgment, and we ignore concomitant changes in the distribution of income, thereby attaching equal weights to the gainers and losers of the change. To do anything else would mean that we could not welcome an increase in measured national income without prior agreement on the social welfare function.

Harberger is not denying that the evaluation of the distributional effects of an economic project forms part of the decision to accept or reject the project. The argument is simply that, instead of incorporating distributional weights into cost-benefit analysis, we should sum the monetary value of costs and benefits algebraically across relevant individuals or groups of individuals, leaving the addition of alternative distributional weights to a later stage. In this way we can show that society may have to pay a price in terms of efficiency for each incremental distributional 'benefit' obtained.

21. Back to the Conflict Between Efficiency and Equity
We end this long and complex story, therefore, by reasserting the old distinction between efficiency and equity which runs right through the entire literature on

welfare economics, as far back as Pareto, Pigou, Marshall and even Ricardo, without which its elaborately constructed apparatus collapses like a house of cards. This is not to say that efficiency questions are 'positive', 'objective' economics, involving no value judgments. Even first-best, Pareto-optimality rests, as we have said, on definite value judgments. Efficiency is necessarily a value-laden concept and cannot be freed from the notion that efficiency is somehow more desirable than inefficiency. Nevertheless, there is little advantage, and much disadvantage, in cluttering up the conclusions of welfare economics by indiscriminately combining the value judgments underlying the concept of Pareto-optimality with those relating to the economic justice of different distributions of income.

Consider, for example, what is implied by the opposite attitude. If we refuse, even in principle, to distinguish allocative efficiency from distributive equity, we must perforce reject the whole of welfare economics and with it any conventional presumption in favour of competitive markets, and, indeed, in favour of the price mechanism as a method of allocating scarce resources. Arguments for co-ordinating economic activity by markets would then have to be expressed in terms of political philosophy – for example, that markets diffuse economic power – and economics would in consequence have to become a totally different subject. Moreover, it is perfectly clear that economists do judge such practical questions as: should parking meters be used to control road congestion?; should public transport be free?; should governments subsidize gasoline, medical care and public housing?; etcetera; by means of sequential reasoning in which the efficiency of various alternatives is judged before considering any possible adverse distributional effects that may or may not be capable of being offset by taxes and transfers. No doubt, most decisions of public policy proceed exactly the other way round: they are expressly designed to aid a favoured group at the expense of every other, the more so as the benefits of economic policies are often extremely visible, whereas the costs are so widely diffused that most people are hardly aware of paying for them. But that is no argument for economists to duplicate the political process. Jacob Viner once defended the economist as 'the special custodian for society of the long view in economic matters'. Similarly, we must insist on the role of the economist as the special custodian for society of the efficiency view of social and economic problems because all the evidence suggests that if economists do not draw attention to the trade-off between efficiency and equity, no one else will.

So Ruggles, Little, Graaff and Wiseman notwithstanding, the theory of MCP is no empty box. Of course, MCP is a method, not a dogma. It is grounded in Pareto-optimality and the maximization of consumers' and producers' surpluses, but then so are all the policy views of economists. In addition, MCP requires empirical judgments on a product-by-product basis about market structure, indivisibilities, externalities and elasticities of demand and supply. It does not furnish, therefore, any simple pronouncements about public pricing, except perhaps that public enterprises should not necessarily be expected to break even, and that almost any pricing rule is better than average cost pricing.

NOTES ON FURTHER READING

Eighty years after its publication, L. Walras' *Elements of Pure Economics* finally appeared in English, superbly translated by W. Jaffé (1954). One would have to look far and wide, even in so abstract a social science as economics, to find a book that moves so consistently on a high level of abstraction. As the translator has observed: 'The argument is progressive, moving deliberately to be a premeditated climax, and unless the reader moves with it in sympathy with the author's intention, the meaning is lost. The book is all the more difficult because the theory, though essentially mathematical, is expressed in primitive mathematics and then paraphrased in crabbed prose'. With a book so imperfectly executed, a reader's guide would seem to be essential. Fortunately, Jaffé's sixty-page, chapter-by-chapter commentary virtually supplies what is needed. The reader is particularly urged to study the following commentaries: on the relation between Marshallian and Walrasian stability conditions, pp. 502–3; on the meanings of *rareté*, marginal utility and *Grenznutzen*, pp. 506–7; on the maximum-satisfactions doctrine, pp. 510–11; on the *rareté* of capital goods, pp. 517–18; on the meaning of *tâtonnement*, pp. 522, 528–9; on Gossen's utility theory, pp. 523–4; on the theory of capital, pp. 531–2. 536–41; on cash balances and the theory of money, pp. 543–7; and, finally, on marginal productivity theory, pp. 549–53.

Jaffé did not live to finish the biography of Walras that he was writing. For a suggestion of the rich harvest that awaits reaping, see his 'Walras, Léon', *IESS*, 16, his biographical essays in *William Jaffé's Essays on Walras*, ed. Walker, and the three fat volumes of *Correspondence of Leon Walras and Related Papers*, ed. W. Jaffé (1965). The latter in particular convey an incomparable impression of Walras' ceaseless activities on behalf of general equilibrium theory: hawking summaries to journal editors; claiming priority for virtually every element in the 'marginal revolution'; lobbying for the Nobel Peace Prize in recognition of his scientific discoveries; and meeting every criticism, however trifling. For reviews of this invaluable addition to the primary literature on the first-generation marginalists, see V. Tarascio, 'Leon Walras: On the Occasion of the Publication of His Correspondence and Related Papers', *SEJ*, July, 1967; and D. A. Walker, 'Leon Walras in the Light of His Correspondence and Related Papers', *JPE*, July/August, 1970.

Walras had planned to write two systematic treatises on applied and social economics but in the end was forced to substitute his collected papers for the systematic works he had earlier envisaged. Because these volumes, *Études d'économie sociale* (1896) and *Études d'économie politique* (1898), have never been translated, his policy views have either been ignored or deprecated on insufficient evidence. W. Jaffé, 'Leon Walras, An Economic Adviser *Manqué*', *EJ*, 1975, reprinted in *William Jaffé's Essays on Walras*, ed. Walker, is an attempt to set the record straight. It led Jaffé eventually towards a totally new evaluation of Walras' intentions in writing the *Elements*: see, in particular, W. Jaffé, 'The Normative Bias in the Walrasian Model: Walras Versus Gossen', *QJE*, 1977, and his 'Walras's Economics As Others See It', *JEL*, 1980, both reprinted in Walker's *William Jaffé's Essays on Walras*. Needless to say, the Jaffé interpretations has not been generally accepted: for example, see M. Morishima, 'W. Jaffé on Léon Walras: A Comment', *JEL*, June, 1980, and D. A. Walker, 'Introduction' to *William Jaffé's Essays on Walras*.

Apart from evaluating Walras' works, Jaffé also traced almost everything we know about the genesis of the Walrasian system. In 'A. N. Isnard, Progenitor of the Walrasian General Equilibrium Model', *HOPE*, 1969, and 'The Birth of Leon Walras's Elements', *ibid.*, 1977, both reprinted in Walker's *William Jaffé's Essays on Walras*, he showed that Walras worked out the mathematical framework of his theory on the basis of Isnard's *Traité des richesses* (1781), a forgotten 18th-century book, and Poinsot's *Eleménts de statique* (1803), a once famous textbook in pure mechanics.

Jaffé's translation of the *Elements* stimulated reappraisals of Walras' work. M. Friedman, 'Léon Walras and His Economic System', *AER*, 1955, reprinted in *EET* and *RHET*, and R. F. Harrod, 'Walras: A Re-Appraisal', *EJ*, June, 1956, take a skeptical view of the final value of

Walras' contributions. For an enthusiastic appraisal, see R. E. Kuenne, 'The Architectonics of Léon Walras', *KYK*, IX, 2, 1956. Similarly, Kuenne's *Theory of General Economic Equilibrium* is a comprehensive review of the main body of general equilibrium theory from Walras to Arrow and Debreu and Part II, which takes up half the book, parallels the main chapters of Walras' *Elements*; however, the level of difficulty in this book is sometimes extremely high. One of the most readable brief discussions of Walras' system is by J. R. Hicks, 'Léon Walras', *Ecom*, 1934, reprinted in *DET*. Stigler, *Production and Distribution Theories*, chap. 9, is particularly useful on Walras' capital theory. For a laudatory nonmathematical treatment in rich detail, see Schumpeter, *History of Economic Analysis*, pp. 998–1026. The student is advised, however, to leave this reading until he has developed a feeling for Walras' analytical devices. A. W. Marget, *The Theory of Prices*, II, chap. 8, part 1, specifically defends Walras against the charge of 'sterility'.

G. Pirou, *Les théories de l'équilibre économique: Walras et Pareto* (3rd edn 1946) represents a general account of the evolution of the Lausanne School. For a brief exposition of the Walrasian system, followed by a superb review of Pareto's contributions to the theory of general equilibrim, see U. Ricci, 'Pareto and Pure Economics', *REStud*, October, 1933. A beautiful article by K. J. Arrow, 'Economic Equilibrium', *IESS*, 4, brings the story of general equilibrium economics from Walras down to the present day. See also the useful historical account by J. S. Chipman, 'The Nature and Meaning of Equilibrium in Economic Theory', *Functionalism in the Social Sciences*, ed. D. Martindale (1965), reprinted in *Penguin Modern Economic Readings: Price Theory*, ed. Townsend. E. R. Weintraub, *General Equilibrium Theory* (1974 in paperback) is a readable introduction for students to the latest developments in general equilibrium theory, including the concept of the 'core' in game theory which have simplified recent existence theorems.

N. Kaldor's article, 'The Determinateness of Equilibrium', *REStud*, 1934, reprinted in his *Essays on Value and Distribution*, is the classic piece on problems of determinacy of equilibrium. For an excellent discussion of existence theorems, see Dorfman, Samuelson, and Solow, *Linear Programming and Economic Activity*, chap. 13; this chapter not only discusses the famous existence proof of Wald but gives an elegant proof of its own. On existence theorems, see also Baumol, *Economic Theory and Operations Analysis*, chap. 23; and J. R. Hicks, 'Linear Theory', *EJ*, December, 1960. E. R. Weintraub, 'On the Existence of a Competitive Equilibrium: 1930–1954', *JEL*, March, 1983, tells in loving detail how the very question of the existence of a general equilibrium solution came back into economics thirty years after Walras thought he had disposed of it.

Patinkin, *Money, Interest, and Prices*, Note B, tries to show that Walras' theory of 'groping' is the first example in the history of economics of true dynamic analysis. W. Jaffé, 'Walras' Theory of *Tâtonnement*: A Critique of Recent Interpretations', *JPE*, 1967, and 'Another Look at Léon Walras's Theory of *Tâtonnement*', *HOPE*, 1981, both reprinted in Walker's *William Jaffé's Essays on Walras*, retraces and reappraises Walras' theory of 'groping' as it developed in successive editions of the *Elements*. See also D. A. Walker's useful review of 'Competitive *Tâtonnement* Exchange Markets', *KYK*, 25, 2, 1972. If Walras' theory of 'groping' is unsatisfactory, the same may be said of Edgeworth's theory of recontracting, as D. A. Walker argues in his paper, 'Edgeworth's Theory of Recontract', *EJ*, March, 1973.

Walras' theory of capital and his monetary theory have given rise to numerous conflicting interpretations. On his theory of capital, see W. Jaffé, 'Walras's Theory of Capital Formation in the Framework of His Theory of General Equilibrium' (1953), translated in Walker's *William Jaffé's Essays on Walras*; and L. Foss, 'Some Notes on Léon Walras' Theory of Capitalization and Credit', *MeEc*, April, 1957. For a textbook treatment of capital theory in strictly Walrasian terms, see M. Friedman, *Price Theory* (1962), chap. 13. The evolution of Walras' monetary theory in successive editions of the *Elements* is traced in two articles by A. W. Marget, 'Léon Walras and the "Cash-Balance Approach" to the Problem of the Value of Money', JPE, October, 1931, and 'The Monetary Aspects of the Walrasian System', *ibid.*, April, 1935. Despite its title, R. E. Kuenne, 'Walras, Leontief, and the Interdependence of Economic

Activities', *QJE*, August, 1954, with 'Comment' by J. M. Henderson and R. E. Quandt, *ibid.*, November, 1955, concentrates on the role of money in the Walrasian system and defends Walras against the charge of dichotomizing the pricing process. Patinkin, *Money, Interest, and Prices*, Note C, is a commentary on lessons 29 and 30 of the *Elements*; Patinkin insists that Walras' treatment does leave absolute prices indeterminate and that Walras cannot be described as an exponent of the cash-balance approach in the accepted sense of the term. For R. E. Kuenne's reply, see 'Patinkin on Neo-Classical Monetary Theory: A Critique in Walrasian Specifics', *SEJ*, October, 1959.

For a defence of Walras against the recent Cambridge critique of neoclassical capital theory, see D. Collard, 'Léon Walras and the Cambridge Caricature', *EJ*, June, 1973. W. D. Montgomery, 'An Interpretation of Walras' Theory of Capital as a Model of Economic Growth', *HOPE*, Fall, 1971, demonstrates that Walras' avowedly static theory can be converted into a theory of growth with very little extra work. For a systematic review of Walras' views on economic policy, see M. Boson, *Léon Walras: Fondateur de la politique économique scientifique* (1951). The chapter on Walras in Hutchison, *Review of Economic Doctrines*, emphasizes Walras' view on applied economics. See also J. O. Clark, 'Walras and Pareto: Their Approach to Applied Economics and Social Economics', *CJE*, November 1942.

Pareto's contributions to economics and sociology are discussed by J. A. Schumpeter, 'Vilfredo Pareto, 1848–1923', *QJE*, 1949, reprinted in *Ten Great Economists*, and Hutchison, *Review of Economic Doctrines*, chap. 14. There is an interesting biography by G. H. Bousquet, *Pareto (1848–1923): le savant et l'homme* (1960). See also V. J. Tarascio, *Pareto's Methodological Approach to Economics* (1967), supplemented by a series of his articles: 'Paretian Welfare Economics: Some Neglected Aspects', *JPE*, January/February, 1969; 'Vilfredo Pareto on Marginalism', *HOPE*, Fall, 1972; 'Pareto on Political Economy', *ibid.*, Winter, 1974; and 'Pareto: A View of the Present Through the Past', *JPE*, February, 1976; all attempting to show how vital Pareto's sociology is to his general conception of economic policy. W. J. Samuels, *Pareto on Policy* (1974) makes much the same point.

V. Pareto's *Manual of Political Economy* (1906) has finally been translated into English by A. S. Schwier and A. N. Page (1971) but not to everyone's satisfaction: see W. Jaffé, 'Pareto Translated: A Review Article', *JEL*, December, 1972, and the exchange between Jaffé, the translators and V. Tarascio in *ibid.*, March, 1974. Chapter 6 of the *Manual* contains a statement of the concept of social optimum. In a mathematical appendix to the book, Pareto develops the marginal conditions, concluding with a demonstration that perfect competition maximizes welfare. Later, he seems to have realized that his argument provides only necessary, not sufficient, conditions for a social optimum. At any rate, the article on 'Mathematical Economics' in the *Encyclopédie des sciences mathématiques* (1911), reprinted in *IEP*, No. 5, 1955, and Baumol and Goldfeld's *Precursors of Mathematical Economics*, contain nothing on the doctrine of maximum satisfaction. E. Barone, 'The Ministry of Production in the Collectivist State' (1908), is available in *Penguin Modern Economics Readings: Socialist Economics*, eds. A. Nove and D. M. Nuti (1972 in paperback). Barone's succinct summary of the conditions of general equilibrium under atomistic competition, and his suggestions of how the planning authorities in a socialist state might duplicate 'the competitive solution' are still worth reading. There is a long history to the question of the possibility of rational allocation under socialism, which is intimately connected with the realism or lack of realism of the Walrasian description of *tâtonnement*. On all this, see K. I. Vaughn's excellent paper, 'Economic Calculation Under Socialism: the Austrian Contribution', *EQ*, October, 1980, supplemented by P. Murrell, 'Did The Theory of Market Socialism Answer the Challenge to Ludwig von Mises? A Reinterpretation of the Socialist Controversy', *HOPE*, Spring, 1983.

V. J. Tarascio, 'A Correction: On the Genealogy of the So-called Edgeworth-Bowley Diagram', *WEJ*, June, 1972, shows that Pareto originated the Edgeworth-Bowley box diagram and that Edgeworth never even used it. W. Jaffé continues the theme in 'Edgeworth's Contract Curve, Part I: A Propaedeutic Essay in Clarification', *HOPE*, Fall, 1974, and 'Edgeworth's Contract Curve, Part 2: Two Figures in its Protohistory: Aristotle and Gossen', *ibid.*, Winter,

1974. See also J. Creedy, 'Some Recent Interpretations of *Mathematical Psychics*', *ibid.*, Summer, 1980. Since the name of Edgeworth has come up so frequently in this book – on Mill's theory of international trade, on Cournot's duopoly theory, on Marshall's demand curve, on the law of diminishing returns, on indifference curves, on entrepreneurship, on the determinacy of equilibrium and many other topics – this is as good a place as any to commend J. Creedy, 'F. Y. Edgeworth, 1845–1926', *Pioneers of Modern Economics in Britain*, eds. O'Brien and Presnell, as the first attempt to do justice in the round to this remarkable if quixotic economist.

There are at least five article-length and five book-length surveys of the new welfare economics, but the most concise and succinct treatment is by F. M. Bator, 'The Simple Analytics of Welfare Maximization', *AER*, 1957, reprinted in *Penguin Modern Economics Readings; Price Theory*, ed. Townsend, and *Readings in Microeconomics*, ed. Kamerschen. This beautiful essay touches on many issues we have passed over: corner tangencies, community indifference curves and dynamical extensions. Moreover, it provides a historical note on the literature and an almost complete bibliography.

Bator's bibliography carries the debate down to 1957. Since then the whole field has been surveyed again by J. de V. Graaff, *Theoretical Welfare Economics* (1957); E. J. Mishan, 'A Survey of Welfare Economics, 1939–1959', *EJ*, 1960, reprinted in his *Welfare Economics. Five Introductory Essays* (1964 in paperback) and in *Surveys of Economic Theory*, I (1965); and S. K. Nath, *A Reappraisal of Welfare Economics* (1969). Graaff's elegant monograph pays particular attention to external effects and the less familiar difficulties of uncertainty and distant-time horizons; Mishan is valuable on such problems as the construction of social indifference maps, consistent social ordering, and second-best optima; and Nath emphasizes the evaluation of compensation payments. All three authors despair of the possibility of practical welfare economics. Paretian welfare economics is restated in activity-analysis terms in the first of T. C. Koopman's *Three Essays on the State of Economic Science* (1957). The educational value of this reading is difficult to exaggerate: it brings the student to the frontiers of modern mathematical economics with surprisingly little pain. Along the same lines, see also Baumol, *Economic Theory and Operational Analysis*, chap. 21. C. E. Ferguson, *Microeconomic Theory* (3rd edn., 1972), chaps. 15, 16, provides one of the most thorough graphic treatments of Paretian welfare economics in the textbook literature. Second-best problems were introduced into welfare economics by R. G. Lipsey and K. Lancaster, 'The General Theory of Second Best', *REStud*, December, 1956.

F. M. Bator, 'The Anatomy of Market Failure', *QJE*, August, 1958, provides an excellent account of the state of the debate on the significance of direct interaction between firms and households before R. H. Coase, 'The Problem of Social Cost', *JLE*, October, 1960, gave a new twist to the debate by introducing the cost of reaching and maintaining agreements between interacting economic agents; see, particularly, pp. 28–39 of Coase's paper on Pigou's *Economics of Welfare*. For an introduction to recent developments in the theory of property rights, stemming from the Coase Theorem, see Ekelund and Hébert, *History of Economic Theory and Method*, chap. 22, and the references cited there.

On public goods, see U. Mazzola, 'The Formation of the Prices of Public Goods' (1890), and K. Wicksell, 'A New Principle of Just Taxation' (1896), both reprinted in *Classics in the Theory of Public Finance*, eds. R. A. Musgrave and A. T. Peacock (1958), with a brief but useful introduction by the editors. M. H. Peston, *Public Goods and the Public Sector* (1972 in paperback), provides an excellent review of more recent developments in the theory of public goods.

On Pigovian welfare economics, see the excellent brief discussion by Hutchison, *Review of Economic Doctrines*, chap. 18, and the critical treatment by Myint, *Theories of Welfare Economics*, chap. 10. Chap. 11 of Myint's book, entitled 'Towards a Broader Concept of Welfare', is one of the few places where the deeper ethical problems of welfare economics are systematically discussed. M. G. O'Donnell shows that Sidgwick is the link between Marshallian and Pigovian welfare economics in 'Pigou: An Extension of Sidgwickian Thought', *HOPE*, Winter, 1979. K. Bharadwaj, 'Marshall on Pigou's *Wealth and Welfare*', *Ec.*, February 1972, gives a fascinating account of Marshall's private reservations about Pigou's treatment of welfare economics.

This brings us, finally, to the question of marginal cost pricing. N. Ruggles, 'The Welfare Basis of the Marginal Cost Pricing Principle', *REStud*, 17, 1, 1949, and 'Recent Developments in the Theory of Marginal Cost Pricing', *ibid.*, 1949, reprinted in *Penguin Modern Economics Readings: Public Enterprise*, ed. R. Turvey (1968 in paperback) are the answer to every student's prayers: a critical survey of a voluminous and diffuse body of literature. The first of these two articles traces the emergence of marginal cost of pricing out of the Marshall-Pigou analysis of decreasing-cost industries and gives an account of the discussion on socialist economics in the 1930s by such writers as Dickinson, Dobb, Durbin, Lange and Lerner. The second article reviews the discussion up to 1950 that was centred on H. Hotelling's famous contribution, 'The General Welfare in Relation to the Problems of Taxation and of Railway and Utility Rates', *Ecom.*, 1938, reprinted in *Readings in Welfare Economics*, eds. Arrow and Scitovsky.

For forgotten earlier contributions to the debate, see the references to Dupuit & company in Notes on Further Reading, chap. 8 of this text; M. Cross and R. B. Ekelund Jr., 'A. T. Hadley on Monopoly Theory and Railway Regulation: An American Contribution to Economic Analysis and Policy', *HOPE*, Summer 1980; J. M. Buchanan, 'Knut Wicksell on Marginal Cost Pricing', *SEJ*, October 1951; and P. Hennipman, 'Wicksell and Pareto: Their Relationship in the Theory of Finance', *HOPE*, Spring, 1982.

The debate on marginal cost pricing entered a second phase in the late 1950s. J. Wiseman, 'The Theory of Public Utility Price – An Empty Box', *OEP*, 1957, reprinted in *L.S.E. Essays on Cost*, eds. J. M. Buchanan and G. F. Thirlby (1973), was answered by M. J. Farrell, 'In Defence of Public-Utility Price Theory', *OEP*, 1958, reprinted in *Penguin Modern Economics Readings: Public Enterprise*, ed. Turvey,. See also W. Vickrey, 'Marginal Cost Pricing', *AER*, 1955, reprinted in *Penguin Modern Economics Readings: Transport*, ed. Munby, and C. J. Oort, *Decreasing Costs as a Problem of Welfare Economics* (1958), especially chap. 3 and Appendix. On the contributions of the French electricity engineers-economists, see J. R. Nelson, ed., *Marginal Cost Pricing in Practice* (1964), R. Turvey, 'Marginal Cost Pricing in Practice', *Ec.*, November 1964, and 'The Second-Best Case for Marginal Cost Pricing', *Public Economics*, eds. J. Margolis and H. Guitton (1969). R. Millward, *Public Expenditure Economics* (1971), chap. 7, is an excellent up-to-date treatment of public utility pricing.

Even this is not the end of the story as W. J. Baumol and D. F. Bradford explain in 'Optimal Departures from Marginal Cost Pricing', *AER*, June 1970. A. Harberger, 'On the Use of Distributional Weights in Social Cost-Benefit Analysis', *JPE*, April 1978, and A. Williams, 'Cost-Benefit Analysis: Bastard Science? And/Or Insidious Poison in the Body Politick', *JPUE*, August, 1972, attack the notion of distributional weights as an integral feature of cost-benefit analysis.

14

Spatial economics and the classical theory of location

Spatial economics concentrates attention on two pervasive features of economic life: distance and area. The role of distance is exemplified by the fact that transport costs affect, not just market prices, but also the location of production facilities. The role of area, on the other hand, implies that the markets for specific goods are subject to definite geographic limits. The great 18th-century writers of economics, such as Cantillon, Steuart and Smith, had much to say about the systematic spatial patterns associated with these twin phenomena of distance and area. Surprisingly enough, however, such problems dropped almost wholly out of sight in the economic treatises written after 1800. Spatial economics, and particularly the theory of the location of economic activity, flourished and matured throughout the 19th century but in almost total isolation of mainstream economics, whether classical or neoclassical. Indeed, it is not too much to say that the whole of mainstream economics was until about 1950 effectively confined to the analysis of an economic world without spatial dimensions.

Here is a major puzzle in the history of economic thought: what was it about spatial economics that prevented its recognition as an integral feature of orthodox economics? But there is another puzzle about the history of spatial economics in general and location theory in particular: it has always been the peculiar province of German economists. Of course, the history of spatial analysis includes French, Swedish, Italian and American names. Nevertheless, all the great treatises in the subject were, until very recently, written by Germans and the overwhelming dominance of German writers in the literature of spatial economics is simply unquestionable. This is a historical curiosity which is probably due to the simple fact that the 'father' of location theory was a German.

1. The Isolated State

The history of location theory begins with the publication of *The Isolated State* by Johann Heinrich von Thünen in 1826. Thünen was not the first writer to analyse the economic phenomena of space but he was the first to treat such phenomena with the aid of a spatial mode of analysis. Unlike the 18th-century writers who had touched on questions of distance and area, Thünen had the vision to postulate an abstract geographical model that highlighted the roles of distance and area by its very construction. On the opening page of *The Isolated State*, he tells us to consider an

614

'ideal' or 'isolated state' – a homogeneous, featureless plain of equal fertility without roads or navigable rivers and restricted to the use of horse-drawn wagons as the only mode of transportation, having a single town at its centre producing all manufactured articles and supplied by the farmers in the plain with all its agricultural products, and closed off to the outside world by being surrounded by an impenetrable wilderness on all sides – and asks us to discover the principles which would, in such circumstances, determine the prices that farmers receive for their products, the rents that are earned by various units of land, and the associated patterns of land use that accompany such prices and rents. This notion of a closed economy in idealised space was a radically new idea, which fully justifies Thünen's claim to the title of 'father' of the economics of space.

Unfortunately, *The Isolated State* is so tortuously constructed that its central message is difficult to discern. The purpose of its severely abstract assumptions was to isolate transport costs as a linear function of distance from all the other factors which influence the location of agricultural production and the patterns of land use, such as climate, topography, soil quality, the demand of town dwellers, the quality of farm management, the technology of food preparation, the inherited transportation network, etcetera. Thünen begins the book by asking: What will be the pattern of agricultural production around the central town in the isolated state? and replies that the pattern will take the form of concentric rings. Having asked the question, however, he immediately breaks it down into two further questions: what crops will be grown in different places as a function of distance from the market and at what intensity will those crops be cultivated in different places as a function of the same distance? He thus has a 'crop theory' and an 'intensity theory'. However, the two questions seem to be hopelessly intertwined because certain crops, such as trees, are by their nature extensive or relatively land-using, whereas others, such as grain, are by their nature intensive or relatively landsaving. It seems difficult, therefore, to separate the problem of what crops to grow where from the problem of how intensively to cultivate those crops. The difficulty is amply demonstrated by Thünen's many generalisations about the forces determining the precise location of different crops, not all of which are consistent with each other, and by the well-known ring-diagram of *The Isolated State* published as an afterthought in the second volume of the book, which does not entirely agree with the text. No wonder that the pattern of crop production in the successive rings of the isolated state has perhaps produced more misunderstanding than any other subject taken up by Thünen – it is virtually *the* Thünen problem.

The standard view is that Thünen taught that so-called 'intensive crops' are always grown near the market, the high price of land near the central town justifying only intensive cultivation, so that the famous concentric rings are really rings of declining crop intensity as we move further and further away from the central town. Undoubtedly, this is Thünen's general rule. It is, however, subject to many exceptions. Some of these arise from the fact that some crops are so bulky or perishable that they must be grown near the market. Others are due to the fact that high crop intensity implies high yields per acre but high yields do not always imply high costs per acre. With so many exceptions, it is difficult to find a general rule and it is even more difficult to find the sense of any single rule.

One of the objects of Thünen's book was to advocate the improved English system of crop rotation whose central feature is the seven-period alternation of cereal crops, root crops and short grasses. Thünen regarded it as generally superior to the medieval three-field system of spring grain, winter grain and a fallow period still common in the Northern Germany of his times. But he was too much of an economist to believe that it was merely ignorance that prevented German farmers from switching over to the improved system and he was therefore concerned to show that the English crop rotation system is only profitable under certain circumstances. The general rule which he gradually develops in the course of the book is that the sites nearest the market will be pre-empted by crops which are capable of achieving the greatest reductions in total costs per unit of output as a result of intensive cultivation, and which therefore produce the highest ground rent by virtue of their particular location.

2. Rent Theory

Indeed, the most striking feature of Thünen's book is the manner in which the entire analysis is geared to the determination of rent, rent being maximized as a result of competition among farmers for the available land. The price of a product like grain in the central town is determined by the production-plus-transportation costs of obtaining grain from the most distant farms whose produce is required to satisfy the town's demand for grain, which, by the way, is simply taken as a given datum. Since grain must sell at the same price regardless of where it is produced and since grain produced on farms near the town enjoys low transportation costs, ground rent will equal the saving in transportation costs on the more favourably situated farms. Ground rent is therefore at a maximum in the first concentric ring, declining with increasing distance from the central town, and reaching zero in the outermost ring at the frontiers of the isolated state. In reality, Thünen observes, differences in the fertility of the soil which are not themselves related to location will give rise to ground rent in the same manner as do differences in proximity to the central town. Thus, starting at the opposite end from Ricardo, and without having read Ricardo at this stage in his life, Thünen nevertheless reached all the Ricardian conclusions by a simpler and more elegant route.

All this refers to what has been called the 'extensive margin' of cultivation. But no one who had thought as deeply about intensive methods of cultivation as Thünen had could miss noticing that ground rent may arise even if all land is equally situated and of equal fertility, owing to the fact that successive applications of capital and labour to the land of a given farm do not yield a constant increment of product. The intramarginal surplus on a given acre of land accrues to the landowner as rent just as much as does the intramarginal surplus among different acres of land. Thus, Thünen might have added (and almost did in the second volume of his book), the phenomenon of rent, whether it be 'locational rent', 'differential rent' or 'scarcity rent', serves the social function of limiting the use of scarce factors like land to the point where its marginal value product is equal in all uses; in consequence, equal additions of investment on more favourably situated, more fertile and more intensively cultivated acres of land will make equal additions to output, and equal units of output will incur identical costs.

3. The Thünen Problem Again

Some of the confusion about the relationship between the 'crop theory' and the 'intensity theory' in Thünen is due to the fact that locational rent and scarcity rent are not always kept separate in the book, which results in fuzzy and oversimplified statements about the succession of crops in different ring zones. In any case, it is clear that for him the 'law' that intensity of cultivation decreases continuously in successive rings as we move away from the central city holds only for the case of a single form of land use for a single product. He recognized that, owing to joint costs and joint processes, any one ring may be devoted to a number of products in combination and the same crop may appear in several successive rings, particularly if there is substitutability between factors in agriculture and if transport costs decline proportionately as distance increases.

It is one thing for us, with the benefit of hindsight, to recognize the merits of Thünen's argument but it was quite another thing for contemporaries to discern the main lines of Thünen's cryptic and disjointed narrative. Even in a science as renowned for its badly written Great Books as economics, there are few parallels to *The Isolated State*: it represents, in fact, a collection of notes, comments, arithmetical examples, and mathematical formulas, which constantly interrupt the flow of its central analysis of an economy governed by transport costs by digressions on various crop-rotation schemes, the effects of diet on the size of the population, the advantages of different methods of sheep rearing, the optimal location of farm buildings on a landed estate, etcetera. Worse still is the fact that, while the theoretical arguments are grounded in clearly stated abstract assumptions, virtually all the functional relationships between relevant variables are expressed in actual calculations derived from Thünen's own farm records, which he continuously revised in the three successive instalments of the book (1826, 1842 and 1850) and which do not always precisely fit the stated assumptions. For example, transport costs are assumed to be strictly proportional to the weights of products and hence are taken to be a linear function of distance but they are actually expressed in bushels of grain, made up of grain to feed the horses on a representative journey and grain paid in kind to the wagoners, which are then converted into silver-money at an assumed market price of grain. When his actual transport cost function is closely inspected, however, it turns out to be slightly nonlinear and this in turn introduces a measure of imprecision into all of his general results. When we add to this the difficulty mentioned earlier of keeping the 'crop theory' distinct from the 'intensity theory', the wonder is not that Thünen's book was neglected in his own day but that there were any contemporaries that gave him his proper due.[1]

---

[1] To be sure, John Bates Clark, Wicksell, Böhm-Bawerk and particularly Marshall all paid their respects to Thünen for discovering the marginal productivity theory of distribution. What they had

4. The Theory of Rings

One of those contemporaries who recognized the value of Thünen's work was
Wilhelm Launhardt, a pioneer of mathematical economics, an important early
contributor to the pure theory of welfare economics, and one of the few German-
engineer economists of his day to carry on the tradition laid down by Rau, Hermann,
Gossen, Mangoldt and Thünen, which is sometimes called German Classical
Economics. His masterpiece was the *Mathematische Begründung der Volkswirtschaftslehre* (1885), the first textbook properly so-called in mathematical economics.
It was written without knowledge of Cournot's path-breaking *Mathematical Principles of Wealth* (1838) and was based instead on a close study of the writings of
Walras and Jevons, whose analysis of durable capital goods and the supply of labour
it both restated and refined. Launhardt's main interests, however, lay elsewhere in
the pricing policies of railways and the associated concept of the location of economic
activity to which the whole of the last third of the *Mathematische Begründung* is
devoted. It is here that he showed how much he had learned from Thünen,
supplementing the latter's supply-determined theory of the location of agricultural
activities by an analysis of the role of market areas in the location of industrial plants.

To convey the flavour of Launhardt's style, we can hardly improve on his
marvelously succinct summary of Thünen in a mere six pages of the *Mathematische
Begründung*. Let us assume, he says, that some agricultural product is produced at a
uniform rate of γ (gamma) units of physical product per unit of land area throughout
an entire homogeneous region. With a single consumption point at the city center of
the region, the supply region of that product will form a circular area of radius z' and
the total quantity of the product will be $Q = \gamma \pi z^2$. If p_0 is the average cost of
production, constant at all levels of output, if f is the average freight rate, constant
per unit of distance, and if p is the delivered market price of the product, then the
boundary of the supply area is defined by the value of the distance radius, z', which
satisfies the equation:

$$p = p_0 + fz^1$$

or

$$z' = (p - p_0)/f$$

The larger the market supply area, the higher must be the delivered price and
therefore the smaller must be the level of demand in the central city. Demand and
supply are equated at some definite size of the supply area, z, at whose boundary
locational rents are zero. Nearer the central city, the landowner receives the same
market price but pays a lower freight charge, thus earning as rent $f(z' - z)$ per unit of
product or $f(\hat{z}' - z)$ per unit of land area. It follows that rents are highest at locations

in mind, however, was the wage and interest theory in the first part of the second volume of *The
Isolated State*, published in 1850, and not the location theory of the first volume, published in 1826
with a second edition in 1842. That first volume was not translated into English until 1966 and it
remains to this day among the least read of the great economic tomes of the nineteenth century; the
name of Thünen conjures up for most modern economists nothing else but the archaic and
mysterious formula: 'the natural wage $= \sqrt{ap}$, which Thünen had engraved on his tombstone [see
chapter 8, section 17].

close to the market and diminish with increasing distance from the market. An increase in the population of the central city extends the market supply area, raises market prices, and increases land rents throughout the region. A reduction of the freight rate works in the opposite direction and also tends to narrow the rent differentials between different locations.

We now introduce competition between different agricultural products. Then as Thünen had shown, says Launhardt, certain products which are highly perishable or heavy and bulky relative to their value will be produced near the central city and others like livestock, where transport costs are small relative to output per unit of land area, will be produced at the boundary of the region. In general, the total supply area will be divided into a number of ring-shaped zones of specialized production regions. In each ring that product is produced which maximizes net profit per unit of land area and which therefore can afford to pay the highest rent. In other words, competition between specialized agricultural producers establishes a pattern of land use which maximizes the generation of ground rent. There follows a diagram, which depicts the rent-gradients for four alternative products.

Figure 14–1

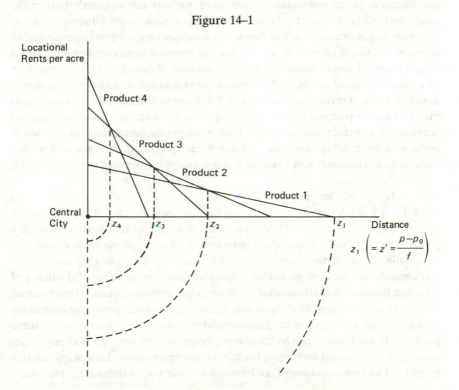

Notes: The lower panel of the diagram translates from lineal to areal terms by rotating the distance axis about the point of origin, thus generating Thünen's concentric circles.

Since rent is expressed net of constant production costs plus transport costs that vary only with distance, the horizon base line of the diagram is the zero-rent line. The zero-rent line, Launhardt might have added but did not, is also the marginal cost line and the equilibrium solution for the 'industry' (there being no distinction here between firm and industry) that maximizes rent is the distance at which marginal rent equals marginal cost, analogous to the modern solution for the conventional monopoly case. At any rate, Launhardt's diagram expresses central city prices and rents per unit of land area for the four products after deducting transport costs as a linear function of distance. By extension of the analysis, Launhardt concluded that the boundaries of the various product zones are only slightly affected by a lowering of transport costs and that cheap imports from outside the isolated state will lower the entire structure of product prices and land rents throughout the region.

Our Figure 14–1 is identical to Fig. 14 in Launhardt's *Mathematische Begründung*, except for the labelling of axes and the lower panel of the diagram. This diagram of what are nowadays called 'rent bid functions' has become the standard method of illustrating Thünen's 'crop theory', which is constantly reproduced in the modern literature on urban and regional economics without any acknowledgement to Launhardt.[2] It is very much a special case because it holds only if the production function of agriculture is linearly homogeneous, if the yield of land is constant at all levels of output, if all factors are available at constant prices everywhere, and if freight rates are strictly linear functions of distance. When any or all of these four conditions are violated, the rent bid functions of different products may be curvilinear, in which case it is perfectly possible for two rent bid functions to cross twice so that the same crop appears in more than one zone. Nevertheless, there is little doubt that the diagram does serve to clarify Thünen's message better than his own words and arithmetical tables ever did. At the same time, it affords us with a neat demonstration of Launhardt's elegance in the exposition of economic ideas.

5. Industrial Plant Location Theory

What is so bewildering about Thünen, the undisputed patron saint of location theory, is that he concentrated attention, not so much on the locational problem of a productive enterprise, as on the phenomenon of rent in association with the value-bulk characteristics of alternative crops; location emerges as a key variable but it is not itself the focus of his analysis. Thünen's analysis has some of the flavor of plant location theory but it essentially resembles the analysis of market-supply areas: the locational decisions in Thünen are those of farmers at given fixed locations choosing both the product to produce and the management pattern of these products. It was Launhardt who first directly addressed the problem of the optimum location of an industrial enterprise. He did so in a frequently-cited article, entitled (in English) 'The Determination of the Practical Location of an Industrial Enterprise'.

---

[2] The rent bid functions are usually spelled out as $R = e(p-a) - efk$, where R = rent per acre, e = yield per acre, p = the fixed market price of the product, a = the production cost of the product, f = the transport rate per unit of distance of the product, and k = the distance from the market. This expression is identical to Launhardt's rent gradient, which in his notation would read: $R = \gamma(p-p_0) - \gamma fz$.

This 1882 paper contains a definitive statement of the so-called 'three-points problem' of classical location theory: how to find an optimum location of a plant that produces a single product at constant costs and faces a given, fixed market outlet and two given, fixed locations where raw materials are extracted, the optimum location being defined as the one that minimizes total transport costs per unit of output. The analysis is then generalized to four or more fixed points with multiple market outlets and multiple raw material sources. Twenty-seven years later, Alfred Weber published his classic book on the *Theory of the Location of Industries* (1909), in which he and his mathematical co-author, George Pick, rediscovered Launhardt's solution of the three-points problem of plant location, without however being aware of Launhardt's writings.

6. The Three-Points Problem

Launhardt begins by observing that his solution of the problem of optimum location abstracts from differences in the prices for site acquisition, the availability of water power or labour, and the rate of wages paid to labour. He then proceeds to state the three-points problem and to solve it in three different ways. The first involves the use of trigonometry and calculus to construct an auxiliary 'weight triangle' formed by sides proportional to the per-mile transport costs of the weights hauled to and from the three respective points, a method which George Pick was to rediscover independently by a more direct route twenty-seven years later. The second involves an 18th-century mechanical model, which treats the lines from the three given points to the unknown optimum location of the plant as if they were lines of mechanical force and uses knotted strings and metal weights to minimize the potential energy of the physical system; this too was rediscovered by George Pick. The third involves the construction of a geometric 'pole' of the consumption point of the locational triangle. This polar-point solution, which is identical to Pick's method of 'three circles', is now familiar from the works of modern writers on location theory but it is not always realized how little these later writers added to Launhardt's original treatment of it.

The polar-point solution is difficult to understand, involving as it does some advanced post-Euclidean geometry. In essence, it consists of laying off arcs on the two points of the sources of raw materials, independent of the precise position of the point of consumption but based on the relative size of the per-mile transport costs between the three points, whose intersection then defines the position of the 'pole'. Once the imaginary polar point is substituted for the consumption point, a circle is circumscribed on the three newly defined points and a straight line is drawn to connect the pole with the consumption point. The optimum location of the plant is determined by the intersection of that straight line with the circumscribed circle. Since this solution is independent of the precise position of the market for consumption, Launhardt extends the argument by finding the optimum plant location point for any possible location of the consumption point relative to the two fixed points of raw materials. He also attempts to generalize the solution for the three-points problem to *n*-points by successive application of the polar construction to trios of points. This procedure, as has often been shown, is invalid but, even if it were valid, it would still be limited to the case of linear transport functions for which the per-mile transport cost is strictly proportional to the weight of goods being hauled. This is a limitation of both the method of 'weight triangles' and the use of the polar principle. To this day, the only perfectly general method for solving the *n*-points problem is that of the mechanical model, although in practice the problem is usually solved by computer algorithms.

There is more still in this 1882 paper. Its closing pages take up the problem of choosing a least-cost access route to reach an established transport network when all routes are straight lines and the transport function is linear. The number of separate, original ideas in this brief paper is quite extraordinary: the first statement of the problem of the least-cost location of an industrial plant relative to a given, fixed market; the first explicit list of the various economic forces other than freight charges which influence the least-cost location; the discovery of all the three methods for solving the three-points problem that were known until the invention of linear programming in our own times; and the first solution of a simple but classic routing problem in railway economics. The effect is only partly spoiled by Launhardt's erroneous claim that he had also solved the *n*-points problem in location theory, that all his solutions relied on linear transport functions, and that he had not touched at all on the question of where to locate the plant when both consumers and suppliers of raw materials are dispersed over space instead of being concentrated at single points.

7. Sales Areas

The last deficiency was made good, however, in the *Mathematische Begründung*, which deals at considerable length with the problem of the optimal sales areas of competing producers, concentrated at single point locations but serving consumers who are scattered continuously over economic space, as well as the Thünen problem of the optimum supply areas of competing consumers concentrated at single point locations but buying from producers dispersed over economic space. Launhardt makes the delivered price of a product to consumers a function of its constant price at the point of production plus a cost of transport that varies proportionately with distance. The quantity demanded at any location is, therefore, a linear function of the local delivered price and, assuming continuously dispersed consumers per unit of area, Launhardt concludes that the total unit sales of a single producer are directly proportional to the cube of the per unit transport costs from the plant to the circular boundary of the market region and inversely proportional to the square of the transport rate. Next, he considers the sales areas of two identical products manufactured at different costs in two different locations, and finds the locus of all points at which the net-mill prices for the two products are equal after deducting the respective transport costs. In a famous diagram (see Figure 14–2) he shows that this locus is a closed oval of the fourth degree, or what Descartes labelled 'an ellipse of the second kind', enclosing the sales region of the 'inferior' product, that is, the product which is heavier for an equivalent value or, as we would say nowadays, for which the transport cost gradient is steeper.

Figure 14–2

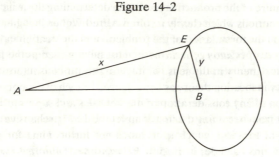

Note: *A* and *B* are the locations of two plants producing competing products. The oval boundary divides the sales region of market *B* from that of market *A* where *B* produces the 'inferior' product. *x* and *y* are the respective distances of the two plants from an arbitrary sales point *E* at which the net-mill prices for the two products are equal.

Launhardt notes that if the two production costs are equal then, whatever the differences in transport costs, the Cartesian oval becomes a perfect circle. Contrariwise, if the two transport costs are equal but the two production costs are not, the market boundary ceases to be a closed curve and becomes a hyperbola with its concave side towards the high-cost location because a hyperbola is a curve for which the difference between the distances from two fixed points is a constant. Lastly, if both production and transport costs are equal, the market boundary becomes the perpendicular bisector of the straight line joining the two given locations. In general, if a single product must compete with a large number of other products emanating from sources which surround it on all sides, the market region assumes the form of a polygon whose sides must be straight lines so as to fill the economic space continuously. Here, in a nutshell, are all the elements that make up the famous 'law of market areas', stated by Marshall in 1890 (and erroneously attributed to Thünen), rediscovered by George Pick in 1909, again rediscovered by Frank Fetter in 1924, and all without the least recognition of Launhardt or of each other.[3] Here, too, is the kernel of the notion of hexagonal market areas, so frequently traced back no further than Christaller and Lösch in the 1930s.

8. New Developments in Location Theory

The years after the *Mathematische Begründung* saw a number of isolated contributions to location theory. Wilhelm Roscher in Germany, Ernest Ross in England and Achille Loria in Italy all speculated on the role of the weight-gaining and

---

[3] All three start from the simple case of equal production and transport costs and then consider the possibility of unequal production costs but equal transport costs, concluding that the market boundary in this case becomes a hyperbola. None of them consider the most general case treated by Launhardt in which both production costs and transport costs are different. Nevertheless, the 'law of market areas' is a striking example of Merton's concept of 'multiple discoveries' in science [see chapter 8, section 5].

weight-losing nature of the productive process in determining the least-cost site of an industrial plant, notions which clearly inspired Alfred Weber (brother of the famous Max Weber) in a new formulation of the problem of plant location in 1909. Weber's book, *Theory of the Location of Industries*, must be regarded as the first successful treatise in location theory in the sense of inspiring continuous interest and ongoing analytical activity in location theory as a specialized branch of economics. Nevertheless, the omission of any consideration of market sales and supply areas in Weber's text prevented it from becoming the first complete and comprehensive analysis of the classical theory of location, which in fact was not forthcoming for another three decades. It was Tord Palander in 1935 in *Beiträge zur Standortstheorie* who finally brought the two sides of plant location theory and market area analysis together and thus consolidated a half-century of theorizing about the spatial location of business enterprises.

Weber had been anticipated in many respects by Launhardt but there is hardly any doubt that he went well beyond Launhardt in introducing the effects of differential labour costs and 'agglomeration' economies. Even in his handling of the three-points problem, he developed a simpler and more general graphic technique than anything available to Launhardt. It is clear from Weber's frequent references in the text to the Mathematical Appendix contributed by George Pick that the mathematical analysis was developed, not as an after-thought, but at an early stage in the preparation of the manuscript. Pick's analysis of the three-points problem invokes the mechanical analogy to the parallelogram of forces from the very beginning, working backwards from the solution of the n-points problem to the three-points problem, instead of forward from the special to the general case as Launhardt had done. The polar principle for solving the three-points problem turns up in Pick as in Launhardt but only as an extra and redundant method for solving the special case. Pick's correct solution of the n-points problem cleared the way for Weber's use of an entirely general, graphic system of 'isodapanes', that is, contours of equal increments in total transfer costs above the level of minimum transfer costs at some initial location, which allowed him to add differentials in labour costs and agglomeration economies to differences in the transport costs of alternative locations.

9. Weber's Theory of Industrial Location

Weber's technical apparatus is too well known from modern textbooks on urban and regional economics to require much explanation. Like Thünen, Weber assumes a uniform, featureless plain with equal, uniform transport rates per ton-mile throughout the region. But instead of assuming a single consumption point, he assumes that there are several known points of consumption and several known sources of power and raw materials. Labour is likewise available in unlimited quantities at a constant wage in several given places. Transportation costs are taken to be a linear function of weight and distance but differences in topography and transportability are allowed for by artificial additions to actual distances. Industrial plants produce single, given products by means of fixed input-output coefficients and the problem is to determine their optimum location in space, which is conceived almost entirely as a matter of minimizing the total transport costs of inputs and outputs. Raw materials are classified into four kinds: (1)'ubiquities' – materials available everywhere; (2) 'localised materials' – materials obtainable only in unique locations; (3) 'pure materials' – localized materials, such as yarn woven into cloth, which enter into the finished product to the full extent of their weights; and (4) 'gross materials' – materials, such as iron ore in the smelting of steel, which lose all or part of their weight in the productive process through combustion or the elimination of waste products. The argument then proceeds by the use of two technical coefficients: (1) the 'material index', namely the ratio of the weight of localized materials to the weight of the finished product; and (2) the 'locational weight', namely the total weight that has to be shipped between all the given locational points expressed per ton of finished product, being one plus the material index. If the productive process is weight-gaining, the material index is less than unity and the locational weight is greater than unity, in consequence of which the location of the plant is pulled towards the points of consumption. On the other hand, if the productive process is weight-losing, the material index is greater than unity, the locational weight is greater than two, and the plant is oriented instead towards the locations at which raw materials are deposited.

This is the case where transport costs are variable but labour costs are constant. When labour costs vary, plant locations deviate from their transport-orientation and become footloose in proportion to the size of their 'labour coefficients' – another Weberian technical term – the ratio between the costs of labour per ton of product and the total weight of both inputs and outputs transported. In addition to transport and labour costs there are agglomeration economies in the form of internal economies of scale, improved marketing outlets, greater proximity to auxiliary industries, and cheaper labour, which create a tendency towards the clustering of plants in city centres. The tendency to centralization is, however, offset by the deglomerating effects of higher rents in congested centers.

The graphic technique of 'isodapanes' made it possible for Weber to illustrate the substitution between outlays on transport and non-transport factors, thus incorporating elements into the least-cost analysis of plant location which Launhardt had had to rule out as exogenous. In the true fashion of Thünen and Launhardt before him, Weber conceives of his analysis as a 'pure' theory of location, that is, one which is independent of special institutional factors, such as differences in interest rates, insurance rates, taxes, the quality of management, etcetera, as well as such general factors as climate and topography. In that sense, he argued that it was applicable to any type of economy so long as perfect competition and profit-maximizing behaviour prevailed.

Criticisms of Weber have become the stock-in-trade of commentaries on location theory. He is constantly accused of neglecting demand; of concentrating on the uninteresting case of producers and consumers concentrated at single or multiple point locations instead of being continuously dispersed over economic space; of operating with linear transport functions and then spuriously generalizing the analysis by the use of purely fictitious 'ideal weights', in which the economies of long-haul shipments are accommodated by artificially foreshortening real distances, and, in general, of casting the entire question of plant location in an engineering rather than an economic context. Weber never replied to any of the criticisms levelled against his theory but for almost twenty years a long list of his pupils continued to apply his ideas to studies of the location of specific German industries. Weber himself turned towards a totally different style of location theory, more in keeping with the historical and evolutionary preoccupations of 18th-century economists and members of the German Historical School in the 19th century. This type of theory is touched upon in the closing chapter of the *Theory of Location of Industries* but it is only fully developed in a lesser known article by him in 1914. Weber lived on until 1958, publishing his last book in 1953, but he never again wrote on location theory. However, the historical-evolutionary approach to location problems lived on in the works of Oskar Engländer, Hans Ritschl and Hans Weigmann, and there are echoes of it even in the more familiar modern works of Christaller, Hoover and Lösch. It represents an entirely different strand of thought from that of partial equilibrium analysis in the writings of Thünen, Launhardt and early Weber, emphasizing as it does the disequilibrating and irreversible forces of historical change.

10. Market Area Analysis

For good or bad reasons, the mainstream of classical location theory paid little attention to the writings of Engländer, Ritschl and Weigmann and instead turned to market area analysis, a topic which had almost dropped out of view since Launhardt, in the effort to develop a general equilibrium treatment of spatial questions. The emergence in the late 1920s of monopolistic competition theory with its notion of spatial differentiation as one of the sources of a firm's monopolistic power of price-making gave impetus to a new analysis of the classical *n*-points problem, in which the consumption vertices of the locational polygon themselves become variables in the determination of the optimum site of a plant. Harold Hotelling, Edward Chamberlin, Abba Lerner, Hans Singer, Tord Palander and Arthur Smithies are some of the leading names associated with this line of development in the modelling of patterns of spatial competition. Christaller's *Central Places in Southern Germany* (1933) gave a new twist to the analysis of market areas by attempting to derive the size, number and distributions of towns in a region from a few elementary assumptions about the behavior of consumers. It was he who first planted the idea that we have already encountered in Launhardt, namely, that nested hexagons are the most likely shape of complementary market boundaries.

Central place theory, and the analysis of market areas under conditions of monopolistic competition, was given further impetus by August Lösch's authoritative treatise on *The Economics of Location* (1939), whose aim was to review and to sum up a century of theorizing about the economics of space from the consistent standpoint of general equilibrium theory. All the leading elements of classical location theory are present in Lösch – Thünen's analysis of areal production serving a punctiform market, Launhardt's analysis of punctiform production serving an areal market, Weber's theory of transport- and labour-orientation in the least-cost siting of industrial plants, Hotelling's analysis of spatial competition under conditions of duopoly and oligopoly, Christaller's theory of regional structures, and even the historical evolutionary theories of the late Weber – but they are subordinate to an almost obsessive interest in the sales areas of competing producers. In fact, Lösch overemphasized demand considerations in spatial decisions almost as much as Weber overemphasized cost considerations and he virtually abandoned the effort to employ location theory to describe and explain actual locational structures. His conjecture that the market areas of competing products always take the form of a network of hexagons has given rise to a highly technical literature, largely concerned with questioning the logical consistency of his axiomatic argument. Lösch achieved a formal superiority over the classical principles and methods of the founding fathers of location theory but only at the expense of increasing remoteness from practical location decisions. Indeed, his book is not, strictly speaking, a work on the economics of location in the classic mould. Its German title, *Die räumliche Ordnung der Wirtschaft*, is literally translated as *The Spatial Organization of the Economic System* and this title comes much closer to capturing its central concern with spatial relationships between economic regions and nation-states. Lösch points towards the macroeconomics of modern urban and regional economics and away from the microeconomics of industrial location theory in the tradition of Launhardt and Weber.

11. Isard's General Equilibrium Theory

Much the same is true of Walter Isard's *Location and Space-Economy* (1956), a book whose main aim was finally to close the century-long gap between classical location theory and mainstream economics. Isard rightly complained that the whole of classical and neoclassical economics had confined itself to 'a wonderland of no spatial dimensions' and he placed part of the blame for this imbalance on the fact that classical location theory was conceived in the outdated language of partial equilibrium, constant coefficients, linear transport rates and given demand configurations. If we define 'transport inputs' as the movement of a unit of weight over a unit of distance and 'transport rates' as the price of these inputs, he argued, the central notion of the equimarginal principle of substitution suffices to obtain a true generalization of location theory. Whatever the concentration or dispersal of sources of inputs and marketing outlets, and whatever the nature of the transport function, profit-maximizing firms will locate so as to equate the marginal rates of substitution between any two transport inputs to the reciprocal of the ratio of their transport rates. From this first-order condition for a maximum, Isard noted, it is possible to derive all the partial location theories of Thünen, Launhardt and Weber.

No doubt, but only by emptying out the baby with the bath-water. We are left with an elegant theorem which places transport inputs as a two-dimensional factor of distance and weight on a par with the other inputs in the productive process, thus dissolving spatial decisions as different in kind from general production decisions. Indeed, the argument can be taken still further. Isard operates with linear production functions, so that the optimum location of a plant is still at the point of minimum transport costs. However, if there is factor substitution between all inputs, the optimum location of a plant will vary with the level of output and almost nothing definite can be said about the location of industrial firms independently of statements about their overall production decisions.

12. Linear Transport Functions

In retrospect, it is evident that classical location theory acquired its *raison d'être* not just from the assumption of linear production functions, separating production from location decisions, but from the notion of linear transport functions, which serve to equate physical distance to economically meaningful distance. It is sometimes argued that this was a realistic assumption in the days of Thünen's horse-drawn wagons and even that the German transport rate structure at the turn of the 19th century was in fact more or less linear. But as we have seen, Thünen's transport functions were not precisely linear and Weber was perfectly aware that freight costs are usually less than proportional to distance. As a matter of fact, it was a well-known dictum of 19th-century railway economics that railway transport costs are always less than proportional to distance owing to terminal loading and unloading costs. The assumption of linear transport functions was adopted to simplify the analysis and to produce clean-cut results, such as concentric production zones, straight-line rent-bid functions, market areas defined in terms of square miles instead of the volume of sales, weights of products as the locational forces that must be equilibrated instead of marginal transfer costs, etcetera.

All locational factors may be summed into three broad groups: (1) transport and certain other transfer costs that vary more or less regularly with distance from any given point of reference; (2) costs associated with labour, power, water, taxes, insurance, interest, climate, topography, and the political environment, which, however stable geographically, do not vary systematically with distance from any given reference point; and (3) general agglomeration and deglomeration economies whose operation is independent of location. Only the first of these three factors imparts regularity to the spatial setting of economic activities and, while all are amenable to formal analysis, only the first lends itself to powerful and significant generalizations. Even these are threatened once we drop the assumption that transport rates are strictly proportional to weight and distance in all directions over straight-line, airplane routes. The increasing unwillingness to base the analysis of industrial location on linear transport functions, and the steady decline of transport costs as a share of the total delivered cost of a product, have contributed more than anything else to the effective demise of classical location theory.

13. What Survives of Classical Location Theory?

Even those who have been most concerned in recent years to commend the classic writings of Thünen, Launhardt, Weber and Lösch have expressed profound misgivings about its operational significance. Classical location theory was posited on the assumption of perfect competition but if firms compete spatially by f.o.b. pricing, the market structure is one of monopolistic, not perfect competition. Unfortunately, monopolistic competition theory offers few unambiguous implications about firm behavior and, indeed, to this day there is little agreement about what is implied by monopolistic competition models of spatial differentiation. Moreover, there is much confusion in the literature as to whether classical location theory was in fact designed to explain all the observed spatial variations in economic activity or, more modestly, to provide what Samuelson has called a 'qualitative calculus', that is, a statement of the algebraic sign of the changes in output and prices that can be expected to result from given changes in spatial circumstances. Recent attacks on location theory from certain radical economists make demands on location theory that no comparative static equilibrium theory could ever satisfy. No wonder that classical locational theory has been swallowed up by so-called 'regional science', which replaces any attempt at a special, coherent theory of spatial location by a veritable portfolio of partial but operational techniques deriving from roots which frequently lie outside economics. Even modern urban and regional economics is largely macroeconomic in spirit and hence has little room for the microeconomic focus of classical agricultural and industrial location theory. In short, classical location theory, despite its promising beginnings, has proved in the fullness of time to be something of a theoretical cul-de-sac, a repository of general maxims about the role of spatial factors, which tells us what to look for once we have arrived at our destination but cannot tell us beforehand what we can expect to find there.

14. The Continued Neglect of Location Theory

It is doubtful whether this negative retrospective assessment throws much light on the continued neglect of spatial economics by mainstream economists until relatively modern times; with the exception of the brief flicker of interest in the 1930s, that neglect largely continues to this day. Despite valiant attempts to explain this neglect by either internal or external factors, it remains one of the great puzzles about the historical development of economics. It is true that much of classical location theory was couched in physical terms alien to the spirit of standard price theory but such was the case even of the first formulations of general equilibrium theory by Walras and Pareto. Moreover, perfect competition, profit-maximization, perfect knowledge, perfect certainty, instantaneous adjustments and equilibrium outcomes characterize the work of all the great figures in location theory as much as they do the work of all the great orthodox economists, and this agreement on methods of analysis should have facilitated, not hindered, the integration of location theory. It is also true that many spatial parameters exhibit indivisibilities and discontinuities (e.g. nodal centres, population clusters, transhipment points, etcetera) which stand in the way of the application of marginal analysis but, on the other hand, most of these were eliminated by assumption in classical location theory. Finally, all the great writers in location theory wrote in German, many of them were never translated in English (and remain untranslated until this day), and economics has remained a predominantly English-speaking subject for over 200 years. But Walras' *Elements of Pure Economics* was only translated for the first time in English in 1954 and that did not prevent Walras from becoming a byword in English and American economics long before that.

In the final analysis, all the attempts to account for the curious disdain of location theory on the part of mainstream economists end up by invoking conservatism and blinkered thinking, which restates the puzzle instead of solving it. Perhaps the solution of the mystery is simpler than anyone has imagined. If Ricardo had based his rent theory on locational advantages instead of fertility differences, if Thünen had been a lucid instead of an obscure writer, and if Launhardt had expressed himself in words instead of equations, is there any reason to doubt that the whole of classical locational theory would have found a place in Marshall's *Principles* and, thereby, in the corpus of received economic doctrine?

NOTES ON FURTHER READING

The fundamental primary source in spatial economics is Thünen's *Isolated State*. This book appeared in four instalments over a 37-year period; volume I was published in 1826 and it is this volume which contains Thünen's major contribution to rent and location theory – it was revised and reprinted in 1842; volume II.1 was published in 1850 as the only part of a projected second volume of *The Isolated State* which Thünen lived to complete; the second part of this second volume appeared posthumously in 1863 in an edition by H. Schumacher, Thünen's official biographer; finally, a third volume, consisting of a dissertation on forestry, also appeared in 1863. The entire work has never been translated in English but a beautiful translation of vol. I, with excerpts from vol. II.1, is available in English: *Von Thünen's Isolated State*, ed. Hall. The whole of vol. II.1 has also been translated by Dempsey, *The Frontier Wage*.

Vol. I of *The Isolated State*, the volume ignored by economists but acclaimed by economic geographers and regional scientists, is one of the most difficult books in the entire history of economic thought. But every student should read chaps. 1–5, 24, 25, and the famous methodological introduction to vol. II.1.

In contrast to Thünen's *Isolated State*, Weber's *Theory of the Location of Industries*, ed. C. J. Friedrich (1929) is extremely readable. The other leading primary sources of spatial economics are, however, almost as demanding as Thünen's *Isolated State* even supposing one is fluent in German: W. Launhardt, *Mathematische Begründung der Volkswirtschaftslehre* (1963), T. Palander, *Beiträge zur Standortstheorie* (1935); A. Lösch, *The Economics of Location* (1954), and W. Isard, *Location and Space-Economy* (1956).

A basic secondary source on eighteenth century spatial economics is P. Dockès, *L'espace dans la pensée économique du XVIe au XVIIIe siècle* (1969). But see also R. F. Hébert, 'Richard Cantillon's Early Contributions to Spatial Economics', *Ec*, February, 1981. An indispensable handbook to Thünen's *Isolated State* is A. Petersen, *Thünens Isolierte Staat. Die Landwirtschaft als Glied der Volkswirtschaft* (1944). A similar detailed gloss on Weber's *Theory of the Location of Industries* is E. Niederhauser, *Die Standortstheorie Alfred Webers* (1944). C. Clark, 'Von Thünen's Isolated State', *OEP*, November, 1967, examines Thünen's calculations of transport costs and crop yields in the light of modern knowledge of agriculture in low-income countries. P. A. Samuelson contributes a useful assessment of 'Thünen at Two Hundred', *JEL*, December, 1983.

For an authoritative history of location theory see C. Ponsard, *History of Spatial Economic Theory* (1983), an expanded and updated version of the original 1958 French edition. In some respects, however, Palander's *Beiträge zur Standortstheorie* is a preferable secondary source for the history of location theory: it provides a critical evaluation of Thünen, Launhardt and Weber; an integrated, graphical treatment of all the standard models in the literature; and a detailed classified bibliography of nineteenth and twentieth century writings on spatial problems. This is a book that should have been translated into English long ago. Similarly, there is an excellent historical account in R. O. Been, *A Reconstruction of the Classical Theory of Location* (1965), which no publisher has seen fit to put into print: it is a University of California, Berkeley Ph.D. thesis, which is only available from University Microfilms in Ann Arbor, Michigan.

J. V. Pinto, 'Launhardt and Location Theory: Rediscovery of a Neglected Book', *JRS*, 17, 1, 1977, provides a splendid account of Launhardt's contributions besides reporting the discovery of a totally unknown book by Launhardt on railway location, which was actually translated into English in 1902. On the law of market areas as a telling instance of 'multiple discoveries', see R. F. Hébert, 'A Note on the Historical Development of the Economic Law of Market Areas', *QJE*, November, 1972, and 'The Theory of Input Selection and Supply Areas in 1887: Emile Cheysson', *HOPE*, February, 1974. C. D. Hyson and W. P. Hyson, 'The Economic Law of Market Areas', *QJE*, May, 1950, provide a modern treatment of the law. M. Blaug, 'The German Hegemony of Location Theory: A Puzzle in the History of Economic Thought', *HOPE*, Spring, 1979, speculates on the causes of the German near-monopoly of spatial economics. R. B. Ekelund Jr. and D. Hooks, 'Joint Demand, Discriminating, Two-Part Tariffs and Location Theory: An Early American Contribution', *WEJ*, March, 1972, discuss the French and American engineer-economist tradition in spatial economics, which owed nothing whatsoever to the writings of Thünen.

Modern books on land use patterns and the location of industrial plants abound in précis of the great figures of spatial economics, not all of which however are historically accurate. However, E. S. Dunn, *The Location of Agricultural Production* (1954), W. Alonso, *Location and Land Use. Toward a General Theory of Land Rent* (1964), and M. Chisholm, *Rural Settlement and Land Use* (1979) are useful in throwing light on Thünen, and E. M. Hoover, *Location Theory and the Shoe and Leather Industry* (1937), M.L. Greenhut, *Plant Location in Theory and Practice* (1956), D. M. Smith, *Industrial Location. An Economic Geographical Analysis* (1971), and E. S. Mills, *Urban Economics* (1972) do the same for Launhardt and Weber. An excellent geographers' treatment is P. E. Lloyd and P. Dicken, *Location in Space: A Theoretical Approach to Economic Geography* (1972). M. Beckmann, *Location Theory* (1968) reworks the entire subject with the aid of linear programming. H. W. Richardson, *Regional Economics. Location Theory, Urban Structure and Regional Change* (1969) is a more standard textbook account. R. D. Dean, W. H. Leahy, and D. L. McKee, eds., *Spatial Economic Theory* (1970) reprints many of the classic papers on spatial economics in the interwar period. A vigorous, radical critique of received location theory is found in S. Holland, *Capital Versus the Regions* (1976), chap. 1.

15

The neoclassical theory of money, interest and prices

This chapter is mercifully brief. All the building bricks were assembled in chapters 1 and 5 and we can, therefore, deal fairly quickly with the neoclassical theory of money, interest and prices. Until the 1930s, the quantity theory of money may be said to have been everybody's theory of money. This is not to say that it was universally accepted: it was attacked, vehemently and repeatedly, by a series of minor writers. But no adequate rival theory was offered in its place and all the leading economists adhered to one of three similar but subtly different versions of the quantity theory: there was the transactions approach popularized by Fisher's *Purchasing Power of Money* (1911); there was the cash balance approach, developed by Marshall, Walras and Wicksell; and lastly, there was the income approach associated with Robertson and the young Keynes, culminating in the explicit introduction of the concept of the income velocity of money in Pigou's *Industrial Fluctuations* (1927).

Fundamentally, the quantity theory drew its strength from the frequently observed correlation between changes in the price level and substantial changes in the quantity of money. As Friedman has put it: 'There is perhaps no other empirical relation in economics that has been observed to recur so uniformly under so wide a variety of circumstances as the relation between substantial changes over short periods in the stock of money and in prices; the one is invariably linked with the other and is in the same direction; this uniformity is, I suspect, of the same order as many of the uniformities that form the basis of the physical sciences'. The use of the quantity theory to predict the reactions of observed prices to dramatic changes in the quantity of money was predicated on the relative stability of the velocity of circulation, V, or the income velocity of money, V_y. But this is not to say that the quantity theorists treated velocity as a natural constant, thus reducing the 'Equation of Exchange $MV = PT$', to an identity rather than an equilibrium relationship. The idea that the old quantity theory of money consisted of nothing more than the obvious equality, $MV = PT$, obvious because T is determined by real forces while V is taken to be an institutional constant, is nothing more than a modern textbook invention. For one thing, such an interpretation of the theory makes nonsense of the equilibrating mechanism by which an increase in the quantity of money acts on prices; in our earlier language of chapter 5, it 'dichotomizes the pricing process' and, therefore, implies 'Say's Identity'. As we shall see, however, Fisher and Wicksell at any rate were perfectly aware of the equilibrating mechanism which alone gives the quantity theory the status of a theory rather than a truism.

1. What is the Quantity Theory of Money?

To convert the quantity equation, $MV = PT$, into a quantity *theory* at least three assumptions or hypotheses appear to be crucial: (1) the direction of causation must be from MV to PT, from the left-hand side to the right-hand side of the equation; (2) V and T must exhibit invariance with respect to changes in M, that is, all changes in V and T must be attributable to non-monetary factors, such as new banking practices, new payment habits, productivity growth in the economy as a whole, etcetera; and (3) the *nominal* stock of money must be exogenously determined, that is, independently of the public's demand for money balances, either because it depends on the output of gold mines and the balance of payments under a gold-specie standard or because it depends on a central bank's control over a narrowly defined base of so-called 'high-powered money' under a convertible or inconvertible paper standard, the issue of checks and notes by the commercial banking system being more or less rigidly linked to the base of high-powered money created by the central bank.

From these three assumptions, a number of propositions follow, which together define the corpus of ideas known as *the* quantity theory of money. First, there is the notion that, given a stable V, P varies in exact proportion to changes in M. This strict version of the quantity theory rules out any function for money except that of a transactions medium and assumes that people are solely concerned with the current purchasing power of their cash balances: they wish to hold a constant quantity of real cash balances, M/P, at the economy's full employment level of real output; hence, to maintain real balances intact, the price level must vary in direct proportion to the nominal money supply. This proportionality theorem refers to an equilibrium condition and therefore implies a dynamic adjustment process that occurs whenever a change in M creates a disequilibrium between M and P. This adjustment process was recognized long ago to involve two distinct transmission mechanisms from M to P: (1) the 'direct mechanism' first expounded by Cantillon and Hume; and (2) the 'indirect mechanism' enunciated by Thornton and repeated by Ricardo. The direct mechanism relies on a disequilibrium between actual and desired real balances to induce the spending that ultimately causes prices to change in proportion to the monetary injection. The indirect mechanism, on the other hand, relies on the fact that extra cash cannot be injected into the economy without a reduction in the market rate of interest, which then stimulates investment spending, exerting an upward pressure on prices until the previous level of the interest rate is restored [see chapter 5, sections 7, 8].

The proportionality theorem is not just a theorem about equilibrium outcomes; it is a theorem about long-run equilibrium outcomes. In long-run equilibrium, money is neutral in the sense that nominal changes in the money supply exert no influence on real economic variables, such as output, employment and the allocation of resources. During the short-run transition to long-run equilibrium, however, monetary changes can exert definite effects on real economic activity. An obvious example is the case in which the monetary injection is not distributed among individuals in exact proportion to their previous shares of money holdings. Another is the case in which there are systematic delays in the adjustment process, causing input costs to lag behind final prices, thus stimulating investment. A third is the one in which debtors form a definite group, such as entrepreneurs, so that the rise in prices favouring debtors at the expense of creditors causes systematic shifts in spending patterns. Finally, there is 'forced saving', which can likewise divert resources from consumption into capital formation [see chapter 5, section 11]. We may label these effects 'short run' and 'transitional' but in point of fact there is no guarantee that these may not have lasting permanent effects on real variables. Thus, an additional proposition may be said to characterize belief in the quantity theory of money, namely, that these and other non-neutral 'transitional' effects are temporary and vanish entirely when the economy has fully adjusted to the monetary change.

All this is to say that a quantity theorist is someone who subscribes to the notion that secular changes in the price level are *principally* due to changes in the stock of money or that any instability of prices stems *fundamentally* from monetary rather than non-monetary causes. That belief is not reducible to the three assumptions about the causal role of M in the determination of absolute prices, the stability of V and the exogeneity of M, or indeed to any firm view about the economic functions of money, but rather to a whole series of empirical hypotheses about the nature of monetary injections, the speed of adjustment processes, the identities of debtors and creditors, the saving and investing propensities of different income recipients, etcetera. No wonder then that it is difficult to pin down *the* quantity theory of money and that even Friedman, the most famous contemporary advocate of the quantity theory, acknowledges that 'The quantity theory of money is a term evocative of a general approach rather than a label for a well-defined theory'.

What complicates matters still further are the three clearly marked stages in the history of the quantity theory of money, which radically altered its meaning over the centuries. Hume clearly grasped the difference between the long-run neutrality but short-run non-neutrality of money and paid almost as much attention to the latter as to the former. The classical economists added to the list of non-neutral effects of a change in M but consistently minimized their significance in reaction to the crude inflationism of their mercantilist predecessors. Whereas Hume conceded the positive output and employment effects of creeping inflation, Ricardo and Mill avoided any suggestion that a monetary injection might generate beneficial real effects; in their hands, the quantity theory of money virtually amounted to the proportionality theorem pure and simple. In the neoclassical period 1870 to 1930, however, the quantity theory gradually retreated from the strict version adopted by Ricardo and Mill.

In fact, the striking characteristic of quantity theorists in this latter period was the emphasis on short-run problems, on the instability of V in disequilibrium situations rather than the proportionality of money to prices in long run. Even Fisher's *Purchasing Power of Money*, which is often taken to be a typical statement of the rigid quantity theory, contains a considerable analysis of 'transition periods' during which both T and V are changing. These 'transition periods' were assumed to last ten years on average and Fisher spent the rest of his life writing on monetary proposals for dealing with the cyclical fluctuations of 'transition periods'. Wicksell, as we shall see, concentrated his attention on the problem of the 'cumulative process' and the cumulative process is essentially a short-run, disequilibrium phenomenon. Likewise, the followers of Marshallian monetary theory, such as Pigou, Robertson, Lavington and the young Keynes, devoted substantial parts of their articles and books on monetary questions to the role of money in industrial fluctuations and, of course, Pigou and Robertson both wrote an entire monograph on the question of the business cycle. This concentration on short-run analysis was even more pronounced among such Chicago quantity theorists of the 1930s as H.C. Simons. What all these writers had in common was a lack of interest in the long-run equilibrium relationship between money and prices and an overwhelming concern with the short-run policy questions of how to stabilize the price level by appropriate monetary action. In short, there was macroeconomics before Keynes because the neoclassical quantity theory of money was, in fact, what we now call macroeconomics. The quantity theory of money in its heyday was no longer what it had once been – a theory of the main causes of the changes in the value or purchasing power of money – but rather a theory of *how* M influenced the *aggregate* demand for goods and services MV, and via MV, the level of prices P and the level of output T.

2. Fisher and Marshall

Popular impression notwithstanding, Fisher stopped well short of anything like a rigid quantity theory. The fact that he devoted a whole chapter to 'the temporary effects during the period of transition', as distinct from what he called 'the permanent or ultimate effects', left no doubt that he meant the equation of exchange to hold only in long-run equilibrium. Furthermore, he admitted the existence of a lagged relationship between the rate of interest and the price level, which allowed T to influence V and M. Nevertheless, he did treat V as determined by slowly changing institutional forces, such as the development of the banking system, the speed of the transport and communication network, the frequency of receipts and disbursements among merchants and traders, the length of the payment period between debtors and creditors, etcetera. For all practical purposes, therefore, he regarded V as an institutional datum, implying a high degree of stability in the demand for money, $1/V$. With a stable demand for money, monetary policy could be expected to exert a powerful, predictable influence on prices and nominal incomes, the more so as T was determined independently by all the real forces tending towards the full-capacity utilization of the economy's resources.

Unfortunately, this very emphasis on the velocity of circulation as a critical variable in monetary analysis focused undue attention on the medium-of-exchange function of money, implying that the existence of positive cash balances is due, not to the utility yielded by money as compared to other asset holdings, but solely to institutional 'frictions' in the economic system. In other words, if perfect efficiency in the circulation of means of payment were somehow achievable, say, by a fully computerized system that instantaneously synchronized all disbursements and receipts, the demand for cash balances would apparently fall to zero. The difficulty here is not just the overemphasis on money as a desirable object to spend as distinct from an object to hold – the 'motion theory' in contrast to the 'rest theory' of velocity – but the failure to formulate the demand for money equation in the same way as the equations for commodity demand.

Marshall and his followers went some way to move the theory of the demand for money in the direction of ordinary demand analysis, first, by relating money to net output or national income rather than the broader category of total transactions, and, second, by shifting from money's rate of turnover to the proportion of annual income that the public wishes to hold in the form of money. In purely formal terms, there is nothing to choose between the Fisherian transaction approach and the Cambridge cash-balance approach, but the Cambridge formulation held out the potential of a genuine portfolio theory of the demand for money, which potential, however, was never fully exploited.

In Fisher, T is the real volume of all market transactions during a period of time and V is the number of money transfers between individuals and firms during the same period of time in connection with all purchases and financial transactions. M stands for coins, bank notes and checking deposits on the assumption that reserve requirements are determined by rigid conventions and that checking deposits bear a stable relationship to hand-to-hand circulation. If, instead, we define Y as real national income per annum, then $V_y = Y/M$ becomes the number of times a unit of money leaves the cash balances of ultimate income receipts during a year. The aggregate amount of money that the public may wish to hold in the form of cash balances can be expressed as a certain proportion k of real annual income. For example, a representative individual may wish to hold enough cash balances to buy one tenth of his real annual income; thus, $k = \frac{1}{10}$, $V_y = 10$, and M circulating 10 times per year would be sufficient to buy Y at the current price level. In this way, we reach the Cambridge equation $M = kPY$. Except for the different definition of T and the associated price index, the cash balance equation is identical to the transaction equation, $M = PT/V$.

The Cambridge formulation implies a demand for money equation, $D_n = kPY$, which contains no variable to represent the opportunity costs of holding cash, namely, the rate of interest or the yield of alternative non-monetary assets, analogous to the relative price arguments of ordinary demand functions. Yet a straightforward application of utility-maximizing principles would have suggested that a rise in interest rates is likely to induce a fall in k as people strive to substitute interest earning assets for passive money balances in their asset portfolios. Similarly, a fall in interest rates, by lowering the opportunity costs of holding money, is likely to cause a rise in k. Strangely enough, however, the Cambridge monetary theory never explicitly recognized the functional dependence of k on either the rate of interest or the rate on all non-monetary assets. After constructing a framework highly suggestive of a study of all the factors influencing cash-holding decisions, the Cambridge writers tended to lapse back to a list of the determinants of κ that differed in no important respects from the list of institutional factors that Fisher had cited in his discussion of V. One can find references in Marshall, Pigou and particularly Lavington to a representative individual striking a balance between the costs of cash holdings in terms of interest forgone (minus the brokerage costs that would have been incurred by the movement into stocks and bonds) and their returns in terms of convenience and security against default but such passages were never systematically integrated with the cash-balance equation. As late as 1923, we find the young Keynes in *A Tract on Monetary Reform* interpreting κ as a stable constant, representing an invariant link in the transmission mechanism connecting money to prices. If only Keynes at that date had read Wicksell instead of Marshall, he might have arrived at a money demand function that incorporates variations in the interest rate years before *The General Theory* (1936).

3. Wicksell's Rehabilitation of the Indirect Mechanism

Marshall's *Evidence and Memoranda* to two Royal Commissions in the late 1880s and particularly an article on 'Remedies for Fluctuations of General Prices' (1887), presents in a short space all the essential elements of his monetary analysis, emphasizing the 'direct mechanism' connecting money and prices in the tradition of Cantillon and Hume; the 'indirect mechanism' is by no means neglected but it is not developed at length. Wicksell's contribution to monetary theory, on the other hand, consists of a careful restatement of the 'indirect mechanism' linking money to prices via the rate of interest. In *Interest and Prices* (1898), the 'direct mechanism' virtually disappears, but in the second volume of the *Lectures* (1906), Wicksell modified his position and combined the 'direct mechanism' involving the real balance effect with a new version of the 'indirect mechanism'. In view of Wicksell's writings, it is surprising that Keynes's chapter on 'The Classical Theory of the Rate of Interest' in the *General Theory* was based entirely on Marshall and Pigou, both of whom paid little attention to the interrelationship between the interest rate and price movements. The Wicksellian theory does appear in Marshall's poorly organised treatise on *Money, Credit and Commerce* (1923), but only in the form in which it is found in J.S. Mill; Mill, in turn, learned it from Thornton. But Wicksell was the first writer after Mill systematically to develop the implications of Thornton's insights.

The expansion of bank credit, Thornton had argued in 1803, can become effective only through a reduction in the bank rate and hence the money rate of interest. As soon as the addition of credit ceases, prices stop rising and the rate of interest returns to its former equilibrium level determined by the unchanged rate of return on real capital. Following this argument, one would expect the interest rate and the general price level to move in opposite directions. But the foremost critic of Ricardian monetary theory, Thomas Tooke, author of the influential *History of Prices*, published in successive volumes between 1838 and 1857, showed that, on the contrary, the market rate of interest and the price level are positively correlated. This finding, corroborated in later days, was dubbed the 'Gibson Paradox' by Keynes in *The Treatise on Money* (1930). The paradox is not hard to explain when it is realized that capital accumulation and technical change tend to alter the real rate independently of monetary forces. The bank rate and hence the money rate of interest will therefore trail behind the real rate of return on capital. What is needed to disprove the theory is, not a positive correlation between prices and the absolute height of the market rate of interest, but a positive correlation between prices and interest differentials. But Tooke's primitive demonstration of the Gibson Paradox seemed to place the entire mechanism in doubt. It was Wicksell's intention to account for the paradox and at the same time to defend the quantity theory against its critics by providing a more detailed explanation of its *modus operandi*. It is a striking fact that when Wicksell sat down to write the second volume of the *Lectures*, he had still not read Thornton's *Nature of the Paper Credit* but knew of Thornton's argument only through its echoes in Ricardo's *Principles*.

4. The Cumulative Process

Wicksell expounds his theory first of all on the assumption of a 'pure cash system': 'money' is coins and paper currency only and, since banks are forced to hold 100 percent of their deposits in the form of metallic reserves, increases in checking deposits may be treated as increases in the velocity of metallic bank reserves. Later, the analysis is carried over to the other extreme, a 'pure credit system', where the only form of bank reserves is central bank credit and 'money' is merely checking deposits.

Assume now that we face a 'pure cash system'. An effective fall in the bank rate – a fall that drives the market rate of interest downward – tends to raise the volume of investment per unit of time. Under perfect competition, the prices of capital goods will rise and the prices of consumer goods will at least not fall. If the economy is fully employed, the entire wage-price level will rise. But this shifts up the demand functions for capital goods and so, at a given reduction in the bank rate, the price rise tends to become 'cumulative'. Provided reserves are held in monetary metals, however, the cumulative process soon comes to a halt. In the inflationary upsurge, there is an external and internal drain into hand-to-hand circulation and banks run up against their reserve requirements; the increase in deposits reduces the reserve ratio but what is even more important is that the internal and external drain depletes absolute reserves. Action will therefore be taken to protect the reserves. The bank rate will be raised to choke off the inflation. Similarly, if the price level declines through an increase in the bank rate, the progressive accumulation of excess reserves induces banks to reduce the bank rate to stimulate borrowing, thus restoring equilibrium.

In a 'pure credit' system, the reining-in effect of limited bank reserves does not exist. Here the process is truly self-generating. Although 'forced saving' and the Real Balance Effect might moderate the price rise [see chapter 5, section 11], the fact is that the monetary authorities can now determine the price level at will by appropriate variations in the bank rate. In the real world, the elasticity of bank credit is neither infinite as in a 'pure credit system' nor zero as in a 'pure cash system'. The monetary authorities can start a cumulative movement but sooner or later they are forced to bring the process to a halt. What Wicksell's cumulative process is all about, therefore, is the determinants of the money supply under various monetary institutions and various regimes of monetary policy.

5. Monetary Equilibrium

In *Interest and Prices*, Wicksell spoke of the market rate and the 'natural' rate of interest. The natural rate of interest seems to refer to the rate of interest that would exist if capital goods were lent *in natura*. This is a confusing concept because there is no *single* rate of interest in a barter economy: in the absence of money, the physical yields of heterogeneous capital goods cannot be reduced to a common denominator and there are as many own-rates of interest as there are capital goods. The natural rate of interest could be taken to refer, however, to a statistical average of the own-rates of different goods. But no such clumsy device is really necessary. There is evidence that Wicksell came to regret his own terminology: on the one occasion when he chose to express his theory in English, he used such phrases as the 'ordinary rate', the 'normal rate', and 'average profits on capital' as synonyms for the 'natural' rate. Let us define the 'natural' rate in Wicksell's words as the 'expected yield of newly created capital' – in short, our old friend the internal rate of return or Keynes's marginal efficiency of capital [see chapter 12, section 20]. A cumulative process is said to be created by a discrepancy between the market rate of interest and this expected yield of investment, or a discrepancy between the cost of borrowing capital and the internal rate of return on new investment options. A cumulative process is thus a disequilibrium situation in which net investment is positive and constantly increasing from period to period. This need not create inflation if the cumulative process also generates additional voluntary savings. The task of the monetary authorities is to check investment at the first signs of inflation by means of raising the bank rate. Thus, if the economy is operating at full employment levels, the rule is that a bank rate that preserves price stability will have to be set at a level to insure that net investment does not exceed voluntary savings.

With a stable price level, the money rate of interest will be a direct expression of the expected yield on investment. At the same time, this rate of return on investment will be equal to the bank rate. We thus have to keep in mind three and not two rates: the rate of return on investment, the money rate of interest and the bank rate. If the bank rate diverges from the going money rate of interest, the price level will begin to change and this will create an additional divergence, as Marshall and Fisher had shown [see chapter 12, section 24], between the money rate and the real rate of return on investment. With a bank rate of 5 percent, a 1 percent rise in prices makes the effective loan rate equal to 4 percent, that is, equal to a 4 percent nominal bank rate at constant prices. Thus, once prices have begun to rise, inflation is aggravated by the fact that debtors always pay back less than the real value of the funds they have borrowed. This also means that the banks are now induced to raise the loan rate lest they suffer capital losses on their loans. In this way we arrive at Wicksell's three criteria of monetary equilibrium: the loan rate of interest is at equilibrium if it is equal to the rate (1) 'which more or less corresponds to the expected yield of newly created capital', (2) 'at which the demand for loan capital and the supply of savings exactly agree', and (3) 'at which the general level of commodity prices has no tendency to move upward or downward'. Together, these three criteria constitute the prerequisites of 'neutral money', a monetary system so managed that the price level remains stable along the economy's growth path.

6. Saving-Investment Concepts

Saving and investment in Wicksell's system are not equal by definition as they are in the Keynesian system: $Y \equiv C + I$, $S \equiv Y - C$, and, therefore, $S \equiv I$. With Keynes of the *General Theory*, saving and investment refer to the same period of time. On the other hand, when Wicksell speaks of an excess of investment over saving as creating inflation, he means an increase in the money value of output that is not translated into disposable income in the time period under consideration. Likewise, when he refers to saving exceeding investment, he is thinking of the attempt to postpone consumption, which produces a cumulative fall in prices and a reduction in the money value of output. Perhaps Robertson's schema comes closest to systematizing Wicksell's conception of saving and investment. If we let the superscripts e and d refer to earned and disposable income and the subscripts refer to the appropriate time periods, we have

$$Y_t^e \equiv C_t + I_t. \tag{1}$$

$$S_t \equiv Y_t^d - C_t \equiv Y_{t-1}^e - C_t. \tag{2}$$

Equation (1) states that today's earned income is spent today. Equation (2) states that today's saving is equal either to today's disposable income minus today's consumption or to yesterday's earned income not consumed today.

From equation (2), we have

$$Y_{t-1}^e = S_t + C_t. \tag{3}$$

Subtracting equation (3) from equation (1), we therefore have

$$Y_t^e - Y_{t-1}^e = I_t - S_t. \tag{4}$$

Thus, when $I_t > S_t$, income is rising, and when $S_t > I_t$, income is falling.

The now familiar distinction between planned and realized saving and investment, with realized saving and investment always equal by definition but planned saving and investment equal only in equilibrium, is derived from Myrdal and Lindahl, the Swedish heirs of Wicksell's monetary theory. In this set-up, planned consumption is always realized but *ex ante* saving and investment need not equal *ex post* magnitudes. Writing subscripts p and r for planned and realized values, the strategic definitional identities are as follows:

$$S_p \equiv Y_p - C. \tag{1}$$

$$Y_r \equiv I_r + C. \tag{2}$$

$$C \equiv Y_r - I_r. \tag{3}$$

Subtracting I_p from equation (1) we have

$$S_p - I_p \equiv (Y_p - C) - I_p. \tag{4}$$

Substituting equation (3) into equation (4), we obtain

$$\begin{aligned} S_p - I_p &\equiv [Y_p - (Y_r - I_r)] - I_p \\ &\equiv (Y_p - Y_r) + (I_r - I_p). \end{aligned} \tag{5}$$

Therefore

$$Y_p - Y_r \equiv (S_p - I_p) - (I_r - I_p).$$

Thus, an excess of planned saving over planned investment implies either a deficiency of realized as compared with planned income or, since investors' capital equipment spending plans are always assumed to be carried out, an unintended increase in inventories, or both.

7. Price Stabilization

To return to Wicksell's argument: the three criteria of monetary equilibrium must be satisfied simultaneously. The market rate of interest is determined by the demand and supply of loanable funds. The demand for loanable funds consists of investment demand *plus* demand for inactive cash balances. The supply of loanable funds consists of personal and business savings *plus* bank credit. If planned saving and planned investment are in equilibrium, a stable price level implies that net credit creation is absorbed into inactive balances. Lerner's graphic treatment (Figure 15–1) of the loanable funds theory of interest brings this out. $S + \Delta M$ is the total supply of loanable funds; S is the supply out of planned private and business savings, and ΔM is the supply through net credit creation. $H + I$ is the total demand for loanable funds; I is the investment demand and H is the net demand for purposes of 'hoarding' inactive balances.[1] All functions are defined for a given income (and are drawn as linear functions strictly for convenience) and all variables are defined per unit of time. In equilibrium, $H + I = S + \Delta M$ or $I - S = \Delta M - H$. Thus S can exceed I but only if $\Delta M < H$ (as is the case at r in Figure 15–1); likewise, I can exceed S but only if $\Delta M > H$. When $I = S$ in equilibrium, $\Delta M = H$, and this can mean only that the bank rate is equal to the market rate of interest and that the latter, in turn, is equal to the real rate of return on investment. No matter where we begin, we always end up having to satisfy all three criteria before we can conclude that the money market is in equilibrium.

A new difficulty now presents itself. As Wicksell's friend Davidson pointed out, economic growth involves continuous increases in productivity via technical change. If prices are to be kept stable, the money supply will have to increase with the rate of increase in productivity. Thus, the bank rate will have to be low enough to induce a net inflow of money into circulation through bank loans or open market operations. But then the bank rate that stabilizes prices will be below the rate at which the

[1] The distinction between this theory and Keynes's liquidity preference theory is analogous to the distinction between investment theory and capital theory. Liquidity preference theory is concerned with an asset-holding equilibrium in which the demand and supply of stocks of money are equal. Loanable funds theory considers hoarding and dishoarding as a flow of funds that are non-zero in value when the stocks are in disequilibrium. In equilibrium the two theories yield identical results.

Figure 15–1

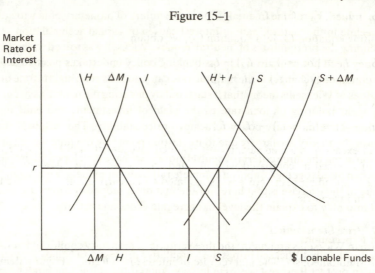

demand for investment funds equals the supply of savings. To state Davidson's point in another way: to preserve monetary equilibrium, banks should always tailor their lending solely to the demand for inactive balances; but if they obey this rule, prices will fall with every increase in productivity, thus disturbing the established equilibrium. It is not even necessary to assume technical change, Davidson might have added. The fact that investment is capacity-creating will produce the same difficulty. In every period, net investment will increase the potential output of subsequent periods. If net investment and net saving do not change, prices will fall unless the bank rate is lowered to encourage the expansion of output.

Furthermore, when the bank rate is lowered to prevent a decline in prices resulting from productivity improvements, the upward cumulative movement encourages the construction of real capital. Owing to the gestation period of construction projects, the boom may be halted by an increase in the bank rate before capital projects have been completed. It is unlikely that the abandoned projects will be resumed in the next upward movement. Instead, new ones will be started. Thus, the attempt to damp down cumulative movements by monetary policy may give rise to an increasing collection of unfinished capital projects. This is the basis of Hayek's charge in *Prices and Production* that price stabilization involves a·waste of economic resources.

It is beginning to be apparent that the simple Wicksellian criteria do not constitute an adequate guide to monetary management. A central bank interested in preserving price stability will get little help from the maxim that it ought to maintain equality between the market rate of interest and the average rate of profit on capital. In fairness to Wicksell, however, we should note that he himself pointed out the difficulties of estimating the net yield of investment, the inadequacy of most existing price indices, and the impossibility therefore of measuring anything but a gross divorce between the market rate and the natural rate of interest. Moreover, he used his own theory primarily to explain secular changes, such as the deflationary movement of the Great Depression of 1873–97. Such secular swings in the price level, he argued, were fundamentally due to the failure of monetary policy to adjust to the decline in the 'natural' rate of interest caused by capital accumulation.

By defining the prerequisites of 'neutral' money, Wicksell was forced to recognize that money need not be neutral. Unless banking policy undertakes positive action, purely spontaneous changes in the 'natural' rate can lead to oversaving. It is one of the peculiarities of Wicksell's theory that it starts out by picturing the banking system as a passive agent tailoring its loan rate to the yield of investment, and ends up by advocating active monetary policy to achieve price stability. The technical short-comings of the theory are largely due to its starting point. By the time we reach the conclusion about the three criteria of neutral money, we have developed all the pieces which, when fitted together, supply a complete rationale for monetary management. The value of the exercise is that here, for the first time, monetary forces are clearly brought into play to explain the level of aggregate economic activity.

8. Expectations

We noted earlier that Wicksell brings the 'cumulative process' to a halt by the actions of banks to protect their reserves. He largely ignored the stabilizing tendencies of forced saving and the Real Balance Effect. Furthermore, he paid no attention to changing expectations. We must now ask whether the idea of a cumulative movement is not in fact dependent on certain assumptions about the state of expectations.

Wicksell starts from a situation of static equilibrium and then deduces the effects of a reduction in the bank rate. In static equilibrium, expectations are determined by the results of previous periods. Wicksell assumes that this is also the case during the cumulative process. Given the background of static equilibrium, it is reasonable to assume that producers regard the rise in the price level as temporary. This means that while the current prices of capital goods are above normal levels, the price of output accruing in the future is expected to fall back to normal levels. Hence, the calculated net yield of current investment must fall, causing investment to sink below normal. To be sure, the cost of borrowing has declined, but since producers also expect the price of capital goods to fall back in the future, they will postpone investment. In short, when expectations are governed by normal price situations, we will get alternative swings of investment and prices around the normal level instead of a cumulative process.

Wicksell's analysis implicitly assumes that expectations are not governed in the way described above. Indeed, his system is entirely dependent on what Hicks has called an 'elasticity of expectations of unity', meaning that a change in current prices is expected to change future prices in the same direction and in the same proportion. The argument really has nothing to do with a peculiarity of monetary equilibrium. Whenever future prices are expected to move just as spot prices do, any disturbance from equilibrium sets off a cumulative movement. If every time we demanded more bread, not only the spot price of bread but also bread prices expected in the future were to rise, equilibrium in the bread market could never be established. Wicksell did at one point admit that producers may begin to anticipate price increases – the case of relatively elastic expectations – in which case the cumulative process 'creates its own draft' even when money is 'neutral'. But he did not realize that the very notion of cumulative instability rests on the assumption that people expect future prices to rise as fast as current prices.

Wicksell's defense of the quantity theory of money pointed forward to all subsequent developments in monetary economics: the prominent role of the rate of interest in explaining the adjustment of aggregate demand to changes in the money supply; the crucial role of monetary policy in preventing irreversible inflation; the emphasis on the equality or inequality of saving and investment in determining the level of aggregate demand; and even the vital role played by expectations in an inflationary process. Nonetheless, Wicksell too failed explicitly to incorporate cost or yield variables into the money demand function – the main shortcoming of all quantity theorizing in the 19th century – and he implicitly addressed his arguments to an economy that is operating at the full employment ceiling, so that monetary-induced changes in spending manifest themselves largely in price level changes rather than changes in output and employment.

9. Keynes and Wicksell

In this context, Keynes's *General Theory* may be construed, partly as a wholesale rejection of the quantity theory tradition in which Wicksell was writing, and partly as an analysis of the case Wicksell had ignored, namely, that of an economy operating at less than full employment. When there are idle resources to draw on, changes in spending are more likely to affect output and employment rather than prices and hence, in much of his analysis, Keynes reversed the assumptions of the quantity theory, treating prices as fixed and output as flexible. Moreover, Keynes denied the stability of V or k and argued that a rise in M might well be offset by a fall in V, leaving nominal income or total spending, PT, unchanged, the more so because he regarded investment as typically unresponsive to variations in the interest rate. In general, Keynes's model drew on the contraquantity theory of Tooke in emphasizing expenditure flows rather than the stock of money as the causal agent of economic changes, while replacing the 'direct mechanism' of the quantity theory by a new non-monetary adjustment mechanism, the multiplier. Finally, the chief policy implication of Keynesian theory – the superiority of fiscal over monetary policy in combating depressions – marked a striking contrast to the central role of monetary management in the writings of quantity theorists.

Keynes's theory of interest, however, may be interpreted as rectifying the traditional quantity theory formulation of the demand for money and, even so, not going far enough in that direction. Keynes separated the demand for money into two distinct parts: a transactions demand for active cash balances, M_t, and a precautionary and speculative demand for inactive cash balances, M_s [see chapter 5, section 7]. His treatment of M_t is identical to that of his predecessors in the Cambridge school: transactions balances exhibit a simple, linear relationship to nominal income and are not responsive to cost and yield considerations. The total quantity of money demanded only varies inversely with the interest rate in Keynes because the speculative demand for money is a function of the relationship between the current rate of interest and the expected 'normal' or permanently maintainable rate of interest. Here, for almost the first time in the history of economic thought, we have an explicit consideration of the rate of interest as the cost of holding cash in the money demand function.

10. The Demand for Money after Keynes

In giving explicit consideration to the yields on assets that compete with money, Keynes became one of the founders of the portfolio balance approach to monetary analysis. However, it is Hicks rather than Keynes who ought to be regarded as the true founder of the view that the demand for money is simply an aspect of the problem of choosing an optimum portfolio of assets. In a remarkable paper published a year before the appearance of *The General Theory*, modestly entitled 'A Suggestion for Simplifying the Theory of Money', Hicks argued that money held at least partly as a store of value must be considered a type of capital asset. Hence, the demand for money equation must include total wealth and expected rates of return on non-monetary assets as explanatory variables. Because individuals can choose to hold their entire wealth portfolios in the form of cash, the wealth variable represents the budget constraint on money holdings. The yield variables, on the other hand, represent both the opportunity costs of holding money and the substitution effects of changes in relative rates of return. Individuals optimize their portfolio balances by comparing these yields with the imputed yield in terms of convenience and security of holding money. By these means, Hicks in effect treated the demand for money as a problem of balance sheet equilibrium among assets analyzed along the same lines as those employed in ordinary demand theory.

It was Milton Friedman who carried this Hicksian analysis of money as a capital asset to its logical conclusion. In a 1956 essay, he set out a precise and complete specification of the relevant constraints and opportunity cost variables entering a household's money demand function. His independent variables included wealth or 'permanent income' – the present value of expected future receipts from all sources, whether personal earnings or the income from real property and financial assets – the ratio of human to nonhuman wealth, the expected rates of return on stocks, bonds and real assets, the nominal interest rate, the actual price level, and, finally, the expected percentage change in the price level. Like Hicks, Friedman specified wealth as the appropriate budget constraint but his concept of wealth was much broader than that adopted by Hicks. Whereas Keynes had viewed bonds as the only asset competing with cash, Friedman regarded all types of wealth as potential substitutes for cash holdings in an individual's balance sheet; thus, instead of a single interest variable in the Keynesian liquidity preference equation, we get a whole list of relative yield variables in Friedman. An additional novel feature, entirely original with Friedman, is the inclusion of the expected rate of change of P as a measure of the anticipated rate of depreciation in the purchasing power of cash balances.

This formulation of the money demand function was offered in a paper entitled 'The Quantity Theory of Money: A Restatement'. Friedman claimed not only that the quantity theory of money had always been a theory about the demand for money but also that his reformulation corresponded closely to what some of the great Chicago monetary economists, such as H.C. Simons and L.W. Mints, had always meant by *the* quantity theory. It is clear, however, from our earlier discussion that the quantity theory of money, while embodying an implicit conception of the demand for money, had always stood first and foremost for a theory of the determination of prices and nominal income; it contained much more than a particular theory of the demand for money. Be that as it may, however, Friedman went on to claim that his demand for money equation was a stable functional relationship defined on a limited number of empirically specifiable variables. From this claim, subsequently supported by a number of empirical studies and a massive historical survey, *A Monetary History of the United States, 1867–1960* (1963), written jointly with A. Schwartz, Friedman went on to launch what has been aptly called the 'Monetarist Counterrevolution' to Keynes.

Keynes had argued that monetary policy is relatively ineffective in stimulating economic activity. In so far as it works at all, it does so through an indirect interest rate mechanism rather than through the direct spending of money on goods. However, owing to the high elasticity of substitution between cash and bonds and the low interest-elasticity of investment demand, this indirect mechanism cannot be expected to have substantial effects. Friedman, on the other hand, argued that since money is a substitute, not just for bonds, but also for a wide range of goods and services, changes in the quantity of money will spill over into the market for consumer and producer goods, adding a direct effect on spending to the indirect effect on investment. Since the linkages connecting money to spending are numerous, the full impact of a monetary change is likely to be transmitted to prices and nominal incomes. In short, since the link between money and nominal income is strong and relatively stable, the old quantity theory view that changes in the money stock will always have a powerful impact on economic activity is rehabilitated.

There is much more to monetarism than this. So far we have only recorded the first phase of the monetarist counterattack on Keynesian economics. But Phases II and III are better postponed until we have looked at Keynes.

READER'S GUIDE TO WICKSELL'S 'LECTURES', VOLUME II

The presentation of Wicksell's own monetary theory is squeezed in between long sections on earlier monetary theory, monetary history and various currency systems. This is true both of the presentation in *Interest and Prices* and in the *Lectures*. The latter, however, took into account some of the criticisms that the earlier volume had received. In the last year of his life, Wicksell made further concessions in an article with the title 'The Monetary Problem of Scandinavian Countries', appended to the English edition of *Interest and Prices*.

11. Velocity

The second volume of the *Lectures* opens with an excellent introduction on the various functions of money. Wicksell assumes that the money system is a 'properly functioning one': savings are immediately converted into investment via the intermediary activity of banks and there is no hoarding of coins or bank notes. The second chapter, containing historical material, may be passed over without much loss. **Chapter 3** takes up the crucial problem of the demand for cash balances as reflected in the magnitude of V. Given the quantity of money, 'the average period of idleness', k, is the reciprocal of V, the transactions velocity of money. The determination of V presents profound problems, Wicksell notes, because it varies with the payment habits and the degree of vertical integration in an economy. The motives for holding cash consist of transactions and precautionary motives (page 71). The use of credit amounts to a 'virtual' transfer of currency; credit increases the transactions velocity of a given stock of money (page 67). In a 'pure cash economy', V would be an institutional constant and the rigid quantity theory of money would hold without qualification. But with the introduction of credit, V becomes a function of economic variables governing the degree of liquidity preference.

The evolution of banking institutions is pictured in terms of the progressive substitution of credit for metallic currency (pages 71–87). Ultimately, this leads to the 'ideal bank', the case of a 'pure credit system': all money is in the form of demand deposits and bank notes (pages 84–7). There is no longer any danger of an internal drain from credit expansion and the banks can bring about any specified price level by an appropriate discount policy. One difficulty of the pure credit system is the need for gold in international settlements. This leads Wicksell to a discussion of banking policy under gold standard conditions (pages 91–122). The statement of the 'characteristic features' of the modern banking system (page 80) does not mention the power to 'create' deposits but Wicksell nevertheless seems to be aware of the phenomenon (see pages 86–7). Wicksell fails to distinguish between one bank, which cannot 'create' deposits unless they are backed by excess reserves, and all banks, which can together 'create' unbacked deposits. This crucial distinction appears in some of the older literature but was not forcefully brought home to the profession until the publication of Phillips' *Bank Credit* (1920) [see chapter 11, section 41].

12. The Demand Curve for Money

The traditional problems of index number theory are discussed in the opening pages of chapter 4. Next, Wicksell proceeds to a masterful defense of the quantity theory of money, considered as a long-run proposition about the proportionality of money and prices. In holding that the exchange value of money varies inversely with its quantity, quantity theorists, he notes, assume that the market equilibrium curve is a rectangular hyperbola (page 142). Wicksell does not make the mistake of supposing, as did Marshall and Pigou, that the demand curve for paper money or for gold in its monetary use is a rectangular hyperbola. Wicksell's curve varies both the amount of money and the level of prices; it is a locus of the observed intersections of the demand and supply curves of money [see chapter 5, section 7]. The reason that the demand curve for money has less than unitary elasticity is, of course, that the typical individual will reduce his nominal money balances to buy more goods when prices fall at given levels of real income. This is the Real Balance Effect, which Wicksell states in so many words (pages 142–3).

Marshall and Pigou confused the curve along which money balances and prices are always in equilibrium with the true demand schedule for cash balances: as Pigou put it in his *Essays in Applied Economics* (1923), 'an increase in the supply of legal tender ought always, since the elasticity of demand [for legal tender] is equal to unity, to raise prices in the proportion in which the supply has increased'. This confusion may well be due to the fact that they always placed price on the vertical axis irrespective of whether it was the dependent or the independent variable in the argument. Wicksell, who always followed the traditional mathematical practice of measuring the independent variable on the horizontal axis, was less likely to become confused between individual and market demand schedules, price being an independent variable in the first case and a dependent variable in the second.

The proposition that market demand curves for money are necessarily rectangular hyperbolas is tantamount to postulating the rigid quantity theory. It amounts to saying that T/V is always a constant and hence sets up the identity $MV \equiv PT$. The point of the real balance effect is to show that the public's desire to 'hoard' at a given money supply is not the same regardless of the level of prices and the rate of interest. As Wicksell justly observes: 'It will be readily seen that the whole dispute [about the quantity theory] turns ultimately on this last point: whether the velocity of circulation of money is of an autonomous or merely subordinate significance for the currency system' (pages 143–4).

It is worth quoting a passage from *Interest and Prices* in which the Real Balance Effect is more clearly stated than anywhere in the *Lectures*: 'Now let us suppose that for some reason . . . the stock of money is diminished while prices remain temporarily unchanged. The cash balances will gradually appear to be *too small in relation to the new level of prices* . . . I therefore seek to enlarge my balance. This can only be done – neglecting for the present the possibility of borrowing, etc. – through a *reduction* in my *demand* for goods and services, or through an *increase* in the *supply* of my own commodity (forthcoming either earlier or at a lower price than would otherwise have been the case), or through both together. The same is true for all other owners and consumers of commodities. But in fact nobody will succeed in realizing the object at which each is aiming – to increase his cash balance; for the sum of individual cash balances is limited by the amount of the available stock of money, or rather is identical with it. On the other hand, the universal reduction in demand and increase in supply of commodities will necessarily bring about a continuous fall in all prices. This can only cease when prices have fallen to the level at which the cash balances are regarded as *adequate*'. (pages 39–40).

Similar passages could be quoted from Fisher's *Purchasing Power of Money*, Marshall's *Money, Credit and Commerce*, and Pigou's *Essays in Applied Economics*.

13. The Direct and Indirect Mechanism
The difficulties of testing the quantity theory of money are briefly discussed (pages 144–5). There is a mention of Cassel's 'Law of 3 per cent': using 1850–1910 data,

Cassel argued that the annual increase in the stock of gold must be of the order of 3 percent to keep prices stable (page 145). Cassel's method of analysis has been much criticized: it was shown subsequently that there was little if any correlation in the last half of the 19th century between the rate of increase in the supply of gold and the rate of expansion in bank notes and deposits.

Under a gold standard, Wicksell agrees, the relative cost of producing the monetary metal determines the supply of money. International price levels are governed by the comparative 'cost of obtaining gold' (pages 146–8). Contrary to Marx's belief, a commodity theory of money is perfectly compatible with the quantity theory (page 149). But the dangers of the commodity theory are the tendency to overlook *V* or to regard it as a purely passive variable (pages 149–51) and the failure to explain the value of an inconvertible currency (pages 151–2). Absolute prices cannot be explained by propositions about relative prices (pages 154–5). Ricardo showed that a rise of wages in all industries, including the gold industry, cannot raise absolute prices but merely alters relative shares (pages 156–7). The classical proposition that a 'higher standard of living' implies higher absolute prices, inasmuch as the higher standard suggests a greater efficiency in 'obtaining gold', must be qualified by the nature of imports and exports and by transport costs (pages 157–8). A general rise in prices implies excess demand for money or excess supply of commodities. 'This may sound paradoxical', Wicksell comments, in the light of Say's Law. But Say's Law refers only to the 'ultimate' state of equilibrium (page 159). 'Any theory of money worthy of the name must be able to show how and why the monetary or pecuniary demand for goods exceeds or falls short of the supply of goods in given conditions' (page 160). Notice the recognition of the Real Balance Effect in the reference to Hume's exposition of the 'direct mechanism' (pages 160–1).

The effect of the discovery of new gold fields is brilliantly analyzed (pages 161–4). The gold-mining country will incur an import surplus through an upswing in activity, which will tend to distribute gold to the rest of the world. Prices will rise in the gold-receiving countries and, in consequence, the demand for investable funds as well as the real rate of return on investment will rise in these countries. If the banks are 'fully loaned up' before the gold discoveries, they will now find it necessary to raise the bank rate. Not only will the rise in prices precede the rise in the rate of interest, it may even precede the increase in the money supply. Since the gold producers import on credit, the increased demand for imports may raise prices everywhere before gold has actually started to flow between countries. Once prices and interest rates have risen, the subsequent arrival of gold merely serves to keep prices up (pages 164–5; see also pages 197–8, 215). For such transitional periods, Tooke's objection that periods of rising prices are periods of rising not falling interest rates, and that the rise in prices generally precedes the increase in the money supply, is sustained. Nevertheless, in the long run, the increase in the money stock is accompanied by a secular decline in interest rates. Notice the passing comment on the distinction between the nominal and the real rate of interest (page 168).

The reliance on convertibility as a check to excessive note issue constitutes the essence of the 'currency principle' (page 171). As has been so often pointed out, this ignores the possibility of expanding credit through checking deposits (page 172). The 'banking principle', on the other hand, leans heavily on the discredited real bills doctrine (page 173). Tooke's contraquantity theory, with its distinction between note issue against government bonds and note issue against commercial loans, is disputed (pages 173–4). J. S. Mill argued correctly that restriction of discounts to 'real' bills would not ensure stability in either the quantity of money or the volume of credit (pages 174–5).

14. The Two Rates

The concept of a divergence between the market and the 'natural' rate of interest is now introduced by way of discussion of Ricardo's and Tooke's monetary doctrines. Wicksell shows how Ricardo's preoccupation with the causes of the premium of bullion over paper, as well as the existence of the Usury Laws, stood in his way in analyzing the relationship between the interest rate and the price level (pages 176–82. Tooke's stress on the cost aspects of interest at the expense of every other consideration led him to absurdities: the money market turns out always to be in unstable equilibrium (pages 182–7). Notice the assumption that the elasticity of expectations is 'normally' unity (page 185). Now we are ready for the 'positive solution'. The money rate of interest is at its 'normal' or 'natural' rate if it corresponds to the rate of return on real capital, equates the supply and demand for real savings, and is neutral in its effect on the price level (pages 192–3). All this assumes full employment of resources (page 195). As long as bank credit is perfectly elastic, any divergence of the market rate from the real rate brings about a cumulative process (pages 196–7). The only limit to the process is an internal and perhaps also an external drain (pages 198, 200–1). If the banks lower the market rate, the rise in prices may be arrested by forced saving; but forced saving will have to outweigh the reduction in voluntary saving caused by the decline in the market rate of interest (page 199). Davidson's objection that price stabilization may throttle growth is obscurely contested (page 199).

Now, finally, Wicksell resolves the Gibson Paradox. All variations in the level of prices not brought about by changes in gold production have their origin in a passive bank rate trailing behind the active real rate of interest. Statistics about prices and interest rates fail to reveal the dynamics of the process (pages 202–8).

15. Business Cycles

A theory of the trade cycle involving overinvestment in the boom is sketched very tersely (pages 209–14). (Wicksell's article referred to on page 209 has now been translated under the title of 'The Enigma of the Business Cycle', reprinted in *IEP*, No. 3, 1953.) It is noteworthy that Wicksell repudiates a monetary theory of the business cycle (page 209). These pages and a reading of Wicksell's article will dispel the idea that he was one of those so-called 'classical' economists who argued that price and wage flexibility would automatically banish the problem of cyclical unemployment.

16. Currency Reform

In the last pages of the book, Wicksell tries to reconcile his previous argument for internal price stabilization with the international gold standard mechanism. As long as a country is on the gold standard, its central bank is not free to stabilize internal prices irrespective of the relationship between domestic and world prices. His way out of this dilemma is the concept of an international clearings union to divorce the value of money from that of gold: the central banks of different countries must agree to redeem each other's currencies at par in their respective national currencies. Moreover, they must agree to follow a common discount policy with reference to an index of international prices (pages 119–26, 216–17, 221, 223). Significant changes in gold production under gold standard conditions are not the only causes of price movements beyond the control of banks. Countries on an inconvertible paper standard may inflate by fiat issues of paper notes or by large-scale government borrowing from the central bank (pages 166–8). The latter, as well as rapid changes in productivity, constitutes the most important causes of changes in the price level in recent decades. And it is precisely on these points that Wicksell's theory of monetary equilibrium as a guide to banking policy broke down.

NOTES ON FURTHER READING

Apart from K. Wicksell's *Lectures II* and Wicksell's *Interest and Prices*, the reader should consult the following sources to make up his mind about the quantity theory of money 'as it really was': I. Fisher, *The Purchasing Power of Money* (2nd edn, 1913, reprinted 1963), chaps. 1–8; A. Marshall, *Money, Credit and Commerce* (1923, reprinted 1960), Book I, chap. 4; A. C. Pigou, 'The Value of Money', *QJE*, 1917, reprinted in *Readings in Monetary Theory*, eds. F. A. Lutz and L.W. Mints (1951), and slightly revised as 'The Exchange Value of Legal Tender Money' in his *Essays in Applied Economics* (1923); D. H. Robertson, *Money* (1922); F. Lavington, *The Trade Cycle* (1922); and, lastly, J. M. Keynes, *A Tract on Monetary Reform* (1923), chap. 3.

There has certainly been a great deal of controversy about what really was the neoclassical theory of money. We might begin with D. Patinkin's charge that the neoclassical writers dichotomized the pricing process: *Money, Interest and Prices*, chaps. 8 and 15. Patinkin's book also contains several valuable historical notes. Note D deals with the bogey of 'circularity', which has prevented one writer after another from applying marginal utility analysis to money. Note E discusses Wicksell's monetary theory. Note F quotes Fisher on the Real Balance Effect. Note G deals with the Marshallian notion that the demand curve for money has unitary elasticity. Note H dissects the third book of G. Cassel's *Theory of Social Economy* (1918), a notorious example of dichotomization, and Note J demonstrates the awareness of both classical and neoclassical economists of the permanent influence of a monetary change on the rate of interest via forced saving. P. A. Samuelson, 'What Classical and Neoclassical Monetary Theory Really Was', *CJE*, 1968, reprinted in *The Scientific Papers of Paul A. Samuelson*, III; D. Patinkin, 'Reflections on the Neoclassical Dichotomy', *ibid.*, 1972, reprinted in his *Essays On and In the Chicago Tradition* (1981); and a reply by P. A. Samuelson, *ibid.*, May, 1972, remind us of the difference between literary and mathematical statements of economic propositions: mathematical versions of the quantity theory in Divisia, Cassel and Fisher do dichotomize the pricing process but the literary statements of the theory in Marshall, Fisher, Pigou and Robertson are much less guilty on this score. See also R. Clower, 'What Traditional Monetary Theory Really Wasn't', *ibid.*, May, 1969.

In an influential essay, 'The Quantity Theory of Money – A Restatement', *Studies in the*

Quantity Theory of Money, ed. M. Friedman (1956), reprinted in *Readings in Macroeconomics*, ed. M. G. Mueller (1966 in paperback), and restated in 'Money: Quantity Theory', *IESS*, 10, reprinted in *Penguin Modern Economics Readings: Money and Banking*, ed. A. A. Walters (1973 in paperback), M. Friedman claimed that his restatement was nothing more than the University of Chicago 'oral' tradition. That claim was effectively destroyed by D. Patinkin, 'The Chicago Tradition, the Quantity Theory, and Friedman', *JMCB*, 1969, reprinted in his *Studies in Monetary Economics* (1972) and *Essays On and In the Chicago Tradition*. This splendid essay was shortly followed by three other articles by Patinkin, which together constitute a veritable monograph on 'what the neoclassical quantity theory of money really was': 'On the Short-Run Non-Neutrality of Money in the Quantity Theory', *BNQR*, March, 1972; 'Keynesian Monetary Theory and the Cambridge School', *ibid.*, June, 1972, reprinted in *Issues in Monetary Economics*, eds. H. G. Johnson and A. R. Nobay (1972); and 'Friedman on the Quantity Theory and Keynesian Economics', *JPE*, September/October, 1972. See also T. M. Humphrey, 'Role of Non-Chicago Economists in the Evolution of the Quantity Theory of Money in America, 1930–1950', *SEJ*, July, 1971, with comments and discussions, *ibid.*, January, 1973; and G. S. Tavlas, 'Some Further Observations on Monetary Economics and Non-Chicagoans', *ibid.*, April, 1976.

The fundamental content of the quantity theory is admirably expressed by Hegeland, *The Quantity Theory of Money*, chap. 10; and T. M. Humphrey, 'The Quantity Theory of Money: Its Historical Evolution and Role in Policy Debates', *ERV*, 1974, reprinted in his *Essays on Inflation*. Schumpeter's treatment covers a broader front and is particularly useful in correcting misconceptions about Fisher's version of the theory: *History of Economic Analysis*, chap. 8, pp. 1074–1122. For a brief description of the income approach to monetary theory, see Hutchison, *Review of Economic Doctrines*, chap. 21. The history of the income approach is discussed in great detail by Marget, *Theory of Prices*, I, chaps. 12–13. For a beautiful study of the growth of empirical techniques in 20th-century economics via attempts to test a simplified version of the quantity theory of money, see T. M. Humphrey, 'Empirical Tests of the Quantity Theory of Money in the United States, 1900–1930', *HOPE*, Fall, 1973. C. Chen, 'Bimetallism: Theory and Controversy in Perspective', *ibid.*, Spring, 1972, is a fascinating analysis of the issues involved in one of the greatest controversies ever to rage through the economic profession.

A summary of Wicksell's ideas in his own words is to be found in 'The Influence of the Rate of Interest on Prices', *EJ*, 1907, reprinted in *ETHA*. Keynes pays tribute to Wicksell in a famous chapter of the *Treatise on Money* (1930), entitled 'The "Modus Operandi" of the Bank Rate'. For a typical example of the development of Wicksell's ideas into a monetary overinvestment theory of business cycles, see G. Cassel, 'The Rate of Interest, the Bank Rate, and the Stabilization of Prices', *QJE*, 1928, reprinted in the Lutz-Mints *Readings in Monetary Theory*. Marget, *Theory of Prices*, I, chaps. 7–9, provides *inter alia* a detailed analysis of the various meanings assignable to the concept of the 'natural' rate of interest. The publication of G. Myrdal's *Monetary Equilibrium* (1939) gave rise to a reexamination of Wicksell's criteria of monetary equilibrium; see, in particular, T. Palander, 'On the Concepts and Methods of the Stockholm School', *ET*, 1941, reprinted in *IEP*, No. 3, 1953, a brilliant critique of the operational significance of Wicksell's theory for practical monetary policy. See also T. M. Humphrey, 'Interest Rates, Expectations, and the Wicksellian Policy Rule', *ERV*, 1976, and 'The Interest Cost-Push Controversy', *ERV*, 1979, both reprinted in his *Essays on Inflation*; R. V. Eagly, 'A Wicksellian Monetary Model', *SJPE*, June, 1966; and Hicks's marvellously succinct statement of the indeterminacy of the absolute prices in Wicksell's model of the cumulative process: *Value and Capital*, pp. 251–4.

The evolution of Wicksell's ideas on monetary policy in the course of the debate with Davidson are traced in great detail in Uhr, *Economic Doctrines of Knut Wicksell*, chaps. 10–11. 'Explanations of the Great Depression', by such leading economists as Marshall, Wicksell, Fisher and Cassel are canvassed by W. W. Rostow, *British Economy of the Nineteenth Century* (1948). We chose Wicksell to expound neoclassical monetary theory. We might equally well have chosen Marshall. In a useful book, *From Marshall to Keynes. An Essay on the Monetary*

Theory of the Cambridge School (1963 in paperback), E. Eshag demonstrates that all of Marshall's ideas on money go back to Thornton, Ricardo and Mill; even his theory of interest is thoroughly classical. The book succeeds better than most in tracing the gradual emergence of saving-investment analysis in the monetary writings of Marshall's pupils.

The present status of the theory of the demand for money is canvassed by D. E. W. Laidler, *The Demand for Money: Theories and Evidence* (2nd edn. 1976 in paperback); and T. M. Humphrey, 'Evolution of the Concept of the Demand for Money', *ERV*, 1973, reprinted in his *Essays on Inflation*. J. R. Hicks's seminal article, 'A Suggestion for Simplifying the Theory of Money', *Ec.*, 1935, is reprinted in his *Critical Essays in Monetary Theory* (1967) and *Money, Interest and Wages. Collected Essays on Economic Theory*, II (1982).

Nothing proves the arrival of a new appealing doctrine so clearly as the hunt among historians of economic thought for forerunners and predecessors. Thus, we are not surprised that the monetarist counterrevolution has produced a rash of historical articles. For example, G. S. Tavlas, 'Some Initial Formulations of the Monetary Growth-Rate Rule', *HOPE*, Winter, 1977; W. R. Allen, 'Irving Fisher, F. D. R., and The Great Depression', *ibid.*; G. Garvy, 'Carl Snyder, Pioneer Economic Statistician and Monetarist', *ibid.*, Fall, 1978; T. F. Cargill, 'Clark Warburton and the Development of Monetarism Since the Great Depression', *ibid.*, Fall, 1979; P. B. Trescott, 'Discovery of the Money-Income Relationship in the United States, 1921–1944', *ibid.*, Spring, 1982; and G. S. Tavlas, 'Notes on Garvy, Snyder and the Doctrinal Foundations of Monetarism', *ibid*. But all these are topped by T. Mayer, 'David Hume and Monetarism', *QJE*, August, 1980: of the twelve elements that he identifies as characterizing modern monetarism, Mayer finds five of them stated explicitly in Hume's writings.

For a critical review of Friedman's work on the history of money in the USA, see J. Tobin, 'A Monetary Interpretation of History (A Review Article)', *AER*, 1965, reprinted in J. Tobin, *Essays in Economics, Part I: Macroeconomics* (1971). See also P. Temin, *Did Monetary Factors Cause the Depression?* (1976), a rebuttal of the positive answers to that question offered by Friedman. A very useful paper on Friedman's monetarism, stressing the continuity with the 19th-century quantity theory of money, is J. H. Wood, 'The Economics of Professor Friedman', *Essays in Contemporary Fields in Economics*, eds. G. Horwich and J. P. Quirk (1981).

16

Macroeconomics

THE KEYNESIAN SYSTEM

The evolution of the quantity theory of money, particularly in it Wicksellian version, led naturally to a consideration of the role of saving and investment in the determination of national income. This idea in fact makes its appearance in a number of monetary economists writing in the 1920s in particular Dennis Robertson's *Banking Policy and the Price Level* (1926) and Keynes's *Treatise on Money* (1930). Nevertheless, in all these works the focus of attention is still that of the determination of prices, not national income, and the key price that is said to equilibrate saving and investment is the rate of interest. What marks the break in Keynes' thinking between the *Treatise* and the *General Theory* (1936) is, firstly, the switch from prices to real output as the central variable to be explained and, secondly, the entirely novel suggestion that it is variations in output or income rather than variations in the rate of interest that work to equate saving to investment. With it came the equally novel idea that it is investment and not saving that sparks off changes in income: instead of starting with the public's willingness to save and then showing how investment adapts itself to saving via the interest rate, Keynes posited a largely autonomous flow of investment and shows how savings will be generated via the multiplier to satisfy that level of investment.

But even these theoretical innovations would not have added up to the Keynesian Revolution without the proposition that the equilibrium level of income which equates saving to investment is not necessarily the level of income which secures full employment. The idea that the competitive process continually drives the economy back towards a steady state of full employment whenever it falls below the full-capacity utilization of the capital stock permeated all macroeconomic thinking before Keynes. Indeed, it was so widely held that it was frequently implied rather than argued explicitly. If there is anything profoundly new in Keynes it is this deliberate assault on the faith in the inherent recuperative powers of the market mechanism. Once having read Keynes, one might deny every separate element in his reasoning, and even the logical consistency of the entire Keynesian schema, but one could not continue to believe in the automatic tendency of the free market economy to generate full employment. There were those who thought that Keynes had failed to make the case in theoretical terms but even they agreed that he had proved his point as a matter of practice. In either case, the Keynesian Revolution marked the true end of the 'doctrine of laissez faire'.

Moreover, this was a genuine revolution in economic thought: a sudden and amazingly rapid transformation in a whole body of theoretical ideas, including the metaphysical 'vision' of the economic process from which all theorizing begins. And it was not just a revolution in thinking about economic policy, namely, the notion that governments can cure depression and unemployment by discretionary spending and taxation – for there was nothing new in that – but a revolution in the theory that lay behind such recommendations. This is not to say that all the precise features of that theory gained immediate consent. On the contrary, the first printing of the *General Theory* was hardly exhausted before the arguments about the details of Keynes's message had begun – and they have never ceased since. What soon happened to Keynes is precisely what happened to Ricardo and Marx and Walras and Marshall: he was dissected, interpreted, reinterpreted, standardized, simplified, reduced to graphs and alternative mathematical models of Keynes I, Keynes II, etcetera, becoming in the process someone that everybody quotes but no one actually reads.

The content of the *General Theory* provided all the ammunition for such quarrels about what Keynes 'really' meant. Like the treatises of Ricardo, Marx, Walras and Marshall, the *General Theory* was an ambiguous and undigested book, full of digressions and undeveloped themes, running in all directions. In Samuelson's golden words: 'the *General Theory* . . . is a badly written book, poorly organized . . . It abounds in mares' nests and confusions . . . In it the Keynesian system stands out indistinctly . . . Flashes of insight and intuition intersperse tedious algebra. An awkward definition suddenly gives way to an unforgettable cadenza. When it is finally mastered, we find its analysis to be obvious and at the same time new. In short, it is a work of genius'.

1. The Hicks-Hansen Income-Expenditure Model

The first and still most widely accepted interpretation of Keynes's meaning is the so-called 'income-expenditure model' associated with the names of John Hicks and Alvin Hansen. Hicks' 1937 article on 'Mr Keynes and the "Classics"' set the pattern by inventing the *IS-LM* diagram as a representation of the essence of Keynesian economics. But this diagram contains no reference to the labour market and yet other commentators found the heart of the Keynesian system to lie in Keynes's redefinition of the labour supply function. It was Hansen, spurred on perhaps by Franco Modigliani's influential paper, 'Liquidity Preference and the Theory of Interest and Money' (1944), who more than anyone else popularized the income-expenditure conception of the Keynesian system, incorporating the famous *IS-LM* diagram but adding labour demand and supply equations. If we ignore the government sector and the complications of the balance of payments, this Hicks-Hansen model of Keynes can be represented by five equations:

The income function: $Y = C(Y,r) + I(Y,r)$. (1)

The demand for real balances: $D_n = L(Y,r)$. (2)

The aggregate production function: $Y = f(N)$ with $f'(N) > 0$ and $f''(N) < 0$. (3)

The demand for labour: $f'(N) = F\left(\dfrac{w}{p}\right)$. (4)

The supply of labour: $N = N\left(\dfrac{w}{p}\right)$ when $w \geq w'$. (5)

Y has hitherto referred to total money income. It will simplify the notation in this chapter if we now let it stand for the net national product at constant prices or total money income divided by a price index of goods and services entering into NNP. We have used C before to mean fixed capital. But traditional usage demands that we use it now for real consumption. All the other variables have the same meanings as before. labour is the only variable factor of production and the labour demand schedule is derived by taking the first derivative of the aggregate production function. The demand and the supply of labour are functions of the _real_ wage rate, and indeed all the equations are functions of 'real' values; the proviso 'if $w \geq w'$' will be explained in the course of our argument.

Figure 16–1

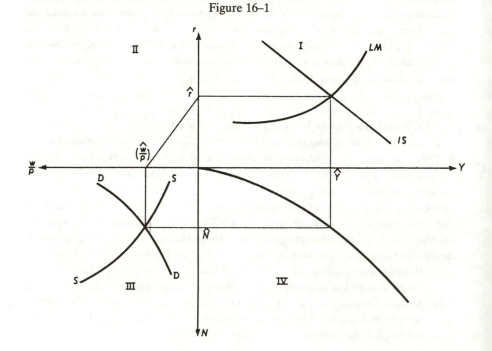

The entire model is depicted in Figure 16–1, where $\hat{N}$, $\hat{Y}$, $\hat{r}$, etc., refer to the full employment values of variables. Beginning with equation (3), the aggregate production function appears in quadrant IV. Quadrant III plots equations (4) and (5), which together determine the level of employment and the real wage rate at full employment levels. Quadrant II gives the ratio of the interest rate to the wage rate. The figure in quadrant I is the Hicks-Hansen diagram of monetary equilibrium in the Keynesian system. This *IS* curve in quadrant I represents equation (1) and shows the relationship between the rate of interest and the equilibrium level of income as determined by the equality of planned saving and planned investment – more of this anon. Given the money supply, an exogenous variable determined by the monetary authorities, equation (2) in quadrant I is represented by the *LM* curve and depicts the equilibrium relationship between the demand and supply of money at the prevailing price level. The heart of the Keynesian system is tucked away behind these last two schedules. Before we can make use of our diagrammatic construction, therefore, we must be certain that we grasp why the *IS* and *LM* curves have the shapes and slopes that they have.

According to the income function (1), saving as well as investment is a function of both Y and r. Keynes himself, however, viewed saving solely as a function of income and investment solely as a function of the rate of interest. However, the more general form of our income function is capable of producing Keynesian conclusions, as we shall see, provided saving is more responsive to variations in income than to variations in the interest rate, and provided the exact opposite is true of investment. We therefore draw the investment function as steeply inclined with respect to r in the upper left-hand panel and as gently inclined with respect to Y in the lower right-hand panel of Figure 16–2. We add to I the consumption function, depicted for convenience as a linear relationship, taking the form $C = a + bY$, in which the intercept a and the slope of the line b, the marginal propensity to consume, are both taken as positive constants. The saving function is derived from the consumption function by subtracting the consumption function from the 45° line, which represents Keynes' aggregate supply function. $C + I$ represents Keynes' aggregate demand function and the intersection of the two functions yields Y_e, the equilibrium level of income.

Given the rate of interest, there is a level of income that will equate planned saving to planned investment. Therefore, the Hicks-Hansen *IS* curve is simply the locus of all possible combinations of r and Y that are consistent with the equality of planned saving and planned investment.

The verbal explanation of the negative slope of the *IS* curve is that when the rate of interest is high, investment is low; if investment is low, so is income in consequence of the multiplier; with income low, saving is low. On the other hand, high income levels yield high saving levels; the interest rate must then be low to produce an equivalent amount of planned investment.

We turn now to the positive slope of the *LM* curve. Keynes decomposed the demand curve for money into $D_n = L_1(Y) + L_2(r)$, where $L_1(Y)$ represents the demand for transactions and precautionary balances and $L_2(r)$ represents the demand for speculative balances. The desire to hold money in order to speculate in

Figure 16–2

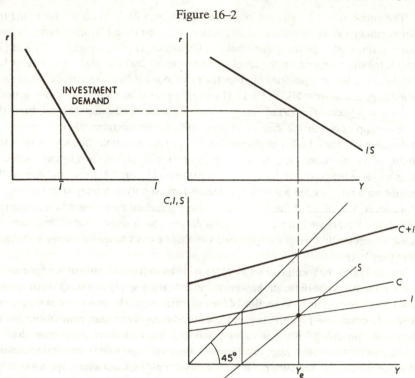

bond markets is alleged to be the only source of the interest-elasticity of the money demand function. Active balances to finance foreseen transactions and to provide a precautionary reserve against unforeseen discrepancies between receipts and expenditures vary solely with the level of money income. It is the speculative demand for inactive balances that alone creates a link between the demand for money and the interest rate.

Keynes's argument goes like this: at any time there exists a concept of a 'normal' rate of interest; a change in the current market rate of interest is not believed to mean an equivalent change in the expected future rate; in other words, the elasticity of expectations of the interest rate is typically less than unity. Given each wealth-owner's idea of the 'normal' rate, a high current rate of interest discourages cash holding and encourages bond holding, not just because of the high opportunity cost of holding cash but also because of the negligible risk of capital losses through a further rise in the rate of interest and, hence, a further fall in the price of bonds. Likewise, a decline in the rate of interest increases the risk of capital losses on bond holdings by increasing the probability of a subsequent rise and therefore encourages a shift out of bonds into money; at very low interest rates and high bond prices, almost everyone will expect a rise in the rate of interest and will therefore prefer to hold cash. This is the essence of Keynes's speculative demand for money.

Figure 16–3

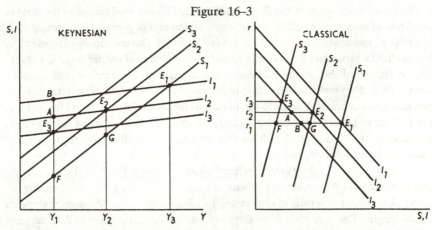

Given the supply of money, the Keynesian money demand function implies that monetary equilibrium will always involve a definite relationship between Y and r. Thus, in Figure 16–3a, we draw a family of Keynesian demand curves for money, each curve corresponding to a given level of income. Given the money stock and the price level, we can then derive the LM curve, showing all the possible combinations r and Y that make the public willing to hold the stock of money in existence (see Figure 16–3). Rising income levels are associated with higher interest rates at each price level because as income rises, the transactions and precautionary demand for money increases, leaving less of the fixed real money supply to satisfy the speculative demand for idle balances; hence, the rate of interest must rise to choke off speculative demand.

Figure 16–4

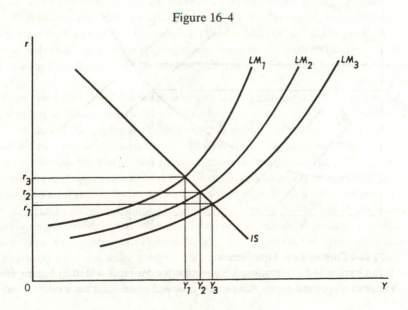

The intersection point of the *IS* and *LM* curves (Figure 16–4) satisfies the double condition of monetary equilibrium: planned saving equals planned investment and, in addition, the desired amount of money is equal to the actual supply of money. As long as the *IS* curve cuts the *LM* curve from above, this equilibrium point is a stable one. A rightward shift to the *LM* curve is due either to an increase in the money supply or a downward shift in the underlying liquidity preference schedule, or possibly a fall in prices. Owing to the nature of the speculative demand for money, the *LM* curve becomes increasingly elastic at lower rates of interest. Thus, equal increases in the money stock will lead to successively smaller reductions in *r* and successively smaller increases in *Y*.

A rightward shift in the *IS* curve reflects either an upward shift in the underlying investment demand function or a downward shift in the saving function (see Figure 16–5). A reduced propensity to save raises the *IS* curve by a uniform amount along its whole length. This will raise *Y* moderately and *r* substantially if the *LM* curve is inelastic; if the *LM* curve is elastic, it will on the contrary raise *Y* substantially and *r* slightly. In verbal terms: a reduced propensity to save raises income through an increased demand for consumer goods, leading to further increases in consumption and investment via the multiplier. A larger amount of money is now tied up in transactions and precautionary balances, diverting funds from speculative balances through a rise in the rate of interest. How far the rate of interest will have to rise to bring the demand for money into equality with the unchanged supply of money depends on the elasticity of the L_2 curve.

Figure 16–5

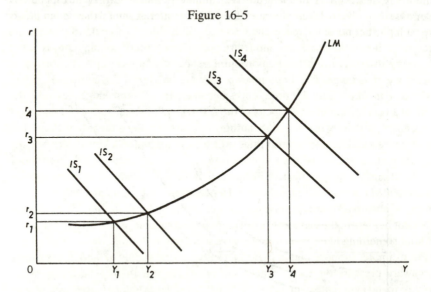

2. Full Employment Equilibrium

We come back now to our original Keynesian model represented in Figure 16–1. With flexible wages and prices, full employment will be automatically maintained. If real wages exceed ($\hat{w}/p$), money wages will fall due to the excess supply of labour. This reduces costs and lowers prices, thus increasing the real value of cash balances. This in turn shifts the *LM* curve to the right by releasing active balances to satisfy the demand for inactive balances, lowering r and expanding investment demand until the output corresponding to full employment has been absorbed. Abstracting entirely from the dynamic effects of falling prices, it follows that income is established at the full employment level in the labour market, the interest rate then equates saving and investment on the *IS* curve at this income level, and, finally, the price level adjusts so as to satisfy liquidity requirements at this rate of interest.

This argument so far is entirely in the neoclassical tradition. The rate of interest is determined solely by the saving-investment process, independently of monetary forces. Monetary forces serve to determine, not the rate of interest, but the level of prices and an increase in the quantity of money has no lasting effect on real income and employment. We now introduce the three Keynesian specifics that make possible an 'unemployment equilibrium': (1) the 'liquidity trap', (2) the low interest-elasticity of investment, and (3) the stickiness of money wages.

3. The Liquidity Trap

Keynes suggested that liquidity preferences may become satiated in a severe depression when shrinking income has reduced the transactions and precautionary demand for money-to-hold and monetary policy has already pushed down the interest rate and thus encouraged the holding of cash for speculative motives. The liquidity preference schedule now becomes infinitely elastic owing to the unanimous expectation of investors that the rate of interest cannot fall any further; bond prices are so high that no one expects them to rise still higher. Consequently, everyone prefers to 'hoard' idle cash and monetary policy is put out of commission. It is not necessary to assume that the liquidity preference schedule is perfectly horizontal over some of its range. The 'liquidity trap' (Robertson's term; Keynes himself called it the case in which liquidity preferences become 'virtually absolute') may take the form of a very high interest elasticity of the *LM* schedule. Open market purchases of government bonds by the monetary authorities can push down the interest rate, but only minute reductions in interest rates suffice to induce individuals to hold virtually any amount of additional cash injected into the system. Increases in the money supply, therefore, are ineffective in reducing interest rates and thus in stimulating investment via the interest rate channel. Hence, even if the monetary authorities are willing to absorb all bonds in private hands in exchange for cash, thus becoming the sole debt holders in the economy, a full employment income level cannot be reached without something like the 'comprehensive socialisation of investment'.

For example, suppose that at (w/p) there is an excess supply of labour, exerting a downward pressure on money wages and prices (Figure 16–6). The fall in prices would expand aggregate demand by shifting the *LM* curve to the right, thus lowering the rate of interest, which in turn would cause an upward shift in the *IS* curve. But the *IS* curve cannot shift *IŜ* because the low interest elasticity of the *LM* schedule prevents r from falling. With *IS*, the rate of interest required to equate planned

Figure 16–6

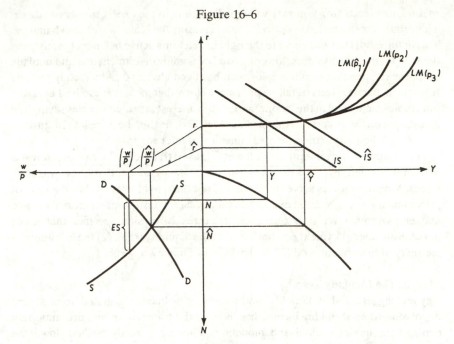

saving and investment at the full employment level of income $\hat{Y}$ is $\hat{r}$ and that is less than the prevailing r. The result is that Y and N are prevented from rising to the level $\hat{Y}$ and $\hat{N}$ by inadequate demand. The real wage will stay put at level $(w/p) > (\hat{w}/p)$. Competition for employment will reduce money wages, costs and prices but the falling price level, while increasing the quantity of money in real terms, has no influence on the rate of interest and hence cannot stimulate investment demand. The system is in equilibrium at less than full employment.

4. Interest-Inelastic Investment Demand
We have drawn the *IS* curve as a straight line. It is reasonable to assume, however, that investment demand becomes increasingly unresponsive to a falling rate of interest. Hence, whatever is assumed about the elasticity of the *LM* curve, full employment may not be achievable and the reader can write his own version of the argument (see Figure 16–7). If the *IS* curve becomes perfectly inelastic, falling wages and prices would merely reduce the rate of interest without expanding income in any way. Another possibility is that a negative rate of interest is required to equate investment to full-employment savings; the *IS* curve cuts the income axis to the left of the income level corresponding to full employment. As long as it costs nothing to hold money, the money rate of interest cannot become negative. Hence, the *LM* schedule has a floor at a zero rate of interest. In consequence, the *IS* and *LM* curves can never intersect at a full employment income level. Once again, the only kind of equilibrium possible is unemployment equilibrium.

Figure 16–7

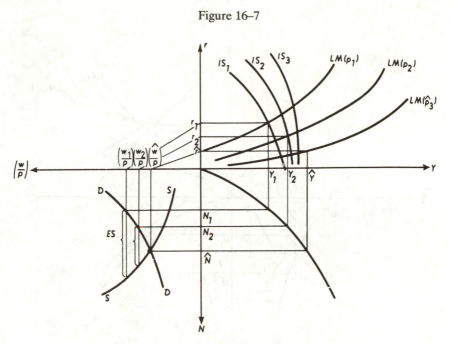

5. Wage Rigidities

Keynes is supposed to have assumed that money wages are rigid downward because workers are subject to a 'money illusion': they are not willing to work at reduced money wages but they are willing to work at lower real wages brought about by a rise in prices. The supply of labour thus depends in effect on nominal and not on real wages; hence, the proviso 'when $w \geq w''$ to equation (5) of our neo-Keynesian income-determination model [see above, section 1].

Powerful trade unions or minimum wage laws will do just as well as a 'money illusion' in the labour supply function to account for the downward rigidity of money wages at w' (see Figure 16–8). The labour supply function in effect becomes perfectly elastic at w': although the labour market is in equilibrium because the real wage rate (w'/p_1) is equal to the marginal product of labour at A, while the marginal utility of the real wage is equal to the marginal disutility of labour at B, there is 'involuntary unemployment' $= ES$. In order to achieve full employment, we need a lower real wage, which implies a rise of the price level from p_1 to $\hat{p}$. But a higher level of prices would push the LM curve to the left and thus aggravate the situation. Hence, full employment cannot be achieved despite the fact that the initial situation is one of unemployment *equilibrium*. If output and employment are at Y_2 and N_2 with a price level p_1 to establish the real wage rate appropriate to N_2, the LM curve will be at the equilibrium level $LM(p_1)$ but $Y_2 < \hat{Y}$, $N_2 < \hat{N}$, and $r_2 > \hat{r}$.

Figure 16–8

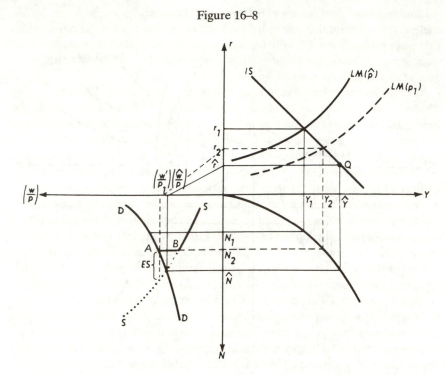

6. Unemployment Equilibrium

The essence of the Keynesian argument is the possibility of 'unemployment equilibrium': the demonstration that there exists no mechanism in a competitive economy that guarantees full employment. We have cited three Keynesian specifics that will produce this result. Just which of these did Keynes himself emphasize? It is strange that this very simple question has been answered by commentators in many different ways. According to Hicks's famous 1937 article on 'Mr. Keynes and the "Classics"', the Keynesian demonstration of unemployment equilibrium consists fundamentally of certain arguments about the shapes of the relevant functions: the liquidity preference schedule is too interest-elastic and the investment schedule is too interest-inelastic to permit a fall in the rate of interest to generate full employment; this is 'Mr. Keynes's *special* theory'. This is fair enough, inasmuch as this is precisely how Keynes himself sums up his argument in chapter 18 of his book, 'The General Theory of Employment Restated', a chapter which *precedes* the discussion of the alleged inflexibility of money wages.

Other commentators, however, argue that Keynes 'proved' the possibility of *competitive* unemployment equilibrium by virtue of the assumption that money wages are rigid downward. But if this were all there was to Keynes, it would hardly warrant a break with neoclassical economics: Pigou's *Industrial Fluctuations* (1927) has a chapter on 'The Part Played by Rigidity in Wage-Rates', asserting that institutional wage rigidities are perfectly capable of causing unemployment. Nevertheless, it is apparent that one of Keynes's intentions was to deny the presumption that wage cutting, even if it were feasible, would increase effective demand and he worked hard to show that his neoclassical predecessors had in fact advocated wage cutting as a remedy for unemployment.

Keynes's argument on the economics of wage cutting in chapter 19 of the *General Theory*, entitled 'Changes in Money-Wages', went something like this: (1) the demand for labour and the level of employment is indeed determined by real wages, not money wages, exactly as we were taught by neoclassical economists; (2) a cut in money wages is always followed by an equivalent cut in real wages, since prices are competitively determined by marginal prime costs, which in the short run consist entirely of labour costs; (3) since real consumption is a unique function of real income and since the marginal propensity to consume of workers is, like everyone else's, less than unity, workers will spend less on consumption after the fall in real wages than before, possibly offset to some extent by the fact that employers will spend more; (4) although labour costs and prices have now fallen, the resulting decline in the rate of interest fails to stimulate investment, either because of the liquidity trap or because of the low interest elasticity of investment demand or because falling wages and prices generate expectations of further falls in the future; and (5) the cut in money wages in a closed economy thus leads to a fall in aggregate demand and unemployment either increases or at best remains unaffected. This is why wage cutting will not work to reduce unemployment even if it were feasible. But in addition, Keynes contended that it is not feasible because workers are unwilling to increase employment by accepting cuts in money wages. This is not so much because of 'money illusion' in the labour supply function (although Keynes certainly hints at that) but because any policy of wage cutting would necessarily affect some class of workers more than others and wage bargaining, Keynes was convinced, is essentially about *relative* rather than absolute money wages. Keynes cites this 'relative wages hypothesis' as the reason for the downward inflexibility of money wages, not just in chapter 19, but also in the opening pages of the *General Theory*, namely chapter 2 on 'The Postulates of the Classical Economics'. In short, he summed up, 'the maintenance of a stable general level of money-wages is, on a balance of considerations, the most advisable policy for a closed system; whilst the same conclusion will hold good for an open system, provided that equilibrium with the rest of the world can be secured by means of fluctuating exchanges'.

7. The Pigou Effect

In what sense does the Keynesian argument differ from the neoclassical position? The view of the 'classics' was that with flexible wages and prices, the interest rate would establish full employment equilibrium between saving and investment and between the demand and supply of money. Needless to say, if there really is 'money illusion' in the labour supply function, so that money wage cuts are resisted, full employment equilibrium may be unattainable. Provided wage cuts are possible, however, and dismissing extreme values for the elasticities of the *LM* and *IS* curves as implausible, there is always some fall in wages and prices that will both stimulate consumption by increasing the liquidity of the economy and stimulate investment by depressing the interest rate, thus driving the system towards full employment *equilibrium*. It is simply a contradiction in terms to speak of 'unemployment equilibrium'.

The neoclassical view is commonly known today as the Pigou Effect in honour of the first economist to state the principle in relation to Keynesian unemployment equilibrium. But the Pigou Effect has a venerable history and has been described in this book under the Patinkin-label of the Real Balance Effect. Since there is considerable terminological ambiguity in the literature, let us distinguish between (1) the Real Balance Effect, (2) the Pigou Effect, and (3) the Keynes Effect. The Real Balance Effect comprises both the Pigou Effect that shows up only in the *IS* curve and the Keynes Effect that shows up only in the *LM* curve. The Keynes Effect, so named because Keynes himself admitted it as a minor qualification of unemployment equilibrium, concerns the change in the demand for nominal money holdings resulting from a change in prices: since the liquidity preference function shows the demand for real cash balances, a fall in prices reduces liquidity preference in real terms and thereby increases the demand for bonds, causing the rate of interest to fall. In other words, the Keynes Effect states that falling prices will shift the *LM* curve to the right, as we mentioned before.

The Pigou Effect, on the other hand, consists of an asset effect on consumption and depends on that part of the stock of money which reflects the net indebtedness of the government; checking deposits are not relevant to the Pigou Effect because the rise in the real value of such privately held assets from a fall in prices is exactly offset by the rise in the real value of the debts owed by banks to the public. The Pigou Effect rests, therefore, on what Gurley and Shaw have called 'outside money' – gold, fiat paper money and government bonds – as distinct from 'inside money' – checking deposits – where falling wages and prices produce no net effect in the aggregate. Therefore, as wages and prices fall, the ratio of the supply of 'outside' liquid wealth to national income rises – for this reason the Pigou Effect is sometimes called the Wealth-Income Effect – until it begins to satiate the desire to save and thus to stimulate consumption; the Pigou Effect states that falling prices will shift the *IS* curve to the right. Hence, the Real Balance Effect combining both the Pigou Effect and the Keynes Effect, contends that falling wages and prices will shift both the *LM* and *IS* curves to the right until they intersect at $\hat{Y}$; even with a fairly elastic *LM* curve and a fairly inelastic *IS* curve, full employment equilibrium is in principle attainable.

At the level of abstraction of the *General Theory*, no effective reply can be given to this neoclassical argument. The Keynesian model is essentially an exercise in comparative statics with some dynamic glosses, purporting to deny the classical and neoclassical view that a competitive economy tends automatically to generate full employment. It is irrelevant to point out that money wages cannot be cut for institutional reasons and hence that the notion of flexible wages and prices is unrealistic. What Keynes wanted to demonstrate was that there can be *competitive* unemployment equilibrium and, in this context, wage rigidity is an illegitimate assumption. Keynes's theory, far from being a general theory, is really a theory of the special case: the inside-money-case in which the public does not possess a *net* monetary asset because the stock of money outstanding consists entirely of checking deposits; indeed, a Wicksellian 'pure credit economy' [see chapter 15, section 4]. Neoclassical models, on the other hand, are based on the pure outside-money-case in which the real value of the public's monetary assets varies inversely with prices. The Keynesian model can, of course, be altered so as to introduce 'outside money'. Once the Real Balance Effect is admitted, however, the Keynesian model is affected in all of its parts; consumption depends not just on current real income but also on the value of the community's real assets; the transactions and precautionary demand for money depends not just on current real income but also on the real value of the stock of liquid assets; liquidity preferences affect aggregate demand not just through investment via the interest rate but also through consumption; and, most important of all, real income is not determined independently of changes in money wages and prices. The price level now enters decisively into every argument and the first two equations of the Hicks-Hansen model [see chapter 16, section 1] would have to be rewritten as:

$$\text{The income function: } Y = C\left(Y, r, \frac{M}{p}\right) + I\left(Y, r, \frac{M}{p}\right); \tag{1}$$

$$\text{The demand for real balances: } D_n = L\left(Y, r, \frac{M}{p}\right) \tag{2}$$

where M is the money value of currency, checking deposits and government securities held by the public minus the banks' indebtedness to the public.

It is a striking fact that the *General Theory*, which purported to integrate value theory and monetary theory, to overcome the neoclassical dichotomization of the pricing process, and to redress the neoclassical overemphasis on real factors, actually ascribes an almost negligible role to money and fails to take full account of price changes and the changing value of liquid assets. In Keynes, money does not influence total spending, consumption or prices except through the rate of interest and, even so, changes in the rate of interest only affect portfolio holdings of bonds and money. Indeed, the entire burden of adjustment is thrust upon the rate of interest, and at the same time, the rate of interest is said to exert too weak an influence to accomplish all that is asked of it.

9. Keynesian Dynamics

Shall we conclude that Keynes was wrong and that his analysis of unemployment equilibrium was untenable? A Keynesian economist would no doubt agree that the self-regulating character of a market economy can be affirmed by the neoclassical Real Balance Effect. But he would deny that therefore monetary or fiscal policy is unnecessary to induce recovery. Admitting the stimulating influence of an increase in liquidity does not imply indifference toward the amount or rate of price fall necessary to achieve full employment equilibrium. The Real Balance Effect is, after all, a matter of comparative statics: it says nothing about the dynamics of a slow adjustment to gradual deflation with its undesirable distributional consequences – the bulk of liquid assets are held by the well-to-do – and its possible perverse effects on expectations. Even Pigou conceded that the Pigou Effect was of little practical importance and that the dynamic consequences of falling wages and prices on expectations made it impossible to advocate wage cutting as a remedy for depressions.

If this interpretation is accepted, the lesson the Keynesian economics teaches us is that the automatic adjustment mechanism of competition cannot be relied upon to achieve such policy objectives as full employment and price stability. Cutting wages in a slump is politically inexpedient because the relevant magnitudes suggest that the wage cut would have to be enormous; therefore, rigidity of wages is not an economic but a political phenomenon. Similarly, the liquidity trap is really a question about the practical politics of monetary policy in circumstances where the monetary authorities would find themselves absorbing all government bonds in private hands. As Patinkin has put it: 'the main message of Keynesian economics becomes that the automatic adjustment process of the market (even with the real-balance effect – and even when supplemented by monetary policy) is too unreliable to serve as a practical basis of full employment policy. In other words, though the real-balance effect must be taken account of in our *theoretical* analysis, it is too weak – and in some cases (due to adverse expectations) too perverse – to fulfil a significant role in our *policy* considerations.'

9. The Counter-revolution

We have arrived at the conclusion that the main difficulty in grasping Keynes's argument is that of distinguishing in practice between an incompleted static macro-equilibrium, on the one hand, and a protracted dynamic macrodisequilibrium, on the other. By and large, this is how economists appraised the significance of Keynes's ideas around, say, 1965. In 1968, however, the apparently endless debate on what-Keynes-really-meant received a fresh jolt. In that year, Leijonhufvud published a book with the pointed title, *On Keynesian Economics and the Economics of Keynes*, which argued that the standard Hicks-Hansen *IS-LM* diagram, which students had long been taught as a cleaned-up version of what Keynes meant to say, does justice neither to the letter nor to the spirit of the *General Theory*. More specifically, Leijonhufvud claimed that (1) Keynes' economics is not equilibrium economics; (2) Keynes assumes a world of less than perfect information, in consequence of which markets adjust to disturbances first by variations in quantities and only later by variations in prices; (3) Keynes does not assume rigid money wages but rather that all prices change only slowly; and (4) Keynes's model is essentially a two-sector model in which the basic cause of unemployment is that 'relative prices are wrong' – interest rates are too high and long-term asset prices are too low to generate full employment.

Leijonhufvud relies heavily on some earlier work by Clower involving 'the dual-decision hypothesis'. The 'dual-decision hypothesis' distinguishes 'notional' excess demand from 'effective' excess demand. Notional excess demand refers to the excess demand functions for commodities of households who can buy all they wish to buy at the final equilibrium prices announced by the Walrasian auctioneer. If the economic system fails to reach full employment equilibrium, however, some households will find that their 'notional' incomes are less than their actual incomes and they will therefore reduce their consumption expenditures to conform to the constraints imposed by their actual incomes. Excess demand functions which take this constraint into account are 'effective' excess demand functions. Only in a standard Walrasian model will both notional and effective excess demands coincide and be equal to zero. When there is considerable unemployment, the excess supply of labour at the going real wage rate is not matched by an equivalent 'effective' excess demand for goods and services because some 'notional' excess demand has been eliminated by the reallocation of expenditure reflecting the constraints of reduced incomes. These deviations from long-period equilibrium are spread throughout all markets via the multiplier process. Producers now will receive the wrong price signals, which will not necessarily induce the adjustments that lead to final equilibrium. The labour market would be cleared if money wages were reduced but such wage reductions are not communicated to employers as an increase in effective demand for output. In consequence, labour markets are cleared by adjusting employment to wages regarded as 'normal', instead of wages being adjusted to unchanged employment levels. In this way, the consumption function, which Keynes introduced as an *ad hoc* 'psychological law', becomes perfectly intelligible as an 'income-constrained process'. Once we are involved in disequilibrium trading at 'false prices', it makes perfectly good sense to think of the adjustment process as depending more on incomes than on relative prices.

A further shortcoming of the standard Hicks-Hansen model, according to Leijonhufvud, is that the standard model uses a scheme in which there are four markets (consumer goods, labour, money and bonds) and three prices (the price of consumer goods, the wage rate and the interest rate), investment goods and consumption goods being lumped together into a single output variable. But Keynes lumped together, not capital goods and consumer goods, but capital goods and bonds as a single nonmonetary asset, thus focussing attention on the rate of interest as the reciprocal of the price of this nonmonetary asset. For Keynes, full employment depends on the correct relationship between the rate of interest and the wage unit, and full employment is to be achieved by lowering the former rather than by lowering the latter. The fundamental cause of unemployment for Keynes is a long-term interest rate that is too high, and the obstacles to its reduction rest partly on institutional barriers to vigorous open market purchases of government securities.

These ideas are a far cry indeed from what has been traditionally taught as Keynesian economics. For Clower and Leijonhufvud, Keynesian economics is about incomplete and costly information, sluggish price adjustments, quantity rather than price adjustments, the dual-decision hypothesis, income-constrained processes, and false trading at nonequilibrium prices in the absence of a Walrasian auctioneer. What is crucial in neoclassical economics, they seem to be saying, is not the assumption of perfect competition but the much less widely noted assumption that all prices adjust instantaneously to clear markets – for that is what is implied by the notion of a Walrasian auctioneer. Once we get away from the rather special case of instantaneously adjusted prices, there is no longer any presumption that the work-ings of the price system will lead automatically to the elimination of shortages and surplus in all markets and thus to full employment.

10. Rereading Keynes

Although Clower and Leijonhufvud have undoubtedly marked out a promising new line of advance in macroeconomics, it is not at all obvious that they are justified in reading these ideas into the works of Keynes. On rereading the *General Theory*, one is struck by how much of what Keynes says does indeed resemble the supposedly vulgar interpretation of the Hicks-Hansen *IS-LM* apparatus, or what Leijonhufvud calls the 'income-expenditure theory'. If Keynes was really analyzing the problems of disequilibrium, why did he insist again and again on the possibility of 'unemployment *equilibrium*'? Why did he invoke such equilibrium conditions as the equality of the wage rate and the marginal product of labour in defining the concept of 'involuntary unemployment' and the equality of the marginal efficiency of capital and the rate of interest in stipulating the demand for investment? And why, on receipt of a personal copy of Hicks's 'Mr. Keynes and the "Classics"', the *fons et origo* of the standard interpretation, did Keynes find that he had 'next to nothing to say by way of criticism'?

Both Clower and Leijonhufvud invite us to interpret what they are doing as going somewhat beyond Keynes. At the same time, they suggest that Keynes must have had something like the dual-decision hypothesis 'at the back of his mind', while leaving no doubt that the *IS-LM* construction is a misinterpretation of Keynes. In Leijonhufvud's book, in particular, it is hard to tell where the economics of Keynes leaves off and the economics of Leijonhufvud begins, the more so as much of Leijonhufvud's argument rests on combining elements of Keynes's earlier *Treatise on Money* with certain brief and ambiguous passages in the *General Theory*, as if the latter were a mere continuation of the former. As a contribution to disequilibrium economics, Leijonhufvud's book is a resounding success. But as a reassessment of Keynes, it suffers from being too clever by half.

The *General Theory* is simply an untidy book – like Ricardo's *Principles*, Marx's *Capital* and Böhm-Bawerk's *Positive Theory* – that contains not one, not two, but three or four 'models' of the workings of a modern economy. For example, chapter 11 of the *General Theory*, which is concerned with the arithmetic of the marginal efficiency of capital, is followed by a self-contained essay on 'The State of Long-Term Expectations' in which the decision to invest is depicted, not as the outcome of a calculated comparison of the internal rate of return on capital projects with the market rate of interest, but as a simple result of 'animal spirits'. A year after the publication of the *General Theory*, Keynes restated 'The General Theory of Employment' in the pages of the *Quarterly Journal of Economics*, and in the first half of this statement there is an even greater emphasis on the nonprobabilistic nature of the uncertainty that pervades economic life, suggesting that investment is therefore doomed to fluctuate with business confidence in no predictable relationship to any of the standard economic variables. Some modern disciples of Keynes have seen this emphasis on uncertainty, ignorance and incalculable expectations as the essence of the Keynesian Revolution, thus ignoring the fact that Keynes goes on in the second half of the 1937 *QJE* article to underline the consumption function as one of the fundamental building blocks of his theory, implying of course that consumption and saving at any rate are stable functions of current disposable income. Nevertheless, the point is that the indeterminacy of much of economic behavior under the influence of pervasive uncertainty is one of the themes of the *General Theory*. Similarly, there are post-Keynesians who find the heart of the book in chapter 17, 'The Essential Properties of Interest and Money', in which the low elasticity of production and the nearly-zero elasticity of substitution of money for other assets is made almost the only reason for the persistence of unemployment. According to this view, Keynesian economics is necessarily monetary economics, amounting in fact to a sustained attack on the received quantity theory of money. And, to be sure, this too is one of the strands of Keynes's arguments. In short, the *General Theory* is, I think, a book with a central message, namely that saving and investment are brought into equality, not by variations in the rate of interest, but by variations in income and that aggregate equilibrium in this sense is typically achieved at income levels below those of full employment. Nevertheless, this central message of the book is surrounded by a great deal of 'noise' pointing in several different directions.

We may sum up our discussion of alternative interpretations of Keynes by invoking Coddington's useful classification of types of Keynesianisms. What we have called the Hicks-Hansen model, what Leijonhufvud calls the 'income-expenditure theory', Coddington labels 'hydraulic Keynesianism', the view that the economy must be conceived at the aggregate level in terms of homogeneous flows of receipts and expenditures with neither prices nor quantities playing a central role in the analysis. The Clower-Leijonhufvud counterrevolution, Coddington labels as 'reconstituted reductionism', meaning the attempt to get back to the pre-Keynesian idea of reducing market phenomena to the logic of individual choice with the aid of an improved specification of the constraints facing individuals. Finally, there is 'fundamentalist Keynesianism', which takes its point of departure from the opening pages of the 1937 *QJE* article. Its best known advocates are Joan Robinson and G.L.S. Shackle. This point of view rejects both reductionism and reconstituted reductionism, and of course the Hicks-Hansen model as 'bastard Keynesianism', and views Keynes's contribution to economic theory as announcing the final demise, not just of the choice-theoretic analysis of economic behavior, but of the very idea of equilibrium or disequilibrium theorizing.

11. Keynes versus the Classics

Up to this point, our discussion of Keynes has been deliberately ahistorical; we have been concerned with the way economists have tried to make sense out of Keynes ever since 1936 without much attention to time and circumstances. Keynes, however, saw himself as principally engaged in attacking a prevailing orthodoxy called 'classical' economics, which, he implied, had no other answer to the Great Depression than an easy money policy and the reduction of money wages. The gist of his own contribution, in his own eyes and in those of his immediate disciples, was to deny the efficacy of such traditional policy measures, suggesting instead that governments should practise deficit finance by spending on public works. This, and not purely theoretical arguments about assumptions or behavioral equations, was rightly or wrongly taken to be the core of the contrast between Keynesian and orthodox economics. We must now ask whether Keynes's description of neoclassical applied economics was an accurate one. That Keynes's predecessors placed much faith in monetary policy is not open to question. But it is not true that they ignored the need for compensatory public works expenditure. Nor is it true that they generally advocated wage cutting as a practical cure for unemployment. The influence of Keynes on attitudes to these policy questions was one of degree, not of kind: the upshot of Keynesian economics was to strengthen the case for public works and to place the burden of proof on anyone who would seek to remedy unemployment by depressing wages.

11. The Traditional Case for Public Works

The last three decades of the 19th century saw a remarkable diminution of interest on the part of English economists in the problem of unemployment and business cycles. It is only around the turn of the century that systematic work on business cycles begins to appear, first in Germany and France with the works of Juglar, Tugan-Baranowsky, Spiethoff and Aftalion, then in the Anglo-Saxon world with the writings of Mitchell, Hawtrey, Robertson and Pigou. The rigorous case for counter-cyclical public works was stated for the first time in the *Minority Report of the Poor Law Commission* (1909). The *Minority Report*, which was largely the work of the Webbs in association with A. L. Bowley, recommended public works expenditures when unemployment reached 4 percent of the labour force. This idea was endorsed with some qualifications by Beveridge in *Unemployment, A Problem of Industry* (1900), and elaborated by the Webbs in their book, *The Prevention of Destitution* (1911). Public works to relieve the unemployed is an idea as old as the Bible; what made the *Minority Report* a milestone in the history of the public works doctrine was that it advocated public spending to smooth out cyclical fluctuations and to stabilize total economic activity.

In *Wealth and Welfare* (1912), Pigou attacked the old classical doctrine that by increasing public construction, the state was only 'diminishing employment with one hand, while it increased it with the other'. The taxes to finance public spending, he pointed out, draw down on 'funds which would normally have been stored' or 'which would normally have been consumed by the relatively well-to-do'. He had used the same argument to show that public spending can increase aggregate employment as early as 1908 in his inaugural lecture as successor to Marshall at Cambridge. The so-called Treasury View, which he was attacking, had not been heard of since Ricardo's time – although there are faint echoes of it in Mill's *Principles* – but it was apparently being appealed to once again. Hawtrey in *Good and Bad Trade* (1913) used it to dismiss the policy proposals of the *Minority Report*. Pigou returned to the theme in *Unemployment* (1913). In considering the case of an increase in public spending matched by an increase in taxes, he said that 'it is probable that only a part of the extra taxes people pay would be taken from funds they would otherwise have devoted at that time directly or indirectly to wage-payments. Hence, the true result of relief works and so on is not to leave the aggregate amount of unemployment in the country unaltered, but to diminish that amount'. In other words, an increase in taxes reduces spending by (a multiple of) a *fraction* of that increase, while the disbursement of tax receipts on public works construction increases spending by (a multiple of) the *full* amount spent; the net effect is expansionary.

It is evident that Pigou's argument rests on what has come to be known as the 'balanced budget multiplier'. Provided taxpayers and unemployed workers have the same marginal propensity to consume and provided private investment is not sensitive to the level of public spending, the balanced budget multiplier is unity. For example, if the marginal propensity to consume is 0.9, the multiplier or reciprocal of the marginal propensity to save is 10; raising taxes by $10 reduces aggregate demand by 9($10) = $90 but increasing public spending by $10 increases aggregate demand by 10($10) = $100. The net effect is to raise aggregate demand by $10, the exact amount of the increase in the balanced budget. It is true that Pigou speaks, not of a fraction of income spent on consumption, but of a fraction of income devoted to wage payments. This is hardly surprising considering the negligible importance of income taxation in 1913. The failure to make any reference to the concept of a multiplier process deprives his argument of any quantitative precision but does not affect its essential validity. The significance of Pigou's attack on the Treasury View is that it demonstrates the case for countercyclical public works expenditures without resort to the notion of deficit finance. Economists before Keynes generally disapproved of unbalanced budgets. But the idea that this necessarily prevented them from advocating fiscal policy to eliminate unemployment is not supported by the evidence.

Pigou qualified the argument for public works in *Unemployment* by noting that the successful application of a compensatory policy requires that labour is highly mobile between private industry and public construction. Despite these qualifications, however, he left no doubt that public works spending could be expected under normal circumstances to lessen unemployment. This became the standard view of economists after World War I. Hawtrey, alone of all British economists in the 1920s, opposed the case for public works on theoretical grounds. He never tired of insisting that the business cycle is purely a 'monetary phenomenon': 'additional public expenditures can give additional employment . . . only if it increases the rapidity of circulation of money'; hence, 'the true remedy for unemployment is to be found in a direct regulation of credit on sound lines'. Nevertheless, despite the consensus of economic opinion, the Treasury followed Hawtrey and remained hostile to the idea of planned countercyclical public works with or without budgetary deficits. The Conservative Chancellor of the Exchequer, Winston Churchill, told Parliament in 1929 that 'very little additional employment and no permanent additional employment can, in fact, and as a general rule, be created by State borrowing and State expenditure'. This was not just party doctrine: the following year, the Labour Chancellor, Phillip Snowden, declared that 'an expenditure which may be easy and tolerable in prosperous times becomes intolerable in a time of grave industrial depression'. In the United States, Hoover failed to balance the budget in 1931 and 1932, and the Democratic presidential candidate, Franklin Roosevelt, vigorously attacked the Republican Administration in the election of 1932 with the slogan: 'Stop the Deficits'. Ironically enough, that slogan received little support from the leaders of the American economics profession: a long list of names, including Slichter, Taussig, Schultz, Yntema, Simons, Gayer, Knight, Viner, Douglas and J. M. Clark, concentrated mainly at the Universities of Chicago and Columbia but with allies in other American universities, research foundations and government and banking circles, declared themselves in print in the early 1930s in favour of a program of public works, specifically attacking the shibboleth of a balanced budget as barring the way to effective recovery measures. Similarly, in England, names such as Pigou, Layton, Stamp, Harrod, Gaitskell, Meade, E. A. G. Robinson and J. Robinson joined Keynes in coming out publicly in support of compensatory public spending. There were certainly powerful voices that disagreed, such as Hawtrey, Cannan, Robbins and Hayek in England, Schumpeter in the United States, and Cassel in Sweden. But after the collapse of the gold standard in 1931, which largely put an end to the belief that recovery would come via the expansion of world trade, the Treasury View lived on solely in the minds of civil servants and political leaders without intellectual support from the theoretical writings of economists.

13. What Economists Said About Wage Cutting

We turn now to what economists really said about wage cutting before the publication of the *General Theory*. The impression that Keynes conveys is that the 'classical' economists favoured wage cutting on the basis of static microeconomic reasoning, illegitimately generalized to the economy as a whole. For evidence of this characterization of orthodox theory, he pointed to Pigou's *Theory of Unemployment* (1933) as 'the only detailed account of the classical theory of employment which exists'. Pigou's book does argue, in great detail and with considerable care, that all-round reductions in money wages may be expected to stimulate employment. But some contemporary reviewers of Pigou's book praised it for its 'novel contributions' and others found its reasoning at best unclear and at worst questionable.

Pigou's argument was indeed original for instead of relying on the 'indirect' effects, he appealed to the 'direct' stimulus afforded by wage cutting. Now as Keynes himself made clear in chapter 19 of the *General Theory* on 'Changes in Money-Wages', it was orthodox doctrine that money wage cuts cannot *directly* affect employment in the short run because the demand for labour depends on real wages; since in the short run all variable costs are labour costs, prices must fall in the same proportion as wages, leaving real wages the same. Any argument in favour of wage cutting to cure unemployment in the short run must rest either on the *indirect* effects via liquidity, the rate of interest, the balance of payments and tax burdens, or on the *dynamic* effects connected with lags between wage cuts and price reductions and the elasticity of expectations. But Pigou somehow managed to argue in *The Theory of Unemployment* that a decline in money wages would stimulate employment in the short run despite the fact that costs fall as fast as money wages. The argument is difficult to summarize because it does not seem to hang together on comparative static grounds and appears to depend on quasi-dynamic considerations introduced *ad hoc* in an otherwise static context. Pigou had been more cautious about wage cutting in earlier writings. In *Industrial Fluctuations*, he did argue that unemployment was due to real wages being 'too high' but he was not sanguine about the possibility of altering real wages per medium of money wages and pointed out that money wages might have to fall to zero in a deep depression to eliminate unemployment.

Even in his *Theory of Unemployment*, Pigou offered much more than wage cuts as remedies for unemployment. In the Appendix to chapter 19 of the *General Theory*, devoted to a critique of Pigou's book, Keynes singled out the first three parts of the *Theory of Unemployment* as the 'classical' model he was rejecting. Keynes ignored the fourth and fifth parts of the book where Pigou turns from 'real analysis' to 'Monetary Factors Affecting Variations in the Level of the Real Demand for Labour' and 'The Causation of Unemployment and of Changes in Unemployment'. Here Pigou concludes in the orthodox fashion that 'the long-run effect of expansionist State policy . . . does not touch employment', meaning 'not only the undertakings of large-scale public works, but bounties, guarantees of interest, and . . . protective duties'. But, he continues, 'Our conclusion . . . affords, of course, no argument against the State's *temporarily* adopting those devices as "remedies" for unemployment in times of exceptional depression. For here it is not their long-run but their short-run consequences that are significant . . . Moreover, a lasting favourable effect on employment might be produced if the State undertook – and succeeded in undertaking – not merely to make the real demand for labour higher than it would otherwise have been, but to make it progressively higher'.

Turning to other prominent economists writing in the 1920s, we find some conflicting evidence. In *Industrial Fluctuations* (1915), D. H. Robertson dismissed wage reductions in a slump and supported the public works proposals of the *Minority Report*; he never revised his views in later years. The young Keynes and Hawtrey both favoured monetary management as a cure for unemployment and Henry Clay, in reply to Pigou, denied that unemployment could be causally attributed to real wages being 'too high'. Everyone agreed that wage cuts would *in principle* lessen unemployment via the 'indirect' effects on the rate of interest and the balance of payments but the general tenor of informed judgment was that such a remedy was both impractical and inequitable.

There was a wage-cutting school, of which Cannan was probably the outstanding spokesman, but most writers shared the cautious views of Pigou in *Industrial Fluctuations*. Some of the journalists and probably Cannan himself were reacting to the interwar situation in Britain in which the price level was being forced down to maintain gold at the pre-war parity and in which excessive wage rates in certain 'sheltered' industries might have contributed to what we would now call structural unemployment. Nevertheless, it is highly significant that Keynes was unable to find any systematic theoretical exposition of the argument that general unemployment is due to labour 'asking too much' and had to resort to Pigou's tortured *Theory of Unemployment* as a prime example of 'classical' thought.

The American scene is much easier to describe because no single American economist in the years between 1929 and 1936 advocated a policy of wage cutting. One reason for this striking unanimity is that both money wages and retail prices in America did fall precipitously between 1929 and 1933, only recovering in 1934 and 1935, while all the time unemployment remained extremely high, although it too reached a peak in 1933. The American economists, in other words, had no difficulty in seeing that wage cutting was no panacea. By way of contrast, money wages in Britain remained virtually constant between the years 1923 and 1936, although prices declined throughout that period, turning up slightly in 1933. It was not patently obvious to British observers, therefore, that wage cutting could not cure unemployment, which makes it all the more remarkable that so few British economists in the early 1930s advocated a policy of forcing down money wages.

A fair way of summarizing the evidence on both fiscal policy and wage cutting is to say that most economists, at least in the English-speaking countries, were united in respect of practical measures for dealing with the depression but utterly disunited in respect of the theory that lay behind these policy conclusions. What orthodoxy there was in theoretical matters extended only so far as microeconomics. Pre-Keynesian macroeconomics in the spirit of the quantity theory of money presented an incoherent *mélange* of ideas culled from Fisher, Wicksell, Robertson, Keynes of the *Treatise* and Continental writers on the trade cycle. Leaning on this body of ideas, orthodox economists had no difficulty in explaining the persistence of unemployment in the 1930s. The government budget in both the United States and Britain was in surplus during most years in the 1930s and it did not need Keynes to tell economists that this was deflationary. It was also well known that monetary policy between 1929 and 1932 was more often tight than easy; at any rate, neither the United States nor the United Kingdom pursued a consistent expansionary monetary policy. Furthermore, the breakdown of the international gold standard aggravated the crisis. There was, in other words, no lack of explanations for the failure of the slump to turn into a boom but these explanations were all *ad hoc*, leaving intact the full employment equilibrium implications of standard theory.

In that sense, the Keynesian Revolution succeeded because Keynes produced the policy conclusions most economists wanted to advocate anyway but it produced these conclusions as logical inferences from a tightly knit if not always coherent theory, and not as endless epicycles on a full employment model of the economy. If we need any further evidence that that was indeed how contemporary economists saw the significance of Keynes, we have only to glance at American and British reviews of the *General Theory* which appeared in 1936 and 1937; most reviewers questioned the new theoretical concepts of the book but they generally dismissed Keynes' policy conclusions as 'old hat'.

14. Keynes's Contribution to Economics

It appears that the body of ideas discussed under the name of 'classical' economics represented a convenient straw man of Keynes's invention to represent the thinking of his predecessors. For Keynes, a 'classical' economist was any writer who defended Say's Law. By Say's Law, Keynes meant the proposition that any increment in output will automatically generate an equivalent increase in spending and income such as to maintain the economy at full employment [see chapter 5, section 6]. Since the mainstream of economic thought in Keynes's view had never abandoned Say's Law, any orthodox economist from Ricardo to Pigou was condemned as guilty of the sins attributed to 'classical' economists. To hit a target so broadly conceived, it was necessary to simplify. And simplify Keynes did, virtually implying that all previous discussions of business cycles were inconsistent with the corpus of received doctrine.

The difficulty with Keynes's characterization of orthodox theory is not simply that no single economist ever held all the ideas Keynes attributed to the 'classics' but that almost no economist after 1870 considered the type of macroeconomic problem with which Keynes was concerned. The strength of neoclassical theory lay in micro-economic analysis, which was ill-suited to the discussion of remedies for general unemployment. Even the valid case for Say's Law as a long-run proposition had never been stated correctly or with sufficient care to bring out its limited practical significance. Now that the separate strands of the *General Theory* have been carefully unravelled, the contrast between the *nouveau* and the *ancien régime* seems much smaller than Keynes himself could ever have anticipated. But this is the fate that time visits on all theoretical innovations. It is doubtful whether Keynes would have made as much of an impression if he had not oversold his wares.

It is one thing, however, to kill the myth of Keynes as a veritable knight in shining armour riding out against the wage cutters, the advocates of Say's Law and the proponents of the Treasury View, and quite another to deny the genuine novelties of Keynesian economics, as if the *General Theory* were only the special theory in the liquidity trap and rigid wages. There really was a Keynesian Revolution!

The novelties are not necessarily the obvious ones, such as the concepts of the consumption function, the multiplier and the speculative demand for money. The striking novel features of Keynesian economics are, first of all, the tendency to work with aggregates and indeed to reduce the entire economy to four interrelated markets for goods, labour, money and bonds; secondly, to concentrate on the short period and to confine analysis of the long period, which had been the principal analytical focus of his predecessors, to asides about the likelihood of secular stagnation; and thirdly, to throw the entire weight of adjustments to changing economic conditions on output rather than prices. Equilibrium for the economy as a whole now involved 'unemployment equilibrium' and the introduction of this conjunction, an apparent contradiction in terms, involved a profound change in the 'vision', *Weltanschauung*, paradigm – call it what you will – of orthodox economics, which undoubtedly included the faith that competitive forces are capable of driving the economy toward a steady state of full employment without the assistance of governments.

Nor is this all. The contribution of the *General Theory* to modern economics was, not simply to replace the conventional concentration on firms and households with an emphasis on aggregates, nor even to place income and employment at the center of macroeconomics reasoning instead of money and prices, but to formulate theory in terms of models whose key variables and relationships are specified in such a way as to be capable of quantitative measurement and testing. The stimulus which the *General Theory* gave to the construction of testable models of economic behavior is an integral feature of the Keynesian success story. The founding of the Econometric Society predates the *General Theory* by several years but econometrics remained an esoteric branch of economics until Keynes had made his impact. By the end of World War II, econometrics had become the leading growth industry of economics and Keynesian or neo-Keynesian macroeconomic models figure heavily, and indeed increasingly, in the work of econometricians. The greatest tribute that can be paid to an economist is that economics is unimaginable without him. Surely, this is true of Keynes?

MACROECONOMICS SINCE KEYNES

There are numerous hints in Keynes's *General Theory* that the wage and price rigidity that was said to characterize the economy in depression would quickly give way to wage and price flexibility once full employment was approached. In his pamphlet, *How to Pay for the War* (1940), Keynes laid the basis for a Keynesian analysis of inflation, conceived as a situation in which aggregate demand intersects aggregate supply at income levels above those of full employment. Even he realized, however, that such a demand-pull inflation would soon generate cost-push inflation owing to the effects of over-full employment on money wage claims. This would produce a new situation in which economic policy could no longer confine itself to demand management but might have to interfere with the wage bargaining process. Such considerations set the stage for the economic debates of the 1950s in which inflation rather than deflation appeared to be the outstanding economic problem facing policy makers. This debate was soon dominated by a new concept, the so-called 'Phillips curve', so named by Samuelson when he introduced it into the sixth edition of his elementary text *Economics* (1964).

15. The Phillips Curve
The Phillips curve first made its appearance in 1958 when A. W. Phillips fitted an empirical curve to a statistical scatter diagram of British time series data for annual percentage rates of change of money wages and unemployment as a proportion of the labour force over the years 1861–1913. The resulting curve was negatively inclined, indicating an inverse relationship between the two variables (see Figure 16–9). This was hardly a surprising finding: when unemployment is low and the labour market is tight, money wages ought to be rising; when unemployment is high and the labour market is slack, money wages ought to stop rising or even to fall. The chief novelty of the Phillips curve, however, was to show that wage inflation can coexist with a

Figure 16–9

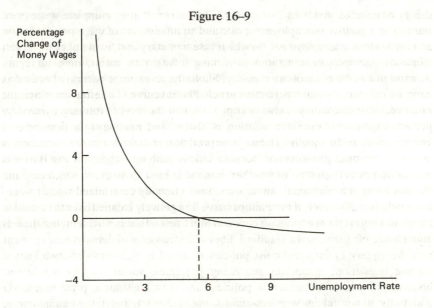

considerable amount of unemployment. According to the Phillips curve, wages in the United Kingdom tended to rise long before absolute full employment was reached; they began to rise at an unemployment rate of just under 5.5 percent, the point at which the Phillips curve crosses the horizontal line of zero wage inflation. Colleagues of Phillips at the London School of Economics soon up-dated the Phillips study to more recent years, which confirmed Phillips's conclusion that the full employment barrier at which wage inflexibility gives way to upward flexibility was much lower than anyone, including Keynes, had imagined.

The original Phillips curve related unemployment to wage changes. Other economists, however, transformed the wage-unemployment relationship into a price-unemployment relationship by subtracting the more or less constant trend rate of increases in labour productivity from the rate of change in money wages, amounting in diagrammatic terms to a downward shift in the original Phillips curve: the new Phillips curve was still negatively inclined and appeared to cross the horizontal line of zero price inflation at an unemployment rate of about 2.5 percent in the U.K. and about 4 percent in the U.S.A. Suffice it to say that this finding killed off the old Keynesian ideal of full employment without inflation as the goal of government policy. Price stability and unemployment were incompatible, conflicting objectives: less unemployment is attainable but only at the cost of faster price inflation and less inflation typically implies more unemployment. Thus, the old hope of simultaneous achievement of stable prices and full employment had to give way to the notion of a trade-off between price stability and full employment.

Moreover, over the relevant range of the Phillips curve, roughly between a 2 and 6 percent unemployment rate, there was no simple way of distinguishing between a demand-pull and a cost-push inflation. A vulgar interpretation of the Keynesian theory of inflation yields an L-shaped Phillips curve, that is, complete wage-price stability at a positive unemployment rate and an infinite rate of wage-price inflation at a zero rate of unemployment, in which case monetary and fiscal policy alone can eliminate unemployment without provoking inflation by maintaining aggregate demand just at the point of full capacity. Similarly, an extreme version of orthodox neoclassical theory yields a perfectly vertical Phillips curve at a zero unemployment rate because the economy is always kept at or near the level of full employment by perfect wage-price flexibility: inflation is always and necessarily a demand-pull phenomenon. In an equally extreme interpretation of orthodox theory, inflation is always a cost-push phenomenon because unions push up wages and Big Business pushes up prices regardless of whether demand is brisk or slack, in which case the Phillips curve is a horizontal line at some institutionally determined rate of wage-price inflation. However, if the Phillips curve is negatively inclined over the relevant range, not only is there a trade-off between inflation and unemployment, but there is also a trade-off between the standard 'liberal' instruments of demand management and the variety of interventionist policies required to fight cost-inflation (union busting legislation, manpower retraining programs, social security legislation, housing policies, job-information policies, anti-trust legislation, price regulation and, lastly, a comprehensive prices-and-incomes policy). In short, the Phillips curve, expressing a truly interdependent relationship between unemployment and wage-price changes, vastly complicates the agenda of economic policy and takes us light-years away from the simplistic conception of economic advice to policy makers that was typical of the Keynesian Revolution.

The Phillips curve gradually came to be interpreted in the 1960s as a frontier of attainable combinations of inflation and unemployment rates along or above which policy makers could move, depending on a 'social welfare function' which assigned relative weights to the twin evils of inflation and unemployment: governments which deplored unemployment more than inflation could select expansionary policies designed to lead the economy to a point on or to the right of the northwest portions of the Phillips curve, while governments which rated inflation as a greater evil than unemployment could instead select contractionary policies, aimed at arriving at the southeast portions of the Phillips curve. The Phillips curve itself was taken to be a stable and consistent relationship, which is not to deny that it is capable of being shifted gradually downwards by such structural policies as manpower training programs and wage-prices guideposts. Nevertheless, in the short to intermediate run, the Phillips curve defined the lower bound of feasible inflation-unemployment trade-offs.

In the late 1960s, however, doubts about the stability of the Phillips curve began to accumulate. Empirical studies of inflation-unemployment data increasingly revealed a large degree of variance of actual inflation-unemployment observations about the fitted Phillips curves and the number of variables that had to be introduced to improve the statistical fit soon exhausted the available degrees of freedom in the data. In addition, the last years of the decade of the 1960s produced rising inflation in many countries without any reduction in unemployment, giving way in the early

1970s both to rising inflation and rising unemployment. Clearly, something was wrong: there was not one stable Phillips curve but rather a whole family of short-run Phillips curves, which shifted over time as a result of influences yet to be determined. One answer of what these influences were was offered by Milton Friedman in his 1967 Presidential address to the American Economic Association. This address, 'The Role Of Monetary Policy' (1968), is easily the most influential paper on macroeconomics published in the post-war era.[1]

16. The Natural Rate of Unemployment

Central to Friedman's argument is the concept of the 'natural rate of unemployment' (NRU), defined in deliberate imitation of Wicksell's 'natural rate of interest' as that level of voluntary unemployment which clears the labour market and which therefore produces a *real* wage rate consistent with multimarket equilibrium. To say that it is the '*natural* rate of unemployment' is not to say that it is immutable because some of its determinants are institutional, for example, the existence of unions, and some legislative, for example, minimum wage laws; it is simply that, given the pattern of demand and supply in the economy, NRU is that rate which holds constant the average real wage rate and, given zero growth in labour productivity, which likewise holds constant the level of prices. It might have been called the 'real' rate of unemployment except that the rate of unemployment is, by definition, a real variable.

Let us suppose that NRU in an economy is 4 percent. For simplicity sake, we assume that productivity growth is zero so that wages and prices change in the same proportion. At 4 percent unemployment, wages and prices are stable and everyone expects on the basis of past experience that they will continue to be stable in the future. We now draw a new kind of Phillips curve through NRU $= U^*$: it is drawn on the assumption that everyone anticipates stable prices ($\dot{p}_e = 0$ in Figure 16–10, where the dot over the price expectations variable indicates the proportional rate of change of prices per unit of time). Suppose now that the government regards $U^* = 4$ percent as too high and launches a monetary and fiscal expansion to lower the unemployment rate. The expansion in aggregate demand bids up both product prices and wage rates but the former responds more rapidly to increased demand than the latter; with prices rising more rapidly than money wages, real wages decline. The fall in real wages induces employers to expand employment; this increase in the demand for labour becomes effective because workers still anticipate stable prices and interpret the rise in money wages as a permanent rise in real wages – the implied asymmetry in the reactions of employers and workers is an essential element in Friedman's story.

Unemployment has now fallen to U_1 – the economy has moved from A to B – but

---

[1] It took 12 years for the Keynesian Revolution to be incorporated into textbooks of elementary economics: the first of many more to follow was P. A. Samuelson, *Economics: An Introductory Analysis* (1948). Friedman's 1967 address invented the so-called 'natural-rate hypothesis': the first textbook in elementary macroeconomics to adopt this idea as the central element in the explanation of inflation appeared 11 years later in 1978; since then, the idea has appeared in virtually every textbook in macroeconomics.

Figure 16–10

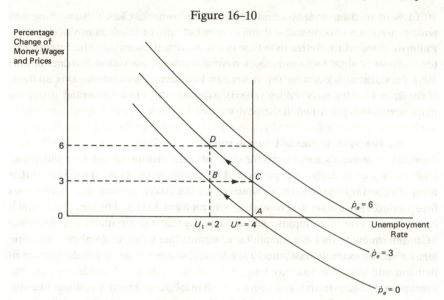

Percentage
Change of
Money Wages
and Prices

wage and price inflation is occurring at the rate of 3 percent which shifts up the 'expectations-augmented' Phillips curve from $\dot{p}_e = 0$ to $\dot{p}_e = 3$. In other words, workers now confidently anticipate 3 percent wage and price inflation and realize that they have been 'fooled' into thinking that their real wages have risen. Hence, they quit their jobs and the economy moves from B to C, restoring NRU = U^*. If the government nevertheless persists in its attempt to reduce unemployment below U^* by expansionary policies, the previous process of 'fooling' workers is repeated at a still higher level of inflation and the expectations-augmented Phillips curve shifts up to $\dot{p}_e = 6$, and so on. It is obvious that the only way in which unemployment can be kept below NRU is to keep prices rising at an ever increasing rate. It is also obvious that the NRU which clears the labour market at an equilibrium real wage rate is consistent with any rate of inflation, provided it is a constant rate of inflation. In the long run, therefore, there is a trade-off between the rate of change of the rate of inflation, the first derivative of $\dot{p}$, and the unemployment rate but there is no trade-off between the level of inflation, $\dot{p}$, and unemployment; in short, the long-run Phillips curve is vertical at U^*, which is the only level of unemployment at which the expected rate of inflation is equal to the actual rate of inflation.

The policy implications of this expectations-augmented view of inflation are startling. The first is already implied in what was said above: governments should refrain from Keynesian demand management designed to achieve a target level of employment which they deem to be 'full employment' because NRU is the lowest unemployment level sustainable over time without inflation. Moreover, this NRU may be crudely estimated by looking at bench-mark years when actual GNP equalled estimated potential GNP. For example, when the American economy operated at what was regarded as maximum capacity, as in the years 1964 and 1972, the observed unemployment rate in the U.S. was 5.2–5.6 percent of the labour force. Thus, an unemployment rate of something like 5.5 percent may be taken to be the empirical value of Friedman's NRU; efforts to push American unemployment below 5.5 percent will produce explosive inflation. The second policy implication of the new view is that, far from policymakers being able to achieve a low rate of unemployment at the price of some constant high rate of inflation, there is no advantage from the point of view of employment to any stable rate of inflation, in which case a zero rate is the optimum policy target. Thirdly, although the transition path to such a policy target of zero inflation is painful, the pain will be short-lived: what is required is a deflationary policy that will keep capacity low and unemployment high and to the right of U^* for as long as it takes to induce people to revise their inflationary expectations downwards to the continuously falling inflation rate. Such a period of high unemployment, we are promised, will not need to last very long – American readers under President Reagan and particularly British readers under Mrs. Thatcher take note! In the meanwhile and perhaps for years thereafter, every effort should be made via microeconomic policies to rid the labour market of 'imperfections', thus permanently lowering NRU.

Friedman subsequently added a new wrinkle to the notion of a vertical long-run Phillips curve. In his Nobel Memorial Lecture in 1976, he noted that 'stagflation', the simultaneous occurrence of unemployment and inflation, had recently given way to 'slumpflation', the simultaneous occurrence of rising unemployment and rising rates of inflation. In short, the vertical Phillips curve had become positively sloped. Friedman conjectured this was happening because inflation was, not only rising in advanced economies, but becoming increasingly volatile. Sharp fluctuations in inflation rates from year to year add an additional element of uncertainty to every market transaction, he suggested, which reduces economic efficiency and so bends the Phillips curve to the right. Nevertheless, he went on to say, the positively sloped Phillips curve will prevail only during a transition period – 'measured by quinquennia or decades, not years' – which will end when expectations and institutional arrangements have once again fully adjusted to the volatility of inflation, say, by complete indexing of all wages and prices, after which the Phillips curve will once again become vertical.

17. How Expectations are Formed

We noted above that the asymmetrical reactions of employers and workers to an expansion of aggregate demand form an essential link in Friedman's argument. It is precisely at this point that criticism was subsequently focussed. Whereas almost everybody was prepared to accept something like a vertical long-run Phillips curve, at least as a thick band rather than a thin line, the real problem was how to justify a short-run negatively inclined Phillips curve when augmented by built-in expectations. Friedman's argument assumes that workers exhibit 'money illusion' and allow money wages to be eroded by inflation, not just once or twice, but on a continuous basis.[2]

---

[2] Friedman slightly altered the argument in 1975, which does not however affect the point being made. Instead of assuming that unanticipated price increases are perceived more quickly by firms

Without persistent money illusion in the labour supply functions, expected price increases feed back completely into money wage bargains and, unless all wage bargaining takes the form of long-term contracts, real wages are maintained at a constant level, in consequence of which there are no short-run Phillips curves.

There are two ways of resolving this dilemma. The first is the Keynesian or neo-Keynesian insistence on the 'relative wage hypothesis' [see chapter 16, section 5]: workers *are* willing to accept reductions in real wages brought about by inflation because they are concerned with relative rather than absolute real wages and inflation is a means of reducing absolute real wages without altering relative wage differentials. So there *is* a trade-off between inflation and unemployment in the short run and the short run may last almost indefinitely if frequent disturbances prevent the economy from ever reaching the long-run vertical Phillips curve. The second is to deny the Friedman argument distinguishing between the expectations of employers and employees, to insist that both groups form wage and price expectations in the same way, but to assert that expectations are based solely on past experience and are only gradually adjusted to present circumstances; hence, in a period of rising inflation, the expected inflation rate always trails behind the actual inflation rate and it is this which restores the possibility of short-run Phillips curves.

This view that people form expectations of future inflation by looking at past rates of inflation was embodied in the modelling of Phillips curves in the late 1960s by adding an adaptive-expectations mechanism to the concept of the expectations-augmented Phillips curve. According to this mechanism, expectations are always adapted to some fraction of the error that occurs when inflation turns out to be different from what is expected. In symbols

$$\dot{p}_e = b(p - p_e) \tag{1}$$

where $(p - p_e)$ is the error in expectations and b is the coefficient of adaptation. Thus, when $b = 0.5$ and the actual and expected rates of inflation are 8 and 4 percent respectively, so that the error in expectations is 4, then the expected rate of inflation will be revised upward per unit of time by 2 percent; this revision will continue from period to period until the expectational error is completely eliminated.

In estimating such a relationship, we have to decide whether to treat all past rates of inflation as having equal weight. It is plausible to assume, however, that people pay more attention to recent prices than to those in the distant past and one way of taking account of this notion is to assume that expected inflation is a geometrically weighted average of all past rates of inflation with the weights summing to one; in short, the weights decline geometrically as time recedes backwards, more quickly if people have short memories and more slowly if they have long memories.

It was in this revised formulation that the natural-rate hypothesis dominated

than by workers, he argued that firms receive information on sales prices before learning of the price of labour services, thus perceiving an unanticipated rise in prices as a rise in the relative price of their own product and hence a *fall* in the real product-wage, whereas workers receive information on nominal wages before learning of the prices they must pay for consumer goods, thus perceiving the rise in wages and prices as a *rise* in real wages [see chapter 12, section 31]. In other words, the old asymmetry between firms and workers is replaced by a new asymmetry.

macroeconomics in the mid-1970s. Why is there a short-run trade-off between inflation and unemployment? Because you can fool all of the people some of the time, at least when the inflation rate is steadily rising or falling over time. However, as inflationary surprises disappear and expectations come to be fully realized, $(p - p_e) = 0$ and unemployment returns to its long-run natural rate. This rate is consistent with all fully-anticipated, steady-state rates of inflation, implying that there is no permanent trade-off between inflation and unemployment and that real economic variables are independent of nominal ones in long-run equilibrium. Note that the terms 'short-run' and 'long-run' are being used here in almost their original Marshallian meaning, that is, a time-period over which one can make adjustments [see chapter 10, section 1]; but instead of businessmen adjusting output partially or fully to a change of demand, everyone is adjusting their price expectations partially or fully to the actual rate of price changes.

Unfortunately, the natural rate hypothesis soon ran into statistical problems because econometric estimates of the expectations-augmented Phillips curve failed to produce the correct numerical value of the coefficient on the price-expectations variable. The expectations-augmented Phillips curve equation may be written as:

$$\dot{p} = a\,(1/U) + \phi\dot{p}_e \tag{2}$$

where $\dot{p}$ is the actual percentage rate of inflation, U is the unemployment rate, a is a coefficient expressing the trade-off between $\dot{p}$ and U, $\dot{p}_e$ is the expected percentage rate of price inflation, and ϕ is the coefficient attached to the price expectations variable. According to the natural rate hypothesis, $\dot{p}_e = \dot{p}$ in long-run equilibrium. Setting $\dot{p}_e = \dot{p}$ in equation (2) and solving for the actual rate of inflation yields:

$$p\,(1 - \phi) = a\,(1/U). \tag{3}$$

To sustain the natural rate hypothesis – no trade-off in the long-run between inflation and unemployment – we require $\phi = 1$ so that equation (3) vanishes. On the other hand, if $\phi < 1$, there is indeed a trade-off between inflation and unemployment in the long run and the original expectations-free Phillips curve, $p = a\,(1/U)$, is restored. In fact, many of the estimated models of inflation incorporating the expectations-augmented Phillips curve equation generated ϕs which were significantly less than unity, thus apparently refuting the natural rate hypothesis.

All of these models used the adaptive-expectations scheme of equation (1) as empirical proxies for the unobservable price expectations variable. Thus, one way of meeting these refutations of the natural rate hypothesis was to deny the adaptive-expectations mechanism as a naïve picture of how people form expectations. Why should people form anticipations solely from a weighted average of past price experience with weights that are fixed and independent of economic conditions and policy actions? Surely, if inflation were steadily accelerating or decelerating, people would soon perceive that their expectations were persistently underestimating or overestimating inflation and would therefore discard the adaptive-expectations mechanism for a more accurate expectations-generating scheme?

The first thing they would do is to focus on current information, such as declared policy intentions, announcements of money growth targets, exchange rate movements and the like, to improve their forecasts of future prices. In short, *rational* economic agents do not form price expectations on the basis of any scheme that is inconsistent with the way inflation is actually generated in the economy and they exploit all the pertinent information about the inflationary process that is available to them, whether past or present data. This means that all systematic and predictable elements influencing the rate of inflation will quickly become known and fully understood, implying paradoxically that people's price expectations are identical to the movement of actual prices. That is to say, people are only surprised by their forecasting errors, 'fooled' by events, because the economy is sometimes subject to random and unforeseen shocks that take time to be digested. It is these shocks which alone account for the momentary appearance of short-run Phillips curves. But for them, the economy would always stick to its long-run Phillips curve.

We have now come full circle and are back to the old Friedman problem of justifying, not the long-run vertical Phillips curve, but any notion of short-run Phillips curves. The concept of 'rational expectations' practically dissolves *any* version of a trade-off between inflation and unemployment that can be exploited by policy makers. Any policy whatsoever, to the extent that it is systematically based on some conception of how the economy works and how the government can interfere with its workings, is predictable and hence will be incorporated into the pricing forecasts of private economic agents; when the policy is applied, it will have no impact on real variables because it will already have been fully discounted, appearing as purely nominal adjustments to wages and prices. The rational-expectations approach, therefore, seems to lead inevitably to the most radical anti-Keynesian conclusion: governments can influence nominal variables like the inflation rate but they are impotent with respect to real variables, such as output and employment; there is no scope whatever for countercyclical stabilization policies. No wonder then that the theory of rational expectations has been labelled as 'the new classical macroeconomics'.

18. Rational Expectations

The theory of rational expectations (RE) first made its appearance in a 1961 article by J. F. Muth on security and commodity markets. Muth asked himself why no rule, formula or model has ever been consistently successful in predicting prices in financial markets, which indeed appear to resemble what is called a 'random walk' process on which 'noise' is superimposed. His answer was, in effect, that all available information capable of maximizing the accuracy of price forecasts is almost instantaneously incorporated into current decisions by speculators, whose forecasts and hence expectations are 'rational' in this precise sense. Traditional Keynesian demand management policies had proved relatively ineffective in the 1970s in solving the macroeconomic problems of the American economy and it occurred simultaneously to a number of economists, in particular R. E. Lucas Jr., T. J. Sargent and N. Wallace, that the reason for this was the same as that advanced by Muth to account for the unpredictability of stock prices: economic agents form their expectations on the basis of exactly the same information that is available to policy makers and, hence, act to neutralize every systematic attempt to intervene in the economy. In effect, economic agents mimic the market by forming forecasts of prices and hence expectations of price changes in the same way that the market determines actual prices. This does not imply that expectations are never mistaken – foresight is not perfect because the economy is subject to random, unpredictable shocks – but that the probability distribution of the subjective expectations of price variables will always have the same mean or 'mathematical expectation' as the objective distribution; a rational forecast or expectation has the property that its expected error is always zero.

In this view, individuals are rational maximizing agents and all markets clear instantaneously to yield an equilibrium price vector at which excess demand is eliminated. What then causes deviations from general equilibrium and full employment? Random error, that is all. However, random errors are not sufficient to account for the more or less regular cyclical fluctuations that are observed in all leading economic time series, such as output, investment and employment. These may be due to some moving average process of random errors but not simply to random errors as such. The standard way in which RE theorists acccount for the business cycle is reminiscent of the way Friedman accounted for the short-run Phillips curves, namely, the relative speed at which suppliers learn of the prices at which they sell compared to the prices at which they buy: everyone mistakenly perceives an unanticipated rise in prices as a rise in the relative price of what they sell, whether goods or services, and therefore supplies more; since on average everyone is making the same mistake, aggregate output rises; subsequently, everyone learns of their mistake, at which point aggregate output falls back to its previous level. In other words, business cycles on this view are essentially due to the limited information provided by price signals. It is difficult not to view this explanation as *ad hoc* and a retreat from the logic of RE. Are we to believe that a peanut producer, who can forecast the price of peanuts over his entire planning horizon with expected error of zero, nevertheless mistakes a global inflation for a local rise in the demand for peanuts?

Be that as it may, it is not difficult in general terms to grasp the essence of the RE approach. What is difficult is to see how one could ever test the notion of rationally formed expectations. Since expectations cannot be directly observed and since they are formed according to this view in exactly the same way as variables are determined in an economic model of the economy, how do we ever discover whether the theory of RE is true or not? We test the theory essentially by drawing out its implications, making sure, hopefully, that similar implications are not deducible from alternative economic theories. For example, one implication of RE is that the 'real' variables of a general equilibrium model of the economy are completely independent of the path of a policy variable, such as the money supply. Another is that only unanticipated changes in the money supply have any influence on the level of unemployment; thus, changes in the unemployment rate should not be capable of being explained by a systematic pattern of the money supply, or indeed policy announcements, interest rates, budgetary deficits, etcetera. A great many such hypotheses have been tested by RE writers but with mixed results: no crushing refutation has yet turned up but, on the other hand, the evidence has only weakly corroborated the concept of RE.

However, all these tests involve much more than just rational expectations: they also involve the assumptions of (1) perfect price flexibility in the sense that all markets clear in every moment of time; (2) costless processing of whatever information is available; and (3) no inequality in information between policy makers and private economic agents. If any of these assumptions are violated – if markets adjust sluggishly, if information costs constrain behavior, if policymakers possess informational advantages – the verification of models embodying RE does not necessarily validate the central policy-neutral implication of RE: expectations may be rationally formed and yet demand management can have lasting effects on real variables.

Much of the appeal of RE is based on its 'reductionism', as Coddington called it, namely, the attempt to treat the formation of expectations in exactly the same way that we treat all economic behavior as a matter of individuals maximizing utility subject to constraints. All rival explanations of expectations, it is argued, either imply that everyone is consistently wrong or that some agents are inexplicably worse at forecasting than others; in either case, such systematic errors create profit opportunities to supply information that is capable of improving private forecasting; these can be relied on to reduce forecasting errors to randomness. In that sense, RE theorists are perfectly justified in labelling their point of view the new *classical* macroeconomics: the idea that only unexpected changes in the money supply, such as originate from currency debasement, the discovery of new gold mines and foreign trade, can influence the real sector of the economy and that only in the short run was a basic tenet of classical monetary theory; it was founded on the unstated premise that fully anticipated changes in public policy are immediately discounted by economic agents and embodied in current decisions. Thus, RE writers may and do invoke tradition to justify their point of view: the reluctance to accept the theory of RE is itself irrational.

In consequence, criticism of RE has focussed more on the assumption of price flexibility and market clearance than on RE as such. But that may be a great mistake. Keynes indeed brought expectations squarely into economics but Keynes never developed a theory of expectations: the proposition that expectations are volatile and incapable of being rationally explained is no theory of expectations. Friedman contributed a number of definite conjectures about how expectations are formed and RE theorists simply carried his arguments to their logical conclusion. Nevertheless, the RE approach has deliberately excluded any discussion of how expectations are actually formed in different markets: it may be that people do not form 'rational' expectations for quite rational reasons, such as informational processing costs or even the sheer abundance of widely conflicting information. The development of alternative market-specific schemes of expectation formation is, surely, the next logical step in macroeconomic theorizing.

19. Monetarism Summed Up

The last quarter of a century of economic thought has been disfigured by a great debate between 'monetarism' and 'fiscalism', which has divided economists as they have not been divided since the 1930s. On the one hand, there are those who agree with Milton Friedman that the most powerful factor influencing economic activity is changes in the money stock and they analyze the income-determination process in terms of some version of the quantity theory of money. On the other side of the debate are the disciples of Keynes who take the view that the basic determinants of the level of economic activity at any given time are the forces which affect the components of aggregate demand and who believe that spending changes can affect the level of real income independently of the quantity of money. The former deny the potency of fiscal policy, while the latter hold that both monetary policy and fiscal policy are capable of exerting substantial effects on income and output. Nevertheless, even here there are disagreements about how quickly and effectively monetary impulses are transmitted and whether indeed changes in the money stock are typically exogenous or are themselves induced by changes in exogenous policy variables.

It is not our object to adjudicate this great controversy but rather to convey a sense of the evolution of the debate over time, which of course remains unresolved to the present day. We noted earlier [see chapter 15, section 10] that monetarism began with Friedman's 1956 formulation of what he understood to be the quantity theory of demand conceived as a statement of the idea that money is one of the many ways of holding wealth and that the demand for money should therefore be viewed as a special aspect of capital theory. Theoretically, he concluded, this demand ought to depend in part on the yield of money relative to other yields but in empirical work he could find no evidence that interest rates actually influenced the demand for money; this strengthened the simple quantity theory with its emphasis on the 'direct' rather than the 'indirect' mechanism [see chapter 15, section 1]. This finding was subsequently rejected by monetarists themselves but since it was peripheral to the main argument, it did little to discredit monetarism.

Next came the massive historical study of monetary history in the United States, purporting to show by means of direct comparisons of the money stock and income changes in twenty business cycles in the USA that monetary changes typically precede income changes by a few months during all stages of the business cycle. Simultaneously, he published (with D. Meiselman) a comparison of a simple 'Keynesian' model and a simple 'monetarist' model in order to demonstrate that the income-velocity of money was a more stable variable than the Keynesian income-multiplier. This claim too was soon refuted as more sophisticated Keynesian models were shown to perform as well as monetarist models. In general, it was concluded that no single-equation estimates, of the type employed by Friedman and Meiselman, were capable of discriminating between Keynesian and monetarist models.

Up to this point, the prevailing complaint of the Keynesian critics of monetarism was that Friedman had provided no theory of the transmission mechanism, that is, the way in which monetary changes are divided between variations in prices and variations in real output. The publication of 'A Theoretical Framework for Monetary Analysis' (1970) was Friedman's reply to such criticisms. In that rebuttal, Friedman chose to express his argument in terms of the Hicks-Hansen *IS-LM* model, arguing that what really divided macroeconomists was, not some fundamental theoretical or ideological differences, but merely empirical questions of the timing and relative speed of adjustment of prices and quantities: 'I regard the description of our position as "money is all that matters for changes in *nominal* income and for short-run changes in real income" as an exaggeration that gives the right flavour of our conclusions. I regard the statement that "money is all that matters", period, as a basic misrepresentation of our conclusions.'

Even before this paper, Friedman had shifted ground from the short run to the long run by the introduction of the natural rate hypothesis. We have already traced the evolution of this expectations-augmented view of the Phillips curve from the original notion that workers form expectations differently from employers to the idea that everyone adapts expectations in terms of a weighted average of past rates of inflation. Friedman consistently adhered to the view that there is a trade-off between inflation and unemployment in the short run and in various places he suggested that the short run was as long as 'eighteen months . . . or two years', in some cases even hinting that it required three years to get back completely to NRU. The RE Revolution removed even this last vestige of Keynesian-type policy making, thus completing the monetarist program in which indeed 'money is all that matters, period'. Friedman himself has studiously avoided commenting on the concept of RE and there is little in his writings that would support the view that the time path of inflation is nowadays generated solely by random shocks, which is what is implied by the RE School.

In the light of these considerations, what then is a 'monetarist'? It is someone who believes in the quantity theory of money. As we noted earlier [chapter 15, section 1], the quantity theory of money consists of a number of interrelated propositions, which commanded wide assent among both classical and neoclassical economists all through the 19th century. We may summarize them once again under five headings: (1) the active and causal role of money in the determination of the price level and hence the level of nominal national income; (2) the neutrality of money in long-run equilibrium, that is, the long-run proportionality between money and prices, grounded on the stability of the demand for money or its reciprocal, the velocity of money; (3) the non-neutrality of money in the short and intermediate run with varying emphases on the length of those runs; (4) the exogeneity of the money supply; and (5) a suspicion of discretionary monetary management and a preference for policy rules, such as tying the note issue rigidly to the gold supply, forcing banks to hold 100 percent of their deposits or reserves, or fixing the annual growth rate of the money supply at a figure corresponding to the long-term growth rate of output. Now, despite all the refinements which have been achieved in monetary economics in recent years and despite the much more sophisticated treatment of the transmission mechanism linking money to spending and the role of expectations in the formation of prices in Friedman compared to, say, Ricardo, Mill, Marshall and Wicksell, we can still discern all the five propositions listed above in the writings of modern monetarists.

For example, the idea that changes in the money stock typically precede and bring about changes in nominal national income, and that both the Great Depression of the 1930s and the inflation of recent decades are fundamentally due to the erratic behavior of the money supply, is at the back of all of Friedman's historical analyses of events in the U.S.A. and the U.K. Likewise, the idea that the long-term path of output and employment in an economy is determined by resource endowments, technology and consumer preferences, so that money is a veil, is a constant note in everything that Friedman has written. It follows that the real rate of interest cannot be permanently altered by monetary action in order to stimulate investment and capital formation, as Keynes believed, because it is determined by the real forces of productivity and thrift. The NRU, to which the economy is constantly returning, is the modern monetarist version of the old classical doctrine of the rigidly proportionate relationship between money and prices in the long run; the sheet anchor of the rate of interest is the stable real demand for cash balances, except that this is now interpreted as including the anticipated rate of inflation as one of its determinants, so that prices may have to rise in greater proportion than the change in money to maintain monetary equilibrium if a steady injection of money has led to a permanent rise in the expected rate of inflation.

There is no disagreement with the Cantillon Effect – the non-neutrality of money in transition periods – although there is a steady tendency in modern monetarism to shorten the length of time over which money is said to have non-neutral effects on real variables, not to mention the fact that the emphasis now falls entirely on the gap between unanticipated and fully anticipated price changes, whereas in Cantillon and Hume the emphasis was on spending lags between incomes and outlays. On the related issue of the transmission mechanism, there is likewise a subtle shift of emphasis from the 'direct' to the 'indirect' mechanism. The motivating force of monetary impulses is still the discrepancy between actual and desired real cash balances but there is increasing stress on the way changes in the money supply are transmitted to prices through numerous interest channels, altering the composition of asset portfolios. Modern monetarists also agree with older quantity theorists on the question of the autonomous source of changes in the money supply, that is, that the supply of money can be effectively controlled by the central bank via control over the monetary base (currency plus bank reserves). It is true that the currency-deposits ratio desired by private individuals is not under the direct control of the monetary authorities but monetarists agree with the old Bullionists and members of the Currency School that the reserve-deposit and currency-deposit ratios are sufficiently stable and predictable to offer control of the total money supply via control of the monetary base. Again, today's monetarists are no less critical of central bank policy than were the Bullionists and writers of the Currency School, rejecting the belief that it is enough to peg the interest rate or to base the currency on gold and then to rely solely on the free convertibility of paper to gold to prevent the excess printing of money. Like the Currency School, modern monetarists argue that the unpredictable lags in the relation between money, income and prices militate against a policy of 'fine tuning' and hence that discretionary monetary policy is at best difficult and at worst destabilizing. Thus, discretionary monetary policy should be replaced by a fixed monetary growth rule.

In all respects, therefore, the quantity theory of money is still alive and well in the works of Friedman and his disciples. But that is not to deny a 'right wing' and a 'left wing' among modern monetarists. The RE writers go much further than Friedman himself and adhere in every case to much stricter versions of our five central propositions; (1) money is practically the only systematic disrupter of economic equilibrium; (2) money and prices always vary nearly proportionately, so that money is not only neutral, it is superneutral; (3) the transition periods between monetary equilibria are momentary; (4) the money supply can be effectively controlled and there are few feedback effects of price and nominal income changes in the money supply; and (5) discretionary monetary management has no discernible influence on output, employment and the real rate of interest and should therefore be replaced by a monetary growth rule. The future will tell whether such 'extremism' is merely a straw in the wind or a harbinger of a new orthodoxy.

NOTES ON FURTHER READING

Every student must sooner or later break his teeth on J. M. Keynes's *General Theory of Employment, Interest and Money* (1936 in paperback or 1973 in hardback as Vol. VII of *The Collected Writings of John Maynard Keynes*, eds. E. Johnson and D. Moggridge); a first reading might omit chaps. 4, 6, 14, 16, 22 and 23, all of which digress from the main argument. An important supplement to the *General Theory* is Keynes's summary restatement of his system a year later, 'The General Theory of Employment', *QJE*, 1937, reprinted in *The General Theory and After: Part II, Defence and Development*, ed. D. Moggridge, Vol. XIV of *The Collected Writings*. Hansen, *A Guide to Keynes*, is still the most useful single book to have on hand while studying *The General Theory*. R. F. Harrod, *The Life of John Maynard Keynes* (1951 in paperback), is the authoritative biography, which however hides the man behind his works and thus makes Keynes out to be almost as dull a person as Marshall. R. Skidelsky, *John Maynard Keynes, Vol. 1, Hopes Betrayed 1883–1920* (1983) promises to be the truly personal biography we have been waiting for but it may be some years before the critical second volume will decide the question. A brief introduction to the man and his works is D. E. Moggridge, *Keynes* (1976 in paperback) with an excellent up-to-date bibliography.

So much has been written on Keynesian economics that only choice items can be mentioned here. For the origins of the standard Keynes-versus-the-Classics argument, see J. R. Hicks, 'Mr. Keynes and the "Classics": A Suggested Interpretation', *Ecom*, 1937, reprinted in the Fellner-Haley *Readings in Income Distribution*, the Mueller *Readings in Macroeconomics*, and *JMKCA*, II; D. H. Robertson, 'A Survey of Modern Monetary Controversy', *MS*, 1938, reprinted in *Readings in Business Cycle Theory*, ed. G. Haberler (1944); and Hansen, *Guide to Keynes*, chap. 7. G. Haberler, 'The General Theory' and W. W. Leontief, 'Keynes and the "Classicists"', *The New Economics: Keynes' Influence on Theory and Public Policy*, ed. S. E. Harris (1947), contain acute comments on the nature of 'classical' economics. A more recent discussion of the problem is by Patinkin in *Money, Interest and Prices*, chaps. 14, 15, and Note K; and G. Ackley, *Macroeconomic Theory* (1961), chaps. 5–15. My exposition of this old debate leans heavily on Patinkin, *Money, Interest and Prices*, chap. 13, and W. L. Smith, 'A Graphical Exposition of the Complete Keynesian System', *SEJ*, 1956, reprinted in the Mueller *Readings in Macroeconomics* and *JMKCA*, III.

Apart from *The New Economics*, ed. Harris, two other collections of essays suffice to depict the wide range of professional reactions to Keynes: *The Critics of Keynesian Economics*, ed. H. Hazlitt (1960), provides a whole battery of anti-Keynesian arguments; and *Keynes' General Theory, Reports of Three Decades*, ed. R. Lekachman (1964), with laudatory and condemnatory essays written in the 1930s, 1940s and 1960s by E. A. G. Robinson, W. B. Reddaway, R. F. Harrod, A. P. Lerner, J. Viner, G. Haberler, P. A. Samuelson and others. All of the latter, and literally a hundred more, are reprinted in the four volumes of *JMKCA*.

W. J. Fellner, 'What is Surviving? An Appraisal of Keynesian Economics on its Twentieth Anniversary', *AER*, 1957, reprinted in *JMKCA*, III; J. R. Hicks, 'A Rehabilitation of "Classical" Economics?', *EJ*, 1957, reprinted with revisions in his *Critical Essays in Monetary Theory* (1967), chap. 8; D. Patinkin, 'Keynesian Economics Rehabilitated: A Rejoinder to Professor Hicks', *EJ*, September, 1959; and H. G. Johnson, '*The General Theory* after Twenty-five Years', *AER*, 1961, reprinted in his *Money, Trade and Economic Growth* (1962 in paperback) and *JMKCA*, II, perfectly convey the consensus that had been reached by the 1960s on the *IS-LM* interpretation of what Keynes is about.

That consensus was rudely shattered by the publication of A. Leijonhufvud, *On Keynesian Economics and the Economics of Keynes: A Study of Monetary Theory* (1968), a book which leaned heavily on a pathbreaking article by R. W. Clower, 'The Keynesian Counter-Revolution: A Theoretical Appraisal', *The Theory of Interest Rates*, eds. F. H. Hahn and F. Brechling (1965), reprinted in a slightly revised form in *Penguin Modern Economics Readings: Monetary Theory*, ed. R. W. Clower (1969 in paperback). Leijonhufvud's book is conveniently summed up by the author in his pamphlet, *Keynes and the Classics* (1969 in paperback). It is criticized, particularly as an interpretation of Keynes, by H. I. Grossman, 'Was Keynes a "Keynesian"? A Review Article', *JEL*, 1972, reprinted in *JMKCA*, III; R. Jackman, 'Keynes and Leijonhufvud', *OEP* 1974, reprinted in *JMKCA*, IV; and C. Bliss, 'The Reappraisal of Keynes' Economics: An Appraisal', *Current Problems in Economics*, eds. M. Parkin and A. R. Nobay (1975). A Leijonhufvud, 'Keynes' Employment Function', *HOPE*, Summer, 1974, constitutes an important revision of the original argument. See also R. W. Clower's profound 'Reflections on the Keynesian Perplex', *ZN*, July, 1975.

I have learnt much from A. Coddington, *Keynesian Economics: The Search for First Principles* (1983) with its useful distinctions between types of Keynesianisms and even more from D. Patinkin's masterful *Anticipations of the General Theory?* (1982) with its insistence that the central notion of income itself as the force that equilibrates aggregate demand and supply is found in Keynes and only in Keynes. On Coddington's 'fundamentalist Keynesianism', see E. R. Weintraub, 'Uncertainty and the Keynesian Revolution', *HOPE*, 1975, reprinted in *JMKCA*, IV; J. A. Kregel, 'Economic Methodology in the Face of Uncertainty: The Modelling Methods of Keynes and the Post-Keynesians', *EJ*, 1976, reprinted in *JMKCA*, IV; and M. Stohs, '"Uncertainty" in Keynes' *General Theory*', *HOPE*, 1980, reprinted in *JMKCA*, II. The struggle to rescue something from the nihilism implicit in 'fundamentalist Keynesianism' and to somehow unite what is left with the neo-Ricardianism of Sraffa in a new Post-Keynesian research program is amply revealed in *Keynes' Economics and the Theory of Value and Distribution*, eds. J. Eatwell and M. Milgate (1983).

The publication of *The Collected Writings of John Maynard Keynes*, in 29 volumes (1971–83) have led to a number of new attempts to trace the evolution of Keynes's thinking up to 1936. See D. E. Moggridge, 'From the *Treatise* to *The General Theory*: an Exercise in Chronology', *HOPE*, Spring, 1973; and D. Patinkin's brilliant *Keynes' Monetary Thought: A Study of Its Development* (1976).

How accurate was Keynes's indictment of received doctrine? Strangely enough, this question has still not been systematically explored, although many of the missing pieces have now been assembled. See Hutchison, *Review of Economic Doctrines*, chap. 24; J. R. Schlesinger, 'After Twenty Years: The General Theory', *QJE*, 1956, reprinted in *JMKCA*, I; K. Hancock, 'Unemployment and the Economists in the 1920s', *Ec*, November, 1960, and 'The Reduction of Unemployment as a Problem of Public Policy, 1920–1929', *EHR*, 1962, reprinted in *The Gold*

Standard and Employment Policies Between the Wars, ed. S. Pollard (1970 in paperback); H. Stein, *The Fiscal Revolution in America* (1969); D. N. Winch, *Economic Thought and Policy* (1969 in paperback), especially chaps. 8 and 9 on the Hayek-Robbins opposition to Keynes; J. R. Davis, *The New Economics and the Old Economists* (1971); W. J. Samuels, 'The Teaching of Business Cycles in 1905–1906: Insight into the Development of Macroeconomic Theory', *HOPE*, Spring, 1972; S. Howson and D. N. Winch, *The Economic Advisory Council, 1930–1939* (1977); G. C. Peden, 'Keynes, the Treasury and Unemployment in the Later Nineteen-Thirties', *OEP*, 1980, reprinted in *JMKCA*, I; and Hutchison, *On Revolutions and Progress in Economic Knowledge*, chap. 6.

The reviews of Pigou's *Theory of Unemployment* (1933) provide interesting reading in the light of Keynes's attack on the book: see R. F. Harrod, *EJ*, March, 1934; R. G. Hawtrey, *Ec*, May, 1934; and P. M. Sweezy, *JPE*, December, 1934. On Pigou, see also T. W. Hutchison, *Economics and Economic Policy in Britain, 1946–1966* (1968), Appendix B. B. A. Corry, 'Keynes in the History of Economic Thought: Some Reflections', *Keynes and Laissez Faire*, ed. A. P. Thirlwall (1978); and D. Collard, 'A.C. Pigou, 1877–1959', *Pioneers of Modern Economics in Britain*, eds. O'Brien and Presnell; and J. Melitz, 'Pigou and the "Pigou Effect". Rendez-Vous With the Author', *SEJ*, October, 1967, shows ironically that Pigou never really stated the effect attributed to him. For a good account of Hawtrey, a friend of Keynes but one who was doctrinally far more opposed to Keynes than Pigou, see E. G. Davis, 'R. G. Hawtrey, 1879–1975', *Pioneers of Modern Economics in Britain*, eds. O'Brien and Presnell.

To show that at least some 'classical' economists believed in wage cutting to cure unemployment, see E. Cannan, 'The Demand for Labour', *EJ*, September, 1932; and J. Rueff, 'L'assurance-chômage cause du chômage permanent', *REP*, avril, 1931. Rueff's article provoked considerable opposition in France even before 1936; for Rueff's unrepentant recent thinking on the question, see his 'Nouvelle discussion sur le chômage, les salaires et les prix', *ibid.*, septembre-octobre, 1951, and 'The Fallacies of Lord Keynes' General Theory', *QJE*, 1947, followed by a debate with J. Tobin, *ibid.*, 1948, all reprinted in *JMKCA*, II. M. Casson, *Economics of Unemployment. An Historical Perspective* (1983) arrived too late to take into account but chaps. 1–3, 7–8 of this fascinating book draws together the writings of Pigou, Cannan and Henry Clay into an account of the pre-Keynesian theory of employment.

On the pre-Keynesian history of 'The Compensatory Theory of Public Works Expenditure' in England and America, see the article by C. J. Anderson, *JPE*, September, 1945; see also S. H. Slichter, 'The Economics of Public Works', *AER*, 1934, reprinted in *Readings in Fiscal Policy*, eds. A. Smithies and J. K. Butters (1955), for a typical example of pre-Keynesian thinking. The significance of the concept of the multiplier, as the quantitative relationship between a net increase in spending and the consequent expansion of income, seems not to have been clearly grasped until Kahn's famous article in *EJ*, June, 1931. It appears in Pigou and still earlier in Bagehot but neither thought it possible to estimate the multiplier in quantitative terms: see H. Hegeland, *The Multiplier Theory* (1954), chaps. 1 and 2; A. L. Wright, 'The Genesis of the Multiplier Theory', *OEP*, June, 1954; and Patinkin, *Anticipations of the General Theory?*, chap. 7. For a fascinating discussion of popular views, see S. S. Alexander, 'Opposition to Deficit Spending for the Prevention of Unemployment', *Income, Employment and Public Policy*, eds. L. A. Metzler, and others (1948 in paperback). G. Garvey, 'Keynes and the Economic Activists of Pre-Hitler Germany', *JPE*, 1975, reprinted in *JMKCA*, II, demonstrates that something like Keynesian policy measures were advocated by a host of German writers in the early 1930s.

One of the historical puzzles of the Keynesian Revolution was the relationship between Keynes and the extremely Keynesian thinking of Swedish policymakers in the early 1930s. Shackle, *The Years of High Theory: Invention and Tradition in Economic Thought, 1926–1939*, chap. 10, goes so far as to claim that Myrdal's *Monetary Equilibrium* (1934) anticipated all the essentials of Keynes's *General Theory*, so that 'had the *General Theory* never been written, Myrdal's work would eventually have supplied almost the same theory'. Similar assertions have also been made about certain works by B. Ohlin, in particular 'On the Formulation of

Monetary Theory' (1933), reprinted in *HOPE*, Fall, 1978, and since then there has been a vigorous debate in Sweden, not just about the claim of the independent discovery of the Keynesian system by members of the Stockholm School, but also about the influence of these indigenous ideas on contemporary Swedish policy making. Patinkin, *Anticipations of the General Theory?*, chap. 2, reviews the entire debate and comes down on the side of those who deny that the Stockholm School anticipated the central message of the *General Theory*.

Other writers who are sometimes regarded as precursors of Keynes, such as Hobson or Foster and Catchings, prove upon examination to be forerunners of the Harrod-Domar growth theory. See D. J. Coppock, 'A Reconsideration of Hobson's Theory of Unemployment', *MS*, January, 1953; and A. H. Gleason, 'Foster and Catchings: A Reappraisal', *JPE*, April, 1959, with a pertinent note by J. A. Carlson: 'Foster and Catchings: A Mathematical Appraisal', *ibid.*, August, 1962. For a discussion of a writer who synthesized saving-investment analysis with ideas rooted in the quantity theory of money almost a decade before the *General Theory*, see J. R. Presley, 'D. H. Robertson, 1890–1963', *Pioneers of Modern Economics in Britain*, eds. O'Brien and Presnell. R. C. Wiles analyzes the views of an American contemporary of Keynes who came at times amazingly close to Keynesian ideas: 'The Macroeconomics of John Maurice Clark', *RSE*, September, 1971. Another forerunner, who started from Marx, Luxemburg and Tugan-Baranovsky to arrive at many of Keynes's conclusions, was Michael Kalecki. On Kalecki's pre-Keynesian ideas, see G. R. Feiwel, *The Intellectual Capital of Michael Kalecki* (1975), chaps. 1 and 2; and Patinkin, *Anticipations of the General Theory?*, chap. 3.

Keynes, whose contributions did so much to stimulate national income accounting, had a highly ambiguous attitude to statistics, not to mention econometrics and mathematical economics. On all this see R. Stone's pamphlet, *Keynes, Political Arithmetic and Econometrics* (1978) and Patinkin's *Anticipations*, chap. 9. For a fascinating chapter in the history of Keynesian economics after Keynes, see P. A. Samuelson, 'The Balanced-Budget Multiplier: A Case Study in the Sociology and Psychology of Scientific Discovery', *HOPE*, Spring, 1975; and H. M. Somers, 'On the Origins of the Balanced-Budget Multiplier Theorem', *ibid.*, Summer, 1977.

We have said nothing about the stagnation thesis: the view put forward parenthetically in the *General Theory*, and later popularized by A. H. Hansen, of increasing secular unemployment due to declining population growth, the closing of 'the frontier' and the disappearance of laboursaving technical change. But see G. Terborgh, *The Bogey of Economic Maturity* (1945), which dealt a death-blow to the thesis; A. H. Hansen, 'The Stagnation Thesis', a collection of writings published in 1941, 1951 and 1954, reprinted in the Smithies-Butters *Readings in Fiscal Policy*; and J. Burkhead, 'The Balanced Budget', *QJE*, 1954, reprinted in *ibid.*

The Phillips curve was introduced by A. W. Phillips, 'The Relationship Between Unemployment and the Rate of Change of Money Rates in the United Kingdom, 1861–1957', *Ec.*, 1968, reprinted in *Penguin Modern Economics Readings, Inflation*, eds. R. J. Ball and P. Doyle (1969), after which it was discovered that the same idea had occurred to I. Fisher long ago: 'A Statistical Relation Between Unemployment and Price Changes' (1926), reprinted under the title, 'I Discovered the Phillips Curve', *JPE*, March/April, 1973.

Following on from Notes on Further Reading, chap. 15, M. Friedman, *The Optimum Quantity of Money and Other Essays* (1969) contains the 1967 Presidential Adress to the American Economic Association, 'The Role of Monetary Policy', *AER*, 1968, as well as other important papers, such as 'The Demand for Money: Some Theoretical and Empirical Results', *JPE*, 1959, which claims to show that the demand for money is interest-inelastic, and 'The Lag in Effect of Monetary Policy', *JPE*, 1961, which lays down the fixed money-growth rule as an alternative to discretionary monetary policy. In addition, there is M. Friedman, 'A Theoretical Framework For Monetary Analysis', *JPE*, 1970, reprinted with a reply to his critics in R. J. Gordon, ed., *Milton Friedman's Monetary Framework* (1974), which employs the *IS-LM* model of income determination to explain the difference between monetarism and Keynesianism. Friedman's Nobel Memorial Lecture, which introduced the concept of a positively sloped Phillips curve, is available as M. Friedman, 'Inflation and Unemployment: The New Dimension of Politics', *JPE*, 1977, reprinted as *Inflation and Unemployment* (1977). The new explanation of the asymmetry between firms and workers, which accounts for deviations from the vertical Phillips curve, is given in M. Friedman, *Unemployment Versus Inflation? An Evaluation of the Phillips Curve* (1975). Finally, there is M. Friedman and D. Meiselman, 'The Relative Stability of Monetary Velocity and the Investment Multiplier in the United States, 1897–1958', Commission on Money and Credit, *Stabilization Policies* (1963), with its comparison between a Mickey Mouse version of Keynes and an equally Mickey Mouse version of monetarism. The controversy which this paper produced is reviewed by W. C. Brainard and R. N. Cooper, 'Empirical Macroeconomics: What Have We Learned in the Last 25 Years?', *AER*, May 1975. For a textbook on macroeconomics incorporting Friedman's natural-rate hypothesis, see R. J. Gordon, *Macroeconomics* (1968, 2nd ed., 1981).

Most of the path-breaking papers on rational expectations are reprinted in R. E. Lucas, Jr., *Studies in Business-Cycle Theory* (1981) and a two-volume anthology, *Rational Expectations and Econometric Practice*, eds. R. E. Lucas, Jr. and T. J. Sargent (1982). The reader is warned, however, that these are almost all extremely difficult essays. The best way to begin grasping the import of the 'new' classical macroeconomics is to read A. M. Santomero and J. J. Seater, 'The Inflation-Unemployment Trade-Off: A Critique of the Literature', *JEL*, June, 1978, followed by B. Kantor, 'Rational Expectations and Economic Theory', *ibid.*, December, 1979, which shows there is nothing new under the sun; R. Maddock and M. Carter, 'A Child's Guide to Rational Expectations', March, 1982, which makes one glad to be childish; and G. K. Shaw's *Rational Expectations. An Elementary Exposition* (1984). In addition, there is R. Maddock's useful paper, 'Rational Expectations Macrotheory: A Lakatosian Case Study in Program Adjustment', *HOPE*, Summer, 1984.

There are many current books on the theory of inflation that cover more or less the content of this chapter. Two good examples are J. A. Trevithick and C. Mulvey, *The Economics of Inflation* (1975) and J. Flemming, *Inflation* (1976). My own favourite, however, is M. Desai, *Testing Monetarism* (1981), particularly chaps. 1, 2 and 4, supplemented by R. G. Lipsey, 'The Understanding and Control of Inflation: Is There a Crisis in Macroeconomics?, *CJE*, November, 1981, both of which are very congenial to my own methodological predilections. As an antidote to Desai and Lipsey, see the enthusiastic account of S. M. Sheffrin, *Rational Expectations* (1983), chaps. 1, 2, and 6.

17

A methodological postscript

How much does economics explain? What are the grounds on which economic theories have been accepted or rejected? What are the characteristics of endurable economic ideas? What practical use is economic knowledge? These were some of the questions posed in the Introduction to this book. Have any or all of them been answered in the course of the text?

Since the days of Adam Smith, economics has consisted of the manipulation of highly abstract assumptions, derived either from introspection or from casual empirical observations, in the production of theories yielding predictions about events in the real world. Even if some of the assumptions involved nonobservable variables, the deductions from these assumptions were ultimately related to the observable world: economists wanted to 'explain' economic phenomena as they actually occur. In short, economists have always regarded the core of their subject as 'science', in the modern sense of the word: the goal was to produce accurate and interesting predictions that were, in principle at least, capable of being empirically falsified. In practice, they frequently lost sight of this scientific objective and the history of economics is certainly replete with tautological definitions and theories so formulated as to defy all efforts at falsification. But no economist writing on methodology, whether in the 19th or in the 20th century, has ever denied the relevance of the now widely accepted demarcation rule of Popper: theories are 'scientific' if they are falsifiable, at least, in principle, and not otherwise. Such methodologists as Senior, J. S. Mill, Cairnes, Sidgwick, Jevons, Marshall, John Neville Keynes, Böhm-Bawerk and Pareto frequently emphasized other matters and, of course, underemphasized the problem of devising appropriate empirical tests of theories, but nothing they wrote denied the idea that to 'explain' is ultimately to predict that such and such will or will not happen.

Robbins's *Essay on the Nature and Significance of Economic Science* (1932) is frequently cited as a prime example of the opposite tendency, emphasizing the irrelevance of empirical testing to the truth of economic theories. But the purpose of Robbins's book was to purge economics of value judgments. It is not clear whether Robbins really wanted economists to abandon welfare economics altogether or merely to separate 'positive' from 'normative' economics, so as to deny scientific status to the latter. Nor is it clear, even after repeated reading, whether he really meant to commit himself to 'radical apriorism', despite the fact that many passages in the book do invite that interpretation. 'Radical apriorism' holds that economic theory is simply a system of logical deductions from a series of postulates derived from introspection, which are not themselves subject to empirical verification. In stark contrast to radical apriorism is 'ultra-empiricism', which refuses to admit any postulates or assumptions that cannot be independently verified; ultra-empiricism, in other words, asks us to begin with facts, not assumptions. But an 'apriorist' may agree that the predicted results deduced from subjective assumptions, if not the subjective assumptions themselves, should be subject to empirical testing. And few 'ultra-empiricists', no matter how much they insist that all scientifically meaningful statements must be falsifiable by observation, go so far as to deny any role whatever to tautologies and identities in scientific work. The controversy is over matters of emphasis and most economists ever since Senior and J. S. Mill, the first methodologists of the subject, have occupied the middle ground between 'radical apriorism' and 'ultra-empiricism'.

1. Falsifiability in Classical Economics

Nevertheless, the striking fact about the history of economics is how often economists have violated both their own and later methodological prescriptions. The classical economists emphasized the fact that the conclusions of economics rest ultimately on postulates derived as much from the observable 'laws of production' as from subjective introspection. Methodological disputes in the classical period took the form of disagreement over the realism and relevance of the underlying assumptions on which the whole deductive structure was built, while everyone paid lip service to the need to check the predictions of logical deductions against experience. The empirical verification of economics was regarded as too simple to require argument: it was simply a matter of 'look and see'. But despite J. S. Mill's authoritative pronouncement that 'we cannot too carefully endeavour to verify our theory, by comparing . . . the results which it would have led us to predict, with the most trustworthy accounts we can obtain of those which have actually been realised', no real effort was made to test classical doctrines against the body of statistical material that had been accumulated by the middle of the 19th century. The debatable issues in Ricardian economics all hinged on the relative weight of forces making for historically diminishing and increasing returns in the production of wage goods. This question was capable of being resolved along empirical lines, given the fact that some information on money wages and the composition of working class budgets had been made available by the 1840s and that the concept of a price index had passed by this time into general currency. Yet, despite the knowledge that population was no longer 'pressing' upon the food supply, that 'agricultural improvements' were winning the race against numbers, that the rise of productivity in agriculture was steadily reducing the real cost of producing wage goods, the classical writers clung to a belief in the imminent danger of natural resource scarcities.

The standard defense was to attribute every contradiction to the strength of 'counteracting tendencies'. In effect, the classical economists treated certain variables that entered into their analysis as exogenously determined, such as the rate of technical improvement in agriculture, the disposition of the working class to practise family limitation, and the supply of entrepreneurship. Instead of confessing their ignorance about the exogenous variables, however, they advanced bold generalizations about their probable variations through time. For the most part, they did not raise the question whether the exogenous variables were really independently determined constants. In addition, they failed to inquire whether the phenomena labeled 'counteracting tendencies' entered, as it were, as additional parameters to the original equations of their model, or whether they in fact altered the structure of the equations themselves. It was because the motives for family limitation were not in fact independent of the outcome of the race between population and 'subsistence' that the Malthusian theory of population predicted so poorly. It was because Ricardian economics failed to deal with the problems of technical change in agriculture – falling back upon the belief, denied by historical experience, that English landlords were not 'improvers' – that the Corn Laws did not entail the harmful effects that Ricardo had predicted. Had the classical economists acted on Mill's urging to 'carefully endeavour to verify our theory', such weaknesses in the structure would have come to light and led to analytical improvements. As it was, the absence of any alternative theory to that of Ricardo, having equal scope and practical significance, discouraged revisions and promoted a defensive methodological attitude.

Marx is another case in point. His tendency to attribute all discrepancies between his theory and the facts to the dialectical 'inner contradictions' of capitalism provided him with a perfect safety valve against refutations. In addition, he was a past master of the 'apocalyptic fallacy' [see chapter 3, section 4]: there were '*laws* of motion' which were confirmed by evidence, unless of course 'counteracting tendencies' were at work, in which case the evidence would soon bear out the law in question. Nevertheless, the ambiguity with which Marx formulated his secular predictions suggests that he was well aware that there is some weight of contrary evidence sufficient to refute any so-called 'law' – 'laws of motion' that are *never* verified do not deserve the label. Thus, even Marx subscribed in the final analysis to the methodological canon that economic theories should be capable of being falsified; it was simply that he could not bring himself to face up to the requirements of this canon.

2. Falsifiability in Neoclassical Economics

The model of perfect competition that evolved in the heyday of the Marginal Revolution owed much to the older welfare propositions of the loosely stated Invisible Hand type. By limiting the scope of the analysis, however, greater rigor in model construction became possible. The argument was typically related to a few continuous variables and it was confined to explaining the direction of small changes in these variables. All the growth-producing factors, such as the expansion of wants, population growth, technical change and even the passage of time itself, were placed in the box of *ceteris paribus*. The remaining system of endogeneous variables was then shown to have a unique steady-state solution. The problem of achieving equilibrium in the first place was passed over by the method of comparative statics: analysis usually began with an equilibrium situation and then traced out the adjustment process to a new stable equilibrium given a change in the value of one or more of the parameters. Walras saw the problem and deceived himself in thinking that he had solved it: his concept of *tâtonnement*, or Edgeworth's analogous notion of recontracting, demonstrated in effect that markets would attain equilibrium by one bold leap from any initial starting point, thus effectively ruling out the disturbances created by disequilibrium trading. Indeterminacy of equilibrium was eliminated by excluding all interdependence among utility and production functions, and stability of equilibrium was insured by placing various restrictions on the underlying functions and by abstracting from ignorance and uncertainty. The entire procedure was justified by the short-run purpose of the analysis, although this did not prevent excursions into welfare economics involving long-run considerations.

The endogenous variables manipulated in neoclassical models were frequently incapable of being observed, even in principle, and most of the theorems that emerged from the analysis likewise failed to be empirically meaningful. Furthermore, the microeconomic character of the analysis made testing difficult in view of the fact that most available statistical data referred to aggregates: the problem of deducing macroeconomic theorems from microeconomic propositions was not faced squarely until Keynes's work revealed that there was a problem. In addition, the rules for legitimately treating certain variables as exogenous – they must be independent of the endogenous variables in the model, or related to them in a unidirectional manner, and they must be independent of each other – were constantly violated. It is obvious that tastes, population and technology, not only affect and are affected by the typical endogeneous variables of neoclassical models, but that they affect each other in turn.

The standard excuse for treating variables as exogenous that clearly are not exogenous is analytical tractability and expository convenience. For a whole range of practical problems, it is in fact a very good excuse. But the temptation to read more significance into the analysis than is inherent in the procedure is irresistible, and most neoclassical writers succumbed to it. Ambitious propositions about the desirability of perfect competition were laid down with insufficient scruple. Of course, it was recognized that competition was a regulatory device of limited applicability. Important differences between private and social costs, the phenomenon of 'natural monopoly' via increasing returns to scale, and ethically undesirable distributions of income – not to mention the existence of 'public goods' and second-best problems – gave scope to government action. But these qualifications were grafted on, rather than incorporated in, the competitive model. Furthermore, the growth-producing factors that were now regarded as noneconomic in character ceased to receive systematic analysis. Having marked the boundaries of economics, neoclassical writers openly confessed noncompetence outside that boundary and were satisfied to throw out a few commonsense conclusions and occasionally a suggestive insight. It takes no effort of historical perspective to realize that the second half of the 19th century invited a complacent attitude to economic growth: it is only natural than an author like Marshall should think that growth would take care of itself, provided that 'free' competition, supported by minimum state controls, would furnish an appropriate sociopolitical environment. Nevertheless, the result was to leave economics without a theory of growth or development other than the discouraging one that the long-period evolution of an economy depends largely on the neglected noneconomic factors.

The besetting methodological vice of neoclassical economics was the illegitimate use of microstatic theorems, derived from 'timeless' models that excluded technical change and the growth of resources, to predict the historical sequence of events in the real world. A leading example of this vice was the explanation of the alleged constancy of the relative shares of labour and capital by the claim that the aggregate production function of the economy is of the Cobb-Douglas type, although the theory in question referred to microeconomic production functions and no reasons were given for believing that Cobb-Douglas microfunctions could be neatly aggregated to form a Cobb-Douglas macrofunction. But we have witnessed numerous other instances of the vice: the argument that welfare can be improved by taxing increasing-cost industries and subsidizing decreasing-cost industries [see chapter 9, section 16; chapter 10, section 6]; the theory that conditions of monopolistic competition lead to excess capacity [see chapter 10, section 9]; the idea that existence of an equilibrium solution ensures stability of equilibrium [see chapter 10, section 21]; the view that factor payments in accordance with marginal productivity provide a clear rule for increasing aggregate employment in the economy and a theory of the determination of relative shares [see chapter 11, section 9]; the notion that the failure of concentration ratios to rise in all industries shows that there is an optimum size of firms [see chapter 11, section 17]; the proposition that the capital intensity or 'average period of production' of an economy is a monotonic function of the rate of interest [see chapter 12, section 18], that capital intensity falls in the upswing and rises in the downswing of a business cycle because of the Ricardo Effect [see chapter 12, section 30], and that revaluation of the capital stock as a change in investment alters the rate of interest is the key to the theory of capital accumulation [see chapter 12, section 41]; the theory that unemployment tends continually to return to a given 'natural' rate because deviations from it are due to the failure of expectations to catch up with events, which failure can only be momentary [see chapter 16, section 16]; and, lastly – the vice writ large – the view that perfect competition is a sufficient condition for allocative efficiency [see chapter 13, section 13].

Since economic activity takes place in time, can any 'timeless' economic theory ever hope to predict anything? We must begin by disenchanting ourselves of the idea that economic predictions must be quantitative in character to qualify as scientific predictions. Clearly, the predictions of most economic models are qualitative rather than quantitative in nature: they specify the directions of change of the endogenous variables in consequence of a change in the value of one or more exogenous variables, without pretending to predict the numerical magnitude of the change. In other words, all neoclassical economics is about the *signs* of first- and second-order partial derivatives, and that is virtually all it is about.

As Samuelson put it in the *Foundations of Economic Analysis*: 'The method of *comparative statics* consists of the study of the response of our equilibrium unknowns to designated changes in the parameters . . . . In the absence of complete quantitative information concerning our equilibrium equations, it is hoped to be able to formulate qualitative restrictions on slopes, curvatures, etc., of our equilibrium equations so as to be able to derive definite qualitative restrictions upon the responses of our system to changes in certain parameters.' This is what he called the 'qualitative calculus', that is, the attempt to predict directions of change without specifying the magnitude of the change. Now it is an obvious fact that the mere presence of an equilibrium solution for a comparative static model does not guarantee that we can apply the 'qualitative calculus': all the marginal equalities in the world may not add up to a testable prediction. This is perfectly familiar from the theory of household behavior: whenever substitution and income effects work in opposite directions, the outcome depends on relative magnitudes and hence on more than the first- and second-order conditions for a maximum. A moment's reflection, therefore, will show that a great many neoclassical theories are empty from the viewpoint of the 'qualitative calculus'; unless they are fed with more facts to further restrict the relevant functions, they tell us only that equilibrium is what equilibrium must be. If that is so, why have economists not abandoned all such empty models?

3. The Limitations of the Falsifiability Criterion in Economics

In 1953, Friedman published an essay on 'The Methodology of Positive Economics' which quickly generated a methodological controversy almost as heated as that produced by Robbins' *Essay* in 1932. Friedman argued that most traditional criticism of economic theory had scrutinized assumptions, instead of testing implications; the validity of economic theory, he contended, is to be established, not by the descriptive 'realism' of its premises, but by the accuracy of the predictions with which it is concerned. Friedman's methodological position would seem to be unassailable – most assumptions in economic theory involve unobservable variables and it is meaningless to demand that such variables should conform to 'reality' – until it is realized that he is insisting on predictive accuracy as the *sole* criterion of validity.

If a theory is rigorously formulated to the extent of being axiomatized, realism of assumptions is logically equivalent to realism of implications. The trouble is that few economic theories have been successfully axiomatized and, in general, economic hypotheses are not tightly linked to their assumptions in an absolutely explicit deductive chain. In that sense, evidence from direct observation of such behavioral assumptions as transitive preference orderings among consumers, or such technical assumptions as the constant-returns-to-scale characteristics of the production function, is capable of shedding additional light on a theory. But precisely because the theory is loosely formulated, such evidence can never do more than to suggest that the theory is worth testing in terms of its falsifiable consequences. In short, Friedman is quite right to attack the view that realism of assumption is a test of the validity of a theory different from, or additional to, the test of predictive accuracy of implications.

At the same time, it must be admitted that the edict: 'test implications, instead of assumptions', is not very helpful by itself. The criterion of falsifiable implications can be interpreted with different degrees of stringency. If the predictions of a theory are not contradicted by events, the theory is accepted with a degree of confidence that varies uniquely with the magnitude of the supporting evidence. But what if it is contradicted? If no alternative 'simple', 'elegant' and 'fruitful' theory explaining the same events is available – for these are the grounds on which we choose between theories predicting the same consequences – frequent contradiction will be demanded. But what degree of frequency of contradictions will prove persuasive? Economists abhor a theoretical vacuum as much as nature abhors a physical one, and in economics, as in the other sciences, theories are overthrown by better theories, not simply by contradictory facts. Since there are few opportunities to conduct controlled experiments in the social sciences, so that contradictions are never absolute, economists are bound to be more demanding of falsifying evidence than, say, physicists. By the standards of accuracy applied to predictions in the natural sciences, economics make a poor showing and hence economists are frequently forced to resort to indirect methods of testing hypotheses, such as examining the 'realism' of assumptions or testing the implications of theories for phenomena other than those regarded as directly relevant to a particular hypotheses. This opens the door to the easy criticism that economics is a failure because most of its typical assumptions – such as transitive preferences, profit maximization at equal risk levels, independence of utility and production functions, and the like – do not conform to behavior observed in the real world. If economics could conclusively test the implications of its theorems, no more would be heard about the lack of realism of its assumptions. But conclusive once-and-for-all testing or strict refutability of theorems is out of the question in economics because all its predictions are probalistic ones.

Once we have accepted the basic idea that the presence of 'disturbing' influences surrounding economic events precludes absolute falsifiability of economic theorems, it is easy to see why economics contains so many nonfalsifiable concepts. Many economic phenomena have not yet lent themselves to systematic theorizing, and yet economists do not wish to remain silent because of some methodological fiat that real science should consist only of falsifiable theorems. A 'theory' is not to be condemned merely because it is as yet untestable, not even if it is so framed as to preclude testing, provided it draws attention to a significant problem and provides a framework for its discussion from which a testable implication may some day emerge. It cannot be denied that many so-called 'theories' in economics have no empirical content and serve merely as filing systems for classifying information. To demand the removal of all such heuristic devices and theories in the desire to press the principle of falsifiability to the limit is to proscribe further research in many branches of economics. It is perfectly true that economists have often deceived themselves – and their readers – by engaging in what Leontief once called 'implicit theorizing', presenting tautologies in the guise of substantive contributions to economic knowledge. But the remedy for this practise is clarification of purpose, not radical and possibly premature surgery.

Furthermore, it is not always easy to draw the line between tautologies and falsifiable propositions. A 'theory' that is obstensibly a mere collection of deductions from 'convenient' assumptions, so framed as to be nonfalsifiable under any conceivable circumstance, may be reinterpretable as a verifiable proposition. After a hundred years of discussion, economists are still not quite agreed as to whether the Malthusian theory of population is nothing but a very complicated tautology that can 'explain' any and all demographic events, or a falsifiable prediction about per capita income in the event of population growth. Whatever Malthus' own intention, the theory can be so restated as to meet the criterion of falsifiability, in which case it has in fact been falsified. The concept of a negatively inclined demand curve in conjunction with an inclusive *ceteris paribus* clause is not a falsifiable concept, because if quantity and price are both observed to decline together in the absence of changes in other prices, incomes and expectations, it is always possible to save the original proposition by the contention that tastes have changed. But the concept can be rendered falsifiable if we hypothesize that tastes are stable over the relevant period of time, or that tastes change in a predictable fashion over time. The assumption of stable tastes is a genuine empirical hypothesis and all work on statistical demand curves has been concerned in one way or another with testing this hypothesis.

The same comments apply to the supply side. The notion of a production function – the spectrum of all known techniques of production – is by itself a concept so general as to be empty. Businessmen have not experienced all known techniques and the cost of obtaining more experience with techniques is not negligible; the vital difference for an individual firm is not between known and unknown but between tried and untried methods of production. The convention of putting all available technical knowledge in one box called 'production functions' and all advances in knowledge in another box called 'innovations' has no simple counterpart in the real world, where most innovations are 'embodied' in new capital goods, so that firms move down production functions and shift them at one and the same time. Nevertheless, the concept of a production function can be given an empirical interpretation if we hypothesize that production functions are stable. This may well be very difficult to verify in practice but in principle it is verifiable and work in recent years on 'embodied' and 'disembodied' capital-growth models, however inconclusive it has proved to be, has been precisely concerned with testing the hypothesis of stable production functions. And so the two fundamental propositions of neoclassical price theory, to wit, positive excess demand leads to a rise in price and an excess of price over cost leads to a rise in output, are both capable of being falsified, despite the fact that they have frequently been laid down as immutable laws of nature.

To drive the point home, let the reader ask himself whether the following familiar propositions – the list is merely suggestive – constitute falsifiable or heuristic statements; if the former, whether they are falsifiable in principle or in practice and, if the latter, whether and in what sense they are defensible as fruitful points of departure for further analysis.

1.   A specific tax on an article will raise its price by less than the tax if the

elasticity of demand is greater than zero and the elasticity of supply is less than infinity.

2. The elasticity of demand for a commodity is governed by the degree of substitutability of that commodity in consumption.

3. The impact effect of a rise in money wages in a competitive industry is to reduce employment.

4. In the absence of technical change, a rise in the average capital-labour ratio of an economy causes wage rates to rise and capital rentals to fall.

5. A laboursaving innovation is one that reduces capital's relative share of output at given factor prices.

6. An 'industry' is a group of firms whose products are perfect or near-perfect substitutes for each other.

7. Perfect competition is incompatible with increasing returns to scale.

8. Profit maximization is a plausible assumption about business behavior because the competitive race ensures that only profit maximizers survive.

9. An equal rise in government expenditures and receipts will raise national income by the amount of that rise if the community's marginal propensity to consume is positive and less than one.

10. A tax imposed on an industry whose production function is linearly homogeneous results in a loss of consumers' surplus greater than the amount of the tax receipts.

11. Increasing or diminishing returns to scale are always due to the indivisibility of some input.

12. Price expectations are always 'rational' in the sense that the expected mean value of the probability distribution of forecasted prices is identical to the mean value of the probability distribution of actual prices.

An hour spent thinking about these propositions will convince anyone that it is not easy to make up one's mind whether particular economic theories are falsifiable or not; it is even more difficult to know what to make of these theories that are not falsifiable; and as for the ones that are indeed falsifiable, it is still more difficult to think of appropriate methods of putting them to the test. In short, empirical testing may be the heart of economics but it is only the heart.[1]

---

[1] A few words about a subject like psychoanalysis will show that the difficulties of applying the falsifiability criterion are not confined to economics. Is psychoanalysis a science or merely a psychic poultice for the rejects of industrial civilization? If it is a science, are its leading concepts – the Oedipus Complex; the division of the mind into id, ego and superego; sublimation; repression; transference; and the like – falsifiable? Despite the fact that psychoanalysis is now over sixty years old, there is still very little agreement on these questions either among analysts or among critics of psychoanalysis. In one sense, the situation in psychoanalysis is much worse than economics. At least economists do agree that economics is a science and that its principles must ultimately stand up to scientific testing. Psychoanalysts, however, sometimes argue that what Freud tried to do was not to explain neurotic symptoms in terms of cause and effect but simply to make sense of them as disguised but meaningful communication; psychoanalysis is, therefore, an art of healing and must be judged in terms of its success in curing patients. Even so, there has been surprisingly little research on psychoanalytic 'cures', and, of course, it is difficult to see how psychoanalysis could cure patients if its interpretations of neurotic behavior did not somehow correspond with reality. At any rate, it would be fair to say that the status of the falsifiability criterion in economics is about halfway between its status in psychoanalysis and its status in nuclear physics.

4. The Role of Value Judgments

Even if all economics could be neatly divided into testable and untestable theories and even if unanimous agreement had been obtained on the *validity* of the testable theories, we would still have to assess their *significance* or *relevance*. This introduces the problem of normative as distinct from positive economics. After a series of attacks on utilitarian welfare economics, a new Paretian welfare economics was erected in the 1930s that purported to avoid interpersonal comparisons of utility. 'Scientific' welfare economics has lately come in for its share of destructive criticism and some economists have echoed once again the old Seniorian cry that economics should be wholly 'positive' in character. But whatever we may think of modern welfare economics, there can be no doubt that the desire to evaluate the performance of economic systems has been the great driving force behind the development of economic thought and the source of inspiration of almost every great economist in the history of economics.

Indeed, it would be difficult to imagine what economics would be like if we succeeded in eliminating all vestiges of welfare economics. For one thing, we would never be able to discuss *efficient* allocation of resources, for the question of efficient allocation of scarce means among competing ends cannot even be raised without a standard of evaluation. The fact that the price system is a particular standard of evaluation, namely, one that counts every dollar the same no matter whose dollar it is, should not blind us to the fact that acceptance of the results of competitive price systems is a value judgment. The price system is an election in which some voters are allowed to vote many times and the only way people can vote is by spending money. Economists are constantly engaged in making the fundamental value judgment that only certain types of individual preferences are to count and, furthermore, to count equally. We all know, of course, why economics has confined its attention to those motives for action that can be evaluated with 'the measuring rod of money' but the fact remains that value judgments are involved at the very foundation of the science.

If economists are necessarily committed to certain value judgments at the outset of analysis, how can it be claimed that economics is a science? This innocent question has been productive of more methodological mischief than any other posed in this chapter. Ever since Max Weber attempted to settle this question by defining the prerequisites of ethical neutrality in social science, there has been an endless debate on the role of value judgments in subjects like sociology, political science and economics. Critics of economics have always been convinced that the very notion of objective economics divorced from value judgments is a vain pretense. Working economists, on the other hand, more or less aware of their own value judgments, and very much aware of the concealed value judgments of other economists with whom they disagree, never doubted that the distinction between positive and normative economics was as clear-cut as the distinction between the indicative and imperative mood in grammar. But how can there be such total disagreement on what appears to be a perfectly straightforward question?

The orthodox Weberian position on *wertfrei* social science is essentially a matter of logic: as David Hume taught us, 'you can't deduce ought from is'. Thus, the descriptive statements or behavioral hypotheses of economics cannot *logically* entail ethical implications. It is for this reason that J. N. Keynes, the leading neoclassical methodologist, could write as long ago as 1891: 'the proposition that it is possible to study economic uniformities without passing ethical judgments or formulating economic precepts seems in fact so little to need proof, when the point at issue is clearly grasped, that it is difficult to say anything in support of it that shall go beyond mere truism'. Nevertheless, time and time again it has been claimed that economics is *necessarily* value-loaded and that, in Myrdal's words, 'a "disinterested social science" has never existed and, for logical reasons, cannot exist'. When we sort out the various meanings that such assertions carry, they reduce to one or more of the following propositions: (1) the selection of questions to be investigated by economics may be ideologically biased: (2) the answers that are accepted as true answers to these questions may be likewise biased, particularly since economics abounds in contradictory theories that have not yet been tested; (3) even purely factual statements may have emotive connotations and hence may be used to persuade as well as to describe; (4) economic advice to political authorities may be value-loaded because means and ends cannot be neatly separated and hence policy ends cannot be taken as given at the outset of the exercise; and (5) since all practical economic advice involves interpersonal comparisons of utility and these are not testable, practical welfare economics almost certainly involves value judgments. Oddly enough, all of these assertions are perfectly true but they do not affect the orthodox doctrine of value-free social science in any way whatsoever.

Proposition (1) simply confuses the origins of theories with the question of how they may be validated. Schumpeter's *History of Economic Analysis* continually reminds the reader that all scientific theorizing begins with a 'Vision' – 'the preanalytic cognitive act that supplies the raw material for the analytic effort' – and in this sense science is ideological at the outset. But that is quite a different argument from the one that contends that for this reason the acceptance or rejection of scientific theory is also ideological. Similarly, both propositions (1) and (2) confuse methodological judgments with normative judgments. Methodological judgments involve criteria for judging the validity of a theory, such as levels of statistical significance, selection of data, assessment of their reliability and adherence to the canons of formal logic, all of which are indispensable in scientific work. Normative judgments, on the other hand, refer to ethical views about the desirability of certain kinds of behavior and certain social outcomes. It is the latter which alone are said to be capable of being eliminated in positive science. As for propositions (3) and (4), it may be granted that economists have not always avoided the use of honorific definitions and persuasive classifications. Nor have they consistently refused to recommend policy measures without first eliciting the policy maker's preference function. But these are abuses of the doctrine of value-free economics and do not suffice to demonstrate that economics is *necessarily* value-loaded. We conclude that when economists make policy recommendations, they should distinguish as strongly as possible between the positive and the normative bases for their recommendations. They should also make it clear whether their proposals represent second-best compromises, or concessions to considerations of political feasibility. But they should not refuse to advise simply because they do not share the policy maker's preference function and they should stoutly resist the argument that economic advice depends entirely on the particular economist that is hired.

Proposition (5) deserves separate comment. Welfare economics, whether pure or applied, obviously involves value judgments, and, as we noted earlier, the idea of value-free welfare economics is simply a contradiction in terms. This question would never have arisen in the first place if the new Paretian welfare economics had not adopted the extraordinary argument that a consensus on certain value judgments renders these judgments 'objective'; apparently, the only value judgments that fail to meet this test involve interpersonal comparisons of utility and these were therefore banned from the discussion.

5. American Institutionalism

Despite obeisance to the concept of 'positive' economics and the principle of verifying predictions by submitting them to evidence, most economists who have had qualms about the value of received doctrine have stilled these qualms, not by searching for tangible evidence of the predictive power of economic theory, but by reading the substantive contributions of leading critics of orthodox analysis. Bad theory is still better than no theory at all and, for the most part, critics of orthodoxy had no alternative construction to offer. One obvious exception to this statement are Marxist critics. Another possible exception are the American Institutionalists. Indeed, no discussion of methodology in economics is complete without a mention of this last but greatest effort to persuade economists to base their theories, not on analogies from mechanics, but on analogies from biology and jurisprudence.

'Institutional economics', as the term is narrowly understood, refers to a movement in American economic thought associated with such names as Veblen, Mitchell and Commons. It is no easy matter to characterize this movement and, at first glance, the three central figures of the school seem to have little in common: Veblen applied an inimitable brand of interpretative sociology to the working creed of businessmen; Mitchell devoted his life to the amassing of statistical data, almost as an end in itself; and Commons analyzed the workings of the economic system from the standpoint of its legal foundations. More than one commentator has denied that there ever was such a thing as 'institutional economics', differentiated from other kinds of economics. But this is tantamount to asserting that a whole generation of writers in the interwar years deceived themselves in thinking that they were rallying around a single banner. Surely, they must have united over certain principles?

If we attempt to delineate the core of 'institutionalism', we come upon three main features, all of which are methodological: (1) dissatisfaction with the high level of abstraction of neoclassical economics and particularly with the static flavor of orthodox price theory; (2) a demand for the integration of economics with other social sciences, or what might be described as 'faith in the advantages of the interdisciplinary approach'; and (3) discontent with the casual empiricism of classical and neoclassical economics, expressed in the proposal to pursue detailed quantitative investigations. In addition, there is the plea for more 'social control of business', to quote the title of J. M. Clark's book, published in 1926; in other words, a favourable attitude to state intervention. None of the four features are found in equal measure in the works of the leading institutionalists. Veblen cared little for digging out the facts of economic life and was not fundamentally opposed to the abstract-deductive method of neoclassical economics. Moreover, he refused to admit that the work of the German Historical School constituted scientific economics. What he disliked about orthodox economics was, not its method of reaching conclusions, but its underlying hedonistic and atomistic conception of human nature – in short, the Jevons-Marshall theory of consumer behavior. Moreover, he dissented vigorously from the central implication of neoclassical welfare economics that a perfectly competitive economy tends, under certain restricted conditions, to optimum results. This amounted to teleology, he argued, and came close to an apologia for the *status quo*. Economics ought to be an evolutionary science, Veblen contended, meaning an inquiry into the genesis and growth of economic institutions; the economic system should be viewed, not as a 'self-balancing mechanism', but as a 'cumulatively unfolding process'. He defined economic institutions as a complex of habits of thought and conventional behavior; it would seem to follow, therefore, that 'institutional economics' comprised a study of the social mores and customs that becomes crystalized into institutions. But what Veblen actually gives the reader is *Kulturkritik*, dressed up with instinct psychology, racist anthropology and a flight of telling adjectives: 'conspicuous consumption', 'pecuniary emulation', 'ostentatious display', 'absentee ownership', 'discretionary control', these are just a few of Veblen's terms that have passed into the English language. It was a mixture so unique and individual to Veblen that even his most avid disciples were unable to extend or develop it. Books like *The Theory of the Leisure Class* (1899) and *The Theory of Business Enterprise* (1940) appear to be about economic theory but they are actually interpretations of the values and beliefs of the 'captains of industry'.

To fully appreciate the difficulty of evaluating Veblen's ideas, let us take one striking example. No matter what book of Veblen we open, we find the idea that life in a modern industrial community is the result of a polar conflict between 'pecuniary employments' and 'industrial employments', or 'business enterprise' and 'the machine process', or 'vendibility' and 'serviceability', making money and making goods, or acquisition and physical production. There is a class struggle under capitalism, not between capitalists and proletarians, but between businessmen and engineers. Pecuniary habits of thought unite bankers, brokers, lawyers and managers in a defense of private acquisition as the central principle of business enterprise. In contrast, the discipline of the machine falls on the workmen in industry and more especially on the technicians and engineers that supervize them. It is in these terms that Veblen describes modern industrial civilization. As we read him, we have the feeling that something is being 'explained'. Yet what are we really to make of it all? Is it a contrast between subjective and objective criteria of economic welfare? Is it a plea to abandon the emphasis on material wealth, implying in the manner of Galbraith that we would be better off with more public goods and less trivia? Is it a demonstration of a fundamental flaw in the price system? Is it a call for a technocratic revolution? There is evidence in Veblen's writings for each of these interpretations but there is also much evidence against all of them. Furthermore, Veblen never tells us how to find out whether his polarities explain anything at all. It is not simply that he never raised the question of how his explanations might be validated but that he is continually hinting that a description is a theory, or, worse, that the more penetrating is the description, the better is the theory.

Mitchell, on the other hand, was a thinker of a different breed. He showed little inclination for methodological attacks on the preconceptions of orthodox economics and eschewed the interdisciplinary approach. His 'institutionalism' took the form of collecting statistical data on the notion that these would eventually furnish explanatory hypotheses. He was the founder of the National Bureau of Economic Research and the chief spokesman of the concept that has been uncharitably described as 'measurement without theory'.

Commons alone wrote a book specifically entitled *Institutional Economics* (1934) which, together with his *Legal Foundations of Capitalism* (1926), analyzed the 'working rules' of 'going concerns' that governed 'individual transactions'; 'transactions', 'working rules', 'the going concern', these were the building blocks of his system. In his own day, Commons was much better known as a student of labour legislation. His theoretical writings are as suggestive as they are obscure and few commentators have succeeded in adequately summarizing them.

Thus, despite certain common tendencies, the *school* of 'institutional economics' was never more than a tenous inclination to dissent from orthodox economics. This may explain why the phrase itself has degenerated into a synonym for 'descriptive economics', a sense in which it may be truly said: 'we are all institutional economists now'. Of course, if we are willing to recast our terms and to include in our net all those that have contributed to 'economic sociology' – which Schumpeter regarded as one of the four fundamental fields of economics, the other three being economic theory, economic history and statistics – we would have to treat Marx, Schmoller, Sombart, Max Weber, Pareto and the Webbs, to cite only a few, as 'institutional economists'. It has been said that if economic analysis deals with the question of how people behave at any time, 'economic sociology' deals with the question of how they come to behave as they do. Economic sociology, therefore, deals with the social institutions that are relevant to economic behavior, such as governments, banks, land tenure, inheritance law, contracts and so on. Interpreted in this way, there is nothing to quarrel with. But this is hardly what Veblen, Mitchell and Commons thought they were doing. Institutional economics was not meant to complement economic analysis as it had always been understood but to replace it.

There are few economists today who would consider themselves disciples of Veblen, Mitchell and Commons; although there is an Association of Evolutionary Economics, publishing its own journal, the *Journal of Economic Issues*, which is determined to revitalize the spirit of the founding fathers of American institutionalism. Nevertheless, the institutionalist movement ended for all practical purposes in the 1930s. This is not to deny that there were lasting influences. Mitchell's contribution to our understanding of the business cycle and in particular to the revolution in economic information that separates 20th- from 19th-century economics is too obvious to call for comment. And the recent interest in cybernetics, operations research, management science, organization theory and general systems analysis, all testifying to a growing concern with integration of the social sciences, may owe something to the frequent attacks of Veblen and Commons on the narrow focus of traditional economics. But in the final analysis, institutionalist economics did not fulfil its promise to supply a viable alternative to neoclassical economics and for that reason, despite the cogency of much of the criticisms of institutionalists, it gradually faded away. The moral of the story is simply this: it takes a new theory, and not just the destructive exposure of assumptions or the collection of new facts, to beat an old theory.

6. Why Bother with the History of Economic Theory?
There are no simple rules for distinguishing between valid and invalid, relevant and irrelevant theories in economics. The criterion of falsifiability can separate propositions into positive and normative categories and thus tell us where to concentrate our empirical work. Even normative propositions can often be shown to have positive underpinnings, holding out the prospect of eventual agreement on the basis of empirical evidence. Nevertheless, a core of normative theorems always remains for which empirical testing is irrelevant and immaterial. Moreover, there is an undetermined body of economic propositions and theorems which appear to be about economic behavior but which do not result in any predictable implications about that behavior. In short, a good deal of received doctrine is metaphysics. There is nothing wrong with this, provided it is not mistaken for science. Alas, the history of economics reveals that economists are as prone as anyone else to mistake chaff for wheat and to claim possession of the truth when all they possess are intricate series of definitions or value judgments disguised as scientific rules. There is no way of becoming fully aware of this tendency except by studying the history of economics. To be sure, modern economics provides an abundance of empty theories parading as scientific predictions or policy recommendations carrying concealed value premises. Nevertheless, the methodological traps are so subtle and insidious that the proving ground cannot be too large. One justification for the study of the history of economics, but of course only one, is that it provides a more extensive 'laboratory' in which to acquire methodological humility about the actual accomplishments of economics. Furthermore, it is a laboratory that every economist carries with him, whether he is aware of it or not. When someone claims to explain the determination of wages without bringing in marginal productivity, or to measure capital in its own physical units, or to demonstrate the benefits of the invisible hand by purely objective criteria, the average economist reacts almost instinctively but it is an instinct acquired by the lingering echoes of the history of the subject. Why bother then with the history of economic theory? Because it is better to know one's intellectual heritage than merely to suspect it is deposited somewhere in an unknown place and in a foreign tongue. As T. S. Eliot put it: 'Someone said: "The dead writers

are more remote from us because we *know* so much more than they did." Precisely, and they are that which we know.'

NOTES ON FURTHER READING

I have dealt at greater length with the issues raised in this chapter in *The Methodology of Economics* (1980), which contains its own 'Suggestions for Further Reading'. B. J. Caldwell, *Beyond Positivism: Economic Methodology in the Twentieth Century* (1982) is an excellent alternative account and an effective counterpoise to my own tendentious interpretation of the issues. T. W. Hutchison, *The Politics and Philosophy of Economics* (1981) contains two useful essays on the old Austrian *Methodenstreit* and the methodology of the modern Austrian School.

For an exhaustive but pretentious study of all the leading American Institutionalist writers, see A. G. Gruchy, *Modern Economic Thought: The American Contribution* (1947): the endless repetition of its central theme, to wit, that all these writers were contributing to a heterodox type of 'holistic economics', is a *tour de force* of interpretation which, unfortunately, collapses the moment it is probed. *Institutional Economics, Veblen, Commons and Mitchell Reconsidered*, eds. J. Dorfman, and others (1963), contains a background article by J. Dorfman, a piece on Veblen by C. E. Ayres, another on Commons by N. W. Chamberlin – which succeeds better than most expositions in clarifying this obscure thinker – a review of Mitchell's contributions by S. Kuznets, and a surprising essay by R. A. Gordon, 'Institutional Elements in Contemporary Economics', depicting Schumpeter as an 'institutionalist'. On Veblen in particular, see the excellent introduction by W. C. Mitchell to *What Veblen Taught: Selected Writings* (1963), reprinted in *DET*; T. Sowell, 'The Evolutionary Economics of Thorstein Veblen', *OEP*, July, 1976; and D. A. Walker, 'Thorstein Veblen's Economic System', *EQ*, April, 1977. See also J. P. Diggins, *The Bard of Savagery. Thorstein Veblen and Modern Social Theory* (1978), a sympathetic but critical account of Veblen's entire output with illuminating comparisons between Veblen, Marx and Weber. On Mitchell, see M. Friedman, 'Wesley C. Mitchell as an Economic Theorist', *JPE*, December, 1950; and A. Hirsch, 'The *A Posteriori* Method and the Creation of New Theory: W. C. Mitchell as a Case Study', *HOPE*, Summer, 1976. See, finally, K. E. Boulding's postmortem, 'A New Look at Institutionalism', *AER*, May, 1957, with some very revealing comments by various discussants.

Source material on the American Institutionalists is readily available: a minimum list is Veblen's famous paper, 'Why Is Economics Not an Evolutionary Science?' *QJE*, 1898, reprinted in *ETHA*; J. R. Commons, 'Institutional Economics', *AER*, 1931, reprinted in *ibid.*, and Veblen's *Theory of the Leisure Class* and *Theory of Business Enterprise*, both available in paperback.

Index of names

713

Index of subjects

Money
demand for; 56, 153, 158–9, 574, 583,
635–6, 645–6; *see also* Excess demand,
for money *and* Money balances
as medium of exchange, 56, 154, 635
as store of value, 19, 150, 154, 180, 269,
583, 645
as unit of account, 150, 154, 548
and needs of trade, 158
neutral, 633, 640, 642–3
outside and inside, 666–7
supply of, 633–4
and transmission mechanism, 637, 646,
689, 691; *see also* Monetary theory,
direct mechanism
velocity of circulation of, 19, 202, 203, 632,
633, 635–6, 644, 646–7, 649
motion versus rest theory of velocity, 153,
198, 636
Money balances
active, 158, 658
inactive, 158, 658
precautionary demand for, 153, 644, 647
demand for real, 153, 159
speculative demand for, 153, 158, 644,
657–60
transactions demand for, 153, 154, 158,
644, 657–8
working, 158
Money illusion, 164, 663, 665, 683–4
Money market equilibrium, 639–40, 641–2,
643–4
Monopolistic competition, 392–6, 410, 412,
419, 428, 443, 448, 549, 563, 626, 628–9,
701
Monopoly; *see also* Oligopoly
bilateral, 310–2
in classical economics, 43–4, 49, 109, 190
in neoclassical economics, 317–18, 321,
414–15, 604
Monopsony, 187, 428–9, 482
Moral restraint; *see* Checks to population
Multiplier, 170, 694; *see also* Balanced
budget, multiplier
Multiple discoveries, in intellectual history,
294, 303–5, 623, 631
Multiple equilibria; *see* Equilibrium, multiple

National Bureau of Economic Research, 710
National income accounting; *see* Income,
concepts of
Natural rate of unemployment; *see*
Unemployment, natural rate of
Natural wage, in Thünen, 322–4, 327
Navigation Laws, 58
Needs-of-trade doctrine; *see* Banking
Neo-Malthusianism; *see* Birth control
Net national product, *see* Income, concepts of
Net product; *see* Physiocratic system

Noncompeting groups, 192, 210
Normative economics, 6–7, 180, 697, 607–8
Numéraire, 573

Occupations
choice of, 48
net advantages of, 48–9
Offer curves, 205
Oligopoly
Chamberlin on, 395–6
Marshall on, 410
Open market operations, 285, 661, 669
Organisation, as a factor of production,
550
Overproduction; *see* Gluts, general

Paralleltheorie; see Wages, and price of food
Pareto optimality; *see* Walfare economics, in
neoclassical economics, Pareto on
Partial equilibrium analysis; *see* Equilibrium
partial
Particular expenses curve, in Marshall, 374,
412–13
Peasant proprietorship, 190, 191, 213, 222
Pecuniary and non-pecuniary rewards, 48–9
Period of production, concepts, 506–23, 568
Phillips curve, 678–86, 690
Physiocratic system, 10
and China, 33
concept of net product in, 28, 54
criticism of mercantilism in, 24
interpretations of, 33
and natural-law doctrine, 33
and Say's Law, 28–9, 33
single tax in, 24
Smith on, 24, 57, 59
Tableau Economique in, 25–8, 32–3
theory of rent in, 28
Pigou Effect; *see* Real Balance Effect
Planned economy, 191, 595
Poor Laws, 49, 117, 221
Population
compound growth of, 69
explosion, 68
Malthusian theory of, 67–77, 91, 190, 192,
220, 295, 402, 423, 699, 704
modern theory of, 76
optimum theory of, 73–4, 75–6, 192, 404
Positive economics, 180, 697
Predictions, economic, 245, 697, 701–5
Price; *see also* Value
absolute and relative, 153, 232, 649
discrimination, 602
effort, 50
market and natural, 38–9
of production, in Marx, 229, 278
reserve, 488–9
short and long period, 39, 197
stability, 642, 648–9